THE NAVAL INSTITUTE GUIDE TO THE
Ships and Aircraft of the U.S. Fleet

FIFTEENTH EDITION

THE NAVAL INSTITUTE GUIDE TO THE Ships and Aircraft of the U.S. Fleet

Norman Polmar

Naval Institute Press
Annapolis, Maryland

To the memory of Carole Keig Wilson

Contents

Preface

This edition of *Ships and Aircraft* appears at a historic moment in U.S. naval development. The Cold War is over, the end of more than 40 years of armed confrontation between the United States and the Soviet Union. The end of the Cold War era, marked by the dissolution of the Soviet Union and the breakdown of the Eastern Bloc, and the U.S. fiscal situation have led to massive reductions in the U.S. armed forces, including the Navy. Simultaneously, a new naval strategy is being developed, based on the principals of "jointness" (i.e., multi-service operations) and littoral operations (i.e., in forward, Third World areas rather than in ocean areas).

At the same time, a number of new ships, aircraft, and weapons are joining the U.S. fleet, the result of programs initiated during the Cold War. Several of these had their combat debut in the brief but violent Gulf War of January–February 1991. But that conflict also marked the final operations of several Navy ships, aircraft, and missiles.

The future of the Navy is not clear. While several previous programs will continue, the long-touted SEAWOLF (SSN 21) submarine program has been cut to only two units, while several aircraft programs as well as the planned airship effort have been cancelled. At the same time, the Coast Guard's sea-based aerostat program has been transferred to the Army, marking the end of lighter-than-air programs by the sea services.

In virtually all categories of naval activity—ships, aircraft, weapons, personnel, and bases—the Navy is being reduced, as is the Marine Corps. However, on a percentage basis the sea services are suffering smaller reductions than the Army and Air Force. Further, some highly controversial naval programs are being supported by the Department of Defense, especially the continued construction of NIMITZ (CVN 68)-class aircraft carriers, a steady building rate for ARLEIGH BURKE (DDG 51)-class destroyers, the funding of large amphibious ships, and the continuation of the very expensive overhaul/refueling of the carrier ENTERPRISE (CVN 65).

This edition describes the fleet of the early 1990s and the on-going naval programs as well as several recent cancellations. The emphasis on sealift ships, including maritime prepositioning, has led to development of a separate chapter to describe those ships (chapter 24). All other chapters have been extensively revised and updated since publication of the 14th Edition of *The Ships and Aircraft of the U.S. Fleet*.

Organization: Effective 2 January 1992 the Navy consolidated most of its laboratory and research activities as well as certain fleet support activities into five major warfare centers. The consolidation effort is intended to reduce overhead expenses, eliminate duplication, provide more cost-effective planning and cost eliminating, and streamline management functions, according to Navy statements.

The older organization terms are generally used in this volume. The new warfare commands and the activities being consolidated under them are:[1]

(1) Naval Air Warfare Center (NAWC)[2]
   Naval Air Development Center, Trenton, N.J.
   Naval Air Development Center, Warminster, Penna.
   Naval Air Development Center, Indianapolis, Ind.
   Naval Air Engineering Center, Lakehurst, N.J.
   Naval Air Test Center, Patuxent River, Md.
   Naval Air Weapons Station, Point Mugu, Calif.
   Naval Air Weapons Station, China Lake, Calif.
   Naval Ordnance Missile Test Station, White Sands, N.M.
   Naval Weapons Center, China Lake, Calif.
   Naval Weapons Evaluation Facility, Albuquerque, N.M.
   Pacific Missile Test Center, Point Mugu, Calif.

(2) Naval Surface Warfare Center (NSWC)[3]
   David Taylor Research Center, Annapolis, Md.
   David Taylor Research Center, Carderock-Bethesda, Md.
   David Taylor Research Center Det., Bayview, Idaho
   David Taylor Research Center Det., Bremerton, Wash.
   Fleet Combat Direction Systems Support Facility, Dam Neck, Va.
   Integrated Combat Systems Test Facility, San Diego, Calif.
   Naval Coastal Systems Center, Panama City, Fla.
   Naval Mine Warfare Engineering Activity, Yorktown, Va.
   Naval Ordnance Station, Indian Head, Md.
   Naval Ordnance Station, Louisville, Ky.
   Naval Ordnance Station Det., McAlester, Okla.
   Naval Ships Systems Engineering Station, Philadelphia, Pa.
   Naval Ship Weapons Systems Engineering Station, Port Hueneme, Calif.
   Naval Surface Warfare Center, Dahlgren, Va.
   Naval Surface Warfare Center Det., Fort Lauderdale, Fla.
   Naval Surface Warfare Center, Washington, D.C.
   Naval Surface Warfare Center, White Oak-Silver Spring, Md.
   Naval Weapons Support Center, Crane, Ind.

---

1. Some of the activities have undergone intermediate name changes from the ones listed below prior to becoming components of the commands indicated.
2. Reports to Commander, Naval Air Systems Command.
3. Reports to Commander, Naval Sea Systems Command.

(3) Naval Undersea Warfare Center (NUWC)[4]
   Naval Sea Combat Systems Engineering Station, Norfolk, Va.
   Naval Torpedo Station, Keyport, Wash.
   Naval Undersea Warfare Center, Washington, D.C.
   Atlantic Undersea Test and Evaluation Center, Andros Island, Bahamas
   Atlantic Undersea Test and Evaluation Center Det., West Palm Beach, Fla.
   Naval Undersea Warfare Center Det., New London, Conn.
   Naval Undersea Warfare Center Div., Newport, R.I.
   Naval Undersea Warfare Engineering Station Det., Hawthorne, Nev.
   Naval Undersea Warfare Engineering Station Det., Indian Island, Wash.
   Naval Undersea Warfare Engineering Station Det., Lualualei, Hawaii
   Naval Undersea Warfare Engineering Station Det., San Diego, Calif.

4. Reports to Commander, Naval Sea Systems Command.

(4) Naval Command, Control and Ocean Surveillance Center (NCCOSC)[5]
   Naval Ocean Systems Center, San Diego, Calif.

(5) Naval Corporate Research Laboratory (NRL)
   Naval Research Laboratory, Washington, D.C.

Photography: Where possible the latest available photography has been used in this edition. This is especially critical with respect to ships, where radar and other antennas and features change periodically. However, in some entries, especially aircraft and missiles, older photography is used that shows specific features.

5. Reports to Commander, Space and Naval Warfare Systems Command.

Acknowledgments

Many individuals and organizations have provided assistance in producing this book. The draft manuscript was reviewed by James Mulquin and M.P. (Blade) Chapman, both of whom made invaluable contributions to this edition. Lt. Comdr. Rick Burgess, USN, editor of *Naval Aviation News* kindly reviewed the aviation material.

As always, Dr. Giorgio Arra—the dean of ship photographers—has taken the majority of the ship photos in this edition. Leo Van Ginderen was unsparing in providing his photos and those of his colleagues, while several provided by Stephan Terzibaschitsch, Dr. Maurizio Del Prete, Wilhelm Donko, and other photographers were invaluable. Peter Mersky, assistant editor of the Navy's *Approach* magazine, has provided a number of his own photos for this edition. Many of the photos submitted to the author and not used in the book were still of value in helping to identify changes to ships.

Comdr. Mark Van Dyke, USN, formerly assistant Chief of Navy Information (CHINFO) for operations, who brought a new perspective to that position, has been most helpful to this effort through his assistants Lts. Taylor Kiland, Becky Brenton, Bob Ross, and Mark Walker. A continuous flow of U.S. Navy photography has been provided by Russ Egnor of CHINFO and his most able assistants Patricia Toombs and JOC Jay Davidson.

Among the persons who provided assistance for this edition were Dr. William Armstrong, historian, Naval Air Systems Command; Terry Arnold, manager, tilt-rotor communications, Bell Helicopter Textron; Comdr. Joe Dan Banker, USN, public affairs officer, Mine Warfare Command; Diane Banks, public relations, Kaman; Thomas Balfour, vice president for marketing, Newport News Shipbuilding; Capt. R.C. Berning, USN, Commander, Patrol Combatant Missile Hydrofoil Squadron 2; Adm. Jeremy (Mike) Boorda, USN, former Chief of Naval Personnel; Dr. Robert M. Browning, Jr., historian, Coast Guard Headquarters; Tom Burgess, public relations, General Dynamics; Comdr. William H. Cahill, USN, Military Sealift Command; Marilyn Carlson, public affairs officer, Special Projects Program Office; M.P. (Blade) Chapman, naval analyst; Comdr. Steve Clawson, USN, public affairs officer, Bureau of Naval Personnel; Adrienne M. Combs, public affairs, U.S. Army Transportation Center; Brad Dease, manning branch, Coast Guard Headquarters; Vice Adm. Richard M. Dunleavy, USN, Assistant Chief of Naval Operations for Air Warfare, and Lt. Comdr. Roxanne Baxter, USN, of his staff; JOC David T. Farmer of the Naval Submarine Base, New London, Conn.; Susan Filli, public affairs, Naval Sea Systems Command; Jean Fitzgerald, for facilitating photography for the book; Wayne R. Fritz, manager, submarine warfare programs, General Electric; Lt. Maureen Ford, USN, public affairs, USS LEXINGTON (AVT 16); CWO Randy L. Gaddo, USMC, public affairs, Headquarters U.S. Marine Corps; John Georg, manager of public relations, Litton Corp. in Washington, D.C.; Col. John Greenwood, USMC (Ret.), editor of the *Marine Corps Gazette;* Fred N. Hallett, public relations, National Steel and Shipbuilding; Capt. R.W. Havel, USN, program manager for combatant and service craft, Naval Sea Systems Command; Margaret Holtz, public affairs officer, Military Sealift Command, and her assistants Tricia Larson, Christine MacKinnon, and Nancy Breen; 1st Lt. Brian Hubbard, USAF, and Staff Sgt. Rick Fligort, USAF, public affairs, Tyndall Air Force Base; Barbara Johnson, division marketing administrator, Electromagnetic Systems Division/Raytheon; Kim Kitson, communications, McDonnell Douglas; Dennis W. Kuklovsky, manager, Phalanx marketing development, General Dynamics; Marc P. Lasky, office of ship construction, Maritime Administration; Shelley M. Lauzon, senior news officer, Woods Hole Oceanographic Institution; Lt. Brian Lippi, USN, public affairs, Special Boat Unit 12; Tom Luichinger, ship analyst, Office of the Chief of Naval Operations; Lt. Comdr. George McEwen, USN, office of the Assistant CNO (Undersea Warfare); Steve Millikin, editor of *The Hook;* Lt. Rob Newell and Lt. Maureen Olson, public affairs office, Bureau of Medicine and Surgery; Penny Norman, historian's office, Joint Chiefs of Staff; Ronald O'Rourke, senior naval analyst, Congressional Research Service; Hank Pangborn, public affairs officer, Naval Undersea Warfare Engineering Station; Rear Adm. Kendall Pease, USN, former public affairs officer, Commander in Chief Atlantic Command/Atlantic Fleet; David L. Perry, regional manager for Navy programs of FMC; Capt. Rosario Rausa, USNR (Ret.), editor of *Wings of Gold;* Capt. Carter B. Refo, USN, commanding officer, USS INDEPENDENCE (CV 62); John Romer, public affairs, Naval Air Warfare Center (Patuxent River, Md.); David J. Rossetti, business development, Electronic Systems Group/Westinghouse Electric; Sandy Russell, managing editor, *Naval Aviation News;* Sam Salem, Loral Defense Systems; Nick Sandiford, Jim Ward, and PA1 David Santos, USCG, of the public affairs office, Coast Guard Headquarters; Lt. Comdr. Kenneth Satterfield, public affairs, Department of Defense; James Schlueter, McDonnell Douglas Missile Systems; Ellen Shapiro, Tom Warring, and Jim Scott of the public affairs office, David Taylor Research Center; Col. Eugene E. Shoults, USMC (Ret.), manager, amphibious warfare and strategic sealift, Naval Sea Systems Command; Harold D. Sisson, director of marketing, Textron Marine Systems; Tommy H. Thomason, formerly with the XV-15/V-22 programs, Bell Helicopter Textron; William Tuttle, public relations, Sikorsky Aircraft; Judy Van Benthuysen, head of research and public inquiries, CHINFO; John Vosilla, public relations, Grumman Aerospace; Capt. Neil P. Walsh, USN, head, Combat Systems Branch, Assistant CNO for Undersea Warfare; Bill A. Warner, manager, photographic services, McDermott, Inc.; Capt. David W. Yeager, former chief of the program services division, NOAA; and Maj. Doug Yurovich, USMC, Naval Air Test Center, Patuxent River, Md.

Most useful in preparing this edition has been the column "Weapons and Technology" by Edward J. Walsh in the magazine *Sea Power,* monthly journal of the U.S. Navy League.

Several members of the Naval Institute staff made major contributions to making this edition a reality, most especially Carol Swartz, who edited the manuscript and provided sage guidance; Mary Lou Kenney, who gave needed encouragement and perspective; Sandra Kaline, who helped with many, many details; and Patty Maddocks, Mary Beth Straight, and Linda Cullen, who undertook photo research and provided friendship.

Steven Llanso of the Naval Institute–sponsored Military Database of the United Communications Group was a constant source of help, while Ted Minter was a constant source of data conformation.

As with many of my projects, I appreciate the guidance of Fred Rainbow, editor in chief of the Naval Institute *Proceedings,* and Dr. Scott Truver, director of studies and analysis at Techmatics, Inc. Robert Anderson, Edward Feege, and John Patrick of Dr. Truver's staff also provided assistance.

Compilation of the next edition of *Ships and Aircraft* begins almost immediately, to be published subsequently. Comments and photographs should be submitted to the author in care of the Naval Institute.

NORMAN POLMAR

THE NAVAL INSTITUTE GUIDE TO THE Ships and Aircraft of the U.S. Fleet

CHAPTER 1

State of the Fleet

The shape of things to come: The ARLEIGH BURKE will be the principal surface combatant produced by the United States for the remainder of this decade and, in modified form, probably well into the twenty-first century. The ship has less combat capability than the TICONDEROGA-class ships. (Giorgio Arra)

The U.S. military establishment is in a state of massive change. The end of the Cold War—signified by the independence of Eastern Europe and the breakup of the Soviet Union—and the U.S. domestic fiscal problems have led to massive reductions in the U.S. armed forces. These reductions, euphemistically called a "build down," will result in a smaller percentage of the U.S. budget being spent on national defense than any time since the beginning of World War II more than 50 years ago.

The Navy's share of this "build down" will see the size of the fleet drop from almost 600 ships in the late 1980s to perhaps as few as 350 ships in the year 2000. At the same time, the number of Navy personnel is scheduled to drop from almost 600,000 in the late 1980s to about 500,000 men and women, and Marine Corps personnel from almost 200,000 to 177,000.

Still, in many respects the Navy is suffering less reduction than the other military services. This is especially true with respect to the investment in surface ship construction, where the Navy's aircraft carrier, destroyer, and amphibious ship programs are continuing at a reasonable pace. As will be discussed below, the Bush administration's six-year shipbuilding program presented in 1992, when compared to the program submitted a year earlier—before the demise of the Soviet Union—represents a net *increase* in surface ship tonnage

Sean O'Keefe, Acting Secretary of the Navy since July 1992, and Admiral Frank B. Kelso, the Chief of Naval Operations since July 1990. (U.S. Navy, PHC Jeff Elliott)

and expenditures. New submarine funding, however, has suffered a staggering blow. No submarines are now scheduled for authorization for seven years, from fiscal year 1991 through 1997.

Thus, the Bush administration appeared to recognize the continued potential importance of naval forces in the troubled world that is anticipated for the 1990s and beyond. That trouble is unlikely to be caused by Russian (née Soviet) aggression and intervention. Rather, regional and local instability, crises, and outright conflict in the Third World will be caused by economic, religious, and personal aggressiveness.

The 1980s saw a parade of such events, several of which required U.S. political-military intervention: the Grenada rescue operation, the assault on Panama, the air strikes against Libya, the futile attempts at peacekeeping in Lebanon, the Persian Gulf conflicts, and the evacuation of Americans and other foreign nationals under serious threat from Liberia and Somalia, were all beyond the scope of U.S.–Soviet competition.[1] In all of these operations, except for Panama, U.S. naval forces had major roles.

Substantive issues concerning the future of the Navy are being affected by the fallout of several sex scandals, especially the manhandling of women (including naval aviators) at the Tailhook Association's fall 1991 symposium. These scandals and the failure of the Naval Investigative Service to conduct an effective inquiry led to the resignation of Secretary of the Navy H. Lawrence Garrett in July 1992. The scandals also led to the reassignment of a number of senior officers, and Congress delayed the promotions of several thousand officers.

In addition to the sexual issues, the Navy's image has been tarnished by allegations about the circumstances of the VINCENNES (CG 49) shootdown of the Iranian Air Bus in 1990, cancellation of several major naval aircraft programs, failure to develop an effective submarine program (reflected in termination of SEAWOLF/SSN 21 construction at two ships), open disagreements between Admiral Bruce DeMars, head of the Navy's nuclear propulsion program, and the Navy's leadership on submarine and carrier issues, and other difficulties.

In this clouded environment, the Navy was suddenly subjected to a major staff reorganization in 1992, with more changes anticipated that will reduce the status and prestige of the Navy's leadership (see chapter 5). All of these issues are having an adverse effect on personnel morale and attitudes, and is in turn affecting virtually all decisions related to the Navy being made by the Navy, Department of Defense, and Congress.

---

1. So, too, was the Argentine-British conflict in the Falklands, which was, in most respects, a maritime conflict.

THE GULF CONFLICT

The Iraqi invasion of Kuwait on 2 August 1990 led to the largest concentration of U.S. naval forces since World War II. Within one hour of the invasion the INDEPENDENCE (CV 62) battle group in the Indian Ocean and the DWIGHT D. EISENHOWER (CVN 69) in the eastern Mediterranean were ordered into the Red Sea and Gulf of Oman, respectively.

The official Department of Defense report on the Gulf War notes that these carrier groups "were the only sustainable U.S. combat forces nearby when Iraq invaded Kuwait."[2] These forces probably had a restraining effect on Saddam Hussein's plans for further aggression into Saudi Arabia and the Gulf States.

The two carriers—each with some 85 combat aircraft—arrived in the area ready to fight. In comparison, the initial land-based tactical aircraft flown from the United States arrived in Saudi Arabia after a 15-hour flight with seven air-to-air refuelings from tanker aircraft; the combat readiness of these F-15 fighters and their pilots was seriously reduced after their trans-ocean deployment. Simulta-

neously, the timely arrival of the 82nd Airborne Division from the United States provided a light infantry force to defend U.S. bases in Saudi Arabia. The arrival a few days later of two Maritime Prepositioning Squadrons (MPS) provided tanks, artillery, and other equipment for two Marine brigades that were airlifted into the area, providing the first U.S. armor capability "in country."

Also significant, on 16 August 1990 the Navy imposed a United Nations–declared blockade on shipping bound for Iraq, with several Coalition navies joining that effort. On 31 August the missile cruiser BIDDLE (CG 34) intercepted and stopped the Iraqi tanker AL KARAMAH, and a combined Navy–Coast Guard team carried out the first ship boarding of the conflict. The tanker was empty and allowed to continue en route to Jordan's port of Aqaba. The Coalition ships soon averaged some 40 ship intercepts and 4 boardings per day; the U.S. destroyer O'BRIEN (DD 975) logged the Coalition's 1,000th ship intercept on 16 September when she stopped the Bahamian-flag tanker DAIMON. Sometimes the Coalition ship had to fire a shot across the bow of a merchant ship when it ignored a flashing light signal to stop. Only once was there active resistance: On 26 December U.S. and Coalition ships stopped the Iraqi-flag freighter IBN HALDOON ("Peace Ship"). After initially refusing requests to

---

2. Department of Defense, *Conduct of the Persian Gulf War—Final Report to Congress* (Washington, D.C.: April 1992), p. 250. This is the most comprehensive unclassified report available on the conflict.

A Tomahawk TLAM missile is launched from the battleship MISSOURI during the Gulf conflict. At left the missile is emerging from one of eight Armored Box Launchers (ABL) on the ship; at right the missile is clear of the launcher, but its wings, fins, and air scoop have not yet deployed. A Phalanx CIWS is in the foreground. (PH3 Brad Dillon, USN)

stop, the ship's crew attempted to prevent a boarding team from coming onto the ship. The U.S. sailors fired warning shots in the air and set off smoke and noise grenades. The resistance was overcome, and a search revealed cargo prohibited by the U.N. embargo.

By the time the war began in mid-January 1991 the Coalition ships had recorded 6,960 intercepts with 832 boardings. Thirty-six ships were diverted from their intended destinations because they carried prohibited cargo. The blockade was extended by the United Nations into 1992; on 13 April a team from the destroyer JOHN HANCOCK (DD 981) conducted the 4,000th boarding of a merchant ship by Coalition naval forces. More than 13,400 ships had been intercepted in the Persian Gulf-Arabian Sea area by that time, with some 250 of those ships having been diverted from their intended destination.

In all, the Coalition naval force numbered some 150 ships at its peak—100 U.S. ships and 50 naval ships from 17 other nations. These ranged from nuclear-propelled aircraft carriers to submarines, amphibious ships, auxiliaries, and minesweepers. The INDEPENDENCE entered the Persian Gulf on 1 October 1990, the first time that an aircraft carrier had entered that waterway since 1974. This operation demonstrated the feasibility of large carrier operations in the Gulf's relatively restricted waters. She was relieved in the Gulf on 1 November by the MIDWAY (CV 41), which had recently celebrated her 45th year in commission. Thereafter, aircraft carriers and battleships sailed regularly into the Gulf, demonstrating the ability of the U.S. "blue-water" fleet to operate in any waters where there is sufficient depth.

(The U.S. Navy did not send submarines into the Gulf, although there were contingency plans to send in nuclear-propelled submarines to lay mines off the Shatt-Al'-Arab waterway, i.e., Iraq's only port on the Persian Gulf. The Royal Navy did operate two diesel-electric submarines of the OBERON class in the Gulf, with one unit conducting at least two "special operations" while in the Gulf.[3])

From August 1990 through mid-January 1991, in Operation Desert Shield, the ships of the Navy's Military Sealift Command (MSC) and chartered merchant ships carried into Saudi Arabia and the Gulf States the equipment, supplies, water, fuel, munitions, and rations for a half-million U.S. troops and some foreign forces. Key ships in this movement were seven SL-7 cargo ships—the world's fastest merchant ships—the MPS ships, and a large number of fairly modern cargo ships that had been procured in the 1980s and laid up in the Ready Reserve Force managed by MSC and the Maritime

Administration.[4] Those ships had been procured with funds that many admirals felt could have been better spent on warships, but without those ships the U.S. military buildup in the Gulf would have taken far longer and suffered more difficulties.

In addition, a flotilla of 31 Navy amphibious ships carried 17,000 Marines into the Gulf in preparation for an amphibious assault. Although the Marines did not make an assault landing, the threat of such an operation did tie down several first-line Iraqi divisions along the coast in anticipation of one.[5] The amphibious ships were protected by U.S. and Coalition escort ships against possible Iraqi interference, while mine countermeasure ships located, swept, or destroyed almost 1,300 mines planted by Iraqi forces. And U.S. Navy SEALs joined the special forces of the U.S. Army and Air Force and other countries in penetrating into Iraqi territory.

4. There are eight SL-7s, but one suffered an engineering casualty on her initial voyage and became inoperative.
5. After the beginning of the Coalition ground assault, a Marine brigade made an "administrative" landing along the coast behind the front line to reinforce U.S. ground forces. Also, on 29 January a Marine battalion did raid an Iraqi-held island, and several feints were made against the coast.

A Navy ordnance disposal expert attaches an explosive charge to an Iraqi-laid LUGM contact mine during Operation Desert Storm. The diver is wearing a Mk 16 underwater breathing apparatus, which has low magnetic and acoustic signatures. (U.S. Navy)

3. Similarly, during the 1982 conflict in the Falklands, the Royal Navy was required to send an OBERON-class diesel submarine into the combat area to conduct special operations. Five British nuclear attack submarines were also employed in that conflict.

An Army OH-58D Kiowa helicopter—fitted with a mast-mounted sight and other special operations features—hovers near the destroyer KIDD (DDG 993) in the Persian Gulf. These helicopters flew from the KIDD and other Navy ships in the Gulf, an example of inter-service cooperation in the conflict. (Courtesy Bell Helicopter Textron)

Once the air campaign began on 17 January 1991—Operation Desert Storm—the Navy's contribution to the fighting began with Tomahawk Land-Attack Missile (TLAM) strikes, which led the air assault against high-priority targets in Iraq. A total of 282 Tomahawks struck targets in Iraq with a high degree of accuracy. They were followed by Coalition land- and carrier-based aircraft. The planes from the six U.S. carriers flew some 20 percent of the sorties in the war. Initially four carriers operated in the Red Sea (RS) and two in the Persian Gulf (PG) with the following air wings:[6]

CV 41	MIDWAY	Carrier Air Wing 5	(PG)
CV 60	SARATOGA	Carrier Air Wing 17	(RS)
CV 61	RANGER	Carrier Air Wing 2	(PG)
CV 66	AMERICA	Carrier Air Wing 1	(RS)
CV 67	JOHN F. KENNEDY	Carrier Air Wing 3	(RS)
CVN 71	THEODORE ROOSEVELT	Carrier Air Wing 8	(RS)

Subsequently, two more carriers—the THEODORE ROOSEVELT and AMERICA—entered the Gulf, putting four carriers in that restricted body of water. In addition to conventional bombs, the aircraft used precision-guided weapons, including the SLAM, which was rushed into the conflict before formally being declared operational. Naval aircraft provided some support for other Coalition aircraft, especially Navy E-2C Hawkeye radar aircraft and Navy and Marine EA-6B Prowler electronic aircraft, the latter employing HARM missiles. Tactical Air-Launched Decoys (TALD) were also used extensively by naval aircraft in the electronic phase of the conflict.

The six carriers flew almost 20,000 sorties during the war, delivering more than 10,500 tons of ordnance. Twenty Marine AV-8B Harriers flew strikes from the helicopter carrier NASSAU

(LHA 4) and other Harriers operated from bases ashore, while other Navy and Marine aircraft flew a variety of combat and combat support missions from shore bases.

Shortly after the air campaign began, Coalition warships began bombarding coastal targets in Kuwait and the offshore islands held by Iraqi forces. The battleships MISSOURI (BB 63) and WISCONSIN (BB 64), the world's last operational dreadnoughts, bombarded the targets with their 16-inch (406-mm) guns. The battleships as well as other naval and ground operations were supported by Pioneer aerial drones, marking their first-time use in a combat environment by U.S. forces.

In general, U.S. naval forces were highly successful in the Gulf conflict. Beyond the combat operations and the blockade, Navy and Coast Guard personnel provided invaluable logistic, support, and security functions. The principal shortfall of U.S. naval activity in the Gulf was in mine countermeasures. Despite the mine problems encountered in the Red Sea in 1984 and in the Persian Gulf in 1988, the Navy was still ill-prepared for the ordeal of countering hundreds of both simple and highly sophisticated Iraqi-laid mines.

Initially, six MH-53E Sea Dragon helicopters were employed to seek out and destroy mines. Additionally, three MSOs and the new AVENGER (MCM 1) were transported to the Gulf by heavy-lift ship for the sweep operation. Coalition navies contributed additional MCM ships. Unfortunately, U.S. mapping and sweeping capabilities lagged behind those of the allies. The Aegis cruiser PRINCETON (CG 59) detonated two mines on 18 February 1991 and was damaged; that same day the helicopter carrier TRIPOLI (LPH 10) struck another mine. The carrier was, at the time, operating MH-53E helicopters and serving as flagship for the mine force. Neither ship was in danger of foundering.[7]

6. The INDEPENDENCE and EISENHOWER had departed the area prior to the outbreak of fighting.

7. That was not the case when the frigate SAMUEL B. ROBERTS (FFG 58) struck a mine in the Gulf in 1988 and came perilously close to sinking.

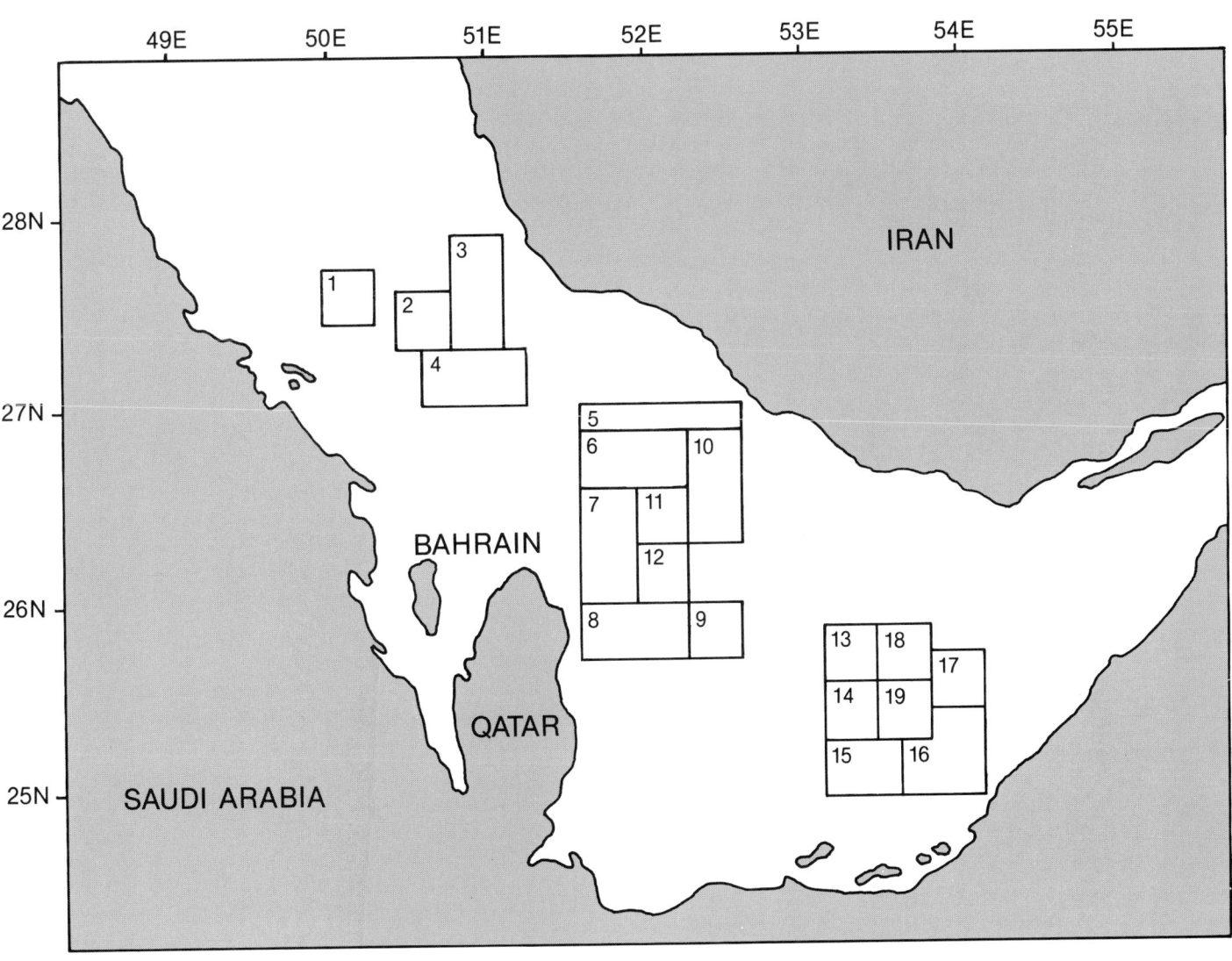

Persian Gulf deployments for Operation Desert Storm, 17 January 1991, courtesy Royal Australian Navy. (William Clipson)

1	*AAW/Combat SAR Station* BUNKER HILL (CG 52) LEFTWICH (DD 984) CURTS (FFG 38) NICHOLAS (FFG 47)	**4**	*AAW/Strike Station* MISSOURI (BB 63) WISCONSIN (BB 64) FIFE (DD 991) CARDIFF (British DDG)	**9**	PAUL F. FOSTER (DD 964)

14	TERRA NOVA (Canadian FF)

10 SYDNEY (Australian FFG)

15 LIBECCIO (Italian FFG)

2 *AAW/Strike Station*
MOBILE BAY (CG 53)

5 MACDONOUGH (DDG 39)

11 *Carrier Battle Group*
MIDWAY (CV 41)
PRINCETON (CG 59)

16 ZEFFIRO (Italian FFG)

6 BRISBANE (Australian DDG)

17 OLFERT FISCHER (Danish FFG)

3 *AAW Station*
WORDEN (CG 18)
GLOUCESTER (British DDG)

7 MARVIN SHIELDS (FF 1066)

12 *Carrier Battle Group*
RANGER (CV 61)
VALLEY FORGE (CG 50)

18 no ship assigned

8 PHILIPS VAN ALMONDE (Dutch FFG)

13 JEAN DE VIENNE (French DD)

19 ATHABASCAN (Canadian DDG)

Still, naval accomplishments were considerable and failures few in the Gulf war. Further, the Navy-Marine forces were deployed into the Gulf area while at the same time continuing a deployment off the coast of Liberia from July 1990 until January 1991 to provide security for the U.S. embassy and to evacuate over 2,400 civilians from the country during a violent insurrection (Operation Sharp Edge). Then, on 3 January 1991, the U.S. embassy in Mogadishu, Somalia, asked for prompt evacuation as the two-week-old civil war was threatening all Westerners in that African country. Armed looters were already in the American embassy compound. Operation Eastern Exit was started immediately, with a Navy amphibious group in the Indian Ocean launching two CH-53E Sea Stallion helicopters carrying 50 Marines plus 10 Navy SEALs and medical personnel.

The ship was 460 nautical miles (851 km) from Mogadishu, and the helicopters required two night aerial refuelings by Marine KC-130 cargo planes flying from Bahrain. The two helicopters landed on the embassy grounds early on 4 January. Some of the Marines they brought in set up a defense of the embassy while the others went into the corpse-littered streets to rescue Americans and other foreigners,

including the Soviet ambassador and his staff. That same day, even as the embassy was being fired on, the CH-53Es took off with 62 evacuees and safely landed on the helicopter carrier GUAM (LPH 9). The next day other helicopters from the carrier began bringing out more evacuees; a total of 260 men, women, and children from ten countries were successfully lifted out of the besieged capital.

The subsequent scope and magnitude of naval operations in the Gulf War were significant. They were overshadowed, however, by the six weeks of dramatic ground and air operations that were—for the first time in history—shown live on television. The coverage and continuous news briefings at Central Command headquarters in Riyadh, Saudi Arabia, and in the Pentagon in Washington, D.C., provided an unprecedented flow of information to the American public and Congress. Those perspectives of the success of the air and ground conflict, abetted by a third-rate U.S. Navy public affairs effort, led to impressions and, indeed, "lessons" of the Gulf War that would greatly influence military planning and budgets in the post–Cold War era.

THE SHIPS

The rapid decline of the U.S. fleet in the 1970s, following the conclusion of the Vietnam War and the retirement of large numbers of wartime-built ships, was arrested in the 1980s during the Reagan administration. Mr. Reagan's Secretary of the Navy, John Lehman, who held that post for six years, demanded and received White House and congressional backing for a 600-ship fleet.[8]

Centering his 600-ship fleet on 15 aircraft carriers and 4 rejuvenated battleships, Mr. Lehman did not fully explain the other 581 so-called "battle force" ships. An analysis of public statements by Mr. Lehman and other Navy officials indicates that the following ships were planned for the year 2000; this was in addition to certain categories of support and sealift ships:[9]

20–36	SSBN	strategic missile submarines
6	AS/AK	SSBN support ships
100	SSN	attack submarines
15	CV/CVN	aircraft carriers
4	BB	battleships
33	CG/CGN	missile cruisers
67	DDG	missile destroyers
100–110	FF/FFG	frigates (26 Naval Reserve)
6	PHM	small missile combatants
31	MCM/MHC	mine countermeasure ships (all Naval Reserve)
75		amphibious ships (5 Naval Reserve)
60		auxiliary ships (10 Naval Reserve)
25+	T-AGOR	ocean surveillance ships

Obviously, such a fleet composition was beyond likelihood, especially the strategic missile submarine force, in view of strategic arms limitation agreements with the Soviet Union.

Regardless, Mr. Lehman's departure from the Pentagon coincided with the end of the Reagan arms buildup in most areas (with the notable exception of the strategic defense initiative or "star

wars"). The subsequent funding cutback for most of the defense programs, the lack of direction by the Navy's leadership, and the feeling in many quarters of the Pentagon that "the Navy got theirs and now it's our turn" combined to impact on the Navy reductions.

The actual number of "battle force" ships reached almost 570 ships for a sustained period in the late 1980s. This included 14 aircraft carriers and 4 battleships.

Afterwards, the number of active ships dropped precipitously—to to 545 ships in late 1990 and 475 in mid-1992. Table 1-1 shows the Navy's early 1992 planning for end-of-fiscal year 1993 and 1995 force levels. But, by the late 1990s a fleet of as few as some *350 ships is probable under current level of "straight-line" budget planning.*

The future U.S. fleet will be smaller than the 600 ships planned under Mr. Lehman, but it will be a relatively modern, effective force. Indeed, as shown in table 1-2, the shipbuilding program that the Bush administration put forward after the collapse of the Soviet Union in late 1991 shows the net loss of seven attack submarines and four surface ships. In the table, the administration proposals made in 1991 are shown to the left of the stroke, and the 1992 proposals are to the right.

The cancellation of the SEAWOLF (SSN 21) program was only marginally related to the end of the Cold War and was, instead, the result of the failure of the U.S. nuclear submarine community to develop an effective submarine program.[10] While there is a net loss of four surface ships, the changes from the 1991 plan to the 1992 plan show an *increase* in both surface ship tonnage and funding.

The "base force" for the armed services proposed by the Bush administration in early 1992, however, is unlikely to be supported by Congress. Indeed Senator Sam Nunn and Representative Les Aspin, the respective chairmen of the Senate and House Armed Services Committees, have put forth alternative force levels for U.S. military forces—all lower than the planned "base force." The proposal from Mr. Aspin proposes four options, shown in Table 1-3. Option D is really irrelevant, having more aircraft carriers and amphibious ships than the base force. Option C is the one endorsed by Mr. Aspin and

8. Mr. Lehman was Secretary of the Navy from February 1981 to April 1987. The only men to serve longer in that position were Claude A. Swanson, from 4 March 1933 until 7 July 1939 (6 years, 4 months), and Josephus Daniels, from 5 March 1913 to 5 March 1921 (8 years).

9. Even in his autobiographic *Command of the Seas* (New York: Scribners, 1988), which had the subtitle "Building the 600 Ship Navy," Lehman did not detail the composition of his planned fleet.

10. Only two SEAWOLFS will be built; see Addenda. A detailed analysis of the current shipbuilding situation is found in Dr. Scott C. Truver, "Tomorrow's Fleet," U.S. Naval Institute *Proceedings* (June 1992), pp. 43–51, and (July 1992), pp. 61–69.

High-mix ships will dominate the smaller, post–Cold War fleet. These are expected to include 62 of the Los Angeles-class attack submarines and 27 of the Ticonderoga-class missile cruisers, two of which are shown here with a British Invincible-class VSTOL carrier. (Giorgio Arra)

TABLE 1-1. POST–COLD WAR FORCE STRUCTURE (END OF FISCAL YEAR)

	1988	1993	1995	2000
Strategic Forces				
strategic missile submarines	37	24	23	18
Combatant Forces				
attack submarines	100*	90	89	66
aircraft carriers	14	13	12	12
surface combatants	217	143	152	132
battleships	3			
cruisers				33
destroyers				64
frigates				35
patrol combatants†	6	6	6	0
amphibious ships‡	63	58	53	~50
mine warfare	4	15	15	15
combat logistics	58	54	51	~30
Support Forces				
auxiliary ships	66	58	50	~30
Totals	565	461	451	~350

*Includes three non-nuclear attack submarines (SS); transport/special operations submarines are included in this category.

†PHM-type hydrofoil missile combatants; special warfare craft are not included.

‡Includes fleet/amphibious command ships (LCC).

Source: 1988, 1993, 1995 data are from *Department of the Navy 1992 Posture Statement* (February–March 1992); year 2000 data estimated by the author. NRF-operated ships are *not* included in this table.

TABLE 1-3. FORCE STRUCTURE OPTIONS

	Base Force	Option D	Option C	Option B	Option A
Attack submarines	80	50	40	40	20
Aircraft carriers	12	14	11	7	5
Amphibious ships	50	82	50	50	50
Totals	450	430	340	290	220

the House-passed version of the defense budget resolution for fiscal 1993.

Note that the carrier and attack submarine levels decline precipitously while amphibious ships remain level at some 50 units. The surface combatant strength—cruisers, destroyers, and frigates—will be reduced in proportion to the carrier force and the overall number of ships. The number of surface ships should probably be *increased* if carriers are reduced, to provide some compensation in firepower (especially Tomahawks) and area coverage. But logic and analyses will have little to do with congressional decisions during the 1990s as political, social, and fiscal concerns will guide defense legislation.

Strategic missile submarines: Under the strategic arms agreements with the late Soviet Union, the United States was limited in the number of weapons that could be deployed. The ultimate U.S. strategic "base force" was to include 18 OHIO (SSBN 726)-class submarines armed with Trident C-4 and D-5 missiles. All earlier SSBNs would be retired by 1997–1998, when the last OHIO-class SSBN will be completed.

When this edition went to press, there were proposals to accelerate the retirement of the 11 remaining SSBNs that had been updated from their original Polaris-Poseidon configurations to carry the Trident C-4 missile. Their earlier (pre-1997) retirement would save considerable operating and maintenance funds.

The 18 Trident SSBNs will constitute the majority of U.S. strategic offensive weapons for the foreseeable future. The "new base force" now proposed will see the land-based ICBM force comprising only 500 Minuteman III missiles, each armed with a single Re-entry Vehicle (RV). While 18 planned Trident submarines will carry a total of 432 missiles with 3,456 separately targeted RVs, a proposed reduction of the sea-based force by one-third could cut the number of RVs to some 2,300. The major strategic missile issues are (1) whether or when the first eight Trident submarines, built with C-4 missiles, will be upgraded to the D-5 missile, and (2) how the proposed one-third RV reduction will be accomplished.

(There will also be a U.S. "strategic" bomber force, but those aircraft will be assigned to primarily conventional/theater strike missions.)

In 22 April of 1992 the Trident missile submarine TENNESSEE (SSBN 734) completed the 3,000th fleet ballistic missile submarine patrol—31 years after the pioneer GEORGE WASHINGTON (SSBN 598) concluded the first such patrol. Such calculations of U.S. deterrent patrols by submarines armed with nuclear-tipped missiles do not take into account the 41 patrols conducted by *guided* missile submarines from mid-1960 to mid-1964. Those patrols were undertaken in the North Pacific by one nuclear-propelled (SSGN) and four diesel-electric (SSG) submarines carrying the surface-launched Regulus missile.

These strategic missile submarine operations were a major factor in the U.S. nuclear deterrent posture during the Cold War.

Attack submarines: The defense budget put forward by the Bush administration in January 1992 cancelled procurement of all submarines of the SEAWOLF class except for two units. This action ended a trouble-plagued program that had suffered large cost increases. The implications of the SEAWOLF cancellation are severe. It means that no additional submarines will be ordered from U.S. shipyards until at least 1997.

The year 2000 attack submarine (SSN) force level will likely consist of the two SEAWOLFS and 62 of the LOS ANGELES (SSN 688) class, plus two older submarines employed in the transport/special operations role. Without new construction, beyond the year 2010 the attack submarine force level will drop rapidly as the LOS ANGELES-class units, completed from 1976 onward at a high production rate, reach the end of their planned 30-year service life.

If the 62 LOS ANGELES-class submarines are retained for 30 years, and if a new SSN design enters production in fiscal 1998, and if a production rate of 2½ SSNs per year could be achieved, the attack submarine force would still decline at the rate of at least two submarines per year after 2010. But that all of these conditions would be met is unlikely, and the rate of decline could be greater.

Thus, the future of the SSN force was far from clear when this edition went to press. Whereas the two previous Chiefs of Naval

TABLE 1-2. SIX-YEAR SHIPBUILDING PLAN (JANUARY 1991/JANUARY 1992 BUDGET REQUESTS)

Type/Class		FY 1992	FY 1993	FY 1994	FY 1995	FY 1996	FY 1997
SSN 21	SEAWOLF	1/0	1/0	1/0	1/0	2/0	1/0
CVN 68	NIMITZ	—	—	—	1/1	—	—
DDG 51	ARLEIGH BURKE	5/5	4/4	3/3	3/4	4/4	3/4
LX		—	—	—	1/1	—	1/1
LHD 1	WASP	—	—	—	—	0/1	—
LSD 49	HARPERS FERRY	1/0	1/0	—	—	—	—
MHC 51	OSPREY	2/3	2/2	1/0	—	—	—
MHC(V)		—	—	—	1/1	—	2/2
AGOR		2/2	2/0	2/2	1/0	—	—
T-AGOS		0/1	1/0	1/1	2/2	—	0/1
AOE 6	SUPPLY	1/1	—	—	—	—	—
AR		—	—	—	—	1/1	—
ARS		—	—	1/0	—	2/0	—

Losses: 7 SSN, 2 LSD, 3 AGOR, 3 ARS.
Gains: 2 DDG, 1 LHD, 1 T-AGOS.

The Australian ASW frigate DARWIN and her S-70B Seahawk helicopter cover a boarding by British troops from a Lynx helicopter during Gulf blockade operations. The DARWIN, a sister ship to the U.S. OLIVER HAZARD PERRY (FFG 7) class, is a low-mix warship. (OS2 John Bouvia, USN)

Operations (James Watkins, 1982–1986, and Carlisle A.H. Trost, 1986–1990) had given unconditional support to the SEAWOLF, labeling it their No. 1 shipbuilding priority, the current CNO, Admiral Frank B. Kelso II, has taken a more balanced view of the situation and refused to give the SEAWOLF his absolute support. As early as August 1990, Admiral Kelso initiated a program known as "The Way Ahead" in response to concerns about future funding that would be available to the Navy.[11] Kelso's memo noted that "the current . . . building rate is not adequate to sustain force levels and the industrial base which require the construction [of] two to three SSNs per year. Therefore, we must commence development of a lower-cost SSN to complement the SSN-688/SSN-21s."

The new design is labeled Centurion (for the next century). The Naval Sea Systems Command soon submitted concepts that strongly resembled the SSN-21. That design was rejected by the Navy's leadership as being unresponsive. The design reflected the attitude of the hard-core nuclear propulsion community—that only the SEAWOLF was acceptable; there could be no compromise. It was precisely this attitude that created the present situation.

A new study/design effort is under way, seeking to develop a lower-cost SSN that will be acceptable to a now-sensitized and fiscally austere Congress.[12] It is to be hoped that the new SSN design will incorporate the new technologies being explored by the Defense Advanced Research Projects Agency (DARPA) and the Navy and will be affordable. And, coupled with the application of cruise missiles, satellite communications, over-the-horizon targeting, and other features, attack submarines should have an even greater role in future political-military operations.

Also critical is the future of the two shipyards that still construct nuclear submarines in the United States, the Electric Boat Division of General Dynamics Corp., in Groton, Conn., and Newport News Shipbuilding, part of the Tenneco organization, in Virginia.[13] The

last of the submarines currently under construction in those two yards will be completed by 1997. After that, Electric Boat, which constructs only submarines, will have only overhaul work until a new submarine program is started. It is unlikely that Electric Boat could survive just on overhauls. (Newport News now constructs aircraft carriers, does both commercial and surface combatant work, and will overhaul-refuel at least three nuclear cruisers in the 1990s.)

Aircraft carriers: The Navy is scheduled to retain 12 aircraft carriers in service plus a training carrier (the FORRESTAL/AVT 59). Keeping that many carriers in commission could be difficult for both political and fiscal reasons, with the Air Force seeking to have manned bombers replace the carrier in the conventional/theater strike roles—to some extent a replay of the infamous carrier-versus-B-36 bomber controversy of the late 1940s. However, so long as "where are the carriers?" continues to be among the first questions asked by White House officials when there is an overseas crisis, a large force of carriers will be retained.

Admiral Kelso has labeled aircraft carriers and amphibious ships as his No. 1 shipbuilding priorities.[14] The Bush administration has decided to continue the costly modernization-refueling of the nuclear carrier ENTERPRISE (CVN 65), and a tenth nuclear carrier is provided in the fiscal 1995 program (the CVN 76). A future reduction in the carrier force is possible, with ten ships (plus a training carrier) the number most often mentioned. Such a force in the late 1990s would consist of ten nuclear ships; or, if one nuclear ship is in long-term overhaul/refueling, it would include the oil-burning INDE-PENDENCE (CV 62), home-ported in Japan.

As critical as the number of carriers is the issue of carrier-based aircraft (see below).

Surface combatants: The planned 27 Aegis cruisers of the TICON-DEROGA class will be completed, while the smaller Aegis destroyers of the BURKE class have survived a number of political-budgetary hurdles with an average of four ships per year planned for the foreseeable future. Along with six under-armed nuclear cruisers (CGN 36–41), the Aegis ships will provide a smaller but highly effective surface combatant force for the future. In total numbers,

11. Enclosure "The Way Ahead" to memorandum from OP-80 dated 4 January 1991.
12. The Department of Defense has directed the Navy to examine also the potential for non-nuclear submarines in the U.S. Navy; based on an official's statement during the February 1992 budget briefings, that subject has already been rejected out of hand by the Navy.
13. In the 1960s the United States had seven shipyards constructing nuclear-propelled submarines.

14. Adm. Kelso, at meeting of the Naval & Maritime Correspondents Circle, Washington, D.C., 17 December 1991. Adm. Kelso, like Watkins and Trost, is a nuclear submarine officer.

this force will probably consist of up to 33 cruisers and 64 destroyers.

The frigate force is being reduced—only a small number are to be retained in active service—with others retained in various levels of reserve availability.

No new surface combatant construction is now envisioned beyond BURKE-class variations, although the issue of a new "low-cost" surface combatant is periodically put forward.

The four battleships of the Reagan-Lehman era have been retired. They were very expensive to operate, and while they did provide effective naval gunfire and launch 18 percent of the Tomahawk missiles used in the Gulf conflict, the value of the shore bombardment was questionable in view of the allied aerial bombardment, while other ships in the area could have provided the 52 Tomahawk missiles that they launched.

Amphibious ships: The long-standing amphibious requirement to carry 1⅓ Marine Expeditionary Forces (MEF) has been reduced, and while the planned amphibious force is being cut (as is the Fleet Marine Force), the "amphib" modernization is continuing. The six-year shipbuilding plan put forth by the Bush administration in 1992 cancels two LSDs, but adds a much larger helicopter carrier (LHD) and continues the procurement of the new LX design.

The helicopter carrier NASSAU operated a largely AV-8B Harrier "air group" in the Gulf conflict, again demonstrating the feasibility of VSTOL operations from amphibious ships. The Navy's current interest in the development of an advanced VSTOL aircraft could have major implications for the future of amphibious ships being employed in broader naval missions.

Mine Countermeasures: The new AVENGER mine countermeasures ship, after some "teething" problems were solved, performed well in the Gulf conflict as did three earlier ocean minesweepers (MSO). The effectiveness of the MH-53E helicopters has been questioned, but a related issue is how well the helicopters were employed and whether the proper equipment was available to them. And, based on Gulf War experience, major mine warfare support ships are to be acquired. The IWO JIMA (LPH 2)-class helicopter carriers are to be converted to MCM support ships; subsequently, one or two heavy lift ships will be acquired for MCM transport.

The post–Gulf War emphasis on mine countermeasure forces in the U.S. Navy will probably be transitory, and will dissipate in the near term as mine warfare continues to be an under-supported activity, with few incentives for a career in this field. With the current "system," this is expected to occur despite recognition of the problem by the current CNO:

> I believe there are some fundamentals about mine warfare that we should not forget. Once mines are laid, they are quite difficult to get rid of. That is not likely to change. It is probably going to get worse, because mines are going to become more sophisticated.[15]

Also, the planned movement of virtually all surface mine warfare ships to Ingleside, Texas, will remove the mine force from the fleet's

operating bases, a factor that will further inhibit the support of the mine force and an understanding of its importance. (At this writing the MCM helicopters were scheduled to remain at their current air stations, but movement of those squadrons to the nearby Corpus Christi Naval Air Station is also being considered.)

The Navy has almost consistently failed to understand the significance—and threat—of mine warfare. As a Marine Corps officer recently wrote in the Navy's professional journal: "If the Navy refuses to solve this problem, the [mine countermeasures] responsibility and resources should be given to those who will."[16] The Coast Guard may be the better service to operate the nation's mine countermeasure forces.

(The Gulf conflict also provided important lessons in the area of mine warfare when the Marine Corps initiated new programs to counter advanced land mines.)

Auxiliary ships: The reduction in the size of the fleet and the proportion of forward deployments will reduce the requirements for auxiliary ships. Also, the decrease of the Russo-Soviet submarine threat has led to the decision to deactivate all 18 of the monohull T-AGOS sonar surveillance ships.

New auxiliary ships are being built, but these will be mostly the larger, more specialized ships (e.g., multi-product replenishment ships and repair ships). Smaller, less sophisticated ships (e.g., tugs and salvage ships) will suffer in future programs.

Also, an increasing number of auxiliary ships will be manned by civilian crews of the Military Sealift Command and, possibly, by the Naval Reserve Force.

Sealift: The success of the Navy's sealift efforts in Desert Shield/Desert Storm has led to additional support for increasing both the Maritime Prepositioning Force and the sealift ships. Special problems identified in the Gulf included obtaining sufficient merchant seamen to man the ships, U.S. and overseas port facilities, and cargo handling. These problems are being addressed, with the Army as well as the Marine Corps, Navy, and Air Force to employ forward-deployed material in future MPS deployments. The Army is particularly interested in the MPS concept following the refusal of Saudi Arabia to allow the prepositioning of U.S. Army equipment in that country. (A small amount of Army equipment is being placed ashore in Kuwait.)

The increasing significance of sealift operations and ships, including the MPS and APF (Afloat Prepositioning Ships) programs, have led to a new chapter, Sealift Ships, being added to this edition of *Ships and Aircraft*. This is in addition to the existing chapter on the Military Sealift Command (called Strategic Sealift in previous editions).

15. "Challenge on the Horizon" [Interview with Adm. Kelso], *Sea Power* (Navy League) (October 1991), p. 14.

16. Col. W.C. Gregson, USMC, commentary, U.S. Naval Institute *Proceedings* (April 1992), p. 34. Also see N. Polmar, "Mine Warfare Problems . . . and a Solution," *Proceedings* (December 1991), pp. 105–106, and Tamara Moser Melia, '*Damn the Torpedoes*'—A Short History of U.S. Naval Mine Countermeasures, 1777–1991 (Washington, D.C.: Naval Historical Center, 1991). Ms. Melia, a naval historian, spent considerable time with the MCM forces in the Gulf.

THE AIRCRAFT

The Navy continues to operate a large land- and carrier-based air arm, as does the Marine Corps. While the Navy has a relatively modern aircraft inventory, the recent cancellation of several programs will probably result in severe shortfalls by the end of the decade.

Recent decisions to cancel procurement of the F-14D Tomcat fighter, the A-12 Avenger attack aircraft, the P-7 maritime patrol aircraft, and the MV-22 Osprey tilt-rotor assault aircraft will have a major impact on naval force capabilities. Especially critical will be carrier-based aircraft, with only the F/A-18 Hornet now planned to be procured in sufficient numbers to meet long-term force requirements. However, the increase in development costs for the advanced E and F models of the F/A-18 could place those aircraft in jeopardy.

The possible reduction of active carrier strength to ten ships could ease the aircraft shortfall. Alternatively, with 12 carriers, air wings could be reduced from the current 84 aircraft to perhaps 65 or 70 planes. The major aircraft limitations facing those air wings will be long-range fighter and strike aircraft.

The decisions by Secretary of Defense Dick Cheney to cancel further F-14 Tomcat procurement and to halt upgrading the existing aircraft to the F-14D configuration will force total reliance on the F/A-18 for fleet air defense and strike escort. Range and radar limitations could limit the F/A-18 in those roles.

The situation is even more critical with respect to long-range strike missions. Even the planned follow-on F/A-18E/F variants will have less range/payload than the A-6E Intruder, and cannot serve as

The F/A-18 Hornet was flown in larger numbers in the Gulf conflict than any other naval aircraft. This is a Navy Hornet firing a Sparrow missile over the Gulf during an exercise. This plane is from VFA-136 aboard the DWIGHT D. EISENHOWER (CVN 69). (Comdr. John Leenhouts, USN)

effectively in a "buddy store" tanker role as the A-6E to extend strike ranges. The Hornet's mission versatility is some compensation, providing the ability to rapidly shift from the fighter to strike role, and vice versa; and, the use of S-3 Viking ASW aircraft as tankers will mitigate the range limitation in *some* scenarios. Thus, the development of the AX attack aircraft could be critical for the future of the carrier in the long-range strike role.

(The availability of Tomahawk land-attack and anti-ship missiles will alleviate the need to send carrier aircraft against some targets. But Tomahawks are relatively expensive. Today they are limited to attacking fixed, pre-designated targets, and they lack other advantages of manned aircraft.)

Carrier aircraft contributed about 20 percent of the Coalition inventory of combat aircraft to the Gulf War and conducted about 20 percent of the sorties flown. The F/A-18 was a clear star, demonstrating—as McDonnell Douglas/Northrop had advertised—that the aircraft could serve equally as a fighter or attack aircraft on the same mission. Other naval air stars included the E-2C Hawkeye and EA-6B Prowler electronic aircraft, while S-3B Viking anti-submarine aircraft, without submarine targets, served primarily as attack planes against shore and ship targets, and as tankers.

The Pioneer Remotely Piloted Vehicle (RPV) also demonstrated its efficacy in the Gulf, launched from ashore and the decks of

battleships by Army, Navy, and Marine personnel. After the Navy's distaste for drones following the experience with Drone Anti-Submarine Helicopters (DASH) in the 1960s, the Pioneer changed many minds about the value of such systems. The Navy also used Tactical Air-Launched Decoys (TALD) in the war to entice the Iraqis to turn on air-defense radars, marking them as targets for HARM anti-radar missiles.

Follow-on Unmanned Aerial Vehicles (UAV) are being pursued for naval use. But the planned development of manned airships to support naval operations has been cancelled, mainly for fiscal reasons. Simultaneously, in early 1992 the Coast Guard's unmanned aerostat surveillance program was transferred to the Army.

Another major issue facing naval aviation relates to the Marine Corps's medium-lift requirement. This requirement is now being met with several hundred CH-46E Sea Knight helicopters, with the Navy flying additional H-46s in the Search-And-Rescue (SAR) and Vertical Replenishment (VERTREP) roles. The V-22 tilt-rotor aircraft was developed for these and other naval roles. However, Secretary of Defense Dick Cheney cancelled that program, primarily on the basis of high cost; the Congress has continued funding the effort and pressing for procurement. The issue has not been resolved while the Marine CH-46Es are approaching the end of their already extended service life.

THE PEOPLE

The Navy deployed more than 80,000 men and women to the Persian Gulf during Operation Desert Shield, most afloat, but large numbers were also ashore, most providing support to the Marine units there. The Marine Corps strength in the Gulf consisted of some 76,000 men and women on the ground and another 17,000 on 31 amphibious ships in the Gulf.

The performance of these naval personnel, as well as the several hundred Coast Guard personnel in the Gulf, was exemplary. Naval personnel were in direct combat—in the air, on the ground, and at sea. Further, naval operations experienced a high degree of safety despite the high tempo of operations, including those during the six weeks of combat in Desert Storm. The impressive safety record contrasted sharply with numerous accidents in the Navy during the late 1980s when the Navy's leadership concentrated on safety, at times at the cost of readiness. The large number of safety problems included the disaster aboard the battleship IOWA in 1989 when powder bags being loaded into a 16-inch gun exploded. Forty-seven men died in that tragedy, which was compounded by the Navy leadership rushing to blame a sailor in an alleged suicide-murder action.[17]

The success of Gulf operations came as the Navy and Marine personnel strengths were being severely reduced. However, morale within the naval services remains high, with retention at an all-time high; reductions are being made primarily through attrition, including early retirement programs, controls on the retention of personnel, and reduced accessions. Attention is being given to the retention of high-quality personnel in key specialties. However, personnel in ratings that are over-manned will have the opportunity to reenlist if they have the right qualifications and are willing to retrain into skills that are not adequately manned. Sailors and Marines who enter civilian life are receiving financial planning, employment assistance, and help in relocating.

The Navy's leadership has made the decision not to suffer the problems created in the rapid reduction of Navy and Marine Corps personnel after the Vietnam War. However, the morale issue discussed above will present problems for the Navy's leadership for several years.

17. The Navy's leadership later conceded that it never had "clear and convincing evidence" with which to blame the sailor.

TACTICS AND OPERATIONS

The reduction of the fleet is causing an adjustment in naval operational concepts. The Navy's No. 1 warfighting priority under Admiral Kelso is tactical training. As a part of this effort, a new level of fleet standardization is being pursued. Over the past decades the Atlantic and Pacific Fleets have diverged in their operating procedures for a variety of reasons. These became apparent in the late 1970s when the two fleets began to share Indian Ocean commitments. Since then, and especially during the Gulf operations, these differences have become more evident.

The current effort will make fleet components the same from an operational and support viewpoint. Thus, ships being assigned to a unified commander (see chapter 4) will be "transparent" in that their training, relative capabilities, and logistics support will be identical.[18]

Similarly, "force packaging" is being considered whereby, for example, a carrier could carry a small number of Marines (perhaps 150–300) and troop helicopters to provide a carrier battle group with a limited assault capability—possibly having more political than military utility. Or, an amphibious group's LHA/LHD would have a squadron of Harriers on board to provide a limited fighter/attack force. Under these concepts, traditional labels for naval forces would have little meaning, while force flexibility for limited contingencies would be enhanced.

In conjunction with the new emphasis on tactical training, new "employment" and maintenance cycles are being developed. Related to the traditional 1-in-3 cycle of forward-deploying most naval surface ships, the Navy has developed the employment cycle shown in figure 1-1. In brief, a ship will spend eight months in refit/maintenance/trials, with the crew engaged in basic training. This will be followed by the ship being assigned to the "ready fleet," with the ship in port or operating with the Second or Third Fleet, and the crew undergoing intermediate and advanced warfare training for a period of six months. While with the "ready fleet," the ships will be able to deploy within four to ten days in response to a crisis.

Subsequently, the ship will be assigned to forward operations under a unified commander for six months. Major overhauls or nuclear refuelings would constitute a fourth phase, when appropriate.

While tactical training is the Navy's No. 1 warfighting priority, the Navy is giving priority to the development of strike weapons (Tomahawk missiles and carrier-based strike aircraft), and within the surface Navy the highest priority is for missile defense—Aegis ships with the SPY-1 radar and Standard missiles, and other missile and radar/fire control systems in non-Aegis ships.

The above emphasis contrasts with that of the late 1980s when anti-submarine warfare was accorded the highest priority. Although the Soviet Union with its large, modern submarine force has ceased to be a direct threat to the United States, the U.S. Navy should still have major concern for submarine activity.

For the past 30 years the U.S. Navy has concentrated on locating nuclear-propelled submarines, believing that if one could find a modern "nuke," locating and destroying diesel–electric submarines would be even simpler. That is not the case, however, as the Royal Navy discovered in the Falklands conflict, when a single Argentine-operated Type 209 submarine successfully evaded British anti-submarine efforts while threatening the British battle force for sustained periods.[19] The proliferation of modern non-nuclear submarines, possibly carrying cruise missiles and mines, demands increased attention to the Third World submarine threats. (Unfortunately, the U.S. Navy rarely trains against non-nuclear submarines because of the lack of such craft in the U.S. Navy for targets.)

Duration	—— 8 months ——	—— 6 months ——		—— 6 months ——
Status	Refit	Ready Fleet		Deployment
Assignment		Second or Third Fleet		Unified Commander*
Readiness	Baseline	Surge		Full
Training	Basic	Intermediate	Advanced	Exercises and Operations
Maintenance				

*Sixth or Seventh Fleet, or Naval Forces Central Command.

FIGURE 1-1. Evolving Employment Cycle

And the progress made by the late Soviet Navy in submarine and anti-submarine development and the unknown future status of Russia and those ex-Soviet naval forces (and the related research and development activities) prevent long-term complacency by the West.

The U.S. Strategic Defense Initiative (SDI) or "star wars" program has survived the Cold War era. That program has been enlarged to include GPALS (Global Protection Against Limited Strike). This component of SDI seeks to provide regional defense against ballistic missile attacks. Responsibility for development of the Anti-Tactical Ballistic Missile (ATBM) aspect of GPALS has been assigned to the Navy's Strategic Systems Program (formerly Strategic Systems Projects Office/Special Projects Office).

The ATBM mission envisions the use of forward-deployed naval forces to provide wide-area defense for specific geographic areas, including amphibious forces standing offshore and for Marines during a landing operation. Employing surveillance satellites and possibly long-endurance, unmanned surveillance aircraft to provide targeting data, the sea-based ATBM would make use of vertical-launch intercept missiles fired from cruisers and destroyers. Also being considered is the potential use of Trident SSBNs to launch intercept missiles if those submarines are no longer required for the strategic deterrent role.[20]

While the future of the world political-economic scene is far from clear, it is apparent that the same regional/local crises and conflicts of the type that have occurred over the past 45 years will continue. Indeed, without the restraints sometimes imposed by superpower rivalry, and with the proliferation of advanced weapons, the incidence of crisis and conflict could increase. In this context, according to the Navy's leadership:

> The Navy and Marine Corps are especially at home in today's fluid, multipolar environment. Although the United States will continue to support its traditional alliances in Europe and the Far East, the National Security Strategy is shifting *from* an emphasis on fixed forward defense against a continental superpower *to* flexible forward positioning of forces designed to shape and influence overseas regional events.[21]

18. A recent exposition of this concept and related considerations is Adm. Paul David Miller, USN, "Doing the Job With a Smaller Fleet," U.S. Naval Institute *Proceedings* (April 1992), pp. 54–59.

19. The Argentine submarine suffered from a faulty fire control computer (improperly wired).

20. The Trident SSBNs are also being considered for reconstituting satellites that might be damaged or destroyed in a future conflict. The 83-inch (210-cm) diameter Trident missile tubes could be used to place a one-ton satellite into orbit.

21. *Department of the Navy Posture Statement* (Washington, D.C.: February–March 1992), pp. 3–4.

CHAPTER 2

Glossary

The Coalition's Mine Countermeasures (MCM) efforts were an important element in the Gulf conflict. This Iraqi-laid horn mine was destroyed before it posed a threat to the battleship MISSOURI (BB 63), the centerpiece of a Surface Action Group (SAG). (PH3 Brad Dillon, USN)

AA	Anti-Aircraft
AAM	Air-to-Air Missile
AAW	Anti-Air Warfare
ABL	Armored Box Launcher
ACLS	Automatic Carrier Landing System
ASM	Air-to-Surface Missile
ASROC	Anti-Submarine Rocket
ASUW	Anti-Surface Warfare
ASW	Anti-Submarine Warfare
barrel	42 U.S. gallons (159.6 liters) fuel
beam	extreme width of hull
bhp	brake horsepower (for diesel engines)
BPDMS	Basic Point Defense Missile System
cal	caliber: (1) the diameter of a gun's bore; U.S. naval guns with a diameter of less than one inch (25.4 mm) are measured in "calibers"—fractions of an inch, as .50 calibers—or millimeters (mm) (2) the nominal length of the gun's bore expressed in multiples of its bore; thus, a 76-mm/62-cal gun has a bore or inner barrel length of 4,712 mm or approximately 185½ inches (4.7 m).
CBR	Chemical-Biological-Radiological
CinC	Commander in Chief
CIWS	Close-In Weapon System
COD	Carrier Onboard Delivery
CORT	Coherent Radar Transmitter
CVBG	Carrier Battle Group
DASH	Drone Anti-Submarine Helicopter
displacement	*light* (ship) is displacement of the ship and all machinery without crew, provisions, fuel munitions, other consumables, or aircraft
	standard is displacement of ship fully manned and equipped, ready for sea, including all provisions, munitions, and aircraft, but without fuels
	full load is displacement of ship complete and ready for service in all respects, including all fuels (aviation as well as ship)
DP	Dual Purpose (for use against air and surface targets)
draft	maximum draft of ship at full load, including fixed projections beneath the keel (e.g., sonar dome)
DWT	Deadweight Tonnage (ship's carrying capacity)
ECM	Electronic Countermeasures
ESM	Electronic Surveillance Measures
EW	Electronic Warfare
extreme width	maximum width at or about a carrier's flight deck, including fixed projections (e.g., "gun tubs")
FBM	Fleet Ballistic Missile (now referred to as SLBM)
FCS	Fire Control System
FLIR	Forward-Looking Infrared
fiscal	Fiscal Year (FY); from 1 October of the calendar year until 30 September of the following year (since June 1976; previously from 1 July through 30 June); the letter *S* in front of the year indicates Supplemental authorization

FRAM	Fleet Rehabilitation And Modernization
GFCS	Gunfire Control System
GRP	Glass-Reinforced Plastic
GRT	Gross Registered Tons (ship's tonnage measured in total cubic contents expressed in units of 100 cubic feet or 2.83 m³)
HTS	High Tensile Steel
HY	High Yield (steel)
IOC	Initial Operational Capability
IR	Infrared
ISAR	Inverse Synthetic Aperture Radar
IVDS	Independent Variable Depth Sonar
LAMPS	Light Airborne Multi-Purpose System (helicopter)
LASH	Lighter Aboard Ship
lbst	pounds static thrust
length	*waterline* indicates length on waterline (this length is generally the same as between perpendiculars [bp])
	overall indicates length overall
Mach	speed of sound at sea level; from the name of German physicist Ernest Mach
mack	[combined] mast and stack
MAD	Magnetic Anomaly Detection
manning	the number of personnel assigned to the ship or craft; the term *complement* is no longer used by the U.S. Navy
MarAd	Maritime Administration
MCLWG	Major Caliber Lightweight Gun
MCM	Mine Countermeasures
MEB	Marine Expeditionary Brigade
MEF	Marine Expeditionary Force
MEU	Marine Expeditionary Unit
Mk	Mark
Mod	Modification
MPS	Maritime Prepositioning Ship
MSC	Military Sealift Command (changed from Military Sea Transportation Service in 1970)
MSTS	Military Sea Transportation Service (established 1 October 1949); changed to MSC in 1970
MTBF	Mean Time Between Failure
NASA	National Aeronautics and Space Administration
NDRF	National Defense Reserve Fleet
n.mile	nautical mile (1.15 statute miles or 1.852 kilometers)
NOAA	National Oceanic and Atmospheric Administration
NOS	National Ocean Survey
NRF	Naval Reserve Force
NTDS	Navy Tactical Data System
NTU	New Threat Upgrade
NVR	Naval Vessel Register[1]

1. The official U.S. Navy listing of ships owned by the Navy.

PAIR   Performance And Integration Retrofit (sonar)

psi   pounds per square inch (kg/cm^2) (boiler pressure)

RAST   Recovery Assistance, Securing, and Traversing System

RCOH   Refueling/Complex Overhaul

reactors   the first letter of the reactor designation indicates the platform (A = Aircraft carrier, C = Cruiser, D = frigate [DL/DLG], S = Submarine); numeral indicates the sequence of the reactor design by specific manufacturer (G = General Electric, W = Westinghouse)

RFA   Royal Fleet Auxiliary (British)

RPV   Remotely Piloted Vehicle

RRF   Ready Reserve Fleet

RWR   Radar Warning Receiver

SAG   Surface Action Group

SAM   Surface-to-Air Missile

SAR   Search And Rescue

SATCOMM   Satellite Communications

SCB   Ships Characteristics Board; sequential number of Navy ship designs reaching the advanced planning stage; numbered in a single sequential series from 1947 (SCB No. 1 was the NORFOLK/CLK 1, later DL 1) through 1964 (SCB No. 252 was the FLAGSTAFF/PGH 1); from 1964 in numbered blocks: 001–009 cruisers, 100 carriers, 200 destroyers/frigates, 300 submarines, 400 amphibious, 500 mine warfare, 600 patrol, 700 auxiliary, 800 service craft, 900 special purpose. The latter numbers have suffixes of fiscal year of prototype, as 400.65 being the LCC of fiscal 1965 design.

SDV   SEAL Delivery Vehicle (formerly Swimmer Delivery Vehicle)

SEAL   Sea-Air-Land (team)

shp   shaft horsepower

SLBM   Submarine-Launched Ballistic Missile

SLEP   Service Life Extension Program

SOSUS   Sound Surveillance System

SRBOC   Super Rapid-Blooming Offboard Chaff

SSM   Surface-to-Surface Missile

Status
- **AA**   Atlantic Active
- AR   Atlantic Reserve
- **GL**   Great Lakes (Coast Guard)
- **PA**   Pacific Active
- PR   Pacific Reserve
- **R&D**   Research and Development
- RRF   Ready Reserve Force
- **TRA**   Training

STOL   Short Takeoff and Landing

STOVL   Short Takeoff/Vertical Landing

SUBROC   Submarine Rocket

SURTASS   Surveillance Towed Array Sonar System

SWATH   Small Waterplane-Area Twin-Hull (ship)

TACAN   Tactical Air Navigation

TACTAS   Tactical Towed Array Sonar

TALD   Tactical Air-Launched Decoy

TAR   Training and Administration of Reserves

TAS   Target Acquisition System

TASM   Tomahawk Anti-Ship Missile

TASS   Towed Array Sonar System

TLAM   Tomahawk Land-Attack Missile

UNREP   Underway Replenishment

USCGC   U.S. Coast Guard Cutter

USNS   U.S. Naval Ship

USS   U.S. Ship

URG   Underway Replenishment Group

VDS   Variable Depth Sonar

VERTREP   Vertical Replenishment

VLA   Vertical-Launch ASROC

VLS   Vertical-Launch System

VOD   Vertical Onboard Delivery

VSTOL   Vertical/Short Take-Off and Landing

Note: Aviation abbreviations are found in chapter 28.

CHAPTER 3

Ship Classifications

A dry deck shelter is loaded onto the submarine SAM HOUSTON (SSN 609). The shelter can house small SEAL delivery vehicles and swimmers. The Navy's transport/special operations submarines are designated SSN although diesel-electric submarines formerly used in that role were designated LPSS. (U.S. Navy)

U.S. Navy ships and small craft, with a few specific exceptions, are classified by type, and by sequence within that type. The list of classifications is issued periodically, updating a system that was begun in 1920.

The following are those classifications on the current list, which was last revised in 1991. Letter prefixes to the basic symbols are used to indicate:

F   being constructed for foreign government
T   assigned to Military Sealift Command (formerly
     Military Sea Transportation Service)
W   Coast Guard cutter

The suffix *N* is used to denote nuclear-propelled ships. For service craft the suffix *N* indicates a non-self-propelled version of a similar self-propelled craft. While the prefix letter *W* on the list indicates that Coast Guard classifications are included in the Navy list of classifications, in fact they are not.

There are many inconsistencies in the current classification list, such as the repair ship (AR) being listed as a *mobile logistic type ship*, but the small repair ship (ARL) is considered a *support type ship*. Indeed, the term *mobile logistic ship* initially referred to replenishment ships, as AE, AO, AOE.

The suffix letter *X*—which does not appear on the classification list—is used unofficially to indicate new designs or classes, as DDX, LHDX, AKX, and ARX. More formal designations often exist for several years in official documents and usage before they appear in the ship classification, as MSH (added to the list in 1982) and LHD (added in 1983).

Parentheses are not used in designations.

In the following list the ships are arranged in the order of the current Navy instruction on classifications; some levels of sub-categorization are deleted here for purposes of readability. Note that combat logistics ships are listed—as combat ships—ahead of mine warfare ships, and separated from other auxiliary ships.

Changes to the previous list of classifications are indicated by asterisks.

WARSHIPS

Aircraft Carrier Type

CV	multi-purpose aircraft carrier
CVA	attack aircraft carrier
CVN	multi-purpose aircraft carrier (nuclear propulsion)
CVS	ASW aircraft carrier

Surface Combatant Type

BB	battleship
CA	gun cruiser
CG	guided missile cruiser
CGN	guided missile cruiser (nuclear propulsion)

DD	destroyer
DDG	guided missile destroyer
FF	frigate
FFG	guided missile frigate
FFT	frigate (Reserve Training)*

Submarine Type

SS	submarine
SSBN	ballistic missile submarine (nuclear propulsion)
SSN	submarine (nuclear propulsion)

OTHER COMBATANTS

Patrol Combatant Type

PG	patrol gunboat
PHM	patrol combatant missile (hydrofoil)*

Amphibious Warfare Type

LCC	amphibious command ship
LHA	amphibious assault ship (general-purpose)
LHD	amphibious assault ship (multi-purpose)
LKA	amphibious cargo ship
LPA	amphibious transport
LPD	amphibious transport dock
LPH	amphibious assault ship (helicopter)
LSD	dock landing ship
LST	tank landing ship

Combat Logistics Type

AE	ammunition ship
AF	store ship
AFS	combat store ship
AO	oiler
AOE	fast combat support ship
AOR	replenishment oiler

Mine Warfare Type

MCM	mine countermeasures ship
MHC	minehunter, coastal
MSO	minesweeper, ocean

Coastal Defense

PC	patrol, coastal*

AUXILIARIES

Mobile Logistic Type

AD	destroyer tender
AR	repair ship
AS	submarine tender

Support Type

ACS	auxiliary crane ship
AG	miscellaneous
AGDS	deep submergence support ship
AGF	miscellaneous command ship
AGFF	auxiliary general frigate*
AGM	missile range instrumentation ship
AGOR	oceanographic research ship
AGOS	ocean surveillance ship
AGS	surveying ship
AGSS	auxiliary research submarine[1]

AH	hospital ship
AK	cargo ship
AKR	vehicle cargo ship
AOG	gasoline tanker
AOT	transport oiler
AP	transport
ARC	cable repairing ship
ARL	repair ship, small
ARS	salvage ship
ASR	submarine rescue ship
ATF	fleet ocean tug
ATS	salvage and rescue ship
AVB	aviation logistic support ship
AVM	guided missile ship
AVT	auxiliary aircraft landing training ship

1. No combat capability in submarines with this designation.

COMBATANT CRAFT

Patrol Type Craft

ATC	mini-armored troop carrier
PB	patrol boat
PBR	river patrol craft
PCF	patrol craft (fast)

Amphibious Warfare Type Craft

LCAC	landing craft, air cushion
LCM	landing craft, mechanized
LCPL	landing craft, personnel, large
LCU	landing craft, utility
LCVP	landing craft, vehicle, personnel
LSSC	light SEAL support craft

SUPPORT TYPE CRAFT

Dry Docks (non-self-propelled)

AFDB	large auxiliary floating dry dock
AFDL	small auxiliary floating dry dock
AFDM	medium auxiliary floating dry dock
ARD	auxiliary repair dock
ARDM	medium auxiliary repair dry dock
YFD	yard floating dry dock

Tugs (self-propelled)

YTB	large harbor tug
YTL	small harbor tug
YTM	medium harbor tug

Tankers (self-propelled)

YO	fuel oil barge
YOG	gasoline barge
YW	water barge

Lighters and Barges
(self-propelled)

YF	covered lighter
YFU	harbor utility craft

(non-self-propelled)

YC	open car lighter
YCF	car float
YCV	aircraft transportation lighter
YFN	covered lighter
YFNB	large covered lighter
YFNX	lighter (special purpose)
YFRN	refrigerated covered lighter
YFRT	range tender
YGN	garbage lighter
YOGN	gasoline barge*
YON	fuel oil barge*
YOS	oil storage barge
YSR	sludge removal barge
YWN	water barge

LWT	amphibious warping tug
MSSC	medium SEAL support craft
SDV	swimmer delivery vehicle
SLWT	side-loading warping tug
SWCL	special warfare craft, light
SWCM	special warfare craft, medium

Mine Warfare Type Craft

MCT[2]	mine countermeasures craft, training*
MSB	minesweeping boat

2. Craft-Of-Opportunity Program (COOP).

Other Craft
(self-propelled)

DSRV	deep submergence rescue vehicle
DSV	deep submergence vehicle
NR	submersible research vehicle (nuclear propulsion)
YAG	miscellaneous auxiliary service craft
YFB	ferry boat or launch
YTT	torpedo trials craft
YM	dredge
YP	patrol craft, training

(non-self-propelled)

APL	barracks craft
YD	floating crane
YDT	diving tender
YFND	dry dock companion craft
YFP	floating power barge
YLC	salvage lift craft
YMN	dredge
YNG	gate craft
YPD	floating pile driver
YR	floating workshop
YRB	repair and berthing barge
YRBM	repair, berthing and messing barge
YRDH	floating dry dock workshop (hull)
YRDM	floating dry dock workshop (machine)
YRR	radiological repair barge
YRST	salvage craft tender

Unclassified Miscellaneous

IX	unclassified miscellaneous unit

COAST GUARD CUTTERS AND BOATS

The cutter designations currently in use for Coast Guard cutters and boats are:

WAGB	Icebreaker
WAGO	Oceanographic cutter
WHEC	High Endurance Cutter (multi-mission; 30 to 45 days at sea without support)
WIX	Training cutter
WLB	Offshore buoy tender (full sea-keeping capability; medium endurance)
WLI	Inshore buoy tender (short endurance)
WLIC	Inland construction tender (short endurance)
WLM	Coastal buoy tender (medium endurance)
WLR	River buoy tender (short endurance)
WLV	Light Vessel
WMEC	Medium Endurance Cutter (multi-mission; 10 to 30 days at sea without support)
WPB	Patrol Boat (multi-mission; 1 to 7 days at sea without support)
WSES	Surface Effect Ship

The Coast Guard uses the term *icebreaker* for a variety of vessels with the following categories:

Type A	late GLACIER (WAGB 4)
Type B	MACKINAW (WAGB 83) and late Wind class (WAGB 281)
Type C	Bay class (WTGB 140)
Type D	medium harbor tugs (WYTM)
Type E	small harbor tugs (WYTL)
Type P	Polar (WAGB 10) class

MARITIME ADMINISTRATION

The following are Maritime Administration design classifications; they were developed in the late 1930s by the Maritime Commission. They are currently assigned only to auxiliary/sealift ships; during World War II the escort aircraft carriers, frigates, and tank landing ships designed by the Maritime Commission also had these design classifications.

The first letter-number series indicates ship type, with the adjacent number indicating size (e.g., C4)

C	Cargo
P	Passenger
R	Refrigerator (reefer)
S	Special type
T	Tanker
VC	Victory-Cargo

The second letter-number series indicates propulsion:

M	Motor (diesel)
ME2	Motor; 2 shafts (diesel)
MET	diesel-electric; 2 shafts
S	Steam
S2	Steam; 2 shafts
SE	turbo-electric
SE2	turbo-electric; 2 shafts
ST	Steam; 2 shafts

The third letter-number series indicates specific ship design, usually beginning with A1 or 1; designs have lower-case suffix letters, as 1b.

CHAPTER 4

Defense Organization

The Gulf War saw the extensive cooperation of the U.S. military services, all under joint direction. Although there were problems in the coordination of forces, in most instances the problems were solved. Here an Air Force KC-135 tanker refuels a Navy A-6E Intruder from VA-35 and F/A-18 Hornet strike-fighters from VFA-83 aboard the carrier SARATOGA (CV 60). (U.S. Navy courtesy Lt. Nick Mongillo, USN)

The United States has a unified defense establishment responsible for the conduct of military operations—in peace and in war—in support of the national security strategy. That strategy has changed dramatically in the past few years with the end of the Cold War as manifested in the demise of the Soviet Union and the termination of Soviet control over Eastern Europe and the Baltic states. President George Bush unveiled this new strategy in a speech at Aspen, Colo., in August 1990, when he said: "Our new strategy must provide the framework to guide our deliberate reductions [of military forces] to no more forces than the forces we need to guard our enduring interests—the forces to exercise forward presence in key areas, to respond effectively to crises, to retain the national capacity to rebuild our forces should this be needed . . . [and to] maintain an effective deterrent."[1]

The President, under the provisions of the Constitution, is the Commander in Chief of the U.S. armed forces. The Secretary of Defense, the President's immediate subordinate, serves as the day-to-day decision maker in defense matters. Together, the President and Secretary of Defense—and in an emergency their designated alternates—comprise the National Command Authority (NCA), empowered to command all U.S. combat forces and to release nuclear weapons for operational use.

1. President Bush's speech, at the Aspen Institute Symposium, was made on 2 August 1990—the day that Iraq invaded Kuwait.

From the President the operational chain-of-command goes through the Secretary of Defense, with orders transmitted to operational commanders through the Chairman of the Joint Chiefs of Staff.

The Secretary of Defense and the Chairman of the Joint Chiefs of Staff are the principal military advisers to the President. In addition, by statute the President is assisted by an advisory body called the National Security Council that provides advice on a broad range of national security and intelligence matters. Chaired by the President, the permanent members of the National Security Council (NSC) are the Vice President, the Secretaries of Defense, State, and Treasury, the Chairman of the Joint Chiefs of Staff, and the Director of Central Intelligence. The official who coordinates NSC activities and directs its staff is known as the President's National Security Adviser.

The principal components of the Defense establishment are (1) the Department of Defense, (2) the Joint Chiefs of Staff, (3) the military departments and their subordinate services, and (4) the unified and specified commands. Four of the U.S. military services are within the Department of Defense; the fifth military service, the Coast Guard, is part of the Department of Transportation. That service has responsibilities to both departments as well as to the Navy (see chapter 32).

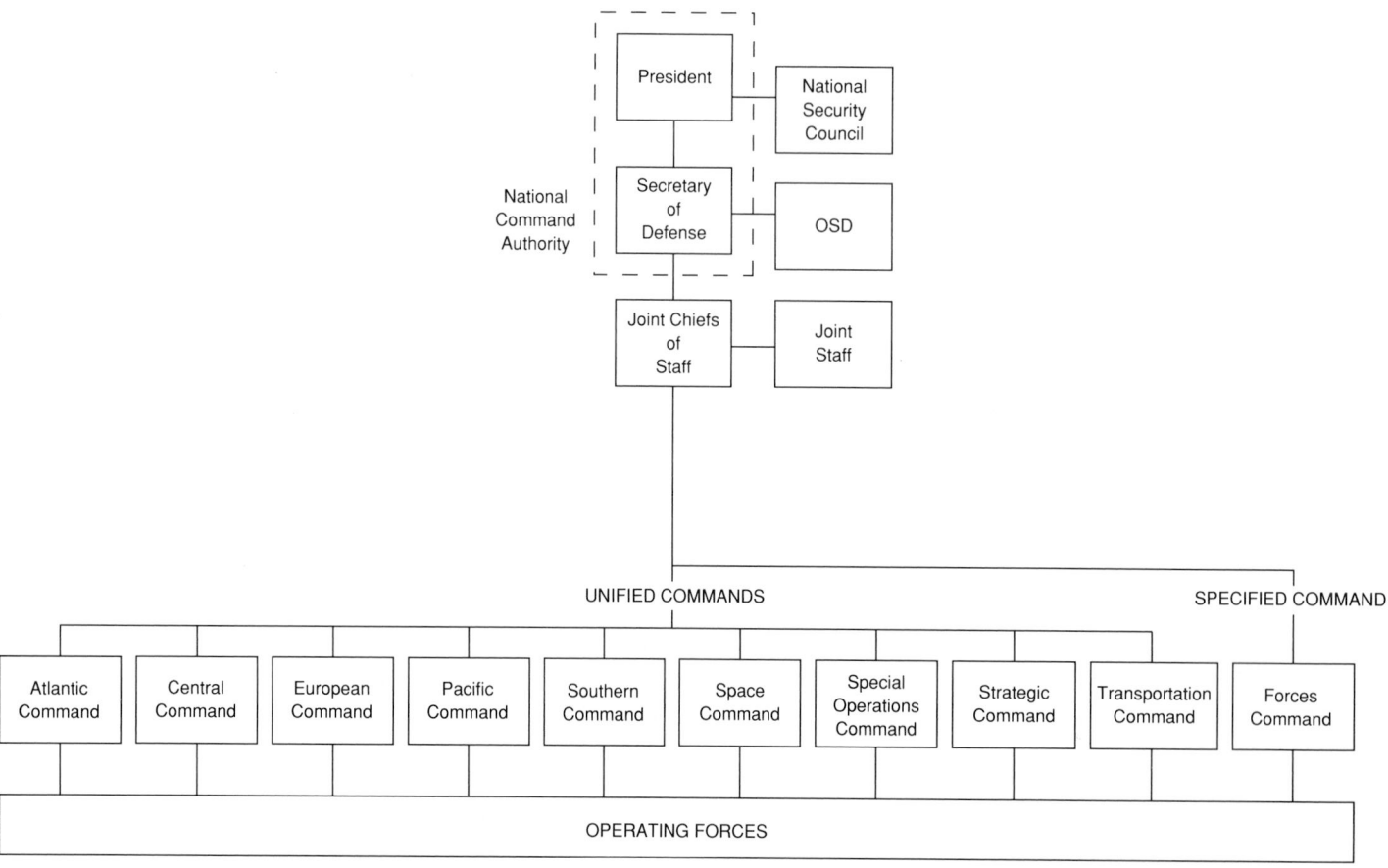

FIGURE 4-1.   U.S. National Defense Command Structure

DEPARTMENT OF DEFENSE

The Department of Defense is headed by the Secretary of Defense, who is a member of the President's cabinet and a member of the National Security Council. By custom the Secretary of Defense is a civilian and not a professional military officer.[2]

The principal deputies to the Secretary of Defense are the Deputy Secretary, the Under Secretary for Policy, and the Under Secretary for Acquisition. The under secretaries, in turn, are supported by Deputy Under Secretaries for Acquisition, Acquisition Planning, and Total Quality Management; 11 Assistant Secretaries; the Comptroller; General Counsel; Inspector General; Director Defense Research and Engineering; and Director Operational Test and Evaluation. The assistant secretaries are responsible for:

- Command, Control, Communications and Intelligence
- Force Management and Personnel
- Health Affairs
- International Security Affairs
- International Security Policy
- Legislative Affairs
- Production and Logistics
- Program Analysis and Evaluation
- Public Affairs
- Reserve Affairs
- Special Operations and Low-Intensity Conflict

The large staff that supports these officials is the Office of the Secretary of Defense (OSD). There are approximately 585 military personal and 1,560 civilians assigned to OSD.

There are 14 separate agencies under the Secretary of Defense that support the Department of Defense and the military services. These agencies generally perform functions that affect all U.S. military activities. Those agencies are:

- Defense Advanced Research Projects Agency
- Defense Audiovisual Agency
- Defense Contract Audit Agency
- Defense Communications Agency
- Defense Intelligence Agency
- Defense Investigative Service
- Defense Logistics Agency
- Defense Mapping Agency
- Defense Nuclear Agency
- Defense Security Assistance Agency
- Inspector General
- National Security Agency
- Office of Small and Disadvantaged Business Utilization
- Strategic Defensive Initiative Organization

The Defense Intelligence Agency, in addition to performing intelligence analysis for OSD, serves as the intelligence staff for the Joint Chiefs of Staff (the equivalent of a J-2 staff). The National Security Agency performs electronic intercept and cryptological activities to support the entire U.S. intelligence community as well as the Defense establishment. That agency also supervises the cryptologic activities of the Army, Navy, and Air Force.

2. The exception was General of the Army George C. Marshall, who was Chief of Staff of the U.S. Army during World War II. He served as Secretary of State (1947–1949) and Secretary of Defense (1950–1951).

Dick Cheney, Secretary of Defense since March 1989, with Marshal of the Soviet Union Dmitri Yazov during a 1990 visit to the Soviet Union. (Helene C. Stikkel/Department of Defense)

Historical. The Congress established the War Department in 1789 and the Navy Department in 1798 (see below). These two departments administered their respective services (with the Navy Department administering the Navy and Marine Corps). The secretaries of these two departments reported directly to the President and were members of the President's cabinet.

The National Security Act of 1947 created the National Military Establishment, which came into being on 18 September 1947, as well as the National Security Council and Joint Chiefs of Staff. The Departments of the Army, Navy, and Air Force were established as cabinet-level departments, with the newly created Secretary of Defense functioning primarily as a coordinator of these military departments.

In 1949, amendments to the National Security Act established the Secretary of Defense as the principal assistant to the President on defense matters and changed the National Military Establishment to the Department of Defense. The amendments also made the three military departments subordinate to the Department of Defense, and removed their secretaries from the cabinet. Subsequent actions by various Secretaries of Defense have taken away much of the decision-making prerogatives of the military departments and assigned them to OSD and the various defense agencies.

The Defense Reorganization Act of 1958 established a new chain of command from the President and Secretary of Defense to the unified and specified commanders, who were given "full operational command" over the forces assigned to them. However, the Secretary of Defense could delegate the Joint Chiefs of Staff to exercise operational control over forces when it was deemed appropriate. Previously, the military departments acted as executive agencies for the control of forces.

JOINT CHIEFS OF STAFF

The Joint Chiefs of Staff (JCS) consists of a Chairman, Vice Chairman, and the military chiefs of the Army, Navy, Air Force, and Marine Corps. The Commandant of the Coast Guard attends JCS meetings when issues of interest to his service are discussed. The Chairman and the Vice Chairman are four-star officers (i.e., full generals or admirals) as are the military service chiefs.[3]

The JCS collectively serve as the principal military advisers to the President, Secretary of Defense, and the National Security. In addition, with passage by Congress of the Goldwater-Nichols Department of Defense Reorganization Act in 1986, the JCS is in the chain-of-command between the National Command Authority and the unified and specified commanders.

Orders and other communications are transmitted to unified and specified commanders through the Chairman of the JCS.

The JCS has a Joint Staff comprised of seven directorates that perform military staff functions for the Joint Chiefs and to some extent for the unified commands. The staff directorates are:

- J-1   Manpower and Personnel
- J-3   Operations
- J-4   Logistics
- J-5   Strategic Plans and Policy
- J-6   Command, Control, and Communications
- J-7   Operational Plans and Interoperability
- J-8   Force Structure, Resource, and Assessment

The directors of these staff directorates are three-star officers (i.e., lieutenant generals or vice admirals). Their staffs are composed mostly of military officers from all services. There are approximately 1,260 military personnel and 260 civilians assigned to the Joint Staff. Unlike the former Soviet General Staff and the staffs of some other

---

3. Of the 13 Chairmen of the Joint Chiefs of Staff since 1942, four have been naval officers:

Fleet Adm. William D. Leahy   June 1942–Mar 1949
Adm. Arthur W. Radford   Aug 1953–Aug 1957
Adm. Thomas H. Moorer   July 1970–June 1974
Adm. William J. Crowe, Jr.   Oct 1985–Sep 1989

Adm. Leahy's official position was Chief of Staff to Presidents Roosevelt and Truman.

---

military establishments, the officers assigned to the Joint Staff are not professional staff officers, but are assigned from the separate services, often without any prior staff experience or education.

Historical. President Franklin D. Roosevelt and Prime Minister Winston Churchill decided at their wartime meeting in Washington during December 1941–January 1942 to create the Anglo-American Combined Chiefs of Staff. The British component already existed as the Chiefs of Staff Committee; there was no comparable U.S. body of senior military officers.

Without specific executive action or congressional legislation, the senior U.S. military officers met as a body for the first time with their British colleagues to form the Combined Chiefs of Staff on 23 January 1942. At the time, the term Joint Chiefs of Staff (JCS) was used for the Americans although several members were not the chiefs of their services. The JCS initially consisted of the Chief of Naval Operations, Commander in Chief U.S. Fleet, Army Chief of Staff, and Chief of the Army Air Forces.[4] In July 1942 retired Admiral William D. Leahy was appointed Chief of Staff to the Commander in Chief (Roosevelt) and became *de facto* Chairman of the JCS. The JCS membership stabilized at four for the remainder of the war. The JCS served as both the U.S. component of the Combined Chiefs of Staff and as the executive body for the direction of U.S. military forces during the war.

The JCS was formally established by the National Security Act of 1947, but not until the 1949 amendments was a chairman authorized. The chairman thereafter rotated, although in no strict order, among the Army, Navy, and Air Force. Some, but certainly not all, of the chairmen were former chiefs of their services.

In 1952 the Commandant of the Marine Corps was authorized to sit with the JCS and vote on issues of direct interest to the Marine Corps. In 1979 the Commandant was made a full member of the JCS.

The position of Vice Chief of the JCS was established in 1987. (Previously, when the chairman was absent, the other members served in his place by rotation.)

---

4. The Chief of the Army Air Forces was changed to Commanding General in March 1942; the position of Chief of Naval Operations was combined with that of CinC U.S. Fleet in March 1942, giving the JCS three members—Army, Army Air Forces, and Navy—plus the chairman.

MILITARY DEPARTMENTS

There are three military departments within the Department of defense—Army, Navy, and Air Force. Each department is headed by a civilian secretary, under secretary, and several assistant secretaries. These are civilian positions although, on occasion, a professional officer has been appointed to one of the assistant secretary positions.

Reporting directly to the civilian secretary is the chief of the service assigned to the department, who is the senior military officer of that department (except for officers assigned as chairman or vice chairman of the JCS, who rank above service chiefs). The Navy Department has two services—the Navy and the Marine Corps.

The military departments are responsible for the training, provision of equipment, and administration of their military services. They do not direct military operations, that function having been taken away by the Defense Reorganization Act of 1958. The influence and prerogatives of the military departments have varied considerably in recent years on the basis of the personality, influence, and attitudes of the service secretaries and, to a lesser degree, on the service chiefs.

Historical. The Second Continental Congress authorized the first increment of national troops on 14 June 1775, with their officers responsible to the Congress. The U.S. Constitution of 1789 provided that the President should be Commander in Chief of the Army and Navy, his powers over them exclusive, limited only "by their nature and by the principles of our institutions." On 7 August 1789 the Congress created the War Department.

The U.S. Navy originated with the decision by General George Washington in 1775 to dispatch vessels to prey on British shipping. In

October of that year the Continental Congress established a naval committee to acquire and fit out vessels for naval operations. (The following month the Continental Congress established the Marine Corps.)

At the end of the American Revolution in 1783, the weak and almost bankrupt Congress ordered the Navy to disband. Although the Constitution, adopted in 1789, directed the Congress "to provide and maintain a navy," a separate Navy Department was not considered necessary, and naval affairs—such as they were—were included under the jurisdiction of the War Department. Not until the Navy Act of 1794, which authorized the procurement of six frigates, was the Navy reestablished.[5] Not until 30 April 1798 did Congress create the Navy Department.

The U.S. Army is believed to have accepted the world's first military aircraft on 2 August 1909. Initially assigned to the Signal Corps, military aviation continued under the Army through World War II, although from 1942 the head of the Army Air Forces served as a full member of the Joint Chiefs of Staff (see above). The U.S. Air Force and the Department of the Air Force were established on 18 September 1947.

The 1949 amendments to the National Security Act removed the secretaries of the three military departments from the cabinet and placed them under the supervision of the Secretary of Defense.

---

5. These frigates included the CONSTITUTION and CONSTELLATION; see chapter 25.

UNIFIED AND SPECIFIED COMMANDS

Essentially all U.S. operating forces are assigned to *unified* or *specified* commands, which plan for military operations, direct exercises and combat operations, and have operational control of specifically assigned U.S. forces. The 1958 reorganization of the Department of Defense established the chain of command of the operating forces from the National Command Authority (President and Secretary of Defense) to the Commanders in Chief of the unified and specified commanders.

Unified commands contain forces from two or more services; most are responsible for specific geographic areas. Whereas the Atlantic and Pacific commands, for example, continually have large forces assigned to them, other unified commands are mainly planning staffs until specific forces are placed under them during an exercise, a crisis, or in wartime. For example, prior to the Iraqi invasion of Kuwait in August 1990, the Central Command was a planning staff of several hundred men and women in the United States. Except for exercises, no major military units were assigned to CENTCOM. When Operation Desert Shield was initiated in early August, CENTCOM took command of the buildup, with more than 500,000 U.S. military personnel and large numbers of ships, aircraft, and ground units being assigned to CENTCOM. Subsequently, CINC-CENT, in coordination with the commander of Saudi forces, directed Operation Desert Storm, the assault on occupied Kuwait and Iraq.

There are nine unified commands, some of which date to World War II. The commanders in chief of the unified forces are four-star officers; some CinC positions rotate among the services while some are assigned to officers of only one service; the incumbent CinC when this edition of *Ships and Aircraft* went to press is indicated by an asterisk. In 1992 there were four unified commands and the single specified command under Army generals, three commands under Air Force generals, two commands under Navy admirals, and one command under a Marine general.

The unified commands are:

U.S. Atlantic Command (USCINCLANT). U.S. forces in the Atlantic area, including the Caribbean. The CinC Atlantic Command is also the NATO Supreme Allied Commander Atlantic and, until 1985, additionally served as CinC Atlantic Fleet.
Headquarters: Norfolk, Va.
Established: December 1947.
CinC: Navy.*

U.S. Central Command (USCINCCENT). U.S. forces operating in the Middle East area. The Central Command directed U.S. military operations in the buildup and war in the Persian Gulf War area in 1990–1991; it is the successor to the Rapid Deployment Force (see 13th Edition/pages 22–25).
Headquarters: MacDill Air Force Base, Tampa, Fla.
Established: January 1983.
CinC: Army, Air Force, Marine Corps.*

U.S. European Command (USCINCEUR). U.S. forces in Europe, including U.S. naval forces in the Mediterranean. The CinC European Command is also the NATO Supreme Allied Command Europe.
Headquarters: Stuttgart-Vaihingen, Germany.
Established: March 1947.[6]
CinC: Army* or Air Force.

U.S. Pacific Command (USCINCPAC). U.S. forces in the Pacific and Indian Ocean areas as well as on the Asian mainland. The CinC Pacific Command additionally served as CinC Pacific Fleet until 1958.
Headquarters: Camp H.M. Smith, Oahu, Hawaii.
Established: January 1947.
CinC: Navy.*

U.S. Southern Command (USCINCSO). U.S. forces in Central America and South America. The command was known as the Caribbean Command (CINCCARIB) until June 1963.
Headquarters: Quarry Heights, Panama.
Established: November 1947.
CinC: Army.*

U.S. Space Command (USCINCSPACE). U.S. activities and forces in space, including the monitoring of foreign space activities.
Headquarters: Peterson Air Force Base, Colorado Springs, Colo.
Established: September 1985.
CinC: Air Force,* Navy.

U.S. Special Operations Command (USCINCSOC). Directs U.S. special forces activities (primarily Air Force Special Operations Command, Army Green Berets and Delta Force, Navy SEALs).
Headquarters: MacDill Air Force Base, Tampa, Fla.
Established: April 1987.
CinC: Army,* Navy, Air Force, Marine Corps.

U.S. Strategic Command (USCINCSTRAT). All U.S. land-based and sea-based strategic forces. The Strategic Air Command (SAC), a specified command with only Air Force components, was abolished in 1992 with most of its resources being assigned to the Strategic Command. Also incorporated into the new Strategic Command was the Joint Strategic Target Planning Staff (JSTPS), a multi-service agency that planned the laydown of U.S. strategic weapons, and various Navy activities related to strategic missile submarine operations. (Despite some writers stating that the new U.S. Strategic Command combined the separate Air Force and Navy strategic commands, in fact the Navy never had a strategic command; previously the naval strategic forces—carrier-based aircraft and ballistic missile submarines—were assigned to the Atlantic, Pacific, and European unified commands and their respective naval component commanders.)
Headquarters: Offutt Air Force Base, Neb.
Established: June 1992.
CinC: Air Force,* Navy.

U.S. Transportation Command. All air and sea transport resources, including the sea transportation assets of the Navy's Military Sealift Command.
Headquarters: Scott Air Force Base, Ill.
Established: July 1987.
CinC: Air Force.*

Specified commands have forces assigned from only one military service, with the CinC being assigned from that service. There is now only one specified command:

Forces Command. Responsible for all U.S. Army forces (active and inactive) in the United States.
Headquarters: Fort McPherson, Ga.
Established: July 1987.
CinC: Army.*

The number of unified and specified commands is not fixed by law or regulation, and may be changed from time to time at the discretion of the President and the Secretary of Defense.

Within most unified commands there are air, ground, and naval component commanders, who direct the operations of their respective services.

Historical. The official history of the U.S. Joint Chiefs of Staff states: "the surprise attack [on Pearl Harbor] indicated dramatically the difficulties inherent in coordinating responsibility for defense of the whole Hawaiian area. It likewise made President Roosevelt and his advisors determine that there be no uncertainty as to responsibility for protection of the Panama Canal."[7] Consequently, on 12

---

6. From March 1947 until July 1952 was Commander in Chief Europe (CINCEUR), largely a U.S. Army command and only nominally unified.

7. Grace Person Hayes, *The History of the Joint Chiefs of Staff in World War II: The War Against Japan* (Annapolis, Md.: Naval Institute Press, 1982), p. 29.

December 1941, meeting with the President, U.S. military leaders established the first unified commands: all U.S. military forces in the Hawaii area were placed under the Commander in Chief Pacific Fleet and those in the Panama area under the CinC Panama (an Army Air Forces officer).

Subsequent U.S. unified commanders were also Allied commanders with responsibility for directing U.S. and British forces in a specific area (with some other Allied forces being present in some commands). The complexity of strategic bombing operations against Germany (including coordination with the British bombers) and later Japan led to the JCS establishing the U.S. Strategic Air Forces in Europe and U.S. Strategic Air Forces in the Pacific. These were all-Army Air Force commands that were operationally outside the control of the respective Allied commanders and, in reality, the first U.S. specified commands.

Unified and specified commanders were in a sort of limbo after World War II as the military departments tended to direct operations of their forces within specific geographic areas. The 1958 defense reorganization gave the unified commands responsibility for all military forces and operations within a specific area and established specified commands when the component forces were all from one service.

JOINT TASK FORCES

Periodically, unified Joint Task Forces (JTF) are organized within unified commands for specific operations. In 1989 several JTFs were established to help combat the influx of illegal drugs into the United States. In 1992 there were three such JTFs engaged in counternarcotic operations:

Unified/Specified Command	Joint Task Force	Area
U.S. Atlantic Command	JTF-4	U.S. East Coast–Caribbean
U.S. Pacific Command	JTF-5	U.S. West Coast
U.S. Forces Command	JTF-6	U.S.–Mexican border

These task forces serve as their respective command's counternarcotic coordinators, with forces from all military services, including the Coast Guard, being assigned to the task forces. The JTFs also coordinate activities with other unified and service commands, and with other government agencies. Coast Guard flag officers currently serve as Commander JTF-4, with headquarters in Key West, Fla., and Commander JTF-5, with headquarters in Alameda, Calif. The Commander JTF-6, an Army officer, has his headquarters in El Paso, Texas.

Historical. The first joint task force of the post–World War II era was JTF-1, established in 1946 to conduct the multi-service atomic bomb tests at the Bikini atoll in the Pacific in July of 1946. Task forces are non-permanent organizations, being formed and disestablished as required.

CHAPTER 5

Navy Organization

The massive Navy organizational structure is being reorganized and reduced. It exists to provide and support ships—such as the Aegis destroyer ARLEIGH BURKE (DDG 51)—aircraft, and Marines to fight potential enemies. (U.S. Navy)

The Navy is responsible for organizing, training, and equipping the Navy and Marine Corps to conduct prompt and sustained combat operations at sea—specifically to seek out and destroy enemy naval forces and to suppress enemy sea commerce, to gain and maintain general naval supremacy, to control vital sea areas, to protect vital sea lines of communication, to establish and maintain local superiority (including air) in an area of naval operations, to seize and defend advanced naval bases, and to conduct such land and air operations as may be essential to the prosecution of a naval campaign.[1]

To carry out these functions, the Navy is part of a dual command structure: (1) an administrative structure that originates with the Secretary of the Navy and the Chief of Naval Operations, and (2) an

1. See "Functions of the Department of Defense and Its Major Components," Department of Defense Directive No. 5100.1 with changes.

OPERATIONAL ORGANIZATION

The operating forces of the Navy and Marine Corps—like those of the Army and Air Force—are subordinate to unified commands. Most naval forces are assigned to the naval component commanders of three unified commands; their basic command structure is shown in figure 5-1.

Unified Command	Naval Component	Operating Fleet
U.S. Atlantic Command	Atlantic Fleet	Second Fleet
U.S. European Command	Naval Forces Europe	Sixth Fleet
U.S. Pacific Command	Pacific Fleet	Third Fleet / Sixth Fleet

These three naval component commanders are full admirals with shore-based staffs.[2]

Atlantic Fleet. The CinC Atlantic Fleet functions in both the administrative and tactical chains of command. Until 1986 the position of CinC Atlantic Fleet was an additional duty of the CinC Atlantic Command (who is additionally NATO Supreme Allied Commander Atlantic). The Second Fleet is the major operational component of the Atlantic Fleet.
Headquarters: Norfolk, Va.

Naval Forces Europe. The CinC Naval Forces Europe is responsible for U.S. naval operations in the European area, including the Sixth Fleet in the Mediterranean. The CinC simultaneously holds the NATO position of CinC Allied Forces Southern Europe, responsible to the NATO Supreme Allied Commander Europe.
The CinC Naval Forces Europe does not have administrative responsibilities for support of U.S. naval forces in Europe, those being under the cognizance of the CinC Atlantic Fleet.
Headquarters: Naples, Italy.

Pacific Fleet. Like CinC Atlantic Fleet, the CinC Pacific Fleet functions in both the administrative and operational chains of command. In the latter role (as a naval component commander) he is responsible for naval operations in the Pacific–Indian Ocean areas. The principal operating commands are the Third Fleet and Seventh Fleet.
Headquarters: Pearl Harbor, Hawaii.

The numbered fleet commanders are vice admirals. Their staffs are normally "split" between the fleet flagship and a component ashore.

Second Fleet. Operating in the Atlantic area, the Second Fleet serves as the NATO strike force, is responsible for anti-submarine operations in the Atlantic, and, increasingly, has operational requirements in the Caribbean area and off Central America. Most ships of

2. All active-duty U.S. Navy admirals and Marine Corps generals are listed, with their current positions, in the May issue of the U.S. Naval Institute *Proceedings* (Naval Review issue).

operational structure that originates with the unified commanders in chief. The administrative structure fulfills the institutional need for civilian control and the balancing of service interests by enabling the Navy to support deployed forces without intervening in combat operations directed by the unified command system. The operational structure relieves the fleet and task force commanders from the administrative and procurement workload that would otherwise distract them from their primary task—the command of combat forces.

The Navy has long had a bilinear organization, with squadron and later fleet commanders and, after 1942, the Chief of Naval Operations exercising military command over the operating forces, while the Secretary of the Navy, through civilian assistants and chiefs of the various bureaus and agencies, directing the business, research and development, procurement, and support activities of the Navy.

the Second Fleet rotate at regular intervals to the Sixth Fleet in the Mediterranean.
Fleet headquarters: Norfolk, Va.
Flagship: MOUNT WHITNEY (LCC 20).

Third Fleet. The Third Fleet operates in the Eastern Pacific and rotates ships to the Seventh Fleet in the Western Pacific–Indian Ocean areas. The Third Fleet has an anti-submarine orientation, derived from its origins as ASW Force Pacific. The growth of Soviet naval capabilities in the Pacific during the 1980s led to an increase in carrier battle force operations in the Third Fleet, with regular North Pacific operations, some within air-strike range of Russian bases in Siberia.
Fleet headquarters: Naval Air Station North Island (San Diego), Calif. Fleet headquarters were shifted from Ford Island in Pearl Harbor, Hawaii, to San Diego in August 1991.
Flagship: CORONADO (AGF 11).

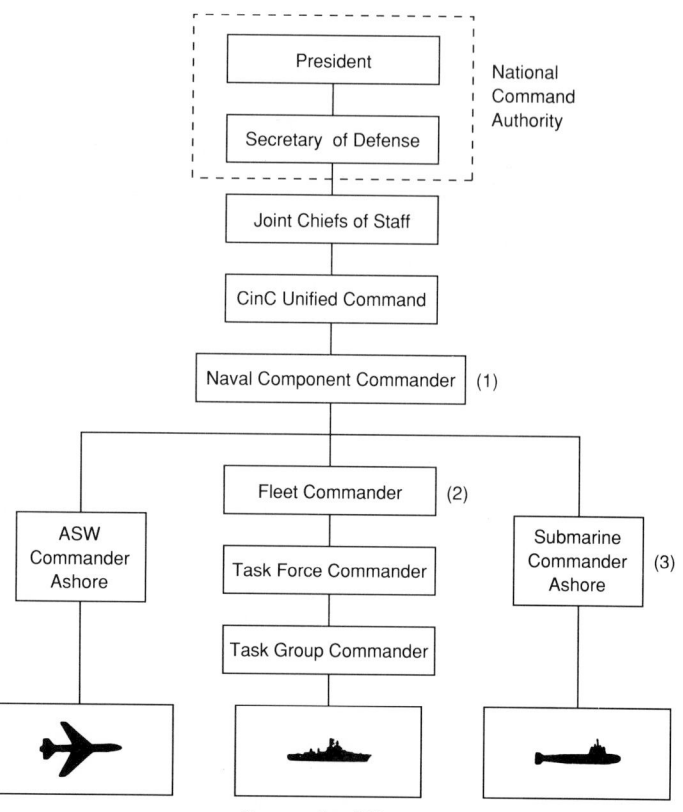

Commanding Officers

(1) Nominally CinC Atlantic Fleet or CinC Pacific Fleet.
(2) Nominally numbered fleet commander.
(3) Nominally Commander Submarine Force Atlantic Fleet or Pacific Fleet.

FIGURE 5-1. Operational Chain of Command

Sixth Fleet. The Sixth Fleet operates in the Mediterranean Sea and has both U.S. and NATO responsibilities, the latter as the NATO Striking and Support Forces, Southern Europe. Several NATO allies provide direct support to the Sixth Fleet in terms of shore bases and ASW and reconnaissance forces.

A few Sixth Fleet support ships and the cruiser flagship are home-ported in the Mediterranean. Most Sixth Fleet ships and aircraft squadrons are on rotation from the Atlantic Fleet; those units normally spend six months in transit and operating in the Mediterranean, and 12 months in their home port and in Atlantic operations.

Fleet headquarters: Gaeta, Italy.
Fleet flagship: BELKNAP (CG 26).

Seventh Fleet. The Seventh Fleet has broad responsibilities for naval operations in the Western Pacific and Indian Ocean areas— from the Kamchatka Peninsula of Russian Siberia to the Persian Gulf. Thus the Seventh Fleet has complex and wide-ranging mission requirements with only limited allied support available. The aircraft carrier INDEPENDENCE (CV 62), a cruiser-destroyer group, and an amphibious group are home-ported in Japan.

During the Persian Gulf operations of 1990–1991 (Desert Shield/Desert Storm), the Commander, Seventh Fleet became the naval component commander for Central Command.

Fleet headquarters: Yokosuka, Japan.
Flagship: BLUE RIDGE (LCC 19).

Naval Forces Central Command. One other unified command has significant naval operating forces assigned, the U.S. Central Command, responsible for combat operations in the Middle East. The Commander, U.S. Naval Forces Central Command is the naval component, with Commander, Middle East Force as the operating command. A rear admiral normally serves as both Commander, U.S. Naval Forces Central Command and Commander, Middle East Force. His flagship is the LA SALLE (AGF 3), based at Mina' Sulman, Bahrain. Several frigate- and destroyer-type ships and minesweepers are currently assigned to the Middle East Force as well as support ships.

ADMINISTRATIVE ORGANIZATION

The administrative organization for the Navy begins with the Secretary of Defense and then goes through the Secretary of the Navy and the Chief of Naval Operations (CNO), as shown in simplified form in figure 5-2. The CNO is "double hatted" as both the uniformed head of the Navy and as a member of the Joint Chiefs of Staff.

The Secretary of the Navy and the CNO—as the uniformed head of the Navy—are essentially managers with tasks of supporting unified commanders. They are responsible for the logistics, maintenance, personnel management, procurement of naval systems and supplies, and research and development.

To accomplish these tasks the Secretary and the CNO each have staff organizations, with the Secretary's mostly composed of civilians and the CNO's mostly of naval personnel. The Secretary of the Navy has the following principal assistants, mostly civilians:[3]

- Under Secretary
- Assistant Secretary (Financial Management)
- Assistant Secretary (Manpower and Reserve Affairs)
- Assistant Secretary (Research, Engineering, and Acquisition)
- Assistant Secretary (Shipbuilding and Logistics)
- General Counsel
- Judge Advocate General (★★)
- Competition Advocate General (★)
- Chief of Information (★)

These officials handle Marine Corps as well as Navy matters within their areas of responsibility. With the CNO and his staff, these officials are jointly responsible for the administration of the 16 major commands of the shore establishment; these commands are all headed by naval officers:

- Bureau of Medicine and Surgery* (★★★)
- Bureau of Naval Personnel* (★★★)
- Naval Air Systems Command (★★★)
- Naval Data Automation Command (captain)
- Naval Education and Training Command (★★★)
- Naval Facilities Engineering Command (★★)
- Naval Intelligence Command (captain)
- Naval Investigative Service Command (★)
- Naval Legal Service Command (★)
- Naval Oceanography Command (captain)
- Naval Sea Systems Command (★★★)
- Naval Security Group Command (★)
- Naval Space Command (★)
- Naval Supply Systems Command (★★)
- Naval Telecommunications Command (captain)
- Space and Naval Warfare Systems Command (★★)

The commanders of two of these commands—indicated by asterisks— are "double hatted" on the staff of the Chief of Naval Operations (see below). The Naval Space Command also serves as the naval component of the U.S. Space Command and is thus an operational as well as administrative organization.

The Chief of Naval Operations has several deputies and assistants and a large staff historically known as the Office of the Chief of Naval Operations (OPNAV). The most far-reaching reorganization of the U.S. Navy headquarters in almost 50 years has changed the OPNAV staff to the Chief of Naval Operations Staff and destroyed the so-called "platform barons," the vice admirals who directed the submarine, surface, and air "communities." The reorganization, revealed on 22 July 1992, also eliminated several flag billets, including four vice admirals, and cut the size of the headquarters staff by about 150 positions.

These changes were made, according to the Navy's statement to Congress, because

> The dramatic changes that have taken place and are continuing to take place in the world situation have dictated a reduction in the force structure of the U.S. Navy. This reduction also requires that the Navy review how its command and administrative structure is organized. Navy leadership has recognized for some time the need to have a tighter, leaner headquarters organization, better tailored and coordinated to deal with [Department of Defense] and [Joint Chiefs of Staff] as well as operational staffs."[4]

However, the reorganization reflected a long-standing desire by Department of Defense officials as well as senior Army and Air Force officers to bring the Navy "into line" with the other services. The new organization brings the Navy into closer alignment to the staff of the Joint Chiefs of Staff as well as to the other services. The principal subordinates to the Chief of Naval Operations under the new setup will be the Vice Chief of Naval Operations (now N9), four Deputy CNOs, and three directors.

The major organizational changes are the elimination of the "barons" or "platform" sponsors at the three-star level—the Assistant CNOs for undersea warfare (OP-02), surface warfare (OP-03), and air warfare (OP-05). The concept of these offices, which sought to control their respective communities as fiefdoms, date to August 1943, when the Deputy CNO for air was established with responsibility for "the preparation, readiness and logistic support" of naval aviation.

Surface and submarine warfare matters were directed by a single Deputy CNO until 1971, who also had general sponsorship responsibilities for aviation ships. Pleading for "equality" by Admiral H.G. Rickover, then head of naval nuclear propulsion, and the submarine

---

3. The rank of military incumbents is shown in parenthesis; ★ = rear admiral (lower half); ★★ = rear admiral; ★★★ = vice admiral; ★★★★ = admiral.

4. Memorandum from Capt. J.R. McCleary, USN, subject: "Reorganization of the Naval Headquarters Staff," 22 July 1922.

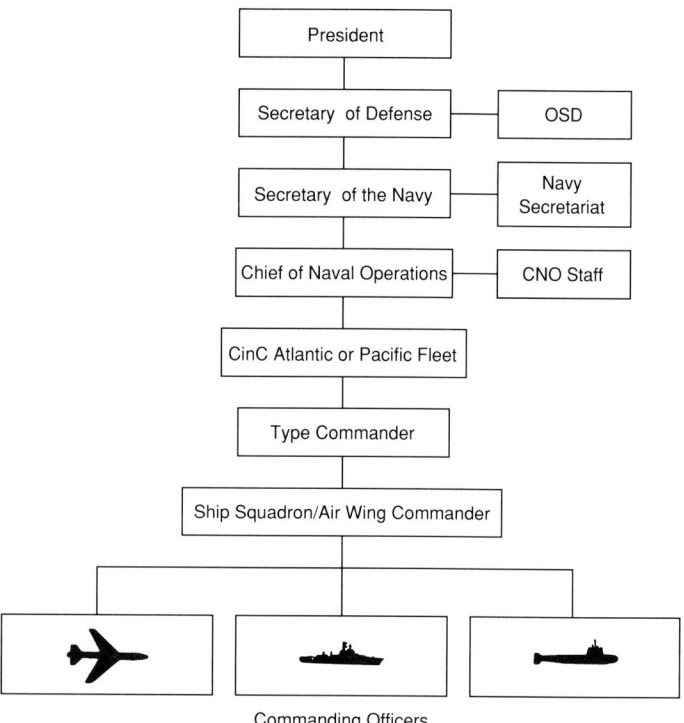

FIGURE 5-2. Administrative Chain of Command

community led the then-CNO, Admiral E.R. Zumwalt, to establish a separate Deputy CNO for submarine warfare (OP-02) in 1971. Zumwalt believed that "Setting up the DCNO for Submarines made it easier to deal with the submarine community and with Rickover."

This move, in turn, led to OP-03 becoming the Deputy CNO for surface warfare, and initiated two decades of intra-Navy or "union" competition as the "platform barons" competed for resources, political position, and even flag billets. For example, prior to the establishment of OP-02, submarine-qualified officers could serve as OP-03 while the air and surface communities worked much more closely together. Beyond the competitive aspects of the new arrangement, it was easy for non-platform specific programs to "fall through the cracks"—to become lost or underfunded, especially mine warfare and certain C³ programs.

The 1992 reorganization, which downgrades the platform barons from three stars to two and inserts the intermediate Deputy CNO for resources, warfare requirements, and assessments (N8), seeks to alleviate the disruptive competition between the air, surface, and submarine "navies." Secretary of the Navy Sean O'Keefe, in announcing the changes, stressed, "one of my primary concerns is ending rivalries and jealousies between the various key warfare fighting communities in the Navy. . . . We believe there can be no jealousy

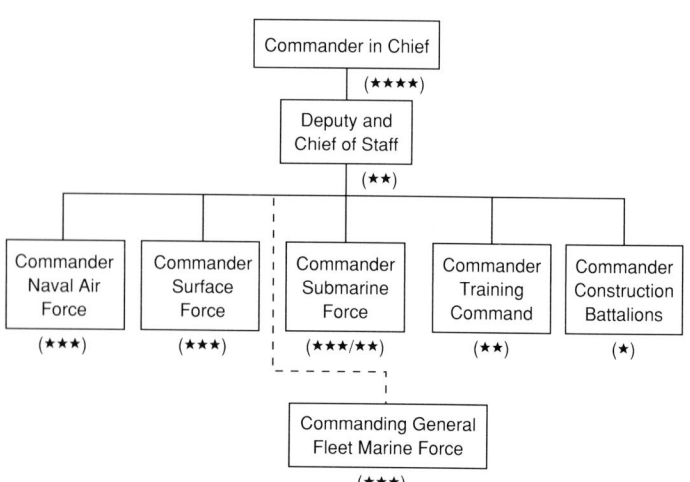

FIGURE 5-3. Fleet Command Administrative Structure

among the fingers of a strong fist. This Navy reorganization will begin the process of bringing our warfare fighters together into a tighter, stronger fist."[5]

The downgrading of platform sponsors at headquarters will lead the Navy to rely more on fleet input to determine requirements rather than driving those requirements from the Washington staffs.

Also downgraded are the former three-star positions of Director, Test and Evaluation and Technology Requirements (OP-091) and the Deputy CNO Navy for Program Planning (OP-08). Other changes include the elevation of the Director of Naval Intelligence to a major staff position (N2), and the double-hatting of the Chief of Naval Education and Training as the Director of Training and Doctrine (N7). Accordingly, the principal offices of the Navy staff are:

N1 DCNO Manpower & Personnel: The former DCNO Manpower, Personnel & Training (OP-01), but with the training functions transferred to N7.

N2 Director of Naval Intelligence: The former Director of Naval Intelligence (OP-92).

N3/5 DCNO Policy, Strategy & Plans: Essentially the former DCNO Plans, Policy & Operations (OP-06).

N4 DCNO Logistics: The same as the former DCNO Logistics (OP-04).

N6 Director Space & C⁴ System Requirements: The former Director Space & Electronic Warfare (OP-094) plus certain OpNav C³ functions.

N7 Director Training and Doctrine: This is the Chief of Naval Education and Training at Pensacola, Florida. The Navy is seeking to establish a doctrine command, as exists in the other services, but has not yet decided how to do so. The N7 will now oversee the doctrine part of the reorganization.

N8 DCNO Resources, Warfare Requirements & Assessments: This office will combine the Director, Test & Evaluation & Technology Requirements (OP-091) as well as the former platform sponsors (OP-02/-03/-05) plus the Navy's financial staff.

The changes announced in July were made through the end of 1992, with the N-staff officially replacing the OPNAV designators in August 1992. Additional were expected in 1993, in part because of the expected retirement of Mr. Gerald Cann, the Assistant Secretary of the Navy for Research, Development, and Acquisition; it is anticipated that his position will be divided (as it was prior to 1990) into the research and development and the acquisition functions. Other changes in the Navy secretariat and in the naval systems commands as well as in the naval staff are expected.

During the discussions prior to the reorganization, the position of Chief of Naval Operations was considered for renaming as the Chief of Staff of the Navy, to bring the Navy into further alignment with the Army and Air Force. However, that change, according to one officer in the Pentagon, was not made but "will probably occur in the future . . . we will see more changes in the headquarters staff and in the type commands."

Another factor driving the Washington area reorganization has been the need to eliminate 34 flag billets, including six vice admirals, by 1995. The Chief of Naval Operations, Admiral Frank B. Kelso, has said that he prefers to cut the flag positions in Washington in order to preserve leadership positions in the fleet. (There are currently some 250 admirals, with a requirement to have 216 by 1995.)

Unfortunately, the reorganization missed opportunities to return anti-submarine warfare programs and mine warfare programs to a realistic staff level, especially when one considers their increasing importance for potential operations in littoral areas. They should have been placed at the same level within N8 as the C³ systems, air, surface, and subsurface offices.

Secretary O'Keefe has declared that at the fleet level the current structures "positively will remain the way they are, because that's where the requirements are driven."[6] But Admiral Kelso added, "I

5. Secretary of the Navy Sean O'Keefe, press conference, the Pentagon, 22 July 1992.
6. O'Keefe, ibid.

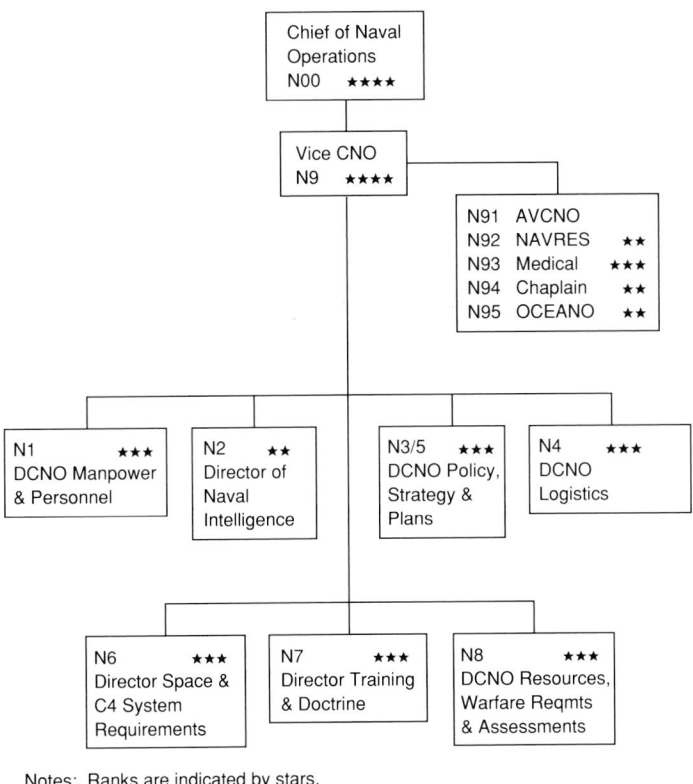

Notes: Ranks are indicated by stars.
  AVCNO   = Assistant Vice Chief of Naval Operatios (captain).
  NAVRES = Chief of Naval Reserve.
  OCEANO = Oceanographer of the Navy.

FIGURE 5-4.   Chief of Naval Operations Staff Organization

think you'll see us do a lot of streamlining and consolidation in the fleet level, particularly in the shore establishment in the years ahead."[7]

No major reorganization of Marine Corps Headquarters is now envisioned, as it already reflects traditional military staff structures. However, the Navy headquarters changes will cause some "disconnects" with the Marine Corps. For example, the Deputy Chief of Staff for aviation in the Marine Corps is a lieutenant general, who in the past served as an assistant DCNO to the head of naval aviation. But the latter is now a two-star position within the N8 organization.

The administrative chain of command flows from the Secretary of the Navy/Chief of Naval Operations to the CinCs of the Atlantic Fleet and Pacific Fleet. Those CinCs have responsibility for the readiness of their forces, which are operationally subordinate to the unified commands. Readiness includes maintenance and logistics as well as the assignment and training of their personnel.

Each of the two fleet commanders in chief has five subordinate "type" commanders who supervise specific categories of forces or activities: Naval Air Force (which includes aircraft carriers as well as aviation units), Naval Surface Force, Submarine Force, Training Command, and Construction Battalions (Seabees). In addition, the Fleet Marine Force (FMF) serves as a *de facto* type commander. These type commanders are based ashore; the Commanders Naval Air Forces and Surface Forces are vice admirals as is Commander Submarine Force Atlantic; Commander Submarine Force Pacific and the Commanders Training Commands are rear admirals, the Commanders Construction Battalions are either captains or rear admirals, and the Commanders Fleet Marine Forces are lieutenant generals.

Type commanders primarily supervise personnel, training, logistics, maintenance, and other support to ships, aircraft, and units. The type commanders do not normally have operational responsibilities, except that the fleets' submarine type commanders do have opera-

7. Adm. Frank B. Kelso, USN, press conference, the Pentagon, 22 July 1992.

tional control of undersea craft and the FMF commanders may be commanders of Marine Expeditionary Forces (see chapter 7). Carrier air wings and air squadrons not on board ship or forward deployed come under the control of their various type commanders. Below the type commanders in the administrative chain of command are officers in charge of groups or squadrons (e.g., Cruiser-Destroyer Group 1), while air squadrons are under administrative wings (e.g., Commander Anti-Submarine Warfare Wing Pacific Fleet at North Island [San Diego], Calif.). At the lower levels some administrative commanders are "double hatted" as operational commanders. At sea this distinction becomes somewhat blurred, and existing command links and staffs may be called upon to simultaneously handle operational as well as administrative matters.

Historical. The Navy Department was formally established by an act of Congress of 30 April 1798, and the first Secretary of the Navy was Benjamin Stoddart, installed on 18 June 1798. As originally established, the Secretary of the Navy exercised direct control over the Navy's shore establishment as well as over the operating forces.

From 1842 onward the Congress established a series of bureaus to provide effective procurement of ships and supplies, to manage personnel, and to operate shore activities. These bureaus, commanded by naval officers, also reported directly to the Secretary of the Navy. This organizational concept continues today, with the original bureaus having evolved into the modern systems commands and bureaus.

The position of Aide for Operation was established from 1909–1915 to provide a flag officer (rear admiral) on the staff of the Secretary of the Navy who would be responsible for ship operations as well as training, planning, intelligence, and logistics, and to recommend officer appointments. In 1915, as a result of the war in Europe, the position was changed to Chief of Naval Operations (with the rank of full admiral, the first appointee being Admiral William S. Benson).

However, the CNO did not direct naval forces afloat. Rather, various squadron and, from 1906, fleet commanders exercised command of ships, with their commands based on geographic areas. In 1919 the position of Commander in Chief U.S. Fleet (CinCUS) was established as the overall commander of U.S. naval forces afloat. The CinCUS reported to the Secretary of the Navy, independent of the Chief of Naval Operations.

The positions of CNO and CinCUS remained separate until Admiral Ernest J. King, who had become Commander in Chief U.S. Fleet in December 1941, was additionally named Chief of Naval Operations in March 1942. From that time on the CNO had *de facto* operational command of forces afloat. At the same time the CNO was also the Navy member of the Joint Chiefs of Staff. The position of Commander in Chief U.S. Fleet (which King had changed to ComInCh—pronounced com-*INCH*) was abolished in October 1945, immediately after World War II.

There have been continuous organizational changes within the Navy. Among the more significant, in 1963 the separate technical

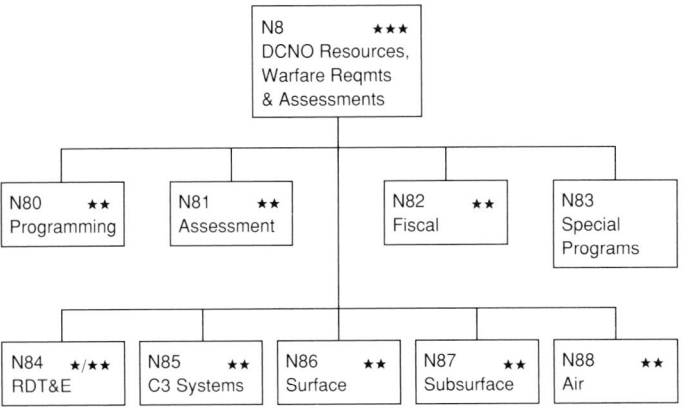

Note: Ranks are indicated by stars.

FIGURE 5-5.   N8 Organization

bureaus were incorporated under a central Naval Material Command headed by the Chief of Naval Material (a full admiral). This had the effect of increasing the influence of the CNO over the bureaus. In 1966 the Secretary of the Navy placed the Naval Material Command (and hence the system commands) directly under the CNO, giving him full responsibility for material, personnel, and medical support of the operating forces. Also in this period, the technical bureaus were redesignated as systems commands—air, ship, ordnance, electronic, supply, etc.

The intermediate administrative organization of the Naval Material Command was abolished in 1985 by Secretary of the Navy John Lehman. Under his revisions, the Secretary and the CNO would jointly exercise direction of the six existing systems commands, at the time the Naval Air Systems Command, Naval Sea Systems Command, Space and Naval Warfare Systems Command, Naval Facilities Engineering Command, and Naval Supply Systems Command.

The Bureau of Naval Personnel and Bureau of Medicine and Surgery had remained outside of the Naval Material Command. Those bureaus survived with those titles until 1978 and 1982 when, respectively, they were renamed the Naval Military Personnel Command and the Naval Medical Command. Those awkward and bureaucratic titles survived only until 1989, when their traditional bureau names were restored.[8]

8. The Bureau of Personnel was created in October 1942, evolving from the Bureau of Navigation (1862) and the predecessor Bureau of Ordnance and Hydrography (1842); the Bureau of Medicine and Surgery was one of the five bureaus originally established by Congress in August 1842.

CHAPTER 6

Fleet Organization

Naval forces are flexible in that they can be easily task-organized for specific missions and operations. Here the replenishment ship NIAGARA FALLS (AFS 3) transfers supplies to the British missile destroyer GLOUCESTER; the anti-submarine destroyer FIFE (DD 991) stands by as the ships steam in a placid Persian Gulf. (PH2 Rob Clare, USN)

The operating forces of the Navy—the ships, submarines, aircraft units, Marine units, construction battalions (Seabees) and other forces—are assigned to two organizational structures: operational and administrative (see chapter 5).

The operational organizations are based primarily on task forces/ groups. The Task Force (TF) organizations shown under the commanders in chief of Atlantic and Pacific Fleets are mainly for contingency operations; exceptions include the respective submarine force commanders, who have both operational and administrative roles. Most of these TF organizations are employed only for exercises or in war.

In the summer of 1992, "permanent" organizations were instituted for the battle groups of the Atlantic and Pacific Fleets. These are "transparent" battle groups in the current vernacular, all with essentially the same composition and capabilities, intended to be easily shifted from one unified command to another. Each of the 12 battle groups nominally consists of one carrier; an embarked carrier air wing; cruiser, destroyer, and frigate units; and two attack submarines. However, there is a two-carrier (one air wing) group organized in the Pacific, while Carrier Air Wing 17 is assigned to both the SARATOGA and WASHINGTON battle groups in the Atlantic.

When this edition went to press, the destroyer, frigate, and submarine assignments for the Pacific Fleet's battle groups had not been completely decided. The assignments will be similar to those in the Atlantic Fleet.

The compositions of these battle groups as they were established are shown in Table 6-5.

Naval administrative organizations are asymmetrical; the hierarchy, organization, and composition of units vary within the fleets and from fleet to fleet. Major organizational changes are taking place in the early 1990s as the size of the active fleet is reduced and organizations are realigned. Ship squadrons that do not have ships assigned are usually operational command staffs that prepare with task forces or groups for forward deployments.

The following tables show a breakdown of naval organizations and nominal ship and aircraft squadron assignments as of 1 January 1992. The assignments are changing with the reduction in Navy force levels. Ships assigned to type commanders are indicated under the administrative organizations. Such assignments change regularly as new ships are commissioned, older ships are stricken, and ships are reassigned for overhaul or modernization. Specific aircraft carriers and fleet flagships are identified by hull number; only aircraft squadrons not assigned to carrier air wings are listed. The ships indicated include active and Naval Reserve Force ships, the latter indicated by asterisks.

Headquarters locations or flagship home ports are indicated, although all ships of a command may not be at the same port. Note that major Atlantic Fleet units often have even numbers and Pacific Fleet units use odd numbers.

Fleet Marine Force organization is described in chapter 7 and operational naval aviation units (air wings and squadrons) are listed in chapter 28.

TABLE 6-1. COMMANDER IN CHIEF PACIFIC FLEET
Operational Organization

CinC Pacific Fleet		Pearl Harbor, Hawaii
TF-10	Temporary Operations Force	
TF-11	Training Force	
TF-12	Anti-Submarine Force	
TF-14	Submarine Force	
TF-15	Surface Force	
TF-16	Maritime Defense Zone[a]	
TF-17	Naval Air Force	
TF-18	Sealift Forces	
TF-19	Fleet Marine Force[b]	
TF-91	Naval Forces Alaska	
TF-199	Naval Support Force Antarctica	
Third Fleet		North Island, Calif./AGF 11
TF-30	Battle Force	
TF-31	Command and Coordination Force	
TF-32	Patrol and Reconnaissance Force	
TF-33	Combat Logistics Support Force	
TF-34	Submarine Force	
TF-35	Surface Combatant Force	
TF-36	Amphibious Force	
TF-37	Carrier Strike Force	
TF-38	Canadian Maritime Force[c]	
TF-39	Landing Force[b]	
Fifth Fleet[d]		
TF-51	Command and Coordination Force	
TF-54	Submarine Force	
TF-55	Coast Guard Area	
Seventh Fleet		Yokosuka, Japan/LCC 19
TF-70	Battle Force	
TF-71	Command and Coordination Force	
TF-72	Patrol and Reconnaissance Force	
TF-73	Logistic Support Force	
TF-74	Submarine Force	
TF-75	Surface Combatant Force	
TF-76	Amphibious Force	
TF-77	Carrier Striking Force	
TF-78	Joint Task Force Middle East[e]	
TF-79	Landing Force[b]	

[a]Commanded by Coast Guard flag officer.
[b]Commanded by Marine Corps general officer.
[c]Commanded by a Canadian officer.
[d]The Fifth Fleet and component task forces do not exist in peacetime.
[e]This is a logistics and administrative support element.

TABLE 6-2. COMMANDER IN CHIEF PACIFIC FLEET
Administrative Organization

CinC Pacific Fleet	Pearl Harbor, Hawaii	
Naval Air Force Pacific	North Island, Calif.	CV 64[a]
		CVN 65[b]
		CVN 72
Carrier Group 1	North Island, Calif.	(no ships)
Carrier Group 3	Alameda, Calif.	CVN 70
Carrier Group 5	Yokosuka, Japan	CV 62
Carrier Group 7	North Island, Calif.	CV 61
		CVN 68
Carrier Air Wing 2	Miramar, Calif.	
Carrier Air Wing 5	Yokosuka, Japan	
Carrier Air Wing 9	Lemoore, Calif.	
Carrier Air Wing 11	Miramar, Calif.	
Carrier Air Wing 14	Miramar, Calif.	
Carrier Air Wing 15	Alameda, Calif.	
ASW Wing Pacific	North Island, Calif.	
VRC-30		
VS-21,41		
VXE-6		
HC-1, 3, 11		
HM-15		
HS-10		
HSL-31, 33, 35, 37, 41, 43, 45, 47, 49		
Fighter-Airborne Early-Warning Wing Pacific	Miramar, Calif.	
VAW-110*		
VC-1		
VF-124, 126		
VX-4		
Light Attack Wing Pacific	Lemoore, Calif.	
VA-122		
VAQ-34		
VFA-125, 127, 303*		
VX-5		
Medium Attack/VAQ Wing Pacific	Whidbey, Wash.	
VA-128		
VAQ-129, 140, 142		
Patrol Wings Pacific	Moffett Field, Calif.	
VP-31		
Patrol Wing 1	Kamiseya, Japan	
(no squadrons assigned)		
Patrol Wing 2	Barbers Point,	
VP-1, 4, 6, 17, 22	Hawaii	
VPU-2		
VQ-3		
Patrol Wing 10	Moffett Field, Calif.	
VP-9, 19, 40, 46, 47, 48, 50		
Fleet Air Western Pacific	Atsugi, Japan	
VC-5		
VRC-50		
VQ-1, 5		
HC-5		
Naval Surface Force Pacific	Coronado, Calif.	1 CG
		1 LSD
		1 MCM
		1 AR
Cruiser-Destroyer Group 1	San Diego, Calif.	5 CGN
		1 CGN
		4 AD
Cruiser-Destroyer Group 3	San Diego, Calif.	6 CG
Cruiser-Destroyer Group 5	San Diego, Calif.	5 CG
Naval Surface Group Long Beach	Long Beach, Calif.	2 CG
		6 FFG*
		2 LST*
		1 ARS*
Naval Surface Group Mid-Pacific	Pearl Harbor, Hawaii	3 CG[e]
		2 AO
Surface Squadron 3	San Francisco, Calif.	
Surface Squadron 5	San Diego, Calif.	2 FFG*
Destroyer Squadron 7	San Diego, Calif.	(no ships)
Destroyer Squadron 9	Long Beach, Calif.	1 DD
		5 FFG
		3 FF
Destroyer Squadron 13	San Diego, Calif.	3 DD
		1 FFG
		6 FF
Destroyer Squadron 15[c]	Yokosuka, Japan	3 DD
		4 FFG

TABLE 6-2. COMMANDER IN CHIEF PACIFIC FLEET
Administrative Organization (continued)

Destroyer Squadron 17	San Diego, Calif.	(no ships)
Destroyer Squadron 21	San Diego, Calif.	(no ships)
Destroyer Squadron 23	San Diego, Calif.	(no ships)
Destroyer Squadron 25	Pearl Harbor, Hawaii	1 DDG
		1 DD
		2 FF
Destroyer Squadron 31	Pearl Harbor, Hawaii[g]	2 DD
		2 FFG
Destroyer Squadron 33	San Diego, Calif.	7 DDG
		4 DD
		2 FFG
		1 FF
Destroyer Squadron 35	Pearl Harbor, Hawaii	1 DDG
		1 DD
		4 FF
Amphibious Group 1[c]	White Beach,	1 LKA
	Okinawa	1 LPD
		1 LST
Amphibious Group 3	San Diego, Calif.	(no ships)
Amphibious Squadron 1	San Diego, Calif.	(no ships)
Amphibious Squadron 3	San Diego, Calif.	(no ships)
Amphibious Squadron 5	San Diego, Calif.	(no ships)
Amphibious Squadron 7	San Diego, Calif.	2 LKA
		5 LSD
		7 LST
Amphibious Squadron 9	San Diego, Calif.	3 LHA
		3 LPH
		6 LPD
Naval Beach Group 1	Coronado, Calif.	
Assault Craft Units 1, 5		
Mine Group 1	Seattle, Wash.	
Mine Division 51	Tacoma, Wash.	2 MSO*
Mine Division 52	San Francisco, Calif.	2 MSO*
Mine Division 53	Seattle, Wash.	3 MSO*
Mine Division 54	San Diego, Calif.	1 MSO*
COOP Mine Squadron 11	Seattle, Wash.	
Explosive Ordnance Group 1	San Diego, Calif.	
Logistics Group 1	Oakland, Calif.	6 AE
		1 AFS
		2 AOE
		4 AOR
Surface Group Western Pacific[c]		LCC 19[d]
		3 CG
		1 AE
		3 AFS
		2 ATS
Combat Support Squadron 5	Pearl Harbor, Hawaii	4 ARS
		(1*)
Submarine Force Pacific	Pearl Harbor, Hawaii	1 AFDM
Submarine Development Group 1	San Diego, Calif.	2 SSN
		1 AGSS
		1 ASR
		2 DSRV
		2 DSV
Submarine Group 9	Bangor, Wash.	1 SSBN
		2 SSN
Submarine Group 5	San Diego, Calif.	2 SSN
Submarine Group 7	Yokosuka, Japan	1 AS[f]
Submarine Squadron 1	Pearl Harbor, Hawaii	8 SSN
		1 ASR
Submarine Squadron 3	San Diego, Calif.	7 SSN
		1 AS
		1 ARD
Submarine Squadron 7	Pearl Harbor, Calif.	7 SSN
Submarine Squadron 11	San Diego, Calif.	7 SSN
		1 AS
		1 ARDM
Submarine Squadron 17	Bangor, Wash.	8 SSBN

[a]Undergoing SLEP modernization at Philadelphia Naval Shipyard.
[b]Undergoing refueling/modernization at Newport News Shipbuilding, Newport News, Va.
[c]All ships home-ported in Western Pacific.
[d]Administrative command for flagship of Commander Seventh Fleet.
[e]One cruiser is home-ported in Yokosuka, Japan.
[f]Submarine tender PROTEUS (AS 19) home-ported at Guam.
[g]Shifted from San Diego to Pearl Harbor in August 1991; DesRon-31 serves as the basis for Pacific Fleet ASW training and tactics development.

TABLE 6-3. COMMANDER IN CHIEF ATLANTIC FLEET
Operational Organization

CinC Atlantic Fleet		Norfolk, Va.
TF-40	Naval Surface Force	
TF-41	Naval Air Force	
TF-42	Submarine Force	
TF-43	Training Command	
TF-44	Coast Guard Forces[a]	
TF-45	Fleet Marine Force[b]	
TF-46	Mine Warfare Force	
TF-47	Naval Construction Battalions	
TF-49	Poseidon Operational Test Force	
TF-80	Naval Patrol and Protection of Shipping	
TF-81	Sea Control and Surveillance Force	
TF-82	Amphibious Task Force	
TF-83	Landing Force[b]	
TF-84	ASW Task Force	
TF-85	Mobile Logistic Support Force	
TF-86	Patrol Air Task Force	
TF-87	Tactical Development and Evaluation and Transit Force	
TF-88	Training Force	
TF-89	Maritime Defense Zone[a]	
TF-134	Naval Forces Caribbean	
TF-137	Eastern Atlantic	
TF-138	South Atlantic Force	
TF-139	Multilateral Special Operations Force	
TF-142	Operational Test and Evaluation Force	
Commander Second Fleet		
TF-20	Battle Force[c]	
TF-21	Sea Control and Surveillance Force[c]	
TF-22	Amphibious Force	
TF-23	Landing Force[b]	
TF-24	ASW Task Force	
TF-25	Mobile Logistics Support Force	
TF-26	Patrol Air Force	
TF-28	Caribbean Contingency Force	

[a]Commanded by Coast Guard flag officer.
[b]Commanded by Marine Corps general officer.
[c]Commander Second Fleet.

TABLE 6-4. COMMANDER IN CHIEF ATLANTIC FLEET
Administrative Organization

CinC Atlantic Fleet	Norfolk, Va.	AVT 59
Naval Air Force Atlantic	Norfolk, Va.	
Helicopter Wings Atlantic	Jacksonville, Fla.	
VX-1		
Helicopter ASW Wing 1	Jacksonville, Fla.	
HS-1		
Helicopter Sea Control Wing 1	Norfolk, Va.	
HSL-30, 32, 34, 36		
Helicopter Sea Control Wing 3	Mayport, Fla.	
HSL-40, 42, 44, 46, 48		
Helicopter Tactical Wing 1	Norfolk, Va.	
VC-6 (no aircraft assigned)		
HC-2, 6, 8, 16		
HM-12, 14		
Tactical Wings Atlantic	Oceana, Va.	
Fighter Wing 1	Oceana, Va.	
VC-8, 10		
VF-43, 101		
Medium Attack Wing 1	Oceana, Va.	
VA-42		
Carrier Airborne Early Warning Wing 12	Norfolk, Va.	
VAW-120		
VRC-40		
Strike Fighter Wings Atlantic	Cecil Field, Fla.	
Light Attack Wing 1	Cecil Field, Fla.	
VAQ-33		
VF-45		
VFA-106		
Sea Strike Wing 1	Cecil Field, Fla.	
VS-27		
Patrol Wings Atlantic	Brunswick, Maine	
VP-30		
VXN-8		
Patrol Wing 5	Brunswick, Maine	
VP-8, 10, 11, 23, 26, 44		
Patrol Wing 11	Jacksonville, Fla.	
VP-5, 16, 24, 45, 49, 56		
Fleet Air Mediterranean[a]		
VR-22, 24		
HC-4		
Carrier Group 2	Norfolk, Va.	CV 66
Carrier Group 4	Norfolk, Va.	CV 67
Carrier Group 6	Mayport, Fla.	CV 60
Carrier Group 8	Norfolk, Va.	CVN 69
		CVN 71
Carrier Air Wing 1	Oceana, Va.	
Carrier Air Wing 3	Cecil Field, Fla.	
Carrier Air Wing 7	Oceana, Va.	
Carrier Air Wing 8	Oceana, Va.	
Carrier Air Wing 17	Cecil Field, Fla.	

[a]HC-4 and VR-24 are based as Sigonella, Sicily, and VR-22 at Rota, Spain.

TABLE 6-4. COMMANDER IN CHIEF ATLANTIC FLEET
Administrative Organization (continued)

Surface Force Atlantic	Norfolk, Va.	
Naval Surface Group Mediterranean	Naples, Italy	CG 26[b]
Naval Surface Group 4	Newport, R.I.	3 FFG
		4 FFG*
		7 FF (3*)
Cruiser-Destroyer Group 2	Charleston, S.C.	2 CG
		1 AD
Cruiser-Destroyer Group 8	Norfolk, Va.	4 CGN
		8 CG
		2 DDG
Cruiser-Destroyer Group 12	Mayport, Fla.	7 CG
		1 AD
Destroyer Squadron 2	Norfolk, Va.	3 DDG
		8 FF
Destroyer Squadron 4	Charleston, S.C.	5 DDG
		6 DD
		2 FF (1*)
		2 AE
Destroyer Squadron 6	Charleston, S.C.	11 FFG (2*)
Destroyer Squadron 8	Mayport, Fla.	2 DD
		12 FFG (2*)
Destroyer Squadron 10	Norfolk, Va.	2 DDG
		8 DD
Destroyer Squadron 12	Mayport, Fla.	3 DDG
		4 FF
		2 MCM
		2 MSO*
Destroyer Squadron 14	Mayport, Fla.	(no ships)
Destroyer Squadron 20	Charleston, S.C.	(no ships)
Destroyer Squadron 22	Norfolk, Va.	(no ships)
Destroyer Squadron 24	Mayport, Fla.	(no ships)
Destroyer Squadron 26	Norfolk, Va.	(no ships)
Destroyer Squadron 32	Norfolk, Va.	(no ships)
Destroyer Squadron 36	Charleston, S.C.	(no ships)
Amphibious Group 2	Norfolk, Va.	
Amphibious Squadron 2	Norfolk, Va.	(no ships)
Amphibious Squadron 4	Norfolk, Va.	(no ships)
Amphibious Squadron 6	Norfolk, Va.	(no ships)
Amphibious Squadron 8	Norfolk, Va.	(no ships)
Amphibious Squadron 10	Little Creek, Va.	6 LSD
		10 LST
Amphibious Squadron 12	Norfolk, Va.	LC 20[c]
		AGF 3[d]
		1 LHD
		2 LHA
		4 LPH
		2 LKA
		6 LPD
Naval Beach Group 2 Assault Craft Units 2, 4		
Patrol Combat Missile Squadron	Key West, Fla.	6 PHM
Mine Squadron 2	Charleston, S.C.	1 MC
		3 MSO (2*)
COOP Mine Squadron 22	Charleston, S.C.	
Mine Division 121	Newport, R.I.	1 MCM
		2 MSO*
Combat Logistics Group	Norfolk, Va.	3 AD
		1 AR
Combat Logistics Squadron 2	Earle, N.J.	3 AE
		2 AOE
Combat Logistics Squadron 4	Norfolk, Va.	3 AFS
		3 AO
		3 AOR
Support Squadron 8	Little Creek, Va.	2 MCM
		3 MSO*
		4 ARS (1*)
		2 ATF
		1 ATS

[b]Home-ported in Gaeta, Italy.
[c]Administrative commander is PhibRon-10; flagship of Commander Second Fleet.
[d]Administrative commander is PhibRon-10; flagship of Commander Middle East Force; home-ported in Bahrain.

TABLE 6-4. COMMANDER IN CHIEF ATLANTIC FLEET
Administrative Organization (continued)

Submarine Force Atlantic	Norfolk, Va.	
Submarine Group 2	Groton, Conn.	3 SSBN
		5 SSN
		NR-1
Submarine Group 6	Charleston, S.C.	2 SSBN
Submarine Group 8	Naples, Italy	(no ships)
Submarine Group 10	Kings Bay, Ga.	1 SSBN
Submarine Squadron 2	Groton, Conn.	8 SSN
		1 ASR
		1 ARD
		1 ARDM
Submarine Squadron 4	Charleston, S.C.	10 SSN
		1 AS
		1 ASR
Submarine Squadron 6	Norfolk, Va.	9 SSN
		1 AS
		1 ASR
Submarine Squadron 8	Norfolk, Va.	17 SSN
		2 AS
		1 AFDM
Submarine Squadron 10	New London, Conn.	5 SSN
Submarine Development Squadron 12	Groton, Conn.	7 SSN[e]
Submarine Squadron 14	Holy Loch, Scotland[f]	6 SSBN[g]
Submarine Squadron 16	Kings Bay, Ga.	9 SSBN
		1 AS
		1 ARDM
Submarine Squadron 18	Charleston, S.C.	4 SSBN
		1 AS
Submarine Squadron 20	Kings Bay, Ga.	2 SSBN
Submarine Squadron 22	La Maddalena, Sardinia	1 AS

[e]Develops tactics for ASW, including Arctic warfare; anti-ship warfare; mine warfare; and tactical strike warfare.
[f]Base closed in 1992.
[g]Submarines are home-ported in Groton, Conn.

TABLE 6-5.   CARRIER BATTLE GROUPS, LATE 1992[1]

PACIFIC FLEET		ATLANTIC FLEET	

INDEPENDENCE BATTLE GROUP
Carrier Group 5
Destroyer Squadron 15
Carrier Air Wing 5

CV 62	INDEPENDENCE
CG 52	BUNKER HILL
CG 53	MOBILE BAY
DD 966	HEWITT
DD 975	O'BRIEN
DD 991	FIFE
FFG 38	CURTS
FFG 41	MCCLUSKY
FFG 43	THACH
FFG 60	RODNEY M. DAVIS

NIMITZ BATTLE GROUP
Carrier Group 7
Destroyer Squadron 23
Carrier Air Wing 9

CVN 68	NIMITZ
CGN 9	LONG BEACH
CG 23	HALSEY
CG 24	REEVES
CG 33	FOX
CGN 35	TRUXTUN
CG 57	LAKE CHAMPLAIN
DDG 994	CALLAGHAN
DDG 996	CHANDLER
DDG 56	JOHN S. MCCAIN
DD 964	PAUL F. FOSTER
DD 971	DAVID R. RAY
DD 984	LEFTWICH
FFG 48	VANDEGRIFT
FFG 54	FORD

AMERICA BATTLE GROUP
Carrier Group 6
Destroyer Squadron 14
Carrier Group 1

CV 66	AMERICA
CGN 37	SOUTH CAROLINA
CG 60	NORMANDY
CG 61	MONTEREY
DDG 39	MACDONOUGH
DDG 42	MAHAN
DDG 995	SCOTT
DD 981	JOHN HANCOCK
DD 988	THORN
FFG 28	BOONE
FFG 34	AUBRY FITCH
FFG 50	JESSE L. TAYLOR
FFG 56	SIMPSON
SSN 694	GROTON
SSN 757	ALEXANDRIA

ROOSEVELT BATTLE GROUP
Carrier Group 8
Destroyer Squadron 22
Carrier Air Wing 8

CVN 71	THEODORE ROOSEVELT
CG 20	RICHMOND K. TURNER
CG 27	JOSEPHUS DANIELS
CGN 40	MISSISSIPPI
CG 47	TICONDEROGA
CG 69	VICKSBURG
DDG 51	ARLEIGH BURKE
DD 978	STUMP
DD 982	NICHOLSON
FFG 47	NICHOLAS
FFG 53	HAWES
FFG 59	KAUFFMAN
SSN 714	NORFOLK
SSN 756	SCRANTON

KITTY HAWK BATTLE GROUP
Cruiser Destroyer Group 5
Destroyer Squadron 17
Carrier Air Wing 15

CV 63	KITTY HAWK
CG 16	LEAHY
CG 18	WORDEN
CG 32	W.H. STANDLEY
CG 62	CHANCELLORSVILLE
CG 63	COWPENS
DDG 54	CURTIS WILBUR
DDG 63	STETHEM
DD 967	ELLIOT
DD 976	MERRILL
FFG 33	JARRETT
FFG 37	CROMMELIN

RANGER/CONSTELLATION BATTLE GROUP
Cruiser Destroyer Group 1
Destroyer Squadron 7
Carrier Air Wing 2

CV 61	RANGER
CV 64	CONSTELLATION
CG 21	GRIDLEY
CG 29	JOUETT
CG 30	HORNE
CG 50	VALLEY FORGE
CG 65	CHOSIN
CG 73	PORT ROYAL
DDG 60	PAUL HAMILTON
DD 965	KINKAID
DD 972	OLDENDORF
FFG 30	REID
FFG 46	RENTZ

KENNEDY BATTLE GROUP
Carrier Group 2
Destroyer Squadron 20
Carrier Air Wing 3

CV 67	JOHN F. KENNEDY
CG 28	WAINWRIGHT
CG 55	LEYTE GULF
CG 64	GETTYSBURG
CG 71	CAPE ST. GEORGE
DD 983	JOHN RODGERS
DD 987	O'BANNON
DD 990	CARON
FFG 8	MCINERNEY
FFG 31	STARK
FFG 36	UNDERWOOD
FFG 40	HALYBURTON
SSN 669	SEAHORSE
SSN 706	ALBUQUERQUE

SARATOGA BATTLE GROUP
Cruiser Destroyer Group 8
Destroyer Squadron 24
Carrier Air Wing 17

CV 60	SARATOGA
CG 19	DALE
CG 34	BIDDLE
CG 51	THOMAS S. GATES
CG 58	PHILIPPINE SEA
DD 968	ARTHUR W. RADFORD
DD 970	MOOSBRUGGER
DD 974	COMTE DE GRASSE
DD 997	HAYLER
FFG 24	JACK WILLIAMS
FFG 26	GALLERY
FFG 29	STEPHEN W. GROVES
FFG 32	JOHN L. HALL
SSN 676	BILLFISH
SSN 705	CITY OF CORPUS CHRISTI

LINCOLN BATTLE GROUP
Carrier Group 3
Destroyer Squadron 21
Carrier Air Wing 11

CVN 72	ABRAHAM LINCOLN
CG 31	STERETT
CGN 36	CALIFORNIA
CGN 39	TEXAS
CG 59	PRINCETON
CG 67	SHILOH
DDG 53	JOHN PAUL JONES
DDG 62	FITZGERALD
DD 973	JOHN YOUNG
DD 990	INGERSOLL
FFG 51	GARY
FFG 61	INGRAHAM

VINSON BATTLE GROUP
Cruiser Destroyer Group 3
Destroyer Squadron 5
Carrier Air Wing 14

CVN 70	CARL VINSON
CG 22	ENGLAND
CGN 41	ARKANSAS
CG 49	VINCENNES
CG 54	ANTIETAM
CG 70	LAKE ERIE
DDG 59	RUSSELL
DD 985	CUSHING
DD 986	HARRY W. HILL
DD 992	FLETCHER
FFG 57	REUBEN JAMES

EISENHOWER BATTLE GROUP
Cruiser Destroyer Group 12
Destroyer Squadron 32
Carrier Air Wing 7

CVN 69	DWIGHT D. EISENHOWER
CGN 38	VIRGINIA
CG 48	YORKTOWN
CG 68	ANZIO
CG 72	VELLA GULF
DD 969	PETERSON
DD 977	BRISCOE
DD 979	CONOLLY
FFG 42	KLAKRING
FFG 49	ROBERT G. BRADLEY
FFG 55	ELROD
FFG 58	SAMUEL B. ROBERTS
SSN 712	ATLANTA
SSN 723	OKLAHOMA CITY

WASHINGTON BATTLE GROUP
Cruiser Destroyer Group 2
Destroyer Squadron 26
Carrier Air Wing 17

CVN 73	GEORGE WASHINGTON
CG 17	HARRY E. YARNELL
CGN 25	BAINBRIDGE
CG 56	SAN JACINTO
CG 66	HUE CITY
DDG 993	KIDD
DD 963	SPRUANCE
DD 989	DEYO
FFG 39	DOYLE
FFG 45	DE WERT
FFG 52	CARR
SSN 667	BERGALL
SSN 709	HYMAN G. RICKOVER

1. See chapter 28 for the composition of carrier air wings.

CHAPTER 7

Fleet Marine Force

Marines on the move in Kuwait during the 100-hour ground-war phase of Operation Desert Storm; an oil well burns in the distance. The Marines are considered light forces, and for the ground war had to be reinforced by British Army and, subsequently, U.S. Army heavy tanks. (U.S. Marine Corps)

The Marine Corps is a separate service (with the Navy) within the Department of the Navy. The primary mission of the Marine Corps is to provide the Fleet Marine Forces of the Atlantic and Pacific Fleets with combat-ready air-ground task forces to conduct amphibious operations.

In addition to maintaining the Fleet Marine Forces, the Marine Corps provides:

- Afloat detachments in aircraft carriers and some submarine tenders.[1]
- Security detachments for selected Navy shore installations in the United States.
- Security detachments for U.S. embassies and diplomatic missions abroad.

The U.S. Marine Corps is the world's largest "naval infantry force," with a current strength of approximately 182,000 officers and enlisted men and women.[2] This strength is down from a post–Vietnam War peak of approximately 200,000 in the late 1980s. Under current planning the Marines will decline to some 159,000 by 1995. The Fleet Marine Force (FMF)—the "muscle of the Corps"—will be reduced from 116,000 troops to 89,000. All units are expected to be reduced in size from the nominal strengths listed in this chapter.

About 96.5 percent of the Marine officers are male and 3.5 percent female; for the enlisted troops, some 95 percent are male and 5 percent female. Thus, the Marine Corps has the highest ratio of male-to-female personnel of any of the military services.

The Marine Corps is a "combined arms" force possessing armor and heavy artillery, and a large tactical air arm including fixed-wing aircraft and helicopters. The Marine Corps is the only such service with its own air arm, except for a small number of helicopters and light fixed-wing aircraft flown by the British and Russian Marines. (The U.S. Marine Corps aviation structure is described in chapter 28 and Marine aircraft in chapter 29).

The Marine Corps is nominally organized into three ground divisions and three aircraft wings, with a large combat support force formed into three service support groups. The basing structure of the FMF is shown in table 7-1. The Marine Corps Reserve consists of an additional division and aircraft wing. However, these divisions and wings can be considered primarily as an administrative structure as Marine units deployed in Marine Air-Ground Task Force (MAGTF) formations (pronounced "*mag*-taf").

The Marine Corps follows a basic triangular organization, with each division having three infantry regiments (plus an artillery regiment), each infantry regiment having three rifle battalions, and each battalion having three rifle companies (and a weapons company).[3] Marine divisions are the world's largest, with a total strength of 17,883 Marines and 932 Navy personnel. (Figures 7-2 through 7-4 at the end of this chapter show the nominal Marine division organization; the division totals will vary in actual units because of differing organizations of artillery regiments, tank battalions, and assault amphibian battalions.)

1. Previously, Marine detachments were provided to battleships as well as some large cruisers.
2. At the time of the demise of the Soviet Union, in December 1991, the Soviet Naval Infantry consisted of some 18,000 troops. However, in the late 1980s four motorized rifle divisions of the Soviet Ground Forces had been transferred to the Navy, with the Naval Infantry and Navy-controlled Coastal Missile-Artillery Force (some 14,000 troops), to form the Coastal Defense Force within the naval establishment.
   The next largest Marine forces are those of China, with an estimated 50,000+ troops, Taiwan with 39,000, Vietnam with 27,000, South Korea with 25,000, and Thailand with 20,000; Britain's Royal Marines has a strength of some 7,700.
3. In 1988–1989 eight Marine battalions, designated as MEU (Special Operations Capability), were provided with a fourth rifle company. However, the drawdown of Marine strength forced a reduction to three rifle companies in those battalions during 1991.

TABLE 7-1. MARINE CORPS BASING

Camp H.M. Smith, Hawaii
Headquarters, FMF Pacific
Headquarters, 1st Marine Expeditionary Brigade
Kaneohoe, Hawaii
　　3rd Marines* (infantry)
　　Marine Aircraft Group 24
Camp Pendleton, Calif.
Headquarters, I Marine Expeditionary Force
1st Marine Division
　　1st, 5th Marines (infantry)
　　11th Marines (artillery)
　　Marine Aircraft Group 39
1st Force Service Support Group
Twenty-nine Palms, Calif.
　　7th Marines (infantry)
El Toro, Calif.
3rd Marine Aircraft Wing
　　Marine Aircraft Group 11
Tustin, Calif.
　　Marine Aircraft Group 16
Camp Butler, Okinawa
Headquarters, III Marine Expeditionary Force
3rd Marine Division
　　4th, 9th Marines (infantry)
　　12th Marines (artillery)
1st Marine Aircraft Wing
　　Marine Aircraft Group 36
3rd Force Service Support Group
Iwakuni, Japan
　　Marine Aircraft Group 12
Norfolk, Va.
Headquarters, 4th Marine Expeditionary Brigade (Little Creek)
Camp Lejeune, N.C.
Headquarters, FMF Atlantic†
Headquarters, II Marine Expeditionary Force
2nd Marine Division
　　2nd, 6th, 8th Marines (infantry)
　　10th Marines (artillery)
2nd Force Service Support Group
Cherry Point, N.C.
2nd Marine Aircraft Wing
　　Marine Aircraft Groups 14, 26, 29, 32
Beaufort, S.C.
　　Marine Aircraft Group 31

---

*Marine regiments are referred to as "Marines."
†Formerly at Norfolk, Va. (Camp Elmore); moved in 1992; the Deputy Commanding General FMF Atlantic and a small staff remain at Norfolk.

Marine divisions can be considered as "light" or "mechanized" combat units. While one tank battalion and one light armored vehicle battalion is assigned to each division, the limited number of tanks (51 or 68 tanks per battalion) and the lack of armored personnel carriers limits the effectiveness of Marine units against heavily armored forces. The Marines do use tracked amphibian vehicles (AAV) for battlefield transport; however, those vehicles are limited in that role (see chapter 20).

The Marine Corps does not have medical, dental, or chaplain personnel, but relies upon the Navy to provide these services. These Navy personnel are fully integrated into Marine units and, when in the field, dress in Marine uniforms. In turn, Marine representatives are assigned to all appropriate Navy staffs, including those of the Secretary of the Navy and the Office of the Chief of Naval Operations (OPNAV); for example, the Marine Deputy Chief of Staff/Aviation also served as a Deputy Assistant Chief of Naval Operations (Air Warfare) to ensure the full integration and coordination of the two services' air arms. (The DCNO for Air Warfare was changed to Director of Air Warfare in 1992.)

FLEET MARINE FORCE ORGANIZATION

The Fleet Marine Force (FMF) is the land assault component of what are now called Naval Expeditionary Forces—Marine assault units, amphibious ships, supporting carrier task forces, and other forces required to project American military power by sea.

The Marine Corps is a "combined armed" force, with deploying forces called Marine Air-Ground Task Forces (MAGTF) that each contain components of the ground divisions, aircraft wings, and support groups. These MAGTFs can be tailored to the size and composition required to meet a broad range of operational requirements, and for transport by various methods.

There are four generic types of MAGTFs; from smallest to largest they are:

Marine Expeditionary Unit (MEU)
Marine Expeditionary Brigade (MEB)
Marine Expeditionary Force (MEF)
Special-Purpose Force (SPF)

During the 1980s some MEUs underwent special training and qualifications and were designated as Special Operations Capable (SOC); that qualification was dropped in late 1991. Each MAGTF has four fundamental elements that are drawn from the ground divisions, aircraft wings, and support groups as needed; those elements are shown in figure 7-1.

The buildup of MAGTFs from the component "building blocks" is not linear. For example, while a Marine regiment and aircraft group are the ground and air elements of a Marine Expeditionary Brigade, a division-wing team cannot form three MEBs because of the shortfall of command and support units.

Thus, the Fleet Marine Force, with three divisions and three wings, can effectively deploy two MEFs or perhaps four MEBs, plus some smaller units. Table 7-2 describes the structure of the various MAGTFs.

The Special-Purpose Force (SPF) units are employed for both conventional and "unconventional" operations; they can be deployed by aircraft, surface ships, or the Navy's transport submarines.

Originally the MAGTFs, when established in the late 1970s, were not permanent organizations, but were to be "task organized for a specific mission and, after completion of that mission, . . . dissolved."[4]

4. Commanding General, Marine Corps Development and Educational Command, *Marine Air-Ground Task Force Doctrine* (FMFM 0-1) (Quantico, Va., June 1978), pp. 1–5.

Gen. Carl Mundy, Jr., Commandant of the Marine Corps since July 1991.

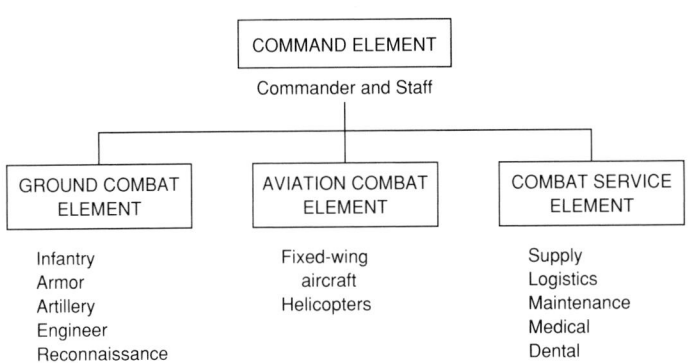

FIGURE 7-1. **Notional MAGTF Structure**

TABLE 7-2. **MAGTF ORGANIZATIONS**

	Marine Expeditionary Unit (MEU)	Marine Expeditionary Brigade (MEB)	Marine Expeditionary Force (MEF)	Special Purpose Force (SPF)
Total personnel	1,000–4,000	4,000–18,000	30,000–60,000	100–1,000
Commander	colonel	brigadier general	lieutenant general	varies
Ground combat element	infantry battalion	infantry regiment	one or more divisions	rifle company
Aviation combat element	composite squadron (helicopters + VSTOL)	aircraft group	aircraft wing	aviation detachment
Combat service support element	MEU service support group	brigade service support group	force service support group	combat service
Self-sustainment capability*	15 days	30 days	60 days	as required
Amphibious lift	4–6 ships	21–26 ships	approx. 50 ships	varies
Major equipment	5 tanks	17 tanks	70 tanks	
	8 155-mm howitzers	30 155-mm howitzers	108 155-mm howitzers	
	8 81-mm mortars	6 8-inch (203-mm) howitzers	12 8-inch (203-mm) howitzers	
	9 60-mm mortars	24 81-mm mortars	72 81-mm mortars	
	32 Dragon anti-tank launchers	27 60-mm mortars	81 60-mm mortars	
	8 TOW anti-tank launchers†	96 dragon anti-tank launchers	288 Dragon anti-tank launchers	
	12 assault amphibian vehicles	48 TOW anti-tank launchers	144 TOW anti-tank launchers	
	5 Stinger SAM teams	47 assault amphibian vehicles	208 assault amphibian vehicles	
	6 fixed-wing aircraft (VSTOL)	36 light armored vehicles	147 light armored vehicles	
	~ 20 helicopters	6 Hawk SAM launchers	24 Hawk SAM launchers	
		15 Stinger SAM teams	75 Stinger SAM teams	
		~ 75 fixed-wing aircraft	~ 150 fixed-wing aircraft	
		~ 100 helicopters	~ 150 helicopters	

*Varies with tactical situation, level of combat, etc.
†Additional TOW launchers are mounted on AH-1W SeaCobra helicopters.

Marines during an amphibious exercise. The Marine Corps continues to develop improved techniques for over-the-beach assaults, although the Marine capability for helicopter assault appears to be more practical in many scenarios. (U.S. Marine Corps)

But in the 1980s the MAGTF units took on an increasingly permanent structure. This shift came in large part because of commitments to "marrying" Marine combat units with weapons and material in Maritime Prepositioning Ships (MPS) deployed in various ocean areas, and prepositioned ashore in Norway. The permanent assignment of MAGTFs to specific prepositioned equipment and to specific geographic areas has reduced the flexibility of Marine units.

During 1992, as a consequence of force-level reductions and the lessons learned in Desert Shield and Desert Storm, the Marine Corps began to reform their MAGTF structure. Since 1982 a total of 15 permanent MAGTF command elements had been formed—3 MEFs, 6 MEBs, and 6 MEUs. With the cutback in personnel strength, all six standing brigade-level command elements are being deactivated, the last scheduled for fiscal 1994.

(Note: The MEB command elements are being abolished because of the reductions in manpower and force restructuring; similarly, Marine divisions are being reorganized. See addenda.)

In the future, as Marine units larger than MEUs deploy, they will be commanded by a forward element of the MEF command element. In a related move, the staffs of the I and II MEF headquarters are being expanded; the III MEF will be deactivated and will be replaced by I MEF (Forward), which will retain all of the functions now found in III MEF.

While Marine strength is being reduced, the quality of personnel continues to improve. Here a Marine with an M16 rifle mounting a grenade launcher stands at the ready in the Kuwaiti desert. (CWO Ed Bailey, USN)

MARINE SECURITY FORCES

The Marine Corps Security Force (MCSF) provides security force detachments on board all operational aircraft carriers, some submarine tenders, at various ammunition storage sites, at major bases in the United States and overseas, and at U.S. embassies and consulates abroad. A total of almost 7,000 men and women are assigned to the MCSF mission.[5]

On board ship the Marines primarily provide security for nuclear weapons, serve as the cadre for a landing force, and perform ceremonial functions. The standard detachment on aircraft carriers is two officers and 64 enlisted men; on battleships during the 1980s it was two officers and 53 enlisted men; and on certain submarine tenders it is one officer and 53 enlisted men.

The security companies, detachments, and "barracks" at more then 100 locations vary considerably in size. The largest such unit is the Marine barracks at the Guantánamo Bay (Cuba) naval base; commanded by a colonel, that unit has 21 officers and 323 enlisted personnel. In addition to base security, that barracks has the responsibility for safeguarding Haitian refugees who are interned at

the base. The other MCSF units that survive as barracks are at the Naval Academy in Annapolis, Md.; Washington, D.C.; Guam; Hawaii; and Yokosuka, Japan. (The Marine barracks at Subic Bay in the Phillipines was disestablished with the U.S. withdrawal from the Philippines in 1992.)

The current MCSF structure was established in late 1987 in response to a directive by the Secretary of the Navy for the reorganization of naval security forces "to meet the growing threat of terrorism . . . [and] strengthen its ability to detect and defeat attacks targeted at Service members and their families." The Marine Corps responded by creating two MCSF battalions—Atlantic and Pacific—to supervise the operations of companies and detachments at shore bases around the world. The Atlantic battalion has its headquarters at Norfolk, Va., and the Pacific battalion is at Mare Island, Calif.

In addition to the companies and detachments that safeguard various shore facilities, each battalion also has a Fleet Anti-terrorism Security Team (FAST) company. The FAST units are especially trained and equipped to rescue hostages and contain terrorists. The Atlantic FAST company has a strength of 233 Marines, and the Pacific FAST company has 345. Each battalion has a special school to instruct personnel in counter-terrorist operations.

5. This does not include some 1,000 men and women assigned to the Marine Barracks in Washington, D.C., who perform a variety of duties and functions at various area installations.

FLEET MARINE FORCE MOBILITY

Mobility is a principle of naval operations and is a key characteristic of the Fleet Marine Force. There are several aspects to FMF mobility:

Forward afloat forces. Marine units are normally afloat in amphibious ships in forward areas. Normally one MEU is afloat in the Mediterranean area and one in the Pacific–Indian Ocean area; at times additional MEUs or larger formations are at sea, in transit to relieve forward-deployed MEUs, or for exercises. As a crisis begins to evolve, the afloat MEUs, like other naval forces, can be dispatched to the problem area without creating an intrusion in foreign territory or air space.

Amphibious assault. The Marines have a significant amphibious assault capability employing helicopters, landing craft and vehicles from the Navy's amphibious ships (see chapter 19). The existing amphibious force has a theoretical lift capacity of the assault echelon of approximately one MEF, i.e., a reinforced division and the helicopter and VSTOL portions of an aircraft wing. (The "assault echelon" is the portion of the force that makes the actual landing: about two-thirds of the troops, one-half the vehicles, and one-quarter of the cargo of the unit.)[6]

Near-term fleet reductions will see a decline in the lift capacity to only 2½ MEBs, i.e., reinforced regiments. Further budget reductions could further reduce this lift capacity.

Maritime prepositioning. Three squadrons of Maritime Prepositioning Ships (MPS) are forward deployed, one in the Atlantic, one off Diego Garcia in the Indian Ocean, and one off the Mariana Islands in the Western Pacific. Each MPS squadron carries weapons, vehicle equipment, munitions, and provisions for a MEB (see chapter 8). These ships can be sent into a port to be "married" with Marines flown into the area by transport aircraft. While this force does not have the ability to make a forcible entry but requires a friendly port or sheltered unloading area and nearby airfield, the viability of the MPS concept was demonstrated in Operation Desert Shield in August 1990.

Airlift. Marines, as other light combat forces, can be airlifted into an area by transport aircraft. The Marine Corps has a small force of C-130 Hercules transport-tanker aircraft, but a sizeable troop commitment would require the use of U.S. Air Force transport aircraft.

6. A recent, simplified exposition on this subject is Congressional Budget Office, *Moving the Marine Corps by Sea in the 1990s* (Washington, D.C.: October 1989).

MARINE OPERATIONS

The Marines had a major role in the U.S. buildup in the Middle East from August 1990 (Operation Desert Shield) and the subsequent war with Iraq in early 1991 (Operation Desert Storm). With fears that Iraq would launch an assault on Saudi Arabia immediately after consolidating its position in Kuwait, in early August 1990 the President ordered the deployment of U.S. combat forces into Saudi Arabia.

The first squadron of prepositioning ships arrived at the port of Al Jubayl, Saudi Arabia, on 15 August 1990 and were met by troops of the 7th MEB (based on the 7th Marines), airlifted from Twenty-nine Palms, Calif.[7] Additional Marines followed, by air and sea, with all three MPS squadrons unloading their material in Saudi Arabia. When the Gulf War began on 17 January 1991, there were 76,000

7. These were the ships of Maritime Prepositioning Squadron 2. They had been anchored at Diego Garcia in the Indian Ocean and were ordered to get under way for the Persian Gulf on 8 August.

Marines "in country" in the 1st and 2nd Marine Divisions, with a massive Marine air force consolidated under the 3rd Marine Aircraft Wing and a large support establishment designated as the 1st Force Service Support Group. The Marine air component in Desert Storm—both on amphibious ships and ashore—totaled 20 fixed-wing and 24 helicopter squadrons, plus detachments of other aviation units.

The entire Marine force within Saudi Arabia was under the command of the I Marine Expeditionary Force, with the commanding general, Lieutenant General Walter E. Boomer, also serving as Commander U.S. Marine Corps Central Command (MARCENT), the Marine component of the "unified" Southern Command. Separate from this command were 17,000 Marines on board 31 amphibious ships in the Persian Gulf. This afloat force consisted of two separate Marine brigades (4th and 5th MEBs) plus a separate MEU; for political reasons there was no overall Marine commander assigned for the afloat force. This represented the largest amphibious task force since World War II. (Another 5,000 Marines were embarked in amphibious ships in the eastern Mediterranean.)

During the ground assault against occupied Kuwait and Iraq, the I MEF was to the right of the allied line and saw considerable combat. The Marines' shortfall in armored vehicles was a major consideration to allied planners, however, and an Army tank brigade was attached to the I MEF and, in the field, some Marine units also exchanged their M60A1 tanks for the new M1A1 Abrams tank.[8]

Although the 17,000 afloat Marines were not employed in an amphibious assault, the threat of such a landing did force the Iraqi high command to maintain several front-line divisions along the coast of Kuwait and away from the main line of defense along the Kuwaiti border. During January the 5th MEB was landed some 20 miles (32 km) south of the Kuwait-Saudi border, behind the advancing I MEF. Eight air-cushion landing craft (LCAC) and helicopters brought

8. The Marine Corps completed transition from the M60 to the M1A1 tank in mid-1992; there are now 221 tanks in Marine service, including reserve units, and 30 in each of the three MPS squadrons.

MARINE CORPS RESERVE

The Marine Corps Reserve consists of the 4th Marine Division and the 4th Marine Aircraft Wing. These units generally parallel active units in organization, but in some categories have older equipment and lack several service support components. Based on command problems during the reserve callup in Desert Shield and Desert Storm, the Marine Corps in 1992 reorganized its reserves under one command structure. Known as the Marine Reserve Forces, the new organization will oversee the training, equipping, and leadership of the 4th Marine Division, the 4th Marine Aircraft Wing, and the 4th Force Service Support Group.

Marine reservists have training sessions on a weekly or monthly basis, and for two weeks' duration during the summer. The latter periods include participation in exercises with active units in the United States and overseas.

As of March 1991 the Marine Corps Reserve had 3,772 officers and 41,560 enlisted personnel assigned to reserve units. The reserve force is expected to be reduced to some 34,900, resulting in a reduction in the size of all major reserve units.

ashore 7,300 Marines along with almost 2,400 tons of vehicles and weapons in less than 24 hours; the ship-to-shore transfer required 55 trips by the LCACs, made in heavy seas with 40-knot winds. Portions of the 4th MEB were subsequently brought ashore.

Eighty-five percent of the Fleet Marine Force was deployed to the Persian Gulf area; 25,710 men and women of the Marine Corps Reserve—61 percent—were mobilized in that period, with many of them sent into the desert with their active-duty counterparts. Then-Commandant A.M. (Al) Gray declared: "There are four kinds of Marines: those in Saudi Arabia, those going to Saudi Arabia, those who want to go to Saudi Arabia, and those who don't want to go to Saudi Arabia but are going anyway!"

Simultaneous with Desert Shield, a Navy-Marine amphibious force conducted an extensive rescue operation off the coast of strife-torn Liberia, and on the eve of Desert Storm another Navy-Marine team carried out a dramatic rescue in Somalia. (Described in chapter 1.)

Following Operation Desert Shield, Navy-Marine amphibious forces were engaged in humanitarian assistance to Kurds in northern Iraq and assisting survivors of the flooding in Bangladesh.

Historical. The Marine Corps was established on 10 November 1775 by the Continental Congress, with two battalions of men being raised who were "good seamen, or so acquainted with maritime affairs as to be able to serve to advantage by sea, when required." Subsequently, Marines have fought at sea and ashore in almost all American conflicts. The Corps reached a peak strength of 485,000 men and women during World War II, with six divisions and four aircraft wings (plus numerous separate squadrons).

During the 1950s the United States began the practice of maintaining batallion landing teams (and later MEUs) afloat on board amphibious ships in the Mediterranean, Western Pacific, and, at times, in the Caribbean area.

From its beginning, the Marine Corps has been a separate service within the Navy Department. The senior Marine officer, the Commandant, has the rank of full general. He is a member of the Joint Chiefs of Staff (JCS), and while responsible for the readiness and training of the Marine Corps, he does not have operational command of Marine combat forces except as specifically assigned by the JCS or the Secretary of Defense. Rather, the senior organizational commands of the Marine Corps—Fleet Marine Force (FMF) Atlantic and Pacific—are essentially "type" commands within the Atlantic and Pacific Fleets.

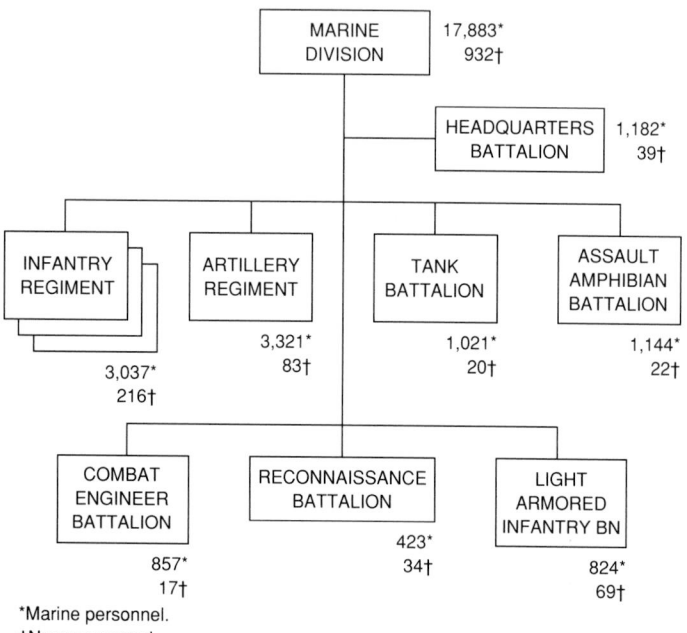

*Marine personnel.
†Navy personnel.

FIGURE 7-2. Marine Division

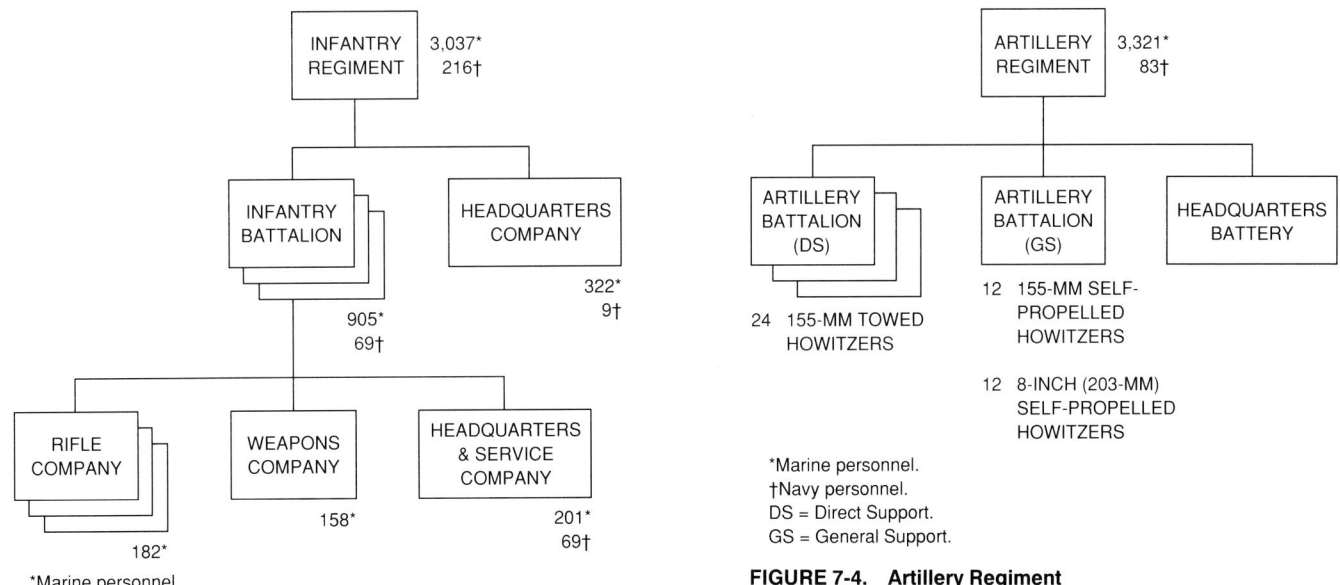

*Marine personnel.
†Navy personnel.

FIGURE 7-3. Infantry Regiment

*Marine personnel.
†Navy personnel.
DS = Direct Support.
GS = General Support.

FIGURE 7-4. Artillery Regiment

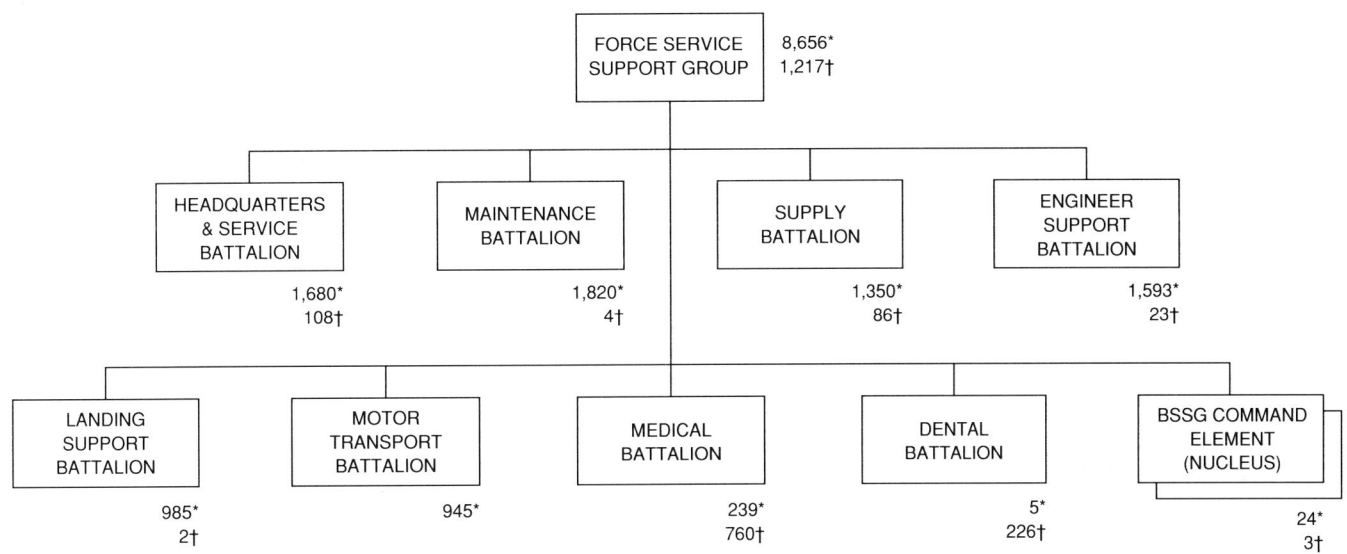

*Marine personnel.
†Navy personnel.
BSSG = Brigade Service Support Group.

FIGURE 7-5. Force Service Support Group

CHAPTER 8

Military Sealift Command

The fast sealift ship ALGOL (T-AKR 287) loads U.S. Army combat vehicles. The ALGOL and seven sister ships of the SL-7 design are the fastest cargo ships ever built. The Military Sealift Command controls a massive cargo fleet and operates a variety of naval auxiliary and special-mission ships. (U.S. Navy)

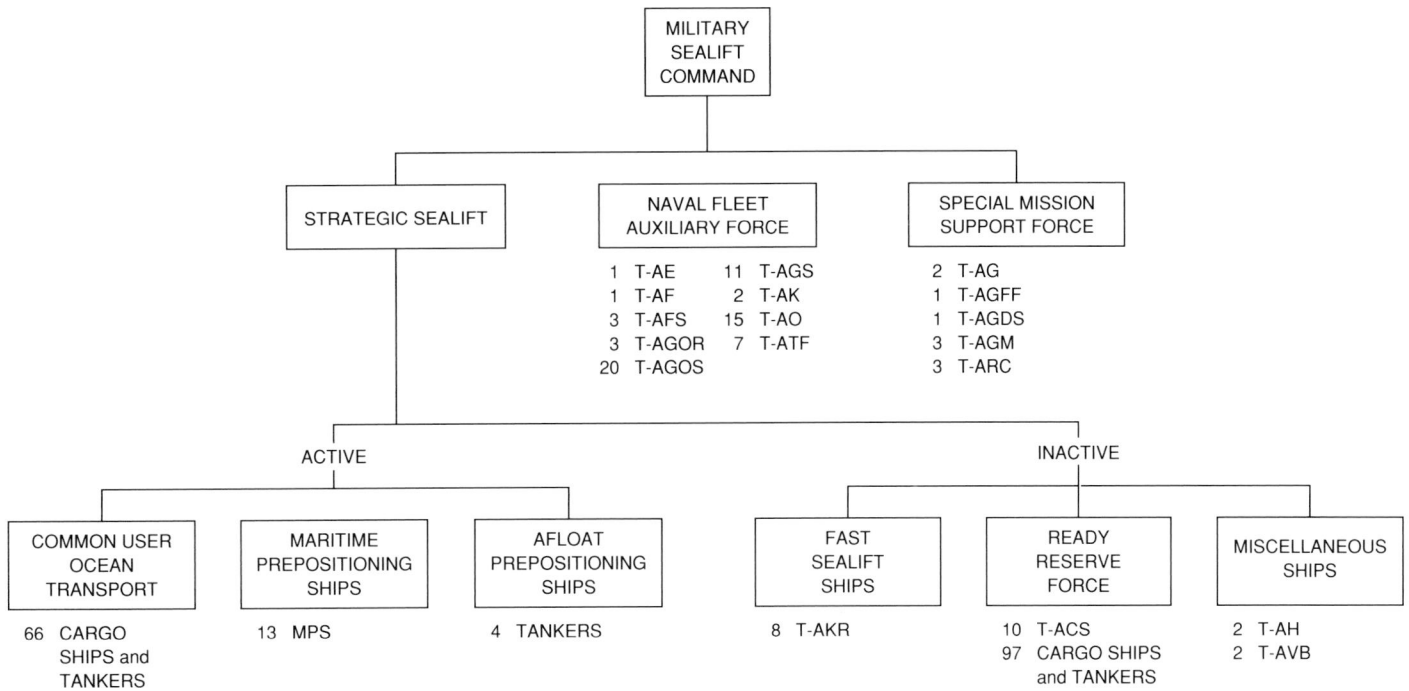

FIGURE 8-1. **Military Sealift Command**

The Military Sealift Command (MSC) operates a variety of ships for the Department of Defense and for the Navy. Under this dual-command concept, the Military Sealift Command is responsible for the operation of several categories of ships: (1) strategic sealift, (2) naval fleet auxiliary force, and (3) special mission support force. These are three diverse, relatively large, and important maritime activities.

STRATEGIC SEALIFT

The Military Sealift Command is responsible for the ocean transport of all Department of Defense materials and supplies. This mission is the command's predominate task in terms of numbers of ships and people and dollars expended. The U.S. sealift program was in a state of flux when this edition of *Ships and Aircraft* went to press, with several studies being conducted to determine future requirements. There will probably be an expansion of the specialized maritime prepositioning ships as the Army and possibly the Marine Corps seek to have more forward-deployed equipment for use in rapid response to overseas crises and conflicts.

The strategic sealift fleet can be considered in three basic categories:

Active. When the Persian Gulf crisis began in August 1990 the MSC strategic sealift fleet consisted of 11 dry-cargo ships and 26 tankers that were operational and at sea under long-term charter, 13 Maritime Prepositioning Ships (MPS), and 11 Afloat Prepositioning Force (APF) ships—a total of 61 privately owned U.S. flagships. One year after the conflict in the Persian Gulf began—in January 1992—the number of active sealift ships stood at 82 (see chapter 24).

Inactive. At the start of the Persian Gulf crisis the inactive MSC fleet consisted of eight Fast Sealift Ships (FSS), which are 33-knot Roll-On/Roll-Off (RO/RO) ships specifically configured for carrying heavy Army equipment and vehicles; 96 merchant ships in the Ready Reserve Force (RRF) that were routinely maintained so that they could be activated within 5, 10, or 20 days; and four specialized ships—two hospital ships (T-AH) and two aviation support ships (T-AVB).

During the Gulf War the eight FSS ships, most of the RRF ships, and the four specialized ships were reactivated and employed in supporting U.S. forces.

The current inactive fleet is about the same size as in mid-1990.

National Defense Reserve Fleet. There were also 116 ships laid up in the Maritime Administration's National Defense Reserve Fleet (NDRF) when the Persian Gulf crisis erupted. These ships consist of 71 World War II–built Victory cargo ships and 45 others of varying age and time in reserve status. The latter ships include two highly flexible vehicle/railroad cargo ships (see chapter 24).

These NDRF ships receive far less maintenance than the RRF ships and required between 30 and 120 days of work to reactivate. In a 1985 test two ships, the AMERICAN VICTORY and HATTIESBURG VICTORY, were reactivated in 60 days and 108 days, respectively; those were, however, among the Victory ships in best condition in the NDRF. Still, because of their limited cargo capacity, slow speed, and generally poor condition, most of these non-RRF ships are being scrapped.[1]

During the U.S. buildup in the Middle East from August 1990 to January 1991 (Operation Desert Shield), MSC-operated or -chartered ships carried 95 percent (by weight) of the war material moved into the Middle East from the United States and Europe. Undertaken in five months and without hostile interference, it was the largest U.S. military buildup of the post–World War II era.

In addition to those sealift ships already in active MSC service, numerous ships were activated from the Ready Reserve Force (RRF) and other, privately owned ships were taken up on charter from commercial service. "Sail orders" were issued on 7 August to the MPS squadrons at Diego Garcia and at Guam to steam for the Persian Gulf to support Desert Shield. The ships of MPS Squadron 2 began unloading on 15 August and the ships from MPS Squadron 1 reached Saudi Arabia on 26 August. Although the Marines units were relatively "light," the ships did carry M60 tanks and 155-mm howitzers as well as light armored vehicles and amphibian tractors that could serve as armored personnel carriers in the desert. The 11 afloat prepositioning ships that were at Diego Garcia began arriving in the Gulf on 17 August to unload their Army and Air Force cargoes. At the same time, MPS Squadron 3 in the Atlantic set course for the Gulf.

---

1. When in good condition, the Victory ships could attain 17 knots.

Vice Adm. Frank Donovan, Commander, Military Sealift Command, from March 1990 to June 1992 (left), and Vice Adm. Michael P. Kalleres, Commander, MSC, from June 1992. (U.S. Navy)

In the United States the eight Fast Sealift Ships (FSS) that had been procured specifically to move heavy Army equipment to a crisis, the RO/RO ships of the SL-7 class, began loading the Army's 24th Mechanized Infantry Division at Savannah, Ga. The SL-7s, with a maximum speed of 33 knots, were intended to be ready to receive cargo within 96 hours; the first of these RO/RO ships was ready in just 48 hours, and all seven met the 96-hour goal. The eighth fast RO/RO ship was in a shipyard for overhaul; she was hastily "put back together" and sailed ten days after the call.

On 27 August—12 days after the first MPS ships had arrived—the first fast sealift ships began unloading M1A1 tanks of the 24th Division in Saudi Arabia. There followed a continuous flow of ships carrying U.S. military equipment. The major bottlenecks in the sealift effort were the lack of shore facilities; for example, there were only two loading berths at Savannah to embark the 24th Division, while the massive shipping effort from several U.S. and overseas ports had to be unloaded through only five berths at the Saudi port of Ad Dammam and two at the port of Al Jubail.

More merchant ships followed; on 28 September 1990 the Desert Shield sealift reached a peak with 90 ships at sea—69 were en route to the Middle East from the United States and Europe, and 21 "empties" were returning for more cargo. Had the ships been evenly spaced on the route from the U.S. East Coast to the Persian Gulf, there would have been one ship every 100 n.miles (185 km). When the "phase II" of Desert Shield was undertaken in November 1990 to build up a U.S. offensive force in the Persian Gulf, a peak of 172 ships at sea was reached on 2 January 1991.

Following the successful campaign against Iraq, MSC supervised the return of masses of equipment, weapons, and munitions to the United States. Labeled Operation Desert Sortie, this effort continued until 17 April 1992, the date the cargo ship LESLIE LYKES left Saudi Arabia (she arrived at Bayonne, N.J., on 12 May 1992).

In addition to the "common user ocean transport" ships that were already operational under the aegis of MSC, for Desert Shield/Desert Storm all of the maritime prepositioning ships and afloat prepositioning ships, the eight fast RO/RO ships (one of which broke down), several ships from the ready reserve force, and 206 operating commercial merchant ships (29 U.S. flag and 177 foreign flag) were chartered by MSC between 10 August 1990 and 18 January 1991 to support Gulf operations. Also activated by MSC and sent to the Gulf were the two hospital ships and two aviation support ships maintained in standby reserve (see chapter 23).

The rapid response and the volume of cargoes carried fully justified the massive Navy investment in the 1980s to build up a strategic sealift capability. That success has caused the initiation of several programs to further enhance the strategic sealift capability, including additional forward maritime prepositioning ships.

All of the types of sealift efforts are periodically exercised.

NAVAL FLEET AUXILIARY FORCE

The Military Sealift Command operates more than 40 naval auxiliary ships that provide direct support to the fleet. This force includes underway replenishment ships (AE-AF-AFS-AO types), the cargo ships that support strategic missile submarine tenders (AK), fleet tugs (ATF), and the Navy's ocean surveillance ships (AGOS). While the number of surveillance ships will be reduced in the near future, several additional replenishment ships will be shifted from the active Navy to MSC operation, including all seven MARS (AFS 1)-class ships, beginning in 1993. (MSC already operates the three former British ships, the T-AFS 8–10.)

These ships are operated by civil service mariners, most ships having a small Navy detachment on board to provide communications and to support ordnance handling and helicopter operations. During Operations Desert Shield/Desert Storm, MSC-operated replenishment ships regularly operated in the Persian Gulf area to support fleet operations.

(Note that the two hospital ships and two aviation support ships are considered to be sealift vice auxiliary ships by the Military Sealift Command.)

SPECIAL MISSION SUPPORT FORCE

This MSC mission provides and operates ships to support specialized military activities, especially oceanographic and hydrographic surveys, undersea surveillance, acoustic research, missile range instrumentation, and the collection of telemetry intelligence against foreign missile tests. A total of 24 ships in this category are operated by MSC (AG-AGDS-AGFF-AGM-AGOR-AGS-ARC types). These include the former frigate GLOVER (now T-AGFF 1), placed in MSC service in 1990, the first warship to be operated by the command. With her weapons inactivated, the ship is employed as a sonar trials ship to support ASW projects.

These ships support a number of Defense agencies as well as the Navy and Air Force.

ORGANIZATION

The headquarters for MSC is located in Washington, D.C., with MSC area commands in London, England; Bayonne, N.J.; Oakland, Calif.; and Yokosuka, Japan. Smaller, sub-area commands are located in other ports.

The Commander MSC is a Navy vice admiral; his executive staff comprises both Navy and civilian personnel. In all, MSC has more than 5,700 civilian employees and almost 1,000 uniformed personnel ashore and afloat, plus approximately 2,500 contract mariners employed on MSC ships during normal peacetime operations.

In wartime, MSC's command structure would be augmented by almost 2,300 reserve personnel who would serve at MSC Headquarters and various area and sub-area offices. During Operation Desert Shield a total of 274 reservists were called to active duty to assist in chartering and scheduling activities. Another 130 reservists performed their annual active training duty in support of MSC.

The Commander MSC is "double hatted" as the single manager for ocean transportation on the staff of the Chief of Naval Operations. In this role, Commander MSC fulfills certain Department of Defense requirements for the centralized control of shipping.

Historical. The Military Sealift Command was established in response to a directive issued by the Secretary of Defense in August 1949 making the Secretary of the Navy the single manager for ocean transportation for the Defense establishment. Accordingly, the Military Sea Transportation Service was established within the Navy on 1 October 1949. The ships of the Naval Ocean Transport Service (NOTS) were provided for the new service. The following year oceangoing cargo ships and transports of the Army Transportation Corps were transferred to MSTS. Through 1950 additional Army ships were transferred to the Navy agency.

Under the aegis of MSTS some of these ships were manned by Navy crews (designated USS) and others were civilian manned (USNS); initially, only the civilian-manned and then all of the ships had the prefix *T-* added to their designations. Some of the Navy-manned ships were armed. The last Navy crew went ashore in the 1960s.

On 1 August 1970 the MSTS was renamed the Military Sealift Command to bring the name in line with the Air Force's Military Airlift Command (MAC). The Military Airlift Command, however, was a specified command within the Defense establishment, while MSC remained a Navy command, reporting to the Chief of Naval Operations.

On 1 July 1987 the unified U.S. Transportation Command (USTRANSCOM) was established, with the Military Sealift Command as well as the Military Airlift Command as its principal components. The Commander MSC is "double hatted" as a component commander of USTRANSCOM while also reporting to the Chief of Naval Operations because of MSC's specialized ship operations.

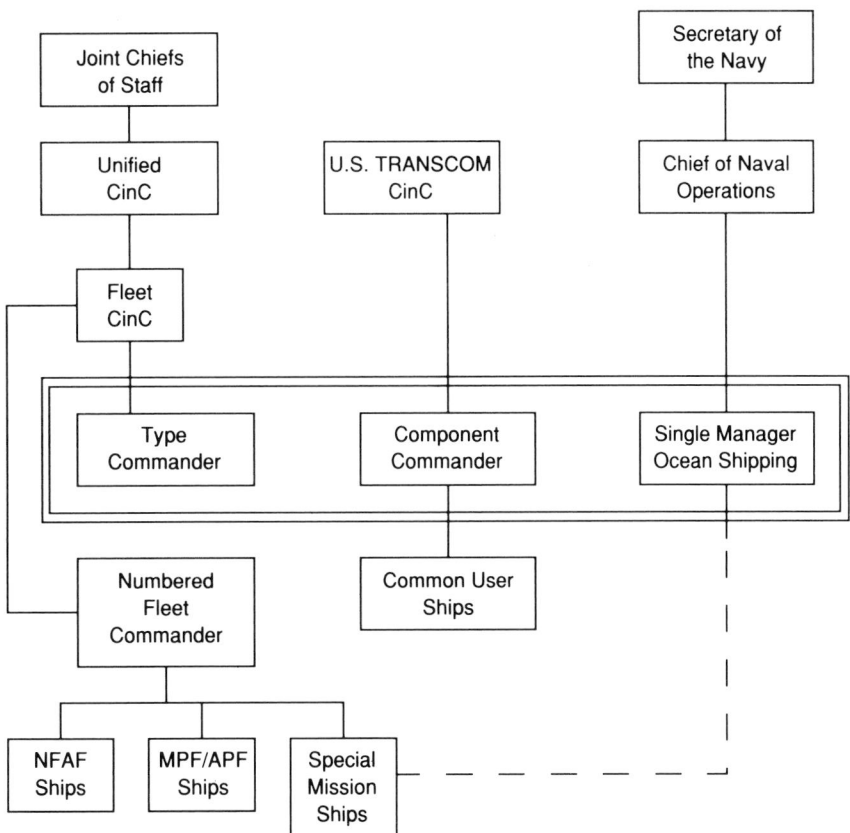

FIGURE 8-2.   MSC Command Relationships

CHAPTER 9

Naval Personnel

Navy men and women operate surface ships, submarines, small craft, and aircraft of varying sizes and types. Here the harbor tug TUSKEGEE (YTB 806) lies alongside a nuclear-propelled attack submarine. Men and women serve in service craft and many types of surface ships; submarine crews are all male. (U.S. Navy)

U.S. naval personnel strength is declining rapidly as the size of the active fleet is reduced. At the same time, the closure of a large number of shore installations and realignment of others will result in additional personnel reductions, although the major cutbacks in personnel will come from the reduction in operating ships and aircraft wings and squadrons. Navy personnel strength will be reduced by about 15 percent from 1990 to 1997—the smallest percentage reduction in that period of the four military services in the Department of Defense; the Army is being reduced by almost 29 percent, the Air Force by 18 percent, and the Marine Corps by just over 16 percent.

The Navy is scheduled to have an active-personnel strength of 536,000 officers and enlisted men and women by the fall of 1993. This is a net reduction of 15,400 from the current (fall 1992) strength and more than 56,000 men and women from the peak Navy strength of the Reagan naval buildup of almost 593,000 personnel in the late 1980s.[1] (See table 9-1).

With currently planned fleet reductions, the Navy's personnel strength should decline to about 501,200 by 1997. However, the size of the active fleet can be expected to decline beyond current plans, with a resulting further reduction in personnel.

Reductions in personnel strength are being achieved by cutting back on new accessions, and by retiring a number of officers and enlisted personnel who have reached 20 years or more of service, the minimum time that can be served to earn a retirement income. In addition, a selective early-retirement program has been implemented to encourage Navy personnel with 20 years or more to retire immediately (rather than wait for the allowable 30-year mark). A temporary "exit deal" has also been implemented to encourage enlisted personnel who have served more than 6 years but less than 20 on active duty to retire with an "exit payment." In addition, in 1991 the Navy designated 442 active-duty commanders and captains with more than 20 years of service who had to retire, with another 350 named in 1992; about 400 per year are to be named through 1995.

Related to the general personnel reductions, the number of flag officers on active duty is also being reduced. There were some 300 admirals on active duty during the 1980s; in late 1992 there were 267 flag officers on active duty, with the number scheduled to decline to 216 by 1995. Not included in these totals are reserve admirals on active duty or retired admirals recalled to active duty. Table 9-2 lists the mid-1992 flag officers on active duty in the Navy; several of the selectees are authorized to assume the title and wear the uniform of a rear admiral (lower half) because of the positions that they hold; however, they are paid as captains. (Note that there are ten full, four-star admirals on active duty although, by law, the Navy is allowed only nine; the tenth is the vice chief of the Joint Chiefs of Staff, who is not counted against the Navy total while in that position.[2]

In the mid-1980s Congress passed several laws affecting flag and general officers. One required them to have unified or joint duty (or duty with allied staffs) before being selected for flag rank; another required them to serve a minimum of 24 months in an assignment (the Navy average in fiscal 1990 was 28.8 months).

The Navy is an all-volunteer force. The current personnel cutbacks permit the Navy to accept enlistees, 97 percent of whom are high-school graduates, men and women with a high aptitude for technical training.[3] The other 3 percent are not high-school graduates, a conscious Navy decision to permit certain high achievers with low academic grades to have an opportunity for naval service.

Quality is also being improved through a continued reduction in first-term attrition (i.e., the loss of sailors who leave after their first enlistment), desertion, and unauthorized absence rates. Improvement in these areas leads to an overall improvement in the quality of personnel. The Navy saves resources each time a sailor reenlists or each time the desertion rate or unauthorized absence rate falls since

1. The planned 600-ship fleet of the Reagan administration would have required some 622,000 personnel for full manning.
2. The names and assignments of flag officers are listed annually in the May (Naval Review) issue of the Naval Institute *Proceedings*.
3. By comparison, 89 percent of the Navy's enlisted intake were high school graduates in 1989 and 92 percent in 1990.

TABLE 9-1. ACTIVE NAVAL PERSONNEL (End of fiscal year)*

	FY 1988 Actual	FY 1989 Actual	FY 1990 Actual	FY 1991 Actual	FY 1992 Planned	FY 1993 Planned
Officers	72,400	72,100	73,100	71,000	69,500	67,600
Enlisted†	520,200	520,500	509,800	498,700	481,900	468,400
Total	592,600	592,700	582,900	569,700	551,400	536,000

*Totals are rounded.
†Includes approximately 4,500 midshipmen in the late 1980s, declining to about 4,000 by 1995.

TABLE 9-2. NAVY FLAG OFFICERS (Mid-1992)

Rank	Category	Number
Admirals	Line	10
Vice Admirals	Line	26
	Engineering	1
	Aerospace Engineering	1
	Intelligence	1
	Medical Corps	1
Rear Admirals	Line	55
	Engineering	5
	Aerospace Engineering	1
	Cryptology	1
	Intelligence	1
	Medical Corps	6
	Dental Corps	1
	Supply Corps	6
	Chaplain Corps	1
	Civil Engineer Corps	3
	Judge Advocate General's Corps	2
Rear Admirals (lower half)	Line	74
	Engineering	5
	Aerospace Engineering	3
	Intelligence	1
	Public Affairs	1
	Oceanography	1
	Medical Corps	6
	Dental Corps	1
	Medical Service Corps	1
	Nurse Corps	1
	Supply Corps	7
	Chaplain Corps	1
	Civil Engineer Corps	2
	Judge Advocate General's Corps	1
Selectees		
Rear Admirals	Line	27
	Engineering	3
	Cryptology	2
	Intelligence	1
	Medical Corps	1
	Dental Corps	1
	Supply Corps	5
	TAR*	2
Recall to Active Duty		
Rear Admirals	Line	1

*Training and Administration of Reserves (Naval Reserve on active duty).

time, energy, and money are not spent to find and train a replacement sailor.

But the Navy still has significant shortfalls in certain areas:

Aviation. The Navy has a major pilot shortfall, currently lacking about 1,100 pilots. However, the major reductions taking place in Navy air wings and squadrons are a mitigating factor to this problem. The effects of several Navy pay incentives for pilots are also taking hold, while the naval air successes in Operation Desert Storm and the turmoil in the civilian aviation industry may also have a positive impact. The Navy's personnel managers are watching to see how much the excitement and thrill of military aviation will be offset by factors of career security and family separation.

Nuclear. The Navy continues to suffer a shortfall of some 25 percent of officers in the ranks of lieutenant commander through captain in the nuclear community, principally nuclear submarine officers. This shortage is most severe in the post-command officer ranks, reflecting poor submarine personnel policies in the past and the lengthy submarine tour assignments. As a result of the shortfall, the Navy must extend sea tours or assign them back-to-back.

"The Good, The Bad . . ." At left, a sailor returns to a homecoming embrace at Norfolk after Operation Desert Storm. At right, sailors take a break during ammunition replenishment aboard ship. Most naval service at sea is physically strenuous. Such efforts along with lengthy deployments make naval service arduous. (PH1 Mike Flynn, USN)

The submarine officer situation is also being exacerbated by the congressionally mandated requirements for unified and joint staff service, which were caused, in large part, by the failure of submarine officers to have that broadening experience. While submarine officers currently have an exemption to such staff assignments, it is questionable if Congress will permit the exemptions to continue indefinitely.

At the same time, nuclear-trained officers are highly sought after in the civilian nuclear community. Efforts to retain these critically needed officers through bonus programs and by reducing submarine operational tempo are having positive results. The reduction in attack submarine and strategic missile submarine force levels will also lessen the shortfall.

Medical. The retention of medical personnel—physicians and nurses—continues to be a problem, in large part because of higher pay and family stability in the civilian sector. There have been modest improvements in this field in the past few years, in large part through incentive pay/bonus programs.

WOMEN IN THE NAVY

Just over 10 percent of the officers and 10 percent of the enlisted personnel in the Navy are women. These are smaller percentages than in the respective categories of the Army and Air Force, but significantly higher portions than in the Marine Corps (see chapter 7). The Navy has three active-duty rear admirals and one admiral selectee who are women.[4]

Women have long served at sea in U.S. Navy hospital ships and transports. Since 1979 women have also been assigned to non-combatant ships and craft, mostly tenders, repair ships, and fleet oilers. Of the 60,000 women currently on active duty in the Navy, some 330 officers and 8,100 enlisted women are assigned to ships, and several score officers and 4,100 enlisted women are assigned to shore-based aviation squadrons.

The first woman to head a Navy aircraft squadron took command of Electronic Warfare Squadron (VAQ) 34 in July 1990, and in December 1990 the first woman took command of a U.S. Navy ship, the salvage ship OPPORTUNE (ARS 41); subsequently, female commanding officers have been named to other ships.[5] Recent Department of Defense policy changes have opened more seagoing and aviation billets to women, and the number of women at sea will certainly increase despite the overall manpower and fleet reductions.

Of concern to Navy personnel managers is the impact of large increases of women in the Navy—numbers as high as 50 percent have been speculated. This could cause major problems in regard to the impact of pregnancy on crew stability and the Navy's currently stringent policy of assigning service husbands and wives to the same base or station.

With respect to pregnancy, in 1991 in 19 forward-deployed ships with women crew members, the average rate of pregnancy which required women to be transferred was 5.2 percent, or 7.6 percent if the number is adjusted for an annual rate. A 1990 Navy report on women showed that 16.2 percent of the enlisted women assigned to sea duty in a given year will get pregnant. During an eight-month deployment in 1990 the destroyer tender ACADIA (AD 42), which operated in the Persian Gulf during the Desert Shield buildup, had an 8 percent pregnancy rate among the ship's 450 women crew members. (Of the 36 women who were pregnant, 9 had become pregnant before the ship deployed but did not realize it until the ship was under way.) The YELLOWSTONE (AD 41), which also deployed to the Gulf, had a pregnancy rate of 4 percent—20 women out of 479 in the crew.

A high pregnancy rate among Navy women, especially those in ships' crews, can disrupt operations and also increase medical-care requirements.

About 10,200 or 17 percent of the Navy's women are married to Navy men. While the Navy attempts to station couples at the same installation, that policy will become increasingly difficult to implement as the number of Navy couples increases.

4. The distaff flag officers are two line officers, holding the positions of Assistant Chief of Naval Personnel for Personnel, Readiness, and Community Support, and Vice Chief of Naval Education and Training; and one nurse officer who is Assistant Chief of the Bureau of Medicine and Surgery for Personnel Management and Director of the Naval Nurse Corps.

5. Lt. Comdr. Darlene M. Iskra took command after the ship's commanding officer was taken off in a medical emergency; the OPPORTUNE had an all-male crew at the time.

CHAPTER 10

Naval Reserve

Active-duty or reserve personnel? It is increasingly difficult to tell the difference as reservists and active personnel share many roles. Reserve surface and air units operate mainly first-line ships and aircraft. There is no submarine reserve force. (U.S. Navy)

The role of the Naval Reserve has continued to increase since the early 1980s when the Navy began to provide its reserves with first-line equipment and increase its functions. The Naval Reserve currently has approximately 23,000 TAR (Training and Administration of Reserve) personnel and 130,400 selected reservists—a total of some 153,400 men and women. There are additional men and women in the individual ready reserve and inactive reserve.

The selected reserve operates numerous ships, as well as aircraft units; it provides staff augmentation and mans construction battalions and other specialized units. These people normally train 48 days per year and serve two weeks on active duty, and most receive pay for their services. The TAR personnel, along with some other reservists, are on full-time active duty, most in conjunction with training reserves. (See table 10-1.)

During their drill periods, some ready reserve personnel participate in Navy day-to-day operational activities. For example, reserve patrol squadrons routinely conduct ASW patrols from bases in the United States and overseas during their training periods. These and other reserve air units have regularly flown drug-interdiction missions in the Caribbean and off the U.S. East and West coasts, while reserve transport aircraft regularly carry personnel and cargo between the United States and overseas points.

The Navy activated 21,109 reservists during Operations Desert Storm/Desert Shield, or almost 16 percent of the ready reserve force. Reportedly, 134,000 reservists requested active duty in conjunction with the Gulf buildup. These reservists were called up mainly for their individual skills, with medical reservists (physicians, nurses, medical service, corpsmen) accounting for almost one-half of those reservists activated. Many of the medical personnel were used to "backfill" positions at U.S. medical facilities while the active-duty personnel were sent to the Persian Gulf, and to two reserve field hospitals and two hospital ships deployed in the Gulf area. Cargo handling, construction (Seabee), and Mobile Inshore Undersea Warfare units (MIUW) were sent to the Gulf. Table 10-2 shows the reservists activated for the Gulf.

No reserve-manned ships were deployed to the Gulf area; however, portions of nine reserve aircraft squadrons were deployed to Europe and the Middle East (see chapter 28).

Some Navy reservists were activated after the cease-fire in Iraq to provide logistics support in the redeployment of personnel and equipment to the United States.

TABLE 10-1. NAVAL RESERVE PERSONNEL (End of fiscal year)*

	FY 1988 Actual	FY 1989 Actual	FY 1990 Actual	FY 1991 Actual	FY 1992 Planned	FY 1993 Planned
TAR officers	2,170	2,304	2,340	2,317	2,287	2,198
TAR enlisted	19,596	19,683	20,367	20,914	19,758	18,915
Total	21,766	21,987	22,707	23,231	22,045	21,113
Selected Reserve officers	26,816	26,796	26,924	26,701	24,939	23,646
Selected Reserve enlisted	103,793	103,813	103,768	103,702	87,616	82,341
Total	130,609	130,609	130,692	130,403	112,555	105,987

*Totals are rounded.

TABLE 10-2. NAVAL RESERVISTS ACTIVATED 1990–1991*

Category	Available†	Activated‡
Medical	19,986	10,452
Ship augmentees	18,687	1,838
Construction	14,731	2,475
Aviation	16,736	1,111
Cargo handling	1,924	961
Military sealift	1,885	469
Other	49,644	3,803
Total	123,593	21,109

*Source: General Accounting Office, *Operation Desert Shield/Desert Storm: Use of Navy and Marine Corps Reserve* (Washington, D.C.: 14 June 1991), p. 3.
†Data as of 31 December 1990.
‡Data as of 6 June 1991.

ORGANIZATION

The Chief of Naval Reserve (rear admiral) manages the Naval Reserve Programs. He also serves on the staff of the Chief of Naval Operations as the Director of Naval Reserve.

The surface ships of the Naval Reserve Force (NRF) report directly to the active fleet commanders, and the Naval Air Reserve Force (tactical air units) report through the Commander Naval Air Reserve Force to the Chief of Naval Operations. The Chief of Naval Reserve has certain administrative and recruiting functions that support these forces.

The headquarters of the Chief of Naval Reserve and the Commander Naval Air Reserve are located in New Orleans, La.

Those Naval Reserve activities that report directly to the Chief of Naval Reserve are:

> Naval Reserve Air Centers
> Naval Reserve ASW Training Center
> Naval Reserve Construction Force/1st Naval Construction
>   Brigade
> Naval Reserve Intelligence Program
> Naval Reserve Readiness Regions

There are 23 Naval Reserve Air Centers, most located at Naval Air Stations with tactical air units assigned. The 1st Naval Construction Battalion Brigade consists of 17 mobile construction battalions—the famed "seabees." These provide two-thirds of the Navy's total construction battalion force.

The Naval Reserve Intelligence Program provides one-third of the Navy's intelligence personnel.

SURFACE NAVAL RESERVE

The surface Naval Reserve operates a large number of ships of frigate size and smaller. As of late 1992 the following ships were operated by composite active-duty/reserve crews under the NRF:

> 16 FFG OLIVER HAZARD PERRY class
> 8   FF   KNOX class
> 3   LST NEWPORT class
> 14 MSO ACME/AGILE/AGGRESSIVE classes
> 2   ARS BOLSTER class

There are also four reserve Small Boat Units (SBU) that operate small craft (see chapter 21). In addition, several COOP-type minesweepers are operated by the Naval Reserve; the Navy plans to phase out this program (see chapter 22).

The surface reserve program is undergoing a major change with the decommissioning from active service of all 40 KNOX-class frigates. The NRF will operate 8 ships as training frigates (FFT), with the remaining 32 ships laid up in reserve; the latter would be reactivated in a crisis or war, employing reserve personnel trained aboard the FFTs. This program has been dubbed the Innovative Naval Reserve Concept (INRC).

Previous plans to transfer other auxiliary ships to the Naval Reserve have been discarded as were plans to shift all MHC/MCM-type mine craft to the reserves after one year in the active fleet. However, the latter policy may change as the entire MHC/MCM fleet becomes operational and the active-personnel strength is reduced. The size and composition of the NRF, like the active fleet, was far from clear when this edition of *Ships and Aircraft* went to press.

NAVAL AIR RESERVE

The Naval Air Reserve consists of two carrier air wings (RCVW) plus a large number of land-based squadrons that largely mirror the active fleet in organization and aircraft:

2	RCVW	carrier air wings
2	VFC	fighter composite squadrons
13	VP	patrol squadrons
14	VR	fleet logistics support squadrons
2	HCS	helicopter combat SAR/special-warfare support squadrons
2	HM	mine countermeasures squadrons
2	HS	helicopter ASW squadrons
3	HSL	light helicopter ASW squadrons

The number of patrol squadrons is being reduced, possibly to nine by 1993–1994; at the same time, reserve VP squadrons have been reduced from nine to eight aircraft. Other squadron reductions are in the offing, with the final numbers still being decided.

Most reserve air squadrons fly the same type of aircraft as their active-duty counterparts. The principal exceptions are the lack of fixed-wing ASW aircraft (S-3 Viking) and the SH-60B/F ASW helicopters in the HS/HSL squadrons; the latter units, however, are intended to operate primarily from KNOX-class frigates that cannot operate the SH-60B, but only the SH-2 LAMPS I helicopter.

In 1984 the Navy established the first Squadron Augment Units (SAU) in the active-fleet readiness squadrons (VP-30 and VP-31) to train reservists for P-3 Orion squadrons. These were followed by a Master Augment Unit (MAU) established at NAS Brunswick, Maine, flying P-3C Orions on loan from the active fleet; subsequently, SAUs were established with F-14A Tomcat, F/A-18 Hornet, A-6E Intruder, E-2C Hawkeye, S-3A Viking, SH-3H Sea King, and C-2A Greyhound squadrons. These units were intended to augment active squadrons with reserve personnel to permit high-tempo operations. The MAU/SAU program was disestablished in 1990–1991.

Historical. The naval reserve concept can be traced to the American Revolution when several of the colonies employed armed merchant ships to resist British military activities within their state's waters. By the time of the signing of the Declaration of Independence in July 1776 there were 11 colonies with some form of navy.

During the next century there were various forms of state volunteers, with a volunteer force established in the Union Navy during the Civil War. Then, beginning in 1888, several states established naval components as part of their state militias. These naval militias were intended for harbor and coastal defense; they had no federal standing, and rules for applicants and the level of competence varied considerably.

Beginning in 1891 the Navy offered to allow state militias to participate in some fleet exercises, and there was soon federal cooperation in a number of training areas. Two years later the training ship NEW HAMPSHIRE (launched in 1864 although laid down 45 years earlier!) was transferred from the Navy to the New York State Naval Militia.

By the eve of the Spanish-American War of 1898 there were more than 4,000 men in state naval militias. When the conflict erupted, the militias were used to patrol the coasts (there was a perceived threat of a Spanish assault) while thousands more militiamen were taken into the Navy. Their outstanding service in the war led to Navy Department recommendations for the creation of a national Naval Reserve. This was opposed—mostly by state interests—until 1914 when Congress passed legislation that largely placed the naval militias under supervision of the Navy Department. In time of war they would become part of the Navy (as the state National Guard units would become part of the Army). A year later, in 1915, the U.S. Naval Reserve was established, a reserve force to be composed of men honorably discharged from the active Navy.

With the U.S. entry into World War I in April 1917, the militias were mobilized as the National Naval Volunteers, with almost the total strength of just over 10,000 men coming onto active duty in the Navy. By September 1917 their ranks had grown to almost 17,000 men. These volunteers were consolidated with the Naval Reserve in July 1918, creating the current U.S. Naval Reserve organization. (The states of California, Illinois, and New York continue to maintain state naval forces, whose members are additionally in the Naval Reserve.)

The Naval Reserve had major roles in World War II, the Korean War, and the Vietnam War, as well as periodic operations in NRF and active Navy ships during normal "peacetime" naval operations.

CHAPTER 11

Strategic Missile Submarines

Strategic missile submarines, the most survivable of U.S. strategic forces, have a limited mission in the post–Cold War era. By the end of this decade only the 18 OHIO-class submarines, like the KENTUCKY shown here, will remain in U.S. service as SSBNs. (1992, Giorgio Arra)

The U.S. strategic missile submarine (SSBN) force in late 1992 consists of 25 operational nuclear-propelled undersea craft, 13 of modern construction and each armed with 24 Trident missiles, and 11 older submarines, each carrying 16 Trident missiles.[1] Additional submarines are in the process of being decommissioned and dismantled, according to terms of U.S.–Soviet Strategic Arms Reduction Talks (START) and Strategic Arms Limitation Talks (SALT) agreements. Five more SSBNs are under construction, to be completed by 1997.

The 488 Submarine-Launched Ballistic Missiles (SLBM) carried in the operational submarines, each with eight thermo-nuclear warheads, constitute the majority of the U.S. strategic missile warheads.

Under current planning the SSBN force will decline to 18 submarines of the OHIO class with 432 missiles by the late 1990s. The Navy's submarine community had sought a force of up to 24 Trident submarines (576 missiles) as late as September 1990. That month the Secretary of Defense agreed to a congressional proposal to halt the program at 18 submarines. The Navy's proposals for 24 SSBNs included a recommendation that up to 72 missiles on three submarines would be considered exempt from strategic arms limitation agreements if those submarines were in overhaul. In the current political-military climate the number of SSBNs in commission in the year 2000 could be fewer than 18.

During the Reagan administration, the proposed 600-ship fleet of Secretary of the Navy John Lehman (1981–1987) included a force of 40 SSBNs, although there was no attempt to provide for such a force level in the Lehman-era shipbuilding programs. Indeed, on at least two occasions, Lehman had sought to have an SSBN deleted from an annual shipbuilding program to make the funds available for other programs. While Lehman supported a construction rate of one SSBN per year, he did attempt to qualify the Newport News Shipbuilding yard in Virginia to build Trident SSBNs in addition to the General Dynamics/Electric Boat yard in Connecticut, which has built all Trident SSBNs.[2] Realistically, however, building only one SSBN per year with a finite number of missile submarines in sight gave limited value to this effort.

There was a steady decline in SSBN numbers and launch tubes from the period 1967–1980, when the sea-based "leg" of the U.S. strategic Triad consisted of 41 SSBNs armed with 656 Polaris and later missiles. This major reduction in submarines and launch tubes is compensated in certain respects by the increased number of Multiple Independently targeted Re-entry Vehicles (MIRV) and major improvements in accuracy with the Poseidon and then Trident missiles. (These weapons are described in chapter 30.)

The older SSBNs are being retired under the provisions of the U.S.–Soviet SALT agreements as more OHIO-class submarines are completed. The LAFAYETTE-class submarines armed with Poseidon missiles ceased operations on 15 October 1991, with the return from patrol of the KAMEHAMEHA and ULYSSES S. GRANT to New London, Conn. The ten Poseidon submarines then began deactivation except for two units being converted into special operations/transport submarines.

The 12 LAFAYETTE-class submarines that have been rearmed with Trident C-4 missiles will be retired by the mid-1990s.

Dismantling of these submarines requires more than a year, with the SSBNs "standing down" prior to being decommissioned.

In addition to the submarines listed here, a number of attack submarines (SSN) carrying Tomahawk Land-Attack Missiles (TLAM) with nuclear warheads could have a limited strategic role in future conflicts. (No nuclear-armed TLAMs are currently in the fleet, but are retained at U.S. storage sites.)

---

1. The strategic submarine "system" is also known as the Fleet Ballistic Missile (FBM) system.
2. The Newport News yard demonstrated its ability to handle Trident submarines when it conducted the post-shakedown availability (overhaul) of the Trident submarine NEVADA in 1987.

TABLE 11-1. U.S. STRATEGIC FORCE STRUCTURE

	1 Jan 1992	FY 1992 Base Force*	New Base Force†
Aircraft		75 B-2	20 B-2
	97 B-1B	97 B-1B	97 B-1B
	95 B-52H	95 B-52H	95 B-52H
	44 B-52G		
ICBM	50 MX Peacekeeper	50 Peacekeeper	
	500 Minuteman III	500 Minuteman III (partially downloaded)	500 Minuteman III (all downloaded to one warhead)
	450 Minuteman II (being deactivated)		
SLBM	120 Trident D-5	240 Trident D-5	240 Trident D-5
	384 Trident C-4	192 Trident C-4	192 Trident C-4

Notes: *The U.S. strategic force planned in FY 1992 for the late 1990s based on the implementation of START agreements.
†A "substantial" portion of the bomber force will be oriented primarily to the conventional role.

Of the 18 submarines that will be at sea in the late 1990s, 10 will be armed with the improved D-5 variant of the Trident missile, also referred to as the Trident II. In the early 1980s the decision was made by then-Secretary of the Navy John Lehman to complete the 9th through 18th Trident submarines with the D-5 missile, and to retrofit the 8 earlier units with the D-5 when those units came in for major overhaul/refueling. However, fiscal constraints led to the subsequent decision to retain the C-4 missile in the first eight submarines.

Assuming the 18th Trident SSBN is completed in 1997, and all of their C-4 and D-5 missiles are loaded with eight warheads, the SSBN force would provide 3,456 re-entry vehicles. These would constitute over 70 percent of the U.S. strategic warheads. Under the U.S. proposal announced in January 1992, the number of strategic warheads would be reduced to about 4,700, a reduction of over one-half from the 11,100-warhead ceiling that START would have imposed. The so-called "new base force," which would be based on specific reductions of Russian MIRV missiles, would see a radically changed U.S. strategic force, as shown in table 11-1.

The Bush administration, however, has proposed that the 3,456 warheads in the 18 Trident submarines could be reduced by approximately one-third by downloading some missiles or leaving empty tubes in SSBNs. This would leave some 2,300 warheads in the Trident force. The administration has also proposed that one-half of the land-based Intercontinental Ballistic Missiles (ICBM) should be rapidly retired and that the 500 Minuteman III weapons retained should be downloaded to a single warhead. This would reduce the temptation for an enemy to strike at the fixed ICBMs in a preemptive attack, seeking to have perhaps two attacking MIRVs destroy an ICBM carrying up to 10 re-entry vehicles (i.e., 1 on each Minuteman II, 3 on each Minuteman III, and 10 on each MX).

The sea-based Trident SLBMs—which are considered highly survivable and essentially immune to a preemptive strike—would then constitute the majority of the nation's strategic offensive force.

There had been efforts to initiate a new SSBN program to complement or succeed the Trident program. For example, the President's Commission on Strategic Forces, reporting in April 1983, urged that to modernize U.S. strategic programs,

research begin now on smaller ballistic-missile carrying submarines, each carrying fewer missiles than the Trident, as a potential follow-on to the Trident submarine force. The objective of such research should be to design a submarine and missile system that would, as much as possible, reduce the value of each platform and also present radically different problems to a Soviet attacker than does the Trident submarine force. This work should proceed in such a way that a decision to construct and deploy such a submarine force could be rapidly implemented should Soviet progress in anti-submarine warfare so dictate.[3]

---

3. The Commission included among its members Mr. R. James Woolsey, former Under Secretary of the Navy, and Vice Admiral Levering Smith, former head of the Navy's Special Projects Office.

In partial response to this proposal, the Los Alamos National Laboratory sought to develop a set of parameters for a future strategic missile submarine program. However, this and other, less-comprehensive efforts have been emasculated or forced to abort by pressure from the Navy submarine community. For example, while the Los Alamos effort was funded by the Department of Energy and the laboratory is a non-Defense activity, the submarine community succeeded in controlling personnel appointments and forbidding the study panel from addressing platform (submarine) size or propulsion concepts. This attitude by the submarine community was due primarily to a fear of a reduction in Trident production numbers and a "not invited here" paranoia.

All ten strategic missile submarines of the earlier GEORGE WASHINGTON and ETHAN ALLEN classes have been laid up or discarded. Details of the disposition of these submarines are provided in chapter 12.

In addition, two retired LAFAYETTE-class SSBNs have been modified for use as Moored Training Ships (MTS) for nuclear propulsion operators at Charleston, S.C. These ships are also listed in chapter 12.

Builders: The Electric Boat Division of General Dynamics in Groton, Conn., is the only shipyard currently constucting strategic missile submarines. (See also chapter 12.)

Manning: All operational U.S. SSBNs are assigned two complete crews (designated Blue and Gold crews). While one crew is at sea, the other is engaged in training (mostly with system simulators), leave, medical treatment, and other shore activities.

Missiles: The Polaris and Poseidon missiles have been retired from the U.S. submarine fleet. The last Polaris A-1 patrol was completed in October 1965, the last A-2 patrol in June 1974, and the last A-3 patrol in April 1981.

The Polaris A-3 missile with a British-developed nuclear warhead remains in service in the four Royal Navy SSBNs of the RESOLUTION class (Chevaline A3TK version); those submarines have not been upgraded to fire the Poseidon or Trident C-4 missile, but will be replaced by new-construction submarines of the VANGUARD class armed with the Trident C-4 missile carrying British warheads.

The last Poseidon C-3 patrols were completed in October 1991 (see chapter 30 for missile characteristics).

Names: The 41 Polaris strategic missile submarines completed from 1960 to 1967 were named for "famous Americans," although several were in fact named for persons who were never in the American colonies or United States.

The subsequent Trident submarines completed from 1981 are named for the states of the Union, beginning with the OHIO. Previously, state names were assigned to battleships. The exception to the latter name source for SSBNs was made on 27 September 1983, when the RHODE ISLAND was renamed for Senator Henry M. "Scoop" Jackson immediately after his death and just prior to the submarine's launching.

Operational: Polaris-Poseidon-Trident submarines had completed 2,916 deterrent patrols through June 1991. The GEORGE WASHINGTON began the first U.S. strategic submarine deployment on 15 November 1960, carrying 16 Polaris A-1 missiles.

The all-Trident force of the late 1990s will be based at Bangor, Wash., for operations in the North Pacific, and at Kings Bay, Ga., for deployments in the North Atlantic. The LAFAYETTE-class SSBNs in the Atlantic were based at Holy Loch, Scotland, and at Kings Bay; the former base was closed in 1992. Holy Loch had been established in 1961, followed by SSBN support bases at Rota, Spain, and Apra Harbor, Guam, both of which have now closed.

The Navy has continued to test the reliability and flexibility of strategic submarines through the SSBN Continuity of Operations Program (SCOOP). These exercises have involved the replenishment and refit of strategic missile submarines at remote ports and anchorages, employing Army, Navy, Air Force, and Coast Guard assistance; at times submarine tenders have been involved, at other times miscellaneous small craft.

TABLE 11-2. STRATEGIC MISSILE SUBMARINE FORCE LEVELS [late 1992]

Type	Class/Ship	Commission	Active	Building	Missiles
SSBN 726	OHIO	1989–	5	5	24 Trident D-5
SSBN 726	OHIO	1981–1986	8	—	24 Trident C-4
SSBN 616	LAFAYETTE	1965–1967	11	—	16 Trident C-4

13 + 5 NUCLEAR-PROPELLED STRATEGIC MISSILE SUBMARINES: "OHIO" CLASS

Number	Name	FY	Builder	Laid down	Launched	Commissioned	Status
SSBN 726	OHIO	74	General Dynamics/Electric Boat	10 Apr 1976	7 Apr 1979	11 Nov 1981	**PA**
SSBN 727	MICHIGAN	75	General Dynamics/Electric Boat	4 Apr 1977	26 Apr 1980	11 Sep 1982	**PA**
SSBN 728	FLORIDA	75	General Dynamics/Electric Boat	9 June 1977	14 Nov 1981	18 June 1983	**PA**
SSBN 729	GEORGIA	76	General Dynamics/Electric Boat	7 Apr 1979	6 Nov 1982	11 Feb 1984	**PA**
SSBN 730	HENRY M. JACKSON	77	General Dynamics/Electric Boat	19 Jan 1981	15 Oct 1983	6 Oct 1984	**PA**
SSBN 731	ALABAMA	78	General Dynamics/Electric Boat	27 Aug 1981	19 May 1984	25 May 1985	**PA**
SSBN 732	ALASKA	78	General Dynamics/Electric Boat	9 Mar 1983	12 Jan 1985	25 Jan 1986	**PA**
SSBN 733	NEVADA	80	General Dynamics/Electric Boat	8 Aug 1983	14 Sep 1985	16 Aug 1986	**PA**
SSBN 734	TENNESSEE	81	General Dynamics/Electric Boat	9 June 1986	13 Dec 1986	17 Dec 1988	**AA**
SSBN 735	PENNSYLVANIA	83	General Dynamics/Electric Boat	2 Mar 1987	23 Apr 1988	9 Sep 1989	**AA**
SSBN 736	WEST VIRGINIA	84	General Dynamics/Electric Boat	18 Dec 1987	14 Oct 1989	20 Oct 1990	**AA**
SSBN 737	KENTUCKY	85	General Dynamics/Electric Boat	18 Dec 1987	11 Aug 1990	13 July 1991	**AA**
SSBN 738	MARYLAND	86	General Dynamics/Electric Boat	18 Dec 1987	10 Aug 1991	13 June 1992	**AA**
SSBN 739	NEBRASKA	87	General Dynamics/Electric Boat	18 Dec 1987	15 Aug 1992	1993	Building
SSBN 740	RHODE ISLAND	88	General Dynamics/Electric Boat		1993	1994	Building
SSBN 741	MAINE	89	General Dynamics/Electric Boat		1994	1995	Building
SSBN 742	WYOMING	90	General Dynamics/Electric Boat		1995	1996	Building
SSBN 743	. . . . . .	91	General Dynamics/Electric Boat		1996	1997	Building

Displacement:	16,764 tons standard
	18,750 tons submerged
Length:	560 feet (170.7 m) overall
Beam:	42 feet (12.8 m)
Draft:	36¼ feet (11.05 m)
Propulsion:	2 steam turbines (General Electric); 1 shaft
Reactors:	1 pressurized-reactor S8G (General Electric)
Speed:	28 knots surface
	approx. 30 knots submerged
Manning:	approx. 172 (16 officers + 156 enlisted)
Missiles:	24 tubes for Trident C-4 SLBM in SSBN 726–733
	24 tubes for Trident D-5 SLBM in SSBN 734–743
Torpedo tubes:	4 21-inch (533-mm) tubes Mk 68 (amidships)

ASW weapons:	Mk 48 torpedoes
Radars:	BPS-15B surface search in SSBN 726–740
	BPS-16 surface search in SSBN 741–743
Sonars:	BQQ-6 bow mounted
	TB-16 towed array; to also have TB-29
	BQR-19 navigation
	BQS-13 active
	BQS-15 under ice
Fire control:	1 CCS Mk 2 Mod 3
	1 Mk 98 missile FCS
	1 Mk 118 torpedo FCS
EW systems:	WLR-8(V)5

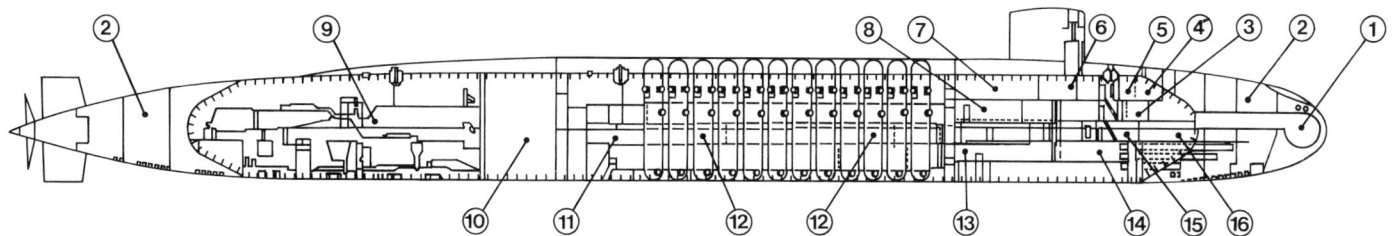

1. sonar sphere   2. ballast tanks   3. computer room   4. radio room   5. sonar room   6. command and control center   7. navigation center   8. missile control center   9. reactor compartment   10. engine room   11. auxiliary machinery   12. crew's berthing   13. crew's mess   14. torpedo room   15. wardroom   16. CPO quarters (William Clipson)

These are the largest submarines to be built in the United States and second in size only to the six Russian Typhoon-class SSBNs, which are at least half again as large. The OHIO was laid down nine years after completion of the previous U.S. strategic missile submarine, the WILL ROGERS.

Incorporation of the D-5 missile in the SSBN 734–736 resulted in a one-year delay in their construction; the SSBN 737 was ordered as a D-5 ship.

Class: The basis for the Trident program was the Department of Defense–sponsored STRAT-X study of 1967–1968 to determine future strategic weapon requirements. The study recommended two land-based and two sea-based strategic systems, with one of the latter being the Underwater Long-range Missile System (ULMS). This evolved into the Trident system, the name being changed from ULMS to Trident on 16 May 1972.

The Trident program is considerably behind the schedule established in May 1972 when the weapon system was approved for development. The lead submarine was funded in fiscal 1974 with a schedule put forward at that time for constructing an initial series of ten Trident SSBNs at an annual rate of 1-3-3-3, with these ten submarines to have been completed by 1982.

The first Trident submarine was ordered on 25 July 1974, with a planned delivery of 30 April 1979. However, the shipyard agreed to attempt to make delivery in December 1977 because of the high priority of the program. Subsequent delays caused by the Navy management of the project, design changes, and problems at the shipyard resulted in the late deliveries of the early submarines, with authorizations for the first ten submarines covering a ten-year period vice four years.

Builders: Note that four submarines of this class were laid down at the Electric Boat yard on the same date.

Cost: The FY 1991 shipbuilding program provided $1.282 *billion* for the SSBN 743, the last submarine of this class.

Design: SCB No. 304.74. The largest submarines yet built in the West, their size was determined primarily by their reactor plant. These submarines have a conservative design with the bow sonar dome and amidships torpedo tubes of later attack submarine designs. These are the only 24-tube strategic missile submarines built by any nation, with the Russian Typhoon-class SSBNs each having 20 tubes.

The ships have comfortable accommodations for their crew, which is only slightly larger than for previous American SSBNs. Three logistic hatches, in the forward (control-accommodation section), center (missile), and after (engineering) compartments have escape trunks that can be removed when in port to provide large, six-foot (1.8-m) diameter resupply and repair openings. These provide for the rapid transfer of supply pallets, equipment replacement modules, and even machinery components, permitting a

significant reduction in the time required for replenishment and maintenance. (The standard U.S. submarine hatches are 26 inches/ 0.66 m in diameter.)

These submarines are reported to have a 985-foot (300-m) operating depth.

Electronics: These submarines carry the Mk 57 MOSS (Mobile Submarine Simulator). The first 15 submarines will be backfitted with the BPS-16 radar beginning about 1997.

Engineering: The S8G reactor plant was originally intended to provide up to 60,000 shp, having been based on an earlier design for a large, high-speed cruise missile submarine. Its actual horsepower is publicly reported as being in excess of 30,000 shp, but significantly less than the 60,000 goal.

The S7G reactor plant, a land-based prototype of the OHIO plant, is installed at West Milton, N.Y.

Reportedly, the OHIO is significantly quieter than the ship's design goals for self-quieting, and at low speeds (i.e., when using natural convection rather than pumps for the circulation of pressurized water in the primary loop) the OHIO may be the quietest nuclear submarine yet constructed.

Manning: The crews of these submarines vary; the Blue/Gold crews each have 13 to 18 officers and 148 to 164 enlisted men assigned.

Missiles: The OHIO fired the first Trident C-4 to be launched from this class on 17 January 1982.

Names: SSBN 730 was originally named RHODE ISLAND; renamed for Senator "Scoop" Jackson, long-time supporter of nuclear and defense programs, on 27 September 1983, following his death earlier that month.

Operational: The OHIO made the first operational patrol of this class from 1 October 1982 to 10 December 1982.

The first squadron of eight submarines operates in the Pacific, based at Bangor, Wash. (Submarine Squadron 17), established on 5 January 1981. The second Trident submarine squadron (SubRon 16) operates in the Atlantic, based at Kings Bay, Ga. The early 1980s planning for a class of at least 20 OHIO-class SSBNs provided for 10 to operate out of each base.

These submarines are intended to conduct 70-day patrols interrupted by 25-day overhaul/replenishment periods, during which time the blue/gold crews change over. Under this schedule the submarines undergo a lengthy overhaul and reactor refueling (and conversion of the first eight submarines to the D-5 missile) every ten years.

Sonar: The BQQ-6 sonar is similar to the BQQ-5 in attack submarines less the active sonar elements. Although fitted with high-definition, under-ice sonar, these submarines are neither configured nor intended to operate in the polar ice pack.

The WEST VIRGINIA being assisted by civilian tugs at Port Everglades, Fla. The upper portions of the missile tubes are covered by a ''turtle back'' structure, with 24 missile hatches faired into the deck structure. (1991, Giorgio Arra)

The WEST VIRGINIA at speed, showing the classic lines of U.S. strategic missile submarines. This basic configuration has been used in all of the world's SSN/SSBNs except for the Russian Typhoon class of six units. (1991, Giorgio Arra)

11 STRATEGIC MISSILE SUBMARINES: "LAFAYETTE" CLASS

Number	Name	FY	Builder	Laid down	Launched	Commissioned	Status
SSBN 616	LAFAYETTE	61	General Dynamics/Electric Boat	17 Jan 1961	8 May 1962	23 Apr 1963	decomm. 12 Aug 1991
SSBN 617	ALEXANDER HAMILTON	61	General Dynamics/Electric Boat	26 June 1961	18 Aug 1962	27 June 1963	decomm. 1992
SSBN 619	ANDREW JACKSON	61	Mare Island Naval Shipyard	26 Apr 1961	15 Sep 1962	3 July 1963	decomm./str. 6 Sep 1989
SSBN 620	JOHN ADAMS	61	Portsmouth Naval Shipyard	19 May 1961	12 Jan 1963	12 May 1964	decomm./str. 30 Sep 1989
SSBN 622	JAMES MONROE	S61	Newport News Shipbuilding	31 July 1961	4 Aug 1962	7 Dec 1963	decomm./str. 25 Sep 1990
SSBN 623	NATHAN HALE	S61	General Dynamics/Electric Boat	2 Oct 1961	12 Jan 1963	23 Nov 1963	decomm./str. 3 Nov 1986
SSBN 624	WOODROW WILSON	S61	Mare Island Naval Shipyard	13 Sep 1961	22 Feb 1963	27 Dec 1963	decomm. 1992
SSBN 625	HENRY CLAY	S61	Newport News Shipbuilding	22 Oct 1961	30 Nov 1962	20 Feb 1964	decomm./str. 6 Nov 1990
SSBN 626	DANIEL WEBSTER	S61	General Dynamics/Electric Boat	28 Dec 1961	27 Apr 1963	9 Apr 1964	decomm.; to MTS 626
SSBN 627	JAMES MADISON	62	Newport News Shipbuilding	5 Mar 1962	15 Mar 1963	28 July 1964	decomm. 1992
SSBN 628	TECUMSEH	62	General Dynamics/Electric Boat	1 June 1962	22 June 1963	29 May 1964	decomm. 1992
SSBN 629	DANIEL BOONE	62	Mare Island Naval Shipyard	6 Feb 1962	22 June 1963	23 Apr 1964	**AA**
SSBN 630	JOHN C. CALHOUN	62	Newport News Shipbuilding	4 June 1962	22 June 1963	15 Sep 1964	**AA**
SSBN 631	ULYSSES S. GRANT	62	General Dynamics/Electric Boat	18 Aug 1962	2 Nov 1963	17 July 1964	decomm. 12 June 1992
SSBN 632	VON STEUBEN	62	Newport News Shipbuilding	4 Sep 1962	18 Oct 1963	30 Sep 1964	**AA;** to decomm. 1993
SSBN 633	CASIMIR PULASKI	62	General Dynamics/Electric Boat	12 Jan 1963	1 Feb 1964	14 Aug 1964	**AA**
SSBN 634	STONEWALL JACKSON	62	Mare Island Naval Shipyard	4 July 1962	30 Nov 1963	26 Aug 1964	**AA**
SSBN 635	SAM RAYBURN	62	Newport News Shipbuilding	3 Dec 1962	20 Dec 1963	2 Dec 1964	decomm./str. 31 July 1989; to MTS 635
SSBN 636	NATHANAEL GREENE	62	Portsmouth Naval Shipyard	21 May 1962	12 May 1964	19 Dec 1964	decomm. 12 Dec 1986; str. 31 Jan 1987
SSBN 640	BENJAMIN FRANKLIN	63	General Dynamics/Electric Boat	25 May 1963	5 Dec 1964	22 Oct 1965	**AA**
SSBN 641	SIMON BOLIVAR	63	Newport News Shipbuilding	17 Apr 1963	22 Aug 1964	29 Oct 1965	**AA**
SSBN 642	KAMEHAMEHA	63	Mare Island Naval Shipyard	2 May 1963	16 Jan 1965	10 Dec 1965	to transport submarine
SSBN 643	GEORGE BANCROFT	63	General Dynamics/Electric Boat	24 Aug 1963	20 Mar 1965	22 Jan 1966	**AA**
SSBN 644	LEWIS AND CLARK	63	Newport News Shipbuilding	29 July 1963	21 Nov 1964	22 Dec 1965	decomm. 27 June 1992
SSBN 645	JAMES K. POLK	63	General Dynamics/Electric Boat	23 Nov 1963	22 May 1965	16 Apr 1966	to transport submarine
SSBN 654	GEORGE C. MARSHALL	64	Newport News Shipbuilding	2 Mar 1964	21 May 1965	29 Apr 1966	decomm. 24 Sep 1992
SSBN 655	HENRY L. STIMSON	64	General Dynamics/Electric Boat	4 Apr 1964	13 Nov 1965	20 Aug 1966	**AA;** to decomm. 1993
SSBN 656	GEORGE WASHINGTON CARVER	64	Newport News Shipbuilding	24 Aug 1964	14 Aug 1965	15 June 1966	decomm. 1992
SSBN 657	FRANCIS SCOTT KEY	64	General Dynamics/Electric Boat	5 Dec 1964	23 Apr 1966	3 Dec 1966	**AA**
SSBN 658	MARIANO G. VALLEJO	64	Mare Island Naval Shipyard	7 July 1964	23 Oct 1965	16 Dec 1966	**AA**
SSBN 659	WILL ROGERS	64	General Dynamics/Electric Boat	20 Mar 1965	21 July 1966	1 Apr 1967	decomm. 1992

Displacement:	6,650 tons light
	7,250 tons standard
	8,250 tons submerged
Length:	425 feet (129.6 m) overall
Beam:	33 feet (10.06 m)
Draft:	31½ feet (9.6 m)
Propulsion:	2 steam turbines; 15,000 shp; 1 shaft
Reactors:	1 pressurized-water S5W (Westinghouse)
Speed:	approx. 20 knots surface
	approx. 25 knots submerged
Manning:	approx. 150 (15 officers + 135 enlisted)
Missiles:	16 tubes for Poseidon C-3 SLBM in SSBN 616, 617, 619, 620, 622–626, 628, 631, 635, 636, 642, 644, 645, 654, 656, 659 (19 units); no missiles carried
	16 tubes for Trident C-4 SLBM in SSBN 627, 629, 630, 632–634, 640, 641, 643, 655, 657, 658 (12 units)
Torpedo tubes:	4 21-inch (533-mm) Mk 65 (bow)
Torpedoes:	Mk 48
Radars:	BPS-15D surface search
Sonars:	BQR-7 passive detection
	BQR-15 towed array
	BQR-19 navigation
	BQR-21 passive array
	BQS-4 active/passive detection
Fire control:	Mk 113 torpedo/missile FCS

These submarines were built to carry the Polaris SLBM, with all subsequently being modified to carry the Poseidon C-3 missile; 12 were upgraded to fire the Trident C-4 missile.

Originally a class of 31 submarines, only 11 that have been rearmed with Trident C-4 missiles remain in commission; most of the other 20 submarines—19 armed with the Poseidon missile and 1 with Trident—have been or are in the process of being retired. However, the SAM RAYBURN and DANIEL WEBSTER are being modified (and immobilized) to serve as Moored Training Ships (MTS) to train nuclear propulsion plant operators, and the KAMEHAMEHA and JAMES K. POLK are being converted to special operations/transport submarines; see chapter 12. The others are being retired, although a few may serve briefly in the attack role (SSN).[4] The 12 submarines of this class armed with the Trident C-4 missile will be retired by the late 1990s. The JAMES MADISON was the first to be decommissioned.

Class: Thirty-five submarines of this class were originally programmed with four proposed in the fiscal 1965 shipbuilding program to complete the then-planned 45 submarine program (five squadrons of nine submarines each). The additional submarines were cancelled by Secretary of Defense Robert McNamara.

Five submarines were authorized under a supplemental program (S61).

The last 12 submarines of this design are officially the BENJAMIN FRANKLIN class (see Design notes).

Design: SCB No. 216. These submarines are enlarged and improved versions of the previous ETHAN ALLEN class. Like the ETHAN ALLEN class, the pressure hulls are constructed of HY-80 steel.

The last 12 submarines of this class have quieter machinery installations and other minor differences.

Electronics: All active submarines of this class now have the BPS-15D search radar.

Manning: The crews of these submarines mostly vary from 13 to 17 officers and from 122 to 144 enlisted men.

Missiles: The first eight submarines of this class initially deployed with the Polaris A-2 missile and the 23 later units with the Polaris A-3 missile. All were converted during 1970–1978 to launch the Poseidon C-3 missile. Subsequently, the last 12 of these submarines were selected for modification to launch the Trident C-4 missile. Their dates of conversion are listed in table 11-3; those modifications made

4. Several submarines of the ETHAN ALLEN and GEORGE WASHINGTON classes served briefly in the SSN role during the 1980s; they were not successful as SSNs because of their relatively high self-noise levels, limited sonar capability, and few torpedo reloads.

The GEORGE MARSHALL of the LAFAYETTE class—externally similar in appearance, but significantly smaller than the OHIO class. Note the height of the fully extended BRD-series radio direction finding antenna at the after end of the sail structure. (1988, Giorgio Arra)

The LEWIS AND CLARK entering port, with line handlers on deck and safety rails rigged; note the small sonar dome forward. (1991, Giorgio Arra)

at Cape Canaveral, Fla., were undertaken by technicians from the Norfolk Naval Shipyard. The more lengthy modifications periods indicate the work being accomplished during an overhaul.

The FRANCIS SCOTT KEY made the first Trident C-4 deployment, beginning on 20 October 1979.

Operational: All operational submarines are assigned to the Atlantic Fleet, operating out of Kings Bay, Ga.

These submarines were designed originally for a 20-year service life, but the Navy determined that they will be able to operate successfully for up to 30 years.

The sail structure of the LEWIS AND CLARK. There is a small sonar dome at the forward edge of the sail; a variety of masts and scopes are raised including the BPS-15D search-and-navigation radar, with a smaller, portable radar fitted forward on the sail. (1991, Giorgio Arra)

Stern aspect of the HENRY L. STIMSON. The light circular areas on the after deck mark air fittings for salvage and rescue; the safety track, for men working on deck when at sea, is also visible. (1991, Giorgio Arra)

TABLE 11-3. TRIDENT CONVERSIONS

SSBN	FY	Yard	
627	79	Newport News Shipbuilding	Aug 1979–Feb 1982
629	80	Cape Canaveral, Fla.	Apr 1980–May 1980
630	80	Cape Canaveral, Fla.	June 1980–Aug 1980
632	80	Newport News Shipbuilding	Jan 1980–May 1982
633	80	Newport News Shipbuilding	July 1980–Dec 1982
634	81	Cape Canaveral, Fla.	Sep 1981–Nov 1981
640	80	Portsmouth Naval Shipyard	Nov 1979–Sep 1981
641	79	Portsmouth Naval Shipyard	Mar 1979–Dec 1980
643	80	Portsmouth Naval Shipyard	June 1980–Mar 1982
655	80	Cape Canaveral, Fla.	Dec 1979–Feb 1980
657	79	Cape Canaveral, Fla.	Sep 1978–Dec 1978
658	79	Cape Canaveral, Fla.	Sep 1979–Nov 1979

STRATEGIC MISSILE SUBMARINES: "ETHAN ALLEN" CLASS

Five ballistic missile submarines of the ETHAN ALLEN (SSBN 608) class were built, being completed in 1961–1963. All were withdrawn from the strategic role in 1980–1981 and employed briefly in the attack submarine role. See chapter 12 for status notes.

STRATEGIC MISSILE SUBMARINES: "GEORGE WASHINGTON" CLASS

The U.S. Navy's first five ballistic missile submarines were based on the SKIPJACK (SSN 585) design, lengthened to provide space for 16 Polaris missile tubes and related equipment. These submarines were completed in 1960–1961 after a remarkably rapid design and construction period. See chapter 12 for status notes.

CHAPTER 12

Submarines

The CHICAGO, a nuclear-propelled attack submarine at high speed on the surface. Underwater she is less visible, although submerged wake is a means of locating and tracking submarines. (1991, Giorgio Arra)

The U.S. Navy's attack submarine force in late 1992 consists of about 75 nuclear-propelled submarines (SSN), including one serving in the research role. All diesel-electric combat attack submarines (SS) have been discarded from the U.S. Navy, although one diesel-electric research submarine (AGSS) is in service.[1] Based on the submarine funding rates of the 1990s and the accelerated retirement of older SSNs, the attack submarine force should decline to about 65 submarines by the year 2000. The Navy's current force-level goal for SSNs is 80 units, down from the goal of 100 SSNs of the 1980s.

Construction of LOS ANGELES-class submarines is coming to an end with only one submarine of the SEAWOLF design to be built. As a result of the January 1992 decision by the Department of Defense to cancel the SEAWOLF program except for the first unit (SSN 21), no new construction SSN will be authorized from 1991 through at least 1997. The 62 LOS ANGELES-class submarines being delivered represent the largest nuclear submarine class to be built by any nation. The subsequent SEAWOLF class will be much smaller—possibly totaling only seven or eight units.

The Navy is now developing a smaller SSN design to succeed the LOS ANGELES class; the new submarine is now being called the "new fast attack submarine." That concept was previously known as the "Centurion" program.[2] In December 1990 the Chief of Naval Operations[3] directed that the Navy undertake the development of a lower-cost SSN, stating:

> Procurement and design cycle for submarines and reactor components likewise require a lengthy cycle. The current SYDP [Six-Year Defense Plan] building rate is not adequate to sustain force levels and the industrial base which require the construction of two to three SSNs per year. Therefore, we must commence development of a lower-cost SSN to complement the SSN 688/SSN 21s. We should commence design of a new SSN to begin delivery in the late 1990s."[4]

In addition, two ex-Poseidon missile submarines are being converted to special operations/transport submarines.

Peacetime SSN missions include intelligence collection and anti-submarine training of air, surface, and other submarine forces. In wartime the primary mission of U.S. attack submarines would be operations against enemy "attack" and strategic missile submarines as well as anti-surface ship, land attack (with Tomahawk), and mining operations. Two LOS ANGELES-class SSNs participated in the Gulf War by firing Tomahawk missiles against targets in Iraq. However, the submarines fired only 12 of the 288 Tomahawks (4 percent) of the ship-launched missiles fired in that conflict, those launches being made primarily for "public relations" purposes, although the launchings were valuable to test the concept.

Several proposals have been made for the U.S. Navy to procure non-nuclear submarines, particularly designs fitted with Air Independent Propulsion (AIP) to supplement the diesel-electric propulsion plant. Such submarines could carry out missions as well as nuclear units, among them anti-submarine training (against non-nuclear submarine targets), special operations in low-threat areas, and research and development. However, the submarine community continues to be adamant against the acquisition of non-nuclear submarines.

All PERMIT-class and earlier submarines have been stricken. However, those submarines are preserved in various conditions at Bremerton, Wash., and Norfolk, Va., while means of disposal are

determined. In total, some 60 U.S. submarine reactors are now awaiting final disposal.[5] All diesel-electric submarines have been discarded except for the deep-diving research submarine DOLPHIN; the last U.S. Navy diesel-electric attack submarine was the BLUE-BACK, stricken on 30 October 1990.

Two former SSBNs converted to Moored Training Ships (MTS) are listed on page 77.

Several submersibles, including the nuclear-propelled NR-1, are also in service; see chapter 26.

Builders: There are currently two U.S. shipyards constructing nuclear-propelled submarines, the Electric Boat Division of the General Dynamics Corp. in Groton, Conn., and Newport News Shipbuilding in Newport News, Va. Their current workload of SSN and SSBN new construction will be completed by 1997. With no new construction authorizations until at least 1998, the future of the two existing submarine construction yards is questionable.

During the 1960s the United States had seven shipyards constructing nuclear-propelled submarines:

> Portsmouth Naval Shipyard, N.H.
> Bethlehem, Quincy, Mass.
> General Dynamics/Electric Boat, Groton, Conn.
> Mare Island Naval Shipyard, Vallejo, Calif.
> New York Shipbuilding, Camden, N.J.
> Newport News Shipbuilding, Va.
> Litton/Ingalls Shipbuilding, Pascagoula, Miss.

Classification: All U.S. submarines were numbered in a single series with the exception of six specialized craft until the advent of the SEAWOLF, which is designated SSN 21—to indicate the 21st century. The six exceptions were numbered in the midget (X), hunter-killer (SSK), and target and training (SST) series; all are listed at the end of this chapter.

Names: Attack submarines have had several name sources. The Navy's first submarine, the HOLLAND (SS 1), was named for its designer, Irish immigrant-schoolteacher John P. Holland, who was living when the craft was accepted by the Navy and named in 1900. Subsequent U.S. submarines were given "fish" names until 1911, when class letters and numerals were assigned (as A-2). This scheme continued until 1931, at which time fish names were again used (in addition to a scheme of class designations and hull numbers).

After World War II the class letter-number names were again used for the small T (training) and K (hunter-killer) submarines, but they were soon given fish names. Postwar submarines continued the use of fish or other marine-life names until 1971, when Admiral H. G. Rickover, then head of the Navy's nuclear propulsion program, instituted the practice of naming attack submarines for deceased members of Congress who had supported nuclear programs. Four SSNs were so named.

The naming source for attack submarines was changed to city names in 1974, the first being the LOS ANGELES. In 1983, however, Secretary of the Navy John Lehman directed that the then-building SSN 705 be named HYMAN G. RICKOVER for Admiral Rickover, whom he had helped force to leave the Navy in January 1982. (This was the second recent U.S. Navy ship to be named for a living person, the first being the carrier CARL VINSON [CVN 70]). Lehman's action was intended to prevent Congress from naming an aircraft carrier for Admiral Rickover.

The SSN 21 class was to revert to fish names for submarines.

Weapons: All U.S. combat submarines (SSBN/SSN) have 21-inch (533-mm) torpedo tubes. This diameter has been the standard in U.S. submarines since the submarine AA-2 (SS 60) completed in

---

1. The four other navies that operate nuclear-propelled submarines (Britain, China, France, and Russia) also operate diesel-electric combat submarines; all but France continue to build those craft, as do several other nations.
2. There has never been a U.S. Navy ship with the name Centurion. The Royal Navy has had nine ships named *Centurion* since 1650, including two battleships.
3. Adm. Frank B. Kelso II, Chief of Naval Operations from 1990.
4. Extract from "The Way Ahead" memorandum, signed on 4 January 1991.

5. One reactor has been permanently disposed of, the original SEAWOLF (SSN 575) liquid-sodium reactor. The reactor, with fuel core removed but still radioactive, was dropped into the Atlantic in April 1959 to a depth of some 9,000 feet (2,744 m) at a point 120 n.miles (222 km) due east of the Delaware-Maryland state lines.

1922. The SEAWOLF will introduce 30-inch (762-mm) diameter torpedo tubes to U.S. submarines. These submarines are still planned to carry only the 21-inch Mk 48 torpedo, but the larger-diameter tubes, fitted with skids, will permit quiet, "swim-out" launch of torpedos.

All U.S. attack submarines are armed with the Harpoon anti-ship missile and Tomahawk anti-ship (TASM) and land-attack (TLAM) missiles. These missiles can be launched from standard 21-inch torpedo tubes, with the later LOS ANGELES-class units additionally having 12 vertical-launch Tomahawk tubes.

An ASW Stand-Off Weapon (SOW) named Sea Lance was under development, ostensibly as a replacement for the outdated SUBROC (Submarine Rocket), an ASW weapon carrying a nuclear depth bomb. That missile was discarded in the late 1980s, and with the subsequent cancellation of the Sea Lance, no ASW stand-off weapon is available to U.S. submarines. (The Sea Lance was to have carried both a nuclear depth bomb and the Mk 50 conventional, lightweight torpedo as a warhead, with the latter having development priority.)

The STURGEON and the later LOS ANGELES submarines can carry Submarine-Launched Mobile Mines (SLMM) in place of torpedoes.

Operational: Asterisks in ship entry lists indicate submarines that participated in Operations Desert Shield/Desert Storm in 1991.

TABLE 12-1. SUBMARINE FORCE LEVELS [late 1992]

Type	Class/Ship	Comm.	Active	Building*	Reserve	Notes
SSN 21	SEAWOLF	1996 (?)	—	1	—	in production
SSN 751	Improved LOS ANGELES	1988–	10	13	—	in production
SSN 688	LOS ANGELES	1976–1989	39	—	—	1 serves in research role
SSN 671	NARWHAL	1969	1	—	—	to be deactivated in 1990s
SSN 637	STURGEON	1967–1975	32	—	4	to be deactivated in 1990s
SSBN 616	LAFAYETTE		—	2	—	undergoing conversion to special operations/transport submarines
AGSS 555	DOLPHIN	1968	1	—	—	deep-diving research submarine

*Ships authorized through fiscal 1992.

NUCLEAR-PROPELLED ATTACK SUBMARINES: CENTURION DESIGN

The development of a lower-cost SSN was initiated in 1990 in response to the increasing costs of the SEAWOLF class. On 19 March 1991, Secretary of the Navy H. Lawrence Garrett III testified before Congress that

> the Navy face[s] a long-term problem of maintaining an adequate force of first line ships when the [SSN] 688 class begins to be retired. As part of an overall effort to seek economies in all our ships and aircraft, I have recently directed the Chief of Naval Operations ... to begin studies for a new submarine that would incorporate the technologies developed for SSN 21 and new technologies, in a smaller, less expensive platform as an option when the LOS ANGELES-class submarines reach the end of their service lives after the year 2000. ... The proposed new submarine will complement the SEAWOLF in the multi-mission environment of the twenty-first century. While the SEAWOLF design strongly emphasizes ASW capability against the very best projected Soviet submarines, this new submarine design will emphasize capability in other kinds of contingencies. Both of these ships will allow us to maintain an adequate force level as we move past the year 2010.

Through mid-1991 the Navy had maintained that the new-design SSN would be a complement to the SEAWOLF rather than a sucessor. In late June 1991, however, there were reports that the SEAWOLF procurement would cease about the year 2000 to permit acceleration of the new SSN design, initially known as the Centurion, but changed by early 1992 to the "new fast attack submarine." The Navy had planned to introduce the new SSN in the fiscal 1998 shipbuilding program with a lead ship completion about 2003. The Navy envisioned that follow-on submarines would be built at the rate of two or three per year beginning with the fiscal 1999 authorization. However, when this edition of *Ships and Aircraft* went to press, there was no Department of Defense–approved plan for SSN construction through fiscal year 1997.

While design of the Centurion is not complete, it was initially believed that the craft would displace some 5,000–6,000 tons, and would have a pressurized-water reactor plant. The cost goal was one-half that of a SEAWOLF-class SSN.

(1) NUCLEAR-PROPELLED ATTACK SUBMARINE; "SEAWOLF" CLASS

Number	Name	FY	Builder	Start*	Launch	Commission	Status
SSN 21	SEAWOLF	89	General Dynamics/Electric Boat	25 Oct 1989		1997 (?)	Building

*The SEAWOLF did not have a formal keel laying; date is for official construction start.

Displacement:	9,150 tons submerged (see Design notes)	Missiles:	Harpoon and Tomahawk SSMs launched from torpedo tubes
Length:	350 feet (106.7 m) overall	Torpedo tubes:	8 30-inch (762-mm) amidships
Beam:	40 feet (12.2 m)	ASW weapons:	Mk 48 torpedoes
Draft:	35 11/12 feet (10.9 m)	Radars:	BPS-16
Propulsion:	2 steam turbines (General Electric); approx. 60,000 shp; 1 shaft/propulsor	Sonars/Fire Control:	BSY-2 with bow-mounted transducers and hull-mounted Wide Aperture Arrays (WAA)
Reactors:	1 pressurized-water S6W (Westinghouse)		TB-16D towed array
Speed:	35 knots submerged (see Propulsion notes)		TB-29 towed array
Manning:	approx. 130	EW systems:	BLD-1
			WLQ-4(V)1
			WLR-8(V)

The SEAWOLF design was intended to succeed the LOS ANGELES class in series production. The SEAWOLF design emphasis was on: (1) improved machinery, (2) quieting, and (3) improved combat systems, both sensors and additional weapons. These submarines will be slightly faster than the LOS ANGELES class and will have more torpedo tubes and more internally stowed weapons; there will be no Tomahawk launch tubes external to the pressure hull, as in the later LOS ANGELES class units. *See Addenda for latest program changes.*

The Navy originally planned to construct 29 submarines of this class in fiscal years 1989 to 2000: one to be authorized in fiscal 1991, two each in fiscal 1991 and 1992, and an average of three and one-third ships in the following years. However, controversy over the design, the issue of concurrent BSY-2 system development and submarine construction, and high costs led to reductions in the program. On 13 August 1990, as a result of a four-month Department of Defense major warship and threat review, the SEAWOLF production rate was reduced to three submarines every two years (i.e., 1.5 per year). The six-year defense plan submitted to Congress in February 1991 reduced the planned procurement rate to one SSN per year through fiscal 1995; after that there would be a 2-1-2-1 pattern starting in fiscal 1996. The SSN 22 was authorized in fiscal 1991 and the SSN 23 in fiscal 1992.

In September 1991 the Chief of Naval Operations, Admiral Frank Kelso, said that he expected only one SEAWOLF per year to be constructed until the lead Centurion SSN was authorized; this indicated that he did not anticipate a total program of more than nine SEAWOLFs.

In January 1992 the Department of Defense announced that the entire SEAWOLF program would be cancelled, with only the first unit to be completed. The funds previously voted by Congress for the SSN 22 and SSN 23 were to be rescinded.

Construction of the lead ship began in November 1989; there was no keel laying as such. The SSN 21 delivery was originally scheduled for November 1994; the delivery of the lead ship was delayed by at least six months (to May 1995) due to changes in the BSY-2 system configuration.[6] On 1 August 1991 the Navy announced that massive weld failures had been discovered in the hull that would undoubtedly delay the lead submarine at least into 1996.

The cracks in the welding, which were first discovered in June 1991, required the replacement of all welds completed up to that time. The SEAWOLF contract was increased by $58,825,590 on 18 December 1991 to cover the costs of the corrections.

Builders: In 1987 the Navy awarded complementary design contracts to General Dynamics/Electric Boat and Newport News Shipbuilding. A fixed-price, incentive-fee contract to build the lead submarine of the class was awarded to Electric Boat on 9 January 1989 and construction began on 25 October 1989 with a scheduled delivery date of May 1995.

6. The first *Naval Sea Systems Command Monthly Progress Report* issued after the construction contract was awarded listed the SSN 21 projected launch date as 28 January 1994 and completion on 26 May 1995.

The Navy awarded a contract for the second submarine of the class of Electric Boat on 3 May 1991. Four days later Newport News Shipbuilding filed a lawsuit protesting the decision, basing its case on a congressional mandate to preserve a two-yard submarine construction capability.[7]

On 31 August 1991 a federal judge voided the contract award to Electric Boat and directed that the Navy let the contract for the second SEAWOLF out for bids again.

Class: The decision to construct a new SSN class was taken in July 1982. This followed a Navy decision one year earlier not to construct a new SSN (see the 13th Edition/page 54). When the SEAWOLF was conceived in 1982, the SSN force-level goal was increased from 90 to 100 submarines.[8] But from the outset of the SEAWOLF effort even a cursory look at the program made it apparent that it would be impossible to procure a 100-submarine force with procurement of the SEAWOLF.

Classification: The Navy has designated this class as SSN 21, indicating an attack submarine for the 21st century. That hull number was previously carried by the submarine F-2 (initially named BARRACUDA), completed in 1912.

Cost: Estimates for the construction of 29 submarines at an eventual production rate of 3 or 4 submarines per year was calculated at $36 *billion* in 1988. The Secretary of the Navy's cost ceiling for the program (in fiscal 1985 dollars) was $1.6 *billion* for the lead ship and $1 *billion* for the fifth and later ships; the latter unit cost excludes the cost of constructing the ninth and later ships with HY-130 steel. (These cost estimates do not take into account the welding problems and resulting delays.)

By mid-1991 the lead submarine was estimated to cost about $2.3 *billion* (including advance procurement funds in FY 1987–1988) plus $1.913 *billion* in direct research and development funds (through FY 1990).

The fiscal 1991 budget appropriation provided $2.1 *billion* for the second unit; the fiscal 1992 appropriation provided $2.38 *billion* for the third unit. Follow-on submarines are expected to cost more than $2 *billion* each in fiscal 1992 dollars.

With cancellation of follow-on units, the actual cost of the SEAWOLF will be in excess of $3 *billion.* The last Department of Defense acquisition report on series production of the SEAWOLF, issued in late 1991, listed the cost of 12 submarines—including the BSY-2 program—at $33.627 *billion* in current-year dollars or an average of $2.8 *billion* per submarine.

Design: The basic SEAWOLF design was established in 1982–1983. This design provides for a smaller length-to-beam ratio than that of

7. On 8 May 1991, the Navy terminated a contract with Newport News Shipbuilding to participate in the design of the Centurion. This was one day after Newport News filed its suit challenging the selection of Electric Boat to build the second SEAWOLF. Navy officials denied that the two events were linked.

8. Ninety attack submarines was the Navy's force goal from 1973 to 1981; that goal was never achieved. Before that a force of 120 attack submarines, both diesel and nuclear, was authorized.

The more obvious features that differ from previous U.S. SSNs include hull-mounted diving planes, a "wedge" at the forward edge of the sail to reduce flow "vortex," and a six-surface tail configuration with the propeller mounted in a circular shroud or duct; the last feature is not shown on this official model. (U.S. Navy)

previous U.S. attack submarine classes. A six-surface tail configuration will be provided with the single propeller shaft common to U.S. SSNs since the late 1950s, but the propeller will have a circular shroud or duct similar to the installation in some British TRAFALGAR-class SSNs and (on a smaller scale) the Mk 48 torpedo. The submarine will have bow-mounted diving planes (vice sail mounted), which will retract into the bow for under-ice operations.

Special emphasis will be given to quieting, especially in isolating machinery from the hull.

The submerged displacement (9,150 tons) listed above is the limit imposed by the Secretary of the Navy. The actual submerged displacement is approximately 9,300 tons. About 150 tons of this comprises the water trapped in the bow sonar dome, which is normally flooded and closed when the submarine is at sea. However, in this class, to keep within the secretary's ceiling, the sonar dome is "open" to the sea when flooded.

The ninth and subsequent units were planned to have HY-130 steel vice HY-100 steel used in the early SEAWOLF-class submarines. All U.S. submarines from the THRESHER through the LOS ANGELES class were constructed of HY-80 steel.[9] (HY-100 steel was originally proposed for the LOS ANGELES class.)

A quarter-scale model of the SEAWOLF is being used to evaluate her design concepts (see page 80).

Electronics: This submarine will have the BSY-2 combat system, previously known as SUBACS for Submarine Advanced Combat System (see chapter 31 for characteristics). In mid-1991 the BSY-2 installation for the lead submarine was estimated to cost $280 million (12 percent of the submarine's estimated cost at that time).

Changes in the design of the BSY-2 caused redesign of portions of the SEAWOLF. In addition to the large bow spherical array, there are three Wide Aperture Array (WAA) panels along each side of the submarine.

Engineering: The maximum submerged speed is reported to be 35 knots, apparently making the SEAWOLF class faster than any previous U.S. submarine design. The SEAWOLF is expected to have a maximum "acoustic speed" in excess of 20 knots (i.e., the speed at which the submarine can transit while maintaining a sufficiently low noise level to still employ passive sonar with a narrow-band capability; a comparative Soviet speed is reported at 6 to 8 knots for submarines built in the 1980s).

Names: The name SEAWOLF was chosen for the lead submarine of this class in 1986 with the assumption that the existing SEAWOLF (SSN 575) would be striken by the time the new craft was launched; the SSN 575 was striken on 10 July 1987.

The previous SEAWOLF was the Navy's second nuclear-propelled submarine. That submarine was built with a liquid-sodium reactor plant (vice pressurized water); it was not considered successful and was removed. A previous submarine named SEAWOLF (SS 197) was the only U.S. submarine sunk by American forces in World War II.

Torpedoes: The Navy originally planned to place the torpedo tubes in the bows of this design, where they would be less vulnerable to water-flow problems during weapon launches at high speed. Following tests, the launch tubes were retained in the amidships position used in all designs since the TULLIBEE and THRESHER classes. Firing tests, however, demonstrated the feasibility of high-speed torpedo firing from amidship tubes and the SEAWOLF design was modified accordingly.

9. HY-80 was used in the SKIPJACK class, but the THRESHER was the first to have a complete HY-80 pressure hull, permitting a deeper operating depth.

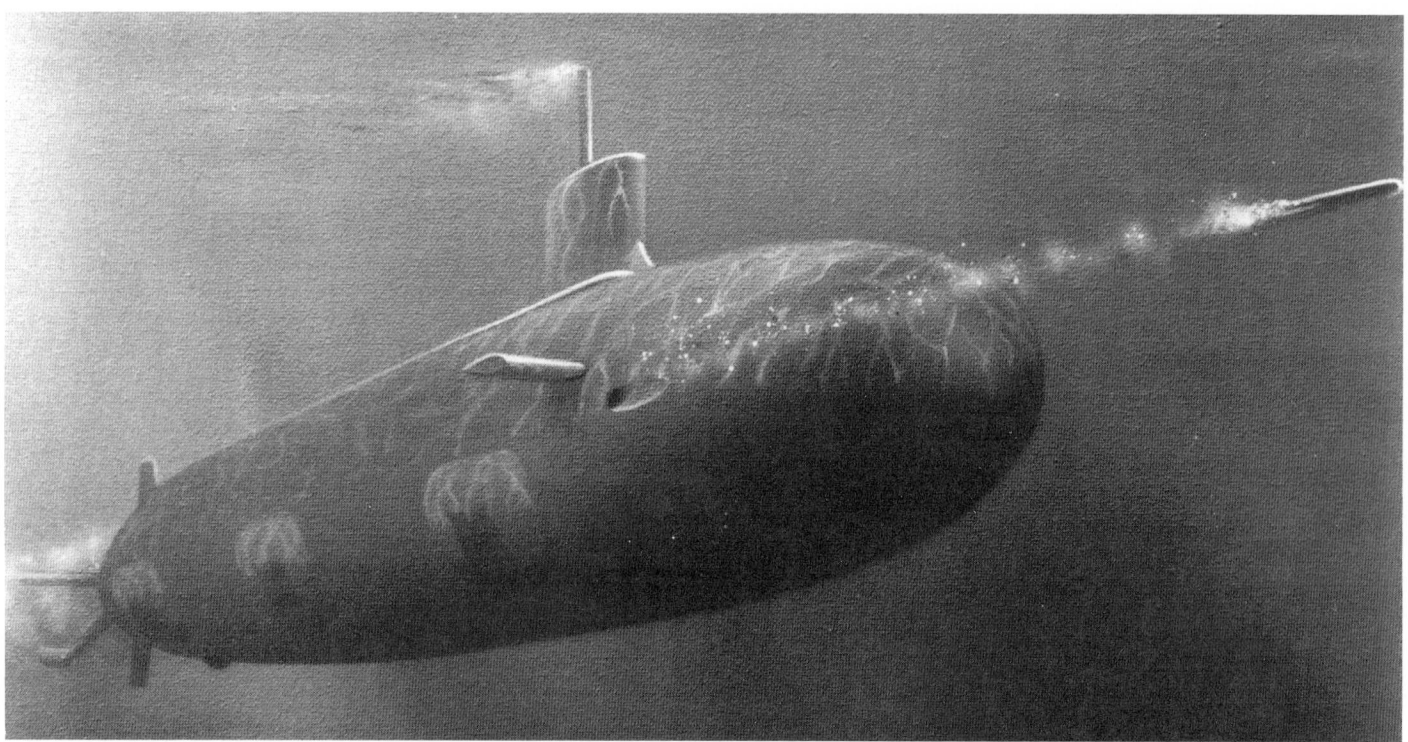

An artist's concept of the SEAWOLF. Design of the controversial undersea craft began in 1982 and has encountered a variety of difficulties. Only a few will be built, having an adverse impact on U.S. attack submarine force levels and submarine construction capabilities. (U.S. Navy)

10 + 13 NUCLEAR-PROPELLED ATTACK SUBMARINES: IMPROVED "LOS ANGELES" CLASS

Number	Name	FY	Builder	Laid down	Launched	Commissioned	Status
SSN 751	SAN JUAN	83	General Dynamics/Electric Boat	16 Aug 1985	6 Dec 1986	6 Aug 1988	**AA**
SSN 752	PASADENA	83	General Dynamics/Electric Boat	20 Dec 1985	12 Sep 1987	11 Feb 1989	**PA**
SSN 753	ALBANY	84	Newport News Shipbuilding	22 Apr 1985	13 June 1987	7 Apr 1990	**AA**
SSN 754	TOPEKA	84	General Dynamics/Electric Boat	13 May 1986	23 Jan 1988	21 Oct 1989	**PA**
SSN 755	MIAMI	84	General Dynamics/Electric Boat	24 Oct 1986	12 Nov 1988	30 June 1990	**AA**
SSN 756	SCRANTON	85	Newport News Shipbuilding	29 Aug 1986	3 July 1989	26 Jan 1991	**AA**
SSN 757	ALEXANDRIA	85	Newport News Shipbuilding	19 June 1987	23 June 1990	29 June 1991	**AA**
SSN 758	ASHEVILLE	85	Newport News Shipbuilding	9 Jan 1987	24 Feb 1990	28 Sep 1991	**AA**
SSN 759	JEFFERSON CITY	85	Newport News Shipbuilding	21 Sep 1987	17 Aug 1990	29 Feb 1992	**AA**
SSN 760	ANNAPOLIS	86	General Dynamics/Electric Boat	15 June 1988	18 May 1991	11 Apr 1992	**AA**
SSN 761	SPRINGFIELD	86	General Dynamics/Electric Boat	29 Jan 1990	4 Jan 1992	1993	Building
SSN 762	COLUMBUS	86	General Dynamics/Electric Boat	7 Jan 1991	1 Aug 1992	1993	Building
SSN 763	SANTA FE	86	General Dynamics/Electric Boat	9 July 1991	1992	1994	Building
SSN 764	BOISE	87	Newport News Shipbuilding	25 Aug 1988	23 Mar 1991	1992	Building
SSN 765	MONTPELIER	87	Newport News Shipbuilding	19 May 1989	6 Apr 1991	1993	Building
SSN 766	CHARLOTTE	87	Newport News Shipbuilding	7 Jan 1990	11 Apr 1992	1994	Building
SSN 767	HAMPTON	87	Newport News Shipbuilding	2 Mar 1990	28 Sep 1991	1993	Building
SSN 768	HARTFORD	88	General Dynamics/Electric Boat	24 Apr 1992	1993	1994	Building
SSN 769	TOLEDO	88	Newport News Shipbuilding	8 Apr 1991	1992	1994	Building
SSN 770	TUCSON	88	Newport News Shipbuilding	20 Sep 1991	1993	1995	Building
SSN 771	COLUMBIA	89	General Dynamics/Electric Boat	1992	1994	1995	Building
SSN 772	GREENEVILLE	89	Newport News Shipbuilding	1992	1993	1995	Building
SSN 773	CHEYENNE	90	Newport News Shipbuilding	1992	1994	1996	Building

Displacement:	6,080 tons standard	Torpedo tubes:	4 21-inch (533-mm) amidships Mk 67
	6,927 tons submerged	ASW weapons:	Mk 48 torpedoes
Length:	360 feet (109.7 m) overall	Radars:	BPS-15A surface search
Beam:	33 feet (10.1 m)	Sonars:	BSY-1 combat system
Draft:	32 feet (9.75 m)		TB-16 and/or TB-29 towed array
Propulsion:	2 steam turbines; approx. 30,000 shp; 1 shaft	Fire control:	1 CCS Mk 2 Mod 2
Reactors:	1 pressurized-water S6G (General Electric)		1 Mk 117 torpedo FCS
Speed:	22 knots surface	EW systems:	BRD-7 direction finder
	30+ knots submerged		WLQ-4(V)
Manning:	approx. 143 (15 officers + 128 enlisted)		WLR-8(V)
Missiles:	Harpoon and Tomahawk SSMs launched from torpedo tubes		WLR-9
	12 vertical launch tubes for Tomahawk SSM		WLR-12

These are improved LOS ANGELES-class submarines being provided with Tomahawk vertical-launch missile tubes, minelaying and under-ice capabilities, and improved machinery quieting. See the LOS ANGELES-class entry for additional information and notes on these submarines.

Class: The LOS ANGELES class is the world's largest series of nuclear-propelled submarines with 62 submarines built and under construction. The "final" program was for 65 units, but the Navy did not request funds for the last four units, supporting the SEAWOLF program instead. The Congress authorized one more LOS ANGELES-class submarines (SSN 773) for a total of 62 units. This is the largest class of submarines built since World War II by any nation except for the Soviet diesel-electric Whiskey class (236 units completed 1949–1957) and Foxtrot class (62 built for Soviet service plus 17 for foreign navies, 1958–1973).

Cost: The last submarine to be authorized, the SSN 773, was funded at $732.9 million in the fiscal 1990 budget; in addition, there

was $35.1 million for outfitting and $7 million for post-delivery costs—a total of $782 million.

The two previous submarines, SSN 771 and SSN 772, were funded at an average of $649.25 million in fiscal 1989 plus $8.85 million each for outfitting and $3.5 million for post-delivery costs.

Electronics: These submarines are fitted with the BSY-1 sonar/fire control "combat system." Major problems were encountered in late 1986 in installing the initial system in the SSN 751, resulting in a completion delay of the submarine.

Manning: The crews for these submarines vary from 12 to 16 officers, and from 125 to 133 enlisted men; not all personnel are on board for long-duration deployments.

Missiles: The Harpoon and Tomahawk missiles can be launched from the torpedo tubes in this class. All have 12 vertical-launch tubes for Tomahawk missiles fitted forward, between the pressure hull and sonar sphere, in space previously used for ballast tanks.

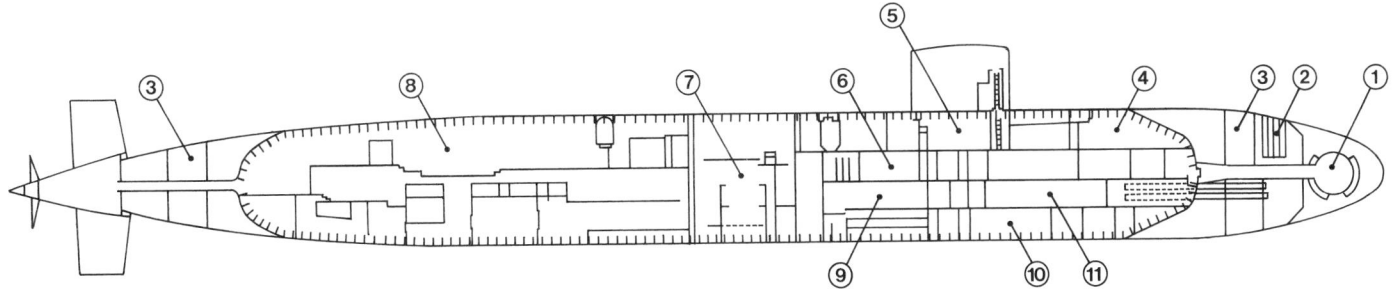

1. sonar sphere   2. vertical-launch tubes   3. ballast tanks   4. sonar room   5. control room/attack center   6. crew's mess   7. reactor compartment
8. engine room   9. auxiliary machinery   10. battery compartment   11. torpedo room (William Clipson)

The MIAMI, an Improved LOS ANGELES-class submarine, externally is similar to the standard SSN 688s except for the absence of sail-mounted diving planes. The bitts and cleats shown on deck retract when the submarine is at sea. (1990, Giorgio Arra)

The MIAMI, bow on, showing the circular cross section of a modern submarine hull. The only other U.S. nuclear-propelled submarine class (i.e., multiple units) built without sail-mounted diving planes was the SKATE class. (1991, Giorgio Arra)

Another view of MIAMI. The sheath-like housing on the starboard side, just below the safety track, is for the TB-series towed sonar array. The darker deck surface running aft from the sail is coated with a non-skid material. (1991, Giorgio Arra)

The bow of the OKLAHOMA CITY showing the 12 Tomahawk vertical-launch tubes. The tubes are fitted in space between the pressure hull and the sonar dome that was previously used for ballast tanks. (1991, PH1 Robert McRoy, USN)

38 NUCLEAR-PROPELLED ATTACK SUBMARINES | "LOS ANGELES" CLASS
1 NUCLEAR-PROPELLED RESEARCH SUBMARINE |

Number	Name	FY	Builder	Laid down	Launched	Commissioned	Status
SSN 688	LOS ANGELES	70	Newport News Shipbuilding	8 Jan 1972	6 Apr 1974	13 Nov 1976	**PA**
SSN 689	BATON ROUGE	70	Newport News Shipbuilding	18 Nov 1972	26 Apr 1975	25 June 1977	**AA**
SSN 690	PHILADELPHIA*	70	General Dynamics/Electric Boat	12 Aug 1972	19 Oct 1974	25 June 1977	**AA**
SSN 691	MEMPHIS	71	Newport News Shipbuilding	23 June 1973	3 Apr 1976	17 Dec 1977	**AA-R&D**
SSN 692	OMAHA	71	General Dynamics/Electric Boat	27 Jan 1973	21 Feb 1976	11 Mar 1978	**PA**
SSN 693	CINCINNATI	71	Newport News Shipbuilding	6 Apr 1974	19 Feb 1977	10 June 1978	**AA**
SSN 694	GROTON	71	General Dynamics/Electric Boat	3 Aug 1973	9 Oct 1976	8 July 1978	**AA**
SSN 695	BIRMINGHAM	72	Newport News Shipbuilding	26 Apr 1975	29 Oct 1977	16 Dec 1978	**PA**
SSN 696	NEW YORK CITY	72	General Dynamics/Electric Boat	15 Dec 1973	18 June 1977	3 Mar 1978	**PA**
SSN 697	INDIANAPOLIS	72	General Dynamics/Electric Boat	19 Oct 1974	30 July 1977	5 Jan 1980	**PA**
SSN 698	BREMERTON	72	General Dynamics/Electric Boat	6 May 1976	22 July 1978	28 Mar 1981	**PA**
SSN 699	JACKSONVILLE	72	General Dynamics/Electric Boat	21 Feb 1976	18 Nov 1978	16 May 1981	**AA**
SSN 700	DALLAS	73	General Dynamics/Electric Boat	9 Oct 1976	28 Apr 1979	18 July 1981	**AA**
SSN 701	LA JOLLA	73	General Dynamics/Electric Boat	16 Oct 1976	11 Aug 1979	24 Oct 1981	**PA**
SSN 702	PHOENIX	73	General Dnyamics/Electric Boat	30 July 1977	8 Dec 1979	19 Dec 1981	**AA**
SSN 703	BOSTON	73	General Dynamics/Electric Boat	11 Aug 1978	19 Apr 1980	30 Jan 1982	**AA**
SSN 704	BALTIMORE	73	General Dynamics/Electric Boat	21 May 1979	13 Dec 1980	24 July 1982	**AA**
SSN 705	CITY OF CORPUS CHRISTI	73	General Dynamics/Electric Boat	4 Sep 1979	25 Apr 1981	8 Jan 1983	**AA**
SSN 706	ALBUQUERQUE	74	General Dynamics/Electric Boat	27 Dec 1979	13 Mar 1982	21 May 1983	**AA**
SSN 707	PORTSMOUTH	74	General Dynamics/Electric Boat	8 May 1980	18 Sep 1982	1 Oct 1983	**PA**
SSN 708	MINNEAPOLIS-SAINT PAUL	74	General Dynamics/Electric Boat	20 Jan 1981	19 Mar 1983	17 Mar 1984	**AA**
SSN 709	HYMAN G. RICKOVER	74	General Dnyamics/Electric Boat	24 July 1981	17 Aug 1983	8 Sep 1984	**AA**
SSN 710	AUGUSTA	74	General Dynamics/Electric Boat	1 Apr 1982	21 Jan 1984	19 Jan 1985	**AA**
SSN 711	SAN FRANCISCO	75	Newport News Shipbuilding	26 May 1977	27 Oct 1979	24 Apr 1981	**PA**
SSN 712	ATLANTA	75	Newport News Shipbuilding	17 Aug 1978	16 Aug 1980	6 Mar 1982	**AA**
SSN 713	HOUSTON	75	Newport News Shipbuilding	29 Jan 1979	21 Mar 1981	25 Sep 1982	**PA**
SSN 714	NORFOLK	76	Newport News Shipbuilding	1 Aug 1979	31 Oct 1981	21 May 1983	**AA**
SSN 715	BUFFALO	76	Newport News Shipbuilding	25 Jan 1980	8 May 1982	5 Nov 1983	**PA**
SSN 716	SALT LAKE CITY	77	Newport News Shipbuilding	26 Aug 1980	16 Oct 1982	12 May 1984	**PA**
SSN 717	OLYMPIA	77	Newport News Shipbuilding	31 Mar 1981	30 Apr 1983	17 Nov 1984	**PA**
SSN 718	HONOLULU	77	Newport News Shipbuilding	10 Nov 1981	24 Sep 1983	6 July 1985	**PA**
SSN 719	PROVIDENCE	78	General Dynamics/Electric Boat	14 Oct 1982	4 Aug 1984	27 July 1985	**AA**
SSN 720	PITTSBURGH*	79	General Dynamics/Electric Boat	15 Apr 1983	8 Dec 1984	23 Nov 1985	**AA**
SSN 721	CHICAGO*	80	Newport News Shipbuilding	5 Jan 1983	13 Oct 1984	27 Sep 1986	**PA**
SSN 722	KEY WEST	80	Newport News Shipbuilding	6 July 1983	20 July 1985	12 Sep 1987	**AA**
SSN 723	OKLAHOMA CITY	81	Newport News Shipbuilding	4 Jan 1984	2 Nov 1985	9 July 1988	**AA**
SSN 724	LOUISVILLE*	81	General Dynamics/Electric Boat	16 Sep 1984	14 Dec 1985	8 Nov 1986	**PA**
SSN 725	HELENA	82	General Dynamics/Electric Boat	28 Mar 1985	28 June 1986	11 July 1987	**PA**
SSN 750	NEWPORT NEWS*	82	Newport News Shipbuilding	3 Mar 1984	15 Mar 1986	3 June 1989	**AA**

Displacement:	6,080 tons standard	Radars:	BPS-15A surface search
	6,927 tons submerged	Sonars:	BQQ-5 multi-function bow mounted (BQQ-5E in later and updated units)
Length:	360 feet (109.7 m) overall		
Beam:	33 feet (10.1 m)		BQR-15 towed array
Draft:	32 feet (9.75 m)		BQR-26 in some submarines
Propulsion:	2 steam turbines; approx. 30,000 shp; 1 shaft		BQS-13 active
Reactors:	1 pressurized-water S6G (General Electric)		BQS-15 under ice/mine detection
Speed:			TB-16 or TB-23 towed array in later and updated units
	30+ knots submerged	Fire control:	1 CCS Mk 2 Mod 0 in SSN 688–719
Manning:	approx. 133 (13 officers + 120 enlisted)		1 CCS Mk 2 Mod 1 in SSN 720–725, 750
	later units 135 (15 officers + 120 enlisted)		1 Mk 117 torpedo FCS
Missiles:	Harpoon and Tomahawk SSMs launched from torpedo tubes	EW systems:	BRD-7 direction finder
	12 vertical-launch tubes for Tomahawk SSM in SSN 719 and later submarines		WLQ-4(V)
			WLR-8(V)
Torpedo tubes:	4 21-inch (533-mm) amidships Mk 67		WLR-9
ASW weapons:	Mk 48 torpedoes		WLR-12

These are large attack submarines, originally developed to counter the Soviet Victor fast-attack submarines that were first completed in 1967–1968. The MEMPHIS is employed as a research and development platform; she retains most of her combat capabilities (see below).

The LOS ANGELES submarines are about five knots faster than the previous U.S. STURGEON class, the higher speed being the principal advantage over the earlier class (see Propulsion notes). However, the LOS ANGELES class is about one-half again as large in terms of displacement and considerably more expensive (see Cost notes). Also, the original LOS ANGELES design lacked the under-ice and minelaying capabilities, vital for modern submarine warfare.

The SAN JUAN and later units are considered an "improved" design (see previous listing).

Class: The MEMPHIS, formerly a "straight" SSN, began operating as a full-time "interim" research-and-development platform in August 1989. She provides an at-sea testing environment for the Defense Advanced Research Projects Agency (DARPA), Navy, and industry. One of the first projects to be evaluated in the MEMPHIS is a non-penetrating periscope (i.e., mounted on a flexible cable employing fiber optics). In 1993–1994 she will undergo more extensive modifications to serve in the research role, including tests of the 30-inch torpedo tube and advanced towed sonar arrays.

The project is the result of congressional criticism of the Navy's failure to pursue advanced submarine technology. There is no plan to reclassify the submarine; properly she should be designated SSAGN.

Classification: Submarine hull numbers 726 through 749 were reserved for Trident SSBNs.

While cost comparisons of ship classes are difficult, the last (37th) STURGEON cost $186 million compared to the 32nd LOS ANGELES, which had an estimated cost of $343 million in same-year dollars. The STURGEON's BQQ-2 and Mk 113 fire control system could be upgraded to the LOS ANGELES' BQQ-5 and Mk 117 for some $22 million in fiscal 1978 dollars.

Design: SCB No. 303. These are large SSNs, the increase in size over the STURGEON class being due primarily to the installation of the larger, more-capable S6G reactor plant in an effort to regain the speed lost in the PERMIT and STURGEON classes. These submarines were designed to be constructed of HY-100 steel; however, they were built with HY-80. The ALBANY and TOPEKA have some hull sections of HY-100 to serve as a materials test bed for the SEAWOLF class; those submarines have not encountered the welding problems sustained by the later submarines.

The LOS ANGELES also has improved sonar and fire control systems (that were being retrofitted to the STURGEON class) compared to previous classes. These submarines are not fitted to carry mines nor are they configured for under-ice operations; these shortcomings are corrected in the Improved LOS ANGELES class.

These submarines originally had berthing for only 95 enlisted men; the remainder used sleeping bags in available space or "hot bunked." Additional berthing has been added, but the ships are considered to be quite crowded in comparison with earlier SSNs.

Electronics: The large towed array passive sonar is carried in a sheathlike housing fitted to the upper starboard side of the hull.

The early submarines were fitted with the Mk 113 (analog) fire control system and could carry the Tomahawk missile, while those with the Mk 117 (digital) cannot carry the SUBROC. All have been refitted with the Mk 117.

Electronics: The ATLANTA evaluated the BPS-16 radar for the SSN 21 and SSBN 726 classes in 1991–1992; that set was to go in the SEAWOLF.

Engineering: The S6G reactor is estimated to have an initial fuel core operating life of 10 to 13 years. According to official Navy statements, with the LOS ANGELES "the speed threshold which had been established by SKIPJACK 18 years earlier was finally surpassed."

The S6G reactor plant is adapted from the D2G plant fitted in eight guided missile cruisers (CGN, previously DLGM). The LOS ANGELES plant is essentially one-half of the cruiser plant.

Missiles: The Harpoon and Tomahawk missiles can be launched from the torpedo tubes in this class. The ATLANTA was the first SSN to deploy with Tomahawk, in November 1983.

Names: Most of the earlier submarines of this class carry names previously borne by cruisers; many later names were carried by lesser warships (e.g., frigates [PF]).

The SSN 705 was originally to be named CHICAGO; it was changed while under construction to CORPUS CHRISTI for the Texas port city. That name was previously borne by the frigate PF 44 (launched in 1943); the seaplane tender ALBEMARLE (AV 5) was converted to a helicopter repair ship (ARVH 1) during the Vietnam War and renamed CORPUS CHRISTI BAY (she was operated by the Military Sealift Command for the Army). After protests from Catholic groups, the SSN 705 was commissioned as the CITY OF CORPUS CHRISTI.

The SSN 708 honors the "twin cities" in Minnesota, which are actually named Minneapolis–St. Paul (vice *Saint* Paul).

The SSN 709 was named for Admiral H. G. Rickover, long-time head of the U.S. Navy's nuclear-propulsion program, on 4 March 1983; the move to honor Rickover while he was still alive was, in part, an effort to resist congressional pressure to name an aircraft carrier for the controversial admiral.

The SSN 719 was named PROVIDENCE in September 1983 to honor the state of Rhode Island after the SSBN 730 was renamed HENRY M. JACKSON (the SSBN having previously been named RHODE ISLAND).

Operational: The AUGUSTA suffered an underwater collision with a Soviet nuclear-propelled submarine in the North Atlantic in October 1986; she struck a Soviet strategic missile submarine (at least one other Soviet submarine was in the area at the time). Repairs to the AUGUSTA cost $2.7 million.

Operational: The LOUISVILLE and PITTSBURGH launched Tomahawk TLAM missiles against targets in Iraq during the 1991 Gulf War. The latter submarine fired the first "war shot" against an enemy by a U.S. submarine since World War II. The LOUISVILLE fired eight missiles, and the PITTSBURGH fired four; this represented 4 percent of the 288 missiles fired in the Gulf War.

The BATON ROUGE collided with a Russian nuclear-propelled attack submarine in the Barents Sea on 11 February 1992. U.S. officials said that the incident occurred in international waters, beyond the 12-n.mile (22.2-km) territorial zone recognized by the United States; Russian officials declared that the collision was off Murmansk, within their territorial waters. Neither submarine was believed to have suffered serious damage, although there was some damage to the Soviet craft's sail structure. No injuries were reported by either submarine.

NUCLEAR-PROPELLED ATTACK SUBMARINE: "GLENARD P. LIPSCOMB"

The one-of-a-kind GLENARD P. LIPSCOMB (SSN 685) was decommissioned and stricken on 11 July 1990. The LIPSCOMB, commissioned in 1974, was constructed to evaluate a Turbo Electric Drive (TED) propulsion plant. Speed was sacrificed to reduce machinery noises. The TULLIBEE, constructed more than a decade earlier, was in part a similar effort to replace reduction gear with electric drive. No additional submarines of this type were built because of a decision to make the faster LOS ANGELES class the Navy's standard SSN design.

See 14th Edition/page 56 for characteristics.

The MINNEAPOLIS-SAINT PAUL on a sun-lit sea. When at sea submarines rarely run on the surface, but remain submerged for weeks or months at a time. They often operate near the surface, however, to employ sensors (periscopes, ESM, radar) and to facilitate radio reception. (1990, Giorgio Arra)

The OKLAHOMA CITY's sail structure shows the submarine's two periscopes partially raised; the mottled camouflage is effective in choppy seas. The snorkel intake head is slightly raised. Acoustic "windows" are at the front and rear edges of the sail, as is the anechoic coating on the deck. (1990, Giorgio Arra)

The SALT LAKE CITY, leaving the characteristic wake of U.S. submarines running at high speed on the surface. The sail-mounted diving planes allow better depth control when near the surface, but are cumbersome for operations in ice and create some drag at high submerged speeds. (1989, Giorgio Arra)

The BALTIMORE entering port with lines and line handlers on deck. There is a rope ladder rigged from the sail, forward of the diving planes. The unusual drying patterns on the hull are caused by the anechoic materials, which absorb active acoustic emissions from torpedo and submarine sonars. (1991 Giorgio Arra)

32 NUCLEAR-PROPELLED ATTACK SUBMARINES: "STURGEON" CLASS

Number	Name	FY	Builder	Laid down	Launched	Commissioned	Status
SSN 637	STURGEON	62	General Dnyamics/Electric Boat	10 Aug 1963	26 Feb 1966	3 Mar 1967	**AA**
SSN 638	WHALE	62	General Dynamics/Electric Boat	27 May 1964	14 Oct 1966	12 Oct 1968	**AA**
SSN 639	TAUTOG	62	Ingalls Shipbuilding	27 Jan 1964	15 Apr 1967	17 Aug 1968	**PA**
SSN 646	GRAYLING	63	Portsmouth Naval Shipyard	12 May 1964	22 June 1967	11 Oct 1969	**AA**
SSN 647	POGY	63	Ingalls Shipbuilding	4 May 1964	3 June 1967	15 May 1971	**PA**
SSN 648	ASPRO	63	Ingalls Shipbuilding	23 Nov 1964	29 Nov 1967	20 Feb 1969	**PA**
SSN 649	SUNFISH	63	General Dynamics, Quincy, Mass.	15 Jan 1965	14 Oct 1966	15 Mar 1969	**AA**
SSN 650	PARGO	63	General Dynamics/Electric Boat	3 June 1964	17 Sep 1966	5 Jan 1968	**AA**
SSN 651	QUEENFISH	63	Newport News Shipbuilding	11 May 1965	25 Feb 1966	6 Dec 1966	decomm. 8 Nov. 1991/str. 8 Nov 1991
SSN 652	PUFFER	63	Ingalls Shipbuilding	8 Feb 1965	30 Mar 1968	9 Aug 1969	**PA**
SSN 653	RAY	63	Newport News Shipbuilding	1 Apr 1965	21 June 1966	12 Apr 1967	decomm. 1992
SSN 660	SAND LANCE	64	Portsmouth Naval Shipyard	15 Jan 1965	11 Nov 1969	25 Sep 1971	**AA**
SSN 661	LAPON	64	Newport News Shipbuilding	26 July 1965	16 Dec 1966	14 Dec 1967	decomm. 25 June 1992
SSN 662	GURNARD	64	Mare Island Naval Shipyard	22 Dec 1964	20 May 1967	6 Dec 1968	**PA**
SSN 663	HAMMERHEAD	64	Newport News Shipbuilding	29 Nov 1965	14 Apr 1967	28 June 1968	**AA**
SSN 664	SEA DEVIL	64	Newport News Shipbuilding	12 Apr 1966	5 Oct 1967	30 Jan 1969	decomm. 16 Oct 1991/str. 16 Oct 1991
SSN 665	GUITARRO	65	Mare Island Naval Shipyard	9 Dec 1965	27 July 1968	9 Sep 1972	decomm. 29 May 1992
SSN 666	HAWKBILL	65	Mare Island Naval Shipyard	12 Dec 1966	12 Apr 1969	4 Feb 1971	**PA**
SSN 667	BERGALL	65	General Dynamics/Electric Boat	16 Apr 1966	17 Feb 1968	13 June 1969	**AA**
SSN 668	SPADEFISH	65	Newport News Shipbuilding	21 Dec 1966	15 May 1968	14 Aug 1969	**AA**
SSN 669	SEAHORSE	65	General Dynamics/Electric Boat	13 Aug 1966	15 June 1968	19 Sep 1969	**AA**
SSN 670	FINBACK	65	Newport News Shipbuilding	26 June 1967	7 Dec 1968	4 Feb 1970	**AA**
SSN 672	PINTADO	66	Mare Island Naval Shipyard	27 Oct 1967	16 Aug 1969	11 Sep 1971	**PA**
SSN 673	FLYING FISH	66	General Dynamics/Electric Boat	30 June 1967	17 May 1969	29 Aug 1970	**AA**
SSN 674	TREPANG	66	General Dynamics/Electric Boat	28 Oct 1967	27 Sep 1969	14 Aug 1970	**AA**
SSN 675	BLUEFISH	66	General Dynamics/Electric Boat	13 Mar 1968	10 Jan 1970	8 Jan 1971	**AA**
SSN 676	BILLFISH	66	General Dynamics/Electric Boat	20 Sep 1968	1 May 1970	12 Mar 1971	**AA**
SSN 677	DRUM	66	Mare Island Naval Shipyard	20 Aug 1968	23 May 1970	15 Apr 1972	**PA**
SSN 678	ARCHERFISH	67	General Dynamics/Electric Boat	19 June 1969	16 Jan 1971	17 Dec 1971	**AA**
SSN 679	SILVERSIDES	67	General Dynamics/Electric Boat	13 Oct 1969	4 June 1971	5 May 1972	**AA**
SSN 680	WILLIAM H. BATES	67	Ingalls Shipbuilding	4 Aug 1969	11 Dec 1971	5 May 1973	**PA**
SSN 681	BATFISH	67	General Dynamics/Electric Boat	9 Feb 1970	9 Oct 1971	1 Sep 1972	**AA**
SSN 682	TUNNY	67	Ingalls Shipbuilding	22 May 1970	10 June 1972	26 Jan 1974	**PA**
SSN 683	PARCHE	68	Ingalls Shipbuilding	10 Dec 1970	13 Jan 1973	17 Aug 1974	**PA**
SSN 684	CAVALLA	68	General Dynamics/Electric Boat	4 June 1970	19 Feb 1972	9 Feb 1973	**PA**
SSN 686	L. MENDEL RIVERS	69	Newport News Shipbuilding	26 June 1971	2 June 1973	1 Feb 1975	**AA**
SSN 687	RICHARD B. RUSSELL	69	Newport News Shipbuilding	19 Oct 1971	12 Jan 1974	16 Aug 1975	**PA**

Displacement:	4,250 tons standard, except SSN 678–687 4,460 tons	**ASW weapons:**	Mk 48 torpedoes
	4,780 tons submerged, except SSN 678–687 4,960 tons	**Radars:**	BPS-14/15 surface search
Length:	292 feet (89.0 m) overall except SSN 678–687 302 feet (92.1 m)	**Sonars:**	BQQ-5 multi-function bow mounted
Beam:	31²⁄₃ feet (9.65 m)		BQR-7 passive in ships with BQQ-2
Draft:	28⅝ feet (8.8 m)		BQR-26 in SSN 666
Propulsion:	2 steam turbines (De Laval or General Electric); 15,000 shp; 1 shaft		BQS-6 active in ships with BQQ-2
Reactors:	1 pressurized-water S5W (Westinghouse)		BQS-12 active on SSN 637–664; BQS-13 in later submarines
Speed:	approx. 15 knots surface		TB-16 or TB-23 towed array
	approx. 30 knots submerged	**Fire control:**	Mk 117 torpedo FCS
Manning:	approx. 142 (16 officers + 126 enlisted)	**EW systems:**	WLQ-4(V)
Missiles:	Harpoon and Tomahawk SSMs launched from torpedo tubes		WLR-4(V)
Torpedo tubes:	4 21-inch (533-mm) amidships Mk 63		WLR-9

These submarines are improved versions of the PERMIT class, the principal visible difference being the taller sail structure and under-ice operational capability (see Design notes). After the LOS ANGELES class this is the largest U.S. series of nuclear-propelled submarines.

The GUITARRO sank alongside a pier at the San Francisco Naval Shipyard on 15 May 1969 while still under construction because of faulty ballasting and workers' errors; there were no casualties. She was raised and rebuilt.

All submarines of this class are scheduled to be decommissioned and stricken by the mid- to late 1990s.

Builders: The POGY was begun by the New York Shipbuilding Corp., Camden, N.J. The contract for her construction was terminated on 5 June 1967, and the unfinished submarine was towed to the Ingalls yard for completion under a contract awarded on 7 December 1967.

Design: SCB No. 188A (through SSN 664) and subsequently SCB No. 300 in the new series. These submarines are similar to the previous PERMIT class, but with several deficiencies of the earlier design being corrected. An improved electronics suite was added as well as a larger sail structure that provides more space for masts, under-ice operational features, and maintenance of specific depth

when near the surface. This resulted in a larger submarine which, with the S5W reactor plant, resulted in a further loss of speed over the PERMIT and SKIPJACK classes.

The under-ice feature include upward- and forward-looking navigational sonars, strengthened sail and rudder caps, and provision for the sail-mounted diving planes to rotate 90° for breaking through ice.

Since 1978 the SSN 679 and 687 have a communications-buoy housing fitted abaft the sail.

Electronics: The original BQQ-2 system has been upgraded to BQQ-5 configuration during overhauls. The HAWKBILL has a protruding BQR-26 sonar fitted in the forward part of her sail structure. A few ships have been fitted with the TB-23 thin-line array.

Many, if not all, of these submarines have an acoustic device known as GNAT fitted just forward of the upper rudder fin.

Fire control: This class was built with the Mk 113 analog fire control system; replaced by Mk 117 digital system during overhauls.

Manning: The crews of these submarine vary, with from 13 to 19 officers and from 119 to 134 enlisted men assigned to each submarine. Not all personnel are embarked for long-duration deployments.

Missiles: The GUITARRO was trials ship for the submarine-launched Tomahawk.

Modifications: The CAVALLA was modified August 1982–December 1982 with fittings provided for carrying a removable Dry Deck Shelter (DDS) hangar that can accommodate a Swimmer Delivery Vehicle (SDV) or lock out a group of commandos/swimmers while fully or partially submerged. There is no reduction of submarine combat capability, except for a slightly reduced speed and higher (flow) noise level when the hangar is installed. Five other "long-hull" submarines were similarly modified in FY 1988–1991 (SSN 678–680, 682, 686).

Names: The SSN 680 was originally to be named REDFIN; she was renamed for a deceased member of Congress on 25 June 1971.

Operational: The QUEENFISH was the first of several submarines of this class to conduct extensive operations under the Arctic ice pack and was the first single-screw submarine of any nation to surface through the ice, in February 1967.[10] The WHALE and PARGO were the first submarines of this class to surface at the North Pole, in April 1969. (The QUEENFISH surfaced there during her July–August 1970 under-ice operations.)

10. See N. Polmar, "Sailing Under the Ice," U.S. Naval Institute *Proceedings* (June 1984): 121–123.

The BILLFISH shows the tall sail structure and short hull area forward of the sail that characterize STURGEON-class submarines. There is a small sonar dome at the after end of the hull. (1991, Giorgio Arra)

The stern of the ARCHERFISH with the upper rudder indicating that the rudder is hard over. In this class the towed-array sheath housing is on the port side of the hull. (1990, Giorgio Arra)

The PARGO in the Arctic demonstrating how the sail-mounted diving planes rotate 90° for surfacing through the ice pack. The subsequent LOS ANGELES class did not have this Arctic operations capability, a shortcoming corrected in the Improved LOS ANGELES and SEAWOLF classes. (1991, U.S. Navy)

1 NUCLEAR-PROPELLED ATTACK SUBMARINE: "NARWHAL"

Number	Name	FY	Builder	Laid down	Launched	Commissioned	Status
SSN 671	NARWHAL	64	General Dynamics/Electric Boat	17 Jan 1966	9 Sep 1966	12 July 1969	**AA**

Displacement:	5,284 tons standard	Missiles:	Harpoon and Tomahawk SSMs launched from torpedo tubes
	5,830 tons submerged	Torpedo tubes:	4 21-inch (533-mm) amidships Mk 63
Length:	314$1\frac{1}{12}$ feet (96.0 m) overall	ASW weapons:	Mk 48 torpedoes
Beam:	37$\frac{3}{4}$ feet (11.5 m)	Radars:	BPS-14 surface search
Draft:	25$1\frac{1}{12}$ feet (7.9 m)	Sonars:	BQQ-5 multi-function bow mounted
Propulsion:	2 steam turbines (General Electric); 17,000 shp; 1 shaft		BQS-14 under ice/mine detection
Reactors:	1 pressurized-water S5G (General Electric)		TB-16 towed array
Speed:	approx. 20 knots surface	Fire control:	Mk 117 torpedo FCS
	approx. 25 knots submerged	EW systems:	BRD-7 direction finder
Manning:	152 (16 officers + 136 enlisted)		WLR-8

The NARWHAL was constructed to evaluate the natural-circulation S5G reactor plant. Weapons, sensors, and other features of the NARWHAL are similar to the STURGEON-class SSNs. She will be decommissioned in the late 1990s.

Design: SCB No. 245.

Fire control: The Mk 117 torpedo fire control system has been installed in place of the original Mk 113.

Reactor: The S5G reactor plant uses natural convection rather than pumps for heat transfer/coolant transfer at slow speeds, thus reducing self-generated machinery noises. This concept is used in the subsequent LOS ANGELES and OHIO (SSBN 726) classes. A land-based prototype of the S5G plant was built at Arco, Idaho.

Sonars: The BQQ-2 has been upgraded to a BQQ-5 configuration.

The one-of-a-kind NARWHAL, departing Portsmouth, England. The NARWHAL's reactor plant was a prototype for natural-circulation reactor plants employed in later U.S. submarines. The NARWHAL is otherwise similar to the STURGEON class. (1987, L. Van Ginderen collection)

(2) TRANSPORT SUBMARINES; CONVERTED SSBNs

Number	Name
SSN 642	Kamehameha
SSN 645	James K. Polk

These submarines are being converted from Poseidon-armed SSBNs (same hull numbers) to transport submarines for SEAL and other special forces. They are replacing the JOHN MARSHALL and SAM HOUSTON (see below). Each is being configured to carry 67 swimmers or troops, with a Dry Deck Shelter (DDS) being fitted to carry SEAL Delivery Vehicles (SDV); see page 78.

Their building yards and construction dates are listed in chapter 11 of this edition.

NUCLEAR-PROPELLED ATTACK SUBMARINES: "THRESHER/PERMIT" CLASS

Number	Name	Status
SSN 593	Thresher	sunk 10 Apr 1963
SSN 594	Permit	decomm. 22 July 1991
SSN 595	Plunger	decomm./str. 3 Jan 1990
SSN 596	Barb	decomm./str. 20 Dec 1989
SSN 603	Pollack	decomm./str. 1 Mar 1989
SSN 604	Haddo	decomm. 12 June 1991/str. 30 Aug 1991
SSN 605	Jack	decomm./str. 11 July 1990
SSN 606	Tinosa	decomm. 15 Jan 1992
SSN 607	Dace	decomm. 2 Dec 1988
SSN 612	Guardfish	decomm. 4 Feb 1992
SSN 613	Flasher	decomm. 1992
SSN 614	Greenling	decomm. 1992
SSN 615	Gato	decomm. 1992
SSN 621	Haddock	decomm. 1992

These submarines established the basic design for subsequent U.S. Navy SSNs and SSBNs, having a deep-diving capability (approx. 1,300 feet/396 m), quiet machinery, and large bow-mounted sonar with torpedo tubes mounted amidships. Fourteen submarines were completed from 1961 through 1967; the later units were delayed following the 1963 loss of the THRESHER, being modified under the so-called "subsafe" program. The THRESHER was lost on post-overhaul sea trials off New England with 112 naval personnel and 17 civilians on board. (Officially called the PERMIT class after the loss of the THRESHER.) All are being stricken.

See 14th Edition/pages 62–64 for characteristics.

STRATEGIC MISSILE/ATTACK SUBMARINES: "ETHAN ALLEN" CLASS

Number	Name	Changed to SSN	Notes
SSBN 608	Ethan Allen	1 Sep 1980	decomm./str. 21 Mar 1986
SSBN 609	Sam Houston	10 Nov 1980	decomm. 6 Sep 1991
SSBN 610	Thomas A. Edison	6 Oct 1980	decomm. 1 Dec 1983/str. 30 Apr 1986
SSBN 611	John Marshall	Feb 1981	decomm. 29 July 1992
SSBN 618	Thomas Jefferson	Apr 1981	decomm. 24 Jan 1985/str. 30 Apr 1986

The five Polaris fleet ballistic missile submarines of the ETHAN ALLEN class, completed 1961–1963, have been retired. All five were reclassified as attack submarines (SSN) after discarding their Polaris missiles. Two, the JOHN MARSHALL and SAM HOUSTON, were extensively converted in 1984–1986 to transport submarines to carry SEALs or other special forces, and to conduct other special operations. (They retained SSN designations, although LPSSN would have been more appropriate.) The SAM HOUSTON was employed in the mid-1980s as a test platform for the UQQ-2 Surveillance Towed Array Sonar System (SURTASS); the SURTASS is carried by T-AGOS surveillance ships (see chapter 23).

STRATEGIC MISSILE/ATTACK SUBMARINES: "GEO. WASHINGTON" CLASS

Number	Name	Changed to SSN	Notes
SSN 598	George Washington	20 Nov 1981	decomm. 24 Jan 1985/str. 30 Apr 1986
SSN 599	Patrick Henry	24 Oct 1982	decomm. 3 Feb 1985
SSBN 600	Theo. Roosevelt	—	decomm./str. 28 Feb 1981
SSN 601	Robert E. Lee	1 Mar 1982	decomm. 1 Dec 1983/str. 30 Apr 1986
SSBN 602	Abraham Lincoln	—	decomm./str. 28 Feb 1981

The five Polaris fleet ballistic missile submarines of the GEORGE WASHINGTON class, completed 1960–1961, have been partially dismantled and are laid up pending ultimate disposal. Three boats were briefly employed in the SSN role after their last Polaris patrols. They are no longer capable of active service (the ROOSEVELT and LINCOLN being actually cut into two sections).

NUCLEAR-PROPELLED ATTACK SUBMARINE: "TULLIBEE"

The one-of-a-kind TULLIBEE (SSN 597) was decommissioned and stricken on 18 June 1988. Built as a specialized hunter-killer (ASW) submarine and completed in 1960, the TULLIBEE was the smallest nuclear-propelled combat submarine to be built except for the French RUBIS class (four units).[11] The construction of additional submarines of the TULLIBEE design was halted in favor of the larger and more versatile THRESHER/PERMIT class. The TULLIBEE was the first U.S. submarine to have bow-mounted sonar with the torpedo tubes fitted amidships, angled out to port and starboard. The TULLIBEE was referred to as a hunter-killer submarine (SSKN), but she was completed as an SSN.

See 14th Edition/page 67 for characteristics.

NUCLEAR-PROPELLED RESEARCH SUBMARINE: "HALIBUT"

The HALIBUT (SSGN 587) was the U.S. Navy's only nuclear-propelled submarine armed with the Regulus strategic cruise missile. Completed in 1960, the HALIBUT was designed and constructed as a guided missile submarine (SSGN). After the phasing out of the

11. The U.S. and Russian fleets have smaller nuclear-propelled *submersibles,* the NR-1 and Xray, respectively; see chapter 26.

The transport submarine SAM HOUSTON fitted with a Dry Deck Shelter (DDS) for swimmer delivery vehicles and SEALs. The SAM HOUSTON and JOHN MARSHALL are being replaced in this role by the KAMEHAMEHA (SSBN 642) and JAMES K. POLK (SSBN 645). (U.S. Navy)

Regulus program, the HALIBUT was reclassified as an attack submarine (SSN) in 1965 and subsequently served as a research submarine until 1976. No additional submarines of this design were built; an improved Regulus II–armed SSGN class was planned, but those submarines were reordered as THRESHER/PERMIT-class SSNs. The HALIBUT was decommissioned on 30 June 1976 and stricken on 30 April 1986.

See 14th Edition/page 68 for characteristics.

NUCLEAR-PROPELLED ATTACK SUBMARINE: "TRITON"

The TRITON (SSRN 586) was the world's only nuclear-propelled radar picket submarine and the only non-Soviet submarine with two reactors. The TRITON was the world's largest undersea craft when completed in 1959, having been developed by Admiral H. G. Rickover specifically as a precursor to multi-reactor surface warships. (The Navy phased out the radar picket submarine program in the late 1950s because of the greater effectiveness of Airborne Early Warning [AEW] aircraft.) The TRITON was reclassified as an SSN in 1961 and was employed in general submarine operations until 1969. She was decommissioned on 29 March 1969 and stricken on 30 April 1986.

See 14th Edition/page 69 for characteristics.

NUCLEAR-PROPELLED ATTACK SUBMARINES: "SKIPJACK" CLASS

Number	Name	Status
SSN 585	SKIPJACK	decomm./str. 19 Apr 1990; str. 1992
SSN 588	SCAMP	decomm. 26 Apr 1988
SSN 589	SCORPION	sunk 27 May 1968
SSN 590	SCULPIN	decomm./str. 3 Aug 1990
SSN 591	SHARK	decomm./str. 15 Sep 1990
SSN 592	SNOOK	decomm./str. 14 Nov. 1986

The SKIPJACK-class submarines were the first to combine nuclear propulsion with the high-speed, "tear-drop" hull design of the experimental submarine ALBACORE. These were the fastest submarines in the U.S. Navy when built; their approximate 33-knot speed was not equalled until the advent of the LOS ANGELES class.

Six units were completed in 1959–1961; five have been decommissioned and stricken. The SCORPION was lost with all 99 men on board on 27 May 1968 while some 400 n.miles (740 km) southwest of the Azores.

See 14th Edition/pages 70–71 for characteristics.

NUCLEAR-PROPELLED ATTACK SUBMARINES: "SKATE" CLASS

Number	Name	Status
SSN 578	SKATE	decomm. 12 Sep 1986; str. 1992
SSN 579	SWORDFISH	decomm./str. 2 June 1989
SSN 583	SARGO	decomm. 26 Feb 1988; str. 21 Apr 1988
SSN 584	SEADRAGON	decomm. 12 June 1984; str. 1992

This class was the first U.S. effort to develop a nuclear-propelled submarine for series production, with four units completed 1957–1959. Additional units were deferred in favor of the high-speed SKIPJACK class. All of the SKATE class except the SWORDFISH were employed extensively in Arctic operations. The SEADRAGON was home-ported in Sasebo, Japan, from November 1964, the first U.S. nuclear submarine to be based overseas.

See 14th Edition/pages 71–72 for characteristics.

NUCLEAR-PROPELLED ATTACK SUBMARINE: "SEAWOLF"

The second U.S. nuclear-propelled submarine, the SEAWOLF (SSN 575) differed from all other Western "nukes" in using liquid-metal (sodium) as a heat-exchange medium for the reactor plant in lieu of pressurized water. Completed in 1957, the SEAWOLF was re-engined in 1959–1960 with a conventional reactor plant and was engaged in research activities from 1969 until decommissioned on 30 March 1987; she was stricken on 10 July 1987.

See 14th Edition/page 73 for characteristics.

NUCLEAR-PROPELLED ATTACK SUBMARINE: "NAUTILUS"

The pioneer nuclear-propelled submarine NAUTILUS (SSN 571), completed in 1954, is now a memorial at Groton, Conn., near the Electric Boat yard where she was built and the submarine base at New London.[12] She became the first ship to reach the North Pole on 3 August 1958, while sailing under the Arctic ice pack. The NAUTILUS was decommissioned on 3 March 1980; she was towed to Groton in 1985 and formally transferred to private control on 6 July 1985.

See 13th Edition/page 74 for characteristics.

ATTACK SUBMARINES: "BARBEL" CLASS

Number	Name	Status
SS 580	BARBEL	decomm. 4 Dec 1989; str. 17 Jan 1990
SS 581	BLUEBACK	decomm. 1 Oct 1990; str. 30 Oct 1990
SS 582	BONEFISH	decomm. 28 Sep 1988; str. 28 Feb 1989

These were the last diesel-electric combat submarines built in the United States and the last in U.S. Navy service. They were the first combat submarines to incorporate the ALBACORE or "tear-drop" high-speed hull design. All three were completed in 1959.

The BARBEL was decommissioned following a diving accident on 1 May 1989. The BONEFISH was severely damaged by fire off the coast of Florida on 24 April 1988; 1 officer and 2 sailors were killed in the blaze; there were 89 survivors.

See 14th Edition/page 75 for characteristics.

ATTACK SUBMARINE: "DARTER"

The DARTER (SS 576) was built to an improved TANG-class design, with the construction of further submarines of this class deferred in favor of a more-capable BARBEL class. Completed in 1956, the DARTER's service life was continually extended several times until decommissioned on 1 December 1989; she was stricken on 17 January 1990. (The GRAYBACK and GROWLER were to have been of this class, but were completed instead as Regulus guided missile submarines, the SSG 574 and SSG 577, respectively.)

See 14th Edition/page 76 for characteristics.

ATTACK SUBMARINES: "TANG" CLASS

Number	Name	Status
SS/AGSS 563	TANG	to Turkey 18 Feb. 1980; str. 6 Aug 1987
SS 564	TRIGGER	str./to Italy 10 July 1973
SS 565	WAHOO	str. 15 July 1983
SS 566	TROUT	str./to Iran 19 Dec 1978 (not transferred)
SS/SSAG 567	GUDGEON	to Turkey 30 September 1983; str. 6 Aug 1987
SS 568	HARDER	str./to Italy 20 Feb. 1974

All six of the TANG-class fast attack submarines, completed in 1951–1952, have been transferred or stricken. Three submarines of this class were to have been transferred to Iran, the TANG, WAHOO, and TROUT; their transfer was cancelled in 1979 after the fall of the Shah. The WAHOO was decommissioned on 27 June 1980, partially stripped and laid up and stricken in 1983. The TROUT was technically transferred to Iran in 1978, but was not formally decommissioned until 6 May 1980, and was then retained by the U.S. Navy; she is laid up at the Philadelphia Naval Shipyard.

See 12th Edition/page 45 for characteristics.

---

12. The Navy had decided to moor the ship at the Washington Navy Yard in the nation's capital. However, President Carter directed that the ship be moored at New London.

1 RESEARCH SUBMARINE: "DOLPHIN"

Number	Name	FY	Builder	Laid down	Launched	Commissioned	Status
AGSS 555	DOLPHIN	61	Portsmouth Naval Shipyard	9 Nov 1962	8 June 1968	17 Aug 1968	**PA**

Displacement:	860 tons standard
	950 tons submerged
Length:	165 feet (50.3 m) overall
Beam:	19⁵/₁₂ feet (5.9 m)
Draft:	16 feet (4.9 m)
Propulsion:	2 diesel engines (General Motors 12V71)
	1 electric motor (Elliott); 1,650 shp; 1 shaft
Speed:	7.5 knots surface
	15 knots submerged

Manning:	47 (5 officers + 42 enlisted)
Missiles:	none
Torpedo tubes:	removed
Radars:	SPS-53 navigation
Sonars:	Deep Submergence Obstacle Avoidance Sonar
Fire control:	none

The DOLPHIN is an experimental, deep-diving submarine. Reportedly, she has operated at greater depths than any other operational U.S. submarine. The DOLPHIN is assigned to Submarine Development Group 1, providing support to the Naval Ocean Systems Center and several other Navy research activities. She has been modified to test HY-130 steel components.

Design: SCB No. 207. The DOLPHIN has a constant-diameter pressure hull with an outside diameter of approximately 15 feet with hemisphere heads at both ends. The submarine has a stepped sail, with the radar antenna, UHF antenna, and single periscope mounted on the upper (rear) step, and the lights, whip antenna, VLF loop antenna, and searchlight mounted on the lower step.

An improved rudder design and other features permit maneuvering without conventional submarine diving planes. There are minimal penetrations of the pressure hull (e.g., only one access hatch) and built-in safety systems that automatically surface the submarine in an emergency.

The experimental torpedo tube that was originally fitted was removed in 1970.

Electronics: Various experimental sonars have been fitted in the DOLPHIN. Her original bow sonar, which had four arrays that could be extended at 90° angles to the submarine's bow-stern axis, has been removed. She subsequently was fitted with a BQS-15 prior to the current system.

Engineering: Submerged endurance is approximately 24 hours; her sea endurance is about 14 days.

Operational: The DOLPHIN's activities have supported research in air–submarine laser communications, deep submergence, sonar, oceanography, and ASW.

The deep-diving research submarine DOLPHIN, showing her unusual sail structure, with a forward overhang. The submarine's SPS-53 radar is mounted at the after end of the sail, behind the periscope. (1985, Giorgio Arra)

2 MOORED TRAINING SHIPS: FORMER "LAFAYETTE" CLASS

Number	Name	Status
MTS 626 (ex-SSBN 626)	DANIEL WEBSTER	decomm. 1991
MTS 635 (ex-SSBN 635)	SAM RAYBURN	decomm./str. 28 Aug 1989

These submarines are former ballistic missile submarines, converted to stationary nuclear reactor operator training ships. The WEBSTER and RAYBURN are both located at Charleston, S.C.

TABLE 12-2. POST–WORLD WAR II SUBMARINES

Number	Name/Class	Comm.	Notes	Number	Name/Class	Comm.	Notes
SS 551	BASS (ex-K-2/SSK 2)	1951	stricken 1 Apr 1965	SSN 594–596	PERMIT class*		
SS 552	BONITA (ex-K-3/SSK 3)	1952	stricken 1 Apr 1965	SSN 597	TULLIBEE		
SS 553	(KINN) Norway OSP		completed 1964	SSBN 598–602	GEORGE WASHINGTON class		
SS 554	(SPRINGEREN) Denmark OSP		completed 1964	SSN 603–607	PERMIT class		
AGSS 555	DOLPHIN	1968		SSBN 608–611	ETHAN ALLEN class		
SS 556–562	not used			SSN 612–615	PERMIT class		
SS 563–568	TANG class			SSBN 616–617	LAFAYETTE class		
AGSS 569	ALBACORE	1953	stricken 1 May 1980	SSBN 618	ETHAN ALLEN class		
AGSS 570	completed as SST 1			SSBN 619, 620	LAFAYETTE class		
SSN 571	NAUTILUS	1954	memorial	SSN 621	PERMIT class		
SSR 572	SAILFISH (later SS)	1956	stricken 30 Sep 1978	SSBN 622–636	LAFAYETTE class		
SSR 573	SALMON (later SS)	1956	stricken 1 Oct 1977	SSN 637–639	STURGEON class		
SSG 574	GRAYBACK (later LPSS/SS)	1958	stricken 16 Jan 1984	SSBN 640–645	LAFAYETTE class		
SSN 575	SEAWOLF	1957	stricken 10 July 1987	SSN 646–653	STURGEON class		
SS 576	DARTER	1956	stricken 17 Jan 1990	SSBN 654–659	LAFAYETTE class		
SSG 577	GROWLER	1958	stricken 30 Sep 1980	SSN 660–670	STURGEON class		
SSN 578, 579	SKATE class			SSN 671	NARWHAL		
SS 580–582	BARBEL class			SSN 672–684	STURGEON class		
SSN 583, 584	SKATE class			SSN 685	GLENARD P. LIPSCOMB		
SSN 585	SKIPJACK class			SSN 686, 687	STURGEON class		
SSRN 586	TRITON (later SSN)			SSN 688–725	LOS ANGELES class		
SSGN 587	HALIBUT (later SSN)			SSBN 726–743	OHIO class		
SSN 588–592	SKIPJACK class			SSBN 744–749	reserved for SSBNs		
SSN 593	THRESHER			SSN 750–773	LOS ANGELES class		

*The SSN 594–596 and 607 were originally ordered as Regulus cruise missile submarines (SSGN with same hull numbers); they were reordered as attack submarines after the Regulus II program was cancelled in December 1958.

U.S. submarine programs reached hull number SS 562 during World War II, with hulls 526–562 being cancelled late in the war. Subsequently, five of these numbers were assigned to postwar submarines, three U.S. submarines and American-financed, foreign-built submarines (Offshore Procurement).

The last war-built submarine on the Naval Register was the transport submarine SEALION (LPSS 315), decommissioned and laid up in 1970 and stricken on 15 March 1977. The last active submarine of World War II construction was the TIGRONE (AGSS 419), which was decommissioned on 30 June 1975 and stricken on 27 June 1975 (i.e., three days before being formally decommissioned).

Note the large number of submarine designs developed and built from the late 1940s into the early 1960s. This was a period of highly innovative thinking in the submarine community, in part while searching for new roles for submarines and exploring the potential impact of emerging technologies on submarine warfare. In particular, the research submarine ALBACORE introduced many of the features found in subsequent undersea craft; in many respects she was the beginning of the modern submarine era.

All postwar U.S. submarines—including ballistic missile craft—have been numbered in the same series except for three small, hunter-killer submarines (SSK), three training submarines (SST), which were in separate series, and the SEAWOLF (SSN 21).

The U.S. Navy's lone midget submarine, the X-1 completed in 1955, was stricken on 16 February 1973. She is on display at the Naval Academy in Annapolis, Md.

TABLE 12-3. HUNTER-KILLER SUBMARINES

Number	Name	Comm.	Notes
SSK 1	BARRACUDA (ex-K-1)	1951	to SST 3
SSK 2	BASS (ex-K-2)	1951	to SS 551
SSK 3	BONITA (ex-K-3)	1952	to SS 552

These purpose-built SSKs were small (1,000-ton, 196-foot/59.75 m) hunter-killer submarines, intended to lie in wait to intercept Soviet submarines off their home ports and in narrow waterways. Several hundred were to have been produced in time of war. They were originally assigned K-number "names" and were given fish names in 1955. The BASS and BONITA were reclassified SS in 1959 for use in the training role; the BARRACUDA was changed to SST in 1959 for the training role.

In addition to the three built-for-the-purpose SSKs, the nuclear-propelled TULLIBEE was built as an SSKN (although designated SSN 597) and seven GATO (SS212)-class diesel submarines were converted to SSKs in the 1950s.

TABLE 12-4. TRAINING SUBMARINES

Number	Name	Comm.	Notes
SST 1	MACKEREL (ex-T-1)	1953	stricken 31 Jan 1973
SST 2	MARLIN (ex-T-2)	1953	stricken 31 Jan 1973
SST 3	BARRACUDA (ex-K-1/SSK 1)	1951	stricken 1 Oct 1973

The SST 1 and 2 were small (310-ton, 133-foot/40.5 m) submarines developed for training and target use. The MACKEREL was ordered as AGSS 570 and completed as the SST 1. Originally assigned T-number "names," they were given fish names in 1956.

SWIMMER DELIVERY VEHICLES

The Navy has about 15 Swimmer Delivery Vehicles (SDV) that can be carried into forward areas in hangars within attack or special-operations submarines. These are Mk VIII and Mk IX "wet" vehicles, which can carry up to six SEALs wearing SCUBA-type breathing apparatuses. These are less than state-of-the-art with respect to propulsion and the capability to support swimmers.

In 1990 the Navy awarded a contract to Unisys Corp. of Great Neck, N.Y., to upgrade the Mk VIII vehicles, but in March 1992 the Navy cancelled it, after spending more than $18 million on the project.

The term Swimmer Delivery Vehicle was changed to SEAL Delivery Vehicle in the early 1990s.

Meanwhile, a study of an Advanced SEAL Delivery System (ASDS), long demanded by Congress, continued. Earlier the Navy began to evaluate the Italian (Maritalia) toroidal-hull submersible 3GST9. That effort was also cancelled.

Thus, when this edition went to press, there was no significant progress in this field despite 15 years of professed Navy needs and major congressional interest.

UNMANNED UNDERWATER VEHICLES

The U.S. Navy is now looking into the potential role of Unmanned Underwater Vehicles (UUVs). In the underwater environment, unmanned craft—either tethered or Autonomous Underwater Vehicles (AUV)—could undertake a number of missions, some considered too dangerous to risk a manned submarine. The missions being considered for UUVs include:

Submarine warfare: A variety of UUV configurations could support friendly submarine operations. A UUV could serve as a decoy to draw out hostile submarines, as a sustained remote communication relay (a link for radio or, in the future, lasers), as an offboard platform for acoustic or wake sensors, or as area search and reconnaissance to expand a submarine's "search horizon"; it could also lay mines, and collect specific intelligence (off an enemy port or in a transit area).

Offboard acoustic sensors, i.e., AUV-carried active and passive systems, would permit submarines to use bi-static and multi-static, low-frequency detection techniques. These are already in use with surface ships that tow active low-frequency sonars.

Anti-submarine warfare: In addition to the above operations, an ASW-configured AUV would perform barrier surveillance, towing a towed array through an area and automatically transmitting detections to another platform (ship, submarine, or satellite). Future technology might enable an AUV to pick up and trail an enemy submarine as it leaves port or transits through a barrier line.

Ocean surveillance: An extension of the ASW mission, in the ocean surveillance role AUVs could be programmed to patrol wide ocean areas with passive sensors. Or they could be employed as an active sound source, the reflections of their acoustic pulses being monitored by fixed underwater Sound Surveillance Systems (SOSUS) or Surface Towed Array Surveillance Systems (SURTASS).

Mine Warfare: A Mine Countermeasures (MCM) vehicle could transit enemy minefields, map them for future reference, or guide a friendly submarine or surface ship through them. Active sonar would be used to detect the mines, while a bottom-matching sonar coupled with an inertial navigation system would provide precise information or the UUV's position.

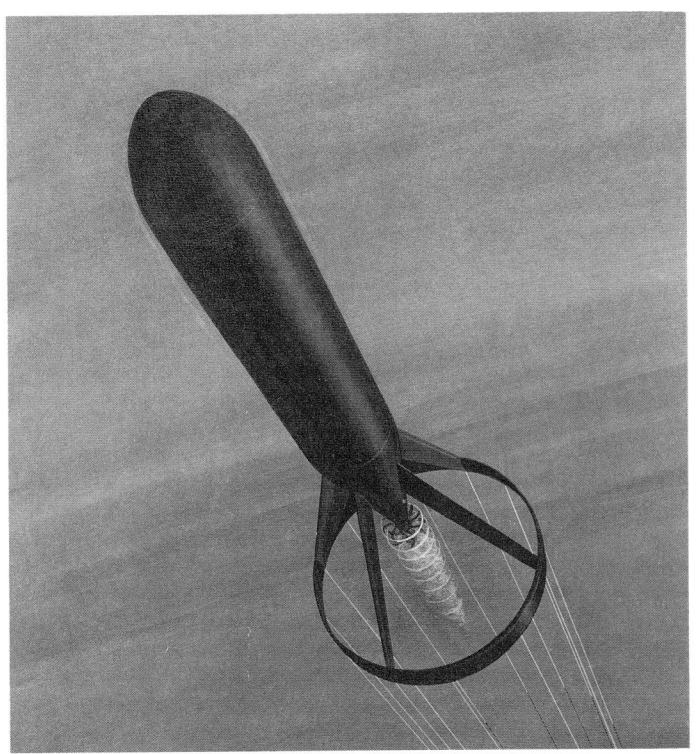

An unmanned underwater vehicle design developed by the Navy's David Taylor Research Center to deploy a towed acoustic array. (U.S. Navy)

A minefield picture would be maintained that could be transmitted back to friendly units via an acoustic datalink or a fiber-optic cable, or it could be retained for physical return of the vehicle to a recovery ship, submarine, or even aircraft. The MCM vehicle could also provide "routine maintenance," periodically transitting a friendly minefield to ensure that an enemy submarine had not penetrated the field to plant mines on the safe routes used by friendly submarines.

And, as noted above, mines could be laid by an AUV. This would be an extension of the existing Mk 67 Submarine-Launched Mobile Mine (SLMM) that can be launched from a standard 21-inch submarine torpedo tube and travel several miles through the water on a preset course before reaching its target and becoming active.

Special warfare: The AUV in this warfare area could perform friendly harbor patrol/defense, beach reconnaissance prior to a clandestine operation, and intelligence collection.

Non-combat operations: These AUV activities are primarily search and recovery of foreign or friendly objects dropped on the ocean floor. These could include satellites and weapons.

A number of unmanned underwater vehicles are already in foreign and U.S. naval use. Since the 1960s the U.S. Navy has used cable-controlled torpedo recovery devices,[13] the Mk 30 submarine target, the Mk 71 MOSS decoy used by ballistic missile submarines, and tethered mine countermeasures vehicles. There have also been classified deep-ocean search and recovery devices used to exploit Soviet objects lost on the ocean floor. (There are also numerous commercial UUV-type vehicles in service, most referred to as ROV for remote operating vehicles. These are used mostly for exploration and support of offshore oilfields. As an indication of the state of the art, some of the commercial vehicles can operate to almost 10,000 feet and have a 350-hour mission duration at 5 or 6 knots.)

The new family of UUVs will expand the "operational envelope" of underwater drones. The Navy and the Defense Advanced Research Projects Agency (DARPA) initiated a joint advanced-technology UUV program in 1986. Through this effort, DARPA has developed two prototypes for test bed/mission hardware demonstrations. One vehicle took the first mission "package"—a tactical acoustic decoy system developed by Martin Marietta—to sea in 1990 and has since been transferred to the Navy for testing. According to a Navy spokesperson, the initial payoff for this UUV would be increased submarine survivability, but it would pave the way for UUV applications to a number of classified submarine scenarios.[14] The second DARPA vehicle, also completed in 1990, has a Lockheed-developed mine search system package. A third mission package for ocean surveillance is also being developed under DARPA contract.

Several Navy laboratories are also working in the UUV field. While most will not discuss their efforts, a notional vehicle for long-duration ocean surveillance is being designed by the David Taylor Research Center (DTRC) in Carderock, Md. This vehicle would be much larger than the torpedo-like DARPA devices—68 feet (20.7 m) long with a tail ring some ten feet in diameter that would stream a multi-line passive acoustic array. Under the DRTC concept, the AUV would operate in the deep ocean powered by a hydrogen liquid-fuel-cell power plant that could provide a mission duration of several weeks. When a contact is made and evaluated as a possible hostile intruder, an expendable communications buoy would be launched, pop up to the surface, and broadcast the data or serve as a datalink.

Obviously, in all of these efforts the key to success will be component or "enabling" technologies: navigation, composite hull materials, guidance, energy source, propulsion, communication links, and signal processing as well the specific mission packages. Advanced autonomous underwater vehicles will require enhanced sensor and decision-making capability; while these are within the scope of near-term technologies, they could be very expensive. (A handful of relatively unsophisticated autonomous vehicles have been used by the U.S. Navy since the early 1960s.)

The operating Navy, however, is cautious about moving toward UUVs. While most vehicles are considered in the context of enhancing submarine operations, that may be the most difficult platform to support a UUV. Limited space, the problem of hull openings, the difficulty of maintenance on vehicles, and other factors make it a problem for submarines to support UUVs. Even if they are sized for torpedo tubes—now 21-inch diameter and 30-inch diameter in the single SEAWOLF SSN—keeping UUVs aboard submarines will displace torpedoes and missiles. A double-hull submarine configuration might more easily accommodate a UUV, but that design concept is anathema to the Navy's nuclear-propulsion leadership. Further, underwater-to-underwater communications will be more difficult than underwater to surface, air, or satellite platforms.

Surface ships, submarines, and even aircraft (fixed-wing and helicopters) could also deploy and recover UUVs. Surface ships would be the most feasible to support UUV operations; however, even a preliminary review of vehicle potential indicates that some UUVs, such as a DTRC-type area surveillance vehicle, would best be supported by surface ships, but for many UUV missions the submarine is the ideal launch/support platform.

---

13. One of these vehicles—a Cable-controlled Underwater Research Vehicle (CURV)—recovered a hydrogen bomb from a depth of 2,800 feet (854 m) off the coast of Palomares, Spain, in 1966.

14. Rear Adm. D. J. Wolkensdorfer, USN, presentation "Joint DARPA/Navy Technology program" at IEEE Conference, Dulles Airport, Va., 5 June 1990.

1 LARGE SCALE VEHICLE: "KOKANEE"

Number	Name	Completed
(none)	KOKANEE	1988

Builders:	Southwest Research Institute, San Antonio, Texas
Weight:	155 tons
Length:	88⅚ feet (27.1 m) overall
Beam:	10⅙ feet (3.1 m)
Draft:	9½ feet (2.9 m)
Propulsion:	1 direct-drive electric motor; 3,000 shp; 1 shaft
Speed:	
Range:	see Engineering notes
Manning:	unmanned

The KOKANEE is a submarine design test vehicle operated in Lake Pend Oreille, Bayview, Idaho, by the David Taylor Research Center's Acoustic research detachment. Known as the Large Scale Vehicle (LSV), the craft has been employed to test variations of submarine propulsors for the submarine SEAWOLF.

The LSV concept was proposed by Dr. M. M. Sevik of DTRC in 1972 as an extension of the Center's model testing program. The construction contract was awarded in February 1984. The completed vehicle was delivered to Bayview in October 1987 and dedicated at ceremonies there on 7 March 1988. She was transported from San Antonio to Bayview by train.

The KOKANEE is the world's largest autonomous, free-swimming submersible.

Cost: Construction cost of the KOKANEE was $65 million.

Design: The KOKANEE has a conventional submarine configuration with a modified sail or fairwater structure (that can be removed); the forward portion of the submarine contains electric storage batteries; the after portion has the DC electric motor and auxiliary machinery as well as data recorders, guidance, and navigation equipment.

The operational depth of the craft is not known; the lake has a maximum depth of 1,150 feet (350 m).

Engineering: The craft is controlled by on-board computers that are programmed before each test run. Lead-acid batteries are employed. Endurance is approximately six hours for medium-power runs and two or three hours for full-power runs.

Names: The KOKANEE is a salmon found in Lake Pend Oreille.

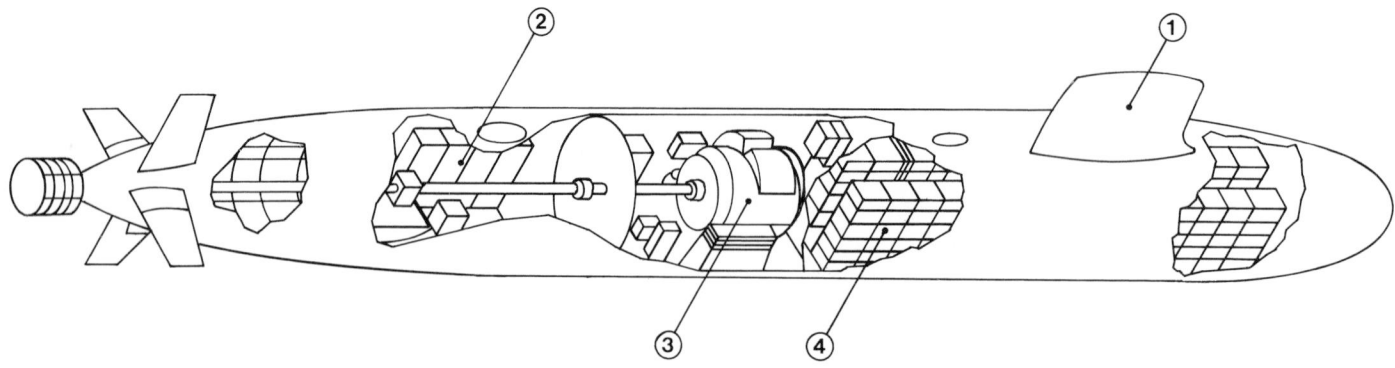

1. removable fairwater   2. data recorders and navigation equipment   3. DC electric motor   4. batteries (William Clipson)

The KOKANEE immediately after surfacing in Lake Pend Oreille, Bayview, Idaho. Note the SSN-like appearance, with a "fillet" at the forward base of the sail structure, to help "blend" the sail into the hull. (U.S. Navy)

CHAPTER 13

Aircraft Carriers

The carrier DWIGHT D. EISENHOWER transits the Suez Canal under the escort of an SH-3H Sea King from Helicopter ASW Squadron (HS) 5. The "Ike" and the carrier INDEPENDENCE brought the first U.S. combat-ready forces into the Persian Gulf area after Iraq's invasion of Kuwait in August 1990, again demonstrating the responsiveness of aircraft carriers. (1990, U.S. Navy, PH3 Frank A. Marquart)

The U.S. carrier force in late 1992 consists of 12 operational carriers—6 nuclear-propelled ships (CVN) and 6 conventional, oil-burning ships (CV). Not included in these numbers are those ships undergoing long-term modernizations (the CONSTELLATION and ENTERPRISE) and a carrier employed as a pilot-training ship (FORRESTAL).

Some proposals from Congress and the Department of Defense have projected as few as eight or ten operational or "deployable" carriers before the year 2000.[1] The term "deployable" has meant an operational carrier at sea or able to go to sea to meet scheduled commitments or an emergency situation, including those ships in a shipyard that could get under way within several weeks. Carriers in normal overhaul were considered deployable but not those carriers undergoing SLEP or RCOH modernizations.[2] In 1991 the Navy ceased using the term "deployable."

Budgetary constraints may force a further decline in carrier force levels, possibly to only ten operational ships according to some budget projections. In late 1992 two additional nuclear-propelled carriers of the NIMITZ class were under construction, and Department of Defense budget planning provides for another NIMITZ-class carrier (No. 9) to be authorized in fiscal 1995 with a 2003 completion. Thus, there is significant flexibility with respect to the potential carrier numbers during the next decade.

When the last NIMITZ-class carrier now authorized (No. 8) is completed in 1998, it will be 25 years after the completion of the lead ship, a remarkable and probably unique life span for a warship design, the preliminary design of the NIMITZ having begun in 1964. (Many minor changes have been made to the design in the 25-year period; see below.) The NIMITZ class also represents the largest number of carriers of any type of any nation built to the same basic design since World War II.

Under the Reagan administration (1981–1988) the force-level goal for carriers was increased to 15 active ships from the 12 ships of the Carter period (1977–1980). Further, President Reagan's Secretary of the Navy, John Lehman, gained congressional approval for two carriers each in fiscal years 1983 and 1988; not since World War II had two or more carriers been authorized in the same fiscal year. Then, in a surprise announcement in January 1987, shortly after Mr. Lehman's departure from the administration but based on his efforts, Secretary of Defense Caspar Weinberger put forward a naval shipbuilding plan that included long-lead components for two additional NIMITZ-class carriers (No. 9 and No. 10), which would be requested in the fiscal 1990 and 1993 shipbuilding programs to maintain a force of at least 15 carriers. However, political and budgetary realities of the next few years have led to a revised plan that provides for only one carrier (CVN 76) with long-lead component funding in fiscal 1993 and full funding in fiscal 1995.

Accordingly, under current planning the carrier force in the year 2000 could consist of eight NIMITZ-class nuclear carriers, the nuclear ENTERPRISE, and the conventional KITTY HAWK, CONSTELLATION, and KENNEDY; but with one CVN undergoing long-term refueling/overhaul, there probably would be only 11 deployable ships.

In addition to these operational carriers, the Navy maintains a pilot-training ship, the FORRESTAL. The FORRESTAL replaced the venerable LEXINGTON, an ESSEX/HANCOCK-class carrier completed in 1943, that served in that role from 1963 to 1990; she, in turn succeeded the ANTIETAM, the first large dedicated training carrier, which served in that role from 1957 to 1962.[3] The FORRESTAL, based at Pensacola, Fla., operates in the Gulf of Mexico. She has only limited aircraft support capabilities or other features that would permit her to operate in a combat role without extensive preparation (requiring about one year).

All World War II–built carriers of the MIDWAY and ESSEX/HANCOCK classes have been discarded, except for the MIDWAY, decommissioned in 1991, which is mothballed. (The full ESSEX/HANCOCK class list is found at the end of this chapter.)

In 1981 the Reagan administration sought to reactivate the ORISKANY or BON HOMME RICHARD (decommissioned in 1971) to increase the deployable carrier force. The preliminary cost estimate for reactivating one of these ships was $503 million (fiscal 1982 dollars). After extensive consideration the Congress refused to fund the ships because of their poor material condition, their limited remaining service life, and the problems in obtaining suitable aircraft for them.

There have been several efforts since 1970 to initiate the construction of smaller aircraft carriers—the Sea Control Ship (SCS), VSTOL Support Ship (VSS), and mid-size carrier (CVV), the last designed to operate conventional fixed-wing aircraft. Such programs have been staunchly opposed by proponents of large nuclear carriers within the Navy and Congress, although such ships could supplement and not necessarily replace the larger ships.[4] In the early 1990s smaller VSTOL carriers of about 30,000 tons and mid-size carriers of about 60,000 tons were being studied by the Navy-sponsored Center for Naval Analyses and the Naval Studies Board of the National Academy of Sciences for construction beyond the planned CVN 76.

The U.S. Navy also has 13 helicopter carriers (LPH/LHA/LHD) in service. These are employed as amphibious assault ships and are listed in chapter 19 of this edition. They could be employed on a limited basis in the sea-control role, i.e., operating helicopters for anti-submarine and other combat roles and AV-8B Harrier VSTOL aircraft in low- to medium-threat environments. A detachment of four to six Harriers is often deployed on board these "amphibs" for forward deployments.

Aircraft: Carrier air wing compositions are described in chapter 28.

Air wings: Air wings vary in types of aircraft and personnel strength; nominal wing strengths are provided in this chapter based on a composition of two fighter squadrons (VF), two strike fighter squadrons (VFA), and single squadrons of medium attack (VA), electronic countermeasure (VAQ), early warning (VAW), fixed-wing ASW (VS), and helicopter ASW (HS) aircraft.

Builders: Newport News Shipbuilding in Newport News, Va., is the only U.S. shipyard now constructing aircraft carriers. The Litton/Ingalls Shipyard in Pascagoula, Miss., constructs carrier-type amphibious ships of some 50,000 tons (see chapter 19).

Design: Displacements of carriers have been continuously increased because of new equipment added during overhauls and modernization. The data below have been updated for this edition.

Electronics: The SLQ-29 is being replaced by the SLQ-32(V)4 in active carriers.

Names: The first carrier was named LANGLEY (CV 1) for aviation pioneer Samuel P. Langley, after which aircraft carriers were traditionally named for older American warships and battles.[5] In 1945 the CVB 42 was named for President Franklin D. Roosevelt, who died in office; later on, the CVA 59 was named for the first Secretary of Defense, James V. Forrestal, who committed suicide soon after leaving office, and the CVA 67 was named for John F. Kennedy, assassinated while in office.

Subsequently, the Navy named the CVN 68 for Fleet Admiral Chester W. Nimitz, who died in 1966, and the naming of carriers became a more political issue.[6] White House intervention led to carriers being named for former President Dwight D. Eisenhower (CVN 69), Representative Carl Vinson (CVN 70), and Senator John C. Stennis (CVN 74).

---

1. The lower number was reportedly contained in a proposal from David Chu, Assistant Secretary of Defense for Program Analysis; cited in "Pentagon tells Navy to plan on eight carriers," *Navy News* (18 March 1991), p. 1.
2. SLEP = Service Life Extension Program; RCOH = Refueling/Complex Overhaul.
3. The ANTIETAM served as a pilot-training ship with the designation CVS (ASW carrier). The LEXINGTON was changed from CVS to CVT (training) on 1 January 1969; subsequently, on 27 June 1978, she was changed to AVT to avoid confusion with operational carrier listings.

4. Spain has built a carrier to the sea control ship configuration; see page 000.
5. The most notable exception to the traditional naming scheme was the SHANGRI-LA (CV 38). When journalists asked where the Doolittle bombers that struck Tokyo and other Japanese cities in April 1942 had flown from, President Franklin D. Roosevelt replied "Shangri-La," referring to the mythical Asian kingdom in James Hilton's novel *Lost Horizon*. The Doolittle bombers had actually flown from the carrier HORNET (CV 8).
6. The Navy's three other Fleet Admirals—William D. Leahy, Ernest J. King, and William F. Halsey—were remembered by guided missile frigates (DLG).

The CVN 71–73 have names previously assigned to ballistic missile submarines (SSBN). The CVN 72 and CVN 73 were named prior to their start, in part to preempt potential congressional pressure to name one of those ships for Admiral H. G. Rickover (the SSN 709 was named for the admiral instead).

The UNITED STATES is named for an early sailing frigate (see below).

Operational: From the late 1940s into the late 1980s the Navy attempted to operate two carriers forward-deployed to the Mediterranean and three and, subsequently, two to the Western Pacific–Indian Ocean region. With the remaining carriers in transit to or from deployment areas, engaged in fleet exercises or other types of training, or in overhaul, there was a 1:3 deployment cycle, which meant a ship was forward-deployed for about six months at a time. Higher deployment rates, as during the Vietnam War and various crises, invariably resulted in lower retention rates, a critical factor in an all-volunteer, high-technology service. Also, the 1:3 cycle did not take into account carriers undergoing the long-term SLEP modernization.

The crises and conflicts of the early 1980s, especially the Soviet invasion of Afghanistan (1979) and the Iran–Iraq War (1980–1988), led to more flexible carrier deployment patterns—called FlexOps. Carriers were withdrawn from some areas and spent more time at sea to provide for multi-carrier exercises or to support special operations, as in the continuing crisis in Lebanon, the invasion of Grenada in October 1983, operations against Libya in 1986, and Operations Desert Shield/Desert Storm (1990–1991). Carrier deployments have thus significantly exceeded the nominal ratio of six months' deployment to 12 months in transit/overhaul/in port/local operations.

The situation has become more exacerbated in the 1990s because of the general concern for the Indian Ocean area in the wake of the Gulf War. That situation is caused not only by the continuing Iraqi situation, but by the buildup of naval and military forces by India. The distances from U.S. ports to the Indian Ocean require on the order of five carriers to maintain one ship on a six-month deployment.

Asterisks in the ship entry lists indicate carriers that participated in Operations Desert Shield/Desert Storm, 1990–1991. The EISENHOWER and INDEPENDENCE arrived in the Gulf area from the Mediterranean and western Indian Ocean, respectively, a few days after Iraq's invasion of Kuwait on 2 August 1990. They provided air cover for the U.S. military buildup in Saudi Arabia, but returned to the United States prior to the outbreak of hostilities. Planes from the carriers AMERICA, KENNEDY, MIDWAY, RANGER, ROOSEVELT, and SARATOGA flew strikes, air cover, reconnaissance, and support missions in the conflict.

TABLE 13-1. CARRIER FORCE LEVELS [late 1992]

Number	Class/Ship	Comm.	Active	Building	Yard	Reserve	Notes
CVN 68	NIMITZ	1975–	6	2	—	—	nuclear-propelled
CV 63	KITTY HAWK	1961–1968	3	—	1	—	1 ship in yard undergoing SLEP modernization
CVN 65	ENTERPRISE	1961	—	—	1	—	nuclear-propelled; in yard undergoing nuclear refueling/overhaul
CV 59	FORRESTAL	1957–1959	3	—	—	—	
AVT 59	FORRESTAL	1956	1	—	—	—	non-deployable pilot-training ship
CV 41	MIDWAY	1945	—	—	—	1	in reserve

6 + 3 MULTI-PURPOSE AIRCRAFT CARRIERS: "NIMITZ" CLASS

Number	Name	FY	Builder	Laid down	Launched	Commissioned	Status
CVN 68	NIMITZ	67	Newport News Shipbuilding	22 June 1968	13 May 1972	3 May 1975	**PA**
CVN 69	DWIGHT D. EISENHOWER*	70	Newport News Shipbuilding	15 Aug 1970	11 Oct 1975	18 Oct 1977	**AA**
CVN 70	CARL VINSON	74	Newport News Shipbuilding	11 Oct 1975	15 Mar 1980	13 Mar 1982	**PA**
CVN 71	THEODORE ROOSEVELT*	80	Newport News Shipbuilding	31 Oct 1981	27 Oct 1984	25 Oct 1986	**AA**
CVN 72	ABRAHAM LINCOLN	83	Newport News Shipbuilding	3 Nov 1984	13 Feb 1988	11 Nov 1989	**PA**
CVN 73	GEORGE WASHINGTON	83	Newport News Shipbuilding	25 Aug 1986	21 July 1990	4 July 1992	**AA**
CVN 74	JOHN STENNIS	88	Newport News Shipbuilding	13 Mar 1991	1994	1996	Building
CVN 75	UNITED STATES	88	Newport News Shipbuilding	1993	1996	1998	Building
CVN 76	. . . . . .	95	Newport News Shipbuilding			2003	Planned

Displacement: CVN 68–70 74,042 tons light
CVN 71–73 77,606 tons light
CVN 74, 75 78,127 tons light
CVN 68–70 95,413 tons full load
CVN 71–73 97,574 tons full load
CVN 74, 75 99,050 tons full load

Length: 1,040 feet (317.2 m) waterline
1,092 feet (332.9 m) overall

Beam: 134 feet (40.85 m)

Flight deck: 250⅝ feet (76.5 m)

Draft: CVN 68–70 37 feet (11.3 m)
CVN 71–73 38⅚₁₂ feet (11.7 m)

Propulsion: 4 steam turbines (General Electric); 280,000 shp; 4 shafts

Reactors: 2 pressurized-water A4W (Westinghouse)

Speed: 30+ knots

Manning:

	Total	Officers	Enlisted
CVN 68	2,903	171	2,732
CVN 69	2,970	158	2,812
CVN 70	2,973	168	2,805
CVN 71	3,162	173	2,989
CVN 72	2,892	154	2,738
CVN 73			
Marines:	66	2	64
Air wing: approx.	2,020	287	1,733

Aircraft: approx. 80

Catapults: 4 steam Mk 13-1 in CVN 68–71
4 steam Mk 13-2 in CVN 72 and later ships

Elevators: 4 deck edge—85 × 52 feet (25.9 × 15.85 m); 130,000-lb (58,500-kg) capacity

Missiles: 3 8-tube NATO Sea Sparrow launchers Mk 29

Guns: 3 20-mm Phalanx CIWS Mk 16 (3 multi-barrel) in CVN 68, 69; 4 guns in later ships

Radars: SPS-10F surface search in CVN 68–70
SPS-48C 3-D air search in CVN 68–73; SPS-48E 3-D air search in CVN 74–76
SPS-49 air search
SPS-64(V) navigation in CVN 71–73
SPS-67(V) surface search in CVN 71–73
TAS Mk 23 threat detection in CVN 72, 73

Sonars: none

Fire control: 3 Mk 91 missile FCS

EW systems: SLQ-29 (SLQ-17 + WLR-8) in CVN 68–71
SLQ-32(V)4 in CVN 72 and later ships
WLR-1H in CVN 72 and later ships

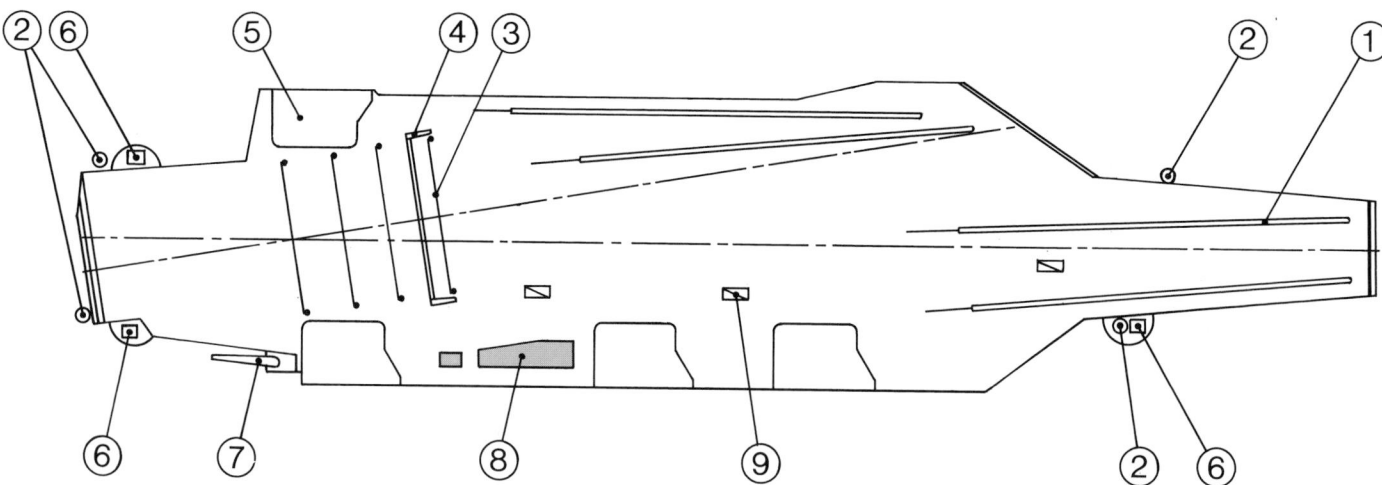

GEORGE WASHINGTON   1. catapults (4)   2. Phalanx CIWS   3. arresting pendants (4)   4. barricade   5. elevators (4)   6. NATO Sea Sparrow launcher
7. crane   8. island structure   9. bomb elevators (3) (William Clipson)

These are the largest warships ever built. Six ships are in commission with two more under construction and another unit planned. The Navy has proposed continued construction of this class to maintain a force of 12 or more aircraft carriers.

Details vary, as improvements have been made with succeeding ships (see Design notes).

Class: A program to construct the first three CVNs of this class was approved by Secretary of Defense Robert S. McNamara during the Vietnam War as replacements for the three MIDWAY-class carriers to provide a force of 12 large carriers (i.e., CV 59–64, 66, 67, and CVN 65, 68–70).

The first three ships were delayed during construction by labor strikes and scheduling problems at the Newport News yard. The NIMITZ was seven years from keel laying to commissioning compared to less than four years for the more complex (eight-reactor) ENTERPRISE.

The CVN 71 was forced on the Carter administration by Congress in 1980; the CVN 72 and CVN 73 were approved through the efforts of Secretary of the Navy John Lehman early in the Reagan administration. The CVN 74 was originally included in the last year of the five-year (FY 1984–1988) shipbuilding program put forward by the Reagan administration in January 1983. That ship, however, was included for "planning" purposes only and appeared to be a backup in the event that Congress declined to authorize one of the two NIMITZ-class ships in the fiscal 1983 program. In mid-1986 several members of Congress urged the construction of CVN 74, but budget limitations and the overall budget deficit prevented serious consideration of the ship. In December 1986 it was learned that the Reagan administration would request two additional CVNs, with Lehman becoming the principal advocate; in January 1987 the fiscal 1988 defense budget proposed the construction of the CVN 74 and CVN 75.

Classification: The NIMITZ and EISENHOWER were ordered as attack aircraft carriers (CVAN); they were changed to multi-mission aircraft carriers (CVN) on 30 June 1975. The VINSON and later ships were ordered as CVNs.

Cost: The ROOSEVELT was completed 17 months ahead of schedule at a reported savings of $80 million.

By simultaneously awarding a contract for the CVN 72 and CVN 73, construction costs were reduced by a total of $750 million for both ships. Total cost of the two ships was estimated at $3.323 *billion* for the CVN 72 and $3.643 *billion* for the CVN 73 at the time of contract award (27 December 1982). In addition, there will be outfitting and other post-delivery costs.

The Department of Defense acquisition report on series production of the NIMITZ class in late 1991 listed the costs in current-year dollars as:

CVN 72 and CVN 73	$6.170 *billion*
CVN 74 and CVN 75	$6.514 *billion*
CVN 76	$4.297 *billion*

The fiscal 1993 budget request provides $832.2 million for long-lead components for the CVN 76.

Design: SCB No. 102. The general arrangement of these ships is similar to the previous KITTY HAWK class with respect to flight deck, hangar, elevators, and island structure (e.g., the island structure is aft of the No. 1 and No. 2 elevators, with the No. 4 elevator on the port side aft of the angled deck and opposite the No. 3 elevator on the starboard side). The angled deck is canted to port at 9°3′ and is 796⅔ feet (242.9 m) long.

The hangar deck is 684 feet (208.5 m) long, 108 feet (32.9 m) wide, and 26½ feet (8.1 m) high.

This class has been in production longer than any other carrier design in history. The uncertainty of future CVN construction and the general excellence of the NIMITZ design precluded major changes in the later ships. The CVN 71 and later ships incorporate improved magazine protection; the CVN 73 and later ships have improved topside ballistic protection; and the CVN 74 and later units were constructed with HSLA-100 steel. There have also been incremental improvements in the ships' electrical and electronics systems.

Payload includes up to 2,970 tons of aviation ordnance and up to 3.5 million gallons (13.2 million liters) of jet fuel (JP-5).

Electronics: Several carrier-landing radars are provided—SPN-41, SPN-43A, and SPN-44; the CVN 68–71 have the SPN-42 Automatic Carrier Landing System (ACLS), and the CVN 72 and later ships have the SPN-46 ACLS. The CVN 68–73 will receive SPS-48E during major overhauls.

Proposals to provide these ships with the SPY-1 radar have been turned down on the basis of cost.

Engineering: These carriers have only two reactors compared to eight in the first nuclear carrier, the ENTERPRISE. The fuel cores in the early ships were estimated to have a service life of at least 13 years (800,000 to 1,000,000 n.miles/1,481,000 to 1,850,350 km); however, the later cores have been pushed out to 23 years. This means that the later ships would be refueled only once during a service life of 45 to 50 years.

Missiles: The CVN 68 and CVN 69 were built with the Sea Sparrow Mk 25 missile launchers (with Mk 115 fire control system); they were rearmed with the NATO Sea Sparrow system.

Names: The CVN 75 is named for one of the six sailing frigates authorized by the Congress in 1794 and the first to be launched; the other ships in that series included the frigates CONSTITUTION and CONSTELLATION. The second UNITED STATES was a battle cruiser (CC 6), laid down in 1920 but cancelled; sister ships were completed as the carriers LEXINGTON (CV 2) and SARATOGA (CV 3). The next UNITED STATES was the first "super carrier" (CVA 58), laid down in 1949 and promptly cancelled, leading to the well-publicized carrier-versus-bomber controversy.

Operational: The VINSON shifted to the Pacific Fleet in 1983, the NIMITZ in 1987, and the LINCOLN in 1990.

The ABRAHAM LINCOLN is one of the latest U.S. aircraft carriers to go to sea. The LINCOLN and five other large carriers participated in the Persian Gulf conflict, but their responsiveness and performance was not sufficient to stem the decline in U.S. carrier forces—possibly to only eight operational carriers by the end of this decade. (1990, PHAN Sean Linehan, USN)

The THEODORE ROOSEVELT—which also participated in the Gulf War—was forced on the Carter administration by a Congress concerned with growing Soviet military power and declining U.S. strengths. Note the sponsons along the starboard side, the foremost supporting a Phalanx CIWS and NATO Sea Sparrow missile launcher. (1990, Giorgio Arra)

The NIMITZ with a fraction of her air wing on deck. The NIMITZ, the first U.S. aircraft carrier to be named for an admiral, is lead ship for the largest class of aircraft carriers constructed in the post–World War II era. (1991, Giorgio Arra)

Atop the island of the LINCOLN are the SPS-48C and SPS-67 radar antennas, with the bar antenna for the SPS-64(V) offset to starboard (almost adjacent to the SPS-64); the large antenna for the SPS-49 is mounted on the tower aft of the island. The SPN-series antennas are aft of the mast. (1990, Giorgio Arra)

3 + 1 MULTI-PURPOSE AIRCRAFT CARRIERS | "KITTY HAWK" CLASS / "JOHN F. KENNEDY"

Number	Name	FY	Builder	Laid down	Launched	Commissioned	Status
CV 63	KITTY HAWK	56	New York Shipbuilding, Camden, N.J.	27 Dec 1956	21 May 1960	29 Apr 1961	**PA**
CV 64	CONSTELLATION	57	New York Naval Shipyard, Brooklyn, N.Y.	14 Sep 1957	8 Oct 1960	27 Oct 1961	Yard
CV 66	AMERICA*	61	Newport News Shipbuilding	9 Jan 1961	1 Feb 1964	23 Jan 1965	**AA**
CV 67	JOHN F. KENNEDY*	63	Newport News Shipbuilding	22 Oct 1964	27 May 1967	7 Sep 1968	**AA**

Displacement:

	Light	Full load
CV 63, 64	61,057 tons	81,985 tons
CV 66	61,174 tons	85,490 tons
CV 67	59,629 tons	81,430 tons

Length: 990 feet (301.9 m) waterline
CV 63, 64 1,045 ⅔ feet (318.8 m) overall
CV 66 1,047½ feet (319.25 m) overall
CV 67 1,052 feet (320.3 m) overall

Beams: 129¹¹⁄₁₂ feet (39.6 m) except CV 67 128½ feet (39.2 m)
Flight deck: 265½ feet (80.9 m) except CV 67 267½ feet (81.5 m)
Draft: 37 feet (11.3 m) except CV 67 36½ feet (11.1 m)
Propulsion: 4 steam turbines (General Electric); 280,000 shp; 4 shafts
Boilers: 8 1,200 psi (83.4 kg/cm²) (Foster Wheeler)
Speed: 30+ knots
Range: 12,000 n.miles (22,225 km) at 20 knots

Manning:

	Total	Officers	Enlisted
CV 63	2,726	140	2,586
CV 66	2,846	141	2,705
CV 67	3,007	153	2,854

Marines: 64 — 2 — 62
Air wing: approx. 2,020 — 287 — 1,733
Aircraft: approx. 80

Catapults: 4 steam C13 in CV 63, 64
3 steam C13 + 1 steam C13-1 in CV 66, 67
Elevators: 4 deck edge—85 × 52 feet (25.9 × 15.9 m) 130,000-lb (58,500-kg) capacity
Missiles: 2 8-tube NATO Sea Sparrow launchers Mk 29 in CV 64; 3 launchers in other ships
Guns: 4 20-mm Phalanx CIWS Mk 16 (3 multi-barrel) in CV 64; 3 guns in other ships
Radars: SPS-10F surface search
SPS-48C 3-D air search in CV 66, 67; SPS-48E 3-D air search in CV 63, 64
SPS-49 air search
Sonars: (removed from CV 66)
Fire control: 3 Mk 91 missile FCS
EW systems: SLQ-29 (SLQ-17 + WLR-8)
WLR-1H
WLR-11

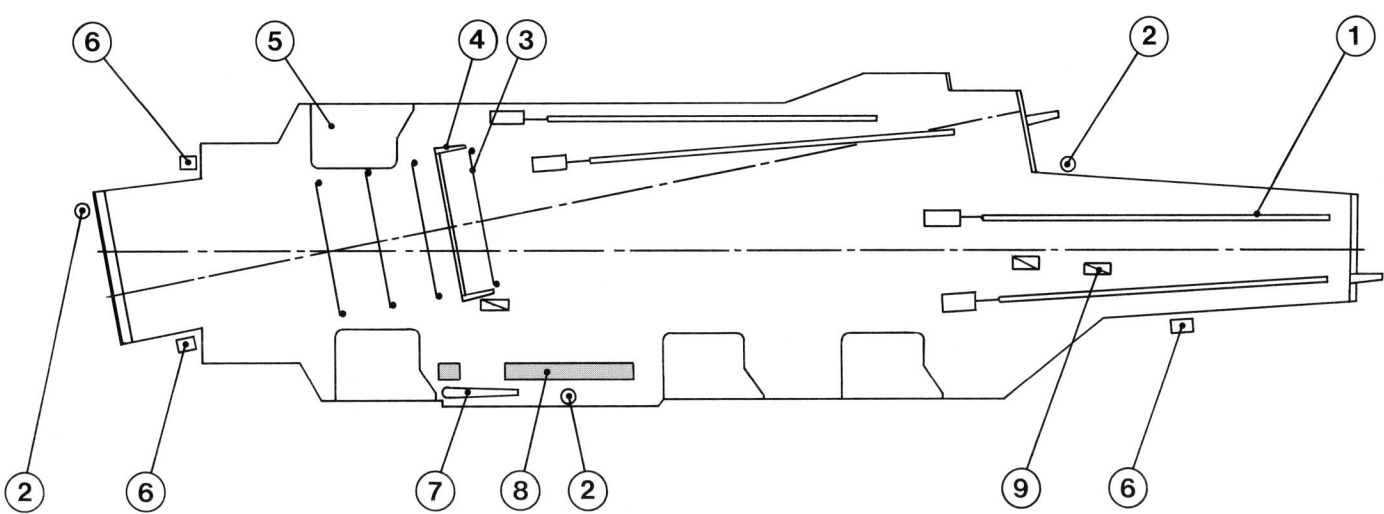

AMERICA 1. catapults (4) 2. Phalanx CIWS 3. arresting pendants (4) 4. barricade 5. elevators (4) 6. NATO Sea Sparrow launcher 7. crane
8. island structure 9. bomb elevators (3) (William Clipson)

These ships have a modified FORRESTAL configuration with improved elevator and flight deck arrangements. The KITTY HAWK was delayed because of shipyard problems; the CONSTELLATION was delayed because of a fire on board while under construction; and the KENNEDY was delayed because of lengthy debates over whether the ship should have nuclear or conventional propulsion. (All subsequent U.S. large carriers have been nuclear-propelled.)

The KITTY HAWK and CONSTELLATION have been modernized under the SLEP upgrade (see below). The AMERICA will not be upgraded and is scheduled to be decommissioned in fiscal 1996; when this edition went to press there were no plans to decommission the KITTY HAWK, CONSTELLATION, or KENNEDY before the year 2000.

The Secretary of Defense in early 1991 cancelled the planned SLEP for the KENNEDY; nevertheless, the Congress placed language in the fiscal 1991 supplemental appropriation to force the SLEP to be undertaken at the Philadelphia Naval Shipyard.[7] But Congress voted only $405 million for the KENNEDY's overhaul, about one-half the estimated cost of a SLEP. Instead, when this edition went to press, the Navy planned only a COH modernization, starting in 1993 and to take some 14 months (vice about three years for a SLEP).

Builders: This is the last class of U.S. aircraft carriers to be built by shipyards other than Newport News.

Class: The KENNEDY is officially a separate, one-ship class. All four ships are often grouped with the FORRESTAL class in force-level discussions.

7. The Philadelphia yard has been scheduled for closure in the mid-1990s. The KENNEDY modernization will probably delay the closing by several months.

Classification: All four ships were originally attack aircraft carriers (CVA). Two ships were changed to multi-mission carriers (CV) when modified to operate ASW aircraft: the KITTY HAWK on 29 April 1973 and the KENNEDY on 1 December 1974. The CONSTELLATION and AMERICA were changed to CV on 30 June 1975, prior to being modified.

Design: SCB No. 127, 127A, 127B, and 127C, respectively. These ships are larger than the FORRESTAL class and have an improved flight deck arrangement, with two elevators forward of the island structure and the port-side elevator on the stern quarter rather than at the forward end of the angled flight deck.

The hangar deck in the first three ships is 740 feet (225.6 m) long, 101 feet (30.8 m) wide, and 25 feet (7.6 m) high; in the KENNEDY the hangar deck is 688 feet (209.75 m) long, 106 feet (32.3 m) wide, and 25 feet (7.6 m) high. The angled deck is canted to port at 11°20′, except the KENNEDY is canted at 11°; the KITTY HAWK's and CONSTELLATION's angled decks are 722$\frac{7}{12}$ feet (220.3 m) long, the AMERICA's is 741 feet (225.9 m) long, and that of the KENNEDY 754 feet (229.9 m) long. The KENNEDY has her stack angled out to starboard to help carry exhaust gases away from the approach path to the flight deck.

Electronics: Several carrier-landing radars are provided in these ships—SPN-35, SPN-41, SPN-42, and SPN-43A. The SPN-46 ACLS is fitted. The KENNEDY is scheduled to receive the SPS-48E radar during her next major overhaul.

The AMERICA and KENNEDY have bow sonar domes, but only the AMERICA has sonar installed. She was the only postwar U.S. carrier so fitted at the time; the set, an SQS-23, was removed in late 1981.

The AMERICA at sea with an SH-3H Sea King landing aboard. On the starboard quarter is the boat and aircraft crane found in all U.S. aircraft carriers; the hangar deck openings for the three starboard deck-edge elevators are visible. (1990, Giorgio Arra)

The JOHN F. KENNEDY, the U.S. Navy's last oil-burning carrier, in the Hudson River, New York. The ship's stem anchor indicates the bow sonar dome, originally intended for SQS-23 sonar. A Phalanx CIWS is visible ahead of the forward edge of the angled flight deck. (1990, Giorgio Arra)

Missiles: The first three ships were built with Terrier missile launchers (Mk 10 Mod 3 on starboard quarters and Mk 10 Mod 4 on port quarter) and SPQ-55B missile control "searchlight" radars. The KENNEDY originally had three Sea Sparrow Mk 25 launchers and Mk 115 FCS.

Modernization: The KITTY HAWK was modernized under the Service Life Extension Program (SLEP) at the Philadelphia Naval Shipyard; the CONSTELLATION is currently undergoing SLEP at the yard. The KENNEDY is scheduled to follow for a limited modernization; the AMERICA will not undergo SLEP because of the reduction of carrier force-level goals.

	Arrival at yard	Conversion started	Conversion completed
CV 63	Apr 1987	Jan 1988	July 1991
CV 64	Apr 1990	July 1990	early 1993

The upgrades add an estimated 15 years to the ships' nominal 30-year service life.

See FORRESTAL class for SLEP details.

The radar arrangement on these ships (as seen here on the JOHN F. KENNEDY) differs from the NIMITZ class, with the SPS-49 antenna atop the bridge (beneath the SPS-10 and SPS-67 antennas) and the SPS-48C antenna on the tower abaft the island structure. (1989, Giorgio Arra)

(1) NUCLEAR-PROPELLED MULTI-PURPOSE AIRCRAFT CARRIER: "ENTERPRISE"

Number	Name	FY	Builder	Laid down	Launched	Commissioned	Status
CVN 65	ENTERPRISE	58	Newport News Shipbuilding	4 Feb 1958	24 Sep 1960	25 Nov 1961	Yard

Displacement: 74,000 tons light
92,377 tons full load
Length: 1,040 feet (317.2 m) waterline
1,101½ feet (335.8 m) overall
Beam: 133 feet (40.5 m)
Flight deck: 248⅓ feet (75.7 m)
Draft: 39 feet (11.9 m)
Propulsion: 4 steam turbines (Westinghouse); approx. 280,000 shp; 4 shafts
Reactors: 8 pressurized-water A2W (Westinghouse)
Speed: 30+ knots
Manning: 2,643 (162 officers + 2,481 enlisted) in full commission
Marines: 64 (2 officers + 62 enlisted)
Air wing: approx. 2,020 (287 officers + 1,733 enlisted)
Aircraft: approx. 80

Catapults: 4 steam C13
Elevators: 4 deck edge—85 × 52 feet (25.9 × 15.9 m); 130,000-lb (58,500-kg) capacity
Missiles: 2 8-tube NATO Sea Sparrow launchers Mk 29
Guns: 3 20-mm Phalanx CIWS Mk 16 (3 multi-barrel)
Radar: SPS-10F surface search
SPS-48C 3-D air search
SPS-49 air search
SPS-65 threat warning
Sonars: none
Fire control: 2 Mk 91 missile FCS
EW systems: SLQ-29 (SLQ-17 + WLR-8)
WLR-1
WLR-11

The ENTERPRISE was the world's second nuclear-propelled surface warship and at the time of her construction was the world's largest and most expensive warship. Estimated construction cost was $444 million (contemporary conventional carrier construction cost in same-year dollars was estimated at $265 million).

The ship operated in the Pacific from 1965 until early 1990. She arrived at Norfolk, Va., on 16 March 1990 in preparation for a three-year Refueling/Complex Overhaul (RCOH) at Newport News Shipbuilding (see Modernization).

Class: Congress provided $35 million in the fiscal 1960 budget for long-lead-time nuclear components for a second aircraft carrier of this type. The Eisenhower administration (1953–1961), however, deferred the project. The next nuclear carrier, the NIMITZ, was not ordered until almost ten years after the ENTERPRISE, with two oil-burning carriers having been constructed in the interim period.

Classification: Originally classified as an attack aircraft carrier (CVAN), the ENTERPRISE was changed to a multi-mission carrier (CVN) on 30 June 1975.

Design: SCB design No. 160. The ENTERPRISE was built to a modified KITTY HAWK design, but in her original configuration she had a distinctive island structure because of the arrangement of "billboard" radar antennas (see Radar notes).

Her hangar deck is 860 feet (262.2 m) long, 107 feet (32.6 m) wide, and 25 feet (7.6 m) high. The angled deck is canted to port at 10°8′44″; the angled deck is 755⅚ feet (230.4 m) long.

Electronics: The ENTERPRISE and cruiser LONG BEACH were the only ships fitted with the Hughes SPS-32 and SPS-33 fixed-array radars. They were difficult to maintain and were replaced during the 1979–1981 modernization with conventional SPS-48 and SPS-49 radars.

Engineering: At the time of her construction the ENTERPRISE was estimated to have a cruising range of more than 200,000 n.miles (370,400 km) without refueling. On her initial fuel cores the ship travelled 207,000 n.miles (383,365 km).

The two-reactor A1W prototype of the ENTERPRISE propulsion plant was constructed at Arco, Idaho.

Missiles: As built, the ENTERPRISE had neither defensive missiles nor guns, the planned Terrier system having been deleted from the design because of cost. Late in 1967 she was fitted with two Sea Sparrow Mk 25 launchers. During her 1979–1982 overhaul the NATO Sea Sparrow launchers were installed as were the Phalanx CIWS. A planned third Sea Sparrow launcher intended for installation on the starboard quarter was not fitted; it is being installed during her current overhaul.

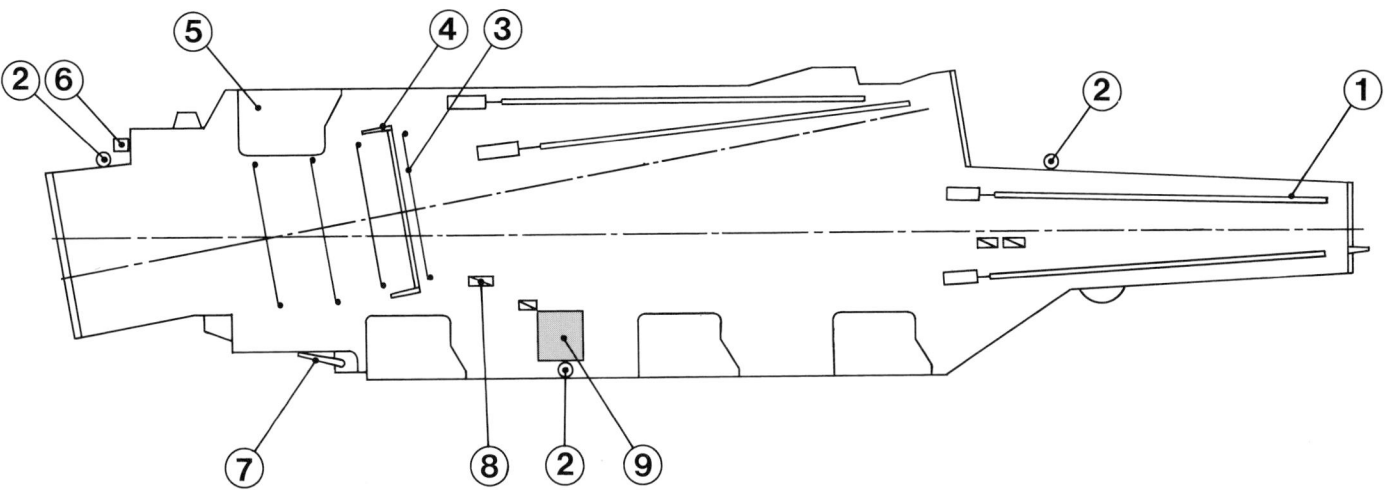

1. catapults (4)   2. Phalanx CIWS   3. arresting pendants (4)   4. barricade   5. elevators (4)   6. NATO Sea Sparrow launcher   7. crane   8. bomb elevators (4)   9. island structure (William Clipson)

The "Big E" prior to entering the Newport News shipyard for her extensive overhaul and refueling. The largest—and most expensive—warship ever built when completed in 1961, the cost of her modernization and refueling has made her extremely controversial 30 years later. (1990, Giorgio Arra)

The stern of the ENTERPRISE with a UH-46 Sea Knight making a Vertical Replenishment (VERTREP) delivery. On her port quarter is a Phalanx CIWS below a NATO Sea Sparrow launcher; on the starboard side her after deck-edge elevator is lowered to the hangar deck level. (1990, Giorgio Arra)

Modernization: The ENTERPRISE underwent a 36-month modernization and overhaul from January 1979 to March 1982 at the Puget Sound Naval Shipyard.

A SLEP-type modernization of some three years is under way at Newport News Shipbuilding, officially referred to as a Refueling/Complex Overhaul (RCOH). Congress authorized $79.5 million in fiscal 1989 and $1.4 *billion* in fiscal 1990 to refuel and upgrade the ship. The actual costs are expected to be approximately $2.5 *billion.* However, the amount of modernization has been reduced because of cost constraints. The refueling is expected to provide cores with a service life of about 20 years, i.e., until about 2115. 2015

The ENTERPRISE modernization and refueling is not called a SLEP for arbitrary reasons at the direction of the Navy's nuclear-propulsion directorate.

The ship completed her last operational cruise on 16 March 1990; she conducted local flight operations through 18 July 1990, followed by a one-day dependents' cruise on 20 July 1990. From 7 to 14 August 1990 she went to sea with a team of engineers to observe the operation of her nuclear plant; the plant was shut down at the Norfolk Naval Base on 15 August 1990 and she was towed to the Newport News yard on 12 October 1990 for modernization. She is scheduled to complete the refueling/overhaul in April 1994.

Operational: During August–October 1964 the ENTERPRISE, in company with the missile-armed cruiser LONG BEACH and frigate BAINBRIDGE (DLGN 25, now CGN 25), formed the all-nuclear Task Force 1. The ships steamed around the world without refueling or replenishing, travelling 32,600 n.miles (60,375 km) in 64 days, including time for port visits in several countries.

The ENTERPRISE shifted to the Pacific Fleet in 1965 and in November of that year began flying air strikes against North Vietnam, becoming the first nuclear ship to enter combat. She remained in the Pacific until 1990, when she returned to the Atlantic in preparation for overhaul at Newport News Shipbuilding.

The ENTERPRISE's island was configured to support the SPS-32/SPS-33 "billboard" radar antennas. It now supports conventional radars, which are to be upgraded during her modernization. Mk 91 missile directors are mounted on all four sides of the island structure. (1990, Giorgio Arra)

3 MULTI-PURPOSE AIRCRAFT CARRIERS } "FORRESTAL" CLASS
1 TRAINING CARRIER

Number	Name	FY	Builder	Laid down	Launched	Commissioned	Status
AVT 59	FORRESTAL	52	Newport News Shipbuilding	14 July 1952	11 Dec 1954	1 Oct 1955	**TRA-A**
CV 60	SARATOGA*	53	New York Naval Shipyard	16 Dec 1952	8 Oct 1955	14 Apr 1956	**AA**
CV 61	RANGER*	54	Newport News Shipbuilding	2 Aug 1954	29 Sep 1956	10 Aug 1957	**PA**
CV 62	INDEPENDENCE*	55	New York Naval Shipyard	1 July 1955	6 June 1958	10 Jan 1959	**PA**

Displacement:	AVT 59	59,098 tons light				
	CV 60–62	61,000 tons light				
	AVT 59	80,662 tons full load				
	CV 60–62	81,500 tons full load				
Length:	990 feet (301.8 m) waterline					
	CV 59, 60	1,040 feet (317.1 m) overall				
	CV 61, 62	1,052 feet (320.7 m) overall				
Beam:	130 feet (39.6 m)					
Flight deck:	CV 59, 60	252⅔ feet (77.0 m)				
	CV 61	238½ feet (72.7 m)				
	CV 62	250 feet (76.2 m)				
Draft:	37 feet (11.3 m)					

Manning:

	Total	Officers	Enlisted
CV 59	2,767	154	2,613
CV 60	2,962	149	2,813
CV 61	2,937	155	2,782
CV 62	2,617	155	2,462
Marines:	64	2	62
Air wing: approx.	2,020	287	1,733

Propulsion: 4 steam turbines (Westinghouse in CV 59, General Electric in CV 60–62); 260,000 shp in CV 59, 280,000 shp in CV 60–62; 4 shafts

Boilers: 8 600 psi (41.7 kg/cm²) (Babcock & Wilcox) in CV 59
8 1,200 psi (83.4 kg/cm²) (Babcock & Wilcox) in CV 60–62

Speed: CV 59 33 knots
CV 60–62 34 knots

Range: 12,000 n.miles (22,225 km) at 20 knots

Aircraft: approx. 80

Catapults: 3 steam C7 + 1 steam C11-1 in CV 59, 60
4 steam C7 in CV 61, 62

Elevators: 4 deck edge—63 × 52 feet (19.2 × 15.9 m); 110,000-lb (49,500-kg) capacity

Missiles: 2 8-tube NATO Sea Sparrow launchers Mk 29 except 3 launchers in CV 61

Guns: 3 20-mm Phalanx CIWS Mk 16 (3 multi-barrel)

Radars: SPS-10 surface search
SPS-48C 3-D air search except SPS-48E in CV 59
SPS-49 air search

Sonars: none

Fire control: 2 Mk 91 missile FCS except 3 in CV 61

EW systems: SLQ-29 (SLQ-17 + WLR-8)
WLR-1
WLR-3
WLR-11

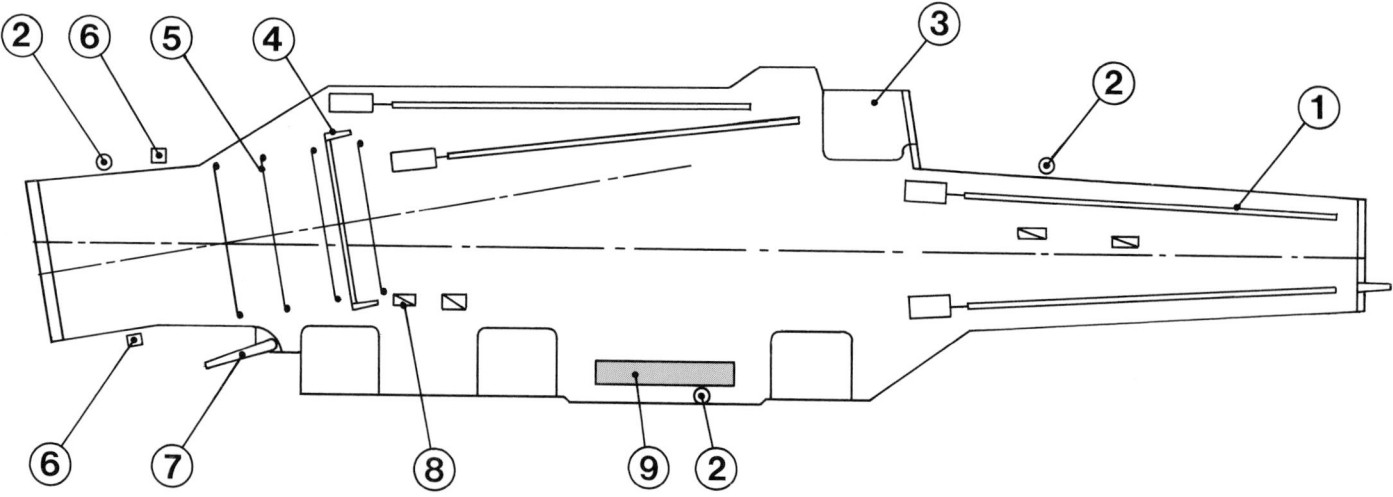

INDEPENDENCE   1. catapults (4)   2. Phalanx CIWS   3. elevators (4)   4. barricade   5. arresting pendants (4)   6. NATO Sea Sparrow launcher
7. crane   8. bomb elevators (4)   9. island structure

These were the world's first aircraft carriers to be constructed from the keel up after World War II. They were intended specifically to operate heavy and high-performance turbojet attack aircraft.

The FORRESTAL made her last operational deployment in mid-1991, after which she became the Navy's pilot-training ship in 1992. She replaced the LEXINGTON in that role and is home-ported at Pensacola, Fla. The FORRESTAL could be reactivated as a fully operational carrier in about 12 months.

The RANGER is scheduled to be decommissioned and placed in reserve in fiscal 1993, the SARATOGA in fiscal 1995, and the INDEPENDENCE in fiscal 1998.

The INDEPENDENCE is home-ported in Yokosuka, Japan, having replaced the MIDWAY as the only U.S. aircraft carrier based overseas; the INDEPENDENCE arrived at Yokosuka on 11 September 1991.

The FORRESTAL, SARATOGA, and INDEPENDENCE have undergone major SLEP modernization; see below. The above manning, weapons, and electronics data are for the FORRESTAL as a CV in 1991.

Classification: The FORRESTAL and SARATOGA were ordered as large aircraft carriers (CVB 59, CVB 60); they were reclassified as attack aircraft carriers (CVA) on 1 October 1952. Two ships were changed to multi-mission aircraft carriers (CV) when modified to operate S-3A Viking ASW aircraft and SH-3 Sea King ASW helicopters: the SARATOGA on 30 June 1972, and the INDEPENDENCE on 28 February 1973. The FORRESTAL and RANGER were changed to CV on 30 June 1975, prior to modification.

The FORRESTAL was changed from CV 59 to AVT 59 on 4 February 1992.

Design: SCB No. 80. These ships incorporated many design features of the aborted carrier UNITED STATES (CVA 58). They were originally designed as axial (straight) deck ships. The FORRESTAL was modified during construction to incorporate the British-developed angled flight deck. As built, the FORRESTAL had a large second mast on her island structure to carry electronic antennas; it has been replaced by a smaller pole mast. Details of these ships differ considerably.

The hangar decks of these ships are 740 feet (225.6 m) long, 101 feet (30.8 m) wide, and 25 feet (7.6 m) high.

Engineering: The SARATOGA was the first U.S. carrier to have 1,200-psi (83.4 kg/cm^2) boilers.[8] The ship has had major problems with her propulsion plant.

Guns: These were the last U.S. aircraft carriers built with a major gun armament. As built, all four ships had eight 5-inch/54-cal DP Mk 42 single guns, mounted in pairs on sponsons, both sides, fore and aft. The forward sponsons were removed early in their service because of damage in heavy seas (except that after deletion of guns, the RANGER retained the forward sponsons—the only ship to be permanently assigned to the Pacific and not have to operate in the rougher seas of the North Atlantic). The after guns were removed as Sea Sparrow launchers became available for these ships.

Modernization: The FORRESTAL, SARATOGA, and INDEPENDENCE have had the SLEP update intended to add 15 years to their nominal 30-year service lives. However, under current planning all will be retired prior to 45 years of service life. The RANGER is not scheduled to undergo SLEP. The SLEP updates were undertaken at the Philadelphia Naval Shipyard:

	Arrival at yard	Conversion started	Conversion completed
CV 59	Jan 1983	Jan 1983	May 1985
CV 60	Sep 1980	Oct 1980	Feb 1983
CV 62	Apr 1985	Apr 1985	mid-1988

The SLEP update includes rehabilitation of the ship's hull, propulsion, auxiliary machinery, and piping systems, with improved radars, communications equipment, and aircraft launch-and-recovery systems provided.

After the SARATOGA's modernization, several problems were found with the yard's work, including improper welding of boiler tubes that cost an additional $8 million to repair. The total SARATOGA SLEP cost was $491.7 million, the FORRESTAL SLEP cost $624 million, and the INDEPENDENCE SLEP cost $690 million.

Operational: The FORRESTAL departed Mayport, Fla., with Carrier Air Wing (CVW) 6 for her last operational deployment (to the Mediterranean) in May 1991; she returned to the United States in December 1991.

8. The four MITSCHER (DL 2)-class frigates, completed 1953–1954, were the first U.S. Navy ships built with 1,200-psi (83.4 kg/cm^2) boilers.

The first supercarrier to be completed, the FORRESTAL is shown while still a multi-purpose carrier. After her late 1991 deployment to the Mediterranean, she became a pilot-training ship. Here the ship is undergoing maintenance at the carrier base at Mayport, Fla. (1989, Giorgio Arra)

The FORRESTAL with the crew manning the rail during a visit to New Orleans, La. The SPS-49 is offset to the starboard side of the island. The radar arrangements in the eight conventional carriers vary greatly. (1988, Giorgio Arra)

1 MULTI-PURPOSE AIRCRAFT CARRIER: "MIDWAY"

Number	Name	FY	Builder	Laid down	Launched	Commissioned	Status
CV 41	MIDWAY*	42	Newport News Shipbuilding	27 Oct 1943	20 Mar 1945	10 Sep 1945	PR

Displacement:	52,972 tons light
	69,873 tons full load
Length:	900 feet (274.3 m) waterline
	976 feet (297.5 m) overall
Beam:	141 feet (43.0 m)
Flight deck:	263½ feet (80.3 m)
Draft:	35 feet (10.7 m)
Propulsion:	4 steam turbines (Westinghouse); 212,000 shp; 4 shafts
Boilers:	12 600 psi (41.7 kg/cm^2) (Babcock & Wilcox)
Speed:	32 knots
Range:	15,000 n.miles (27,780 km) at 15 knots
Manning:	2,534 (123 officers + 2,411 enlisted)
Marines:	64 (2 officers + 62 enlisted)
Air wing:	approx. 1,715 (245 officers + 1,470 enlisted)

Aircraft:	approx. 75
Catapults:	2 steam C13
Elevators:	3 deck edge—63 × 52 feet (19.2 × 15.9 m); 130,000-lb (58,500-kg) capacity
Missiles:	2 8-tube Sea Sparrow Mk 25 launchers
Guns:	2 20-mm Phalanx CIWS Mk 16 (3 multi-barrel)
Radars:	SPS-48C 3-D air search
	SPS-49 air search
	SPS-65 navigation
Sonars:	none
Fire control:	2 Mk 115 missile FCS
EW systems:	WLR-1
	WLR-10
	WLR-11

The MIDWAY was the last World War II–era warship in commission in the U.S. Navy. She was decommissioned in April 1992 and is laid up in reserve. The ship was scheduled to remain as a first-line carrier until the late 1990s, when replaced by the CV 74, to maintain a 15-carrier force. The early 1990s fleet reductions led to her being mothballed immediately after returning from Operation Desert Storm. She is laid up with the capability of replacing the FORRESTAL in the AVT role should the latter ship be returned to operational status.

The MIDWAY was based at Yokosuka, Japan, from 1973 until August 1991, the first U.S. carrier ever to be based in a foreign country. She has been replaced there by the INDEPENDENCE. (Another U.S. carrier was planned for home-porting in Pireaus, Greece, in the early 1970s; that proposal was dropped because of problems within the Greek government.)

The above manning numbers reflect her last year in commission.

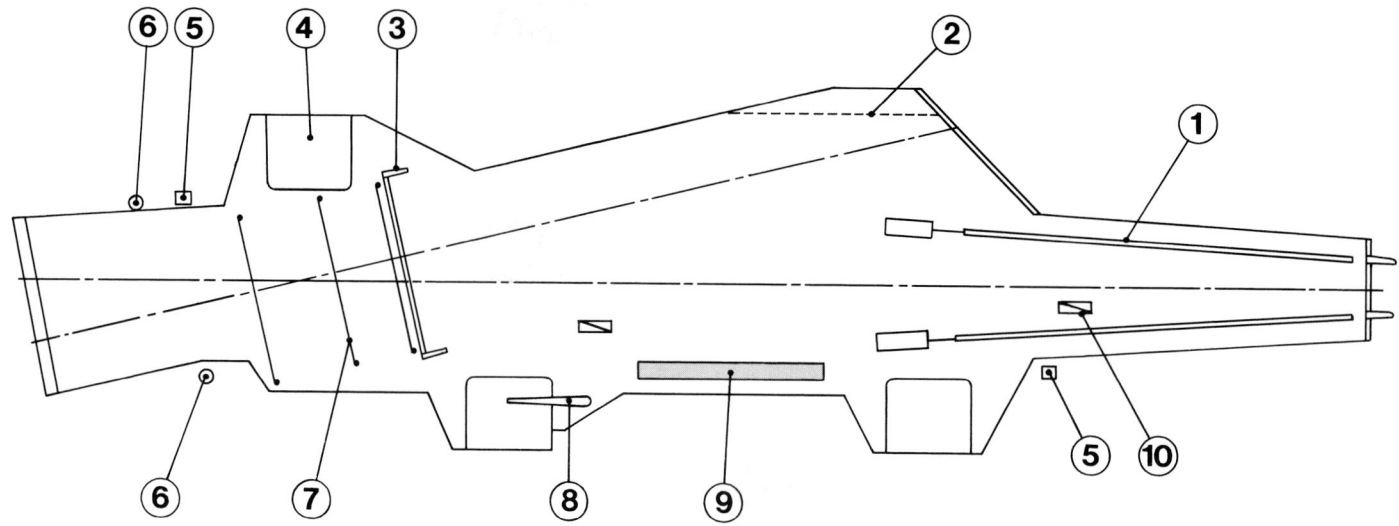

1. catapults (2)   2. removable deck extension   3. barricade   4. elevators (3)   5. BPDMS Sea Sparrow launchers   6. Phalanx CIWS   7. arresting pendants (3)   8. crane   9. island structure   10. bomb elevators (2)

Aircraft: The MIDWAY did not operate F-14 Tomcat fighters or S-3 Viking ASW aircraft because of limited hangar deck space and support facilities. Prior to being mothballed the MIDWAY carried CVW-5 with three F/A-18 Hornet squadrons and two A-6E Intruder squadrons, and an SH-3H Sea King squadron, plus combat support aircraft.

Class: Six ships of this class were authorized in 1942–1945: CVB 41–44, 56, and 57; the CVB 44 was cancelled on 1 November 1943, and the CVB 56 and CV 57 were cancelled on 28 March 1945. None had been laid down.

The FRANKLIN D. ROOSEVELT (CVB 42, later CVA/CV) was commissioned in 1945; active for virtually her entire career, the "FDR" was stricken in 1977 and scrapped. The CORAL SEA (CVB 43, later CVA/CV) was commissioned in 1947; in almost continuous active service, she was decommissioned and stricken on 30 April 1991.

Classification: These ships were built as large carriers (CVB 41–43), sometimes being referred to as "battle" carriers. They were reclassified as attack aircraft carriers (CVA) on 1 October 1952 and as aircraft carriers (CV) on 30 June 1975.

Design: The MIDWAYs were the largest warships designed by the U.S. Navy during World War II, being significantly larger than the previous ESSEX class.[9] They had a larger aircraft capacity and heavier gun battery than their predecessors, and were the first U.S. aircraft carriers with an armored flight deck. As built, each ship had two hydraulic catapults and three elevators (two centerline and one port deck edge). Aircraft capacity was rated at 137 at the time completed. They were the first U.S. warships constructed with a beam too great

9. The original displacements of the major war-built classes are shown below (source: Department of the Navy, *Ships' Data U.S. Naval Vessels*, Vol. I, 15 April 1945 [Confidential]):

		Standard	*Full load*
CVB 41	MIDWAY	45,000 tons	60,100 tons
CV 9	ESSEX	27,100 tons	33,000 tons
BB 61	IOWA	45,000 tons	57,540 tons

to permit passage through the 110-foot (33.5-m)-wide locks of the Panama Canal. (Several U.S. battleships damaged at Pearl Harbor on 7 December 1941 were rebuilt with beam blisters that prevented them from passing through the canal.)

The MIDWAY hangar deck is 692 feet (211 m) long, 85 feet (25.9 m) wide, and 17½ feet (5.3 m) high. Her flight deck is canted 13° to port and is 682 feet (207.9 m) long. In her final configuration the MIDWAY has three deck-edge elevators, one forward and one abaft the island on the starboard side, and one on the port quarter.

Guns: As built, the MIDWAY mounted 18 single 5-inch/54-cal DP Mk 39 guns; these were arranged on both sides at the main-deck level. Her secondary gun armament consisted of 84 40-mm AA guns and 28 20-mm AA guns at completion. The 40-mm and 20-mm guns were replaced by twin 3-inch/50-cal AA gun mounts. The gun armament was reduced until, by the 1970s, she mounted only three 5-inch guns. Subsequently all conventional guns were removed.

Modernization: The MIDWAY has been extensively modernized. Her major modernization, which provided an enclosed ("hurricane") bow, angled flight deck, strengthened flight deck and elevators, and steam catapults was at the Puget Sound Naval Shipyard from September 1955 to September 1957 (SCB 110—old SCB scheme) and at the San Francisco Naval Shipyard from February 1966 to January 1970 (SCB 101—new SCB scheme). The MIDWAY's 1966–1970 modernization was delayed because of the workload for West Coast shipyards during the Vietnam conflict.

During a 1986 overhaul in Japan, the MIDWAY was fitted with blisters to add buoyancy and improve stability. However, the modifications caused a reduction in roll time, i.e., the ship tried to right herself more quickly from a roll with a negative effect on flight operations. During sea trials in December 1986 the ship rolled up to ten degrees at nine knots in four- to six-foot (1.2 to 1.8-m) seas, and took water over the flight deck. (The above beam and draft are as refitted with bulges; see 14th Edition/page 96 for pre-bulge dimensions.)

Operational: The MIDWAY initially operated in the Atlantic–Mediterranean areas. She transferred to the Pacific Fleet in 1955.

The U.S. Navy's last operational carrier of World War II construction, the MIDWAY is shown here during a visit to Sydney, Australia. Her above-waterline configuration was changed several times during her 46-year career, which ended with the Persian Gulf conflict. (1987, L. Van Ginderen collection)

The MIDWAY refueling from the oiler MISSISSINEWA (T-AO 144) during operations in the Indian Ocean. The carrier's SPS-49 radar antenna is offset to the starboard side of the island structure. (1987, L. Van Ginderen collection)

POST–WORLD WAR II AIRCRAFT CARRIER PROGRAMS

World War II aircraft carrier programs reached hull number CVB 57 (a cancelled MIDWAY-class ship). After the war there were several proposals to construct new-design aircraft carriers, but the large number of fleet (CV), light (CVL), and escort (CVE) carriers available precluded any serious consideration of new construction except for "heavy" carriers (CVA) to carry heavy, long-range nuclear-strike aircraft.

HEAVY AIRCRAFT CARRIERS

One CVA was laid down, the UNITED STATES (CVA 58), and although never completed, she served as the progenitor of the FORRESTAL and later large U.S. aircraft carriers. The UNITED STATES design provided for a flush-deck configuration that could simultaneously launch two heavy attack aircraft and two fighters from a pair of forward catapults and a pair of waist catapults. Three deck-edge elevators and one stern elevator would lift aircraft to the flight deck.

Four ships of this class were initially planned, with the UNITED STATES authorized in fiscal 1948. The ship was laid down at Newport News Shipbuilding on 18 April 1949 but cancelled on 23 April 1949. Her SCB number was 6A.

SEA CONTROL SHIPS

Several proposals were put forward in the 1960s for providing ASW helicopters as the primary armament of convoy escorts (with the designations DH, DDH, and DHK being used). Subsequently, in 1970 the Chief of Naval Operations[10] proposed a class of at least eight sea control ships that would carry several SH-3 Sea King ASW helicopters plus a small number of AV-8 Harriers for self-defense. The SCS concept was evaluated at sea from October 1971 to January 1972 with the helicopter carrier GUAM (LPH 9).

The lead ship was planned for the fiscal 1975 shipbuilding program. The Congress refused to authorize such ships, however, because of their limited capability, and was strongly supported by the advocates of large carriers. A modified version of the SCS design was built for the Spanish Navy, the PRINCIPE DE ASTURIAS, launched in 1982.

10. Admiral Elmo R. Zumwalt, Jr., Chief of Naval Operations from 1970 to 1974.

VSTOL SUPPORT SHIPS

During the mid-1970s there was increased U.S. Navy interest in VSTOL aircraft, with a major analysis known as the Sea-Based Air Master Study developing a long-term program for several categories of them. In 1975 the Chief of Naval Operations[11] proposed a VSTOL aircraft carrier of approximately twice the size of the aborted SCS that would be able to operate a number of improved AV-8 Harrier combat aircraft in addition to ASW aircraft. About 50 design alternatives were considered, with some having a small number of catapults and arresting wires to permit the use of E-2 Hawkeye AEW aircraft and S-2 Viking ASW aircraft. The primary aircraft to have been embarked in this ship would have been VSTOL fighter and attack variants.

MEDIUM AIRCRAFT CARRIER

The Ford administration (1974–1977) and Carter administration (1977–1981) both proposed the construction of large-deck conventional aircraft carriers of 50,000 to 60,000 tons designated CVV to be constructed in lieu of additional NIMITZ-class ships at a ratio of about 2:1. A variety of designs was considered under this concept, ranging from about 40,000 tons full-load displacement (i.e., about the size of a HANCOCK-class ship) up to a repeat of the KENNEDY design.

A CVV program was put forth to Congress; however, the ship was strongly opposed by proponents of the nuclear-powered NIMITZ, especially Admiral Rickover, and none was authorized.

"ESSEX" AND "HANCOCK" CLASSES

All ships of the war-built ESSEX and HANCOCK classes have been stricken. These aircraft carriers formed the backbone of U.S. carrier strength from 1943 through the Korean War. They operated alongside the larger MIDWAY- and FORRESTAL-class ships through the Cold War and the Vietnam War. The LEXINGTON was the last active ship, serving as a training carrier until decommissioned on 8 November 1991 (date of ceremony; official decommission date is 26 November 1991). The last fully operational carrier was the ORISKANY, which was decommissioned in 1976.

Most were modernized to different degrees after World War II, with the most extensive mods being designated as the HANCOCK class (see previous editions). Construction of the ORISKANY was suspended in 1946; it was resumed in 1947, and she was completed to a modified design, the prototype for later modernizations.

Twenty-four ships were completed of 32 ordered from 1940 to 1942. Originally designated CV, all were changed to CVA (attack aircraft carrier) in 1952; subsequently, several became ASW carriers (CVS), three became amphibious assault ships (LPH), one a training carrier (CVT/AVT), and several (while in mothballs) were changed to aviation transports (AVT); the ORISKANY reverted to CV in 1975. All except the amphibious assault ships (LPH) and transports (AVT) retained their original CV hull number.

Table 13-2 lists U.S. aircraft carriers from the ESSEX class onward. See 14th Edition/pages 98–101 for characteristics.

11. Admiral James L. Holloway III, CNO from 1974 to 1978.

TABLE 13-2.　AIRCRAFT CARRIERS

Number	Name	Comm.	Classifications	Stricken
CV 9	ESSEX	1942	CVA/CVS	1 June 1973
CV 10	YORKTOWN	1943	CVA/CVS	1 June 1973
CV 11	INTREPID	1943	CVA/CVS	30 Sep 1980
CV 12	HORNET	1943	CVA/CVS	25 July 1989
CV 13	FRANKLIN	1944	CVA/CVS/AVT 8	1 Oct 1964
CV 14	TICONDEROGA	1944	CVA	16 Nov 1973
CV 15	RANDOLPH	1944	CVA/CVS	1 June 1973
CV 16	LEXINGTON	1943	CVA/CVS/CVT/AVT*	
CV 17	BUNKER HILL	1943	CVA/CVS/AVT 9	1 Nov 1966
CV 18	WASP	1943	CVA/CVS	1 July 1972
CV 19	HANCOCK	1944	CVA	31 Dec 1975
CV 20	BENNINGTON	1944	CVA/CVS	20 Sep 1989
CV 21	BOXER	1945	CVA/CVS/LPH 4	1 Dec 1969
CVL 22–30	INDEPENDENCE-class light carriers			
CV 31	BON HOMME RICHARD	1944	CVA	20 Sep 1989
CV 32	LEYTE	1946	CVA/CVS/AVT 10	1 June 1969
CV 33	KEARSARGE	1946	CVA/CVS	1 May 1973
CV 34	ORISKANY	1950	CVA/CV	25 July 1989
CV 35	REPRISAL	cancelled 1945		
CV 36	ANTIETAM	1945	CVA/CVS	1 May 1973
CV 37	PRINCETON	1945	CVA/CVS/LPH 5	30 Jan 1970
CV 38	SHANGRI-LA	1944	CVA	15 July 1982
CV 39	LAKE CHAMPLAIN	1945	CVA/CVS	1 Dec 1969
CV 40	TARAWA	1945	CVA/CVS/AVT 12†	1 June 1967
CVB 41–44	MIDWAY-class large carriers			
CV 45	VALLEY FORGE	1946	CVA/CVS/LPH 8	15 Jan 1970
CV 46	IWO JIMA	cancelled 1945		
CV 47	PHILIPPINE SEA	1946	CVA/CVS/AVT 11	1 Dec 1969
CVL 48, 49	SAIPAN-class light carriers			
CV 50–55	ESSEX class	cancelled 1945		
CVB 56, 57	MIDWAY-class large carriers			
CVA 58	UNITED STATES heavy carrier			
CV 59–64	FORRESTAL and modified FORRESTAL class			
CVAN 65	ENTERPRISE			
CV 66, 67	modified FORRESTAL class			
CVN 68–	NIMITZ class			

*Training carrier; the other AVTs are aviation transports.
†The TARAWA operated as an LPH in the late 1950s, but she was not reclassified (while classified CVS 40).

In March 1991 the Navy ordered a halt to LEXINGTON training operations because of maintenance problems; her last arrested aircraft landing took place in February 1991—landing no. 493,248, undoubtedly more than any other aircraft carrier of any nation. The ship will be on display at Corpus Christi, Texas.

The BUNKER HILL was retained as a moored electronics test ship in San Diego harbor until December 1972 (after being stricken). The INTREPID and YORKTOWN are memorials, as is the light carrier CABOT (CVL 28); see appendix D.

CHAPTER 14

Battleships

Impressive naval power: The battleship WISCONSIN at sea. The massive 16-inch (406-mm) guns and their armored turrets dominate the dreadnought's graceful lines. But the ships proved too expensive to man and operate in relationship to their firepower and limited combat capabilities. (1991, Giorgio Arra)

All four U.S. battleships of the Iowa class, the world's last operational dreadnoughts, have been again decommissioned and are laid up in reserve. These ships, reactivated in the 1980s with considerable fanfare in the Reagan-Lehman naval buildup, had little support in or out of the Navy once more stringent budgets were encountered in the late 1980s.

Two of the ships—the Missouri and Wisconsin—saw extensive service in the gunfire support role and as Tomahawk missile launch platforms in the Gulf War. The New Jersey was in commission longer than any of the others, almost nine years; the Wisconsin's tenure was the shortest, less than three years (see below). The Missouri was retained in active service with a reduced crew into early 1992 to be present at Pearl Harbor on 7 December 1991, for the commemoration of the 50th anniversary of the Japanese attack.

The rationale for retaining the battleships in active service was untenable for several reasons:

(1) Battleships are expensive to operate. The reactivation of the battleships cost "only" some $300 to $500 million each (i.e., enough to buy two or three FFG 7-class frigates). The dreadnoughts each require a crew of some 1,600 men, and cost some $65 million per year to operate. Each battleship's crew is enough to man more than four Aegis missile cruisers or almost eight anti-submarine frigates (albeit these are smaller ships requiring higher skill levels). The expense is considerable for a single-mission warship.

(2) Battleships are too limited in capability. They have no anti-submarine and no effective anti-air capability; they must be escorted in most operational scenarios. An Iowa's main batteries are nine 16-inch (406-mm) guns and 32 Tomahawk cruise missiles. The guns are useful for amphibious gunfire support, but are outdistanced by modern assault methods (helicopters and air-cushion landing craft), and there are too many Third World nations with modern aircraft, mines, submarines, and missiles for the United States to *politically* risk those ships in assault areas. (A few hits with napalm or an under-the-keel torpedo explosion could severely injure them.)

The Tomahawks are a potent weapon. But the Spruance (DD 963)-class anti-submarine destroyers are each being fitted with 61 vertical-launch cells for Tomahawk missiles with no loss of their other capabilities. A Spruance has a crew of some 345 men, making them far more efficient Tomahawk launch platforms.

(3) Battleships are too few in number. With only four battleships, one of which is probably in overhaul at any given time, and the others widely scattered, the probability of a battleship being available at short notice in a crisis area was small. This is partially compensated for by their sustained high speed, although in the face of air or submarine threats they would require escort ships.

As recommissioned in the 1980s, the battleships were intended to undertake forward deployments, operating in place of aircraft carriers in those areas judged to have a low-to-medium air threat (vice the medium-to-high threat areas that would require a carrier battle group). The nominal organization for a battleship-centered Surface Action Group (SAG) was to be one Iowa, one Aegis cruiser (CG 47), and three ASW destroyers (DD 963).

In the post-Vietnam period the issue of reactivating some or all of the Iowa-class ships to supplement carrier deployments was first raised in the early 1970s, but not until the Reagan administration took office in January 1981 was their reactivation given priority by the Navy's leadership, especially Secretary of the Navy John Lehman. The recommissioning of the Iowa class was Mr. Lehman's second highest priority, after the construction of nuclear-propelled aircraft carriers.

During the 1960s and early 1970s there were several proposals to convert the battleships to "commando ships," retaining some or all of their main gun battery with accommodations for several hundred Marines and space for assault helicopters to be embarked. Other configurations suggested in this period were conversion to cruise missile carriers, with several hundred vertical-launch Tomahawk cruise missiles being fitted in place of the after turret, or to a battleship-VSTOL carrier, with the after turret replaced by a flight deck to operate AV-8B Harrier VSTOL aircraft.

In theory the VLS and Harrier configurations were considered for future modification to the ships after their 1980s reactivation. However, funding limitations following the recommissioning of the four ships halted all realistic consideration of further major modifications to the ships. Indeed, funding considerations prevented the ships from being provided with task force/battle group flagship facilities, which would have been a most useful role in view of their space for staff accommodations and working areas.

(In the late 1950s and early 1960s there were also proposals to convert some or all of the Iowa-class ships to strategic "missile monitors" carrying Polaris missiles.)

Names: Battleships were named for states of the Union except for the Kearsarge (BB 5), which was named for a mountain in New Hampshire to honor that state. State names have subsequently been assigned to six nuclear-propelled missile cruisers (CGN 36–41) and the Ohio (SSBN 726)-class strategic missile submarines.

Operational: Two ships indicated by asterisks in the following table participated in Operations Desert Storm/Shield in the Persian Gulf in 1990–1991.

4 BATTLESHIPS: "IOWA" CLASS

Number	Name	Builder	Laid down	Launched	Commissioned	Recommissioned	Decommissioned	Status
BB 61	Iowa	New York Navy Yard	27 June 1940	27 Aug 1942	22 Feb 1943	28 Apr 1984	26 Oct 1990	AR
BB 62	New Jersey	Philadelphia Navy Yard	16 Sep 1940	7 Dec 1942	23 May 1943	28 Dec 1982	8 Feb 1991	PR
BB 63	Missouri*	New York Navy Yard	6 Jan 1941	29 Jan 1944	11 June 1944	10 May 1986	31 Mar 1992	PR
BB 64	Wisconsin*	Philadelphia Navy Yard	25 Jan 1941	7 Dec 1943	16 Apr 1944	22 Oct 1988	30 Sep 1991	AR

Displacement:	48,425 tons standard	Missiles:	16 Harpoon SSM (4 quad canisters Mk 141)
	57,350 tons full load		32 Tomahawk TASM/TLAM (8 quad ABL Mk 143)
Length:	860 feet (262.3 m) waterline	Guns:	9 16-inch (406-mm) 50-cal Mk 7 (3 triple)
	887¼ feet (270.6 m) overall except BB 62 887⁷⁄₁₂ feet (270.7 m) overall		12 5-inch (127-mm) 38-cal DP Mk 28 (6 twin)
			4 20-mm Phalanx CIWS Mk 16 (4 multi-barrel)
Beam:	108⅛ feet (33.0 m)	ASW weapons:	none
Draft:	38 feet (11.6 m)	Radars:	LN-66 navigation except SPS-64(V) in BB 64
Propulsion:	4 steam turbines (General Electric in BB 61, 63; Westinghouse in BB 62, 64); 212,000 shp; 4 shafts		SPS-49 air search
			SPS-67 surface search except SPS-10F in BB 62
Boilers:	8 600 psi (41.7 kg/cm²) (Babcock & Wilcox)	Sonars:	none
Speed:	33 knots (see notes)	Fire control:	4 Mk 37 GFCS with Mk 25 radar
Range:	15,000 n.miles (27,780 km) at 15 knots		2 Mk 38 gun directors with Mk 13 radar
Manning:	approx. 1,570 (70 officers + 1,500 enlisted)		1 Mk 40 gun director with Mk 27 radar
Marines:	55 (2 officers + 53 enlisted)		1 SPQ-9 in BB 61
Helicopters:	landing area	EW systems:	SLQ-25 Nixie
			SLQ-32(V)3

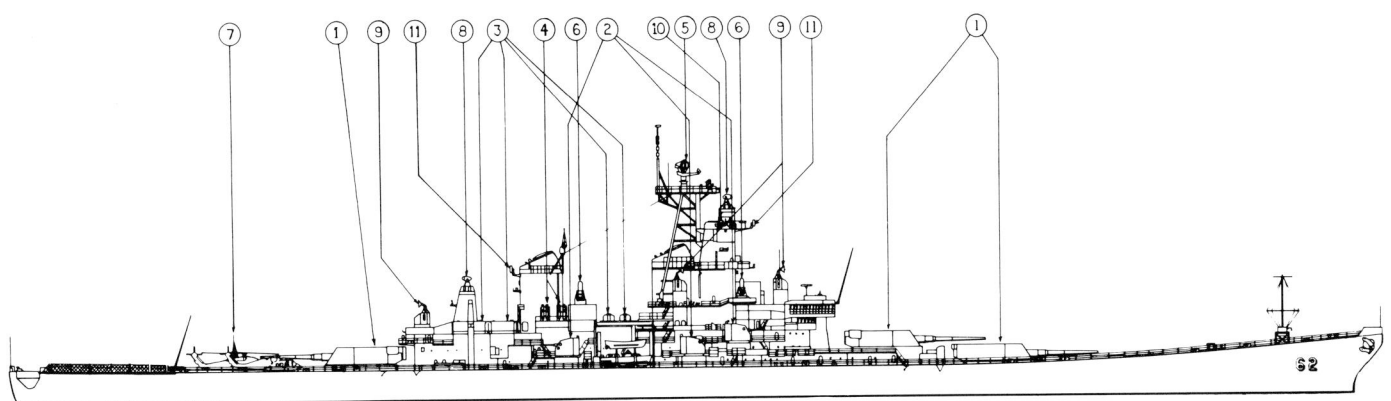

NEW JERSEY: 1. 16-inch/50-cal triple turrets   2. 5-inch/38-cal twin mounts   3. Tomahawk box launchers   4. Harpoon canisters   5. SPS-49 radar
6. Phalanx CIWS   7. helicopter area   8. Mk 38 GFCS with Mk 13 radar   9. Mk 37 GFCS with Mk 25 radar   10. SLQ-32(V)3 ECM   11. OE-82 SATCOMM
antennas (A.D. Baker III)

All four ships were modernized and recommissioned as part of the naval buildup under the Reagan administration. The recommissioning of the WISCONSIN in 1988 marked the first time that four battleships had been in commission since 1955 (see below). All have since been retired. No other battleships of any nation are intact.

The above data reflect the state of the ships at the time of their decommissioning in 1990–1992.

Aircraft: These ships were built with two rotating stern catapults and an aircraft crane for handling floatplanes. Three aircraft were normally embarked for scouting and gunfire spotting. The catapults were beached during the Korean War and the ships were assigned utility helicopters. During the Vietnam War the NEW JERSEY also flew QH-50C "snoopy dash" drones for gunfire spotting.

In early 1984 the NEW JERSEY is reported to have evaluated the Israeli-made Mastiff Remotely Piloted Vehicle (RPV) for reconnaissance/gunfire spotting roles. Subsequently, the IOWA deployed in 1987 with five Pioneer surveillance drones (with control systems including the radome mounted on second funnel). All subsequently were fitted to operate the Pioneer, with the MISSOURI and WISCONSIN flying Pioneer drones for gunfire spotting during the 1991 Gulf War (see chapter 29).

One or two utility helicopters are normally embarked. No elevators or aircraft support facilities are provided.

Class: The IOWAs were the world's last battleships to be constructed, although two ships built in the same period were completed after the war: the British VANGUARD (laid down in 1941 and completed in 1946) and the French JEAN BART (laid down in 1939 and completed in 1955). The U.S. dreadnoughts were exceeded in size and firepower only by the Japanese sister ships YAMATO and MUSASHI, both completed and sunk during World War II. Those ships displaced approximately 70,000 tons full load and had a main battery of nine 18.1-inch (460-mm) guns.

Six ships of the IOWA class were ordered; the ILLINOIS (BB 65) was cancelled on 12 August 1945 when 22 percent complete; construction of the KENTUCKY (BB 66) was suspended on 17 February 1947 when 72.1 percent complete and she was cancelled on 22 January 1950 (although the hull was not stricken from the Naval Register until 9 June 1958). In the early 1950s it was intended to complete the KENTUCKY as a guided missile ship carrying the Terrier missile system; however, no work was undertaken on that project.

Five larger battleships of the MONTANA class (BB 67–71) were ordered on 9 September 1940, but none was laid down and the program was cancelled on 21 July 1943. They were to have had four triple 16-inch gun turrets, displace 58,000 tons standard, and to be 903 feet (275.3 m) long. The construction of the MIDWAY (CVB 41)-class aircraft carriers and other priority naval construction programs as well as the ascendancy of carrier-based aircraft over the battleship gun caused cancellation of the MONTANA class.

There has been speculative press mention of a "super MONTANA" class of some 80,000 tons mounting 20-inch (508-mm) guns with the hull numbers BB 72 to 78; in fact, no battleships beyond the MONTANAs were officially considered by the U.S. Navy.

Design: The design of these ships was constrained by the requirement to transit the Panama Canal (lock width 110 feet).

Armor protection was intended to protect vital areas of the ship from enemy shells fired by guns up to 16-inches. The Class A steel armor belt tapers vertically from 307 mm to 41 mm. There is a lower armor belt of 343 mm aft of the No. 3 main battery turret to protect the propeller shafts (within hull). Turret faces have 432 mm of armor, turret tops 184 mm, turret backs 305 mm, barbettes up to 295 mm, second armor deck 152 mm, conning tower sides 439 mm, and conning tower top 184 mm.

Electronics: During their 1980s reactivation the ships were fitted with a cruiser (CG/CGN) communications suite; the WISCONSIN had the most-capable communications suite of the four ships. However, they lacked NTDS (except for Link 11 receiver) and certain other electronic features of a modern surface combatant.

Three of the ships have a commercial LN-66 navigation radar.

Engineering: All of these ships are reported to have achieved 35 knots in service. Reports that the MISSOURI, which suffered a serious grounding in 1950, and possibly other ships could not achieve 30 knots were incorrect.

Guns: As built during World War II, in addition to the main battery of nine 16-inch guns these ships carried 20 5-inch/38-cal guns (twin), up to 80 40-mm AA guns (quad), and almost 60 20-mm AA guns (twin and single). The 20-mm weapons were removed after the war and the number of 40-mm guns successively reduced. (The NEW JERSEY carried only nine 16-inch and 20 5-inch guns during her brief Vietnam reactivation.)

Postwar plans to provide twin 3-inch/50-cal AA mounts in place of the quad 40-mm mounts were abandoned.

Four of the original ten 5-inch/38-cal twin gun mounts were removed during the ships' 1980s reactivation. Four Phalanx Gatling-type guns were also provided for anti-ship missile defense.

During 1990–1991 the MISSOURI and WISCONSIN were armed with 25-mm Bushmaster "chain" guns, and 20-mm cannon for close-in defense against small craft while operating in the Persian Gulf.

Manning: The NEW JERSEY recommissioning in 1982 marked the first time that Marines had served in a U.S. battleship since the Korean War. The World War II manning of this class was 2,500 to 2,900 men per ship.

Missiles: During the 1970s there was a proposal to provide the IOWAs with the Aegis/SPY-1 AAW weapons system. However, it was discarded at the time as being too costly and was not considered when the ships were recommissioned in the early 1980s. When reactivation plans were being prepared in the 1980s, it was intended to fit the Sea Sparrow PDMS. However, it was determined that the system could not withstand the overpressure when the 16-inch guns were fired.

Modernization: When reactivated in the 1980s these ships underwent a limited modernization, including updated communications and radar equipment; sewage holding tanks and habitability features were provided. The Phalanx CIWS defensive system as well as Harpoon and Tomahawk offensive missiles were fitted.

The MISSOURI—the world's last operational battleship—at sea. The "Mighty Mo" and WISCONSIN participated in the Gulf War as gunfire support ships and Tomahawk "shooters." The ship's broad beam is evident, constrained to permit transiting the 110-foot (33.5-m) locks of the Panama Canal. (1991, Giorgio Arra)

A Phase II modernization was to have added more Tomahawks fired from vertical launchers, removing the after 16-inch gun turret, and making other upgrades. This proposal was dropped in 1983.

There have been several proposals to fit these ships as numbered fleet flagships; however, they have not been so modified or employed.

The NEW JERSEY and MISSOURI were modernized and recommissioned at the Long Beach Naval Shipyard; the IOWA and WISCONSIN were modernized at the Avondale and Litton/Ingalls shipyards.

Operational: All four ships of the class saw extensive combat in the later stages of World War II, mainly as AAW defensive ships for fast carriers. In the Korean War (1950–1953) they served primarily as gunfire support ships; they also served as fleet and force flagships in those conflicts. The MISSOURI, named for the home state of President Harry S Truman, was the scene of the Japanese surrender ceremony in Tokyo Bay on 2 September 1945, officially marking the end of World War II. Three ships were mothballed after the war with the MISSOURI retained in partial commission as a training ship.

During her 1968–1969 reactivation for the Vietnam War the NEW JERSEY made one deployment to the Western Pacific. She was on the "gun line" off South Vietnam for 120 days during which she fired 5,688 rounds of 16-inch ammunition and 14,891 5-inch rounds. (The NEW JERSEY fired a total of 6,200 main-battery rounds in her 1968–1969 commission, including test and training; by comparison, she fired 771 rounds from 1943 to 1948, and 6,671 during her participation in the Korean War and midshipmen cruises from 1950–1957.)

The NEW JERSEY was again reactivated as part of the Reagan administration's naval buildup, followed, in order, by the IOWA, MISSOURI, and WISCONSIN. The NEW JERSEY deployed to the Western Pacific in June 1983, but shortly after arriving in the Far East she was ordered to stand off Central America, and on 12 September 1983 she transited the Panama Canal into the Caribbean. Later that month she made a hurried trip across the Atlantic and through the Mediterranean to operate off the coast of war-torn Lebanon. (This was the first time a U.S. battleship had been in the Mediterranean since the WISCONSIN, in May of 1957.) The NEW JERSEY fired her 16-inch guns against shore targets near Beirut for the first time on 14 December 1983.

The IOWA suffered an explosion in her No. 2 16-inch gun turret on 19 April 1989, while the ship was operating some 330 n.miles (610 km) off Puerto Rico. One officer and 46 enlisted men in the turret and in the below-deck handling spaces were killed in the explosion and flash fire; 11 sailors in lower powder magazines escaped without harm, and those spaces were partially flooded to prevent a powder explosion, which most likely would have destroyed the ship. The damaged gun—center gun of No. 2 turret—was not repaired before the ship was mothballed.

The Navy's investigations concluded that the most probable cause of the disaster was a sabotage-suicide effort by a sailor in the turret. However, subsequent investigation, mainly by the Sandia National Laboratories, concluded that the "foreign materials" the Navy found in the turret that exploded were normal to battleship turrets, that the powder bags were overrammed against the projectile, and that the powder bags were sensitive in that condition. This led to an official Navy apology to the family of the sailor who had been implicated.

The WISCONSIN and MISSOURI participated in Operation Desert Storm in January–February 1991. Operating in the Persian Gulf, the MISSOURI fired 759 16-inch rounds and launched 28 Tomahawk cruise missiles, and the WISCONSIN fired 324 16-inch rounds and

The MISSOURI's superstructure is inundated with antennas, directors, weapons, and chaff launchers. At right are the coffin-like Tomahawk armored box launchers with the Harpoon canisters outboard of the after funnel. There are four Mk 36 SRBOC chaff launchers on each side, next to the port and starboard Mk 37 GFCS. (1991, Giorgio Arra)

The WISCONSIN under way off the Atlantic coast. One of the starboard-side refueling booms is visible aft of the superstructure. Small boats are stacked alongside the after 16-inch turret; an SH-3G Sea King VIP transport from Helicopter Combat Support Squadron (HC) 2 is on the helicopter deck. (1991, Giorgio Arra)

launched 24 missiles. (Thus 18 percent of the 288 Tomahawks launched in the conflict were from the two battleships.)

During their 1980s reactivation period, the four battleships fired the following 16-inch rounds (Desert Storm included):

IOWA	2,034
NEW JERSEY	2,983
MISSOURI	2,602
WISCONSIN	1,408

The last ship to decommission, the MISSOURI, was present at Pearl Harbor on 7 December 1991 for the commemoration of the 50th anniversary of the Japanese attack that caused American entry into World War II. Subsequently, she steamed into the Long Beach Naval Shipyard (Calif.) on 21 December 1991 for deactivation. She was then towed to the Bremerton Naval Shipyard (Wash.) for formal decommissioning on 31 March 1992.

TABLE 14-1. "IOWA"-CLASS ACTIVE SERVICE

Ship	World War II	Korean War	Vietnam War	600-ship Fleet
IOWA	22 Feb 1943–24 Mar 1949	25 Aug 1951–24 Feb 1958	—	28 Apr 1984–26 Oct 1990
NEW JERSEY	23 May 1943–30 June 1948	21 Nov 1950–21 Aug 1957	6 Apr 1968–17 Dec 1969	28 Dec 1982–8 Sep 1991
MISSOURI	11 June 1944	to → 26 Feb 1955	—	10 May 1986–31 Mar 1992
WISCONSIN	16 Apr 1944–1 July 1948	3 Mar 1951–8 Mar 1958	—	22 Oct 1988–30 Sep 1991

The battleships MISSOURI (left) and WISCONSIN refuel from the replenishment ship SACRAMENTO (AOE 1) in the Persian Gulf, immediately before the start of Operation Desert Storm in January 1991. The WISCONSIN's forward turrets are trained to port. Both warships made a major contribution to the conflict and garnered most of the media publicity that the Navy received during the conflict. (1991, U.S. Navy, PH3 Brad Dillon)

CHAPTER 15

Cruisers

The Aegis missile cruisers SAN JACINTO and NORMANDY heading to sea. These ships are representative of the largest cruiser class to be built by any navy since World War II. The TICONDEROGAS are also the most-capable cruisers, with more combat capability than any other cruiser now afloat. (1991, Giorgio Arra)

TABLE 15-1. CRUISER-DESTROYER FORCE-LEVEL OBJECTIVES [1980s Plan]

	CGN	CG 47	DDG 51	DDG 993	DD 963
10 Carrier Battle Groups (CVBG) with 2 carriers	6	21	29		28
1 Carrier Battle Group (CVBG) with 1 carrier		2	2		2
4 Surface Action Groups (SAG) with 1 battleship		4	12		
Amphibious Forces			10	4	
7 Military Convoys					7
10 Underway Replenishment Groups (URG)			10		
Totals	6	27	63	4	37

The U.S. Navy has 48 guided missile cruisers (CG/CGN) in active commission in late 1992 with the TICONDEROGA-class Aegis cruisers continuing in series production. Nine of the active cruisers have nuclear propulsion. One other nuclear-propelled cruiser is being laid up, and at least two other nuclear ships will be retired by the end of the decade.

Cruisers serve primarily as screening ships for carrier battle groups. All U.S. cruisers are armed with anti-aircraft missiles, some ships also having major anti-submarine capabilities. Anti-ship and land-attack capabilities have been belatedly provided to U.S. cruisers; all have been fitted with Harpoon missile canisters, while five nuclear ships and most TICONDEROGA-class ships (CG 52 and later) also have Tomahawk missiles. (On a practical basis the TICONDEROGAS deploy with primarily anti-air weapons.)

A total of 27 TICONDEROGA-class cruisers will be built, the number planned when then-Secretary of the Navy John Lehman designed a 600-ship fleet centered on 15 aircraft carriers and 4 battleships. (The cruiser and destroyer objectives of the 1980s are shown in table 15-1.) Beyond the completion of the TICONDEROGA class, no additional cruisers are under construction or planned.

The TICONDEROGA-class ships are the most-capable surface combatants afloat in most respects. Their Aegis AAW system is undoubtedly the best anti-air missile system in service with any navy, while the ships also have the most-capable ASW suite available in the U.S. Navy, the same as in the SPRUANCE (DD 963)-class destroyers. Because the TICONDEROGAS have the same hull and propulsion plant and some of the same combat systems as the SPRUANCE and KIDD (DDG 993) classes, and essentially the same anti-air system as the ARLEIGH BURKE (DDG 51) class, the blurring of lines between cruisers and destroyers can be seen. The term "cruiser" tends to indicate a ship that is commanded by a captain (vice commander in destroyer) and costs more than a contemporary destroyer (although this may not be true in the case of the ARLEIGH BURKE versus TICONDEROGA).

By the year 2000 the LEAHY and BELKNAP classes and older nuclear ships will begin to leave the fleet. Their nominal replacements, in addition to the TICONDEROGA class, will be the Aegis-fitted BURKE-class destroyers. Shortly after the year 2000 the U.S. cruiser force will consist only of the 27 TICONDEROGA-class ships and the six nuclear-propelled cruisers of the VIRGINIA and CALIFORNIA classes, providing a force level of 33 cruisers.

No "gun ships" remain in active commission. The largest guns in active U.S. cruisers are 5-inch weapons, with ten cruisers (CG 16–24 and CGN 25) having no guns larger than the Phalanx CIWS. Two heavy cruisers (CA) with 8-inch (203-mm) guns were laid up in reserve and were stricken in 1991. At the start of the battleship recommissioning program in the early 1980s, there were proposals to reactivate the two surviving heavy cruisers instead of, or in addition to, the battleships. The Navy rejected those proposals, preferring the larger guns of the more impressive IOWA (BB 61)-class dreadnoughts.

Builders: Both the TICONDEROGA-class missile cruisers and the ARLEIGH BURKE-class missile destroyers are being constructed by the Litton/Ingalls Shipbuilding yard in Pascagoula, Miss. (lead yard for the cruisers), and Bath Iron Works, Bath, Maine (lead yard for the destroyers).

Classification: The Aegis program office within the Naval Sea Systems Command has established its own classification of Aegis ships with variations known as "baselines." The following are the principal baseline characteristics; note that there are some system overlaps in the TICONDEROGA-class cruisers.

Baseline 1:	cruisers	SPY-1A radar
		Mk 26 launchers
		UYK-7 computers
Baseline 2:	cruisers	VLS/Tomahawk
		SQQ-89 ASW system
Baseline 3:	cruisers	SPY-1B radar
		improved communications
Baseline 4:	cruisers	SPY-1B(V) radar
		SQS-53C sonar
		UYK-43/44 computers
	destroyers	SPY-1D radar
		SQS-53C sonar
		UYK-43/44 computers
Baseline 5:	destroyers	SLQ-32(V)3 EW suite
		Standard SM-2 Block IV missile
		JTIDS[1]
Baseline 6:	destroyers	helicopter hangar

Guns: During the 1980s several cruisers were fitted with .50-cal machine guns and 25-mm Bushmaster "chain" guns for close-in defense against small craft; this armament suite was especially important for ships deploying into the Persian Gulf. The weapons are shifted from ship to ship as they forward deploy; accordingly, they are not listed under the specific class entries.

Electronics: All U.S. cruisers now in service are fitted with the Naval Tactical Data System (NTDS).

All older EW sets (i.e., pre-SLQ-32 series) have been deleted from the existing cruiser force.

Engineering: Despite congressional legislation passed in 1974 (U.S. Code Title VIII) directing that all future surface combatants intended for operations with carrier battle groups should be nuclear-propelled, no nuclear surface combatants have been authorized since 1974 and none is planned. A class of nuclear strike cruisers (CSGN) was proposed in the 1970s as was an improved VIRGINIA-class ship fitted with Aegis (CGN 42), but those ships were not built. (See 13th Edition/pages 136–137 for CSGN characteristics.)

The Reagan administration had included a CGN in the last year of the fiscal 1983–1987 shipbuilding plan, but that ship has "slipped" into oblivion. According to Navy officials, the ship was placed in the long-range program for "planning purposes" and will not be pursued. This total lack of support for resuming nuclear-propelled cruiser construction means that the increasing number of nuclear carriers will have mostly conventional escorts. In 1984 there were nine nuclear escorts for four nuclear carriers, essentially a 2-to-1 ratio; in 2000 there will be six nuclear cruisers in service with probably ten nuclear carriers, a 0.6-to-1 ratio.

While the nuclear cruisers have a high-speed endurance far superior to that of the fossil-fuel ships, the TICONDEROGA-class Aegis ships make the few available nuclear cruisers inferior in AAW as well as ASW capabilities. (There were proposals in the 1970s to provide the large cruiser LONG BEACH with Aegis during her "mid-life" modernization and even to complete the then-building ARKANSAS with an Aegis system. But those efforts were halted, in large part through the efforts of Admiral H. G. Rickover, then head of the naval nuclear-propulsion program, who feared that making those ships more capable would reduce the chances of additional cruiser construction. In the event, the Navy lost both ways: Neither the LONG BEACH nor ARKANSAS has Aegis, and no more nuclear cruisers have been built.)

Modernization: The Standard missile system and radars of several cruisers and one destroyer (DDG 42) have undergone the New Threat Upgrade (NTU) modernization. The NTU process enables the ships to employ later variants (blocks) of the Standard missile.

---

1. JTIDS = Joint Tactical Information Distribution System.

Names: U.S. cruisers traditionally had been named for major cities in the United States, with the CANBERRA (CA 70, later CAG 2) being named for an Australian cruiser sunk while operating with U.S. forces in 1942. From 1971 to 1978, six cruisers were assigned state names (DLGN/CGN 36–41).

From 1981 cruisers have been named for famous American battles, although even this scheme was corrupted when the CG 51 was named for a deceased Secretary of the Navy and Secretary of Defense.

Operational: Asterisks in ship entry lists indicate cruisers participating in Operations Desert Shield/Desert Storm in 1990–1991.

TABLE 15-2.   CRUISER FORCE LEVELS [late 1992]

Number	Class/Ship	Comm.	Active	Building*	Reserve
CG 47	TICONDEROGA	1983–	22	5	—
CGN 38	VIRGINIA	1976–1980	4	—	—
CGN 36	CALIFORNIA	1974–1975	2	—	—
CGN 35	TRUXTUN	1967	1	—	—
CG 26	BELKNAP	1964–1967	9	—	—
CGN 25	BAINBRIDGE	1962	—	—	—
CG 16	LEAHY	1962–1964	9	—	—
CGN 9	LONG BEACH	1961	1	—	—

*Ships authorized through fiscal 1992.

The ANZIO, one of the newest Aegis cruisers, showing the unimpressive, above-deck aspect of the forward VLS. The launch systems provide these cruisers and the ARLEIGH BURKE (DDG 51)-class destroyers with more large missiles than any warships except the Soviet KIROV-class battle cruisers, KUZNETSOV-class aircraft carriers, and the carrier BAKU. (1991, Litton/Ingalls Shipbuilding)

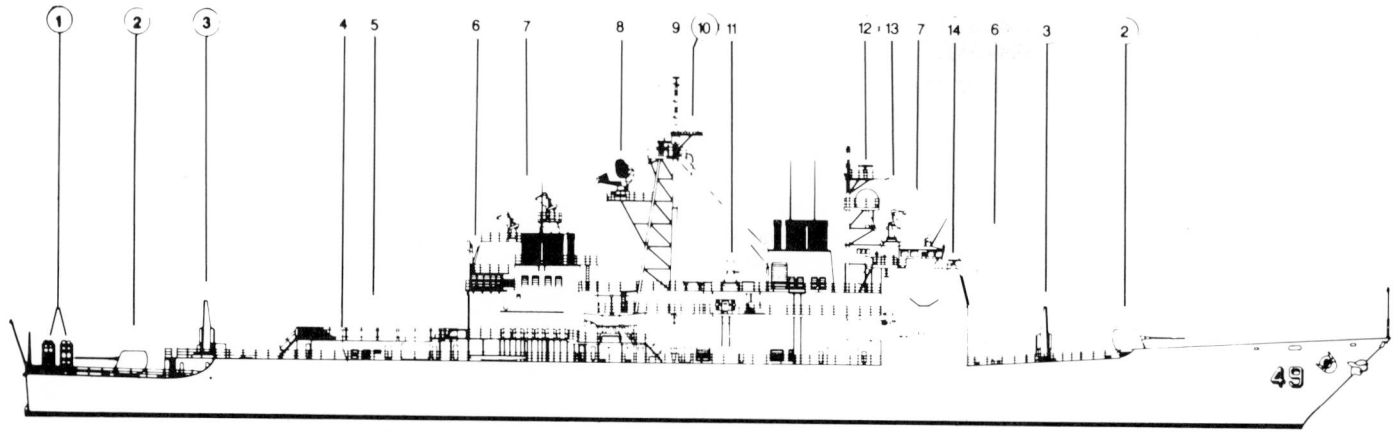

VINCENNES: 1. Harpoon canisters   2. 5-inch/54-cal single gun mount   3. Mk 26 missile launcher   4. Mk 32 torpedo tubes (behind shutters)   5. helicopter deck   6. SPY-1A radar   7. SPG-62 illuminator   8. SPS-49(V)6 radar   9. URN-25 TACAN   10. SQQ-28 LAMPS datalink antenna   11. 20-mm Phalanx CIWS   12. SPS-55 radar   13. SPQ-9A radar   14. SPS-64 radar (A.D. Baker III)

22 + 5 GUIDED MISSILE CRUISERS: "TICONDEROGA" CLASS

Number	Name	FY	Builder	Laid down	Launched	Christened	Commissioned	Status
CG 47	TICONDEROGA*	78	Litton/Ingalls Shipbuilding	21 Jan 1980	25 Apr 1981	16 May 1981	22 Jan 1983	**AA**
CG 48	YORKTOWN	80	Litton/Ingalls Shipbuilding	19 Oct 1981	17 Jan 1983	16 Apr 1983	4 July 1984	**AA**
CG 49	VINCENNES	81	Litton/Ingalls Shipbuilding	20 Oct 1982	14 Jan 1984	18 Apr 1984	6 July 1985	**PA**
CG 50	VALLEY FORGE*	81	Litton/Ingalls Shipbuilding	14 Apr 1983	23 June 1984	29 Sep 1984	11 Jan 1986	**PA**
CG 51	THOMAS S. GATES*	82	Bath Iron Works, Maine	31 Aug 1984	14 Dec 1985	—	22 Aug 1987	**AA**
CG 52	BUNKER HILL*	82	Litton/Ingalls Shipbuilding	11 Jan 1984	11 Mar 1985	19 Apr 1985	20 Sep 1986	**PA**
CG 53	MOBILE BAY*	82	Litton/Ingalls Shipbuilding	5 June 1984	22 Aug 1985	12 Oct 1985	21 Feb 1987	**PA**
CG 54	ANTIETAM*	83	Litton/Ingalls Shipbuilding	15 Nov 1984	14 Feb 1986	19 Apr 1986	6 June 1987	**PA**
CG 55	LEYTE GULF*	83	Litton/Ingalls Shipbuilding	18 Mar 1985	20 June 1986	11 Oct 1986	26 Sep 1987	**AA**
CG 56	SAN JACINTO*	83	Litton/Ingalls Shipbuilding	24 July 1985	14 Nov 1986	24 Jan 1987	23 Jan 1988	**AA**
CG 57	LAKE CHAMPLAIN	84	Litton/Ingalls Shipbuilding	3 Mar 1986	3 Apr 1987	25 Apr 1987	12 Aug 1988	**PA**
CG 58	PHILIPPINE SEA*	84	Bath Iron Works, Maine	8 May 1986	12 July 1987	—	18 Mar 1989	**AA**
CG 59	PRINCETON*	84	Litton/Ingalls Shipbuilding	15 Oct 1986	25 Sep 1987	17 Oct 1987	11 Feb 1989	**PA**
CG 60	NORMANDY*	85	Bath Iron Works, Maine	7 Apr 1987	19 Mar 1988	—	9 Dec 1989	**AA**
CG 61	MONTEREY	85	Bath Iron Works, Maine	19 Aug 1987	23 Oct 1988	—	16 June 1990	**AA**
CG 62	CHANCELLORSVILLE	85	Litton/Ingalls Shipbuilding	24 June 1987	15 July 1988	23 July 1988	4 Nov 1989	**PA**
CG 63	COWPENS	86	Bath Iron Works, Maine	23 Dec 1987	11 Mar 1989	—	9 Mar 1991	**PA**
CG 64	GETTYSBURG	86	Bath Iron Works, Maine	17 Aug 1988	22 July 1989	—	22 June 1991	**AA**
CG 65	CHOSIN	86	Litton/Ingalls Shipbuilding	22 July 1988	1 Sep 1989	14 Oct 1989	12 Jan 1991	**PA**
CG 66	HUE CITY	87	Litton/Ingalls Shipbuilding	20 Feb 1988	1 June 1990	21 July 1990	14 Sep 1991	**AA**
CG 67	SHILOH	87	Bath Iron Works, Maine	1 Aug 1989	8 Sep 1990	8 Sep 1990	18 July 1992	**PA**
CG 68	ANZIO	87	Litton/Ingalls Shipbuilding	21 Aug 1989	2 Nov 1990	10 Nov 1990	2 May 1992	**AA**
CG 69	VICKSBURG	88	Litton/Ingalls Shipbuilding	30 May 1990	2 Aug 1991	12 Oct 1991	1993	Building
CG 70	LAKE ERIE	88	Bath Iron Works, Maine	6 Mar 1990	13 July 1991	—	1993	Building
CG 71	CAPE ST. GEORGE	88	Litton/Ingalls Shipbuilding	19 Nov 1990	10 Jan 1992	11 Apr 1992	1993	Building
CG 72	VELLA GULF	88	Litton/Ingalls Shipbuilding	15 Apr 1991	13 June 1992	25 July 1992	1993	Building
CG 73	PORT ROYAL	88	Litton/Ingalls Shipbuilding	30 Sep 1991	1993	—	1994	Building

Displacement:	CG 47, 48 7,019 tons light	**Guns:**	2 5-inch (127-mm) 54-cal DP Mk 45 (2 single)
	CG 49–51 7,014 tons light		2 20-mm Phalanx CIWS Mk 16 (2 multi-barrel)
	CG 52–73 8,910 tons standard		several light machine guns or cannon
	CG 47, 48 9,589 tons full load	**ASW weapons:**	ASROC fired from Mk 26 launcher in CG 47–51
	CG 49–51 9,407 tons full load		6 12.75-inch (324-mm) torpedo tubes Mk 32 (2 triple)
	CG 52–73 9,466 tons full load	**Radars:**	SPS-49(V)6 air search
Length:	532⅔ feet (162.4 m) waterline		SPS-53 surface search in CG 47, 48
	567 feet (172.9 m) overall		SPS-55 surface search
Beam:	55 feet (16.75 m)		SPS-64 navigation in CG 49–73
Draft:	31½ feet (9.6 m)		(4) SPY-1A multi-function in CG 47–58
Propulsion:	4 gas turbines (General Electric LM 2500); 80,000 shp; 2 shafts		(4) SPY-1B multi-function in CG 59–73
Speed:	30+ knots	**Sonars:**	SQS-53A bow mounted in CG 47–55
Range:	6,000 n.miles (11,110 km) at 20 knots		SQS-53B bow mounted in CG 56–67
Manning:	approx. 385 (29 officers + 356 enlisted)		SQS-53C bow mounted in CG 68–73
Helicopters:	2 SH-2F LAMPS I in CG 47, 48		SQR-19 TACTAS in CG 54–73
	2 SH-60B Seahawk LAMPS III in CG 49–73	**Fire control:**	1 Mk 7 Aegis weapon system
Missiles:	2 twin Mk 26 Mod 1 launchers for Standard-MR SM-2/ASROC (88) in CG 47–51		1 Mk 86 GFCS with SPQ-9A radar
			4 Mk 99 missile directors with SPG-62 radar
	2 61-cell Mk 41 VLS for Standard-MR SM-2 and other weapons in CG 52–73		1 Mk 116 ASW FCS
			SQQ-89(V)3 ASW system in CG 54–73
	8 Harpoon SSM (2 quad canisters Mk 141)	**EW systems:**	SLQ-25 Nixie
			SLQ-32(V)3

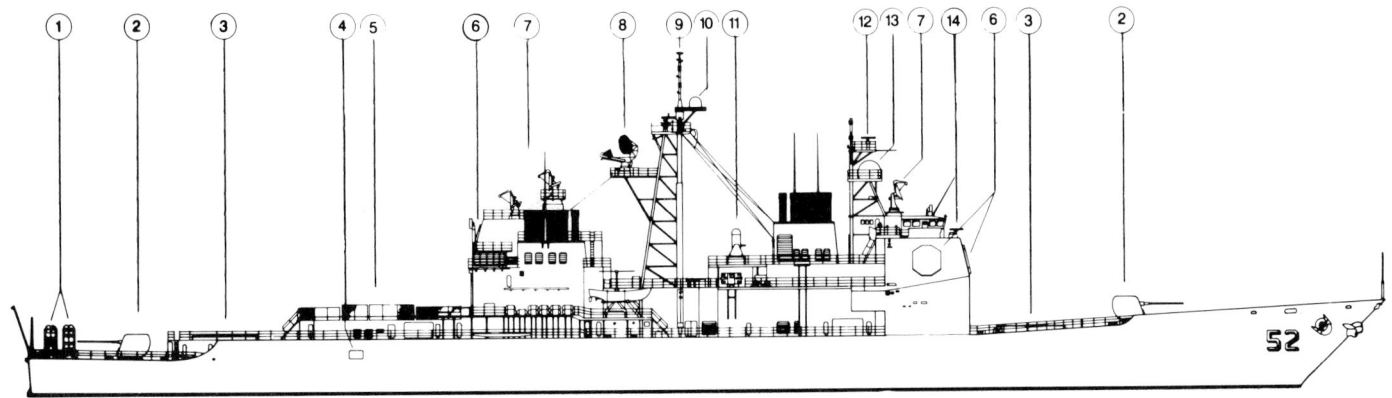

BUNKER HILL: 1. Harpoon canisters   2. 5-inch/54-cal single gun mount   3. Mk 41 Mod 0 vertical missile launcher   4. Mk 32 torpedo tubes (behind shutters)   5. helicopter deck   6. SPY-1A radar   7. SPG-62 illuminator   8. SPS-49(V)6 radar   9. URN-25 TACAN   10. SQQ-28 LAMPS datalink antenna   11. 20-mm Phalanx CIWS   12. SPS-55 radar   13. SPQ-9A radar   14. SPS-64 radar (A.D. Baker III)

These are the world's most capable AAW ships, developed to provide carrier battle group defense against aircraft and anti-ship missiles. In addition, the ships have major ASW and strike capabilities. The BUNKER HILL and later ships are fitted with vertical launchers for the Tomahawk anti-ship/land-attack missiles as well as vertical-launch ASROC and Standard anti-aircraft missiles, making these highly versatile warships.

The Ingalls-built ships are launched from a floating dock; their christening—public relations—ceremony is held at a later date. Some of these ships received administrative commissioning ceremonies at their building yard; their formal commissioning dates are listed above (e.g., the BUNKER HILL was formally commissioned in Boston).

The BUNKER HILL and MOBILE BAY are both home-ported in Yokosuka, Japan.

Class: This is the largest cruiser class built by any Navy in the post–World War II period. The only other cruiser class of this size built by any nation was the 27-ship CLEVELAND (CL 55) class of light cruisers, built for the U.S. Navy, completed 1942–1946.[2]

When conceived, these ships were intended to complement the nuclear-propelled strike cruiser (CSGN), which also was to be fitted with the Aegis AAW system. However, the Congress refused to fund the strike cruiser, and only the conventionally propelled CG 47 class was built. The Aegis system was subsequently fitted in the ARLEIGH BURKE class; see chapter 16.

Classification: These ships were changed from guided missile destroyers (DDG with same hull numbers) to guided missile cruisers on 1 January 1980 to better reflect their capabilities and cost.

Cost: The Department of Defense selected acquisition report for late 1991 gave a current-year program cost for the 27 ships of $23.316 *billion* or an average of $863.55 million per ship.

Design: SCB No. 226. These ships are based on the SPRUANCE design, employing the same hull and propulsion plant. The superstructure has been enlarged to accommodate the Aegis/SPY-1 equipment, with two fixed-array radar antennas on the forward deckhouse facing forward and to starboard, and two on the after deckhouse, facing aft and to port. Internal changes include limited armor plating for the magazine and critical electronic spaces, increases in the ship's service generators from three 2,000 kw to three 2,500 kw, additional accommodations, and additional fuel tanks.

During construction the design was changed to provide higher exhaust stacks and a bow bulwark, the latter required to reduce water over the bow due to the greater draft compared to the SPRUANCE class.

The VINCENNES and later ships have tripod (vice quadrapod) lattice masts, providing a reduction of some nine tons in topside weight.

---

2. In addition, one CLEVELAND was cancelled and nine were converted to light carriers (CVL); nine modified CLEVELANDs were planned, with only two completed in 1945–1946, the CL 106 and CL 107.

Electronics: All ships have the SQR-17 sonar data processor.

Helicopters: The LAMPS III ships have the RAST helicopter-hauldown system (see OLIVER HAZARD PERRY/FFG 7 class). The sizes of the twin helicopter hangars in these ships vary; they are approximately 39 feet (11.9 m) long, 26½ to 29 feet (8.1 to 8.8 m) wide, and 14⅓ to 15½ feet (4.35 to 4.7 m) high.

Manning: The crews for these ships vary from 26 to 34 officers, and from 331 to 382 enlisted.

Missiles: The Vertical Launching System (VLS) provides the later TICONDEROGA-class ships with a Tomahawk launch capability. The BUNKER HILL was the first U.S. naval ship other than the missile test ship NORTON SOUND (AVM 1) to launch a missile from a VLS installation, on 20 May 1986.

All ships have Harpoon canisters.

Modernization: A proposed update for this class includes the provision of five-foot (1.5 m) blisters on either side along about three-fifths of the ship length; this would provide additional side protection from anti-ship missiles. The shear line of the weather deck would be raised. The blisters would increase displacement and reduce maximum speed by less than one knot.

Names: All ships of this class are named for battles except for the CG 51, named for a deceased Secretary of the Navy and Secretary of Defense. (Other Secretaries of the Navy are remembered by destroyers and cruisers, the former having been named for secretaries when they were built as DLG "frigates" in the destroyer family; the only other Secretaries of Defense to have had Navy ships named in their honor were James V. Forrestal, also a former Secretary of the Navy, and George C. Marshall.)

Most of these ships also remember World War II–era aircraft carriers of the ESSEX (CV 9) and INDEPENDENCE (CVL 22) classes (also see WASP/LHD 1 class amphibious ships). The CG 66 is the second U.S. warship to be named for a battle of the Vietnam War; the PELELIU (LHA 5) was originally named DA NANG, but that ship was renamed on 15 February 1978 after the fall of the Republic of (South) Vietnam to Communist forces.

Three ships were renamed during construction; the CG 65 and CG 66 traded names; the CG 69 was originally PORT ROYAL.

Operational: The VINCENNES shot down an Iranian airliner on 3 July 1988 over the southern Persian Gulf. All 290 passengers and crew were killed. The VINCENNES's combat information center had identified the target as probably an Iranian F-14 Tomcat making a dive on the ship. Two Standard missiles were fired.

Seven ships of this class fired 105 Tomahawk missiles during Operation Desert Storm:

BUNKER HILL	28 missiles
MOBILE BAY	22 missiles
LEYTE GULF	2 missiles
SAN JACINTO	14 missiles
PHILIPPINE SEA	10 missiles
PRINCETON	3 missiles
NORMANDY	26 missiles

The YORKTOWN shows the twin Mk 26 missile launchers of the first five cruisers of this class. The stem anchor indicates that the ship has a large bow-mounted sonar dome; there is a second anchor on the starboard side. The substitution of VLS in later ships increases missile payload from 88 to 122 weapons (plus Harpoons). (1991, Giorgio Arra)

The stern of the THOMAS S. GATES—the only U.S. cruiser to be named for a person—showing one of the two large LAMPS hangars open. Note the asymmetrical arrangement of SPY-1A radar antennas on the forward and after deckhouses; an OE-82 satellite antenna is fitted on the starboard side of the hangar. (1991, Giorgio Arra)

These missiles represented 36 percent of the Tomahawks fired during the conflict. Although there were widely circulated reports that the SAN JACINTO, which departed Norfolk, Va., on 15 August 1990, carried only Tomahawk missiles in her VLS, she in fact deployed to Desert Storm with both Standard anti-air and Tomahawk missiles in her launch cells.

During the Gulf War, on 18 February 1991, the PRINCETON struck a bottom-laid influence mine that damaged the ship (a second mine was detonated by the explosion of the first). The damage to the

PRINCETON required her being towed to port, although at no time was the ship in danger of sinking and most of her combat systems remained operational. (The ship could have proceeded under her own power, but the commanding officer decided on the tow to avoid strain on the ship's hull until an examination could be made in a dockyard.) Repairs were made during a seven-week "availability" at Dubai in the United Arab Emirates followed by a two-month yard period in the United States.

4 NUCLEAR-PROPELLED GUIDED MISSILE CRUISERS: "VIRGINIA" CLASS

Number	Name	FY	Builder	Laid down	Launched	Commissioned	Status
CGN 38	VIRGINIA*	70	Newport News Shipbuilding	19 Aug 1972	14 Dec 1974	11 Sep 1976	**AA**
CGN 39	TEXAS	71	Newport News Shipbuilding	18 Aug 1973	9 Aug 1975	10 Sep 1977	**PA**
CGN 40	MISSISSIPPI*	72	Newport News Shipbuilding	22 Feb 1975	31 July 1976	5 Aug 1978	**AA**
CGN 41	ARKANSAS	75	Newport News Shipbuilding	17 Jan 1977	21 Oct 1978	18 Oct 1980	**PA**

Displacement:	10,400 tons light	Guns:	2 5-inch (127-mm) 54-cal DP Mk 45 (2 single)
	11,300 tons full load		2 20-mm Phalanx CIWS Mk 16 (2 multi-barrel)
Length:	585 feet (178.4 m) overall	ASW weapons:	ASROC fired from forward Mk 26 launcher
Beam:	63 feet (19.2 m)		6 12.75-inch (324-mm) torpedo tubes Mk 32 (2 triple)
Draft:	31½ feet (9.6 m)	Radars:	LN-66 navigation
Propulsion:	2 steam turbines; approx. 60,000 shp; 2 shafts		SPS-40B air search in CGN 38, 39
Reactors:	2 pressurized-water D2G (General Electric)		SPS-48C 3-D air search
Speed:	30+ knots		SPS-49(V) air search in CGN 40, 41
Manning:	CGN 38 617 (46 officers + 571 enlisted)		SPS-55 surface search
	CGN 39 568 (36 officers + 532 enlisted)	Sonars:	SQS-53A bow mounted
	CGN 40 630 (42 officers + 588 enlisted)	Fire control:	1 Mk 14 weapon direction system
	CGN 41 581 (48 officers + 533 enlisted)		1 Mk 86 GFCS with SPG-60D and SPQ-9A radars
Helicopters:	VERTREP area only (see notes)		1 Mk 74 missile FCS
Missiles:	2 twin Mk 26 Mod 0/1 launchers for Standard-MR SM-2 SAM (68)		1 Mk 116 ASW FCS
	4 Harpoon SSM (2 quad canisters Mk 141)		2 SPG-51D radar
	16 Tomahawk TASM/TLAM (2 quad ABL Mk 143)	EW systems:	SLQ-25 Nixie
			SLQ-32(V)3

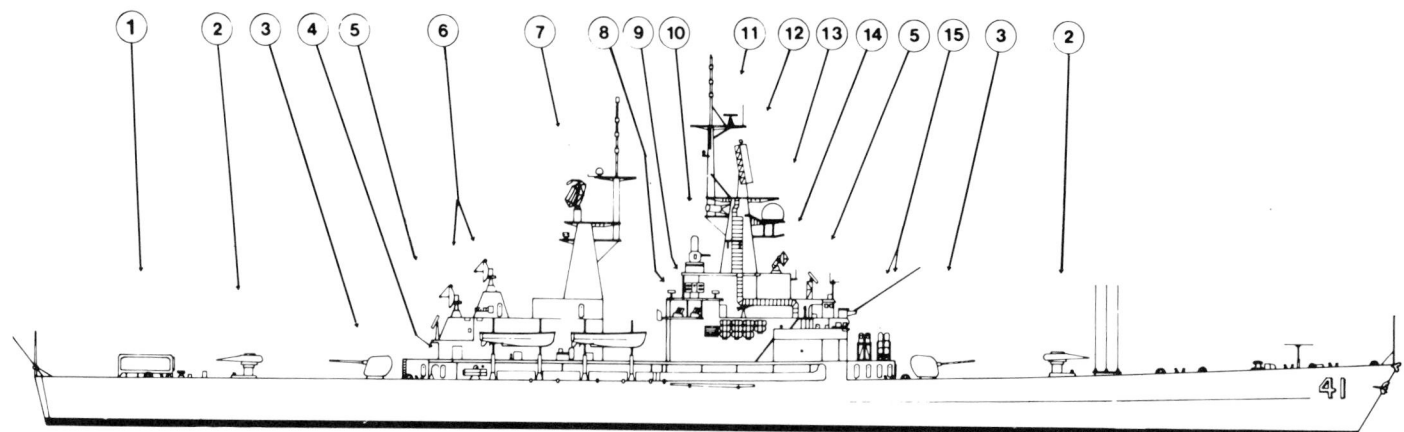

ARKANSAS 1. Tomahawk ABL   2. Mk 26 missile launcher   3. 5-inch/54-cal single gun mount   4. Mk 32 torpedo tubes   5. OE-82 SATCOMM antenna
6. SPG-51D radar director   7. SPS-40B radar   8. Mk 36 SRBOC chaff launchers   9. SLQ-32(V)3 ECM antenna   10. 20-mm Phalanx CIWS   11. SPS-55
radar   12. SPS-48B radar   13. SPQ-9A radar   14. SPG-60D radar director   15. Harpoon canisters

These were the last nuclear-propelled surface combatants to be built for the U.S. Navy.[3] The ARKANSAS and TEXAS were reassigned from the Atlantic to the Pacific in 1983, accompanying the shift of the nuclear carrier VINSON (CVN 70) to the Pacific Fleet.

Class: The number of nuclear fleet escorts proposed for the fleet has varied considerably, apparently reaching a peak of 28 ships in Navy program proposals of 1970—the cruiser LONG BEACH, the four then-DLGN ships already built and under construction plus 23 of the DXGN design, which evolved into the VIRGINIA class. This ambitious program was soon reduced to more fiscally possible numbers, and in May 1971 the Department of Defense decided to hold this class at three ships (then DLGN 38–40), i.e., a total of eight CGN/DLGNs to provide escorts for two all-nuclear carrier groups. Subsequent Navy efforts to garner support for nuclear ships led to congressional funding of a fourth ship (DLGN 41) and for long-lead components of a fifth ship (DLGN 42) that was to be authorized in fiscal 1975. However, Congress then declined to fund the latter ship when the Navy proposed the more-capable strike cruiser (CSGN) for later construction and the DLGN/CGN 42 was never built.

3. From 1980 to 1991 the Soviet Navy completed four guided missile battle cruisers of the 28,000-ton KIROV class. See N. Polmar, *Guide to the Soviet Navy* (Annapolis, Md.: Naval Institute Press, 1991), pp. 148–152.

Classification: CGN 38–40 were originally classified as frigates (DLGN 38–40); they were changed to cruisers on 30 June 1975. The ARKANSAS was ordered as CGN 41.

Design: These ships are of an improved design, superior to the previous CALIFORNIA class with Mk 26 missile launchers and provision for a helicopter hangar and elevator in their stern. These were the first U.S. ships built since World War II to have the latter feature.

Helicopters: As built, the ships had a stern hangar with a folding hatch cover and elevator arrangement to accommodate a single SH-2F LAMPS. The hangar was 42 feet (12.8 m) long, 14 feet (4.3 m) wide, and 14¼ feet (4.3 m) high. The ships encountered problems both in keeping the hangars watertight and with the elevators. Accordingly, in the early 1980s the decision was made to delete the helicopters in favor of the Tomahawk box launchers. The ships have small VERTREP areas forward and on the fantail.

Guns: Two Phalanx CIWS have been installed in each ship.

Missiles: These ships have been fitted with Tomahawk cruise missiles in armored box launchers on the fantail, aft of the second Mk 26 launcher. Earlier proposals to provide a VLS for Tomahawk missiles in place of the hangar were dropped.

The VIRGINIA and her sister ships are attractive warships. The four later nuclear cruisers are easily distinguished from the previous CALIFORNIA class, the earlier ships having a separate ASROC launcher and reload housing forward; the later ships now have Tomahawk box launchers on the fantail (covering over the helicopter hangar). (1990, Giorgio Arra)

Note that the Harpoon canisters are installed forward of the bridge, on the 01 level.

Modernization: From the late 1980s these ships have had a weapons upgrade, although they did not receive a full New Threat Upgrade (NTU) modernization. Their Mk 13 weapons-direction system was replaced by the Mk 14; the SPS-40B radar replaced by the SPS-49(V); and SPS-48B upgraded to the SPS-48C variant.

Three Refueling/Complex Overhauls (RCOH) for this class have been scheduled—the VIRGINIA to be funded in fiscal 1994, the MISSISSIPPI in fiscal 1996, and the ARKANSAS in fiscal 1997. The RCOH—the nuclear community's term for a SLEP-type effort—will include a general modernization, including the full NTU. This work will probably be done at the Newport News yard.

Operational: The VIRGINIA fired two Tomahawk missiles and the MISSISSIPPI launched five during Operation Desert Storm in 1991; these amounted to 2 percent of the TLAM missiles fired in the war. (The only other cruisers to launch Tomahawks in the conflict were TICONDEROGA-class ships.)

The superstructure of the MISSISSIPPI showing the Harpoon canisters crossed forward of the bridge on the 01 level. The Phalanx CIWS are fitted at the after end of the bridge, in an elevated position; the SLQ-32(V)3 ECM antennas are installed below the CIWS mounts. (1988, Giorgio Arra)

The MISSISSIPPI at high speed. The tower-like "macks" (combined masts and stacks) are common to many U.S. and Russian warships; nuclear ships have exhaust stacks for their auxiliary machinery. Although far more capable than the earlier CALIFORNIA-class cruisers, these ships still lack a helicopter capability. (1991, Giorgio Arra)

The stern of the MISSISSIPPI showing Tomahawk ABLs on her fantail. In the 1970s it was proposed to complete the MISSISSIPPI with an Aegis radar/missile system and to backfit some or all of the other ships of the class. The proposal was rejected by supporters of the abortive strike cruiser (CSGN) program. (1988, Giorgio Arra)

2 NUCLEAR-PROPELLED GUIDED MISSILE CRUISERS: "CALIFORNIA" CLASS

Number	Name	FY	Builder	Laid down	Launched	Commissioned	Status
CGN 36	CALIFORNIA	67	Newport News Shipbuilding	23 Jan 1970	22 Sep 1971	16 Feb 1974	**PA**
CGN 37	SOUTH CAROLINA*	68	Newport News Shipbuilding	1 Dec 1970	1 July 1972	25 Jan 1975	**AA**

Displacement:	9,676 tons light		ASW weapons:	1 8-tube ASROC launcher Mk 16
	10,530 tons full load			4 12.75-inch (324-mm) torpedo tubes Mk 32 (4 fixed single)
Length:	596 feet (181.8 m) overall		Radars:	LN-66 navigation
Beam:	61 feet (18.6 m)			SPS-40B air search
Draft:	31½ feet (9.6 m)			SPS-48C 3-D air search
Propulsion:	2 steam turbines; approx. 60,000 shp; 2 shafts			SPS-67 surface search
Reactors:	2 pressurized-water D2G (General Electric)		Sonars:	SQS-26CX bow mounted
Speed:	30+ knots		Fire control:	1 Mk 14 weapon direction system
Manning:	CGN 36 634 (48 officers + 586 enlisted)			2 Mk 74 missile FCS
	CGN 37 639 (48 officers + 591 enlisted)			1 Mk 86 GFCS with SPG-60 and SPQ-9A radars
Helicopters:	VERTREP area only			1 Mk 114 ASW FCS
Missiles:	2 single Mk 13 Mod 3 launchers for Standard-MR SM-1 SAM (80)			4 SPG-51D radar
	4 Harpoon SSM (2 quad canisters Mk 141)		EW systems:	SLQ-25 Nixie
Guns:	2 5-inch (127-mm) 54-cal DP Mk 45 (2 single)			SLQ-32(V)3
	2 20-mm Phalanx CIWS Mk 16 (2 multi-barrel)			

These "double-end" ships are essentially nuclear-propelled versions of guided missile designs proposed in the early 1960s, with the so-called Tartar-D missile system vice the more-capable missile systems of other U.S. cruisers and some destroyer classes. Their construction was delayed because of opposition to nuclear ship construction by Secretary of Defense Robert McNamara and the fiscal demands of the Vietnam War. Funds for their construction were released only after strong congressional pressure.

This was the first class of nuclear-propelled surface warships intended for series production.

Class: A third ship of this design was authorized in fiscal year 1968 but was not built because of rising costs and the development of the more capable VIRGINIA design.

Classification: Both ships originally were classified as guided missile frigates (DLGN); they were cruisers on 30 June 1975.

Design: SCB No. 241. These ships have a large helicopter landing area aft, but no hangar or aviation maintenance facilities. They have a separate ASROC "box" launcher because the Mk 13 launchers cannot accommodate the anti-submarine rockets.

Their SCB number is part of the new SCB series (241.65).

Guns: Unlike earlier CG/CGN-type ships built with 5-inch guns, these ships were not built with a secondary gun battery of 3-inch/50-cal weapons.

Missiles: These are the Navy's only cruisers armed with the SM-1 series Standard missiles (née Tartar-D system).

No Tomahawk missiles are provided. The starboard-firing Harpoon canister is fitted amidships, between the "mack" structures, and the port-firing canister is at the after end of the superstructure, at the 01 level.

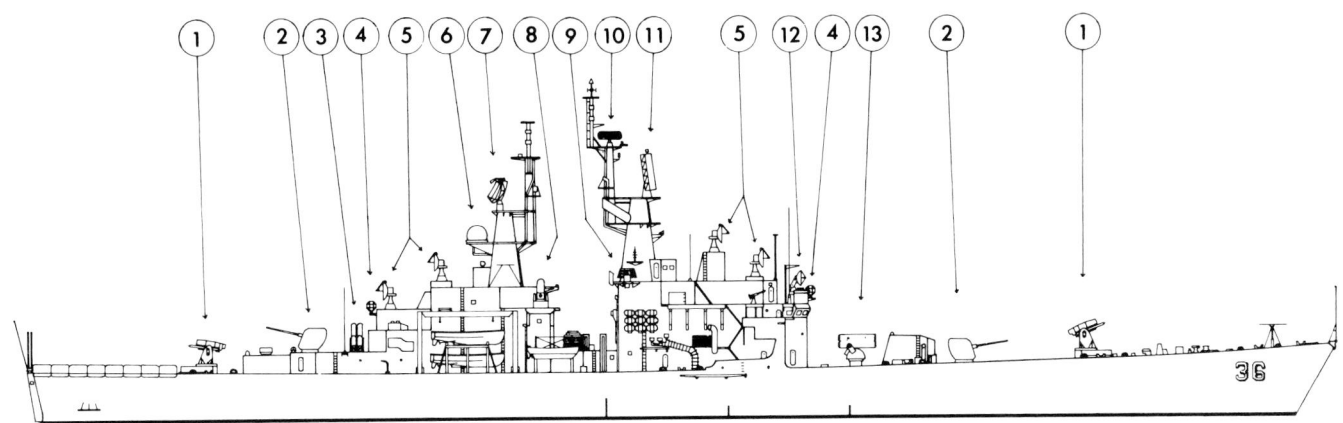

CALIFORNIA 1. Mk 26 missile launcher   2. 5-inch/54-cal single gun mount   3. Harpoon canisters   4. SATCOMM antenna   5. SPG-51D radar directors   6. SPQ-9A radar   7. SPS-40 radar   8. 20-mm Phalanx CIWS   9. SLQ-32(V)3 ECM antenna   10. SPS-10 radar   11. SPS-48C radar   12. SPG-60D radar director   13. ASROC rocket launcher

The SOUTH CAROLINA and her sister ship CALIFORNIA have the smallest missile armament of any U.S. cruisers. Their single-arm Mk 13 launchers for the Standard-MR SM-1 missile are also fitted in destroyers and frigates. The large ASROC launcher/magazine housing is between the 5-inch gun mount and the bridge. (1991, Giorgio Arra)

The SOUTH CAROLINA with an awning spread between her after 5-inch gun and Mk 13 missile launcher. The Harpoon canisters are aft, between the superstructure and the 5-inch gun mount; the Harpoons and gun mount are on the 01 level. Despite their large size, these ships were built without a helicopter hangar. (1991, Giorgio Arra)

1 NUCLEAR-PROPELLED GUIDED MISSILE CRUISER: "TRUXTUN"

Number	Name	FY	Builder	Laid down	Launched	Commissioned	Status
CGN 35	TRUXTUN	62	New York Shipbuilding, Camden, N.J.	17 June 1963	19 Dec 1964	27 May 1967	**AA**

Displacement:	8,322 tons light	ASW weapons:	ASROC fired from Mk 10 missile launcher
	9,127 tons full load		4 12.75-inch (324-mm) torpedo tubes Mk 32 (4 fixed single)
Length:	564 feet (172.0 m) overall	Radars:	LN-66 navigation
Beam:	58 feet (17.7 m)		SPS-40D air search
Draft:	31 feet (9.5 m)		SPS-48C 3-D air search
Propulsion:	2 steam turbines; approx. 60,000 shp; 2 shafts		SPS-67 surface search
Reactors:	2 pressurized-water D2G (General Electric)	Sonars:	SQS-26BX bow mounted
Speed:	30+ knots	Fire control:	1 Mk 14 weapon direction system
Manning:	549 (44 officers + 505 enlisted)		1 Mk 68 GFCS with SPG-53F radar
Helicopters:	1 SH-2F LAMPS I		2 Mk 76 missile FCS
Missiles:	1 twin Mk 10 Mod 8 launcher for Standard-ER SM-2 SAM (60)		1 Mk 114 ASW FCS
	8 Harpoon SSM (2 quad canisters Mk 141)		2 SPG-55C radars
Guns:	1 5-inch (127-mm) 54-cal DP Mk 42	EW systems:	SLQ-25 Nixie
	2 20-mm Phalanx CIWS Mk 16 (2 multi-barrel)		SLQ-32(V)3

The TRUXTUN was the U.S. Navy's fourth nuclear-propelled surface warship. The ship was requested by the Navy as one of seven oil-burning frigates in the fiscal 1962 program; however, the Congress directed that one of the ships have nuclear propulsion.

The ship will be decommissioned and laid up in 1995.

Classification: Originally classified as a guided missile frigate (DLGN); changed to cruiser (CGN) on 30 June 1975.

Design: SCB No. 222. The TRUXTUN was built to a modified BELKNAP-class design with the gun and missile-launcher positions reversed. The ship has a distinctive appearance with "four-legged" lattice masts replacing the "macks" of the oil-burning ships.

Guns: As built, the TRUXTUN additionally carried two 3-inch/50-cal AA single gun mounts amidships. They were deleted and the positions are now used for Harpoon missile canisters.

The Phalanx CIWS are mounted forward of the bridge.

Helicopters: The TRUXTUN's hangar is 40¾ feet (12.4 m) long, 19 feet (5.8 m) wide, and 14 feet (4.3 m) high.

Torpedoes: As built, the ship had two Mk 25 torpedo tubes built into the stern counter with ten reloads provided; they were subsequently removed. The Mk 32 tubes are built into the after deckhouse.

The TRUXTUN alongside a destroyer tender at the sprawling naval base in San Diego. No Harpoon canisters are fitted in the amidships "gun tub" visible on the starboard side. The missile canisters can be easily installed or removed. (1984, Giorgio Arra)

The one-of-a-kind TRUXTUN with two distinctive lattice masts atop the superstructure. The ship has the same armament as the BELKNAP class, but with the Mk 10 missile-launch and gun positions reversed. Both Phalanx CIWS mounts are installed forward of the bridge. (1986, Giorgio Arra)

8 GUIDED MISSILE CRUISERS: "BELKNAP" CLASS

Number	Name	FY	Builder	Laid down	Launched	Commissioned	Status
CG 27	JOSEPHUS DANIELS	61	Bath Iron Works, Maine	23 Apr 1962	2 Dec 1963	8 May 1965	**AA**
CG 28	WAINWRIGHT	61	Bath Iron Works, Maine	2 July 1962	25 Apr 1964	8 Jan 1966	**AA**
CG 29	JOUETT*	62	Puget Sound Naval Shipyard	25 Sep 1962	30 June 1964	3 Dec 1966	**PA**
CG 30	HORNE*	62	San Francisco Naval Shipyard	12 Dec 1962	30 Oct 1964	15 Apr 1967	**PA**
CG 31	STERETT	62	Puget Sound Naval Shipyard	25 Sep 1962	30 June 1964	8 Apr 1967	**PA**
CG 32	WILLIAM H. STANDLEY	62	Bath Iron Works, Maine	29 July 1963	19 Dec 1964	9 July 1966	**PA**
CG 33	FOX	62	Todd Shipyards, San Pedro, Calif.	15 Jan 1963	21 Nov 1964	28 May 1966	**PA**
CG 34	BIDDLE*	62	Bath Iron Works, Maine	9 Dec 1963	2 July 1965	21 Jan 1967	**AA**

Displacement:	6,570 tons standard	ASW weapons:	ASROC launched from Mk 10 missile launcher
	8,065 tons full load	Torpedoes:	6 12.75-inch (324-mm) torpedo tubes Mk 32 (2 triple)
Length:	547 feet (166.8 m) overall	Radars:	LN-66 navigation
Beam:	54¾ feet (16.7 m)		SPS-67 surface search
Draft:	28¾ feet (8.8 m)		SPS-48E 3-D air search
Propulsion:	2 steam turbines (General Electric in CG 27, 28, 32, 34; De Laval in		SPS-49(V)5 air search
	CG 29–31, 33); 85,000 shp; 2 shafts	Sonars:	SQS-26BX
Boilers:	4 1,200 psi (83.4 kg/cm²) (Babcock & Wilcox in CG 27, 28, 32, 34;	Fire control:	1 Mk 14 weapon direction system
	Combustion Engineering in CG 29–31, 33)		1 Mk 68 GFCS with SPG-53F radar
Speed:	33 knots		2 Mk 76 missile FCS
Range:	7,100 n.miles (13,150 km) at 20 knots		1 Mk 114 ASW FCS
Manning:	approx. 489 (29 officers + 460 enlisted)		2 SPG-55D radar
Helicopers:	1 SH-2F LAMPS I		1 SYS-2(V)1 weapon control system
Missiles:	1 twin Mk 10 Mod 7 launcher for Standard-ER SM-2 SAM (60)	EW systems:	T Mk 6 Fanfare
	8 Harpoon SSM (2 quad canisters Mk 141)		in CG 28–30, 32–34
Guns:	1 5-inch (127-mm) 54-cal DP Mk 42		
	2 20-mm Phalanx CIWS Mk 16 (2 multi-barrel)		

These are "single-end" guided missile cruisers built to screen aircraft carriers. Originally a class of nine ships, the BELKNAP is now listed separately in Navy documents because of the ship's extensive reconfiguration as a flagship and lack of AAW/ASW upgrade. All eight ships have undergone an AAW modernization under the New Threat Upgrade (NTU) program; see below.

The nuclear-propelled TRUXTUN is similar.

Classification: These ships were originally classified as guided missile frigates (DLG 27–34); they were changed to CG on 30 June 1975.

Design: SCB No. 212. These ships were built to an improved LEAHY-class design with a 5-inch gun substituted for the after missile launcher. The Mk 10 Mod 7 launcher has three 20-round magazine "rings" compared to two 20-missile rings in the previous class, thus partially compensating for the reduction in launchers.

Guns: Two 3-inch/50-cal AA single gun mounts that were originally mounted amidships have been removed, with quad Harpoon missile canisters fitted in their place. The installation of the Harpoon canisters and Phalanx CIWS are asymmetrical; see photographs.

Helicopters: The helicopter hangar in these ships varies in size; most are approximately 43 feet (13.1 m) long, 14 feet (4.3 m) wide, and 14 feet (4.3 m) high; the JOUETT and STANDLEY have hangars approximately 55 feet (16.8 m) long.

Manning: The crews for these ships vary from 25 to 31 officers, and from 445 to 478 enlisted.

Missiles: The WAINWRIGHT was the first ship to be fitted with the SM-2 version of the Standard missile, conducting evaluation of that missile in 1977.

Modernization: All eight ships have had their AAW capability modernized under the NTU program. The CG 34 completed in 1987, CG 29 and 30 in 1989, CG 28, 32, and 33 in 1990; CG 27 and 31 1991.

The principal changes are:
- SPS-10F radar replaced by SPS-67
- SPS-48C radar replaced by SPS-48E
- installation of SYS-2 weapon control system
- upgrade of missile system to SM-2 NTU

In addition, the CG 28, 30, and 31 were fitted with the tactical flag communications center in 1983–1985.

Torpedoes: As built, these ships had two Mk 25 torpedo tubes in their after superstructure—angled out, one to starboard and one to port. They have been removed.

The JOUETT is typical of the large "single-end" cruisers of the BELKNAP class. The arrangement of Phalanx CIWS and Harpoon canisters on the port and starboard side are asymmetrical—Harpoons forward of the Phalanx on the port side and the reverse to starboard. (1991, Giorgio Arra)

The BELKNAPS have a helicopter landing deck, hangar, and 5-inch gun aft in place of the second Mk 10 missile launcher in the earlier LEAHY class. This stern view of the JOSEPHUS DANIELS shows the helicopter control position on the starboard side of the hangar. (1989, Giorgio Arra)

The BIDDLE was the last fossil-fuel-burning cruiser to be build for the U.S. Navy for 16 years. The large, angled structure behind the Mk 10 missile launcher connects with the three-ring missile magazine below decks. (1988, Giorgio Arra)

1 GUIDED MISSILE CRUISER-FLAGSHIP: "BELKNAP" CLASS

Number	Name	FY	Builder	Laid down	Launched	Commissioned	Status
CG 26	BELKNAP	61	Bath Iron Works, Maine	5 Feb 1962	20 July 1963	7 Nov 1964	**AA**

Displacement:	6,570 tons standard	Guns:	1 5-inch (127-mm) 54-cal DP Mk 42
	8,950 tons full load		2 20-mm Phalanx CIWS Mk 16 (2 multi-barrel)
Length:	547 feet (166.8 m) overall	ASW weapons:	ASROC launched from Mk 10 missile launcher
Beam:	54¾ feet (16.7 m)	Torpedoes:	6 12.75-inch (324-mm) torpedo tubes Mk 32 (2 triple)
Draft:	32 feet (9.75 m)	Radars:	SPS-48C 3-D air search
Propulsion:	2 steam turbines (General Electric) 85,000 shp; 2 shafts		SPS-49(V)3 air search
Boilers:	4 1,200 psi (83.4 kg/cm²) (Babcock & Wilcox)		SPS-67 surface search
Speed:	33 knots	Sonars:	SQS-53A
Range:	7,100 n.miles (13,150 km) at 20 knots	Fire control:	1 Mk 11 weapon direction system
Manning:	512 (26 officers + 486 enlisted)		1 Mk 68 GFCS with SPG-53F radar
Flag:	approx. 160		2 Mk 76 missile FCS
Helicopters:	landing area		1 Mk 116 ASW FCS
Missiles:	1 twin Mk 10 Mod 7 launcher for Standard-ER SM-2 SAM (60)		2 SPG-55D radar
	8 Harpoon SSM (2 quad canisters Mk 141)	EW systems:	SLQ-25 Nixie
			SLQ-32(V)3

The BELKNAP is a "single-end" missile cruiser that has been extensively modified to serve as flagship of the Sixth Fleet in the Mediterranean. She is home-ported at Gaeta, Italy.

The BELKNAP was severely damaged in a collision with the carrier JOHN F. KENNEDY (CV 67) in the Ionian Sea on the night of 22 November 1975. The cruiser was rebuilt at the Philadelphia Naval Shipyard, arriving at the yard on 30 January 1976 and returning to sea in April 1980 (recommissioned on 10 May 1980).

Classification: The ship was originally classified as a guided missile frigate (DLG 26); changed to CG on 30 June 1975.

Conversion: The ship was extensively modified to serve as a numbered fleet flagship at the Norfolk Naval Shipyard from May 1985 to February 1986. On 7 July 1986 the BELKNAP became flagship for the Sixth Fleet in the Mediterranean (replacing the CORONADO/AGF 11).

The ship was provided with a fleet command center (war room), improved communications, drafting and photographic facilities, addi-

tional berthing and messing, an office and reception area for the fleet commander, and expansion of the landing area to permit operation of an SH-3 Sea King helicopter. The ship's hangar has been converted to a berthing area.

The ship will not receive the NTU anti-air warfare modernization.

Design: SCB No. 212. See BELKNAP-class entry (above) for additional data.

Guns: Two 3-inch/50-cal AA single gun mounts that were originally mounted were removed, with quad Harpoon missile canisters fitted in their place. The installation of the Harpoon canisters and Phalanx CIWS are asymmetrical.

Helicopters: The BELKNAP retains a helicopter landing area aft and has a small VERTREP area forward. An SH-3G is usually embarked.

Torpedoes: As built, the BELKNAP had two Mk 25 torpedo tubes in her after superstructure—angled out, one to starboard and one to port. They have been removed.

The BELKNAP as modified to serve as Sixth Fleet flagship. The ship has a large deckhouse amidships and an extension to the front of the bridge, with the helicopter hangar converted to berthing spaces. The other numbered fleets have amphibious-type ships as flagships. (U.S. Navy)

Into the early 1980s the BAINBRIDGE carried an outdated SPS-39 3-D radar forward and an SPS-37 air search radar amidships. In this view the ship has an SPS-48C forward and SPS-49 amidships—both highly capable radars. (1990, L. Van Ginderen collection)

1 NUCLEAR-PROPELLED GUIDED MISSILE CRUISER: "BAINBRIDGE"

Number	Name	FY	Builder	Laid down	Launched	Commissioned	Status
CGN 25	BAINBRIDGE	59	Bethlehem Steel, Quincy, Mass.	15 May 1959	15 Apr 1961	6 Oct 1962	**PA**

Displacement:	8,000 tons light	Guns:	2 20-mm Phalanx CIWS Mk 16 (2 multi-barrel)
	9,100 tons full load	ASW weapons:	1 8-tube ASROC launcher Mk 16
Length:	549$^{11}/_{12}$ feet (167.65 m) waterline	Torpedoes:	6 12.75-inch (324-mm) torpedo tubes Mk 32 (2 triple)
	564$^{5}/_{6}$ feet (172.2 m) overall	Radar:	1 LN-66 navigation
Beam:	57$^{2}/_{3}$ feet (17.6 m)		SPS-48C 3-D air search
Draft:	31$^{1}/_{6}$ feet (9.5 m)		SPS-49(V) air search
Propulsion:	2 steam turbines; 60,000 shp; 2 shafts		SPS-67 surface search
Reactors:	2 pressurized-water D2G (General Electric)	Sonars:	SQQ-23 bow mounted
Speed:	30+ knots	Fire control:	1 Mk 14 weapon direction system
Range:	90,000 n.miles (166,680 km) at 20 knots		4 Mk 76 missile FCS
Manning:	565 (31 officers + 534 enlisted)		1 Mk 111 ASW FCS
Helicopters:	VERTREP area only		4 SPG-55C radars
Missiles:	2 twin Mk 10 Mod 5/6 launchers for Standard-ER SM-2 SAM (80)	EW systems:	SLQ-32(V)3
	8 Harpoon SSM (2 quad canisters Mk 141)		

The BAINBRIDGE was the U.S. Navy's third nuclear-propelled surface escort ship. She differs from the later TRUXTUN in being a "double-end" missile ship and in not having a 5-inch gun and helicopter-support capability.

The ship will be decommissioned in 1996.

Classification: Originally classified as a guided missile frigate (DLGN 25); changed to cruiser on 30 June 1975.

Design: SCB No. 189. No ASROC reloads are provided.

Electronics: The ship received a belated update of electronic systems, especially radars, in a yard period from October 1983 to April 1985.

Guns: The two 3-inch/50-cal AA twin mounts previously fitted amidships have been removed. Single 20-mm guns were mounted as the ship's only gun armament from 1978 until the Phalanx CIWS were installed during the 1983–1985 yard period.

Modernization: The BAINBRIDGE had an AAW upgrade from June 1974–September 1976.

The BAINBRIDGE has a built-up amidships structure to provide more space for berthing and electronics equipment. The lattice masts are less predominant than those in the TRUXTUN. The large SPG-55C missile directors—two forward and two aft—dominate the ship's superstructure. (1988, Giorgio Arra)

The BAINBRIDGE is a "double-end" missile cruiser and the world's smallest nuclear-propelled surface warship. She is similar in appearance to the LEAHY class, but without the "macks" of the oil-burning ships. (1988, Giorgio Arra)

9 GUIDED MISSILE CRUISERS: "LEAHY" CLASS

Number	Name	FY	Builder	Laid down	Launched	Commissioned	Status
CG 16	LEAHY	58	Bath Iron Works, Maine	3 Dec 1959	1 July 1961	4 Aug 1962	**PA**
CG 17	HARRY E. YARNELL	58	Bath Iron Works, Maine	31 May 1960	9 Dec 1961	2 Feb 1963	**AA**
CG 18	WORDEN*	58	Bath Iron Works, Maine	19 Sep 1960	2 June 1962	3 Aug 1963	**PA**
CG 19	DALE	59	New York Shipbuilding, Camden, N.J.	6 Sep 1960	28 July 1962	23 Nov 1962	**AA**
CG 20	RICHMOND K. TURNER*	59	New York Shipbuilding, Camden, N.J.	9 Jan 1961	6 Apr 1963	13 June 1964	**AA**
CG 21	GRIDLEY	59	Puget Sound Bridge & Dry Dock, Wash.	15 July 1960	31 July 1961	25 May 1963	**PA**
CG 22	ENGLAND*	59	Todd Shipyards, San Pedro, Calif.	4 Oct 1960	6 Mar 1962	7 Dec 1962	**PA**
CG 23	HALSEY	59	San Francisco Naval Shipyard	26 Aug 1960	15 Jan 1962	20 July 1963	**PA**
CG 24	REEVES	59	Puget Sound Naval Shipyard	1 July 1960	12 May 1962	15 May 1964	**PA**

Displacement:	6,070 tons light	Guns:	2 20-mm Phalanx CIWS Mk 16 (2 multi-barrel)
	8,200 tons full load	ASW weapons:	1 8-tube ASROC launcher Mk 16
Length:	533 feet (162.5 m) overall		6 12.75-inch (324-mm) torpedo tubes Mk 32 (2 triple)
Beam:	55 feet (16.8 m)	Radars:	SPS-10F or SPS-67 surface search
Draft:	25 feet (7.6 m)		SPS-48C/E 3-D air search
Propulsion:	2 steam turbines (General Electric in CG 16–18, De Laval in CG		SPS-49(V)5 air search
	19–22, Allis-Chalmers in CG 23–24); 85,000 shp; 2 shafts	Sonars:	SQQ-23B PAIR
Boilers:	4 1,200 psi (83.4 kg/cm²) (Babcock & Wilcox in CG 16–18, Foster	Fire control:	1 Mk 14 weapon direction system
	Wheeler in CG 19–24)		4 Mk 76 missile FCS
Speed:	33 knots		1 Mk 114 ASW FCS
Range:	8,000 n.miles (14,815 km) at 20 knots		4 SPG-55B radars
Manning:	approx. 432 (26 officers + 406 enlisted)		1 SYS-2(V)1 weapon control system
Helicopters:	VERTREP area only	EW systems:	SLQ-25 Nixie except T Mk 6 Fanfare in CG 17
Missiles:	2 twin Mk 10 Mod 5/6 launchers for Standard-ER SM-2 SAM (80)		SLQ-32(V)3
	8 Harpoon SSM (2 quad canisters Mk 141)		

These are "double-end" missile cruisers, the smallest U.S. Navy ships currently classified as cruisers. All ships of this class have been modernized under the New Threat Upgrade (NTU) program.

Classification: These ships were built as guided missile frigates (DLG 16–24); they were changed to cruisers on 30 June 1975.

Design: SCB No. 172. This class introduced the "mack" superstructure (combination masts and exhausts stacks) to U.S. warships. No ASROC reloads are provided.

Guns: As built, all ships of this class had two 3-inch/50-cal AA twin mounts amidships. They have been removed, with Harpoon missile canisters fitted in their place.

Manning: The crews for these ships vary from 22 to 33 officers, and from 375 to 442 enlisted men.

Modernization: See BELKNAP-class entry for information on NTU program. The upgrades were completed 1987–1990.

The HARRY E. YARNELL at high speed off Norfolk. The ten ships of this class have been modernized under the NTU program; however, force-level cutbacks may cause their being decommissioned during the 1990s. These ships lack an effective ASW/helicopter capability. (1988, Giorgio Arra)

The YARNELL without Harpoons installed; they are normally fitted on the main deck, immediately behind the Phalanx CIWS. The SLQ-32(V)3 ECM antennas are mounted high in these ships, above the bridge structure. Each ''mack'' has two exhaust stacks. (1988, Giorgio Arra)

The DALE showing the long and relatively lower superstructure of the LEAHY class. These were the U.S. Navy's first new-construction ''double-end'' missile ships; three heavy cruisers (CA) were converted in the same period to double-end missile cruisers of the ALBANY class. (1990, Giorgio Arra)

1 NUCLEAR-PROPELLED GUIDED MISSILE CRUISER: "LONG BEACH"

Number	Name	FY	Builder	Laid down	Launched	Commissioned	Status
CGN 9 (ex-CLGN/CGN 160)	LONG BEACH	57	Bethlehem Steel, Quincy, Mass.	2 Dec 1957	14 July 1959	9 Sep 1961	PA

Displacement:	15,540 tons light	Guns:	2 5-inch (127-mm) 38-cal DP Mk 30 (2 single)
	17,525 tons full load		2 20-mm Phalanx CIWS Mk 16 (2 multi-barrel)
Length:	720¾ feet (219.75 m) overall	ASW weapons:	1 8-tube ASROC launcher Mk 16
Beam:	73¼ feet (22.35 m)		6 12.75-inch (324-mm) torpedo tubes Mk 32 (2 triple)
Draft:	31⅛ feet (9.5 m)	Radars:	LN-66 navigation
Propulsion:	4 steam turbines (General Electric); approx. 80,000 shp; 2 shafts		SPS-48C 3-D air search
Reactors:	2 pressurized-water C1W (Westinghouse)		SPS-49(V)3 air search
Speed:	30.5 knots		SPS-67 surface search
Range:	approx. 90,000 n.miles (166,680 km) at 30 knots	Sonars:	SQQ-23B PAIR keel mounted
	approx. 360,000 n.miles (666,720 km) at 20 knots	Fire control:	1 Mk 14 weapon direction system
Manning:	871 (63 officers + 808 enlisted)		2 Mk 56 GFCS with Mk 35 radar
Flag:	68 (10 officers + 58 enlisted)		4 Mk 76 missile FCS
Helicopters:	landing area only		1 Mk 111 ASW FCS
Missiles:	2 twin Mk 10 Mod 1/2 launchers for Standard-ER SM-2 SAM (120)		4 SPG-55D radars
	8 Harpoon SSM (2 quad canisters Mk 141)		2 SPW-2B radars
	8 Tomahawk TASM/TLAM (2 quad ABL Mk 143)	EW systems:	SLQ-32(V)3
			T Mk 6 Fanfare

The LONG BEACH was the world's first nuclear-propelled surface warship (the Soviet icebreaker LENIN was completed in September 1959). The LONG BEACH was the first U.S. cruiser to be constructed since World War II and the world's first warship to be built with guided missiles as the main battery.

The ship will be decommissioned in 1994 and laid up in reserve.

Classification: The LONG BEACH was ordered as a guided missile light cruiser (CLGN 160) on 15 October 1956, reclassified as a guided missile cruiser (CGN 160) on 6 December 1956, and renumbered CGN 9 on 1 July 1957.

Design: SCB No. 169. The LONG BEACH was initially proposed as a large destroyer or "frigate" (DLGN) of some 7,800 tons (standard displacement); her design subsequently was enlarged to accommodate additional missile systems to take maximum advantage of the benefits of nuclear propulsion.

Twenty ASROC missiles are provided.

Electronics: The ship was built with the fixed-array SPS-32 and SPS-33 radars mounted on the forward, square superstructure. The radars were difficult to maintain.

In the late 1970s it was proposed that the LONG BEACH be fitted with the Aegis weapon system. The fiscal 1978 budget provided $371 million to begin Aegis conversion. The Aegis AAW system would have included the fixed-array SPY-1A radars in the place of the existing SPS-32/33 radars (plus two Mk 26 missile launchers).

However, the conversion was cancelled because of concern that the new cruiser construction program would be reduced.

Instead, during the 1980 modernization the LONG BEACH received SPS-48C and SPS-49(V) radars in place of her SPS-32/33 radars. (The square island structure is retained with 1¾-inch/44.5 mm armor being fitted from the 05 to 08 levels.)

Engineering: The C1W reactors in the LONG BEACH are essentially the same as the A2Ws in the aircraft carrier ENTERPRISE.

Guns: As built, the LONG BEACH had no guns; subsequently, she was fitted with two 5-inch guns to provide minimal defense against attacks by subsonic aircraft or small craft. The Phalanx CIWS were later installed on the after superstructure.

Missiles: The LONG BEACH was built with a twin Talos Mk 12 launcher aft. It was removed in 1979 along with the associated Mk 77 missile FCS and SPG-49B and SPW-2B radars. Harpoon canisters were originally installed aft of the superstructure on the main deck. When the armored box launchers for Tomahawks were installed on the fantail in 1985 the Harpoons were moved to the after structure, on the 02 level alongside the lattice mast.

Mk 26 Standard missile launchers were to have been installed in place of the Mk 10 launchers during the planned Aegis conversion (see Electronics notes).

The original LONG BEACH design provided for the ship to carry the Regulus II strategic cruise missile and, after cancellation of that program in 1958, it was planned to provide launch tubes for eight Polaris SLBMs. In the event, neither weapon was installed.

Modernization: The LONG BEACH was extensively modernized at the Puget Sound Naval Shipyard from October 1980 through March 1983. The ship's two Mk 26 Terrier/Standard missile systems were upgraded as was the ship's combat systems. The SPS-32/33 3-D "billboard" radars were removed and the ship was fitted with conventional radars (as was the carrier ENTERPRISE/CVN 65, the only other ship that was fitted with SPS-32/33 radars).

The LONG BEACH was not followed by further large cruiser construction because of her high cost and the increasing capabilities of the smaller DLG/DLGN-type warships. Her distinctive superstructure was built to mount the fixed-array SPS-32/SPS-33 radars. (1986, Giorgio Arra)

The after superstructure of the LONG BEACH showing, from left, Tomahawk ABL "coffins," stepped Phalanx CIWS, and four Harpoon canisters (starboard side). Fifteen sealed life raft canisters are on the main deck, beneath the Phalanx CIWS. (1986, U.S. Navy)

The LONG BEACH was the world's first nuclear-propelled surface warship and the only U.S. ship actually built to a true cruiser design since World War II. In this view the uppermost portion of the mast has been removed to permit passage under the Coronado bridge at San Diego. (1986, U.S. Navy)

HEAVY CRUISERS: "DES MOINES" CLASS

Number	Name	Status
CA 134	DES MOINES	decomm. 14 July 1961; str. 9 July 1991
CA 139	SALEM	decomm. 30 Jan 1959; str. 12 July 1991
CA 148	NEWPORT NEWS	decomm. 27 June 1975; str. 31 July 1978

These were large, graceful heavy cruisers—the largest ships with 8-inch (203-mm) guns to be built by any nation, displacing 21,500 tons full load and 716½ feet (218.5 m) in length. They carried nine 8-inch gun Mk 16, a rapid-firing weapon that used metal cartridge cases in place of the bagged powder charges used in all other 8-inch and larger guns.

TABLE 15-3. GUIDED MISSILE CRUISERS

Number	Name	Notes
CAG 1	BOSTON (ex-CA 69)	reverted to CA 69; stricken 1973
CAG 2	CANBERRA (ex-CA 70)	reverted to CA 70; stricken 1978
CLG 3	GALVESTON (ex-CL 93)	stricken 1973
CLG 4	LITTLE ROCK (ex-CL 92)	changed to CG 4; stricken 1977
CLG 5	OKLAHOMA CITY (ex-CL 91)	changed to CG 5; stricken 1979
CLG 6	PROVIDENCE (ex-CL 82)	changed to CG 6; stricken 1978
CLG 7	SPRINGFIELD (ex-CL 66)	changed to CG 7; stricken 1978
CLG 8	TOPEKA (ex-CL 67)	stricken 1973
CGN 9	LONG BEACH (ex-CLGN/CGN 160)	
CG 10	ALBANY (ex-CA 123)	stricken 1985
CG 11	CHICAGO (ex-CA 136)	stricken 1984
CG 12	COLUMBUS (ex-CA 74)	stricken 1976
CG 13, 14	BALTIMORE class	conversions cancelled
CG 15	not used	
CG 16–24	LEAHY class (ex-DLG 16–24)	
CGN 25	BAINBRIDGE (ex-DLGN 25)	
CG 26–34	BELKNAP (ex-DLG 26–34)	
CGN 35	TRUXTUN (ex-DLGN 35)	
CGN 36, 37	CALIFORNIA class (ex DLGN 36, 37)	
CGN 38–41	VIRGINIA class (ex-DLGN 38–40)	
CGN 42	VIRGINIA class	cancelled
CG 43–46	not used	
CG 47–73	TICONDEROGA (ex-DDG 47) class	

World War II cruiser programs reached hull number CL 159 (with hulls 154–159 being cancelled in 1945). All heavy (CA), light (CL), and anti-aircraft (CLAA) cruisers were numbered in the same series. Only one ship was added to this series in the postwar period, the LONG BEACH, ordered as CLGN 160, changed to CGN 160, and completed as CGN 9. Further "cruiser" construction was halted in

Completed in 1948–1949, too late for service in World War II, all three ships were employed extensively as fleet flagships during their active careers. The NEWPORT NEWS saw service as a gunfire support ship in the Vietnam War and was the world's last heavy cruiser to see operational service.[4]

Class: Twelve ships of this class were planned, the CA 134, 139–143, and 148–153; only three ships were completed.

See 14th Edition/pages 134–135 for characteristics.

4. The NEWPORT NEWS outlasted by ten months the Spanish heavy cruiser CANARIAS, completed in 1936 with a main battery of eight 8-inch guns; she was paid off on 2 September 1974.

favor of the smaller and comparatively less expensive "frigates," which could carry most of a cruiser's armament.

One cruiser hull, the NORTHAMPTON, was completed as a command ship after the war. Begun as a heavy cruiser (CA 125), she was cancelled in 1945 when partially complete; reordered in 1948 and completed as a tactical command ship in 1953 (CLC 1) and later changed to a national command ship (CC 1). She was stricken on 1 December 1977.

The guided missile cruiser classifications were established in 1952 to reflect the specialized weapons and AAW roles of these ships. In 1975, 25 guided missile frigates (DLG/DLGN) were changed to cruisers, and in 1980 the Aegis-equipped destroyers were reclassified as cruisers; the latter ships began with CG 47, their former DDG number.

Two BALTIMORE (CA 68)-class 8-inch gun cruisers and six CLEVELAND-class 6-inch gun cruisers converted to a gun-missile configuration (CAG and CLG, respectively) have all been stricken, the last being the OKLAHOMA CITY, decommissioned on 15 December 1979 and stricken on 30 August 1982. The CAGs had twin Terrier launchers aft; the CLGs were fitted with either a single Talos or Terrier, with four of the CLGs especially modified to serve as numbered fleet flagships. The two CAGs lost their missile systems and reverted to CA designations during the Vietnam War; four of the CLGs were changed to CG in 1975, although all retained 6-inch and 5-inch guns forward.

Three other heavy cruisers were converted to all-missile configurations (CG 10–12), with two planned conversions being cancelled (CG 13, 14). Known as the ALBANY class, these too have been stricken, the last being the ALBANY on 30 June 1985.

See 13th Edition/page 130 for characteristics.

TABLE 15-4. HUNTER-KILLER CRUISERS

Number	Name	Notes
CLK 1	NORFOLK	completed as DL 1
CLK 2	NEW HAVEN	deferred 1949; cancelled 1951

After World War II the U.S. Navy established the classification of hunter-killer cruiser (CLK) for a planned series of small cruisers intended for ASW operations against high-speed submarines. Only the lead ship, the NORFOLK, was completed; she was reclassified as a frigate (DL) while under construction. She was employed mainly in ASW test and evaluation, being decommissioned on 15 January 1970 and stricken in 1973.

STRIKE CRUISERS

The strike cruiser (CSGN) was an outgrowth of the DLGN concept, developed in 1973–1974 as an enlarged DLGN intended specifically to carry the Aegis weapon system. As more weapons were added, especially the Harpoon and Tomahawk cruise missiles, the ship was enlarged and the twin-reactor D2G propulsion plant was upgraded.

The ship was proposed as a carrier escort, with up to four CSGNs being considered to screen each carrier. The cost of the lead strike cruiser in fiscal 1976 was estimated at $1.371 *billion* and the ship was to have been completed in December 1983. After the ship was ignored by Congress, the Naval Sea Systems Command hurriedly developed a strike cruiser Mk II design retaining the same armament but with a flight deck added, presenting a superficial similarity to the Soviet KIEV-class VSTOL carriers.[5] However, the U.S. ship, with two vertical-launch systems in place of the two Mk 26 launchers, would have had an enlarged island structure with hangars for several Harrier VSTOL aircraft and LAMPS III helicopters (far fewer than the KIEV operates). A further modification of the Mk II design considered a hangar above the main deck, resulting in a design somewhat similar to the Navy's small or light carriers of World War II (CVL 22–30). That ship would have carried about 18 Harriers on a displacement of some 18,000 tons.

See 13th Edition/pages 136–137 for additional strike cruiser details.

5. See N. Polmar, *Guide to the Soviet Navy* (Annapolis, Md.: Naval Institute Press, 1991), pp. 138–144.

TABLE 15-5. FRIGATES

Number	Name	Notes
DL 1	NORFOLK (ex-CLK 1)	comm. 1953; stricken 1973
DL 2	MITSCHER (ex-DD 927)	converted to DDG 35
DL 3	JOHN S. McCAIN (ex-DD 928)	converted to DDG 36
DL 4	WILLIS A. LEE (ex-DD 930)	comm. 1954; stricken 1972
DL 5	WILKINSON (ex-DD 930)	comm. 1954; stricken 1974
DLG 6–15	FARRAGUT class	to DDG 37–46
DLG 16–24	LEAHY class	to CG 16–24
DLGN 25	BAINBRIDGE	to CGN 25
DLG 26–34	BELKNAP class	to CG 26–34
DLGN 35	TRUXTUN	to CGN 35
DLGN 36, 37	CALIFORNIA class	to CGN 36, 37
DLGN 38–40	VIRGINIA class	to CGN 38–40

The frigate classifications (DL/DLG/DLGN) were established after 1951 for large destroyer-type ships that were designed to operate with fast-carrier forces. In general, the emphasis has been on AAW systems, although some ships additionally had the most-capable ASW systems available (i.e., large sonar, ASROC, helicopter). The hunter-killer cruiser NORFOLK was completed as the DL 1, while four MITSCHER-class ships ordered as destroyers were completed as DL 2–5. Note that the missile-armed frigates and all-gun frigates are numbered in the same series; in the cruiser, destroyer, and frigate/destroyer escort categories the missile and non-missile ships were in separate series.

The frigate classification (DL/DLG/DLGN) was abolished on 30 June 1975, and frigate (FF/FFG) was established to indicate smaller escort ships (formerly DE/DEG).

The sterns of the Aegis cruiser VINCENNES (CG 49) and the destroyer CALLAGHAN (DDG 994) exhibit the similarity of the two designs, both based on the SPRUANCE-class ASW destroyer. The DDG's Harpoon missiles are amidships, between the gas turbine exhaust stacks (funnels). (1988, Giorgio Arra)

CHAPTER 16

Destroyers

The ARLEIGH BURKE, progenitor of the only class of surface combatants that will be under construction in the United States at the start of the 21st century. Improved and enlarged versions of the BURKE design have been proposed, but fiscal constraints will inhibit changes for the foreseeable future. (1991, Bath Iron Works)

The U.S. Navy has 38 destroyers (DD/DDG) in active commission in late 1992, a reduction from 68 ships in the late 1980s. The composition of this force is changing rapidly as Aegis-fitted ships of the ARLEIGH BURKE class are being built (at the rate of some four per year) while older destroyers are being retired. At current building rates, by the year 2000 the Navy will have some 33 missile-armed destroyers (all but four having the Aegis system) and 31 ASW destroyers.

The long-delayed and controversial BURKE-class destroyers are in series production with the Department of Defense and Congress supporting a four-per-annum program although the Navy had sought five to six ships per year. However, the reduction in aircraft carrier and battleship force levels makes a more modest destroyer program appropriate, especially when they are complemented by the 27 Aegis cruisers of the TICONDEROGA (CG 47) class.

The so-called flight III was a proposed enhancement of the ARLEIGH BURKE design, the principal changes being the provision of a two-helicopter hangar and reduced radar and infrared signatures. Construction of this configuration was to begin in the late 1990s with the DDG 90, following the 39 BURKE-class flight I/II ships.

By the spring of 1991, however, the Navy realized that the reduced shipbuilding budgets made the Phase III ship too expensive to be procured in significant numbers. Rather, a more modest improved BURKE will probably be built (see below).

Destroyers provide anti-air and anti-submarine defense for other surface forces (see page 000 for assignments under planned force levels). Adding Harpoon missiles to destroyers provides an anti-ship capability, while the provision of vertical-launch missile tubes or armored box launchers in the 31 ships of the SPRUANCE class enables them to launch Tomahawk anti-ship and land-attack (strike) missiles. While the BURKE-class ships have 90 VLS missile cells, the requirement to arm those ships with Standard AAW and possibly VLA ASW missiles will probably preclude their carrying significant numbers of Tomahawk missiles, if any. (All destroyers except the CHARLES F. ADAMS class were fitted with eight Harpoons in canisters; the ADAMS class could fire the Harpoon from the Mk 11/13 missile launchers.)

The BURKE-class ships have a helicopter platform, but no hangar and only limited helicopter support facilities, a major shortcoming in view of the helicopter being the most effective ASW weapon

available to surface ships. The 35 ships of the SPRUANCE and KIDD classes have extensive facilities to operate two ASW helicopters, which can also be used for over-the-horizon targeting of ship-launched missiles and, in the future, themselves launching Penguin anti-ship missiles.

All destroyers have 5-inch (127-mm) guns, the largest weapons now carried in active U.S. Navy warships. The 8-inch (203-mm) Major Caliber Lightweight Gun (MCLWG), at one time proposed for the entire SPRUANCE class, was terminated. The gun was successfully evaluated at sea in the older destroyer HULL in 1975–1979. With the retirement of the four IOWA (BB 61)-class battleships, the issue is again being raised of deploying the MCLWG in the SPRUANCE-class destroyers.

Builders: The BURKE-class ships are being built by the Bath Iron Works in Maine (lead yard) and Litton's Ingalls Shipbuilding yard at Pascagoula, Miss.

Classification: The Aegis program office in the Naval Sea Systems Command has developed its own "baseline" designation scheme for Aegis ships; see page 126.

Modernization: Several destroyers have had AAW modernizations, although only the MAHAN has formally undergone the New Threat Upgrade (NTU) modernization program to the Standard missile system and radars. The NTU process enables the ship to employ later block variants of the Standard missile.

Names: Destroyers have traditionally been named for naval heroes and leaders, including deceased Secretaries of the Navy, admirals, and inventors.

Operational: Destroyers participating in the 1990–1991 buildup and war in the Persian Gulf—Operations Desert Shield/Desert Storm—are indicated by asterisk in the ship entry tables.

TABLE 16-1. DESTROYER FORCE LEVELS [late 1992]

Number	Class/Ship	Comm.	Active	Building*	Reserve
DDG 51	ARLEIGH BURKE	1991–	2	20	—
DDG 993	KIDD	1980–1981	4	—	—
DDG 37	FARRAGUT	1960–1961	1	—	†
DDG 2	CHARLES F. ADAMS	1960–1964	—	—	†
DD 963	SPRUANCE	1975–1983	31	—	—

*Includes ships authorized through fiscal 1992.
†None will be retained; see class entry.

GUIDED MISSILE DESTROYERS: DD(V) PROGRAM

A large number of Navy studies have been conducted to determine the characteristics for a new guided missile destroyer intended for construction to begin with the fiscal 1998 shipbuilding program. After preliminary study efforts, the decision was made that the "affordable follow-on" to the BURKE class would use the BURKE's hull and propulsion plant.

Designated DD(V), the destroyer variants being considered include an anti-air warfare configuration with no sonar or a small sonar of the SQS-56 type, and other reductions in ASW capabilities. Similarly, an anti-submarine variant might be similar to the Phase I/II ships now being built, but with only the SPS-49 two-dimensional radar (vice SPY-1), fewer VLS missile cells, and full facilities for two SH-60B LAMPS III helicopters.

Also considered has been an anti-surface (ASUW) variant, which could include the 8-inch/55-cal (203-mm) Major Caliber Lightweight

Gun (MCLWG) for the shore bombardment role. However, it is considered highly unlikely that the Navy would produce an ASUW variant during an austere budget period.

Construction of the first DD(V) ship could be proposed as early as the fiscal 1996 budget, although 1997–1998 appears more likely. When this edition of *Ships and Aircraft* was being compiled, it appeared likely that the DD(V) would be similar to the Flight I/II ships, but with a capability for two LAMPS.

In mid-1992 the Navy also had a DDS (for Strike) variant under consideration that would have additional VLS cells and possibly only one helicopter.

(The Navy has previously employed the same hull and propulsion plant and related systems for multi-variants of a warship. The most significant effort has been the SPRUANCE/ASW and KIDD/AAW destroyer variants.)

GUIDED MISSILE DESTROYERS: "ARLEIGH BURKE" CLASS FLIGHT III

The planned flight III configuration of the ARLEIGH BURKE has been cancelled (see introductory comments to this chapter). The estimated cost for flight III ships in the mid-1990s was $930 million per unit. The tentative characteristics of the flight III ships were:

Displacement:	10,722 tons full load
Length:	506 feet (154.3 m) overall
Beam:	66$\frac{1}{12}$ feet (20.4 m)[1]
Draft:	
Propulsion:	4 gas turbines (General Electric LM 2500); 100,000 shp; 2 shafts
Speed:	30 knots
Range:	4,400 n.miles (8,150 km) at 20 knots
Manning:	353 (30 officers + 302 enlisted) + helicopter det. 21 (6 officers + 15 enlisted)
Helicopters:	2 SH-60B LAMPS III
Missiles:	90-cell VLS for Standard-MR/Tomahawk/VLA (29 cells forward + 61 cells aft)
	8 Harpoon SSM (2 quad canisters Mk 141)
Guns:	1 5-inch (127-mm) 54-cal DP Mk 45
	2 20-mm Phalanx CIWS Mk 16 (2 multi-barrel)
ASW weapons:	VLA (ASROC)
	6 12.75-inch (324-mm) torpedo tubes Mk 32 (2 triple)

1. The beam at waterline is 59 feet (18.0 m).

Radars:	1 SPS-64 navigation
	1 SPS-67(V)3 surface search
	(4) SPY-1D multi-function
Sonars:	SQS-53C bow mounted
	SQR-19 TACTAS towed array
Fire control:	3 Mk 99 illuminators with SPG-62 radar
	1 Mk 116 ASW control system
	1 GFCS
EW systems:	SLQ-25 Nixie
	SLQ-32(V)3

Design: The SPY-1 radar "faces" were to be mounted one deck higher in these ships than in previous DDG 51 flights to clear the line-of-sight of the helicopter hangar, which was to be fitted immediately behind the second funnel.

Electronics: The flight III ships were to have an improved SPY-1 radar (designated SPY-1E in some publications) and the (V)3 variant of the SLQ-32 EW system.

Propulsion: The fiscal 1990 defense appropriations act as passed by Congress required the Navy to provide electric drive in flight III ships. However, the Navy has stated that if the flight III design was to be "finalized" in 1995 there would not be sufficient time to develop and test the propulsion plant.

2 + 39 GUIDED MISSILE DESTROYERS: "ARLEIGH BURKE" CLASS (FLIGHTS I/II)

Number	Name	FY	Builder	Laid down	Launched	Christened	Commissioned	Status
DDG 51	ARLEIGH BURKE	85	Bath Iron Works	31 July 1986	16 Sep 1989	—	4 July 1991	**AA**
DDG 52	BARRY	87	Litton/Ingalls Shipbuilding	26 Feb 1990	10 May 1991	8 June 1991	12 Dec 1992	**PA**
DDG 53	JOHN PAUL JONES	87	Bath Iron Works	8 Aug 1990	26 Oct 1991	—	1993	Building
DDG 54	CURTIS WILBUR	89	Bath Iron Works	12 Mar 1991	16 May 1992	—	1993	Building
DDG 55	STOUT	89	Litton/Ingalls Shipbuilding	17 June 1991	17 Oct 1992		1994	Building
DDG 56	JOHN S. MCCAIN	89	Bath Iron Works	3 Sep 1991	1992		1994	Building
DDG 57	MITSCHER	89	Litton/Ingalls Shipbuilding	12 Feb 1992	1993		1994	Building
DDG 58	LABOON	89	Bath Iron Works		1993		1994	Building
DDG 59	RUSSELL	90	Litton/Ingalls Shipbuilding		1993		1994	Building
DDG 60	PAUL HAMILTON	90	Bath Iron Works		1993		1995	Building
DDG 61	RAMAGE	90	Litton/Ingalls Shipbuilding		1993		1995	Building
DDG 62	FITZGERALD	90	Bath Iron Works		1994		1995	Building
DDG 63	STETHEM	90	Litton/Ingalls Shipbuilding		1994		1995	Building
DDG 64	CARNEY	91	Bath Iron Works				1996	Building
DDG 65	BENFOLD	91	Litton/Ingalls Shipbuilding				1996	Building
DDG 66	GONZALEZ	91	Bath Iron Works				1996	Building
DDG 67	COLE	91	Litton/Ingalls Shipbuilding				1996	Building
DDG 68	THE SULLIVANS	92	Bath Iron Works				1997	Building
DDG 69	MILIUS	92	Litton/Ingalls Shipbuilding				1997	Building
DDG 70	HOPPER	92	Litton/Ingalls Shipbuilding				1997	Building
DDG 71	. . . . . .	92	Bath Iron Works				1997	Building
DDG 72	. . . . . .	92	Bath Iron Works				1998	Authorized
DDG 73–76	(4 ships)	93						Planned
DDG 77–79	(3 ships)	94						Planned
DDG 80–83	(4 ships)	95						Planned
DDG 84–87	(4 ships)	96						Planned
DDG 88, 91	(4 ships)	97						Planned

Displacement:	DDG 51 6,624 tons light
	later units 6,682 tons light
	DDG 51 8,315 tons full load
	later units 8,373 tons full load
Length:	465$\frac{5}{6}$ feet (142.0 m) waterline
	504$\frac{1}{3}$ feet (153.8 m) overall
Beam:	66$\frac{1}{12}$ feet (20.4 m)[2]
Draft:	30$\frac{7}{12}$ feet (9.3 m)
Propulsion:	4 gas turbines (General Electric LM 2500–30); 100,000 shp; 2 shafts
Speed:	31 knots
Range:	4,400 n.miles (8,150 km) at 20 knots
Manning:	325 (23 officers + 302 enlisted)
Helicopters:	landing deck only

2. The beam at waterline is 59 feet (18.0 m).

Missiles:	90-cell VLS for Standard-MR SM-2/Tomahawk/VLA (ASROC) (29 cells forward + 61 cells aft)
	8 Harpoon SSM (2 quad canisters Mk 141)
Guns:	1 5-inch (127-mm) 54-cal DP Mk 45
	2 20-mm Phalanx CIWS Mk 16 (2 multi-barrel)
ASW weapons:	VLA (ASROC)
	6 12.75-inch (324-mm) torpedo tubes Mk 32 (2 triple)
Radars:	1 SPS-64 navigation
	1 SPS-67(V)3 surface search
	(4) SPY-1D multi-function
Sonars:	SQS-53C bow mounted
	SQR-19 TACTAS towed array
Fire control:	3 Mk 99 illuminators with SPG-62 radar
	1 Mk 116 ASW control system
	1 Mk 160 GFCS
	SQQ-89(V)4 ASW system
EW systems:	SLQ-25 Nixie
	SLQ-32(V)2

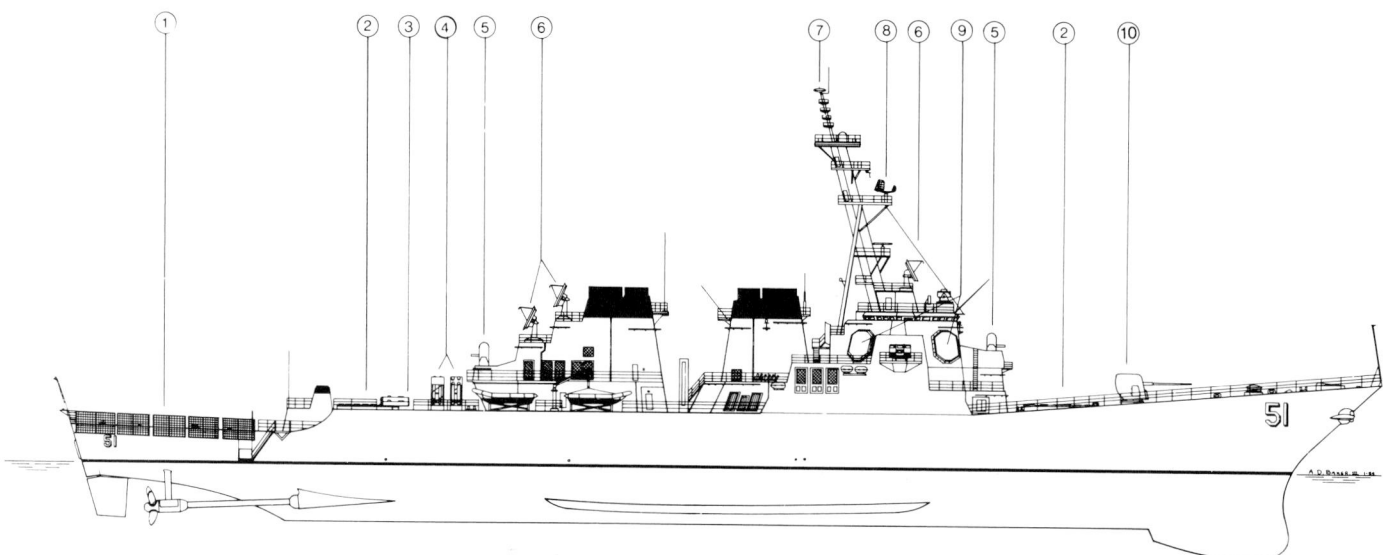

1. helicopter deck   2. Mk 41 Mod 0 vertical-launch system   3. Mk 32 torpedo tubes   4. Harpoon canisters   5. 20-mm Phalanx CIWS   6. SPG-62 radars   7. URN-25 TACAN   8. SPS-67 radar (above SPS-64 radar)   9. SPY-1D radar   10. 5-inch/54-cal single gun mount (A.D. Baker III)

These destroyers emphasize AAW capabilities and are intended to complement Aegis cruisers (CG 47) in the air/missile defense of carrier battle groups. Initial plans for a more-advanced radar and propulsion plant for these ships were dropped in favor of the propulsion plant in the CG 47/DDG 993/DD 963 classes and a derivative of the CG 47 Aegis radar.

The production DDG 51 units were planned to cost approximately 75 percent of a CG 47-class cruiser. The significant differences in the weapons and sensors for the DDG 51 from the CG 47 are:

- three vice four missile illuminators
- 90 vice 122 VLS missiles
- no helicopter hangar
- no AAW commander/coordination facilities

The lead ship of the class was completed 21 months behind schedule, the original contract with Bath Iron Works requiring delivery in October 1989. The Navy states that the delays were caused by: (1) a 90-day labor strike at Bath Iron Works, (2) corrections to government-furnished information for the main reduction gear, (3) Navy changes to engine-room piping, (4) extension of the combat system testing program, and (5) limitations of Bath's design and production capacity.

Class: Original Navy planning provided for 50 to 60 advanced missile destroyers to be authorized in fiscal 1985–1994 to replace about the same number of older cruisers and destroyers. The Carter administration (1977–1980) proposed the construction of 49 ships of this class, while the Reagan administration initially (1981) envisioned a program of 63 ships. For several reasons, including program cost issues, in the mid-1980s the Reagan administration revised the program down to 29 ships. However, it now appears that construction will continue to least through the fiscal 1997 program at the rate of three or four ships per year for a class total of 39 units.

In April 1985 a contract was awarded to Bath Iron Works for detailed design and construction of the lead ship. With 63 ships, the class was planned for construction at two or three shipyards at the average rate of five ships per year. The Litton/Ingalls yard, which is the lead yard for the Ticonderoga-class cruisers, was subsequently selected as the second yard.

The DDG 51–67 are known as "Flight I" ships and the DDG 68 and later ships are designated "Flight II."[3] The later ships have a number of combat capability improvements such as the Joint Tactical Information Distribution System (JTIDS), Tactical Data Information Exchange Subsystem (TADIX), the upgraded SLQ-32(V)3, and the Standard-MR Block 4 missile. The later ships will also have the ability to refuel and rearm helicopters (see below).

The Japanese Yukikaze-class destroyers, being fitted with the Aegis/VLS system, have a similar configuration but are smaller. The lead unit of that four-ship class is scheduled to be completed in 1993.

Classification: The initial Navy study conducted in 1979 leading to the preliminary design of this ship used the designation DDX and subsequently DDGX. (Of the various design/capability options developed in the study, sub-type 3A was selected for development as the DDG 51.)

Cost: Early cost estimates stipulated $550 million per ship (FY 1982 dollars) for the 6,000-ton ship in series production. Subsequently, in February 1983 the Secretary of the Navy established a cost ceiling of $1.1 *billion* for the lead ship and $700 million each for ships nos. 6 through 10. In early 1987, the Navy estimated in FY 1983 dollars that the lead ship would cost $1.048 *billion* and the later ships $677 million each.

The FY 1991 budget provided $3.145 *billion* for four ships (plus $8 million for outfitting and $19.1 million for post-delivery costs; the FY 1992 budget provided $4.064 *billion* for five ships (plus outfitting and post-delivery; and the FY 1993 budget $3.370 *billion* for four ships plus outfitting and post-delivery.

The Department of Defense selected acquisition report for late 1991 reported a current-year program cost for 49 ships of $47.379 *billion* or an average of $966.9 million per ship.

Design: From the outset these ships were directed by the Chief of Naval Operations to be smaller and less expensive than the DDG/CG 47 design. Early design concepts envisioned a ship as small as 6,000 tons full-load displacement.

---

3. Within the Aegis program, the Flight I ships are referred to as Aegis baseline 4 and the Flight III ships as Aegis baseline 5.

The ARLEIGH BURKE has a relatively broad hull form; the angled superstructure and funnels reduce the ship's radar signature, although the tripod mast and various antennas create distinctive radar "spikes." The twin stern openings are for the SLQ-25 Nixie towed torpedo countermeasures. (1991, Giorgio Arra)

The ARLEIGH BURKE has an unusual tripod mast supporting several small radar antennas. There are OE-82 SATCOMM antennas on either side of the mast and SPY-1D radar antennas angled at 45° below the bridge. Two Phalanx CIWS mounts were the only guns in the original DDG 51 design planned for construction. (1991, Giorgio Arra)

These are the first U.S. destroyers of post–World War II construction with steel superstructures; that decision was made as a result of the cruiser BELKNAP (CG 26) colliding with an aircraft carrier in 1975 (and not after the loss of a British destroyer to Argentine-launched Exocet air-to-surface missiles in the 1982 conflict in the Falklands). The steel construction provides increased resistance to blast overpressure, fragment, and fire damage plus Electromagnetic Pulse (EMP) protection. The ships have 130 tons of Kevlar armor plating to protect vital spaces, and for the first time in a U.S. warship an enhanced partial Chemical-Biological-Radiological (CBR) protective system is being fitted from the outset.

The ships have been designed with a significantly reduced radar cross section over previous destroyer-type ships.

The so-called "modular" approach to the DDG 51 design undertaken by the Navy had provided that a twin LAMPS III facility could be installed aft in place of the *entire* after 61-missile VLS battery, i.e., two-thirds of the ship's missile armament!

Electronics: A derivative of the CG 47 Aegis system is provided, with all four SPY-1D radar "faces" mounted on a single, forward deckhouse.

Fitted with NTDS.

Engineering: Essentially the same propulsion plant that is in the CG 47/DD 963/DDG 993 classes is fitted in this class. At congressional urging the Navy looked into the possibility of the Rankin regenerative system to enhance the efficiency of the gas turbines, but that system was found to require too much internal volume to be practical for the class.

The ARLEIGH BURKE reportedly attained 32 knots on sea trials. The sustained horsepower for these ships is approximately 90,000.

Guns: The original DDGX proposal called for a gun armament of only two Phalanx CIWS. Subsequently, a single 76-mm OTO Melara Mk 75 was provided in the design and later the single 5-inch/54-cal Mk 45, in addition to the two CIWS.

Helicopters: The ships have a large helicopter landing area on their fantail and a VERTREP position forward; however, no hangar is provided and helicopters will not normally be deployed in these ships. The DDG 52 and later ships have the RAST hauldown system plus helicopter refueling and rearming capabilities (adding 58 tons to full-load displacement).

Names: In 1983 the not-yet-started DDG 51 was named for Admiral Arleigh Burke, the Chief of Naval Operations from 1955 to 1961. This was the second U.S. ship to be named in recent years for a living person, the first being the CARL VINSON (CVN 70). One other ship of this class honors a former CNO, Admiral Robert B. Carney (CNO from 1951 to 1955). The Navy's leading carrier force commanders of World War II are also venerated by two of these ships, Admirals John S. McCain and Marc Mitscher.

The DDG 52 was originally named JOHN BARRY; it was changed to BARRY on 1 February 1988, back to JOHN BARRY on 9 May 1988, and again back to BARRY on 8 December 1989, and finally christened as JOHN BARRY—further testimony to the rampant confusion in the U.S. Navy ship-naming process.

The ARLEIGH BURKE presents a modern, streamlined look although the ship has significantly less combat capability than the improved TICONDEROGA (CG 47) class, which is slightly more than 1,000 tons heavier. The BURKE design had a long gestation period. (1991, Giorgio Arra)

4 GUIDED MISSILE DESTROYERS: "KIDD" CLASS (FORMER IRANIAN SHIPS)

Number	Name	FY	Builder	Laid down	Launched	Christened	Commissioned	Status
DDG 993	KIDD*	79S	Litton/Ingalls Shipbuilding	26 June 1978	11 Aug 1979	13 Oct 1979	27 July 1981	**AA**
DDG 994	CALLAGHAN	79S	Litton/Ingalls Shipbuilding	23 Oct 1978	1 Dec 1979	19 Jan 1980	29 Aug 1981	**PA**
DDG 995	SCOTT*	79S	Litton/Ingalls Shipbuilding	12 Feb 1979	1 Mar 1980	29 Mar 1980	24 Oct 1981	**AA**
DDG 996	CHANDLER	79S	Litton/Ingalls Shipbuilding	7 May 1979	24 May 1980	24 May 1980	13 Mar 1982	**PA**

Displacement:	6,950 tons light	Radars:	SPS-48E 3-D air search
	9,574 tons full load		SPS-49(V)5 air search
Length:	528⅝ feet (161.2 m) waterline		SPS-55 surface search
	563⅓ feet (171.8 m) overall		SPS-64 navigation
Beam:	55 feet (16.8)	Sonars:	SQS-53A bow mounted
Draft:	33 feet (10.1 m)	Fire control:	1 Mk 14 weapon direction system
Propulsion:	4 gas turbines (General Electric LM 2500); 80,000 shp; 2 shafts		2 Mk 74 missile FCS with SPG-51D radars
Speed:	30+ knots		1 Mk 86 GFCS with SPG-60 and SPQ-9A radars
Range:	6,000 n.miles (11,112 km) at 20 knots		1 Mk 116 ASW FCS
	3,300 n.miles (6,112 km) at 30 knots		1 SYS-2 Integrated Automatic Detection and Tracking (IADT)
Manning:	approx. 357 (23 officers + 334 enlisted)		system
Helicopters:	1 SH-2F LAMPS I	EW systems:	SLQ-25 Nixie
Missiles:	2 twin Mk 26 Mod 0/1 launchers for Standard-MR SM-2 SAM/ASROC (68)		SLQ-32(V)2
	8 Harpoon SSM (2 quad canisters Mk 141)		
Guns:	2 5-inch (127-mm) 54-cal DP Mk 45 (2 single)		
	2 20-mm Phalanx CIWS Mk 16 (2 multi-barrel)		
ASW weapons:	ASROC fired from forward Mk 26 launcher		
	6 12.75-inch (324-mm) torpedo tubes Mk 32 (2 triple)		

These were the most-capable destroyers in U.S. service prior to the advent of the BURKE class, being the guided missile variant of the SPRUANCE class. However, the KIDD design has considerably more ASW capability than the BURKE class.

The four ships were ordered by the government of the Shah of Iran, which fell in 1979. Subsequently, the U.S. Navy sought to acquire the ships that were then under construction. The FY 1979 supplemental budget provided $1.353 *billion* for the purchase of these ships, and they were formally acquired on 24 July 1979.

The ships differ from the contemporary CG 47 Aegis cruisers primarily in not having the Aegis/SPY-1A AAW system.

All have been modernized to the equivalent of the New Threat Upgrade (NTU) configuration.

Class: The Iranian government announced plans to order two AAW ships based on the SPRUANCE design on 15 December 1973, with an announcement for four additional ships on 27 August 1974; two ships were cancelled in June 1976. Four ships were ordered on 23 March 1978 under the U.S. foreign military sales program.

Stern aspect of the KIDD with an SH-2F LAMPS I on the flight deck. The original SPRUANCE-class program provided for similar ships (DXG) to be constructed in large numbers for the U.S. Navy. (1990, Giorgio Arra)

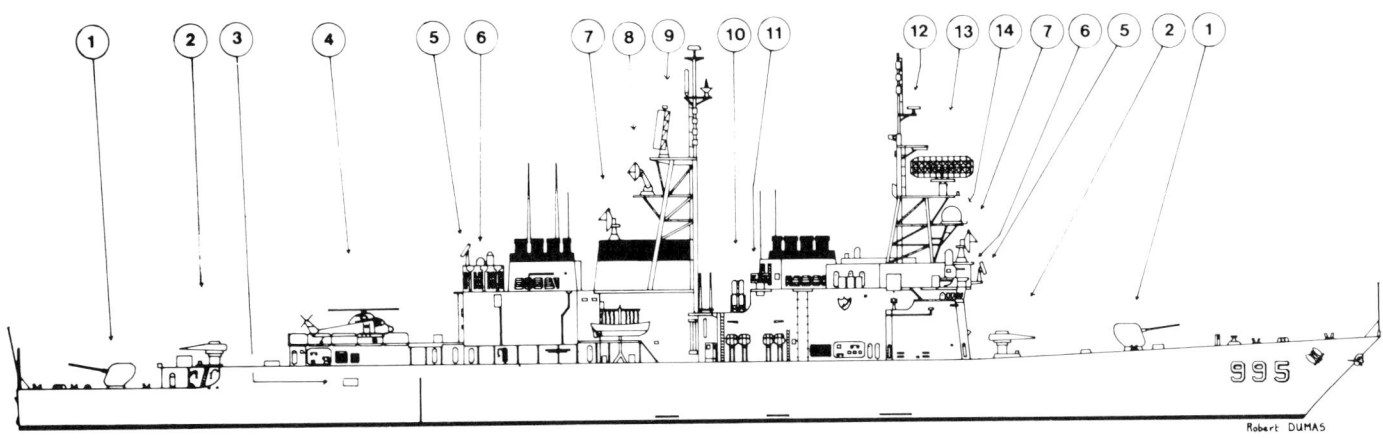

1. 5-inch/54-cal single gun mount.   2. Mk 26 missile launcher   3. Mk 32 torpedo tubes (behind shutters)   4. helicopter deck   5. OE-82 SATCOMM antenna   6. 20-mm Phalanx CIWS   7. SPG-51D radar director   8. SPG-60 gun control radar   9. SPS-48E radar   10. Harpoon canisters   11. SLQ-32(V)2 ECM antenna   12. SPS-55 radar   13. SPS-49(V)2 radar   14. SPQ-9A radar (Robert Dumas)

Classification: These ships were originally ordered as DD 993–996, indicating that they were basically SPRUANCE-class ships. They were changed to DDG with the same non-missile hull numbers on 8 August 1979.

Design: The original SPRUANCE destroyer concept consisted of a missile-armed variant (designated DXG) as well as the basic ASW ship (DX). These are the only ships that were built to the DXG design, none having been ordered for the U.S. Navy.

The Iranian government required that these ships be provided with increased air-conditioning capacity and dust separators for their engine air intakes. See SPRUANCE class for additional notes.

Electronics: The SQR-19A TACTAS towed-array sonar was considered for these ships; however, with existing funding constraints it is unlikely that it will be installed.

Helicopters: The ship's configuration provides for two SH-60B LAMPS III helicopters to be embarked; however, only one SH-2F has been assigned to these ships. It is planned to eventually upgrade the ships to embark two SH-60B LAMPS III helicopters.

Manning: The crews of these ships vary from 20 to 27 officers and from 314 to 366 enlisted.

Missiles: The Mk 26 Mod 0 missile launcher installed forward was provided with a smaller (24-missile) magazine than the after Mk 26 Mod 1 launcher to provide space for possible installation of the 8-inch Mk 71 gun in place of the existing 5-inch gun. The after, 44-missile magazine is used for ASROCs in these ships.

Modernization: The SCOTT completed the NTU modernization in March 1988, KIDD in September 1989, CALLAGHAN in July 1990, and CHANDLER in August 1990.

Names: See table 16-2 for Iranian names.

An SH-2F LAMPS-I from HSL-34 shares the hangar on the KIDD with an Army OH-58D Kiowa during operations in the Persian Gulf. Navy destroyers and frigates worked with Army helicopters during Desert Shield/Desert Storm. The special operations OH-58D is fitted with a rapid-fire Gatling gun. (1991, Lt. Comdr. David Gruber)

The SCOTT and three sister ships were begun for the Imperial Iranian Navy and taken over by the U.S. Navy. Although this DDG variant of the SPRUANCE class was intended for U.S. Navy construction, these were the only ships to be built to this design. (1989, Giorgio Arra)

The KIDD with an SH-2F LAMPS I helicopter on her flight deck. These ships retain the full SPRUANCE-class ASW capabilities while mounting a surface-to-air missile system. As in the SPRUANCE class, the starboard Phalanx CIWS is forward, the port mounting is atop the helicopter hangar. (1990, Giorgio Arra)

The KIDD with an SH-2F LAMPS I helicopter on her flight deck. These ships retain the full SPRUANCE-class ASW capabilities while mounting a surface-to-air missile system. As in the SPRUANCE class, the starboard Phalanx CIWS is forward, the port mounting is atop the helicopter hangar. (1990, Giorgio Arra)

1 GUIDED MISSILE DESTROYER: "FARRAGUT" CLASS

Number	Name	FY	Builder	Laid down	Launched	Commissioned	Status
DDG 37 (ex-DLG 6)	FARRAGUT	56	Bethlehem Steel, Quincy, Mass.	3 June 1957	18 July 1958	10 Dec 1960	AR decomm. 31 Oct 1989
DDG 38 (ex-DLG 7)	LUCE	56	Bethlehem Steel, Quincy, Mass.	1 Oct 1957	11 Dec 1958	20 May 1961	AR decomm. 1 Apr 1991
DDG 39 (ex-DLG 8)	MACDONOUGH*	56	Bethlehem Steel, Quincy, Mass.	15 Apr 1958	9 July 1959	4 Nov 1961	AR decomm. 1992
DDG 40 (ex-DLG 9)	COONTZ	56	Puget Sound Naval Shipyard	1 Mar 1957	6 Dec 1958	15 July 1960	AR decomm. 4 Oct 1989
DDG 41 (ex-DLG 10)	KING	56	Puget Sound Naval Shipyard	1 Mar 1957	6 Dec 1958	17 Nov 1960	AR decomm. 28 Mar 1991
DDG 42 (ex-DLG 11)	MAHAN	56	San Francisco Naval Shipyard	31 July 1957	7 Oct 1959	25 Aug 1960	**AA**
DDG 43 (ex-DLG 12)	DAHLGREN	57	Philadelphia Naval Shipyard	1 Mar 1958	16 Mar 1960	8 Apr 1961	AR decomm. 31 July 1992
DDG 44 (ex-DLG 13)	WILLIAM V. PRATT*	57	Philadelphia Naval Shipyard	1 Mar 1958	16 Mar 1960	4 Nov 1961	AR decomm. 30 Sep 1991
DDG 45 (ex-DLG 14)	DEWEY	57	Bath Iron Works, Maine	10 Aug 1957	30 Nov 1958	7 Dec 1959	AR decomm. 31 Aug 1990
DDG 46 (ex-DLG 15)	PREBLE*	57	Bath Iron Works, Maine	16 Dec 1957	23 May 1959	9 May 1960	PR decomm. 15 Nov 1991

Displacement:	4,700 tons light
	6,150 tons full load
Length:	512⅓ feet (156.2 m) overall
Beam:	52½ feet (16.0 m)
Draft:	25 feet (7.6 m)
Propulsion:	2 steam turbines (De Laval in DDG 37–39, 45–46; Allis-Chalmers in DDG 40–44); 85,000 shp; 2 shafts
Boilers:	4 1,200 psi (83.4 kg/cm²) (Foster Wheeler in DDG 37–39; Babcock & Wilcox in DDG 40–46)
Speed:	33 knots
Range:	4,500 n.miles at 20 knots
	1,500 n.miles at 30 knots
Manning:	DDG 39; 411 (25 officers + 386 enlisted)
	DDG 42; 428 (24 officers + 404 enlisted)
Helicopters:	VERTREP area only

Missiles:	1 twin Mk 10 Mod 0 launcher for Standard-ER SM-2 SAM (40)
	8 Harpoon SSM (2 quad canisters Mk 141)
Guns:	1 5-inch (127-mm) 54-cal DP Mk 42
ASW weapons:	1 8-tube ASROC launcher Mk 16
	6 12.75-inch (324-mm) torpedo tubes Mk 32 (2 triple)
Radars:	SPS-10B surface search
	SPS-48C 3-D air search except SPS-48E in DDG 42
	SPS-49(V)1 air search except SPS-49(V)5 in DDG 42
	SPS-53 surface search or Raytheon 2900 navigation
Sonars:	SQQ-23 PAIR
Fire control:	1 Mk weapon direction system except Mk 14 in DDG 42
	1 Mk 68 GFCS with SPG-53A radar
	2 Mk 76 missile FCS with SPG-55B radar
	1 Mk 111 ASW FCS
EW systems:	T Mk 6 Fanfare in DDG 43, 46
	SLQ-25 Nixie in DDG 42
	SLQ-32(V)2

These ships originally were classified as "frigates" (DLG). Although reclassified as destroyers, they have the Terrier/Standard-ER missile system and Naval Tactical Data System (NTDS) of some U.S. cruiser classes.

Nine ships were decommissioned in 1989–1992 and are being stricken. The MAHAN is scheduled to be decommissioned in 1994; she served as prototype for the NTU program and has the most capable AAW weapons system of this class.

Class: These ships are also referred to as the COONTZ class, that ship being the first ordered with the DLG designation.

Classification: The first three ships of this class were ordered on 27 January 1956 as all-gun frigates (DL 6–8); they were changed to guided missile frigates (DLG 6–8) on 14 November 1956.

All ten ships were classified as DLG 6–15 from the time of their commissioning until 30 June 1975, when they were changed to guided missile destroyers (DDG 37–46). There was some internal Navy debate over whether to classify them as cruisers or destroyers when the frigate (DLG) designation was dropped; a major factor was that their commanding officers were commanders while all other DLG/DLGNs were commanded by captains.

Design: SCB No. 142. At the time they were ordered these ships were to have a second 5-inch gun mount in the "B" position; however, they were fitted with an ASROC launcher in that position before completion. At the same time, the planned SQS-4 sonar was changed to the much-improved SQS-23 (keel mounted). As built, no

ASROC reloads were provided, although the FARRAGUT was subsequently provided with a reload capability.

Electronics: The KING and MAHAN were test ships for the Naval Tactical Data System (NTDS) in 1961–1962.

In 1982 the MAHAN was provided with the first surface combatant NTU modernization, with the SPS-48E and SPS-49(V)5 radars, the Standard-ER SM-2 Block II missile, and other features. The other ships were not upgraded.

Guns: As built, each ship had two 3-inch/50-cal Mk 33 AA twin gun mounts aft of the second funnel; these have been removed from all ships. The COONTZ was fitted with two 20-mm Vulcan (not Phalanx) Gatling guns in 1973–1974 for evaluation. These ships did not receive the Phalanx CIWS because of space and weight limitations.

Missiles: The MAHAN was the first U.S. ship of the class to be fitted with the improved Standard-ER SM-2 missile in 1979. (The cruiser WAINWRIGHT/CG 28 was the first ship fitted with the SM-2, in 1978.) When decommissioned, the ships of this class carried either the SM-1 or SM-2 version of the Standard.

Modernization: All ships underwent AAW modernization between 1968 and 1977 (SCB-243). Radars and fire control systems were updated, NTDS installed (updated in KING and MAHAN), and 3-inch guns removed.

Names: The LUCE was to have been named DEWEY; changed in 1957.

The WILLIAM V. PRATT showing the heavy lattice masts fitted in U.S. missile ships prior to the development of "macks." These were the first U.S. warships to be built to a guided missile configuration. The design originally had a second 5-inch gun in the "B" position; the ships were completed with the ASROC instead. (1990, Giorgio Arra)

The MAHAN is the only ship of the FARRAGUT class to undergo the NTU anti-air warfare modernization. The distinctive SPG-55B radar directors are fitted atop the after superstructure. These are the only U.S. cruiser/destroyer/frigate-type ships without a Phalanx CIWS. (1990, Giorgio Arra)

The Luce at Fort Lauderdale, Fla. Most of the ships of this class are now laid up, with the others to follow soon. They have had minimal modernization during their three decades of active service. (1990, Giorgio Arra)

GUIDED MISSILE DESTROYERS: "CHARLES F. ADAMS" CLASS

Number	Name	FY	Builder	Laid down	Launched	Commissioned	Status
DDG 2	CHARLES F. ADAMS	57	Bath Iron Works, Maine	16 June 1958	8 Sep 1959	10 Sep 1960	AR decomm. 1 Aug 1990
DDG 3	JOHN KING	57	Bath Iron Works, Maine	25 Aug 1958	30 Jan 1960	4 Feb 1961	AR decomm. 30 Mar 1990
DDG 4	LAWRENCE	57	New York SB, Camden, N.J.	27 Oct 1958	27 Feb 1960	6 Jan 1962	decomm. 30 Mar 1990; str. 16 May 1990
DDG 5	CLAUDE V. RICKETTS	57	New York SB, Camden, N.J.	18 May 1959	4 June 1960	5 May 1962	decomm. 31 Oct 1989; str. 1 June 1990
DDG 6	BARNEY	57	New York SB, Camden, N.J.	18 May 1959	10 Dec 1960	11 Aug 1962	AR decomm. 17 Dec 1990
DDG 7	HENRY B. WILSON	57	Defoe Shipbuilding	28 Feb 1958	23 Apr 1959	17 Dec 1960	decomm. 2 Oct 1989; str. 26 Jan 1990
DDG 8	LYNDE MCCORMICK	57	Defoe Shipbuilding	4 Apr 1958	9 Sep 1960	3 June 1961	PR decomm. 1 Oct 1991
DDG 9	TOWERS	57	Todd Shipyards, Seattle, Wash.	1 Apr. 1958	23 Apr 1959	6 June 1961	PR decomm. 1 Oct 1990
DDG 10	SAMPSON*	58	Bath Iron Works, Maine	2 Mar 1959	9 Sep 1960	24 June 1961	AR decomm. 24 June 1991
DDG 11	SELLERS	58	Bath Iron Works, Maine	3 Aug 1959	9 Sep 1960	28 Oct 1961	AR decomm. 31 Oct 1989
DDG 12	ROBISON	58	Defoe Shipbuilding	23 Apr 1959	27 Apr 1960	9 Dec 1961	PR decomm. 1 Oct 1991
DDG 13	HOEL	58	Defoe Shipbuilding	1 June 1960	4 Aug 1960	16 June 1962	PR decomm. 1 Oct 1990
DDG 14	BUCHANAN	58	Todd Shipyards, Seattle, Wash.	23 Apr 1959	11 May 1960	7 Feb 1962	PR decomm. 1 Oct 1991
DDG 15	BERKELEY	59	New York SB, Camden, N.J.	1 June 1960	29 July 1961	15 Dec 1962	PR decomm. 1 May 1992
DDG 16	JOSEPH STRAUSS	59	New York SB, Camden, N.J.	27 Dec 1960	9 Dec 1961	20 Apr 1963	decomm. 1 Feb 1990; to Greece
DDG 17	CONYNGHAM	59	New York SB, Camden, N.J.	1 May 1961	19 May 1962	13 July 1963	decomm. 30 Oct 1990; str. 30 May 1991
DDG 18	SEMMES	59	Avondale Marine, New Orleans	18 Aug 1960	20 May 1961	10 Dec 1962	decomm. 13 Sep 1991; to Greece
DDG 19	TATTNALL*	59	Avondale Marine, New Orleans	14 Nov 1960	26 Aug 1961	13 Apr 1963	AR decomm. 18 Jan 1991
DDG 20	GOLDSBOROUGH*	60	Puget Sound Bridge, Seattle	3 Jan 1961	15 Dec 1961	9 Nov 1963	PR to decomm. 1992
DDG 21	COCHRANE	60	Puget Sound Bridge, Seattle	31 July 1961	18 July 1962	21 Mar 1964	PR decomm. 1 Oct 1990
DDG 22	BENJAMIN STODDERT	60	Puget Sound Bridge, Seattle	11 June 1962	8 Jan 1963	12 Sep 1964	PR decomm. 20 Dec 1991
DDG 23	RICHARD E. BYRD	61	Todd Shipyards, Seattle, Wash.	12 Apr 1961	6 Feb 1962	7 Mar 1964	decomm. 27 Apr 1990; to Greece
DDG 24	WADDELL	61	Todd Shipyards, Seattle, Wash.	6 Feb 1962	26 Feb 1963	28 Aug 1964	str. 1992; to Greece

Displacement:	3,570 tons light 4,825 tons full load	Guns:	2 5-inch (127-mm) 54-cal DP Mk 42 (2 single)
Length:	419⅝ feet (128.0 m) waterline 436⅝ feet (133.2 m) overall	ASW weapons: Torpedoes:	1 8-tube ASROC launcher Mk 16 6 12.75-inch (324-mm) torpedo tubes Mk 32 (2 triple)
Beam:	47 feet (14.3 m)	Radars:	LN-66 navigation
Draft:	27¼ feet (8.3 m)		SPS-10F surface search except SPS-10D in DDG 19, 20, 22
Propulsion:	2 steam turbines (General Electric in DDG 2, 3, 7, 8, 10–13, 15–22; Westinghouse in DDG 4–6, 9, 14, 23, 24); 70,000 shp; 2 shafts		SPS-40B/C/D air search SPS-52B 3-D air search except SPS-52C in DDG 19, 20, 22
Boilers:	4 1,200 psi (84.4 kg/cm²) (Babcock & Wilcox in DDG 2, 3, 7, 8, 10–13, 20–22; Foster Wheeler in DDG 4–6, 9, 14; Combustion Engineering in DDG 15–19)	Sonars: Fire control:	SQS-23A or SQQ-23A PAIR keel mounted except bow mounted in DDG 20–24 1 Mk 4 weapon direction system except Mk 13 weapon direction system in DDG 9, 12, 15, 19–22
Speed:	31.5 knots		1 Mk 68 GFCS with SPG-53A/F radar except Mk 86 with SPG-60 and SPQ-9A radar in DDG 19, 20, 22
Range:	4,500 n.miles at 20 knots 1,600 n.miles at 30 knots		2 Mk 74 missile FCS with SPG-51C radar except SPG-51D in DDG 19, 20, 22
Manning:	varies; 356 (22 officers + 334 enlisted)		1 Mk 111 ASW FCS in DDG 2–15; Mk 114 ASW FCS in DDG 16–24
Helicopters:	VERTREP area only	EW systems:	SLQ-20
Missiles:	1 twin Mk 11 Mod 0 launcher for Tartar/Standard-MR SM-1 SAM and Harpoon SSM (42) in DDG 2–14		SLQ-32(V)2 T Mk 6 Fanfare in DDG 12, 14, 15, 18–20, 24
	1 single Mk 13 Mod 0 launcher for Tartar/Standard-MR SAM and Harpoon SSM (40) in DDG 15–24		

These are highly capable destroyers for their relatively small size although they lack helicopter facilities. Numerically this was the largest class of missile-armed surface warships to be constructed for the U.S. Navy prior to the FFG 7 class.

The class began to decommission in 1990, with only three ships remaining in commission by the end of 1991; all are being stricken. The last to be decommissioned were the modernized BERKELEY, GOLDSBOROUGH, and WADDELL. The CONYNGHAM suffered a major fire off the Virginia Capes on 8 May 1990; the ship was not repaired (one officer was killed).

Anti-submarine: These ships were built without ASROC reloads; many units subsequently were provided with a four-reload ASROC magazine on the starboard side of the forward stack.

Class: Three additional ships of this class were built for Australia (assigned U.S. hull numbers DDG 25–27) and three for West Germany (DDG 28–30).

As part of the 8 July 1990 agreement for the renewal of U.S. military bases in Greece, it was announced that four decommissioned ADAMS-class destroyers would be transferred to Greece: WADDELL, SEMMES, BYRD, and STRAUSS (transferred 1991–1992).

Classification: The first eight ships of this class were authorized as all-gun/ASW destroyers (DD 952–959); changed to guided missile ships and reclassified DDG 952–959 on 16 August 1956; they were changed to DDG 2–9 on 26 June 1957.

Design: SCB No. 155. The ADAMS design is based on an improved FORREST SHERMAN arrangement, with a Tartar missile-launching system in place of the SHERMAN's aftermost 5-inch gun. The last five ships have their sonar in the improved, bow position.

Engineering: The STRAUSS established a speed record of 35.2 knots in 1979. At that time the ship was 16 years old.

Missiles: These ships can fire the Harpoon anti-ship missile from the Mk 11 or Mk 13 launcher. The HOEL and LAWRENCE evaluated the Army Chapparal anti-aircraft missile during the 1960s.

Modernization: The Navy had planned to modernize all 23 ships of this class, extending their useful service life for 15 years beyond the nominal 30 years. The modernizations were to be funded in fiscal 1980–1983. However, increasing costs and congressional interest in constructing new destroyer-type ships rather than upgrading older units has led to a cutback in the modernization program, limiting it to the last ten ships and then to only three ships—the DDG 19 modified from August 1981 to November 1982, DDG 20 from November 1983 to July 1984, and DDG 22 from April 1984 to August 1985. Some other ships have had their radars upgraded (see previous editions for earlier electronic configurations).

Planned sonar upgrades were not undertaken.

The CHARLES F. ADAMS-class destroyers are being rapidly retired as part of the post–Cold War fleet reductions. They were highly capable ships despite their lack of a helicopter capability. The SLQ-32(V)2 ECM antennas are fitted above the bridge, outboard of the tripod mast. (1991, Giorgio Arra)

Names: The DDG 5 was originally named BIDDLE; renamed CLAUDE V. RICKETTS on 28 July 1964 (with the DLG/CG 34 subsequently named BIDDLE).

Operational: A boarding team, including a Coast Guard law-enforcement detachment, from the GOLDSBOROUGH made the first seizure of an Iraqi freighter in Operation Desert Shield on 16 September 1990. The seizure of the ZANOOBIA occurred in the North Arabian Sea; the ship was detained and then escorted to Muscat, Oman.

The SEMMES has the single-arm Mk 13 Tartar/Standard-MR missile launcher fitted in the later ADAMS-class destroyers. The missile launcher replaced a third 5-inch gun fitted in the FORREST SHERMAN class, from which the DDG design evolved. (1990, Giorgio Arra)

The twin-arm Mk 11 missile launcher was fitted in the first 13 ships of the Adams class. The single-arm launcher is lighter than the Mk 11 system but has a similar missile capacity and rate of fire. (1988, Giorgio Arra)

The Conyngham has the lines of the early post–World War II destroyer designs. The SPS-49 air search radar is on the tripod mast; the SPS-52 3-D radar is on a platform attached to the second funnel. (1990, George Nassiopoulos)

31 DESTROYERS: "SPRUANCE" CLASS

Number	Name	FY	Builder	Laid down	Launched	Commissioned	Status
DD 963	SPRUANCE*	70	Litton/Ingalls, Pascagoula, Miss.	27 Nov 1972	10 Nov 1973	20 Sep 1975	**AA**
DD 964	PAUL F. FOSTER*	70	Litton/Ingalls, Pascagoula, Miss.	6 Feb 1973	23 Feb 1974	21 Feb 1975	**PA**
DD 965	KINKAID	70	Litton/Ingalls, Pascagoula, Miss.	19 Apr 1973	25 May 1974	10 July 1976	**PA**
DD 966	HEWITT	71	Litton/Ingalls, Pascagoula, Miss.	23 July 1973	24 Aug 1974	25 Sep 1976	**PA**
DD 967	ELLIOT	71	Litton/Ingalls, Pascagoula, Miss.	15 Oct 1973	19 Dec 1974	22 Jan 1977	**PA**
DD 968	ARTHUR W. RADFORD	71	Litton/Ingalls, Pascagoula, Miss.	14 Jan 1974	1 Mar 1975	16 Apr 1977	**AA**
DD 969	PETERSON	71	Litton/Ingalls, Pascagoula, Miss.	29 Apr 1974	21 June 1975	9 July 1977	**AA**
DD 970	CARON*	71	Litton/Ingalls, Pascagoula, Miss.	1 July 1974	24 June 1975	1 Oct 1977	**AA**
DD 971	DAVID R. RAY*	71	Litton/Ingalls, Pascagoula, Miss.	23 Sep 1974	23 Aug 1975	19 Nov 1977	**PA**
DD 972	OLDENDORF*	72	Litton/Ingalls, Pascagoula, Miss.	27 Dec 1974	21 Oct 1975	4 Mar 1978	**PA**
DD 973	JOHN YOUNG	72	Litton/Ingalls, Pascagoula, Miss.	17 Feb 1975	7 Feb 1976	20 May 1978	**PA**
DD 974	COMTE DE GRASSE	72	Litton/Ingalls, Pascagoula, Miss.	4 Apr 1975	26 Mar 1976	5 Aug 1978	**AA**
DD 975	O'BRIEN*	72	Litton/Ingalls, Pascagoula, Miss.	9 May 1975	8 July 1976	3 Dec 1977	**PA**
DD 976	MERRILL	72	Litton/Ingalls, Pascagoula, Miss.	16 June 1975	1 Sep 1976	11 Mar 1978	**PA**
DD 977	BRISCOE	72	Litton/Ingalls, Pascagoula, Miss.	21 July 1975	18 Dec 1976	3 June 1978	**AA**
DD 978	STUMP	72	Litton/Ingalls, Pascagoula, Miss.	22 Aug 1975	21 Mar 1977	19 Aug 1978	**AA**
DD 979	CONOLLY	74	Litton/Ingalls, Pascagoula, Miss.	29 Sep 1975	3 June 1977	14 Oct 1978	**AA**
DD 980	MOOSBRUGGER*	74	Litton/Ingalls, Pascagoula, Miss.	3 Nov 1975	23 July 1977	16 Dec 1978	**AA**
DD 981	JOHN HANCOCK	74	Litton/Ingalls, Pascagoula, Miss.	16 Jan 1976	28 Sep 1977	10 March 1979	**AA**
DD 982	NICHOLSON	74	Litton/Ingalls, Pascagoula, Miss.	20 Feb 1976	29 Nov 1977	12 May 1979	**AA**
DD 983	JOHN RODGERS*	74	Litton/Ingalls, Pascagoula, Miss.	12 Aug 1976	25 Feb 1978	14 July 1979	**AA**
DD 984	LEFTWICH*	74	Litton/Ingalls, Pascagoula, Miss.	12 Nov 1976	8 Apr 1978	25 Aug 1979	**PA**
DD 985	CUSHING	74	Litton/Ingalls, Pascagoula, Miss.	2 Feb 1977	17 June 1978	20 Oct 1979	**PA**
DD 986	HARRY W. HILL*	75	Litton/Ingalls, Pascagoula, Miss.	1 Apr 1977	10 Aug 1978	17 Nov 1979	**PA**
DD 987	O'BANNON	75	Litton/Ingalls, Pascagoula, Miss.	24 June 1977	25 Sep 1978	15 Dec 1979	**AA**
DD 988	THORN	75	Litton/Ingalls, Pascagoula, Miss.	29 Aug 1977	14 Nov 1978	16 Feb 1980	**AA**
DD 989	DEYO	75	Litton/Ingalls, Pascagoula, Miss.	14 Oct 1977	20 Jan 1979	22 Mar 1980	**AA**
DD 990	INGERSOLL	75	Litton/Ingalls, Pascagoula, Miss.	16 Dec 1977	10 Mar 1979	12 Apr 1980	**PA**
DD 991	FIFE*	75	Litton/Ingalls, Pascagoula, Miss.	6 Mar 1978	1 May 1979	31 May 1980	**PA**
DD 992	FLETCHER	75	Litton/Ingalls, Pascagoula, Miss.	24 Apr 1978	16 June 1979	12 July 1980	**PA**
DD 997	HAYLER	78	Litton/Ingalls, Pascagoula, Miss.	22 Oct 1980	27 Mar 1982	5 Mar 1983	**AA**

Displacement:	5,916 tons light	Guns:	2 5-inch (127-mm) 54-cal DP Mk 45 (2 single)
	8,040 tons full load		2 20-mm Phalanx CIWS Mk 16 (2 multi-barrel)
Length:	528¹¹⁄₁₂ feet (161.25 m) waterline	ASW weapons:	1 8-tube ASROC launcher Mk 16 (being removed from ships receiving VLS)
	563⅙ feet (171.7 m) overall		6 12.75-inch (324-mm) torpedo tubes Mk 32 (2 triple)
Beam:	55 feet (16.8 m)	Radars:	Mk 23 TAS in most ships
Draft:	29 feet (8.8 m)		SPS-40B/C/D air search except SPS-49(V) in DD 997
Propulsion:	4 gas turbines (General Electric LM 2500); 80,000 shp; 2 shafts		SPS-53 or LN-66 navigation
Speed:	32.5 knots		SPS-55 surface search
Range:	6,000 n.miles (11,112 km) at 20 knots	Sonars:	SQS-53B bow mounted except SQS-53C in 6 ships
	3,300 n.miles (6,112 km) at 30 knots		SQR-19 TACTAS towed array
Manning:	approx. 342 (21 officers + 321 enlisted)	Fire control:	1 Mk 86 GFCS with SPG-60 and SPQ-9A radars
Helicopters:	2 SH-60B Seahawk LAMPS III		1 Mk 91 missile FCS
Missiles:	1 8-tube NATO Sea Sparrow launcher Mk 29		1 Mk 116 ASW FCS
	8 Harpoon SSM (2 quad canisters Mk 141)		SQQ-89(V)1 ASW system
	8 Tomahawk TASM/TLAM (2 quad ABL Mk 143) in DD 974, 976, 979, 983, 984, 989, 990 (7 ships)	EW systems:	SLQ-25 Nixie
	61-cell VLS for Tomahawk/VLA (ASROC) (Mk 41 Mod 1) in 24 ships		SLQ-32(V)2

The SPRUANCES were originally built as specialized ASW ships, with only point-defense missiles for the AAW role. However, they have been provided with an anti-ship capability with the Harpoon missile and are being provided with an anti-ship/land-attack capability with the Tomahawk missile. (These are the only ships rated as "destroyers" to carry the Tomahawk.)

The four KIDD-class missile destroyers and TICONDEROGA-class missile cruisers have the same hull, propulsion, and auxiliary systems. The SPRUANCE class represents the largest destroyer class built by any Western navy since World War II.

Builders: The entire SPRUANCE class was contracted with a single shipyard to facilitate design and mass production. A contract for the development and production of 30 ships was awarded on 23 June 1970 to a new yard established by the Ingalls Shipbuilding Division of Litton Industries at Pascagoula, Miss. Labor and technical problems delayed the construction of these ships. The 31st ship was placed under contract in 1979 (see below).

Class: The SPRUANCE-class destroyers were developed as replacements for the large number of World War II–built general-purpose destroyers of the ALLEN M. SUMNER (DD 692) and GEARING (DD 710) classes that reached the end of their service lives in the mid-1970s. In addition to these 31 ships, four similar ships were ordered with the Mk 26/Standard AAW missile system for the Iranian Navy, but were completed as the USS KIDD class, accounting for hull numbers DD 993–996.

One additional ship of this class was ordered on 29 September 1979 (DD 997). This ship was one of two authorized (one funded) by Congress with the proviso that, in the wording of the Senate Committee on Armed Services, "The committee does not intend for these funds to be used for acquisition of two standard DD 963-class destroyers; rather, it is the committee's intention that these ships be the first element in a new technology approach to the problems of designing surface escorts. The standard [DD] 963 class design should be modified to substantially increase the number of helicopter aircraft carried." This feature could permit the eventual modification of the ships to operate VSTOL aircraft as well. However, the Navy chose to build the ship as a standard SPRUANCE, and no additional ships were funded by Congress. (The ship was initially listed as DDH 997 in Navy working papers.)

Design: SCB No. 224. The original concept for this class provided for an AAW missile version (DXG) as well as the ASW version (DX); these designs became the KIDD and SPRUANCE classes, respectively.

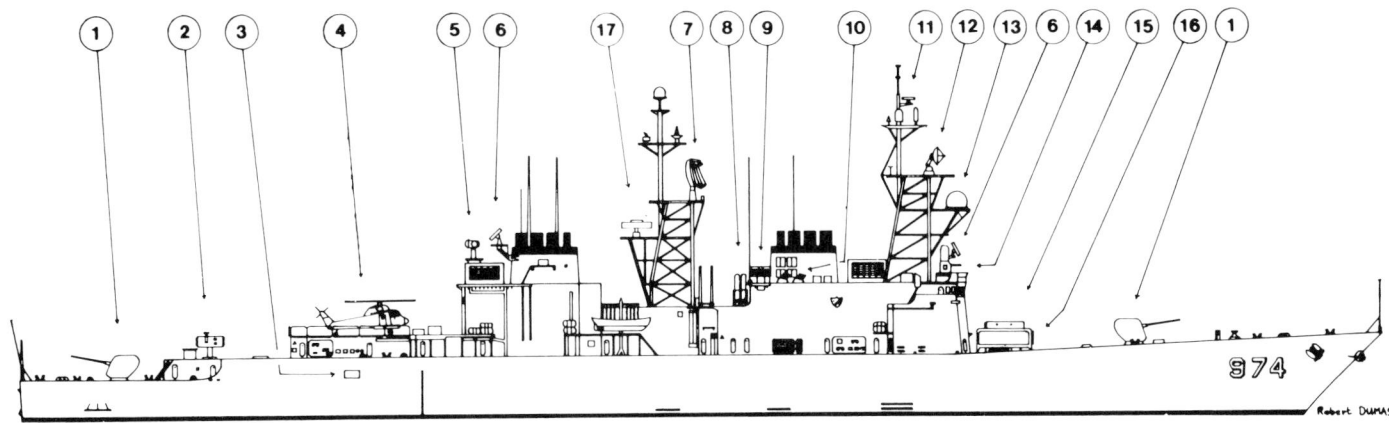

COMTE DE GRASSE: 1. 5-inch/54-cal single gun mount   2. NATO Sea Sparrow launcher   3. Mk 32 torpedo tubes (behind shutters)   4. helicopter deck   5. radar for Mk 91 missile director   6. OE-82 SATCOMM antenna   7. SPS-40 radar   8. Harpoon canisters   9. SLQ-32(V)2 ECM antenna   10. SPS-55 radar   11. 20-mm Phalanx CIWS   12. SPG-60 gun control radar   13. SPQ-9A radar   14. 20-mm Phalanx CIWS   15. ASROC rocket launcher   16. Tomahawk ABL   17. Mk 23 TAS radar (Robert Dumas)

The SPRUANCE design provided for the subsequent installation of additional weapon systems, specifically the Mk 26 missile launcher (and subsequently the Mk 41 VLS) forward with removal of the ASROC launcher and aft with removal of the Sea Sparrow launcher (see Missiles notes). In addition, the forward 5-inch gun could be replaced by the now-cancelled 8-inch Mk 71 Major Caliber Lightweight Gun.

The ASROC launcher is automatically reloaded, with a vertical magazine providing 16 reloads. A total of 24 Sea Sparrow missiles are normally carried.

Electronics: Original plans provided for these ships to have the SQS-35 Independent Variable Depth Sonar (IVDS) in addition to their bow-mounted SQS-53. The IVDS was deleted because of the effectiveness of the SQS-53.

These ships are now fitted with the SQR-19 TACTAS towed-array sonar. The STUMP was fitted with the engineering development model of the SQS-53C sonar; the MOOSBRUGGER was refitted with the SQS-53B sonar and was the first Navy ship to have the SQQ-89 system.

Four ships were fitted with the SQR-15 TASS; removed by 1992.

Engineering: These are the first U.S. Navy surface combatants to have gas-turbine propulsion. Gas turbines previously were installed in Navy patrol combatants (PGM/PG 84 class) and in the Coast Guard HAMILTON (WHEC 715) class as well as some RELIANCE (WMEC 615)-class cutters.

The SPRUANCE-class ships have four LM 2500 gas turbines, which are modified TF39 aircraft turbofan engines. Their maximum horsepower is about 86,000. One engine can propel the ships at about 19 knots, two engines at about 27 knots, and three and four engines can provide speeds in excess of 30 knots. The engines have a maximum rating of 86,000 shp; 80,000 shp is the sustained rating.

Helicopters: The sizes of the twin helicopter hangars in these ships vary; they are 49 to 54 feet (14.9 to 16.5 m) long, 21 to 23½ feet (6.4 to 7.2 m) wide, and at least 16 feet (4.9 m) high.

Manning: Crews vary from 19 to 26 officers and 291 to 361 enlisted.

Missiles: The MERRILL was fitted with armored box launchers for eight Tomahawk anti-ship cruise missiles in October 1982, the first U.S. surface ship to carry that weapon. The ABLs are mounted forward of the superstructure, alongside the ASROC launcher and aft of the 5-inch gun mount.

The Mk 41 Mod 1 VLS installation replaces the ASROC launcher and magazine. The VLS installation can launch the vertical-launch ASROC. The last VLS ship is scheduled to complete installation in 1996.

Names: The DD 974 carries the *title* of the admiral who led the French fleet that protected American forces from the British fleet and reinforcements in the Battle of Yorktown (1781), the last major battle in the American Revolution. The admiral's full name was Comte [Count] François Joseph Paull, Marquis de Grasse-Tilly.

Operational: Five ships of this class fired Tomahawk missiles during Operation Desert Storm:

CARON	2 missiles
FIFE	60 missiles
LEFTWICH	8 missiles
PAUL F. FOSTER	40 missiles
SPRUANCE	2 missiles

These 112 missiles were 39 percent of the Tomahawks fired during the Gulf War. The FOSTER fired the first Tomahawk missile and hence the "opening shot" of the Gulf War on 17 January 1991. While the FIFE had 61 missile cells, the Navy would not comment on whether a 61st missile was carried, or if it failed to launch, or was simply not required.

The ARTHUR W. RADFORD's 61-cell VLS installation. SPRUANCE-class destroyers fired more Tomahawk cruise missiles than any other ship types during the Persian Gulf conflict. The DDG variant of the SPRUANCE class—the KIDD class—has Mk 26 launchers forward and aft. (1990, Giorgio Arra)

The ARTHUR W. RADFORD as refitted with the Mk 41 Mod 0 vertical launcher system forward of the bridge; the ASROC box launcher is deleted, with the VLS being capable of firing the Vertical-Launch ASROC (VLA) if that weapon is procured in quantity. (1990, Giorgio Arra)

The CONOLLY with a Mk 29 NATO Sea Sparrow missile launcher between the helicopter deck and the after 5-inch gun mount. These are the only U.S. cruiser/destroyer-type ships fitted with the Sea Sparrow missile; it provides a limited air/missile-defense capability. (1990, Giorgio Arra)

The JOHN RODGERS is one of seven SPRUANCE-class destroyers fitted with two armored box launchers, each holding four Tomahawk cruise missiles. The ABLs are installed forward of the bridge, flanking the ASROC launcher; the ABLs open and elevate to fire. (1989, Giorgio Arra)

The MOOSBRUGGER with a partially lowered stem anchor. An SH-60B LAMPS III helicopter rests on the flight deck. The large quadrapod-lattice masts seem to be a revision to earlier surface combatant designs. (1990, Giorgio Arra)

DESTROYERS: "FORREST SHERMAN" CLASS

Number	Name	Comm.	Status
DD 931	FORREST SHERMAN	1955	str. 27 July 1990
DD 932	JOHN PAUL JONES	1956	to DDG 32; str. 30 Nov 1985
DD 933	BARRY	1956	str. 31 Jan 1983
DD 936	DECATUR	1956	to DDG 31; str. 16 Mar 1988
DD 937	DAVIS	1957	str. 27 July 1990
DD 938	JONAS INGRAM	1957	str. 15 June 1983
DD 940	MANLEY	1957	str. 1 June 1990
DD 941	DU PONT	1957	str. 1 June 1990
DD 942	BIGELOW	1957	str. 1 June 1990
DD 943	BLANDY	1957	str. 27 July 1990
DD 944	MULLINNIX	1958	str. 26 July 1990
DD 945	HULL	1958	str. 15 Oct 1983
DD 946	EDSON	1958	str. 31 Jan 1989
DD 947	SOMERS	1959	to DDG 34; str. 26 Apr 1988
DD 948	MORTON	1959	str. 7 Feb 1990
DD 949	PARSONS	1959	to DDG 33; str. 15 May 1984
DD 950	RICHARD S. EDWARDS	1959	str. 7 Feb 1990
DD 951	TURNER JOY	1959	str. 13 Feb 1990

These were the first U.S. Navy ships to be completed with the designation of "destroyer" after World War II; the four large destroyers of the MITSCHER class were built earlier, but they were completed with the classification "frigate" (DL). Further construction of this class was deferred in favor of the missile-armed CHARLES F. ADAMS class, which had the same general arrangement, but with a Tartar missile launcher in place of the third 5-inch gun.

All have been stricken. The last to be decommissioned was the EDSON, which served as an Officer Candidate School/NRF training ship at Newport, R.I.; she was assigned to NRF on 1 April 1977 and decommissioned and stricken on 15 December 1988. The BARRY is preserved as a memorial-museum ship at the Washington Navy Yard; the EDSON was transferred to the INTREPID (CVS 11) Sea-Air-Space Museum in New York City on 30 June 1989. The INGRAM, stripped of weapons and radars, serves as a test hulk at the Philadelphia Naval Shipyard.

Originally a class of 18 ships, four were converted to a guided missile configuration (DDG 31-34); further conversions were cancelled, primarily because of cost. The 14 others were scheduled for ASW modernization, but only eight were completed.

See 14th Edition/pages 156–158 for DD characteristics; see 13th Edition/pages 146–147 for DDG characteristics; previous editions contain decommissioning dates.

The FORREST SHERMAN-class destroyer BARRY—stricken in 1983—is now a memorial-museum ship at the Washington Navy Yard. The Navy Yard, which built 22 vessels from 1804 to 1879, is now an administrative and logistics complex for the Navy and several other agencies. The BARRY has an ASROC launcher aft, in place of the original No. 2 5-inch gun. (U.S. Navy)

TABLE 16-2. POST–WORLD WAR II DESTROYERS

Number	Name	Notes
DD 927–930	MITSCHER class	completed as DL 2–5
DD 931–933	FORREST SHERMAN class	
DD 934	ex-Japanese HANAZUKI	
DD 935	ex-German T-35	
DD 936–938	FORREST SHERMAN class	
DD 939	ex-German Z-39	
DD 940–951	FORREST SHERMAN class	
DD 952–959	CHARLES F. ADAMS class	completed as DDG 2–9
DD 960	(AKIZUKI)	Japan OSP 1960
DD 961	(TERUZUKI)	Japan OSP 1960
DD 962	(ex-British CHARITY)	to Pakistan 1958 (SHAH JAHAN)
DD 963–992	SPRUANCE class	
DD 993	(ex-Iranian KOUROSH)	completed as U.S. DDG 993
DD 994	(ex-Iranian DARYUSH)	completed as U.S. DDG 994
DD 995	(Iranian ARDESHIR)	cancelled June 1976
DD 996	(ex-Iranian NADER)	completed as U.S. DDG 995
DD 997	(Iranian SHAPOUR)	cancelled June 1976; reassigned to SPRUANCE class
DD 998	(ex-Iranian ANOUSHIRVAN)	completed as U.S. DDG 996

U.S. World War II destroyer programs reached hull number DD 926 (with hulls DD 891–926 being cancelled in 1945). Many ships built during the war were subsequently reclassified as escort destroyers (DDE), hunter-killer destroyers (DDK), radar picket destroyers (DDR), and experimental destroyers (EDD). One GEARING-class ship was converted to a missile configuration (DDG 712) to evaluate the Terrier system in a destroyer-size ship; changed to DDG 1. All except the DDG retained their DD hull numbers in their new roles.

All surviving special-configuration destroyers reverted to "straight" DD classification except for six DDRs during the early 1960s. Most ships were updated under the FRAM (Fleet Rehabilitation And Modernization) program of the early 1960s.

As indicated above, several war prizes and foreign-built ships (offshore procurement) had DD-series hull numbers, as did one British destroyer transferred to Pakistan with U.S. funds.[4]

4. While three Axis destroyers were given DD numbers, the Japanese battleship NAGATO, the German heavy cruiser PRINZ EUGEN, and several German and Japanese submarines acquired after World War II were not given warship designations. The German CA was assigned the designation IX 300 (sunk in Bikini atomic bomb tests of 1946 along with the NAGATO). The German supply ship CONECUH became the IX 301 and, subsequently, saw U.S. Navy service as the AO/AOR 110.

Six missile-armed ships of the SPRUANCE class ordered by Iran were assigned DD hull numbers by the U.S. Navy. The four ships actually built went to the U.S. Navy with DDG designations but with their DD-series hull numbers. The two other ships were cancelled, with one of their hull numbers being subsequently assigned to the thirty-first SPRUANCE-class ship.

TABLE 16-3. GUIDED MISSILE DESTROYERS

Number	Name	Comm.	Notes
DDG 1	GYATT (ex-DD 712)	1956	stricken (as DD 712)
DDG 2–24	CHARLES F. ADAMS class		
DDG 25	(Australian PERTH)	1965	
DDG 26	(Australian HOBART)	1965	
DDG 27	(Australian BRISBANE)	1967	
DDG 28	(German LÜTJENS)	1969	
DDG 29	(German MÖLDERS)	1969	
DDG 30	(German ROMMEL)	1970	
DDG 31	DECATUR (ex-DD 936)	1956	stricken 16 Mar 1988
DDG 32	JOHN PAUL JONES (ex-DD 932)	1956	stricken 1985
DDG 33	PARSONS (ex-DD 949)	1959	stricken 1984
DDG 34	SOMERS (ex-DD 947)	1959	stricken
DDG 35	MITSCHER (ex-DL 2)	1968	stricken 1978
DDG 36	JOHN S. MCCAIN (ex-DL 3)	1969	stricken 1978
DDG 37–46	FARRAGUT class (ex-DLG 6–15)		
DDG 47–50	TICONDEROGA class		changed to CG 47–50
DDG 51	ARLEIGH BURKE class		

The guided missile destroyer (DDG) classification was established in 1956. The first DDG was the GEARING-class destroyer GYATT (DD 712), fitted with a twin Terrier SAM launcher aft, replacing the ship's after 5-inch twin gun mount. The GYATT became DDG 712 on 3 December 1956 and DDG 1 on 23 April 1957. Subsequent DDGs were fitted with the smaller Tartar (later Standard-MR) missile system until the FARRAGUT-class frigates were reclassified as destroyers in 1975, those ships being armed with the Terrier/Standard-ER missile. Six ADAMS-class DDGs built for Australia and West Germany in U.S. shipyards were assigned the hull numbers DDG 25–30.

CHAPTER 17

Frigates

The REID is one of 35 OLIVER HAZARD PERRY-class frigates scheduled to remain in full commission in the late 1990s; another 16 are NRF ships manned by composite active-reserve crews. This class comprised one-half the U.S. frigate force of the 1980s, built to counter the massive Soviet submarine force. (1991, Giorgio Arra)

The Navy has 43 guided missile frigates (FFG) in active commission in late 1992 plus 16 ships assigned to the Naval Reserve Force (NRF) with composite active-reserve crews. This is an overall reduction of almost 65 ships from the Navy's active/NRF frigate strength of the late 1980s. All of the KNOX-class ships are being laid up in reserve (mothballs) except for eight ships that will be employed in the training role (designated FFT). This will reduce the total frigate force to 35 active ships and 16 NRF ships of the OLIVER HAZARD PERRY class by the mid-1990s. No additional frigates are planned for construction during the 1990s.

Frigates are primarily ASW ships, with the PERRY class intended to provide limited AAW defense to amphibious and replenishment groups and convoys. Despite the higher speed and missile capabilities of the PERRY class, these ships are still not capable of serving as effective escorts for carrier battle groups in wartime. These ships can also fire Harpoon anti-ship missiles from their Mk 13 missile launcher, albeit at the expense of anti-air missiles.

The large PERRY class has been controversial, having been initiated in the early 1970s together with the planned Sea Control Ship (SCS) to provide a viable capability for defending Sea Lines Of Communications (SLOC) against Soviet air and submarine attacks. Subsequent Navy planning has emphasized other missions, and while there are inadequate numbers of frigates to provide SLOC defense in the face of a Soviet attack, frigates are the only U.S. warship category in which the planned forces will exceed the force-level goals. The following table indicates the assignment of frigates to reach the frigate force-level goals under the Reagan administration's planned 600-ship fleet; the previous 92-frigate force-level objective is shown in parentheses.

Amphibious Forces	8 frigates (5)
7 Military Convoys	63 frigates (63)
10 Underway Replenishment Groups (URG)	30 frigates (24)
Totals	101 frigates (92)

These figures included both active and NRF ships, with a total of 26 frigates of the PERRY and KNOX classes scheduled for assignment to the reserves at the time.

All frigates of the earlier BROOKE and GARCIA classes have been discarded, and the two BRONSTEIN-class ships have been laid up.

In the mid-1980s the Navy began the design of an advanced frigate (FFX) for construction in the 1990s to replace the KNOX and previous frigate classes. That effort, however, was cancelled in 1986 by the Deputy Chief of Naval Operations (Surface Warfare) because of the large size of those designs (see below).

A smaller frigate (FFX) intended specifically for NRF service was planned by the Carter administration in the late 1970s, but was not built; neither will the long-gestation surface-effects-ship frigate (FFGS) be built.[1]

The Coast Guard's HAMILTON (WHEC 715)-class ships have frigate capabilities.

Classification: This type of warship was classified as destroyer escort (DE) from its inception in the U.S. Navy in 1941 until the early 1950s, when DE was changed to "ocean escort." (At that time the term "frigate" was applied to large destroyer-type ships—DL/DLG.)

Subsequently, missile-armed escort ships were designated DEG, and the escort research ship GLOVER became AGDE. All escort ships were changed to "frigate" (FF/FFG/AGFF) on 30 June 1975.

Guns: During the 1990–1991 Persian Gulf crisis several PERRY class frigates were fitted with .50-cal machine guns and 25-mm Bushmaster "chain" guns for close-in defense against small craft. The FAHRION and NICHOLAS were the first to carry the 25-mm weapon. The weapons are shifted from ship to ship as they forward deploy; accordingly, they are not listed under the specific class entries.

Names: The frigate ship type evolved from the World War II–era destroyer escort (DE), so frigates have destroyer-type names. The HAROLD E. HOLT remembers the deceased Australian prime minister who supported U.S. policy in the Vietnam War.

Operational: Frigates that participated in Operation Desert Shield/Desert Storm in 1990–1991 are indicated by asterisks in the ship entries.

TABLE 17-1. FRIGATE FORCE LEVELS [late 1992]

Number	Ship/Class	Comm.	Active	NRF	Reserve
FFG 7	OLIVER HAZARD PERRY	1977–1989	35	16	—
FFG 1	BROOKE	1966–1967	—	—	2*
FF 1052	KNOX	1969–1974	8	8	24
FF 1040	GARCIA	1964–1968	—	—	2*
FF 1037	BRONSTEIN	1963	—	—	2*

*These ships can be expected to be leased to foreign navies or otherwise disposed of in the near future.

1. In 1989–1990 The Soviet Navy completed the first Dergach-class guided missile surface effects ship, a heavily armed corvette-type ship of some 760 tons full load. See N. Polmar, *Guide to the Soviet Navy* (Annapolis, Md.: Naval Institute Press, 1991), p. 192.

GUIDED MISSILE FRIGATES: ADVANCED DESIGN

A low-level Navy design program to develop a multi-purpose frigate for construction in the 1990s was cancelled in April 1986 because of dissatisfaction with the efforts to date. Those efforts had produced preliminary designs of some 7,000 tons for a monohull ship and 9,200 tons for a SWATH (Small Waterplane Area Twin-Hull) design.

The SWATH configuration would have been approximately 300 feet (91.5 m) in length and, in some versions, could accommodate large helicopters (H-46/H-53 series) or the V-22 Osprey tilt-rotor aircraft.

The ships were considered too large and too expensive for the anticipated ship construction budgets of the 1990s.

51 GUIDED MISSILE FRIGATES: "OLIVER HAZARD PERRY" CLASS

Number	Name	FY	Builder	Laid down	Launched	Commissioned	Status (date to NRF)
FFG 7	OLIVER HAZARD PERRY	73	Bath Iron Works, Maine	12 June 1975	25 Sep 1976	17 Dec 1977	**NRF-A** (31 May 1984)
FFG 8	MCINERNEY*	75	Bath Iron Works, Maine	16 Jan 1978	4 Nov 1978	15 Dec 1979	**AA**
FFG 9	WADSWORTH	75	Todd Shipyards, San Pedro, Calif.	13 July 1977	29 July 1978	2 Apr 1980	**NRF-P** (30 June 1985)
FFG 10	DUNCAN	75	Todd Shipyards, Seattle, Wash.	29 Apr 1977	1 Mar 1978	24 May 1980	**NRF-P** (13 Jan 1984)
FFG 11	CLARK	76	Bath Iron Works, Maine	17 July 1978	24 Mar 1979	9 May 1980	**NRF-A** (30 Sep 1985)
FFG 12	GEORGE PHILIP	76	Todd Shipyards, San Pedro, Calif.	14 Dec 1977	16 Dec 1978	15 Nov 1980	**NRF-P** (18 Jan 1986)
FFG 13	SAMUEL ELIOT MORISON	76	Bath Iron Works, Maine	4 Dec 1978	14 July 1979	11 Oct 1980	**NRF-A** (30 June 1986)
FFG 14	SIDES	76	Todd Shipyards, San Pedro, Calif.	7 Aug 1978	19 May 1979	30 May 1981	**NRF-P** (9 Aug 1986)
FFG 15	ESTOCIN	76	Bath Iron Works, Maine	2 Apr 1979	3 Nov 1979	10 Jan 1981	**NRF-A** (30 Sep 1986)
FFG 16	CLIFTON SPRAGUE	76	Bath Iron Works, Maine	30 July 1979	16 Feb 1980	21 Mar 1981	**NRF-A** (31 Aug 1984)
FFG 19	JOHN A. MOORE	77	Todd Shipyards, San Pedro, Calif.	19 Dec 1978	20 Oct 1979	14 Nov 1981	**NRF-P** (30 Jan 1987)
FFG 20	ANTRIM	77	Todd Shipyards, Seattle, Wash.	21 June 1978	27 Mar 1979	26 Sep 1981	**NRF-A** (30 Jan 1987)
FFG 21	FLATLEY	77	Bath Iron Works, Maine	13 Nov 1979	15 May 1980	20 June 1981	**NRF-A** (30 Nov 1987)
FFG 22	FAHRION	77	Todd Shipyards, Seattle, Wash.	1 Dec 1978	24 Aug 1979	16 Jan 1982	**NRF-A** (30 Sep 1988)
FFG 23	LEWIS B. PULLER	77	Todd Shipyards, San Pedro, Calif.	23 May 1979	15 Mar 1980	17 Apr 1982	**NRF-P** (1 June 1987)
FFG 24	JACK WILLIAMS	77	Bath Iron Works, Maine	25 Feb 1980	30 Aug 1980	19 Sep 1981	**AA**
FFG 25	COPELAND	77	Todd Shipyards, San Pedro, Calif.	24 Oct 1979	26 July 1980	7 Aug 1982	**NRF-P** (30 Sep 1989)
FFG 26	GALLERY	77	Bath Iron Works, Maine	17 May 1980	20 Dec 1980	5 Dec 1981	**AA**
FFG 27	MAHLON S. TISDALE	78	Todd Shipyards, San Pedro, Calif.	19 Mar 1980	7 Feb 1981	13 Nov 1982	**NRF-P** (31 Jan 1988)
FFG 28	BOONE	78	Todd Shipyards, Seattle, Wash.	27 Mar 1979	16 Jan 1980	13 Nov 1982	**AA**
FFG 29	STEPHEN W. GROVES	78	Bath Iron Works, Maine	16 Sep 1980	4 Apr 1981	17 Apr 1982	**AA**
FFG 30	REID*	78	Todd Shipyards, San Pedro, Calif.	8 Oct 1980	27 June 1981	19 Feb 1983	**PA**
FFG 31	STARK	78	Todd Shipyards, Seattle, Wash.	24 Aug 1979	30 May 1980	23 Oct 1982	**AA**
FFG 32	JOHN L. HALL*	78	Bath Iron Works, Maine	5 Jan 1981	24 July 1981	26 June 1982	**AA**
FFG 33	JARRETT*	78	Todd Shipyards, San Pedro, Calif.	11 Feb 1981	17 Oct 1981	2 July 1983	**PA**
FFG 34	AUBREY FITCH	78	Bath Iron Works, Maine	10 Apr 1981	17 Oct 1981	9 Oct 1982	**AA**
FFG 36	UNDERWOOD	79	Bath Iron Works, Maine	3 Aug 1981	6 Feb 1982	29 Jan 1983	**AA**
FFG 37	CROMMELIN	79	Todd Shipyards, Seattle, Wash.	30 May 1980	1 July 1981	18 June 1983	**PA**
FFG 38	CURTS*	79	Todd Shipyards, San Pedro, Calif.	1 July 1981	6 Mar 1982	8 Oct 1983	**PA**
FFG 39	DOYLE	79	Bath Iron Works, Maine	23 Oct 1981	22 May 1982	21 May 1983	**AA**
FFG 40	HALYBURTON*	79	Todd Shipyards, Seattle, Wash.	26 Sep 1980	13 Oct 1981	7 Jan 1984	**AA**
FFG 41	MCCLUSKY	79	Todd Shipyards, San Pedro, Calif.	21 Oct 1981	18 Sep 1982	12 Oct 1983	**PA**
FFG 42	KLAKRING	79	Bath Iron Works, Maine	19 Feb 1982	18 Sep 1982	20 Aug 1983	**AA**
FFG 43	THACH	79	Todd Shipyards, San Pedro, Calif.	6 Mar 1982	18 Dec 1982	17 Mar 1984	**PA**
FFG 45	DE WERT	80	Bath Iron Works, Maine	14 June 1982	18 Dec 1982	19 Nov 1983	**AA**
FFG 46	RENTZ	80	Todd Shipyards, San Pedro, Calif.	18 Sep 1982	16 July 1983	30 June 1984	**PA**
FFG 47	NICHOLAS*	80	Bath Iron Works, Maine	27 Sep 1982	23 Apr 1983	10 Mar 1984	**AA**
FFG 48	VANDEGRIFT*	80	Todd Shipyards, Seattle, Wash.	13 Oct 1981	15 Oct 1982	24 Nov 1984	**PA**
FFG 49	ROBERT G. BRADLEY	80	Bath Iron Works, Maine	28 Dec 1982	13 Aug 1983	11 Aug 1984	**AA**
FFG 50	TAYLOR*	81	Bath Iron Works, Maine	5 May 1983	5 Nov 1983	1 Dec 1984	**AA**
FFG 51	GARY	81	Todd Shipyards, San Pedro, Calif.	18 Dec 1982	19 Nov 1983	17 Nov 1984	**PA**
FFG 52	CARR	81	Todd Shipyards, Seattle, Wash.	26 Mar 1982	26 Feb 1983	27 July 1985	**AA**
FFG 53	HAWES*	81	Bath Iron Works, Maine	22 Aug 1983	17 Feb 1984	9 Feb 1985	**AA**
FFG 54	FORD*	81	Todd Shipyards, San Pedro, Calif.	16 July 1983	23 June 1984	29 June 1985	**PA**
FFG 55	ELROD	81	Bath Iron Works, Maine	21 Nov 1983	12 May 1984	6 July 1985	**AA**
FFG 56	SIMPSON	82	Bath Iron Works, Maine	27 Feb 1984	31 Aug 1984	9 Nov 1985	**AA**
FFG 57	REUBEN JAMES	82	Todd Shipyards, San Pedro, Calif.	19 Nov 1983	8 Feb 1985	22 Mar 1986	**PA**
FFG 58	SAMUEL B. ROBERTS*	82	Bath Iron Works, Maine	21 May 1984	8 Dec 1984	12 Apr 1986	**AA**
FFG 59	KAUFFMAN	83	Bath Iron Works, Maine	8 Apr 1985	29 Mar 1986	21 Feb 1987	**AA**
FFG 60	RODNEY M. DAVIS	83	Todd Shipyards, San Pedro, Calif.	8 Feb 1985	11 Jan 1986	9 May 1987	**PA**
FFG 61	INGRAHAM	84	Todd Shipyards, San Pedro, Calif.	30 Mar 1987	25 June 1988	5 Aug 1989	**PA**

Displacement:	2,769 tons light except 3,210 tons for ships with LAMPS III modification	Missiles:	1 single Mk 13 Mod 4 launcher for Standard-MR SM-1 SAM/ Harpoon SSM (40)
	3,658 tons full load except 3,900–4,100 tons for ships with LAMPS III modification	Guns:	1 76-mm/62-cal DP Mk 75
			1 20-mm Phalanx CIWS Mk 16 (multi-barrel) in active ships and FFG 13
Length:	413 feet (125.9 m) waterline	ASW weapons:	6 12.75-in (324-mm) torpedo tubes Mk 32 (2 triple)
	445 feet (135.6 m) overall except 455¼ feet (138.8 m) for ships with LAMPS III modification	Radars:	SPS-49(V)4 air search except SPS-49(V)5 in FFG 50 and FFG 61
Beam:	45 feet (13.7 m)		SPS-55 surface search
Draft:	21¹¹/₁₂ feet (6.7 m)	Sonars:	SQS-56 keel mounted
Propulsion:	2 gas turbines (General Electric LM 2500); 40,000 shp; 1 shaft		SQR-19 towed array in active ships except FFG 24 and 26
Speed:	29 knots (sustained; see notes)	Fire control:	1 Mk 13 weapon direction system
Range:	5,000 n.miles (9,260 km) at 18 knots		1 Mk 92 weapons FCS
	4,200 n.miles (7,778 km) at 20 knots		1 STIR radar
Manning:	active ships approx. 214 (16 officers + 198 enlisted)		SQQ-89(V)2 ASW system in active ships except FFG 24 and 26
	NRF ships approx. 114 active (11 officers + 103 enlisted) + 76 reserve (4 officers + 72 enlisted)		SYS-2(V)2 Integrated Automatic Detection and Tracking (IADT) system in FFG 50 and FFG 61
Helicopters:	2 SH-60B Seahawk LAMPS III in FFG 8, 36–61	EW systems	SLQ-25 Nixie
	1 SH-2F LAMPS I in FFG 7, 9–35		SLQ-32(V)2 except SLQ-32(V)5 Sidekick in FFG 30, 53, and several other units

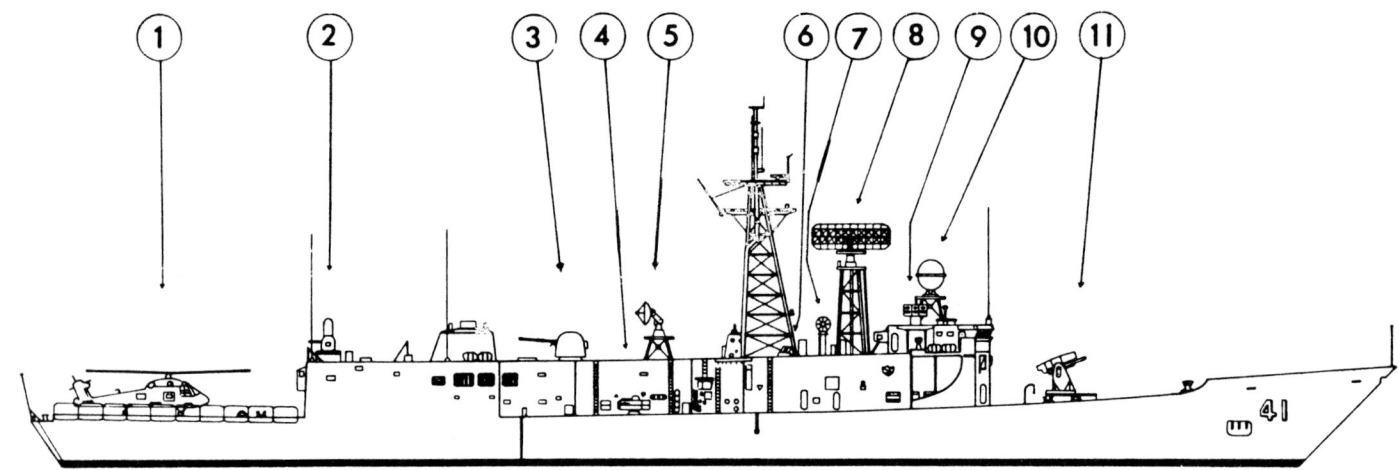

McCLUSKEY: 1. helicopter deck   2. 20-mm Phalanx CIWS   3. 76-mm/62-cal single gun mount   4. Mk 32 torpedo tubes   5. STIR fire control radar
6. SRBOC chaff launchers   7. OE-82 SATCOMM antennas   8. SPS-49(V)2 radar   9. SLQ-32(V)2 ECM antenna   10. Mk 92 fire control radome
11. Mk 13 missile launcher (Robert Dumas)

This is the second largest class of major surface warships to be built by any nation since World War II; only the Soviet SKORYY destroyer class was larger, with 72 ships completed between 1950 and 1954. Sixteen of the PERRY-class frigates are operated by the Naval Reserve Force; the others are in active service.

These ships were constructed to provide a frigate force to escort merchant ships, especially tankers carrying Middle East petroleum, during a prolonged campaign against Western shipping. After the cutback of the DX/DXG program, i.e., SPRUANCE (DD 963) class, the FFG 7 class was additionally looked upon as a replacement for the surviving GEARING (DD 710)-class destroyers.

These ships lack the large, hull-mounted active/passive sonar and ASROC launcher of previous frigate classes. However, their towed array and ability to support two large LAMPS III helicopters make them useful ASW ships. In addition, they have a surface-to-air missile system, a feature lacking in all but six of the previous U.S. post–World War II frigates.[2] And despite their relatively light construction, according to the reference work *Combat Fleets of the World,* "The soundness of the design has permitted the expansion [of capabilities], and the ships have proven remarkably sturdy."[3]

The CURTS, McCLUSKY, THACH, and RODNEY M. DAVIS are home-ported in Yokosuka, Japan.

The PERRY's gun, fire control, and sonar systems were evaluated in the frigate TALBOT.

Anti-submarine: The only ship-mounted ASW weapons are torpedo tubes; the SH-60B helicopters are their primary ASW weapon. These are the first U.S. surface combatants built without ASROC since that weapon became available in the early 1960s.

Class: Early U.S. Navy planning provided for approximately 75 ships of this class. Shipbuilding programs of the early 1970s reduced the number of ships to be built in "later" years, in part because of the planned FFX, a smaller frigate intended specifically for NRF operation (see page 151).

The last Carter administration five-year plan, for fiscal 1982–1986, deleted all FFG 7 construction after one ship in the 1983 program. However, the Reagan administration's shipbuilding program put forward in January 1982 for fiscal 1983–1987 provided for 12 additional FFGs:

FY 1983	2 ships
FY 1984	2 ships
FY 1985	2 ships
FY 1986	3 ships
FY 1987	3 ships

The Congress voted the two ships in the fiscal 1983 budget, but the Reagan administration's subsequent five-year plan (FY 1984–1988)

deleted all further frigate construction, thus halting the FFG 7 program at 50 ships. Congress subsequently funded one additional ship in the fiscal 1984 budget for construction at the Todd San Pedro yard (FFG 61).

The Todd-Seattle yard built four ships of this class for the Australian Navy (given the U.S. designations FFG 17, 18, 35, and 44), delivered from 1980 to 1983. Additional ships of this design are being constructed in Australia and in Spain for their respective navies; a modified PERRY design is also being built by Taiwan (CHENG KUNG class).

Classification: When conceived these ships were classified as "patrol frigates" (PF), a designation previously applied to a series of smaller World War II–era ships (PF 1–102) and postwar coastal escorts that were constructed specifically for foreign transfer (PF 103–108). The PERRY was designated PF 109 until changed to "frigate" FFG 7 on 30 June 1975.

Design: SCB design No. 261. During their design phase the Chief of Naval Operations[4] placed constraints on the ships' cost, displacement, and crew size:

- $50 million in then-year dollars
- 3,530 tons full load
- 185 crew (17 officers + 168 enlisted); see Manning notes

All were exceeded, although the design did arrest the upward trend in frigate (DE/FF) cost, size, and manning requirements.

These ships were designed specifically for modular assembly and mass production. All major components were tested at sea or in land facilities before completion of the lead ship. Space and weight were reserved for fin stabilizers, which were installed during construction in FFG 36 and later units. Early designs provided for a single hangar aft with twin funnels ("split" by the hangar). The design was revised to provide separate, side-by-side hangars to accommodate two SH-60B helicopters (see Helicopter notes).

The hangars vary in size. They are approximately 41 to 46 feet (12.5 to 14 m) long, each 13⅔ to 16 feet (4.2 to 4.9 m) wide, and 13½ to 15½ feet (4.1 to 4.7 m) in height. In addition to the fantail landing area, the ships have a VERTREP area forward.

Electronics: The STIR (Separate Target Illumination Radar) is a modified SPG-60 radar. The Sperry Corporation (now Unisys) had lobbied Congress and the Navy to install a phased-array radar in the later ships of this class, with a backfit to the earlier ships. However, the cost was considered prohibitive by the Navy.

The INGRAHAM was completed with an improved combat system developed by Sperry/Unisys, referred to as CORT (Coherent Receiver/Transmitter). It consists of the Mk 92 Mod 6 fire control system with the SYS-2(V)2 automatic tracking system. The ship's SPS-49(V)5 digital radar has enhanced ECM capabilities. A similar CORT refit of the TAYLOR was completed in 1991, and the GARY and UNDERWOOD were to complete in late 1992.

---

2. The point-defense missile system fitted in a number of previous frigates does have a limited anti-air capability, but is intended primarily to defeat incoming Styx-like cruise missiles.
3. Bernard Prézelin and A.D. Baker III, *Combat Fleets of the World 1990/1991* (Annapolis, Md.: Naval Institute Press, 1990), p. 805.

4. Adm. Elmo R. Zumwalt, CNO from 1970 to 1974.

The ANTRIM, an NRF ship, shows the long, boxy superstructure of this class. The low gas-turbine exhaust stack (funnel) is fitted between the hangars, forward of the Phalanx CIWS. The ship does not have the RAST extension. (1991, Giorgio Arra)

The Sidekick ECM installation provides an active countermeasures capability to the otherwise passive SLQ-32(V)2.

The SQR-18A towed sonar array is fitted in the NRF ships, and the SQR-19 towed sonar array is provided in the active units. The first ship to be built with the SQR-19 was the ELROD, with the array to be backfitted in the earlier ships. The severely limited capabilities of hull-mounted SQS-56 will make these ships rely primarily on the towed array for effective ASW. Several ships were provided with the so-called Kingfisher modification for mine detection; some ships employed it in that role during Operation Desert Storm.

The SQQ-89I ASW combat system was intended for installation in this class. The plan was cancelled in 1990 because of budgetary constraints. (The system is being installed in cruisers and destroyers.)

Engineering: These ships have two LM 2500 gas turbine main-propulsion engines and can attain 25 knots on one engine. On trials some ships reportedly have reached 36 knots. The maximum rated horsepower is 41,000; the sustained shp is shown above.

The ships have two 350-hp electric-drive, retractable auxiliary propulsion pods for precise maneuvering; they also provide a "come-home" capability at six knots in the event of main propulsion failure. They are fitted with four 1,000-kilowatt diesel ship's service generators, thus lacking the elaborate silencing of the SPRUANCE-class destroyers, which have gas turbine generators.

Guns: Early designs addressed a variety of guns for these ships, among them a twin 35-mm rapid-fire gun in place of the later 76-mm gun and CIWS. These are the first U.S. surface combatants built since the early 1960s without a 5-inch gun.

Helicopters: These are the first U.S. ships fitted with a helicopter haul-down system. The MCINERNEY tested the helicopter hauldown system and conducted FFG sea trials with the SH-60B in 1981. The hauldown system is designated RAST (Recovery Assistance, Securing, and Traversing system).[5] It permits the recovery of helicopters with the ship rolling through 28° and pitching up to 5°. RAST was backfitted in those ships completed prior to the TAYLOR (ships that have LAMPS III capability), with that ship being the first to be completed with the RAST system.

Except for the MCINERNEY, the first 26 ships will retain their SH-2F/LAMPS I capability for the foreseeable future.

The DOYLE served as trials ship for the Canadair CL-227 Sentinel unmanned aerial reconnaissance vehicle, a peanut-shaped Vertical Take-Off and Landing (VTOL) aircraft.

Manning: The original complement was to be 179 (12 officers + 167 enlisted); it was increased to 185 by the time the design was completed (17 officers + 168 enlisted). The crews of active ships vary considerably, from 13 to 19 officers and from 184 to 215 enlisted.

Operational: While operating in the Persian Gulf the STARK was struck by two Exocet missiles launched by an Iraqi Mirage F1 aircraft on the night of 17 May 1987 that mistook the frigate for an Iranian ship. The STARK suffered 37 dead as one of the missile warheads detonated, with unexpended fuel in both setting fires and causing heavy damage. The STARK was able to return to the United States under her own power and underwent 15 months of repairs at the Litton/Ingalls yard. The repairs cost an estimated $90 million.

The SAMUEL B. ROBERTS struck an Iranian-laid mine in the Persian Gulf on 14 April 1988. The ship suffered a 22-foot (6.7-m) gash in her side, a 9-foot (2.7-m) tear in her bottom, cracked superstructure, gas turbines knocked from their mountings, and heavy flooding; ten sailors were injured, but there were no fatalities. After emergency repairs, on 1 July 1988 the crippled ROBERTS departed the Gulf on the Dutch-flag heavy-lift ship MIGHTY SERVANT 2; the frigate was brought back to the United States and underwent 18 months of repairs at Bath Iron Works. The repairs cost an estimated $37.5 million.

The stern of the "long-hull" NICHOLAS, which has been refitted with RAST. During Operations Desert Shield/Desert Storm, the NICHOLAS joined other Navy ships in operating Army OH-58 special-operations helicopters as well as their own LAMPS I/III helicopters against Iraqi forces. (1991, Giorgio Arra)

5. The RAST system was developed for the Canadian Navy; it has been used in U.S. Navy ships since the late 1980s.

The UNDERWOOD and other PERRY-class frigates differ from the previous 67 U.S. Navy frigates in not having a large, bow-mounted sonar of the SQS-26 series. Rather, these ships rely primarily on the SQR-19 towed array and helicopter-launched sonobuoys for long-range passive detection. (1991, Giorgio Arra)

The REID's Mk 13 Standard-MR missile launcher sits atop a cylindrical, rotary magazine, similar to those of the Mk 11 launcher and several Russian shipboard missile systems. The SLQ-32(V)2 ECM antennas are outboard of the Mk 92 radome; the OE-82 SATCOMM antennas are immediately behind them. (1991, Giorgio Arra)

The stern of the "long-hull" UNDERWOOD. The hangars are separated by a passageway and the gas-turbine exhaust uptakes. There is a helicopter control station between the hangar doors. Twin openings for the SLQ-25 Nixie towed torpedo countermeasures and one for the towed array penetrate the stern counter. (1991, Giorgio Arra)

2 GUIDED MISSILE FRIGATES: "BROOKE" CLASS

Number	Name	Status
FFG 1	BROOKE	decomm. 16 Sep 1988; to Pakistan 1989
FFG 2	RAMSEY	PR decomm. 1 Sep 1988
FFG 3	SCHOFIELD	PR decomm. 8 Sep 1988
FFG 4	TALBOT	decomm. 30 Sep 1988; to Pakistan 1989
FFG 5	RICHARD L. PAGE	decomm. 30 Sep 1988; to Pakistan 1989
FFG 6	JULIUS A. FURER	decomm. 10 Nov 1988; to Pakistan 1989

These were the Navy's first ASW frigates armed with surface-to-air missiles with a Tartar/Standard launcher in place of the second 5-inch gun of the similar GARCIA class. Six ships were completed in 1966–1967. Additional ships of this configuration were planned but not built because of the significantly higher costs of the missile variants compared to all-gun ASW frigates.

These and the GARCIA-class all-gun frigates were the first ships to be taken out of active service after Secretary of the Navy John Lehman stepped down from that office in 1987, ending the effort to build a 600-ship fleet. Four ships have been leased to Pakistan. The RAMSEY and SCHOFIELD were to go to Turkey but were rejected by that Navy; they are stored at Bremerton, Wash., awaiting final disposition.[6]

See 14th Edition/pages 168–169 for characteristics.

6. See appendix D for dates of lease.

46 FRIGATES: "KNOX" CLASS

Number	Name	FY	Builder	Laid down	Launched	Commissioned	Status
FF 1052	KNOX	64	Todd Shipyards, Seattle, Wash.	5 Oct 1965	19 Nov 1966	12 Apr 1969	PR decomm. 14 Feb 1992
FF 1053	ROARK	64	Todd Shipyards, Seattle, Wash.	2 Feb 1966	24 Apr. 1967	22 Nov 1969	PR decomm. 14 Dec 1991
FF 1054	GRAY	64	Todd Shipyards, Seattle, Wash.	19 Nov 1966	3 Nov 1967	4 Apr 1970	PR decomm. 29 Sep 1991
FF 1055	HEPBURN	64	Todd Shipyards, San Pedro, Calif.	1 June 1966	25 Mar 1967	3 July 1969	PR decomm. 20 Dec 1991
FF 1056	CONNOLE	64	Avondale Shipyards, New Orleans, La.	23 Mar 1967	20 July 1968	30 Aug 1969	AR decomm. Aug 1992
FF 1057	RATHBURNE	64	Lockheed SB & Constn., Seattle, Wash.	8 Jan 1968	2 May 1969	16 May 1970	PR decomm. 14 Feb 1992
FF 1058	MEYERKORD	64	Todd Shipyards, San Pedro, Calif.	1 Sep 1966	15 July 1967	28 Nov 1969	PR decomm. 14 Dec 1991
FF 1059	W. S. SIMS	64	Avondale Shipyards, New Orleans, La.	10 Apr 1967	4 Jan 1969	3 Jan 1970	AR decomm. 6 Sep 1991
FF 1060	LANG	64	Todd Shipyards, San Pedro, Calif.	25 May 1967	17 Feb 1968	28 May 1970	PR decomm. 12 Dec 1991
FF 1061	PATTERSON	64	Avondale Shipyards, New Orleans, La.	12 Oct 1967	3 May 1969	14 Mar 1970	AR decomm. 30 Sep 1991
FF 1062	WHIPPLE	65	Todd Shipyards, Seattle, Wash.	24 Apr 1967	12 Apr 1968	22 Aug 1970	PR decomm. 14 Feb 1992
FF 1063	REASONER*	65	Lockheed SB & Constn., Seattle, Wash.	6 Jan 1969	1 Aug 1970	31 Jul 1971	PR decomm. July 1992
FF 1064	LOCKWOOD	65	Todd Shipyards, Seattle, Wash.	3 Nov 1967	5 Sep 1968	5 Dec 1970	**PA** decomm. 1993
FF 1065	STEIN	65	Lockheed SB & Constn., Seattle, Wash.	1 June 1970	19 Dec 1970	8 Jan 1972	PR decomm. 19 Mar 1992
FF 1066	MARVIN SHIELDS*	65	Todd Shipyards, Seattle, Wash.	12 Apr 1968	23 Oct 1969	10 Apr 1971	**PA** decomm. 1993
FF 1067	FRANCIS HAMMOND*	65	Todd Shipyards, San Pedro, Calif.	15 July 1967	11 May 1968	25 July 1970	PR decomm. 2 July 1992
FF 1068	VREELAND*	65	Avondale Shipyards, New Orleans, La.	20 Mar 1968	14 June 1969	13 June 1970	decomm. 30 June 1992; lease
FF 1069	BAGLEY	65	Lockheed SB & Constn., Seattle, Wash.	22 Sep 1970	24 Apr 1971	9 May 1972	PR decomm. 26 Sep 1991
FF 1070	DOWNES	65	Todd Shipyards, Seattle, Wash.	5 Sep 1968	13 Dec 1969	28 Aug 1971	PR decomm. 5 June 1992
FF 1071	BADGER	65	Todd Shipyards, Seattle, Wash.	17 Feb 1968	7 Dec 1968	1 Dec 1970	PR decomm. 20 Dec 1991
FF 1072	BLAKELY	65	Avondale Shipyards, New Orleans, La.	3 June 1968	23 Aug 1969	18 July 1970	AR decomm. 15 Nov 1991
FF 1073	ROBERT E. PEARY	65	Lockheed SB & Constn., Seattle, Wash.	20 Dec 1970	23 June 1971	23 Sep 1972	decomm. 7 Aug 1992; lease
FF 1074	HAROLD E. HOLT	65	Todd Shipyards, San Pedro, Calif.	11 May 1968	3 May 1969	26 Mar 1971	PR decomm. 2 July 1992
FF 1075	TRIPPE	65	Avondale Shipyards, New Orleans, La.	29 July 1968	1 Nov 1969	19 Sep 1970	decomm. 30 July 1992; lease
FF 1076	FANNING	65	Todd Shipyards, San Pedro, Calif.	7 Dec 1968	24 Jan 1970	23 July 1971	**PA** decomm. 1993
FF 1077	OUELLET	65	Avondale Shipyards, New Orleans, La.	15 Jan 1969	17 Jan 1970	12 Dec 1970	**PA** decomm. 1993
FF 1078	JOSEPH HEWES	66	Avondale Shipyards, New Orleans, La.	15 May 1969	7 Mar 1970	24 Apr 1971	to FFT 15 Dec 1991
FF 1079	BOWEN	66	Avondale Shipyards, New Orleans, La.	11 July 1969	2 May 1970	22 May 1971	to FFT 15 Dec 1991
FF 1080	PAUL	66	Avondale Shipyards, New Orleans, La.	12 Sep 1969	20 June 1970	14 Aug 1971	AR decomm. 15 Aug 1992
FF 1081	AYLWIN	66	Avondale Shipyards, New Orleans, La.	13 Nov 1969	29 Aug 1970	18 Sep 1971	AR decomm. 15 May 1992
FF 1082	ELMER MONTGOMERY*	66	Avondale Shipyards, New Orleans, La.	23 Jan 1970	21 Nov 1970	30 Oct 1971	**AA** decomm. 1993
FF 1083	COOK	66	Avondale Shipyards, New Orleans, La.	20 Mar 1970	23 Jan 1971	18 Dec 1971	PR decomm. 30 Apr 1992
FF 1084	McCANDLESS	66	Avondale Shipyards, New Orleans, La.	4 June 1970	20 Mar 1971	18 Mar 1972	to FFT 31 Dec 1991
FF 1085	DONALD B. BEARY	66	Avondale Shipyards, New Orleans, La.	24 July 1970	20 May 1971	22 July 1972	to FFT 15 Dec 1991
FF 1086	BREWTON*	66	Avondale Shipyards, New Orleans, La.	2 Oct 1970	24 July 1971	8 July 1972	decomm. 2 July 1992; lease
FF 1087	KIRK	66	Avondale Shipyards, New Orleans, La.	4 Dec 1970	25 Sep 1971	9 Sep 1972	**PA** decomm. 1993; lease
FF 1088	BARBEY*	67	Avondale Shipyards, New Orleans, La.	5 Feb 1971	4 Dec 1971	13 Nov 1972	PR decomm. 19 Mar 1992
FF 1089	JESSE L. BROWN	67	Avondale Shipyards, New Orleans, La.	8 Apr 1971	18 Mar 1972	17 Feb 1973	to FFT 31 Dec 1991
FF 1090	AINSWORTH	67	Avondale Shipyards, New Orleans, La.	11 June 1971	15 Apr 1972	31 Mar 1973	to FFT 15 Dec 1991
FF 1091	MILLER	67	Avondale Shipyards, New Orleans, La.	6 Aug 1971	3 June 1972	30 June 1973	AR decomm. 15 Oct 1991
FF 1092	THOMAS C. HART*	67	Avondale Shipyards, New Orleans, La.	8 Oct 1971	12 Aug 1972	28 July 1973	**AA** decomm. 1993
FF 1093	CAPODANNO	67	Avondale Shipyards, New Orleans, La.	12 Oct 1971	21 Oct 1972	17 Nov 1973	**AA** decomm. 1993
FF 1094	PHARRIS	67	Avondale Shipyards, New Orleans, La.	11 Feb 1972	16 Dec 1972	26 Jan 1974	AR decomm. 11 Apr 1992
FF 1095	TRUETT	67	Avondale Shipyards, New Orleans, La.	27 Apr 1972	3 Feb 1973	1 June 1974	to FFT 31 Dec 1991
FF 1096	VALDEZ	67	Avondale Shipyards, New Orleans, La.	30 June 1972	24 Mar 1973	27 July 1974	AR decomm. 16 Dec 1991
FF 1097	MOINESTER	67	Avondale Shipyards, New Orleans, La.	25 Aug 1972	12 May 1973	2 Nov 1974	to FFT 31 Dec 1991

Displacement:	3,075 tons light	Helicopters:	1 SH-2F LAMPS I
	4,260 tons full load	Missiles:	1 8-tube Sea Sparrow BPDMS launcher Mk 25 in FF 1052–1069,
Length:	414$^{11}/_{12}$ feet (126.5 m) waterline		1071–1083
	439½ feet (134.0 m) overall		Harpoon SSM fired from ASROC launcher
Beam:	47 feet (14.3 m)	Guns:	1 5-inch (127-mm) 54-cal DP Mk 42
Draft:	24¾ feet (7.55 m)		1 20-mm Phalanx CIWS Mk 16 (multi-barrel)
Propulsion:	1 steam turbine (Westinghouse); 35,000 shp; 1 shaft	ASW weapons:	1 8-tube ASROC launcher Mk 16
Boilers:	2 1,200 psi (83.4 kg/cm²) (Combustion Engineering except		4 12.75-inch (324-mm) torpedo tubes Mk 32 (4 single)
	Babcock & Wilcox in FF 1056, 1057, 1061, 1063, 1065, 1072,	Radars:	1 LN-66 or CRP-series Pathfinder or SPS-53 navigation
	1073, 1075, 1077)		1 SPS-10 or SPS-67 surface search
Speed:	27+ knots		1 SPS-40B air search
Range:	4,300 n.miles (7,964 km) at 20 knots		1 SPS-58 threat warning in some ships
Manning:	active ships approx. 283 (20 officers + 263 enlisted)	Sonars:	SQS-26CX bow mounted
	FFT ships 177 active (14 officers + 163 enlisted) + 61 reserve		SQS-35 IVDS in FF 1052, 1056, 1063–1071, 1073–1076,
	(4 officers + 57 enlisted)[7]		1078–1097
	NRF ships vary—175 active (10 officers + 165 enlisted)		SQR-18A (see Electronics notes)
	+ 136–164 reserve (9 officers + 127–155 enlisted)	Fire control:	1 Mk 1 target designation system
			1 Mk 68 GFCS with SPG-53A/D/F radar

7. The active personnel include 9 officers + 67 enlisted who are designated as TAR (Training and Administration of Reserves); the reservists are on two-year active-duty training, and will then go into the regular reserve force (drilling on weekends and for two weeks per year). In addition, each weekend and for cruises another 61 reservists will be on board—4 officers + 57 enlisted.

	1 Mk 114 ASW FCS
	1 Mk 115 Missile FCS in ships with Sea Sparrow
	SQR-17 sonar processor/data link
EW systems:	SLQ-32(V)1/2
	T Mk 6 Fanfare in FF 1074, 1079–1081, 1086, 1087, and 1097

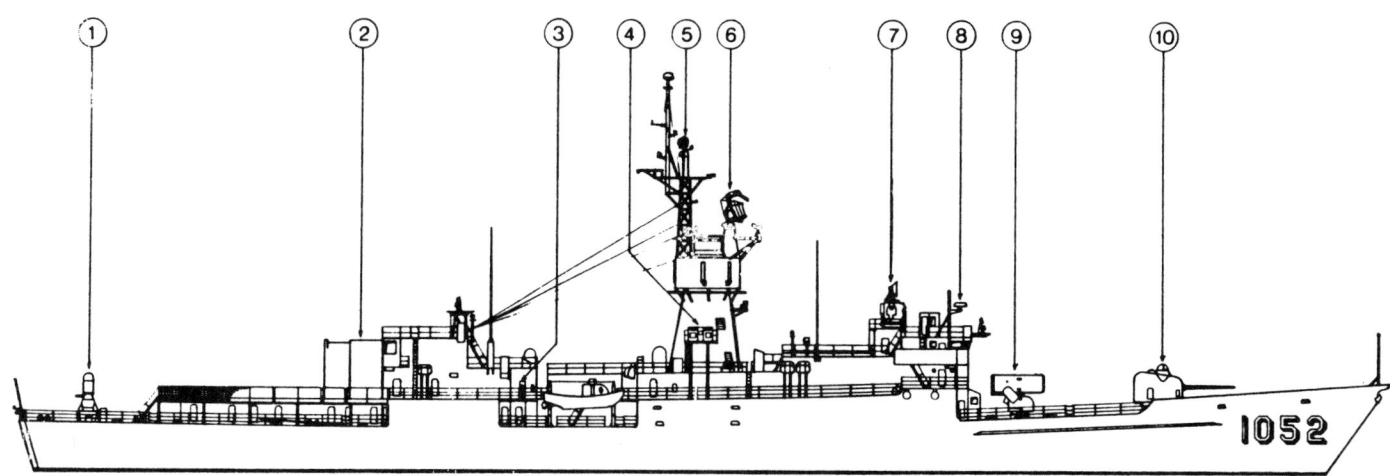

KNOX: 1. 20-mm Phalanx CIWS   2. telescoping helicopter hangar   3. Mk 32 torpedo tubes (in deckhouse)   4. SLQ-32(V)2 ECM antenna   5. SPS-10 radar   6. SPS-40 radar   7. Mk 68 GFCS   8. navigation radar   9. ASROC rocket launcher   10. 5-inch/38-cal single gun mount (A.D. Baker III)

This was the largest class of surface combatants to be constructed in the West since World War II prior to the PERRY-class frigates. The KNOX-class ships have been highly criticized for their large size (comparable to World War II–era destroyers) with a single propeller shaft and limited AAW/ASUW capabilities. The latter limitation has been partially corrected with the Harpoon missile fired from the ASROC launcher.

In 1991, in conjunction with the massive fleet reductions, the decision was made to take the entire KNOX class out of active service: 6 ships are being leased to other navies; 32 ships will be kept in a state of "reduced maintenance" (mobilization category B); and 8 ships have been designated as training frigates (FFT), to be NRF-operated to train nucleus crews for the other 32 ships. It is estimated that the reduced maintenance ships could be returned to full operational capability—if crews and industrial facilities are available—within 180 days. In addition, the ships would require some 60 to 90 days of at-sea training before they could be considered fully operational. All FFTs except AINSWORTH became NRF ships immediately prior to becoming FFTs.

The 32 laid up ships will be stowed in an "as is" condition, with the radar antennas removed and stowed on deck, but with their Phalanx CIWS and SLQ-32 systems removed and stored ashore.

Class: Ten additional ships were authorized in the fiscal 1968 budget (DE 1098–1107); the construction of the last six ships (DE 1102–1107) was deferred in 1968 in favor of the more-capable

SPRUANCE-class destroyers, and three other ships (DE 1099–1101) were deferred later that year to help pay for cost overruns of nuclear submarines; one shp (DE 1098) was deferred in 1969. Note that hull number 1098 was reassigned to the *earlier* GLOVER (formerly AGDE/AGFF 1; now AGFF 1).

Five similar ships were built in Spain with a SAM launcher amidships, designated DEG 7–11 for U.S. Navy record purposes.

Thirteen ships had been assigned to the NRF through early 1991, when the decision was made to take the entire class out of service:

FF 1053	to NRF	1 June 1987
FF 1054	to NRF	15 July 1982
FF 1055	to NRF	1 Oct 1989
FF 1058	to NRF	30 Sep 1989
FF 1059	to NRF	30 Sep 1990
FF 1060	to NRF	17 Jan 1982
FF 1061	to NRF	15 June 1983
FF 1072	to NRF	11 June 1983
FF 1083	to NRF	1 Oct 1989
FF 1088	to NRF	15 Jan 1991
FF 1090	to NRF	30 Sep 1990
FF 1091	to NRF	17 Jan 1982
FF 1096	to NRF	14 Aug 1982

The TRIPPE showing the bow bulwark and spray strake forward to reduce wetness on the forecastle. Although designed for convoy escort, the KNOX-class ships have been employed in fleet operations. (1991, Giorgio Arra)

The KIRK (FF 1087) was scheduled to shift to NRF status prior to being decommissioned about August 1993; at that time the ship will be available for foreign lease.

Classification: These ships were built as ocean escorts (DE); they were changed to frigates on 30 June 1975.

Electronics: The VDS ships have the SQR-18A(V)1 towed array fitted to their variable-depth sonar "fish" (transducer); the other ships have the SQR-18A(V)2 variant.

Engineering: The cancelled DE 1101 was to have had gas-turbine propulsion to evaluate that plant for future use in surface combatants. The BARBEY and PATTERSON evaluated controllable-pitch propeller configurations for subsequent use with LM 2500 gas-turbine propulsion plants.

During the late 1980s it was proposed to refit these ships with LM 2500 gas turbines in place of their steam propulsion plants as part of the upgrade package. In the event, the massive force cutbacks of the early 1990s halted these considerations.

Guns: The design originally provided for a single 5-inch/38-cal gun forward, but the improved 5-inch/54-cal Mk 42 became available and was installed in all ships.

These ships are all to be fitted with a single Phalanx CIWS; the ships with the Sea Sparrow BPDMS are having the CIWS installed in place of the missile launcher, beginning with the FF 1087 in 1983, with all 46 ships subsequently armed with the close-in weapon.

Manning: Crews of the active ships vary from 16 to 25 officers and from 183 to 269 enlisted.

Missiles: Thirty-one ships were fitted after completion with Sea Sparrow point-defense systems. Installations of the Sea Chapparal, adopted from an Army SAM system, was planned for 14 other ships but was not undertaken.

The DOWNES served as evaluation ship for the NATO Sea Sparrow missile. It was fitted with Mk 29 missile launcher aft and Mk 23 TAS (Target Acquisition System) in place of SPS-40 radar; both systems were removed in 1983 with CIWS fitted aft.

Modernization: During the late 1980s there were several proposals to upgrade these ships and extend their nominal 30-year service life by 10 years. Proposals included fitting a vertical-launched missile system, adding a second Phalanx CIWS forward, replacing the steam turbine and boilers with LM 2500 gas turbines, and upgrading the electronics. In the event, funding constraints and then the 1990–1991 retirement decisions ended consideration of major upgrades.

Operational: Each of the eight operational NRF ships will be responsible for nucleus crew training for four laid-up ships. The reservists will train on board the operational ship one weekend per month and be under way on board for two weeks every year.

The eight FFTs will be based in three ports:

> Staten Island, N.Y. (FFT 1079, 1085, 1090)
> Mobile, Ala. (FFT 1089, 1097)
> Inglewood, Texas (FFT 1078, 1084, 1095)

Torpedoes: The original design called for two Mk 25 torpedo tubes to be fitted in the stern counter (with 12 torpedoes carried); they were not installed. The Mk 32 tubes are fitted in the after superstructure.

Design: FF 1052–1061 were assigned SCB No. 199C; the later ships were given SCB No. 200 in the new series.

These ships are considerably larger than the previous BROOKE and GARCIA classes because of the use of non-pressure-fired boilers. The superstructure is topped by a distinctive cylindrical "mack" that combines mast and stacks, which was to mount an advanced electronic warfare suite (that was not developed). A portside anchor is fitted at the bow and a larger anchor retracts into the after end of the bow sonar dome fairing. Anti-roll fin stabilizers are provided. The Prairie-Masker system, fitted to bleed bubbles through hull and propeller tips, reduces ship-generated noises.

The original DASH hangar has been enlarged to accommodate the LAMPS I helicopter. Hangars vary in size from 41½ feet (12.7 m) to 47⅙ feet (14.4 m) in length and 14½ to 18¼ feet (4.4 to 5.6 m) in width; height is 14 to 20 feet (4.3 to 6.1 m).

As built, the ships took water over their bows in rough seas. Beginning in 1980 they have had raised bulwarks and spray strakes fitted forward. These changes added 9.1 tons and extended their overall length from the original 438⅙ feet (133.6 m).

An ASROC reload capability is provided along with a total of 16 rockets and Harpoon missiles—8 in the launcher and 8 in the below-deck magazine (with automatic reload).

The THOMAS C. HART showing the expandable hangar, permitting the original DASH hangar to accommodate an SH-2 LAMPS I helicopter. Note that the Phalanx CIWS rises some five feet (1.5 m) above the helicopter deck. (1991, Giorgio Arra)

The KNOX design was the most numerous surface combatant class built for the U.S. Navy since World War II; that distinction now belongs to the PERRY class. The BARBEY shows the boxy lines of the class, with the massive "mack" structure placed exactly amidships. An SH-2 LAMPS I helicopter is barely visible on the flight deck. (1991, Giorgio Arra)

The TRIPPE's stern showing the opening for streaming the SQS-35 IVDS/ SQR-18A towed array combination. The more effective Phalanx CIWS has replaced the previously installed Sea Sparrow box launcher. (1991, Giorgio Arra)

The hinged openings for the Mk 32 torpedo tubes on the starboard side of the JOSEPH HEWES; there are two tubes on each side of the after super-structure for launching Mk 46/Mk 50 ASW torpedoes. The chain railing at right is lowered to fire the tubes (and to lower the adjacent launch). (1989, Giorgio Arra)

2 FRIGATES: "GARCIA" CLASS

Number	Name	Status
FF 1040	GARCIA	decomm. 10 Nov 1988; to Pakistan 1989
FF 1041	BRADLEY	decomm. 30 Sep 1988; to Brazil 1989
FF 1043	EDWARD MCDONNELL	AR decomm. 30 Sep 1988
FF 1044	BRUMBY	decomm. 31 Mar 1989; to Pakistan 1989
FF 1045	DAVIDSON	decomm. 31 Dec 1988; to Brazil 1989
FF 1047	VOGE	AR decomm. 23 Aug 1989
FF 1048	SAMPLE	decomm. 23 Sep 1988; to Brazil 1989
FF 1049	KOELSCH	decomm. 31 May 1989; to Pakistan 1989
FF 1050	ALBERT DAVID	decomm. 18 Sep 1989; to Brazil 1989
FF 1051	O'CALLAHAN	decomm. 20 Dec 1988; to Pakistan 1989

The ten ships of the GARCIA class were commissioned between 1964 and 1968. All have been decommissioned, with eight leased to other navies; the two others will also be disposed of. These ships are similar to the contemporary BROOKE-class frigates but have a second 5-inch gun in place of the missile ships' Mk 22 launcher.

The planned transfer of the McDONNELL and VOGE to Turkey was cancelled.

See 14th Edition/pages 176–177 for characteristics.

2 FRIGATES: "BRONSTEIN" CLASS

Number	Name	Status
FF 1037	BRONSTEIN	PR decomm. 13 Dec 1990
FF 1038	MCCLOY	AR decomm. 14 Dec 1990

Both frigates of the BRONSTEIN class, completed in 1963, have been decommissioned and can be expected to be stricken in the near future. These ships were the prototype for a new generation of ASW ocean escorts, featuring large bow-mounted sonar, ASROC, and a DASH capability. These features were provided in the next 63 escort ships built by the U.S. Navy as well as in several foreign ASW ships. However, the BRONSTEIN class was too slow and lacked the seakeeping and range necessary for effective ASW to counter contemporary Soviet submarine designs. During the 1970s and 1980s they were employed extensively to evaluate the Towed Array Surveillance System (TASS) and were used to monitor Soviet naval activities.

See 14th Edition/pages 177–178 for characteristics.

FFX DESIGN

During the late 1970s the Navy proposed the construction of a class of small frigates (designation FFX) for use by the Naval Reserve Force. These ships were intended to augment the FFG 7 force in the ASW role in low-threat areas. A class of approximately 12 ships was planned, with the lead ship intended for authorization in FY 1984. For reasons not fully clear, although such ships would have had only marginally effective ASW capabilities, the FFX class was not started. Subsequently, the Naval Reserve Force has been provided with frigates of the KNOX and PERRY classes to replace the aging GEARING (DD 710)-class ships previously assigned to the NRF.

The tentative characteristics of the FFX were provided in the 13th Edition/page 176.

TABLE 17-2. POST–WORLD WAR II ESCORT/FRIGATES

Number	Ship/Class	Comm.	Notes
DE 1006	DEALEY	1954	to Uruguay 1952
DE 1007	(French LE NORMAND)	OSP 1956	
DE 1008	(French LE LORRAIN)	OSP 1956	
DE 1009	(French LE PICARD)	OSP 1956	
DE 1010	(French LE GASCON)	OSP 1957	
DE 1011	(French LE CHAMPENOIS)	OSP 1957	
DE 1012	(French LE SAVOYARD)	OSP 1957	
DE 1013	(French LE BOURGUIGNON)	OSP 1957	
DE 1014	CROMWELL	1954	str. 1972
DE 1015	HAMMERBERG	1955	str. 1973
DE 1016	(French LE CORSE)	OSP 1952	
DE 1017	(French LE BRESTOIS)	OSP 1952	
DE 1018	(French LE BOULONNAIS)	OSP 1953	
DE 1019	(French LE BORDELAIS)	OSP 1953	
DE 1020	(Italian CIGNO)	OSP 1957	
DE 1021	COURTNEY	1956	str. 1973
DE 1022	LESTER	1957	str. 1973
DE 1023	EVANS	1957	str. 1973
DE 1024	BRIDGET	1957	str. 1973
DE 1025	BAUER	1957	str. 1973
DE 1026	HOOPER	1958	str. 1973
DE 1027	JOHN WILLIS	1957	str. 1972
DE 1028	VAN VOORHIS	1957	str. 1972
DE 1029	HARTLEY	1957	to Colombia 1972
DE 1030	JOSEPH K. TAUSSIG	1957	str. 1972
DE 1031	(Italian CASTORE)	OSP 1957	
DE 1032	(Portuguese PERO ESCOBAR)	OSP 1957	
DE 1033	CLAUD JONES	1959	to Indonesia 1974
DE 1034	JOHN R. PERRY	1959	to Indonesia 1973
DE 1035	CHARLES BERRY	1959	to Indonesia 1974
DE 1036	MCMORRIS	1960	to Indonesia 1974
DE 1037, 1038	BRONSTEIN class		
DE 1039	(Portuguese ALMIRANTE PEREIRA DA SILVA)	OSP 1966	
DE 1040, 1041	GARCIA class		
DE 1042	(Portuguese ALMIRANTE GAGO COUTINHO)	OSP 1967	
DE 1043–1045	GARCIA class		
DE 1046	(Portuguese ALMIRANTE MAGALHAES CORREA)	OSP 1967	
DE 1047–1051	GARCIA class		
DE 1052–1097*	KNOX class		

*The hull number FF 1098 subsequently was reassigned to the GLOVER (former AGFF/AGDE 1).

U.S. World War II destroyer-escort programs reached hull number DE 1005 (with DE 801–1005 being cancelled). After the war several destroyer escorts were converted to radar picket escorts (DER), a few for the tactical fleet role, but most for strategic early warning of bomber attack against the continental United States. A few also were modified to an escort control (DEC) configuration to support amphibious landings.

The first postwar DEs were actually envisioned as successors to the war-built, steel-hulled submarine chasers (PC). With the start of the postwar programs in the early 1950s, these ships were reclassified as ocean escorts (DE), partly to avoid confusion with escort destroyers (DDE).

U.S. hull numbers were assigned to 17 ships built in Europe with American funding (Offshore Procurement or OSP). Thirteen U.S. ships were completed between 1954 and 1957, built to the similar DEALEY and COURTNEY designs, and four ships to the CLAUD JONES design. These designs were intended for mass production in wartime. However, the two-ship BRONSTEIN class introduced the ASROC and large SQS-26 sonar, the principal features of the next 63 escort ships/frigates of the BROOKE, GARCIA, and KNOX classes.

The GLOVER was built as an experimental frigate with a modified propeller configuration. The ship was commissioned in 1965 as the AGDE 1, subsequently changed to AGFF 1 and then FF 1098; she was again changed to the research role with the auxiliary designation T-AGFF 1 on 15 June 1990 (see chapter 23).

CHAPTER 18

Command Ships

The LA SALLE—flagship for Commander U.S. Middle East Force—steaming through the placid waters of the Persian Gulf with most of her crew on deck. The LA SALLE carries on the tradition of a white-painted U.S. Navy ship serving as a flagship in the Gulf area since 1949. (U.S. Navy)

The U.S. Navy has five fleet-level command ships in service: the guided missile cruiser BELKNAP (CG 26), flagship of Commander, Sixth Fleet in the Mediterranean; the former amphibious command ships BLUE RIDGE, flagship of Commander, Seventh Fleet in the Western Pacific, and MOUNT WHITNEY, flagship of Commander, Second Fleet in the Atlantic; and the former amphibious transport docks LA SALLE, flagship of the Commander, U.S. Naval Forces Central Command and Middle East Force, and CORONADO, flagship of Commander, Third Fleet in the Eastern Pacific.

The four numbered fleets generally had cruisers for flagships from the end of World War II until the 1970s. The cruisers now in service do not have major flag facilities and accommodations, except for the BELKNAP, which was partially converted in 1986 to accommodate a portion of the Sixth Fleet staff. The BELKNAP retains a full missile cruiser capability and is listed in chapter 15 of this edition.

The IOWA (BB 61)-class battleships reactivated in the 1980s were not fitted to serve as major flagships.

Data on other types of command ships are listed at the end of this chapter.

Classification: The BLUE RIDGE and MOUNT WHITNEY retain their amphibious command ship LCC designation in the fleet command ship role; the miscellaneous flagships (AGF) retain their previous LPD hull numbers with their AGF designation.

Names: Amphibious command ships (AGC/LCC) have traditionally been assigned the names of American mountains and mountain ranges. The AGFs retain their amphibious ship names.

2 AMPHIBIOUS COMMAND SHIPS: "BLUE RIDGE" CLASS

Number	Name	FY	Builder	Laid down	Launched	Commissioned	Status
LCC 19	BLUE RIDGE*	65	Philadelphia Naval Shipyard	27 Feb 1967	4 Jan 1969	14 Nov 1970	**PA**
LCC 20	MOUNT WHITNEY	66	Newport News Shipbuilding, Va.	8 Jan 1969	8 Jan 1970	16 Jan 1971	**AA**

Displacement:	16,790 tons light		Troops:	LCC 19 16 (1 officer + 15 enlisted)
	18,646 tons full load		Helicopters:	landing area only
Length:	579¹¹⁄₁₂ feet (176.8 m) waterline		Missiles:	2 8-tube Sea Sparrow BPDMS launchers Mk 25
	636⁵⁄₁₂ feet (194.0 m) overall		Guns:	4 3-inch (76-mm) 50-cal AA Mk 33(2 twin)
Beam:	82 feet (25.0 m)			2 20-mm Phalanx CIWS Mk 16 (2 multi-barrel)
Extreme width:	108 feet (32.9 m)		Radars:	SPS-40E air search
Draft:	28⅝ feet (8.8 m)			SPS-48C 3-D search
Propulsion:	1 steam turbine (General Electric); 22,000 shp; 1 shaft			SPS-64 navigation
Boilers:	2 600 psi (41.7 kg/cm²) (Foster Wheeler)			SPS-67 surface search
Speed:	22 knots		Fire control:	2 Mk 115 missile FCS
Range:	13,500 n.miles (25,000 km) at 16 knots		EW systems:	SLQ-25 Nixie
Manning:	LCC 19 753 (47 officers + 706 enlisted)			SLQ-32(V)3
	LCC 20 861 (44 officers + 817 enlisted)			ULQ-16
Flag:	LCC 19 226 (54 officers + 172 enlisted)			
	LCC 20 191 (63 officers + 128 enlisted)			

These are large command ships, the only ships to be designed from the outset specifically for the amphibious command ship role. The Navy's earlier command ships could not operate with the 20-knot amphibious ships built from the 1960s onward. Both ships are now employed as fleet flagships.

The BLUE RIDGE is home-ported in Yokosuka, Japan, having relieved the cruiser OKLAHOMA CITY (CG 5) in October 1979 as flagship of the Seventh Fleet; the MOUNT WHITNEY is based at Norfolk, Va., having relieved the cruiser ALBANY (CG 10) as flagship of the Second Fleet in January 1981.

Class: A third ship of this class (AGC 21) was planned; she was to have been configured for service as both an amphibious flagship and fleet flagship.

Classification: These ships were originally classified as amphibious force flagships (AGC); they were changed to amphibious command ships (LCC) on 1 January 1969.

Design: SCB No. 400. The hull and propulsion machinery are similar to that of the IWO JIMA (LPH 2)-class helicopter carriers. The command ship facilities originally provided in this class were for a Navy amphibious task force commander and a Marine assault force commander and their staffs. Their designed flag/staff accommodations were for 200 officers and 500 enlisted.

The ships have large, open deck areas to provide for optimum antenna placement. There is a helicopter landing area aft, but no hangar. (A small-vehicle hangar is serviced by an elevator.) Davits provide stowage for five LCPL/LCVP-type personnel craft plus a ship's launch.

Electronics: Fitted with Naval Tactical Data System.

Engineering: Maximum sustained speed is 20 knots.

Guns: The early designs for this ship provided for an additional pair of twin 3-inch/50-cal AA mounts forward, on the forecastle; they were not installed.

Phalanx CIWS were long scheduled for installation in these ships; two CIWS were provided in the BLUE RIDGE in 1985, mounted forward on a small deckhouse fitted on the main deck and a sponson at the stern (increasing length approximately 16 feet/4.9 m); fitted in MOUNT WHITNEY in 1987.

Helicopters: An SH-3D Sea King is usually assigned to each ship.

Missiles: The Sea Sparrow BPDMS launchers were fitted in 1974.

Operational: In addition to the Seventh Fleet staff (54 officers + 172 enlisted), the BLUE RIDGE carries a Marine communications detachment. For exercises the BLUE RIDGE normally embarks the staffs of Commander Amphibious Group 1/Amphibious Force Seventh Fleet (48 officers + 95 enlisted) and the Commander III Marine Expeditionary Force/Landing Force Seventh Fleet (80 officers + 127 enlisted).

The MOUNT WHITNEY, in addition to the Second Fleet staff (37 officers + 81 enlisted), carries for exercises the staff of Amphibious Group 2 (26 officers + 47 enlisted) and a Marine communications detachment (1 officer + 15 enlisted).

The MOUNT WHITNEY presents an ungainly stern aspect as she heads toward port. Note the large bridge "wings" and Phalanx CIWS at the stern; there is another at the bow. The stern gun has a very restricted field of fire. (1990, Giorgio Arra)

The large and stately BLUE RIDGE and MOUNT WHITNEY retain their amphibious-ship classification of LCC although they are primarily employed as numbered fleet flagships. The ships have a limited self-defense capability with 3-inch/50-cal guns, 20-mm Phalanx CIWS, and Sea Sparrow missiles plus EW systems. (1990, Giorgio Arra)

The MOUNT WHITNEY arrives at Antwerp, Belgium, with an SH-3G Sea King of squadron HC-2 on her helicopter deck. A stern sponson was added to accommodate the Phalanx CIWS; the amidship sponsons house small boats. The after tower for electronic antennas resembles the taller ''macks'' of the KNOX (FF 1052)-class frigates. (1989, L. Van Ginderen collection)

The MOUNT WHITNEY at sea showing the ship's unusual configuration with an amidship island structure and most of the flat deck used as an "antenna farm." There is a helicopter deck aft but, unfortunately, no helicopter hangar was provided. Life raft canisters are fitted forward. (U.S. Navy)

AMPHIBIOUS COMMAND SHIPS

Amphibious command ships—originally called amphibious force flagships—reached hull number AGC 18 during World War II. The type comprised a variety of ships—15 C2 merchant ships completed as AGCs, a converted liner, a converted seaplane tender, and a converted Coast Guard cutter. The last was one of six 327-foot (99.7-m) cutters of the Secretary class (WPG 31, 32, 34–37) that served as amphibious flagships, although only the DUANE (WPG 33) was reclassified (AGC 6).

Five surviving ships were changed from AGC to LCC on 1 January 1969. The last war-era AGC to see active naval service was the ELDORADO (AGC/LCC 11), decommissioned in 1973. She and the others were transferred to the Maritime Administration for disposal.

The yacht WILLIAMSBURG, which served as a gunboat (PG 56) from 1941 to 1945, was assigned as the presidential yacht after World War II, being redesignated AGC 369 on 10 November 1945. She served in that role for Presidents Truman and (for one cruise) Eisenhower. The WILLIAMSBURG was decommissioned in 1953 until stricken in 1962. (The ship was then employed as a civilian oceanographic research ship from 1962 to 1968.)

1 MISCELLANEOUS FLAGSHIP: CONVERTED "AUSTIN" CLASS

Number	Name	FY	Builder	Laid down	Launched	Commissioned	Status
AGF 11 (ex-LPD 11)	CORONADO	64	Lockheed SB & Constn., Seattle, Wash.	3 May 1965	30 July 1966	23 May 1970	**PA**

Displacement:	11,050 tons light	Helicopters:	1 SH-3 Sea King
	16,912 tons full load	Missiles:	none
Length:	568¾ feet (173.4 m) overall	Guns:	4 3-inch (76-mm) 50-cal AA Mk 33 (2 twin)
Beam:	84 feet (25.6 m)		2 20-mm Phalanx CIWS Mk 16 (2 multi-barrel)
Draft:	23⁷⁄₁₂ feet (7.2 m)	Radars:	LN-66 navigation
Propulsion:	2 steam turbines (De Laval); 24,000 shp; 2 shafts		SPS-10 surface search
Boilers:	2 600 psi (41.7 kg/cm²) (Foster Wheeler)		SPS-40 air search
Speed:	21 knots	Fire control:	local control only
Range:	7,700 n.miles (14,260 km) at 20 knots	EW systems:	SLQ-32(V)2
Manning:	461 (25 officers + 436 enlisted)		WLR-1H
Flag:	approx. 50		

The CORONADO was built and served as a dock landing ship until 1980 when she was modified to serve as a temporary flagship to permit the Middle East flagship LA SALLE to undergo a lengthy overhaul at the Philadelphia Naval Shipyard. Subsequently, after overhaul in 1983–1984, the CORONADO replaced the destroyer tender PUGET SOUND (AD 38) as Sixth Fleet flagship in August 1985 and was home-ported in Gaeta, Italy.

In June 1986, with the BELKNAP assigned as Sixth Fleet flagship, the CORONADO departed the Mediterranean and the following month shifted to the Pacific to become flagship for Commander, Third Fleet (then based at Pearl Harbor). Prior to breaking his flag in the CORONADO on 26 November 1986, the Commander, Third Fleet had flown his flag ashore since the end of World War II. In August

1991 the Commander, Third Fleet, sailing on board the CORONADO, shifted her home port to North Island Naval Air Station at San Diego, Calif.

Classification: Changed from LPD 11 to AGF 11 on 1 October 1980.

Conversion: See LA SALLE for description of LPD conversion to flagship. The CORONADO's telescoping hangar is 49½ feet (15.1 m) long, 18½ feet (5.6 m) wide, and 17⅔ feet (5.4 m) high; it expands to a length of about 75 feet (22.9 m).

Design: SCB No. 187C. See AUSTIN (LPD 4) listing for additional details. The ship is similar to, but larger than, the LA SALLE.

Guns: Phalanx CIWS have been installed on an extension of the bridge structure, forward to port, and amidships, starboard.

The CORONADO departing Pearl Harbor for her new home port of NAS North Island, San Diego, Calif. Her two 3-inch/50-cal twin gun mounts and two Phalanx CIWS mounts are staggered, one of each forward and one of each at the after end of the superstructure. The other light-colored domes are satellite radomes. (1991, OS2 John Bouvia, USN)

The CORONADO with her crew manning the rail entering San Francisco. Note the gun arrangement and telescoping hangar; the flight deck has two helicopter landing spots. Both LPDs converted to flagships retain their docking well. (1988, Giorgio Arra)

The CORONADO moored at San Francisco. A sponson has been added to the port side, amidships. The antenna rigs on the various command ships change periodically. Two rows of life raft canisters line the sides of the CORONADO's superstructure. (1988, Giorgio Arra)

1 MISCELLANEOUS FLAGSHIP: CONVERTED "RALEIGH" CLASS

Number	Name	FY	Builder	Laid down	Launched	Commissioned	Status
AGF 3 (ex-LPD 3)	LA SALLE*	61	New York Naval Shipyard	2 Apr 1962	3 Aug 1963	22 Feb 1964	**Middle East**

Displacement:	8,040 tons light	Manning:	604 (29 officers + 575 enlisted)
	14,650 tons full load	Flag:	238 (67 officers + 171 enlisted)
Length:	500 feet (152.4 m) waterline	Helicopters:	1 SH-3 Sea King
	521¾ feet (159.0 m) overall	Missiles:	none
Beam:	84 feet (25.6 m)	Guns:	4 3-inch (76-mm) 50-cal AA Mk 33 (2 twin)
Draft:	22 feet (6.7 m)		2 20-mm Phalanx CIWS Mk 16 (2 multi-barrel)
Propulsion:	2 steam turbines (De Laval); 24,000 shp; 2 shafts	Radars:	LN-66 navigation
Boilers:	2 600 psi (41.7 kg/cm²) (Babcock & Wilcox)		SPS-10 surface search
Speed:	21.6 knots (20 knots sustained)		SPS-40E air search
Range:	9,600 n.miles (17,780 km) at 16 knots	Fire control:	local control only
	16,500 n.miles (30,558 km) at 10 knots	EW systems:	SLQ-32(V)2
			WLR-1

The LA SALLE was converted from an amphibious transport dock specifically to serve as flagship for the Commander, U.S. Middle East Force, now also Commander, Naval Forces Central Command. The LA SALLE initially served as an amphibious ship.

Class: The LA SALLE is one of three RALEIGH (LPD 1)-class amphibious transport docks.

Classification: Built as LPD 3 and served as an amphibious ship until 1 July 1972 when changed to AGF 3.

Conversion: The ship was converted to a flagship in 1972, being fitted with command and communication facilities, a helicopter hangar, and additional air conditioning. The amidships hangar is 47⁵⁄₁₂ feet (14.6 m) long, 18¹⁄₁₂ feet (5.5 m) wide, and 19¹⁄₃ feet (5.9 m) high.

Design: SCB No. 187A.

Guns: Phalanx CIWS have been installed amidships, port and starboard.

Operational: The LA SALLE operated in the Persian Gulf–Indian Ocean area from 1972 to 1980, when she was relieved by the CORONADO. The LA SALLE underwent an extensive overhaul at the Philadelphia Naval Shipyard from December 1980 to September 1982. After that overhaul she in turn relieved the CORONADO as flagship of the Middle East Force on 16 June 1983 at Mina' Sulman, Bahrain.

Prior to the conversion of the LA SALLE the flagship of the Commander, Middle East Force had been a small seaplane tender of the BARNEGAT (AVP 10) class from the time that command was established in the late 1940s (see below).

The LA SALLE steaming in the Middle East. She has both 3-inch/50-cal twin gun mounts forward and the Phalanx CIWS fitted amidships. The red "E" and two chevrons on the forward funnel indicate engineering excellence for three years. The Gulf conflict put the Navy's three white ships into the Persian Gulf—the LA SALLE and two hospital ships. (1991, OS2 John Bouvia, USN)

The LA SALLE showing the small hangar on the port side of her flight deck and her LPD stern gate. Both of her sister ships of the RALEIGH (LPD 1) class are being mothballed. (1991, OS2 John Bouvia, USN)

FLEET/NATIONAL COMMAND SHIPS

In addition to the two amphibious command ships (AGC/LCC) listed above, in the post–World War II era the Navy has built one ship and converted another specifically for use as major command ships. A third such ship was planned for conversion.

The heavy cruiser NORTHAMPTON (CA 125) was cancelled on 11 August 1945 while under construction (about 50 percent complete). She was subsequently reordered in 1948 as a tactical light command ship (CLC 1) and completed in that configuration in 1953. After operating as a fleet flagship, she was reconfigured to serve as a National Emergency Command Post Afloat (NECPA) in 1961 and reclassified as CC 1. She was decommissioned in 1970 and laid up in reserve until stricken in 1977.

The light carriers WRIGHT (originally CVL 49) and SAIPAN (CVL 48) were similarly designated for conversion to the NECPA role. The WRIGHT, also designated AVT 7 while in reserve, was converted in 1962–1963 and became CC 2; she operated in the NECPA role until 1970 when she was laid up in reserve. She was stricken in 1977.

The SAIPAN, designated AVT 6 while in reserve after World War II, began conversion to CC 3 in 1964, but was instead completed as a major communications relay ship in 1966 (renamed ARLINGTON and designated AGMR 2).

In the NECPA role these ships were to provide afloat facilities for the President in the event of a national emergency or war. (A more interesting, although not undertaken, proposal was to convert the large, nuclear-propelled submarine TRITON/SSRN 586 to an underwater NECPA.)

After World War II the unfinished large cruiser HAWAII (CB 3) was considered for conversion to a fleet command ship (CBC), but no work was undertaken on that project.

MISCELLANEOUS FLAGSHIPS

From 1949 until 1965 the Navy rotated small seaplane tenders (AVP) as flagship for U.S. forces in the Persian Gulf area—the DUXBURY BAY (AVP 38), GREENWICH BAY (AVP 41), and VALCOUR (AVP 55). Subsequently, the VALCOUR was reclassified as a miscellaneous flagship (AGF 1) on 15 December 1965 specifically for that role and home-ported in Bahrain. She was replaced in that role by the LA SALLE in 1972.

The Middle East flagships are painted white to help counter the intense heat in the Persian Gulf area.

CHAPTER 19

Amphibious Ships

A Marine Corps CH-53E Super Stallion from squadron HMH-464 operates from the RALEIGH in the North Arabian Sea during Desert Shield/Desert Storm. Other "amphibs" steam behind her, a portion of the 31 amphibious ships that operated in the area carrying some 17,000 Marines by the start of the allied assault on occupied Kuwait and Iraq. It was the largest amphibious force concentration since World War II. (1990, Capt. Richard Mullen, USMC)

The U.S. Navy's amphibious lift consists of 57 ships in active service in late 1992 plus three tank landing ships operated by the Naval Reserve Force (NRF). Four additional amphibious ships (LCC/LPD types) are employed as command ships for fleet/force commanders and are not readily available to support amphibious landings (see chapter 18).

Currently under construction are additional large helicopter-dock ships (LHD) and dock landing ships (LSD). Two new amphibious assault ships are being designed (design designations LVX and LX); the first LX is planned for the fiscal 1995 budget and the second in fiscal 1997.

The existing "amphibs" have a theoretical lift capacity of the assault elements of approximately one Marine Expeditionary Force (MEF), i.e., a reinforced division. In 1991 the Commandant of the Marine Corps told Congress that the Marine operational requirement was to have enough shipping to lift two MEFs simultaneously.[1] At the same time, the Chief of Naval Operations explained that the ongoing force reductions would reduce the lift capacity to only 2½ Marine Expeditionary Brigades (MEB), i.e., reinforced regiments.[2]

The current one-MEF lift capacity is theoretical in the sense that the ships are about evenly divided between the Atlantic and Pacific fleet areas, and with several ships undergoing overhaul or modernization at any given time, the actual lift available is less than that needed to lift the assault elements of a division. More likely, with a buildup period measured in weeks, the most probable capability would be the landing of a MEB in a specific ocean area.

The amphibious-ship force objective in the 1980s was 72 ships to provide lift for the assault elements of one Marine Expeditionary Force plus one Marine Expeditionary Brigade. Delays in planned construction and modernization programs meant a delay in achieving the lift goal of MEF + MEB until 1997—if the planned construction programs were completed. (This lift capacity is shown in table 19-1).

TABLE 19-1.   PROPOSED MEF + MEB LIFT CAPACITY

Ships	Troops	Vehicle Space (square feet)	Cargo Space (cubic feet)	Helicopter Spots	LCAC Spots
5 LHD 1	9,300	100,000	505,000	210	15
5 LHA 1	8,500	125,000	544,000	190	5
7 LPH 2	14,000	23,000	279,000	189	—
5 LKA 113	1,000	167,000	343,000	—	—
11 LPD 4	8,500	124,000	430,000	44	11
6 LSD 41CV	2,700	80,000	240,000	—	12
8 LSD 41	4,000	100,000	40,000	—	32
5 LSD 36	1,500	79,000	7,000	—	15
20 LST 1179	8,000	380,000	65,000	—	—
Totals	57,500	1,178,000	2,453,000	633	90

Three classes of amphibious ships were initiated in the late 1970s: the new WASP-class helicopter carriers, at over 40,000 tons almost the same displacement as the Russian KIEV-class VSTOL aircraft carriers; the WHIDBEY ISLAND-class dock landing ships; and a modification of this LSD design with increased cargo capacity (designated LSD 41CV for *Cargo Variant*).

Twenty ships of these three classes were scheduled for construction in the fiscal 1981–1993 shipbuilding programs. At the same time, 20 amphibious ships that were constructed during the 1960s will reach the end of their nominal 30-year service life in the 1990s. In late January 1992 the Department of Defense cancelled two LSD 41CV-class ships, one having been cancelled earlier. However, an

additional LHD was added (with more than twice the displacement of an LSD).

The Reagan administration's buildup of amphibious shipping was the third major "spurt" of amphibious ship construction since World War II. The first, during the Korean War, produced the LSD 28 and LST 1156 classes (23 ships); the second, in the Kennedy-Johnson administrations of the early 1960s, produced the LCC 19, LHA 1, LKA 112, LPD 12, LSD 36, and LST 1179 classes (49 ships).

The third postwar amphibious ship programs began with the WHIDBEY ISLAND, the first amphibious ship authorized for the U.S. Navy in a decade. That ship was funded by the Congress in fiscal 1981 over the objections of the Carter administration. With the advent of the Reagan administration the major program of amphibious ship construction began.

The early 1990s cutbacks in fleet strength have affected the amphibious force. The LHD program has been halted at five ships (as the LHA program had been curtailed more than two decades earlier). By the late 1990s the amphibious force will probably decline to some 57 ships, including the three NRF-operated LSTs (but not the command ships).

Aircraft: A normal LHA "air wing" consists of a Marine composite squadron of 18 CH-46 Sea Knights, 4 CH-53 Sea Stallions, and 4 AH-1 SeaCobra helicopters, plus a couple of UH-1N Huey command/ utility helicopters. Beginning in the mid-1980s each LHA/LPH-type ship was assigned an UH-1N Huey to provide Search-And-Rescue (SAR) capabilities during Marine flight operations.

No catapults or arresting gear are fitted to the LHD/LHA/LPH– type ships.

Guns: During the 1980s LSD- and LPD-type amphibious ships were fitted with .50-cal machine guns, 25-mm Bushmaster "chain" guns, and 20-mm cannon for close-in defense against small craft; this armament suite was especially important for ships deploying into the Persian Gulf. The weapons are shifted from ship to ship as they forward deploy; accordingly, they are not listed under the specific class entries.

Names: Amphibious assault ships (LHA/LPH) are named for battles fought by Marines; the LHD series, however, carries the names of World War II–era aircraft carriers, a further perversion of the Navy's nomenclature scheme.

Amphibious cargo ships (LKA) and tank landing ships (LST) are named for counties and parishes, the latter being the equivalent of counties in the state of Louisiana.[3]

Amphibious transport docks (LPD) are named for cities that honor explorers and pioneers.

Dock landing ships (LSD) carry the names of historic sites and cities.

Operational: The current amphibious force is organized into seven Amphibious Squadrons (PhibRons). One PhibRon is normally deployed to the Mediterranean, serving as an Amphibious Readiness Group with a Marine Expeditionary Unit (MEU) embarked, and a second PhibRon is similarly deployed to the Western Pacific–Indian Ocean area with a MEU embarked. Periodically, a third amphibious squadron operates in the Caribbean area and a fourth in the Western Pacific. Including PhibRons that are en route to and from deployments, or on special exercises, a significant fraction of the Navy's amphibious lift capability is at sea in widely separated areas at any given time. (This peacetime deployment pattern could inhibit the rapid assembly of a large number of amphibious ships in time of crisis or war.)

Asterisks in the ship entry lists indicate ships that participated in Operations Desert Shield/Desert Storm in 1990–1991.

1. Gen. A.M. Gray, USMC, testimony before the House Armed Services Committee, 21 February 1991.
2. Adm. Frank B. Kelso II, USN, Chief of Naval Operations, testimony before the House Armed Services Committee, 21 February 1991. These Marine Corps organizations are described in chapter 7.

3. When LSTs were first assigned names on 1 July 1955, all names had the suffix county or parish. This naming scheme was continued until the naming of the NEWPORT and several of her sister ships, which do not have suffixes.

TABLE 19-2. AMPHIBIOUS WARFARE SHIPS [late 1992]

Type	Class/Ship	Comm.	Active	NRF	Building*	Reserve
LHD 1	WASP	1989–	2	—	3	—
LHA 1	TARAWA	1976–1980	5	—	—	—
LPH 2	IWO JIMA	1961–1970	7	—	—	—
LKA 113	CHARLESTON	1968–1970	4	—	—	1
LPD 12	AUSTIN	1965–1971	11	—	—	—
LPD 1	RALEIGH	1962–1963	—	—	—	2
LSD 49	HARPERS FERRY	1994–	—	—	3	—
LSD 41	WHIDBEY ISLAND	1984–1992	8	—	—	—
LSD 36	ANCHORAGE	1969–1972	5	—	—	—
LSD 28	THOMASTON	1954–1957	—	—	—	4
LST 1179	NEWPORT	1969–1972	15	3	—	2

*Ships authorized through fiscal 1992.

AMPHIBIOUS ASSAULT SHIPS: LVX DESIGN

The LVX is planned as a replacement for the LHA-type ships as they reach the end of their projected 35-year service life (although they will probably serve longer with SLEP/modernization work). The principal difference from the LHA/LHD will be replacement of the docking well with a "dry-well" for three LCACs or other vehicles. It would be unloaded via a stern ramp.

The first LVX would be completed about 2011 under current planning.

(2+) AMPHIBIOUS ASSAULT SHIPS: LX DESIGN

Number	Name	FY	Status
LX 1	. . . . . .	95	Planned
LX 2	. . . . . .	97	Planned

Displacement:	approx. 23,000 tons full load
Length:	approx. 600 feet (182.9 m) overall
Beam:	
Draft:	
Propulsion:	gas turbines
Speed:	
Range:	
Manning:	
Helicopters:	2 H-46 or CH-53 or MV-22 type
Missiles:	
Guns:	20-mm Phalanx CIWS Mk 16 (multi-barrel)
Radars:	

The LX is planned as a functional replacement for 38 ships of the LPD/LSD/LST types. Construction of the lead ship is proposed for authorization in fiscal 1995, with the first unit to be completed about the year 2000. The Navy had proposed to construct 27 LX-type ships to operate with 17 LSD and 15 LHD/LHA ships to provide a MEF + MEB lift capability; however, the reduced amphibious lift goals will probably lead to fewer ships being built.

Design: These will have an internal docking well that can accommodate two LCACs or Amphibian Assault Vehicles (AAV); no bow doors/ramp will be fitted.

2 + 4 AMPHIBIOUS ASSAULT SHIPS: "WASP" CLASS

Number	Name	FY	Builder	Laid down	Launched	Christened	Commissioned	Status
LHD 1	WASP	84	Litton/Ingalls SB, Pascagoula, Miss.	30 May 1985	4 Aug 1987	19 Sep 1987	29 July 1988	**AA**
LHD 2	ESSEX	86	Litton/Ingalls SB, Pascagoula, Miss.	20 Mar 1989	7 Jan 1991	16 Mar 1991	19 Oct 1992	**PA**
LHD 3	KEARSARGE	88	Litton/Ingalls SB, Pascagoula, Miss.	6 Feb 1990	26 Mar 1992	16 May 1992	1993	Building
LHD 4	BOXER	89	Litton/Ingalls SB, Pascagoula, Miss.	8 Apr 1991			1994	Building
LHD 5	BATAAN	91	Litton/Ingalls SB, Pascagoula, Miss.				1996	Building
LHD 6	. . . . . .	96						Planned

Displacement:	28,233 tons light
	40,530 tons full load
Length:	777⅝ feet (237.1 m) waterline
	844 feet (257.3 m) overall
Beam:	106 feet (32.3 m) waterline
Extreme width:	140 feet (42.7 m)
Draft:	26⅔ feet (8.1 m)
Propulsion:	2 steam turbines; 70,000 shp; 2 shafts
Boilers:	2 600 psi (41.7 kg/cm²)
Speed:	24 knots
Range:	9,500 n.miles (17,594 km) at 20 knots
Manning:	LHD 1 1,082 (73 officers + 1,009 enlisted)
Troops:	1,875 (see notes)
Aircraft:	amphibious role: approx. 30 CH-46 Sea Knight and CH-53 Sea Stallion helicopters + 6 AV-8B Harrier VSTOL
	carrier role: approx. 20 AV-8B Harrier VSTOL + up to 6 SH-60B/F ASW helicopters

Elevators:	2
Missiles:	2 8-tube NATO Sea Sparrow missile launchers Mk 29
Guns:	3 20-mm Phalanx CIWS Mk 16 (3 multi-barrel)
	8 12.7-mm machine guns (8 single)
Radars:	Mk 23 TAS
	SPS-48E 3-D air search in LHD 2–6
	SPS-49(V)5 air search
	SPS-52C 3-D air search in LHD 1
	SPS-64(V)9 navigation
	SPS-67 surface search
Fire control:	2 Mk 91 missiles FCS
	1 SYS-2(V)3 weapon control system
EW systems:	SLQ-32(V)3

These ships and the similar TARAWA class are the world's largest amphibious ships. The only larger amphibious ships were the converted ESSEX (CV 9)-class fleet carriers that operated in the LPH role; see below. The WASP class was initially planned as helicopter-carrying amphibious ships that would be smaller and less costly than the TARAWA class. In the event, the basic LHA design was adopted with the following principal differences: (1) increased Harrier VSTOL aircraft support capability; (2) movement of the stern elevator to the starboard side of the flight deck; (3) redesign of the docking well to accommodate three LCAC with an LPD/LSD stern gate vice the sectional, "split" gate of the LHA; and (4) modification of the self-defense armament.

Class: The Navy's long-range planning provided for a sixth ship (LHD 6) in the fiscal 1993 shipbuilding program as the first replacement for the IWO JIMA-class LPHs. The sixth ship has been delayed until the fiscal 1996 program. The Marine Corps had, at times, expressed plans for up to ten of these ships to replace the IWO

JIMA-class LPHs; it was unlikely that a force of 15 LHA/LHD-type ships would have been approved, even in the high-budget years of the early 1980s.

Classification: During the preliminary design stage these ships were designated LHDX. They should correctly have been designated in the LHA series.

Cost: The fiscal 1991 shipbuilding program provided $1.123 *billion* for the LHD 5, including outfitting and post-delivery costs.

Design: The basic configuration of these ships is similar to the LHA 1 class; however, they have less vehicle storage space and bulk cargo space, only 22,000 square feet (1,980 m²) and 101,000 cubic feet (3,030 m³), but carry more aircraft, and the arrangement of the docking well permits more air-cushion landing craft to be embarked (three LCACs can be embarked); the LHDs also have communications and certain command spaces moved into the hull (vice island structure) for better protection. These ships are configured to facilitate AV-8B Harrier VSTOL operations.

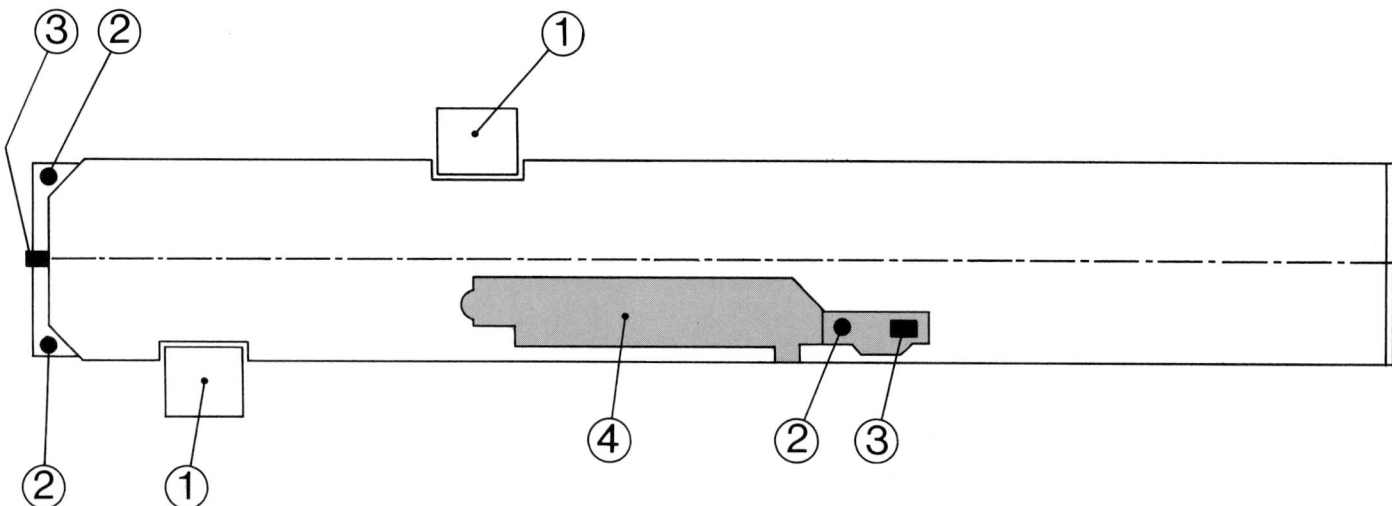

1. deck-edge elevator   2. 20-mm Phalanx CIWS   3. NATO Sea Sparrow launcher   4. island structure

The docking well is 267 feet (81.4 m) long, 50 feet (15.2 m) wide, and has a clear height of 28 feet (9.5 m).

Although intended from the outset to operate Harriers as well as helicopters, these ships will not have ski-jump ramps to assist VSTOL operations because the size of the flight deck is considered sufficiently large to enable rolling takeoffs for heavily laden VSTOL aircraft.

Medical facilities include beds for 600 patients with four main operating rooms and extensive emergency and dental facilities.

Electronics: Fitted with SPN-35A and SPN-43B aircraft approach/control systems.

Engineering: Maximum horsepower is indicated above; the sustained is 70,000.

Names: The first five ships honor World War II–era fleet carriers (CV/CVL), the WASP remembering both the CV 7, which was sunk in 1942, and her namesake, the CV 18.

Troops: Approximately 200 additional troops can be embarked for short transits (i.e., several days).

The LHD/LHA amphibious ships are large and impressive. The WASP is larger than any warship built since World War II except for U.S. and Russian aircraft carriers. There is a boat-and-aircraft crane abaft the island structure, as in larger aircraft carriers. (1990, Giorgio Arra)

The WASP at sea. She resembles a straight-deck aircraft carrier but with the after portion of her hull squared off because of the large, internal docking well. The massive internal volume provides a large troop, helicopter, vehicle, and landing craft capacity. (1989, R. Elias, Litton/Ingalls Shipbuilding)

The WASP entering Portsmouth, Va. Mounted across her stern are two Phalanx CIWs and a NATO Sea Sparrow; the second Sea Sparrow launcher is just visible forward of the island structure. These ships lack the 5-inch/54-cal guns installed in the similar TARAWA class. (1990, L. Van Ginderen collection)

The Essex being fitted out at the Litton/Ingalls yard. She is larger than the World War II carrier of that name. In this view the starboard deck-edge elevator is lowered to the hangar deck; the stern gate is open (but the ship is not ballasted down). (1991, Litton/Ingalls Shipbuilding)

The Wasp electronics configuration differs from that of the Tarawa class, most noticeably by the Wasp class having the 3-D radar (SPS-52C or SPS-48E) forward on the island structure with the long-range search radar (SPS-49) aft; in the Tarawa class the SPS-52B 3-D radar is aft and the SPS-40B is immediately behind the forward lattice mast. (1990, Giorgio Arra)

5 AMPHIBIOUS ASSAULT SHIPS: "TARAWA" CLASS

Number	Name	FY	Builder	Laid down	Launched	Christened	Commissioned	Status
LHA 1	Tarawa*	69	Litton/Ingalls SB, Pascagoula, Miss.	15 Nov 1971	1 Dec 1973	1 Dec 1973	29 May 1976	**PA**
LHA 2	Saipan	70	Litton/Ingalls SB, Pascagoula, Miss.	21 July 1972	18 July 1974	20 July 1974	15 Oct 1977	**AA**
LHA 3	Belleau Wood	70	Litton/Ingalls SB, Pascagoula, Miss.	5 Mar 1973	11 Apr 1977	11 June 1977	23 Sep 1978	**PA**
LHA 4	Nassau*	71	Litton/Ingalls SB, Pascagoula, Miss.	13 Aug 1973	21 Jan 1978	28 Jan 1978	28 July 1979	**AA**
LHA 5	Peleliu	71	Litton/Ingalls SB, Pascagoula, Miss.	12 Nov 1976	25 Nov 1978	6 Jan 1979	3 May 1980	**PA**

Displacement:	25,120 tons light	Aircraft:	approx. 30 CH-46 Sea Knight and CH-53 Sea Stallion + 6 AV-8B
	39,300 tons full load		Harrier VSTOL
Length:	777⅔ feet (237.1 m) waterline	Elevators:	1 deck edge—50 × 34 feet (15.2 × 10.3 m)
	833¾ feet (254.2 m) overall		1 stern—59¾ × 34¾ feet (18.2 × 10.6 m)
Beam:	106 feet (32.3 m)	Missiles:	see notes
Extreme width:	132 feet (40.2 m)	Guns:	2 5-inch (127-mm) 54-cal DP Mk 45 (2 single)
Draft:	26 feet (7.9 m)		2 20-mm Phalanx CIWS Mk 16 (2 multi-barrel)
Propulsion:	2 steam turbines (Westinghouse); 70,000 shp; 2 shafts		6 20-mm AA Mk 67 (6 single)
Boilers:	2 600 psi (41.7 kg/cm²) (Combustion Engineering)	Radars:	SPS-10F surface search
Speed:	24 knots (22 knots sustained)		SPS-40B air search
Range:	10,000 n.miles (18,520 km) at 20 knots		SPS-52B 3-D air search
Manning:	LHA 1 926 (60 officers + 866 enlisted)		SPS-53 surface search
	LHA 2 964 (63 officers + 901 enlisted)	Fire control:	1 Mk 86 GFCS with SPG-60 and SPQ-9A radars
	LHA 3, 5 927 (59 officers + 868 enlisted)		2 Mk 115 missile FCS
	LHA 4 923 (62 officers + 861 enlisted)	EW systems:	SLQ-32(V)3
Troops:	1,900		

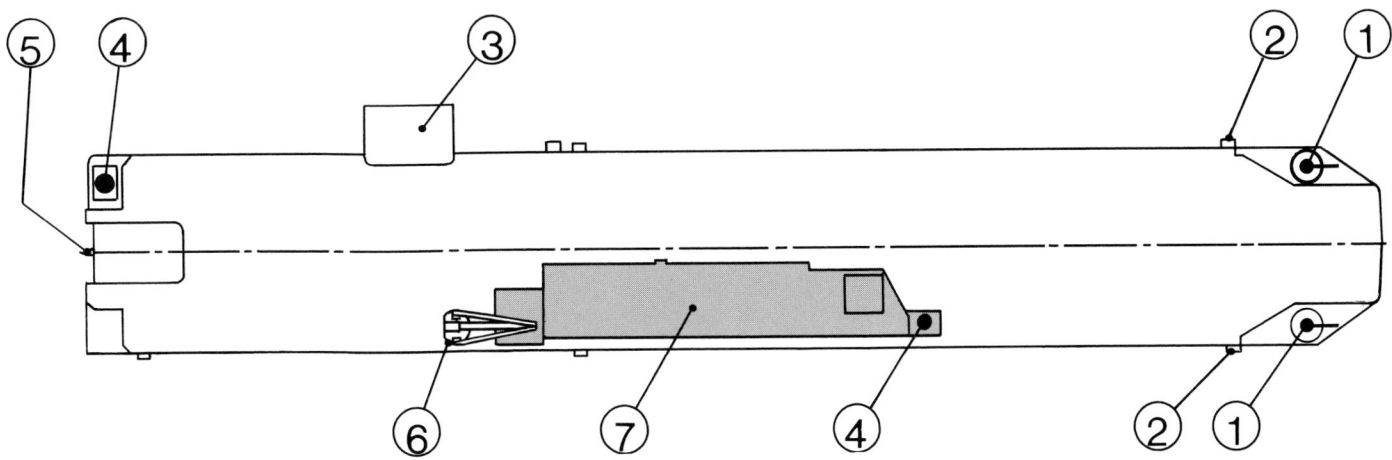

1. 5-inch/54-cal single gun mount   2. 3 20-mm cannon   3. deck-edge elevator   4. 20-mm Phalanx CIWS   5. stern elevator   6. crane   7. island structure

These and the WASP-class LHDs are the largest amphibious ships ever built. The TARAWA-class ships were intended to combine the capabilities of several types of amphibious ships in a single hull. In addition, these ships periodically have operated AV-8 Harrier VSTOL aircraft and OV-10 Bronco STOL aircraft.

Note that the TARAWA was christened on the same date that she was launched ("floated off" her assembly dock).

Class: Nine ships of this class were originally planned in the early 1960s. The Navy announced on 20 January 1971 that LHA 6–9 would not be constructed.

Design: SCB No. 410. Special features of this class include an 18-foot (5.5-m) section of the mast that is hinged to permit passage under bridges; a 5,000-square-foot (450-m²) training and acclimatization room to permit troops to exercise in a controlled environment; approximately 30,000 square feet (2,700 m²) of vehicle-storage decks connected by ramps to the flight deck and docking well; five cargo elevators that move equipment between the holds and flight deck; and approximately 110,000 cubic feet (3,300 m³) of space for bulk cargo. Extensive command and communications facilities are provided for an amphibious force commander.

The hangar deck is 820 feet (250 m) long and 78 feet (27.8 m) wide with a 20-foot (6.1-m) overhead.

The stern docking well is 268 feet (81.7 m) long and 78 feet (23.8 m) wide and can accommodate 4 LCU 1610 landing craft or 2 LCUs and 3 LCM(8)s or 17 LCM(6)s or 45 AAV/LVTP-7 amphibian vehicles. Because of the arrangement of the docking well, only one LCAC can be carried. In addition, 35 amphibian vehicles can be carried on the third deck of an LHA.

Extensive medical facilities are provided, including three operating rooms and bed space for 300 patients.

Electronics: SPN-35 aircraft approach/control system fitted.

Engineering: Maximum horsepower is indicated above; the sustained is 70,000. A 900-hp through-tunnel thruster is fitted in the forward part of the hull to assist in maneuvering while launching landing craft.

The ships' boilers are the largest ever manufactured in the United States.

Guns: These are the only U.S. amphibious ships currently armed with 5-inch guns. As built, three 5-inch guns were fitted; the 5-inch gun originally mounted aft, starboard side, has been replaced by drone (RPV) aircraft controls.

The 20-mm Mk 67 weapons are manually operated and intended for defense against swimmers and small craft.

Missiles: These ships originally had two Sea Sparrow BPDMS Mk 25 launchers (one in LHA 2); they have been deleted. PELELIU and subsequently BELLEAU WOOD were fitted in 1992 with two RAM (Rolling Airframe Missile) launchers; the other ships will follow.

Operational: The NASSAU evaluated the "sea control" configuration of these ships during a 1981 deployment when she successfully operated 19 AV-8A Harrier VSTOL aircraft; that same year the TARAWA made the first extended deployment of an amphibious ship with Harriers on board, carrying six AV-8A aircraft during a deployment to the Western Pacific. Subsequent studies showed that an LHA in the sea control role could effectively operate 20 Harriers plus 4 to 6 SH-60B LAMPS III helicopters. Also see Operational notes for GUAM, page 667.

The NASSAU with a Phalanx CIWS forward of the island structure, replacing a Sea Sparrow launcher. The starboard SLQ-32(V)3 ECM antenna is mounted between the funnels; beneath it hang underway refueling hoses. The SPS-40B radar is hidden by the lattice mast. (1989, Giorgio Arra)

The BELLEAU WOOD entering port. The Phalanx CIWS forward of the island structure is fitted on a tower to improve the defensive coverage. There are single 5-inch/54-cal gun mounts forward, port and starboard; these are the only U.S. amphibious ships that have 5-inch weapons. (1989, Giorgio Arra)

The NASSAU with AV-8B Harriers on her flight deck; she operated a Marine AV-8B Harrier squadron in the Persian Gulf conflict. The large black opening in the stern is the elevator well; there is a Phalanx CIWS on the port quarter, replacing the Sea Sparrow missile launcher originally fitted. (1989, Giorgio Arra)

A portrait of the NASSAU at sea, with crewmen lining the edge of the flight deck. The port-side, deck-edge elevator is at the flight deck level. The configurations of the WASP and TARAWA classes are similar; having a five-ship program of each class with the same hull numbers is confusing. (1989, Giorgio Arra)

7 AMPHIBIOUS ASSAULT SHIPS: "IWO JIMA" CLASS

Number	Name	FY	Builder	Laid down	Launched	Commissioned	Status
LPH 2	IWO JIMA*	58	Puget Sound Naval Shipyard, Wash.	2 April 1959	17 Sep 1960	26 Aug 1961	**AA**
LPH 3	OKINAWA*	59	Philadelphia Naval Shipyard, Penna.	1 Apr 1960	14 Aug 1961	14 Apr 1962	**PA**
LPH 7	GUADALCANAL	60	Philadelphia Naval Shipyard, Penna.	1 Sep 1961	16 Mar 1963	20 July 1963	**AA**
LPH 9	GUAM*	62	Philadelphia Naval Shipyard, Penna.	15 Nov 1962	22 Aug 1964	16 Jan 1965	**AA**
LPH 10	TRIPOLI*	63	Ingalls SB, Pascagoula, Miss.	15 June 1964	31 July 1965	6 Aug 1966	**PA**
LPH 11	NEW ORLEANS*	65	Philadelphia Naval Shipyard, Penna.	1 Mar 1966	3 Feb 1968	16 Nov 1968	**PA**
LPH 12	INCHON	66	Ingalls SB, Pascagoula, Miss.	8 Apr 1968	24 May 1969	20 June 1970	**AA**

Displacement:	11,000 tons light
	18,300 tons full load
Length:	556 feet (169.5 m) waterline
	602¼ feet (183.6 m) overall
Beam:	83⅔ feet (25.5 m) waterline
Extreme width:	104 feet (31.7 m)
Draft:	26 feet (7.9 m)
Propulsion:	1 steam turbine (Westinghouse); 23,000 shp; 1 shaft
Boilers:	2 600 psi (41.7 kg/cm²) (Combustion Engineering, except Babcock and Wilcox in LPH 9
Speed:	23 knots (21 knots sustained)
Range:	16,600 n.miles (30,743 km) at 11.5 knots
	10,000 n.miles (18,520 km) at 20 knots
Manning:	LPH 2 673 (51 officers + 622 enlisted)
	LPH 3 700 (50 officers + 650 enlisted)
	LPH 7 681 (47 officers + 634 enlisted)
	LPH 9 667 (49 officers + 618 enlisted)
	LPH 10 690 (49 officers + 641 enlisted)
	LPH 11 656 (46 officers + 610 enlisted)
	LPH 12 682 (51 officers + 631 enlisted)

Troops:	1,900
Aircraft	approx. 25 CH-46 Sea Knight and CH-53 Sea Stallion helicopters
Elevators:	2 deck edge—50 × 34 feet (15.2 × 10.4 m)
Missiles:	2 8-tube Sea Sparrow BPDMS launchers Mk 25 except none in LPH 3
Guns:	4 3-inch (76-mm) 50-cal AA Mk 33 (2 twin)
	2 20-mm Phalanx CIWS Mk 16 (2 multi-barrel) in most ships
	4 to 8 12.7-mm machine guns (4 to 8 single)
Radars:	LN-66 navigation except CRP-1900B Pathfinder in LPH 9
	SPS-10 surface search
	SPS-40 air search
Fire control:	2 Mk 115 missile FCS
	local control only for 3-inch guns
EW systems:	SLQ-32(V)3

These ships were the first ships of any navy to be constructed specifically to operate helicopters. Unlike the Royal Navy's commando carriers of the 1960s and 1970s, and the later TARAWA/WASP classes, the LPHs do not carry landing craft (except for the LCVP davits in the INCHON).

The IWO JIMA is scheduled to be decommissioned in 1993.

Design: SCB No. 157. These ships represent an improved World War II–type escort carrier design with accommodations for a Marine battalion and supporting helicopter squadron. The INCHON has davits for two LCVPs. The ships have approximately 3,000 square feet (270 m²) of vehicle space and 40,000 cubic feet (1,200 m³) of space for bulk cargo.

These ships have extensive medical facilities with a 300-bed sick bay.

Electronics: SPN-35 and SPN-43 aircraft approach/control systems fitted in these ships.

Guns: As built, these ships had four 3-inch twin gun mounts, two forward of the island structure and two on the after corners of the flight deck. Between 1970 and 1974 all ships had two 3-inch gun mounts replaced by Sea Sparrow launchers (one forward of the island and one on the port quarter); subsequently removed from the OKINAWA.

These ships have been fitted with two Phalanx CIWS. The OKINAWA had her forward Sea Sparrow launcher replaced by a Phalanx mount; all others have one Phalanx on a sponson on the starboard side, forward of the Sea Sparrow launcher. The second Phalanx is fitted on a sponson on the port side, aft.

All gun FCS have been removed and only local control is now available for the 3-inch guns.

Helicopters: The ships have the capability of operating up to seven CH-46 Sea Knight or four CH-53 Sea Stallion helicopters on their flight decks. The hangar deck can accommodate 19 Sea Knights or 11 Sea Stallions or various mixes of these and other aircraft.

Operational: The GUAM operated as an interim Sea Control Ship (SCS) from 1972 to 1974 to evaluate the concept of flying VSTOL aircraft and ASW helicopters from a ship of about this size in the convoy defense role. She operated AV-8A Harriers and SH-3 Sea Kings. The ship subsequently reverted to an amphibious assault role.

These ships have also operated H-53 helicopters in the mine countermeasures role off North Vietnam and in the Suez Canal. In December 1990, upon arrival in the Middle East, the TRIPOLI became flagship of the U.S. mine countermeasures group for operations in the Persian Gulf and took aboard Mine Countermeasures Squadron (MH) 14. On 18 February 1991 the TRIPOLI struck a moored contact mine in the Gulf that blasted a 20 × 30-foot (6.1 × 9.1-m) hole in the ship's starboard side, below the waterline. None of the crew were killed and injuries were slight.

The TRIPOLI was repaired in a dry dock in Bahrain; after repairs, which took one month, she returned to MCM duties in the Gulf, with her last helicopter mine mission being flown on 18 June 1991, after which she departed the Gulf on 23 June and returned to the United States.

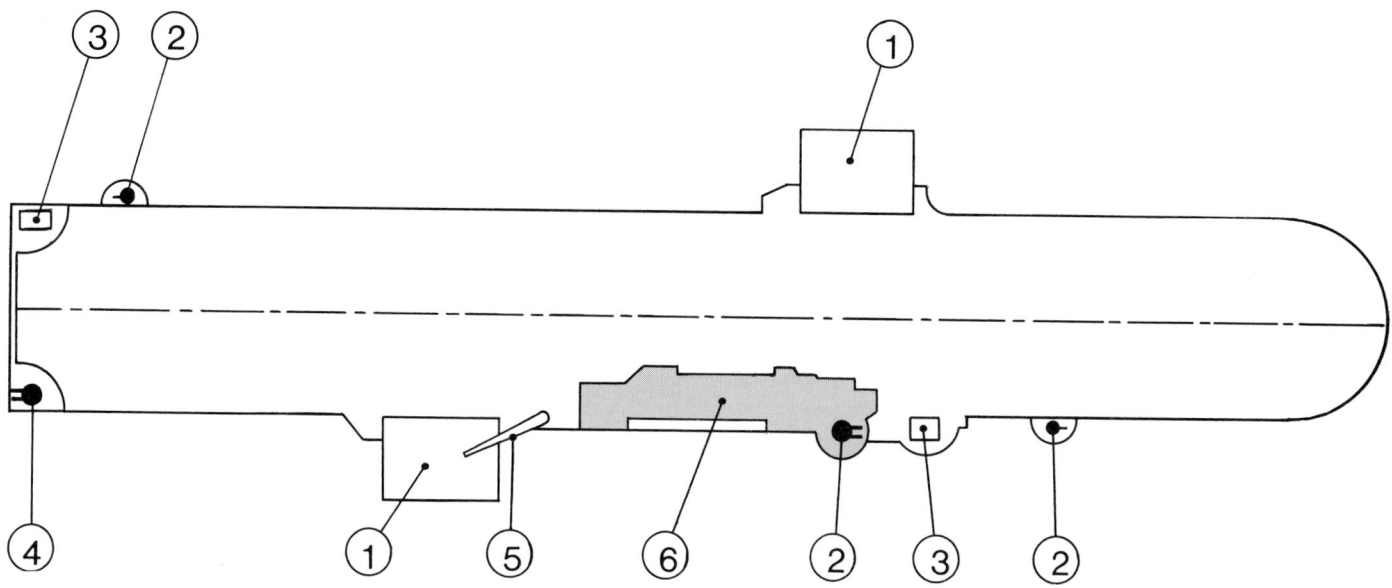

1. deck-edge elevator   2. 20-mm Phalanx CIWS   3. Sea Sparrow launcher   4. 3-inch/50-cal twin gun mount   5. crane   6. island structure (There are armament variations; see text.)

The TRIPOLI with four Navy and Marine helicopters of different types on her flight deck. She has a small island structure, giving her an appearance similar to the escort or "jeep" carriers of World War II. (1991, Giorgio Arra)

The narrow, single-screw stern configuration of the LPHs is evident in this view of the NEW ORLEANS. Just below the flight-deck level she has a Sea Sparrow launcher to port and a twin 3-inch gun mount to starboard. (1989, Giorgio Arra)

The GUAM at New Orleans, La., with Marine CH-53 Sea Stallion helicopters on her after flight deck. The starboard deck-edge elevator is folded against the hull; the elevators fold up to facilitate docking operations and passage through the Panama Canal. (1990, Giorgio Arra)

TABLE 19-3. AMPHIBIOUS ASSAULT SHIPS

Number	Name	Notes
LPH 1	BLOCK ISLAND (ex-CVE 106)	conversion cancelled
LPH 2, 3	IWO JIMA class	
LPH 4	BOXER (ex-CV/CVA/CVS 21)	to LPH 1959; str. 1969
LPH 5	PRINCETON (ex-CV/CVA/CVS 37)	to LPH 1959; str. 1970
LPH 6	THETIS BAY (ex-CVE 90)	to CVHA 1/LPH 1956; str. 1966
LPH 7	IWO JIMA class	
LPH 8	VALLEY FORGE (ex-CV/CVA/CVS 45)	to LPH 1961; str. 1970
LPH 9–12	IWO JIMA class	

The LPH classification was established in 1955. The World War II–era escort carrier BLOCK ISLAND was to have been LPH 1, but her conversion was cancelled. Three ESSEX (CV 9)-class aircraft carriers subsequently were modified to LPHs as was the escort carrier THETIS BAY. The smaller ship had been designated as a helicopter assault carrier (CVHA 1) at the start of her 1955–1956 conversion; she was changed to LPH to avoid confusion and budget competition with the CV-type aircraft carriers.

In addition to the three ESSEX-class ships changed to LPH, the TARAWA (CVS 40) operated extensively with Marine helicopters in the late 1950s.

The designation LPH has *never* signified "Landing Platform Helicopter," as used in some documents.

The TRIPOLI in dry dock in Bahrain showing damage caused by an Iraqi mine during the Gulf conflict. She was operating minesweeping helicopters at the time of her misfortune. The ship was able to continue operations after damage-control teams stopped flooding caused by the explosion. (1991, JO1 Joe Gawlowicz, USN)

The INCHON's island showing the ship's forward twin 3-inch gun mount, Sea Sparrow launcher, and Phalanx CIWS. The OKINAWA has had her Sea Sparrow launchers deleted and has the forward Phalanx CIWS forward of the 3-inch gun mount. (1989, Giorgio Arra)

5 AMPHIBIOUS CARGO SHIPS: "CHARLESTON" CLASS

Number	Name	FY	Builder	Laid down	Launched	Commissioned	Status
LKA 113	CHARLESTON	65	Litton/Ingalls SB, Pascagoula, Miss.	5 Dec 1966	2 Dec 1967	14 Dec 1968	AR
LKA 114	DURHAM*	65	Litton/Ingalls SB, Pascagoula, Miss.	10 July 1967	29 Mar 1968	24 May 1969	**PA**
LKA 115	MOBILE*	65	Litton/Ingalls SB, Pascagoula, Miss.	15 Jan 1968	19 Oct 1968	29 Sep 1969	**PA**
LKA 116	SAINT LOUIS	65	Litton/Ingalls SB, Pascagoula, Miss.	3 Apr 1968	4 Jan 1969	22 Nov 1969	**PA**
LKA 117	EL PASO	66	Litton/Ingalls SB, Pascagoula, Miss.	22 Oct 1968	17 May 1969	17 Jan 1970	**AA**

Displacement:	10,000 tons light		Troops:	approx. 225
	18,600 tons full load		Helicopters:	landing area only
Length:	549¾ feet (167.6 m) waterline		Missiles:	none
	576 feet (175.6 m) overall		Guns:	6 3-inch (76-mm) 50-cal AA Mk 33 (3 twin) except 4 guns in
Beam:	62 feet (18.9 m)			LKA 113, 117
Draft:	27¹¹⁄₁₂ feet (8.5 m)			2 20-mm Phalanx CIWS Mk 16 (2 multi-barrel) in LKA 113, 117
Propulsion:	1 steam turbine (Westinghouse); 22,000 shp; 1 shaft		Radars:	LN-66 navigation
Boilers:	2 600 psi (41.7 kg/cm²) (Combustion Engineering)			CRP-2900 Pathfinder in LKA 113
Speed:	20 knots			SPS-10 surface search
Range:			Fire control:	local control only for 3-inch guns
Manning:	approx. 363 (25 officers + 338 enlisted)		EW systems:	SLQ-32(V)1

These ships carry heavy equipment and supplies for amphibious assaults. They are configured for rapid unloading of equipment into landing craft and helicopters.

The SAINT LOUIS is home-ported at Sasebo, Japan. The CHARLESTON was decommissioned on 27 April 1992 and the MOBILE is scheduled to be decommissioned in 1993.

During 1979–1981 four of the ships were shifted to the NRF; they were returned to active Navy service in the early 1980s to improve amphibious readiness in response to the crises in the Persian Gulf, Lebanon, and Caribbean areas:

Ship	To NRF	Return to Active Fleet
LKA 113	21 Nov 1979	18 Feb 1983
LKA 114	1 Oct 1979	1 Oct 1982
LKA 115	1 Sep 1980	30 Sep 1983
LKA 117	1 Mar 1981	1 Oct 198?

Classification: These ships were ordered as attack cargo ships (AKA). The CHARLESTON was changed to LKA on 14 December 1968, and the others were changed to LKA on 1 January 1969.

Design: SCB No. 403. This is the first class of ships designed specifically for this role; all previous ships of the LKA/AKA type were converted from or built to merchant designs.

These ships have a large helicopter landing area aft, but no hangar or maintenance facilities. They have approximately 33,000 square feet (2,970 m²) of vehicle storage space and almost 70,000 cubic feet (2,100 m³) of bulk cargo space. There are two 78-ton-capacity booms, two 40-ton booms, and eight 15-ton booms.

The ships normally carry as deck cargo 4 LCM(8)s, 5 LCM(6)s, 2 LCVPs, and 2 LCPLs.

Engineering: Maximum horsepower is shown above; sustained horsepower is 19,250.

Despite the development of amphibious ships with helicopter and docking-well features, the Navy still requires amphibious cargo ships to carry break-bulk cargo for landing operations. The EL PASO is at anchor, lowering LCM-type landing craft. (1991, Giorgio Arra)

The CHARLESTON with LCMs alongside and a Marine CH-46 Sea Knight hovering over the flight deck. All amphibious ships have helicopter decks; most can hangar helicopters. (1986, Giorgio Arra)

Guns: As built, four 3-inch twin gun mounts were provided. One mount, as well as the Mk 56 GFCS, was removed from each ship in 1977–1978; a second 3-inch twin mount is being removed for the installation of the CIWS.

Two Phalanx CIWS are planned for installation in these ships. In the CHARLESTON and EL PASO, the first ships so fitted, one Phalanx CIWS is fitted forward, to the left of the remaining forward 3-inch gun mount, and the other Phalanx is fitted on the superstructure in place of the starboard 3-inch gun mount.

Manning: The crews of these ships vary from 22 to 29 officers and 316 to 353 enlisted.

Operational: These ships are being replaced by LHD/LHA types.

AMPHIBIOUS CARGO SHIP: MARINER TYPE (C4-S-1a)

The Navy's only other post–World War II amphibious cargo ship, the TULARE (AKA/LKA 112), was stricken on 1 August 1981 and placed in NDRF. She was made available for sale in 1989 but, at this writing, remains in the mothball fleet at Suisun Bay, Calif.

The LKA 112, LPA 248, and LPA 249 were acquired by the Navy while under construction as Mariner-class merchant ships; two others became support ships for the Polaris program (AG 153, AG 154).[4] One ship of this design remains on the Naval Vessel Register

as a missile range instrumentation ship, the OBSERVATION ISLAND (T-AGM 23); see chapter 23.

See 12th Edition/page 141 for TULARE characteristics.

AMPHIBIOUS TRANSPORTS: MARINER TYPE (C4-S-1a)

The Navy had two postwar-built amphibious transports, the PAUL REVERE (APA/LPA 248) and FRANCIS MARION (APA/LPA 249); both ships were stricken on 1 January 1980 and sold to Spain in January 1980 and July 1980, respectively.

See 11th Edition/page 131 for characteristics.

4. Thirty ships were completed to this design for commercial use in 1952–1955. The design was developed by the Maritime Administration to compete with the foreign trend toward larger and faster cargo ships.

11 AMPHIBIOUS TRANSPORT DOCKS: "AUSTIN" CLASS

Number	Name	FY	Builder	Laid down	Launched	Commissioned	Status
LPD 4	AUSTIN	62	New York Naval Shipyard	4 Feb 1963	27 June 1964	6 Feb 1965	**AA**
LPD 5	OGDEN*	62	New York Naval Shipyard	4 Feb 1963	27 June 1964	19 June 1965	**PA**
LPD 6	DULUTH	62	New York Naval Shipyard	18 Dec 1963	14 Aug 1965	18 Dec 1965	**PA**
LPD 7	CLEVELAND	63	Ingalls SB, Pascagoula, Miss.	30 Nov 1964	7 May 1966	21 Apr 1967	**PA**
LPD 8	DUBUQUE*	63	Ingalls SB, Pascagoula, Miss.	25 Jan 1965	6 Aug 1966	1 Sep 1967	**PA**
LPD 9	DENVER*	63	Lockheed SB & Constn., Seattle, Wash.	7 Feb 1964	23 Jan 1965	26 Oct 1968	**PA**
LPD 10	JUNEAU*	63	Lockheed SB & Constn., Seattle, Wash.	23 Jan 1965	12 Feb 1966	12 July 1969	**PA**
LPD 12	SHREVEPORT*	64	Lockheed SB & Constn., Seattle, Wash.	27 Dec 1965	25 Oct 1966	12 Dec 1970	**AA**
LPD 13	NASHVILLE	64	Lockheed SB & Constn., Seattle, Wash.	14 Mar 1966	7 Oct 1967	14 Feb 1970	**AA**
LPD 14	TRENTON*	65	Lockheed SB & Constn., Seattle, Wash.	8 Aug 1966	3 Aug 1968	6 Mar 1971	**AA**
LPD 15	PONCE	65	Lockheed SB & Constn., Seattle, Wash.	31 Oct 1966	30 May 1970	10 July 1971	**AA**

Displacement:	11,050 tons light		Flag:	90 in LPD 7–10, 12, 13
	16,585 to 17,595 tons full load		Helicopters:	landing area and hangar, except no hangar in LPD 4
Length:	568¾ feet (173.4 m) overall		Missiles:	none
Beam:	84 feet (25.6 m)		Guns:	4 3-inch (76-mm) 50-cal AA Mk 33 (2 twin), except 2 guns in LPD 10
Draft:	23 to 23⁷⁄₁₂ feet (7.0 to 7.2 m)			2 20-mm Phalanx CIWS Mk 16 (2 multi-barrel) in LPD 4, 12–15
Propulsion:	2 steam turbines (De Laval); 24,000 shp; 2 shafts		Radars:	LN-66 navigation
Boilers:	2 600 psi (41.7 kg/cm²) (Foster Wheeler, except Babcock & Wilcox			SPS-10F surface search
	in LPD 5, 12)			SPS-40C air search
Speed:	21 knots		Fire control:	local control only for 3-inch guns
Range:	7,700 n.miles (14,260 km) at 20 knots		EW systems:	SLQ-32(V)1
Manning:	approx. 402 (28 officers + 374 enlisted)			
Troops:	930 in LPD 4–6, 14, 15			
	840 in LPD 7–10, 12, 13			

These ships are enlarged versions of the previous RALEIGH-class LPDs. They carry Marines into forward areas and unload them by landing craft and vehicles carried in their docking well, and by using helicopters provided mainly from amphibious assault ships. The general configuration of these ships is similar to dock landing ships, but with a relatively smaller (covered) docking well and additional space for troop berthing and vehicle parks.

The DUBUQUE is home-ported at Sasebo, Japan.

Aircraft: These ships have deployed with up to six CH-46 Sea Knights embarked for short-term operations. They are rated as being able to deploy with up to four cargo helicopters (CH-46 or CH-53), but this can only be done with a helicopter carrier in company to provide maintenance and other support on a sustained basis.

Builders: The DULUTH was completed at the Philadelphia Naval Shipyard after the closing of the New York Naval Shipyard; she was reassigned to Philadelphia on 24 November 1965.

Class: An additional ship of this class (LPD 16) was provided for in the fiscal 1966 shipbuilding program, but construction was deferred in favor of the LHA program and was officially cancelled in February 1969.

The CORONADO (LPD 11) of this class was modified for use as a flagship in late 1980 and reclassified AGF 11; see chapter 18.

Design: LPD 4–10 are SCB No. 187B, LPD 11–13 No. 187C, changed to No. 402 for LPD 14 and 15 under the new SCB numbering scheme.

The LPD 7–13 are configured as amphibious squadron flagships and have an additional bridge level plus flag berthing space and communications equipment. The docking well in these ships is 168 feet long (51.2 m) and 50 feet (15.2 m) wide. The well deck can accommodate 1 LCU and 3 LCM(6)s or 9 LCM(6)s or 4 LCM(8)s or 28 AAV/LVTP-7 amphibian vehicles.

The ships have about 12,000 square feet (1,080 m²) of vehicle storage space and 40,000 cubic feet (1,200 m³) of bulk cargo space. One 30-ton-capacity crane and six 4-ton cranes are provided.

These ships have a fixed flight deck above the docking well with two landing spots. All except the AUSTIN are fitted with a hangar varying from 58 to 64 feet (17.7 to 19.5 m) in length, 18½ to 24 feet (5.6 to 7.3 m) in width, and 17½ to 19 feet (5.3 to 5.8 m) in height; the hangars have an extension that can expand to provide a length of approximately 80 feet (24.4 m).

Guns: As built, these ships had eight 3-inch guns in twin mounts. The number was reduced to four in the late 1970s, and the associated Mk 56 and Mk 63 GFCS were removed. All are to be fitted with two Phalanx CIWS.

Manning: Crews of these ships vary from 25 to 31 officers and 351 to 389 enlisted.

Modernization: A Service Life Extension Program (SLEP) has been developed for these ships to permit them to operate beyond a nominal 30-year service life by 10 to 15 years. In addition to general improvements, they were to be fitted with the SPS-67 radar vice SPS-10 and modified to carry two LCACs; their aviation capabilities were also to be improved. However, budgetary constraints make these modernizations unlikely to occur.

Operational: During U.S. minesweeping operations in the Persian Gulf in 1988 the TRENTON served as tender to six ocean minesweepers (MSO).

The DULUTH in a floating dry dock at San Diego, Calif. The docking well is open; the twin screws and rudders are visible. (1981, L. Van Ginderen collection)

The NASHVILLE with two Phalanx CIWS mounted forward; amidships she has two 3-inch/50-cal twin gun mounts. She and five sister ships are configured as amphibious squadron flagships with an additional bridge level. (1988, Giorgio Arra)

The TRENTON with her telescoping hangar fully extended. Her 3-inch gun mounts are lost in the clutter atop her island structure (the port-side mount is forward of the helicopter control station). Her SATCOMM antenna arrangement is different from the NASHVILLE's with a tower amidships. (1991, Giorgio Arra)

2 AMPHIBIOUS TRANSPORT DOCKS: "RALEIGH" CLASS

Number	Name	FY	Builder	Laid down	Launched	Commissioned	Status
LPD 1	RALEIGH*	59	New York Naval Shipyard	23 June 1960	17 Mar 1962	8 Sep 1962	AR
LPD 2	VANCOUVER*	60	New York Naval Shipyard	19 Nov 1960	15 Sep 1962	11 May 1963	PR

Displacement:	8,491 tons light		Manning:	LPD 1 397 (24 officers + 373 enlisted)
	14,865 tons full load			LPD 2 401 (27 officers + 374 enlisted)
Length:	500 feet (152.4 m) waterline		Troops:	1,140
	521½ feet (159.0 m) overall		Helicopters:	landing area only
Beam:	84 feet (25.6 m)		Missiles:	none
Draft:	22 feet (6.7 m)		Guns:	6 3-inch (76-mm) 50-cal AA Mk 33 (3 twin)
Propulsion:	2 steam turbines (De Laval); 24,000 shp; 2 shafts			2 20-mm Phalanx CIWS Mk 16 (2 multi-barrel)
Boilers:	2 600 psi (41.7 kg/cm²) (Babcock & Wilcox)		Radars:	LN-66 navigation
Speed:	21.6 knots (20 knots sustained)			SPS-10 surface search
Range:	16,500 n.miles (30,558 km) at 10 knots			SPS-40 air search
	9,600 n.miles (17,780 km) at 16 knots		Fire control:	local control only for 3-inch guns
			EW systems:	SLQ-32(V)1

The LPD is a development of the dock landing ship (LSD) concept with increased troop and vehicle capacity and a relatively small docking well. The RALEIGH was decommissioned on 13 December 1991 and the VANCOUVER on 27 March 1992.

Class: The third ship of this class, the LA SALLE (LPD 3), was converted to a flagship and reclassified as AGF 3; see chapter 18.

Design: SCB No. 187. There is a fixed helicopter deck fitted over the docking well in these ships. The well is 168 feet (51.2 m) long and 50 feet (15.2 m) wide; see AUSTIN class for well-deck capacity. In addition, 2 LCM(6)s or 4 LCVP/LCPLs are normally carried on the

helicopter deck; up to 16 amphibian vehicles can be parked on the main deck (slightly more in the LPD 4 class). The ships have 12,500 square feet (1,125 m²) of vehicle storage space.

No helicopter hangar or support facilities are provided, but there is a large helicopter landing area.

Guns: These ships were built with eight 3-inch/50-cal guns in twin mounts. These were reduced to three mounts and, with installation of the Phalanx CIWS, to two mounts. Their Mk 56 and Mk 51 GFCS were removed when the 3-inch gun battery was reduced in 1977–1978.

The first LPD—her crew proclaiming her "the mother of all LPDs"—returning to Norfolk, Va., after Operation Desert Storm. These ships have large boat cranes with several landing craft stowed in place of the hangar in later LPDs. Both ships of this class have been mothballed. (1991, Giorgio Arra)

The RALEIGH showing traditional LSD/LPD lines: the hull joins the fixed flight deck in the LPDs; the LSDs have an opening beneath the flight deck, sections of which can be removed. Both types are extremely flexible "amphibs" and the progenitors of the LHA/LHD designs. (1991, Giorgio Arra)

(3) DOCK LANDING SHIPS: "HARPERS FERRY" CLASS

Number	Name	FY	Builder	Laid down	Launched	Commission	Status
LSD 49	HARPERS FERRY	88	Avondale Industries, New Orleans, La.	15 Apr 1991	20 June 1992	1994	Building
LSD 50	CARTER HALL	90	Avondale Industries, New Orleans, La.	8 Nov 1991	1993	1995	Building
LSD 51	OAK HILL	91	Avondale Industries, New Orleans, La.	1992	1993	1995	Building

Displacement:	11,894 tons light		Helicopters:	landing area
	16,695 tons full load		Missiles:	none
Length:	579¹¹⁄₁₂ feet (176.8 m) waterline		Guns:	2 20-mm Phalanx CIWS Mk 16 (2 multi-barrel)
	609⁵⁄₁₂ feet (185.8 m) overall			2 20-mm Bushmaster rapid-fire cannon Mk 88 (2 single)
Beam:	84 feet (25.6 m)			8 12.7-mm machine guns (8 single)
Draft:	19¾ feet (6.0 m)		Radars:	1 SPS-49(V) air search
Propulsion:	4 diesel engines (Colt-Pielstick 16 PC2.5V400); 41,600 bhp; 2 shafts			1 SPS-64(V)9 navigation
Speed:	22 knots			1 SPS-67 surface search
Range:	approx. 8,000 n.miles (14,816 km) at 20 knots		Fire control:	none
Manning:	approx. 410		EW systems:	SLQ-32(V)2
Troops:	approx. 500			

These ships will be similar to the WHIDBEY ISLAND-class LSDs, but will have a smaller docking well to provide for increased troop, vehicle, cargo, and helicopter capacity. Navy planning documents refer to the class as LSD 41CV for *Cargo Variant*.

During the design stage the class was designated LPDX, indicating that the design was originally considered as an amphibious transport dock; however, it will instead be a modified dock landing ship.

Class: The Navy originally planned a class of six ships: the three above ships plus two in fiscal 1992 and one in fiscal 1993. In 1991 the planned 1992 program was reduced to one ship, and in late January 1992 the Department of Defense cancelled the remaining two ships, ending the program with the acquisition of only three ships.

Cost: The fiscal 1991 ship was funded at $238.7 million with an additional $25 million in the fiscal 1992 program.

Design: The ship's docking well will accommodate two LCACs or ten LCM(6) landing craft. They will have approximately 13,000 square feet (1,170 m²) of vehicle storage space and 40,000 cubic feet (1,200 m³) of bulk cargo space.

Engineering: Maximum horsepower is given above; sustained horsepower is 33,600.

Names: LSDs are named for historic sites. Harpers Ferry, W.Va., was the site of a government arsenal that insurrectionist-abolitionist John Brown captured in 1859, a prelude to the American Civil War.

8 DOCK LANDING SHIPS: "WHIDBEY ISLAND" CLASS

Number	Name	FY	Builder	Laid down	Launched	Commissioned	Status
LSD 41	WHIDBEY ISLAND	81	Lockheed SB, Seattle, Wash.	4 Aug 1981	10 June 1983	9 Feb 1985	**AA**
LSD 42	GERMANTOWN*	82	Lockheed SB, Seattle, Wash.	5 Aug 1982	29 June 1984	8 Feb 1986	**PA**
LSD 43	FORT MCHENRY*	83	Lockheed SB, Seattle, Wash.	10 June 1983	1 Feb 1986	8 Aug 1987	**PA**
LSD 44	GUNSTON HALL*	84	Avondale Industries, New Orleans, La.	26 May 1986	27 June 1987	22 Apr 1989	**AA**
LSD 45	COMSTOCK	85	Avondale Industries, New Orleans, La.	27 Oct 1986	16 Jan 1988	3 Feb 1990	**PA**
LSD 46	TORTUGA	85	Avondale Industries, New Orleans, La.	23 Mar 1987	15 Sep 1988	17 Nov 1990	**AA**
LSD 47	RUSHMORE	86	Avondale Industries, New Orleans, La.	9 Nov 1987	6 May 1989	1 June 1991	**PA**
LSD 48	ASHLAND	86	Avondale Industries, New Orleans, La.	4 Apr 1988	11 Nov 1989	9 May 1992	**AA**

Displacement:	11,854 tons standard		Troops:	560
	17,745 tons full load		Helicopters:	landing area
Length:	580 feet (176.8 m) waterline		Missiles:	none
	609$\frac{5}{12}$ feet (185.8 m) overall		Guns:	2 20-mm Phalanx CIWS Mk 15 (2 multi-barrel)
Beam:	84 feet (25.6 m)			2 20-mm Bushmaster rapid-fire cannon Mk 67 (2 single)
Draft:	19$\frac{7}{12}$ feet (6.0 m)			8 12.7-mm machine guns (8 single)
Propulsion:	4 diesel engines (SEMT-Pielstick 16 PC2.5 V400); 41,600 bhp; 2 shafts		Radars:	SPS-64(V)9 navigation
				SPS-49 air search
Speed:	22 knots			SPS-67 surface search
Range:	8,000 n.miles (14,816 km) at 20 knots		Fire control:	none
Manning:	approx. 334 (23 officers + 311 enlisted)		EW systems:	SLQ-32(V)1

These ships were built to replace the THOMASTON-class LSDs and to provide increased lift for air-cushion landing craft.

Class: Navy planning in the early 1980s called for nine or ten ships of this class to replace the LSD 28 class; the number was subsequently increased to 12 ships through the fiscal 1988 shipbuilding program. However, the decision was made in the mid-1980s to produce instead eight LSD 41s plus six LSD 41 cargo variants (HARPERS FERRY class) in place of 12 units of this design.

Design: The docking well is 440 feet (134.1 m) long and 50 feet (15.2 m) wide and can accommodate 4 LCACs or 3 LCUs or 21 LCM(6) landing craft or 64 AAV/LVTP-7 amphibian vehicles. In addition, several LCVP/LCPL-type landing craft are normally carried on deck. These ships have a heavy lattice mast.

There is approximately 12,500 square feet (1,080 m²) of vehicle storage space and 5,000 cubic feet (450 m³) of space for bulk cargo. Fitted with one 60-ton-capacity crane and one 20-ton crane.

No helicopter hangar or support facilities are provided.

Engineering: These are the first U.S. ships powered by medium-speed diesel engines. Of French design, the diesels are produced under license by the Fairbanks Morse Division of Colt Industries.

Maximum horsepower is given above; sustained horsepower is 33,600.

Manning: Crews vary in these ships, from 22 to 27 officers and from 289 to 352 enlisted.

The latest LSD design to enter service, the WHIDBEY ISLAND class has been succeeded on the building ways by the similar HARPERS FERRY class, the latter having additional cargo space and a smaller docking well. These ships have two large boat cranes to handle cargo and landing craft. (1991, Giorgio Arra)

The GUNSTON HALL from astern. The docking well can accommodate four LCACs while the large helicopter deck can permit CH-53E and smaller helicopters to land, or can be used to store vehicles, containers, or other equipment. (1991, Giorgio Arra)

The GUNSTON HALL and her sister ships have a massive superstructure "block" to house troops and crews. Two Phalanx CIWS are atop the superstructure; along with the WASP-class LHDs, these are the only amphibious ships not armed with 3-inch or 5-inch guns. (1990, George Nassiopoulos)

5 DOCK LANDING SHIPS: "ANCHORAGE" CLASS

Number	Name	FY	Builder	Laid down	Launched	Commissioned	Status
LSD 36	ANCHORAGE*	65	Ingalls Shipbuilding, Pascagoula, Miss.	13 Mar 1967	5 May 1968	15 Mar 1969	**PA**
LSD 37	PORTLAND*	66	General Dynamics, Quincy, Mass.	21 Sep 1967	20 Dec 1969	3 Oct 1970	**AA**
LSD 38	PENSACOLA*	66	General Dynamics, Quincy, Mass.	12 Mar 1969	11 July 1970	27 Mar 1971	**AA**
LSD 39	MOUNT VERNON*	66	General Dynamics, Quincy, Mass.	29 Jan 1970	17 Apr 1971	13 May 1972	**PA**
LSD 40	FORT FISHER	67	General Dynamics, Quincy, Mass.	15 July 1970	22 Apr 1972	9 Dec 1972	**PA**

Displacement:	8,600 tons light	Troops:	approx. 330
	14,000 tons full load	Helicopters:	landing area
Length:	534 feet (162.8 m) waterline	Missiles:	none
	553¼ feet (168.66 m) overall	Guns:	6 3-inch (76-mm) 50-cal AA Mk 33 (3 twin) except 4 guns in LSD 37–39
Beam:	85 feet (25.9 m)		
Draft:	20 feet (6.1 m)		2 20-mm Phalanx CIWS Mk 16 (2 multi-barrel) in LSD 37–39
Propulsion:	2 steam turbines (De Laval); 24,000 shp; 2 shafts	Radars:	LN-66 navigation
Boilers:	2 600 psi (Foster Wheeler, except Combustion Engineering in LSD 36)		SPS-10 surface search
			SPS-40 air search
Speed:	22 knots (20 knots sustained)	Fire control:	local control only for 3-inch guns
Range:		EW systems:	SLQ-32(V)1
Manning:	approx. 358 (20 officers + 338 enlisted)		

These LSDs were part of the large amphibious ship construction program of the early 1960s and were to supplement the LPDs and LHAs by carrying additional landing craft to the assault area.

Design: SCB No. 404. The docking well is 430 feet (131.1 m) long and 50 feet (15.2 m) wide; it can accommodate 3 LCACs or 3 LCUs or 9 LCM(8)s or 52 AAV/LVTP-7 amphibian vehicles. Another 15 AAV/LVTPs can be stowed on a "mezzanine" deck. A removable helicopter deck is fitted over the docking well. Total vehicle storage space (outside of docking well) is 15,800 square feet (1,422 m²).

Two 50-ton-capacity cranes are fitted.

No helicopter hangar or support facilities are provided.

Guns: As built, these ships had eight 3-inch guns in twin mounts; one amidships mount and the Mk 56 and Mk 63 GFCS were removed in 1977. One additional 3-inch gun mount was deleted with installation of the two Phalanx CIWS in the 1980s.

Manning: Crews vary in these ships from 18 to 22 officers and from 322 to 351 enlisted.

The PORTLAND at Fort Lauderdale, Fla. She retains two 3-inch/50-cal twin gun mounts, one forward and one aft on the superstructure, and has two Phalanx CIWS atop the superstructure; she also has the SLQ-32(V)1 ECM suite. (1989, Giorgio Arra)

The ANCHORAGE with a single, enclosed 3-inch/50-cal twin gun mount forward; the two mounts amidships are open. No CIWs has been fitted in two of these ships. Budget reductions will probably force the retirement of these ships in the late 1990s, as the HARPERS FERRY class is completed. (1987, Giorgio Arra)

4 DOCK LANDING SHIPS: "THOMASTON" CLASS

No.	Name	Status
LSD 28	THOMASTON	PR decomm. 5 Sep 1984
LSD 29	PLYMOUTH ROCK	decomm. 30 Sep 1983 to MarAd 8 Nov 1989
LSD 30	FORT SNELLING	decomm. 28 Sep 1984 to MarAd 7 Sep 1989
LSD 31	POINT DEFIANCE	PR decomm. 30 Sep 1983
LSD 32	SPIEGEL GROVE	AR decomm. 2 Oct 1980
LSD 33	ALAMO	decomm. 28 Sep 1990 to Brazil 1990
LSD 34	HERMITAGE	decomm. 2 Oct 1989 to Brazil 1989
LSD 35	MONTICELLO	PR decomm. 1 Oct 1985

This was the first class of docking-well ships to be built after World War II, with eight ships completed in 1954–1957. All will be discarded in the near future.

See 14th Edition/pages 204–205 for characteristics.

20 TANK LANDING SHIPS: "NEWPORT" CLASS

Number	Name	FY	Builder	Laid down	Launched	Commissioned	Status
LST 1179	NEWPORT	65	Philadelphia Naval Shipyard	1 Nov 1966	3 Feb 1968	7 June 1969	AR
LST 1180	MANITOWOC*	66	Philadelphia Naval Shipyard	1 Feb 1967	4 June 1969	24 Jan 1970	**AA**
LST 1181	SUMTER	66	Philadelphia Naval Shipyard	14 Nov 1967	13 Dec 1969	20 June 1970	**AA**
LST 1182	FRESNO	66	National Steel & SB, San Diego	16 Dec 1967	20 Sep 1968	22 Nov 1969	**NRF-P**
LST 1183	PEORIA*	66	National Steel & SB, San Diego	22 Feb 1968	23 Nov 1968	21 Feb 1970	**PA**
LST 1184	FREDERICK*	66	National Steel & SB, San Diego	13 Apr 1968	8 Mar 1969	11 Apr 1970	**PA**
LST 1185	SCHENECTADY*	66	National Steel & SB, San Diego	2 Aug 1968	24 May 1969	13 June 1970	**PA**
LST 1186	CAYUGA*	66	National Steel & SB, San Diego	28 Sep 1968	12 July 1969	8 Aug 1970	**PA**
LST 1187	TUSCALOOSA	66	National Steel & SB, San Diego	23 Nov 1968	6 Sep 1969	24 Oct 1970	**PA**
LST 1188	SAGINAW*	67	National Steel & SB, San Diego	24 May 1969	7 Feb 1970	23 Jan 1971	**AA**
LST 1189	SAN BERNARDINO*	67	National Steel & SB, San Diego	12 July 1969	26 Mar 1970	27 Mar 1971	**PA**
LST 1190	BOULDER	67	National Steel & SB, San Diego	6 Sep 1969	22 May 1970	4 June 1971	**NRF-A**
LST 1191	RACINE	67	National Steel & SB, San Diego	13 Dec 1969	15 Aug 1970	9 July 1971	**NRF-P**
LST 1192	SPARTANBURG COUNTY*	67	National Steel & SB, San Diego	7 Feb 1970	11 Nov 1970	1 Sep 1971	**AA**
LST 1193	FAIRFAX COUNTY	67	National Steel & SB, San Diego	28 Mar 1970	19 Dec 1970	16 Oct 1971	**AA**
LST 1194	LA MOURE COUNTY*	67	National Steel & SB, San Diego	22 May 1970	13 Feb 1971	18 Dec 1971	**AA**
LST 1195	BARBOUR COUNTY*	67	National Steel & SB, San Diego	15 Aug 1970	15 May 1971	12 Feb 1972	PR
LST 1196	HARLAN COUNTY	67	National Steel & SB, San Diego	7 Nov 1970	24 July 1971	8 Apr 1972	**AA**
LST 1197	BARNSTABLE COUNTY	67	National Steel & SB, San Diego	19 Dec 1970	2 Oct 1971	27 May 1972	**AA**
LST 1198	BRISTOL COUNTY	67	National Steel & SB, San Diego	13 Feb 1971	4 Dec 1971	5 Aug 1972	**PA**

Displacement:	4,793 tons light	Manning:	active ships approx. 253 (15 officers + 238 enlisted)
	8,450 tons full load	Troops:	430
Length:	522⅛ feet (159.2 m) overall	Helicopters:	landing area
	561⅚ feet (171.3 m) over derrick arms	Guns:	4 3-inch (76-mm) 50-cal AA Mk 32 (2 twin)
Beam:	69½ feet (21.2 m)		1 20-mm Phalanx CIWS Mk 16 (multi-barrel) in some ships (see notes)
Draft:	5¹¹/₁₂ feet (1.8 m) forward		2 or 4 12.7-mm machine guns (2 or 4 single)
	17½ feet (5.3 m) aft	Radars:	LN-66 navigation
Propulsion:	6 diesel engines (General Motors 16-645-E5 in LST 1179–1181; Arco 16-251 in others); 16,500 bhp; 2 shafts		SPS-10F surface search
		Fire control:	local control only for 3-inch guns
Speed:	22 knots (20 knots sustained)	EW systems:	none
Range:			

These ships represent the "ultimate" design in landing ships that can be "beached." However, they generally unload onto pontoon causeways. They depart from the traditional LST bow-door design to obtain a hull design for a sustained speed of 20 knots.

Three ships have been assigned to the Naval Reserve Force:

LST 1182	30 September 1990
LST 1190	1 December 1980
LST 1191	15 January 1981

The SAN BERNARDINO is home-ported in Sasebo, Japan.

The BARBOUR COUNTY was decommissioned on 30 March 1992 and the NEWPORT on 30 September 1992.

Class: Seven additional ships were planned for the fiscal 1971 shipbuilding program; they were cancelled.

Design: SCB No. 405. The design provides bow and stern ramps for unloading tanks and other vehicles. The aluminum bow ramp is 112 feet (34.1 m) long and is handled over the bow by the twin, fixed derrick arms. Vehicles can be driven between the main deck forward and aft through a passage in the superstructure. The stern ramp permits unloading AAV/LVTP-type amphibious vehicles directly into the water while the ships are under way or by "mating" the LST to landing craft or a pier. The ships have 17,300 square feet (1,557 m²) of vehicle storage space; they can carry 2,000 tons of cargo but only 500 tons when beaching. The tank (lower) deck can accommo-

date 23 AAV/LVTP-7 amphibian vehicles or 41 2½-ton 6x6 cargo trucks; another 29 trucks can be carried on the main (upper) deck. Two 10-ton-capacity cranes are fitted amidships.

Four LCVP/LCPL-type landing craft are carried in amidship davits. Four pontoon causeway sections can be carried alongside the hull, amidships.

There is a large helicopter landing area aft, but no hangar or support facilities.

Electronics: In the 1970s the Navy planned to provide the SLQ-32(V)1 in these ships; however, EW systems will not be installed (nor will SRBOC launchers).

Guns: These ships were built with four 3-inch/50-cal guns in twin mounts atop the superstructure; their Mk 63 GFCS were removed in 1977–1978. The 3-inch guns were scheduled to be replaced by two 20-mm Phalanx CIWS; however, beginning in the mid-1970s the Atlantic Fleet ships were fitted with a single Phalanx CIWS. Installation of the second CIWS is unlikely in view of budget constraints.

Manning: The crews of the active ships vary from 12 to 17 officers and from 226 to 252 enlisted.

Missiles: Proposals to mount the Army's Assault Ballistic Rocket System (ABRS) on some or all of these ships have been dropped.

Names: Note that the first 13 ships do not have county or parish name suffixes, as had all previously named LSTs.

The MANITOWOC showing the unusual "bow horns" for handling the 111½-foot (34-m) aluminum ramp, passed through the upper section of the bow, which hinges open. The ramp can carry 75-ton loads. Note the opening for the drive-through tunnel in the superstructure. (1991, Giorgio Arra)

The FAIRFAX COUNTY shows the stern ramp, which can be used for unloading vehicles into landing craft, or for launching amphibious vehicles. A stern anchor is fitted to kedge the ship out of shallow water. (1988, Giorgio Arra)

The FAIRFAX COUNTY carrying four pontoon causeways on her after hull. These ships have a single Phalanx CIWS with two 3-inch/50-cal twin gun mounts on the after superstructure. They have asymmetrical funnels. (1990, George Nassiopoulos)

Assault amphibian vehicles spew forth from the stern of the BRISTOL COUNTY during an amphibious exercise off South Korea. The AAVs can be launched while the LST is under way. The BRISTOL COUNTY's stern anchor is down to hold her steady; her deck is filled with Marine vehicles and equipment. (1984, U.S. Navy)

TANK LANDING SHIPS: "TERREBONNE PARISH" CLASS

Number	Name*	Status
LST 1156	TERREBONNE PARISH	to Spain 1971
LST 1157	TERRELL COUNTY	to Greece 1977
LST 1158	TIOGA COUNTY	str. 1 Nov 1973 (NDRF)
LST 1159	TOM GREEN COUNTY	to Spain 1972
LST 1160	TRAVERSE COUNTY	str. 1 Nov 1973; to Peru 1984
LST 1161	VERNON COUNTY	to Venezuela 1973
LST 1162	WAHKIAKUM COUNTY	str. 11 Jan 1973 (NDRF)
LST 1163	WALDO COUNTY	str. 1 Nov 1973; to Peru 1984
LST 1164	WALWORTH COUNTY	str. 1 Nov 1973; to Peru 1984
LST 1165	WASHOE COUNTY	str. 1 Nov 1973; to Peru 1984
LST 1166	WASHTENAW COUNTY	to MSS 2 (str. 30 Aug 1973)
LST 1167	WESTCHESTER COUNTY	to Turkey 1974
LST 1168	WEXFORD COUNTY	to Spain 1971
LST 1169	WHITFIELD COUNTY	to Greece 1977
LST 1170	WINDHAM COUNTY	to Turkey 1973

*County and parish names were assigned to 158 existing LSTs on 1 July 1955 (36 Japanese-manned T-LSTs were not named). All subsequent LSTs have been assigned names when built.

These 15 ships were built during the Korean War, completing in 1952–1954. They were the Navy's first post–World War II LST design. All were in Navy service until decommissioned in 1970, except WALWORTH COUNTY in 1971; the LSTs 1158, 1160, 1162–1165 then served with the Military Sealift Command in 1972–1973 (designated T-LST). Upon being laid up the ex–T-LSTs were retained in NDRF for possible future use; two remain. Most transferred to other navies (lease or sale); four ships were leased to Peru on 7 August 1984.

The WASHTENAW COUNTY was reclassified as a minesweeper support ship before being stricken; see chapter 22.

See 14th Edition/pages 210–211 for characteristics.

TABLE 19-4. POST–WORLD WAR II TANK LANDING SHIPS

Number	Name	Notes
LST 1153	TALBOT COUNTY	stricken 1973
LST 1154	TALLAHATCHEE COUNTY	to AVB 2
LST 1155	cancelled 1946	
LST 1156–1170	TERREBONNE PARISH class	
LST 1171	DE SOTO COUNTY class	
LST 1172	cancelled 1955	
LST 1173–1178	DE SOTO COUNTY class	
LST 1179–1198	NEWPORT class	

Through June 1945 a total of 1,052 LSTs were completed for the U.S. Navy (numbered LST 1–1152 with 100 units cancelled). All were of the same basic design, with the later 611 ships (LST 542 onward) having minor improvements over the earlier series. Three larger, improved LSTs with steam-turbine propulsion were ordered late in the war with two being completed, the LST 1153 and LST 1154 in 1947 and 1949, respectively; the third ship was cancelled. (All other U.S. LSTs have had diesel propulsion.)

FIRE SUPPORT SHIP PROGRAMS

In World War II numerous production landing ships were modified during construction or converted to the fire-support role for amphibious landings (LCIG, LCIM, LCIR, LSMR), and the LCSL was constructed specifically for that role. One inshore fire support ship was constructed after the war—the CARRONADE (IFS 1), an improved LSMR with a single 5-inch gun and rapid-fire rocket launchers. Her designation was changed to LRF on 1 January 1969 along with the surviving war-built LSMRs. The CARRONADE was commissioned in 1955 and stricken in 1973.

There have been subsequent proposals to build fire support ships (IFS/LFR/LFS), but none has been authorized. The recommissioning of the four IOWA (BB 61)-class battleships made consideration of such ships superfluous in the 1980s, while funding constraints will probably negate construction efforts in the 1990s.

TANK LANDING SHIPS: "DE SOTO COUNTY" CLASS

Number	Name	Notes
LST 1171	DE SOTO COUNTY	to Italy 1972
LST 1172	. . . . . .	cancelled 1955
LST 1173	SUFFOLK COUNTY	str. 16 Feb 1989
LST 1174	GRANT COUNTY	to Brazil 1973
LST 1175	YORK COUNTY	to Italy 1972
LST 1176	GRAHAM COUNTY	to AGP 1976
LST 1177	LORAIN COUNTY	str. 16 Feb 1989
LST 1178	WOOD COUNTY	str. 16 Feb 1989

The seven ships of this class were completed in 1957–1959. All have been stricken. The last three, which had been in NDRF since 1972, were stricken in 1989 and transferred to the Maritime Administration for disposal.

These were the last U.S. Navy LSTs to be built with the traditional bow doors and ramp, and superstructure aft. The GRAHAM COUNTY (LST 1176) was converted to a gunboat support ship to support the ASHEVILLE (PG 84)-class ships operating in the Mediterranean. The WOOD COUNTY was to have been converted to support the PEGASUS (PHM 1)-class hydrofoil missile craft; her conversion was deferred in 1977 (to have been designated AGHS).

See 14th Edition/page 209 for characteristics.

CHAPTER 20

Landing Craft and Vehicles

The first LCAC skims into the water while carrying four Marine Corps Light Armored Vehicles (LAV). U.S. Navy LCACs are considerably smaller than their Russian counterparts, but the U.S. craft can be transported by larger amphibious ships. (U.S. Navy)

The U.S. Navy operates several hundred landing craft. The larger air-cushion landing craft (LCAC) and utility landing craft (LCU) are usually identified by hull numbers.

All landing craft are operated by Navy personnel. The smaller landing craft are identified by the ship, unit, or base to which they are assigned. The assault amphibian vehicles (formerly amphibious tractors) operated by the Marine Corps are listed in the latter section of this chapter.

Several LCUs have been transferred to other navies, reclassified, or stricken; others serve as test support craft (IX), ferry boats (YFB), and harbor utility craft (YFU); they are described in chapter 25. The Army operates several LCUs in the same designation series as the Navy craft as well as LCMs, and the Air Force operates several LCMs; see chapter 34.

The amphibious forces also operate two warping tugs (LWT) and three side-loading warping tugs (SLWT), which are used to move pontoon causeways in amphibious areas. They can be transported to forward areas by amphibious ships.

Operational: In the Pacific Fleet, Naval Beach Group 1, based at the Naval Amphibious Base Coronado (San Diego), Calif., has Assault Craft Unit (ACU) 1 that operates conventional landing craft and ACU-5 that operates LCACs; in the Atlantic Fleet, Naval Beach Group 2 at Little Creek (Norfolk), Va., has ACU-2 for conventional landing craft and ACU-4 for LCACs.

49 + 35 LANDING CRAFT AIR CUSHION: LCAC TYPE

Number	FY	In service	Assignment	Number	FY	In service	Assignment
LCAC 1	82	Dec 1984	ACU-5	LCAC 43	89	Feb 1992	ACU-5
LCAC 2	82	Feb 1986	ACU-5	LCAC 44	89	Feb 1992	ACU-5
LCAC 3	82	June 1986	ACU-5	LCAC 45	89	Mar 1992	ACU-4
LCAC 4	83	Aug 1986	ACU-5	LCAC 46	89	May 1992	ACU-4
LCAC 5	83	Nov 1986	ACU-5	LCAC 47	89	June 1992	ACU-5
LCAC 6	83	Dec 1986	ACU-5	LCAC 48	89	June 1992	ACU-5
LCAC 7	84	Mar 1987	ACU-4	LCAC 49	90	Oct 1992	ACU-4
LCAC 8	84	June 1987	ACU-4	LCAC 50	90	Building	
LCAC 9	84	June 1987	ACU-4	LCAC 51	90	Building	
LCAC 10	84	Oct 1987	ACU-4	LCAC 52	90	Building	
LCAC 11	84	Dec 1987	ACU-4	LCAC 53	90	Building	
LCAC 12	84	Dec 1987	ACU-4	LCAC 54	90	Building	
LCAC 13	85	Sep 1988	ACU-5	LCAC 55	90	Building	
LCAC 14	85	Nov 1988	ACU-5	LCAC 56	90	Building	
LCAC 15	85	Sep 1989	ACU-4	LCAC 57	90	Building	
LCAC 16	85	Jan 1990	ACU-5	LCAC 58	90	Building	
LCAC 17	85	Feb 1990	ACU-5	LCAC 59	90	Building	
LCAC 18	85	Nov 1988	ACU-5	LCAC 60	90	Building	
LCAC 19	85	June 1990	ACU-4	LCAC 61	91	Building	
LCAC 20	85	Sep 1990	ACU-4	LCAC 62	91	Building	
LCAC 21	85	Mar 1989	ACU-4	LCAC 63	91	Building	
LCAC 22	86	Nov 1990	ACU-5	LCAC 64	91	Building	
LCAC 23	86	June 1991	ACU-5	LCAC 65	91	Building	
LCAC 24	86	Mar 1990	ACU-5	LCAC 66	91	Building	
LCAC 25	86	June 1990	ACU-4	LCAC 67	91	Building	
LCAC 26	86	June 1990	ACU-4	LCAC 68	91	Building	
LCAC 27	86	Aug 1990	ACU-4	LCAC 69	91	Building	
LCAC 28	86	Oct 1990	ACU-4	LCAC 70	91	Building	
LCAC 29	86	Dec 1990	ACU-5	LCAC 71	91	Building	
LCAC 30	86	Dec 1990	ACU-5	LCAC 72	91	Building	
LCAC 31	86	Feb 1991	ACU-5	LCAC 73	92	Building	
LCAC 32	86	May 1991	ACU-5	LCAC 74	92	Building	
LCAC 33	86	June 1991	ACU-5	LCAC 75	92	Building	
LCAC 34	89	Mar 1991	ACU-5	LCAC 76	92	Building	
LCAC 35	89	Mar 1992	ACU-5	LCAC 77	92	Building	
LCAC 36	89	Apr 1992	ACU-4	LCAC 78	92	Building	
LCAC 37	89	July 1991	ACU-4	LCAC 79	92	Building	
LCAC 38	89	Sep 1991	ACU-4	LCAC 80	92	Building	
LCAC 39	89	Sep 1991	ACU-4	LCAC 81	92	Building	
LCAC 40	89	Nov 1991	ACU-4	LCAC 82	92	Building	
LCAC 41	89	Nov 1991	ACU-4	LCAC 83	92	Building	
LCAC 42	89	Dec 1991	ACU-5	LCAC 84	92	Building	

Builders:	Bell-Aerospace/Textron Marine Systems, New Orleans, La., except LCAC 15–23, 34–36, 49–51 by Avondale Gulfport Marine, La.	
Displacement:	102.2 tons light	
	169 tons full load	
	184 tons overload	
Length:	81 feet (24.7 m) overall (structure)	
	87$^{11}/_{12}$ feet (26.8 m) on cushion	
Beam:	43$^2/_3$ feet (13.3 m) (structure)	
	47 feet (14.3 m) (cushion)	
Draft:	3 feet (0.9 m) structure	
Propulsion/lift:	4 gas turbines (Avco-Lycoming TF-40B); 15,820 shp; 2 shrouded propellers and 2 bow thrusters/4 centrifugal lift fans	
Speed:	50 knots maximum on cushion	
	40+ knots with payload on cushion in sea state 2	
	30+ knots with payload on cushion in sea state 3	
	25 knots maximum on hull	
Range:	200 n.miles at 40 knots with payload	
Manning:	5 (enlisted)	
Troops:	24	
Guns:	(see notes)	
Radars:	modified LN-66 navigation	

These landing craft are the first advanced-technology surface ships to be produced in series by the U.S. Navy. They carry heavy vehicles and cargo from amphibious ships onto the beach at higher speeds and for longer distances than can conventional landing craft.

Congress authorized 24 LCACs in fiscal 1992 in lieu of the 12 units requested by the Bush administration. In the event, only the 12 are being built, the contract awarded on 22 May 1992.

All 84 units should be completed by 1995.

Builders: Lockheed Shipyard in Seattle, Wash., was originally the second source for LCAC construction; however, beginning in June 1988 that firm divested itself of shipbuilding activities and the Gulfport Marine division of Avondale Industries took over the Lockheed contracts.

Class: The original Navy-Marine plan was for 107 LCACs to support an amphibious assault by a MEF + MEB. In early 1984 the Department of Defense announced a plan for "at least 90" units, although the 107 force-level goal was listed in official documents through fiscal 1991. The fiscal 1992 Department of Defense budget request provided for the final 12 LCACs for a total of 84 units.

Costs: The fiscal 1991 budget provided $263.4 million for 12 units, with $264.8 million for the final 12 units in fiscal 1992.

Design: The Navy began development of air-cushion craft in 1960 (see appendix A). The production LCACs are based on the JEFF(B), one of two competitive prototypes delivered to the Navy in 1977.

The LCAC has a modular design, which facilitates construction, maintenance, and damage repairs. The craft are fully "skirted"; they are amphibious and can clear land obstacles up to four feet (1.2 m) high. Bow and stern ramps are fitted. The cargo deck area is 81 feet (24.7 m) × 27 feet (8.2 m) totaling 1,809 square feet (162.8 m²).

The design payload is 120,000 pounds (54,545 kg) with a maximum overload of 150,000 pounds (68,182 kg). An LCAC can accommodate one M60-series tank or four Light Armored Vehicles (LAV) or three AAV/LVTP-7 amphibian vehicles (two AAVs if appliqué armor is fitted), or two M198 155-mm towed howitzers.

The control compartment is located on the starboard side, with an aircraft-type cockpit with the operator seated on the far right, the engineer in the center, and the navigator on the left.

Design problems occurred with the early craft when operational tests revealed that the craft shipped water that could cause electrical shorts and interrupt operations. The early craft have been modified and the Navy did not request additional units in the fiscal 1987–1988 budgets because the five units completed at that time would require additional testing before modifications could be developed.

All units were built with composite (ceramic tile) armor for the control station module. The LCAC 34 and later units have one engine on each side armored, with the LCAC 61 and subsequent units having additional engine armor. Armor, modular arrangement, and redundancy provide a relatively high degree of survivability.

Electronics: The modified LN-66 is combined with a Unisys-developed system to provide multiple functions.

Engineering: The gas turbines are fitted in modules, two per side, in the port and starboard sides. The clutch/gearbox system permits a high degree of flexibility. Two engines are normally employed for propulsion and two for lift; under emergency conditions one engine can provide propulsion and one can provide lift. The craft have a high degree of maneuverability and can turn 180° within their own length.

The propellers are four-bladed, 11¾-foot (3.6-m) diameter, reversible, each fitted with two rudders; the lift fans are 5¼ feet (1.6 m) in diameter.

Guns: No armament is fitted. However, three mounting positions are provided: one for a 7.62-mm M60 machine gun and two for a 7.62-mm or .50-cal M2 machine gun or 40-mm Mk 19 grenade launcher.

Operational: Each LCAC is commanded by a craftmaster, a chief petty officer who also pilots the craft; the other crewmen are the engineer, navigator, load master, and deck seaman.

The LCACs are assigned in approximately equal numbers to Assault Craft Unit 4 at Little Creek (Norfolk), Va., and Assault Craft Unit 5 at Camp Pendleton, Calif. ACU-4 was established in 1987 and ACU-5 in 1983.

The LCACs can be carried by the following amphibious ships: LHD (3), LHA (1), LSD 41 (4), LSD 41CV (2), LSD 36 (3), and LPD (1).

In 1988 the Navy evaluated the LCAC in the mine countermeasures role; the LCAC 12 was employed in these tests, being fitted with helicopter-type MCM equipment.

Seventeen LCACs were deployed on board amphibious ships participating in Operation Desert Storm in January–February 1991. All were "mission-ready" and operated in day and night exercises and administrative (non-combat) landings.

An LCAC rests in the docking well of the PENSACOLA (LSD 38). The LCACs can be transported by four types of amphibious ships fitted with docking wells. However, LCACs can be embarked only at the cost of other landing craft or amphibious vehicles. (U.S. Navy)

The LCAC 24 at high speed. The craft has bow and stern ramps; the control compartment, with an aircraft-type cockpit for three operators, is located on the starboard side. The engines are located in the side structures, a modular and compact design. (1990, Textron Marine Systems)

The LCAC 10 of Assault Craft Unit 4 at rest at Norfolk, Va. Twin directional control vanes are fitted to each shrouded propeller. The craft are fast and highly maneuverable; they can operate in an emergency or in the event of battle damage with only two engines providing both lift and propulsion. (1988, U.S. Navy)

45 UTILITY LANDING CRAFT: "LCU 1610" CLASS

Number	Assignment*		Number	Assignment*
LCU 1611 ex-YFU 97			LCU 1647	NUSC, Andros range, Caribbean
LCU 1613	PMTC, San Diego, Calif.		LCU 1648	ACU-1
LCU 1614	NADC, Key West, Fla.		LCU 1649	
LCU 1616	ACU-1		LCU 1650	
LCU 1617	ACU-1		LCU 1651	ACU-1
LCU 1619	ACU-1		LCU 1652	ACU-1
LCU 1621	NAB Coronado (San Diego), Calif.		LCU 1653	ACU-2
LCU 1623	Naval Special Warfare Group 2		LCU 1654	ACU-2
LCU 1624	ACU-1		LCU 1655	ACU-2
LCU 1627	ACU-1		LCU 1656	ACU-2
LCU 1629	ACU-1		LCU 1657	ACU-2
LCU 1630	ACU-1		LCU 1658	
LCU 1631	ACU-1		LCU 1659	ACU-2
LCU 1632	ACU-1		LCU 1660	ACU-2
LCU 1633	ACU-1		LCU 1661	ACU-2
LCU 1634	ACU-1		LCU 1662	ACU-2
LCU 1635	ACU-1		LCU 1663	ACU-2
LCU 1637	NS, Roosevelt Roads, Puerto Rico		LCU 1664	ACU-2
LCU 1641	Mine Division 126, Mayport, Fla.		LCU 1665	fleet activities, Sasebo, Japan
LCU 1643	ACU-2		LCU 1666	ACU-1
LCU 1644	ACU-2		LCU 1680	reserve training, Buffalo, N.Y.
LCU 1645	ACU-2		LCU 1681	reserve training, Tampa, Fla.
LCU 1646	ACU-1			

*Notes: NAB = Naval Amphibious Base; NADC = Naval Air Development Center; PMTC = Pacific Missile Test Center;
NS = Naval Station; NUSC = Naval Underwater Systems Center;

Builders:	Defoe SB, Bay City, Wisc.: LCU 1646–1666
	General Ship & Engine Works, East Boston, Mass.: LCU 1627, 1628, 1631–1635
	Gunderson Bros, Portland, Ore.: LCU 1616–1619, 1623, 1624
	Marinette Marine, Marinette, Wisc.: LCU 1643–1645
	Moss Point Marine, Escatawpa, Miss.: LCU 1680, 1681
	Southern SB, Slidell, La.: LCU 1626, 1629, 1630
Displacement:	190 tons light
	390 tons full load, except LCU 1680, 1681 404 tons
Length:	134¾ feet (41.1 m) overall
Beam:	29¾ feet (9.1 m)
Draft:	6¹¹⁄₁₂ feet (2.1 m)
Propulsion:	4 diesel engines (General Motors Detroit 6-71); 1,200 bhp; 2 Kort-nozzle propellers (except LCU 1646 and later units 4 General Motors 12V71N, 1,840 bhp)
Speed:	11 knots
Range:	1,200 n.miles (2,222 km) at 8 knots with payload
Manning:	6 (enlisted)
Troops:	8
Guns:	2 20-mm cannon or 2 .50-cal machine guns (2 single) (see notes)
Radars:	LN-66 or SPS-53 navigation

These are improved LCUs with 15 units (LCU 1610–1624) completed in 1959–1960 and the remainder from 1967 to 1976, except LCU 1680 and LCU 1681 in 1984–1985.

Class: This class originally consisted of hull numbers LCU 1610–1624 and 1627–1681. The LCU 1637 is a prototype all-aluminum craft, otherwise identical to the LCU 1610 class; no additional aluminum units were built. The LCU 1680 and LCU 1681 had a modified design.

The LCU 1621, 1623, and 1628 have been converted to auxiliary swimmer delivery vehicles (ASDV) to support diving operations; see below.

Classification: LCU 1611 is the former YFU 97; she was changed back to LCU on 15 June 1990.

Design: The LCU 1610–1624 were SCB No. 149; the LCU 1627 and later units were SCB No. 149B (new series SCB No. 406).

These LCUs have a "drive-through" configuration with bow and stern ramps, and a small, starboard-side island structure housing controls and accommodations. Previous LCU/LCT-type landing craft had a small deck structure aft. They are welded-steel construction; the mast folds down for entering well decks of amphibious ships.

Cargo capacity is two or three M60-series Abrams tanks or up to about 190 tons of cargo or, for short distances, 350 troops.

Engineering: The LCU 1621 had vertical shafts fitted with vertical-axis, cycloidal six-bladed propellers. All other units have Kort-nozzle propellers. The LCU 1680 and 1681 were built with improved engines; LCU 1646 and higher have been backfitted.

Guns: Weapons are not normally fitted in these craft.

Operational: Most LCUs are assigned to Assault Craft Units 1 and 2, as indicated above.

The LCU 1641, used as a training minelayer, is fitted with mine rails and a recovery crane.

The LCU 1647 employed as a test support craft at the Atlantic Undersea Test and Evaluation Center operated by the Naval Undersea Systems Center at Andros Range in the Caribbean. (1991, Giorgio Arra)

The LCU 1614 configured as a support barge for the Naval Air Development Center facility at Key West, Fla. A large crane is fitted amidships. (1989, Giorgio Arra)

The LCU 1627 represents the Navy's standard LCU design. These craft are invaluable for moving troops, vehicles, and bulky equipment from ship to shore. They are still needed for amphibious operations despite the advent of helicopters and air-cushion landing craft. (1988, Giorgio Arra)

The stern of the LCU 1635 showing the stern ramp, which permits "drive-through" operation of vehicles from one craft to another and stern loading. The folding navigation radar "pot" is raised; the mast is lowered to permit the craft to enter ship docking wells. (1988, Giorgio Arra)

The LCU 1641 as configured as a practice minelayer; there are rails over the stern ramp and a small crane (starboard side) for mine recovery. (1984, Giorgio Arra)

2 UTILITY LANDING CRAFT: "LCU 1466" CLASS

Number	Assignment
LCU 1564	PMTC, Point Mugu, Calif.
LCU 1590	Mobile Diving and Salvage Unit 2

Builders:	
Displacement:	180 tons light
	360 tons full load
Length:	119 feet (39.0 m) overall
Beam:	34 feet (10.4 m)
Draft:	6 feet (1.8 m)
Propulsion:	3 geared diesel engines (Gray Marine); 675 bhp; 3 shafts
Speed:	8 knots
Range:	
Manning:	6 (enlisted)
Troops:	8
Guns:	removed
Radars:	navigation

These are the survivors of a large series of LCUs; they are smaller than the later LCU 1610 and have a deckhouse-aft configuration.

Class: This class covered hull numbers LCU 1466–1609 with 14 units constructed in Japan under the offshore procurement program for foreign service (LCU 1594–1601 built for Taiwan and LCU 1602–1607 for Japan, all completed in 1955). Other ships of this design were built for the U.S. Army.

Numerous units were transferred to other nations; others became service craft (YFU).

Classification: The LCU 1466–1503 were ordered as utility landing ships (LSU) on 31 October 1951; they were reclassified as LCUs on 15 April 1952.

A unit of the LCU 1466 class carrying three Marine M48 Patton tanks (with turrets turned to the rear) during a landing exercise. Several of these craft are operated by the Army (see chapter 34). There is only a bow ramp; twin 20-mm cannon are fitted on either side of the bridge. (U.S. Navy)

Design: SCB-25.

Guns: Built with gun "tubs" on either side of the bridge structure for .50-cal machine guns or 20-mm cannon.

POST–WORLD WAR II TANK LANDING CRAFT

The tank landing craft designs LCT(1), (2), (3), and (4) were British. The first U.S. design was the LCT(5) with No. 1–500 being completed in 1942; many were transferred to Great Britain. The LCT(6) followed, with No. 501–1465 being completed in 1943–1944; a few went to Britain and six became coastal minehunters, designated AMc(U) 1–6.[1] The LCT(6) had an "island" structure on the port side, introducing the "drive-through" design to landing craft.

The American LCT(7) No. 1501–1830 were oceangoing craft, completed as medium landing ships (LSM/LSMR). The British LCT(8) was a similar, oceangoing craft.

In 1949 the surviving LCT(6)s were reclassified as utility landing ships (LSU) with their LCT hull numbers. Landing craft No. 1466–1503 were ordered in 1951 as LSUs but changed to LCU in May 1952. Subsequent LCUs follow in sequence, ignoring the numbers initially assigned to the LCT(7) series.

MECHANIZED LANDING CRAFT: LCM(8) MOD 3/4 TYPES

Weight:	34 tons light
	121 tons full load
Length:	73⁷/₁₂ feet (22.4 m) overall
Beam:	21 feet (6.4 m)
Draft:	4⁷/₁₂ feet (1.4 m) aft
Propulsion:	4 diesel engines (General Motors Detroit 6-71); 1,300 bhp; 2 shafts (see notes)
Speed:	12 knots
Range:	150 n.miles (278 km) at 12 knots
Manning:	5 (enlisted)
Guns:	none (see notes)

These are standard landing craft intended to carry vehicles and cargo. Capacity is one M60-series Abrams tank or 58 tons of cargo. No accommodations are provided in these or other LCM-type craft. More than 100 are in service, some on board Maritime Prepositioning Ships (MPS)—58 Mk 4 units delivered 1967–1979, 1985–1988, and 1991–1992.

Guns: A pair of .50-cal machine guns can be fitted.

Engineering: Most have four GM 6-71 diesels; a few have two of the larger GM 12V71 diesels. The last 20 units (delivered 1991–1992) have GM 8V92N engines.

1. AMc(U) = minesweeper, coastal (underwater locator). See chapter 22.

MECHANIZED LANDING CRAFT: LCM(8) MOD 2 TYPE

Weight:	36.5 tons light
	106.75 tons full load
Length:	74¹/₁₂ feet (22.6 m) overall
Beam:	21¹/₁₂ feet (6.4 m)
Draft:	4½ feet (1.4 m)
Propulsion:	4 diesel engines (General Motors); 1,300 bhp; 2 shafts
Speed:	12 knots
Range:	150 n.miles (278 km) at 12 knots
Manning:	5 (enlisted)
Guns:	none

The Mod 2 is an aluminum version of the steel-hulled LCM(8) developed for use with the CHARLESTON (LKA 113)-class amphibious cargo ships. About 20 are in service; 6 were transferred to Bangladesh in the early 1990s.

Another 12 aluminum units are under construction for the U.S. Navy at Swiftships.

Design: These craft are constructed of welded aluminum. They can carry one M60-series Abrams tank or 65 tons of cargo.

Engineering: Some units have been refitted with Kort nozzles.

MECHANIZED LANDING CRAFT: LCM(8) MOD 1 TYPE

Only a few of these craft remain in service, employed as work boats; see 13th Edition/page 211 for characteristics.

An LCM(8) assigned to the Naval Amphibious Base in Coronado (San Diego), Calif. Bow ramps vary in these craft. The mast protruding from the conning position holds a navigation light. (1985, Giorgio Arra)

An LCM(8) from Assault Craft Unit 2 off Norfolk, Va. There is a glass-enclosed cover installed over the conning position. LCMs and smaller landing craft are identified by their parent unit, base, or ship. (1985, Giorgio Arra)

An aluminum LCM(8) being loaded aboard the MOBILE (LKA 115). With the layup of the ships of this class, the existing aluminum LCM(8)s are being discarded; others, however, are being built for the Navy. (1988, L. Van Ginderen collection)

MECHANIZED LANDING CRAFT: LCM(6) TYPE

Weight:	26.7 tons light
	62.35 tons full load
Length:	56 feet (17.1 m) overall
Beam:	14⅓ feet (4.4 m)
Draft:	3⅚ feet (1.2 m)
Propulsion:	2 diesel engines (Gray Marine 64HN9 or General Motors 8V71); 625 bhp; 2 shafts
Speed:	12 knots
Range:	130 n.miles (240 km) at 9 knots
Manning:	5 (enlisted)
Guns:	none

About 100 of these craft are in service. Numerous LCMs of this type were converted to riverine combat craft during the Vietnam War. Older LCMs are employed as work boats.

Design: Welded steel construction. They can carry 34 tons of cargo or, for short distances, 120 troops.

Engineering: Above horsepower and speed for GM engines; those with Gray Marine have 450 bhp and can make 10 knots.

LANDING CRAFT VEHICLE AND PERSONNEL (LCVP): MK 7

Weight:	13.5 tons full load
Length:	35¾ feet (10.9 m) overall
Beam:	10½ feet (3.2 m)
Draft:	3½ feet (1.1 m)
Propulsion:	1 diesel engine (Gray Marine 64HN9); 225 bhp; 1 shaft
Speed:	10 knots
Range:	110 n.miles (204 km) at 8 knots
Manning:	2 or 3 (enlisted)
Guns:	none

These small landing craft can be carried by all U.S. amphibious ships. About 135 are in service.

Design: These craft are built of wood or fiberglass-reinforced plastic. They have a bow ramp and can carry light vehicles or four tons of cargo or 40 troops.

A "short-hull" LCM(6), showing the wear and tear on these craft; LCMs are usually heavily dented from being smashed against the docking-well walls in amphibious ships. (1983, Giorgio Arra)

An LCM(6) modified to serve as a tender at the Naval Surface Warfare Center in Florida. There is a liferaft canister installed alongside the elevated pilothouse. (1990, Giorgio Arra)

LCVP from the BLUE RIDGE (LCC 19). (Giorgio Arra)

LCVP from the MOUNT WHITNEY (LCC 20). (Giorgio Arra)

LANDING CRAFT PERSONNEL LIGHT (LCPL): MK 11/12 TYPES

Weight:	10 tons full load
Length:	36 feet (11.0 m) overall
Beam:	13 feet (4.0 m)
Draft:	3½ feet (1.1 m)
Propulsion:	1 diesel engine (General Motors 8V71); 350 bhp; 1 shaft (see notes)
Speed:	17 knots
Range:	150 n.miles (278 km) at 15 knots
Manning:	3 (enlisted)
Guns:	none (see notes)

These small landing craft are used for passenger transport, for the control of other landing craft, and to transport light cargo. More than 200 are built or under construction, with several being constructed by Bollinger.

Design: These craft are built of fiberglass-reinforced plastic. They carry 17 passengers.

Engineering: The newest LCPLs have Cummins lightweight engines fitted.

Guns: During the Vietnam War several LCPLs were armed with one or more .50- and .30-cal machine guns and employed for inshore patrol (some with a navigation radar fitted).

3 AUXILIARY SWIMMER DELIVERY VESSELS: MODIFIED LCUs

Number	Built	Assignment
ASDV 1 (ex-LCU 1610)	1960	Naval Amphibious Base, Coronado, (San Diego), Calif.
ASDV 2 (ex-LCU 1623)	1960	Naval Special Warfare Group 2
ASDV 3 (ex-LCU 1628)	1967	SBU-12

These are former utility landing craft modified to support training operations for combat swimmers/SEALs. See page 000 for basic characteristics of these craft.

They are fitted with a decompression chamber and associated air compressors, storage flasks, and an electrical generator. Manning varies from 10 to 14 enlisteds, depending upon whether or not the mission requires use of the decompression chamber. A crane is fitted for handling swimmer delivery vehicles, small boats, and underwater equipment. Sleeping quarters are provided for embarked personnel.

Operational: ADSV 2 operates in the Caribbean.

AMPHIBIOUS WARPING TUGS AND SIDE LOADING WARPING TUGS

The amphibious warping tugs (LWT) and side loading warping tugs (SLWT) are listed at the end of chapter 25 in this edition of *Ships and Aircraft.*

LANDING VEHICLES

Assault amphibian vehicles (AAV) are used by the Marine Corps for assault landings and for subsequent movement ashore. The Marine Corps currently operates 1,323 assault amphibian vehicles of the AAV7 series. Most of these are troop carriers (AAVP7) with 106 configured as command vehicles (AAVC7) and 64 as recovery/repair vehicles (AAVR7).[2]

The AAV7 series was previously designated landing vehicle tracked, personnel LVTP-7. The term AAV was adopted in the 1970s as a "sexy" designation for the next generation of assault amphibian vehicle. In 1985 the designation LVTP and the terms amphibious tractors or "amtrac" were discarded for the AAV terminology.

Increasingly, the Marines have employed these vehicles on land as well as for ship-to-shore movement. However, some authorities—both Marine and non-Marine—believe that the AAV/LVT is not an effective armored personnel carrier because of (1) its high noise level, (2) height of the vehicle, (3) treads that are vulnerable to heavy land use, (4) slow speed over certain terrain, and (5) light armor. Also, there is now no effective method of protecting the troops in the AAV7 vehicles from chemical/biological weapons attack.

An Advanced Assault Amphibian Vehicle (AAAV) is under development, although the procurement of this vehicle is not yet assured. Indeed, the reduction in defense budgets coupled with the need to develop a new medium-lift aircraft to replace the H-46 Sea Knight helicopter series, and the availability of the LCAC for ship-to-shore movement makes the procurement of the AAAV questionable.

The Marine Corps has three battalions that operate amphibian tractors. These battalions are:

- 1st Armored Assault Battalion on Okinawa supporting the 3rd Marine Division (2 amphibian companies)

2. Two AAV7s were heavily damaged during the Gulf War in 1991; they may be rehabilitated.

ASDV 1 off San Diego. (1983, Giorgio Arra)

ASDV 3 off San Diego. (1983, Giorgio Arra)

- 2nd Assault Amphibian Battalion at Camp Lejeune, N.C., supporting the 2nd Marine Division (4 amphibian companies)
- 3rd Assault Amphibian Battalion at Camp Pendleton, Calif. (3 amphibian companies)
- Company D, 3rd Assault Amphibian Battalion, at Twentynine Palms, Calif.
- Detachment A, 3rd Assault Amphibian Battalion (2 platoons), at Kaneohe Bay, Hawaii

Note that the battalion on Okinawa is an *armored* unit, with two tank companies in addition to the amphibian companies. The standard amphibian battalion has a total of 1,166 personnel and 208 amphibian vehicles—187 AAVP7s, 15 AAVC7s, and 6 AAVR7s (Fig. 20-21).

The 2nd and 3rd Battalions are each capable of simultaneously lifting the assault elements of a Marine Expeditionary Brigade (i.e., regiment), while the 1st Battalion can provide lift for a Marine Expeditionary Unit (i.e., battalion).

There are another 327 AAVs forward deployed on board the 13 maritime pre-positioning ships. Additional AAVs are pre-positioned with Marine material in Norway, and the remaining vehicles are assigned to the Marine Corps Reserve or are in the pipeline for maintenance, training, etc.

The service life of the present AAV7 "family" of vehicles was expected to end in the mid-1980s. However, the failure to gain approval for a follow-on amphibian vehicle led the Marines to embark on an extensive Service Life Extension Program (SLEP) for existing vehicles (with modified vehicles receiving the designation suffix A1).

There have been two previously proposed successors to the AAV7/LVTP-7, the landing assault vehicle (LVA), initiated in 1973 and cancelled in 1979, followed by the advanced tracked landing vehicle, designated LVT(X). The abortive LVT(X), which was cancelled in 1985, is described in the 13th Edition/page 212.

Modernization: The AAV7 SLEP upgrade program includes the following changes:

- Replacing the existing gun turret mounting a single .50-cal M85 machine gun with an electric-drive turret mounting a 40-mm Mk 19 grenade launcher as well as the older but more-reliable .50-cal M2 machine gun.
- An advanced mine-clearing system, firing explosive "snakes" for detonating ground mines; the system—including a possible later version with fuel-air explosive—can be installed on top of a tractor.
- Limited Chemical-Biological-Radiological (CBR) alarm and protection system.
- Appliqué steel armor that can be bolted onto the vehicle by the crew. This P-900 armor will defeat 14.7-mm gunfire. The armor weighs 3,500 pounds (1,591 kg), which the vehicle can easily handle—in fact, the weight actually improves water stability of the craft. A lighter, improved armor is in development.

- A bow plane is being fitted that extends when the craft is in the water to reduce the tendency to push down into seas.
- An automatic fire sensor and suppression system is being installed to reduce the possibility of fuel fires in the troop compartment.
- An improved transmission and suspension.
- A magnetic heading device.

These improvements add weight to the vehicle, which is not a concern because of the craft's great payload. More critical is space, with the changes reducing the troop capacity to perhaps 21 riflemen; if crew-served weapons, such as mortars, are carried, the troop capacity is less.

An advanced propulsion system is being considered, which will provide enhanced mobility. An engine of about 750 hp with all-electric drive is being considered for the so-called block III upgrade to the AAV7.

Marines scramble from an AAVP7A1 during a landing exercise. These are highly mobile vehicles although they suffer from several limitations. (FMC Corp.)

ADVANCED AMPHIBIAN ASSAULT VEHICLE

Weight:	62,000 to 72,000 pounds (28,182 to 32,727 kg) full load
Length:	
Beam:	
Draft:	
Propulsion:	probably diesel engine + gas turbine; 2,500 to 3,000 hp
Speed:	
	20 knots water
Range:	
Manning:	3
Troops:	17 or 18
Guns:	25-mm or 30-mm rapid-fire cannon

The development of a more advanced amphibian assault vehicle (AAV) "remains our primary developmental research effort," according to the Commandant of the Marine Corps.[3] This development program—referred to as AAAV for advanced amphibious assault—

3. Gen. A.M. Gray, USMC, testimony before the House Armed Services Committee, 21 February 1991.

seeks to provide a high-speed tracked vehicle to move assault troops from amphibious ships beyond the horizon to inland objectives.

The Marine AAAV envisions a so-called "high-speed" sea craft with the land mission capabilities of the U.S. Army's Bradley Armored Fighting Vehicle (AFV). The new craft is intended to be able to move at speeds in excess of 20 knots through three-foot (0.9-m) seas.

The Marine Corps plans to procure about 900 AAAVs to replace the 1,300 AAV7s. Two groups, the FMC Corporation's Ground Systems Division (which built all AAV7s) and General Dynamics' Land Systems Division teamed with AAI Corp., are competing in the development of the new vehicle. Following tests with demonstration vehicles, one firm will be chosen to produce 15 prototype vehicles: 13 troop carriers and 2 command and control vehicles. Initial production would then begin about 2002–2003 with an IOC of 2004–2005.

Design: The FMC design will have a hydrofoil-assisted planing hull, a concept that demonstrated 33-knot speeds in a half-scale demonstrator model. The GD design has a planing hull.

Propulsion: The advanced AAV program has a goal of producing an assault vehicle that can travel 20 knots through water. In 1991 an AAI-developed, 17-ton propulsion-system demonstration vehicle fitted with a combined gas-turbine/diesel power plant generating 2,215 horsepower reached a water speed of 27 knots.[4]

4. The propulsion demonstration vehicle is fitted with a Cummins VTA 903T diesel engine and a General Electric LM 120/T700/CT7 gas-turbine engine (for high-speed water operation). The program is run by the Navy's David Taylor Research Center.

The Propulsion System Demonstrator (PSD) developed as part of the Advanced Amphibian Assault Vehicle (AAAV) program. This craft attained a water speed of 27 knots on trials. (1991, David Taylor Research Center)

1,153 PERSONNEL VEHICLES: AAVP7A1 SERIES (formerly LVTP-7)

Weight:	38,450 pounds (17,477 kg) empty
	50,350 pounds (22,886 kg) loaded
Length:	26 feet (7.9 m) overall
Width:	10¾ feet (3.3 m)
Height:	10¼ feet (3.1 m)
Draft:	5⅔ feet (1.7 m)
Propulsion:	turbo-supercharged diesel engine (Cummins VT400);
	400 hp; tracked running gear on land
	2 waterjets in water (3,025 lbst each)
Speed:	40 mph maximum, 20–30 mph cruise on land
	8.4 mph maximum, 8 mph cruise in water
Range:	300 miles at 25 mph on land
	approx. 55 miles at 8 mph in water
Crew:	3
Troops:	21
Guns:	1 .50-cal machine gun M2
	1 40-mm grenade launcher Mk 19

The AAVP7 is a full-tracked, amphibian vehicle, providing an over-the-beach capability for landing troops and equipment through heavy surf. It is the world's only vehicle capable of operating in rough seas and plunging surf (up to ten feet high). Several hundred are being modernized and are designated AAV7A1 (see below).

These vehicles were designed and manufactured by the Ordnance Division of FMC Corporation, San Jose, Calif. They are also used by the marine forces of Argentina, Brazil, Italy, South Korea, Spain, and Thailand.

Armament: The LVTP-7 was designed to mount a 20-mm cannon coaxially with a machine gun; because of development problems, however, the cannon was deleted. The current .50-cal machine gun is co-mounted with a 40-mm grenade launcher in a 360° powered turret; the turret holds 200 .50-cal rounds and 98 40-mm rounds.

A mine-clearance kit can be fitted for clearing beach obstacles. This consists of a rack launcher firing three 350-foot-long explosive line charges. Detonation is controlled by wire from within the vehicle.

Class: The prototypes for the LVTP-7 design were 15 LVTPX-12 vehicles delivered to the Marines in 1967–1968. These were followed by a production run of 965 LVTP-7s delivered from 1970 to 1974 plus the specialized LVTC and LVTR vehicles described below. In addition, one LVTE-7 prototype of an assault engineer/mine clearance vehicle was delivered in 1970, but none were series produced. Additional vehicles have been produced for use by the maritime pre-positioning forces.

Design: The LVTP-7 was designed to replace the LVTP-5 series amtracs and offered increased land and water speeds and more range with less vehicle weight. In lieu of troops, the newer vehicle can carry 10,000 pounds (4,545 kg) of cargo. The LVTP-7 has a rear door and ramp for loading/unloading troops and cargo; it can turn 360° within its own length on land or in water.

Modernization: The SLEP upgraded vehicles were designated LVTP-7A1 prior to the change to AAV7A1. The first updated vehicles were delivered to the Marine Corps on 24 October 1983.

An "amtrac" carrying Marines in the assault on occupied Kuwait during the Gulf conflict. The troops have hung their gear from the vehicle. "Pressure Point" is the vehicle's name. (1991, CWO2 Ed Bailey, USN)

The turret of an AAVP7A1 showing the .50-cal machine gun and 40-mm grenade launcher. Previous generations of "amtracs" included vehicles armed with heavier guns and howitzers up to 105 mm. (1991, CWO2 Ed Bailey, USN)

An AAVP7A1 "buttoned up" and fitted with appliqué steel armor. The vehicle has been fitted with racks to carry troop gear. The Israeli firm of Rafael won a 1988 competition to provide the Enhanced Appliqué Armor Kit (EAAK) to the Marine Corps. (Rafael)

An AAVP7A1 employed as an armored personnel carrier; the roof plates are open, and Marines with M16 rifles are at the ready in the troop compartment. (FMC Corp.)

An AAVP7A1 fitted with a mine-clearance kit; the three-rocket launcher for deploying explosive line charges is in the raised position at the rear of the vehicle. (U.S. Marine Corps)

106 COMMAND VEHICLES: AAVC7A1 SERIES (formerly LVTC-7)

Weight:	40,187 pounds (18,267 kg) empty
	44,111 pounds (20,050 kg) loaded
Crew:	12 (3 vehicle crew, 5 radiomen, 4 unit commander) and staff
Troops:	none
Guns:	1 7.62-mm machine gun M60D

Except as indicated above, the AAVC7 command vehicle characteristics are similar to those of the basic AAV7 series. Eighty-five of these vehicles were originally procured for use as command vehicles in amphibious landings. Additional vehicles were procured in the 1980s.

These vehicles are fitted with radios, crypto equipment, and telephones. Seventy-seven of the original vehicles are being modernized to the 7A1 configuration.

64 RECOVERY/REPAIR VEHICLES: AAVR7A1 SERIES (formerly LVTR-7)

Weight:	47,304 pounds (21,502 kg) empty
	49,583 pounds (22,660 kg) loaded
Crew:	5 (3 vehicle crew, 2 mechanics)
Troops:	none
Guns:	1 7.62-mm machine gun M60D

Except as indicated above, the characteristics of the recovery/repair vehicle are similar to the AAV7 series. Sixty of these vehicles were originally procured for the recovery of damaged amtracs during amphibious landings. Additional units were procured during the 1980s.

They are fitted with a 6,000-pound (2,727-kg)-capacity telescoping boom-type crane and a 30,000-pound (13,636-kg) pull winch, plus maintenance equipment.

POST–WORLD WAR II AMPHIBIOUS TRACTORS

The U.S. Marine Corps procured 18,620 "amtracs" of various LVT/LVTA models during World War II. The first postwar LVT design produced for the Marine Corps was the LVTP-5 troop carrier and the derivative LVTH-6, the latter mounting a 105-mm howitzer, LVTE-1 engineer vehicle, LVTC-1 command vehicle, and LVTR-1 recovery vehicle. A total of 1,332 of these vehicles were manufactured between 1951 and 1957.

This series was followed by the LVT-7 (now AAV7) series.

An AAVR7A1 vehicle with the crane raised. There is a towing winch at the rear of the vehicle, above the ramp. (FMC Corp.)

An AAVR7A1 showing the equipment compartment open. Inside are a power generator, air compressor, welder power supply, and battery charger. (U.S. Marine Corps)

CHAPTER 21

Patrol and Special Warfare Craft

Navy SEALs drive a 33-foot (10-m) Setton boat on patrol in the Persian Gulf during Desert Storm. A variety of small craft are operated by the Navy's special warfare forces with several types under development. The new PC-series will fill a serious void in requirements for a larger craft for patrol and special warfare operations. (1991, U.S. Navy)

The U.S. Navy is now building a class of small combatants intended for coastal interdiction and to support special warfare operations. This program for 13 ships follows a long period of difficulty in procuring such craft.

The Navy also operates six hydrofoil missile craft (PHM) plus a large number of inshore and special warfare craft, with many of the latter operated by the Naval Reserve Force. The PHMs operate in the Caribbean area, primarily in anti-drug operations; the other craft primarily support Navy SEAL activities.[1]

Many of these craft are approaching the end of their useful service life and, by foreign standards, are inferior to contemporary designs. There were several small combat craft/special warfare craft designs developed in the early 1980s with the designations PBM, PCM, SWCM (Sea Viking), and PXM, the last being a hydrofoil patrol craft.[2] None were procured; several other advanced special warfare craft are now planned (see below).

The U.S. Navy has historically shown little interest in small combatants in peacetime, in part because of the emphasis on long-range, blue-water operations that support the Navy's primary missions, and because of the belief that the tactics and craft needed for coastal and inshore operations can be rapidly developed in wartime.

All of the ASHEVILLE-class patrol gunboats and the fast patrol boats—the PTF-series—produced in the 1960s have been discarded, although a few are employed as research craft (see chapters 25 and 34). The Navy had evaluated several advanced technology combat craft in that decade, with several being used in the Vietnam War. These too have been mostly discarded (see appendix A). During the Vietnam War the lack of a capability in small combatant craft forced the Navy to procure Norwegian-built fast patrol boats and to adopt commercial designs for naval use. Subsequently, the Navy has sought to keep abreast of small craft design, and during the early 1980s U.S. yards delivered a series of Navy-designed missile craft (PCG/PGG types) to Saudi Arabia as well as smaller, inshore and riverine combat craft to several other navies.

The proposed transportable fast attack craft (TFAC) effort to develop a small combat craft that could be easily transported by amphibious ships or maritime pre-positioning ships has been abandoned.

The ASDV-type support craft employed for combat swimmer/SEAL training are listed in chapter 20.

Armament: No anti-submarine weapons are carried by U.S. patrol craft.

Classification: The smaller, unnamed patrol boats and craft are individually designated by their hull length, hull type, calendar year of construction, and consecutive hull of that type built during the year. Thus, 65PB776 indicates the sixth 65-foot PB-type craft built in 1977. The first two letters in this scheme generally reflect the craft's designation except RP is used for PBRs.

Operational: Most of the Navy's smaller combat craft are assigned to Special Boat Units (SBU) under Special Boat Squadron 1 at the Naval Amphibious Base Coronado (San Diego), Calif., and Special Boat Squadron 2 at Naval Amphibious Base Little Creek (Norfolk), Va.

Squadron 1 has one SBU-12 active and Naval Reserve Force (NRF) SBU-11 and SBU-13, plus a Western Pacific detachment; Squadron 2 has active SBU-20 and reserve SBU-22 and SBU-24.

The active SBUs regularly deploy detachments overseas. (The special boat squadrons are components of naval special warfare groups; see chapter 6.)

1. SEALs—for Sea-Air-Land—are the Navy's special operations forces, akin to the U.S. Army's Green Berets.
2. See 13th Edition/page 221 and 14th Edition/pages 227–228 for characteristics.

ADVANCED SPECIAL WARFARE CRAFT

The Navy's Surface Warfare Plan through 1989 had proposed a series of advanced special warfare craft in addition to the PC series, described below. However, with the drastic budget reductions of the early 1990s the procurement of these craft is doubtful. These craft were:

SWCX: The Navy planned to procure 20 special warfare craft designated SWCX, to be delivered from 1994 to 1998. These craft, smaller than the PBC/PC design, were intended specifically to "insert" SEAL teams into hostile territory. Thus, they were to have had an enhanced "stealth" capability.

RIB: The rigid inflatable boat, a 30-foot (9.1-m) craft, and an undefined high-speed interceptor craft were intended to replace the Seafox special warfare craft–light. The RIB was to be a lightweight, highly seaworthy craft that could be easily launched from an amphibious ship or a surface combatant.

SWCR: The special warfare craft–riverine was intended as a shallow-draft boat to replace the existing 32-foot (9.75-m) PBRs.

MATCX: This was to be a replacement for the mini-armored troop carrier (mini-ATC).

1 + 12 COASTAL PATROL SHIPS: NEW CONSTRUCTION

Number	Name	FY	Commission	Status
PC 1	CYCLONE	90	1992	**AA**
PC 2	TEMPEST	90	1993	Building
PC 3	HURRICANE	90	1993	Building
PC 4	MONSOON	90	1993	Building
PC 5	TYPHOON	90	1993	Building
PC 6	SCIROCCO	90	1993	Building
PC 7	SQUALL	90	1993	Building
PC 8	ZEPHYR	90	1993	Building
PC 9–13	. . . . . .	91	1994	Building

Builders:	Bollinger Machine Shop & Shipyard, Lockport, La.
Displacement:	315 tons full load
Length:	170½ feet (52.0 m) overall
Beam:	25 feet (7.6 m)
Draft:	7⅝ feet (2.4 m)
Propulsion:	4 diesel engines (Paxman Ventura); 13,400 bhp; 4 shafts
Speed:	35 knots
Range:	2,000 n.miles (3,700 km) at 12 knots
Manning:	28 (4 officers + 24 enlisted)
Troops:	9 (SEALs or other passengers)
Missiles:	Stinger SAM
Guns:	2 25-mm Bushmaster cannon Mk 38 (2 single)
	2 .50-cal machine guns (2 single)
	2 7.62-mm machine guns M60 (2 single)
	2 40-mm grenade launchers Mk 19 (2 single)
Radars:	Sperry RASCAR surface search
Sonars:	Wesmar side-scanning
EW systems:	(passive)

This is a series of small combatants intended for coastal interdiction and special warfare (SEAL) operations. They are specifically intended as replacements for the Navy's overage PB Mk III craft.

These ships are successors to a series of small combatant designs that were proposed in the late 1980s; the previous PCC and special warfare craft–coastal (SWCC) requirements were merged into the PBC/PC design. The PC 1 will be significantly larger than these designs.[3]

The lead ship was laid down on 22 June 1991; launched on 1 February 1992; and christened on 15 February 1992.

Armament: These ships are intended to eventually be fitted with the Stabilized Weapon Platform System (SWPS), to be installed on the fantail. The SWPS will launch a variety of missiles, including the Hellfire, Stinger, and Hydra-70, with a co-mounted 25-mm or 30-mm cannon, a television camera, laser rangefinder and designator, and Forward-Looking Infrared (FLIR) sensor.

3. See 13th Edition/page 221 and 14th Edition/pages 227–228 for characteristics.

An artist's concept of the new CYCLONE-class coastal patrol ship. These craft are intended to fulfill several roles; a number of previous attempts to develop small craft for these roles have been aborted, reflecting the U.S. Navy's continued failure in this area. (Bollinger)

Class: The Navy planned to construct 16 of these ships (PBC) when the program was defined in the late 1980s; by the time the lead ship was ordered, the program had been reduced to 13 units.

Bollinger was awarded a contract for the construction of eight ships with an option for five additional units in August 1990; the five-ship option was exercised in July 1991.

Classification: These ships were originally to be designated PBC for coastal patrol boats. In June 1991 they were reclassified as PC—coastal patrol ships.

The classification PC originated in World War I as the *hull numbers* for a series of 110-foot (33.5-m) wood-hull submarine chasers given *names* in an SC series. Beginning in 1940 a series of steel-hull submarine chasers were built with PC designations, and in October 1942 all wood-hull submarine chasers were given SC hull numbers.

The World War II steel-hull program reached hull number PC 1603 (completed through 1944); most were 173-foot (52.7-m) ocean-going craft, although the PC/PCE/PCS/SC types shared the same numbering series.

U.S. and foreign-built ships stretched the PC/SC series to No. 1646, all being transferred to other navies. The PC 1647 and 1648 were cancelled; thus, the new-construction U.S. PCs should begin with No. 1651.

Design: The PC hull/propulsion design is based on the Vosper Thornycroft–built RAMADAN-class missile craft for the Egyptian Navy (six units completed 1981–1982).

The hulls of the U.S. ships are built of steel with aluminum superstructures. The ship construction process is modular. Endurance will be ten days.

Operational: Upon completion these ships will be assigned to special boat units.

The CYCLONE, fitting out after being launched at the Bollinger yard on 1 February 1992; she was formally christened two weeks later. The TEMPEST was launched on 4 April 1992, with subsequent ships scheduled to come off the "production line" at two-month intervals. The last launching will occur in early 1994. (U.S. Navy)

6 PATROL COMBATANTS–MISSILE (HYDROFOIL): "PEGASUS" CLASS

Number	Name	FY	Builder	Laid down	Launched	Commissioned	Status
PHM 1	Pegasus	73	Boeing Marine, Seattle, Wash.	10 May 1973	9 Nov 1974	9 July 1977	AA
PHM 2	Hercules	76	Boeing Marine, Seattle, Wash.	12 Sep 1980	13 Apr 1982	15 Jan 1983	AA
PHM 3	Taurus	75	Boeing Marine, Seattle, Wash.	30 Jan 1979	8 May 1981	10 Oct 1981	AA
PHM 4	Aquila	75	Boeing Marine, Seattle, Wash.	10 July 1979	16 Sep 1981	26 June 1982	AA
PHM 5	Aries	75	Boeing Marine, Seattle, Wash.	7 Jan 1980	5 Nov 1981	18 Sep 1982	AA
PHM 6	Gemini	75	Boeing Marine, Seattle, Wash.	13 May 1980	17 Feb 1982	13 Nov 1982	AA

Displacement:	198 tons light 241 tons full load, except PHM 1 235 tons
Length:	118$\frac{1}{12}$ feet (36.0 m) waterline 147$\frac{1}{6}$ feet (44.9 m) overall, foils retracted 131$\frac{1}{2}$ feet (40.1 m) overall, foils extended
Beam:	28$\frac{1}{6}$ feet (8.6 m)
Extreme width:	47$\frac{7}{12}$ feet (14.5 m) over after foils
Draft:	6$\frac{1}{6}$ feet (1.9 m) foils retracted 23$\frac{1}{6}$ feet (7.1 m) foils extended
Propulsion:	2 diesel engines (MTU 8V331 TC81); 1,630 bhp; 2 waterjets hullborne 1 gas turbine (General Electric LM 2500); 19,416 shp except PHM 1 16,000 shp; 1 waterjet foilborne
Speed:	10 knots hullborne 40+ knots foilborne
Range:	1,225 n.miles (2,270 km) at 11 knots hullborne 600+ n.miles (1,111 km) at 40+ knots foilborne
Manning:	approx. 25 (5 officers + 20 enlisted)
Missiles:	8 Harpoon SSM (2 quad canisters Mk 141)
Guns:	1 76-mm 62-cal AA Mk 75
Radars:	(see Fire control) SPS-64(V)1 navigation, except APS-137 in PHM 2
Sonars:	none
Fire control:	1 Mk 92 weapon FCS except Mk 94 in PHM 1
EW systems:	TAC-105, except ALR-66 in PHM 6

These are high-speed, heavily armed missile craft, originally intended to conduct sea-control operations in restricted seas. However, from their completion they have been employed in anti-drug operations in the Caribbean area.

At one time the Hercules was to have been completed without armament because of fiscal problems; subsequently, the Congress funded a full weapons suite for the craft.

The Hercules was originally authorized in fiscal 1973 and laid down on 30 May 1974; however, all work on her halted in August 1975 to fund cost increases of the Pegasus. The ship was reauthorized in fiscal 1976 and begun a second time in 1980. She was originally placed in commission on 15 January 1983 upon completion in Seattle; she was formally commissioned a second time in ceremonies upon her arrival at Key West on 12 March 1983.

Class: This design was one of the new warship types initiated by Admiral Zumwalt when Chief of Naval Operations (1970–1974). A class of at least 30 missile craft of this type were planned. When Zumwalt left office, the Navy reduced the program to only the prototype; however, congressional pressure led the first "flight" of six ships, already funded, to be completed.

Design: SCB No. 602. In November 1972 the governments of West Germany, Italy, and the United States signed a memorandum of understanding in which the three nations agreed to share the development costs of the PHM, with procurement planned for all three navies. After the reduction of the planned U.S. Navy procurement to one (later six) craft the other nations withdrew from the program. The foreign units were to be similar, with the addition of light guns on the bridge structure.

The PHM design provides for fully submerged canard foils, with approximately 32 percent of the dynamic lift provided by the single bow foil and 68 percent by the double-strut after foil. The foils retract forward (into a bow recess) and rearward, respectively. Steep flaps are fitted to the training edges of the bow and after foils to provide control and lift augmentation. The ships are very stable platforms at high speeds.

The superstructure and hull are all aluminum; the struts and foils are stainless steel; and the foil-borne weight-bearing trunnions are made of titanium.

Electronics: The PHM 1 has the earlier Mk 94 Mod 1, American version of the Hollandse Signaal Apparaaten WM-28 weapons control system; the other ships have the later Mk 92 Mod 1 version.

The previously mounted SPS-63, an Americanized version of the Italian SMA 3TM 20-H navigation radar, was fitted on a small stand between the bridge and the Mk 92 radome or "eggshell." The SPS-64 is mounted on a small platform on the mast.

Engineering: Combination Diesel Or Gas (CODOG) turbine propulsion. Foilborne propulsion consists of a single waterjet driven through reduction gears from the gas turbine engine. The foil-mounted propulsor is capable of pumping 141,000 gallons (535,800 liters) per minute. Foilborne speeds exceeding 40 knots are possible in 8- to 13-foot (2.4- to 4-m) seas. When hullborne, the PHM is propelled by twin waterjets powered by two diesel engines. Each of these waterjets can pump 30,000 gallons (114,000 liters) per minute. A maximum speed of 55 knots has been achieved by these ships.

A through-bow thruster is provided for low-speed maneuvering.

Guns: No secondary gun battery is provided. The PHM design provided for two 20-mm Mk 20 single gun mounts to be fitted abaft the mast; it was never installed.

Manning: These craft are normally commanded by commanders or lieutenant commanders. This is a relatively senior rank for the CO of a small combat craft. The other officers are the executive, combat systems, engineer, and operations officers.

The original manning was 4 officers and 17 enlisted.

Missiles: The original PHM design provided for two single Harpoon tubes fitted aft; the design was revised to provide two quad canisters on the fantail.

Names: The PHM 1 was originally named Delphinus; she was renamed Pegasus on 26 April 1974.

Operational: The six Pegasus-class PHMs are assigned to Patrol Combat Missile Hydrofoil Squadron 2 based at Key West, Fla. The last of the six craft arrived at Key West in mid-1983.

Earlier plans to deploy the PHMs to the Mediterranean, supported by a specially configured LST, have been discarded; their support ship was to have been the Wood County (LST 1178).

The Pegasus on her hull, showing the exhaust stack aft of the superstructure and the amidships hinges for the after foil. The bridge has all-around visibility. (1991, Giorgio Arra)

The HERCULES and TAURUS cruise in the Gulf of Mexico. These highly effective craft were never employed in Cold War operations, but found their niche in anti-drug patrols. Note the bow thruster immediately aft of the forward strut; the SPS-64(V)1 was not fitted in the HERCULES when this photo was taken. (1989, U.S. Navy, PH2 Mark Kettenhofen)

The AQUILA leads a trio of PHMs nested at their home port of Key West, Fla. All have a bar-type SPS-64 antenna mounted on the mast, above the Mk 92 radome. Their eight Harpoon missile canisters are for "show" in the anti-drug war. (1989, U.S. Navy, PH2 Mark Kettenhofen)

The HERCULES at high speed shows the clean, compact design of the PHM. These and the PERRY (FFG 7)-class frigates are the only U.S. Navy ships armed with the 76-mm/62-cal OTO Melara gun. (1989, U.S. Navy, PH2 Mark Kettenhofen)

SUBMARINE CHASER (HYDROFOIL): "HIGH POINT"

The hydrofoil submarine chaser HIGH POINT (PCH 1) was the U.S. Navy's first operational hydrofoil. She was built to evaluate structural and hydrodynamic features of hydrofoils, as well as to develop ASW concepts for hydrofoils. She was placed in service in 1963. After extensive Navy evaluation, she was transferred to the Coast Guard in 1975 for evaluation by that service (designated WMEH 1); she was subsequently returned to the Navy for continued test and evaluation work.

The HIGH POINT was taken out of service in October 1978. She was at Boeing's hydrofoil facility for several years and was sold on 29 March 1990 to a private firm.

PATROL GUNBOATS: "ASHEVILLE" CLASS

The Navy commissioned 17 ASHEVILLE-class patrol gunboats from 1966 to 1970. Fourteen have been stricken, loaned to other U.S. government or state agencies, transferred to other nations, or are laid up; the three other ships, the CHEHALIS, GRAND RAPIDS, and DOUGLAS, have been stripped of armament and are employed by the David Taylor Research Center (see chapter 25).

These ships were originally classified as motor gunboats (PGM) and were changed to patrol combatants (PG) on 1 April 1967; they retained their PGM hull numbers, which repeated World War II–era gunboat (PG) numbers. (The post–World War II built PGM 33–83, 91, and 102–124 were gunboats built in the United States or overseas from 1955 onwards specifically for transfer to foreign navies; none served in the U.S. Navy.)

The last two U.S. Navy units in service as combat craft, the TACOMA and WELCH, were used in the late 1970s to train Saudi Arabian naval personnel at Norfolk, Va.

See the 12th Edition/page 165 for details and characteristics.

TABLE 21-1. "ASHEVILLE"-CLASS PATROL GUNBOATS

Number	Name	Notes
PG 84	ASHEVILLE	str. 31 Jan 1977; to Massachusetts Maritime Academy 15 Dec 1976
PG 85	GALLUP	str. 15 Dec 1976*
PG 86	ANTELOPE	to Environmental Protection Agency Jan 1978
PG 87	READY	str. 6 Jan 1977; to Massachusetts Maritime Academy Mar 1978
PG 88	CROCKETT	to Environmental Protection Agency Apr 1977
PG 89	MARATHON	str. 31 Jan 1977; to Massachusetts Maritime Academy Apr 1977
PG 90	CANON	str. 15 Dec 1976*
PG 92	TACOMA	to Colombia May 1983
PG 93	WELCH	to Colombia May 1983
PG 94	CHEHALIS	reclassified as research ship; now ATHENA I
PG 95	DEFIANCE	to Turkey June 1973
PG 96	BENICIA	to South Korea Oct 1971
PG 97	SURPRISE	to Turkey Feb 1973
PG 98	GRAND RAPIDS	reclassified as research ship; now ATHENA II
PG 99	BEACON	stricken 1 Apr 1977†
PG 100	DOUGLAS	str. 1 Oct 1977; reclassified as research ship; now LAUREN
PG 101	GREEN BAY	str. 1 Apr 1977†

*Both units were restored to the Naval Vessel Register on 17 July 1981 and placed in reserve at Bremerton, Wash. They were temporarily returned to the NVR (date not recorded in official records) pending foreign military sale; they were "permanently" stricken on 9 October 1984.

†Both retained in storage at Little Creek, Va., for possible foreign sale.

MISCELLANEOUS PATROL/SPECIAL WARFARE CRAFT

The Navy also operates several other types of small patrol and special warfare craft. During Operation Desert Storm the SEAL units deployed to the Persian Gulf used, among other craft, high-speed patrol boats of the 33-foot (10-m) type produced by the now defunct Setton Boatyard of Miami, Fla.

Navy and Marine Corps units also have a variety of combat rubber raiding craft (CRRC), Boston Whaler rigid raiding craft (RRC), and rigid inflatable boats (RIB). All are propelled by outboard motors.

3 PATROL BOATS: PB MK IV TYPE (SEA SPECTER)

Number	Launched	Completed	Assignment
68PB851	23 Sep 1985	1 Feb 1986	SBU-26
68PB852	11 Nov 1985	1 Feb 1986	SBU-26
68PB853	31 Dec 1985	15 Feb 1986	SBU-26

Builders:	Atlantic Marine, Ft. George Island, Fla.
Displacement:	42.25 tons full load
Length:	68 5/12 feet (20.85 m) overall
Beam:	18 1/12 feet (5.5 m)
Draft:	3½ feet (1.1 m)
Propulsion:	3 diesel engines (General Motors 12V71 TI); 1,950 bhp; 3 shafts
Speed:	30 knots
Range:	
Manning:	5 (1 officer + 4 enlisted) minimum
Guns:	1 25-mm Bushmaster cannon Mk 88
	1 20-mm cannon
	1 81-mm mortar Mk 2/1 .50-cal machine gun M2
	2 40-mm grenade launchers Mk 19 (2 single)
Radars:	navigation

These are slightly enlarged variants of the PB Mk III series. They are referred to by the design name Sea Specter. They were intended specifically for patrol operations in the Panama Canal area. Aluminum construction.

Authorized in fiscal 1985, with the original intention of being used in the Panama Canal Zone area.

Guns: Originally armed with two 20-mm cannon; one gun replaced by the rapid-fire Bushmaster cannon in 1987.

The 68PB851 with a lengthened deckhouse; 20-mm cannon are mounted fore and aft in this view, plus machine guns. PB armaments can be easily changed. (1986, U.S. Navy)

The 68PB851 at high speed; there is a life raft canister fitted amidships. (1986, U.S. Navy)

15 PATROL BOATS: PB MK III TYPE (SEA SPECTER)

Number	Built	Assignment
65PB731	1974	SBU-20
65PB734	1975	SBU-20
65PB735	1975	SBU-24
65PB736	1976	SBU-12
65PB737	1976	SBU-12
65PB751	1976	SBU-12
65PB753	1976	SBU-13
65PB755	1976	SBU-13
65PB757	1976	SBU-13
65PB758	1977	SBU-24
65PB759	1977	SBU-20
65PB775	1979	SBU-12
65PB776	1979	SBU-12
65PB777	1979	SBU-20
65PB778	1979	SBU-24

Builders:	Peterson Builders, Sturgeon Bay, Wisc.
Displacement:	28 tons light
	36.7 tons full load
Length:	64¹¹⁄₁₂ feet (19.8 m) overall
Beam:	18¹⁄₁₂ feet (5.5 m)
Draft:	5⅝ feet (1.8 m)
Propulsion:	3 diesel engines (General Motors 8V71); 1,950 bhp; 3 shafts
Speed:	26 knots
Range:	2,000 n.miles at slow speeds
	450 n.miles at 26 knots
Manning:	5 (1 officer + 4 enlisted) minimum
Missiles:	(see notes)
Guns:	1 20-mm Bushmaster cannon Mk 88
	1 or 2 7.62-mm machine gun (1 or 2 single)
	(see notes)
Radars:	navigation

The PB Mk III was developed as a multi-mission inshore warfare craft for U.S. and foreign naval service. The U.S. craft are operated by the active Small Boat Units (SBU). These craft are named Sea Specter, but are generally referred to simply as PB Mk IIIs.

These craft are scheduled to be discarded by the end of 1993.

Class: Twenty-two of these craft were built for the U.S. Navy and four for the Philippines. PB Mk IIIs were procured from Peterson Builders as well as Marinette Marine Corp., Wisc.

Classification: These craft are also designated as special warfare craft—medium (SWCM). The Naval Sea Systems Command designates these craft as PB Mk 3; however, they are listed as Mk III in most Navy documentation.

Design: The Mk III is a modified commercial craft used to support offshore drilling platforms in the Gulf of Mexico. These craft are of all-aluminum construction with their pilothouse offset to starboard to provide maximum deck space for weapons and equipment. The craft has a low radar cross section and quiet engines for clandestine operations. Mission duration is up to five days.

Engineering: Note that these craft have three engines; the centerline engine is specially silenced for slow, quiet operations.

Guns: These craft were originally fitted with an automatic 40-mm Bofors cannon or a manually operated 20-mm cannon forward and up to four .50-cal machine guns on pintle mountings. There are hard points on the deck for fitting other guns as well as missiles. They can also be rigged to carry mines, torpedoes, or minesweeping gear.

Missiles: The PB III was used to evaluate the Norwegian-developed Penguin SSM with four stowage/launcher containers being fitted

A PB Mk III with several shields for machine guns fitted. Two search radar antennas are installed. (1991, Giorgio Arra)

A PB Mk III with canvas-covered 40-mm gun forward; note the circular magazine atop the gun. The lifting pads are visible on the starboard side. (1986, Giorgio Arra)

A PB Mk III configured as test craft for the Norwegian-developed Penguin anti-ship missile. There were two penguin canisters aft, a massive radome atop the deck structure, and a 40-mm grenade launcher and machine guns forward. (1982, Giorgio Arra)

1 PATROL BOAT: PB MK I TYPE

Number	Built	Assignment
65PB722	1973	Kings Bay, Ga.

Builders:	Sewart Seacraft, Berwick, La.
Displacement:	26.9 tons light
	36.3 tons full load
Length:	65 feet (19.8 m) overall
Beam:	16 feet (4.9 m)
Draft:	4⅚ feet (1.5 m)
Propulsion:	2 diesel engines (General Motors 12V71 T1); 1,200 bhp; 2 shafts
Speed:	20 knots
Range:	
Manning:	8 (2 officers + 6 enlisted)
Missiles:	none
Guns:	small arms
Radars:	navigation

The 65PB722 is assigned for security duties at the submarine base at Kings Bay, Ga. There is a machine gun mount aft of the bridge, but no guns are fitted. (1989, Giorgio Arra)

The PB Mk I series were prototype patrol boats developed as replacements for the "Swift" PCFs. The Mk Is were completed in 1972 and delivered to the Navy in 1973 for evaluation. They were subsequently transferred to the NRF and were operated by SBU-24 at Little Creek until 1990. No. 722 was assigned for security duties at the submarine base at Kings Bay, Ga., in January 1991; No. 721 is employed as a pilot boat. Both have been disarmed.

Armament: Originally fitted with 1 81-mm mortar Mk 2/1 .50-cal machine gun M2 in addition to other light guns.

Class: The Navy's 65-foot (19.8-m) small combatants originated with the Sewart/Swiftships firm of Morgan City, La. A variety of military and commercial craft were produced to this general design. Production for the U.S. Navy began in the 1960s, for use in the Vietnam War. Most of the PB Mk I-type craft—possibly as many as 200—were produced for other countries with only two, 65PB721 and 65PB722, being built for the U.S. Navy (authorized in fiscal 1972).

No PB Mk II was built.

Design: These craft are based on a commercial offshore support craft. They differ from the Mk III in size and in having a centerline superstructure.

Guns: Configured for a twin .50-cal machine gun mount atop the pilothouse and a .50-cal machine gun/81-mm mortar mount aft, plus pintle-mounted .30-cal machine guns.

2 PATROL CRAFT—FAST: PCF MK II TYPE

Displacement:	17.5 tons light
	22.2 tons full load
Length:	51⁵⁄₁₂ feet (15.7 m) overall
Beam:	14¹¹⁄₁₂ feet (4.6 m)
Draft:	3½ feet (1.1 m)
Propulsion:	2 diesel engines (General Motors); 960 bhp; 2 shafts
Speed:	28 knots
Range:	350 n.miles (648 km) at 28 knots
Manning:	
Guns:	removed
Radars:	navigation

All of the so-called Swift boats (PCF) have been discarded from first-line Navy service. These two craft are operated by SBU-12 for support of the gunnery range at San Clemente Island (Calif.). The last of a handful of PCF Mk I and Mk II craft operated by the Naval Reserve Force were discarded in early 1987.

Armament: As patrol craft their standard armament was an 81-mm mortar co-mounted with a .50-cal M2 machine gun aft with a twin .50-cal machine gun mount atop the deckhouse.

Class: These PCFs are the survivors of 139 units built from 1965 onward. Most were used by the U.S. Navy in Vietnam, with 104 being transferred to South Vietnam in 1968–1970. Others were built specifically for South Korea, the Philippines, and Thailand.

Variations used by the U.S. Navy were a torpedo weapons recovery craft (TWR) and utility/rescue craft.

Design: The configuration of these all-metal craft was adopted from an oil-rig crew boat used to support offshore drilling rigs in the Gulf of Mexico.

A PCF Mk II zips along. The portholes in the deckhouse differ from the windows of the earlier but similar, 50-foot (15-m) PCF Mk I, which was widely used in the Vietnam War. This craft is fully armed. (U.S. Navy)

29 RIVERINE PATROL BOATS: PBR MK 2 TYPE

Number	Built	Assignment
31RP664	1965	SBU-11
31RP66137	1966	SBU-11
31RP673	1967	SBU-22
31RP674	1967	SBU-11
31RP6881	1968	SBU-11
31RP6883	1968	SBU-22
31RP6884	1968	SBU-22
31RP6887	1968	SBU-26
31RP6889	1968	SBU-11
31RP6893	1968	SBU-26
31RP6894	1968	SBU-26
31RP6923	1969	SBU-11
31RP6924	1969	SBU-11
31RP7021	1970	SBU-26
31RP7118	1972	SBU-22
31RP7210	1972	SBU-11
31RP721	1972	SBU-22
31RP722	1972	SBU-11
31RP723	1972	SBU-11
31RP724	1972	SBU-11
31RP7329	1979	SBU-22
31RP7330	1982	SBU-22
31RP7331	1974	SBU-22
31RP7332	1974	SBU-11
31RP7333	1974	SBU-11
31RP7334	1974	SBU-22
31RP7335	1974	SBU-22
31RP7336	1974	SBU-11
31RP7337	1974	SBU-22

Builders:	Uniflite, Bellingham, Wash.
Displacement:	7.5 tons light
	8.9 tons full load
Length:	32 feet (9.75 m) overall
Beam:	11⅔ feet (3.6 m)
Draft:	2⁷⁄₁₂ feet (0.8 m)
Propulsion:	2 diesel engines (General Motors 6V53 or 6V53T or 4-53N); 430 bhp; 2 waterjets
Speed:	24 knots
Range:	
Manning:	4 or 5 (enlisted)
Missiles:	none
Guns:	1 60-mm mortar Mk 4 in some units
	1 40-mm grenade launcher Mk 19
	3 .50-cal machine guns (1 twin, 1 single)
Radars:	navigation

A PBR Mk 2 under way in San Francisco Bay. The Coast Guard aids-to-navigation boat 55101 is in the background. Several of the PBRs were used in the Persian Gulf from the late 1980s. (1988, Giorgio Arra)

A PBR Mk 2. These craft were also widely used in the Vietnam War. (1988, Giorgio Arra)

These heavily armed craft were developed for riverine warfare in Vietnam. All U.S. survivors are operated by the NRF.

Class: More than 500 PBRs were built in 1965–1973, with most transferred to South Vietnam after being used by the U.S. Navy.

Additional units were built for the U.S. Navy in the early 1980s (with GM 4-53N diesel engines). Subsequently, replacement hulls have been procured commercially for refit/replacement of existing boats in a one-for-one "swap" procedure. The newer boats are being provided with GM 6V53T engines.

Design: These craft have fiberglass hulls and ceramic armor.

Engineering: The waterjet propulsion enables the boats to operate in shallow and debris-filled water with a very high degree of maneuverability.

30 SPECIAL WARFARE CRAFT—LIGHT: SEAFOX TYPE

Number	Built	Assignment
36SW801	1981	SBU-20
36SW803	1982	SBU-24
36SW804	1982	SBU-12
36SW805	1982	SBU-24
36SW807	1982	SBU-24
36SW808	1982	SBU-13
36SW811	1983	SBU-24
36SW8110	1983	SBU-12
36SW8111	1983	SBU-24
36SW8112	1983	SBU-12
36SW812	1982	SBU-13
36SW813	1982	SBU-24
36SW814	1982	SBU-12
36SW815	1982	SBU-20
36SW817	1982	SBU-24
36SW818	1983	SBU-13
36SW819	1983	SBU-20
36SW821	1983	SBU-20
36SW829	1983	SBU-20
36SW8210	1983	SBU-12
36SW8211	1983	SBU-24
36SW8212	1983	SBU-13
36SW8214	1983	SBU-12
36SW8215	1983	SBU-24
36SW8216	1984	SBU-12
36SW822	1983	SBU-12
36SW823	1983	SBU-24
36SW824	1983	SBU-12
36SW826	1983	SBU-12
36SW828	1983	SBU-12

Builders:	Uniflite, Bellingham, Wash.
Displacement:	21,200 lbs light
	23,700 lbs hoisting weight
	13 tons full load
Length:	36 feet (10.8 m) overall
Beam:	9⅞ feet (3.0 m)
Draft:	2⅞ feet (0.85 m)
Propulsion:	2 diesel engines (General Motors 6V92 TA); 890 bhp; 2 shafts
Speed:	32 knots
Range:	
Manning:	3 (enlisted)
Troops:	12 (SEALs)
Guns:	2 .50-cal machine guns (2 single)
	2 7.62-mm machine guns M60 (2 single)
Radars:	LN-66 navigation

These are small, high-speed craft intended primarily to support SEAL operations. They replaced a variety of small craft previously used by SEALs. One prototype (built in 1976–1977) plus 36 operational units were built for the U.S. Navy; others were built for foreign service.

Design: These craft can carry SEALs under shelter and a rubber landing craft (atop deckhouse). They are constructed of glass-reinforced plastic, reportedly with kevlar armor.

Electronics: Fitted with several radios, IFF, and echo-sounder.

A Seafox under way with a couple of SEALs atop the after canopy. A rubber landing craft can be carried on the canopy. (1988, Giorgio Arra)

A rare sight: A Seafox at rest, with an officer and two enlisted men in "whites." This unit was at Hong Kong with a forward-deployed SEAL team. (1985, Giorgio Arra)

A covey of Seafoxes from Small Boat Unit 12 at San Diego. The unit at far left does not have a canopy rigged. Although intended for stealthy operations, these craft have a large radar cross section and high infrared signatures, while use of their radar also reveals their presence. (1991, U.S. Navy)

23 ARMORED TROOP CARRIERS: MINI-ATC TYPE

Number	Built	Assignment
36AT721	1972	SBU-22
36AT7213	1972	SBU-22
36AT7214	1973	SBU-22
36AT7215	1973	SBU-22
36AT7216	1973	SBU-22
36AT7217	1973	SBU-22
36AT722	1973	SBU-11
36AT723	1973	SBU-11
36AT724	1973	SBU-11
36AT725	1973	SBU-11
36AT726	1973	SBU-11
36AT727	1973	SBU-11
36AT728	1973	SBU-11
36AT729	1973	SBU-11
36AT7212	1973	SBU-11
36AT76008	1977	
36AT763	1977	SBU-22
36AT764	1977	SBU-11
36AT768	1977	SBU-22
36AT783	1979	SBU-11
36AT784	1979	SBU-22
36AT785	1979	SBU-22
36AT786	1979	SBU-22

Builders:	Marinette Marine, Wisc.
	Tacoma Boatbuilding, Wash.
Displacement:	11 tons light
	14.75 tons full load
Length:	36 feet (11.0 m) overall
Beam:	12¾ feet (3.9 m)
Draft:	3½ feet (1.0 m)
Propulsion:	2 diesel engines (General Motors 8V53N); 566 bhp; 2 waterjets
Speed:	28 knots
Range:	
Manning:	2 (enlisted)
Troops:	16
Guns:	2 .50-cal machine guns (2 single)
Radars:	LN-66 navigation

These craft were developed from lessons learned in the Vietnam War and are intended for clandestine operations during riverine campaigns. They have low radar signatures and quiet engines.

Design: The mini-ATCs have aluminum hulls and ceramic armor. At high speed they have a one-foot (0.3-m) draft. They can carry two tons of cargo.

Additional weapons can be mounted.

A mini-ATC in San Francisco Bay. (1988, Giorgio Arra)

A mini-ATC without a radar "pot." (1986, Giorgio Arra)

75 HARBOR SECURITY BOATS

Number	Built
24HS8701–24HS8750 24HS87801–24HS8825	1988–1989

Builder:	Peterson Builders, Sturgeon Bay, Wisc.
Displacement:	2.5 tons light
	3.8 tons full load
Length:	24 feet (7.3 m) overall
Beam:	7⁷⁄₁₂ feet (2.3 m)
Draft:	5⅛ feet (1.6 m)
Propulsion:	2 diesel engines (Volvo Penta AGAD 41A); 2 outboard drives
Speed:	22.5 knots
Range:	
Manning:	4 (enlisted)
Guns:	(see notes)
Radars:	none

These craft are employed for harbor patrol. Aluminum construction. No armament is provided, but light machine guns can be mounted.

A harbor security boat in the Persian Gulf, patrolling against Iraqi swimmers or floating mines. (1991, U.S. Navy)

A harbor security boat approaches the Middle East flagship LA SALLE (AGF 3) during operations in the Persian Gulf. (1991, U.S. Navy)

COASTAL PATROL AND INTERDICTION CRAFT

A single CPIC was built for the U.S. Navy as prototype for a craft to succeed the PT/PTF-type small combatants in U.S. service and for foreign sales. The prototype CPIC was launched in 1974 and, after exhaustive trials, was transferred to South Korea on 1 August 1975. (Additional craft of this type were built in South Korea.)

The CPIC was returned to U.S. custody in the Philippines in 1981 and brought back to San Diego in 1982. After being surveyed, the craft was rated unsuitable for further evaluation or service and was discarded.

See 13th Edition/page 226 for characteristics.

FAST PATROL BOATS

The classification fast patrol boat (PTF) was established in 1963 for a fast seagoing craft to conduct clandestine operations off the coast of Vietnam. The PTF 3–16 were Nasty-class boats built in Norway and taken over by the U.S. Navy upon completion in 1962–1965. The first four units had been assigned Norwegian names in preparation for service in that Navy. The subsequent PTF 17–22 were built by John Trumpy yacht builders (Annapolis, Md.) to the Nasty design, and the PTF 23–26, built by Sewart Seacraft, were of a different design.

Most saw combat service in Vietnam; all have been stricken, with some expended as targets.

See the 13th Edition and previous volumes for details and characteristics.[4]

4. A revealing article on PTF operations in the Vietnam War was written by Steve Edwards, "Stalking The Enemy's Coast," Naval Institute *Proceedings* (February 1992), pp. 56–64.

POST–WORLD WAR II MOTOR TORPEDO BOATS

U.S. motor torpedo boat construction in World War II reached hull number PT 809 with 774 units being completed through 1945 (another 34 were cancelled before completion). Many survivors served with allied fleets after the war.

Four competitive prototype PT-boats of advanced designs were completed in 1950–1951: the PT 809 by Electric Boat, PT 810 by Bath Iron Works, PT 811 by Trumpy, and PT 812 by the Philadelphia Naval Shipyard. They were reclassified (as PTs) from patrol vessels to service craft on 13 April 1951. All were stricken, but the PT 810 and 811 were reinstated in service (vice in commission) as the PTF 1 and PTF 2 on 21 December 1962 for Vietnam service. The PT 809 was reinstated in service for use by the Secret Service and subsequently by the Navy and served as the drone recovery craft RETRIEVER (DR-1); see chapter 25.

RIVERINE AND INSHORE COMBAT CRAFT

During the Vietnam War (1963–1972) the U.S. Navy operated several hundred riverine and inshore combat craft built for the purpose or converted from landing craft. These were used mainly for Operation Market Time (coastal surveillance), Game Warden (river patrol), and operations with U.S. Army troops in the Rung Sat Special Zone. About 650 river and coastal craft were turned over to South Vietnamese forces in 1970–1971 as the United States withdrew from the conflict.

In addition to the PCF and PBR types listed above, the principal Vietnam-era small craft were:

ASPB	assault support patrol boat
ATC	armored troop carrier
CCB	command and control boat (converted LCM)
MON	monitor (converted LCM)
PACV	patrol air-cushion vehicles (see appendix A)

All of the above craft were produced in large numbers except for the air-cushion craft. Several other craft were also developed and evaluated during the war.

1 GUIDED MISSILE CRAFT: EX-SOVIET TARANTUL I CLASS

Number	Name	Commissioned
185NS9201	(unnamed; see notes)	2 Apr 1985

Builders:	Volodarskiy Shipyard (No. 341), Rybinsk (USSR)
Displacement:	480 tons standard
	540 tons full load
Length:	172 1/6 ft (52.5 m) waterline
	185 1/3 ft (56.5 m) overall
Beam:	34 5/12 ft (10.5 m)
Draft:	8 1/4 ft (2.5 m)
Propulsion:	COGAG: 2 gas turbines (NK-12M); 24,000 shp + 2 gas turbines; 8,000 shp = 32,000 shp; 2 shafts
Speed:	46 knots
Range:	400 n.miles at 36 knots
Complement:	39
Missiles:	4 SS-N-2c Styx anti-ship (2 twin)
	4 SA-N-5 anti-air launcher (1 quad)
Guns:	1 76.2-mm/59-cal DP
	2 30-mm/65-cal close-in (2 multi-barrel)
ASW weapons:	none
Torpedoes:	none
Mines:	none
Radars:	1 Bass Tilt (fire control)
	1 Plank Shave (targeting)
	1 TSR-333 (navigation)
Sonars:	none
EW systems:	4 . . . . . . (passive)
	1 Square Head IFF
	1 High Pole-B IFF

This Soviet-built missile craft was transferred upon completion to East Germany, one of five such craft to enter that navy. Following the reunification of Germany in 1990, this was the only ship of the five to be placed in German service. She was transferred to the U.S. Navy in November 1991 for trials and evaluation; she was transported to the United States on a heavy-lift ship in early 1992. The craft was placed on the Navy list of small craft on 14 February 1992.

The improved Tarantul II continued in production for Russian naval service at least into 1991; the Tarantul I/II variants in Russian service carry the Styx missile (as above); the Tarantul III variant has four SS-N-22 anti-ship missiles in place of the Styx.[5]

Class: Two Tarantul I-class units are believed to be in Russian service with units having been built for East Germany, India, and Poland, with additional units being constructed in India.

Design: The Tarantul hull is similar to the Pauk-class ASW corvette, but with a different propulsion system. The craft has seven watertight hull compartments.

The Tarantul I and II/III designs differ primarily in electronics, and the Tarantul III has a more capable anti-ship missile.

Fitted with a Chemical-Biological-Radiological (CBR) protective system.

Names: In East German service the craft was named RUDOLF EGELHOFER; she was renamed HIDDENSEE by the unified German Navy (Hiddensee is an island in the Baltic Sea).

5. See N. Polmar, *Guide to the Soviet Navy*/5th Edition (Annapolis, Md.: Naval Institute Press), pp. 192-193.

A former East German Tarantul I-class missile corvette during U.S. Navy trials in Chesapeake Bay. She is one of five ships of this class built in the Soviet Union for East Germany; the four others are being sold—sans armament—by the unified German government. (1992, U.S. Navy)

CHAPTER 22

Mine Countermeasures Ships and Craft

The old and the new: The AVENGER and ADROIT about to be unloaded from the Dutch heavy lift ship SUPER SERVANT 3 off Bahrain in the Persian Gulf. The ships are similar in concept and design despite the 30-year interval in their construction. The U.S. Navy is now seeking an improved capability for providing support to forward-deployed mine craft. (1991, U.S. Navy, Comdr. John C. Roach)

The Navy's Mine Countermeasures (MCM) force is undergoing a long-delayed modernization, with new ships (MCM and MHC types) and helicopters (MH-53E) entering the fleet.

After extensive use of U.S. minesweepers in the Persian Gulf in the late 1980s, as the Navy escorted Kuwaiti tankers and other merchant ships during the Iran-Iraq conflict, and again in 1991 during the Desert Shield/Desert Storm operations, the Navy's minesweeper strength has declined rapidly. By late-1992 the surface MCM force consists of 10 outdated MSO-type ships (1 active and 9 Naval Reserve Force), 9 of the new AVENGER-class MCMs, and the first of the OSPREY-class coastal minehunters (MHC). Thus, there is a qualitative improvement of the surface MCM force although the numbers are declining.

By the year 2000 the surface MCM force is expected to consist of the 14 AVENGER-class ships and 11 smaller, coastal minehunters of the OSPREY class, a modification of the Italian LERICI design. These 25 ships will fall short of providing the Navy's minimum goal for mine countermeasure capabilities. That goal, as stated in 1991, was 45 new MCM/MHC ships plus helicopters. (Studies of wartime requirements indicate a need for between 60 and 300 minesweepers, much too large a force for American peacetime budgets—or interest.)

Prior to the Persian Gulf conflict of January–February 1991, the Navy had planned a follow-on class of coastal minehunters, tentatively designated MHC(V). These ships would have a self-deploying capability, i.e., be able to forward deploy. After the Gulf War the Navy decided not to build additional MHCs but to instead procure two mine countermeasure support ships (MCS) that could sustain existing MHCs and mine countermeasure helicopters in a forward area (see below).

However, the fiscal 1992–1997 shipbuilding plan submitted to Congress by the Department of Defense in late January 1992 still contained the MHC(V) program, with the lead ship planned for the fiscal 1995 budget. While it appeared unlikely that the Navy would support the MHC(V) effort, the final outcome of that program was not clear when this edition of *Ships and Aircraft* went to press. This was another indication of the continuing disarray in the Navy's mine countermeasure program.

In addition, the Navy operates three active and two reserve airborne MCM squadrons, flying the MH-53E Sea Dragon and RH-53D Sea Stallion, respectively. The helicopters can be self-deployed (i.e., fly to a forward area with in-flight refueling) or be flown overseas by C-5 transport aircraft and operated from various amphibious ships.

MCM forces have the primary mission of clearing U.S. waters and strategic choke points, and clearing a path for amphibious assaults in time of war. It should be noted, however, that the helicopters have a limited night-flying capability and cannot effectively counter bottom-laid mines.

The current MCM force buildup was initiated under the Reagan-Lehman naval regime. After an almost 30-year hiatus in the series production of minesweepers, two new ship classes were initiated in the early 1980s—the AVENGER-class MCM ships and the CARDINAL-class air-cushion minehunters (MSH). Both the MCM and MSH encountered major construction problems. As described below, the AVENGER class suffered major engine problems before completion of the first ship. The CARDINAL's design and material problems were so great that, in 1986, the entire program was cancelled before the completion of the first ship.

In place of the MSH, the Navy adopted a modification of the Italian LERICI-class coastal minehunter (MHC), now known as the OSPREY class. Interestingly, the U.S. Navy had earlier rejected an enlarged version of the LERICI proposed by the Marinette shipyard as being too large and too costly for this same role.

The problems in the belated MCM and MSH programs, the mining of the supertanker BRIDGETON in the first convoy escorted by U.S. forces in the Gulf in 1987, the mining of the U.S. frigate SAMUEL B. ROBERTS in the Persian Gulf in 1988 (see page 145), and the damage inflicted by mines on a U.S. helicopter carrier and an Aegis cruiser in the Gulf in 1991 have raised questions about the fundamental ability of the U.S. Navy to cope with modern mine warfare issues. According to the then-Deputy Chief of Naval Operations (Surface Warfare), speaking in 1983, "No segment of Naval Warfare has been under funded for so many years as has the Mine Warfare community.

TABLE 22-1. MINE WARFARE SHIPS AND CRAFT (late 1992)

Type	Ship/Class	Comm.	Active	Building*	NRF
MHC 51	OSPREY	1993–	—	10	—
MCM 1	AVENGER	1987–	8	5	—
MSO 508	ACME	1957–1958	—	—	1
MSO 421	AGILE/AGGRESSIVE	1954–1956	1	—	8
CT	COOP		19	—	—

*Ships authorized through fiscal 1992.

threat."[1]

Despite the large stockpiles of sophisticated modern mines possessed by the Soviets, we have only recently begun to respond to the

The Persian Gulf minings—like the U.S. experiences in the Korean War (1950–1953)—demonstrate that even Third World nations can effectively employ sea mines. This lack of understanding came to the fore in 1987 when a U.S. Navy captain, at a press briefing, observed that the Iranians "have some potential capability to moor mines . . . but nothing that we would think of as minelaying capability in military terms and no modern mines. . . . So we would say that their mine warfare capability is limited."[2] A month later an Iranian-laid mine damaged the supertanker BRIDGETON, embarrassing the United States and questioning U.S. ability to escort reflagged Kuwaiti tankers.

Even with the demise of the Soviet Union as a military threat for at least the next few years, sea mines remain a major threat to U.S. and other maritime operations. The Department of Defense report on the Persian Gulf conflict states:

> Operation Desert Shield and Desert Storm highlighted the dangers that sea mines pose to naval forces. Mines will continue to pose a difficult problem. Refocusing our national defense strategy away from the European theater and toward regional contingencies has exposed a gap in U.S. mine warfare capability that our European allies were previously expected to fill.[3]

Minesweeping: The MCM and MHC classes use hull-mounted Variable Depth Sonar (VDS) as their primary means of mine detection and cable-controlled SLQ-48 Mine Neutralization System (MNS) for examination and clearance of the mines.[4] These vehicles are described at the end of this chapter.

Names. The larger minesweepers have militant characteristic names and smaller units have bird names. The latter names date to World War I, having been the name source for all minesweepers until the 1950s, except that the larger, destroyer-minesweepers (DMS series) retained their destroyer names.

Operational. The entire U.S. Navy surface ship/craft mine countermeasures force was scheduled to be operated by the Naval Reserve Force. However, following the mine countermeasures effort in Operation Desert Storm, the decision was made to retain all AVENGER-class ships in the active fleet. The smaller OSPREY-class ships will be operated by the NRF with composite active-reserve crew.

The Navy sent four MSOs as well as MSBs to the Persian Gulf in 1988, and the AVENGER and three MSOs into the Gulf in 1990. Ships that participated in Operations Desert Shield/Desert Storm in 1990–1991 are indicated by an asterisk.

The Navy announced in March 1992 the approval of a plan under which virtually all surface mine countermeasure ships (MCM/MHC) would be based at Ingleside (Corpus Christi), Texas, which would also become headquarters for the Commander, Mine Warfare Command. The exceptions will be two MCMs based in Astoria, Ore., and two MCMs at Pearl Harbor, Hawaii. The MCM helicopters will eventually move to NAS Corpus Christi.

(While certain advantages will accrue to consolidating their home ports, the shift will demand long transit times to the important operating areas off the U.S. East and West coasts.)

1. Vice Adm. Robert L. Walters, USN, Deputy CNO (Surface Warfare), statement before the House Appropriations Committee, 20 April 1983.
2. Press conference, Pentagon, Washington, D.C., 18 June 1987.
3. Department of Defense, *Conduct of the Persian Gulf Conflict* (Washington, D.C.: July 1991), pp. 6–9.
4. The MNS was previously referred to as MNV for Mine Neutralization Vehicle.

(2) MINE COUNTERMEASURES SUPPORT SHIPS

The fiscal 1992 budget provides $10 million to begin the development of a mine countermeasures support or "mother" ship. The Navy supporters of this program have sought a ship that could (1) support and provide underway replenishment for mine countermeasures ships, (2) provide command and control facilities for MCM operations, and (3) carry and operate MH-53E helicopters. In mid-1992 the Navy decided to convert an IWO JIMA (LPH 2)-class helicopter carrier to this role (see chapter 19). A second LPH conversion will follow during the late 1990s. These ships will undergo modification to provide the support capabilities described above.

Earlier the Navy had considered the conversion of two AUSTIN (LPD 4)-class dock landing ships for this role. The LPD conversions would have provided a limited transport capability for MHC-type ships. However, their command and control and helicopter support facilities were too limited for the MCS role.

The Navy is also considering the acquisition of two large, Float-On/Float-Off (FLO/FLO) ships to serve as MHC/MCM transports; those ships would not provide support or replenishment capabilities for mine countermeasures forces. These ships would probably be assigned to the MSC Ready Reserve Force (RRF) and maintained with civilian cadre crews.

TABLE 22-2. MINE WARFARE COMMAND AND SUPPORT SHIPS

Number	Name	Comm.	MCM Comm.	Notes*
MCS 1	CATSKILL	1944	1967	ex-LSV 1, CM 6, AP 106
MCS 2	OZARK	1944	1967	ex-LSV 2, CM 7, AP 107
MCS 3	OSAGE	1944	—	ex-LSV 3, AN 3, AP 108
MCS 4	SAUGUS	1945	—	ex-LSV 4, AN 4, AP 109
MCS 5	MONITOR	1944	—	ex-LSV 5
MCS 6	ORLEANS PARISH	1945	1959	ex-LST 1069
MCS 7	EPPING FOREST	1943	1962	ex-LSD 4

*LSV = landing ship vehicle; CM = minelayer; AP = transport; LST = tank landing ship; LSD = dock landing ship.

The designation MCS was established in 1956 for mine countermeasure ship; subsequently changed to mine warfare command and support ship. The CATSKILL and OZARK were converted in 1963–1967; their near-sister ships LSV 3–5 were not converted and remained laid up in "mothballs" while carrying the MCS designation. The ORLEANS PARISH supported minesweepers for several years with an LST designation before being changed to MCS.

ADVANCED COASTAL MINEHUNTERS

In early 1991 the Navy put forth proposals to procure an enlarged coastal minehunter, the first unit being planned for the fiscal year 1995 shipbuilding program. These ships—tentatively designated MHC 51(V)—were to be larger than the modified LERICI class and would be capable of long-range deployments. However, by the fall of 1991 the proposal was dropped by the Navy in favor of having the planned mine countermeasures mother ship transport the existing LERICI-class MHCs. However, the six-year (FY 1992–1997) shipbuilding plan presented to Congress in late January 1992 by the Department of Defense provided for the construction of the lead ship of the new MHC class in the fiscal 1995 budget with two follow-on ships in fiscal 1997. Approximately eight ships are planned for construction.

This class, probably fabricated of glass-reinforced plastic, was to have had both the SQQ-32 minehunting sonar and the SLQ-48 mine neutralization system.

(11) COASTAL MINEHUNTERS: MODIFIED "LERICI" CLASS

Number	Name	FY	Builder	Start*	Launched	Commissioned	Status
MHC 51	OSPREY	86	Intermarine USA, Savannah, Ga.	16 May 1988	23 March 1991	1993	Building
MHC 52	HERON	89	Intermarine USA, Savannah, Ga.	7 Apr 1989	21 March 1992	1993	Building
MHC 53	PELICAN	89	Avondale Industries, New Orleans, La.	6 May 1991		1993	Building
MHC 54	ROBIN	90	Avondale Industries, New Orleans, La.			1994	Building
MHC 55	ORIOLE	91	Avondale Industries, New Orleans, La.	8 May 1991		1994	Building
MHC 56	KINGFISHER	91	Avondale Industries, New Orleans, La.			1994	Building
MHC 57	CORMORANT	92	Avondale Industries, New Orleans, La.			1995	Building
MHC 58	· · · · · ·	92	Avondale Industries, New Orleans, La.			1995	Authorized
MHC 59	· · · · · ·	92	Avondale Industries, New Orleans, La.				Authorized
MHC 60	· · · · · ·	93					Authorized
MHC 61	· · · · · ·	93					Planned

*These ships do not have a formal keel laying.

Displacement:	895 tons full load	Speed:	approx. 15 knots
Length:	174⅙ feet (53.1 m) waterline	Range:	1,500 n. miles (2,780 km) at 10 knots
	187¾ feet (57.2 m) overall	Manning:	51 (5 officers + 46 enlisted)
Beam:	35¹¹/₁₂ feet (10.95 m)	Guns:	1 or 2 .50-cal machine guns (1 or 2 single)
Draft:	36½ feet (11.0 m)	Radar:	SPS-64(V)9 navigation
Propulsion:	2 diesel engines (Isotta-Fraschini ID 36 SS 6V-AM) 1,160 bhp; 2 cycloidal propellers	Sonar:	SQQ-32 mine detection
	2 180-shp hydraulic motors for quiet operation		

The OSPREY after launching. She is designed for coastal operations against moored and bottom mines from continental U.S. bases. However, in the post–Cold War environment the MHCs will undoubtedly be used in overseas areas. (1991, Intermarine)

These ships are intended for harbor clearance, port breakout, and deep-water coastal mine countermeasures. This class is being developed in place of the cancelled CARDINAL-class of air-cushion minehunters.

These ships are much larger and more capable than the CARDINAL design (see below). Fiscal 1986 funds originally authorized for the aborted MSH program were used to procured the lead MSH at a cost of approximately $120 million.

Class: The Congress added one ship to the Bush administration's request for two MHCs each in the fiscal 1992 and 1993 programs, reflecting an increase in concern over the U.S. Navy's mine countermeasure capabilities. Still, only 11 MHCs will be procured under current planning although the initial program was planned at 17 units.

The Italian LERICI class continues in series production at the Intermarine shipyard at Sarzana. The Italian lead ship was laid down in 1978 and completed in 1985. (She displaces 520 tons full load with a length of 164 feet/50.0 m; diesel propulsion provides a maximum speed of 15 knots. The U.S. ship is slightly larger to accommodate U.S. sonars, MNS, and navigation gear; also, a different propulsion system is provided.)

Ships of the Italian LERICI class are also in service in the Indonesian and Nigerian navies.

Classification: The MHC designation originated in the 1950s as AMC(U)—mine vessel underwater locator. Those ships were intended to locate and plot mines for subsequent destruction by minesweepers. The BITTERN (MHC 43), completed in 1957, was built for the purpose on a 144-foot (43.9-m) MSC hull with a full load displacement of 350 tons; the planned series production of similar MHCs was cancelled. The AMC(U) 1–6 were converted LCT(6)s; the AMC(U) 7–11, 15–33, 35–42 were former LSI(L)s; the AMC(U) 12 and 13 were converted coastal surveying ships (AGSC); the MHC 34 and 44–50 were converted from YMS/AMS minesweepers; and the MHC 14 is a former AMC/PCS. Some of the LSI(L) conversions were not completed.

The designation AMC(U) was changed to coastal minehunter (MHC) in 1955.

Cost: The fiscal 1992 budget contains $349.6 million for the MHC 57–59 and the fiscal 1993 budget request asks $246.2 million for the two final units of this class, the MHC 60 and MHC 61.

Design: These ships are fabricated of Glass-Reinforced Plastic (GRP), a material long used in foreign mine countermeasure craft. The hull has a monocoque design, with no longitudinal or transverse framing.

One Mine Neutralization Vehicle (MNV) is carried (see page 217).

Engineering: Fitted with a 180-shp bow thruster.

Operational: Beginning in 1993, one MHC will be retained in the active fleet, and all others will be transferred to the NRF.

AIR-CUSHION MINE HUNTERS: "CARDINAL" CLASS

The planned minesweeper hunter (MSH) program was a failure and was halted by the Navy on 25 August 1986 and formally cancelled on 24 November 1986. That program had envisioned the construction of 17 air-cushion minehunters of some 470 tons displacement to be authorized from fiscal 1984 through 1989. (See 13th Edition/page 230.)

The lead ship, CARDINAL (MSH 1), was authorized in fiscal 1984, and a contract was awarded to Bell-Halter of New Orleans for construction of the ship. Subsequently the MSH 2–5 were authorized in fiscal 1986 and MSH 6–9 were requested in fiscal 1987. However, explosive shock testing of a 103-ton fiberglass MSH hull section caused the fiberglass to delaminate. There were other problems as well, several with the Isotta-Fraschini diesel engines (also being used in the MCM class). The then-Assistant Secretary of the Navy for Shipbuilding, Everett Pyatt, admitted: "The Navy wasn't very good. The naval architect was terrible. And the shipbuilders weren't very good."

The lead ship, which was laid down on 13 February 1986, was not completed.

9 + 5 MINE COUNTERMEASURES SHIPS: "AVENGER" CLASS

Number	Name	FY	Builders	Laid down	Launched	Commissioned	Status
MCM 1	AVENGER*	82	Peterson Builders, Sturgeon Bay, Wisc.	3 June 1983	15 June 1985	12 Sep 1987	**AA**
MCM 2	DEFENDER	83	Marinette Marine, Marinette, Wisc.	1 Dec 1983	4 Apr 1987	30 Sep 1989	**AA**
MCM 3	SENTRY	84	Peterson Builders, Sturgeon Bay, Wisc.	8 Oct 1983	20 Sep 1986	6 Oct 1990	**PA**
MCM 4	CHAMPION	84	Marinette Marine, Marinette, Wisc.	28 June 1984	15 Apr 1989	8 Feb 1991	**PA**
MCM 5	GUARDIAN	84	Peterson Builders, Sturgeon Bay, Wisc.	8 May 1985	20 June 1987	16 Dec 1989	**AA**
MCM 6	DEVASTATOR	85	Peterson Builders, Sturgeon Bay, Wisc.	9 Feb 1987	11 June 1988	6 Oct 1990	**AA**
MCM 7	PATRIOT	85	Marinette Marine, Marinette, Wisc.	31 Mar 1987	15 May 1990	18 Oct 1991	**AA**
MCM 8	SCOUT	85	Peterson Builders, Sturgeon Bay, Wisc.	8 June 1987	20 May 1989	15 Dec 1990	**AA**
MCM 9	PIONEER	85	Peterson Builders, Sturgeon Bay, Wisc.	5 June 1989	25 Aug 1990	late 1992	**AA**
MCM 10	WARRIOR	86	Peterson Builders, Sturgeon Bay, Wisc.	25 Sep 1989	8 Dec 1990	1993	Building
MCM 11	GLADIATOR	86	Peterson Builders, Sturgeon Bay, Wisc.	7 May 1990	29 June 1991	1993	Building
MCM 12	ARDENT	90	Peterson Builders, Sturgeon Bay, Wisc.	22 Oct 1990	16 Nov 1991	1993	Building
MCM 13	DEXTROUS	90	Peterson Builders, Sturgeon Bay, Wisc.	11 Mar 1991	20 June 1992	1994	Building
MCM 14	CHIEF	90	Peterson Builders, Sturgeon Bay, Wisc.	19 Aug 1991	1992	1994	Building

Displacement:	1,195 tons light	Speed:	13.5 knots
	1,312 tons full load	Range:	2,500 n. miles (4,630 km) at 10 knots
Length:	212¾ feet (64.85 m) waterline	Manning:	81 (6 officers + 75 enlisted)
	224¼ feet (68.4 m) overall	Guns:	2 .50-cal machine guns M2 (2 single)
Beam:	38¹¹⁄₁₂ feet (11.9 m)	Radars:	SPS-55 surface search
Draft:	11¼ feet (3.4 m)		SPS-66 surface search
Propulsion:	MCM 1, 2 4 diesel engines (Waukesha L-1616); 2,280 bhp;	Sonars:	SQQ-30 mine detection in MCM 2–5
	2 shafts		SQQ-32 mine detection in MCM 1, 6–14
	MCM 3–9 4 diesel engines (Isotta-Fraschini ID36 SS 6V-AM);		
	2,600 bhp; 2 shafts (see notes)		
	2 low-speed motors (Hansome); 400 shp (geared to propellers)		

These are relatively large mine countermeasures ships intended to locate and destroy mines that cannot be countered by conventional minesweeping techniques.

The AVENGER class has suffered a number of design and construction problems. The first two ships were fitted with American engines from existing stocks; they were installed improperly and subsequently tests revealed potential fire hazard from lubricating oil leakage through the turbocharger into the exhaust stack. (This engine design had been blamed for a series of fires in previous minesweepers.) The Italian engines planned for the later MCMs then failed in their endurance tests.

The MCMs are also overweight; one of two planned DC generators for sweep gear and mine hunting had to be deleted because of space/weight problems, and the ships have had electronic interference problems. During Operation Desert Storm in 1991 the AVENGER suffered generator problems as she hunted mines in the Gulf, while there was evidence that her acoustic signature was greater than expected.

The AVENGER was ordered on 29 June 1982 and laid down on 3 June 1983, the first large minesweeper under construction for the U.S. Navy since the ASSURANCE (MSO 521) was completed in 1958. The AVENGER was almost two years behind her original contract schedule and the DEFENDER more than 15 months behind contract schedule.

Class: The Navy originally planned a two-year "program gap" between the fiscal 1982 lead ship and four ships in fiscal 1984. Subsequently, the Navy sought to accelerate the program with four ships in fiscal 1983. The Congress, citing problems with the MCM design, instead funded only one ship in fiscal 1983 and directed the Navy to develop a second source shipyard (i.e., Marinette).

Cost: The three ships authorized in the fiscal 1990 program had an average cost of $112.4 million plus $933,333 for outfitting and $2.33 million post-delivery costs; additional funds in the latter category were provided in the fiscal 1991 budget for those ships, approximately $5.26 million each. Thus, the total cost per ship is on the order of $121 million.

Design: The current MCM design is similar to previous MSO classes. Their hulls are constructed of fiberglass-sheathed wood (laminated oak framing, Douglas fir planking and deck sheathing with reinforced fiberglass covering). One MNV is carried in addition to conventional sweep gear.

The MCM concept has undergone several changes in the past few years, originally being proposed in the late 1970s as an oceangoing ship to protect U.S. strategic missile submarines from Soviet deep-ocean mines. A Small Waterplane Area Twin Hull (SWATH) design was considered to provide improved seakeeping in northern waters. Under that concept the MCMs would have operated in pairs, towing a sweep gear between them. Nineteen of these ships were proposed, to have displaced 1,640 tons and with a length of 265 feet (80.8 m).

Electronics: Fitted with SSN-2 precise navigation system.

The first five ships were fitted with the SQQ-30 variable-depth minehunting sonar. This equipment, an upgraded SQQ-14, has severe limitations and is replaced in later ships by the SQQ-32. It was planned to backfit the SQQ-32 into the earlier ships; in 1990 the AVENGER was hurriedly refitted with the engineering development model of the SQQ-32 for operations in the Persian Gulf. Deployed to the Gulf (with several MSOs), the AVENGER detected the first Manta bottom mine to be discovered, but the ship then suffered mechanical and power-generation problems and was forced to withdraw from the mined area.

Engineering: All ships have four very-low-magnetic diesel engines for propulsion; electrical power for minesweeping gear is provided by gas turbines. The low-speed motors are geared to the propellers. A bow thruster of 350 hp is fitted for precise maneuvering. Maximum mine hunting speed is five knots.

Congress directed that the MCM 10–14 would have American-made diesel engines.

Operational: The AVENGER was deployed to the Persian Gulf for Operations Desert Shield/Desert Storm, transported to the area on board the heavy-lift ship SUPER SERVANT 3 along with three MSOs. The AVENGER returned to the United States in June 1991 under her own power. She was relieved in the Gulf by the GUARDIAN.

The Scout shows the distinctive appearance of the MCM design with a tripod mast and raked funnel. Forward of the bridge is the winch for the variable-depth minehunting sonar. The SPS-55 and SPS-66 radars have bar-type antennas. (1991, Giorgio Arra)

The stern of the Scout shows the floats or "pigs" for the SLQ-37(V) magnetic/acoustic influence and SLQ-38 mechanical minesweeping systems. The crowded fantail also has a pair of derricks for handling sweep gear, cable and reels, and other gear. (1991, Giorgio Arra)

The stern of the SCOUT. These are relatively large mine countermeasure ships—55 feet (16.8 m) longer than the European Tripartite-class MCMs; the U.S. ships have a greater range and payload. (1991, Giorgio Arra)

1 OCEAN MINESWEEPER: "ACME" CLASS

Number	Name	FY	Builder	Laid down	Launched	Commissioned	Status
MSO 511	AFFRAY	54	Frank L. Sample, Jr., Boothbay Harbor, Maine	24 Aug 1955	18 Dec 1956	8 Dec 1958	**NRF-A**

Displacement:	682 tons light	Range:	3,300 n.miles at 10 knots
	818 tons full load	Manning:	approx. 82 (8 officers + 37 enlisted active; 4 officers + 33 enlisted
Length:	173 feet (52.7 m) overall		reserve)
Beam:	36 feet (11.0 m)	Guns:	2 .50-cal machine guns (1 twin)
Draft:	14 feet (4.3 m)	Radars:	SPS-64(V)9 navigation
Propulsion:	4 diesel engines (Packard 1D-1700); 2,280 bhp; 2 shafts	Sonars:	SQQ-14 mine detection
Speed:	14 knots		

This ship is an improved version of the AGILE and AGGRESSIVE classes. She is fitted as a mine division flagship. The AFFRAY is operated by the Naval Reserve Force.

Class: Four ships were built to this design for the U.S. Navy (MSO 508–511) and seven for allied navies (MSO 512–518). The ADROIT was stricken on 12 December 1991.

Design: SCB No. 45A. See previous class notes.

The ADROIT on a hazy day in the Persian Gulf. The multinational Coalition mine countermeasures force found approximately 1,300 Iraqi-laid mines in the Gulf, two of which damaged U.S. warships. The ADROIT was stricken in December 1991; all MSOs will be discarded by 1995. (1991, U.S. Navy, JO1 Joe Gawlowicz)

9 OCEAN MINESWEEPERS: "AGILE" AND "AGGRESSIVE" CLASSES

Number	Name	FY	Builder	Laid down	Launched	Commissioned	Status
MSO 427	CONSTANT	51	Fulton Shipyard Co., Antioch, Calif.	16 Aug 1951	14 Feb 1953	8 Sep 1954	**NRF-P**
MSO 439	EXCEL	51	Higgins Inc., New Orleans, La.	9 Feb 1953	25 Sep 1953	24 Feb 1955	**NRF-P**
MSO 440	EXPLOIT	51	Higgins Inc., New Orleans, La.	28 Dec 1951	10 Apr 1953	31 Mar 1954	**NRF-A**
MSO 441	EXULTANT	51	Higgins Inc., New Orleans, La.	22 May 1952	6 June 1953	22 June 1954	**AA**
MSO 446	FORTIFY	51	Higgins Inc., New Orleans, La.	30 Nov 1951	14 Feb 1953	16 July 1954	**NRF-A**
MSO 455	IMPLICIT	52	Wilmington Boat Works Inc., Calif.	29 Oct 1951	1 Aug 1953	10 Mar 1954	**NRF-P**
MSO 488	CONQUEST	53	J.M. Martinac SB Corp., Tacoma, Wash.	26 Mar 1953	20 May 1954	20 July 1955	**NRF-P**
MSO 489	GALLANT	53	J.M. Martinac SB Corp., Tacoma, Wash.	21 May 1953	4 June 1954	14 Sep 1955	**NRF-P**
MSO 492	PLEDGE	53	J.M. Martinac SB Corp., Tacoma, Wash.	24 June 1954	20 July 1955	20 Apr 1956	**NRF-P**

Displacement:	716 tons light	Range:	3,300 n.miles (6,112 km) at 10 knots
	853 tons full load	Manning:	active ships approx. 81 (6 officers + 75 enlisted)
Length:	171¹¹⁄₁₂ feet (52.4 m) overall		NRF ships approx. 82 (5 officers + 52 enlisted active + approx. 25
Beam:	36 feet (11.0 m)		reserve)
Draft:	13¾ feet (4.2 m)	Guns:	2 .50-cal machine guns (twin)
Propulsion:	4 diesel engines (Packard except Waukesha L-1616 in MSO 441,	Radars:	SPS-64(V)9 navigation
	488); 2,400 bhp; 2 shafts	Sonars:	SQQ-14 mine detection
Speed:	15.5 knots		

These ocean minesweepers and the later ACME class are the survivors of the massive U.S. minesweeper construction programs started during the Korean War as a result of extensive North Korean use of Soviet-supplied mines. Large numbers of these ships were built for the U.S. Navy and several NATO navies.

They are fitted for sweeping contact, magnetic, and acoustic mines, but lack the capability of countering modern mines.

Of the surviving ships, two are in active Navy service and the remainder are NRF ships. The active ships serve as mine countermeasure test platforms and also perform operational minesweeper training and exercises.

The EXULTANT was changed from NRF to active status on 31 July 1989.

Class: Fifty-eight ships of this class were built for the U.S. Navy (MSO 421–449, 455–474, 488–496); another 28 ships were built for allied navies (MSO 450–454, 475–487, 498–507), with the MSO 497 being cancelled.

All three ships of the similar ABILITY class (MSO 519–521) built for the U.S. Navy have been discarded. The MSO 522 of this design

was also for foreign use. Sixteen additional MSOs of an improved version of this general design were funded in the fiscal 1966–1968 shipbuilding programs but were not built.

The following are ships that were decommissioned/stricken since the 14th Edition of *Ships and Aircraft:*

MSO 433	ENGAGE (NRF)	stricken 30 Dec 1991
MSO 437	ENHANCE (NRF)	stricken 31 Dec 1991
MSO 438	ESTEEM (NRF)	stricken 20 Sep 1991
MSO 442	FEARLESS (NRF)	stricken 28 Oct 1990
MSO 443	FIDELITY	stricken 16 June 1989
MSO 448	ILLUSIVE to NRF 31 July 1989;	stricken 1 June 1990
MSO 449	IMPERVIOUS* (NRF)	stricken 12 Dec 1991
MSO 456	INFLICT*	stricken 23 May 1990
MSO 464	PLUCK	stricken 16 Jan 1991
MSO 490	LEADER*	stricken 12 Dec 1991

The remaining ships will be stricken as the new MCM/MHC types become available, the last being scheduled for disposal in 1995.

Classification: All MSOs originally were classified as minesweepers (AM with same hull numbers); they were changed to MSO on 7 February 1955.

Design: SCB No. 45A. These ships are of lightweight wooden construction with laminated timbers; the fittings and machinery are of stainless steel (non-magnetic) and bronze. Magnetic items are reduced to a minimum.

Electronics: These ships originally had UQS-1 mine-detecting sonar; all surviving units have been refitted with the more-capable SQQ-14 sonar. The latter is a variable-depth sonar, lowered on a rigid rod from within the hull, forward of the deck structure.

The PLUCK was test ship in the mid-1970s for the SSN-2 precise navigation system fitted in the subsequent MCM and MHC classes.

Guns: As built these ships had one 40-mm gun and two .50-cal machine guns. Most were rearmed with provisions for mounting a 20-mm mount forward, originally a twin-barrel Mk 24 and subsequently a single-barrel Mk 68 cannon. The smaller 20-mm mount was required in modernized ships to permit installation of the larger, retractable SQQ-14 sonar in the forward hull. Most now have .50-cal machine guns.

Modernization: In fiscal 1968 a program was begun to modernize the existing MSOs (SCB No. 502). New engines, communications, and sonar were installed and improved sweep gear provided. However, increasing costs and shipyard delays caused the program to be halted after only 13 ships had been fully modernized—MSO 433, 437, 438, 441–443, 445, 446, 448, 449, 456, 488, and 490. Subsequently, some of these features, especially the improved sonar, were fitted to several additional ships.

Operational: The MSO 437, 439, and 442 were deployed to the Persian Gulf in 1987 (along with several MSBs). The MSO 449, 490, and 509 were deployed to the Persian Gulf in 1990 (Desert Shield/Desert Storm).

The IMPERVIOUS—now stricken—while clearing mines off the coast of Kuwait. Eight countries contributed mine countermeasure forces to the Gulf campaign; four U.S. minesweepers and six MH-53E helicopters swept or neutralized some 15 percent of the known Iraqi mines. (1991, U.S. Navy, JO1 Joe Gawlowicz)

The FORTIFY is one of the few surviving MSOs, ships that comprised the preponderance of U.S. mine countermeasures capability for some 35 years. In the Vietnam War they were also employed for offshore patrol and arms interdiction. (1991, Giorgio Arra)

MINESWEEPING BOATS

The Navy's long-serving minesweeping boats (MSB) have all been discarded from the MCM role. These craft, which saw extensive service in the Vietnam War and in the Persian Gulf in the late 1980s, were assigned to Mine Division 125 at Charleston, S.C. That formation was disestablished on 1 April 1992, and the last of the MSBs were stripped of their sweep gear and assigned to utility duties (see chapter 25). LCU 1641 was also assigned to Mine Division 125.

See 14th Edition/pages 241–242 for hull numbers and characteristics.

Operational: Four of these boats were carried by LPD to the Persian Gulf in 1987 to help counter mines while the U.S. Navy was escorting merchant ships during the Iran-Iraq war.

CRAFT OF OPPORTUNITY PROGRAM

The Navy developed the COOP plan in the 1980s to provide a harbor mine countermeasures capability for U.S. ports. Each of 22 planned COOP sweepers was to have four reserve (NRF) crews for a total of 88. In wartime up to 66 previously identified civilian, trawler-type craft would be taken over by the Navy, manned by the 66 additional crews, and employed in the harbor sweep role.

The COOP craft have towed side-looking sonar; they would locate enemy bottom mines and then direct larger minecraft or swimmers to place charges next to them.

The COOP effort was essentially cancelled by the Navy in 1990 (zero funded), but funds were again requested in 1991 (fiscal 1992 budget).

With the end of the Cold War and the apparent end of the danger of Russian submarines mining U.S. ports, the Navy has sought to discard the COOP program. However, the effort has generally been supported by the Congress; the House Armed Services Committee report on fiscal 1993 Navy programs (May 1992) states:

> The committee continues to believe that the COOP program provides a significant deterrent to, and capability in response to, terrorism in United States Harbors. The COOP program also provides a cost-effective and useful means of mine countermeasures training for both active and reserve forces.
>
> Accordingly, the committee directs the Secretary of the Navy to continue the COOP program in the Naval Reserve and to maintain 15 units geographically dispersed on the Atlantic, Pacific, and Gulf coasts.

While the Navy is now opposed to the COOP effort, it appears to have been successful. For example, a former Commander, Mine Warfare Command, stated in 1989 that in a recent test the Navy had laid 30 bottom mines and COOP craft had found 29 of them on the first pass, "just dragging [a trawler net]...." He concluded his description of the COOP effort with the evaluation "it works well."[5]

Classification: Note that CT (for COOP trainer) is not an "official" designation; a hyphen is used in the designation. Five CT numbers have been used twice while others were not used within the series.

Manning: Each COOP craft has a nine-man enlisted operating crew, with four reserve crews assigned. These crews (designated Blue, Gold, Red, and Green) were to alternate weekends operating the craft. In addition, each craft has two active enlisted personnel assigned plus an administrative staff of two officers and two enlisted.

Operational: Squadron/base assignments are listed below; the craft are based at various ports along the Atlantic, Gulf, and Pacific coasts.

Mine Group 11 headquarters at Seattle, Wash., and Mine Squadron 22 at Charleston, S.C., previously directed COOP operations. The 1992 Mine Warfare Command reorganization abolished these groups.

5. Rear Adm. Charles F. Horne III, U.S. Naval Institute symposium "Mine Warfare: Which Platform?" Charleston, S.C., 26 February 1987.

12 COOP MINESWEEPERS: CONVERTED YP TRAINING CRAFT

Number	Assignment*
CT-1 (ex-YP 675)	Mine Squadron 22
CT-2 (ex-YP 668)	Mine Squadron 22
CT-4 (ex-YP 669)	Mine Squadron 22
CT-5 (ex-YP 654)	Mine Squadron 22
CT-6 (ex-YP 664)	Mine Squadron 22
CT-8 (ex-YP 661)	Mine Squadron 22
CT-9 (ex-YP 660)	Mine Squadron 22
CT-10 (ex-YP 659)	Mine Squadron 22
CT-11 (ex-YP 666)	Mine Squadron 22
CT-12 (ex-YP 665)	not employed as COOP
CT-13 (ex-YP 663)	not employed as COOP
CT-15 (ex-YP 662)	Mine Squadron 22
CT-16 (ex-YP 670)	not employed as COOP
CT-17 (ex-YP 671)	not employed as COOP
CT-18 (ex-YP 672)	NAS Patuxent River, Md.
CT-19 (ex-YP 673)	not employed as COOP
CT-20 (ex-YP 674)	NAS Patuxent River, Md.

*Notes: NAS = Naval Air Station.

Builders:	YP 654–662 Stephen Brothers, Stockton, Calif.
	YP 664 Elizabeth City Shipbuilders, N.C.
	YP 666–675 Peterson Brothers, Sturgeon Bay, Wisc.
Displacement:	60 tons light
	71 tons full load
Length:	80⅓ feet (24.5 m) overall
Beam:	18⅓ feet (5.6 m)
Draft:	5⅓ feet (1.7 m)
Propulsion:	2 diesel engines (General Motors 6-71); 660 bhp; 2 shafts
Speed:	13.5 knots
Range:	
Manning:	9 to 11 (enlisted)
Guns:	none
Radars:	Raytheon 1220 navigation
Sonar:	C Mk 2 side-scan towed sonar

7 COOP MINESWEEPERS: CONVERTED FISHING CRAFT

Number	Built	Acquired	Length	Assignment
CT-2 (ex-Tiki)	1960	1983	65 ft	Mine Group 11
CT-12 (unnamed)	1976	1990	58 ft	Mine Squadron 22
CT-18 (ex-Widgeon)	1971	1987	53 ft	Mine Group 11
CT-19 (ex-Falcon)	1978	1987	56 ft	Mine Group 11
CT-20 (ex-Sisod)	1974	1987	60 ft	Mine Group 11
CT-21 (ex-Frigate Bird)	1989	1989	56 ft	Mine Group 11
CT-22 (ex-Albatross)	1989	1989	56 ft	Mine Group 11

These are converted trawlers; they tow a modified trawler net with a chain "footrope" and side-scan sonar for examining and mapping harbor bottoms. The towed sonar has about a 50-yard sweep width.

The CT-1 (ex-Ida Green) was returned to her owners in October 1986. The CT-3 was the minesweeping shrimp boat (MSSB 1).

UNMANNED CATAMARAN MINESWEEPERS

Name	Completed	Acquired
Gerry (ex-SAM 03)	1983	5 Feb 1991
Peggy (ex-SAM 05)	1983	5 Feb 1991

Builders:	Karlskronavarvet, Karlskrona (Sweden)
Displacement:	15 tons light
	20 tons full load
Length:	59 feet (18.0 m)
Beam:	20 feet (6.1 m)
Draft:	5¼ feet (1.6 m) over propellers
	2⅓ feet (0.7 m) hulls
Propulsion:	1 diesel engine (Volvo Penta TAMD 70D); 210 bhp; 1 rotating propeller
Speed:	8 knots
Range:	330 n.miles (611 km) at 7 knots
Manning:	unmanned

The CT-6 at high speed; she is a converted YP. The COOP effort has had mixed reviews; originally praised by the Navy, it is now being criticized despite its apparent success. Several other nations employ craft-of-opportunity in the mine countermeasure role. (1991, Giorgio Arra)

Seventeen former Naval Academy seamanship training craft (YP) were to be adopted for the COOP effort. In the event, only 12 were modified in 1989; the five others were subsequently assigned to the Naval Postgraduate School at Monterey, Calif., as training craft.

Class: This YP class originally consisted of YP 654–675 (originally SCB No. 139; changed to No. 800 in the new SCB series). They were completed between 1965 and 1979.

Electronics: A modified SQQ-14 sonar was considered for later installation in these craft.

MINESWEEPING SHRIMP BOAT

The prototype for the COOP effort was the so-called minesweeping shrimp boat Robin Gail II (designated MSSB 1 and later CT-3 by the Navy). It was acquired in 1980 under rental contract to evaluate the feasibility of configuring such small fishing craft for MCM activities. Placed in service in 1985, the 101-foot (30.8-m) craft had been seized by the U.S. Customs Service in February 1980 while carrying marijuana. An additional electric generator, minesweeping gear, a small sonar (WQS-1), and other special equipment were installed for the craft to be evaluated.

The craft was subsequently given the small boat designation 103WB831; she was discarded in 1986.

The Navy purchased two unmanned, remote-controlled catamaran minesweepers from the Swedish Navy just after the outbreak of the Gulf War in early 1991. They were employed in Gulf operations.

The craft—known as SAM from their Swedish acronym—perform several functions; according to their manufacturer, they perform "magnetic minesweeping by hull-integrated coils; acoustic minesweeping by a towed acoustic transmitter; clearing the way to get a higher security for minesweepers and minehunters; and marking out of 'free passages' with buoys on board."

Eight swept-channel marker buoys are carried.

Several of these craft are in Swedish service. The former Swedish designations are indicated above.

Design: The platform and superstructure are made of aluminum.

Engineering: Fitted with a Schottel-type propeller.

Names: The craft were named for relatives of the U.S. Navy project manager.

The U.S. Navy used two unmanned, Swedish-developed catamaran minesweepers in the Persian Gulf campaign. There is an ongoing U.S.–Swedish development program in this area. Here the PEGGY (foreground) and GERRY are maneuvered by U.S. sailors; the discs on their fantail are on marker buoys. (1991, U.S. Navy, Capt. Joseph Davis)

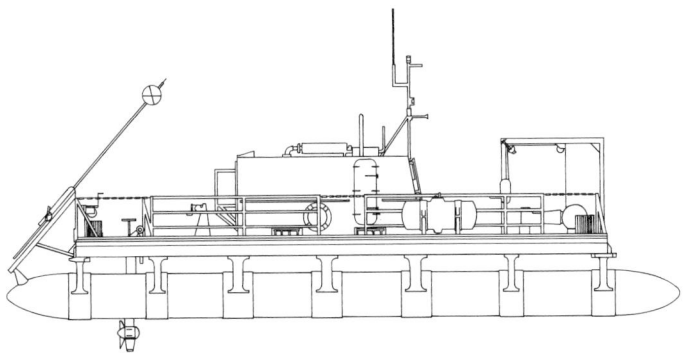

Drawing of Swedish-built SAM used by U.S. Navy in the Persian Gulf. Courtesy Karlskronavarvet. (William Clipson)

POST–WORLD WAR II MINESWEEPERS

A large number of minesweepers of various types were acquired by the U.S. Navy during the past 35 years, beginning with the massive ocean minesweeper (AM/MSO) and coastal minesweeper (AMS/MSC) series built in the early 1950s. During the 1960s a large number of smaller, riverine sweep craft were developed for use in the Vietnam War (all of which have been discarded, as have all previous craft except for the MSO type listed in this edition).

The various types of post–World War II minesweepers are discussed in the 13th Edition/pages 236–237 and previous editions of *Ships and Aircraft.*

MINE NEUTRALIZATION SYSTEM

Mine Neutralization Systems (MNS) are carried on board U.S. MCM and MHC mine countermeasure ships. The vehicle is approximately 12½ feet (3.8 m) long, three feet (0.9 m) high, and weighs 2,500 pounds. Two electric motors in the vehicle are powered through control/power cables. A closed-circuit television and close-range sonar will provide viewing of objects detected by shipboard sonar; the vehicle can then cut cables for moored mines or plant a small explosive charge to detonate bottom mines. The umbilical cable is 3,500 feet (1,067 m) long.

The MNS is built by Honeywell and is designated SLQ-48.
22-opener—ID

An SLQ-48(V) MNS vehicle showing the sonar and cable cutters at left. The TV camera is aft, between the ducted thrusters. The umbilical to the surface ship feeds into the structure atop the MNS; the other lines are for handling the vehicle aboard ship. (Honeywell)

CHAPTER 23

Auxiliary Ships

On a distant sea the oiler CIMARRON refuels the frigate BREWTON (FF 1086). Fleet auxiliaries—increasingly manned by civilian crews under the aegis of the Military Sealift Command—permit the fleet to maintain forward operations largely independent of land bases. (1991, OS2 John Bouvia, USN)

TABLE 23-1. NAVAL AUXILIARY SHIPS

Type		Operational					Building†	Reserve
		Total	Navy	MSC	Academic*	NRF		
AD	Destroyer Tenders	9	9	—	—	—	—	—
AE	Ammunition Ships	13	12	1	—	—	—	—
AF	Store Ships	1	—	1	—	—	—	—
AFS	Combat Store Ships	10	7	3	—	—	—	—
AG	Miscellaneous Auxiliaries	2	—	2	—	—	—	1
AGDS	Deep Submergence Support Ships*	1	—	1	—	—	—	—
AGFF	Sonar Trials Ship	1	—	1	—	—	—	—
AGM	Missile Range Instrumentation Ships	3	—	3	—	—	—	—
AGOR	Oceanographic Research Ships	8	—	2	6	—	1	—
AGOS	Ocean Surveillance Ships	18	—	18	—	—	3	2
AGS	Surveying Ships	11	—	11	—	—	3	—
AH	Hospital Ships	—	—	—	—	—	—	2
AK	FBM Supply Ships	2	—	2	—	—	—	1
AO	Oilers	18	5	13	—	—	5	16
AOE	Fast Combat Support Ships	4	4	—	—	—	3	—
AOR	Replenishment Oilers	7	7	—	—	—	—	—
AR	Repair Ships	1	1	—	—	—	—	1
ARC	Cable Repair Ships	2	—	2	—	—	—	1
ARS	Salvage Ships	8	8	—	—	2	—	1
AS	Submarine Tenders	10	10	—	—	—	—	2
ASR	Submarine Rescue Ships	4	4	—	—	—	—	1
ATF	Fleet Tugs	7	—	7	—	—	—	8
ATS	Salvage and Rescue Ships	3	3	—	—	—	—	—
AVB	Aviation Logistic Ships	—	—	—	—	—	—	2

*Academic-operated ships that are Navy built and/or owned.
†Ships authorized through fiscal 1992.

Auxiliary ships provide support to the "fighting fleet." There are a large number of different types of specialized auxiliary ships in U.S. naval service. Sealift ships—although nominally considered to be auxiliary ships—are described in chapter 24 of this edition.

The Reagan-Lehman naval programs of the 1980s emphasized the construction of underway replenishment ships to support battle groups. This effort, and the procurement of large numbers of sealift ships, were undertaken while several planned (and needed) destroyer tenders and repair ships were deleted from shipbuilding programs of the 1980s.

Auxiliary ships are listed in this chapter alphabetically according to classification. The U.S. Navy arranges auxiliary ships according to function with the categories being:

(1) Mobile Logistic Type Ships
Ships that have the capability to provide underway replenishment to fleet units and/or provide direct material support to other deployed units operating far from home base.
   (a) Underway Replenishment: AE, AF, AFS, AO, AOE, AOR
   (b) Material Support: AD, AR, AS

(2) Support Type Ships
Ships designed to operate in the open ocean in a variety of sea states to provide general support to either combatant forces or shore-based establishments. (Includes smaller auxiliaries that by the nature of their duties rarely leave inshore waters.)
   (a) Fleet Support: ARS, ASR, ATA, ATF, ATS
   (b) Other Auxiliaries: AG, AGDS, AGF, AGM, AGOR, AGS, AH, AK, AKR, AOG, AOT, AP, ARC, ARL, AVM, AVT

While overly simplistic, this Navy scheme, initiated in 1978, does attempt to indicate the types of support the various auxiliaries provide to the fleet.

Several ships officially classified as auxiliaries are listed elsewhere in this volume and are not included in the following table:

AGF	miscellaneous command ship	Chapter 18
AGSS	auxiliary submarine	Chapter 12
ASDV	auxiliary swimmer delivery vehicles	Chapter 20
AVT	landing training ship	Chapter 13

Guns: None of the ships operated by the Military Sealift Command are armed. Most Navy-manned auxiliaries have a minimal armament of 20-mm or .50-cal guns and 40-mm grenade launchers for self-defense. The major underway replenishment ships, which in wartime would provide direct support to battle groups, have 20-mm Phalanx CIWS and/or Sea Sparrow point-defense missiles as well as SLQ-32 electronic countermeasures gear.

No active auxiliary ships retain the 5-inch guns that were placed on such ships from the late 1930s onward; a large number of auxiliary ships still carry 3-inch/50-cal AA guns.

Missiles: The AOE/AOR-type replenishment ships are the only U.S. Navy auxiliary ships that are armed with guided missiles.

Names: The historic naming scheme for auxiliary ships, like that for combatants, has undergone a considerable degree of corruption during the past few years, mainly for political purposes.

Destroyer tenders (AD) are named for geographic areas, except for the SAMUEL GOMPERS (AD 37), which honors a labor leader.

Ammunition ships (AE) carry the names of explosives and volcanoes.

Store ships (AF) are named for star constellations.

Combat store ships (AFS), fast combat support ships (AOE), and replenishment oilers (AOR) have city names, except that the MARS (AFS 1) honors the Roman god of war while the SUPPLY (AOE 6)-class ships carry the names of an earlier ammunition ship (RAINIER/AE 5), store ship (ARCTIC/AF 7), and aviation store ship (SUPPLY/IX 147).

Missile range instrumentation ships (AGM) have carried a variety of names, including cities (WHEELING/T-AGM 8), "range" names (RANGE SENTINEL/T-AGM 22), and missile project names (REDSTONE/T-AGM 20), while the ships formerly "owned" by the Air Force honor generals (GENERAL H.H. ARNOLD/T-AGM 9).

Oceanographic research ships (AGOR) and surveying ships (AGS) are generally named for oceanographers and Navy oceanographic officers. The PATHFINDER (T-AGS 60) commemorates the Coast and Geodetic Survey ship of that name that was operated by the Navy (AGS 1) during World War II.

Surveillance ships (AGOS) have names that convey traits of capability or accomplishment.

Hospital ships (AH) are assigned "mercy" names.

Cargo ships (AK) mostly have star and constellation names.

Oilers (AO) historically have been named for rivers with Indian names. The lead ship of the latest class, the HENRY J. KAISER (T-AO 187), is named for an American industrialist and World War II master shipbuilder; the succeeding eight ships of the class are named for industrialists, engineers, and naval architects—after which Indian names were assigned to the final nine ships of the class.

Repair ships (AR/ARL) and cable ships (ARC) are assigned mythological names.

Salvage ships (ARS) are named for terms related to salvage activity.

Submarine tenders (AS) have a variety of name sources—mostly mythological (PROTEUS/AS 19) and submarine pioneers (SIMON LAKE/AS 33).

Submarine rescue ships (ASR) have historically had bird names, with the first ASRs having been converted World War I–era minesweepers with bird names.

Tugs (ATA/ATF) have Indian names. The salvage and rescue ships (ATS) carry the names of American cities with English namesakes, a reasonable scheme for ships that were constructed in Britain.

Aviation logistic ships (AVB) are named for aviation pioneers.[1]

1. The first two AVBs were converted LSTs and continued to carry their landing ship names after conversion to aviation base ships.

Operational: Auxiliary ships are operated by (1) the active Navy, (2) the Military Sealift Command (MSC) with civil service or contractor civilian crews, (3) the Naval Reserve Force (NRF) with composite active-reserve crews, or (4) by academic institutions on loan from the Navy. The MSC ships have the prefix USNS for U.S. Naval Ship and the prefix T- is appended to their hull numbers; the active and NRF ships have the prefix USS.

AUXILIARY CRANE SHIPS

The auxiliary crane ships (ACS) are listed with sealift ships; see chapter 24. The Navy's one previous ship in this general category was the CRANE SHIP NO. 1 (designation AB 1, previously IX 16), the immobilized former battleship KEARSARGE (BB 5). Completed in 1900, the KEARSARGE was converted in 1920 and fitted with a 250-ton-capacity crane. She was non-self-propelled as a crane ship.

DESTROYER TENDERS

6 DESTROYER TENDERS: "SAMUEL GOMPERS" CLASS

Number	Name	FY	Launched	Commissioned	Status
AD 37	SAMUEL GOMPERS	64	14 May 1966	1 July 1967	**PA**
AD 38	PUGET SOUND	65	16 Sep 1966	27 Apr 1968	**AA**
AD 41	YELLOWSTONE	75	27 Jan 1979	28 June 1980	**AA**
AD 42	ACADIA	76	28 July 1979	6 June 1981	**PA**
AD 43	CAPE COD	77	2 Aug 1980	17 Apr 1982	**PA**
AD 44	SHENANDOAH	79	6 Feb 1982	15 Aug 1983	**AA**

Builders:	AD 37, 38	Puget Sound Naval Shipyard
	AD 41–44	National Steel & Shipbuilding, San Diego, Calif.
Displacement:	AD 37, 38	13,600 tons light
	AD 41–44	13,318 tons light
	AD 37, 38	20,500 tons full load
	AD 41–44	20,224 tons full load
Length:	643⅝ feet (196.3 m) overall	
Beam:	85 feet (25.9 m)	
Draft:	22½ feet (6.9 m)	
Propulsion:	1 steam turbine (De Laval); 20,000 shp; 1 shaft	
Boilers:	2 600 psi (41.7 kg/cm²) (Combustion Engineering)	
Speed:	20 knots (18 knots sustained)	
Range:		
Manning:	AD 37	578 (45 officers + 533 enlisted)
	AD 38	680 (43 officers + 637 enlisted)
	AD 41	676 (43 officers + 633 enlisted)
	AD 42	631 (47 officers + 584 enlisted)
	AD 43	640 (44 officers + 596 enlisted)
	AD 44	608 (45 officers + 563 enlisted)
Helicopters:	landing area (see Design notes)	
Guns:	2 40-mm grenade launchers Mk 19 (2 single)	
	2 20-mm cannon Mk 67 (2 single) except 4 guns (4 single) in AD 37, 38	
Radars:	LN-66 navigation	
	SPS-10 surface search	

The PUGET SOUND arriving in port, with crew manning the rail and a tug assisting. The heavy cranes handle parts, weapons, and the ship's boats. Note the side ports for easy access to ships moored alongside. (1991, Giorgio Arra)

The Navy's first post–World War II destroyer tenders, these ships are designed to support modern surface combatants, including ships with nuclear and gas-turbine propulsion.

The PUGET SOUND served as flagship of the U.S. Sixth Fleet from May 1980 to August 1985, when relieved by the command ship CORONADO (AGF 11). When serving as the Sixth Fleet flagship, the PUGET SOUND was home-ported at Gaeta, Italy; she has since shifted home port to Norfolk, Va. As fleet flagship the PUGET SOUND carried some 225 flag personnel.

Class: The AD 39 was authorized in the fiscal 1969 shipbuilding program but was cancelled prior to the start of construction because of cost overruns in other new ship programs. The AD 40 was authorized in fiscal 1973 but was not built. An AD 45 was planned for the fiscal 1980 program but was not funded. Two additional tenders planned for fiscal 1987 and 1988 were deleted from the five-year program of January 1984.

The AD 41 and later ships are officially considered the YELLOWSTONE class. The SHENANDOAH was placed in "commission special" at San Diego on 15 August 1983 and in full commission at Norfolk on the date shown above.

Design: The GOMPERS was SCB No. 244; subsequent ships were No. 700 in the new SCB series. These ships are similar to the L.Y. SPEAR (AS 36)-class submarine tenders.

A landing platform and hangar for DASH helicopters were provided in the AD 37 and 38. The hangar on the GOMPERS has been converted to a repair shop; the PUGET SOUND's hangar is 54⅓ feet (16.55 m) long, 22⅓ feet (6.8 m) wide, and 16 feet (4.9 m) high; she also has TACAN.

The ships have two 30-ton-capacity cranes and two 6½-ton cranes.

Guns: As built the AD 37 and 38 had a single 5-inch/38-cal DP gun forward with a Mk 56 GFCS; this armament was removed. Plans to install NATO Sea Sparrow missile launchers in these ships have been dropped.

The CAPE COD showing the massive structure of modern fleet tenders. They carry repair shops, parts, provisions, and weapons for surface combatants. These ships are Navy-manned with a relatively large portion of female personnel. (1991, Giorgio Arra)

The PUGET SOUND is the only destroyer tender that still has a helicopter hangar, although none is embarked in the ship. Hangars were provided in the 1960s to destroyer tenders for serving DASH helicopters. (1991, Giorgio Arra)

3 DESTROYER TENDERS: "DIXIE" CLASS

Number	Name	Launched	Commissioned	Status
AD 15	PRAIRIE	9 Dec 1939	5 Aug 1940	**PA**
AD 18	SIERRA	23 Feb 1943	20 Mar 1944	**AA**
AD 19	YOSEMITE	16 May 1943	25 May 1944	**AA**

Builders:	AD 15 New York Shipbuilding, Camden, N.J.
	AD 18, 19 Tampa Shipbuilding, Fla.
Displacement:	9,450 tons standard
	17,190 tons full load
Length:	520 feet (158.5 m) waterline
	530½ feet (161.7 m) overall
Beam:	73⅓ feet (22.35 m)
Draft:	25⁷⁄₁₂ feet (7.8 m)
Propulsion:	2 steam turbines (Parsons in AD 15, Allis Chalmers in AD 18, 19);
	11,000 shp; 2 shafts
Boilers:	4 403 psi (28 kg/cm²) (Babcock & Wilcox)
Speed:	19.6 knots
Range:	12,200 n.miles (22,594 km) at 12 knots
Manning:	AD 15 527 (53 officers + 474 enlisted)
	AD 18 548 (40 officers + 508 enlisted)
	AD 19 560 (42 officers + 518 enlisted)
Helicopters:	VERTREP area
Guns:	4 20-mm cannon Mk 68 (4 single)
Radars:	LN-66 navigation
	SPS-10 surface search

The PRAIRIE is the oldest U.S. Navy ship in commission except for the relic CONSTITUTION (ex-IX 21). These ships have been modernized to support surface warships fitted with ASROC, improved electronics, etc. They were among three classes of large tender-type ships begun in the late 1930s, the others being the VULCAN (AR 5) and FULTON (AS 11) classes.

Class: Five destroyer tenders were built to this design (AD 14, 15, 17–19); the DIXIE (AD 14) was stricken on 15 June 1982 and the PIEDMONT (AD 17) was stricken on 30 September 1982 and transferred to Turkey on 18 October 1982. (The later NEW ENGLAND/AD 32, ex-AS 28, cancelled in 1945, was of a different design.)

The YOSEMITE is typical of the World War II–built large tenders and repair ships. Her bridge has been enlarged, her heavy gun battery deleted, and her shops upgraded to permit her to support modern surface ships. Still, the 1940s lines are unmistakable. (1991, Giorgio Arra)

Guns: As completed these ships had four 5-inch/38-cal DP guns and eight 40-mm AA guns; armament was reduced up to the mid-1970s, when minimal 20-mm armament was provided.

Helicopters: In the 1960s these ships were modified to support the DASH helicopter program with small flight decks installed aft. They are now suitable only for VERTREP operations, although the PRAIRIE's fantail landing area is rated for manned helicopter landings.

DESTROYER TENDERS: "KLONDIKE" CLASS

The last ship of this class, the EVERGLADES (AD 24), was striken on 24 May 1989. Thirteen destroyer tenders were built to a modified C3 configuration: the KLONDIKE class (AD 22–25) and the SHENANDOAH class (AD 26–29, 31, 36), and the similar AD 16, 20, and 21; three additional ships were cancelled in 1945 (AD 30, 33, 35). The KLONDIKE (AD 22) and GRAND CANYON (AD 28) were reclassified as repair ships (changed to AR) in 1960 and 1971, respectively.

See 14th Edition/page 250 for characteristics.

The YOSEMITE in port with one of her launches swung outboard. Tenders carry several boats, to support ships being serviced and to carry their liberty crews. There are 20-mm cannon (covered in canvas) mounted on the ship's VERTREP deck. (1991, Giorgio Arra)

AMMUNITION SHIPS

AMMUNITION SHIPS: MODIFIED "KILAUEA" CLASS

The planned ammunition ships of the modified KILAUEA class (AE 36–40) were deferred in favor of the construction of additional AOE-type replenishment ships. With the lead ship initially planned for the fiscal 1986 shipbuilding program, the ships were continually delayed until; when the program was halted, one ship was planned for fiscal 1991, one for fiscal 1992, two for fiscal 1993, and one for fiscal 1994.

These ships were to have been slightly larger than the KILAUEA class with gas-turbine propulsion (two LM 2500s); see 14th Edition/ pages 250–251 for characteristics.

8 AMMUNITION SHIPS: "KILAUEA" CLASS

Number	Name	FY	Launched	Commissioned	Status
AE 26	KILAUEA	65	9 Aug 1967	10 Aug 1968	**MSC-PA**
AE 27	BUTTE	65	9 Aug 1967	29 Nov 1968	**AA**
AE 28	SANTA BARBARA	66	23 Jan 1968	11 July 1970	**AA**
AE 29	MOUNT HOOD	66	17 July 1968	1 May 1971	**PA**
AE 32	FLINT	67	9 Nov 1970	20 Nov 1971	**PA**
AE 33	SHASTA	67	3 Apr 1971	26 Feb 1972	**PA**
AE 34	MOUNT BAKER	68	23 Oct 1971	22 July 1972	**AA**
AE 35	KISKA	68	11 Mar 1972	16 Dec 1972	**PA**

Builders:	AE 26, 27	General Dynamics, Quincy, Mass.
	AE 28, 29	Bethlehem Steel, Sparrows Point, Md.
	AE 32–35	Ingalls Shipbuilding, Pascagoula, Miss.
Displacement:	9,238 tons light	
	19,937 tons full load	
Length:	563⅚ feet (171.9 m) overall	
Beam:	81 feet (24.7 m)	
Draft:	27¹¹/₁₂ feet (8.5 m)	
Propulsion:	1 steam turbine (General Electric); 22,000 shp; 1 shaft	
Boilers:	3 600 psi (41.7 kg/cm²) (Foster Wheeler)	
Speed:	22 knots (20 sustained)	
Range:	18,000 n.miles (33,336 km) at 11 knots	
	10,000 n.miles (18,520 km) at 20 knots	

Manning:	Navy ships approx. 409 (21 officers + 388 enlisted)
	T-AE 26 123 civilian + 67 Navy
Helicopters:	2 UH-46 Sea Knight
Guns:	4 3-inch (76-mm) 50-cal AA Mk 33 (2 twin) except none in T-AE 26
	2 20-mm Phalanx CIWS Mk 16 (2 multi-barrel) in AE 32–35
Radars:	LN-66 navigation
	SPS-10 surface search
EW systems:	SLQ-32(V)1

These are high-capability underway replenishment ships, fitted with the FAST system for the rapid transfer of missiles and other munitions. The KILAUEA was transferred to MSC on 1 October 1980; no additional transfers are planned.

Design: SCB No. 703. The KILAUEA design provides for the ship's main cargo spaces forward of the superstructure with a helicopter landing area aft. A hangar approximately 50 feet (15.2 m) long, 15½ to 17½ feet (4.7 to 5.3 m) wide, and 16⅔ to 17¾ feet (5.1 to 5.4 m) high is built into the superstructure. Cargo capacity is approximately 6,500 tons.

Guns: As built, the ships had eight 3-inch guns in twin mounts with two Mk 56 GFCS. Their armament was reduced during the late 1970s. Two Phalanx CIWS are scheduled for installation in the AE 27–29.

The SANTA BARBARA with a UH-46D Sea Knight from Helicopter Combat Support Squadron (HC) 8 on her fantail. The helicopter control position is above the twin hangars. The top of the mast is folded to permit passage under a bridge. (1989, Giorgio Arra)

The SANTA BARBARA with a UH-46D Sea Knight hovering over the helicopter deck. Forward she has a twin 3-inch/50-cal AA gun mount to port and a Phalanx CIWS to starboard; the arrangement is reversed for the guns atop the superstructure. There are small boat davits forward of the bridge. (1990, Giorgio Arra)

The KISKA displays the unusual configuration of the KILAUEA class, with cargo holds forward, superstructure amidships, and helicopter facilities aft. Motor launch positions are "notched" into the superstructure. This design has been very successful. (1989, U.S. Navy, PH2 P. Mucutt)

5 AMMUNITION SHIPS: "SURIBACHI" CLASS

Number	Name	FY	Launched	Commissioned	Status
AE 21	SURIBACHI	54	2 Nov 1955	17 Nov 1956	**AA**
AE 22	MAUNA KEA	54	3 May 1956	30 Mar 1957	**PA**
AE 23	NITRO	56	25 June 1958	1 May 1959	**AA**
AE 24	PYRO	56	5 Nov 1958	24 July 1959	**PA**
AE 25	HALEAKALA	57	17 Feb 1959	3 Nov 1959	**PA**

Builders:	Bethlehem Steel, Sparrows Point, Md.
Displacement:	10,000 tons light
	AE 21, 22 17,000 tons full load
	AE 23–25 17,450 tons full load
Length:	512 feet (156.1 m) overall
Beam:	72 feet (22.0 m)
Draft:	29 feet (8.8 m)
Propulsion:	1 steam turbine (Bethlehem); 16,000 shp; 1 shaft
Boilers:	2 600 psi (41.7 kg/cm^2) (Combustion Engineering)
Speed:	20.6 knots
Range:	12,000 n.miles (22,224 km) at 15 knots
	10,000 n.miles (18,520 km) at 20 knots
Manning:	approx. 346 (21 officers + 325 enlisted)
Helicopters:	landing area only
Missiles:	none
Guns:	4 3-inch (76-mm) 50-cal AA Mk 33 (2 twin)
	4 .50-cal machine guns (4 single) in some ships
Radars:	LN-66 navigation
	SPS-10 surface search
EW systems:	SLQ-32(V)1 in AE 21

These ships were designed specifically for underway replenishment of munitions. The MAUNA KEA was transferred to the Naval Reserve Force on 1 October 1979 and the PYRO on 1 September 1980; however, the heavy operating tempo in the Indian Ocean-Persian Gulf areas in the early 1980s led to their being returned to the active fleet on 1 January 1982 and 1 June 1982, respectively.

Class: The three later ships are also referred to as the NITRO class.

Design: AE 21 and AE 22 are SCB No. 114; AE 23–25 are No. 114A. Cargo capacity is 7,500 tons.

Guns: These ships were completed with eight 3-inch guns in twin mounts (see Modernization notes). The arrangement of the forward guns varies; some ships have 3-inch mounts side-by-side and others in a tandem arrangement. The Mk 56 and Mk 63 GFCS have been removed.

Modernization: All five ships were extensively modernized during the 1960s (SCB project No. 232). They were fitted to carry and transfer guided missiles; their after 3-inch gun mounts were removed and a helicopter deck installed. No hangar is provided.

The SURIBACHI transits the Suez Canal en route to the Red Sea and Persian Gulf during Operation Desert Shield. The twin 3-inch/50-cal AA guns are in open, tandem mounts, all forward. This class does not have Phalanx CIWS fitted. (1990, U.S. Navy, PH3 Frank A. Marquart)

The PYRO has the later SURIBACHI gun arrangement with side-by-side enclosed 3-inch/50-cal AA mounts forward. Cargo holds are forward and aft; there is a large helicopter deck but no hangar. (1989, Giorgio Arra)

STORE SHIPS

1 STORE SHIP: "RIGEL" CLASS (R3-S-4a)

Number	Name	FY	Launched	Completed	Status
T-AF 58	RIGEL	53	15 Mar 1955	2 Sep 1955	**MSC-AA**

Builders:	Ingalls Shipbuilding, Pascagoula, Miss.
Displacement:	9,696 tons light
	15,540 tons full load
Deadweight:	8,112 tons
Length:	502 feet (153.1 m) overall
Beam:	72 feet (22.0 m)
Draft:	29 feet (8.8 m)
Propulsion:	1 steam turbine (General Electric); 16,000 shp; 1 shaft
Boilers:	2 600 psi (41.7 kg/cm²) (Combustion Engineering)
Speed:	21 knots
Range:	15,000 n.miles (27,780 km) at 15 knots
	10,000 n.miles (18,520 km) at 21 knots
Manning:	113 civilian + 19 Navy
Helicopters:	landing area

Missiles:	none
Guns:	removed
Radars:	Raytheon 1650/CX navigation
	SPS-10 surface search

The RIGEL is the last refrigerated store ship in U.S. naval service. She was assigned to MSC on 23 June 1975.

Class: Two ships of this class were constructed, the RIGEL and VEGA (AF 59). They were built specifically for naval service as "reefers," with the RIGEL laid down on 15 March 1954.

Design: SCB No. 97. Cargo capacity is 4,650 tons.

Guns: The RIGEL was completed with eight 3-inch AA guns Mk 33 in twin mounts. The two after mounts were removed for installation of a helicopter platform. The forward guns and associated Mk 56 and Mk 63 GFCS were removed when the ship was assigned to MSC.

The only refrigerated store ship or "reefer" in U.S. naval service is the RIGEL, operated by MSC in direct fleet support. This specialized ship type has been succeeded in the Navy by the multi-product replenishment ships. She has a large helicopter landing area aft. (U.S. Navy)

COMBAT STORE SHIPS

3 COMBAT STORE SHIPS: EX-BRITISH STORE SUPPORT SHIPS

Number	Name	Launched	Completed	U.S. In Service	Status
T-AFS 8	SIRIUS	7 Apr 1966	22 Dec 1966	17 Jan 1981	**MSC-AA**
T-AFS 9	SPICA	22 Feb 1967	21 Mar 1967	4 Nov 1981	**MSC-PA**
T-AFS 10	SATURN	16 Sep 1966	10 Aug 1967	30 Sep 1984	**MSC-AA**

Builders:	Swan Hunter & Wighman Richardson, Wallsend-on-Tyne (England)
Displacement:	9,010 tons light
	16,792 tons full load
Length:	489⅝ feet (149.35 m) waterline
	523¼ feet (159.5 m) overall
Beam:	72 feet (22.0 m)
Draft:	25½ feet (7.8 m)
Propulsion:	1 turbo-charged diesel engine (Wallsend-Sulzer 8RD76); 12,700 bhp; 1 shaft

Speed:	19 knots
Range:	27,500 n.miles (50,930 km) at 12 knots
	11,000 n.miles (20,372 km) at 19 knots
Manning:	110–125 civilian + approx. 47 Navy (5 officers + 42 enlisted)
Helicopters:	2 UH-46 Sea Knight
Guns:	none
Radars:	2 navigation

These ships are former Royal Navy replenishment ships, acquired by the U.S. Navy because of the increased logistics demands of maintaining two carrier battle groups in the Persian Gulf-Indian Ocean area following the crises and conflicts in that region that began with the Iranian Revolution of 1979. The ships were all previously operated as Royal Fleet Auxiliaries (RFA) with civilian crews.

With the purchase of the third British ship, the Navy dropped plans to construct an additional AFS under the fiscal 1987 shipbuilding program.

Class: This was a three-ship class, their British names being LYNESS, TARBATNESS, and STROMNESS, respectively. The LYNESS was originally acquired by the U.S. government on a bare-boat charter for one year on 17 January 1981, at which time she was placed in U.S. service (renamed SIRIUS); acquired by the Navy on 1 March 1982.

The TARBATNESS was acquired on time charter on 30 September 1981; changed to bare-boat charter on 4 November 1981 and at that time placed in U.S. service (renamed SPICA); acquired by the Navy on 30 September 1982.

The STROMNESS was acquired on 1 October 1983 (renamed SATURN).

The SIRIUS and SPICA were purchased under the fiscal 1982 program at a total cost of $37 million. The SATURN was purchased in fiscal 1984 for $13 million (plus $3.1 million in spare parts for the entire class).

Modernization: In U.S. service the ships have been modernized with the provision of improved communication and UNREP facilities, plus automated data processing. All have now been fitted with twin helicopter hangars.

The SATURN in MSC service still shows the lines of her British origins as a Royal FLeet Auxiliary; contrast them with the U.S. MARS class. A large helicopter hangar has been installed aft. Note that her three king-post-like transfer rigs are separated by deck structures. (1989, L. Van Ginderen Collection)

The rounded stern is typical of British replenishment ships. The SPICA has large cranes amidships and forward; the double hangar has a special antenna installed on its roof, forward of the helicopter control station. These are considered comfortable ships and highly successful in the AFS role. (1988, L. Van Ginderen Collection)

7 COMBAT STORE SHIPS: "MARS" CLASS

Number	Name	FY	Launched	Commissioned	Status
AFS 1	MARS	61	15 June 1963	21 Dec 1963	**PA**
AFS 2	SYLVANIA	62	15 Aug 1963	11 July 1964	**AA**
AFS 3	NIAGARA FALLS	64	26 Mar 1966	29 Apr 1967	**PA**
AFS 4	WHITE PLAINS	65	23 July 1966	23 Nov 1968	**PA**
AFS 5	CONCORD	65	17 Dec 1966	27 Nov 1968	**AA**
AFS 6	SAN DIEGO	66	13 Apr 1968	24 May 1969	**AA**
AFS 7	SAN JOSE	67	12 Dec 1969	23 Oct 1970	**PA**

Builders:	National Steel & Shipbuilding, San Diego, Calif.
Displacement:	9,200–9,400 tons light
	16,070 tons full load
Length:	529⅝ feet (161.5 m) waterline
	580⅝ feet (177.1 m) overall
Beam:	79 feet (24.1 m)
Draft:	24 feet (7.3 m)
Propulsion:	1 steam turbine (De Laval except Westinghouse in AFS 6); 22,000 shp; 1 shaft
Boilers:	3 600 psi (41.7 kg/cm²) (Babcock & Wilcox)
Speed:	21 knots
Range:	18,000 n.miles (33,336 km) at 11 knots
	10,000 n.miles (18,520 km) at 20 knots
Manning:	approx. 432 (28 officers + 404 enlisted)
Helicopters:	2 UH-46 Sea Knight
Guns:	4 3-inch (76-mm) 50-cal AA Mk 33 (2 twin)
	2 20-mm Phalanx CIWS Mk 16 (2 multi-barrel) in AFS 2, 4
Radars:	LN-66 navigation
	SPS-10 surface search
EW systems:	SLQ-32(V)1

These are large, built-for-the-purpose underway replenishment ships combining the capabilities of store ships (AF), store-issue ships (AKS), and aviation store ships (AVS). They do not carry bulk petroleum products as do the AOE-AOR replenishment ships.

These ships are being transferred to MSC operation with civilian crews in 1993–1994.

Class: Three additional ships that were originally planned in the fiscal 1977–1978 shipbuilding programs were not requested by the administration in those years.

Design: The AFS 1–3 were SCB No. 208; the later ships were No. 705 in the later SCB series. These ships have five cargo holds (one refrigerated) with a 7,000-ton cargo capacity. A large helicopter deck is fitted with a hangar 46¾ to 51 feet (14.25 to 15.5 m) in length and 16 to 23 feet (4.9 to 7 m) wide.

Engineering: Two boilers are normally used for full-power steaming with the third shut down for maintenance.

Guns: These ships were completed with four 3-inch twin gun mounts with one pair of mounts forward and a second pair abaft the funnel. Two mounts were deleted from all ships but the WHITE PLAINS during the late 1970s; all ships lost their Mk 56 GFCS as well as their SPS-40 air-search radar.

The WHITE PLAINS carried eight 3-inch guns until the mid-1980s when she beached two twin mounts in favor of two Phalanx CIWS. The other ships were to be similarly rearmed, but only the SYLVANIA was so armed prior to transfer to MSC operation.

The SAN DIEGO, riding at anchor, represents the ultimate "store ship" design. She has four sets of heavy replenishment masts plus a refueling mast forward on the starboard side (compare with photo of SYLVANIA). All of these ships are shifting to civilian manning under MSC. (1989, Giorgio Arra)

The SYLVANIA is one of two MARS-class ships with Phalanx CIWS, installed atop the superstructure behind the funnel. All of the class have two 3-inch/50-cal AA twin mounts forward; armament will be removed when the ships are civilian manned. (1989, Giorgio Arra)

MISCELLANEOUS AUXILIARIES

1 SOUND TRIALS SHIP: "HAYES"

Number	Name	FY	Launched	Commissioned	Status
T-AG 195 (ex-T-AGOR 16)	HAYES	67	2 July 1970	21 July 1971	**MSC-AA**

Builders:	Todd Shipyards, Seattle, Wash.
Displacement:	2,329 tons light
	4,037 tons full load
Length:	220 feet (67.1 m) waterline
	246⁵⁄₁₂ feet (75.1 m) overall
Beam:	75 feet (22.9 m)
Draft:	22 feet (6.7 m)
Propulsion:	diesel-electric (3 Caterpillar 3516 geared diesels); 5,400 shp; 2 shafts
Speed:	12 knots
Range:	6,000 n.miles (11,112 km) at 12 knots
Manning:	36 civilian + 30 technicians
Helicopters:	no facilities
Guns:	none
Radars:	Raytheon TM 1650/6X navigation
	Raytheon TM 1660/12S navigation

The HAYES is a catamaran, built specifically for use as an oceanographic research ship. She has been converted to an acoustic research ship to replace the sound barge MONOB ONE (YAG 61) in support of noise measuring of nuclear-propelled submarines. In her new role the HAYES can transport, deploy, and retrieve acoustic arrays, and conduct acoustic research. She is operated by an MSC civilian crew.

Following service as an oceanographic research ship (T-AGOR 16), the HAYES was laid up from 1983 until her conversion to a sound trials ship began in 1989 with completion in May 1992.

The HAYES operates in the Exuma Sound in the Bahama Islands under sponsorship of the David Taylor Research Center. She is home-ported at Port Canaveral, Fla.

Classification: Changed from T-AGOR 16 to T-AG 195 on 20 March 1989.

Conversion: The HAYES was to have been converted to a sound trials ship under a contract awarded on 20 February 1987 to the Tacoma Boatbuilding Co., in Tacoma, Wash. Conversion began on 27 August 1989, but the contract with Tacoma was terminated and the ship towed to the Puget Sound Naval Shipyard on 1 December 1990 for completion at that yard. Placed in MSC service in 1992.

Design: SCB No. 726. The HAYES has two hulls, each with a 24-foot (7.3-m) beam, spaced 27 feet (8.2 m) apart for an overall ship beam of 75 feet (22.9 m). Berthing and messing spaces are located in the forward superstructure "block," and the laboratories are located aft.

This ship and the two PIGEON (ASR 21)-class submarine rescue ships are the Navy's only oceangoing catamarans. The catamaran design provides a stable work platform with a large, open deck area; also, a centerline well makes it possible to lower research equipment into sheltered water between the two hulls. Some seakeeping problems were encountered in the design and it has not been repeated. In particular, the HAYES suffered excessive pitching in her AGOR role.

Electronics: The ship conducts noise measurements with a towed array, with a towing speed of 3 to 10 knots.

Engineering: The AG conversion included providing a high degree of automation in the engineering spaces; the original four high-speed diesel engines driving controllable-pitch propellers were replaced. An auxiliary 165-hp diesel engine is provided in each hull to permit a "creeping" speed of 2 to 4 knots with main propulsion shut down.

The HAYES with name displayed on both of the ships' sterns; there are MSC blue-and-gold color bands and MSC insignia on both funnels. Note the array of cranes and other lift gear to handle oceanographic research equipment. (1981, L. Van Ginderen Collection)

NAVIGATION RESEARCH SHIP: CONVERTED OILER

The research ship VANGUARD (T-AG 194, formerly T-AGM 19) is listed in this edition on page 236.

The HAYES in the Firth of Clyde as an AGOR, prior to her conversion to a sound trials ship. She was not successful as an oceangoing research ship; the subsequent SWATH design has been considerably more effective for ocean operations. (1981, L. Van Ginderen Collection)

1 HEAVY LIFT SHIP: "GLOMAR EXPLORER"

Number	Name	Launched	Completed	Status
AG 193	GLOMAR EXPLORER	14 Nov 1972	July 1973	NDRF

Builders:	Sun Shipbuilding and Dry Dock, Chester, Pa.
Displacement:	63,300 tons full load
Tonnage:	39,705 DWT
	27,445 GRT
	18,511 tons net
Length:	556¹¹⁄₁₂ feet (169.8 m) waterline
	618¾ feet (188.7 m) overall
Beam:	115⅔ feet (35.3 m)
Draft:	46¹¹⁄₁₂ feet (14.3 m)
Propulsion:	diesel-electric (5 Nordberg diesel engines; 6 General Electric motors); 13,200 shp; 2 shafts
Speed:	10.8 knots
Range:	
Manning:	approx. 180 civilian
Helicopters:	landing area
Guns:	none
Radars:	2 navigation

The GLOMAR EXPLORER was built and operated by the Central Intelligence Agency specifically to lift the remains of a Soviet Golf-class ballistic missile submarine (SSB) that sank in the mid-Pacific in 1968. The ship lifted the forward portion of the submarine from a depth of three miles (4.8 km) in 1974 in a clandestine operation given the code name Jennifer. (The ship's cover story was a seafloor mining operation under the aegis of millionaire Howard Hughes through the Summa Corporation for his Global Marine Development firm.)

The ship was acquired by the Navy on 30 September 1976; she was transferred to the Maritime Administration on 17 January 1977 and laid up in the National Defense Reserve Fleet in Suisun Bay, Calif.

Subsequent Navy efforts to sell the ship failed, and in 1978 she was leased to Global Marine Development, Inc., for a commercial seafloor mining venture; she was to be operated by the Lockheed Missiles and Space Company in that role. However, that lease was terminated and the ship was returned to Navy control on 25 April 1980 and again assigned to the Maritime Administration on the same date.

In late 1979 it was planned to provide the ship to the National Science Foundation as a deep-sea drilling ship. After modification she was to have the capability of drilling into the earth at an operating depth of approximately 15,000 feet (4,573 m). That project was not funded.

The ship remains on the Naval Vessel Register (NVR) and is laid up in Suisun Bay, Calif.

Classification: When acquired by the Navy in 1976 the GLOMAR EXPLORER was assigned hull number AG 193.

Cost: The cost of the ship at the time of construction was estimated at approximately $350 million. Certain related equipment and the cost of the HMB-1 submersible barge plus personnel brought the total project cost to an estimated $550 million.

Design: The ship was designed specifically to lift the sunken Golf-class submarine from a depth of 16,500 feet (5,030 m), employing a heavy lift system including a grappling claw that could be attached to the ship clandestinely by a submersible barge (designated HMB-1). Reportedly, the barge would also be used to hide the Soviet submarine had the entire 330-foot (100.6-m) submarine been salvaged. In the event, the portion salvaged could be accommodated in a large underwater hangar or "moon pool" within the GLOMAR EXPLORER.

Engineering: Three bow and two stern thrusters are fitted with an automatic position-keeping system to permit precise maneuvering or holding directly over an object on the ocean floor.

Name: As built, the ship was named HUGHES GLOMAR EXPLORER; it was changed when acquired by the Navy.

Operational: The GLOMAR EXPLORER arrived at the submarine lift site on 4 July 1974 and during the month-long operation lifted the forward portion of the submarine. The amidships section containing three SS-N-5 ballistic missiles with nuclear warheads was not salvaged. However, torpedos were recovered, including two reported to have nuclear warheads. The remains of the submarine were studied within the GLOMAR EXPLORER, then cut apart and packaged for further analyses or jettisoned.

This was the deepest and most complex salvage operation ever undertaken.

SURVEYING SHIP: "S.P. LEE"

The small surveying ship S.P. LEE (AG 192, formerly AGS 31) was loaned to the U.S. Geological Survey in February 1974; the ship is carried in the NVR in a "lease" status. See chapter 34.

HYDROGRAPHIC RESEARCH SHIP: VICTORY TYPE (VC2-S-AP3)

The hydrographic research ship KINGSPORT (T-AG 164, formerly T-AK 239) was striken from the NVR on 31 January 1984 *and again* on 20 August 1990 due to a Navy records error. She remains laid up in the James River (Va.) group of the NDRF.

See 14th Edition/pages 259–260 for characteristics.

PRESIDENTIAL YACHT: "SEQUOIA"

The presidential yacht SEQUOIA (ex-AG 23) is noted under Service Craft (chapter 25).

The deep-sea salvage ship GLOMAR EXPLORER at sea. Efforts to employ her as a seafloor exploration/drilling ship have failed, and there is little likelihood that she will ever again be employed in the salvage role. A photo of her current configuration, as laid up in NDRF, appears in the 13th Edition/page 249.

1 SONAR TRIALS SHIP: "GLOVER"

Number	Name	FY	Launched	Commissioned	Status
T-AGFF 1	GLOVER	61	17 Apr 1965	13 Nov 1965	**MSC-AA**

Builders:	Bath Iron Works, Maine
Displacement:	2,643 tons standard
	3,426 tons full load
Length:	390 feet (118.9 m) waterline
	414½ feet (126.4 m) overall
Beam:	44⅛ feet (13.5 m)
Draft:	24 feet (7.3 m)
Propulsion:	1 steam turbine (Westinghouse); 35,000 shp; 1 shaft
Boilers:	2 1,200 psi (83.4 kg/cm²) (Foster Wheeler)
Speed:	27 knots
Range:	4,000 n.miles (7,408 km) at 20 knots
Manning:	69 civilian + 21 Navy
Helicopters:	no facilities
Guns:	removed
ASW weapons:	removed
Radars:	SPS-10 surface search
	SPS-40 air search
Sonars:	SQS-26AXR bow mounted
	SQS-35
Fire control:	removed
EW systems:	removed

The GLOVER is an experimental sonar trials ship operated by the MSC. She was built as an experimental frigate with a modified propeller configuration. The ship was originally authorized in the fiscal 1960 program but postponed until fiscal 1961. She was used primarily for research into the 1970s, after which she served as an operational frigate. In 1990 she was reconfigured as trials ship for the wide-aperture array sonar and placed in MSC service on 15 June 1991.

She is operated by MSC under the sponsorship of the Naval Sea Systems Command.

The GLOVER was laid down on 29 July 1963.

Armament: As built, the ship had a single 5-inch/38-cal DP gun forward, an eight-cell ASROC launcher, and two sets of 12.75-inch (324-mm) triple ASW torpedo tubes. The removal of these weapons and related munitions caused a reduction in displacement; full load displacement was 3,630 tons as FF 1098.

Classification: The GLOVER was authorized as a miscellaneous auxiliary (AG 163), completed as an escort research ship (AGDE 1), and changed to a frigate research ship (AGFF 1) on 30 June 1975. The ship was redesignated as a frigate (FF 1098) on 1 October 1979, being assigned the hull number of a cancelled KNOX-class frigate.

She was again changed to AGFF and designated T-AGFF 1 on 14 May 1990.

Design: SCB No. 198. The ship was similar to the BROOKE (FFG 1) and GARCIA (FF 1040) frigate classes, but with a modified hull and propulsor. The ship had no after weapon (i.e., 5-inch gun or Mk 22 missile launcher); there is a raised platform aft 2⅔ feet (0.8 m) above the main deck, for a VDS housing. A DASH hangar was provided, but the ship was not modified to operate a LAMPS I helicopter.

Engineering: A pumpjet (shrouded) propeller is fitted.

Torpedoes: Two Mk 25 torpedo tubes with 12 torpedoes were originally fitted into the stern (in addition to the Mk 32 tubes). They were subsequently removed.

The GLOVER, again employed as a research ship, now in the sonar trials role with a civilian crew. She is the only "warship" operated by the Military Sealift Command, a further demonstration of that organization's flexibility. (1991, Giorgio Arra)

The stern aspect of the GLOVER shows her unique stern configuration with the sliding stern door originally intended for the variable-depth sonar. There are equipment "blisters" along the hull—above and below the waterline—as well as a stern crane and other, below-decks modifications. (1991, Giorgio Arra)

INTELLIGENCE COLLECTION SHIPS

INTELLIGENCE COLLECTION SHIP: EX-REPAIR SHIP

The SPHINX (ARL 24, ex-LST 963) was the last of several score LSTs converted to various types of repair and support ships to be operated by the U.S. Navy. Originally completed in 1944, the SPHINX was decommissioned and stricken from the NVR on 19 June 1989. She was laid up in reserve from 1947 to 1950, 1956 to 1967, and a third time from 1971 to 1985; she was recommissioned on 26 July 1985, reportedly for employment as an intelligence collection ship to operate off Central America to intercept radio and radar emissions from Marxist Nicaragua.

For her intelligence collection role the SPHINX was fitted with electronic intercept and direction-finding gear; a helicopter platform was installed.

The ship had previously served as a small craft repair ship in World War II, the Korean War, and in Vietnam, one of 39 tank landing ships converted to the ARL configuration to repair and support landing craft in advanced areas: ARL 1–24, 26–33, and 35–41, with the ARL 25 and 34 cancelled. Several of these ships survive in foreign navies with the INDRA (ARL 37, ex-LST 1147), which was stricken on 31 December 1977, remaining at the Norfolk Naval Shipyard as an accommodations hulk.

See 14th Edition/pages 316–317 for characteristics.

ENVIRONMENTAL RESEARCH SHIP: "PUEBLO"

The ill-fated "spy ship" PUEBLO (AGER 2) remains on the NVR. The ship is listed as "active, in commission" although she has been interned since being captured on 23 January 1968 some 12 miles off the coast of Wonsan in international waters.

The PUEBLO was a former U.S. Army cargo ship (FS 344), transferred to the Navy in 1966 and named PUEBLO (AKL 44); she was converted in 1966–1967 specifically for the intelligence collection role. Eighty-three men were captured when the ship was taken; one U.S. crewman was fatally injured in the boarding. The others were held in prison and brutalized for 11 months, being released on 23 December 1968 after a U.S. apology.

Three ships of this type (AGER 1–3) and five larger, converted Liberty- and Victory-type ships, classified as technical research ships (AGTR 1–5), were operated in the intelligence collection role. Two smaller cargo-type ships were also employed in the intelligence role in the 1960s, the PRIVATE JOSEPH E. VALDEZ (AG 169) and SERGEANT JOSEPH E. MULLER (AG 171).

MISSILE RANGE INSTRUMENTATION SHIPS

1 MISSILE-TEST SUPPORT SHIP: "POINT LOMA" (S2-ST-23a)

Number	Name	Launched	T-AKD in service	AGDS Comm.	Status
T-AGDS 2 (ex-T-AKD 1)	POINT LOMA	25 May 1957	29 May 1958	26 Feb 1976	**MSC-PA**

Builders:	Maryland Shipbuilding & Dry Dock, Baltimore, Md.
Displacement:	8,000 tons light
	9,478 tons standard
	12,430 tons full load
Length:	475 feet (144.8 m) waterline
	492 feet (150.0 m) overall
Beam:	74 feet (22.6 m)
Draft:	19 feet (5.9 m)
Propulsion:	2 steam turbines (Westinghouse); 6,000 shp; 2 shafts
Boilers:	2 (Foster Wheeler)
Speed:	15 knots
Range:	8,800 n.miles (16,298 km) at 10 knots
Manning:	44 civilian
Helicopters:	no facilities
Guns:	none
Radars:	SPS-10 surface search
	SPS-53 surface search

The POINT LOMA was built as a "wet well" dock cargo ship (originally the POINT BARROW, T-AKD 1) to carry vehicles, supplies, and landing craft to support U.S. radar installations in the Arctic. She was assigned to MSTS after completion and operated in the cargo role until 1965. The ship was modified that year to carry Saturn missile boosters and other space-program equipment from California to Cape Kennedy and served in that role until 1970. (She also made some trips to Vietnam carrying landing craft during that period.)

The ship was laid up in 1971–1972 and then returned to general cargo work under the Military Sealift Command.

The ship was shifted to Navy operational control on 28 February 1974 and was converted in 1974–1976 to transport and support the research submersible TRIESTE and, subsequently, to support other submersibles (placed in commission on 30 April 1975). During her 1980–1982 overhaul the POINT LOMA was modified to serve as the support ship for operational test firings of Trident submarine missiles, being fitted with extensive tracking gear. (The submersible support capability was retained.)

The POINT LOMA was transferred back to MSC operation in 1986 (see below). She currently supports Trident missile tests under the sponsorship of the Navy's Strategic Systems Programs.[2]

The POINT LOMA was operated by Navy personnel as the AGDS 2 in the submersible support role until 1 October 1986, when she was assigned to the Military Sealift Command and her designation changed to T-AGDS 2.

Classification: The classification AGDS was established on 3 January 1974. The previous TRIESTE II support ship, the modified floating dry dock WHITE SANDS (ARD 20), was briefly assigned the hull number AGDS 1.

Conversion: The ship was converted in 1974–1976 specifically for use with the TRIESTE II with tankage provided for approximately 100,000 gallons (380,000 liters) of aviation gasoline used for flotation by the TRIESTE II and the lead shot that is used by the submersible for ballast.

She was modified in 1980–1982 at the Mare Island Naval Shipyard to support the DSVs TURTLE and SEA CLIFF and to carry out deep-sea recovery operations as well as to support Trident missile test launches. At that time the aviation gasoline handling capability was deleted and deep-sea recovery gear was installed.

For Trident support the POINT LOMA has four missile tracking and telemetry vans; additional HF/UHF/satellite communications equipment; a variable-depth sonar tracking system; and berthing for technical support personnel.

Bow and stern thrusters were installed in 1984 for precise ship positioning.

Design: The ship was originally ice-strengthened and winterized for Arctic supply operations. She is no longer "winterized" because of the removal of the hull steam jacket system and conversion of the fire main from dry to wet operation.

2. Formerly Strategic Systems Projects Office and, before that, Special Projects Office.

The POINT LOMA has had a long and unusual career. Her design is an adaptation of the LSD configuration. Originally a single-stack ship, the second was installed for diesel generator exhausts. (1986, Giorgio Arra)

The Point Loma's stern showing the gate to her docking well. She has a fixed, heavy-lift crane amidships for handling submersibles and their equipment. There are OE-82 SATCOMM antennas mounted on the after deck structure. (1985, Giorgio Arra)

The bow of the Point Loma with four spherical missile tracking antennas. They are designated LAS (Launch Area Support) and provide telemetry data for Trident missile flight tests; they are generally referred to as "golf balls." (1986, Giorgio Arra)

1 MISSILE RANGE INSTRUMENTATION SHIP: MARINER TYPE (C4-S-1a)

Number	Name	Launched	Commissioned	Status
T-AGM 23 (ex-AG 154)	Observation Island	15 Aug 1953	5 Dec 1958	**MSC-PA**

Builders:	New York Shipbuilding, Camden, N.J.
Displacement:	13,060 tons light
	16,076 tons full load
Length:	563 feet (171.6 m) overall
Beam:	76 feet (23.2 m)
Draft:	29⅚ feet (9.1 m)
Propulsion:	1 steam turbine (General Electric); 22,000 shp; 1 shaft
Boilers:	2 600 psi (41.7 kg/cm²) (Combustion Engineering)
Speed:	20 knots
Range:	
Manning:	80 civilian + 60 technicians
Helicopters:	no facilities
Guns:	none
Radars:	Raytheon 1650/9X navigation
	Raytheon 1660/12S navigation
	SPQ-11 missile tracking
	...... missile tracking

The Observation Island is a former missile test ship now employed as a range instrumentation ship, primarily to monitor Soviet missile flights in the Pacific.

The ship was built for commercial cargo service, being completed in February 1954; after operating she was laid up in the National Defense Reserve Fleet in November 1954. She was transferred to the Navy on 10 September 1956 for conversion to a missile test ship for the Polaris SLBM, being commissioned in 1958; she was subsequently modified to launch the Poseidon missile. After completion of the Poseidon development program, the ship was decommissioned on 25 September 1972 and again laid up in the NDRF.

The Observation Island was reacquired for conversion to a missile range instrumentation ship on 18 August 1977. Converted in 1979–1981, she is now operated by MSC with a civilian crew in support of Strategic Arms Limitation Talks (SALT) agreements, i.e., monitoring Russian missile tests.

Class: Five Mariner-class merchant ships were acquired by the Navy, with three being converted to amphibious assault ships (AKA 112, APA 248, APA 249) and two to support ships for the Polaris program, the Compass Island (AG 153) and Observation Island. A third Mariner was planned to support the Polaris effort (AG 155), but was not acquired. The Compass Island was configured to test strategic missile submarine navigation systems; she was laid up in 1980 and stricken on 1 October 1981 (correction to previous edition).

Classification: The Observation Island was originally classified YAG 57 for naval service; changed to AG 154 on 19 June 1956, being listed as EAG 154 until 1 April 1968 when the ship was "reclassified" as AG 154 to avoid confusion. The ship was changed to T-AGM 23 on 1 May 1979.

Conversion: Converted to AGM configuration at the Maryland Shipbuilding & Dry Dock Co., Baltimore, Md., from July 1977 to April 1981. She was fitted with the Cobra Judy phased-array radar (SPQ-11) aft, and two radar spheres were installed atop her superstructure.

Design: As an AG she was fitted with two SLBM launch tubes.

Engineering: Two bow thrusters are fitted for precise position-keeping.

Names: Her merchant name was Empire State Mariner.

The OBSERVATION ISLAND is one of five Mariner-class merchant ships acquired by the Navy for conversion to amphibious and research roles. She is now a missile range instrumentation ship. The forward antenna mast was changed in the 1980s; see earlier photo. (1987, L. Van Ginderen Collection)

The OBSERVATION ISLAND with her massive Cobra Judy phased-array radar facing to port. This photo was taken before the addition of a conventional tracking antenna at the after end of the deckhouse and the installation of a king-post-type mast forward. (1981, U.S. Navy)

1 MISSILE RANGE INSTRUMENTATION SHIP: VICTORY TYPE (VC2-S-AP5)

Number	Name	Launched	APA Comm.	T-AGM in service	Status
T-AGM 22 (ex-APA 205)	RANGE SENTINEL	10 July 1944	20 Sep 1944	14 Oct 1971	**MSC-AA**

Builders:	Permanente Metals, Richmond, Calif.
Displacement:	11,860 tons full load
Tonnage:	8,306 GRT
	5,301 DWT
Length:	436½ feet (133.1 m) waterline
	455 feet (138.8 m) overall
Beam:	62 feet (18.9 m)
Draft:	28⅝ feet (8.8 m)
Propulsion:	1 steam turbine (Westinghouse); 8,500 shp; 1 shaft
Boilers:	2 465 psi (32.3 kg/cm²) (Combustion Engineering)
Speed:	17.7 knots
Range:	10,000 n.miles (18,520 km) at 15 knots
Manning:	68 civilian + 27 technicians
Helicopters:	no facilities
Guns:	none
Radars:	Raytheon TM 1650/9X navigation
	Raytheon TM 1660/12S navigation
	SPQ-7 missile tracking
	3 ...... missile tracking

The RANGE SENTINEL is a former Navy attack transport converted to a missile range instrumentation ship. She served in the amphibious role during World War II, being subsequently laid up and stricken on 1 October 1958. She was reacquired from the Maritime Administration on 22 October 1969 for conversion to an AGM.

The ship operates in support of Trident missile firings in the Atlantic under the sponsorship of the Navy's Strategic Systems Programs.

Class: A total of eight Victory-type merchant ships served in various AGM configurations (T-AGM 1, 3–8, 22).

Classification: Changed from APA 205 to AGM 22 on 16 April 1971.

Converted: Converted between October 1969 and October 1971 to a support ship for Poseidon and later Trident test firings.

Names: The ship's name as APA 205 was SHERBURNE; renamed on 26 April 1971.

The RANGE SENTINEL is one of only two Victory-type merchant ships remaining in U.S. naval service, the other being an FBM supply ship (see MARSHFIELD, below). The array of tracking antennas previously mounted on the foredeck has been removed; see 14th Edition/page 263. (1989, Giorgio Arra)

1 NAVIGATION RESEARCH SHIP
1 MISSILE RANGE INSTRUMENTATION SHIP | CONVERTED OILERS (T2-SE-A2)

Number	Name	Launched	Acquired	T-AGM in service	Status
T-AG 194 (ex-T-AGM 19, AO 122)	VANGUARD	25 Nov 1943	21 Oct 1947	28 Feb 1966	**MSC-AA**
T-AGM 20 (ex-AO 114)	REDSTONE	28 Feb 1944	22 Oct 1947	30 June 1966	**MSC-AA**

Builders:	Marine Ship, Sausalito, Calif.
Displacement:	16,800 tons light
	T-AG 194 21,478 tons full load
	T-AGM 20 24,700 tons full load
Length:	595 feet (181.4 m) overall
Beam:	75 feet (22.9 m)
Draft:	25 feet (7.6 m)
Propulsion:	1 steam turbine with turbo-electric drive (General Electric); 8,700 shp; 1 shaft
Boilers:	2 600 psi (41.7 kg/cm²) (Babcock & Wilcox)
Speed:	16 knots
Range:	27,000 n.miles (50,000 km) at 16 knots
Manning:	T-AG 194 200 civilian
	T-AGM 20 90 civilian + 110 technicians

Helicopters:	no facilities
Guns:	none
Radars:	Raytheon 1650/9X navigation
	Raytheon 1660/12S navigation
	2 missile tracking in T-AGM 20

These ships are former Mission-class oilers that were extensively converted for the missile range instrumentation role. The VANGUARD was subsequently modified for use as a navigation test ship for Trident strategic missile submarines.

Both ships initially served as merchant oilers and were then acquired by the Navy (dates above) and placed in service as oilers (AO) with the Naval Ocean Transportation Service (NOTS); they were transferred to MSTS service when that service was created on 1 October 1949. Subsequently, both ships were in and out of service as the oiler/tanker requirements changed:

T-AO 114: to NDRF on 23 September 1949; reacquired by Navy on 21 July 1950; to NDRF on 15 November 1954; stricken from NVR on 22 June 1955; reacquired on 6 July 1956 and placed in MSTS service; stricken and returned to NDRF on 13 March 1958; reacquired by Navy on 19 September 1964 to become AGM 20. Converted and employed as AGM (see Conversion notes).

T-AO 122: to NDRF on 10 May 1946; reacquired by Navy on 21 October 1947 and placed in NTS/MSTS operation; to NDRF on 24 May 1955; stricken from NVR on 22 June 1955; reacquired by Navy on 21 June 1956; stricken and returned to NDRF on 4 September 1957; reacquired by the Navy on 28 September 1964 for conversion to AGM 19. Converted and employed as AGM (see Conversion notes).

The T-AO 122 was assigned to the Navy's Strategic Systems Programs on 1 October 1978 for conversion to a navigation research ship to replace the COMPASS ISLAND (AG 153). She initially served as T-AGM 19 but was changed to T-AG 194 on 30 September 1980.

Class: A third ship of this type, the MERCURY (T-AGM 21), was stricken on 28 April 1970; sold for commercial service.

Conversions: These ships were extensively converted in 1964–1966 to the AGM configuration at the General Dynamics yard in Quincy, Mass. A 72-foot (21.95-m) section was installed amidships, increasing the ships' original length and beam from 523½ feet (159.6

m) and 68 feet (20.7 m), respectively; they were fitted with missile/space tracking systems, extensive communications equipment, and accommodations for a large technical staff. Their configurations differed as AGMs.

The VANGUARD was converted to a navigation research ship at the Todd Corporation's San Francisco yard in 1980.

Names: The VANGUARD was built as the MISSION SAN FERNANDO; renamed MUSCLE SHOALS on 8 April 1965, and then VANGUARD on 1 September 1965. The REDSTONE was built as the MISSION DE PALA; changed to JOHNSTOWN on 8 April 1965 and to REDSTONE on 1 September 1965.

Operational: These ships were converted specifically to support the Apollo lunar flight program, with the MERCURY operating in the Indian Ocean, the VANGUARD in the Atlantic, and the REDSTONE in the Pacific during manned flights to the moon.

The VANGUARD now serves as Trident navigation test ship, and the REDSTONE supports Trident missile test flights in the Atlantic; both ships are operated by MSC under the sponsorship of the Navy's Strategic Systems Programs.

The REDSTONE retains the classic AGM appearance with large radomes housing missile tracking radars; the superstructure aft reveals her tanker origins. (1989, Giorgio Arra)

The REDSTONE's funnel has two exhaust "arms" to carry stack gasses away from electronic equipment. The hangar is used for sounding balloons. There are numerous communications antennas visible. (1989, Giorgio Arra)

The VANGUARD has lost her large radomes and has been refitted with several navigation antennas. Both the VANGUARD and REDSTONE have their navigation bridge forward, larger superstructure and funnel aft. (1989, Giorgio Arra)

MISSILE RANGE INSTRUMENTATION SHIPS: EX-TRANSPORTS (C4-S-A1)

The large converted troop transport GENERAL H.H. ARNOLD (T-AGM 9, ex-AP 139) was transferred to MarAd and laid up in NDRF on 23 February 1982; stricken on 1 March 1982. The GENERAL HOYT S. VANDENBERG (T-AGM 10, ex-AP 145) was transferred to MarAd on 8 February 1983 and remains in NDRF.

These World War II–built ships had been converted to support Air Force ICBM tests, with the VANDENBERG later supporting Navy SLBM test firings.

See 13th Edition/pages 254–255 for characteristics.

OCEANOGRAPHIC RESEARCH SHIPS

The oceanographic research ships perform a broad spectrum of basic ocean research. A major U.S. oceanographic research/surveying ship construction program has been initiated to replace the large number of such ships procured in the 1960s. The older ships have reached the end of their effective service life and are technologically inadequate for modern oceanographic operations. Their replacement ships will be multi-mission designs.

The decision to retire the majority of the ocean surveillance ships (T-AGOS) may lead to some of those units being converted to oceanographic research ships in lieu of new construction.

The former oceanographic research ship HAYES (T-AGOR 16) has been reclassified as the T-AG 195; see page 229.

None of these ships is armed.

Operational: All of these ships are operated by civilian crews under the aegis of MSC (T-AGOR) or by academic institutions under the Navy's University National Oceanographic Laboratory System (UNOLS).

1 + 7 OCEANOGRAPHIC RESEARCH SHIPS: "T. G. THOMPSON" CLASS

Number	Name	FY	Launched	In service	Status
(AGOR 23)	THOMAS G. THOMPSON	87	27 July 1990	9 May 1991	**Academic**
(AGOR 24)	· · · · · ·	90			Building
(AGOR 25)	· · · · · ·	90			Authorized
AGOR 26	· · · · · ·	90			Authorized
AGOR 27	· · · · · ·	92			Authorized
AGOR 28	· · · · · ·	92			Authorized
AGOR 29	· · · · · ·	94			Planned
AGOR 30	· · · · · ·	94			Planned

Builders:	AGOR 23 Trinity Marine, Halter Shipyard, Moss Point, Miss.
Displacement:	2,100 tons light
	3,250 tons full load
Length:	274 feet (83.5 m) overall
Beam:	52 feet (15.85 m)
Draft:	17 feet (5.2 m)
Propulsion:	diesel-electric (6 diesel generators, 2 electric motors); 6,000 shp; 2 azimuth propellers
Speed:	15 knots
Range:	12,000 n.miles (22,224 km) at 12 knots
Manning:	20 civilian + 35 scientists and technicians
Helicopters:	no facilities
Radars:	navigation
Sonar:	Krupp-Atlas seafloor mapping

This is a new class of oceanographic research ships, especially suited to support Navy research laboratories, academic institutions, and commercial contractors involved in Navy projects (replacing the CONRAD-class ships). The program was designated AGX during the design phase.

Some ships will be Navy/MSC operated, and at least two units will be assigned to academic institutions under the Navy's University National Oceanographic Laboratory System (UNOLS).

The lead ship, the THOMPSON, was laid down on 29 March 1989; delivered to the University of Washington on 8 July 1991.

Cost: Two AGORs are funded in the fiscal 1992 plan for an average of $49.9 million each.

Design: The ships are being built to commercial standards. They are especially designed for extended at-sea operations. One or more ships may be configured for supporting deep submergence vehicles. They are fitted with a dynamic positioning system to maintain station during research activities. Four laboratory/accommodation vans can be carried on deck. Endurance is 60 to 70 days.

The AGOR 23 is configured for oceanographic research and coastal survey.

Engineering: The ships are fitted with azimuth or Z-drives with 360° rotating propellers; there is also a rotating 360°, 1,100-shp bow thruster to provide precise station keeping.

Names: The AGOR 23 was initially to be named EWING.

Operational: The AGOR 23 is operated by the University of Washington (state), replacing her namesake, the former AGOR 9 (subsequently IX 517); the AGOR 24 and AGOR 25 will be operated by the Scripps Institution of Oceanography in La Jolla, Calif.

The THOMAS G. THOMPSON, the Navy's newest oceanographic research ship, has neat but boxy lines; the ship is one of several designs now being constructed to upgrade the Navy's ocean science fleet. In addition, several T-AGOS ocean surveillance ships are expected to be converted to research configurations. (1991, Trinity-Halter Marine)

2 OCEANOGRAPHIC RESEARCH SHIPS: "GYRE" CLASS

Number	Name	FY	Launched	Delivered	Status
(AGOR 21)	GYRE	71	25 May 1973	14 Nov 1973	**Academic**
(AGOR 22)	MOANA WAVE	71	18 June 1973	16 Jan 1974	**Academic**

Builders:	Halter Marine, New Orleans, La.
Displacement:	946 tons light
	1,190 tons full load
Length:	AGOR 21 176 feet (53.7 m) overall
	AGOR 22 204⅙ feet (62.25 m) overall
Beam:	36 feet (11.0 m)
Draft:	14½ feet (4.4 m)
Propulsion:	2 geared diesel engines (Caterpillar); 1,700 bhp; 2 shafts
Speed:	12.5 knots (sustained 11.5 knots)
Range:	8,000 n.miles (14,816 km) at 10 knots
Manning:	AGOR 21 10 civilian + 19 scientists
	AGOR 22 13 civilian + 19 scientists
Helicopters:	no facilities
Radars:	navigation

These are small "utility" research ships built specifically for use by academic research institutions. They are operated for the Oceanographer of the Navy by Texas A&M University and the Hawaii Institute of Geophysics, respectively; they were assigned to those institutions upon completion. During the early 1980s the MOANA WAVE was employed for at-sea testing of the T-AGOS/SURTASS towed sonar array.

Both ships were laid down on 9 October 1972.

Design: SCB No. 734. These ships are based on the design of a commercial offshore oil-rig resupply ship. The open deck aft provides space for special-purpose vans and research equipment. Endurance is 40 to 50 days.

Engineering: A 175-hp bow thruster is fitted.

Modifications: The MOANA WAVE conducted trials in 1979–1984 with satellite communications equipment and with the towed SURTASS array for the T-AGOS program. In 1984–1985 the ship was lengthened, with a deckhouse built aft.

The MOANA WAVE in her current configuration. She was previously employed as a test ship for the T-AGOS/SURTASS program; see 14th Edition/page 266. She now has a large housing amidships for lowering equipment into the sea, as well as cranes and other lifting gear aft. (1991, L. Van Ginderen Collection)

2 OCEANOGRAPHIC RESEARCH SHIPS: "MELVILLE" CLASS

Number	Name	FY	Launched	Commissioned	Status
(AGOR 14)	MELVILLE	66	10 July 1968	27 Aug 1969	**Academic**
(AGOR 15)	KNORR	66	21 Aug 1968	14 Jan 1970	**Academic**

Builders:	Defoe Shipbuilding, Bay City, Mich.
Displacement:	1,915 tons standard
	2,670 tons full load
Tonnage:	2,100 GRT
Length:	279 feet (85.1 m) overall
Beam:	46⅓ feet (14.1 m)
Draft:	15 feet (4.6 m)
Propulsion:	diesel-electric (4 diesel generators); 3,000 shp; 3 azimuth propellers (1 forward retractable, 2 aft)
Speed:	14 knots
Range:	12,000 n.miles (22,224 km) at 12 knots
Manning:	24 civilian + 34 scientists
Helicopters:	no facilities
Radars:	navigation

These are large research ships. They were extensively modified from 1988 to 1991 (see Engineering notes).

The MELVILLE is operated by the Scripps Institution of Oceanography and the KNORR by the Woods Hole Oceanographic Institution, both for the Office of Naval Research under the technical control of the Oceanographer of the Navy. They were assigned to those institutions upon completion.

The MELVILLE was laid down on 12 July 1967 and the KNORR on 9 August 1967.

Class: The AGOR 19 and AGOR 20 were authorized in the fiscal 1968 program, but their construction was cancelled.

Design: SCB No. 710. Although these ships have the same SCB number as the CONRAD class, they are quite different. A bow observation dome is fitted. Endurance is 35 to 40 days.

Engineering: These ships were built with a single diesel engine driving two cycloidal (vertical) propellers through long, internal shafts; the forward propeller is located just behind the bow observation dome, and the after propeller is just in front of the rudder. The ships could hold a fixed position in heavy seas with winds up to 35 knots. Cycloidal propulsion—controlled by a "joystick"—allowed the ship to be propelled in any direction and to turn up to 360° in their own length. This type of propulsion also allowed precise station keeping and slow speeds without the use of auxiliary propulsion units.

The ships experienced transmission system difficulties with their original propulsion plant. They were reengined in 1988–1991 to the configuration described above. They have azimuth or Z-drives with 360° rotating propellers.

Modernization: Both ships were extensively modernized when reengined. See 14th Edition/page 267 for original characteristics.

Operational: The KNORR located the wreck of the British liner TITANIC in the North Atlantic on 1 September 1985 using a remote-controlled search vehicle.

The MELVILLE (above) and the similar KNORR have an unusual configuration. Their "mack"—combined mast and stack—structure is amidships, with an enclosed observation platform. The ships are well equipped for their academic role. (1989, Giorgio Arra)

3 OCEANOGRAPHIC RESEARCH SHIPS: "CONRAD" CLASS

Number	Name	FY	Launched	In service	Status
(AGOR 10)	THOMAS WASHINGTON	63	1 Aug 1964	17 Sep 1965	**Academic**
T-AGOR 12	DE STEIGUER	65	21 Mar 1966	28 Feb 1969	**MSC-PA**
T-AGOR 13	BARTLETT	65	24 Mar 1966	31 Mar 1969	**MSC-AA**

Builders:	AGOR 7 Marietta Manufacturing, Point Pleasant, West Va.
	AGOR 10 Marinette Marine, Wisc.
	AGOR 12, 13 Northwest Marine Iron Works, Portland, Ore.
Displacement:	varies; approx. 1,200 tons standard, 1,643 tons full load
Length:	195⅝ feet (59.7 m) waterline
	208⅝ feet (63.7 m) overall
Beam:	37 feet (11.4 m)
Draft:	approx. 20⅔ feet (6.3 m)
Propulsion:	diesel-electric (2 Cummins diesel engines); 1,000 bhp; 1 shaft
Speed:	13.5 knots
Range:	varies 9,000 n.miles (16,668 km) at 12 knots
	8,500 n.miles (15,742 km) at 9.5 knots
Manning:	T-AGOR 7 30 civilian + 20 scientists
	AGOR 10 23 civilian + 22 scientists
	T-AGOR 12 29 civilian + 20 scientists
	T-AGOR 13 30 civilian + 20 scientists
Helicopters:	no facilities
Radars:	AGOR 7, 12, 13 Raytheon 1650/SX navigation
	Raytheon 1660/12S
	others 1 or 2 navigation

These are small but capable oceanographic research ships. Three ships are operated by MSC; the THOMPSON by the University of Washington (state), and the WASHINGTON by the Scripps Institution of Oceanography. All are under the sponsorship of the Naval Oceanographic Command. The institution-operated ships were assigned upon completion.

Class: Originally a class of nine similar ships built for U.S. naval and academic service.

Three ships of this class have been transferred on loan to other nations—JAMES M. GILLISS (AGOR 4) to Mexico on 15 June 1983, CHARLES H. DAVIS (AGOR 5) to New Zealand on 10 Aug 1970, and SANDS (AGOR 6) to Brazil on 1 July 1974.

The BARTLETT and other ships of the CONRAD class all differ in detail and equipment. The radome housing a satellite antenna atop the superstructure has been changed between the time these two photos were taken. (1992, Giorgio Arra)

The ROBERT D. CONRAD (AGOR 3) was transferred to MarAd on 26 July 1989 for layup and disposal.

The LYNCH (T-AGOR 7) was stricken on 6 November 1991.

The THOMAS G. THOMPSON (AGOR 9) was reclassified as IX 517 on 11 December 1989; see chapter 25.

Design: The early ships were SCB No. 185; the AGOR 12 and 13 were changed to the new series No. 710. These ships vary in detail, each with differing bridge, side structure, mast, and laboratory arrangements.

Engineering: The large stacks contain a small diesel exhaust funnel and provide space for the small, 620-hp gas-turbine engine used in these ships to provide "quiet" power when noise generated by the main propulsion machinery could interfere with research activities. The gas turbine can be linked to the propeller shaft for speeds up to 6.5 knots. There is also a retractable, bow propeller pod that allows precise maneuvering and can propel the ship at speeds up to 4.5 knots.

The BARTLETT's stern is crammed with winches, cranes, and other gear. The port and starboard sides differ. There is a second radome atop the bridge and a bar-type navigation radar antenna atop the forward mast. (1989, Giorgio Arra)

The DE STEIGUER is one of four CONRAD-class ships still in naval-academic service, survivors of an original class of nine small AGORs. (U.S. Navy)

The LYNCH has a tripod mast forward and less superstructure than the BARTLETT. The RSB-1 is moored off the starboard of the LYNCH as the ship enters Fort Lauderdale, Fla. (1989, Giorgio Arra)

OCEANOGRAPHIC RESEARCH SHIPS: EX-CARGO SHIPS (C1-ME2-13a)

The two oceanographic research ships of this type, extensively converted from Arctic cargo ships, have been stricken from the NVR. Three ships of this design were completed in 1957–1958 specifically to carry cargo for U.S. military projects in the Arctic area.

The ELTANIN (T-AGOR 8, ex-T-AK 270), was on loan to Argentina from 1972 to 1979; returned to the United States and laid up, she was stricken on 19 April 1988 and turned over to MarAd for disposal.

The MIZAR (T-AGOR 11, ex-T-AK 272) was stricken on 10 January 1990 and transferred to MarAd for layup (in James River NDRF).

The MIRFAK (T-AK 271) served only as a cargo ship; she is laid up in the NDRF (see chapter 24).

See 14th Edition/pages 269–270 for characteristics.

The MIZAR shortly before being stricken and laid up in the National Defense Reserve Fleet. The converted Arctic cargo ship had key roles in the searches for the sunken submarines THRESHER (SSN 593), SCORPION (SSN 589), and the Soviet Golf-class SSB lost in the mid-Pacific in 1968; also the hydrogen bomb lost off Palomares, Spain, in 1966, and the French submarine EURYDICE, sunk in 1970. (1989, Giorgio Arra)

OCEANOGRAPHIC RESEARCH SHIP: "ACANIA"

The ACANIA (no hull number), which served as an oceanographic research ship for the U.S. Naval Postgraduate School at Monterey, Calif., was sold in August 1986. Launched in 1929 as a private yacht, she was acquired by the Coast Guard in 1942 for use as a patrol boat, being named NELLWOOD (designated WPYc 337). Subsequently returned to private ownership in 1947, she was later reacquired by the government and from 1971 to late 1985 served as a research vessel (designated R/V vice USS or USNS). She was not carried in the NVR.

See 13th Edition/page 260 for characteristics.

OCEAN SURVEILLANCE SHIPS

The Surveillance Towed Array Sensor System (SURTASS) is a submarine detection system towed by slow surface ships to supplement the seafloor Sound Surveillance System (SOSUS). These ships operate where SOSUS coverage is inadequate or where the seafloor arrays are damaged or destroyed. The SURTASS data is sent via satellite link to shore facilities for processing and further transmission to ASW forces; however, the ships can provide "raw" acoustic data to ASW ships in the area. (The SURTASS concept differs from the tactical TACTAS system in that the latter consists of tactical hydrophone arrays towed by warships to supplement hull-mounted sonars.)

The initial Navy planning for the T-AGOS/SURTASS program called for 18 ships. This was later reduced to 12 ships because of fiscal constraints; however, because of the success of the early ships and the increasing Soviet submarine threat, in the mid-1980s the Navy sought a much larger program, i.e., these 18 monohull ships plus at least nine SWATH-configured ships.[3] These are the U.S. Navy's first SWATH ships except for the research/range support ship KAIMALINO (see chapter 25). The SWATH design was adopted because the monohull T-AGOS ships experienced difficulties in northern latitudes during winter.

Electronics: The UQQ-2 SURTASS array is a flexible, tube-like structure some 2,600 feet (793 m) long containing numerous hydrophones towed with a 6,000-foot (1,829-m) cable. It is neutrally buoyant when at depth, with the depth being varied to compensate for environmental conditions. Typical array operating depths are 500 to 1,500 feet (152 to 457 m).

Data from the hydrophone array are generated at a very high data rate. They are "pre-processed" on board the T-AGOS and sent at a much lower rate, reduced by a factor of ten, via satellite to shore stations. The data rate from ship to shore is about 32,000 bits (32 kilobits) per second.

In January 1992, based on the reduction of the former Soviet submarine threat, the Navy revealed plans to decommission the 18 surveillance ships of the STALWART class. They will be taken out of service at the rate of three ships per year through 1997. Several will be retained by the Navy in research roles, and some may be transferred to other government agencies and to other countries for service as research and surveying ships.

These ships are not armed.

3. SWATH = Small Waterplane Twin-Hull design; see appendix A.

(5) OCEAN SURVEILLANCE SHIPS: SWATH-A DESIGN

Number	Name	FY	Launched	In service	Status
T-AGOS 23	IMPECCABLE	90		1994	Building
T-AGOS 24	......	92			Planned
T-AGOS 25	......	94			Planned
T-AGOS 26	......	95			Planned
T-AGOS 27	......	95			Planned

Builders:	T-AGOS 23 Tampa Shipbuilding, Fla.
Displacement:	5,362 tons full load
Length:	281½ feet (85.8 m) overall
Beam:	95¾ feet (29.2 m)
Draft:	26 feet (7.9 m)
Propulsion:	diesel-electric (4 diesel generators); 5,000 shp; 2 shafts
Speed:	12 knots sustained
Range:	8,000 n.miles (14,816 km) at 15 knots
Manning;	26 civilian + 19 Navy technicians
Helicopters:	no facilities
Radars:	navigation
Sonars:	UQQ-2 SURTASS

These are enlarged SWATH ships to support SURTASS missions in higher sea states. The hull form is based on the T-AGOS 19 design.

The planned production of these ships has been slowed. The lead ship was ordered from the Tampa shipyard on 28 March 1991. When this edition went to press five ships were proposed.

Endurance will be 50 to 60 days.

Cost: The fiscal 1992 ship is proposed at a cost of $148.5 million.

Engineering: To be fitted with two 360° thrusters for station keeping.

2 + 2 OCEAN SURVEILLANCE SHIPS: "VICTORIOUS" CLASS (SWATH-P)

Number	Name	FY	Launched	In service	Status
T-AGOS 19	VICTORIOUS	87	2 May 1990	13 Aug 1991	**MSC-PA**
T-AGOS 20	ABLE	89	14 Feb 1991	1992	**MSC-AA**
T-AGOS 21	EFFECTIVE	89	12 Oct 1991	1992	Building
T-AGOS 22	LOYAL	89	1992	1993	Building

Builders:	McDermott, Morgan City, La.
Displacement:	2,676 tons light
	3,438 tons full load
Length:	190⅔ feet (58.1 m) waterline
	234½ feet (71.5 m) overall
Beam:	93½ feet (28.5 m)
Beam of "box":	80½ feet (24.5 m)
Draft:	25 feet (7.6 m)
Propulsion:	diesel-electric (4 Caterpillar-Kato 3512-TA diesel generators; 2 General Electric motors); 3,200 shp; 2 shafts
Speed:	16 knots; 9.6 knots array towing speed
Range:	3,000 n.miles (5,556 km) at 10 knots
Manning:	25 civilian + 12 Navy technicians
Helicopters:	no facilities
Radars:	navigation
Sonars:	UQQ-2 SURTASS

These are improved, twin-hull SURTASS ships.

A contact was awarded to the McDermott firm in October 1986 for the detailed design and construction of the lead ship of this class; the lead ship, the VICTORIOUS, was laid down on 12 April 1988.

The SWATH ships are intended specifically for operations in high-latitude areas; they are intended to operate through sea state 6 on all headings, and sea state 7 on best heading.

Design: These will be the world's first operational military ships with the Small Waterplane-Area Twill-Hull design; previously the U.S. Navy has operated a range support ship of this design, the KAIMALINO (see chapter 25).

The Navy's first SWATH surveillance ship, the VICTORIOUS, on sea trials. The twin, submerged-hull configuration provides enhanced seakeeping characteristics in northern waters. With the retirement of T-AGOS 1-18, the SURTASS force will consist entirely of SWATH ships according to current plans. (1990, McDermott)

The SWATH design of the VICTORIOUS provides extensive working space aft. A fixed, guide device extending from the stern keeps the towed-array cable clear of the twin propellers. No helicopter deck is provided. (1990, McDermott)

The design has two fully submerged hulls that support the deck and superstructure. The design differs from a catamaran hull, which has two conventional hulls. The SWATH design offers a high degree of stability and a large deck working area in comparison with conventional-hull designs. There is an outrigger device aft to move the tow point behind the propellers.

Mission endurance is 90 days.

Engineering: The ships' steering system uses a pair of angled rudders aft and a pair of angled canards forward; two azimuth thrusters are fitted forward.

Names: The T-AGOS 17 originally was named INTREPID; renamed while under construction.

Operational: The SURTASS data is transmitted from the T-AGOS via satellite link to shore facilities for processing and further transmission to ASW forces; however, the ships can provide "raw" acoustic data to ASW ships in the area. (The SURTASS concept differs from the tactical TACTAS in that the latter is a tactical hydrophone array towed by warships to supplement hull-mounted sonars.)

The twin, submerged hulls of the VICTORIOUS have stabilizing fins facing inward both forward and aft. Two anchors are set into the bow of the ship (not installed in this view). (1990, McDermott)

The stern of the VICTORIOUS showing the twin, five-blade propellers. The torpedo-like submerged hulls have a streamlined appearance, but a SWATH is built for stability and not speed characteristics. (1990, McDermott)

18 OCEAN SURVEILLANCE SHIPS: "STALWART" CLASS

Number	Name	FY	Launched	In service	Status
T-AGOS 1	STALWART	79	11 July 1983	9 Apr 1984	**MSC-AA**
T-AGOS 2	CONTENDER	79	20 Dec 1983	29 July 1984	**MSC-PA**
T-AGOS 3	VINDICATOR	80	1 June 1984	20 Nov 1984	**MSC-AA**
T-AGOS 4	TRIUMPH	81	7 Sep 1984	19 Feb 1985	**MSC-PA**
T-AGOS 5	ASSURANCE	81	12 Jan 1985	1 May 1985	**MSC-PA**
T-AGOS 6	PERSISTENT	81	6 Apr 1985	14 Aug 1985	**MSC-AA**
T-AGOS 7	INDOMITABLE	81	16 July 1985	1 Dec 1985	**MSC-PA**
T-AGOS 8	PREVAIL	81	7 Dec 1985	5 Mar 1986	**MSC-AA**
T-AGOS 9	ASSERTIVE	82	20 June 1986	12 Sep 1986	**MSC-PA**
T-AGOS 10	INVINCIBLE	82	1 Nov 1986	30 Jan 1987	**MSC-AA**
T-AGOS 11	AUDACIOUS	82	28 Jan 1989	18 June 1989	**MSC-PA**
T-AGOS 12	BOLD	82	22 May 1989	20 Oct 1989	**MSC-AA**
T-AGOS 13	ADVENTUROUS	85	23 Sep 1987	19 Aug 1988	**PR**
T-AGOS 14	WORTHY	85	6 Feb 1988	7 Apr 1989	**MSC-AA**
T-AGOS 15	TITAN	86	18 June 1988	8 Mar 1989	**MSC-PA**
T-AGOS 16	CAPABLE	86	28 Oct 1988	9 June 1989	**PR**
T-AGOS 17	TENACIOUS	87	17 Feb 1989	29 Sep 1989	**MSC-R&D**
T-AGOS 18	RELENTLESS	87	12 May 1989	12 Jan 1990	**MSC-AA**

Builders:	T-AGOS 1–12 Tacoma Boatbuilding, Wash.
	T-AGOS 13–18 Halter Marine, New Orleans, La.
Displacement:	1,600 tons light
	2,285 tons full load
Tonnage:	1,584 GRT
	786 DWT
Length:	203⅔ feet (62.1 m) waterline
	224 feet (68.3 m) overall
Beam:	43 feet (13.1 m)
Draft:	15 feet (4.6 m)
Propulsion:	diesel-electric (4 Caterpillar D-398B diesel generators with General Electric motors); 3,200 bhp; 2 shafts
Speed:	11 knots; 3 knots array towing speed
Range:	3,000 n.miles (5,556 km) at 11 knots + 90 days on station at 3 knots
Manning:	19 civilian + 10 Navy technicians
Helicopters:	no facilities
Radars:	2 navigation
Sonars:	UQQ-2 SURTASS

These are monohull SURTASS ships. The program has suffered from significant cost increases over original estimates and equipment failures, resulting in at least a several-year delay over the original 1974 schedule. All will be taken out of service as surveillance ships through 1997. The ADVENTUROUS and CAPABLE were taken out of service in 1992; the TENACIOUS was modified in 1992 to serve as a SURTASS trials ship under the sponsorship of the Space and Naval Warfare Systems Command (operated by MSC).

The other ships will be taken out of service at the rate of three units per year.

The lead ship, the STALWART, was laid down on 3 November 1982.

Design: The T-AGOS hull is similar to that of the T-ATF 166 class. There is a high degree of crew habitability provided, including single staterooms for all crewmembers with three single and four double staterooms for technicians. There are four additional berths in the T-AGOS 1–12 and seven additional berths in the later ships. The T-AGOS 13–18 also have a larger SURTASS operations center and modified machinery layout.

Endurance is rated at 98 days (see below).

Engineering: The four diesel generators drive two main propulsion motors. A bow thruster powered by a 550-hp electric motor is fitted for station keeping. There are special features to reduce machinery noise.

Names: T-AGOS 11 originally named DAUNTLESS, T-AGOS 12 originally named VIGOROUS, and T-AGOS 17 originally named INTREPID; all renamed during construction.

Operational: Early Navy planning provided for the ships to have 90-day patrol periods plus 8 days in transit, resulting in more than 300 days at sea per year. This intensity of operations was rejected by MSC as impractical and unrealistic with a patrol duration to 60 to 74 days now planned although the ships do have the higher endurance capability.

The WORTH, typical of the 18 STALWART-class surveillance ships. All 18 of these ships—the last completed in 1990—will be taken out of service by 1997. Some will be employed in research roles by the Navy and by other government and possibly academic agencies. (1992, Giorgio Arra)

The RELENTLESS in Navy grey. The T-AGOS ships were originally painted white. Shown in the view are the SURTASS control station above the cable reel, the tripod mast carrying the SATCOMM radome, twin funnels, and a bar-type radar antenna forward. (1990, Giorgio Arra)

SURVEYING SHIPS

Surveying ships conduct ocean surveys and collect data in support of fleet operations and systems development. All Navy surveying ships are operated by the Military Sealift Command under the sponsorship of the Naval Oceanographic Command.

The confusion in the numbering of AGS-series ships requires that a list be provided for the convenience of readers of this volume; see table 23-2 at the end of this section.

None of these ships is armed.

(3) OCEAN SURVEYING SHIPS: "PATHFINDER" CLASS

Number	Name	Launch	In service	Status
T-AGS 60	PATHFINDER	1993	1994	Building
T-AGS 61	SUMNER	1993	1994	Building
T-AGS 62	. . . . . .		1995	Planned

Builders:	Trinity Marine, Halter Shipyard, Moss Point, Miss.
Displacement:	4,762 tons full load
Length:	328 feet (100.0 m) overall
Beam:	58 feet (17.7 m)
Draft:	19 feet (5.8 m)
Propulsion:	diesel engines; 8,000 bhp; 2 azimuth propellers
Speed:	16 knots
Range:	
Manning:	60 civilian
Helicopters:	no facilities
Radars:	navigation

This is a new class of ships for long-range ocean survey and research. Research for a variety of ocean sciences will be conducted. Their design is based on the T-AGOR 23, with the third ship having special features for ice operations.

The PATHFINDER and SUMNER were laid down on 30 January 1991. The T-AGS 62 was ordered in June 1992 for $46.2 million.

Engineering: These ships will be propelled and steered through a Z-drive arrangement to azimuth thrusters. Retracting bow-thrusters will also be fitted.

The RELENTLESS end-on reveals the open stern with a roller for passing through the SURTASS cable; the reel is covered with canvas. (1990, Giorgio Arra)

(2) COASTAL SURVEYING SHIPS: "JOHN MCDONNELL" CLASS

Number	Name	FY	Launched	In service	Status
T-AGS 51	JOHN MCDONNELL	87	13 Dec 1990	1992	**MSC-AA**
T-AGS 52	LITTLEHALES	87	14 Feb 1991	1992	**MSC-AA**

Builders:	Trinity Marine, Halter Shipyard, Moss Point, Miss.
Displacement:	2,000 tons full load
Length:	208⅙ feet (63.5 m) overall
Beam:	45 feet (13.7 m)
Draft:	14 feet (4.3 m)
Propulsion:	diesel engines; 1 shaft
Speed:	16 knots sustained
Range:	13,800 n.miles (25,535 km) at 16 knots
Complement:	23 civilian + 10 scientists
Helicopters:	no facilities
Radars:	navigation

These coastal surveying ships were laid down on 10 November 1988. They are intended to collect bathymetric/hydrographic data in shallow and deep water. They carry small survey launches.

The keel for the MCDONNELL was laid down on 3 August 1989 and that of the LITTLEHALES on 25 October 1989.

The JOHN MCDONNELL on builder's trials. The ship is typical of the several new research and surveying ships being built for the Navy and Navy-sponsored academic institutions that are replacing the older, less capable ships. Although MSC-operated, research ships are mostly painted white. (1991, Halter Marine)

The LITTLEHALES at high speed during builders' trials in the Gulf of Mexico. These ships have several cranes and other lifting devices for survey gear. (1991, Halter Marine)

The MCDONNELL's low, squared-off stern facilities lowering and raising survey equipment. (1991, Halter Marine)

(1) SURVEYING SHIP: "WATERS"

Number	Name	FY	Launched	In service	Status
T-AGS 45	WATERS	90	1992	1993	Building

Builders:	Avondale Industries, New Orleans, La.
Displacement:	12,208 tons full load
Length:	442 feet (134.75 m) overall
Beam:	69 feet (21.0 m)
Draft:	21⅛ feet (6.45 m)
Propulsion:	diesel-electric; 7,400 shp; 2 shafts
Speed:	13.2 knots sustained
Range:	
Complement:	62 civilian + 6 Navy + 21 technicians
Helicopters:	no facilities
Radars:	navigation

This is a large, multi-function surveying ship intended to replace the MIZAR (T-AGOR 11). The new ship will be capable of performing bathymetric, oceanographic, and hydrographic surveys. She will be able to launch and recover a variety of remotely operated vehicles.

The keel for the WATERS was laid down on 21 May 1991.

Design: Fitted with bow and stern thrusters for precise maneuvering during survey work.

2 OCEAN SURVEYING SHIPS: "MAURY" CLASS

Number	Name	FY	Launched	In service	Status
T-AGS 39	MAURY	85	4 Sep 1987	31 Mar 1989	**MSC-AA**
T-AGS 40	TANNER	85	3 Mar 1988	27 Aug 1990	**MSC-AA**

Builders:	Bethlehem Steel, Sparrows Point, Baltimore, Md.
Displacement:	8,810 tons light
	15,821 tons full load
Length:	462$\frac{1}{12}$ feet (140.9 m) waterline
	499$\frac{5}{8}$ feet (152.4 m) overall
Beam:	72 feet (22.0 m)
Draft:	30$\frac{1}{2}$ feet (9.3 m)
Propulsion:	2 diesel engines (Transamerica Delaural Enterprise R5-V16); 25,000 bhp; 1 shaft
Speed:	20 knots
Range:	17,820 n.miles (33,000 km) at 20 knots
Manning:	56 civilian + 32 Navy (3 officers + 29 enlisted) + 20 scientists
Helicopters:	no facilities
Radars:	2 navigation
Sonars:	SQN-17 BOTOSS
	BQN-3 narrow-beam mapping

These are built-for-the-purpose ocean survey ships, replacing the outdated BOWDITCH and DUTTON. They surpass the CHAUVENET and HARKNESS as the largest purpose-built U.S. Navy research ships. The ships conduct primarily hydrographic, magnetic, and gravity surveys.

Until November of 1983 the Navy had planned to convert the 20-year-old merchant ships MORMACPRIDE and MORMACSCAN, completed in 1960 and 1961, respectively, to this role; both ships were laid up in NDRF (MarAd C3-S-33a type). However, congressional direction caused the Navy to instead construct two new survey ships.

The keels for the MAURY and TANNER were laid down on 29 July 1986 and 22 October 1986, respectively.

Electronics: Fitted with SQN-17 Bottom Topography Survey System (BOTOSS) multi-beam, wide-angle precision sonar for continuous charting of a broad strip of ocean floor under the ship's track. The ships are also fitted with two BQN-3 narrow-beam sonars with precision depth recorders. (Also provided with gravity and magnetic measuring systems.)

Cost: Requested in fiscal 1985 at a cost of $245 million to construct both ships.

Names: These names were previously assigned to the Navy's first major surveying ships of the post–World War II era, the TANNER (AGS 15) and MAURY (AGS 16); both were converted attack cargo ships (AKA).

The MAURY at high speed. Most of her hull volume—except for engineering spaces—is largely voids with 7,339 tons of water ballast being carried. Working spaces and accommodations are in the superstructure. (1989, Bethlehem Steel, C. Snyder)

Carrying the name of Matthew Fontaine Maury, one of the most distinguished scientists of the U.S. and Confederate Navies, the MAURY is one of the most ungainly ships ever built. However, the ship does carry a battery of modern survey gear. (1989, U.S. Navy)

1 SURVEYING SHIP: "H.H. HESS" (C4-S-1sa)

Number	Name	Launched	In service	Status
T-AGS 38	H.H. HESS	30 May 1964	16 Jan 1976	**MSC-PA**

Builders:	National Steel and Shipbuilding, San Diego, Calif.
Displacement:	13,525 tons light
	21,255 tons full load
Tonnage:	12,720 GRT
Length:	527⅝ feet (160.3 m) waterline
	563½ feet (171.81 m) overall
Beam:	76 feet (23.2 m)
Draft:	31½ feet (9.6 m)
Propulsion:	1 steam turbine (General Electric); 19,250 shp; 1 shaft
Boilers:	2 600 psi (41.7 kg/cm²) (Foster Wheeler)
Speed:	21 knots
Range:	14,000 n.miles (25,928 km) at 20 knots

Manning:	30 civilian + 75 Navy technicians
Helicopters:	no facilities
Radars:	Raytheon TM 1650/6X navigation
	Raytheon TM 1660/12S navigation

This ship is a former merchant ship, acquired by the Navy on 9 July 1976 for conversion to a surveying ship to replace the MICHELSON (T-AGS 23). She is operated by MSC for the Oceanographer of the Navy.

Classification: Classified as an AGS and renamed on 1 November 1976.

Conversion: Converted to a surveying ship from March 1977 to January 1978 by National Steel and Shipbuilding, San Diego, Calif.

Names: Merchant name was CANADA MAIL.

The Navy's largest surveying ship is the H.H. HESS, here visiting Southampton, England. The HESS was built to a modern break-bulk cargo design with seven king posts retained in the T-AGS role. (1986, L. Van Ginderen Collection)

4 SURVEYING SHIPS: "SILAS BENT" CLASS

Number	Name	FY	Launched	In service	Status
T-AGS 26	SILAS BENT	63	16 May 1964	23 July 1965	**MSC-PA**
T-AGS 27	KANE	64	20 Nov 1965	19 May 1967	**MSC-AA**
T-AGS 33	WILKES	67	31 July 1969	28 June 1971	**MSC-AA**
T-AGS 34	WYMAN	67	30 Oct 1969	3 Nov 1971	**MSC-AA**

Builders:	T-AGS 26 American Shipbuilding, Lorain, Ohio
	T-AGS 27 Christy Corp., Sturgeon Bay, Wisc.
	T-AGS 33, 34 Defoe Shipbuilding, Bay City, Mich.
Displacement:	1,790 to 1,935 tons light
	T-AGS 26, 27 2,558 tons full load
	T-AGS 33 2,540 tons full load
	T-AGS 34 2,420 tons full load
Length:	265 feet (80.8 m) waterline
	285⅓ feet (87.0 m) overall
Beam:	48 feet (14.6 m)
Draft:	15 feet (4.6 m)
Propulsion:	diesel-electric (2 Alco diesel engines; Westinghouse or General Electric motors); 3,600 shp; 1 shaft
Speed:	14 knots
Range:	5,800–6,300 n.miles (10,742–11,668 km) at 14 knots
	8,000 n.miles (14,816 km) at 13 knots
Manning:	50 civilian + 26 scientists except
	41 civilian + 20 scientists in T-AGS 34
Helicopters:	no facilities
Radars:	Raytheon TM 1650/9X navigation
	Raytheon TM 1660/12S
Sonars:	BQN-17 BOTOSS in T-AGS 34

These ships were designed specifically for surveying operations. They differ in detail. All four ships are operated by MSC. Some support the Navy's SOSUS program.

Design: The first two ships are SCB No. 226; the WILKES is No. 725 in the new series and WYMAN No. 728.

Electronics: WYMAN fitted with SQN-17 bottom survey system.

Engineering: These ships have 350-hp bow propulsion units for precise maneuvering and station keeping.

The WYMAN and the other ships of the SILAS BENT class bear a superficial resemblance to the smaller CONRAD-class AGORs. (1991, Giorgio Arra)

The KANE showing some of the wear-and-tear of an oceanographic research cruise. The ship's sides differ from port to starboard, the latter being more open for handling research gear over the side. (1988, Giorgio Arra)

The SILAS BENT showing the crane and other lifting gear fitted aft. (1991, Giorgio Arra)

2 SURVEYING SHIPS: "CHAUVENET" CLASS

Number	Name	FY	Launched	In service	Status
T-AGS 29	CHAUVENET	65	13 May 1968	13 Nov 1970	**MSC-PA**
T-AGS 32	HARKNESS	66	12 June 1968	29 Jan 1971	**MSC-PA**

Builders:	Upper Clyde Shipbuilders, Glasgow (Scotland)
Displacement:	3,540 tons standard
	4,830 tons full load
Tonnage:	2,890 GRT
	1,030 DWT
Length:	333¹¹/₁₂ feet (101.8 m) waterline
	393⅙ feet (119.9 m) overall
Beam:	54 feet (16.5 m)
Draft:	16 feet (4.9 m)
Propulsion:	diesel-electric (2 Alco diesel engines; Westinghouse electric motors); 3,600 shp; 1 shaft
Speed:	15 knots

Range:	12,000 n.miles (22,224 km) at 15 knots
Manning:	69 civilian + 12 scientists + 74 Navy
Helicopters:	2 HH-2D Seasprite
Radars:	2 navigation

The CHAUVENET and HARKNESS were built specifically for the research role by the U.S. Navy. Both ships are operated by MSC. The Navy personnel include a 19-person helicopter detachment.

Builders: These ships and the EDENTON (ATS 1)-class salvage and rescue ships were the first ships to be constructed since World War II in British yards for the U.S. Navy. Subsequently, the Navy has acquired three British-built combat store ships (T-AFS).

Design: SCB No. 723. This is the only AGOR/AGS class with a full helicopter support capability. The hangar is 45½ feet (13.9 m) long and 12 feet (3.65 m) wide.

The HARKNESS (shown here) and the CHAUVENET are large ships, capable of conducting extensive hydrographic surveys and preparing charts on board. There are helicopter facilities—the only AGS/AGOR-type ships that operate helicopters—and davits for several survey launches. (1983, Giorgio Arra)

The HARKNESS with both helicopter hangars open. UH-2D Seasprites can be embarked to assist survey operations. (1983, Giorgio Arra)

SURVEYING SHIPS: VICTORY TYPE (VC2-S-AP3)

All three former Victory-type merchant ships, acquired by the Navy in 1957 and converted for seafloor charting and magnetic surveys to support the Navy's SSBN programs, have been stricken.

The BOWDITCH (T-AGS 21) was stricken on 26 May 1987 and transferred to the Maritime Administration. The ship had been heavily damaged during a hurricane while anchored in Rio de Janeiro, Brazil, in January 1987, being rammed by two ships that broke loose from their moorings during the storm.

The DUTTON (T-AGS 22) was transferred to MarAd on 25 October 1989 pending disposal; stricken on 14 February 1990.

The MICHELSON (T-AGS 23) was stricken on 15 April 1975.

See 14th Edition/page 277 for characteristics.

TABLE 23-2. POST–WORLD WAR II SURVEYING SHIPS

Number	Name	AGS Comm.	Notes (MarAd type)
AGS 15	TANNER	1946	ex-AKA 34 (S4-SE2-BE1)
AGS 16	MAURY	1946	ex-AKA 36 (S4-SE2-BE1)
AGS 17	PURSUIT	1950	ex-MSF 108
AGS 18	REQUISITE	1950	ex-MSF 109
AGS 19	SHELDRAKE	1952	ex-AM 62
AGS 20	PREVAIL	1952	ex-MSF 107
AGS 21	BOWDITCH	1958	(VC2-S-AP3)
AGS 22	DUTTON	1958	(VC2-S-AP3)
AGS 23	MICHELSON	1958	(VC2-S-AP3)
AGS 24	SERRANO	1960	ex-ATF 112
AGS 25	KELLAR	1968	to Portugal 1972
AGS 26, 27	SILAS BENT class		
AGS 28	TOWHEE	1964	ex-MSF 388
AGS 29	CHAUVENET	1970	
AGS 30	SAN PABLO	1948	ex-AVP 30
AGS 31	S.P. LEE	1968	to AG 192 (see above)
AGS 32	HARKNESS	1971	
AGS 33, 34	SILAS BENT class		
AGS 35	SGT. GEORGE D. KEATHLEY	1967	ex-APc 117 (C1-M-AV1)
AGS 36	COASTAL CRUSADER	1969	ex-AGM 16
AGS 37	TWIN FALLS	1964	ex-AGM 11 (VC2-S-AP3)
AGS 38	H.H. HESS	1976	(C4-SA)
AGS 39	MAURY	1989	
AGS 40	TANNER	1990	
AGS 41–44	not used		
AGS 45	WATERS	1993	
AGS 46–49	not used		
AGS 50	REHOBOTH	1948	ex-AVP 50
AGS 51	JOHN MCDONNELL	1992	
AGS 52	LITTLEHALES	1992	
AGS 53–59	not used		
AGS 60–62	PATHFINDER class		

World War II–era surveying ships reached AGS 14. The designations AGSc 11–14 were used for coastal surveying ships (assigned in same series as AGS). The SAN PABLO and REHOBOTH retained their AVP numbers as surveying ships, throwing the AGS numbering scheme out of sequence and causing later confusion with hull number assignment.

HOSPITAL SHIPS

During the early 1980s the Department of Defense decided to provide two hospital ships to support the deployment of U.S. forces overseas in conventional combat operations. Several alternatives were considered, both merchant ship conversions and new construction.

The proposed conversion included converting the super liner UNITED STATES, laid up since her final transatlantic voyage in November 1969. The 990-foot (301.8-m) liner, completed in 1952, carried up to 2,000 passengers and was designed from the outset for conversion to a transport for 14,000 troops. As an AH she would have had 2,000 to 2,500 beds. The UNITED STATES averaged 35.59 knots on her maiden transatlantic voyage, and reached 38.32 knots on her sea trials—the fastest merchant ship ever built.

2 HOSPITAL SHIPS: CONVERTED TANKERS (T8-S-100b)

Number	Name	Launched	In service	Status
T-AH 19	MERCY*	1976	15 Dec 1986	MSC-RRF-P
T-AH 20	COMFORT*	1976	1 Dec 1987	MSC-RRF-A

Builders:	National Steel and Shipbuilding, San Diego, Calif.
Displacement:	24,752 tons light
	69,360 tons full load
Length:	854⅝ feet (260.6 m) waterline
	894 feet (272.6 m) overall
Beam:	105¾ feet (32.25 m)
Draft:	32⅝ feet (10.0 m)
Propulsion:	1 steam turbine (General Electric); 24,500 shp; 1 shaft
Boilers:	2
Speed:	17.5 knots
Range:	13,400 n.miles (24,817 km) at 17.5 knots
Manning:	approx. 68 civilian + 1,191 Navy (see notes)
Patients:	1,000 beds (see notes)
Helicopters:	landing area
Radars:	navigation
	SPS-67 surface search

These ships are former commercial tankers that have been fully converted to support the Rapid Deployment Joint Task Force. They are the first ships of the type in U.S. service since the SANCTUARY was decommissioned in March 1974; at that time the SANCTUARY was serving as a naval dependents support ship. The COMFORT was placed in service for Desert Shield/Desert Storm on 14 August 1990 and the MERCY on 15 August 1990; they were subsequently returned to RRF status in 1992.

The ships are intended to be based at U.S. ports; in crisis or wartime they would be assigned medical staffs from military hospitals and go to sea with five days' notice as part of the MSC Ready Reserve Force (RRF). The MERCY is based at Oakland, Calif., and the COMFORT at Baltimore, Md.

Their cadre medical crew consists of 5 officers and 28 enlisted personnel.

Conversion: Both ships were converted at the National Steel and Shipbuilding yard in San Diego; the T-AH 19 conversion was authorized in fiscal 1983 (begun July 1984) and the T-AH 20 in fiscal 1984 (begun April 1985).

As hospital ships they have 12 operating rooms, four X-ray rooms, and an 80-bed intensive-care facility, with a bed-care casualty capacity of about 1,000 patients; up to 1,000 additional patients can be accommodated for limited care. The ships are intended to handle a peak admission rate of 300 patients in 24 hours with surgery required by 60 percent of the admissions and an average patient stay of five days.

The ships are designed to take aboard casualties primarily by helicopter; there is a limited capability to take on casualties from boats on the port side.

There are facilities for preparing 7,500 meals daily and distilling 75,000 gallons (285,000 liters) of fresh water daily.

Manning: The planned Navy manning for these ships when activated is:

Medical Corps officers	60
Dental Corps officers	6
Medical Service Corps officers	22
Nurse Corps officers	183
Non-medical officers	16
Hospital/enlisted	674
Hospital/dental enlisted	16
Non-hospital/dental enlisted	214
Total	1,191

Operational: The MERCY operated in the Philippines as a hospital facility from March to June 1987. She was staffed with 375 medical personnel from all of the U.S. military services as well as from civilian organizations. The ship treated almost 63,000 patients during the three-month period.

Both ships were activated in August 1990 in response to the Kuwaiti crisis. They departed their respective home ports on 13 August; the COMFORT arrived in the Persian Gulf on 8 September and the MERCY on 14 September. They were manned by some 450 medical personnel who were assigned from the naval hospitals at Oakland, Calif., and Bethesda, Md.; they were subsequently augmented by about 700 additional personnel from the hospitals who were flown to the Middle East to rendezvous with the ships. Both ships were in the Persian Gulf during Operations Desert Shield/Desert Storm.

Names: The merchant names of the ships were WORTH and ROSE CITY, respectively.

HOSPITAL SHIPS: "HAVEN" CLASS

The last surviving hospital ship of the World War II–built HAVEN class, the SANCTUARY (AH 17), was stricken from the NVR on 16 February 1989; she was transferred to Life International on 18 September 1989 for use as a civilian hospital facility in Africa.

In 1980 the SANCTUARY was considered for reactivation to support the prepositioning of U.S. military equipment in the Indian Ocean. Instead, the decision was made to acquire and convert two merchant ships.

See 14th Edition/page 278 for characteristics.

Coalition allies in the Persian Gulf: The hospital ship COMFORT and the Australian replenishment oiler SUCCESS during an UNREP operation. Two Australian Navy surgical teams and one Army officer joined the COMFORT during the Gulf campaign. (1991, Royal Australian Navy)

The MERCY showing her numerous life boats and large helicopter landing deck; helicopters are the principal method of accepting casualties. Both of the massive ships served in Desert Shield/Desert Storm, although Coalition casualties were very light. (1986, National Steel and Shipbuilding)

FBM SUPPLY SHIPS

These ships transported missiles, spare parts, provisions, and other equipment to forward-deployed FBM tenders at Holy Loch, Scotland; Rota, Spain; and Guam when those bases were active.

1 FBM SUPPLY SHIP: CONVERTED MORMAC CARGO SHIP (C3-S-33a)

Number	Name	Launched	In service	Status
T-AK 286	VEGA	May 1960	4 Mar 1983	**MSC-AA**

Builders:	Sun Shipbuilding and Dry Dock, Chester, Pa.
Displacement:	16,363 tons full load
Length:	457⅝ feet (139.6 m) waterline
	485¹¹⁄₁₂ feet (148.15 m) overall
Beam:	68 feet (20.7 m)
Draft:	28½ feet (8.7 m)
Propulsion:	1 steam turbine (General Electric); 11,000 shp; 1 shaft
Boilers:	2 600 psi (41.7 kg/cm²) (Combustion Engineering)
Speed:	19 knots
Range:	14,000 n.miles (25,928 km) at 18 knots
Manning:	68 civilian + 7 Navy
Helicopters:	no facilities
Radars:	Raytheon TM 1650/6X
	Raytheon TM 1660/12S

The VEGA was a commercial cargo ship built for Moore-McCormack Lines; after merchant service she was laid up in NDRF. She was acquired by the Navy in April 1981 for conversion to an FBM/SSBN supply ship to replace the VICTORIA (T-AK 281). Two other ships of this class were acquired as cargo ships (see chapter 24), and two additional ships were acquired for conversion to surveying ships (T-AGS 39 and T-AGS 40), but the Congress directed new construction ships for the latter role.

The naval personnel are a security detachment.

Conversion: The VEGA was converted to transport 16 Trident missiles and other submarine stores and supplies from U.S. ports to forward-deployed submarine tenders; fitted with eight 10-ton-capacity booms, four 5-ton booms, and one 75-ton boom. The missiles are stowed vertically in the No. 3 hold. She was converted at Boland Marine and Manufacturing, New Orleans, La., from May 1982 to March 1983. She was placed on the NVR on 15 October 1981.

Names: The VEGA's merchant name was MORMACBAY. She was to have been named KING'S BAY in naval service.

The VEGA is one of the two cargo ships modified to support FBM submarine tenders that are still in service. Their fate is uncertain as all SSBN operations are being concentrated at two continental bases, Kings Bay, Ga., and Bangor, Wash. The VEGA's No. 3 hold—immediately forward of the bridge—is fitted to carry SLBMs. (1985, Giorgio Arra)

1 CABLE TRANSPORT SHIP / 1 FBM SUPPLY SHIP: VICTORY TYPE (VC2-S-AP3)

Number	Name	Launched	In service	Status
T-AK 280	FURMAN	6 Mar 1945	18 Sep 1963	NDRF
T-AK 282	MARSHFIELD	15 May 1944	28 May 1970	**MSC-AA**

Builders:	Oregon Shipbuilding, Portland, Ore.
Displacement:	6,700 tons light
	11,150 tons full load
Tonnage:	7,491 GRT
	9,649 DWT
Length:	436½ feet (133.05 m) waterline
	455 feet (138.8 m) overall
Beam:	62 feet (18.9 m)
Draft:	24 feet (7.3 m)
Propulsion:	1 steam turbine (General Electric in T-AK 280, Westinghouse in T-AK 282); 8,500 shp; 1 shaft
Boilers:	2
Speed:	16.5 knots
Range:	20,000 n.miles (37,040 km) at 16.5 knots
Manning:	T-AK 280 35 civilian
	T-AK 282 70 civilian + 7 Navy
Helicopters:	no facilities
Guns:	none
Radars:	T-AK 282 Raytheon TM 1650/6X navigation
	Raytheon TM 1660/12S navigation

These are former merchant ships taken over by the Navy specifically for conversion into supply ships to support FBM/SSBN tenders. With the reduction in the Navy's SSBN force and overseas basing, the FURMAN was further modified in 1982–1983 at the Atlantic Dry Dock Corp., Fort George Island, Fla., to transport undersea cable. The ship was operated by MSC under the sponsorship of the Naval Space and Warfare Systems Command; she was temporarily laid up in the NDRF (Beaumont, Texas) from 22 October 1986 until October 1987.

Class: The NORWALK (T-AK 279) of this type was stricken on 1 Aug 1979 and the VICTORIA (T-AK 281) on 31 March 1986.

Three earlier converted Victory-type FBM supply ships have been stricken, the ALCOR (T-AK 259) in 1968, BETELGEUSE (T-AK 260) in 1974, and NORWALK (T-AK 279) in 1979.

Conversion: The ships were fitted to carry 16 Polaris and later Poseidon ballistic missiles plus 430,000 gallons (1,634,000 liters) of black oil (for tenders), 355,000 gallons (1,273,000 liters) of diesel fuel, bottled gases, dry and frozen provisions, packaged petroleum products, spare parts, and torpedoes. The No. 3 hold was configured for vertical storage of 16 missiles. Also fitted for carrying radioactive waste. Conversion was SCB No. 234.

Names: Former merchant names were T-AK 280 ex-FURMAN VICTORY and T-AK 282 ex-MARSHFIELD VICTORY.

Operational: The FURMAN supported the Polaris SSBN tender PROTEUS (AS 19) based at Guam; the other ships of this type operated in the Atlantic. With the withdrawal of the Polaris missile submarines from active service, the FURMAN was laid up in reserve in August 1981 and scheduled to be stricken on 30 September 1981. However, she was retained for use as a cable transport ship.

The MARSHFIELD also remained in service when this edition of *Ships and Aircraft* went to press. The SLBM missile storage tubes are forward of the bridge. These ships carry a variety of supplies and provisions for FBM submarine tenders. (1984, U.S. Navy)

The FURMAN has been converted to serve as a cable transport ship. Her heavy boom for lifting missiles does not have the same arrangement as that of her sistership MARSHFIELD. Also, the MARSHFIELD's superstructure has been enlarged. (1980, U.S. Navy)

OILERS

Oilers—sometimes referred to as fleet oilers—provide underway replenishment to naval forces. These ships differ from tankers, which provide point-to-point transfer of fuels, at times replenishing oilers at sea (see chapter 24).

The fleet oiler PASSUMPSIC refuels the carrier RANGER (CV 61) and the French destroyer LATOUCHE-TRÉVILLE in the Persian Gulf during Operation Desert Storm. Oilers and the AOE/AOR replenishment ships fuel warships in forward areas; tankers (T-AOT), in turn, restock the UNREP ships. (1991, U.S. Navy, PH3 Russell Bos)

13 + 5 FLEET OILERS: "HENRY J. KAISER" CLASS

Number	Name	FY	Launched	In service	Status
T-AO 187	HENRY J. KAISER	82	5 Oct 1985	19 Dec 1986	**MSC-AA**
T-AO 188	JOSHUA HUMPHREYS	83	22 Feb 1986	3 Apr 1987	**MSC-AA**
T-AO 189	JOHN LENTHALL, JR.	84	9 Aug 1986	25 June 1987	**MSC-AA**
T-AO 190	ANDREW J. HIGGINS	84	17 Jan 1987	22 Oct 1987	**MSC-PA**
T-AO 191	BENJAMIN ISHERWOOD	85	15 Aug 1988	7 Dec 1991	**MSC-PA**
T-AO 192	HENRY ECKFORD	85	14 Aug 1989	1992	**MSC**
T-AO 193	WALTER S. DIEHL	85	10 Oct 1987	13 Sep 1988	**MSC-PA**
T-AO 194	JOHN ERICSSON	86	21 Apr 1990	19 Mar 1991	**MSC-PA**
T-AO 195	LEROY GRUMMAN	86	3 Dec 1988	2 Aug 1989	**MSC-AA**
T-AO 196	KANAWHA	87	22 Sep 1990	10 Dec 1991	**MSC-AA**
T-AO 197	PECOS	87	23 Sep 1989	13 July 1990	**MSC-PA**
T-AO 198	BIG HORN	88	2 Feb 1991	1992	**MSC-AA**
T-AO 199	TIPPECANOE	88	16 May 1992	1993	Building
T-AO 200	GUADALUPE	89	5 Oct 1991	1992	**MSC-PA**
T-AO 201	PATUXENT	89	1992	1993	Building
T-AO 202	YUKON	89	1992	1993	Building
T-AO 203	LARAMIE	89	1993	1994	Building
T-AO 204	RAPPAHANNOCK	89	1993	1994	Building

Builders:	Avondale Shipyards, New Orleans, La., except T-AO 191 and 192 by Tampa Shipbuilding, Fla.
Displacement:	9,500 tons light
	40,700 tons full load
Tonnage:	26,500 DWT
Length:	649¾ feet (198.1 m) waterline
	677½ feet (206.6 m) overall
Beam:	97½ feet (29.7 m)
Draft:	36 feet (11.0 m)
Propulsion:	2 diesel engines (Colt-Pielstick 10PC4.2V); 32,540 bhp; 2 shafts
Speed:	20 knots
Range:	6,000 n.miles (11,112 km) at 20 knots
Manning:	95 civilian + 21 Navy
Helicopters:	landing area
Guns:	none (see notes)
Radars:	2 navigation
EW systems:	(see notes)

These fleet oilers are being built to civilian specifications. Although civilian manned, they operate regularly with forward-deployed battle groups. By the mid-1990s these ships will provide the majority of the Navy's fleet oiler strength.

The lead ship was laid down on 22 August 1984.

Builders: Contracts for the construction of T-AO 191, 192, 194, and 196 were awarded to the Pennsylvania Shipbuilding Co. in 1985–1986; those contracts were cancelled on 31 August 1989 for default. The first two ships were towed to the Philadelphia Naval Shipyard in October 1989, and subsequently the ships were transferred to the Tampa shipyard for completion; they were reordered on 16 November 1989. The two later ships, for which assembly had not yet begun, were awarded to Avondale for construction.

Design: These are mid-size petroleum carriers with a 180,000-barrel cargo capacity; in addition, they can carry 25,000 gallons (95,000 liters) of lubrication oil as bulk cargo plus 105,000 gallons (399,000 liters) of potable water and 88,000 gallons (334,400 liters) of boiler feed water.

The ships have a limited UNREP capacity for dry stores as well as fuels with a tunnel for fork-lift trucks running through the superstructure to permit cargo to be carried aft to the helicopter deck. Crew requirements have been increased by about ten from the early designs with space also provided for another ten transient personnel.

Electronics: Space and weight are reserved for the SLQ-25 Nixie torpedo countermeasures. However, no SLQ-32 installation is planned (compare with AOE/AOR systems).

Guns: There are provisions to mount 20-mm Phalanx CIWS on the bow and after superstructure in wartime.

The JOHN ERICSSON and other ships of this class have a large helicopter deck aft, but no oilers have helicopter hangars or support facilities. Note the refueling hoses on the five alongside refueling stations; there are also two solid-store transfer stations. (1991, Avondale Shipyards)

The LEROY GRUMMAN is typical of the new, mid-size fleet oilers that carry dry stores as well as ship and aviation fuels. The GRUMMAN has the forward fore-castle sides plated in; they are open on earlier ships (forward area with open ports). (1989, U.S. Navy)

5 FLEET OILERS: "CIMARRON" CLASS

Number	Name	FY	Launched	Commissioned	Status
AO 177	CIMARRON	76	28 Apr 1979	10 Jan 1981	**PA**
AO 178	MONONGAHELA	76	4 Aug 1979	5 Sep 1981	**AA**
AO 179	MERRIMACK	77	17 May 1980	14 Nov 1981	**AA**
AO 180	WILLAMETTE	78	18 July 1982	18 Dec 1982	**PA**
AO 186	PLATTE	78	30 Jan 1982	5 Feb 1983	**AA**

Builders:	Avondale Shipyards, New Orleans, La.
Displacement:	37,866 tons full load
Length:	708⅓ feet (215.95 m) overall
Beam:	83 feet (25.3 m)
Draft:	33⅓ (10.2 m)
Propulsion:	1 steam turbine; 24,000 shp; 1 shaft
Boilers:	2 600 psi (41.7 kg/cm²) (Combustion Engineering)
Speed:	19.4 knots
Range:	
Manning:	approx. 226 (16 officers + 210 enlisted)
Helicopters:	landing area
Guns:	2 20-mm Phalanx CIWS Mk 16 (2 multi-barrel)
Radars:	LN-66 navigation
	SPS-55 surface search
EW systems:	SLQ-25 Nixie
	SLQ-32(V)1

These fleet oilers are designed to provide two complete refuelings to a conventional aircraft carrier and six to eight accompanying escort ships. All five ships have been lengthened or "jumboized."

These are the only "straight" oilers (AO) that are Navy manned.

Classification: The AO hull numbers 182–185 were assigned to the Falcon-class transport tankers (T-AOT) and the USNS PO-TOMAC is T-AOT 181; see chapter 24.

Conversion: All five ships have undergone a "jumbo" conversion to increase their cargo capacity to 183,000 barrels of petroleum products (from 72,000) and to fit self-defense CIWS guns and EW systems. The ships were lengthened by 117 feet (35.7 m), with a reduction in speed of 0.6 knots. The conversions were carried out at Avondale Industries.

The conversions were:

AO 177	June 1990 to Mar 1992
AO 178	Jan 1990 to Oct 1991
AO 179	Mar 1989 to Dec 1990
AO 180	Oct 1989 to May 1991
AO 181	Nov 1990 to Sep 1992
AO 186	Nov 1990 to Oct 1992

See 14th Edition/pages 295–296 for previous characteristics.

Design: SCB No. 739. The ships have an elliptical underwater bow for improved seakeeping. A Vertical Replenishment (VERTREP) platform is provided aft, but no helicopter hangar or support facilities is installed.

Manning: Original Navy manning was to be approximately 135; it was increased to provide improved maintenance self-sufficiency for prolonged deployments.

The PLATTE and her sister ships of the CIMARRON class are the only Navy-manned fleet oilers; all others are civilian-manned MSC ships. These ships have a Phalanx CIWS and EW systems to provide a minimal defense when operating in forward areas. (1989, Giorgio Arra)

The PLATTE has similar lines to the HENRY J. KAISER class, but the later ships are significantly larger and have a greater payload. The large bridge wings are vital for alongside UNREP operations. (1989, Giorgio Arra)

6 FLEET OILERS: "NEOSHO" CLASS

Number	Name	FY	Launched	Commissioned	Status
T-AO 143	Neosho	52	10 Nov 1953	24 Sep 1954	NDRF
T-AO 144	Mississinewa	52	12 June 1954	18 Jan 1955	NDRF
T-AO 145	Hassayampa	52	12 Sep 1954	19 Apr 1955	NDRF
T-AO 146	Kawishiwi	52	11 Dec 1954	6 July 1955	NDRF
T-AO 147	Truckee	52	10 Mar 1955	23 Nov 1955	NDRF
T-AO 148	Ponchatoula	52	9 July 1955	12 Jan 1956	NDRF

Builders:	T-AO 143 Bethlehem Steel, Quincy, Mass.
	T-AO 144–148 New York Shipbuilding, Camden, N.J.
Displacement:	11,750 tons light
	36,840 tons full load
Length:	639⅝ feet (195.1 m) waterline
	655⅔ feet (200.0 m) overall
Beam:	86 feet (26.2 m)
Draft:	35 feet (10.7 m)
Propulsion:	2 steam turbines (General Electric); 28,000 shp; 2 shafts
Boilers:	2 600 psi (41.7 kg/cm²) (Babcock & Wilcox)
Speed:	20 knots
Range:	34,000 n.miles (62,968 km) at 12 knots
	14,000 n.miles (25,928 km) at 19 knots
Manning:	approx. 125 civilian + approx. 23 Navy (1 officer + 22 enlisted)
Helicopters:	landing area in T-AO 143, 144, 147
	VERTREP area in T-AO 145, 146
	no facilities in T-AO 148
Guns:	removed
Radars:	Raytheon TM 1650/6X or 12X navigation
	SPS-10 surface search

These were the first fleet oilers built for the U.S. Navy after World War II. All were originally active Navy-manned ships; AO 144 transferred to MSC for civilian manning on 15 November 1976; AO 143 on 25 May 1978; AO 145 on 17 November 1978; AO 146 and 147 on 30 January 1980; and AO 148 on 5 September 1980.

T-AO 145 laid up on 2 October 1991; T-AO 147 on 21 October 1991; T-AO 144 on 30 July 1991; T-AO 148 on 1 April 1992; T-AO 143 on 9 June 1992; T-AO 146 on 31 July 1992.

Design: SCB No. 82. Cargo capacity is approximately 180,000 barrels of petroleum products. Limited flag accommodations were provided for the ships to serve as flagships for service squadrons. Three ships have had a helicopter platform fitted aft; the after superstructure has been extended forward and the T-AO 143 has a deck structure forward.

Guns: As built, these ships mounted two 5-inch/38-cal DP guns in single mounts plus 12 3-inch/50-cal AA guns in twin mounts. The former were removed in the late 1960s and the latter subsequently reduced until most had only four guns (two mounts) installed when transferred to MSC and disarmed. When Navy-manned and fully armed their complement was approximately 360.

5 FLEET OILERS: "MISPILLION" CLASS (T3-S2-A3)

Number	Name	Launched	Commissioned	Status
T-AO 105	Mispillion	10 Aug 1945	29 Dec 1945	NDRF
T-AO 106	Navasota	30 Aug 1945	27 Feb 1946	NDRF
T-AO 107	Passumpsic	31 Oct 1945	1 Apr 1946	NDRF
T-AO 108	Pawcatuck	19 Feb 1945	10 May 1946	NDRF
T-AO 109	Waccamaw	30 Mar 1946	25 June 1946	NDRF

Builders:	Sun Shipbuilding and Dry Dock, Chester, Pa.
Displacement:	9,486 tons light
	35,090 tons full load
Tonnage:	19,294 GRT
	23,250 DWT
Length:	646 feet (197.0 m) overall
Beam:	75 feet (22.9 m)
Draft:	35½ feet (10.8 m)
Propulsion:	2 steam turbines (Westinghouse); 13,500 shp; 2 shafts
Boilers:	4 450 psi (31.3 kg/cm²) (Babcock & Wilcox)
Speed:	16 knots
Range:	
Manning:	approx. 110 civilian + approx. 21 Navy (1 officer + 20 enlisted) in some ships
Helicopters:	landing area (forward)
Guns:	removed
Radars:	Raytheon TM 1650/6X navigation
	SPS-10 surface search

These ships were built during World War II as Navy fleet oilers. They were enlarged under the "jumbo" process in the mid-1960s to increase their cargo capacity, forming a new five-ship class. The ships were transferred from the active Navy to MSC civilian manning: AO 105 on 26 July 1973; AO 106 on 13 August 1975; AO 107 on 24 July 1975; AO 108 on 15 July 1975; and AO 109 on 24 February 1975.

The T-AO 109 transferred to the Maritime Administration for layup on 22 October 1989; T-AO 105 on 9 February 1990; and T-AO 106 on 19 November 1991; T-AO 107 on 18 December 1991; and T-AO 108 on 19 September 1991.

Design: They were "jumboized" in the mid-1960s with the addition of a 93-foot (28.35 m) midsection, increasing their cargo capacity to approximately 150,000 barrels (from 142,500). A helicopter landing area is located forward, but it is used primarily for vertical replenishment. No hangar is provided.

Guns: These ships had a designed armament of one 5-inch/38-cal DP gun, four 3-inch/50-cal AA guns, and eight 40-mm AA guns. This armament was successively reduced until only four 3-inch single mounts remained when the ships were transferred to MSC operation and completely disarmed.

The Truckee was one of the first class of fleet oilers built by the Navy after World War II. All six ships have been retired after three decades of naval service. As built, they had a heavy armament of 5-inch/38-cal DP and 3-inch/50-cal AA guns. (1988, Giorgio Arra)

The PAWCATUCK was one of two of the MISPILLION-class oilers still in active service when this edition of *Ships and Aircraft* went to press. These ''jumboized'' T2s are the oldest oilers in U.S. naval service. Some ships had the king post forward of the bridge removed. (1990, Giorgio Arra)

The PAWCATUCK and other ships of this design have a helicopter landing area forward, retaining their conventional T2 tanker configuration aft; the navigation bridge is amidships. (1989, Giorgio Arra)

3 FLEET OILERS: "ASHTABULA" CLASS (T3-S2-A1)

Number	Name	Launched	Commissioned	Status
AO 51	ASHTABULA	22 May 1943	7 Aug 1943	NDRF
AO 98	CALOOSAHATCHEE	2 June 1945	10 Oct 1945	AR
AO 99	CANISTEO	6 July 1945	3 Dec 1945	NDRF

Builders:	Bethlehem Steel, Sparrows Point, Md.
Displacement:	9,769 tons light
	36,500 tons full load
Length:	644 feet (196.4 m) overall
Beam:	75 feet (22.9 m)
Draft:	31½ feet (9.6 m)
Propulsion:	1 steam turbine (Bethlehem); 13,500 shp; 2 shafts
Boilers:	4 450 psi (31.28 kg/cm²) (Foster-Wheeler)
Speed:	18 knots
Range:	16,000 n.miles (29,632 km) at 11 knots
Manning:	approx. 370 (20 officers + 350 enlisted)

Helicopters:	VERTREP area
Guns:	2 3-inch (76-mm) 50-cal AA Mk 26 (2 single)
Radars:	Raytheon TM 1650/6X navigation
	SPS-10 surface search

These oilers were built for naval service; they were "jumboized" to increase their cargo capacity. The ASHTABULA was Navy-manned until decommissioned on 30 September 1982 and laid up in the National Defense Reserve Fleet; the Navy-manned CALOOSA-HATCHEE was decommissioned on 28 February 1990; and the CANISTEO was transferred to MarAd for layup on 5 November 1990.

Conversion: These three ships were converted in the mid-1960s under the "jumbo" program (SCB No. 224); an additional 91-foot (27.7-m) midsection was installed, increasing their cargo capacity to approximately 143,000 barrels along with a limited capacity for stores and munitions. A small VERTREP area is provided forward.

Guns: See the MISPILLION class for data on original armament.

The CANISTEO and her two "jumboized" T3 sister oilers could be distinguished from the MISPILLION T2s by their having two king posts forward of the bridge. There is a small VERTREP area forward. (1986, Giorgio Arra)

2 FLEET OILERS: "CIMARRON" CLASS (T3-S2-A1)

Number	Name	Launched	Commissioned	Status
T-AO 57	MARIAS	21 Dec 1943	12 Feb 1944	NDRF
T-AO 62	TALUGA	10 July 1944	25 Aug 1944	NDRF

Builders:	Bethlehem Steel, Sparrows Point, Md.
Displacement:	7,470 tons light
	24,450 tons full load
Tonnage:	12,000 GRT
	18,400 DWT
Length:	525 feet (160.0 m) waterline
	553 feet (168.6 m) overall
Beam:	75 feet (22.9 m)
Draft:	33⅛ feet (10.1 m)
Propulsion:	2 steam turbines (Bethlehem); 13,500 shp; 2 shafts
Boilers:	4 450 psi (31.28 kg/cm²) (Foster-Wheeler)
Speed:	18 knots
Range:	14,000 n.miles (25,928 km) at 13 knots
	10,000 n.miles (18,520 km) at 18 knots
Manning:	105 civilian + 16 Navy
Helicopters:	VERTREP area

Guns:	removed
Radars:	Raytheon TM 1650/9X navigation
	SPS-10 surface search

These ships are the survivors of a large number of twin-screw fleet oilers built during World War II. Ships of this design that have been enlarged under the "jumbo" process are listed separately.

The TALUGA was transferred from active naval service to MSC on 4 May 1972 and the MARIAS on 2 October 1973. The MARIAS was laid up on 15 August 1982 and the TALUGA on 29 August 1983; they were transferred to MarAd for layup in the NDRF on 29 November 1982 and 22 November 1983, respectively.

Class: The lead ship for this design was the CIMARRON (AO 22), the first Maritime Commission tanker acquired by the Navy (upon completion in 1939). Four ships of this class were converted to escort aircraft carriers (CVE 26–29); this basic design served as the basis for later war-built oilers and the COMMENCEMENT BAY (CVE 105) class of carriers.

Design: Cargo capacity is approximately 115,000 barrels of petroleum products. A VERTREP platform is fitted forward.

Guns: See MISPILLION class for notes on original armament.

The MARIAS was typical of the large number of T2 and T3 oilers built during World War II for military service. (Giorgio Arra)

FAST COMBAT SUPPORT SHIPS: IMPROVED DESIGN

These ships are intended to operate as part of fast carrier battle groups, providing petroleum products, munitions, and other supplies to aircraft carriers and their screening surface combatants.

An improved multi-product store ship—tentatively designated AOE(V)—was being designed as a follow-on to the SUPPLY class. The later ship was to be slightly larger, with enhanced munitions carrying capacity. The design effort was cancelled in 1991. Sixteen AOE(V)s were provided in preliminary planning for the class, with the first unit to be requested in the fiscal 1993 budget, to be completed in 1997. These ships were to replace the ammunition ships (AE) of the NITRO and SURIBACHI classes, and, subsequently, the combat store ships (AFS) of the MARS and LYNESS classes.

(4) FAST COMBAT SUPPORT SHIPS: "SUPPLY" CLASS

Number	Name	FY	Launched	Commission	Status
AOE 6	SUPPLY	87	6 Oct 1990	1993	Building
AOE 7	RAINIER	89	28 Sep 1991	1993	Building
AOE 8	ARCTIC	90	1993	1994	Building
AOE 9	. . . . . .	92		1997	Authorized

Builders:	National Steel, San Diego, Calif.
Displacement:	19,700 tons light
	48,800 tons full load
Length:	754¾ feet (230.1 m) overall
Beam:	107 feet (32.6 m)
Draft:	39 feet (11.9 m)
Propulsion:	4 gas turbines (General Electric LM 2500); 100,000 shp; 2 shafts
Speed:	26 knots
Range:	
Manning:	approx. 660 (35 officers + 625 enlisted)
Helicopters:	3 UH-46 Sea Knight
Missiles:	1 8-tube NATO Sea Sparrow launcher Mk 29
Guns:	2 20-mm Phalanx CIWS Mk 16 (2 multi-barrel)
	2 25-mm cannon Mk 88 (2 single)
Radars:	SPS-64(V)9 navigation
	SPS-67 surface search
Fire control:	1 Mk 25 TAS
	2 Mk 91 missile FCS
EW systems:	SLQ-32(V)3

These are large, multi-product replenishment ships. They are based on the SACRAMENTO design, the principal difference in the two classes being in their propulsion plants. The lead ship, the SUPPLY, was laid down on 24 February 1989.

The first three ships have suffered major delays, caused mainly by delays in delivery of reduction gears, a major propulsion system component. The original and early 1992 estimated ship delivery dates are:

The lead ship of a new series of AOEs, the SUPPLY slides down the building ways at National Steel & Shipbuilding Co. in San Diego. These ships have large bow "bulbs" to enhance seakeeping; they have a "bulky" design, reflecting their configuration as floating storehouses and fuel dumps. (1990, National Steel)

	Original	*Current*
AOE 6	Apr 1991	Feb 1993
AOE 7	July 1992	Aug 1993
AOE 8	Aug 1993	June 1994

Related to these delays has been a major increase in cost. In August 1991 the Navy stated that the ships will cost 30 percent more than original estimates. When this edition went to press the Navy had not exercised its option for AOE 9, and it is unlikely that the ship will be procured in view of the cutback in carrier battle groups.

Cost: The AOE 9 is funded in the fiscal 1992 budget at $499.1 million.

The RAINIER as launched at San Diego. The principal difference between this class and the AOE 1–4 series will be their propulsion systems, with the later ships having an elongated after superstructure with tandem funnels. (1991, Kim Lee, National Steel)

Design: Cargo capacity is 156,000 barrels of petroleum products plus 1,800 tons of munitions, 400 tons of refrigerated provisions, and 250 tons of dry stores.

This is the second class of U.S. Navy ships to be built with the so-called Level III collective protection features against CBR attack, the first having been the ARLEIGH BURKE (DDG 51)-class destroy-

ers. Level III provides the maximum protection possible within a ship, including berthing, medical, and control spaces.

Names: The AOE 7 was originally named PAUL HAMILTON; changed while under construction, with the former name being assigned to the destroyer DDG 60.

4 FAST COMBAT SUPPORT SHIPS: "SACRAMENTO" CLASS

Number	Name	FY	Launched	Commissioned	Status
AOE 1	SACRAMENTO	61	14 Sep 1963	14 Mar 1964	**PA**
AOE 2	CAMDEN	63	29 May 1965	1 Apr 1967	**PA**
AOE 3	SEATTLE	65	2 Mar 1968	5 Apr 1969	**AA**
AOE 4	DETROIT	66	21 June 1969	28 Mar 1970	**AA**

Builders:	AOE 1, 3, 4 Puget Sound Naval Shipyard, Bremerton, Wash.
	AOE 2 New York Shipbuilding, Camden, N.J.
Displacement:	18,700 tons light
	53,600 tons full load
Length:	707⅝ feet (215.8 m) waterline
	794¾ feet (242.4 m) overall
Beam:	107 feet (32.6 m)
Draft:	38 feet (11.6 m)
Propulsion:	2 steam turbines (General Electric); 100,000 shp; 2 shafts
Boilers:	4 600 psi (41.7 kg/cm²) (Combustion Engineering)
Speed:	27.5 knots (26 knots sustained)
Range:	10,000 n.miles (18,520 km) at 17 knots
	6,000 n.miles (11,112 km) at 26 knots
Manning:	AOE 1 639 (35 officers + 604 enlisted)
	AOE 2 620 (28 officers + 592 enlisted)
	AOE 3 611 (26 officers + 585 enlisted)
	AOE 4 595 (20 officers + 575 enlisted)
Helicopters:	2 UH-46 Sea Knight
Missiles:	1 8-tube NATO Sea Sparrow launcher Mk 29
Guns:	2 20-mm Phalanx CIWS Mk 16 (2 multi-barrel)
	4 .50-cal machine guns (4 single)
Fire control:	1 Mk 91 missile FCS
	1 Mk 23 TAS in AOE 3
Radars:	SPS-10 surface search
	SPS-40 air search in AOE 1, 2
	SPS-53 surface search
EW systems:	SLQ-25 Nixie
	SLQ-32(V)3

These are the world's largest underway replenishment ships, designed to provide a carrier battle group with full fuels, munitions, dry and frozen provisions, and other supplies. (The largest foreign UNREP ship is the one-of-a-kind Russian BEREZINA, completed in 1977, which displaces some 40,000 tons full load.)

Class: The AOE 5 of this class was planned for the fiscal 1968 program but cancelled on 4 November 1968.

Design: SCB No. 196. These ships can carry 156,000 barrels of fuels, 2,100 tons of munitions, 250 tons of dry stores, and 250 tons of refrigerated stores. The ships have highly automated cargo-handling equipment.

A large helicopter deck is fitted aft with a three-bay hangar for VERTREP helicopters. Each bay is 47 to 52 feet (14.3 to 15.85 m) long, 17 to 19 feet (5.2 to 5.8 m) wide, and 18 to 18½ feet (5.5 to 5.6 m) high.

Electronics: The hull has provision for SQS-26 sonar, but it has not been installed. The earlier WLR-1 ECM systems have been replaced by SLQ-32 systems.

Engineering: The first two ships were provided with the machinery produced for the cancelled battleship KENTUCKY (BB 66).

Guns: As built, these ships were armed with eight 3-inch guns in twin mounts and associated Mk 56 GFCS. They were reduced in the mid-1970s and a NATO Sea Sparrow launcher was installed forward. The remaining 3-inch guns have been removed with two Phalanx CIWS being fitted to each ship.

The SACRAMENTO only superficially resembles a fleet oiler, with a larger hull form and heavy superstructure blocks. A NATO Sea Sparrow launcher is fitted forward, in place of two 3-inch/50-cal AA twin gun mounts that were originally provided. (1982, L. Van Ginderen Collection)

The DETROIT shows the twin hangars and landing deck for UH-46 Sea King helicopters employed in VERTREP operations. The two Phalanx CIWS are fitted outboard of the helicopter hangars. A major EW suite is provided. (1983, Giorgio Arra)

7 REPLENISHMENT OILERS: "WICHITA" CLASS

Number	Name	FY	Launched	Commissioned	Status
AOR 1	WICHITA	65	18 Mar 1968	7 June 1969	**PA**
AOR 2	MILWAUKEE	65	17 Jan 1969	1 Nov 1969	**AA**
AOR 3	KANSAS CITY	66	28 June 1969	6 June 1970	**PA**
AOR 4	SAVANNAH	66	25 Apr 1970	5 Dec 1970	**AA**
AOR 5	WABASH	67	6 Feb 1971	20 Nov 1971	**PA**
AOR 6	KALAMAZOO	67	11 Nov 1972	11 Aug 1973	**AA**
AOR 7	ROANOKE	72	7 Dec 1974	30 Oct 1976	**PA**

Builders:	AOR 1–6 General Dynamics, Quincy, Mass.
	AOR 7 National Steel and Shipbuilding, San Diego, Calif.
Displacement:	12,500 tons light, except AOR 7: 13,000 tons
	41,350 tons full load
Length:	659 feet (200.9 m) overall
Beam:	96 feet (29.3 m)
Draft:	33⅙ feet (10.1 m)
Propulsion:	2 steam turbines (General Electric); 32,000 shp; 2 shafts
Boilers:	3 600 psi (41.7 kg/cm²) (Foster Wheeler)
Speed:	20 knots
Range:	10,000 n.miles (18,520 km) at 17 knots
	6,500 n.miles (12,038 km) at 20 knots
Manning:	approx. 461 (26 officers + 435 enlisted)
Helicopters:	2 UH-46 Sea Knight
Missiles:	1 NATO Sea Sparrow launcher Mk 29 in AOR 2–7
Guns:	2 20-mm Phalanx CIWS Mk 16 (2 multi-barrel) in AOR 2–7
	2 20-mm cannon Mk 67 (2 single) in AOR 2
Fire control:	1 Mk 25 TAS in AOR 6
	2 Mk 91 missile FCS in AOR 2–7
Radars:	LN-66 or SPS-53 navigation
	SPS-10 surface search
EW systems:	SLQ-25 Nixie in AOR 4–6
	SLQ-32(V)3 in AOR 4–6

These are smaller variations of the AOE-type ships. The WICHITA and MILWAUKEE are scheduled to be decommissioned in 1993 and laid up.

Classification: The AOR classification was established in 1952 as fleet replenishment tanker to provide "one stop" fuel and munitions replenishment. The German war prize CONECUH, formerly the U-boat tender DITHMARSCHEN, previously designated IX 301 and then AO 110, was changed to AOR 110. The CONECUH was decommissioned in 1956 and stricken in 1960, with the designation AOR then being dropped. The WACCAMAW (AO 109) was to be similarly modified, but she remained a "straight" fleet oiler. The classification AOR was reestablished as replenishment oiler in 1964.

Design: SCB No. 707. These ships can carry 175,000 barrels of petroleum, 600 tons of munitions, 200 tons of dry stores, and 100 tons of refrigerated stores. All ships except the ROANOKE were built with helicopter decks but without hangars (see below).

Engineering: The ships can steam at 18 knots on two boilers while the third is being maintained.

Guns: The AOR 1–6 were built with an armament of two 3-inch/50-cal twin AA gun mounts aft and the Mk 56 GFCS. The 3-inch guns were removed from all ships when helicopter hangars were installed. A minimal 20-mm gun armament was installed in some ships prior to installation of the Phalanx CIWS (which are planned for all units). The WICHITA remained unarmed when this edition went to press.

Helicopters: The ROANOKE was built with a twin-bay helicopter hangar aft. The other ships have been similarly fitted; the hangar bays are 61½ to 63 feet (18.75 to 19.2 m) long, 18 to 21 feet (5.5 to 6.4 m) wide, and 17¾ to 18⅓ feet (5.4 to 5.6 m) high.

Missiles: NATO Sea Sparrow launchers and the associated Mk 91 missile FCS are fitted to five ships of the class (atop the hangar structure, aft of the funnel).

The KALAMAZOO shows off the AOR lines. The AOEs and AORs are configured for the underway transfer of ''solid'' as well as liquid cargo, the former including bombs, missiles, provisions, and spare parts. (1991, Giorgio Arra)

The KALAMAZOO has twin helicopter hangars and a large flight deck for UH-46 helicopters. Six of these ships have been refitted with Phalanx CIWs (forward) and a NATO Sea Sparrow launcher (between the helicopter hangars). (1991, Giorgio Arra)

REPAIR SHIPS

(1+) REPAIR SHIPS: NEW CONSTRUCTION

The Navy plans a new class of repair ships to replace the VULCAN-class ships. The lead ship of this long-delayed replacement program is planned for the fiscal 1996 budget.

2 REPAIR SHIPS: "VULCAN" CLASS

Number	Name	Launched	Commissioned	Status
AR 5	VULCAN	14 Dec 1940	16 June 1941	AR
AR 8	JASON	3 Apr 1943	19 June 1944	**PA**

Builders:	AR 5 New York Shipbuilding, Camden, N.J.
	AR 8 Los Angeles Shipbuilding, Calif.
Displacement:	9,325 tons light
	16,245 tons full load
Length:	520 feet (158.5 m) waterline
	AR 5 529⅓ feet (161.4 m) overall
	AR 8 530 feet (161.6 m) overall
Beam:	73⅓ feet (22.4 m)
Draft:	23⅓ feet (7.1 m)
Propulsion:	2 steam turbines (Allis Chalmers in AR 8; New York Shipbuilding in AR 5); 11,000 shp; 2 shafts
Boilers:	4 400 psi (28 kg/cm²) (Babcock & Wilcox)
Speed:	19.2 knots
Range:	18,000 n.miles (33,336 km) at 12 knots
Manning:	AR 5 593 (23 officers + 570 enlisted)
	AR 8 888 (35 officers + 853 enlisted)
Helicopters:	VERTREP area
Guns:	4 20-mm cannon Mk 67 (4 single)
Radars:	SPS-10 surface search
	CRP 1500 navigation

The new ship, which may be a modified SAMUEL GOMPERS (AD 37)-class design, will have an H-53E helicopter capability (including hangar) and facilities for Tomahawk missile stowage and rearming.

These are large, highly capable repair ships although they lack the ability to support more sophisticated weapon and electronic systems.

Class: Originally a class of four ships completed in 1941–1944. The VULCAN was decommissioned on 30 September 1991; AJAX (AR 6) decommissioned on 31 December 1986 and stricken on 16 May 1989; and HECTOR (AR 7) decommissioned on 31 March 1987 and transferred to Pakistan on 20 April 1989.

Classification: The JASON was completed as a heavy hull repair ship (ARH 1); she was reclassified as AR 8 on 9 September 1957.

Design: A very small VERTREP station is provided forward. Two 10-ton-capacity cranes are fitted.

Guns: As built, these ships carried four 5-inch/38-cal DP guns and eight 40-mm AA guns. The 5-inch weapons were retained into the 1970s when they were beached in favor of minimal 20-mm armament.

Operational: Consideration was given in the mid-1980s to assigning some or all of these ships to NRF operation; none was transferred.

The VULCAN at sea prior to being decommissioned. She is one of the large, 1940s-era fleet support ships, similar to the DIXIE and FULTON classes. All have twin, 20-ton-capacity cranes amidships; some war-era tenders had 30-ton cranes. (1990, Giorgio Arra)

The VULCAN and her sister ships are being retired without immediate replacement, as the Navy's replacement AR program has lagged considerably. (1990, Giorgio Arra)

CABLE REPAIR SHIPS

The Navy's cable ships support SOSUS and other underwater cable activities. In addition to supporting these undersea projects, cable ships conduct special oceanographic and acoustic surveys in support of the Space and Naval Warfare Systems Command under the Oceanographer of the Navy. (Commercial ships are also used under contract to support U.S. seafloor cable installations.)

The Navy's three cable ships are operated by the Military Sealift Command.

1 CABLE REPAIR SHIP: "ZEUS"

Number	Name	FY	Launched	In service	Status
T-ARC 7	ZEUS	79	30 Oct 1982	19 Mar 1984	**MSC-PA**

Builders:	National Steel and Shipbuilding, San Diego, Calif.
Displacement:	8,297 tons light
	14,157 tons full load
Length:	454 feet (138.4 m) waterline
	502½ feet (153.2 m) overall
Beam:	73⅛ feet (22.3 m)
Draft:	23⅝ feet (7.3 m)
Propulsion:	diesel-electric (5 General Motors EMD diesel engines); 12,500 shp; 2 shafts
Speed:	15.8 knots
Range:	10,000 n.miles (18,520 km) at 15 knots
Manning:	88 civilian + 8 Navy + 32 technicians
Helicopters:	no facilities
Guns:	none
Radars:	2 navigation

The ZEUS is the first cable ship built specifically for the U.S. Navy. Two ships of this type were planned, originally to replace the now-stricken THOR (ARC 4) and AEOLUS (ARC 3). The second ship, planned for the fiscal 1986 budget, was not requested.

The ZEUS was delayed because of design and construction problems; her keel was laid down 1 June 1981.

The Navy personnel are communications specialists.

Design: The ship can lay up to 1,000 miles (1,610 km) of cable in depths down to ten miles (16 km).

Electronics: The ZEUS and other T-ARCs are fitted with the SSN-2 precise seafloor navigation system.

Engineering: Two 1,200-hp bow and two 1,200-hp stern thrusters are fitted for station keeping while handling cables.

The ZEUS is the only cable ship to be constructed specifically for U.S. naval use. Older naval ships and commercial cable ships also support the Navy's seafloor acoustic detection and Air Force missile impact arrays. (1991, Giorgio Arra)

The ZEUS has cable sheaves forward and aft with large holds for cable stowage. Her machinery-aft design has tandem funnels. No helicopter deck is fitted. (1991, Giorgio Arra)

2 CABLE REPAIR SHIPS: "NEPTUNE" CLASS (S3-S2-BP1)

Number	Name	Launched	Commissioned	Status
T-ARC 2	NEPTUNE	22 Aug 1945	1 June 1953	NDRF
T-ARC 6	ALBERT J. MEYER	7 Nov 1945	13 May 1963	**MSC-PA**

Builders:	Pusey and Jones, Wilmington, Del.
Displacement:	5,818 tons light
	T-ARC 2 8,625 tons full load
	T-ARC 6 8,510 tons full load
Length:	321¾ feet (98.1 m) waterline
	370 feet (112.8 m) overall
Beam:	47 feet (14.3 m)
Draft:	24¹¹⁄₁₂ feet (7.6 m)
Propulsion:	diesel-electric (4 General Electric diesel engines); 4,000 shp; 2 shafts
Speed:	13 knots
Range:	10,000 n.miles (18,520 km) at 13 knots
Manning:	T-ARC 6 88 civilian + 6 Navy (enlisted) + 18 technicians
Helicopters:	VERTREP area in T-ARC 2
Guns:	none
Radars:	Raytheon TM 1650/6X navigation
	Raytheon TM 1660/12S navigation

These are built-for-the-purpose cable ships initially intended for Army use. Both ships were completed in 1946 and laid up in Maritime Administration reserve. The MEYER was acquired by the Navy in 1952 and the NEPTUNE in 1953 to support the SOSUS program; they were placed in Navy commission (ARC) and operated as commissioned ships (USS); the MEYER was transferred outright to the Navy and the NEPTUNE on loan until permanently acquired in September 1966. Both ships were transferred to the MSC operation on 8 November 1973 (T-ARC).

The ships were extensively modernized 1979–1982. Both are operated by MSC with civil service personnel. The Navy personnel are communications specialists.

The NEPTUNE was taken out of service on 24 September 1991.

Design: The NEPTUNE no longer has a VERTREP position aft (removed during 1980–1982 modernization).

Engineering: These were the last ships in U.S. government service with reciprocating engines; they have been re-engined (see below).

Modernization: The ships have been extensively modernized, the MEYER at Bethlehem Steel, Baltimore, Md., from March 1978 to May 1980, and the NEPTUNE at General Dynamics, Quincy, Mass., from February 1980 to February 1982. Their propulsion machinery was replaced along with all appropriate piping and wiring, and their superstructures were rebuilt.

Name: The NEPTUNE was to have had the merchant name WILLIAM H.G. BULLARD.

The ALBERT J. MEYER is one of two outdated cable ships still in U.S. naval service. The MEYER and NEPTUNE have cable sheaves forward, not aft. These ships have been extensively rebuilt since their completion—a decade apart. (1989, L. Van Ginderen Collection)

The cable sheaves of the MEYER show the distinct configuration of cable ships. A spherical marker buoy (with radar reflector) is located aft of the sheaves. (1988, Giorgio Arra)

CABLE REPAIR SHIPS: "AEOLUS" CLASS

The cable repair ship AEOLUS (T-ARC 3) was stricken from the NVR on 28 March 1985. Built in 1945 as the attack cargo ship TURANDOT (AKA 47), she was laid up in reserve from 1946 until converted to a cable ship in 1955. The ship was Navy-manned from 1955 until 1973, when transferred to MSC for operation by civil service personnel.

A sister ship, the THOR (T-ARC 4, formerly AKA 49), was stricken on 1 March 1978.

SALVAGE SHIPS

In addition to naval salvage activities, the Navy has a national responsibility for the salvaging of all U.S. ships, both government and private (Public Law 80-513).

These ships as well as the ASR rescue ships and ATS-type tugs are the principal diver-support ships of the Navy. Note that the ATS-type ships are listed in this section because of their role, although they have a "tug" designation.

SALVAGE SHIPS: NEW CONSTRUCTION

A new class of ARS-type ships was planned to replace the older ARS/ASR-type ships in salvage, heavy towing, and diving roles. The lead ship was scheduled for authorization in the fiscal 1994 shipbuilding program. The entire program was cancelled by the Department of Defense in January 1992.

4 SALVAGE SHIPS: "SAFEGUARD" CLASS

Number	Name	FY	Launched	Commission	Status
ARS 50	SAFEGUARD	81	12 Nov 1983	17 Aug 1985	**PA**
ARS 51	GRASP	82	21 Apr 1984	14 Dec 1985	**AA**
ARS 52	SALVOR	82	28 July 1984	14 June 1986	**PA**
ARS 53	GRAPPLE	83	8 Dec 1984	15 Nov 1986	**AA**

Builders:	Peterson Builders, Sturgeon Bay, Wisc.
Displacement:	2,725 tons light
	3,193 tons full load
Length:	240 feet (73.15 m) waterline
	254$^{11}/_{12}$ feet (77.7 m) overall
Beam:	51 feet (15.5 m)
Draft:	15$^{5}/_{12}$ feet (4.7 m)
Propulsion:	4 geared diesel engines (Caterpillar D399 BTA); 4,200 bhp; 2 shafts (Kort-nozzles)
Speed:	13.5 knots
Range:	8,000 n.miles (14,816 km) at 12 knots
Manning:	approx. 103 (7 officers + 94 enlisted)
Helicopters:	VERTREP area
Guns:	2 .50-cal machine guns (2 single)
Radars:	SPS-64(V) navigation

These ships replaced several of the long-serving salvage ships of the ESCAPE class in the salvage and towing role. The three large ATS-type tugs plus these four ships will permit the continuous peacetime deployment of one salvage-capable ship in the Western Pacific and one in the Mediterranean.

Design: Fitted for towing and heavy lift, with a limited diving-support capability. A 30-ton-capacity boom is fitted aft and a 10-ton boom is located forward.

Engineering: A 500-hp bow thruster is provided.

Operational: In July 1990 the GRASP salvaged an S-3B Viking anti-submarine aircraft off the coast of Virginia from a depth of more than 10,000 feet (3,049 m). The aircraft had crashed at sea during a takeoff from the carrier JOHN F. KENNEDY (CV 67) on 7 October 1989.

The GRAPPLE shows the unusual SAFEGUARD-class design. The bow configuration facilitates deep-sea, four-point mooring to keep the ship over a salvage target. There are booms forward and aft, with a pair of work boats stowed amidships. (1991, Giorgio Arra)

The GRASP's stern aspect shows the all-around bridge views of these ships, a valuable feature for mooring and salvage operations. Her fantail work area is relatively small, reflecting the compact design of these highly capable ships. (1989, Giorgio Arra)

7 SALVAGE SHIPS: "DIVER" AND "BOLSTER" CLASSES

Number	Name	Launched	Commissioned	Status
ARS 8	PRESERVER	1 Apr 1943	11 Jan 1944	AR
ARS 38	BOLSTER	23 Dec 1944	1 May 1945	**NRF-P**
ARS 39	CONSERVER	27 Jan 1945	9 June 1945	**PA**
ARS 40	HOIST	31 Mar 1945	21 July 1945	**AA**
ARS 41	OPPORTUNE	31 Mar 1945	5 Oct 1945	**AA**
ARS 42	RECLAIMER	25 June 1945	20 Dec 1945	**NRF-P**
ARS 43	RECOVERY	4 Aug 1945	15 May 1946	**AA**

Builders:	Basalt Rock Co., Napa, Calif.
Displacement:	1,530 tons standard
	2,045 tons full load except ARS 8 1,970 tons
Length:	207 feet (63.1 m) waterline
	213½ feet (65.1 m) overall
Beam:	43 feet (13.1 m) except ARS 8 39 feet (11.9 m)
Draft:	13 feet (4.0 m)
Propulsion:	diesel-electric (4 Cooper Bessemer diesel engines except Caterpillar in ARS 38, 39, 42); 3,000 bhp; 2 shafts
Speed:	16 knots except ARS 8; 14.8 knots
Range;	20,000 n.miles (37,040 km) at 7 knots
	9,000 n.miles (16,668 km) at 14 knots
Manning:	approx. 103 (7 officers + 94 enlisted)
Helicopters:	VERTREP area
Guns:	2 20-mm cannon Mk 68 (2 single) except Mk 67 in ARS 39, 41
Radars:	SPS-10 search radar in ARS 40, 41, 43
	SPS-53 surface search in ARS 8, 38, 39, 42
	Raytheon 3400 navigation in ARS 43

The RECOVERY and some of her sister ships will shoulder on indefinitely as the construction of replacement salvage ships continues to be delayed. The ship has OE-82 SATCOMM antennas atop the bridge. (1991, Giorgio Arra)

These ships are fitted for salvage and towing operations.

Four ships were transferred to NRF: the PRESERVER on 1 November 1979, BOLSTER on 30 June 1983, and HOIST and RE-CLAIMER on 30 September 1986; they were manned by composite active-reserve crews.

The PRESERVER and CONSERVER were decommissioned on 30 September 1986; both were recommissioned on 26 September 1987 for salvage and anti-drug patrol duties in the Caribbean. The PRESERVER then shifted to NRF in exchange for the HOIST on 30 April 1989, with the latter returning to active service. The PRESERVER again decommissioned on 7 August 1992.

The ESCAPE (ARS 6) was reactivated from NDRF and transferred to the Coast Guard on 4 December 1980. The CLAMP (ARS 33), stricken in 1963, was reacquired from NDRF in 1973 but not reactivated and was again stricken.

Class: These classes originally included 21 ships, the ARS 5–9, 19–28, 38–43, plus the cancelled ARS 44–49. The lead ship of this design was the DIVER (ARS 5); after she was sold in 1949, the Navy listed ESCAPE as the class name. The BOLSTER (ARS 38) and later ships are considered a separate class; the differences are minimal (e.g., beam, fuel capacity).

Two of these ships were converted to oceanographic ships, the AGOR 17 ex-ARS 20 and AGOR 18 ex-ARS 27; three others serve with the Coast Guard: WMEC 167 ex-ARS 9, WMEC 168 ex-ARS 26, and WMEC 6 ex-ARS 6.

Guns: The original armament consisted of two or four 20-mm guns in twin mounts. After World War II most of the active ships carried a single 40-mm AA gun atop the superstructure.

Historical: In December 1990 the OPPORTUNE became the first U.S. naval ship to be commanded by a woman.

At anchor, the RECOVERY shows the low stern and after boom of these tug-type salvage ships. The short funnel is lost in the clutter atop the superstructure. The ship's port work boat is alongside. (1991, Giorgio Arra)

3 SALVAGE AND RESCUE SHIPS: "EDENTON" CLASS

Number	Name	FY	Launched	Commissioned	Status
ATS 1	EDENTON	66	15 May 1968	23 Jan 1971	AA
ATS 2	BEAUFORT	67	20 Dec 1968	22 Jan 1972	PA
ATS 3	BRUNSWICK	67	14 Oct 1969	10 Dec 1972	PA

Builders:	Brooke Marine, Lowestoft (England)
Displacement:	2,650 tons standard
	3,200 tons full load
Length:	264 feet (80.5 m) waterline
	288⅔₃ feet (88.0 m) overall
Beam:	50 feet (15.25 m)
Draft:	15⅙ feet (4.6 m)
Propulsion:	4 diesel engines (Paxman 12 YLCM); 6,000 bhp; 2 shafts
Speed:	16 knots
Range:	10,000 n.miles (18,520 km) at 13 knots
Manning:	ATS 1 117 (8 officers + 109 enlisted)
	ATS 2 118 (9 officers + 109 enlisted)
	ATS 3 104 (9 officers + 95 enlisted)
Helicopters:	VERTREP area
Guns:	ATS 1 4 20-mm cannon Mk 24 (2 twin)
	ATS 2, 3 2 20-mm cannon Mk 68 (2 single)
Radars:	SPS-53 surface search
	SPS-64(V)9 navigation

These are tug-type ships with extensive salvage and diving capabilities. They are one of two classes of auxiliary ships to be constructed in British shipyards for the U.S. Navy, the other being the two CHAUVENET (T-AGS 29)-class ships. The more recently acquired British-built stores ships (T-AFS) were constructed for RFA service.

Class: The ATS 4 was authorized in fiscal 1972 and the ATS 5 in fiscal 1973. Their construction was deferred in 1973 and plans for additional ships of the class were cancelled because of their high cost. Instead, the less-capable ATF 166 class was procured.

Classification: ATS originally indicated salvage tug; changed to salvage and rescue ship on 16 February 1971.

Design: SCB No. 719. These ships have large open work spaces forward and aft. Four mooring buoys are carried (as in submarine rescue ships) to assist in four-point moors for diving and salvage activities. A 10-ton-capacity crane is fitted forward and a 20-ton crane aft. The ships have compressed-air diving equipment (not helium-oxygen).

Engineering: The ships have a through-bow thruster for precise maneuvering and station keeping.

The BEAUFORT at Hong Kong, showing the bow layout for deep-sea mooring, the forward, 10-ton-capacity crane, and the mooring buoys and work boat carried on the starboard side. The supports for the forward crane flank the bridge face. (1986, Giorgio Arra)

The BEAUFORT's stern showing a large working area, the heavy, 20-ton-capacity crane, and the centerline stern anchor. (1986, Giorgio Arra)

SUBMARINE TENDERS

Submarine tenders have extensive maintenance shops for various submarine systems and equipment as well as extensive weapon and provision storage. Tenders also provide extensive hospital facilities as well as extra berths for submarine relief personnel.

The FBM tenders can carry 20 submarine-launched ballistic missiles, stowed in a vertical position.

These are improved versions of the L.Y. SPEAR-class tenders with the later ships fitted specifically to support the LOS ANGELES (SSN 688)-class attack submarines. Up to four SSNs can be supported alongside simultaneously.

Design: SCB No. 737. Fitted with a 30-ton-capacity crane and two 5-ton travelling cranes. Medical facilities include an operating room, dental clinic, and 23-bed ward.

3 SUBMARINE TENDERS: "EMORY S. LAND" CLASS

Number	Name	FY	Launched	Commissioned	Status
AS 39	EMORY S. LAND	72	4 May 1977	7 July 1979	AA
AS 40	FRANK CABLE	73	14 Jan 1978	5 Feb 1980	AA
AS 41	McKEE	77	16 Feb 1980	15 Aug 1981	PA

Builders:	Lockheed Shipbuilding and Construction, Seattle, Wash.
Displacement:	13,842 tons light
	22,650 tons full load
Length:	645⅔ feet (196.9 m) overall
Beam:	85 feet (25.9 m)
Draft:	25½ feet (7.8 m)
Propulsion:	1 steam turbine (De Laval); 20,000 shp; 1 shaft
Boilers:	2 650 psi (43.6 kg/cm²) (Combustion Engineering)
Speed:	20 knots (18 knots sustained)
Range:	7,600 n.miles (14,075 km) at 18 knots
Manning:	AS 39, 40 558 (56 officers + 502 enlisted)
	AS 41 588 (52 officers + 536 enlisted)
Flag:	69 (25 officers + 44 enlisted)
Helicopters:	VERTREP area
Guns:	4 20-mm cannon Mk 67 (4 single)
	2 40-mm grenade launchers Mk 19 (2 single)
Radars:	SPS-10 surface search
	1 navigation

The FRANK CABLE entering port with the crew manning the rail. The EMORY S. LAND-class tenders resemble the SAMUEL GOMPERS-class destroyer tenders, although their internal arrangement and shops are quite different. (1991, Giorgio Arra)

The FRANK CABLE passing under the Cooper River Bridge at Charleston, S.C. Tenders have numerous cranes and work boats to support ships being serviced alongside. A minimal armament is fitted in contrast to the heavy gun batteries of World War II. (1984, Giorgio Arra)

2 SUBMARINE TENDERS: "L.Y. SPEAR" CLASS

Number	Name	FY	Launched	Commissioned	Status
AS 36	L.Y. SPEAR	65	7 Sep 1967	28 Feb 1970	**AA**
AS 37	DIXON	66	20 June 1970	7 Aug 1971	**PA**

Builders:	General Dynamics, Quincy, Mass.
Displacement:	12,770 tons light
	23,493 tons full load
Length:	645⅔ feet (196.9 m) overall
Beam:	85 feet (25.9 m)
Draft:	24⅔ feet (7.5 m)
Propulsion:	1 steam turbine (General Electric); 20,000 shp; 1 shaft
Boilers:	2 650 psi (43.6 kg/cm²) (Foster Wheeler)
Speed:	20 knots (18 knots sustained)
Range:	7,600 n.miles (14,075 km) at 18 knots
Manning:	AS 36 547 (56 officers + 491 enlisted)
	AS 37 559 (55 officers + 504 enlisted)
Flag:	69 (25 officers + 44 enlisted)
Helicopters:	VERTREP area in AS 36
	landing area in AS 37
Guns:	4 20-mm cannon Mk 67 (4 single)
Radars:	SPS-10 surface search
	1 navigation

These were the Navy's first submarine tenders designed specifically to support nuclear-propelled attack submarines; they can support four submarines alongside at one time.

Class: The AS 38 of this design was authorized in the fiscal 1969 budget but was not built because of funding shortages in other ship programs; cancelled on 9 April 1969.

Design: SCB No. 702.

Guns: As built, these ships each had two 5-inch/38-cal DP guns. They were deleted in favor of the minimal 20-mm gun armament.

The L.Y. SPEAR and DIXON were the first submarine tenders constructed by the U.S. Navy specifically to service nuclear-propelled attack submarines. Their heavy cranes handle spare parts and are used to load torpedoes and cruise missiles into SSNs. (1990, Giorgio Arra)

The L. Y. SPEAR showing the stern anchor and mooring features common to submarine tenders. Tenders have several side ports for laying gangplanks and conveyors to ships moored alongside. (1990, Giorgio Arra)

2 FBM SUBMARINE TENDERS: "SIMON LAKE" CLASS

Number	Name	FY	Launched	Commissioned	Status
AS 33	SIMON LAKE	63	8 Feb 1964	7 Nov 1964	**AA**
AS 34	CANOPUS	64	12 Feb 1965	4 Nov 1965	**AA**

Builders:	AS 33 Puget Sound Naval Shipyard, Bremerton, Wash.
	AS 34 Ingalls Shipbuilding, Pascagoula, Miss.
Displacement:	12,000 tons light
	AS 33 19,934 tons full load
	AS 34 21,089 tons full load
Length:	643¾ feet (196.3 m) overall
Beam:	85 feet (25.9 m)
Draft:	28½ feet (8.7 m)
Propulsion:	1 steam turbine (De Laval); 20,000 shp; 1 shaft
Boilers:	2 650 psi (43.6 kg/cm²) (Combustion Engineering)
Speed:	18 knots
Range:	7,600 n.miles (14,075 km) at 18 knots
Manning:	AS 33 598 (56 officers + 542 enlisted)
	AS 34 615 (58 officers + 557 enlisted)
Helicopters:	VERTREP area
Guns:	4 3-inch (76-mm) 50-cal AA Mk 33 (2 twin)
Radars:	LN-66 navigation
	SPS-10 surface search

These tenders are designed to service fleet ballistic missile submarines. The SIMON LAKE was the last submarine tender to be based at Holy Loch, Scotland, where the U.S. Navy had maintained an SSBN base from 1961 until 1992; she departed on 6 March 1992.

Class: The AS 35 of this design was authorized in fiscal 1965, but construction was deferred and the ship was not built. The ship would have provided one tender for each of five Polaris SSBN squadrons with a sixth ship in overhaul or transit. However, the Polaris SSBN program was reduced from the proposed 45 to 41 submarines and only four squadrons were formed (four tenders built [AS 31–34] plus one conversion [AS 19]).

The SIMON LAKE with a red "E" for engineering excellence on the funnel. Chevrons under the "E" are used to indicate additional awards. The SIMON LAKE and CANOPUS retain their 3-inch/50-cal AA gun mounts alongside the funnel. (1985, Giorgio Arra)

Design: SCB No. 238. Two 30-ton-capacity cranes and four 5-ton travelling cranes are fitted.

These ships were originally built to support the Polaris missile; the SIMON LAKE was modified in 1970–1971 and the CANOPUS in 1969–1970 to support the Poseidon missile; the SIMON LAKE has subsequently been modified to handle the Trident C-4 missile.

Guns: Note that the 3-inch guns have been retained, making these the only tender-type ships with guns larger than 20-mm. Two Mk 63 directors for the 3-inch guns have been removed.

The SIMON LAKE off Charleston, S.C., with the carrier YORKTOWN (CV 10) and nuclear-propelled merchant ship SAVANNAH moored at Patriots Point in the background. Note the funnel-aft design used in later SSN tenders. (1985, Giorgio Arra)

2 FBM SUBMARINE TENDERS: "HUNLEY" CLASS

Number	Name	FY	Launched	Commissioned	Status
AS 31	HUNLEY	60	28 Sep 1961	16 June 1962	**AA**
AS 32	HOLLAND	62	19 Jan 1963	7 Sep 1963	**AA**

Builders:	AS 31 Newport News Shipbuilding, Va.
	AS 32 Ingalls Shipbuilding, Pascagoula, Miss.
Displacement:	11,000 tons light
	19,819 tons full load
Length:	599 feet (182.7 m) overall
Beam:	83 feet (25.3 m)
Draft:	24¼ feet (7.4 m)
Propulsion:	diesel-electric (10 Fairbanks-Morse 38D⅛ diesel engines); 15,000 shp; 1 shaft
Speed:	19 knots
Range:	10,000 n.miles (18,520 km) at 12 knots
Manning:	AS 31 568 (53 officers + 515 enlisted)
	AS 32 632 (60 officers + 572 enlisted)
Helicopters:	VERTREP area
Guns:	4 20-mm cannon Mk 67 (4 single)
Radars:	LN-66 navigation
	SPS-10 surface search

Commercial tugs assist the HOLLAND entering port. The HOLLAND has "AS" painted on her stern (not bows); virtually all other auxiliary ships have the "A" deleted. The stern anchor is not fitted in this view. (1989, Giorgio Arra)

The HUNLEY and HOLLAND were the first tenders designed specifically to service fleet ballistic missile submarines. With the reduction of U.S. SSBNs, in 1991 the HUNLEY was reassigned to support attack submarines (at Norfolk, Va.).

Design: SCB No. 194. As built, they could support the Polaris missile; the HUNLEY was modified in 1973–1974 and the HOLLAND in 1974–1975 to support Poseidon-armed submarines.

As built, the ships had a 32-ton-capacity hammerhead crane fitted aft. It has been replaced in both ships by two amidships cranes, as in the later SIMON LAKE class; these are 30-ton-capacity devices.

Guns: The original armament for these ships was four 3-inch/50-cal AA guns in twin mounts.

The HUNLEY's amidships funnel reveals the diesel-electric propulsion of all four purpose-built SSBN tenders; the later tenders have steam turbine propulsion. Both ships of this class are being laid up. (1989, Giorgio Arra)

1 SUBMARINE TENDER: CONVERTED "FULTON" CLASS

Number	Name	Launched	Commissioned	Status
AS 19	PROTEUS	12 Nov 1942	31 Jan 1944	PR

Builders:	Moore Shipbuilding and Dry Dock, Oakland, Calif.
Displacement:	14,195 tons standard
	20,295 tons full load
Length:	563⅝ feet (171.9 m) waterline
	574½ feet (175.2 m) overall
Beam:	73 feet (22.25 m)
Draft:	27½ feet (8.4 m)
Propulsion:	diesel-electric (8 General Motors 16-248 diesel engines); 11,520 shp; 2 shafts
Speed:	15.4 knots
Range:	26,000 n.miles (48,152 km) at 10 knots
Manning:	578 (53 officers + 525 enlisted)
Helicopters:	VERTREP area
Guns:	4 20-mm cannon Mk 68 (4 single)
Radars:	LN-66 navigation
	SPS-10 surface search

The PROTEUS originally was a submarine tender of the FULTON class. She was in active service from 1944 to 26 September 1947, when she was decommissioned and placed "in service." The ship provided support submarines at New London, Conn., until January 1955 when she was taken in hand for conversion to support Polaris fleet ballistic missile submarines; she was recommissioned on 8 July 1960.

During the 1980s the PROTEUS was employed in general repair and support activities for surface ships and submarines; inactivated on 11 July 1992 and decommissioned on 30 September 1992.

Conversion: The ship was converted at the Charleston Naval Shipyard to become the first U.S. FBM submarine tender beginning 15 January 1959. A 44-foot (13.4-m) amidships section was added to provide space for additional shops and support facilities as well as vertical storage for Polaris missiles. The "insert" was six decks high and weighed about 500 tons. A thwartships travelling missile crane was installed and also vertical stowage for 20 Polaris missiles. During conversion the gun battery was reduced to two 5-inch/38-cal DP guns, both forward. These guns were removed in the mid-1970s.

The conversion was SCB No. 190.

Operational: The PROTEUS accomplished her first SSBN refit at New London, Conn., from 20 January to 21 February 1961, after which she deployed to Holy Loch, Scotland, arriving there in March 1961 to establish a Polaris submarine base. In February 1963, after an overhaul in the United States, she established a second overseas Polaris submarine base at Rota, Spain, in February 1964. She then established the third overseas Polaris submarine base at Apra Harbor, Guam, in November 1964.

From 1981 the ship has been based at Guam in the Mariana Islands; she has periodically deployed to Diego Garcia in the Indian Ocean.

The PROTEUS wearing World War II–era camouflage markings for her two-month deployment to Australia in the spring of 1992 to commemorate the 50th anniversary of the Battle of the Coral Sea. The venerable PROTEUS was relieved as the "station tender" at Guam in mid-1992 by the HOLLAND. (1992, U.S. Navy)

2 SUBMARINE TENDERS: "FULTON" CLASS

Number	Name	Launched	Commissioned	Status
AS 11	FULTON	27 Dec 1940	12 Sep 1941	AR
AS 18	ORION	14 Oct 1942	30 Sep 1943	AA

Builders:	AS 11 Mare Island Navy Yard
	AS 18 Moore Shipbuilding and Dry Dock, Oakland, Calif.
Displacement:	9,734 tons light
	18,000 tons full load
Length:	520 feet (158.5 m) waterline
	529½ feet (161.5 m) overall
Beam:	73⅓ (22.4 m)
Draft:	25½ feet (7.8 m)
Propulsion:	diesel-electric (8 General Motors 16-248 diesel engines); AS 11: 11,500 shp, AS 18: 11,200 shp; 2 shafts
Speed:	15 knots
Range:	32,000 n.miles (59,264 km) at 15 knots
Manning:	AS 11 575 (53 officers + 522 enlisted)
	AS 18 527 (53 officers + 474 enlisted)
Helicopters:	VERTREP area
Guns:	4 20-mm cannon Mk 68 (4 single)
Radars:	LN-66 navigation
	SPS-10 surface search

These tenders are similar to the contemporary DIXIE (AD 14)-class destroyer tenders and VULCAN (AR 5)-class repair ships. The ships have been modernized but have a limited capability to support nuclear-propelled attack submarines.

The ORION has been home-ported at La Maddalena, Sardinia, since 1 June 1980 to service U.S. submarines in the Mediterranean; to be decommissioned in 1993.

Class: The FULTON class originally consisted of six ships completed in 1941–1944 (AS 11, 12, 15, 16, 18, 19) plus the NEREUS (AS 17), completed in 1960. The PROTEUS is listed separately; of the others: SPERRY (AS 12) decommissioned and stricken on 30 September 1982; BUSHNELL (AS 15) stricken on 15 November 1980 (sunk as Mk 48 torpedo target on 3 June 1983); HOWARD W. GILMORE (AS 16) stricken on 1 December 1980; and NEREUS stricken on 27 October 1971 (survived as a hulk into 1990s).

Guns: As built, the armament installed in these ships was four 5-inch/38-cal DP guns and eight 40-mm AA guns.

Operational: The FULTON was moored at the State Pier in New London, Conn., supporting Submarine Squadron 10 from the time she was recommissioned in 1951 until decommissioned 40 years later.

The ORION at Piraeus, Greece. She is based at La Maddalena, Sardinia, supporting surface ships of the U.S. Sixth Fleet as well as SSNs. (1986, L. Van Ginderen Collection)

SUBMARINE RESCUE SHIPS

2 SUBMARINE RESCUE SHIPS: "PIGEON" CLASS

Number	Name	FY	Launched	Commissioned	Status
ASR 21	PIGEON	67	13 Aug 1969	28 Apr 1973	**PA**
ASR 22	ORTOLAN	68	10 Sep 1969	14 July 1973	**AA**

Builders:	Alabama Dry Dock and Shipbuilding, Mobile, Ala.
Displacement:	3,411 tons light
	4,570 tons full load
Length:	251 feet (76.5 m) overall
Beam:	86 feet (26.2 m)
Draft:	21¼ feet (6.5 m)
Propulsion:	4 diesel engines (Alco); 6,000 bhp; 2 shafts
Speed:	15 knots
Range:	8,500 n.miles (15,742 km) at 13 knots
Manning:	ASR 21 193 (10 officers + 183 enlisted)
	ASR 22 182 (11 officers + 171 enlisted)
Helicopters:	landing area
Guns:	2 20-mm cannon Mk 68 (2 single)
Radars:	SPS-53 surface search
	LN-66 navigation in ASR 21
	Raytheon navigation in ASR 22
Sonars:	SQQ-25

These ships were constructed specifically to carry the DSRV submarine rescue vehicles and support deep-ocean diving operations (see chapter 26). For the latter they have the Mk II Deep Diving System that can support up to eight divers operating to depths of 1,000 feet (305 m) in helium-oxygen saturation conditions. They are the Navy's only saturation diving ships other than the ELK RIVER (IX 501) and can support divers indefinitely under pressure, lowering them to the ocean floor in pressurized transfer chambers for open-sea work periods. They can also carry the McCann Submarine Rescue Chamber (SRC).[4]

These ships were delayed by problems in design, construction, and fitting out.

4. The McCann chamber was developed in the late 1930s for rescuing crewmen trapped in submarines at depths to 850 feet (259 m). The chamber is tethered and winches itself down to the escape hatches of bottomed submarines while the ASR is moored above the craft. After the THRESHER (SSN 593) sinking in 1963, the McCann capability was increased slightly, but still short of the 1,000-foot-plus operating depths of U.S. submarines, whose "crush" depth is about half-again their operating depth.

The ORTOLAN, showing the catamaran hull design of these submarine rescue ships. The large mooring buoys on the bows are called "spuds"; the fish insignia above the bow anchors indicates a submerged submarine—a symbol dating back to early in this century. (1990, Giorgio Arra)

The massive travelling cranes on the PIGEON and ORTOLAN can lift a Deep Submergence Rescue Vehicle (DSRV) and diving chamber and lower it between the catamaran hulls; both the DSRV and chamber can be mated with two decompression chambers in the ships. (1990, Giorgio Arra)

Class: The Navy had planned to build at least three ships of this class to support six DSRVs at three rescue-unit home ports. In the mid-1960s long-term planning called for ten ships as replacements for the older ASR force. In the event, only these two ships were funded and built. Additional ASRs are not planned.

Design: SCB No. 721. These are the Navy's largest catamaran ships, being larger than the research ship HAYES (T-AG 195/T-AGOR 16). Each ASR hull is 26 feet (7.9 m) wide with a separation of 34 feet (10.4 m) between hulls. The separation facilitates the lowering and raising of DSRVs and diving chambers between the hulls.

The ships have a precision three-dimensional sonar tracking system for directing DSRV operations. A helicopter deck is situated aft, but is suitable primarily for VERTREP operations.

Accommodations are provided for a salvage staff of 14 and a DSRV operations and maintenance team of 24.

Engineering: Through-bow thrusters are fitted in each hull for maneuvering and station keeping during diving and salvage operations. (The ships are not moored when operating DSRVs.)

Guns: As built, the PIGEON had two 3-inch/50-cal AA guns in two "tubs" forward on her hulls. After their removal the large mooring buoys ("spuds") were mounted in their place; previously she had two buoys forward of the bridge and two between the hulls aft.

3 SUBMARINE RESCUE SHIPS: "CHANTICLEER" CLASS

Number	Name	Launched	Commissioned	Status
ASR 13	KITTIWAKE	10 July 1945	18 July 1946	**AA**
ASR 14	PETREL	26 Sep 1945	24 Sep 1946	AR
ASR 15	SUNBIRD	3 Apr 1946	23 June 1950	**AA**

Builders:	ASR 9 Moore Shipbuilding and Dry Dock, Oakland, Calif.
	ASR 13–15 Savannah Machine and Foundry, Ga.
Displacement:	1,670 tons standard
	2,015 tons full load
Length:	240 feet (73.2 m) waterline
	251⅓ feet (76.6 m) overall
Beam:	42 feet (12.8 m)
Draft:	16½/₁₂ feet (4.9 m)
Propulsion:	diesel-electric (4 General Motors 12-278A diesel engines except Alco 539 in ASR 9); 3,000 shp; 1 shaft
Speed:	15 knots
Range:	
Manning:	approx. 108 (8 officers + 100 enlisted)
Helicopters:	no facilities
Guns:	2 20-mm cannon Mk 68 (2 single)
Radars:	LN-66 navigation
	SPS-53 surface search

These are large tug-type ships fitted for salvage and helium-oxygen diving operations. They have a limited submarine rescue capability when carrying the McCann chamber.

The SUNBIRD was accepted by the Navy on 15 January 1947 and towed (inactivated) to the Charleston Naval Shipyard; she was not commissioned for 3½ years. The FLORIKAN (ASR 9) was decommissioned on 2 August 1991 and stricken on 3 September 1991; the PETREL was decommissioned on 30 September 1991.

The KITTIWAKE is one of the World War II–era submarine rescue ships still in service. Although fitted for rescue and salvage, they have far less capability than newer ships of the ARS/ASR/ATS types. Mooring buoys are fitted outboard of the funnel. (1991, Giorgio Arra)

Class: Originally there were eight ships in this class, ASR 7–11 and 13–15, plus the cancelled ASR 16–18.

Design: A pair of cylindrical mooring buoys is carried on both sides of the deck structure, and a tripod mast aft supports three booms.

Guns: The design armament of these ships was two 3-inch/50-cal AA guns in single mounts and two 20-mm single guns.

The SUNBIRD with a McCann Submarine Rescue Chamber (SRC) on her fantail. The device rescued 33 from the crew of the submarine SQUALUS (SS 192) when she foundered in 1939; 26 trapped crewmen were lost. It was the only operational use of the SRC. (1989, Giorgio Arra)

OCEANGOING TUGS

The ATS-series salvage and rescue ships (formerly salvage tugs) are listed as salvage ships in this edition of *Ships and Aircraft;* see page 272.

7 FLEET TUGS: "POWHATAN" CLASS

Number	Name	FY	Launched	In service	Status
T-ATF 166	POWHATAN	75	24 June 1978	15 June 1979	**MSC-AA**
T-ATF 167	NARRAGANSETT	75	28 Nov 1978	9 Jan 1979	**MSC-PA**
T-ATF 168	CATAWBA	75	22 Sep 1979	28 May 1980	**MSC-PA**
T-ATF 169	NAVAJO	75	20 Dec 1979	13 June 1980	**MSC-PA**
T-ATF 170	MOHAWK	78	5 Apr 1980	16 Oct 1980	**MSC-AA**
T-ATF 171	SIOUX	78	30 Oct 1980	12 May 1981	**MSC-PA**
T-ATF 172	APACHE	78	20 Dec 1980	30 July 1981	**MSC-AA**

Builders:	Marinette Marine, Wisc.
Displacement:	2,000 tons standard
	2,260 tons full load
Length:	225¹¹/₁₂ feet (68.9 m) waterline
	240¹/₁₂ feet (73.2 m) overall
Beam:	42 feet (12.8 m)
Draft:	15 feet (4.6 m)
Propulsion:	diesel-electric (2 General Motors EMD 20-645X7 diesel engines); 4,500 shp; 2 shafts (Kort-nozzle propellers)
Speed:	15 knots
Range:	10,000 n.miles (18,520 km) at 13 knots
Manning:	16 civilian + 4 Navy (enlisted) + 20 transients
Helicopters:	VERTREP area
Guns:	none
Radars:	SPS-53 surface search
	Raytheon TM 1660/12S navigation

These are oceangoing tugs based on a commercial design. They have replaced the war-built ATFs in the active fleet. The new ATF differs from the ASR and ATS types in that it lacks the salvage and diving equipment of the earlier ships and has a limited towing capability. A portable Mk 1 Mod 1 diving/decompression module can be loaded on the stern of these ships.

Design: SCB No. 744. These craft are easily distinguished by their side-by-side funnels and low, open sterns. The Navy personnel are communications specialists, and the transients are salvage and diving specialists. There is a 10-ton-capacity electrohydraulic crane.

In wartime two 20-mm guns and two .50-cal machine guns can be fitted.

Engineering: The ships have a 300-hp bow thruster.

The APACHE has the lines of a commercial off-shore oil-drilling support ship. The masts are especially fitted to carry lights and shapes to indicate towing operations. These ships have no organic diver support capabilities but can carry portable gear. (1990, Giorgio Arra)

The APACHE's low stern, fitted with a cable roller in the transom, has a large working area. This class of seven MSC-operated ships represents the entire U.S. Navy force of "straight" oceangoing tugs. (1990, Giorgio Arra)

8 FLEET TUGS: "CHEROKEE" CLASS

Number	Name	Launched	Commissioned	Status
ATF 91	SENECA	2 Feb 1943	30 Apr 1943	Trials
ATF 105	MOCTOBI	25 Mar 1944	25 July 1944	NDRF
ATF 110	QUAPAW	15 May 1943	6 May 1944	NDRF
ATF 113	TAKELMA	18 Sep 1943	3 Aug 1944	NDRF
ATF 149	ATAKAPA	11 July 1944	8 Dec 1944	NDRF
ATF 158	MOSOPELEA	7 Mar 1945	28 July 1945	NDRF
ATF 159	PAIUTE	4 June 1945	27 Aug 1945	NDRF
ATF 160	PAPAGO	21 June 1945	3 Oct 1945	NDRF

Builders:	ATF 105, 149, 158, 159, 160 Charleston Shipbuilding and Dry Dock, S.C.
	ATF 110, 113 United Engineering, Alameda, Calif.
	ATF 91 Cramp Shipbuilding, Philadelphia, Pa.
Displacement:	1,235 tons standard
	1,640 tons full load
Length:	195 feet (59.45 m) waterline
	205 feet (62.5 m) overall
Beam:	38½ feet (11.7 m)
Draft:	15½ feet (4.7 m)
Propulsion:	diesel-electric (4 Caterpillar D399 diesel engines); 3,000 shp; 1 shaft
Speed:	16.5 knots
Range:	15,000 n.miles (27,780 km) at 8 knots
	6,500 n.miles (12,038 km) at 15 knots
Manning:	approx. 93 (8 officers + 85 enlisted men)
Helicopters:	no facilities
Guns:	removed

These are large oceangoing tugs, many of which saw extensive combat service in World War II. All of the above ships are on the NVR and laid up in NDRF except the SENECA, which was reacquired from NDRF on 21 November 1985 for use as an immobilized trials craft at the David Taylor Research Center, Annapolis, Md.

The MOCTOBI was decommissioned on 30 September 1985; the QUAPAW decommissioned on 30 August 1985; TAKELMA decommissioned on 30 September 1983; ATAKAPA and MOSOPELEA on 1 October 1981; PAIUTE on 23 August 1985; and PAPAGO on 28 June 1985.

The PAIUTE and PAPAGO were recommissioned into active naval service for anti-drug patrols in the Caribbean on 23 August 1985 and 28 June 1985, respectively; the PAIUTE was decommissioned on 7 August 1992 and the PAPAGO on 28 July 1992.

Class: The AT 64–76 and 81–118 were built to the same basic design (see Engineering notes). The class was officially known as the CHEROKEE (ATF 66) after the loss of the NAVAJO (AT 64) in 1943 and the SEMINOLE (AT 65) in 1942. Later ships are unofficially referred to as the ABNAKI (ATF 96) class.

Of recent disposals, the NARRAGANSETT (ATF 88), WENATCHEE (ATF 118), and ACHOMAWI (ATF 148) were sold to Taiwan 30 October 1990; the TENINO (ATF 115) was reacquired from NDRF on 18 August 1986 for use as a salvage training hulk. Several other ships formerly in NDRF have now been disposed of.

Ships of this class serve with the U.S. Coast Guard as well as in several foreign navies.

Classification: These ships were all ordered with the AT designation. The AT 66 and later ships were changed to ATF on 15 May 1944.

Design: These are steel-hulled ships. They are fitted with a 10- or 20-ton-capacity boom. Most have compressed-air diving equipment.

Engineering: Ships numbered below ATF 96 have four diesel engines, four generators, and four electric motors driving through a gear to a single propeller shaft. The later ships have only one very large electric motor.

The early ships also have a short, squat exhaust funnel; the later ships have waterline exhausts for their diesels and a tall, thin galley funnel (i.e., "Charlie Noble").

The surviving ships were reengined before being laid up.

Guns: As built, these ships were armed with one 3-inch/50-cal AA gun and up to two 40-mm AA guns, plus machine guns.

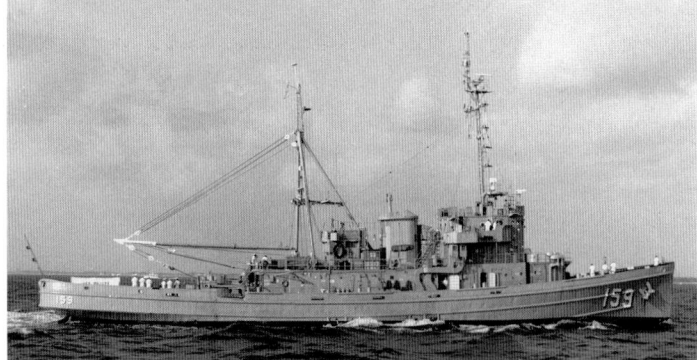

The PAIUTE is a large-funnel ATF; some ships of this design had tall, slender diesel exhausts. All of the surviving war-built ATFs remaining in U.S. service are laid up, except for the SENECA. Several serve in the U.S. Coast Guard and foreign navies. (1990, Giorgio Arra)

The PAPAGO showing the ship's crane arrangement and stern working area. (1991, Giorgio Arra)

The SENECA is employed as a stationary experimental/trials ship at the David Taylor Research Center in Annapolis. She wears the center's previous name—David Taylor Naval Ship Research and Development Center—in this photo. (1986, U.S. Navy, P. Fairall)

AUXILIARY TUGS: "SOTOYOMO" CLASS

All tugs of this series (ATA 121–125, 146, 170–213, and 219–238) have been stricken; none is retained in NDRF. Four hulks are employed as salvage-training platforms, periodically scuttled and then salved: the TUNICA (ATA 178), ACCOKEEK (ATA 181), NAVIGATOR (ATA 203), and KEYWADIN (ATA 213).

See 14th Edition/page 330 for characteristics.

AVIATION LOGISTIC SHIPS

2 AVIATION LOGISTIC SHIPS: CONVERTED "SEABRIDGE" CLASS (C5-S-78a)

Number	Name	Built	In service	Status
T-AVB 3	WRIGHT	1970	14 May 1986	MSC-RRF-A
T-AVB 4	CURTISS	1969	18 Aug 1987	MSC-RRF-P

Builders:	Ingalls Shipbuilding, Pascagoula, Miss.
Displacement:	12,409 tons light
	27,580 tons full load
Length:	559⅚ feet (170.7 m) waterline
	600¹¹⁄₁₂ feet (183.2 m) overall
Beam:	90 feet (27.4 m)
Draft:	34 feet (10.4 m)
Propulsion:	2 steam turbines (General Electric); 30,000 shp; 1 shaft
Boilers:	2 (Combustion Engineering)
Speed:	23.6 knots
Range:	9,000 n.miles (16,668 km) at 23.6 knots
Manning:	39 civilian
Troops:	300+
Helicopters:	landing area (forward)
Guns:	none
Radars:	2 navigation

These ships were converted from RO/RO-container ships to provide maintenance and logistic support for Marine aircraft in forward areas. Providing peacetime support for Marine aviation, the ships are normally in the United States and partially loaded with a Marine intermediate maintenance unit; the WRIGHT is normally based at Philadelphia, Penna., and the CURTISS at Port Hueneme, Calif. During war or crisis periods, the remainder of the unit and personnel are loaded on board and the ships deployed to forward areas to support Marine tactical aircraft.

The majority of the maintenance unit's facilities used ashore are packaged in standard freight containers. Access ladders, scaffolding, and shipboard electrical power and other services will permit the unit to function while embarked in the ship.

Most of the embarked troops are associated with the maintenance unit; the remainder are communications and support personnel.

Class: The previous AVB 1 and AVB 2 were tank landing ships converted to support land-based patrol aircraft from unimproved airfields and seaplanes in the Mediterranean area; they were Navy-manned in the AVB role. The ALAMEDA COUNTY (LST 32) became the AVB 1 and, after she was stricken in 1962, the TALLAHATCHIE COUNTY (LST 1154) became the AVB 2.

Conversion: Both ships were converted at Todd Shipyards in Galveston, Texas, the WRIGHT from December 1984 to May 1986, and the CURTISS from December 1985 to August 1987.

Design: The ships are combination RO/RO and self-sustaining container ships. The conversion included fitting a helicopter deck above the two forward holds; the deck can be removed to permit full access to the holds with the use of off-board cranes.

There are seven cargo holds, with the No. 7 hold, aft, having troop berthing and mess facilities installed above it. As a maintenance ship the AVB can embark 300 standard containers plus 52 access modules; in the resupply role 684 containers can be carried. There are 35,000 square feet (3,150 m²) of vehicle storage space provided.

They are fitted with ten 30-ton-capacity booms (which can be joined to form 60-ton lifts), and a single 70-ton Stuelcken boom is also installed.

Names: Original merchant names were YOUNG AMERICA and GREAT REPUBLIC, respectively; they were changed when acquired by the Navy for conversion to AVB.

The CURTISS (above) and her sister ship WRIGHT provide extensive maintenance and parts stowage facilities for Marine fixed-wing aircraft and helicopters. The amidships deck can be stacked with aviation support containers. (U.S. Navy)

The WRIGHT with a Marine CH-53 helicopter on her flight deck. The T-AVBs are generally considered to be in the category of sealift ships, being intended primarily to support forward-deployed Marine aviation units. (U.S. Navy)

GUIDED MISSILE SHIPS

GUIDED MISSILE SHIP: "NORTON SOUND"

The long-serving test and evaluation ship NORTON SOUND (AVM 1, ex-AV 11) was stricken on 26 January 1987. Built as a seaplane tender and commissioned in 1945, she served as a gun/missile/electronics test ship from 1948 until decommissioned on 11 December 1986.

See 14th Edition/pages 334–335 for characteristics.

TRAINING SHIPS

The U.S. Navy has no dedicated training ships except for eight KNOX (FF 1052)-class frigates now designated FFT (see chapter 17) and the COOP minecraft (see chapter 22).

In 1986 then-Secretary of the Navy Lehman proposed the construction of a sail-training ship for the Navy. Beyond training, the ship was to "serve as a national symbol and a demonstration of the maritime heritage of our nation."[5] The proposed ship, to have been named UNITED STATES, was to have cost an estimated $20 million and have a completion date of 1990. She would have been a three-masted, square-rigged sailing ship, with a steel hull; displacement would have been about 1,380 tons, with a length between 220 and 238 feet (67.1 to 72.6 m). She would have had an auxiliary diesel engine capable of moving the ship at ten knots.

A large number of small sail-training vessels are operated by the U.S. Naval Academy, and the Coast Guard has the training bark EAGLE (WIX 327).

UNCLASSIFIED MISCELLANEOUS SHIPS

These ships (designated IX) are officially considered to be service craft; see chapter 25.

5. Quoted in James A. Russell, "Tall Ship Wars," *Navy News & Undersea Technology* (11 August 1986), p. 1.

CHAPTER 24

Sealift Ships

Maritime prepositioning ships moored in a Middle East country during a recent exercise. The prepositioning concept originated in the early 1960s, when then-Secretary of Defense Robert S. McNamara initiated a program of C-5 transport aircraft and Fast Deployment Logistics Ships (FDL); only the aircraft were procured. (U.S. Navy)

Sealift ships provide point-to-point transportation of troops and cargo for all of the U.S. military services, including both dry and liquid cargoes. Also included in this category are the forward or prepositioned merchant ships that carry guns, vehicles, munitions, provisions, fuels, field hospitals, and other supplies for U.S. troops who will be flown into forward areas to "marry up" with the matériel.

All sealift ships are operated by civilian crews under contract to the Military Sealift Command (MSC). The official categories of sealift ships are described in chapter 8.

As discussed below, two specialized sealift ships have been designed for future construction. These ships and others will be procured in the near future, although the Navy, Military Sealift Command, U.S. Transportation Command, and Maritime Administration as well as Congress were engaged in discussions of future sealift acquisitions when this edition of *Ships and Aircraft* went to press.

The Joint Chiefs of Staff released portions of a comprehensive "Mobility Requirements Study" on 23 January 1992 that proposed a program to acquire 20 large Roll-On/Roll-Off (RO/RO) ships of the CSP/CSS type listed below and to lease two container ships (2,000-container-capacity each) for the maritime prepositioning role. Table 24-1 shows the planned delivery schedule for these ships.

Under the JCS plan, 9 ships will be assigned to carry Army prepositioned equipment, and 11 ships will be used for the rapid deployment of heavy Army divisions from the United States (to be added to eight ships current employed in this role). In addition to these new acquisitions (plus the two container ships), the Ready Reserve Force (RRF) would be increased from the current 96 ships to 142 ships by fiscal 1999, of which 104 would be dry cargo ships and the remainder tankers and several specialized ships.

TABLE 24-1. PLANNED SEALIFT ACQUISITION PROGRAM (DELIVERIES)

	FY 1993	FY 1994	FY 1995	FY 1996	FY 1997	FY 1998	FY 1999	Total
Prepositioning	—	4	—	4	1	—	—	9
Fast sealift	—	—	—	2	5	4	—	11
Container	—	2	—	—	—	—	—	2

Maritime prepositioned material was used by all of the U.S. military services in the Persian Gulf conflict of 1990–1991. The first U.S. ground combat units brought into Saudia Arabia with tanks, heavy artillery, etc., were two Marine Expeditionary Brigades (MEB) that married up with Maritime Prepositioning Ship (MPS) squadrons (see chapter 7). The third MPS squadron followed. In addition, several Afloat Prepositioning Force (APF) ships were at Diego Garcia, loaded with Navy field hospitals, Air Force and Army equipment, and potable water.

The three MPS squadrons consist of the 13 specialized maritime prepositioning ships of the new-construction BOBO class, the converted Waterman class, and the converted Maersk type. Each squadron carries weapons, munitions, and 30 days of supplies for a 16,500-man MEB. The cargo holds of all 13 ships are temperature and humidity controlled. Six to eight civilian technicians permanently assigned to each ship regularly check the equipment on board and conduct routine maintenance. Each ship returns to Jacksonville, Fla., about every 2½ years for the equipment to be offloaded, checked, and repaired. In addition, the ships are periodically exercised in offloading at forward locations.

The 13 ships of the current three MPS squadrons were initially deployed in 1985–1986. The present MPS program began in 1980 when standard merchant ships were loaded with weapons and supplies for a single Marine Amphibious Brigade (MAB) and deployed to Diego Garcia as Near-Term Prepositioning Ships (NTPS) until 1985.[1]

The MPS ships and other prepositioned merchant ships carrying munitions, equipment, fuels, and provisions are collectively referred to as the Afloat Prepositioning Force (APF).

In addition, the Navy and Maritime Administration control eight Fast Sealift Ships (FSS), which are modified SL-7-type merchant ships intended specifically to carry Army mechanized and tank divisions, and several general cargo ships that are laid up for rapid "breakout" in time of crisis or war. The latter include several auxiliary crane ships (ACS), which were standard cargo ships fitted with heavy cranes to permit unloading at unimproved ports or into barges and landing craft.

Most of these ships were acquired under the aegis of then-Secretary of the Navy John Lehman in the 1980s. During the 1980s the Navy spent almost $7 *billion* for sealift improvement, including:[2]

   8 Fast Sealift Ships (FSS)
  25 Maritime/Near-Term Prepositioning Ships (MPS/NTPS)
  96 Ready Reserve Force (RRF) ships

In addition to the above sealift ships, there are 116 older merchant ships laid up in the National Defense Reserve Fleet (NDRF) that are expected to be scrapped in the next few years. These ships, of limited military value and questionable condition, consist of 71 Victory-type cargo ships built in World War II and 45 other ships. None of these ships was activated for Operations Desert Shield/Desert Storm in 1990–1991.

There are NDRF mothball groups at Beaumont, Texas; James River, Va.; and Suisun Bay, Calif. However, Ready Reserve Force (RRF) ships are moored at several other ports as well as with these mothball groups. Called "outporting," when possible the RRF ships are moored near the ports that they would load from.

In this chapter, ships are arranged in the following order:

> Auxiliary Crane Ships
> Maritime Prepositioning Ships
> Vehicle Cargo Ships
> Barge Carrying Ships
> Cargo Ships
> Transport Oilers/Tankers
> Gasoline Tankers
> Troop Transports

Within those categories ships are listed in the order of the Maritime Administration design designations. The Maritime Administration code scheme is explained in chapter 3.

Designations: There are two types of hull numbers used in this chapter—the multiple-digit Navy Ships and Aircraft Supplementary Data Tables (SASDT) numbers that are assigned for accounting purposes and are not actual hull numbers in the normal context and the one- to three-digit numbers that are traditional Navy hull numbers, assigned when the ship is ordered and part of the ship designation scheme that began in 1920.

Sealift ships that are listed in the Naval Vessel Register (NVR) are indicated in this chapter by the arrow (↑) symbol. Note that the MPS units are *not* on the NVR. The NICOR CLIPPER is designated AGDS although used in a cargo role.

Guns/Missiles: These ships are not armed.

Helicopters: Only the 13 MPS ships and the eight converted SL-7 fast sealift ships have explicit helicopter landing decks plus two C4-S-58a cargo ships. Some other sealift ships have open areas that could be used in an emergency.

Names: The crane ships have state nicknames; the MPS ships have names of Marine heroes. See table 24-2 at the end of this chapter for former merchant names of these ships.

Status: U.S. Naval Ships (USNS) are indicated under Status notes; all others have the prefix SS (steamship) or MV (motor vessel). State maritime academy training ships are usually designated TS.

Ships that are not active are mostly assigned to the RRF, where they are maintained and kept ready for rapid reactivation, or to the Maritime Administration's NDRF. The RRF ships are planned for reactivation in 5, 10, or 20 days; the NDRF ships would take considerably longer to reactivate.

---

1. The Marine Corps redesignated the Marine Amphibious Brigade as the Marine Expeditionary Brigade in 1988; see chapter 7.

2. This amount included funding for two aviation supply ships (T-AVB) listed in chapter 23.

SEALIFT SHIPS: NEW CONSTRUCTION

Beginning with the fiscal 1990 defense budget, the Congress has added funds for the construction of additional sealift ships, both multi-purpose cargo ships and tankers. However, the Navy has been reluctant to spend the funds, having traditionally given relatively little support to sealift programs.

Following continued congressional interest, on 2 August 1991 the Naval Sea Systems Command issued to industry a request for proposals for the design of two sealift ships that would be suitable for series production. The designs are designated CSP-24 for Conventional Sealift ship, Prepositioned, and CSS-24 for Conventional Sealift Ship. The proposed preliminary characteristics for the ships are:

Length:	CSP-24 approx. 950 feet (289.6 m) overall
	CSS-24 approx. 700 feet (213.4 m) overall
Beam:	105½ feet (32.2 m)
Draft:	35 feet (10.7 m)
Propulsion:	gas turbine *or* diesel
Speed:	24 knots sustained
Range:	12,000 n.miles (22,200 km) at 24 knots
Manning:	
Helicopters:	landing area
Radars:	. . . . . . navigation

During the planning stage these ships are referred to as T-AKR(X). They will be combination Roll-On/Roll-Off (RO/RO) and container ships with moveable decks to permit maximum cargo flexibility. Their requirements include 20,580 square feet (1,852 m^2) of deck space for vehicles and containers.

According to Navy statements, a detailed design and construction contract could be awarded by the end of 1992 or early 1993. The $1.27 *billion* appropriated by Congress for fast sealift in fiscal 1990 and 1991 could pay the construction costs for four to six ships. Estimates of possible numbers of these ships to be constructed range from 10 to 40 units.

AUXILIARY CRANE SHIPS

These ten ships are intended to provide an unloading capability for other sealift ships when port facilities are not available. Moored alongside a loaded merchant ship, the T-ACS can lift cargo onto a pier or into landing craft or barges alongside.

Each crane ship has two or three pairs of 30-ton cargo cranes; the cranes can be paired to lift 60 tons. Thus, one crane can lift a fully loaded container; two cranes an M60-series main battle tank; and four cranes working together can lift a 105-ton floating causeway. (The standard TEU container is 8 × 8 × 20 feet/2.4 × 2.4 × 6.1 m.)[3]

The Navy had planned to have 12 crane ships. The conversion of the BEAVER STATE to T-ACS 10 (below) was cancelled; however, she was expected to resume conversion during 1992. The C6-S-1 container ship AMERICAN BANKER was to become the T-ACS 11 and another, undesignated ship was to have become the T-ACS 12.

3. TEU = Twenty-foot (6.1-m) Equivalent Unit.

1 AUXILIARY CRANE SHIP / 1 CONTAINER SHIP: C6-S-60b TYPE

Number	Name	Launched	Status
T-ACS 9	GREEN MOUNTAIN STATE †	20 Aug 1964	MSC-RRF
T-ACS 10	BEAVER STATE †	14 Jan 1965	MSC-RRF

Builders:	Ingalls Shipbuilding, Pascagoula, Miss.
Displacement:	16,600 tons light
	22,900 tons full load
Tonnage:	14,000 GRT (as built)
	12,763 DWT (as built)
Length:	634⅚ feet (193.55 m) waterline
	665¾ feet (203.0 m) overall
Beam:	75 1/12 feet (22.9 m)
Draft:	31½ feet (9.6 m)
Propulsion:	2 steam turbines (General Electric); 19,000 shp; 1 shaft
Boilers:	2 (Combustion Engineering)
Speed:	21 knots
Range:	17,000 n.miles (31,485 km) at 20 knots
Manning:	
Radars:	. . . . . . navigation

The GREEN MOUNTAIN STATE was converted to an ACS configuration; the BEAVER STATE was transferred to MarAd for layup on 9 April 1990 following cancellation of her ACS conversion on 12 January 1990. The conversion was to be resumed in 1992 at the Charleston Naval Shipyard; she will complete conversion in December 1993.

As container ships they could accommodate 649 standard containers.

Conversion: The T-ACS 9 was converted at Norfolk Shipbuilding Co., Va., in February–March 1989. She was fitted with three sets of twin 30-ton-capacity cranes.

Engineering: Fitted with highly automated engineering plants. Several ships of this design exceeded 24 knots when new.

2 AUXILIARY CRANE SHIPS: C6-S-1qu TYPE

Number	Name	Launched	To RRF	Status
T-ACS 7	DIAMOND STATE †	8 Aug 1961	Feb 1989	MSC-RRF
T-ACS 8	EQUALITY STATE †	6 Jan 1962	May 1989	MSC-RRF

Builders:	Todd Shipyards, San Pedro, Calif.
Displacement:	15,138 tons light
Tonnage:	16,518 GRT (as built)
	19,871 DWT (as built)
Length:	632 11/12 feet (192.95 m) waterline
	667⅚ feet (203.6 m) overall
Beam:	76 feet (23.2 m)
Draft:	33¼ feet (10.1 m)
Propulsion:	2 steam turbines (General Electric); 22,000 shp; 1 shaft
Boilers:	2 (Combustion Engineering)
Speed:	20 knots
Range:	14,000 n.miles (25,930 km) at 20 knots
Manning:	
Radars:	. . . . . . navigation

Former container ships that could accommodate 625 standard containers.

Conversion: The T-ACS 7 was converted November 1987–December 1988 and T-ACS 8 converted January 1988–February 1989 at the Tampa (Fla.) Shipbuilding Co. Fitted with three sets of twin 30-ton-capacity cranes.

The DIAMOND STATE loaded with Army vehicles. Note the manner in which the cranes can be paired for very heavy lift operations and the amidships super-structure position. (1991, L. Van Ginderen Collection)

3 AUXILIARY CRANE SHIPS: C5-S-73b TYPE

Number	Name	Launched	To RRF	Status
T-ACS 4	GOPHER STATE ↑	8 July 1972	Oct 1987	MSC-RRF
T-ACS 5	FLICKERTAIL STATE ↑	11 May 1968	Feb 1988	MSC-RRF
T-ACS 6	CORNHUSKER STATE ↑	2 Oct 1968	Apr 1988	MSC-RRF

Builders:	Bath Iron Works, Maine
Displacement:	15,060 tons light
	25,000 tons full load
Tonnage:	17,902 GRT (as built)
Length:	581⅔ feet (177.35 m) waterline
	609⅚ feet (185.9 m) overall
Beam:	91⅙ feet (27.8 m)
Draft:	30 feet (9.1 m)
Propulsion:	2 steam turbines; 17,500 shp; 1 shaft
Boilers:	2 (Babcock & Wilcox)
Speed:	20 knots
Range:	9,340 n.miles (17,300 km) at 20 knots
Manning:	
Radars:	. . . . . . navigation

Former container ships.

Conversion: All three ships were converted at Norfolk Shipbuilding Co. (Va.)—the T-ACS 4 from October 1986 to October 1987, T-ACS 5 from December 1986 to February 1988, and T-ACS 6 from March 1987 to April 1988. They were fitted with two sets of twin 30-ton-capacity cranes.

Operational: The T-ACS 4, as the mercantile EXPORT LEADER, served as test ship for the Arapaho project of operating and supporting military helicopters from a merchant ship. The 1982 evaluation was totally successful, albeit conducted on a limited scale. (During a 40-hour at-sea period, 178 day and 45 night landings were logged by several helicopter types.)

In early 1990 the FLICKERTAIL STATE and GOPHER STATE were activated and fitted with collective protection spaces for defense against CBR effects. They then carried more than 100,000 artillery projectiles filled with nerve agents from Nordenham, Germany, to Johnston Island in the Pacific. The voyage, from 22 September to 6 November 1990 (via Cape Horn), was under the escrot of two guided missile cruisers and was made without incident. The ships were subsequently employed in Desert Shield.

The GOPHER STATE at Norfolk, her paired cranes operating together. These ships can speed the unloading of sealift ships at locations that do not have shore cranes or other heavy lift equipment. (1988, Giorgio Arra)

3 AUXILIARY CRANE SHIPS: C6-S-1qd TYPE

Number	Name	Launched	To RRF	Status
T-ACS 1	KEYSTONE STATE ↑	2 Oct 1965	May 1984	MSC-RRF
T-ACS 2	GEM STATE ↑	22 May 1965	Oct 1985	MSC-RRF
T-ACS 3	GRAND CANYON STATE ↑	23 Jan 1965	Oct 1986	MSC-RRF

Builders:	National Steel and Shipbuilding Co., San Diego, Calif.
Displacement:	28,660 tons full load
Tonnage:	17,128 GRT
	13,600 DWT
Length:	632¹¹⁄₁₂ feet (192.95 m) waterline
	668½ feet (203.8 m) overall
Beam:	76⅙ feet (23.2 m)
Draft:	33 feet (10.1 m)
Propulsion:	2 steam turbines (General Electric); 19,250 shp; 1 shaft

Boilers:	2 (Foster Wheeler)
Speed:	20 knots
Range:	13,000 n.miles (24,075 km) at 20 knots
Manning:	64 civilian
Radars:	2 . . . . . . navigation

These ships can each accommodate 303 standard containers.

Conversion: The T-ACS 1 was converted by Bay Shipbuilding, Sturgeon Bay, Wisc., from March 1983 to May 1984; T-ACS 2 by Continental Marine, San Francisco, Calif., from October 1984 to October 1985; and T-ACS 3 from October 1985 to October 1987 by Dillingham Corp., San Francisco.

All have been fitted with three sets of twin 30-ton-capacity cranes.

The KEYSTONE STATE's configuration has two sets of paired cranes forward and one set aft. Several containers are on her deck. Special racks called "sea-sheds" permit equipment and vehicles to be carried in place of containers; see chapter 8. (U.S. Navy)

MARITIME PREPOSITIONING SHIPS

These 13 ships were constructed or converted specifically to carry Marine Corps equipment in the three MPS squadrons.

5 MARITIME PREPOSITIONING SHIPS: "BOBO" CLASS (C8-M-MA134j)

Number	Name	Launched	In service	Status
T-AK 3008	2ND LT JOHN P. BOBO	19 Jan 1985	14 Feb 1985	**MSC-MPS**
T-AK 3009	PFC DEWAYNE T. WILLIAMS	18 May 1985	6 June 1985	**MSC-MPS**
T-AK 3010	1ST LT BALDOMERO LOPEZ	26 Oct 1985	21 Nov 1985	**MSC-MPS**
T-AK 3011	1ST LT JACK LUMMUS	22 Feb 1986	6 Mar 1986	**MSC-MPS**
T-AK 3012	SGT WILLIAM R. BUTTON	17 May 1986	18 May 1986	**MSC-MPS**

Builders:	General Dynamics, Quincy, Mass.
Displacement:	22,700 tons light
	40,846 tons full load
Tonnage:	44,543 GRT
	26,523 DWT
Length:	673 feet (205.2 m) overall
Beam:	105½ feet (32.2 m)
Draft:	29½ feet (9.0 m)
Propulsion:	2 diesels (Stork Werkspoor 18TM410V); 26,400 bhp; 1 shaft
Speed:	17.7 knots
Range:	11,100 n.miles (20,557 km) at 17.7 knots
Manning:	30 civilian + 25 maintenance personnel (civilian)
Flag:	7 (Navy-civilian) + 8 Navy communications in 1 ship
Helicopters:	landing area
Radar:	2 navigation

These new-construction ships were classified T-AKX during planning stages. Each of them carries equipment and supplies for about a quarter of a MEB for 30 days. Although built specifically for the MPS role, they are under 25-year charter.

The first two ships were laid down in 1983; others in 1984.

Design: These ships have 162,500 square feet (14,625 m²) of vehicle deck space and can carry 1,605,000 gallons (6 million liters) of break-bulk petroleum products plus 81,770 gallons (310,726 liters) of potable water. Up to 522 standard containers can be carried. A stern ramp is fitted for unloading vehicles into landing craft and onto piers, and there are five 39-ton-capacity cranes fitted.

Engineering: These ships achieved 18.8 knots on trials; above is their sustained speed. A 1,000-hp bow thruster is fitted to permit maneuvering alongside a pier without the aid of tugs.

Manning: All MPS ships will have berthing for a Marine "surge team" that can be embarked to assist in preparation of vehicles and unloading—about 100 troops in these ships and the Waterman ships, and up to 77 in the Maersk ships.

The Sgt William R. Button is typical of the 13 maritime prepositioning ships, characterized by heavy cranes, a stern vehicle ramp, helicopter deck, and large capacity for vehicles and material. These ships now have MSC funnel markings—blue and gold bands. (1988, Giorgio Arra)

The Sgt William R. Button riding high in the water with a light load. The large superstructure blocks for these ships contain comfortable living spaces for their civilian mariner crews. There is a control station at the forward end of the helicopter deck. (1988, Giorgio Arra)

3 MARITIME PREPOSITIONING SHIPS: CONVERTED WATERMAN CLASS (C7-S-133a)

Number	Name	Launched	Start Conv.	In service	Status
T-AK 3005	SGT MATEJ KOCAK	1981	Mar 1983	5 Oct 1984	**MSC-MPS**
T-AK 3006	PFC EUGENE A. OBREGON	1982	Nov 1982	15 Jan 1985	**MSC-MPS**
T-AK 3007	MAJ STEPHEN W. PLESS	1983	Mar 1983	1 May 1985	**MSC-MPS**

Builders:	Sun Shipbuilding and Dry Dock, Chester, Penna., except PLESS by General Dynamics, Quincy, Mass.
Displacement:	15,000 tons light
	48,754 tons full load
Length:	821 feet (250.3 m) overall
Beam:	105½ feet (32.2 m)
Draft:	32⅙ feet (9.8 m)
Propulsion:	2 steam turbines; 30,000 shp; 1 shaft
Boilers:	2
Speed:	20 knots
Range:	13,000 n.miles (24,076 km) at 20 knots
Manning:	29 civilian + 25 maintenance personnel (civilian)
Flag:	7 (Navy-civilian) + 8 Navy communications in 1 ship
Helicopters:	landing area
Radars:	2 . . . . . . navigation

These ships were previously commercial container ships operated by the Waterman Corp. They were acquired specifically for conversion to the MPS role. They were designated T-AKX during the planning stage; they are under 25-year charter.

Conversion: As built, these ships were 695 feet (211.9 m) overall with a full-load displacement of 38,975 tons. A 126-foot (38.4-m) midbody section was inserted, and the ships were reconfigured for 152,524 square feet (13,727 m²) of vehicle cargo space, 540 standard cargo containers, and to carry 1,544,000 gallons (5.8 million liters) of bulk fuels and 94,780 gallons (360,164 liters) of potable water. The ships are fitted with vehicle ramps and cranes to provide a self-unloading capability.

All three ships were converted to the MPS role by the National Steel yard in San Diego, Calif.

The SGT MATEJ KOCAK anchored off Norfolk. The ship has two sets of paired heavy cranes forward as well as a travelling crane for lifting containers. (1988, Giorgio Arra)

The PFC EUGENE A. OBREGON with clear cargo decks forward. Two helicopter landing spots are marked on the flight deck. Cargo helicopters offload high-priority material from these ships. (1989, Giorgio Arra)

5 MARITIME PREPOSITIONING SHIPS: CONVERTED MAERSK TYPE

Number	Name	Launched	Start Conv.	In service	Status
T-AK 3000	CPL LOUIS J. HAUGE JR.	3 Aug 1979	Jan 1984	7 Sep 1984	**MSC-MPS**
T-AK 3001	PFC WILLIAM B. BAUGH JR.	8 Dec 1978	Jan 1983	30 Oct 1984	**MSC-MPS**
T-AK 3002	PFC JAMES ANDERSON JR.	23 Mar 1979	Oct 1983	26 Mar 1985	**MSC-MPS**
T-AK 3003	1ST LT ALEX BONNYMAN JR.	3 Aug 1979	Jan 1984	26 Sep 1985	**MSC-MPS**
T-AK 3004	PVT HARRY FISHER	12 Oct 1979	Apr 1984	12 Sep 1985	**MSC-MPS**

Builders:	Odense Staalskibsvaerft, Lindo (Denmark)
Displacement:	28,249 tons light
	46,484 tons full load
Length:	755½ feet (230.3 m) overall
Beam:	90¹⁄₁₂ feet (27.5 m)
Draft:	32¹⁄₁₂ feet (9.8 m)
Propulsion:	1 diesel (Sulzer 7RND 76M); 16,800 bhp; 1 shaft
Speed:	17.5 knots
Range:	10,800 n.miles (20,000 km) at 17.5 knots
Manning:	27 civilian + 20 maintenance personnel (civilian)
Flag:	7 (Navy-civilian) + 8 Navy communications in BONNYMAN
Helicopters:	landing area
Radars:	2 . . . . . . navigation

These are former Maersk Line combination container and RO/RO vehicle cargo ships that were acquired by the U.S. government specifically for conversion to the MPS role. The ships were designated T-AKX during the design stage.

Conversion: During conversion a new 157½-foot (48-m) midsection was added to each ship (original length 598¹⁄₁₂ feet/182.3 m with a deadweight tonnage of 29,182 tons). In the MPS role they have 120,080 square feet (10,807 m²) of vehicle storage space and can carry up to 332 standard freight containers, 1,283,000 gallons (4.8 million liters) of bulk fuels, and 65,000 gallons (247,000 liters) of potable water. Ramps and cranes provide a limited self-unloading capability.

The HAGUE, ANDERSON, and FISHER were converted by the Bethlehem Steel yard at Sparrows Point, Md.; the BAUGH and BONNYMAN by the Bethlehem Steel yard in Beaumont, Texas.

Names: ALEXANDER BONNYMAN JR. was changed to ALEX BONNYMAN JR. on 4 March 1986. The PVT HARRY FISHER was to have been changed to PVT FRANKLIN S. PHILLIPS, the former being the pseudonym used by Phillips when he won the Medal of Honor; however, the original name has been retained.

The LOUIS J. HAUGE has three sets of paired cranes forward, permitting the MPS ship to unload without port facilities. Note the ship's bulbous bow, visible in this view of the ship riding high in the water. (1991, L. Van Ginderen Collection)

The Pfc William B. Baugh Jr. during a visit to Portsmouth, England. The stern vehicle ramp in these ships is offset to starboard. (1990, L. Van Ginderen Collection)

VEHICLE CARGO SHIPS

These are Roll-On/Roll-Off (RO/RO) ships with strengthened cargo decks for carrying heavy vehicles and side and/or stern ramps for unloading vehicles.

8 FAST SEALIFT SHIPS: CONVERTED SL-7 TYPE

Number	Name	Launched	In service	Status
T-AKR 287	Algol ↑	22 Sep 1972	19 June 1984	MSC-FSS
T-AKR 288	Bellatrix ↑	30 Sep 1972	10 Sep 1984	MSC-FSS
T-AKR 289	Denebola ↑	10 May 1973	7 Oct 1985	MSC-FSS
T-AKR 290	Pollux ↑	18 May 1973	31 Mar 1986	MSC-FSS
T-AKR 291	Altair ↑	28 Apr 1973	13 Nov 1985	MSC-FSS
T-AKR 292	Regulus ↑	18 Dec 1972	28 Aug 1985	MSC-FSS
T-AKR 293	Capella ↑	9 Sep 1971	1 July 1984	MSC-FSS
T-AKR 294	Antares ↑	13 May 1972	12 July 1984	MSC-FSS

Builders:	T-AKR 287, 289, 293 Rotterdamsche Dry Dock Maats, Rotterdam (Netherlands)
	T-AKR 288, 291 Rheinstahl Nordseewerke, Emden (West Germany)
	T-AKR 290, 292, 294 A.G. Weser, Bremen (West Germany)
Displacement:	31,017 tons light
	55,425 tons full load
Tonnage:	
Length:	946⅛ ft (288.5 m) overall
Beam:	105½ feet (32.2 m)
Draft:	36⅔ feet (11.2 m)
Propulsion:	2 steam turbines (General Electric); 120,000 shp; 2 shafts
Boilers:	2 (Foster-Wheeler)
Speed:	33 knots
Range:	12,200 n.miles (22,594 km) at 27 knots
Manning:	49 civilian + 56 or 57 troops
Helicopters:	landing area
Radars:	2 . . . . . . navigation

The Algol with her decks empty. She can carry containers, equipment, or vehicles aft; the helicopter deck is forward, which can also be used for cargo. These ships load/unload vehicles through large, amidships side ports. (U.S. Navy)

These are former high-speed merchant ships of the SL-7 class built for the SeaLand Corporation in European shipyards. They have been converted to Fast Sealift Ships (FSS) and carry U.S. military cargoes with an extensive Roll-On/Roll-Off (RO/RO) capability. These are not maritime prepositioning ships, but are maintained in U.S. Atlantic and Gulf Coast ports, ready for rapid loading of Army or Marine equipment and sailing to crisis/war areas. They are operated by civilian charter crews.

Classification: During the planning stage these ships were designated T-AKRX. Upon acquisition they were designated T-AK and assigned hull numbers in the cargo ship (AK) series; however, upon conversion to RO/RO configuration they were changed to T-AKR but retained the AK-series hull numbers.

T-AK 287 changed to T-AKR on 19 June 1984; T-AK 288 to T-AKR on 10 September 1984; T-AK 289–292 to T-AKR on 1 November 1983; and T-AK 293 and 294 to T-AKR on 30 June 1984.

The fast sealift ship CAPELLA. These ships have been extensively converted from their merchant configuration to carry heavy Army equipment, especially tanks, armored personnel carriers, and trucks. All eight ships were employed early in Operation Desert Shield although the ANTARES suffered an engineering breakdown. (1991, L. Van Ginderen Collection)

Conversion: Four ships were converted with fiscal 1982 funds and four with fiscal 1984 funds: the T-AKR 287, 288, and 292 at National Steel and Shipbuilding Co., San Diego, Calif.; T-AKR 289 and 293 at Pennsylvania Shipbuilding, Chester, Penna.; and T-AKR 290, 291, and 294 at Avondale Shipyards, New Orleans, La.

These ships have approximately 185,000 square feet (16,650 m²) of vehicle space. A major container capability remains aft, with provisions for special racks for loading heavy material, including trucks and tanks (being lifted on and off vice RO/RO). Side ports and heavy ramps are provided on both sides of the ship. Twin 35-ton-capacity cranes are fitted forward and twin 50-ton cranes aft. Through limited arcs they can provide a combined lift of 70 and 100 tons, respectively.

A helicopter landing deck is provided amidships that can accommodate the largest U.S. military helicopters (Marine/Navy CH-53E, Army CH-47 Chinook). The four cargo decks beneath the landing deck are connected by ramps and can accommodate helicopters, the first deck with a height of 19½ feet (5.95 m) and the others with 13½ feet (4.1 m).

In addition to the RO/RO and helicopter space, the ships can each accommodate other vehicles plus 78 35-foot (10.7-m) flatracks and 46 standard containers. There is a tunnel for trucks up to 5-ton capacity in the amidships deck structure to permit passage between the forward and after cargo areas.

Design: As built, the 33-knot SL-7s were the fastest cargo ships ever constructed for the U.S. merchant service.

Names: These ships are assigned traditional Navy cargo ship names (i.e., stars and constellations), reflecting their acquisition on bare-boat charter versus the time charter of MPS ships. Most names were previously carried by store ships (AF).

Operational: All eight ships participated in Operations Desert Shield/Desert Storm in 1990–1991, being activated in August 1990. The ANTARES, which had suffered previous machinery problems, had an engine breakdown in the eastern Atlantic during the initial lift of Desert Shield, in August 1990. She was towed into a Spanish port, and her cargo was shifted to other sealift ships.

Status: These ships are U.S. Naval Ships.

The ANTARES showing the after set of paired heavy cranes; another set is fitted forward. The SL-7s are the fastest cargo ships ever built. (1988, Giorgio Arra)

4 VEHICLE CARGO SHIPS: C7-S-95a TYPE

Number	Name	Launched	To RRF	Status
T-AKR 0010 (T-AKR 10)	MERCURY ↑	21 Dec 1976		**MSC-Active**
T-AKR 0011 (T-AKR 11)	JUPITER ↑	1 Nov 1975	Apr 1986	MSC-RRF
T-AKR 5062	CAPE ISABEL	15 May 1976	June 1986	MSC-RRF
T-AKR 5076	CAPE INSCRIPTION	24 May 1975	Sep 1987	MSC-RRF

Builders:	Bath Iron Works, Maine
Displacement:	14,222 tons light
	33,765 tons full load
Tonnage:	13,156 GRT
	19,172 DWT
Length:	639⅝ feet (195.1 m) waterline
	684¾ feet (208.8 m) overall
Beam:	102 feet (31.1 m)
Draft:	32¹/₁₂ feet (9.8 m)
Propulsion:	2 steam turbines (General Electric); 37,000 shp; 2 shafts
Boilers:	2 (Babcock & Wilcox)
Speed:	24 knots
Range:	12,600 n.miles (23,335 km) at 23 knots
Manning:	29 to 33 civilian except 21 in MERCURY
Radars:	2 . . . . . . navigation

These ships were built for commercial service by the Lykes Brothers Steamship Co. (all named with prefix Lykes). The MERCURY and JUPITER were acquired by the Navy on long-term charter in 1980 for use as prepositioning ships in the Indian Ocean. Note that they were assigned standard Navy hull designations; placed in service on 3 June 1980 and 7 May 1980, respectively.

Design: These ships are RO/RO vehicle carriers, with side ports and a stern ramp for rapidly loading and unloading vehicles. They can also carry standard containers.

Status: The MERCURY and JUPITER are U.S. Naval Ships.

The AKR 11 was transferred to MarAd (Suisun Bay) on 23 April 1986; assigned to RRF on 2 May 1986.

The stern ramp gives way to the large, garage-like interior of the MERCURY as the ship loads U.S. Army vehicles at Antwerp. RO/RO ships are vital to moving military equipment, as was demonstrated in the Gulf War. (1990, L. Van Ginderen Collection)

The RO/RO ship MERCURY loading vehicles at Antwerp. The large crane forward of the bridge is on the shore. The stern ramp is offset to starboard. (1990, L. Van Ginderen Collection)

1 VEHICLE CARGO SHIP: C4-ST-67a TYPE

Number	Name	FY	Launched	Commissioned	Status
T-AKR 0009 (T-AKR 9)	METEOR ↑	63	18 Apr 1965	19 May 1967	MSC-RRF

Builders:	Lockheed Shipbuilding and Construction, Seattle, Wash.
Displacement:	9,154 tons light
	21,480 tons full load
Tonnage:	16,467 GRT
	12,326 DWT
Length:	540 feet (164.7 m) overall
Beam:	83⅔ feet (25.5 m)
Draft:	29 feet (8.8 m)
Propulsion:	2 steam turbine (De Laval); 19,400 shp; 2 shafts
Boilers:	2
Speed:	22 knots
Range:	10,000 n.miles (18,520 km) at 20 knots
Manning:	33 civilian
Radars:	2 . . . . . . navigation

The METEOR, originally named SEA LIFT, was built specifically as a RO/RO ship for naval service. Laid down on 19 May 1964.

Classification: Authorized as T-AK 278 but changed to T-LSV 9 while under construction; changed again to vehicle cargo ship T-AKR 9 on 14 August 1969.

The LSV 1 through 6 were World War II–built vehicle landing ships, all of which served under other designations. The TAURUS (LSV 8) was the former AK 273; she had been begun as the FORT SNELLING (LSD 23). Note that the later SL-7 conversions to rapid response ships have AK-series hull numbers with the prefix AKR type designation.

Design: The METEOR was one of the few ships to have both an SCB (No. 236) and Maritime Administration design designation.

The ship has four side ramps and a stern ramp. She has 87,735 square feet (7,896 m^2) of vehicle space.

Names: Changed from SEA LIFT to METEOR on 12 September 1975 to avoid confusion with the Sealift-class tankers.

Status: The METEOR was a U.S. Naval Ship until transferred to the RRF on 30 October 1985.

The METEOR is rigged with king posts as a general cargo ship in addition to her RO/RO capability. The ship has two thin funnels, tandem behind the bridge (the port funnel is partly obscured by smoke). (1984, Giorgio Arra)

1 VEHICLE CARGO SHIP: C3-ST-14a TYPE

Number	Name	Launched	In service	Status
T-AKR 0007 (T-AKR 7)	COMET ↑	31 July 1957	27 Jan 1958	MSC-RRF

Builders:	Sun Shipbuilding and Dry Dock, Chester, Penna.
Displacement:	8,175 tons light
	18,286 tons full load
Tonnage:	13,792 GRT
	10,111 DWT
Length:	499 feet (152.2 m) overall
Beam:	78 feet (23.8 m)
Draft:	29⅙ feet (8.9 m)
Propulsion:	2 steam turbines (General Electric); 13,200 shp; 2 shafts
Boilers:	2 (Babcock & Wilcox)
Speed:	19 knots
Range:	13,000 n.miles (24,076 km) at 18 knots
Manning:	33 civilian
Radars:	2 Raytheon navigation

The COMET was built specifically for naval service. Laid down on 15 May 1956.

Classification: The COMET originally was classified T-AK 269; she was changed to vehicle cargo ship T-LSV 7 on 1 June 1963 and again to T-AKR 7 on 1 January 1969.

Design: The COMET can accommodate some 700 vehicles in her two after holds, with the two forward holds intended for general cargo. Vehicle space totals 83,613 square feet (7,525 m^2).

Status: The COMET was a U.S. Naval Ship prior to transfer to MarAd on 15 March 1985; assigned to RRF in March 1985.

The RO/RO ship COMET, with her side ports visible. Like the METEOR, she is rigged to carry break-bulk cargo as well as vehicles. (1982, L. Van Ginderen Collection)

2 VEHICLE/RAILROAD CARGO SHIPS: CONVERTED T2-SE-A2 TYPE

Number	Name	Launched	To RRF	Status
T-AK 5020	WASHINGTON	14 March 1944	Feb 1978	NDRF
T-AK 5021	MAINE	10 Oct 1943	June 1979	NDRF

Builders:	Marinship, Sausalito, Calif.
Displacement:	WASHINGTON 21,240 tons full load
	MAINE 21,177 tons full load
Tonnage:	WASHINGTON 8,039 GRT
	12,292 DWT
	MAINE 8,025 GRT
	12,249 DWT
Length:	538¹¹/₁₂ feet (164.3 m) waterline
	559¾ feet (170.7 m) overall
Beam:	67¹¹/₁₂ feet (20.7 m)
Draft:	27 feet (8.2 m)
Propulsion:	1 steam turbine (General Electric); 10,000 shp; 1 shaft
Boilers:	2 (Babcock & Wilcox)
Speed:	16.5 knots
Range:	12,000 n.miles (22,224 km) at 16 knots
Manning:	27 civilian
Radars:	. . . . . . navigation

The WASHINGTON is one of two seatrain-type ships that have demonstrated highly flexible cargo capabilities, including carrying aircraft. However, they will be discarded soon because of their age. They were not activated for Operations Desert Shield/Desert Storm. (1990, Giorgio Arra)

These are former Mission-type tankers, converted to carry railway cars, containers, vehicles, and aircraft. They are invariably referred to as "seatrains."

Formerly assigned to RRF; both ships are deteriorating because of age and are expected to be stricken in the near future.

Class: The WASHINGTON was built as the merchant tanker MISSION SAN DIEGO; acquired by the Navy on 17 October 1947 and designated AO 121 (name retained). She was stricken on 22 June 1955; reacquired on 3 July 1956, she served in MSC until again stricken on 16 October 1957.

The MAINE was built as the Navy tanker TOMAHAWK, designated AO 88. Commissioned on 16 April 1944, she served in the Pacific during 1944–1945 (earning six battle stars). She was decommissioned on 5 January 1946 and stricken on 21 January 1946; she was then acquired for MSTS operation until transferred to the Maritime Administration in September 1961 and laid up.

Conversion: Both ships were converted by the Maryland Shipbuilding and Dry Dock in 1966–1967; they then served as combination train carriers and container ships (renamed with Seatrain prefixes). The conversion made use of sections of several tankers, with the tanker names retained according to their propulsion sections.

The superstructure/machinery aft configuration of the WASHINGTON reveals her origins as a Mission-type tanker. (1990, Giorgio Arra)

2 VEHICLE CARGO SHIPS: CANADIAN BUILT

Number	Name	Launched	To RRF	Status
T-AKR 5077	CAPE LAMBERT	1973	Nov 1987	MSC-RRF
T-AKR 5078	CAPE LOBOS	1972	Mar 1988	MSC-RRF

Builders:	Port Weller Dry Dock, St. Catharines, Ontario (Canada)
Displacement:	30,375 tons full load
Tonnage:	15,005 GRT
	16,382 DWT
Length:	621⅓ feet (189.4 m) waterline
	681⅚ feet (207.9 m) overall
Beam:	75⅙ feet (22.9 m)

Draft:	30½ feet (9.3 m)
Propulsion:	2 diesel engines (Crossley-Pielstick); 18,000 bhp; 2 shafts
Speed:	19 knots
Range:	6,000 n.miles (11,112 km) at 17.5 knots
Manning:	27 civilian
Radars:	. . . . . . navigation

These ships were built as newsprint and vehicle carriers. They are ice-strengthened for operations on the Great Lakes.

Design: The ships have side doors with two vehicle ramps. They have 189,937 square feet (17,094 m²) of vehicle space.

The CAPE LOBOS as laid up in the James River reserve group. The king posts are on the ship moored alongside. RRF ships are moored in Maritime Administration reserve fleets as well as in ports near their potential cargoes. (1989, L. Van Ginderen Collection)

1 VEHICLE CARGO SHIP: SWEDISH BUILT

Number	Name	Launched	To RRF	Status
T-AKR 5069	CAPE EDMONT	1971	Apr 1987	MSC-RRF

Builders:	Eriksberg M/V, Lindholmen (Sweden)
Displacement:	approx. 32,000 tons full load
Tonnage:	13,355 GRT
	20,224 DWT
Length:	602½ feet (183.7 m) waterline
	652¹¹⁄₁₂ feet (199.0 m) overall
Beam:	94 feet (28.65 m)
Draft:	30⅝ feet (9.4 m)

Propulsion:	3 diesel engines; 25,920 bhp; 1 shaft
Speed:	20.7 knots
Range:	20,000 n.miles (37,040 km) at 17 knots
Manning:	31 civilian
Radars:	. . . . . . navigation

Combination vehicle and container ship; 1,212 standard containers can be carried. Assigned to the RRF on 10 April 1987.

Design: The ship has 118,325 square feet (10,649 m²) of vehicle space.

3 VEHICLE CARGO SHIPS: JAPANESE-NORWEGIAN BUILT

Number	Name	Launched	To RRF	Status
T-AKR 5066	Cape Hudson	1979	Nov 1986	MSC-RRF
T-AKR 5067	Cape Henry	1979	Sep 1986	MSC-RRF
T-AKR 5068	Cape Horn	1979	Dec 1986	MSC-RRF

Builders:	T-AKR 5066	Mitsubishi, Nagasaki (Japan)
	T-AKR 5067	Kaldnes Mek., Versted A/S Tønsberg (Norway)
	T-AKR 5068	Tangen Verft, Kragerø (Norway)
Displacement:	approx. 47,200 tons full load	
Tonnage:	T-AKR 5066	21,976 GRT
	T-AKR 5067	21,747 GRT
	T-AKR 5068	22,090 GRT
Length:	693¾ feet (211.5 m) waterline	
	749½ feet (228.5 m) overall	
Beam:	105⅝ feet (32.3 m)	
Draft:	35⁵⁄₁₂ feet (10.8 m)	
Propulsion:	1 diesel engine (Mitsubishi-Sulzer in Cape Henry; Burmeister & Wain in others); 30,150 bhp (30,700 bhp in Norwegian-built ships); 1 shaft	
Speed:	21 knots	
Range:	24,300 n.miles (45,000 km) at 17 knots	
Manning:	28 to 34 civilian	
Radars:	. . . . . . navigation	

These are combination RO/RO-container ships. They can carry vehicles or 1,607 to 1,626 standard containers.

The Cape Hudson, showing the ships superstructure-aft design, large stern vehicle ramp offset to starboard, and forward pedestal crane. She is one of numerous foreign-built ships in the sealift fleet, acquired in the 1980s when there was a world shipping glut. (1990, L. Van Ginderen Collection)

Design: Details vary. They all have one 40-ton-capacity crane forward (superstructure aft).

5 VEHICLE CARGO SHIPS: FRENCH-SWEDISH BUILT

Number	Name	Launched	To RRF	Status
T-AKR 5051	Cape Ducato		Dec 1985	MSC-RRF
T-AKR 5052	Cape Douglas		Nov 1985	MSC-RRF
T-AKR 5053	Cape Domingo		Oct 1985	MSC-RRF
T-AKR 5054	Cape Decision		Oct 1985	MSC-RRF
T-AKR 5055	Cape Diamond		Oct 1985	MSC-RRF

Builders:	T-AKR 5051, 5052, 5054	Eriksberg M/V, Lindholmen (Sweden)
	T-AKR 5053, 5054	Ch. de France, Dunkerque (France)
Displacement:	35,173 tons full load	
Tonnage:	23,972 to 24,437 GRT	
	21,299 to 21,398 DWT	
Length:	633⅝ feet (193.2 m) waterline	
	680¼ feet (207.4 m) overall	
Beam:	97 feet (29.6 m)	
Draft:	31½ feet (9.6 m)	
Propulsion:	*French built:* 3 diesel engines (Ch. d'Atlantic-Pielstick); 28,890 bhp; 1 shaft	
	Swedish built: 3 diesel engines (Lindholmen-Pielstick); 27,000 bhp; 1 shaft	
Speed:	22 knots	
Range:	19,000 n.miles (35,188 km) at 18 knots	
Manning:	27 civilian except Cape Ducato 30	
Radars:	. . . . . . navigation	

These are combination ships, able to carry heavy vehicles as well as 1,327 standard containers.

The Cape Diamond, showing her stern ramp, offset to starboard; the structures on deck are ventilators to circulate air on the vehicle decks. Although generally similar to the Japanese- and Norwegian-built ships in the previous entry, these ships have a conventional funnel configuration. (1990, L. Van Ginderen Collection)

3 VEHICLE CARGO SHIPS: SWEDISH BUILT

Number	Name	Launched	Status
T-AK 2044	AMERICAN EAGLE	1981	**MSC-Active**
T-AKR 9672	AMERICAN FALCON	1981	**MSC-Active**
T-AKR 9673	AMERICAN CONDOR	1981	**MSC-Active**

Builders:	Kockums, Mälmo (Sweden)
Displacement:	
Tonnage:	AMERICAN EAGLE 15,632 GRT
	others 15,636 GRT
	AMERICAN FALCON 20,394 DWT
	others 20,404 DWT
Length:	593 feet (180.8 m) waterline
	635¼ feet (199.2 m) overall
Beam:	91⅝ feet (28.0 m)

Draft:	29½ feet (9.0 m)
Propulsion:	2 diesel engines (Cegielski-Sulzer 6RND68M); 21,500 bhp; 1 shaft
Speed:	22 knots
Range:	16,000 n.miles (29,632 km) at 19 knots
Manning:	21 civilian
Radars:	. . . . . navigation

These are large ships with their bridge forward and twin funnels aft. The AMERICAN EAGLE can carry 1,040 standard containers or vehicles, with 116,669 square feet (10,500 m²) of vehicle parking area; the other ships are similar.

Design: There are two bow thrusters to assist docking operations. Vehicles are loaded/unloaded via stern ramps.

The AMERICAN EAGLE, an unusual split-superstructure design with tandem funnels aft. There are tandem stern ramps. (U.S. Navy)

1 VEHICLE CARGO SHIP: "CALLAGHAN"

Number	Name	Launched	In Service	Status
T-AKR 1001	ADM. WM. M. CALLAGHAN	17 Oct 1967	19 Dec 1967	MSC-RRF

Builders:	Sun Shipbuilding and Dry Dock, Chester, Penna.
Displacement:	26,573 tons full load
Tonnage:	13,500 GRT
	24,471 DWT
Length:	694¼ feet (211.66 m) overall
Beam:	92 feet (28.1 m)
Draft:	29 feet (8.8 m)
Propulsion:	2 gas turbines (General Electric LM 2500); 40,000 shp; 2 shafts
Speed:	26 knots
Range:	12,000 n.miles (22,224 km) at 20 knots
Manning:	30 civilian
Radars:	1 . . . . . . navigation

The CALLAGHAN was an early RO/RO ship, and the first built for the U.S. Navy but operated under charter to MSC rather than outright ownership. The ship was operated by MSTS/MSC in that status for almost two decades until purchased outright in 1986.

Design: The ship has 167,537 square feet (15,078 m²) of vehicle storage space with four side ports and a stern ramp for rapid loading and unloading. She can offload some 750 vehicles in 27 hours. Fitted with two 120-ton-capacity booms and 12 booms with a capacity of 5 to 10 tons.

Engineering: The CALLAGHAN was the first all-gas-turbine ship constructed for the U.S. Navy. The engines were originally two Pratt & Whitney FT-4 (rated at 25,000 shp each); replaced in 1977 by the widely used LM 2500s.

Name: The ship is named for Admiral William M. Callaghan, first commander of the Military Sea Transportation Service (predecessor to MSC), from 1949 to 1952. He was retired and employed by American Export lines, which built the ship, when she was named in his honor by the firm.

Status: Taken out of service and transferred to RRF on 31 May 1987 after almost 20 years of continuous MSC service. Transferred to MarAd on 25 June 1987 for layup.

5 VEHICLE CARGO SHIPS: SHORT-TERM CONTRACTS

The vehicle cargo ships LYRA, PONCE, SENATOR, STRONG TEXAN, and STRONG AMERICAN were under commercial contract to MSC when this edition went to press.

The ADM. WM. M. CALLAGHAN was the first RO/RO ship acquired by the U.S. Navy to move Army vehicles between the United States and Europe. She also served as a gas-turbine trials ship for the Navy. She has cargo holds forward; vehicles are loaded/unloaded through side ports as well as through a stern ramp. (1985, L. Van Ginderen Collection)

BARGE-CARRYING SHIPS

These ships carry barges that are preloaded with military equipment. The term LASH indicates Lighter Aboard Ship; SEABEE is slang for the Sea Barge. The LASH ships use heavy-lift cranes to load and unload their barges; the SEABEE ships have a large stern lift to raise and lower the barges.

4 LASH CARGO SHIPS: C9-S-81d TYPE

Number	Name	Launched	To RRF	Status
T-AK 1015	GREEN ISLAND	1975		**MSC-Active**
T-AKR 5070	CAPE FLATTERY	1973	May 1987	MSC-RRF
T-AKR 5073	CAPE FAREWELL	1973	Apr 1987	MSC-RRF
T-AK 9651	AMERICAN KESTREL	1974		**MSC-Active**

Builders:	Avondale Shipyards, New Orleans, La.
Displacement:	62,314 tons full load
Tonnage:	T-AK type 32,278 GRT
	T-AKR type
	T-AK type 46,152 DWT
	T-AKR type
Length:	797⅙ feet (243.0 m) waterline
	893⅓ feet (272.35 m) overall
Beam:	100 feet (30.5 m)
Draft:	40⅚ feet (12.4 m)

Propulsion:	2 steam turbines (De Laval); 32,000 shp; 1 shaft
Boilers:	2 (Combustion Engineering)
Speed:	22.75 knots
Range:	15,000 n.miles (27,780 km) at 19 knots
Manning:	27 to 29 civilian
Radars:	2 . . . . . . navigation

These LASH ships can carry 89 preloaded barges. A small tug is also embarked to help maneuver barges alongside.

Class: A third ship was procured by MSC in January 1988, the DELTA SUD, to have become the CAPE FEAR. However, she suffered major machinery damage during an MSC-sponsored overhaul and is expected to be scrapped.

Design: A 455-ton-capacity travelling crane is fitted for moving barges.

The AMERICAN KESTREL is a sleek-looking ship, with two large travelling cranes to handle lighters. The engine exhaust stacks are built into the sides, amidships (seen aft of the second crane), somewhat similar to LSD/LPD designs. (U.S. Navy)

3 SEABEE SHIPS: C8-S-82a TYPE

Number	Name	Launched	To RRF	Status
T-AKR 5063	CAPE MAY	1972	July 1986	MSC-RRF
T-AKR 5064	CAPE MENDOCINO	1972	Oct 1986	MSC-RRF
T-AKR 5065	CAPE MOHICAN	1973	Sep 1986	MSC-RRF

Builders:	General Dynamics, Quincy, Mass.
Displacement:	18,880 tons light
	57,290 tons full load
Tonnage:	21,667 GRT
	38,410 DWT
Length:	721⅓ feet (219.9 m) waterline
	873¾ feet (266.39 m) overall
Beam:	105⅝ feet (32.3 m)
Draft:	39¹¹⁄₁₂ feet (11.9 m)
Propulsion:	2 steam turbines (General Electric); 36,000 shp; 1 shaft
Boilers:	2 (Babcock & Wilcox)
Speed:	20.5 knots
Range:	14,300 n.miles (26,484 km) at 19.25 knots
Manning:	40 civilian
Radars:	. . . . . . navigation

These ships can each carry 38 cargo barges.

Design: Fitted with a 2,000-ton-capacity elevator at the stern for loading and unloading fully laden barges. In addition, these ships can carry 4,000 barrels (CAPE MOHICAN 11,000 barrels) of liquid cargo.

The CAPE MAY at Antwerp shows the long, straight lines of this barge-carrying design; the bridge straddles the barge well, and machinery is fitted into the sidewalls. (1991, L. Van Ginderen Collection)

The open stern of the CAPE MAY shows the barge-carrying well of the ship; the stern elevator lifts barges from the water to storage deck levels. (1991, L. Van Ginderen Collection)

5 LASH SHIPS: C8-S-81b TYPE

Number	Name	Launched	To RRF	Status
T-AK 1005	AUSTRAL RAINBOW	1972		**MSC-Active**
T-AK 2064	GREEN HARBOUR	1972		**MSC-Active**
T-AK 5061	AUSTRAL LIGHTNING	1971	May 1985	MSC-RRF
T-AK 5071	CAPE FLORIDA	1971	Feb 1987	MSC-RRF
T-AKR 1192	LASH ATLANTICO	1972		**MSC-Active**

Builders:	Avondale Shipyards, New Orleans, La.
Displacement:	44,606 tons full load
Tonnage:	LASH ATLANTICO 26,404 GRT
	others 26,456 GRT
	29,820 DWT
Length:	723⅝ feet (220.7 m) waterline
	819⅝ feet (249.9 m) overall
Beam:	100 feet (30.5 m)
Draft:	40¾ feet (12.4 m)

Propulsion:	2 steam turbines (De Laval); 32,000 shp; 1 shaft
Boilers:	2 (Babcock & Wilcox)
Speed:	22.5 knots
Range:	13,000 n.miles (24,076 km) at 22.5 knots
Manning:	27 to 29 civilian
Radars:	. . . . . . navigation

These are former LASH barge carriers that were modified (prior to MSC charter) to combination barge/container ships. They can carry 71 standard cargo barges or some 840 standard containers, except GREEN HARBOUR can carry 1,000.

Design: These were highly innovative ships (11 built).

A 30-ton-capacity travelling crane is fitted for handling containers and a 446-ton-capacity travelling barge crane. Two 5-ton cranes are also installed.

These ships are similar to the larger C9-S-81d barge carriers.

The AUSTRAL RAINBOW (ex-AMERICAN VETERAN) is similar to the C9-type LASH ships, but smaller. These ships can carry preloaded barges or containers; in this view two small tugs are being carried to move barges. (U.S. Navy)

CARGO SHIPS

1 ULTRA-HEAVY-LIFT SHIP: CONVERTED TANKER

Number	Name	Launched	Status
T-AK 2062	AMERICAN CORMORANT	1975	**MSC-Active**

Builders:	Eriksbergs Mek. Verkstads, Gothenberg (Sweden)
Tonnage:	10,195 GRT
	51,269 DWT
Length:	738⅙ feet (225.1 m) overall
Beam:	135 feet (41.15 m)
Draft:	32⅔ feet (10.0 m); flooded 65¾ feet (20.05 m)
Propulsion:	1 diesel engine (Eriksberg/Burmeister & Wain 10K84EF); 25,000 bhp; 1 shaft
Speed:	16 knots
Range:	23,700 n.miles (43,892 km) at 13 knots
Manning:	22 civilian
Radars:	2 . . . . . . navigation

The AMERICAN CORMORANT is a semi-submersible, ultra-heavy-lift ship (sometimes referred to as a "flo/flo" for float-on/float-off). The ship has a lifting deck 394 feet (120.1 m) long and 135 feet (41.15 m) wide that can be submerged by ballasting the ship to about 65 feet (19.8 m), at which point the lifting deck is 26 feet (7.9 m) below the surface. Small craft, heavy equipment, and barges up to a total of approximately 45,000 tons can then be positioned over the ship which is then deballasted. The ship can also carry 25 long (40-foot/12.2-m) containers on her fantail.

This unusual ship was built as a tanker (133,000 deadweight tons). She was laid up almost immediately because of the international shipping glut; she was converted in 1981–1982 at the Gotaverken Cityvarvet yard in Sweden to her current configuration. During the modification process she was lengthened by 180 feet (54.9 m).

Status: The ship was purchased by the U.S. firm American Automar in 1985 (and renamed). Chartered by MSC in October 1985.

The "flo/flo" ship AMERICAN CORMORANT loaded with Army barges, floating cranes, landing craft, and tugs. The ship has operated in both the afloat prepositioning role, to assist in unloading Army equipment from merchant ships, and in special cargo service. (American Automar)

1 CARGO SHIP: C6-S-60c TYPE

Number	Name	Launched	Status
T-AK 2037	MALLORY LYKES	1965	**MSC-Active**

Builders:	
Displacement:	
Tonnage:	14,081 GRT
Length:	634⅝ feet (193.55 m) waterline
	665¾ feet (203.0 m) overall
Beam:	75 1/12 feet (22.9 m)

Draft:	31½ feet (9.6 m)
Propulsion:	2 steam turbines; 19,000 shp; 1 shaft
Boilers:	2
Speed:	21 knots
Range:	
Manning:	
Radars:	. . . . . . navigation

Container ship.

2 COMBINATION CARGO SHIPS: C5-S-78a TYPE

Number	Name	Launched	To RRF	Status
T-AK 1013	ROVER	28 Apr 1969		**MSC-Active**
T-AK 1014	CAPE NOME	26 Sep 1969	Dec 1987	MSC-RRF

Builders:	Ingalls Shipbuilding, Pascagoula, Miss.
Displacement:	27,980 tons full load
Tonnage:	11,757 GRT
	15,694 DWT
Length:	559⅝ feet (170.7 m) waterline
	601⅓ feet (183.3 m) overall
Beam:	90 feet (27.4 m)
Draft:	34 feet (10.4 m)
Propulsion:	2 steam turbines (General Electric); 30,000 shp; 1 shaft

Boilers:	2 (Combustion Engineering)
Speed:	23.6 knots
Range:	12,000 n.miles (22,224 km) at 23.6 knots
Manning:	ROVER 25 civilian
	CAPE NOME 37 civilian
Radar:	. . . . . . navigation

Combination break-bulk/container ships with a capacity of 70 standard containers. The ROVER is employed primarily to ship ammunition.

These are especially attractive superstructure-aft ships with three king posts supporting cargo booms.

Note that the MSC also operates a tanker named ROVER.

Design: Fitted with a stern door for vehicle loading/unloading.

The ROVER and CAPE NOME (above) are combination break-bulk and container ships. Here containers are stacked above the CAPE NOME's cargo holds. Increasingly, military equipment and munitions are packaged in containers. (1992, L. Van Ginderen Collection)

2 CARGO SHIPS: C5-S-75a TYPE

Number	Name	Launched	To RRF	Status
T-AK 2039	CAPE GIRARDEAU	1968	Apr 1988	MSC-RRF
T-AK 5051	CAPE GIBSON	1968	Apr 1988	MSC-RRF
T-AK 851	CLEVELAND	1969		**MSC-Active**

Builders:	Newport News Shipbuilding, Va.
Displacement:	31,995 tons full load
Tonnage:	15,949 GRT
	CAPE GIRARDEAU 22,273 DWT
	CAPE GIBSON 22,216 DWT
	CLEVELAND 22,180 DWT
Length:	582⅓ feet (177.55 m) waterline
	604⅝ feet (184.4 m) overall
Beam:	82⅙ feet (25.05 m)

Draft:	35 feet (10.7 m)
Propulsion:	2 steam turbines (General Electric); 24,000 shp; 1 shaft
Boilers:	2 (Babcock & Wilcox)
Speed:	21 knots
Range:	14,000 n.miles (25,928 km) at 21 knots
Manning:	36 civilian except CLEVELAND 21 civilian
Radars:	. . . . . . navigation

These break-bulk cargo ships can carry 409 standard containers as well as dry and refrigerated cargo, and 17,000 barrels of liquid cargo. Accommodations for 22 passengers.

Design: One 70-ton-capacity boom and 20 20-ton and 4 15-ton cranes.

The CAPE GIRARDEAU is one of several multi-cargo ships in MSC service and the RRF. The ship has seven king posts of three variations. (1991, L. Van Ginderen Collection)

4 CARGO SHIPS: C5-S-37e TYPE

Number	Name	Launched	Status
T-AK 9123	JOHN LYKES	1960	**MSC-Active**
T-AK 9808	JOSEPH LYKES	1960	**MSC-Active**
T-AK 9783	NANCY LYKES	1961	**MSC-Active**
T-AK 9838	LESLIE LYKES	1962	**MSC-Active**

Builders:	Bethlehem Steel, Sparrows Point, Baltimore, Md.
Displacement:	
Tonnage:	11,891 GRT
	14,301 DWT except LESLIE LYKES 14,526 DWT
Length:	592½ feet (180.6 m) overall

Beam:	69 feet (21.0 m)
Draft:	30 feet (9.1 m)
Propulsion:	steam turbine; 1 shaft
Boilers:	2
Speed:	17 knots
Range:	18,800 n.miles (34,818 km) at 16 knots
Manning:	32 civilian
Radars:	. . . . . . navigation

Container ships.

The JOSEPH LYKES in light condition at Antwerp. (1990, L. Van Ginderen Collection)

1 CARGO SHIP: C4-S-69b TYPE

Number	Name	Launched	Status
T-AK 1010	SANTA VICTORIA	1969	**MSC-Active**

Builders:	Avondale Shipyards, New Orleans, La.
Displacement:	21,617 tons full load
Tonnage:	13,053 GRT
	13,074 DWT
Length:	544⅓ feet (166.0 m) waterline
	578⅝ feet (176.5 m) overall
Beam:	82 feet (25.0 m)
Draft:	32 feet (9.8 m)

Propulsion:	2 steam turbines (General Electric); 24,000 shp; 2 shafts
Boilers:	2 (Babcock & Wilcox)
Speed:	23 knots
Range:	12,000 n.miles (22,224 km) at 23 knots
Manning:	29 civilian
Radars:	. . . . . . navigation

General cargo ship with limited container capability.

Design: Fitted with one 70-ton-capacity crane, eight 20-ton, eight 10-ton, and eight 5-ton cranes.

The SANTA VICTORIA anchored off Diego Garcia in the Indian Ocean. (U.S. Navy)

7 CARGO SHIPS: C4-S-66a TYPE

Number	Name	Launched	To RRF	Status
T-AK 2043	LETITIA LYKES	1968		**MSC-Active**
T-AK 5056	CAPE BRETON	4 June 1966	May 1985	MSC-RRF
T-AK 5057	CAPE BOVER	12 Feb 1966	Apr 1985	MSC-RRF
T-AK 5058	CAPE BORDA	16 Apr 1966	Apr 1985	MSC-RRF
T-AK 5059	CAPE BON	16 July 1965	July 1985	MSC-RRF
T-AK 5060	CAPE BLANCO	10 July 1965	July 1985	MSC-RRF
T-AK 2045	TAMPA BAY	1966		**MSC-Active**

Builders:	Avondale Shipyards, New Orleans, La.
Displacement:	21,840 tons full load
Tonnage:	10,723 GRT
	14,662 DWT
Length:	514¾ feet (156.9 m) waterline
	539⅝ feet (164.6 m) overall

Beam:	76 feet (23.2 m)
Draft:	32⅔ feet (9.95 m)
Propulsion:	2 steam turbines (De Laval or Westinghouse); 15,500 shp; 1 shaft
Boilers:	2 (Foster Wheeler)
Speed:	21 knots
Range:	13,660 n.miles (25,300 km) at 20 knots
Manning:	28 to 30 civilian except TAMPA BAY 44 civilian
Radars:	. . . . . . navigation

Break-bulk cargo ships. They carry 4,000 barrels of liquid cargo in addition to dry cargo. The LETITIA LYKES carries a 1,000-bed Navy field hospital.

Design: Fitted with one 80-ton capacity boom and 20 small booms.

The CAPE BOVER, showing the unusual king-post arrangement of this cargo variant. There are numerous other details that differ from the C5-type Lykes ships. (1991, Giorgio Arra)

5 CARGO SHIPS: C4-S-58a TYPE

Number	Name	Launched	To RRF	Status
T-AK 5009	CAPE ANN	12 May 1962	Mar 1980	MSC-RRF
T-AK 5010	CAPE ALEXANDER	7 July 1962	Apr 1980	MSC-RRF
T-AK 5011	CAPE ARCHWAY	15 Sep 1962	Apr 1980	MSC-RRF
T-AK 5012	CAPE ALAVA	24 Mar 1962	Apr 1980	MSC-RRF
T-AK 5013	CAPE AVINOF	8 Dec 1962	Apr 1980	MSC-RRF

Builders:	Ingalls Shipbuilding, Pascagoula, Miss.
Displacement:	18,560 tons full load
Tonnage:	11,309 GRT
	12,932 DWT
Length:	540$\frac{11}{12}$ feet (164.9 m) waterline
	571$\frac{5}{6}$ feet (174.35 m) overall
Beam:	75$\frac{1}{6}$ feet (22.9 m)
Draft:	30$\frac{5}{6}$ feet (9.4 m)
Propulsion:	2 steam turbines (General Electric or Westinghouse); 16,500 shp; 1 shaft
Boilers:	2
Speed:	21.5 knots

Range:	13,300 n.miles (24,632 km) at 20 knots
Manning:	32 civilian
Helicopters:	landing deck in CAPE ANN and CAPE AVINOF
Radars:	. . . . . . navigation

Large break-bulk cargo ships built for Farrell Lines.

Design: These ships were built specifically for the East African trade with special dehumidifying equipment to prevent cargo sweating and odor permeation. Originally six ships in class.

Fitted with one 60-ton-capacity boom, six 10-ton and 14 5-ton cranes. Two ships fitted with helicopter deck aft and other enhancements upon being taken over by MSC.

Engineering: Normal horsepower is indicated above; maximum is 19,250 shp. Several ships exceeded their designed speed (above); the AFRICAN NEPTUNE (now T-AK 5011) averaged 22.48 knots on the 6,786-n.mile (12,568-km) trip from New York to Cape Town, South Africa.

The CAPE ALEXANDER, emitting smoke, under way. These ships have unusual king-post-crane-boom arrangements. The CAPE ALEXANDER has not been fitted with a helicopter deck. (1991, L. Van Ginderen Collection)

3 CARGO SHIPS: C4-S-57a TYPE

Number	Name	Launched	To RRF	Status
T-AK 2016	PIONEER COMMANDER	20 Dec 1962	June 1982	MSC-RRF
T-AK 2018	PIONEER CONTRACTOR	22 Mar 1963	Sep 1981	MSC-RRF
T-AK 2019	PIONEER CRUSADER	30 July 1963	Sep 1981	MSC-RRF

Builders:	Bethlehem Steel, Quincy, Mass.
Displacement:	21,053 tons full load
Tonnage:	11,164 GRT except COMMANDER 11,105 GRT
	13,535 DWT
Length:	560¹¹/₁₂ feet (171.0 m) overall
Beam:	75¹/₁₂ feet (22.9 m)
Draft:	32⅙ (9.8 m)
Propulsion:	2 steam turbines (Bethlehem); 16,500 shp; 1 shaft
Boilers:	2 (Foster Wheeler)

4 CARGO SHIPS: C4-S-1u TYPE

Number	Name	Launched	To RRF	Status
T-AK 5022	SANTA ANA	18 Aug 1962	May 1980	MSC-RRF
T-AK 5029	CALIFORNIA	28 July 1961	Dec 1980	MSC-RRF
T-AK 5075	CAPE JOHNSON	5 May 1962	June 1988	MSC-RRF
T-AK 5077	CAPE JUBY	9 Feb 1962	July 1988	MSC-RRF

Builders:	T-AK 5022, 5075, 5077 National Steel and Shipbuilding, San Diego, Calif.
	T-AK 5029 Newport News Shipbuilding, Va.
Displacement:	22,629 tons
Tonnage:	SANTA ANA 12,724 GRT
	SANTA ANA 14,376 DWT
	CAPE JOHNSON 12,724 GRT
	CAPE JOHNSON 14,467 DWT
	others 12,691 GRT
	others 14,321 DWT

Speed:	21 knots
Range:	12,000 n.miles (22,224 km) at 21 knots
Manning:	43 civilian
Radars:	. . . . . navigation

Details of these ships differ. Built for the United States Lines. They carry a mixed load of dry cargo, refrigerated provisions, and 8,000 barrels of liquid cargo.

Design: They have one 70-ton boom and several smaller cranes.

Engineering: Normal horsepower is indicated above; maximum is 18,150 shp. The merchant AMERICAN CHARGER of this design set a 1963 speed record of 24.9 knots across the Atlantic (3,718 n.miles/ 6,886 km).

Length:	528⁵/₁₂ feet (161.1 m) waterline
	565 feet (172.25 m) overall
Beam:	76 feet (23.2 m)
Draft:	32 feet (9.75 m)
Propulsion:	2 steam turbines (General Electric); 17,500 shp; 1 shaft
Boilers:	2 (Foster Wheeler)
Speed:	20.75 knots
Range:	12,600 n.miles (23,335 km) at 20 knots
Manning:	30 to 33 civilian
Radars:	. . . . . navigation

Break-bulk cargo ships originally built for States Steamship Co. or Moore-McCormack Lines.

Design: One 60-ton-capacity boom, ten 20-ton cranes, two 10-ton cranes, and ten 5-ton cranes.

Engineering: Normal horsepower is indicated above; maximum is 19,200 shp.

The CAPE JUBY is a typical break-bulk ship. (1991, L. Van Ginderen Collection)

The long, clean lines of the SANTA ANA show the standard break-bulk configuration. (1991, L. Van Ginderen Collection)

3 CARGO SHIPS: C4-S-66a TYPE

Number	Name	Launched	Status
T-AK 2048	LOUISE LYKES	1965	**MSC-Active**
T-AK 9720	GALVESTON BAY	1966	**MSC-Active**
T-AK 9636	RUTH LYKES	1966	**MSC-Active**

Builders:	Avondale Shipyards, New Orleans, La.
Displacement:	
Tonnage:	10,954 GRT except GALVESTON BAY 10,718 GRT
	14,662 DWT
Length:	540 feet (164.6 m) overall
Beam:	76 feet (23.2 m)

Draft:	33 feet (10.1 m)
Propulsion:	steam turbine; 15,500 shp; 1 shaft
Boilers:	2
Speed:	19 knots
Range:	
Manning:	27 to 30 civilian
Radars:	. . . . . . navigation

Break-bulk ships built for Lykes Brothers.

Design: Fitted with one 8-ton-capacity boom and several lesser booms.

The LOUISE LYKES at San Diego, where the Navy has a major supply center. (1985, Giorgio Arra)

3 CARGO SHIPS: C3-S-76a TYPE

Number	Name	Launched	To RRF	Status
T-AK 5026	DEL VIENTO	9 Dec 1968	Apr 1984	MSC-RRF
T-AK 5049	DEL MONTE	21 June 1968	July 1984	MSC-RRF
T-AK 5050	DEL VALLE	7 Oct 1968	July 1984	MSC-RRF

Builders:	Ingalls Shipbuilding, Pascagoula, Miss.
Displacement:	19,285 tons full load
Tonnage:	10,396 GRT
	13,039 DWT
Length:	521⅚ feet (159.1 m) overall
Beam:	69⅚ feet (21.3 m)
Draft:	30⅚ feet (9.4 m)

Propulsion:	2 steam turbines (General Electric); 11,700 shp; 1 shaft
Boilers:	2 (Babcock & Wilcox)
Speed:	20 knots
Range:	13,600 n.miles (25,187 km) at 18.6 knots
Manning:	DEL MONTE 36 civilian
	DEL VALLE 31 civilian
Radars:	. . . . . . navigation

Break-bulk cargo ships built for the Delta Line. They can carry 11,000 barrels of liquid cargo.

Design: Fitted with one 75-ton-capacity boom and several smaller booms.

3 CARGO SHIPS: C3-S-46a TYPE

Number	Name	Launched	To RRF	Status
T-AK 2033	BUYER	1962	Jan 1988	MSC-RRF
T-AK 5008	BANNER	1961	Jan 1983	MSC-RRF
T-AK 5019	COURIER	1962	Aug 1983	MSC-RRF

Builders:	National Steel and Shipbuilding, San Diego, Calif., except COURIER by Sun Shipbuilding and Dry Dock, Chester, Penna.
Displacement:	19,400 tons full load
Tonnage:	10,659 GRT except COURIER 11,000 GRT
	BUYER 12,529 DWT
	BANNER 12,629 DWT
	COURIER 12,705 DWT
Length:	469¹¹⁄₁₂ feet (143.3 m) waterline
	493 feet (150.3 m) overall
Beam:	73 feet (22.25 m)
Draft:	30½ feet (9.3 m)
Propulsion:	2 steam turbines (General Electric); 13,750 shp; 1 shaft

Boilers:	2 (Babcock & Wilcox)
Speed:	20 knots
Range:	18,000 n.miles (33,336 km) at 18.5 knots
Manning:	32 civilian except BUYER 30 civilian
Radars:	. . . . . . navigation

Break-bulk cargo ships built for American Export/Isbrandtsen Lines. The COURIER has been modified to carry containers in addition to break-bulk cargo.

Design: Machinery and large superstructure aft ships with amidships bridge structure. Fitted with one 60-ton-capacity boom and 20 smaller booms and cranes.

Engineering: Normal horsepower is indicated above; maximum is 13,750 shp.

Names: Note that there is also a tanker named COURIER in MSC service.

The BUYER, one of the relatively small but highly useful break-bulk cargo ships in the RRF. Most military equipment and supplies still come in "pieces" and are not containerized. (1988, L. Van Ginderen Collection)

4 CARGO SHIPS: C3-S-38a TYPE

Number	Name	Launched	To RRF	Status
T-AK 5005	ADVENTURER	9 July 1960	Feb 1980	MSC-RRF
T-AK 5006	AIDE	4 June 1960	Apr 1980	MSC-RRF
T-AK 5007	AMBASSADOR	23 Apr 1960	Dec 1980	MSC-RRF
T-AK 5008	AGENT	30 Jan 1960	Feb 1980	MSC-RRF

Builders: T-AK 5005, 5007 New York Shipbuilding, Camden, N.J.
               T-AK 5006, 5008 National Steel and Shipbuilding, San Diego, Calif.
Displacement: 17,570 tons full load
Tonnage: 7,848 GRT
              11,020 DWT, except ADVENTURER 10,813 tons, AGENT 11,089 tons
Length: 492$^{11}/_{12}$ feet (150.3 m) overall

Beam: 73 feet (22.25 m)
Draft: 27$^{11}/_{12}$ feet (8.5 m)
Propulsion: 1 steam turbine (General Electric); 12,500 shp; 1 shaft
Boilers: 2 (Babcock & Wilcox)
Speed: 19 knots
Range: 12,000 n.miles (22,224 km) at 18.5 knots
Manning: 32 civilian
Radars: . . . . . . navigation

Break-bulk cargo ships originally built for the American Export/Isbrandtsen Lines.

Design: Fitted with a 50-ton-capacity boom and several lesser cranes.

Tugs maneuver the AGENT at Portsmouth, Va. The RRF ships are periodically taken in hand, reactivated, and used for exercises or, on occasion, general cargo work. This photo was taken shortly before the massive Desert Shield sealift operation. (1990, L. Van Ginderen Collection)

5 CARGO SHIPS: C3-S-37d TYPE

Number	Name	Launched	To RRF	Status
T-AK 2035	Gulf Shipper	15 Feb 1964	Aug 1984	MSC-RRF
T-AK 2036	Gulf Trader	28 Dec 1963	Nov 1984	MSC-RRF
T-AK 5044	Gulf Banker	5 Oct 1963	Nov 1984	MSC-RRF
T-AK 5045	Gulf Farmer	3 Aug 1963	Nov 1984	MSC-RRF
T-AK 5046	Gulf Merchant	16 May 1964	Nov 1984	MSC-RRF

Builders:	Avondale Shipyards, New Orleans, La.
Displacement:	17,210 tons full load
Tonnage:	8,988 GRT except T-AK 5044, 5055 8,970 GRT
	11,368 DWT except T-AK 5044, 5055 11,367 DWT
Length:	494⅔ feet (150.8 m) overall
Beam:	69⅙ feet (21.1 m)
Draft:	30¹⁄₁₂ feet (9.2 m)
Propulsion:	2 steam turbines (Westinghouse except T-AK 5044, 5055 have General Electric); 10,000 shp; 1 shaft
Boilers:	2 (Combustion Engineering)
Speed:	18.75 knots
Range:	12,000 n.miles (22,224 km) at 17.75 knots
Manning:	30 to 36 civilian
Radars:	. . . . . . navigation

Break-bulk cargo ships built for the Gulf and South American Steam Ship Co.

Design: These ships have twin risers resembling king posts that serve as stacks. Their machinery spaces are well aft. Fitted with one 66-ton-capacity boom, two 15-ton, two 10-ton, and ten 5-ton derricks.

Engineering: Normal horsepower is indicated above; maximum is 11,000 shp.

The Gulf Trader; she has an unusual king-post/boom configuration, with twin risers behind the bridge. (1990, Giorgio Arra)

8 CARGO SHIPS: C3-S-37c TYPE

Number	Name	Launched	To RRF	Status
T-AK 5036	Cape Chalmers	6 Dec 1962	Nov 1984	MSC-RRF
T-AK 5037	Cape Canso	13 Oct 1962	Aug 1984	MSC-RRF
T-AK 5038	Cape Charles	16 May 1963	Nov 1984	MSC-RRF
T-AK 5039	Cape Clear	14 Aug 1963	Nov 1984	MSC-RRF
T-AK 5040	Cape Canaveral	11 May 1963	Aug 1984	MSC-RRF
T-AK 5041	Cape Cod	11 July 1962	Nov 1984	MSC-RRF
T-AK 5042	Cape Carthage	9 Mar 1963	Sept 1984	MSC-RRF
T-AK 5043	Cape Catoche	22 Dec 1962	Nov 1984	MSC-RRF

Builders:	T-AK 5036, 5038, 5039, 5041 Bethlehem Steel, Sparrows Point, Baltimore, Md.
	T-AK 5037, 5040, 5042, 5043 Avondale Shipyards, New Orleans, La.
Displacement:	18,560 tons full load
Tonnage:	9,296 GRT
	12,684 DWT
Length:	494¾ (150.8 m) overall
Beam:	69⅙ feet (21.1 m)
Draft:	32 feet (9.75 m)
Propulsion:	2 steam turbines (General Electric); 11,000 shp; 1 shaft
Boilers:	2 (Combustion Engineering or Foster Wheeler)
Speed:	18.75 knots
Range:	18,300 n.miles (33,892 km) at 17.75 knots
Manning:	30 to 37 civilian
Radars:	. . . . . . navigation

Break-bulk cargo ships built for the Lykes Brothers Steamship Co. They can carry 8,000 barrels of liquid cargo. This was the first series of U.S. oceangoing cargo ships to be built after World War II by a private shipping company.

Design: Twin risers resembling king posts serve as stacks. Fitted with one 60-ton-capacity boom and 20 smaller booms.

6 CARGO SHIPS: C3-S-33a TYPE

Number	Name	Launched	To RRF	Status
T-AK 0284 (T-AK 284)	NORTHERN LIGHT ↑	Apr 1961	Oct 1964	MSC-RRF
T-AK 0285 (T-AK 285)	SOUTHERN CROSS ↑	Nov 1961	Feb 1985	MSC-RRF
T-AK 5016	LAKE	5 Jan 1961	Mar 1977	MSC-RRF
T-AK 5017	PRIDE	1 Feb 1960	Feb 1977	MSC-RRF
T-AK 5018	SCAN	21 Mar 1961	Feb 1977	MSC-RRF
T-AK 5074	CAPE CATAWBA	1960	Feb 1987	MSC-RRF

Builders:	Sun Shipbuilding and Dry Dock, Chester, Penna., except T-AK 5074 by Todd Shipyards, San Pedro, Calif.
Displacement:	18,365 tons full load
Tonnage:	T-AK 284 9,361 GRT
	12,537 DWT
	T-AK 285 9,259 GRT
	12,519 DWT
Length:	457⅝ feet (139.6 m) waterline
	485¹¹⁄₁₂ feet (148.15 m) overall
Beam:	68 feet (20.7 m)
Draft:	28½ feet (8.7 m)
Propulsion:	1 steam turbine (General Electric); 11,000 shp; 1 shaft
Boilers:	2 (Combustion Engineering)
Speed:	19 knots
Range:	14,000 n.miles (25,928 km) at 18 knots
Manning:	32 to 36 civilian
Radars:	1 . . . . . . navigation

These were commercial cargo ships built for Moore-McCormack Lines. After merchant service they were laid up in NDRF. The NORTHERN LIGHT and SOUTHERN CROSS were acquired by the Navy in April 1980 for use as prepositioning ships in the Indian Ocean; they were placed in service on 22 April 1980 and 1 May 1980. Their sister ship VEGA was acquired in April 1981 for conversion to an SSBN supply ship (T-AK 286); see chapter 23.

Two other ships were acquired for conversion to surveying ships, but instead the Congress directed new-construction ships.

The NORTHERN LIGHT laid up by MSC on 26 April 1984 and the SOUTHERN CROSS on 13 September 1984 (correction to previous edition).

Design: The T-AK 284 has a modified bow that makes her slightly longer than other ships of this design. Both ex-T-AK ships are ice-strengthened for Arctic operations.

Engineering: Normal horsepower is shown above; maximum is 12,100 shp.

Status: The NORTHERN LIGHT and SOUTHERN CROSS were U.S. Naval Ships when active.

The NORTHERN LIGHT is representative of another series of small break-bulk cargo ships in the RRF. A sister ship, the VEGA, serves as an FBM resupply ship. (U.S. Navy)

1 ARCTIC CARGO SHIP: "ELTANIN" CLASS (C1-ME2-13a)

Number	Name	Launched	Commissioned	Status
T-AK 271	MIRFAK	5 Aug 1957	30 Dec 1957	NDRF

Builders:	Avondale Marine, New Orleans, La.
Displacement:	2,022 tons light
	4,800 tons full load
Length:	266 feet (81.1 m) overall
Beam:	51½ feet (15.7 m)
Draft:	23 feet (7.0 m)
Propulsion:	diesel-electric (4 Alco diesels; Westinghouse electric motors); 3,200 shp; 2 shafts
Speed:	13 knots
Range:	14,000 n.miles (25,930 km) at 13 knots
Manning:	48 civilian
Radars:	2 . . . . . . navigation

The MIRFAK is the survivor of a trio of cargo ships designed for Arctic operations. Her two sister ships were converted to oceanographic research ships and had distinguished careers in that role. The MIRFAK's potential usefulness is virtually nil. (U.S. Navy)

The MIRFAK was one of three small cargo ships built specifically for Arctic supply operations. She was operated by MSTS (later MSC) with a civilian crew until laid up in the NDRF in November 1979.

Class: Sister ships ELTANIN (AK 270) and MIZAR (AK 272) were converted to oceanographic research ships, the AGOR 8 and 11, respectively.

Design: The ship has a strengthened hull, icebreaking prow, enclosed crow's nest and control spaces, and other features for Arctic operations.

1 CARGO SHIP: JAPANESE CONSTRUCTION

Number	Name	Launched	Status
T-AK 9652	ADVANTAGE	1977	**MSC-Active**

Builders:	Nippon Kokan, Tsurumi (Japan)
Displacement:	27,750 tons full load
Tonnage:	11,675 GRT
	22,180 DWT
Length:	542½ feet (165.4 m) waterline
	560¹¹⁄₁₂ feet (171.0 m) overall
Beam:	86½ feet (26.4 m)
Draft:	32¾ feet (10.0 m)
Propulsion:	1 diesel engine (Mitsubishi-Sulzer); 14,000 bhp; 1 shaft
Speed:	17.5 knots
Range:	
Manning:	22 civilian
Radars:	. . . . . . navigation

The ADVANTAGE is employed as a prepositioned ammunition ship, carrying Air Force ordnance. She has a 762-container capacity.

Chartered from October 1988 onward.

Design: Fitted with one 150-ton-capacity, four 16-ton, and ten 10-ton cranes.

The ADVANTAGE with her cargo hatches swung open. The superstructure-aft ship has a double 150-ton-capacity crane amidships. (U.S. Navy)

1 CARGO SHIP: NORWEGIAN CONSTRUCTION

Number	Name	Launched	Status
T-AK 9653	NOBLE STAR	1977	**MSC-Active**

Builders:	Kaldnes M/V A/S Tonsberg (Norway)
Displacement:	24,000 tons full load
Tonnage:	10,472 GRT
	15,922 DWT
Length:	534⅔ feet (163.0 m) waterline
	562¼ feet (171.4 m) overall
Beam:	83⁵/₁₂ feet (25.4 m)
Draft:	34⁷/₁₂ feet (10.55 m)
Propulsion:	1 diesel engine (Nylands/Burmeister & Wain) 13,100 bhp; 1 shaft

Speed:	17.5 knots
Range:	
Manning:	21 civilian
Radars:	. . . . . . navigation

This ship was chartered on 31 December 1988 and loaded with a 500-bed deployable field hospital (330 standard containers); she was deployed to Diego Garcia in November 1989 as part of the Afloat Prepositioning Force.

The ship has a capacity of 570 containers.

Design: This superstructure-aft ship has one 150-ton-capacity crane, six 10-ton, four 16-ton, and one 5-ton cranes.

The NOBLE STAR has been employed to carry a largely containerized Navy field hospital. (1990, U.S. Navy)

2 COMBINATION CARGO SHIPS: GERMAN BUILT

Number	Name	Launched	Status
(none)	GREEN RIDGE	12 Jan 1979	**MSC-Active**
T-AK 2050	GREEN WAVE	10 Jan 1980	**MSC-Active**

Builders:	Howaldtswerke (HDW), Kiel (West Germany)	
Displacement:	18,178 tons full load	
Tonnage:	GREEN RIDGE	5,805 GRT
		9,549 DWT
	GREEN WAVE	9,521 GRT
		12,487 DWT
Length:	479¹/₁₂ feet (146.1 m) waterline	
	507 feet (154.6 m) overall	
Beam:	69¾ feet (21.25 m)	

Draft:	24½ feet (7.45 m)
Propulsion:	2 diesels (Krupp-MaK); 10,000 bhp; 1 shaft
Speed:	18 knots
Range:	14,400 n.miles (26,669 km) at 17 knots
Manning:	22 civilian
Radars:	. . . . . . navigation

Combination break-bulk and container ships, chartered by MSC mainly for Greenland and Antarctic resupply. Each can carry 543 standard containers.

Design: Similar but not identical sister ships. Both ships have ice-strengthened hulls. Fitted with six 25-ton-capacity cranes, four of which can be "ganged" to lift 80-ton loads from hold No. 4.

The GREEN WAVE in Arctic waters. Note the height of containers on her deck and the large cranes that provide a self-unloading capability; the bulbous bow is partially visible in this view. (1988, U.S. Navy)

1 COMBINATION CARGO SHIP: DANISH BUILT

Number	Name	Launched	Status
T-AK 9656	MAERSK CONSTELLATION	1980	**MSC-Active**

Builders:	Odense Staalskibsvaerft A/S, Lindo (Denmark)
Displacement:	
Tonnage:	29,750 DWT
Length:	551¾ feet (168.2 m) waterline
	598 feet (182.3 m) overall
Beam:	90 feet (27.4 m)
Draft:	32 feet (9.75 m)
Propulsion:	2 diesel engines (Sulzer); 15,960 bhp; 1 shaft
Speed:	18.5 knots
Range:	
Manning:	21 civilian
Radars:	. . . . . . navigation

Combination container/vehicle ship. Fitted with stern ramp.

1 RANGE SUPPORT SHIP

Number	Name	Launched	Status
T-AGDS 9642	NICOR CLIPPER	20 Apr 1982	**MSC-Active**

Builders:	Moss Point Marine, Escatawpa, Miss.
Displacement:	
Tonnage:	428 GRT
	1,200 DWT
Length:	253¹¹⁄₁₂ feet (77.4 m) overall
Beam:	44 feet (13.4 m)
Draft:	13 feet (4.0 m)
Propulsion:	2 diesel engines (General Motors EMD 12-567C); 2,700 bhp; 2 shafts
Speed:	10 knots
Range:	
Manning:	
Radars:	. . . . . . navigation

This is a small, open-deck cargo ship employed to support U.S. space tracking and research facilities on Caribbean islands.

Design: Built as an offshore oil rig supply vessel. A stern ramp is fitted for carrying small vehicles.

A bow thruster is fitted.

CARGO SHIP: "AMERICAN TROJAN" (C4-S-69)

The self-loading container ship AMERICAN TROJAN (T-AK 1010) suffered a flooded engine room off Diego Garcia on 15 December 1982. The ship was declared a total loss; the charter was terminated by the Navy and the ship was scrapped.

See 14th Edition/pages 286–287 for characteristics.

HEAVY-LIFT CARGO SHIP: "BROSTROM" CLASS (C4-S-B1)

The heavy-lift cargo ship MARINE FIDDLER (T-AK 267) was stricken from the NVR on 31 March 1986. Built for merchant service and completed in 1945, she was laid up from 1946 to 1952; reactivated in 1952 for commercial service but acquired by the Navy for MSTS operation. Converted to a heavy-lift ship in 1954. She remained in MSTS (later MSC) service until 1973 when again laid up in NDRF.

See 13th Edition/page 274 for characteristics.

CARGO SHIP: EX-ATTACK CARGO SHIP (C2-S-B1)

The former attack cargo ship WYANDOT (T-AK 268/AKA 92) of the ANDROMEDA (AKA 15) class was stricken from the NVR on 1 July 1960, but reacquired the following year because of the Berlin crisis. She was recommissioned in November 1961 and in March 1963 assigned to MSTS as a cargo ship (designated T-AKA 92); changed to AK 283 in 1969. She was laid up in the NDRF in 1975 until stricken on 31 March 1986.

See 13th Edition/page 272 for characteristics.

TRANSPORT OILERS/TANKERS

4 TRANSPORT TANKERS: T6-M-98 TYPE

Number	Name	Launched	Status
T-AOT 1001	PATRIOT	1976	**MSC-Active**
T-AOT 1002	RANGER	1976	**MSC-Active**
T-AOT 1006	ROVER	1977	**MSC-Active**
T-AOT 1007	COURIER	1977	**MSC-Active**

Builders:	Todd Shipyards, San Pedro, Calif.
Displacement:	44,150 tons full load
Tonnage:	21,572 GRT
	35,100 DWT
Length:	710¾ feet (216.7 m) overall
Beam:	84 feet (25.6 m)
Draft:	37 feet (11.3 m)
Propulsion:	2 diesel engines (Fairbanks-Morse); 14,000 bhp; 1 shaft
Speed:	16 knots
Range:	12,000 n.miles (22,224 km) at 16 knots
Manning:	21 civilian
Radars:	. . . . . .navigation

These tankers are under long-term MSC charter. Cargo capacity is 308,000 barrels.

These ships were originally chartered by MSC in 1981–1982.

Names: Note that there are also cargo ships named COURIER and ROVER in the sealift fleet.

The ROVER at high speed and deep in the water. Sealift tankers carry fuels for all U.S. defense activities, including naval special fuel oil and aviation fuel for further transfer to Navy replenishment ships in forward areas. Here the ROVER still carries her original name, ZAPATA ROVER. (U.S. Navy)

5 TRANSPORT OILERS: MODIFIED T5 TYPE

Number	Name	Launched	In service	Status
T-AOT 1121	GUS W. DARNELL	10 Aug 1985	11 Sep 1985	**MSC-Active**
T-AOT 1122	PAUL BUCK	1 June 1985	11 Sep 1985	**MSC-Active**
T-AOT 1123	SAMUEL L. COBB	2 Nov 1985	15 Nov 1985	**MSC-Active**
T-AOT 1124	RICHARD G. MATTHIESEN	15 Feb 1986	18 Feb 1986	**MSC-Active**
T-AOT 1125	LAWRENCE H. GIANELLA	19 Apr 1986	22 Apr 1986	**MSC-Active**

Builders:	American Shipbuilding, Tampa, Fla.
Displacement:	9,000 tons light
	39,624 tons full load
Tonnage:	19,037 GRT
	30,150 DWT
Length:	587⅓ feet (179.1 m) waterline
	614⅝ feet (187.45 m) overall
Beam:	90 feet (27.4 m)
Draft:	34 feet (10.4 m)
Propulsion:	1 diesel (Mitsubishi or Ishikawajima-Sulzer 5RTA-76); 15,300 bhp; 1 shaft
Speed:	16 knots
Range:	12,000 n.miles (22,224 km) at 16 knots
Manning:	23 or 24 civilian
Radars:	1 . . . . . . navigation

These are build-and-charter oilers constructed specifically for naval service although initially contracted for commercial service. The lead ship was laid down on 26 December 1983.

Builders: Major components for these ships were built by the American Shipbuilding Co. at Lorain, Ohio, and Nashville, Tenn.

Design: Modified T-5 design with ice-strengthened hulls. Cargo capacity is 238,400 barrels in first three ships; 239,500 barrels in last two units.

Propulsion: Mitsubishi diesels in first two ships and Ishikawajima in others.

The RICHARD G. MATTHIESEN and other ships of this series have ice-strengthened hulls for Arctic operations. (U.S. Navy)

1 TRANSPORT OILER: T5-S-RM2a TYPE

Number	Name	Launched	In service	Status
T-AOT 165	AMERICAN EXPLORER ↑	11 Apr 1958	27 Oct 1959	MSC-RRF

Builders:	Ingalls Shipbuilding, Pascagoula, Miss.
Displacement:	8,400 tons light
	32,628 tons full load
Tonnage:	14,984 GRT
	22,908 DWT
Length:	615 feet (187.5 m) overall
Beam:	80 feet (24.4 m)
Draft:	32 feet (9.75 m)
Propulsion:	1 steam turbine (De Laval); 22,000 shp; 1 shaft
Boilers:	2 (Babcock & Wilcox)
Speed:	20 knots
Range:	14,000 n.miles (25,928 km) at 20 knots
Manning:	32 civilian
Radars:	. . . . . . navigation

The AMERICAN EXPLORER was built for merchant use but upon completion she was acquired by the Navy. She is similar to the MAUMEE-class ships. The AMERICAN EXPLORER was contractor-operated for MSC with a civilian crew. She was laid up in NDRF in June 1984 (still on Naval Vessel Register).

Laid down on 9 July 1957.

Cargo capacity is 174,000 barrels.

Class: This design was intended to serve as a prototype for wartime production of large tankers. In the event, only this one ship was built to this design.

Design: This design was popularly known as the 20-20-20 vessel, for the combination of approximate DWT, horsepower, and speed. At the time built, the AMERICAN EXPLORER was the world's fastest merchant tanker.

Status: To RRF in June 1984.

The AMERICAN EXPLORER—a type originally known as the 20-20-20 design for her tonnage, horsepower, and speed. Only one ship of this exact type entered naval service, although the MAUMEE class is similar. (1981, L. Van Ginderen Collection)

2 TRANSPORT OILERS

Number	Name	Launched	In service	Status
T-AOT 5084	CHESAPEAKE	18 Aug 1964	20 July 1991	MSC-RRF
T-AOT 9101	PETERSBURG	2 Apr 1963	1 Aug 1991	MSC-RRF

Builders:	Bethlehem Steel, Sparrows Point, Baltimore, Md.	
Displacement:	approx. 65,000 tons full load	
Tonnage:	CHESAPEAKE	27,015 GRT
		50,826 DWT
	PETERSBURG	27,469 GRT
		50,072 DWT
Length:	704⅝ feet (214.9 m) waterline	
	736⅙ feet (224.4 m) overall	

Beam:	102⅝ feet (31.2 m)
Draft:	39¾ feet (12.1 m)
Propulsion:	2 steam turbines (Bethlehem); 15,000 shp; 1 shaft
Boilers:	2
Speed:	15 knots
Range:	
Manning:	
Radars:	. . . . . . navigation

Large merchant tankers and, with the similar MOUNT VERNON and MOUNT WASHINGTON, the largest ships in MSC in terms of displacement.

2 TRANSPORT OILERS

Number	Name	Launched	To RRF	Status
T-AOT 5076	MOUNT WASHINGTON		Oct 1989	MSC-RRF
T-AOT 5083	MOUNT VERNON	27 Oct 1960	Mar 1990	MSC-RRF

Builders:	Bethlehem Steel, Quincy, Mass.
Displacement:	approx. 65,800 tons full load
Tonnage:	27,412 GRT
	47,751 DWT
Length:	706⅝ feet (215.5 m) waterline
	736⅙ feet (224.4 m) overall
Beam:	102⅝ feet (31.2 m)

Draft:	40¼ feet (12.3 m)
Propulsion:	2 steam turbines (Bethlehem); 21,500 shp; 1 shaft
Boilers:	2
Speed:	17.5 knots
Range:	
Manning:	
Radars:	. . . . . . navigation

These are large commercial tankers, similar to the CHESAPEAKE and PETERSBURG (see above), but with more powerful turbines.

1 TRANSPORT OILER

Number	Name	Launched	To RRF	Status
T-AOT 5075	American Osprey		June 1987	**MSC-APF**

Builders: Bethlehem Steel, Sparrows Point, Baltimore, Md.
Displacement: 44,840 tons full load
Tonnage: 20,143 GRT
34,723 DWT
Length: 660 11/12 feet (201.5 m) overall
Beam: 89 11/12 feet (27.4 m)
Draft: 36 1/12 feet (11.0 m)
Propulsion: 2 steam turbines (Bethlehem); 15,000 shp; 1 shaft
Boilers: 2 (Foster Wheeler)
Speed: 17 knots
Range: 14,000 n.miles (25,928 km) at 17 knots
Manning: 30 civilian
Radars: . . . . . . navigation

Former merchant tanker, modified at Alabama Dry Dock Co. in 1987–1988 to carry a barge-launching device and four-point mooring system to be used when transferring fuel to shore without pier facilities; fitted with almost four miles (6.4 km) of flexible floating pipeline.

The American Osprey at Norfolk; visible on her deck is the fuel transfer system that enables the Osprey and other tankers moored alongside to transfer fuel ashore through a flexible pipeline. (1988, Giorgio Arra)

1 TRANSPORT OILER

Number	Name	Launched	To RRF	Status
T-AOT 5005 (T-AOT 182)	Mission Capistrano	12 Sep 1970	Mar 1988	MSC-RRF

Builders: Ingalls Shipbuilding, Pascagoula, Miss.
Displacement: 45,877 tons full load
Tonnage: 20,751 GRT
37,874 DWT
Length: 637 5/6 feet (194.5 m) waterline
672 1/6 feet (204.9 m) overall
Beam: 89 1/6 feet (27.2 m)
Draft: 36 1/4 feet (11.0 m)
Propulsion: 2 diesel engines (Crossley-Pielstick 15 PC-2V400); 16,000 bhp; 1 shaft
Speed: 16.5 knots
Range: 16,000 n.miles (29,632 km) at 16.5 knots
Manning: 23 civilian
Radars: . . . . . . navigation

This ship served on MSC charter from 1974 to 1983 under the name Columbia (designated T-AOT 182); see class notes and 13th Edition/page 288 for additional data. Cargo capacity is 303,000 barrels.

Class: Three other tankers of this class were returned to their owners in 1983–1984 after MSC service: Neches (T-AOT 183), Hudson (T-AOT 184), and Susquehanna (T-AOT 185).

This ship should not be confused with the earlier Mission Capistrano (AO 112, later AG 162), a World War II–built T2-SE-A2 oiler.

Classification: The ship was designated T-AO 182 upon being chartered by MSC but changed to T-AOT in 1979.

3 TRANSPORT TANKERS: OVERSEAS CLASS

Number	Name	Launched	In service	Status
T-AOT 1203	Overseas Alice	1967	Aug 1982	**MSC-APF**
T-AOT 1204	Overseas Valdez	1967	Aug 1982	**MCS-Active**
T-AOT 1205	Overseas Vivian	1968	Aug 1982	**MSC-Active**
T-AO 9659	Omi Champion	9 July 1969		**MSC-APF**

Builders: Bethlehem Steel, Sparrows Point, Baltimore, Md.
Displacement: 46,243 tons full load
Tonnage: 20,879 GRT
38,421 DWT
Length: 629 5/6 feet (192.0 m) waterline
660 1/6 feet (201.3 m) overall
Beam: 90 1/6 feet (27.5 m)
Draft: 36 2/3 feet (11.2 m)
Propulsion: 2 steam turbines (General Electric); 15,000 shp; 1 shaft
Boilers: 2 (Foster Wheeler)
Speed: 16.25 knots
Range: 13,000 n.miles (24,076 km) at 16 knots
Manning: 21 to 25 civilian
Radars: . . . . . . navigation

Cargo capacity is 336,000 barrels.

The OVERSEAS VALDEZ is one of four large tankers employed by MSC for the long-distance hauling of petroleum and as afloat prepositioning ships. (1992, Giorgio Arra)

The heavily laden OVERSEAS ALICE shows the typical lines of a large tanker. (U.S. Navy)

1 TRANSPORT OILER

Number	Name	Launched	To RRF	Status
T-AOT 1012	MISSION BUENAVENTURA	14 June 1968	Oct 1987	MSC-RRF

Builders: Bethlehem Steel, Sparrows Point, Baltimore, Md.
Displacement: 46,243 tons full load
Tonnage: 20,947 GRT
           38,851 DWT
Length: 629¹¹/₁₂ feet (192.0 m) waterline
        660 feet (201.2 m) overall
Beam: 90⅙ feet (27.5 m)

Draft: 38¼ feet (11.7 m)
Propulsion: 2 steam turbines (Bethlehem); 15,000 shp; 1 shaft
Boilers: 2 (Foster Wheeler)
Speed: 16.5 knots
Range: 12,000 n.miles (22,224 km) at 16.5 knots
Manning: 27 civilian
Radars: . . . . . . navigation

Cargo capacity is 326,000 barrels.

9 TRANSPORT OILERS: SEALIFT CLASS

Number	Name	Launched	In service	Status
T–AOT 168	SEALIFT PACIFIC ↑	13 Oct 1973	14 Aug 1974	**MSC-Active**
T–AOT 169	SEALIFT ARABIAN SEA ↑	26 Jan 1974	6 Feb 1975	**MSC-Active**
T–AOT 170	SEALIFT CHINA SEA ↑	20 Apr 1974	19 May 1975	**MSC-Active**
T–AOT 171	SEALIFT INDIAN OCEAN ↑	27 July 1974	29 Aug 1975	**MSC-Active**
T–AOT 172	SEALIFT ATLANTIC ↑	26 Jan 1974	26 Aug 1974	**MSC-Active**
T–AOT 173	SEALIFT MEDITERRANEAN ↑	9 Mar 1974	6 Nov 1974	**MSC-Active**
T–AOT 174	SEALIFT CARIBBEAN ↑	8 June 1974	10 Feb 1975	**MSC-Active**
T–AOT 175	SEALIFT ARCTIC ↑	31 Aug 1974	22 May 1975	**MSC-Active**
T–AOT 176	SEALIFT ANTARCTIC ↑	26 Oct 1974	1 Aug 1975	**MSC-Active**

Builders:	T-AOT 168–171 Todd Shipyards, San Pedro, Calif.
	T-AOT 172–176 Bath Iron Works, Maine
Displacement:	6,487 tons light
	33,000 tons full load
Tonnage:	27,217 DWT
Length:	587 feet (179.0 m) overall
Beam:	84 feet (25.6 m)
Draft:	34⅓ feet (10.5 m)
Propulsion:	2 turbo-charged diesel engines (Colt-Pielstick 14PC-2V400); 14,000 bhp; 1 shaft
Speed:	16 knots
Range:	12,000 n.miles (22,224 km) at 16 knots
Manning:	25 civilian + 2 cadets
Radars:	2 . . . . . . navigation

These ships were built specifically for MSC to replace World War II–era tankers of the T2 type. The ships are contractor-operated under "bareboat" charter for MSC with civilian crews.

Classification: Assigned T-AOT in place of T-AO designations on 30 September 1978.

Design: These ships have a cargo capacity of 225,154 barrels.

Engineering: A bow thruster is fitted to assist in docking operations.

The SEALIFT ARABIAN SEA is one of nine Navy-built tankers intended specifically for MSC operations. (U.S. Navy)

SEALIFT CHINA SEA. (1990, Giorgio Arra)

SEALIFT MEDITERRANEAN. (1992, Giorgio Arra)

1 COASTAL TANKER: NORWEGIAN BUILT

Number	Name	Launched	Status
T-AOG 9622	BRAVADO	1977	**MSC-Active**

Builders:	Fosen Mek. Verksteder, Fevag (Norway)
Displacement:	5,995 tons full load
Tonnage:	2,110 GRT
	4,330 DWT
Length:	304¹/₁₂ feet (92.7 m) overall
Beam:	47¹¹/₁₂ feet (14.6 m)
Draft:	22 feet (6.7 m)

Propulsion:	1 diesel engine (MaK); 2,800 bhp; 1 shaft
Speed:	12.5 knots
Range:	6,000 n.miles (11,112 km) at 12 knots
Manning:	16 civilian
Radars:	. . . . . . navigation

The BRAVADO is a coastal tanker under long-term charter to MSC; she replaces MSC-operated gasoline tankers (T-AOG). Cargo capacity is 28,000 barrels.

The small tanker BRAVADO, one of the smallest operated by MSC. Smaller tankers and cargo ships are handy for operating in small ports or restricted waters where U.S. forces may be required to operate. (U.S. Navy)

1 COASTAL TANKER

Number	Name	Launched	Status
T-AO 9657	NEWBRIDGE		**MSC-Active**

Builders:	Ira S. Bushey, New York
Displacement:	
Tonnage:	1,488 GRT
	2,286 DWT
Length:	242½ feet (73.9 m) waterline
	243 feet (74.1 m) overall

Beam:	40¹/₆ feet (12.25 m)
Draft:	16 feet (4.9 m)
Propulsion:	1 diesel engine (Fairbanks-Morse 38D8¹/₈); 1,200 bhp; 1 shaft
Speed:	12 knots
Range:	
Manning:	
Radars:	. . . . . . navigation

This is a coastal tanker; she operates in the Persian Gulf to support U.S. naval forces operating in that area.

1 TRANSPORT OILER: "POTOMAC"

Number	Name	Launched	In service	Status
T-AOT 181	POTOMAC ↑	(see notes)	12 Jan 1976	**MSC-APF**

Builders:	Sun Shipbuilding and Dry Dock, Chester, Penna.
Displacement:	7,333 tons light
	34,800 tons full load
Tonnage:	15,739 GRT
	27,908 DWT
Length:	591⅛ feet (180.2 m) waterline
	619⅝ feet (189.0 m) overall
Beam:	83½ feet (25.5 m)
Draft:	33⁷/₁₂ feet (10.2 m)
Propulsion:	1 steam turbine (Westinghouse); 20,460 shp; 1 shaft
Boilers:	2 (Combustion Engineering)
Speed:	18.5 knots
Range:	18,000 n.miles (33,336 km) at 18 knots
Manning:	37 civilian
Radars:	2 . . . . . . navigation

The POTOMAC was constructed with the mid-body and bow sections built to mate with the stern section of an earlier tanker named POTOMAC (T-AO 150). The "new" tanker was named SHENANDOAH and operated under commercial charter to MSC for several years until she was purchased on 12 January 1976. At that time the ship was renamed POTOMAC and designated T-AO 181; changed to T-AOT 181 on 30 September 1978.

The ship was contractor-operated by MSC with a civilian crew; taken out of service on 26 September 1983 and placed in RRF on 5 March 1984.

(The original POTOMAC was launched on 8 October 1956; she was partially destroyed by fire on 3 October 1961, but the stern section and machinery were relatively intact; she was originally T5-S-12a type.)

Cargo capacity is 200,000 barrels.

She has been modified to transfer fuel ashore without pier facilities and is fitted with a four-mile (6.5-km) flexible floating pipeline.

Status: She was a U.S. Naval Ship prior to transfer to RRF.

3 TRANSPORT OILERS: "MAUMEE" CLASS (T5-S-12a)

Number	Name	Launched	In service	Status
T-AOT 149	MAUMEE ↑	16 Feb 1956	12 Dec 1956	NDRF
T-AOT 151	SHOSHONE ↑	7 Jan 1957	15 Apr 1957	MSC-RRF
T-AOT 152	ex-YUKON ↑	16 Mar 1956	17 May 1957	NDRF

Builders:	T-AOT 149, 152	Ingalls Shipbuilding, Pascagoula, Miss.
	T-AOT 151	Sun Shipbuilding and Dry Dock, Chester, Penna.
Displacement:	7,761 tons light	
	32,953 tons full load	
Tonnage:	15,626 GRT	
	26,943 DWT	
Length:	620 feet (189.1 m) overall	
Beam:	83½ feet (25.5 m)	
Draft:	32 feet (9.75 m)	
Propulsion:	1 steam turbine (Westinghouse); 20,460 shp; 1 shaft	
Boilers:	2 (Combustion Engineering)	
Speed:	18 knots	
Range:	18,000 n.miles (33,336 km) at 18 knots	
Manning:	30 or 31 civilian	
Radars:	2 . . . . . . navigation	

These ships were built specifically for naval use as MSTS/MSC tankers. Cargo capacity is 187,000 barrels.

Class: Originally sister ships of the POTOMAC (T-AO 150), which was extensively rebuilt, becoming the T-AO/T-AOT 181.

Classification: Built as T-AO; changed to T-AOT on 30 September 1978.

Hull numbers AO 166, 167 were reserved for planned Mission-class (T2-SE-A2) "jumbo" conversions; the T-AO 153–164 were T2-SE-A1 tankers acquired during the 1956 Suez crisis and stricken in 1957–1958.

Design: The MAUMEE has an ice-strengthened bow.

Names: The T-AOT 152 dropped the name YUKON on 9 May 1989 to make the name available for the T-AO 202.

Status: The MAUMEE (T-AOT 149) and YUKON (T-AOT 152) were taken out of service on 2 and 20 October 1985, respectively. They were assigned to RRF on 15 and 20 October 1985. Both ships were transferred from the RRF to MarAd for layup on 2 April 1987; in National Defense Reserve Fleet.

The SHOSHONE was assigned to RRF in February 1985.

The YUKON travelling with a light load, down slightly by the stern. She is now officially listed as the "ex-YUKON," her name having been assigned to a new fleet oiler. (1983, Giorgio Arra)

1 TRANSPORT OILER: "SUAMICO" CLASS (T2-SE-A1)

Number	Name	Launched	Commissioned	Status
T-AOT 75	SAUGATUCK ↑	7 Dec 1942	19 Feb 1943	NDRF

Builders:	Sun Shipbuilding and Dry Dock, Chester, Penna.
Displacement:	5,782 tons light
	21,880 tons full load
Tonnage:	10,296 GRT
	16,500 DWT
Length:	502⅚ feet (153.3 m) waterline
	523½ feet (159.7 m) overall
Beam:	68 feet (20.7 m)
Draft:	30⅚ feet (9.4 m)
Propulsion:	turbo-electric drive (Westinghouse turbine) 6,600 shp; 1 shaft
Boilers:	2 (Babcock & Wilcox)
Speed:	15 knots
Range:	13,000 n.miles (24,076 km) at 14.5 knots
Manning:	43 civilian
Radars:	. . . . . . navigation

The ships of this class were begun as merchant tankers but were acquired by the Navy in 1942–1943 and completed as fleet oilers (AO) and Navy manned. After World War II they were employed in the tanker role by MSTS (later MSC). Only the SAUGATUCK remains.

Cargo capacity 141,000 barrels.

Class: The TALLULAH (T-AOT 50), CACHE (T-AOT 67), MILLICOMA (T-AOT 73), and SCHUYLKILL (T-AOT 76) were stricken on 4 March 1988 (approved for disposal on 31 March 1986).

Classification: Changed from T-AO to T-AOT on 30 September 1978 (while laid up).

Guns: As built, this class was armed with one 5-inch/38-cal DP gun, four 3-inch/50-cal AA guns, and eight 40-mm AA guns. All ships were disarmed after World War II when employed in the tanker role.

Status: The SAUGATUCK was laid up in NDRF on 5 November 1974.

The SCHUYLKILL was one of the last T2-type tankers in U.S. naval service. Her sister ship SAUGATUCK remains in the NDRF, but can be expected to be discarded in the near future. (U.S. Navy)

1 TUG/BARGE TANKER

Number	Tug Name/Barge Name	Status
(none)	SENECA/Barge 255	**MSC-Active**

Builders:	
Displacement:	(unknown)/695 tons
Length:	110 feet (33.5 m)/250 feet (76.2 m) overall
Beam:	34⅙ feet (10.4 m)/76 feet (23.2 m)
Draft:	12⅓ feet (3.75 m)/13⁵⁄₁₂ feet (4.1 m)
Propulsion:	diesel
Speed:	8 knots
Range:	
Manning:	10 civilian

Combination tug/barge tanker. Cargo capacity is 43,296 barrels.

A tug/barge tanker combination operating off Hawaii, similar to the type employed by MSC. This concept has been proposed for other naval roles, including tenders and repair ships, which rarely get under way. (U.S. Navy)

1 TUG/BARGE TANKER

Number	Tug Name	Barge Name	Status
T-ATF 414	MALANAE	PUMA HELE	**MSC-Active**

Builders:	
Displacement:	425 tons/5,120 tons
Length:	113 (34.45 m)/248 feet (75.6 m) overall
Beam:	32 feet (9.75 m)/56 feet (17.0 m)

Draft:	13⁷/₁₂ feet (4.15 m)/18 feet (5.5 m)
Propulsion:	diesel
Speed:	
Range:	4,000 n.miles (7,410 km)
Manning:	7 civilian

These combination tug/barges are employed in the Pacific area, based in Hawaii. Cargo capacity of the PUMA HELE is 32,082 barrels.

2 TRANSPORT OILERS: SHORT-TERM CONTRACTS

The oilers VALIANT and PACIFIC TRADER were under commercial contract to MSC when this edition of *Ships and Aircraft* went to press.

TRANSPORT OILERS: T6-M-136A TYPE

The modified Falcon-class ships FALCON LEADER (T-AOT 1208) and FALCON CHAMPION, both launched in 1983, were built specifically for MSC service. They were taken off charter in August 1988 and January 1989, respectively.

TRANSPORT OILERS: MISSION TYPE (T2-SE-A2)

The MISSION SANTA YNEZ (T-AOT 134) was the last survivor retained in reserve of the Mission series of merchant tankers built late in World War II and acquired by the Navy after the war. Delivered as a merchant tanker on 13 March 1944 and acquired by the Navy for use as a tanker on 22 October 1947, she was laid up in NDRF on 6 March 1975 (changed to T-AOT on 30 September 1978); stricken on 1 November 1990.

Class: The Mission class encompassed AO 111–137; other fleet oilers and tankers (transport oilers) of this design were in naval service during and after World War II.

See 14th Edition/page 310 for characteristics.

GASOLINE TANKERS

These are small tankers, originally intended to carry gasoline and aviation fuels for aircraft, motor torpedo boats, and other special craft.

2 GASOLINE TANKERS: "ALATNA" CLASS (T1-MET-24a)

Number	Name	FY	Launched	In service	Status
T-AOG 81	ALATNA	55	6 Sep 1956	July 1957	MSC-RRF
T-AOG 82	CHATTAHOOCHEE	55	4 Dec 1956	Oct 1957	MSC-RRF

Builders:	Bethlehem Steel, Staten Island, N.Y.
Displacement:	2,275 tons light
	5,720 tons full load
Length:	302 feet (92.1 m) overall
Beam:	61 feet (18.6 m)
Draft:	19 feet (5.8 m)
Propulsion:	diesel-electric (4 Alco diesels; Westinghouse electric motors); 4,000 shp; 2 shafts
Speed:	13 knots
Range:	5,760 n.miles (10,667 km) at 10 knots
Manning:	
Radars:	1 . . . . . . navigation

This two-ship class was built specifically for operation in support of U.S. military activities in the Arctic. Both ships were operated by MSTS (later MSC) until taken out of service on 8 August 1972 and laid up in the NDRF.

Design: These ships have ice-strengthened hulls and icebreaking prows and other features for Arctic operation (similar to T-AK 270 class). Cargo capacity is 30,000 barrels of petroleum products plus some 2,700 tons of dry cargo. A small helicopter platform was fitted aft in their original configuration.

The ALATNA at Aukland, New Zealand. These two AOGs were the liquid-cargo versions of the ELTANIN-class Arctic cargo ships. (1982, L. Van Ginderen Collection)

Status: The ships were reacquired by the Navy on 10 May 1979 and 24 May 1979, respectively, and reactivated for MSC service to replace older AOGs; the ALATNA was placed in MSC service on 3 February 1983 and the CHATTAHOOCHEE on 11 January 1982. Both were taken out of service on 25 January 1985 and placed in MSC Ready Reserve Force in April 1985 and January 1985, respectively (berthed in Japan).

1 GASOLINE TANKER: "TONTI" CLASS (T1-M-BT2)

Number	Name	Launched	In service	Status
T-AOG 78	NODAWAY	15 May 1945	7 Sep 1950	MSC-RRF

Builders:	Todd Shipyards, Houston, Texas
Displacement:	2,060 tons light
	5,984 tons full load
Length:	325⅙ feet (99.2 m) overall
Beam:	48⅙ feet (14.7 m)
Draft:	19 feet (5.8 m)
Propulsion:	2 diesels (Nordberg); 1,400 bhp; 1 shaft
Speed:	10 knots
Range:	5,500 n.miles (10,186 km) at 10 knots
Manning:	45 civilian
Radars:	2 . . . . . . navigation

The NODAWAY is the lone survivor in U.S. service of a once numerous type of small gasoline tankers. Five ships of this specific design were built as merchant tankers, all of which were acquired by the Navy in 1950 and assigned to MSTS, later Military Sealift Command.

The RINCON (T-AOG 77), now stricken, was a sister ship of the NODAWAY. These ships had a standard oiler/tanker configuration despite their small size; there is a short, squat funnel aft. (U.S. Navy)

The NODAWAY was taken out of service on 22 July 1984 and assigned to MSC-RRF on 30 September 1985. Berthed in San Francisco.

Class: This class originally consisted of the T-AOG 76–80, with the AOG 64–75 being similar (BT1 design).

Design: Cargo capacity is 30,000 barrels.

TROOP TRANSPORTS

1 TROOP TRANSPORT: S5-S-MA1ua TYPE

Number	Name	Launched	Status
T-AP 1001	EMPIRE STATE VI	16 Sep 1961	**Academic**

Builders:	Newport News Shipbuilding and Dry Dock, Va.
Displacement:	22,629 tons full load
Tonnage:	9,298 GRT (before conversion)
	12,691 DWT (before conversion)
Length:	528⅓ feet (161.1 m) waterline
	564¹¹⁄₁₂ feet (172.2 m) overall
Beam:	76⅙ feet (23.2 m)
Draft:	31⁷⁄₁₂ feet (9.6 m)
Propulsion:	2 steam turbines (General Electric); 17,500 shp; 1 shaft
Boilers:	2 (Foster Wheeler)
Speed:	20 knots
Range:	12,600 n.miles (23,335 km) at 20 knots
Manning:	
Radars:	. . . . . . navigation

A cargo ship acquired on 14 October 1988 from the National Defense Reserve Fleet for conversion to a training ship for the New York State Maritime Academy, replacing the former USNS BARRETT (T-AP 196). She was converted by Bay Shipbuilding, Bay City, Wisc. Refitted with classrooms and berthing for students; troop capacity would be small.

The ship is fully operational.

The ship was laid down on 1 March 1961. MSC has several cargo ships of this design.

2 + 1 TROOP TRANSPORTS: P2-S1-DN3 TYPE

Number	Name	Launched	In Service	Status
T-AP 196	EMPIRE STATE V (USNS BARRETT)	27 June 1950	15 Dec 1951	NDRF
T-AP 197	BAY STATE (USNS GEIGER) ↑	9 Oct 1950	13 Sep 1952	hulk
T-AP 198	STATE OF MAINE (USNS UPSHUR) ↑	19 Jan 1951	20 Dec 1952	**Academic**

Builders:	New York Shipbuilding, Camden, N.J.
Displacement:	17,600 tons standard
	19,600 tons full load
Length:	533 feet (162.5 m) overall
Beam:	73 feet (22.3 m)
Draft:	27 feet (8.2 m)
Propulsion:	1 steam turbine; 13,750 shp; 1 shaft
Boilers:	2
Speed:	19 knots
Range:	
Manning:	
Troops:	1,500 + 400 cabin passengers (as transports)
Radars:	. . . . . . navigation

Three ships of this design were begun as combination passenger-cargo liners for the American President Lines; they were taken over by the Navy during construction and completed as troop transports.

All placed in service in 1951–1952 with MSTS (and subsequently MSC) and operated by civilian crews.

All three ships were laid up in the NDRF in 1973, having been the last transports operated by the Military Sealift Command. They were subsequently transferred on loan to state maritime schools: the BARRETT to the New York Maritime Academy, GEIGER to the Massachusetts Maritime Academy, and UPSHUR to the Maine Maritime Academy. All renamed with the prefix Training Ship (TS) by their schools, with the Navy names retained on U.S. Government documents.

The ex-BARRETT was returned to MarAd for layup on 4 April 1990. The ex-GEIGER (renamed BAY STATE) was severely damaged by fire in 1981 and has not been returned to service.

Design: All troop cabins, mess, and recreation spaces are fully air-conditioned. Some 1,000 additional troops can be carried (total 2,500) by converting recreation areas into high-density berthing spaces. Cabin spaces are for officers and dependents.

Engineering: The BARRETT attained 21.5 knots on trials.

Names: Merchant names were to have been T-AP 196 PRESIDENT JACKSON, T-AP 197 PRESIDENT ADAMS, and T-AP 198 PRESIDENT HAYES.

The ex-USNS BARRETT while employed as a state training ship, shortly before being laid up. The funnels are in a tandem arrangement. (1989, Giorgio Arra)

1 TROOP TRANSPORT: S5-S1-MA49c TYPE

Number	Name	Launched	Status
T-AP 1000	PATRIOT STATE	30 July 1963	**Academic**

Builders:	Bethlehem Steel, Sparrows Point, Baltimore, Md.
Displacement:	approx. 20,500 tons full load
Tonnage:	11,188 GRT
	9,376 DWT
Length:	508⁵⁄₁₂ feet (155.0 m) waterline
	544¹¹⁄₁₂ feet (166.1 m) overall
Beam:	79⅛ feet (24.1 m)
Draft:	29 feet (8.9 m)
Propulsion:	2 steam turbines (General Electric); 19,800 shp; 2 shafts
Boilers:	2 (Babcock & Wilcox)
Speed:	20 knots
Range:	7,000 n.miles (12,964 km) at 20 knots
Manning:	
Radars:	. . . . . . navigation

Former passenger/cargo liner modified for use as a school ship by the Massachusetts Maritime Academy. She is one of four similar ships constructed for the Grace Lines.

The ship is fully operational.

The ship was laid down on 29 October 1962.

Class: One of four similar ships completed in 1963 for the Grace Lines for the Central–South American trade.

Design: As built, the ship was a combination passenger-cargo ship with accommodations for 119 passengers.

Engineering: Above horsepower is maximum; normal is 18,000 shp.

The Massachusetts state training ship PATRIOT STATE at Portsmouth, England. In an emergency, the state training ships could be employed as troop transports, although such employment is unrealistic in most potential conflicts or crises. (1986, L. Van Ginderen Collection)

TROOP TRANSPORTS: ADMIRAL TYPE[4] (P2-SE2-R1)

All transports of this design have been stricken. Ten ships were completed in 1944–1945 (AP 120–129). They could carry up to 5,000 troops. Two units were modified to serve as barrack ships: GEN. HUGH J. GAFFEY (IX 507, ex-T-AP 121) and GEN. WILLIAM O. DARBY (IX 510, ex-T-AP 127); see chapter 25.

4. As built, these ships had "admiral" names; they were transferred to the Army in 1946 and renamed for generals; they were transferred to the Navy on 1 March 1950, following establishment of the Military Sea Transportation Service under the Navy. They retained their Army-assigned names.

The last units stricken were laid up in NDRF: GEN. ALEXANDER M. PATCH (T-AP 122), GEN. SIMON B. BUCKNER (T-AP 123), and GEN. MAURICE ROSE (T-AP 126) stricken on 20 August 1990. The GEN. NELSON M. WALKER (T-AP 125) was stricken on 25 January 1981; the ship was donated to Life International for conversion to a civilian hospital ship; when this edition went to press she remained laid up in the James River NDRF.

See 14th Edition/page 313 for characteristics.

TROOP TRANSPORTS: GENERAL TYPE (P2-S2-R2)

All transports of this design have been stricken. Eleven ships were completed from 1943 to 1945 (AP 110–119 and 176). They could accommodate up to 5,300 troops.

The last units stricken were laid up in NDRF: GEN. A.E. ANDERSON (T-AP 111) stricken on 11 December 1958; GEN. W.A. MANN (T-AP 112), GEN. WILLIAM MITCHELL (T-AP 114), and GEN.

J.C. BRECKINRIDGE (T-AP 176) stricken on 1 December 1966; GEN. W.H. GORDON (T-AP 117) and GEN. WILLIAM WEIGEL (T-AP 119) stricken on 31 March 1986; GEN. JOHN POPE (T-AP 110) stricken on 26 October 1990.

See 14th Edition/pages 313–314 for characteristics.

TABLE 24-2. SEALIFT SHIP NAMES

Number	Name(s)
T-AKR 1001	ADM. WM. M. CALLAGHAN
T-AK 9652	ADVANTAGE, ex-TACNA II, THERMOPYLAE, CONFIDENCE, BARBER THERMOPYLAE
T-AK 5005	ADVENTURER, ex-EXPORT ADVENTURER
T-AK 5008	AGENT, ex-EXPORT AGENT
T-AK 5006	AIDE, ex-EXPORT AIDE
T-AOG 81	ALATNA
T-AKR 287	ALGOL, ex-SEA-LAND EXCHANGE
T-AKR 291	ALTAIR, ex-SEA-LAND FINANCE
T-AK 5007	AMBASSADOR, ex-EXPORT AMBASSADOR
T-AKR 9673	AMERICAN CONDOR, ex-ZENIT EXPRESS
T-AK 2062	AMERICAN CORMORANT, ex-FERNCARRIER, KOLLBRIS
T-AK 2044	AMERICAN EAGLE, ex-ZENIT EAGLE, FINNEAGLE
T-AOT 165	AMERICAN EXPLORER
T-AKR 9672	AMERICAN FALCON, ex-ZENIT CLIPPER
T-AK 9651	AMERICAN KESTREL, ex-LASH PACIFICA
T-AOT 5075	AMERICAN OSPREY, ex-GULF PRINCE
T-AKR 294	ANTARES, ex-SEA-LAND GALLOWAY
T-AK 5061	AUSTRAL LIGHTNING, ex-LASH ESPAÑA
T-AK 1005	AUSTRAL RAINBOW, ex-AMERICAN VETERAN, AUSTRAL MOON, AUSTRALIAN BEAR, PHILIPPINE BEAR
T-AK 5008	BANNER, ex-EXPORT BANNER
T-AP 197	BAY STATE, ex-GEIGER (USNS)
T-ACS 10	BEAVER STATE, ex-AMERICAN DRACO, MORMACDRACO
T-AKR 288	BELLATRIX, ex-SEA-LAND TRADE
T-AOG 9687	BLUETANK STARLET
T-AOG 9622	BRAVADO
T-AK 2033	BUYER, ex-EXPORT BUYER
T-AK 5029	CALIFORNIA, ex-SANTA RITA
T-AK 5012	CAPE ALAVA, ex-COMET, AFRICAN COMET
T-AK 5010	CAPE ALEXANDER, ex-METEOR, AFRICAN METEOR
T-AK 5009	CAPE ANN, ex-MERCURY, AFRICAN MERCURY
T-AK 5011	CAPE ARCHWAY, ex-NEPTUNE, AFRICAN NEPTUNE
T-AK 5013	CAPE AVINOF, ex-SUN, AFRICAN SUN
T-AK 5060	CAPE BLANCO, ex-MASON LYKES
T-AK 5059	CAPE BON, ex-VELMA LYKES
T-AK 5058	CAPE BORDA, ex-HOWELL LYKES
T-AK 5057	CAPE BOVER, ex-FREDERICK LYKES
T-AK 5056	CAPE BRETON, ex-DOLLY TURMAN
T-AK 5040	CAPE CANAVERAL, ex-ALLISON LYKES
T-AK 5037	CAPE CANSO, ex-AIMEE LYKES
T-AK 5042	CAPE CARTHAGE, ex-MARGARET LYKES
T-AK 5074	CAPE CATAWBA, ex-CAPE, MORMACCAPE
T-AK 5043	CAPE CATOCHE, ex-CHRISTOPHER LYKES
T-AK 5036	CAPE CHALMERS, ex-ADABELLA LYKES
T-AK 5038	CAPE CHARLES, ex-CHARLOTTE LYKES
T-AK 5039	CAPE CLEAR, ex-MAYO LYKES
T-AK 5041	CAPE COD, ex-SHELDON LYKES
T-AKR 5054	CAPE DECISION, ex-TOMBARRA
T-AKR 5055	CAPE DIAMOND, ex-TRICOLOR
T-AKR 5053	CAPE DOMINGO, ex-TARAGO
T-AKR 5052	CAPE DOUGLAS, ex-LALANDIA
T-AKR 5051	CAPE DUCATO, ex-BARRANDUNA
T-AKR 5069	CAPE EDMONT, ex-PARRALLA
T-AKR 5073	CAPE FAREWELL, ex-AMERICAN MAR
T-AKR 5070	CAPE FLATTERY, ex-DELTA NORTE
T-AK 5071	CAPE FLORIDA, ex-DELTA CARIBE, LASH TURKEY
T-AK 5051	CAPE GIBSON, ex-PRESIDENT JACKSON, INDIAN MAIL
T-AK 2039	CAPE GIRARDEAU, ex-PRESIDENT ADAMS, ALASKAN MAIL
T-AKR 5067	CAPE HENRY, ex-BARBER PRIAM
T-AKR 5068	CAPE HORN, ex-BARBER TØNSBERG
T-AKR 5066	CAPE HUDSON, ex-BARBER TIAF
T-AKR 5076	CAPE INSCRIPTION, ex-TYSON LYKES, MAINE
T-AKR 5062	CAPE ISABEL, ex-CHARLES LYKES, NEVADA
T-AK 5075	CAPE JOHNSON, ex-MORMACSAGA, M.M. DANT
T-AK 5077	CAPE JUBY, ex-MORMACSEA, HAWAII
T-AKR 5077	CAPE LAMBERT, ex-FEDERAL LAKES, AVON FOREST
T-AKR 5078	CAPE LOBOS, ex-FEDERAL SEAWAY, LAURENTIAN FOREST, GRAND ENCOUNTER
T-AKR 5063	CAPE MAY, ex-ALMERIA LYKES
T-AKR 5064	CAPE MENDOCINO, ex-DOCTOR LYKES
T-AKR 5065	CAPE MOHICAN, ex-TILLIE LYKES
T-AK 1014	CAPE NOME, ex-RAPID, AMERICAN RAPID, RED JACKET, MORMACSTAR
T-AKR 293	CAPELLA, ex-SEA-LAND MCLEAN
T-AOG 82	CHATTAHOOCHEE
T-AOT 5084	CHESAPEAKE, ex-HESS-VOYAGER
T-AK 851	CLEVELAND, ex-PRESIDENT CLEVELAND
T-AKR 0007	COMET (T-AKR 7)
T-ACS 6	CORNHUSKER STATE, ex-STAGHOUND
T-AK 5019	COURIER, ex-EXPORT COURIER
T-AOT 1007	COURIER, ex-ZAPATA COURIER
T-AK 3000	CPL LOUIS J. HAUGE JR., ex-ESTELLE MAERSK
T-AK 5049	DEL MONTE, ex-DELTA BRAZIL
T-AK 5050	DEL VALLE, ex-DELTA URUGUAY
T-AK 5026	DEL VIENTO, ex-DELTA MEXICO
T-AKR 289	DENEBOLA, ex-SEA-LANE EXCHANGE
T-ACS 7	DIAMOND STATE, ex-PRESIDENT TRUMAN, JAPAN MAIL
T-AK 2040	ELIZABETH LYKES
T-AP 1001	EMPIRE STATE VI, ex-CAPE JUNCTION, MORMACTIDE, OREGON
T-AP 196	EMPIRE STATE V, ex-BARRETT (USNS)
T-ACS 8	EQUALITY STATE, ex-AMERICAN BUILDER, PHILIPPINE MAIL, SANTA ROSA, PRESIDENT ROOSEVELT, WASHINGTON MAIL
T-AK 3003	1ST LT ALEX BONNYMAN JR., ex-EMILIE MAERSK
T-AK 3010	1ST LT BALDOMERO LOPEZ
T-AK 3011	1ST LT JACK LUMMUS
T-ACS 5	FLICKERTAIL STATE, ex-LIGHTNING
T-AK 9720	GALVESTON BAY
T-ACS 2	GEM STATE, ex-PRESIDENT MONROE
T-ACS 4	GOPHER STATE, ex-EXPORT LEADER
T-ACS 3	GRAND CANYON STATE, ex-PRESIDENT POLK
T-AK 2064	GREEN HARBOUR, ex-WILLIAM HOOPER, AUSTRAL RAINBOW, CHINA BEAR
T-AK 1015	GREEN ISLAND, ex-GEORGE WYTHE

TABLE 24-2. SEALIFT SHIP NAMES (CONTINUED)

Number	Name(s)		Number	Name(s)
T-ACS 9	GREEN MOUNTAIN STATE, ex-AMERICAN ALTAIR, MORMACALTAIR		T-AOT 1122	PAUL BUCK, ex-OCEAN FREEDOM
(none)	GREEN RIDGE, ex-WOERMAN MERCUR, CAROL MERCUR, SLOMAN MERCUR		T-AOT 9101	PETERSBURG, ex-SINCLAIR TEXAS, CHARLES KURZ, KEYSTONE
T-AK 2050	GREEN WAVE, ex-WOERMAN MIRA, SLOMAN MIRA		T-AK 3009	PFC DEWAYNE T. WILLIAMS
T-AK 5044	GULF BANKER		T-AK 3006	PFC EUGENE A. OBREGON, ex-THOMAS HEYWOOD
T-AK 5045	GULF FARMER		T-AK 3002	PFC JAMES ANDERSON JR., ex-EMMA MAERSK
T-AK 5046	GULF MERCHANT		T-AK 3001	PFC WILLIAM B. BAUGH JR., ex-ELEO MAERSK
T-AK 2035	GULF SHIPPER		T-AK 2016	PIONEER COMMANDER, ex-AMERICAN COMMANDER
T-AK 2036	GULF TRADER		T-AK 2018	PIONEER CONTRACTOR, ex-AMERICAN CONTRACTOR
T-AOT 1121	GUS W. DARNELL, ex-OCEAN CHAMPION		T-AK 2019	PIONEER CRUSADER, ex-AMERICAN CRUSADER
T-AK 9723	JOHN LYKES		T-AKR 290	POLLUX, ex-SEA-LAND MARKET
T-AK 9808	JOSEPH LYKES		T-AKR 9831	PONCE, ex-PONCE DE LEON
T-AKR 0011	JUPITER (T-AKR 11) ex-LIPSCOMB LYKES, ARIZONA		T-AOT 181	POTOMAC (T-AO 150), ex-SHENANDOAH, POTOMAC
T-ACS 1	KEYSTONE STATE, ex-PRESIDENT HARRISON		T-AK 5017	PRIDE, ex-MORMACPRIDE
T-AK 5016	LAKE, ex-MORMACLAKE		T-AK 3004	PVT HARRY FISHER, ex-EVELYN MAERSK
T-AKR 1192	LASH ATLANTICO		T-AOT 1002	RANGER, ex-ZAPATA RANGER
T-AOT 1125	LAWRENCE H. GIANELLA, ex-OCEAN STAR		T-AKR-292	REGULUS, ex-SEA-LAND COMMERCE
T-AK 9838	LESLIE LYKES		T-AOT 1124	RICHARD G. MATTHIESEN, ex-OCEAN SPIRIT
T-AK 2043	LETITIA LYKES		T-AK 1013	ROVER, ex-AMERICAN ROVER, DEFIANCE, MORMACSEA
T-AK 2048	LOUISE LYKES		T-AOT 1006	ROVER, ex-ZAPATA ROVER
T-AKR 112	LYRA, ex-REICHENFELS		T-AK 9636	RUTH LYKES
T-AK 5021	MAINE, ex-SEATRAIN MAINE, TOMAHAWK		T-AOT 1123	SAMUEL L. COBB, ex-OCEAN TRIUMPH
T-AK 9656	MAERSK CONSTELLATION, ex-ELIZABETH MAERSK		T-AK 5022	SANTA ANA, ex-C.E. DANT
T-AK 3007	MAJ STEPHEN W. PLESS, ex-CHARLES CARROLL		T-AK 1010	SANTA VICTORIA, ex-AMERICAN TROJAN, MONTANA
T-ATF 414	MALANAE/PUNA HELE		T-AOT 75	SAUGATUCK, ex-NEWTON
T-AK 2037	MALLORY LYKES		T-AK 5018	SCAN, ex-MORMACSCAN
AOT 149	MAUMEE		T-AOT 176	SEALIFT ANTARCTIC
T-AKR 0010	MERCURY (T-AKR 10), ex-ILLINOIS		T-AOT 169	SEALIFT ARABIAN SEA
T-AKR 0009	METEOR (T-AKR 9), ex-SEALIFT (USNS)		T-AOT 175	SEALIFT ARCTIC
T-AK 271	MIRFAK		T-AOT 172	SEALIFT ATLANTIC
T-AOT 1012	MISSION BUENAVENTURA, ex-SPIRIT OF LIBERTY		T-AOT 174	SEALIFT CARIBBEAN
T-AOT 5005	MISSION CAPISTRANO (T-AOT 182), ex-COLUMBIA, FALCON LADY		T-AOT 170	SEALIFT CHINA SEA
T-AOT 5083	MOUNT VERNON, ex-MOUNT VERNON VICTORY		T-AOT 171	SEALIFT INDIAN OCEAN
T-AOT 5076	MOUNT WASHINGTON		T-AOT 173	SEALIFT MEDITERRANEAN
T-AK 9783	NANCY LYKES		T-AOT 168	SEALIFT PACIFIC
T-AO 9657	NEWBRIDGE, ex-CHRISTIAN F. REINAUER, N.W. GOKEY		T-AK 3008	2ND LT JOHN P. BOBO
T-AGDS 9642	NICOR CLIPPER		T-AKR 9731	SENATOR
			(none)	SENECA/BARGE 255
T-AK 9653	NOBLE STAR, ex-CONCORDIA STAR, HOEGH STAR, COSTA ATLANTICA		T-AK 3005	SGT MATEJ KOCAK ex-JOHN B. WATERMAN
T-AOG 78	NODAWAY, ex-BELRIDGE		T-AK 3012	SGT WILLIAM R. BUTTON
T-AK 0284	NORTHERN LIGHT (T-AK 284), ex-MORMACCOVE		T-AOT 151	SHOSHONE
T-AO 9659	OMI CHAMPION, ex-OGDEN CHAMPION, PENN CHAMPION		T-AK 2085	SOUTHERN CROSS (T-AK 285), ex-TRADE, MORMACTRADE
T-AOT 1203	OVERSEAS ALICE		T-AP 198	STATE OF MAINE, ex-UPSHUR (USNS)
T-AOT 1204	OVERSEAS VALDEZ, ex-OVERSEAS AUDREY		T-AKR 9716	STRONG AMERICAN
T-AOT 1205	OVERSEAS VIVIAN		T-AK 9670	STRONG TEXAN
T-AOT 1001	PATRIOT, ex-ZAPATA PATRIOT		T-AK 2045	TAMPA BAY
T-AP 1000	PATRIOT STATE, ex-SANTA MERCEDES		T-AK 5020	WASHINGTON, ex-SEATRAIN WASHINGTON, MISSION SAN DIEGO
			T-AOT 152	ex-YUKON

The AMERICAN CORMORANT is partially submerged as the ultra-heavy-lift ship loads a former East German Tarantul I-class missile craft at Portsmouth, England. The missile craft was transferred to the U.S. Navy for evaluation (see chapter 21). The U.S. Navy is considering the procurement of similar heavy-lift ships to transport mine countermeasures ships to forward areas. (1992, Maritime Photographic)

CHAPTER 25

Service Craft

The large harbor tug SHABONEE welcomes the aircraft carrier SARATOGA (CV 60) to Mayport, Fla., after Operation Desert Storm. A large variety of service craft are required to support the fleet and related research and development efforts. (U.S. Navy, 1991)

The U.S. Navy operates several hundred service craft, both self-propelled and non-self-propelled. Most service craft are at naval bases in the United States with a few overseas. These craft perform a variety of fleet and base-support services.

Only the self-propelled craft are described here as well as the Navy's miscellaneous unclassified ships (IX designation), which are officially listed as service craft. Four barges designated IX are non-self-propelled craft. Although the relic CONSTITUTION has dropped her IX designation, she is included below in her sequential position for historical reasons. (The sailing corvette CONSTELLATION, formerly IX 20, is not listed in this volume; she is neither owned by the U.S. government nor is she the original frigate built in 1797; see below.)

The Navy's manned submersibles and floating dry docks, officially classified as service craft, are listed in subsequent chapters.

The diving tenders PHOEBUS (YDT 14, ex-YF 294) and SUITLAND (YDT 15, ex-YF 336), listed in the previous edition of *Ships and Aircraft*, are non-self-propelled craft.

Classification: Most service craft have Y-series designations, that letter having been established when these were considered yard craft; they were also known as district craft, from being assigned to the now defunct naval districts.

Only Y-series service craft are listed in the Naval Vessel Register (NVR). All service craft are found in the Service Craft And Boat Accounting Report (SABAR).

Most service craft have hull numbers (Y-series) or hull registry numbers (length + type designation + serial); a few have both.

Guns: Service craft are not armed. The seamanship training craft (YP) can be armed with light weapons for use as harbor patrol craft, while some of the utility cargo carriers (YFU) and barracks ships (APB) were armed for service in the Vietnam War. The IX 515/SES-200 has carried out trials with a number of weapons.

Helicopters: The "mini-carrier" IX 514 and the SWATH research craft KAIMALINO are the only service craft that have a helicopter platform.

Operational: Most service craft are Navy manned; those assigned to the Naval Ocean Systems Center (NOSC), San Diego, Calif., and a few others are manned by civilian–civil service personnel.

UNCLASSIFIED AUXILIARY SHIPS

Unclassified ship designations reached IX 235 at the end of World War II. The series was continued after the war with the German heavy cruiser PRINZ EUGEN designated IX 300; the series reached No. 310 (creating a gap in Nos. 236–299). After the ELK RIVER, formerly LSMR 501, was placed in this category and classified IX with her previous hull number all subsequent ships and craft were assigned in the 500-series, with total disregard for the IX numerical scheme, which dated back to December 1941. (The IX symbol for unclassified vessels was used by the Navy from 1920 without hull numbers being assigned.)

The IX 511 (formerly LST 399) of World War II construction was deactivated and stricken on 1 November 1973; she was laid up in NDRF until reacquired by the Navy on 25 November 1980 for use as a range support ship on the Pacific Missile Range, Point Mugu, Calif. She was classified as IX and placed in service on 30 September 1982; stricken on 15 June 1985.

The acoustic support craft MONOB ONE, formerly IX 309, was changed to YAG 61.

1 EX-OCEANOGRAPHIC RESEARCH SHIP

Number	Name	Launched	In service
IX 517 (ex-AGOR 9)	THOMAS G. WASHINGTON	18 July 1964	4 Sep 1965

This former CONRAD (AGOR 3)-class research ship was redesignated IX 517 on 11 December 1989. She is at the Mare Island Naval Shipyard, Vallejo, Calif.; expected to be disposed of in the near future. See page 000.

1 CLASSROOM BARGE

Number	Name	In service
IX 516	(none)	1988

Displacement:
Length: 303 feet (92.4 m) overall
Beam: 90 feet (27.4 m)
Draft: 22 feet (6.7 m)
Propulsion: non-self-propelled
Manning:

The IX 516 is a classroom barge employed at the Charleston Naval Shipyard (S.C.). There is a three-story deckhouse on the barge containing classrooms; the structure is 241 feet (73.5 m) long, 72 feet (21.95 m) wide, and 35 feet (10.7 m) high.

The IX 516 is a floating classroom barge that supports the former missile submarines employed as Moored Training Ships (MTS) at Charleston, S.C. The craft normally uses shore power, but has emergency power generators. (1990, U.S. Navy)

1 SURFACE EFFECTS SHIP: "SES-200"

Number	Name	Launched	In service
IX 515 (ex-SES-200, WSES 1)	(unnamed)	Dec 1978	Feb 1979

Builder:	Bell-Halter, New Orleans, La.
Displacement:	187 tons light
	243 tons full load
Length:	159$\frac{1}{12}$ feet (48.5 m) overall
Beam:	42$\frac{7}{12}$ (13.0 m)
Draft:	6 feet (1.8 m) on hull
	5 feet (1.5 m) on cushion
Propulsion:	2 diesel engines (MTU 16V396 TB94); 5,720 bhp 2 waterjets
Lift:	2 diesel engines (MTU 6V396 TB83); 1,400 bhp; 4 centrifugal fans
Speed:	16 knots on hull in sea state 0
	14 knots on hull in sea state 3
	40+ knots on cushion in sea state 0
	27 knots on cushion in sea state 3
Range:	2,950 n.miles (5,463 km) at 30 knots in sea state 0
	2,400 n.miles (4,445 km) at 25 knots in sea state 3
Manning:	22 (2 officers + 20 enlisted)
Guns:	(see notes)
Radars:	2 Decca navigation

The U.S. Navy's experimental surface effects ship SES-200 after her latest modification. The U.S. Navy has not proceeded with SES development, as has the Russian Navy, which has developed a corvette-size SES, the Dergach class. (Textron Marine Systems)

The SES-200 was built as a prototype for U.S. Navy and Coast Guard evaluation. The craft was designed by Bell Aerospace and built by Halter Marine. After completion, the craft was leased to the U.S. Coast Guard for trials (beginning January 1980) and then transferred back to the U.S. Navy (from 1982) for continued trials. Following her conversion (see below), the craft was again evaluated by the Coast Guard in late 1984.

In Coast Guard service the craft was named DORADO and designated WSES-1. (Subsequently, the Coast Guard purchased three similar craft; see chapter 32.)

The craft was again placed in U.S. Navy service on 24 September 1982. She is assigned to the David Taylor Research Center and based at the Naval Air Station Patuxent River, Md.[1]

Classification: The hull number IX 515 was assigned on 11 May 1987; previously the craft was listed as "floating equipment."

SES-200. (1989, Giorgio Arra)

Conversion: In January 1982 the craft was returned to Bell-Halter where she was cut in half and a 50-foot (15.2-m) midships section was installed. The modified craft was accepted by the Navy on 24 September 1982.

Two additional lift fans were installed in 1984. Her propulsion plant was upgraded from September 1987 through 1988, with the older propulsion system being replaced by the current diesel engine and waterjet propulsion in 1990.

Engineering: The original characteristics and propulsion plant are described in the 14th Edition/pages 355–356. The waterjet propulsion is the Swedish KaMeWa system.

Guns: The ship was fitted in 1986–1987 with an Ex-25 25-mm Sea Vulcan rotary-barrel (Gatling) gun to evaluate the effectiveness of such weapons on high-speed craft, especially against slow-moving targets.

Missiles: In 1989 the craft evaluated the LTV-developed Crossbow weapons pedestal, which can be used to launch a variety of short-range missiles.

Names: The ship carried the unofficial name JAEGER during her 1985–1986 European tour.

Operational: In 1985–1986 the craft carried out trials and demonstrations in several European countries and Canada. The craft conducted visits to several South American ports in 1987.

SES-200. (1989, Giorgio Arra)

1. Formerly the Naval Ship Research and Development Center, with headquarters at Bethesda, Md.

1 HELICOPTER TRAINING CRAFT: EX-YFU TYPE

Number	Name	Completed	IX in service
IX 514 (ex-YFU 79)	(none)	1968	Mar 1986

Builders:	Pacific Coast Engineering, Alameda, Calif.
Displacement:	220 tons light
	380 tons full load
Length:	125 feet (38.1 m) overall
Beam:	36 feet (11.0 m)
Draft:	7½ feet (2.3 m)
Propulsion:	2 diesel engines (General Motors 6–71); 1,000 bhp; 2 shafts
Speed:	8 knots
Manning:	
Radars:	1 Decca navigation

Converted in 1985–1986 for use as a helicopter landing ship to train helicopter pilots. Placed in service on 31 March 1986, she operates in the Gulf of Mexico, based at Pensacola, Fla.

Classification: Changed from YFU to IX on 31 March 1986.

Helicopters: The flight deck landing area is 57⅚ feet (17.6 m) long and 28 feet (8.5 m) wide. There is no helicopter parking area or hangar on the craft; no refueling capability is provided. Lighting is provided for night landings.

1 RADIATION TEST BARGE

Number	Name	In service
IX 513	(none)	1988

Builders:	Eastern Marine, Panama City, Fla.
Displacement:	approx. 4,400 tons full load
Length:	120 feet (36.6 m) overall
Beam:	90 feet (27.4 m)
Draft:	15 feet (4.6 m)
Propulsion:	non-self-propelled

The IX 513 is an unmanned barge used to produce an electric pulse to evaluate ships' Electro-Magnetic Pulse (EMP) protection under a program termed Empress II. The craft has a 150-foot (45.7-m), four-leg support structure for a 188½-foot (57.5-m) diameter pulse transmission antenna ring. A pulse of 7 million volts can be generated by the craft's two diesel generators.

Delayed by builder problems and environmental impact concerns, the barge began pulse tests against warships in June 1988 off the coast of North Carolina; it was subsequently moved to the Gulf of Mexico, with testing planned to be conducted 26 n.miles (48 km) offshore.

1 MISSILE TEST BARGE

Number	Name	Completed	IX in service
IX 512 (ex-BD 6651)	(none)	1954	Sep 1983

Builders:	Gwater & Zimmerman
Displacement:	approx. 1,000 tons full load
Length:	142 feet (43.3 m) overall
Beam:	58 feet (17.7 m)
Draft:	5¹⁄₁₂ feet (1.55 m)
Propulsion:	non-self-propelled
Manning:	

A former U.S. Army floating crane converted for simulation of Trident missile launches. Known as the Simulated Underwater Partial Launch System (SUPLS II), the craft is fitted with a single Trident missile tube. The 52-ton-capacity crane is retained.

The craft is operated off San Clemente, Calif.

The helicopter landing training craft IX 514 off Pensacola, Fla. The TH-57C SeaRanger is flown by student pilots to practice shipboard landings. (1986, Bell Helicopter Textron)

The Empress II radiation test barge IX 513. Tests to determine electromagnetic effects on ships have been most controversial because of the efforts of environmental groups. (1990, L. Van Ginderen Collection)

The Trident missile test barge IX 512 at the Naval Command, Control and Ocean Surveillance Center at San Diego, Calif. (Formerly the Naval Ocean Systems Center.) (1986, Giorgio Arra)

2 BARRACKS SHIPS: EX-TROOP TRANSPORTS (P2-SE2-R1)

Number	Name	Launched	AP Comm.
IX 507 (ex-AP 121)	Gen Hugh J. Gaffey	20 Feb 1944	18 Sep 1944
IX 510 (ex-AP 127)	ex-Gen William O. Darby	4 June 1945	27 Sep 1945

Builders:	Bethlehem Steel, Alameda, Calif.
Displacement:	12,657 tons light
	22,574 tons full load
Length:	573 feet (174.7 m) waterline
	608$^{11}/_{12}$ feet (185.6 m) overall
Beam:	75½ feet (23.0 m)
Draft:	26$^{5}/_{12}$ feet (8.05 m)
Propulsion:	turbo-electric (2 General Electric turbines); 18,000 shp; 2 shafts
Boilers:	4 600 psi (41.7 kg/cm²) (Combustion Engineering)
Speed:	19 knots
Range:	
Manning:	

The Gen William O. Darby at Newport News Shipbuilding, Va. (1983, Giorgio Arra)

Gen William O. Darby. (1983, Giorgio Arra)

These are immobilized barrack ships. Built for naval service, they were transferred to the Army in 1946; they were assigned to the Navy's newly established Military Sea Transportation Service (MSTS) on 1 March 1950.

The Gaffey was stricken from the NVR on 9 January 1969; the ship was reacquired by the Navy on 1 November 1978 for conversion to a barracks ship and reclassified IX 507 on that date at the Bremerton Naval Shipyard for crews of aircraft carriers undergoing conversion and modernization.

The Darby was operational as a transport from completion until laid up in NDRF ready reserve status on 1 July 1967; she was reacquired from the NDRF on 27 October 1981 (reclassified IX 510 on that date) for use as a barracks ship; after being modified, she was towed to Norfolk Navy Yard to house crews of ships undergoing conversion and modernization.

Only their accommodations and messing spaces have been rehabilitated. The ships are not capable of steaming in their current condition.

Design: As troop transports the AP 121 could carry 4,680 troops and the AP 127 4,985.

Names: The Gaffey was named Adm W.L. Capps in naval service and the Darby was the Adm W.S. Sims; both transferred to the Army in 1946 and were renamed for generals. The name Darby was officially deleted from the IX 510 on 6 July 1976, but it is still used to refer to the ship.

The former troop transport Gen Hugh J. Gaffey, now the IX 507, moored at Yokosuka, Japan. (1986, L. Van Ginderen Collection)

1 EXPLOSIVES DAMGE-CONTROL BARGE

Number	Name	Completed	IX in service
IX 509	(none)	1942	Nov 1979

Builders:	Norfolk Navy Yard
Displacement:	3,000 tons full load
Length:	184 feet (56.1 m) overall
Beam:	
Draft:	
Propulsion:	non-self-propelled

Barge configured to support explosive testing. Operated for the David Taylor Research Center at Portsmouth, Va. Assigned an IX designation on 1 December 1979.

A 60-ton-capacity crane is fitted.

The IX 509 carrying the unofficial designation UEB-1 for Underwater Explosives Barge. (1988, L. Van Ginderen Collection)

1 TEST OPERATIONS SUPPORT SHIP: EX-LCU TYPE

Number	Name	Completed
IX 508 (ex-LCU 1618)	ORCA	1959

Builders:	Gunderson Bros., Portland, Ore.
Displacement:	190 tons light
	390 tons full load
Length:	134¾ feet (41.1 m) overall
Beam:	29¾ feet (9.1 m)
Draft:	6⅝ feet (2.1 m)
Propulsion:	4 diesel engines (General Motors 6-71); 1,200 bhp; 2 shafts (Kort-nozzles)
Speed:	11 knots
Range:	1,200 n.miles (2,222 km) at 11 knots
Manning:	

This craft is configured to support test operations at the Naval Ocean Systems Center (NOSC) at San Diego. Formerly an LCU 1610-class landing craft, she served for several years in the test support role before being changed to IX 508 on 1 December 1979.

Electronics: Modified in 1978 to conduct trials with the NAVSTAR satellite global positioning system.

IX 508. (1990, U.S. Navy)

IX 508. (1986, Giorgio Arra)

1 RESEARCH SUPPORT SHIP: EX-YFU TYPE

Number	Name	Completed
IX 506 (ex-YFU 82)	(none)	1968

Builders:	Pacific Coast Engineering, Alameda, Calif.
Displacement:	220 tons light
	380 tons full load
Length:	136 feet (41.5 m) overall
Beam:	36 feet (11.0 m)
Draft:	5½ feet (1.7 m)
Propulsion:	4 diesel engines (General Motors 6-71); 1,000 bhp; 2 shafts
Speed:	8 knots
Manning:	12 civilian
Torpedoes:	3 12.75-inch (324-mm) tubes Mk 32 (triple)

This former harbor utility craft was converted for use as a research platform by the NOSC San Diego (replacing the YTM 759). Her bow was rebuilt, with a forecastle added; a center well permits lowering test gear to depths of 900 feet (274 m). She was converted in 1978–1982.

Classification: Changed from YFU 82 to IX 506 on 1 April 1978.

IX 506. (1985, Giorgio Arra)

3 SELF-PROPELLED BARRACKS SHIPS: MODIFIED LST DESIGN

Number	Name	Launched	Commissioned
IX 502 (ex-APB 39)	MERCER	17 Nov 1944	19 Sep 1945
IX 503 (ex-APB 40)	NUECES	6 May 1945	30 Nov 1945
IX 504 (ex-APB 37)	ECHOLS	30 July 1945	(1 Jan 1947)

Builders:	Boston Navy Yard
Displacement:	2,190 tons light
	3,640 tons full load
Length:	328 feet (100.0 m) overall
Beam:	50 feet (15.25 m)
Draft:	11 feet (3.4 m)
Propulsion:	2 diesel engines (General Motors 12-267); 1,600 bhp; 2 shafts
Speed:	10 knots
Manning:	198 (12 officers + 186 enlisted) as APB
Troops:	approx. 900
Guns:	removed

These ships were built to provide accommodations and support for small craft. All three were completed as barracks ships (APL, later APB). They were modified in 1975–1976 to serve at shipyards for crews of ships being built or in overhaul; changed from APB to IX at that time.

IX 506. (1985, Giorgio Arra)

Two ships were placed in commission upon original completion; the ECHOLS was placed in service. All three ships were laid up in reserve after World War II. The MERCER and NUECES were recommissioned in 1968 for service in the Vietnam War. They were rearmed at that time with two 3-inch/50-cal AA guns (single), eight 40-mm AA guns (quad), and several machine guns. As modified to support riverine forces in South Vietnam they had crews of 12 officers and 186 enlisted men and could accommodate 900 troops and small-craft crewmen. Both ships were again laid up from 1969–1971 until reactivated in 1975 as barracks ships on the West Coast; they are now at San Diego.

The ECHOLS was reactivated and placed in service on 1 February 1976 as a barracks ship for the crews of new-construction SSBNs at the General Dynamics/Electric Boat yard in Groton, Conn.

Their propulsion plants are not operational.

Class: There were originally 14 ships of this class, APB 35–48.

1 BARRACKS SHIP: EX-SUPPORT SHIP

Number	Name	Launched	Commissioned
IX 501 (ex-LSMR 501)	ELK RIVER	21 Apr 1945	27 May 1945

Builders:	Brown Shipbuilding, Houston, Texas
Displacement:	1,280 tons full load
Length:	230 feet (70.1 m) overall
Beam:	50 feet (15.25 m)
Draft:	9⅞ feet (3.0 m)
Propulsion:	2 diesel engines (General Motors 16-278A); 1,400 bhp; 2 shafts
Speed:	11 knots
Manning:	71 (20 officers + 51 enlisted)

The ELK RIVER was converted from a rocket landing ship to a test and training ship for deep-sea diving and salvage. She was operated in that role by NOSC at San Diego from 1969 until 1986. The large gantry crane (see below) and other equipment were removed in October 1986, and the ship was relegated to service as a barracks hulk.

The ship was laid down on 24 March 1945.

Class: The ELK RIVER was one of 48 medium landing ships (LSM) completed as or converted to rocket fire support ships (LSMR 401–412 and 501–536). All other ships of this type have been stricken,

1 SONAR TEST BARGE

Number	Name	IX in service
IX 310	(none)	1 Apr 1971

The IX 310 consists of two non-self-propelled barges moored in Lake Seneca, N.Y., for sonar research by the Naval Underwater Sound Laboratory at Newport, R.I.

1 TORPEDO TRIALS SHIP: EX-CARGO SHIP

Number	Name	Completed
IX 308 (ex-AKL 17)	NEW BEDFORD	Mar 1945

Builders:	Wheeler Shipbuilding, Long Island, N.Y.
Displacement:	549.5 tons light
	940 tons full load
Length:	176½ feet (53.8 m) overall
Beam:	32¾ feet (10.0 m)
Draft:	10 feet (3.0 m)
Propulsion:	2 diesel engines (General Motors 6-278A); 1,000 bhp; 2 shafts
Speed:	12 knots
Range:	3,200 n.miles (5,926 km) at 11 knots
Torpedoes:	1 21-inch (533-mm) tube
	3 12.75-inch (324-mm) tubes Mk 32 (triple)
Manning:	approx. 25

Classification: APL/APB 39 changed to IX 502 and APL/APB 40 to IX 503 on 1 November 1975; APL/APB 37 to IX 504 on 1 February 1976.

Guns: As built, these ships had eight 40-mm AA guns (quad mounts).

The barracks ships MERCER at San Francisco. Barrack ships—most non-self-propelled—provide mess and berthing facilities for crews of ships undergoing construction, overhaul, or conversion. (1985, Giorgio Arra)

the last three LSMRs having been used in the Vietnam War (redesignated IFS for inshore fire support ships with their LSMR hull numbers).

A total of 558 LSM-type ships were completed 1944–1946; originally designated LCT(7), these ships had open tank decks to carry five M4 Sherman medium tanks or six LVT amphibious tractors. The LSMRs had 5-inch (127-mm) spin-stabilized rocket launchers and 5-inch/38-cal DP guns plus lighter weapons.

Conversion: The ship was converted to a test range support ship in 1967–1968 at Avondale Shipyards and the San Francisco Naval Shipyard. The basic 203½-foot (62-m) LSMR hull was lengthened, and eight-foot (2.4-m) sponsons were added to both sides to improve the ship's stability and increase working space. A superstructure was added forward and an open center well was provided for lowering and raising equipment. The 65-ton gantry crane runs on tracks above the opening to handle small submersibles and diver-transfer chambers. An active precision positioning system is installed for position holding without mooring.

The prototype Mk II Deep Diving System (DDS) was installed in the ship. It can support eight divers operating at depths to at least 1,000 feet (305 m) in helium-oxygen saturation conditions. This system is installed in the two PIGEON (ASR 21)-class ships.

Names: The 48 LSMRs were given river names on 1 October 1955.

SOUND TRIALS SHIP: "MONOB ONE"

The MONOB ONE (ex-IX 309, YW 87) has been reclassified as the YAG 61.

The NEW BEDFORD was built as an Army freight and supply ship (FS 289) and was operated by the Coast Guard for the Army; she was acquired by the Navy on 1 March 1950 for use as a cargo ship and operated by MSTS as the T-AKL 17. The ship was later converted for torpedo testing in 1963 and since then has been operated by the Naval Undersea Warfare Engineering Station, Keyport, Wash. (formerly the Naval Torpedo Station). The NEW BEFORD is fitted with the CURV torpedo recovery device.[2]

She is being replaced by a YTT 9-class torpedo trials craft.

Classification: Originally U.S. Army FS 289; operated by MSTS as T-AKL 17. Changed to IX 308 in October 1971.

2. CURV = Cable-controlled Underwater Research Vehicle.

The torpedo trials ship NEW BEDFORD, which is being replaced by the new construction YTT series. (1978, U.S. Navy)

1 SAILING FRIGATE: "CONSTITUTION"

Number	Name	Launched	Commissioned
(ex-IX 21)	CONSTITUTION	21 Oct 1797	1798

Builders:	Hartt's Shipyard, Boston, Mass.
Displacement:	2,200 tons standard
Length:	175 feet (53.35 m) waterline
	204 feet (62.2 m) billet head to taffrail
Beam:	43½ feet (13.3 m)
Draft:	22½ feet (6.85 m)
Masts:	fore 198 feet (60.4 m)
	main 220 feet (67.0 m)
	mizzen 172½ feet (52.6 m)
Speed:	13+ knots (under sail)
Manning:	54 (2 officers + 52 enlisted) as relic; up to 500 as frigate (including 55 Marines)
Guns:	several smooth-bore cannon (see notes)

The CONSTITUTION is the oldest U.S. ship in Navy commission and the oldest known warship still afloat. Her original commissioning date is not known; she first put to sea on 23 July 1798. She is now moored as a relic at the Boston Naval Shipyard. (She is afloat, unlike the older VICTORY, Admiral Lord Nelson's flagship at the Battle of Trafalgar, which is preserved in concrete at Portsmouth, England.)

The CONSTITUTION hosts more than one million visitors per year.

As a sail frigate the CONSTITUTION fought in the Quasi-War with France, against the Barbary pirates, and in the War of 1812 against Great Britain. She has been rebuilt several times and is now restored as much as possible to her original configuration.

No sails are fitted; her designed sail area was 42,710 ft² (3,844 m²). Once a year, usually on 4 July, she is taken out into Boston Harbor under tow and "turned around," so that her masts do not bend from the effects of sun and wind. At noon on 4 July the CONSTITUTION traditionally fires a 21-gun salute from her forward 24-pounder long guns.

Class: The CONSTITUTION was one of six sail frigates built under an act of Congress of 1794. The CONSTELLATION (38 guns), built under the same act and launched on 7 September 1797, was broken

TORPEDO TRIALS SHIP: EX-CARGO SHIP

The IX 306, a former Army freight and supply ship (FS 221), employed as a torpedo trials ship, was stricken on 30 November 1988.

See 14th Edition/page 340 for characteristics.

up at the Gosport Shipyard (Norfolk), Va., in 1852–1853; almost simultaneously, a sailing corvette of that name was built in the same yard. That ship served in the Navy (designated IX 20 in 1941) until her transfer in 1954 to a private group in Baltimore, Md., where she is maintained.[3]

Classification: The CONSTITUTION was classified as an "unclassified" ship in 1920 (IX without a hull number). She became IX 21 on 8 December 1941 and carried that classification until 1 September 1975 when it was withdrawn because, according to Navy officials, the designation "tended to demean and degrade the CONSTITUTION through association with a group of insignificant craft of varied missions and configurations."

Design: Three-masted sail frigate designed by Joshua Humphreys. The ship was built at Edmond Hartt's shipyard in Boston; rebuilt several times, but her basic lines and configuration have been retained.

Guns: The CONSTITUTION was authorized as a 44-gun frigate, but was in fact completed with a larger gun battery. The ship was usually overgunned, with an early armament consisting of 30 long 24-pounders, 20 to 22 long 12-pounders, and 2 long 24-pounder chase guns. This heavy armament overloaded and strained the ship; still, she could have accommodated up to 60 guns.

The number and types of guns varied considerably during her service as a frigate.

Names: From 1 December 1917 until 4 July 1925 the ship was named OLD IRONSIDES while the name CONSTITUTION was assigned to a battle cruiser (CC 5); the cruiser was never completed and the name reverted to this ship.

Operational: The ship has been at Boston since 7 May 1934, following a sailing tour of 90 ports on the U.S. Atlantic, Pacific, and Gulf coasts from 1931 to 1934.

3. Until 1991 the preserving organization contended that the Baltimore CONSTELLATION was the frigate of 1797, despite much evidence to the contrary. The issue was decisively addressed and the Baltimore ship proven to be the 1853 vessel in an analysis published in 1991 by Dana M. Wegner, et al., of the Navy's David Taylor Research Center (*Fouled Anchors: The* Constellation *Questions Answered,* September 1991).

The sailing frigate CONSTITUTION, during her annual "turn-around cruise" in Boston Harbor. (1986, Robert Selly)

1 SOUND TRIALS SHIP

Number	Name	Completed
YAG 62	DEER ISLAND	1966

Builders: Halter Marine, New Orleans, La.
Displacement: approx. 400 tons full load
Length: 120 feet (36.6 m) overall
Beam: 30 feet (8.5 m)
Draft: 7 feet (2.1 m)
Propulsion: 2 diesel engines; 2 shafts
Speed: 10.5 knots
Range: 6,200 n.miles (11,482 km) at 10.5 knots
Manning: 20 civilian

The DEER ISLAND is a former oilfield supply ship; she was acquired on 15 March 1982 and classified as YAG 62, retaining her commercial name. The craft is used for sound testing by the David Taylor Research Center; based at Port Everglades, Fla.

1 SOUND TRIALS SHIP: YAG TYPE

Number	Name	Launched	Completed
YAG 61 (ex-IX 309, YW 87)	MONOB ONE	3 Apr 1943	Nov 1943

Builders: Zenith Dredge Co., Duluth, Minn.
Displacement: 1,390 tons full load
Length: 173⅝ feet (53.0 m) overall
Beam: 33⅛ feet (10.1 m)
Draft: 15¾ feet (4.8 m)
Propulsion: 1 diesel engine (Caterpillar D398); 850 bhp; 1 shaft (swiveling propeller)
Speed: 11 knots
Range: 2,500 n.miles (4,630 km) at 9 knots
Manning: 20 civilian

The MONOB ONE—for *Mobile Noise Barge*—was originally completed in 1943 as a self-propelled water barge (YW 87). She was converted to a sound trials configuration in 1969 and placed in service in June 1970 for the David Taylor Research Center; assigned to Port Canaveral, Fla.

She is scheduled to be replaced by the USNS HAYES (T-AG 195, ex-T-AGOR 16).

Classification: Changed from YW 87 to IX 309 in 1969; changed to YAG 61 on 1 July 1970.

DEER ISLAND at Fort Lauderdale, Fla. (1989, Giorgio Arra)

DEER ISLAND. (1988, Giorgio Arra)

The long-serving MONOB ONE at Fort Lauderdale, Fla. She has an orange hull and white superstructure. (1988, Giorgio Arra)

MONOB ONE. (1988, Giorgio Arra)

TORPEDO TRIALS CRAFT: "YF 852" CLASS

All torpedo trials craft modified from YF 852-class self-propelled covered lighters have been discarded; the YF 862 (unnamed) was stricken on 15 February 1985, the KODIAK (YF 866) stricken in 1989, and the KEYPORT (YF 885) stricken in July 1990.

See 14th Edition/page 343 for characteristics.

4 FERRYBOATS: EX-"LCU 1610" CLASS

Number	YFB in service
YFB 88 (ex-LCU 1636)	1969
YFB 89 (ex-LCU 1638)	1969
YFB 90 (ex-LCU 1639)	1969
YFB 91 (ex-LCU 1640)	1969

Builders:	
Displacement:	approx. 390 tons full load
Length:	134¾ feet (41.0 m) overall
Beam:	29¾ feet (9.0 m)
Draft:	6 feet (1.8 m)
Propulsion:	4 diesel engines (General Motors); 2,000 bhp; 2 shafts
Speed:	11 knots
Manning:	6 (enlisted)

These are former LCU 1610-class utility landing craft modified for use as ferryboats. Their designation was changed from LCU to YFB on 1 September 1969. All are active.

Ferryboat YFU 90 at the naval base, Guantánamo Bay, Cuba. (L. Van Ginderen Collection)

1 FERRYBOAT: YFB TYPE

Number	Name	Completed
YFB 87	MOKU HOLO HELE	May 1970

Builders:	Western Boat
Displacement:	773 tons full load
Length:	162 feet (49.4 m) overall
Beam:	59 feet (18.0 m)
Draft:	12 feet (3.7 m)
Propulsion:	2 diesel engines (General Motors); 860 bhp; 2 shafts
Speed:	
Manning:	

Built-for-the-purpose ferryboat. Active at Pearl Harbor, Hawaii.
Name: The craft's name in Hawaiian means "Ship that goes back and forth."

The MOKU HOLO HELE, heavily laden with trucks and cars, at Pearl Harbor. (1985, U.S. Navy)

1 FERRYBOAT: YFB TYPE

Number	Name	Completed
YFB 83	WA'A HELE HONUA	Apr 1949

Builders:	John H. Mathis Co., Camden, N.J.
Displacement:	500 tons full load
Length:	180 feet (54.9 m) overall
Beam:	46 feet (14.0 m)
Draft:	
Propulsion:	2 diesel engines; 400 bhp; 1 shaft
Speed:	8.5 knots
Manning:	

Built-for-the-purpose ferryboat. Active at Pearl Harbor.
Name: The craft's name means "A canoe that travels on land."

The WA'A HELE HONUA at Pearl Harbor. (1985, U.S. Navy)

6 SPECIAL-PURPOSE LIGHTERS: YFNX TYPE

Number	Completed	YFNX in service
YFNX 24 (ex-YFN 1215)	1965	1966
YFNX 25 (ex-YFN 1224)	1965	1965
YFNX 26 (ex-YFN 1225)	1965	1970
YFNX 31 (ex-YFN 1249)	1970	1970
YFNX 32 (ex-YRBM 7)	1961	1973
YFNX 33 (ex-YFN 1192)	1952	1974

Builders:	
Displacement:	
Length:	126 feet (38.4 m) overall
Beam:	32⅝ feet (10.0 m)
Draft:	
Propulsion:	diesel engines
Speed:	
Manning:	

These are self-propelled special-purpose craft that have been converted from non-self-propelled lighters. All are active.

1 SPECIAL-PURPOSE LIGHTER: YFNX TYPE

Number	Name	Completed	YFNX in service
YFNX 30 (ex-YFN 1186)	SEA TURTLE	1952	1973

Builders:	Long Beach Naval Shipyard
Displacement:	200 tons light
Length:	111½ feet (34.0 m) overall
Beam:	32⅝ feet (10.0 m)
Draft:	5⁷⁄₁₂ feet (1.7 m)
Propulsion:	diesel engines; cyclonic propulsion (Voith Schneider)
Speed:	4 knots
Manning:	9 civilian

The YFNX 30, unofficially named SEA TURTLE, operated by the Naval Command, Control and Ocean Surveillance Center (formerly NOSC). There are three MK 32 torpedo tubes on the 01 level (covered with canvas). (1990, U.S. Navy)

The SEA TURTLE is the only named YFNX-type craft. She is assigned to the Naval Ocean Systems Center, San Diego, and supports the CURV II recovery vehicle.

SEA TURTLE. (1986, Giorgio Arra)

6 SPECIAL-PURPOSE LIGHTERS: YFNX TYPE

Number	Completed	YFNX in service
YFNX 4	1942	1965
YFNX 7	1942	1967
YFNX 15 (ex-YNg 22)	1942	1965
YFNX 20	1952	1965
YFNX 22	1941	1965
YFNX 23 (ex-YFN 289)	1941	1969

Builders:	YFNX 15 Dravo Corp., Wilmington, Del.
Displacement:	
Length:	109¹¹⁄₁₂ feet (33.5 m) overall

Beam:	32⅝ feet (10.0 m)
Draft:	5⁷⁄₁₂ feet (1.7 m)
Propulsion:	diesel engines
Speed:	
Manning:	

These are self-propelled special-purpose craft, having been converted from non-self-propelled lighters. The YFNX 7 is in reserve; the others are active.

The YFNX 15 was built as a non-self-propelled gate craft (originally YNg 22).

3 TORPEDO TRIALS CRAFT: CONVERTED LIGHTERS

Number	Completed	YFRT in service
YFRT 287 (ex-YF 287)	1941	1965
YFRT 451 (ex-YF 451)	1944	1965
YFRT 520 (ex-YF 520)	1943	1965

Builders:	YFRT 287 Norfolk Navy Yard, Va.
	YFRT 451 Basalt Rock Co., Napa, Calif.
	YFRT 520 Erie Concrete & Steel, Penna.
Displacement:	300 tons light
	650 tons full load
Length:	133 feet (40.5 m) overall
Beam:	30 feet (9.1 m)
Draft:	9 feet (2.7 m)
Propulsion:	2 diesel engines (Caterpillar D379); 600–800 bhp; 2 shafts
Speed:	9.5 knots
Torpedoes:	3 12.75-inch (324-mm) tubes Mk 32 (triple)
Manning:	

The YFRT 451 at Keyport, Wash. Being replaced by the YTTs, this craft still carries her original "straight" YF designation. (1990, U.S. Navy)

Converted from YF-type lighters to a torpedo trials configuration. All are active. They are being replaced by the YTT 9-class torpedo craft.

Class: YFRT 523 was stricken on 3 April 1986.

3 HARBOR UTILITY CRAFT: "LCU 1610" CLASS

Number	Completed
YFU 83	1971
YFU 100 (ex-LCU 1610)	1963
YFU 102 (ex-LCU 1642)	1969

Builders:	Defoe Shipbuilding, Bay City, Mich.
Displacement:	190 tons light
	390 tons full load
Length:	134¾ feet (41.0 m) overall
Beam:	29¾ feet (9.0 m)
Draft:	6 feet (1.8 m)
Propulsion:	4 diesel engines (General Motors 6–71); 2,000 bhp; 2 shafts (Kort-nozzles)
Speed:	11 knots
Manning:	6 (enlisted)

These are converted utility landing craft except for the YFU 83, which was built as a harbor utility craft. All are active.

Class: The class originally consisted of the YFU 83 and 97–102. YFU 101 stricken on 3 March 1986; YFU 98 stricken on 10 March 1986. The YFU 97 was reclassified as LCU 1611 on 21 June 1990.

1 HARBOR UTILITY CRAFT: "LCU 1608" CLASS

Number	Completed
YFU 91 (ex-LCU 1608)	1957

Builders:	Defoe Shipbuilding, Bay City, Mich.
Displacement:	351 tons full load
Length:	115⅙ feet (35.1 m) overall
Beam:	34 feet (10.4 m)
Draft:	5 feet (1.5 m)
Propulsion:	3 diesels (Gray Marine 64 HN12); 675 bhp; 3 shafts (Kort-nozzles)
Speed:	8 knots
Manning:	

Coastal cargo craft. Cargo capacity 183 tons. Active.

1 HARBOR UTILITY CRAFT: "YFU 71" CLASS

Number	Completed
YFU 81	1968

Builders:	Pacific Coast Engineering Co., Alameda, Calif.
Displacement:	220 tons light
	380 tons full load
Length:	125 feet (38.1 m) overall
Beam:	38 feet (11.0 m)
Draft:	7½ feet (2.4 m)
Propulsion:	2 diesel engines (General Motors 6–71); 1,000 bhp; 2 shafts (Kort-nozzles)
Speed:	8 knots
Manning:	

This craft was constructed specifically for use as a coastal cargo craft in the Vietnam War. Twelve units were built to a modified commercial design (YFU 71–82), completed in 1967–1968. Cargo capacity is 300 tons. In reserve since October 1978.

Class: The YFU 71–77 and 80–82 were transferred to the U.S. Army in 1970 for use in South Vietnam; they were returned to the Navy in 1973. YFU 74 and YFU 75 were stricken on 30 September 1986. YFU 71, 72, 76, and 77 were transferred to the Department of the Interior on 1 December 1984; YFU 76 and 77 subsequently transferred to the government of the Marshall Islands in 1987.

The YFU 82 became the IX 506 and the YFU 79 became the IX 512.

Guns: During their service in Vietnam waters these craft each had two or more .50-cal machine guns fitted.

The YFU 97 of this type under way off West Palm Beach, Fla. AUTEC indicates the Atlantic Undersea Test and Evaluation Center prior to her being redesigned as an LCU. A container is loaded on her after deck. (1988, Giorgio Arra)

YFU 91. (1991, Giorgio Arra)

The YFU 75 of the YFU 71 class. (U.S. Navy)

1 HARBOR UTILITY CRAFT: "LCU 1466" CLASS

Number
119WB8501 (ex-YFU 50, LCU 1486)

This former landing craft now has the above designation. She is operated by the Naval Station Roosevelt Roads, Puerto Rico. See page 187 for data.

8 FUEL-OIL BARGES: "YO 65" CLASS

Number	Completed
YO 129	Apr 1944
YO 203	Aug 1945
YO 220	Aug 1945
YO 223	Sep 1945
YO 224	Oct 1945
YO 225	Oct 1945
YO 228	Nov 1945
YO 230	Dec 1945

Builders:	YO 129	Pensacola Shipyard and Engine, Fla.
	YO 203	Manitowoc Shipbuilding, Wisc.
	YO 220–230	Jeffersonville Boat and Machinery, Ind.
Displacement:	440 tons light	
	1,390 tons full load	
Length:	174 feet (53.1 m) overall	
Beam:	33 feet (10.0 m)	
Draft:	13 feet (4.0 m)	
Propulsion:	1 diesel engine (General Motors); 560 bhp; 1 shaft	
Speed:	10.5 knots	
Manning:	11 (enlisted)	

These are coastal tankers with a cargo capacity of 6,570 barrels. All except the YO 228 are active; she is in reserve.

Class: The YO 241 was stricken on 31 January 1987.

The fully loaded YO 203 off San Diego. The gun tub aft of the island reflects the craft's World War II design. (1985, Giorgio Arra)

3 SELF-PROPELLED DREDGES: YM TYPE

Number	Completed
YM 17	1934
YM 33	1970
YM 35	1970

These are small dredges; characteristics vary. The YM 17 and 35 are operational; the YM 33 is in reserve.

Class: YM 38 stricken on 31 January 1987; YM 32 stricken on 17 January 1990.

1 FUEL OIL BARGE: "YO 153" CLASS

Number	Completed
YO 153	1943

Builders:	Ira S. Bushey and Sons, Brooklyn, N.Y.
Displacement:	370 tons light
	1,095 tons full load
Length:	156¼ feet (47.6 m) overall
Beam:	30⁷⁄₁₂ feet (9.3 m)
Draft:	11¾ feet (3.6 m)
Propulsion:	1 diesel engine (Fairbanks-Morse) 525 bhp; 1 shaft
Speed:	10 knots
Manning:	15 (enlisted)

The YO 153 is the only survivor in U.S. service of a class of coastal and harbor tankers. Her cargo capacity is 6,000 barrels. The craft is laid up in reserve.

1 FUEL-OIL BARGE: "YO 46" CLASS

Number	Name	Completed
YO 47	CASING HEAD	Nov 1942

Builders:	Lake Superior Shipbuilding, Superior, Wisc.
Displacement:	950 tons light
	2,660 tons full load
Length:	235 feet (71.6 m) overall
Beam:	37 feet (11.3 m)
Draft:	16½ feet (5.0 m)
Propulsion:	2 diesel engines (Enterprise); 820 bhp; 2 shafts
Speed:	9 knots
Manning:	34

This is the only named YO. Cargo capacity is 10,000 barrels. Laid up in reserve since 1971.

5 GASOLINE BARGES: "YOG 5" CLASS

Number
YOG 58
YOG 78
YOG 88
YOG 93
YOG 196 (ex-YO 196)

Builders:	YOG 58, 88, 93	R.T.C. Shipbuilding, Camden, N.J.
	YOG 78	Puget Sound Navy Yard, Bremerton, Wash.
	YOG 196	Manitowoc Shipbuilding, Wisc.
Displacement:	440 tons light	
	1,390 tons full load	
Length:	174 feet (53.0 m) overall	
Beam:	33 feet (10.1 m)	
Draft:	13 feet (4.0 m)	
Propulsion:	1 diesel engine (General Motors except Union in YOG 58); 640 bhp	
	except 560 bhp in YOG 58; 1 shaft	
Speed:	11 knots	
Manning:		

27 SEAMANSHIP TRAINING CRAFT: "YP 676" CLASS

Number	Launched	In service
YP 676	9 Apr 1984	17 Nov 1984
YP 677	23 June 1984	19 Dec 1984
YP 678	3 Nov 1984	13 May 1985
YP 679	11 Dec 1984	3 June 1985
YP 680	23 Mar 1985	30 July 1985
YP 681	1 June 1985	11 Oct 1985
YP 682	3 Aug 1985	19 Nov 1985
YP 683	19 June 1986	21 Oct 1986
YP 684	14 Aug 1986	21 Oct 1986
YP 685	25 Sep 1986	25 Nov 1986
YP 686	25 Oct 1986	8 Dec 1986
YP 687	17 Mar 1987	22 May 1987
YP 688	13 Mar 1987	22 May 1987
YP 689	20 Mar 1987	10 June 1987
YP 690	17 Apr 1987	10 June 1987
YP 691	19 May 1987	2 July 1987
YP 692	18 June 1987	27 July 1987
YP 693	14 Aug 1987	22 Sep 1987
YP 694	21 Sep 1987	27 Oct 1987
YP 695	26 Oct 1987	1 Dec 1987
YP 696	31 Mar 1988	9 May 1988
YP 697	1 Apr 1988	26 May 1988
YP 698	29 Mar 1988	16 June 1988
YP 699	11 Apr 1988	30 June 1988
YP 700	12 May 1988	2 July 1988
YP 701	14 June 1988	9 Aug 1988
YP 702	19 July 1988	2 Sep 1988

Builders:	YP 676–682	Peterson Builders, Sturgeon Bay, Wisc.
	YP 683–702	Marinette Shipbuilding, Marinette, Wisc.
Displacement:	172 tons full load	
Length:	101⅔ feet (31.0 m) waterline	
	108 feet (32.9 m) overall	
Beam:	24 feet (7.3 m)	
Draft:	5¾ feet (1.75 m)	
Propulsion:	2 diesel engines (General Motors 12V71N); 875 bhp; 2 shafts	
Speed:	12 knots	
Range:	1,500 n.miles (2,778 km) at 12 knots	
Manning:	6 (2 officers + 4 enlisted) + 24 students	
Radars:	SPS-64 navigation	

These are seamanship training craft. They have wooden hulls; the deckhouse and pilothouse are aluminum. The YP 686 is fitted for oceanographic research studies.

Class: YP 676 authorized in fiscal 1982, YP 677–682 (6 units) in fiscal 1983, YP 683–688 (6 units) in fiscal 1984, YP 689–695 (7 units) in fiscal 1985, and YP 696–702 (7 units) in fiscal 1986.

Electronics: Fitted with NAVSAT and Loran C receivers as well as navigation radar and fathometer.

Operational: YP 676–695 assigned to Naval Academy, Annapolis, Md.; YP 696–702 assigned to Naval Education and Training Center, Newport, R.I. (location of Surface Warfare Officers School and Officer Candidate School).

These are self-propelled gasoline barges with a cargo capacity of 6,570 barrels. Built in 1944–1946. They are virtually identical to the 174-foot fuel-oil barges. The YOG 78, 88, and 196 are in service; the YOG 58 and 93 are in reserve.

Class: YOG 79 stricken on 30 August 1987; YOG 68 stricken on 28 September 1989.

The YOG 88 at San Diego. (1985, Giorgio Arra)

YP 680. (1990, Giorgio Arra)

YP 679. (1990, Giorgio Arra)

5 SEAMANSHIP TRAINING CRAFT: "YP 654" CLASS

Number	Launched	Completed
YP 655	Aug 1957	Mar 1958
YP 656	Aug 1957	Apr 1958
YP 657	Aug 1957	June 1958
YP 658	Nov 1957	June 1958
YP 667	Apr 1966	Jan 1967

Builders:	YP 655–658 Stephen Brothers, Stockton, Calif.
	YP 667 Peterson Brothers, Sturgeon Bay, Wisc.
Displacement:	approx. 60 tons light
	approx. 71 tons full load
Length:	80⁵⁄₁₂ feet (24.5 m) overall
Beam:	18¾ feet (5.7 m.)
Draft:	5¼ feet (1.6 m)
Propulsion:	2 diesel engines (General Motors 6–71); 590 bhp; 2 shafts
Speed:	13 knots
Range:	400 n.miles (740 km) at 12 knots
Manning:	10 (2 officers + 8 enlisted) + 20 students
Radars:	LN-66 navigation

YP 658. (1988, Giorgio Arra)

These are seamanship training craft.

Class: Seventeen units of this class have been reclassified as mine countermeasures craft under the COOP program (YP 654, 659–666, 668–675); however, five are not employed as mine craft (see chapter 22).

Electronics: Fitted with navigation radar and fathometer.

Names: The YP 658 is named PERSEVERANCE.

Operational: The YP 676 and YP 677 are assigned to the Naval Academy, Annapolis; the others to the Surface Warfare Officers School, San Diego.

3 SEAPLANE WRECKING DERRICKS: "YSD 11" CLASS

Number	Completed
YSD 39	1943
YSD 63	1944
YSD 74	1944

Builders:	YSD 39 Norfolk Navy Yard
	YSD 63 Sonle Steel, San Francisco, Calif.
	YSD 74 Pearl Harbor Navy Yard
Displacement:	240 tons light
	270 tons full load
Length:	104 feet (31.7 m) overall
Beam:	31⅛ feet (9.5 m)
Draft:	4 feet (1.2 m)
Propulsion:	2 diesels (Superior); 640 bhp; 2 shafts
Speed:	6 knots
Manning:	13–15 (enlisted)

The "Mary Ann" YSD 63 chugging along at Subic Bay. (1977, Giorgio Arra)

These are small, self-propelled floating cranes. They have a 10-ton-capacity crane. All are active. YSDs are called "Mary Anns."

Class: YSD 53 was stricken in May 1991.

LARGE HARBOR TUGS: "YTB 839" CLASS

Plans to construct 28 large harbor tugs beginning in 1983 were cancelled in favor of contracting private tug services.

75 LARGE HARBOR TUGS: "YTB 760" CLASS

Number	Name	Number	Name
YTB 760	NATICK	YTB 800	EUFAULA
YTB 761	OTTUMWA	YTB 801	PALATKA
YTB 762	TUSCUMBIA	YTB 802	CHERAW
YTB 763	MUSKEGON	YTB 803	NANTICOKE
YTB 764	MISHAWAKA	YTB 804	AHOSKIE
YTB 765	OKMULGEE	YTB 805	OCALA
YTB 766	WAPAKONETA	YTB 806	TUSKEGEE
YTB 767	APALACHICOLA	YTB 807	MASSAPEQUA
YTB 768	ARCATA	YTB 808	WENATCHEE
YTB 769	CHESANING	YTB 809	AGAWAM
YTB 770	DAHLONEGA	YTB 810	ANOKA
YTB 771	KEOKUK	YTB 811	HOUMA
YTB 774	NASHUA	YTB 812	ACCOMAC
YTB 775	WAUWATOSA	YTB 813	POUGHKEEPSIE
YTB 776	WEEHAWKEN	YTB 814	WAXAHACHIE
YTB 777	NOGALESEN	YTB 815	NEODESHA
YTB 778	APOPKA	YTB 816	CAMPTI
YTB 779	MANHATTAN	YTB 817	HYANNIS
YTB 780	SAUGUS	YTB 818	MECOSTA
YTB 781	NIANTIC	YTB 819	IUKA
YTB 782	MANISTEE	YTB 820	WANAMASSA
YTB 783	REDWING	YTB 821	TONTOCANY
YTB 784	KALISPELL	YTB 822	PAWHUSKA
YTB 785	WINNEMUCCA	YTB 823	CANONCHET
YTB 786	TONKAWA	YTB 824	SANTAQUIN
YTB 787	KITTANNING	YTB 825	WATHENA
YTB 788	WAPATO	YTB 826	WASHTUENA
YTB 789	TOMAHAWK	YTB 827	CHETEK
YTB 790	MENOMINEE	YTB 828	CATAHECASSA
YTB 791	MARINETTE	YTB 829	METACOM
YTB 792	ANTIGO	YTB 830	PUSHMATAHA
YTB 793	PIQUA	YTB 831	DEKANAWIDA
YTB 794	MANDAN	YTB 832	PETALESHARO
YTB 795	KETCHIKAN	YTB 833	SHABONEE
YTB 796	SACO	YTB 834	NEWAGEN
YTB 797	TAMAQUA	YTB 835	SKENANDOA
YTB 798	OPELIKA	YTB 836	POKAGON
YTB 799	NATCHITOCHES		

Builders:	YTB 760, 761	Jakobson Shipyard, Oyster Bay, N.Y.
	YTB 762	Commercial Iron Works, Portland, Ore.
	YTB 763–766, 799–802	Southern Shipbuilding, Slidell, La.
	YTB 767–771	Mobile Ship Repair, Ala.
	YTB 774–798, 816–836	Marinette Marine, Wisc.
	YTB 803–815	Peterson Builders, Sturgeon Bay, Wisc.

Displacement:	283 tons light
	356 tons full load
Length:	109 feet (33.2 m) overall
Beam:	30½ feet (9.3 m)
Draft:	13½ feet (4.1 m)
Propulsion:	1 diesel engine (Fairbanks-Morse 38D8 ⅛); 2,000 bhp; 1 shaft
Speed:	12.5 knots
Range:	2,000 n.miles (3,704 km) at 12 knots
Manning:	10–14 (enlisted)

These tugs were completed during 1961–1975. All of them are in active service.

Class: The similar YTB 837 and YTB 838 were transferred to Saudi Arabia in 1975.

Design: SCB No. 147A. These and other Navy harbor tugs are used for towing and for maneuvering ships in harbors. Their masts fold down to facilitate working alongside large ships.

Tugs are also equipped for firefighting.

Names: Named tugs honor American towns and small cities.

The METACOM assists the attack submarine WHALE (SSN 638) at the New London submarine base; note the comparative freeboards and the "padding" on the YTM 829 to avoid "hurting" her charge. (1991, U.S. Navy, JOSN Connie Sanders)

The SANTAQUIN showing the three roller-fenders fitted on the starboard side; there are another three to port. The tug's stub mast is lowered to avoid damage when coming alongside a "big boy." (1991, Giorgio Arra)

The DAHLONEGA under way. Note the radar "pot" atop the bridge; other YTBs have a bar-type antenna or both types fitted. (1990, L. Van Ginderen Collection)

4 LARGE HARBOR TUGS: "YTB 756" CLASS

Number	Name	Completed
YTB 756	PONTIAC	1960
YTB 757	OSHKOSH	1960
YTB 758	PADUCAH	1961
YTB 759	BOGALUSA	1961

Builders:	Southern Shipbuilding, Slidell, La.
Displacement:	311 tons light
	409 tons full load
Length:	109 feet (33.2 m) overall
Beam:	30 feet (9.1 m)
Draft:	14 feet (4.3 m)
Propulsion:	1 diesel engine (Fairbanks-Morse); 1,800 bhp; 1 shaft
Speed:	12 knots
Manning:	10–12 enlisted

All of these craft are active.

Design: SCB No. 147 (less streamlined superstructure than similar SCB No. 147A design).

OSHKOSH. (1991, Giorgio Arra)

2 LARGE HARBOR TUGS: "YTB 752" CLASS

Number	Name	Completed
YTB 752	EDENSHAW	1959
YTB 753	MARIN	1960

Builders:	Christy Corp., Sturgeon Bay, Wisc.
Displacement:	275 tons light
	375 tons full load
Length:	101 feet (30.8 m) overall
Beam:	29 feet (8.8 m)
Draft:	16 feet (4.9 m)
Propulsion:	1 diesel engine (Alco); 1,800 bhp; 1 shaft
Speed:	12 knots
Manning:	11 or 12 (enlisted)

The EDENSHAW helping a PERRY (FFG 7)-class frigate. The tug has a squared-off funnel compared to later YTBs. (1983, Giorgio Arra)

1 SMALL HARBOR TUG: "YTL 422" CLASS

Number	Name	Completed
YTL 602	(none)	1945

Builders:	Robert Jacob, City Island, N.Y.
Displacement:	70 tons light
	80 tons full load
Length:	66⅛ feet (20.2 m) overall
Beam:	17 feet (5.2 m)
Draft:	5 feet (1.5 m)
Propulsion:	1 diesel engine (Hoover); 375 bhp; 1 shaft
Speed:	10 knots
Manning:	5 (enlisted)

The YTL 602 is the survivor of several hundred small tugs built during World War II. Many serve in foreign navies. The YTL 602 is active.

Most surviving YTL and YTM type tugs were stricken in 1985.

Classification: These craft were originally classified YT with the same hull number. YTL originally meant harbor tug, *little*.

1 HARBOR TUG: EX-ARMY CRAFT

Number	Name
143WB8401 (ex-LT 535)	PACIFIC ESCORT

Builders:	
Displacement:	566 tons light
	807 tons full load
Length:	133⅔ feet (40.7 m) waterline
	143⅓ feet (43.7 m) overall
Beam:	33 feet (10.1 m)
Draft:	14 feet (4.3 m)
Propulsion:	diesel-electric (2 diesel engines); 1,530 shp; 1 shaft
Speed:	11.5 knots
Range:	5,000 n.miles (9,260 km) at 11.5 knots
Manning:	

Former U.S. Army tug acquired in 1984. Based at the Mare Island Naval Shipyard, Calif. Reportedly employed in research activities.

MEDIUM HARBOR TUGS

All surviving YTM-type tugs have been stricken except the ex-YTM 404, which is now designated 100WB8501 and serves at the Naval Station Roosevelt Roads, Puerto Rico.

Table 25-1 lists the disposals since the last edition of *Ships and Aircraft*. The former LT-series tugs were Army craft.

Plans to construct additional YTMs (initially YTM 800–802, authorized in fiscal 1973) were deferred in favor of additional YTB construction.

See 14th Edition/pages 350–351 for YTM characteristics.

4 TORPEDO TRIALS CRAFT: "YTT 9" CLASS

Number	Name	Launched	In service
YTT 9	CAPE FLATTERY	5 May 1989	30 May 1991
YTT 10	BATTLE POINT	17 Aug 1989	30 Nov 1991
YTT 11	DISCOVERY BAY	22 Feb 1990	30 May 1992
YTT 12	AGATE PASS	6 Sep 1990	30 Oct 1992

Builders:	McDermott Shipyard, Morgan City, La.
Displacement:	1,000 tons light
	1,200 tons full load
Length:	186½ feet (56.85 m) overall
Beam:	40 feet (12.2 m)
Draft:	10½ feet (3.2 m)
Propulsion:	diesel-electric (1 Cummins VTA-28 diesel engine); 1,250 shp; 3 azimuth drives (1 forward, 2 aft)
Speed:	11 knots
Torpedoes:	2 21-inch (533-mm) tubes Mk 59 (fixed single; submerged)
	3 12.75-inch (324-mm) tubes Mk 32 (triple)
Manning:	25 (enlisted) + 4–12 technicians

TABLE 25-1. MEDIUM HARBOR TUG DISPOSALS

Number	Name	Notes
YTM 189	NEPANET	str. 15 May 1986
YTM 265	HIAWATHA	str. 15 May 1986
YTM 268	RED CLOUD	str. 15 May 1986
YTM 359	PAWTUCKET	str. 15 May 1986
YTM 364	SASSBA	str. 15 May 1986
YTM 381	CHEPANOC	str. 15 May 1986
YTM 382	COATOPA	str. 15 May 1986
YTM 383	COCHALI	str. 15 May 1986
YTM 397	YANEGUA	str. 31 July 1986
YTM 398	NATAHKI	str. 15 May 1986
YTM 400	OTOKOMI	str. 31 July 1986
YTM 404	COSHECTON	to 100WB8501 in 1986
YTM 406	KITTATON	str. 15 May 1986
YTM 415	SECOTA	sunk 22 March 1986*
YTM 417	TACONNET	str. 31 July 1986
YTM 534	NADLI	str. 15 May 1986
YTM 544	YATANOCAS	str. 28 Feb 1987
YTM 545	ACCOHANOC	str. 28 Feb 1987
YTM 546	TAKOS	str. 15 May 1986
YTM 549	MIGADAN	str. 28 Feb 1987
YTM 748 (ex-LT 2078)	(none)	str. 15 May 1986
YTM 750 (ex-LT 2089)	HACKENSACK	str. 9 June 1986
YTM 759 (ex-LT 2077)	(none)	to IX 508 on 1 Nov 1975†
YTM 760 (ex-YTB 772)	MASCOUTAH	str. 9 June 1986
YTM 761 (ex-YTB 773)	MENASHA	str. 9 June 1986
YTM 768 (ex-YTB 502)	APOHOLA	str. 15 May 1986
YTM 776 (ex-YTB 513)	HIAMONEE	str. 30 Nov 1986; sold to the Philippines 30 June 1990

*Sunk in collision with the GEORGIA (SSBN 729) off Midway Island.
†Former U.S. Army tug employed to support research activities; stricken on 1 December 1977.

The BATTLE POINT and CAPE FLATTERY at Keyport, Wash. These highly capable torpedo trials craft are replacing several outdated ships. Note the mast configuration and the two bar-type radar antennas atop the wide bridge structure. (1990, U.S. Navy)

These are specialized torpedo trials craft that are replacing the IXYF and YFRT craft now employed in this role. Electric drive on batteries permits quiet operation for launching acoustic-homing torpedoes. They can operate remote (cable)-controlled unmanned underwater vehicles. Fitted with precision mooring system. Provided with an 11-ton-capacity crane and smaller cranes and winches.

These craft are assigned to the Naval Undersea Warfare Engineering Station, Keyport, Wash.

Class: The classification YTT originally indicated torpedo testing barge. The YTT 1–4 were built in 1912–1916; the YTT 5–7 were of World War II construction. All were non-self-propelled barges. The designation YTT 8 was not assigned.

Classification: Originally planned as YFRT type, but built as YTT.

The CAPE FLATTERY. The craft has torpedo recovery cranes forward and amidships, with a broad working area aft. (1990, U.S. Navy)

2 WATER BARGES: "YW 83" CLASS

Number	Launched	Completed
YW 98	Sep 1945	Nov 1945
YW 127	May 1945	July 1945

Builders:	YW 98 Geo. Lawley and Son, Neponset, Mass.
	YW 127 Leatham D. Smith Shipbuilding, Sturgeon Bay, Wisc.
Displacement:	440 tons light
	1,282 tons full load
Length:	174 feet (53.0 m) overall
Beam:	32 feet (9.7 m)
Draft:	15 feet (4.6 m)
Propulsion:	1 diesel engine (General Motors 8–2784) 560 bhp; 1 shaft
Speed:	8 knots
Manning:	22 (enlisted)

These craft are similar to the YO/YOG types; they are employed to carry fresh water for ships. Cargo capacity is 200,000 gallons (760,000 liters). The YW 98 is in reserve and the YW 127 is active.

Class: YW 123 stricken on 15 February 1984; YW 108 stricken on 15 October 1985 (to Maritime Academy, Kings Point, N.Y.); YW 83, YW 86, YW 101, and YW 126 stricken on 15 April 1988.

The now discarded YW 119, typical of the large number of water barges that once serviced the fleet. The two surviving units are similar. (Giorgio Arra)

1 RESEARCH SUPPORT BOAT: "RSB-1"

Number	Name	In service
RSB-1	ex-A.B. WOOD II	1966

Builders:	Bishop Marine Service
Displacement:	291 tons full load
Length:	157 feet (47.85 m) overall
Beam:	36 feet (11.0 m)
Draft:	11 feet (3.4 m)
Propulsion:	2 diesel engines; 1,530 bhp; 2 shafts
Speed:	13 knots
Manning:	5 civilian

This craft is operated by the Naval Surface Weapons Center at Ft. Lauderdale, Fla., to recover space-launch booster rockets.

The craft was built in 1966 specifically to support deep-sea work and recovery operations.

Classification: Assigned service craft hull No. 157NS762.

Design: The craft has a bow thruster and is fitted with a 35-ton-capacity hydraulic telescoping boom plus winches for recovering the boosters from depths to 7,000 feet (2,134 m).

RSB-1. (1991, Giorgio Arra)

RSB-1. (1989, Giorgio Arra)

3 RESEARCH CRAFT: "ASHEVILLE" CLASS

Number	Name	Launched	PG Commission	To DTRC
165NS761 (ex-PG 94)	ATHENA I	8 June 1968	8 Nov 1969	21 Aug 1975
165NS762 (ex-PG 98)	ATHENA II	4 Apr 1970	5 Sep 1970	3 Oct 1977
165NS763 (ex-PG 100)	LAUREN	19 June 1970	6 Feb 1970	

Builders:	Tacoma Boatbuilding, Wash.
Displacement:	approx. 265 tons full load
Length:	164½ feet (50.2 m) overall
Beam:	23¾ feet (7.2 m)
Draft:	9½ feet (2.9 m)
Propulsion:	CODOG: 2 diesel engines (Cummins VT12-875M), 1,400 bhp; 1 gas turbine (General Electric LM 1500), 12,500 shp; 2 shafts
Speed:	16 knots on diesel engines; 40+ knots on gas turbines
Range:	2,400 n.miles (4,445 km) at 14 knots on diesel engines
	325 n.miles (602 km) at 37 knots on gas turbines
Manning:	(civilian contractor)

These are former ASHEVILLE-class patrol combatants/gunboats employed in the research role. They are the last of a class of 17 in U.S. naval service (see chapter 21). The three above units were transferred to the David Taylor Research Center for use in various offshore research projects; based at Panama City, Fla.

The DOUGLAS (PG 100) was stricken on 1 October 1977 for transfer to DTRC to be placed in service as the ATHENA III. However, she was instead discarded in 1984 but retained in storage at Little Creek, Va., for possible foreign transfer. She was "reacquired" and converted in 1991–1992 for use as a test ship in the Athena program, although given the name LAUREN.

All weapons have been removed.

Classification: When assigned to the David Taylor Research Center these ships were reclassified as service craft without specific hull designations.

Design: Aluminum hulls with fiberglass superstructures.

Names: Their former names were PG 94 CHEHALIS, PG 98 GRAND RAPIDS, and PG 100 DOUGLAS.

Operational: These ships have participated in a variety of research projects. Possibly the most unusual was one in which the ATHENA II, at maximum speed, towed an in-flight MH-53E helicopter backwards to help assess flight envelope characteristics. Other trials have included sonars and mine countermeasures gear.

The ex-PG 100 undergoing a long-delayed conversion to a research craft, renamed LAUREN. The 3-inch/50-cal enclosed gun mount is still installed forward in this view. (1991, Giorgio Arra)

The ATHENA I showing the extension forward of the bridge. The ATHENA I and II have orange hulls and white superstructures. The ATHENA I does not have the "I" after her name. (1991, Giorgio Arra)

The ATHENA II with a rounded bridge face. All three craft are employed for a variety of tests and research for the David Taylor Research Center. (1991, Giorgio Arra)

The ATHENA II pulling away from the pier. There is a laboratory van amidships; winches and lift equipment aft. (1989, Giorgio Arra)

1 SONOBUOY TRAILS CRAFT

Number	Name
180WB8701	ACOUSTIC PIONEER

Builders:
Displacement: approx. 1,500 tons full load
Length: 179¹¹/₁₂ feet (54.9 m) overall
Beam: 40 feet (12.2 m)
Draft: 14 feet (4.3 m)
Propulsion: 2 diesel engines (General Motors); 2 shafts
Speed
Manning:

Former oilfield supply boat acquired by the Navy in 1987 and employed by the Naval Avionics Development Center at St. Croix in the Virgin Islands for sonobuoy testing. Also designated NADC 38.

1 SONOBUOY TRIALS CRAFT

Number	Name
161NS8801	ACOUSTIC EXPLORER

Former oilfield supply boat acquired by the Navy in 1988 and employed by the Naval Avionics Development Center at St. Croix in the Virgin Islands for sonobuoy testing.

1 RANGE SUPPORT SHIP (SWATH): "KAIMALINO"

Number	Name	Launched	In service
90WB8701	KAIMALINO	7 March 1973	1973

Builders: Coast Guard Yard, Curtis Bay, Md.
Displacement: 228 tons full load
Length: 88⅓ feet (26.9 m) overall
Beam: 46½ feet (14.2 m)
Draft: 15¼ feet (4.65 m)
Propulsion: CODOG: 2 diesel engines (General Motors 6–71), 160 bhp; 2 gas turbines (General Electric T64-6B), 5,000 shp; 2 shafts
Speed: 22 knots
Range: 1,500 n.miles (2,778 km) at 5 knots on diesel engines
                450 n.miles (833 km) at 17 knots on gas turbines
Manning: 10 civilian + 6 scientists
Radars: Raytheon 3610
                Raytheon R40

The Stable Semi-submerged Platform (SSP) KAIMALINO is an experimental SWATH craft employed in the range support role by NOSC on the center's underwater test range in Hawaii. After several years of successful trials and work activities, during 1980–1981 the KAIMALINO was modified (see Conversion notes). She was again placed in service on 24 September 1982.

Classification: The craft is also known as SSP 1 for semi-submerged platform.

Conversion: The KAIMALINO was modified at the Dillingham Shipyard in Hawaii in 1980–1981. The craft was enlarged from 190 to 228 tons through the addition of fiberglass buoyancy modules. Plans to further enlarge the ship to some 600 tons were not carried out.

Design: The SSP is a Small Waterplane Area Twin-Hull (SWATH) craft developed to test this hull concept. The SSP/SWATH concept differs from that of a catamaran, which has two conventional ship hulls joined together. The SWATH design provides a comparatively large deck area with a minimum of heave, pitch, and roll.

The craft has two fully submerged, torpedo-shaped hulls, each 6½ feet (2.0 m) in diameter, with vertical struts penetrating the water to support the superstructure and flight deck. The flight deck area is 3,400 square feet (306 m²).

ACOUSTIC PIONEER. (1991, Giorgio Arra)

ACOUSTIC PIONEER. (1991, Giorgio Arra)

The KAIMALINO with an SH-2F LAMPS I helicopter on board during flight trials of the SWATH. (1976, U.S. Navy)

The KAIMALINO has a hull-stabilizing fin connecting the two submerged hulls and two small canard fins forward, one inboard on each hull. There is an opening in the craft's main deck for lowering research and recovery devices. (The opening is covered over for helicopter operations.) The beam listed above is the maximum over both hulls.

Up to 16 tons of mission equipment can be carried.

Engineering: Two T64-GE-6B aircraft-type gas-turbine engines provide propulsion power. Two Detroit diesel engines (8V-71T) are installed for auxiliary propulsion.

Helicopters: The KAIMALINO conducted tests on the feasibility of landing helicopters on SSP/SWATH-type ships in high sea states at speeds up to 25 knots in 1976. The operations with an SH-2F LAMPS were completely successful.

Torpedoes: In 1982 the KAIMALINO was fitted with triple Mk 32 torpedo tubes for tests of lightweight torpedoes.

KAIMALINO with the SH-2F. (1976, U.S. Navy)

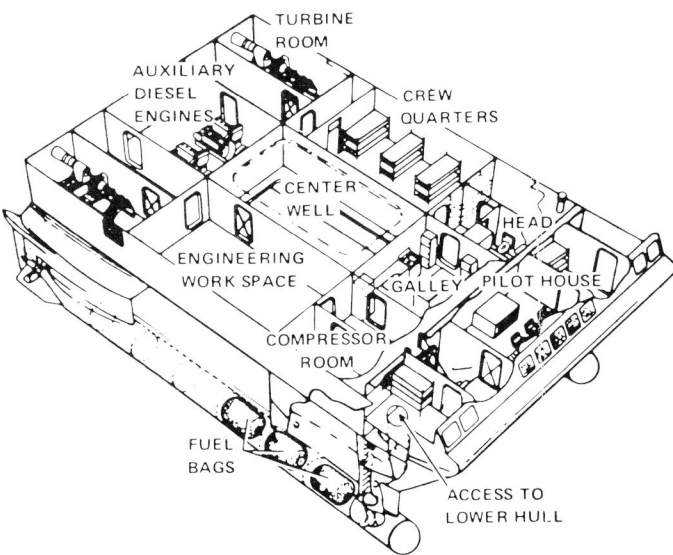

KAIMALINO interior arrangement.

The KAIMALINO in dry dock showing her twin, torpedo-like submerged hulls. Compare this configuration with the SWATH T-AGOS surveillance ships (chapter 23). (1973, U.S. Navy)

1 CONSTRUCTION PLATFORM

Number	Name	Launched	Completed
(none) (ex-YFNB 330)	SEACON	22 Mar 1945	25 Oct 1945

Builders:	Missouri Valley Bridge and Iron, Ind.
Displacement:	2,780 tons full load
Length:	260 feet (79.25 m) overall
Beam:	48 feet (14.6 m)
Draft:	9½ feet (2.9 m)
Propulsion:	3 diesel engines (2 General Motors 6–71, 1 GM 12–71); 1,020 bhp; 3 shafts (Voith-Schneider vertical cylindrical propellers)
Speed:	7 knots
Manning:	50

This craft was converted to transport rockets for NASA; subsequently converted 1974–1976 by the Norfolk Shipbuilding and Dry Dock Co. to serve as a seagoing work ship. The craft is towed to work positions and can use her own engines for propulsion and maneuvering in the work area.

Used to lay cable and do other deep-sea work. Fitted with a 25-ton-capacity A-frame gantry crane and a 22-ton travelling crane.

1 OCEANOGRAPHIC SUPPORT CRAFT

Number	Name	Completed
105UB821	ERLINE	1965

Builders:	Equitable Equipment Co., New Orleans, La.
Displacement:	96 tons light
	120 tons full load
Length:	105 feet (32.0 m) overall
Beam:	20⅔ feet (6.3 m)
Draft:	5¹¹⁄₁₂ feet (1.8 m)
Propulsion:	2 diesel engines; 2 shafts
Speed:	10 knots
Manning:	

The ERLINE, formerly the commercial ORRIN, is a former oilfield crew boat employed by the Naval Underwater Systems Center; based at Tudor Hill, Bermuda.

1 PROPULSION TRIALS CRAFT: "JUPITER II"

Number	Name
(none)	JUPITER II

Builders:
Displacement:
Length: 65 feet (129.8 m) overall
Beam: 17 feet (5.18 m)
Draft: 6 feet (1.83 m)
Propulsion: 2 diesel engines; 550 bhp + gas turbine with 3,000 shp superconductive system; 3 shafts
Speed:
Range:
Manning: 3

Acquired by the Navy in 1976 and operated by the David Taylor Research Center in Annapolis, Md., for trials of superconducting electric motor technology.

The JUPITER II was originally an offshore oil-industry work boat named PRYER. She was converted to her current configuration at the Coast Guard Yard at Curtis Bay, Md., in 1976.

Engineering: The first superconducting system tested in the JUPITER II was a turbine-driven 300-kw superconductive generator that produced 400 horsepower. Subsequently, in 1983 a larger superconductive system generating 3,000 horsepower was installed.

There are two diesel engines for primary power, with two shafts above the shaft connected to the superconductive plant.

Names: The first JUPITER was a collier (AC 3); completed in 1913, she was the first U.S. Navy ship to have electric drive. She was converted to the Navy's first aircraft carrier in 1920–1922 and renamed LANGLEY (CV 1, later AV 3).

The propulsion trials craft JUPITER II under way in Chesapeake Bay; the destroyer DEYO (DD 970) is in the background. (1984, U.S. Navy)

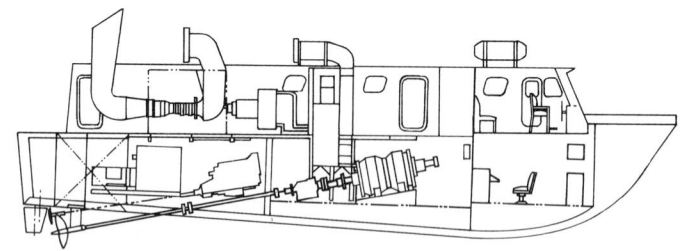

JUPITER II interior arrangement. (William Clipson)

TORPEDO RETRIEVERS

Names assigned to these craft are unofficial.

7 TORPEDO WEAPON RETRIEVERS: 120-FOOT TYPE

Number	Name	Launched	In service
TWR 821	SWAMP FOX	17 Oct 1984	4 Nov 1985
TWR 822		18 Oct 1984	20 Nov 1985
TWR 823		4 May 1985	6 Dec 1985
TWR 825		8 Aug 1985	6 Dec 1985
TWR 833		4 Apr 1986	3 July 1986
TWR 841		15 Aug 1986	18 Oct 1986
TWR 842		22 Sept 1986	24 Dec 1986

Builders: Marinette Marine, Wisc.
Displacement: 174 tons full load
Length: 120 feet (36.6 m) overall
Beam: 25 feet (7.6 m)
Draft: 12 feet (3.65 m)
Propulsion: 2 diesel engines (Caterpillar D 3512); 2,350 bhp; 2 shafts
Speed: 16 knots
Manning: 15 (1 officer + 14 enlisted)

These are improved torpedo retrievers capable of recovering and carrying up to 14 Mk 48 torpedoes.

Class: Originally a class of ten units, TWR 821–825, 831–833, 841, and 842. Two units were sunk by hurricane Hugo at Roosevelt Roads, Puerto Rico; one was sunk in a storm at Pearl Harbor.

Design: A stern ramp and crane are provided for torpedo recovery. Endurance is seven days.

TWR 823. (1986, Giorgio Arra)

TWR 823. (1986, Giorgio Arra)

3 TORPEDO WEAPON RETRIEVERS: 100-FOOT TYPE

Number	Name
TR 681	
TR 711	
TR 771	PHOENIX

Builders:	Peterson Builders, Sturgeon Bay, Wisc.
Displacement:	110 tons light
	165 tons full load
Length:	102 feet (31.1 m) overall
Beam:	21 feet (6.4 m)
Draft:	7¾ feet (2.4 m)
Propulsion:	4 diesel engines (General Motors 12V–149); 1,600 bhp; 2 shafts
Speed:	18 knots
Range:	1,920 n. miles (3,556 km) at 10 knots
Manning:	15 (enlisted)

These torpedo retrievers are based on the PGM 59-class motor gunboat design. Completed in 1969–1970.

Design: Steel construction. Fitted with stern recovery ramp. Can carry 17 tons of torpedoes.

The white-painted TR 711 assigned to AUTEC. (1988, Giorgio Arra)

5 TORPEDO RETRIEVERS: 85-FOOT TYPE

Number	Number	Number
TR 651	TR654	TR762
TR 653	TR761	

Builders:	Tacoma Boatbuilding, Wash.
Displacement:	
Length:	85 feet (25.9 m) overall
Beam:	18⅔ feet (5.7 m)
Draft:	5⅔ feet (1.7 m)
Propulsion:	2 diesel engines (General Motors 16V–71); 2 shafts
Speed:	20 knots
Manning:	8 (enlisted)

Aluminum construction. Can carry eight torpedoes (22,000 pounds/9,979 kg).

100-foot TR showing the open stern for retrieving torpedoes; several Mk 48 torpedoes are on deck. (1984, Giorgio Arra)

4 TORPEDO RETRIEVERS: 72-FOOT MK 2 TYPE

Number
TR 645
TR 652
TR 653
TR 642

Builders:	
Displacement:	53 tons full load
Length:	72⅙ feet (22.0 m) overall
Beam:	17 feet (5.2 m)
Draft:	4⅓ feet (1.3 m)
Propulsion:	8 diesel engines; 1,300 bhp; 2 shafts
Speed:	18 knots
Range:	180 n.miles (333 km) at 18 knots
Manning:	7 (enlisted)

These TRs were completed 1958–1966. They are being replaced by the new, 120-foot craft. Can carry 24,000 pounds (10,886 kg) of torpedoes.

Wood construction.

85-foot TWR type at San Diego. (1985, Giorgio Arra)

6 TORPEDO RETRIEVERS: 65-FOOT TYPE

Number	
TR 671	
TR 672	
TR 673	
TR 674	
TR 675	HARRIER
TR 676	PEREGRINE

Builders:
Displacement:	34.8 tons full load
Length:	65 feet (19.8 m) overall
Beam:	17¼ feet (5.25 m)
Draft:	3⅝ feet (1.2 m)
Propulsion:	2 diesel engines (General Motors 12V71); 800 bhp; 2 shafts
Speed:	18.7 knots
Range:	280 n.miles (518 km) at 18.7 knots
Manning:	6 (enlisted)

These TRs were completed in 1967–1968. The basic 65-foot design was also used for Navy utility and air-sea rescue boats. Aluminum construction. The craft can carry four long torpedoes (11,000 pounds).

72-foot TR type at San Diego. (1986, Giorgio Arra)

65-foot TR at San Diego. (1986, Giorgio Arra)

DRONE RECOVERY BOAT: EX-MOTOR TORPEDO BOAT

The RETRIEVER (DR-1, ex-PT 809), the Navy's last PT boat, was stricken in 1986. The craft, completed in 1950, was one of four post–World War II motor torpedo boats built as competitive prototypes. After extensive trials and limited service, the PT 809 was laid up in reserve.

She was later reactivated and employed to carry Secret Service agents screening the presidential yacht on the Potomac River (based at the Washington Navy Yard), being named GUARDIAN in that role. In December 1974 the craft was transferred to Fleet Composite Squadron (VC) 6, based at Little Creek, Va., for operation as a recovery boat for aerial target drones and a control boat for surface target drones. She was designated DR-1 (for Drone Recovery) and named RETRIEVER.

See 14th Edition/page 356 for characteristics.

65-foot TR at San Diego. A Mk 48 torpedo rests in the open stern; a single liferaft canister is atop the pilothouse. (1986, Giorgio Arra)

RESEARCH SHIPS: EX-MINESWEEPERS

The only two inshore minesweepers operated by the U.S. Navy, the COVE (MSI 1) and CAPE (MSI 2), have been discarded. Completed in 1958–1959, the two craft served for several years in the MSI role, after which they were assigned to research tasks, the COVE operated by the Naval Ocean Systems Center (NOSC) at San Diego and the CAPE by the Applied Physics Laboratory of the Johns Hopkins University. The COVE was sold in August 1986.

Similar units were built for the Iranian and Turkish navies.

See 13th Edition/page 334 for characteristics.

CHARTERED SUPPORT CRAFT

The following are commercial craft that are under charter to the Navy to provide specific support services. They are civilian-manned.

1 SUBMERSIBLE TENDER

Name
LANEY CHOUEST

Builders:	North American Shipbuilding, Larose, La.
Displacement:	approx. 2,600 tons full load
Tonnage:	497 GRT
	1,200 DWT
Length:	212⅔ feet (64.85 m) waterline
	234 feet (71.33 m) overall
Beam:	50 feet (15.2 m)
Draft:	14⅙ feet (4.33 m)
Propulsion:	3 diesel engines (General Motors); 3 shafts
Speed:	16 knots
Manning:	

Former oilfield support craft chartered by the Navy to support the submersibles DSV 3 and DSV 4 in Submarine Development Group 1 at San Diego.

Design: The craft has a large lifting device aft and an ice-strengthened hull. Three thrusters are fitted for station keeping.

LANEY CHOUEST. (1989, Giorgio Arra)

1 TORPEDO TRIALS CRAFT

Name
RANGER

Builders:	
Displacement:	
Length:	192 feet (58.5 m) overall
Beam:	
Draft:	
Propulsion:	2 diesel engines; 2 shafts
Speed:	12 knots
Manning:	

Chartered by the Naval Undersea Systems Center and based at Tudor Hill, Bermuda.

RANGER. (1988, Giorgio Arra)

WARPING TUGS

The Navy operates a large number of these craft, which are fabricated from pontoon sections. They are used to ferry material from amphibious and Maritime Prepositioning Ships (MPS) to shore, to install amphibious fuel and water transfer systems, and to maneuver and support causeways. One warping tug (SLWT) and three or four powered causeway sections (CSP) are carried by each MPS vessel; with some equipment removed and the A-frame lowered, the tugs can be side loaded on tank landing ships of the NEWPORT (LST 1179) class.

The tugs are operated by Amphibious Construction Battalions (ACB) under the Commanders, Naval Beach Group 1 (Coronado, California) and Naval Beach Group 2 (Norfolk, Virginia).

SIDE LOADING WARPING TUGS

Number
SLWT-series

Weight:	110 tons loaded
Length:	84 feet (25.6 m) overall
Beam:	21¼ feet
Draft:	2⅔ feet (0.8 m)
Propulsion:	2 turbocharged diesel engines (Detroit Diesel 8V71TI); 850 bhp; 2 waterjet propulsion units with 360° rotating nozzles with 12,500 lbs (5,625 kg) thrust
Speed:	8.5 knots
Range:	75 n.miles (140 km)
Manning:	8 (enlisted)

These side loading warping tugs (SLWT) are modular, consisting of 33 replaceable pontoon "cans" that are bolted together, plus three engine modules, a small control station, and an A-frame lifting device. They can be connected as "pushers" to one to six unpowered pontoon causeways to form barge ferries; each causeway can carry 100 tons of containerized cargo or vehicles. Without the A-frame and minor modifications, these craft are designated as causeway section, powered (CSP); that designation is not found on the Navy's ship classification list (see chapter 3).

The SLWT has a double-drum, diesel-powered A-frame/winch (turbocharged Detroit Model 4-53T) with a lifting capacity of

12 tons. Fitted with a 1,120-pound (504-kg) stern anchor. Fuel capacity is 625 gallons (2,375 liters).

Classification: In the fleet these craft are (incorrectly) referred to as side-loadable warping tugs (SLWT).

AMPHIBIOUS WARPING TUGS

The LWT 1 and LWT 2 have been stricken. Two units, built by Campbell Machine Works, San Diego, Calif., were delivered in 1970. Series production of this design was not undertaken.

An SLWT from Amphibious Construction Battalion 1 beaching at San Diego. Note the control station (offset to starboard), removable mast, and A-frame. (1992, U.S. Navy, Tom Hollinberger)

The SLWT 35 from ACB-1 serving as pusher for pontoon causeways. (1992, U.S. Navy, Tom Hollinberger)

The SLWT 35 from ACB-1 pushing two pontoon causeways loaded with several Marine trucks. More than 40 SLWTs and CSPs are currently in service in the Pacific Fleet. (1992, U.S. Navy, Tom Hollinberger)

CHAPTER 26

Submersibles

The WILLIAM H. BATES (SSN 680) under way with the rescue vehicle AVALON. The BATES has luminescent paint on the front and top of her sail, on her diving planes, and on her deck to help in underwater mating operations with the DSRV. The DSRV submersibles are among the most advanced of any in the world and are capable of a number of roles in addition to submarine rescue. (1985, Giorgio Arra)

Six manned submersibles are operated by the U.S. Navy to support search, rescue, research, and deep-ocean recovery activities. These craft have also been employed to maintain sea-floor test range and acoustic surveillance equipment.

Submarine Development Group 1 at Point Loma (San Diego), Calif., operates the rescue submersibles AVALON and MYSTIC, and the research submersibles SEA CLIFF and TURTLE. SubDevGru-1 also controls the submarines PARCHE (SSN 683), RICHARD B. RUSSELL (SSN 687), and DOLPHIN (AGSS 555), and the submarine rescue ship PIGEON (ASR 21).

Submarine Group 2 at the Naval Submarine Base New London (Groton, Conn.) operates the nuclear submarine NR-1 as well as a number of attack submarines. (The NR-1 is home-ported at the Portsmouth Naval Shipyard, N.H.)

The Navy-owned research submersible ALVIN is operated by the Woods Hole Oceanographic Institution in Massachusetts.

In addition to the manned submersibles listed here, the Navy also has several deep-ocean, tethered research and work submersibles. Some of these are surface controlled/supported, while others can be operated from submerged submarines (see chapter 12).

Operational: The submersible SEA CLIFF can dive to 20,000 feet (6,100 m), which provides access to 98 percent of the ocean floor. The only other vehicle in the West that has that depth capability is the French submersible NAUTILE, also a three-man craft; the two Finnish-built submersibles of the MIR type operated by Russia have a similar operating depth.

1 NUCLEAR-PROPELLED RESEARCH SUBMERSIBLE: "NR-1"

Number	Name	Launched	In service
NR-1	(none)	25 Jan 1969	27 Oct 1969

Builders:	General Dynamics/Electric Boat, Groton, Conn.
Displacement:	372 tons submerged
Length:	136⁵⁄₁₆ feet (41.6 m) overall
Beam:	12⁵⁄₁₂ feet (3.8 m)
Draft:	15¹⁄₁₂ feet (4.6 m)
Propulsion:	electric motors; 2 shafts
Reactors:	1 pressurized-water
Speed:	4.6 knots surface
	3.6 knots submerged
Operating depth:	approx. 3,000 feet (915 m)
Crew:	5 (2 officers + 3 enlisted) + 2 scientists*

*A total of 6 officers and 23 enlisted personnel are assigned to the NR-1.

The NR-1 was originally built as a test platform for a small submarine nuclear power plant. The craft has subsequently been employed as a deep-ocean research and recovery vehicle.

The craft was funded as a nuclear-propulsion effort and was laid down on 10 June 1967. She is commanded by an officer-in-charge rather than a commanding officer.

Classification: NR-1 indicates Nuclear Research vehicle although the craft is listed as a "submersible research vehicle" in the NVR.

Costs: The estimated cost of the NR-1 in 1965 was $30 million, using "state-of-the-art" equipment. Subsequently, specialized equipment had to be developed, and a hull larger than the one originally intended was designed, with congressional approval of a cost of $58

The NR-1 under way. The crewmen give an indication of the submarine's size. (1982, U.S. Navy)

million being given in 1967. The estimated cost of the NR-1 when launched in 1969 was $67.5 million, plus $19.9 million for oceanographic equipment and sensors and $11.8 million for research and development, a total cost of $99.2 million. No final cost data have been released by the Navy.

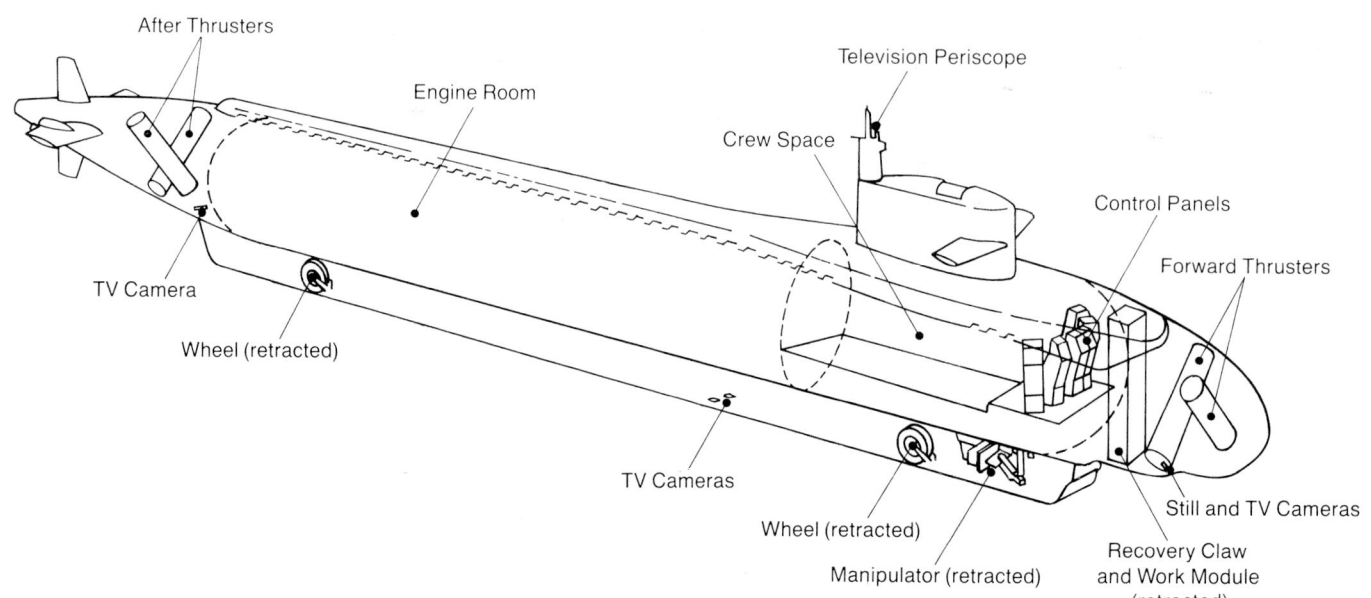

Nuclear-propelled research submersible NR-1.

The NR-1 under tow. The submarine has limited mobility and is generally towed—on the surface or submerged—to operating areas. The NR-1 has been most useful for underwater search, recovery, and seafloor equipment maintenance activities. Her sail, diving planes, and upper rudder are painted international orange. (1982, U.S. Navy)

Design: The hull is constructed of HY-80 steel. The NR-1 does not have periscopes, but instead has a fixed mast with a top-mounted television camera. The craft is fitted with external lights, a remote-control manipulator, and recovery devices.

Three bunks are provided; crew endurance is limited to 30-day missions. There is a warming oven for frozen foods and a hot-drink dispenser.

Electronics: Provided with forward- and side-looking sonar, and a doppler sonar to measure over-bottom speed.

Engineering: The NR-1 is propelled by twin propellers driven by electric motors outside of the pressure hull. Four ducted thrusters—two horizontal and two vertical—give the NR-1 a capability for precise maneuvering. Bottom wheels are installed. The craft is also fitted with lead shot ballast (22,000 pounds/9,978 kg).

Operations: Published reports credit the NR-1 with having been used to maintain sea-floor equipment and to recover items sunk at great depths.

In 1976 the NR-1 helped to recover an F-14 Tomcat fighter armed with a Phoenix missile that rolled off the deck of the carrier JOHN F. KENNEDY (CV 67) and came to rest at a depth of 1,960 feet off the coast of Scotland.

In 1986 the NR-1 was employed in the search for wreckage from the crashed space shuttle *Challenger* off Cape Kennedy, Fla.

NUCLEAR-PROPELLED RESEARCH VEHICLE: HTV/NR-2 DESIGN

The so-called Hull Test Vehicle (HTV) was originally proposed as the NR-2 in 1976 by Admiral H.G. Rickover, then head of the Navy's nuclear-propulsion program, to provide a deep-ocean (i.e., 3,000+ ft/915+ m) test platform for a nuclear reactor and a work submersible. Subsequently, the craft was redesignated HTV to emphasize the use of HY-130 steel. But in the event neither the Navy nor Congress would support the NR-2 at that time.

Subsequently, about 1978 the Navy's leadership decided to proceed with the craft as a hull test vehicle to test the suitability of

HY-130 steel for submarines. (HY-140 steel was used for the small pressure capsules of the DSRV rescue vehicle; see below.) However, in 1983 the Navy's leadership decided that instead of constructing the nuclear-powered HTV, sections of HY-130 would be added to the conventional deep-diving research submarine DOLPHIN. In addition, the Navy has fabricated several portions of a submarine hull of HY-130 steel in preparation for construction of the SEAWOLF (SSN 21) class.

2 DEEP SUBMERGENCE RESCUE VEHICLES: "MYSTIC" CLASS

Number	Name	Launched	Completed
DSRV 1	MYSTIC	24 Jan 1970	6 Aug 1971
DSRV 2	AVALON	1 May 1971	28 July 1

Builders:	Lockheed Missiles and Space Co., Sunnyvale, Calif.
Weight:	37 tons
Length:	49⅔ feet (15 m) overall
Diameter:	8 feet (2.4 m)
Propulsion:	electric motor, 1 propeller-mounted in control shroud (see Engineering notes)
Speed:	4 knots
Operating depth:	5,000 feet (1,524 m)
Manning:	3 + 24 rescuees

These submersibles were developed after the loss of the submarine THRESHER (SSN 593) in 1963 to provide a capability for rescuing survivors from submarines disabled on the ocean floor above their hull collapse depth.

After lengthy tests and evaluation, both DSRVs were declared fully operational in late 1977.

Class: Initially 12 rescue vehicles were planned, each capable of carrying 12 survivors. Subsequently, the vehicle capability was increased to 24 survivors, and the proposed number of DSRVs was reduced to six. Only two units were built.

The DSRVs were developed by the Navy's Deep Submergence Systems Project, which also had responsibility for the non-propulsion aspects of the NR-1 and had planned a set of deep submergence search vehicles (DSSV) that were to have had a 20,000-foot operating capability. The DSSVs were designed, but neither funded nor built.

Costs: The estimated construction cost of the DSRV 1 was $41 million and the DSRV 2 cost $23 million. The total development, construction, test, and support for these craft have cost in excess of $220 million.

Design: The DSRV consists of three interconnected personnel spheres, each 7½ feet (2.3 m) in diameter, constructed of HY-140 steel, encased in a fiberglass-reinforced plastic shell. The forward sphere contains the vehicle's controls and is manned by the pilot and co-pilot; the center and after spheres can accommodate 24 survivors and a third crewmember.

The AVALON on the deck of the CAVALLA (SSN 684). The DSRV is carried atop the after escape hatch of an SSN when deployed by submarine; it can also be carried by the PIGEON (ASR 21)-class rescue ships. (1981, U.S. Navy)

The DSRVs can mate with all U.S. submarines except the DOLPHIN and NR-1.

The DSRV is configured to be launched and recovered by a submerged attack submarine or by a PIGEON (ASR 21)-class submarine rescue ship. After launching, the DSRV can descend to the disabled submarine, "mate" with one of the submarine's escape hatches, take on board up to 24 survivors, and return to the "mother" submarine or ASR. The submersible can be air-transported in C-141 or C-5 cargo aircraft, and ground-transported by a special trailer. It is fitted with a remote-control manipulator.

Electronics: The DSRVs are fitted with elaborate search and navigation sonars, closed-circuit television, and optical viewing devices for locating a disabled submarine and mating with the stricken craft's escape hatches.

Engineering: The DSRVs have a single propeller driven by a 15-hp electric motor for forward propulsion. The propeller is in a rotating control shroud that alleviates the need for rudders and diving planes (which could interfere with a rescue mission). Four ducted thrusters, two vertical and two horizontal, each powered by a 7½-hp electric motor, provide precise maneuvering. The craft has an endurance of 5 hours at a speed of 4 knots.

Names: Names were assigned in 1977.

Operational: The DSRV rapid-deployment concept has been tested periodically from U.S. nuclear attack submarines, and in 1979 the AVALON was flown by C-5 cargo aircraft from San Diego to Glasgow, Scotland, for deployment on board the British SSBN REPULSE.

The DSRVs are based at the North Island Naval Air Station in San Diego.

The AVALON is lowered onto the CAVALLA; the DSRV's mating skirt will fit securely over the after escape hatch, permitting the passage of personnel and supplies between the DSRV and submarine while submerged. (1981, U.S. Navy)

An Air Force C-5A Galaxy transport devours the AVALON during a fly-away exercise. The mating skirt has been removed from the DSRV for road/air transport. Note the AVALON's shrouded propeller or "propulsor." (1981, U.S. Navy)

2 RESEARCH SUBMERSIBLES: MODIFIED "ALVIN" CLASS

Number	Name	Launched	Completed
DSV 3	TURTLE	11 Dec 1968	1969
DSV 4	SEA CLIFF	11 Dec 1968	1969

Builders:	General Dynamics/Electric Boat, Groton, Conn.
Weight:	TURTLE 21 tons
	SEA CLIFF 29 tons
Length:	TURTLE 26 feet (7.9 m) overall
	SEA CLIFF 30⅝ feet (9.4 m)
Beam:	8 feet (2.4 m); 12 feet (3.7 m) over propeller pods
Propulsion:	electric motor, 1 propeller (see Engineering notes)
Speed:	2.5 knots
Operating depth:	TURTLE 10,000 feet (3,048 m)
	SEA CLIFF 20,000 feet (6,096 m)
Manning:	2 + 1 scientist

These are small submersibles used for deep-ocean research. They were originally constructed using an HY-100 steel test sphere and an HY-100 replacement sphere originally fabricated for the ALVIN. Their operating depth with the HY-100 spheres was 6,500 feet (1,980 m); subsequently, in 1979 the TURTLE was refitted with a modified sphere providing a 10,000-foot (3,050-m) operating depth, and the SEA CLIFF was fitted with a titanium sphere in 1981–1983 for 20,000-foot (6,100-m) operations.

Classification: These craft were designated DSV 3 and DSV 4 on 1 June 1971.

Design: The original HY-100 steel spheres were seven (2.1 m) feet in diameter. A light, fiberglass outer hull is fitted to the spheres. The craft have closed-circuit television, external lights, sonars, cameras, and hydraulic remote-control manipulators.

These craft can be transported by C-5 cargo aircraft.

Engineering: A single stern propeller is fitted for ahead propulsion and two pod-mounted external electric motors rotate for maneuvering. No thrusters are fitted. Endurance is one hour at 2.5 knots and eight hours at one knot.

Names: During construction these submersibles were named the AUTEC I and II, respectively, because they were initially to be used to support the Navy's Atlantic Undersea Test and Evaluation Center (AUTEC). The names TURTLE and SEA CLIFF were assigned at their joint launching.

1 RESEARCH SUBMERSIBLE: "ALVIN"

Number	Name	Launched	Completed
DSV 2	ALVIN	5 June 1964	1965

Builders:	General Mills Inc., Minneapolis, Minn.
Weight:	16 tons
Length:	22½ feet (6.9 m) overall
Beam:	8 feet (2.4 m); 12 feet (3.7 m) over propeller pods
Speed:	2 knots
Operating depth:	13,124 feet (4,000 m)
Manning:	1 + 2 scientists

The ALVIN is operated by the Woods Hole Oceanographic Institution for the Office of Naval Research, which sponsored construction of the craft.

The ALVIN accidentally sank in 5,051 feet (1,540 m) of water on 16 October 1968, and her sphere was flooded (there were no casualties).

The submersible SEA CLIFF in the docking well of the POINT LOMA (AGDS 2) en route to the Atlantic Trench off the coast of Guatemala for a 20,000-foot dive. Note the work/recovery arms and sample basket in front of the vehicle. (1985, U.S. Navy, Gary Ballard)

Operational: The SEA CLIFF dived to 20,000 feet for the first time on 10 March 1985. That was the deepest depth achieved by a U.S. submersible except for the discarded bathyscaph TRIESTE (see below). The SEA CLIFF deep dive was made in the Middle America Trench off the Pacific coast of Central America.

In September–October 1990, after eight dives carried out in a 17-day period, the SEA CLIFF recovered both halves of a cargo door that tore away from a Boeing 747 jet aircraft in 1989. They were recovered from a depth of 14,000 feet (4,297 m) approximately 87 n.miles (161 km) southwest of Hawaii.

She was raised in August 1969 and refurbished from May 1971 to October 1972, and became operational in November 1972. (The research ship MIZAR/T-AGOR 11 and the commercial submersible ALUMINAUT effected the salvage of the ALVIN.)

Classification: Classified DSV 2 on 1 June 1971.

Design: As built, the ALVIN had a single, 7-foot-diameter pressure sphere made of HY-100 steel, which gave her a 6,000-foot operating depth. She was refitted with a titanium sphere in 1971–1972, which increased her capabilities. She is fitted with a remote-control manipulator.

Engineering: See the TURTLE and SEA CLIFF for propulsion and maneuvering arrangement.

Operational: In 1988, the ALVIN aided in the location and photographing of the sunken ocean liner TITANIC. On 22 March of that year the ALVIN made her 2,000th dive.

The ALVIN being lowered into the water from her mother ship, the research vessel ATLANTIS II, operated by the Woods Hole Oceanographic Institution. (WHOI, Rod Catanach)

The ALVIN being lifted aboard the FORT SNELLING (LSD 30). (U.S. Navy)

ALVIN. (Woods Hole Oceanographic Institution)

BATHYSCAPH: "TRIESTE II"

The deep-diving (20,000-foot) bathyscaph TRIESTE II was taken out of service on 18 May 1984 and stricken on 1 April 1985. Designated X 2 and, subsequently, DSV 1, this craft was in U.S. Navy service from 1966.[2] Some of her components had been used in the original bathyscaph TRIESTE, built in 1953 and in service with the U.S. Navy from 1958 until rebuilt into the TRIESTE II. The earlier float and one of two spheres built for the TRIESTE are on exhibit at the Washington Navy Yard.

2. The X-1 was the U.S. Navy's only midget submarine; see page 78.

CHAPTER 27

Floating Dry Docks

Floating dry docks have long been invaluable in the support of the U.S. fleet. The SHIPPINGPORT, shown here being towed into the submarine base at New London, Conn., by a commercial tug, has been modified to support nuclear-propelled attack submarines. (1991, U.S. Navy, JOSN Connie Sanders)

The U.S. Navy operates floating dry docks at several bases in the United States and overseas for the repair and maintenance of surface ships and submarines. These are non-self-propelled docks, but have electrical generators to provide power for their lighting, tools, and equipment. Normally they operate with a flotilla of non-self-propelled barges that provide specialized services, such as messing and berthing for ships being dry docked.

All U.S. Navy floating dry docks are open-ended, through-type docks except for the ARD-series. The ARDs are distinctive in having a ship-like form, closed at one end by a ship-shaped bow. The exterior surfaces of these docks are faired to a considerable extent to facilitate towing and have a stern gate.[1]

The larger docks are sectional, to facilitate towing (and originally for passage through the Panama Canal). Mounted on their hull sections—which are called "pontoons"—the large AFDB (former ABSD) docks have side walls that fold down for storage or towing. These "wing" walls can be easily shifted between pontoons in the event of damage.

The floating docks are arranged in this chapter alphabetically, according to their classification. Floating dry docks are officially considered to be service craft.

The docks in active Navy service have their locations indicated; several others are operated by foreign navies and commercial firms on lease from the Navy; the Army and Coast Guard also have ex-Navy floating dry docks.

Class totals are docks in U.S. Navy or Coast Guard service or laid up in reserve. Floating dry docks are listed in both the Naval Vessel Register (NVR) and Service craft And Boat Accounting Report (SABAR).

Design: Lift capacity for sectional docks is for all sections when assembled, except where indicated.

Guns: No floating dry docks are armed, although many were designed to mount light anti-aircraft guns.

Names: Dry docks that service nuclear-propelled submarines have been given the names of towns and cities associated with nuclear power; the others that are named have positive trait names. The AFDB 8 is an exception.

Operational: Operational Navy docks are manned by Navy personnel and civilian employees of the Navy.

1 LARGE AUXILIARY FLOATING DRY DOCK: CIVILIAN BUILT

The two-section AFDB 9 was taken over by the Navy and placed on the Naval Vessel Register effective 12 July 1990. The dock had been operated by the Pennsylvania Shipbuilding Co., but was taken over when that firm defaulted on Navy contracts.

The dock was initially towed to the Philadelphia Naval Shipyard, pending transfer to the National Defense Reserve Fleet James River, Va. The dock is available for commercial lease.

1. The ARD-type docks are also referred to as Camel docks, for a ship of that name that was gutted and fitted with a stern gate to serve as a dock in 1700 at the Russian harbor of Kronshtadt (off St. Petersburg, later renamed Leningrad and, again, St. Petersburg). The project was undertaken by a captain in the Royal Navy because of the lack of docking facilities at Kronshtadt (which is now a major Russian naval base).

1 LARGE AUXILIARY FLOATING DRY DOCK: GERMAN BUILT

Number	Name	Completed	In USN service
AFDB 8	MACHINIST	1980	5 Aug 1985

Builders:	Seebeckwerft, Bremerhaven (West Germany)
Lift capacity:	39,300 tons
Length:	824¾ feet (251.5 m)
Width:	175⁷⁄₁₂ feet (53.5 m)
Width clear inside:	140¼ feet (42.8 m)
Draft:	
Manning:	

The AFDB 8 is large, one-piece floating dry dock purchased by the Navy from the builder on 5 August 1985 and towed to Subic Bay in the Philippines for operation beginning in March 1986. In 1992, with the withdrawal of U.S. forces from the Philippines, the dock was towed to Pearl Harbor and laid up.

The MACHINIST while still at Subic Bay in the Philippines. This is the last dock acquired for U.S. Navy service. The two large cranes ride on rails along the dock walls. (1986, U.S. Navy, Ferdie R. Mendoza)

The MACHINIST servicing the frigate KNOX (FF 1052) at Subic Bay. (1987, U.S. Navy, PHC Chet King)

1 LARGE AUXILIARY FLOATING DRY DOCK: "AFDB 4" CLASS

Number	Name	In service
AFDB 7	LOS ALAMOS	Mar 1945

Builders:	Mare Island Navy Yard, Vallejo, Calif.[2]
Sections:	4 (A-B-C-D) in service
	2 (E-G) in reserve
Lift capacity:	31,000 tons with 4 sections
Length:	413 feet (125.9 m)
Width:	240 feet (73.2 m)
Width clear inside:	119½ feet (36.4 m)
Draft:	8⅔ feet (2.6 m) light
	67⅓ feet (20.5 m) max submerged
Manning:	197 (5 officers + 192 enlisted)

The operational sections of this dock were at Holy Loch, Scotland, to support U.S. Navy SSBNs; they were to be retired with the withdrawal of Submarine Squadron 14 from Holy Loch in 1992.

Four sections were normally at Holy Loch with two sections in reserve, although there are only four sets of dock walls available. The sections were periodically rotated, two at a time, to permit overhaul of the pontoons. The E and G sections were in the James River National Defense Reserve Fleet.

Originally a seven-section dock (A through G). Section F was transferred to the U.S. Army in 1966 for use at Kwajalein Atoll in conjunction with anti-ballistic missile tests.[3]

---

2. The ABSD sections were erected and assembled at Mare Island; they were fabricated by commercial firms.
3. The dock was fitted with gas-turbine generators to serve as a floating power plant.

Class: The Navy constructed seven advanced-base sectional docks (ABSD) in World War II:

	sections	lift capacity
ABSD 1, 2	10	90,000 tons
ABSD 3	9	81,000 tons
ABSD 4–7	7	55,000 tons

The ABSD 1 was completed in 1943, the ABSD 2–6 in 1944, and the ABSD 7 in 1945. A planned eighth ABSD was cancelled.

The ABSD 1–3 had the capacity to lift any World War II–era U.S. warship, including the MIDWAY (CVB 41)-class large aircraft carriers. The ABSD 4–7 could lift IOWA (BB 61)-class battleships and ESSEX (CV 9)-class aircraft carriers.

ARTISAN (AFDB 1) sections B-C-D-E stricken 27 October 1986; they are laid up at Pearl Harbor.

AFDB 3 (unnamed) was transferred to the state of Maine in 1982 for use by the Bath Iron Works at Portland, Maine. The AFDB 5 (unnamed) was transferred to the city of Port Arthur, Texas, in 1984 for use by the Todd Shipyards Corp.

AFDB 4 (unnamed) sections A through G were stricken on 15 April 1989; for sale.

Classification: Originally designated ABSD with same hull numbers; reclassified AFDB in August 1946.

Design: Steel construction. The large wing walls can support cranes and, as built, anti-aircraft guns (authorized armament when built was a twin 40-mm Bofors AA mount on each section).

Names: Names were not assigned to these ships until the 1960s.

Operational: Sections A-B-C-D were reactivated from the reserve fleet in 1961 and towed across the Atlantic in February–March 1961 for use at the Holy Loch SSBN refit base; thus, AFDB 7 sections were in use at Holy Loch for 30 years.

1 LARGE AUXILIARY FLOATING DRY DOCK: "AFDB 1" CLASS

Number	Name	In service
AFDB 2	(unnamed)	Apr 1944

Builders:	Mare Island Navy Yard, Vallejo, Calif.
Sections:	1 (D) in service
	4 (E-F-H-I) laid up
Lift capacity:	40,000 tons
Length:	approx. 472 feet (143.9 m)
Width:	240 feet (73.2 m)
Width clear inside:	119½ feet (36.4 m)
Draft:	9 feet (2.7 m) light
	78 feet (23.8 m) max submerged
Manning:	

Originally a ten-section dock of which only one section remains operational, at Pearl Harbor. Previously four sections were operational at Subic Bay. The laid-up sections are also at Pearl Harbor.

Sections D-E-F-H-I were stricken on 27 October 1986 but reacquired in March 1987; sections A-B-G-J stricken on 15 April 1989; to be sold.

The now-retired ARTISAN, with six sections, at Subic Bay. Another AFDB section—with sidewalls raised—is being overhauled within the dock. All AFDBs were similar except for fully assembled size. (U.S. Navy, Ferdie R. Mendoza)

Two sections of an AFDB (top) and the ADEPT at Subic Bay. The wing walls of the AFDB sections fold down for towing and storage. The AFDL 23 still has gun tubs that held anti-aircraft guns during World War II. (U.S. Navy)

2 SMALL AUXILIARY FLOATING DOCKS: "AFDL 1" CLASS

Number	Name	In service
AFDL 6	DYNAMIC	Mar 1944
AFDL 25	UNDAUNTED	May 1944

Builders:	AFDL 6 Chicago Bridge and Iron, Calif.
	AFDL 25 Doulut, Ewin
Sections:	1
Lift capacity:	1,000 tons
Length:	200 feet (61.0 m)
Width:	64 feet (19.5 m)
Width clear inside:	45 feet (13.7 m)
Draft:	3 5/12 feet (1.0 m) light
	28 1/2 feet (8.7 m) max submerged
Manning:	AFDL 6 24 (1 officer + 23 enlisted)

These are steel docks. The AFDL 6 is operational at Little Creek, Va., and the AFDL 25 is operational at Guantánamo Bay, Cuba. (The AFDL 25, which had been stricken earlier, was reacquired in June 1984 for service at Guantánamo Bay, replacing the dry dock ENDEAVOR.)

Class: AFD/AFDL 1–33 were completed during World War II. The ENDEAVOR (AFDL 1) has been on lease to the Dominican Republic since 8 March 1986; the RELIANCE (AFDL 47) is on commercial lease (both remain on the NVR). Several docks previously on lease to commercial yards were sold on 1 October 1981 (see previous editions); of more recent disposals:

AFDL 10 on lease to the Philippines was stricken 13 July 1987.

AFDL 21 on commercial lease was stricken on 31 March 1989 for transfer to another government agency.

AFDL 22, on loan to South Vietnam since 1971, was stricken on 30 July 1985.

AFDL 40 on commercial lease was stricken on 30 June 1987; transferred to Philippines on 30 June 1990.

AFDL 41 sold in 1983.

DILIGENCE (AFDL 48) on commercial lease was stricken on 28 August 1986 and sold.

Classification: Originally AFD designation was assigned to units No. 1–30 except AFDL 7, 22, and 23.

Design: All AFDLs were of one-piece, steel construction, except for the DILIGENCE (built after World War II) fabricated of concrete. The AFDL 1 type was intended to service minesweeper-size ships (AM, later MSO).

1 SMALL AUXILIARY FLOATING DRY DOCK: MODIFIED "AFDL 1" CLASS

Number	Name	In service
AFDL 23	ADEPT	Dec 1944

Builders:	George D. Auchter
Sections:	1
Lift capacity:	1,900 tons
Length:	288 feet (87.8 m)
Width:	64 feet (19.5 m)
Width clear inside:	45 feet (13.7 m)
Draft:	3¼ feet (1.0 m) light
	31⅓ feet (9.6 m) max submerged
Manning:	

A steel, one-piece dock originally intended to service destroyer escorts (DE), tugs, and minesweepers. Operational at Subic Bay in the Philippines until towed to Guam in February–March 1992.

The ADEPT at Subic Bay. There was a Philippine Navy corvette in the dock when this photo was taken. (1987, U.S. Navy, PHC Chet King)

1 MEDIUM AUXILIARY FLOATING DRY DOCK: "AFDM 14"

Number	Name	Completed
AFDM 14 (ex-YFD 71)	STEADFAST	July 1945

Builders:	Pollock-Stockton Shipbuilding, Calif.
Sections:	3
Lift capacity:	14,000 tons
Length:	598 feet (182.3 m)
Width:	118 feet (36.0 m)
Width clear inside:	87 feet (26.5 m)
Draft:	3⁵⁄₁₂ feet (1.1 m) light
	45¾ feet (13.9 m) max submerged
Manning:	70 (3 officers + 67 enlisted)

This three-piece, steel dock is operational at the Naval Station San Diego, Calif.

Reclassified as an AFDM on 1 February 1983 and named on 9 May 1983.

5 MEDIUM AUXILIARY FLOATING DRY DOCKS: "AFDM 3" CLASS

Number	Name	In service
AFDM 5 (ex-YFD 21)	RESOURCEFUL	Feb 1943
AFDM 6 (ex-YFD 62)	COMPETENT	June 1944
AFDM 7 (ex-YFD 63)	SUSTAIN	Jan 1945
AFDM 8 (ex-YFD 64)	RICHLAND	Dec 1944
AFDM 10 (ex-YFD 67)	RESOLUTE	1945

Builders:	Everett Pacific Shipbuilding, Everett, Wash., except AFDM 8 Chicago Bridge and Iron, Calif.
Sections:	3
Lift capacity:	18,000 tons
Length:	622 feet (189.6 m)
Width:	124 feet (37.8 m)
Width clear inside:	93 feet (28.35 m)
Draft:	6⅙ feet (1.9 m) light
	52¾ feet (16.1 m) max submerged
Manning:	AFDM 5
	AFDM 6 155 (5 officers + 150 enlisted)
	AFDM 7 143 (4 officers + 139 enlisted)
	AFDM 10 150 (6 officers + 144 enlisted)

All of these three-piece steel docks are operational. The AFDM 5 is in reserve, the AFDM 6 is at the Naval Submarine Base Pearl Harbor, the AFDM 7 is at Norfolk, the AFDM 8 is at Guam, and the AFDM 10 is assigned to SubRon-8 at Norfolk; all are operational except the RESOURCEFUL, which was at Subic Bay until 1992. She is at Pearl Harbor.

Class: The AFDM 1, formerly on commercial lease, was stricken on 15 December 1986; AFDM 3 is on commercial lease; and AFDM 9, formerly on lease, was stricken on 31 December 1987.

Classification: These docks were initially classified as floating dry docks (YFD).

Design: Originally intended to dock destroyers, light cruisers, and escort carriers.

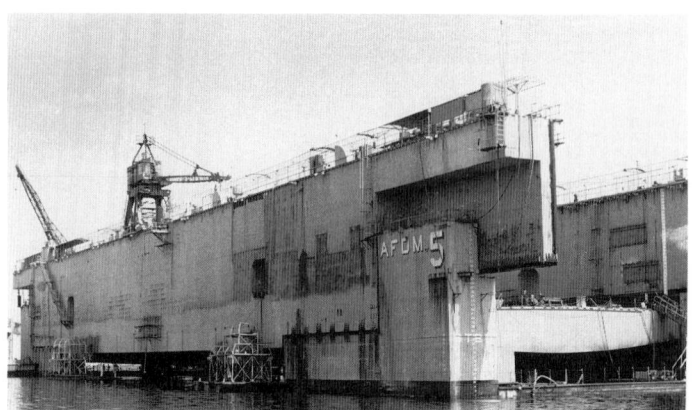

The RESOURCEFUL at Subic Bay. (187, U.S. Navy, PHC Chet King)

The combat stores ship SAN JOSE (AFS 7) in the RICHLAND at Guam. With the abandonment of the U.S. naval base at Subic Bay, the importance of Guam to U.S. operations in the Pacific–Indian Ocean areas has increased. (U.S. Navy)

The RESOLUTE at Norfolk, Va., with the attack submarine BIRMINGHAM (SSN 695) undergoing maintenance. (1984, W. Donko)

1 MEDIUM AUXILIARY FLOATING DRY DOCK: "AFDM 1" CLASS

Number	Name	In service
AFDM 2 (ex-YFD 4)	(none)	Oct 1942

Builders:	
Sections:	3
Lift capacity:	15,000 tons
Length:	615⅔ feet (187.7 m) overall
Width:	116 feet (35.4 m)
Width clear inside:	87½ feet (26.7 m)
Draft:	5¾ feet (1.75 m) light
	49¾ feet (15.2 m) max submerged

The AFDM 2 has been laid up in the National Defense Reserve Fleet (NDRF) at Portsmouth, Va., since 1987. Steel construction.

Design: Originally intended to dock cruisers and escort carriers.

1 AUXILIARY REPAIR DRY DOCK: "ARD 12" CLASS

Number	Name	In service
ARD 30	SAN ONOFRE	Aug 1944

Builders:	Pacific Bridge, Alameda, Calif.
Sections:	1
Lift capacity:	3,500 tons
Length:	494 feet (150.6 m)
Width:	81 feet (24.7 m)
Width clear inside:	59 feet (18.0 m)
Draft:	5⅔ feet (1.7 m) light
	32⅚ feet (10.0 m) max submerged
Manning:	104 (5 officers + 99 enlisted)

One-piece, steel dock active at the Naval Submarine Base (Point Loma) San Diego.

Design: Originally intended to service destroyers and submarines.

1 AUXILIARY REPAIR DRY DOCK: "ARD 2" CLASS

Number	Name	In service
ARD 5	WATERFORD	June 1942

Builders:	Pacific Bridge, Alameda, Calif.
Sections:	1
Lift capacity:	4,100 tons
Length:	485⅔ feet (148.1 m)
Width:	71 feet (21.6 m)
Width clear inside:	49 feet (14.9 m)
Draft:	5¼ feet (1.6 m) light
	32⁷⁄₁₂ feet (9.9 m) maximum submerged
Manning:	131 (6 officers + 125 enlisted)

This is a one-piece, steel dry dock. The WATERFORD is operational at the Naval Submarine Base New London, Conn.

Class: The ARD 6 is on loan to Pakistan, and the ARD 12 is on loan to Turkey.

The WEST MILTON (ARD 7) was transferred to the MarAd on 16 July 1981 and laid up; stricken on 23 August 1990.

The WATERFORD under tow. The dock has a ship-type bow, three anchors, and "navigating" bridge. (U.S. Navy, Jean Russell)

The docking well of an ARD 2-class dry dock. Note the keel blocks, which are adjusted to the specific hull lines of ships being docked. The stern gate is open in this view. (U.S. Navy)

2 MEDIUM AUXILIARY REPAIR DOCKS: "ARDM 4" CLASS

Number	Name	In service
ARDM 4	SHIPPINGPORT	1979
ARDM 5	ARCO	Feb 1986

Builders:	ARDM 4	Bethlehem Steel, Sparrows Point, Md.
	ARDM 5	Todd Shipyards, Seattle, Wash.
Sections:	1	
Lift capacity:	7,800 tons	
Length:	492 feet (150.0 m)	
Width:	96 feet (29.3 m)	
Width clear inside:	64 feet (19.5 m)	
Draft:	54½ feet (16.6 m) max submerged	
Manning:	ARDM 4	131 (6 officers + 125 enlisted)
	ARDM 5	130 (5 officers + 125 enlisted)

These were the first floating dry docks built for the U.S. Navy since the World War II programs. They were designed to support nuclear-propelled attack submarines. The SHIPPINGPORT is operational at the Naval Submarine Base New London, and the ARCO is operational at the Naval Submarine Base (Point Loma) San Diego.

Class: Authorized in the fiscal 1975 and 1983 naval shipbuilding programs. A third, similar dock planned for fiscal year 1984 was not built.

The SHIPPINGPORT, being maneuvered by a commercial tug at New London. (1991, U.S. Navy, JOSN Connie Sanders)

1 MEDIUM AUXILIARY REPAIR DRY DOCK: "ARDM 1" CLASS

Number	Name	In service
ARDM 3 (ex-ARD 18)	ENDURANCE	Feb 1944

Builders:	Pacific Bridge, Alameda, Calif.
Sections:	1
Lift capacity:	5,500 tons
Length:	512 7/12 feet (156.25 m)
Width:	81 feet (24.7 m)
Width clear inside:	61 feet (18.6 m)
Draft:	7 1/8 feet (2.2 m) light
	41 3/4 feet (12.7 m) max submerged
Manning:	

The ENDURANCE was modified in 1969 to support nuclear-propelled submarines. She is active at the Charleston Naval Shipyard, S.C.

The dock differs from the two other units of this type that remain in U.S. service.

The ENDURANCE laid up, without masts, cranes, or other fittings. (U.S. Navy)

2 MEDIUM AUXILIARY REPAIR DOCKS: "ARDM 1" CLASS

Number	Name	In service
ARDM 1 (ex-ARD 19)	OAK RIDGE	Mar 1944
ARDM 2 (ex-ARD 26)	ALAMAGORDO	June 1944

Builders:	Pacific Bridge, Alameda, Calif.	
Sections:	1	
Lift capacity:	8,000 tons	
Length:	541 feet (164.9 m)	
Width:	81 feet (24.7 m)	
Width clear inside:	58 feet (17.7 m)	
Draft:	7 feet (2.1 m) light	
	45 5/8 feet (13.1 m) max submerged	
Manning:	ARDM 1	181 (5 officers + 176 enlisted)
	ARDM 2	191 (5 officers + 186 enlisted)

The OAK RIDGE is active at the Naval Submarine Base Kings Bay, Ga., and the ALAMAGORDO is active at Charleston, S.C.

The ALAMAGORDO at Charleston, S.C. Floating dry docks invariably have small craft and barges alongside to assist in the maintenace work. (U.S. Navy)

The OAK RIDGE when at Rota, Spain, servicing an SSBN. Note the two large travelling cranes on the dock walls. (U.S. Navy)

1 YARD FLOATING DRY DOCK: FORMER AFDL

Number	Name	In service
YFD 83 (ex-AFDL 31)	(unnamed)	Dec 1943

Builders:	Foundation Co., Kearny, N.J.
Sections:	1
Lift capacity:	1,000 tons
Length:	200 feet (61.0 m)
Width:	64 feet (19.5 m)
Width clear inside:	45 feet (13.7 m)
Draft:	3 5/12 feet (1.1 m) light
	28 1/8 feet (8.7 m) max submerged
Manning:	10 civilians

The YFD 83 is a one-piece steel dock. She has been operational at the Coast Guard Yard at Curtis Bay, Md., since 1943.

CHAPTER 28

Naval Aviation

Carrier air wings (CVW) of 80-plus aircraft provide versatile and potent tactical air forces. Here most of CVW-5 and CVW-14 are shown on the flight decks of the carriers MIDWAY (left) and INDEPENDENCE as the carriers transferred air wings in Pearl Harbor in August 1991. (PH3 Mauka Fiegener, USN)

The strength and structure of U.S. naval aviation are in a state of flux. When this edition of *Ships and Aircraft* went to press, the "end strength" of naval aviation—that is, its projected strength in some five years—was uncertain because of major questions over the number of carriers and carrier air wings that would be operated, and questions over aircraft procurement in several categories.

U.S. naval aviation has over 5,000 aircraft, more than any of the world's air forces except for those of the United States, Russia, and China. This total includes "pipeline," research, and training aircraft, and those operated by the U.S. Marine Corps. The current active aircraft inventory is listed in table 28-1. (U.S. Coast Guard aircraft are listed separately; see chapter 32.)

NAVAL AIR ORGANIZATION

All naval aviation units belong to an administrative organization, with most units also under tactical organizations. An attack squadron is administratively under an attack functional or "type" wing while at its home base; while forward deployed on a carrier the squadron would come under the carrier air wing commander embarked in that ship. Similarly, a patrol squadron is under the patrol "type" wing commander while in the United States, but if deployed in a forward area would be under a fleet commander and his subordinate air commander.

The administrative organization is headed by the Assistant Chief of Naval Operations (Air Warfare) and extends through the Commander, Naval Air Force Atlantic Fleet (NavAirLant) and Commander, Naval Air Force Pacific Fleet (NavAirPac), and their respective wing "type" commanders. Details of naval air organizations are provided in chapter 6.

Wings and squadrons are officially "established and disestablished" and are not in commission; however, records and ceremonies continually use the terms "commission" and "decommissioned," especially for wings. Accordingly, the latter terms are used for wings and the former for squadrons in this volume.

UNIT CODES

Most naval aviation organizations have two-letter identification codes that are displayed on aircraft tail fins and, in some marking schemes, on wings; training wings have single-letter designations, while air stations and other special organizations use a number-letter scheme.

Beginning in 1946 the Navy used single-letter codes to identify specific ships to which the planes were attached, as B for BOXER (CV 21) and F for FRANKLIN D. ROOSEVELT (CVB 42), with land-based units having two-letter codes. The system was revised in 1957 to provide the current fleet "split," with the first letter indicating the fleet assignment: A to M for Atlantic and N to Z for Pacific. The letters I and O are not used to avoid confusion with numerals. The unit code AF was dropped because of confusion with Air Force (previously used by Carrier Air Group 6, which then took code letters AE).

TABLE 28-1. NAVAL AIRCRAFT (fall 1992)

Aircraft		Total	Active Navy	Naval Reserve	Active Marine	Marine Reserve	Pipeline
Attack							
A-4E/F/M	Skyhawk	108	46	15	—	36	11
TA-4F	Skyhawk	13	1	7	—	—	5
A-6E	Intruder	329	259	20	20	—	30
KA-6D	Intruder	27	12	8	—	—	7
AV-8B	Harrier	185	7	—	178	—	—
TAV-8B	Harrier	21	1	—	15	—	5
Fighter							
F-5E/F	Tiger II	39	26	—	—	13	—
F-14A/B/D	Tomcat	335	251	48	—	—	36
F-16N	Fighting Falcon	22	22	—	—	—	—
F/A-18	Hornet	722	387	48	192	36	59
Patrol–ASW							
P-3B/C	Orion	329	206	104	—	—	19
S-3A/B	Viking	129	99	—	—	—	30
Electronic–Special Purpose							
E-2C	Hawkeye	100	74	8	—	—	18
E-6A	Mercury	18	16	—	—	—	2
EA-6A	Intruder	13	8	—	—	—	5
EA-6B	Prowler	118	86	8	18	6	11
EC-130Q	Hercules	11	4	—	—	—	7
EP-3A/B/E	Orion	19	14	—	—	—	5
EP-3J	Orion	2	2	—	—	—	—
ES-3A	Viking	7	7	—	—	—	—
RP-3A/D	Orion	13	12	—	—	—	1
Observation							
OV-10D	Bronco	58	—	—	37	12	9
Cargo-Transport							
C-2A	Greyhound	39	35	—	—	—	4
C-9B	Skytrain	29	2	27	—	—	—
C-20D	Gulfstream III	2	2	—	—	—	—
CT-39	Sabreliner	13	4	4	3	2	—
C-130F/T	Hercules	11	5	4	—	—	2
KC-130	Hercules	74	4	—	42	20	8
TC-130G	Hercules	1	—	—	1	—	—
Utility							
UC-12B	Huron	65	42	9	10	4	—
Training							
T-2C	Buckeye	170	158	—	—	—	12
T-34C	Mentor	295	260	—	—	—	35
T-38A/B	Talon	7	6	—	—	—	1
T-39	Sabreliner	3	3	—	—	—	—
T-44	King Air	57	54	—	—	—	3
T-45	Goshawk	2	2	—	—	—	—
TA-4J	Skyhawk	197	186	—	—	—	11
TC-4C	Academe	8	8	—	—	—	—
TF-16N	Fighting Falcon	4	4	—	—	—	—
Helicopters							
AH-1W	SeaCobra	123	4	10	84	—	25
UH-1N	Huey	125	17	—	84	24	2
SH-2F/G	LAMPS I	99	74	24	—	—	1
SH-3D/H	Sea King	129	87	12	—	—	30
VH-3D	Sea King	11	—	—	11	—	—
H-46	Sea Knight	319	65	—	219	24	11
CH-53A/D	Sea Stallion	113	4	10	63	6	30
H-53E	Super Stallion/ Sea Dragon	153	50	—	96	—	7
TH-57B/C	SeaRanger	140	126	—	—	—	14
SH-60B	Seahawk	139	137	—	—	—	2
SH-60F	Seahawk	60	60	—	—	—	—
HH-60H	Seahawk	18	4	14	—	—	—
VH-60N	Seahawk	9	—	—	9	—	—

Side number	Squadron	Color code	Aircraft
100 series	fighter	insignia red	F-14
200 series	fighter	orange-yellow	F-14
300 series	strike fighter	light blue	F/A-18
400 series	strike fighter	international orange	F/A-18
500 series	medium attack	light green	A-6E, KA-6D
600–603 or 600–604	AEW	black	E-2C
604–607 or 620–624	EW	black	EA-6B
610 series	helicopter ASW	black	SH-3H, SH-60F, HH-60H
700 series	fixed-wing ASW	black	S-3

The code letters AD and NJ are carried by several fleet readiness/ transition squadrons. The letters were formally assigned to Combat Readiness Carrier Air Wing 4 and Combat Readiness Carrier Air Wing 12, respectively; both of those wings were disestablished on 1 June 1970, but their squadrons survive in the Atlantic and Pacific Fleets.

Within carrier air wings the squadrons are identified by blocks of numbers and colors, with the individual aircraft identified by num-

bers within the block. The "number" 00 is used by the wing commander and the block numbers (e.g., 100, 200) by the squadron commanders. The color code is rarely used because of the current low-visibility paint scheme.

The numbering of E-2C and EA-6B aircraft varies, depending upon whether four or five aircraft of each type are embarked.

CARRIER AIR WINGS

The Navy currently has 11 active carrier air wings (CVW). During the 1980s the Navy briefly had 14 wings as part of the Reagan-Lehman naval buildup; a fifteenth wing was planned but not activated. There are two reserve carrier air wings (CVWR) that fly mostly first-line aircraft and are suitable for deployment on board carriers. In addition, most Marine Corps combat aircraft are carrier-capable and all Marine aviators carrier trained.

The composition of carrier air wings is changing. Into the 1980s the standard wing had two fighter squadrons (24 F-14A), two light attack squadrons (24 A-7E), and one medium attack squadron (10 A-6E + 4 KA-6D tankers), in addition to specialized Anti-Submarine Warfare (ASW), Airborne Early Warning (AEW), and electronic warfare aircraft.

In the 1980s, with the introduction of the F/A-18 Hornet strike fighter, the Navy developed the so-called "ROOSEVELT air wing," with double the number of A-6E Intruder aircraft, provided by reducing the numbers of fighters and strike fighters (the F/A-18 having replaced the A-7E). Under this plan, the A-6Es would be succeeded in service by improved models of the Intruder (A-6F or A-6G) and, subsequently, by the A-12 Avenger. The cancellation of the A-12 in early 1991 and overall budget reductions have forced the Navy to drop this plan. The standard air wing in the 1990s is a composite of the 1980s and the ROOSEVELT wings although, as discussed below, there will be significant variations based on aircraft availability.

Squadron assignments to carrier air wings change periodically. Also, on 13 January 1992, the Secretary of the Navy directed that the Navy and Marine Corps more closely integrate Marine tactical aviation into carrier air wings. The memorandum directed that the Navy and Marine Corps "undertake innovative measures to enhance the efficiency of naval aviation through the closer integration. . ." especially of Marine fighter-attack (VMFA) and electronic warfare (VMAQ) squadrons, to reduce naval aircraft requirements by at least 140 planes in those categories.

(Marine tactical squadrons have periodically operated from aircraft carriers since November 1931, when Marine scouting squadron VS-15M went aboard the carrier LEXINGTON/CV 2 and VS-14M went aboard the SARATOGA/CV 3 for fleet operations; they remained in those carriers until November 1934.)

With the procurement of follow-on fighter and attack aircraft questionable, and "affordable" approach to carrier air wing modernization was put forward in 1991 by the head of naval aviation.[1] Additional F/A-18s will be procured, including the extended range F/A-18E/F variants. Thus, the typical carrier wing in the year 2010 is estimated to consist of 42 F/A-18s and 18 advanced medium attack aircraft (now designated AX).[2] Anti-submarine (VS and HS), electronic warfare (VAQ), and airborne early warning (VAW) aircraft will also be embarked. (See table 28-2.)

In addition to wing aircraft, forward-deployed carriers generally operate two ES-3A Viking aircraft in the ELINT role, these being assigned from fleet air reconnaissance squadrons VQ-5 in the Pacific area and VQ-6 in the Atlantic-Mediterranean area.

TABLE 28-2. NAVAL AVIATION UNIT DESIGNATIONS*

CVW	Carrier Air Wing
CVWR	Reserve Carrier Air Wing
HC	Helicopter Combat Support Squadron
HCS	Helicopter Combat Search and Rescue/Special Warfare Support Squadron
HM	Helicopter Mine Countermeasures Squadron
HMAL	(Marine) Attack–Light Helicopter Squadron
HMH	(Marine) Heavy Helicopter Squadron
HMM	(Marine) Medium Helicopter Squadron
HMX	(Marine) Helicopter Squadron
HS	Helicopter Anti-Submarine Squadron
HSL	Light Helicopter Anti-Submarine Squadron
HT	Helicopter Training Squadron
MAG	Marine Aircraft Group
MAW	Marine Aircraft Wing
VA	Attack Squadron
VAQ	Tactical Electronic Warfare Squadron
VAW	Carrier Airborne Early-Warning Squadron
VC	Fleet Composite Squadron
VF	Fighter Squadron
VFA	Strike Fighter Squadron
VFC	Fighter Composite Squadron
VMA	(Marine) Attack Squadron
VMA (AW)	(Marine) Attack (All Weather) Squadron
VMAQ	(Marine) Electronic Warfare Squadron
VMFA	(Marine) Fighter-Attack Squadron
VMGR	(Marine) Refueler-Transport Squadron
VMO	(Marine) Observation Squadron
VP	Patrol Squadron
VPU	Patrol Squadron—Special Projects Unit
VQ	Fleet Air Reconnaissance Squadron
VR	Fleet Logistics Support Squadron
VRC	Fleet Logistics Support (COD) Squadron†
VS	Air Anti-Submarine Squadron
VT	Training Squadron
VX	Air Test and Evaluation Squadron
VXE	Antarctic Development Squadron
VXN	Oceanographic Development Squadron

*Marine squadrons add the letter T as a suffix for readiness/transition units.
†COD = Carrier On-board Delivery.

Historical: The designation carrier air wing (CVW) was established on 20 December 1963 in place of carrier air groups (CVG).[3] Air group designations had reached No. 153 with several gaps in the series. The designation ASW carrier air group (CVSG) was established on 1 April 1960 for aircraft assigned to ASW carriers (CVS); those ships were phased out in the late 1960s and early 1970s, the last CVSG being disestablished on 30 June 1973. The ASW groups were numbered from CVSG-50 to CVSG-62.

Replacement air groups (RAG) became combat readiness air wings (CRAW) in 1963, but these were phased out over the next few years, the last on 30 June 1973. Their squadrons survive, known officially as fleet readiness squadrons, also called "replacement" or RAG squadrons. They provide transition training to fleet aircraft and are generally assigned to the specialized aircraft "type" commands under NavAirLant or NavAirPac. When the ASW carrier air groups were phased out in the 1960s and early 1970s, the fixed-wing and

1. Vice Adm. Dick Dunleavy, USN, Assistant Chief of Naval Operations (Air Warfare), "The Shape of Wings to Come," *Naval Aviation News* (May–June 1991), p. 1.
2. Historical descriptions of carrier air group/wing development are found in Norman Polmar, *Aircraft Carriers* (New York: Doubleday, 1969), and in the quarterly journal *The Hook,* published by the Tail Hook Association.

3. The term CAG (for Commander Air Group) is still used to refer to an air wing commander.

helicopter ASW aircraft went aboard the larger attack aircraft carriers (which became simply CV/CVN vice CVA/CVAN). The CV/CVN concept originally provided for the "swing wing" concept, whereby a carrier could be loaded with an emphasis on fighter, attack, or ASW aircraft. In practice this has not been followed, as standard wings have been organized to the extent possible for all carriers. However, in a demonstration of the swing-wing concept, in October 1971 the carrier SARATOGA operated 37 ASW aircraft—21 S-2E Trackers and 16 SH-3D Sea Kings—plus 20 fighters, 9 attack aircraft, and 8 special-mission aircraft.[4]

Carrier-based ASW squadrons now fly the S-3A/B Viking (VS units) and SH-3H Sea King (HS units), with the SH-60F Seahawk being procured to replace the latter aircraft. Two HH-60H rescue variants are now being assigned to the SH-60F squadrons.

Specialized reconnaissance aircraft were phased off carrier decks in the late 1970s as the RA-5C Vigilante and RF-8G Photo Crusader were retired, the active fleet's last "recce" squadrons being RVAH-7, disestablished on 30 September 1979, and VFP-63, disestablished on 30 June 1982, respectively. Marine RF-4B Phantoms then provided a limited photographic reconnaissance capability on some carriers pending the availability in the early 1980s of the Tactical Air Reconnaissance Pod System (TARPS) for the F-14A Tomcat on the larger carriers. (The Naval Air Reserve flew the RF-8G Photo Crusader until early 1987). The TARPS pod, however, flown by non-specialized reconnaissance pilots, does not provide the quality or quantity of tactical reconnaissance that was possible with the RA-5C; this shortfall was keenly felt during Operation Desert Storm (1991). According to the U.S. Director of Naval Intelligence, the TARPS "was totally inadequate" in providing sufficient and timely bomb-damage assessment during Operation Desert Storm.[5]

The personnel strength of air wings varies; the nominal carrier squadron strengths are:

VA	medium attack	37 officers + 226 enlisted
VAQ	electronic	27 officers + 167 enlisted
VAW	early warning	32 officers + 127 enlisted
VF	fighter	36 officers + 216 enlisted
VFA	strike fighter	21 officers + 187 enlisted
VS	air ASW	41 officers + 212 enlisted
HS	helicopter ASW	26 officers + 178 enlisted

Carrier air wing staffs number about 10 officers + 17 enlisted, except that Japan-based CVW-5 has 15 officers and 25 enlisted assigned. Most CVW staffs also have one- to three-officer detachments assigned to their home air base.

Operational: Asterisks indicate wings and squadrons that participated in the air war in Operation Desert Storm, January–February 1991. The DWIGHT D. EISENHOWER and INDEPENDENCE arrived in the Gulf area in early August 1990 to help deter further Iraqi aggression following the invasion of Kuwait. They returned to the United States prior to the start of Desert Storm in January 1991. Air wings from six carriers participated in Desert Storm. See separate squadron entries for asterisks indicating the squadrons that participated.

4. In 1960–1961, in an earlier example of a swing-wing concept, in response to Soviet "saber-rattling," U.S. carriers in the Mediterranean and Far East unloaded fighter aircraft to embark more nuclear strike aircraft.
5. Rear Adm. Thomas A. Brooks, USN, comments at luncheon of Naval & Maritime Correspondents Circle, Washington, D.C., 15 July 1991.

Air Wing	Code	Ship	Squadrons	
CVW-1*	AB	AMERICA	VF-33	VAQ-137
			VF-102	VAW-123
			VFA-82	VS-32
			VFA-86	HS-11
			VA-85	
CVW-2*	NE	RANGER	VF-1	VAQ-131
			VF-2	VAW-116
			VA-145	VS-38
			VA-155	HS-14
CVW-3*	AC	JOHN F. KENNEDY	VF-14	VAQ-130
			VF-32	VAW-126
			VFA-37	VS-22
			VFA-105	HS-7
			VA-75	

CVW-3 was reorganized in 1983 to evaluate an all A-6E attack capability, with the KENNEDY embarking two F-14 squadrons and two A-6E Intruder squadrons (a total of 25 medium attack aircraft) and no light attack squadrons (A-7 or F/A-18). Subsequently, in 1989, CVW-3 was provided with two A-7E squadrons, VA-46 and VA-72, which were the last Corsair squadrons in the fleet. They flew with CVW-3 during Operation Desert Storm, after which they were replaced by VFA-37 and VFA-105 flying the F/A-18 Hornet.

CVW-2 on the RANGER had a KENNEDY-type wing during the 1980s.

CVW-4	Decommissioned 1 June 1970			
CVW-5*	NF	INDEPENDENCE	VF-21	VAQ-136
			VF-154	VAW-115
			VFA-192	VS-21
			VFA-195	HS-12
			VA-115	

CVW-5 previously flew from the carrier MIDWAY, being based at NAF Atsugi, Japan. When assigned to the MIDWAY, the wing did not have F-14 Tomcats or S-3 Vikings because of the ship's size and lack of an ASW command center. A detachment of three Marine RF-4B Phantoms from VMFP-3 had provided the ship with a photo-reconnaissance capability until 1986, when the MIDWAY wing shifted from F-4 Phantom fighters to F/A-18 Hornets. From 1986 until going aboard the INDEPENDENCE in 1991, the wing had eight squadrons: 3 VFA, 2 VA (flying the A-6E), 1 VAQ, 1 VAW, and 1 HS.

Upon joining the "Indy" in August 1991, CVW-5 lost VFA-151 and VA-185; it gained two F-14 squadrons and an S-3 squadron, becoming the last wing to receive those aircraft.

CVW-6	AE	FORRESTAL	Decommissioned 1 Apr. 1992	
			VF-11	VAQ-133
			VF-31	VAW-122
			VFA-132	VS-28
			VFA-137	HS-15
			VA-176	

This wing previously served in the INDEPENDENCE, shifting to the FORRESTAL in 1986 when the "Indy" began her long-term SLEP modernization. After SLEP, the INDEPENDENCE went to the Far East, taking on CVW-5. The wing was decommissioned with the shift of the FORRESTAL to a training role (AVT). See individual squadrons for their disposition.

CVW-7*	AG	Dwight D. Eisenhower	VF-142	VAQ-140
			VF-143	VAW-121
			VFA-131	VS-31
			VFA-136	HS-5
			VA-34	

CVW-7 flew from the Eisenhower during Operation Desert Shield in 1990, but not Desert Storm.

CVW-8*	AJ	Theodore Roosevelt	VF-41	VAQ-141
			VF-84	VAW-124
			VFA-15	VS-24
			VFA-87	HS-3
			VA-36	
			VA-65	

This wing deployed to the Western Pacific with the Nimitz when that carrier departed Norfolk on 30 December 1986 for a six-month deployment prior to assignment to a new home port at Bremerton, Wash. Upon completion of the deployment, CVW-8 returned to the East Coast for subsequent assignment to the Theodore Roosevelt.

CVW-9	NG	Nimitz	VF-24	VAQ-138
			VF-211	VAW-112
			VFA-146	VS-33
			VFA-147	HS-2
			VA-165	

Formerly embarked in the Kitty Hawk, CVW-9 was reassigned to the Nimitz in mid-1986 after the nuclear carrier shifted to the Pacific Fleet. The Kitty Hawk, in turn, entered the Philadelphia Naval Shipyard for her SLEP modernization.

| CVW-10 | Decommissioned 1 June 1988 |

This wing was commissioned on 1 November 1986 as the Navy's 14th carrier air wing. The previous CVW-10 was decommissioned on 20 November 1969.

CVW-11	NH	Abraham Lincoln	VF-114	VAQ-135
			VF-213	VAW-117
			VFA-22	VS-29
			VFA-94	HS-6
			VA-95	

CVW-11 remained on the West Coast to embark in the Lincoln when the Enterprise shifted to the East Coast in early 1990 for her extended modernization and refueling at Newport News Shipbuilding.

| CVW-12 | Decommissioned 1 June 1970 |
| CVW-13 | Decommissioned 1 January 1991 |

CVW-13 had been established on 1 March 1984 at NAS Oceana, Va., for assignment to the Coral Sea following her transfer to the Atlantic Fleet in 1983. The previous CVG-13 had been disestablished on 1 October 1962. The new wing made three Mediterranean deployments in the Coral Sea from 1986 to 1989 before being decommissioned.

CVW-14*	NK	Carl Vinson	VF-11	VAQ-139
			VF-131	VAW-113
			VFA-25	VS-35
			VFA-113	HS-8
			VA-196	

The wing was previously on board the Constellation, shifting to the Independence when the "Connie" entered the Philadelphia Naval Shipyard for SLEP. The wing flew from the "Indy" during Desert Shield (not Desert Storm), after which the Independence took on CVW-5 when she was home-ported in Japan in September 1991. The wing subsequently operated from the Midway during her transit back to the West Coast prior to going aboard the Vinson.

CVW-15	NL	Kitty Hawk	VF-51	VAQ-134
			VF-111	VAW-114
			VFA-27	VS-37
			VFA-97	HS-4
			VA-52	

VS-37 shifted to CVW-15 from CVW-14 in April 1991, replacing VS-29.

CVW-16	Decommissioned 30 June 1971			
CVW-17*	AA	Saratoga	VF-74	VAQ-132
			VF-103	VAW-125
			VFA-81	VS-30
			VFA-83	HS-9
			VA-35	

CVW-17 shifted from the Forrestal to the Saratoga when the former ship began SLEP modernization at the Philadelphia Naval Shipyard in 1982, ending three decades of the wing operating from CVA/CV 59.

CVW-18	Not used
CVW-19	Decommissioned 30 June 1977
CVWR-20	Reserve Air Wing
CVW-21	Decommissioned 12 December 1975
CVW-22 to 30	Not used
CVWR-30	Reserve Air Wing

PATROL WINGS

Patrol Wings (PatWings) direct the operations of the Navy's patrol squadrons (VP), with East Coast squadrons assigned to Patrol Wings Atlantic (PatWingsLant) at NAS Norfolk, Va., and West coast squadrons assigned to Patrol Wings Pacific (PatWingsPac) at NAS Moffett Field, south of San Francisco, Calif.

Under PatWingsLant are PatWing-5 at Brunswick, Maine, and PatWing-11 at Jacksonville, Fla. Their P-3 Orion squadrons operate in the Atlantic, Caribbean, and Mediterranean areas. PatWingsLant has administrative control of the Atlantic P-3 readiness squadron (VP-30) and the oceanographic squadron that flies RP-3 Orions (VXN-8). PatWing-5 is the administrative command for VPU-1.

Patrol Wings Pacific directs Pacific and Indian Ocean VP operations through PatWing-2 at Barbers Point on Oahu and PatWing-10 at Moffett; PatWing-1 at Kamiseya, Japan, directs the VP squadrons that rotate to the Western Pacific. PatWing-2 also has administrative control of two specialized squadrons, VPU-2 and VQ-3. Squadron VP-31, the Pacific Fleet's P-3 readiness training squadron, is directly subordinate to ComPatWingsPac.

See chapter 6 for patrol squadron assignments.

UNIT DESIGNATIONS

Naval Aviation units are designated in two systems of abbreviations: pronounceable acronyms and simpler, letter-number combinations. Accordingly, Fighter Squadron 1 is known as both FitRonOne and VF-1.

The V prefix for naval aircraft types and subsequently for aviation units dates from 1922 when V was used to indicate heavier-than-air and Z for lighter-than-air airships. VF indicates a fighter squadron, VA an attack squadron, ZP an airship patrol squadron, etc. (The last U.S. Navy airship, a Goodyear ZPG-2W, was taken out of service in 1962.) Subsequently, H was introduced as the helicopter type letter for aircraft (HNS-1) in 1943 and for squadrons in 1947 (the first

squadron was Marine Corps HMX-1, followed in 1948 by Navy HU-1 and HU-2). Marine units have the letter M added as the second letter of aviation unit designations.[6]

Current U.S. naval aviation unit designations are listed in table 28-3.

6. The H, V, and Z are also used for ship designations, hence CV for aircraft carrier, AV for seaplane tender, and AZ for airship tender. Subsequently, H was used in CVHA, CVHE, LPH, LHA, and LHD for helicopter-carrying ships.

TABLE 28-3. CARRIER AIR WINGS

Standard Air Wing (1980s)			ROOSEVELT Air Wing (1980s)			1990s Air Wing			2010 Air Wing		
2 VF	24 F-14A/D	Tomcat	2 VF	20 F-14A/D	Tomcat	2 VF	20 F-14A/D	Tomcat			
2 VA or VFA	24 A-7E F/A-18	Crusader Hornet	2 VFA	20 F/A-18	Hornet	2 VFA	20 F/A-18A/C	Hornet	4 VFA	42 F/A-18E/F	Hornet
1 VA	10 A-6E +4 KA-6D	Intruder tankers	2 VA	20 A-6E	Intruder	1 VA	16 A-6E	Intruder	2 VA	18 AX*	(attack)
1 VAQ	4 EA-6B	Prowler	1 VAQ	5 EA-6B	Prowler	1 VAQ	5 EA-6B	Prowler	1 VAQ	5 ATSA†	
1 VAW	4 E-2C	Hawkeye	1 VAW	5 E-2C	Hawkeye	1 VAW	5 E-2C	Hawkeye	1 VAW	5 ATSA†	
1 VS	10 S-3A	Viking	1 VS	10 S-3B	Viking	1 VS	6 S-3B	Viking	1 VS	6 ATSA†	
1 HS	6 SH-3H	Sea King	1 HS	6 SH-3H	Sea King	1 HS	6 SH-60F	Seahawk	1 HS	6 SH-60F	Seahawk
	86			86			2 HH-60H	Seahawk		2 HH-60H	Seahawk
							80			84	

*These squadrons will initially fly seven AX aircraft, to be increased to nine per squadron by 2010.
†Advanced Tactical Support Aircraft.

ATTACK SQUADRONS

Squadron	Aircraft	Name/Notes†	Squadron	Aircraft	Name/Notes†
VA-12	A-7E	disestablished 1 Oct 1986	VA-94	A-7E	to VFA-94 on 28 June 1990
VA-15	A-7E	to VFA-15 on 1 Oct 1986	VA-95	A-6E, KA-6D	Green Lizards
VA-22	A-7E	to VFA-22 on 4 May 1990	VA-97	A-7E	to VFA-97 on 25 Jan 1991
VA-25	A-7E	to VFA-25 on 1 July 1983	VA-105	A-7E	to VFA-105 on 17 Dec 1990
VA-27	A-7E	to VFA-27 on 25 Jan 1991	VA-113	A-7E	to VFA-113 on 25 Mar 1983
VA-34*	A-6E, KA-6D	Blue Blasters	VA-115*	A-6E	Eagles
VA-35*	A-6E, KA-6D	Black Panthers	VA-122	A-7E	disestablished 31 May 1991
VA-36*	A-6E	Road Runners	VA-125	A-7E	disestablished 1 Oct 1977
VA-37	A-7E	to VFA-37 on 28 Nov 1990	VA-127	A-4F, TA-4J	to VFA-127 on 1 Nov 1987
VA-42	A-6E, TC-4C, T-34C	Green Pawns (AD)	VA-128	A-6E, TC-4C	Golden Intruders (NJ)
VA-46*	A-7E	disestablished 30 June 1991	VA-145*	A-6E, KA-6D	Swordsmen
VA-52	A-6E, KA-6D	Knightriders	VA-146	A-7E	to VFA-146 on 21 July 1989
VA-56	A-7E	disestablished 31 Aug 1986	VA-147	A-7E	to VFA-147 on 20 July 1989
VA-65*	A-6E	Fighting Tigers	VA-153	A-7E	disestablished 3 Sep 1977
VA-66	A-7E	disestablished 1 Oct 1986	VA-155*	A-6E, KA-6D	Silver Foxes
VA-72*	A-7E	disestablished 30 June 1991	VA-165	A-6E, KA-6D	Boomers
VA-75*	A-6E, KA-6D	World Famous Sunday Punchers	VA-174	A-7E	disestablished 30 June 1988
VA-81	A-7E	to VFA-81 on 4 Feb 1988	VA-176	A-6E, KA-6D	disestablished 1992
VA-82	A-7E	to VFA-82 on 15 July 1987	VA-185*	A-6E, KA-6D	disestablished on 30 Aug 1991
VA-83	A-7E	to VFA-83 on 1 Mar 1988	VA-192	A-7E	to VFA-192 on 10 Jan 1985
VA-85*	A-6E, KA-6D	Buckeyes	VA-195	A-7E	to VFA-195 on 1 Apr 1985
VA-86	A-7E	to VFA-86 on 15 July 1987	VA-196*	A-6E	World Famous Main Battery
VA-87	A-7E	to VFA-87 on 1 May 1986	VA-215	A-7E	disestablished 30 Sep 1977
VA-93	A-7E	disestablished 31 July 1986			

†Data based in part on Lt. Mark L. Morgan, USN, "No Slack in Light Attack," The Hook (Fall 1991), p. 31.

All existing attack squadrons fly the A-6E Intruder, and some also fly the KA-6D tanker. All A-7E squadrons have been disestablished or converted to VFA units flying the F/A-18 Hornet. VA-46* and VA-72* in the Atlantic were the Navy's last A-7E Corsair squadrons; their demise was delayed because of the Gulf War (flying from the KENNEDY); they were disestablished on 30 June 1991 (ceremonies were held on 23 May 1991, confusing the records).[7] VA-27 and VA-97 were the Pacific Fleet's last A-7 fleet squadrons, being redesignated VFA on 24 January 1991 (they had flown with CVW-15 aboard the VINSON). VA-122, the A-7 readiness/transition squadron, was disestablished in May 1991, the last of three such units (the others being VA-125 and VA-174). This ended the 25-year career of the Corsair II as a first-line attack aircraft.

All carrier air wings now have one A-6E squadron. Squadron size varies from eight to 20 aircraft, with some squadrons also having four

7. The A-7D variant is still flown by the Air Force Reserve; several other countries also fly A-7 variants.

KA-6D Intruder tankers; the tankers are being discarded and replaced by "buddy" refueling stores on A-6Es and S-3s.

VA-55 was established on 7 October 1983 for CVW-13. (The previous VA-55 had been disestablished in 1975.) The squadron was again disestablished on 22 February 1991. VA-185* was established in December 1986 as a second attack squadron for CVW-5; it was disestablished in August 1991.

Atlantic Fleet A-6E squadrons are based at Oceana, Va., under Medium Attack Wing 1; in the Pacific the A-6E units (as well as EA-6B Prowlers) are at NAS Whidbey Island, Wash., under Medium Attack/VAQ Wing Pacific. The VA fleet readiness-training squadrons are VA-42 at Oceana and VA-128 at Whidbey Island.

The Naval Strike Warfare Center at NAS Fallon, Nev., provides strike training to Navy and Marine fliers and planners. "Strike U," as it is called, flies A-6E, F/A-18, and SH-3H aircraft.

Historical: Attack squadrons were established on 15 November 1946, replacing the previous carrier-based bombing-fighting (VBF), bombing (VB), and torpedo (VT) squadrons.

TACTICAL ELECTRONIC WARFARE SQUADRONS

Squadron	Aircraft	Name
VAQ-33	EA-6A, P-3B, EP-3J	Firebirds
VAQ-34	F/A-18 A/B	Flashbacks
VAQ-35	EA-6B	Grey Wolves
VAQ-129	EA-6B	Vikings (NJ)
VAQ-130*	EA-6B	Zappers
VAQ-131*	EA-6B	Lancers
VAQ-132*	EA-6B	Scorpions
VAQ-133	EA-6B	disestablished 1 June 1992
VAQ-134	EA-6B	Garudas
VAQ-135	EA-6B	Black Ravens
VAQ-136*	EA-6B	Gauntlets
VAQ-137*	EA-6B	Rooks
VAQ-138	EA-6B	Yellowjackets
VAQ-139*	EA-6B	Cougars
VAQ-140*	EA-6B	Patriots
VAQ-141*	EA-6B	Shadowhawks
VAQ-142	EA-6B	disestablished 31 Mar 1991

There are 11 deploying fleet tactical EW squadrons, with a four- or five-plane squadron normally assigned to each carrier air wing. These squadrons fly the EA-6B Prowler, with VAQ-132 the first to receive the aircraft, in July 1971. VAQ-129 provides all EA-6B readiness training. The last squadron to be established was VAQ-142 on 1 June 1988; however, when the wings were cut back to 12, that squadron was disestablished on 31 March 1991.

All active EA-6B squadrons and one of two reserve units are based at NAS Whidbey Island, Wash., except for VAQ-136, based at NAF Atsugi, Japan.

All tactical EW squadrons report administratively to Medium Attack/VAQ Wing Pacific. VAQ-33, 34, and 35 operate under the Fleet Tactical Readiness Group (FTRG), formerly the Fleet Electronic Warfare Support Group (FEWSG), with headquarters at the Naval Amphibious Base Little Creek (Norfolk), Va. The FTRG squadrons simulate potential enemy electronic/jamming activities. VAQ-33 is at Key West; VAQ-34 at the Naval Air Weapons Center Pt. Mugu, Calif. (formerly Pacific Missile Test Center); and VAQ-35 at NAS Whidbey Island, Wash. All three squadrons have FTRG's tail code GD. (FTRG also operates two NKC-135A and one EC-24 aircraft; see chapter 29.)

Historical: VAQ-33 (formerly VAW/VA[AW]/VC-33) was originally established on 31 May 1949, VAQ-34 was established on 1 March 1983, and VAQ-35 was established on 1 June 1991. (In July 1990, VAQ-34 became the first U.S. military aviation squadron to be commanded by a woman.)

VAQ-129, 131, and 132 were previously heavy attack squadrons (VAH-10, 4, and 2, respectively); they changed to VAQ in 1968–1970, when they shifted from EKA-3B Skywarriors to EA-6B aircraft. VAQ-130 is formerly early-warning squadron VW-13, redesignated VAQ in 1968. Most of the other VAQs were built up from EKA-3B detachments that operated from forward-deployed carriers.

A pair of EA-6B Prowlers from VAQ-140 over the Mediterranean. These aircraft escort carrier-based strikes to detect and identify hostile ground and shipboard radars; they can also attack radar transmitters with HARM missiles. (Comdr. John Leehouts, USN)

AIRBORNE EARLY-WARNING SQUADRONS

Squadron	Aircraft	Name
VAW-110	E-2C, C-2A	Firebirds (NJ)
VAW-111	E-2C	disestablished 1991
VAW-112	E-2C	Golden Hawks
VAW-113*	E-2C	Black Eagles
VAW-114	E-2C	Hormel Hawgs
VAW-115*	E-2C	Sentinels
VAW-116*	E-2C	Sun Kings
VAW-117	E-2C	Wall Bangers
VAW-120	E-2C, C-2A	Hummers (AD)
VAW-121*	E-2C	Bluetails
VAW-122	E-2C	disestablished 1992
VAW-123*	E-2C	Screwtops
VAW-124*	E-2C	Bear Aces
VAW-125*	E-2C	Tiger Tails
VAW-126*	E-2C	Sea Hawks
VAW-127	E-2C	disestablished 30 Sep 1991

Airborne early-warning aircraft have become a vital component of air combat, both offensive and defensive. The AEW function aboard U.S. aircraft carriers is performed by the E-2C Hawkeye. This one, aboard the SARATOGA, is folded up, ready to be tucked down on the hangar deck. (U.S. Navy)

Each carrier air wing has a four- or five-plane AEW squadron flying the E-2C Hawkeye. Three squadrons stood down in 1991–1993, reducing the deploying VAW squadrons to 11. Fleet readiness training is provided by VAW-110 for the Pacific Fleet and by VAW-120 for Atlantic squadrons; these squadrons also provide transition training for the C-2A Greyhound COD aircraft. The two readiness squadrons were designated RVAW until 1 May 1983, when they dropped the R prefix; they were the only readiness squadrons with that prefix.

West Coast squadrons are based at NAS Miramar, Calif., under Fighter/AEW Wing Pacific; East Coast units are at NAS Oceana under Carrier AEW Wing 12, a functional wing of Commander, Tactical Wings Atlantic.

In addition to regular carrier deployments, VAW aircraft have operated from Keflavik, Iceland, to provide AEW coverage of the Greenland–Iceland–United Kingdom (GIUK) gap, and in Operation Thunderbolt, the U.S. Customs Service's effort to intercept drug smugglers off the U.S. coasts.

Historical: The first carrier AEW squadrons were VAW-1 and VAW-2, commissioned in 1948 to provide aircraft detachments to Pacific and Atlantic carriers, respectively. (AEW aircraft had earlier flown from carriers, and a land-based squadron, VPW-1, had been established in 1948.)

The current VAW structure dates from 1967, when seven AEW squadrons, numbered in sequence, were established. Previously VAW-11, 12, 13, and 33 provided AEW detachments to carriers, while until 1965 Barrier Squadron Pacific and AEW Wing Atlantic operated land-based WV-series/EC-121 Warning Star aircraft as part of the North American air defense efforts.

VAW-110's Detachment 4 flew the Navy's last E-1B Tracers from the FRANKLIN D. ROOSEVELT (CV 42) in 1976–1977.

FLEET COMPOSITE SQUADRONS

Squadron	Code	Aircraft	Name
VC-1	UA	A-4E, TA-4J	Blue Alii
VC-5	UE	A-4E, TA-4J, SH-3G	Checkertails
VC-6*	JG	none assigned	Skeeters
VC-8	GF	TA-4J, SH-3G	Redtails
VC-10	JH	TA-4J	Challengers

Composite squadrons provide utility services for the fleet, including "dissimilar" Air Combat Maneuvering (ACM), noncombat photography, aerial target services, radar calibration, and transport. Two VC squadrons have combat missions: VC-1 and VC-10 had A-4E and TA-4J Skyhawks that have the additional role of air defense for the Hawaiian islands and Guantánamo Bay, Cuba, respectively. VC-1 was disestablished on 30 September 1992 and VC-5 on 31 August 1992.

VC-6 at NAS Norfolk, Virginia, flies no aircraft, but operates air and surface target drones. There are permanent VC-6 detachments at the Fleet Combat Training Center in Dam Neck, Va., and at the Naval Amphibious Base, Little Creek, Va. Five smaller, mobile detachments operate in the Atlantic-Mediterranean areas and periodically deploy with U.S. ships operating around South America in the UNITAS exercises. VC-1 was located at Barbers Point, Hawaii; VC-5 at Cubi Point in the Philippines, with a detachment at Poro Point; VC-8 at Roosevelt Roads, Puerto Rico; and VC-10 at Guantánamo Bay. VC-10 has been at "Gitmo" since April 1945 (originally as VU-16, changed to VU-10 in August 1946). All squadrons provide local SAR capability. The future of VC-5 after the withdrawal of U.S. forces from the Philippines was not decided when this edition was compiled. The squadron had long served at Cubi Point.

Historical: The current VC squadrons comprise the third series of composite squadrons in the fleet. From 1943 to 1945 the Navy had 83 composite squadrons (VC) that operated from escort carriers in the ASW role.

Beginning in 1949, six VC squadrons were formed with nuclear-strike aircraft (P2V-3C Neptunes and AJ Savages); those squadrons became heavy attack squadrons (VAH) in 1955–1956. At the same time, several ASW squadrons were formed but were redesignated VS (see page 383).

On 1 July 1965 the Navy's utility squadrons (VJ and later VU) were changed to VC, with VU-1, -5, -6, -8, and -10 being redesignated as fleet composite squadrons (VC). VC-1 could trace its origins to Utility Squadron (VJ) 1 established on 5 October 1925 at San Diego; although the squadron was disestablished on 30 April 1949 and a new squadron was established on 20 July 1951 as Utility Squadron (VU) 1; still, VJ/VU/VC-1 is often considered to be the Navy's oldest aviation squadron.[8] VC-2 (Oceana) and VC-7 (Miramar) were disestablished in 1980, and VC-3 (North Island) was disestablished in 1981. The last squadron flew DC-130A Hercules to launch aerial drones.

Operational: VC-6 detachments operated Pioneer drones from the battleships MISSOURI (BB 63) and WISCONSIN (BB 64) during the Gulf War. See chapter 29.

8. The official Navy publication *United States Naval Aviation 1910–1980* (NAVAIR 00-80P-1, 1981) notes: "Once a squadron is decommissioned that ends its history. If a new squadron is commissioned with the same designation it does not have any relationship with the previous squadron of the same designation."

FIGHTER SQUADRONS

Squadron	Aircraft	Name
VF-1*	F-14A	Wolfpack
VF-2*	F-14A	Bounty Hunters
VF-11	F-14D	Red Rippers
VF-14*	F-14A	Tophatters
VF-21*	F-14A	Freelancers
VF-24	F-14B	Fighting Renegades
VF-31	F-14D	Tomcatters
VF-32*	F-14A	Swordsmen
VF-33*	F-14A	Starfighters
VF-41*	F-14A	Black Aces
VF-43	F-5E/F, A-4E/F, F-16N, TF-16N, T-2C	Challengers (AD)
VF-45	F-5E/F, A-4E/F, TA-4J, F-16N, TF-16N	Blackbirds (AD)
VF-51	F-14A	Screaming Eagles
VF-74*	F-14B	Bedevilers
VF-84*	F-14A	Jolly Rogers
VF-101	F-14A/B	Grim Reapers (AD)
VF-102*	F-14A	Diamondbacks
VF-103*	F-14B	Sluggers
VF-111	F-14A	Sundowners
VF-114	F-14A	World Famous Fighting Aardvarks
VF-124	F-14A/D, T-34C	Gunfighters (NJ)
VF-126	A-4E/F, TA-4J, F-16N, TF-16N, T-2C	Bandits (NJ)
VF-142*	F-14B	Ghostriders
VF-143*	F-14B	World Famous Puckin' Dogs
VF-154*	F-14A	Black Knights
VF-191	F-14A	disestablished 30 Apr 1988
VF-194	F-14A	disestablished 30 Apr 1988
VF-211	F-14B	Fighting Checkmates
VF-213	F-14A	Black Lions

All carrier air wings have two F-14A/B/D[9] Tomcat fighter squadrons (VF); CVW-5 when assigned to the MIDWAY did not fly F-14s but F-4 Phantoms and then F/A-18 Hornets in the fighter role. Most VF squadrons now have 10 or 12 aircraft assigned; in one of the two F-14 squadrons on each carrier there are three aircraft wired for the TARPS reconnaissance package, which can be installed or removed in a few hours. VF-211 was the first squadron to deploy with TARPS, in early 1982 on board the CONSTELLATION.

West Coast F-14 squadrons are at Miramar under Fighter/AEW Wing Pacific; East Coast units are at NAS Oceana under Fighter Wing 1.

Fleet readiness training is provided for the F-14 by VF-101 at Oceana and VF-124 at Maramar; adversary training is provided by VF-43 at Oceana, VF-45 at Key West, and VF-136 at Miramar, the last also providing instrument training. VA-45 changed to VF-45 on 7 February 1985. The adversary training squadrons fly the F-16N and TF-16N Fighting Falcon, F-5E/F Tiger II, TA-4J and A-4E/F Skyhawk, and T-2C Buckeye. VF-43 previously flew the F-21A Kfir.

The Navy's Fighter Weapons School at Miramar flies the F-16N, TF-16N, F-14A, A-4E/F, and TA-4F/J aircraft. Known as Top Gun, the school was established in September 1969 to develop realistic adversary tactics and training for Navy fliers; it was begun as a department of VF-121 and became a separate command on 1 July 1972.[10]

---

9. The F-14B is the former F-14A+; redesignated in 1991.
10. Officially the designation is Topgun (one word); however, it is almost universally known as Top Gun.

These F-14 Tomcats are the only "straight" fighters aboard Navy carriers. It is unlikely that the Navy version of the Advanced Tactical Fighter will be procured, resulting in the F/A-18 Hornet being the Navy's standard fighter by about 2015. (U.S. Navy)

The MIDWAY flew the Navy's last two active Phantom squadrons (VF-151 and VF-161), which stood down as Phantom units in 1986; the squadrons then became VFA-151 and VFA-161 flying the F/A-18. The last Phantom fleet readiness squadron was VF-171, which was disestablished on 1 June 1984 with all fleet readiness training in the Phantom then being undertaken by VMFAT-101 at MCAS Yuma. (VF-121, the West Coast F-4 readiness squadron, was disestablished on 26 September 1980; it had been the Navy's first F-4 squadron.)

VF-191 and VF-194 were established in 1986 for the Navy's 14th carrier air wing. However, the two squadrons were disestablished in 1988. Plans to establish "new" VF-191 and VF-194 as F-14D squadrons were cancelled when VF-11 and VF-31 became available with the decommissioning of CVW-6 when the FORRESTAL became a training carrier; those squadrons have shifted to the West Coast.

STRIKE FIGHTER SQUADRONS

Squadron	Aircraft	Name	Notes
VFA-15*	F/A-18C	Valions	former VA-15
VFA-22	F/A-18C	Fighting Redcocks	former VA-22
VFA-25*	F/A-18C	Fist of the Fleet	former VA-25
VFA-27	F/A-18C	Chargers	former VA-27
VFA-37	F/A-18C	Bulls	former VA-37
VFA-81*	F/A-18C	Sunliners	former VA-81
VFA-82*	F/A-18C	Marauder	former VA-82
VFA-83*	F/A-18C	Rampagers	former VA-83
VFA-86*	F/A-18C	Sidewinders	former VA-86
VFA-87*	F/A-18C	Golden Warriors	former VA-87
VFA-94	F/A-18C	Mighty Shrikes	former VA-94
VFA-97	F/A-18C	Warhawks	former VA-97
VFA-105	F/A-18C	Gunslingers	former VA-105
VFA-106	F/A-18, T-34C	Gladiators (AD)	former VA-106
VFA-113*	F/A-18C	Stingers	former VA-113
VFA-125	F/A-18, T-34C	Rough Riders (NJ)	former VA-125
VFA-127	F-SE/F, F/A-18A	Cylons (NJ)	former VA-127
VFA-131*	F/A-18C	Wildcats	
VFA-132	F/A-18A	Privateers	disestablished 1 June 1992
VFA-136*	F/A-18C	Knighthawks	
VFA-137	F/A-18A	Kestrels	
VFA-146	F/A-18C	Blue Diamonds	former VA-146
VFA-147	F/A-18C	Argonauts	former VA-147
VFA-151*	F/A-18A	Fighting Vigilantes	former VF-151
VFA-192*	F/A-18C	World Famous Golden Dragons	former VA-192
VFA-195*	F/A-18C	Dambusters	former VA-195

Navy F/A-18s are assigned to strike fighter squadrons, with most carriers operating two squadrons; CVW-2 on the RANGER is the only wing without F/A-18s. VFAs have nine to 12 aircraft.

The first F/A-18 squadron was Fighter Attack Squadron 125, established on 13 November 1980 as the F/A-18 readiness squadron for training Navy and Marine pilots and ground crews; VFA-125's first aircraft was delivered in February 1981. The squadron is located at Lemoore. A second F/A-18 readiness squadron, VFA-106, subsequently "stood up" in October 1985 at NAS Cecil Field (Jacksonville, Fla.) as the East Coast F/A-18 transition squadron. VFA-127 provides adversary training at NAF Fallon, Nev.

VFA-75 and VFA-113 were the Navy's first F/A-18 fleet squadrons, shifting from the A-7E Corsair to F/A-18 in March–June 1983. Most F/A-18 squadrons are former A-7E Corsair units (VA), with two F-14 squadrons (VF-151 and VF-161) transitioning to F/A-18s.

VFA-161, formerly VF-161, was disestablished on 1 April 1987.

Historical: The Marine Corps has had fighter-attack squadrons (VMFA) since the introduction of the F-4 Phantom into squadron service in 1963. The Navy designation VFA originally indicated fighter attack squadron; changed in 1983 to strike fighter to emphasize the attack role.

PATROL SQUADRONS

Squadron	Code	Name
VP-1*	YB	Screaming Eagles
VP-4*	YD	Skinny Dragons
VP-5*	LA	Mad Foxes
VP-6	PC	Blue Sharks
VP-8*	LC	Tigers
VP-9	PD	Golden Eagles
VP-10	LD	Red Lancers
VP-11*	LE	Proud Pegasus
VP-16	LF	Eagles
VP-17	ZE	White Lightnings
VP-19*	PE	disestablished 31 Aug 1991
VP-22	QA	Blue Geese
VP-23*	LJ	Sea Hawks
VP-24	LR	Batmen
VP-26	LK	Tridents
VP-30	LL	Pro's Nest
VP-31	RP	Black Lightnings
VP-40*	QE	Fighting Marlins
VP-44	LM	disestablished 31 May 1991
VP-45	LN	Pelicans
VP-46*	RC	Grey Knights
VP-47	RD	Golden Swordsmen
VP-48	SF	disestablished 31 Aug 1991
VP-49	LP	Woodpeckers
VP-50	SG	disestablished 30 June 1992
VP-56	LQ	disestablished 28 June 1991

The Navy's 19 first-line patrol squadrons each fly eight P-3C Orion aircraft, a reduction from the nine planes per squadron in the 1980s. The last active P-3B was retired from VP-22 on 11 September 1990. There were 24 active VP squadrons from the early 1970s until 1991. Budgetary limitations forced reductions and led to four squadrons standing down in 1991.

Four VP squadrons "stood down" in 1991 and one in 1992. VP-6 is scheduled to be disestablished in 1993, leaving an active force of 18 patrol squadrons. P-3 transition/readiness training is currently performed by VP-30 at NAS Jacksonville and by VP-31 at NAS Moffett Field. Currently both squadrons have 24 aircraft; in addition to "straight" P-3C aircraft, VP-30 has VP-3A, UP-3A, and TP-3A variants; VP-31 has UP-3A and TP-3A variants. VP-31 is scheduled to merge with VP-30 in 1993 as Moffett Field is closed and the VP community is reduced.

Historical: VP indicated patrol squadrons from 1922 to 1944, when patrol and multi-engine land-based bombing squadrons were redesignated patrol bombing squadrons (VPB). The squadrons reverted to VP on 15 May 1946.

PATROL SQUADRONS—SPECIAL PROJECTS UNIT

Squadron	Code	Aircraft	Name
VPU-1	OB	P-3B	Old Buzzards
VPU-2	SP	P-3B, UP-3A	Wizards

These two squadrons fly specially modified electronic surveillance variants of the Orion. They appear to fly with the tail codes of other squadrons. VPU-1 is based at NAS Brunswick and VPU-2 at NAS Barbers Point.

VPU-1's tail code OB is unofficial, indicating Old Buzzards.

ELECTRONIC RECONNAISSANCE SQUADRONS

Squadron	Code	Aircraft	Name
VQ-1*	PR	P-3B, EP-3E	World Watchers
VQ-2*	JQ	P-3B, EP-3E	Batmen
VQ-5	SS	S-3A, ES-3A	Sea Shadows
VQ-6	ET	S-3A, ES-3A	Black Ravens

These units are officially designated fleet air reconnaissance squadrons; they provide electronic surveillance in direct support of fleet operations and carry out special reconnaissance along the borders of foreign territories. VQ-1 at Agana, Guam, and VQ-2 at Rota, Spain, each fly six ELINT-configured EP-3E Orions. Those squadrons previously flew EA-3B Skywarrior ELINT aircraft as well, with the "Whales" operating from forward-deployed carriers. VQ-2 retired the last EA-3B operated by a VQ squadron in September 1991.

VQ-5 was established at Agana on 15 April 1991 and VQ-6 at Cecil Field on 8 August 1991. They fly the new ES-3A Viking, which succeeds the EA-3B as the fleet's carrier-based ELINT aircraft.

Historical: VQ-1 was established as Electronic Countermeasures Squadron 1 at NAS Iwakuni, Japan, on 1 June 1955, initially flying P4M-1Q Mercator aircraft; VQ-2 was established as ECM Squadron 2 on 1 September 1955 at Port Lyautey, Morocco, first flying the P4M-1Q and A3D-1Q (EA-3B) aircraft. VQ was changed to fleet air reconnaissance squadron on 1 January 1960.

Operational: VQ-1 flew EP-3Es, and VQ-2 flew both EP-3s and EA-3Bs in support of Desert Shield/Desert Storm; the latter were the last operational combat-environment flights by the venerable Skywarrior.

STRATEGIC COMMUNICATION SQUADRONS

Squadron	Code	Aircraft	Name
VQ-3	TC	E-6A	Ironmen
VQ-4*	HL	E-6A, EC-130Q, TC-130Q	Shadows

These units, officially designated fleet air reconnaissance squadrons, provide LF/VLF communications relay to strategic missile submarines under a program known as TACAMO (Take Charge And Move Out). VQ-3 completed transition from the EC-130Q Hercules to the E-6A Mercury in 1990; VQ-4 is now getting the E-6A. Sixteen E-6A aircraft are being flown by these squadrons, replacing 22 EC-130Q aircraft. VQ-3 is the Navy's largest aviation squadron, with more than 750 officers and enlisted.

VQ-3 was based at Barbers Point and VQ-4 was at Patuxent River; both squadrons moved to Tinker Air Force Base in Oklahoma in 1992, where they are part of U.S. Strategic Communications Wing 1, established on 1 May 1992.

Subsequently, the 16 Navy E-6 aircraft will be employed as airborne command posts for the new U.S. Strategic Command in addition to their role as LF/VLF communications relay platforms. In the role of airborne command posts, the Navy aircraft and specialized truck convoys in the continental United States will replace 27 Air Force EC-135 aircraft that have been used in that role. The Air Force planes were operated by the former Strategic Air Command and were called "Looking Glass."

The TACAMO airborne alert—which kept some of these aircraft always in the air—ended in the spring of 1992. Some aircraft are now maintained continuously on runway alert.

FLEET LOGISTIC SUPPORT SQUADRONS

Squadron	Code	Aircraft	Name
VR-22*	JL	C-130F, KC-130F	Medriders
VR-24*	JM	CA-2A, CT-39G	Lifting Eagles
VRC-30*	RW	C-2A, UC-12B, CT-39E	Truckin' Traders
VRC-40*	CD	C-2A	Rawhides
VRC-50*	RG	C-2A, US-3A, C-130F	Foo Dogs

These squadrons carry passengers and high-priority cargo in direct support of fleet operations. Inter-theater support for the Navy is provided mainly by the Air Force–operated Military Airlift Command (MAC), while Navy transport requirements within the United States are fulfilled by the Naval Air Reserve, which regularly operates overseas as well.

The KC-130F "Herks" of VR-22 are the Navy's only land-based tanker aircraft. VRC-50 flies the Navy's four US-3A Viking COD aircraft.

The CT-39G and C-130 are land-based aircraft; the turboprop C-2A is not based aboard carriers because of the aircraft's size. The piston-engine C-1A has been retired. VR-24 previously flew RH-53D Sea Stallion helicopters to provide Vertical Onboard Delivery (VOD) capability for the Sixth Fleet. In December 1983 that role was taken over by the newly commissioned HC-4 at NAS Sigonella, Sicily.

Historical: The first transport squadron was VR-1, established on 9 March 1942; it was disestablished in October 1978. The designation VR subsequently became both air transport squadron and fleet tactical support squadron (depending upon role), and then fleet logistics support squadron.

VR-24 is based at Sigonella and VR-22 at Rota, Spain, with both squadrons assigned to Fleet Air Mediterranean; VRC-30 at North Island under ASW Wing Pacific; VRC-40 at Norfolk under Carrier AEW Wing 12; and VRC-50, previously at Cubi Point in the Philippines, is being shifted elsewhere in the Pacific (under Fleet Air Western Pacific).

VAW-110 and VAW-120 took over readiness training for the C-2 from VRC-30; subsequently, VRC-30 provided transition/readiness training for the UC-12 Super King Air for the Navy.

Historical: The VR squadrons were originally transport squadrons (VR), changed to fleet tactical support squadrons (VR) on 15 July 1957. They became fleet logistic support squadrons on 1 April 1976.

The first COD squadron, VRC-40, was established at Norfolk on 1 July 1960.

AIRCRAFT FERRY SQUADRONS

The Navy's last aircraft ferry squadron, VRF-31 (nicknamed Storkline), was disestablished on 1 October 1986. The squadron was originally established on 1 December 1943.

Ferry squadrons provided pilots to transfer Navy and Marine Corps aircraft throughout the world. In 1982 the role of VRF-31, the last such unit, was changed to one of coordinating aircraft movements, with fleet units conducting the actual ferry missions. VRF-31 was based at Norfolk under Fleet Tactical Support Wing 1.

AIR ANTI-SUBMARINE SQUADRONS

Squadron	Aircraft	Name
VS-21	S-3B	Fighting Redtails
VS-22*	S-3B	Checkmates
VS-24*	S-3B	Scouts
VS-27	S-3B	Seawolves (AD)
VS-28	S-3B	disestablished 1992
VS-29	S-3B	Vikings
VS-30*	S-3B	Diamond Cutters
VS-31*	S-3B	Topcats
VS-32*	S-3B	Maulers
VS-33	S-3A	Screwbirds
VS-35	S-3B	Blue Wolves
VS-37*	S-3B	Sawbucks
VS-38*	S-3A	Red Griffins
VS-41	S-3A/B	Shamrocks (NJ)

The Navy's 12 operational air ASW squadrons each fly six aircraft, a reduction from the ten aircraft assigned to these squadrons in the 1980s. Most aircraft are being upgraded to the S-3B configuration.

VS-41 at North Island and VS-27 at Cecil Field provide readiness training for the S-3 community. (VS-30 was an S-2 Tracker readiness training squadron; it became an operational squadron upon transitioning to the S-3A in 1976.) On 20 February 1974 the first S-3A Viking was delivered to VS-41, with the first fleet squadron, VS-21, shifting to the S-3A in June 1974. The last Viking squadron to be formed was VS-35 on 4 April 1991.

East Coast Viking squadrons are assigned to Sea Strike Wing 1 at Cecil Field, and those on the West Coast are under ASW Wing Pacific at North Island.

Historical: Specialized carrier-based ASW squadrons were formed in World War II, most designated as composite squadrons (VC). In April 1950 eight VC squadrons were changed to air anti-submarine squadrons (VS); each flew 18 TBM-3E Avengers. Four of the squadrons had previously been attack units (VA), which were changed to VC on 1 September 1948.

Operational: In the 1991 war in the Gulf, the six S-3B squadrons operating from carriers in the Gulf and Red Sea flew bombing missions with 500-pound (254-kg) "iron bombs" and served as tankers for other strike and fighter aircraft.

AIR TEST AND EVALUATION SQUADRONS

Squadron	Code	Aircraft	Name
VX-1	JA	P-3C, S-3A/B, SH-2F, SH-3H, SH-60B/F	ASW Pioneers
VX-4	XF	TA-4J, F-14A/D, F/A-18A	Evaluators
VX-5	XE	TA-4J, A-6E, EA-6B, AV-8B, F/A-18, AH-1W	Vampires

These squadrons test and evaluate air weapon systems. VX-1 at NAS Patuxent River, Md., specializes in operational test and evaluation of airborne ASW under the cognizance of Sea-Based ASW Wings Atlantic. VX-4 at Point Mugu, Calif., specializes in fighter weapons and tactics under Fighter/AEW Wing Pacific. VX-5 at the Naval Weapons Center China Lake, Calif., supports air-to-surface weapons and tactics, and electronic countermeasures programs under the administrative control of Light Attack Wing Pacific. VX-5 also flew A-7E Corsairs until 1991.

The VX squadrons fly a variety of aircraft. Two specialized development squadrons—VXE-6 and VXN-8—are numbered in the basic VX series (see below).

Historical: An aircraft experimental and development squadron was established at NAS Anacostia in Washington, D.C., on 13 August 1942; this was the predecessor of VX-1.

TRAINING SQUADRONS

Squadron	Code	Aircraft	Name	Training
VT-2	E	T-34C	The Doer Birds	Primary/Intermediate
VT-3	E	T-34C	Red Knights	Primary/Intermediate
VT-4	F	T-2C	Rubber Ducks	E-2/C-2 carqual
VT-6	E	T-34C		Primary/Intermediate
VT-7	A	TA-4J	Eagles	Strike
VT-9	A	T-2C	Tigers	disestablished 1 Nov 1987
VT-10	F	T-2C, T-34C, T-39N	Cosmic Cats	Basic/Intermediate NFO
VT-19	A	T-2C	Fighting Frogs	Intermediate
VT-21	B	TA-4J T-45	Red Hawks	Strike
VT-22	B	TA-4J	King Eagles	Strike
VT-23	B	T-2C	The Professionals	Intermediate
VT-24	C	TA-4J	Bobcats	disestablished 1992
VT-25	C	TA-4J	Cougars	disestablished 1992
VT-26	C	T-2C	Tigers	disestablished May 1992
VT-27	G	T-34C	Boomers	Primary/Intermediate
VT-28	G	T-44A	Rangers	Maritime patrol
VT-31	G	T-44A	Wise Owls	Maritime patrol
VT-86	F	T-2C T-39N	Sabre Hawks	Advanced NFO

These 18 squadrons provide fixed-wing training for Navy, Marine Corps, Coast Guard, and foreign pilots and air crewmen under the direction of the Naval Air Training Command. The single-letter tail codes indicate training wings:

Code	Wing	Location
A	TraWing-1	NAS Meridian, Miss.
B	TraWing-2	NAS Kingsville, Texas
E	TraWing-5	NAS Whiting Field, Fla.
F	TraWing-6	NAS Pensacola, Fla.
G	TraWing-4	NAS Corpus Christi, Texas

TraWing-4 changed from the letter D to G in 1983. TraWing-3 (code letter C) was disestablished on 31 August 1992.

The T-45A, TA-4J, and T-2C aircraft are carrier capable and enable students to practice landings aboard the carrier training ship in the Gulf of Mexico. VT-21 began operating the long-delayed T-45 Goshawk in mid-1992; the plane will eventually replace the surviving TA-4J Skyhawks in VT-22 and VT-23.

VT-4 changed its role in 1986 from intermediate strike training (with T-2C and TA-4J aircraft) to prepare pilots for E-2 and C-2 carrier qualification ("carquals") (with VAW-110 and VAW-120). VT-86 ceased flying the TA-4J in late 1991 (flown by the squadron since 1974); it was replaced by the T-2C.

VT-7 is the largest squadron in the Navy, with some 60 Skyhawks. The T-39Ns of TraWing-6 are refurbished Sabreliners used to train Naval Flight Officers (NFO). They are flown and maintained by contractor personnel, replacing T-47A aircraft that were operated under a similar arrangement.

Historical: The letters T and HT (helicopter) have been used for naval aircraft designations since shortly after World War II; however, VT and HT were not used for squadron designations until 1 May 1960, when 17 training units were redesignated as training squadrons (VT).[11]

---

11. From the 1920s until 15 November 1946, VT indicated torpedo squadron.

ANTARCTIC DEVELOPMENT SQUADRONS

Squadron	Code	Aircraft	Name
VXE-6	XD	LC-130F/R, UH-1N	Puckered Penguins

VXE-6, home-ported at Point Mugu, provides air support of U.S. Antarctic programs sponsored by the National Science Foundation. The squadron flies from McMurdo when operating in Antarctica. It flies six UH-1N Huey helicopters plus two LC-130F and four LC-130R ski-equipped Hercules (a seventh aircraft will become available in 1993; see page 430).

Historical: The U.S. Navy has had aviation interests in the Antarctic since 1928 when retired Commander Richard E. Byrd took four civilian aircraft on his first expedition to the South Pole.[12] Major Navy support began with Byrd's 1939–1940 expedition, and on his 1947–1948 expedition there were 19 Navy fixed-wing aircraft and 4 helicopters, including six R4D/C-47 transports that took off from the aircraft carrier PHILIPPINE SEA (CV 47).

Squadron VXE-6 was originally established as Air Development Squadron 6 (VX-6) on 17 January 1955, specifically for Antarctic operations (Operation Deepfreeze); the squadron was redesignated VXE-6 on 1 January 1969.

OCEANOGRAPHIC DEVELOPMENT SQUADRONS

Squadron	Code	Aircraft	Name
VXN-8	JB	RP-3D	World Travelers

VXN-8 at NAS Patuxent River operates five RP-3D Orion aircraft in support of worldwide research projects; one RP-3D is assigned to each of the three projects: Project Magnet is a gravity and geomagnetic study; Project Birdseye is an ice reconnaissance and physical oceanography study; and Project Seascan is an aerial oceanographic effort.[13] Two RP-3D aircraft are provided for multi-mission research. The squadron, assigned to Patrol Wings Atlantic, previously flew the RP-3A and UP-3A, the last of the earlier Orions being retired in 1991.

In addition, the Naval Research Laboratory in Washington, D.C., operates four research-configured P-3 aircraft in support of worldwide scientific research projects. Based at NAS Patuxent River, Md., these Orions are an EP-3A (gravimetric and ocean floor spreading studies), EP-3B (EW research), RP-3A (space sensing applications), and modified P-3B (various research activities); the aircraft have "NRL" and the American flag on their tail fins (no code letters).

Historical: VXN-8 had its beginnings as Airborne Early Warning Training Unit Atlantic, which in 1951 was assigned Project Magnet. Projects Birdseye and Outpost Seascan were assigned in 1962 and Project Jenny in July 1965. The last was to provide radio and television broadcasts to South Vietnam pending the completion of ground facilities. Subsequently, the unit became the Oceanographic Airborne Survey Unit and, on 1 July 1967, Air Development Squadron (VX) 8. It was changed to VXN-8 in January 1969.

12. While Byrd was on the expedition, on 21 December 1928 Congress promoted him to the rank of rear admiral on the retired list.
13. These aircraft are named "Roadrunner," "El Coyote," and "Arctic Fox," and are emblazoned with distinctive cartoon characters on their fuselages.

FLIGHT DEMONSTRATION TEAMS

Code	Aircraft	Name
BA	F/A-18A/B, TC-130G	Blue Angels

The Blue Angels is the Navy-Marine Corps flight demonstration team, performing throughout the United States to encourage aviation recruiting. The unit currently flies six early-model F/A-18A Hornets (eight F/A-18A and one two-seat F/A-18B). The F/A-18s are not carrier capable, have had their gun removed, and are provided with smoke generators, improved flight control systems, and additional navigation equipment. A Marine-owned TC-130G Hercules known as "Fat Albert" is assigned to the team as a support aircraft.

The tail code BA is not shown on Blue Angels aircraft; they have blue-and-gold livery with large numerals indicating the aircraft place in formation.

Historical: Established in 1946, the "Blues" have flown a succession of first-line naval aircraft: F6F Hellcat, F8F Bearcat, F9F-2 and F9F-5 Panther, F9F-6 Cougar, F11F Tiger, F-4J Phantom, A-4F Skyhawk, and, since November 1986, the F/A-18 Hornet.

An F/A-18 of the Blue Angels flight demonstration team releases colored smoke during an air show. These aircraft are painted blue and gold, with their formation numbers on the tail fin. The team is popularly referred to as "the Blues." (PH1 Bruce R. Trombecky, USN)

HELICOPTER COMBAT SUPPORT SQUADRONS

Squadron	Code	Aircraft	Name
HC-1*	UP	SH-3G, CH-53E	Pacific Fleet Angels
HC-2*	HU	SH-3G/H, H-53E, VH-3A	Circuit Riders
HC-3	SA	HH-46D, CH-46D, UH-46D	Packrats
HC-4*	HC	CH-53E	Black Stallions
HC-5*	RB	HH-46D	Providers
HC-6*	HW	CH-46D, HH-46D, UH-46A/D	Chargers
HC-8*	BR	CH-46D, HH-46D, UH-46D	Dragon Whales
HC-11*	VR	CH-46D, HH-46D	Gunbearers
HC-16	BF	SH-3D, HH-1N	Bullfrogs

Most of these squadrons provide helicopter detachments for Search And Rescue (SAR) and replenishment (VERTREP/VOD) operations in direct support of the fleet. HC-1, based at NAS North Island, provides utility helicopters for the command ship BLUE RIDGE (LCC 19) as well as for fleet logistic support and provides readiness/transition training. HC-2 at NAS Norfolk, established in April 1987, has SH-3G Sea Kings for VIP transport as well as two CH-53E Super Stallions for fleet replenishment; the squadron uses Sea Kings for a regular VIP ferry service between Norfolk and the Pentagon. HC-3 and HC-11 are also at NAS North Island, near the center of San Diego, with HC-3 conducting all Navy readiness/transition training for the H-46 Sea Knight. HC-3 was established in 1967. HC-4,

established in 1983 at NAS Sigonella, Sicily, provides logistics support for the Sixth Fleet with six CH-53Es. HC-5 at NAS Agana provides detachments to the Seventh Fleet for VERTREP operations; the squadron, with 12 Sea Knights, also flies a variety of secondary missions on Guam, including SAR, medical evacuation, VIP transport, and support of local police agencies. HC-6 and HC-8 at NAS Norfolk support Atlantic Fleet ships.

HC-16 is at NAS Pensacola; previously designated HCT-16 from 1974 to 1977, the squadron provided readiness training for Sea Knight crewmen until 1983, when HC-3 took over that role, in turn giving the Pacific Fleet's seagoing VERTREP duties to HC-5 and HC-11. HC-16 then became the readiness squadron for all Navy UH-1N Hueys in addition to providing SAR helicopters for the training carrier in the Gulf of Mexico.

Historical: The genesis of these squadrons was VX-3, the Navy's first helicopter squadron, established in 1947.[14] The following year VX-3 was split into helicopter utility squadrons HU-1 and HU-2, on the West and East Coasts, respectively. All helicopter utility squadrons (HU) were changed to combat support squadrons (HC) on 1 July 1965.

14. During World War II all U.S. Navy helicopter development was undertaken by the Coast Guard.

CH-46 Sea Knight helicopters from HC-5 transfer supplies from the replenishment ship SAN JOSE (AFS 7) to the missile cruiser VINCENNES (CG 49) during UNREP operations in the Indian Ocean. VERTREP operations can be conducted at much greater ranges, if necessary. (U.S. Navy)

HELICOPTER MINE COUNTERMEASURES SQUADRONS

Squadron	Code	Aircraft	Name
HM-12	DH	CH/MH-53E	Seadragons
HM-14*	BJ	MH-53E	Vanguard
HM-15*	TB	MH-53E	Blackhawks

Squadron HM-12 at Norfolk is the Airborne Mine Countermeasures (AMCM) readiness training with HM-14 at Norfolk and HM-15 at NAS Alameda deployable AMCM squadrons. Originally HM-14 and HM-16 were established in 1978 for operational deployments, but HM-16 was subsequently disestablished and HM-15 established at Alameda for Pacific deployments.

HM-14 has 11 MH-53E Sea Dragon helicopters and HM-15 has 12, with 4 assigned to HM-15. Eventually the two deploying squadrons are to have eight each with five in the readiness squadron. (Another 17 aircraft will be in the pipeline for test and evaluation.) The earlier RH-53D Sea Stallion serves in reserve HM squadrons pending the acquisition of additional MH-53E variants for those units.

HM-12 provides training for VERTREP/VOD helicopter operations as well as mine countermeasures.

Historical: The Navy employed helicopters for mine-spotting in the Korean War (1950–1953), and beginning in September 1966 squadrons HC-6 and HC-7 provided RH-3A Sea King detachments for mine countermeasure operations. Those helicopters flew from the USS CATSKILL (MCS 1) and OZARK (MCS 2).

HM-12 was established on 1 April 1971 as the world's first helicopter mine countermeasures squadron. Initially flying Navy and Marine CH-53A Sea Stallions and then the specialized RH-53D, HM-12 operated off North Vietnam in 1972 (Operation Endsweep), at the northern end of the Suez Canal in 1974 (Nimbus Star) and again in 1975 (Nimbus Stream), and in the Red Sea in 1984. These squadrons flew MH-53E helicopters in the Persian Gulf area in the late 1980s (escorting Kuwaiti merchant ships) and in Operation Desert Storm and the subsequent mine cleanup.

HELICOPTER ANTI-SUBMARINE SQUADRONS

Squadron	Aircraft	Name
HS-1	SH-3G/H, SH-60F	Seahorses (AR)
HS-2	SH-60F, HH-60H	Golden Falcons
HS-3*	SH-60F, HH-60H	Tridents
HS-4	SH-60F, HH-60H	Black Knights
HS-5*	SH-3H	Night Dippers
HS-6	SH-60F, HH-60H	Indians
HS-7*	SH-3H	Shamrocks
HS-8*	SH-3H	Eight Ballers
HS-9*	SH-3H	Sea Griffins
HS-10	SH-60F	Task Masters (RA)
HS-11*	SH-3H	Dragon Slayers
HS-12*	SH-3H	Wyverns
HS-14*	SH-3H	Chargers
HS-15	SH-60F, HH-60H	Red Lions

Helicopter ASW squadrons are assigned to all carrier air wings, with most currently flying six SH-3H Sea Kings; HS-5 had eight SH-3H Sea Kings in 1990–1991. All are converting to the SH-60F, the first fleet squadron to receive the SH-60F being HS-2, taking delivery in March 1990. Beginning with HS-6 in September 1990, these squadrons were additionally provided with two HH-60H combat SAR helicopters in addition to six SH-60B variants.

The last squadrons to be formed were HS-17, established in 1984, and HS-16, in 1987. With the decommissioning of CVW-10 and CVW-13, HS-16 was disestablished on 1 June 1988, and HS-17 was disestablished on 2 July 1991. Readiness/transition training for HS squadrons is provided by HS-1 at NAS Jacksonville and by HS-10 at NAS North Island (San Diego). Atlantic Fleet HS and HSL squadrons report to Helicopter Wings Atlantic and the Pacific squadrons to ASW Wing Pacific.

Historical: The first helicopter ASW squadron was HS-1, established on 3 October 1951, flying Sikorsky HO4S-1 helicopters.

LIGHT HELICOPTER ANTI-SUBMARINE SQUADRONS

Squadron	Code	Aircraft	Name
HSL-30	HT	SH-2F	Neptune's Horsemen
HSL-31	TD	SH-2F	Archangels
HSL-32*	HV	SH-2F	Tridents
HSL-33*	TF	SH-2F	Sea Snakes
HSL-34*	HX	SH-2F	Green Checkers
HSL-35*	TG	SH-2F	Magicians
HSL-36*	HY	SH-2F	Lamp Lighters
HSL-37*	TH	SH-2F, SH-60B	Easy Riders
HSL-40	HK	SH-60B	Airwolves
HSL-41	TS	SH-60B	Seahawks
HSL-42*	HN	SH-60B	Proud Warriors
HSL-43*	TT	SH-60B	Battlecats
HSL-44*	HP	SH-60B	Swamp Foxes
HSL-45*	TZ	SH-60B	Wolfpack
HSL-46*	HQ	SH-60B	Grand Masters
HSL-47*	TY	SH-60B	Saberhawks
HSL-48*	HR	SH-60B	Vipers
HSL-49*	TX	SH-60B	Scorpions
HSL-51	TA	SH-60B	Warlords

The HSL squadrons provide detachments of ASW helicopters for deployments on board cruisers, destroyers, and frigates. Each operational squadron has 10 to 13 aircraft. Squadrons HSL-30 at Norfolk and HSL-31 at North Island provided SH-2F readiness training for the Atlantic and Pacific squadrons, respectively. HSL-31 was disestablished on 31 July 1992, with all LAMPS I training being shifted to HSL-30.

The first Seahawk squadron was HSL-41, established on 21 January 1983 at NAS North Island as the SH-60B readiness training squadron; the first SH-60B fleet squadrons were established the following year. The last Atlantic squadron (HSL-49) was established on 23 March 1990; HSL-51 was established on 1 October 1991 to operate helicopters from Japan-based ships, flying from Atsugi, Japan. HSL-37 at NAS Barbers Point became the only composite SH-2F/SH-60B squadron in early 1992 to support LAMPS operations aboard Pearl Harbor–based ships. HSL-40 is the Atlantic SH-60B readiness squadron.

The improved SH-2G had been developed to succeed the SH-2F in the LAMPS role; however, that program was cancelled in early 1992.

Historical: The first SH-2D LAMPS were assigned to helicopter combat support squadrons HC-4 and HC-5, which were redesignated HSL-30 and HSL-31, respectively, on 1 March 1972.

HELICOPTER TRAINING SQUADRONS

Squadron	Code	Name	Aircraft	Training
HT-8	E	(none)	TH-57C	Basic Helicopter
HT-18	E	(none)	TH-57C	Advanced Helicopter

These squadrons provide helicopter training for Navy, Marine Corps, Coast Guard, and foreign pilots. Students first fly fixed-wing T-34 aircraft before going into helicopters. The squadrons are numbered in the same series as VT squadrons and are part of Training Wing 5.

HT-18 previously operated variants of the UH-1 Huey in addition to TH-57A SeaRanger helicopters.

Historical: HT-8 traces its history to HTU-1 established in 1950, changed to HTG-1 in 1957, and to HT-8 in 1960. HT-18 was established in 1972.

NAVAL AIR STATIONS/NAVAL AVIATION ACTIVITIES

Code	Activity
4L	Naval Air Warfare Center Lakehurst, N.J.
4M	NAS Memphis, Tenn.
7A	NAS Patuxent River, Md.
7C	NAS Norfolk, Va.
7E	NAS Jacksonville, Fla.
7F	NAS Brunswick, Me.
7G	NAS Whidbey Island, Wash.
7H	NAS Fallon, Nev.
7J	NAS Alameda, Calif.
7K	NAS Memphis, Tenn.
7L	Naval Air Warfare Center Point Mugu, Calif.
7M	NAS North Island, San Diego, Calif.
7N	NAF Washington, D.C.*
7P	Naval Air Warfare Center China Lake, Calif.
7Q	NAS Key West, Val.
7R	NAS Oceana, Va.
7S	NAS Lemoore, Calif.
7T	Naval Air Warfare Center Patuxent River, Md.
7U	NAS Cecil Field, Fla.
7V	NAS Glenview, Ill.
7W	NAS Willow Grove, Penna.
7X	NAS New Orleans, La.
7Y	NAF Detroit, Mich.
7Z	NAS New South Weymouth, Mass.
8A	NAF Atsugi, Japan
8B	NAS Cubi Point, Philippines
8C	NAS Sigonella, Sicily
8D	Naval Station Rota, Spain
8E	Naval Station Roosevelt Roads, P.R.
8F	NAS Guantánomo, Cuba
8G	NAF Mildenhall, England
8H	NAF Kadena, Okinawa
8J	Naval Station Guam, Marianas
8K	Middle East Force, Bahrain
8M	NAF Misawa, Japan
8N	NAF El Centro, Calif.
8P	NAS Guantánamo, Cuba
8U	NAF Mayport, Fla.

*NAF Washington is located at Andrews Air Force Base near the Washington suburb of Suitland, Md.

These number-letter codes are given to utility and light transport aircraft assigned to the bases and other activities indicated above. The Strike Directorate of the Flight Test and Engineering Group at Patuxent River, Md., is assigned the code SD.

In a far-ranging reorganization of Navy research activities, in 1991–1992 the Naval Air Test Center at Lakehurst, Pacific Missile Test Center at Point Mugu, Naval Weapons Center at China Lake, and Naval Air Test Center at Patuxent River all became components of the new Naval Air Warfare Center.

NAVAL AIR RESERVE

The Naval Air Reserve operates approximately 450 aircraft. These are organized primarily into 2 carrier air wings, 13 maritime patrol squadrons, and 9 helicopter squadrons plus several support and transport squadrons.

Under the direction of Secretary of the Navy John Lehman, a reserve naval aviator, there was a major upgrading of reserve aircraft in the 1980s. An earlier Navy plan to decommission up to 12 squadrons (HAL, HS, VC, VR) in the 1980s was halted by congressional pressure.

All air reserve units are assigned to the Commander, Naval Air Reserve Force based at New Orleans, La. The major air reserve subordinate commands are Reserve Patrol Wing Atlantic and Reserve Patrol Wing Pacific that control the VP squadrons; the Reserve Helicopter Wing that directs reserve HCS, HM, HSL, and HS squadrons; and the Reserve Tactical Support Wing that supervises VFC and VR squadrons.

Squadrons within the two reserve carrier air wings, except for the AEW squadrons, are designated in sequence based on the wing designation. Non-carrier air wing squadrons have designations in the standard Navy squadron numberical series. The VF, VFA, and VA squadrons are normally assigned 12 aircraft each, the VAQ and VAW squadrons four aircraft each.

The two reserve carrier air wings (CVWR) were commissioned on 1 April 1970. There are no ASW aircraft (S-3 Viking, SH-3 Sea King, or SH-60 Seahawk) assigned to these wings.[15] However, current planning provides for the existing HS (SH-3H) squadrons to be reassigned to the carrier wings in wartime if the units are not needed elsewhere (i.e., to compensate for a shortfall of LAMPS helicopters in active fleet destroyers and cruisers). Three of the helicopter anit-submarine squadrons have converted from SH-3G Sea Kings to the SH-2F LAMPS I helicopters, which operate from NRF frigates. Three reserve HAL/HC squadrons have been merged to form two combat support (HCS) squadrons.

15. When CVWR-20 and CVWR-30 were commissioned, the Navy established two reserve ASW air groups, CVSGR-70 and CVSGR-80 on 1 May 1970.

RESERVE CARRIER AIR WINGS

Wing	Codes	Squadron	Aircraft	Location
CVWR-20	AF	VF-201	F-14A	NAS Dallas, Texas
		VF-202	F-14A	NAS Dallas, Texas
		VFA-203	F/A-18A	NAS Cecil Field, Fla.
		VFA-204	F/A-18A	NAS New Orleans, La.
		VA-205	A-6E, KA-6D	NAS Atlanta, Ga.
		VAQ-209	EA-6B	NAF Washington, D.C.
		VAW-78	E-2C	NAS Norfolk, Va.
CVWR-30	ND	VF-301	F-14A	NAS Miramar, Calif.
		VF-302	F-14A	NAS Miramar, Calif.
		VFA-303	F/A-18A	NAS Lemoore, Calif.
		VA-304	A-6E, KA-6D	NAS Alameda, Calif.
		VFA-305	F/A-18A	NAS Point Mugu, Calif.
		VAQ-309	EA-6B	NAS Whidbey Island, Wash.
		VAW-88	E-2C	NAS Miramar, Calif.

ATTACK SQUADRONS

Six reserve VA squadrons—three per wing—flew the A-7, the last being VA-204, which became VFA-204 on 1 May 1991. Two squadrons traded in their Corsairs for A-6E and KA-6D Intruders; the four others shifted to F/A-18 Hornets (see below). Earlier, all six squadrons flew the trouble-plagued A-7B model, and before that the A-4 Skyhawk.

The KA-6D tankers are assigned to these units to replace the KA-3B Skywarrior in the in-flight refueling role.

FIGHTER SQUADRONS

All four reserve fighter squadrons now fly the F-14A Tomcat, having replaced the F-4 Phantom. VF-301 became the first fully operational reserve F-14A squadron in October 1986. The last naval squadron to fly the Phantom was VF-202, which transitioned from the F-4S to the F-14A in early 1987; the Phantom flew in the Marine air reserve until January 1992.

ATTACK/STRIKE FIGHTER SQUADRONS

The F/A-18 Hornet has replaced the A-7E Corsairs in four attack squadrons. VA-303 became the first Naval Reserve squadron to fly the F/A-18 Hornet, acquiring its first aircraft in 1985. With the F/A-18 these units became VFA squadrons vice VA.

FIGHTER COMPOSITE SQUADRONS

Squadron	Code	Aircraft	Location
VFC-12	JY	A-4F	NAS Oceana, Va.
VFC-13	UX	A-4F	NAS Miramar, Calif.

These squadrons provide ACM training for reserve and active fighter and attack squadrons. Each VFC squadron flies 12 aircraft; they have discarded their TA-4J Skyhawks.

The squadrons were previously designated VC-12 and VC-13, respectively; changed to VFC on 22 April 1988 to reflect the emphasis on adversary training.

RECONNAISSANCE SQUADRONS

The last specialized Navy reconnaissance squadron, VFP-206 flying the RF-8G Photo Crusader, was disestablished on 1 April 1987. This was a light photo-reconnaissance squadron. The unit was based at NAF Washington, D.C. One reserve F-14 squadron in each wing provides a photo-reconnaissance capability with TARPS pods.

TACTICAL AERIAL REFUELING SQUADRONS

The two reserve tanker squadrons (VAK) have been disestablished, VAK-308 on 30 September 1988, and VAK-208 on 30 September 1989. They were changed from tactical EW squadrons (VAQ) to tanker units on 1 October 1979, reflecting the primary role of their Skywarriors. They flew KA-3B Skywarriors. (The active Navy did not have specialized tanker squadrons.)

Refueling for reserve units is now undertaken by KA-6D Intruders in VA-205 and VA-304.

TACTICAL ELECTRONIC COUNTERMEASURES SQUADRONS

These two VAQ squadrons were established in 1977 and 1979, respectively, to provide the reserve air wings with an organic ECM capability. The reserve VAQ squadrons flew the EA-6A Intruder until 1989, when they began to fly the more-capable EA-6B Prowler.

AIRBORNE EARLY-WARNING SQUADRONS

The first E-2C variant of the Hawkeye to be flown by the reserves was assigned to VAW-78 in 1983; VAW-88 began receiving the E-2C in 1986. These squadrons have assisted in U.S. drug enforcement surveillance efforts, as have active AEW squadrons.

Note that VAW-78 and VAW-88, both established in 1970, are not numbered in the standard CVWR designation scheme of assigning squadron designations related to air wing number. They were formerly assigned to the now established reserve ASW groups.

PATROL SQUADRONS

Squadron	Code	Aircraft	Location
VP-60	LS	P-3B	NAS Glenview, Ill.
VP-62	LT	P-3C	NAS Jacksonville, Fla.
VP-64	LU	P-3B	NAS Willow Grove, Penna.
VP-65	PG	P-3C	NAS Point Mugu, Calif.
VP-66	LV	P-3B	NAS Willow Grove, Penna.
VP-67	PL	P-3B	NAS Memphis, Tenn.
VP-68	LW	P-3C	NAF Washington, D.C.
VP-69	PJ	P-3B	NAS Whidbey Island, Wash.
VP-90	LX	P-3B	NAS Glenview, Ill.
VP-91*	PM	P-3C	NAS Moffett, Calif.
VP-92	LY	P-3C	NAS South Weymouth, Mass.
VP-93	LH	P-3B	NAF Detroit, Mich.
VP-94	LZ	P-3B	NAS New Orleans, La.

These squadrons each fly eight Orion patrol aircraft (previously nine). The reserve P-3s regularly supplement active squadrons in U.S. and overseas operational deployments. The reserve VP force, long with a strength of 13 squadrons, will be reduced to nine by 1993 if Congress approves the reductions.

Five squadrons fly the P-3C variant, the others P-3B; the first to transition to the P-3C was VP-62. The last reserve-flown P-3A was retired by VP-69 in October 1990. VP-67 was the last squadron to fly the SP-2H Neptune, completing transition to the Orion in 1979. VP-68 shifted from NAS Patuxent to NAF Washington in 1985.

Two VP master Augmentation Units (VP-MAU) were based at NAS Brunswick (code LB) and NAS Moffett Field (code PS). These units—with P-3C, UP-3A, and TP-3A Orions—trained crews to augment fleet VP squadrons and often operated detachments overseas, with VP-MAU Moffett Field operating one aircraft and crew in Desert Storm. The two units were disestablished in 1991.

FLEET LOGISTICS SUPPORT SQUADRONS

Squadron	Code	Aircraft	Location
VR-46	JS	DC-9	NAS Atlanta, Ga.
VR-48	RJ	C-130T	NAF Washington, D.C.
VR-51	RV	C-9B	NAS Glenview, Ill.
VR-52	JT	DC-9	NAS Willow Grove, Penna.
VR-53*	WV	C-130T	NAF Washington, D.C.
VR-54	CW	C-130T	NAS New Orleans, La.
VR-55*	RU	C-9B	NAS Alameda, Calif.
VR-56	JU	C-9B	NAS Norfolk, Va.
VR-57*	RX	C-9B	NAS North Island, Calif.
VR-58*	JV	C-9B	NAS Jacksonville, Fla.
VR-59*	RY	C-9B	NAS Dallas, Texas
VR-60	RT	DC-9	NAS Memphis, Tenn.
VR-61	RS	DC-9	NAS Whidbey Island, Wash.
VR-62	JW	DC-9	NAF Detroit, Mich.

These squadrons provide transport support for active Navy and reserve activities within the United States and, on a limited basis, overseas. Most of the 13 squadrons have two or three C-9B aircraft or ex-commercial DC-9 aircraft. VR-54, established on 1 June 1991, has six C-130T Hercules, the first "Herks" in reserve service, followed by VR-53 as a C-130T operator. VR-48 flew the C-131H Samaritan, the last one being retired in mid-1990. These squadrons have multiple crews for their aircraft.

VR-53 is scheduled to move to Martinsburg, W.Va.; however, there has been strong congressional opposition to the move.

The C-118 Liftmaster aircraft, long flown by the Naval Reserve, has been discarded; the last C-118B retired in 1985. (The C-118 was originally designated R6D by the Navy; changed in the 1962 redesignation action.)

HELICOPTER COMBAT SAR/SPECIAL WARFARE SUPPORT SQUADRONS

Squadron	Code	Aircraft	Location
HCS-4*	NW	HH-60H	NAS Norfolk, Va.
HCS-5*	NW	HH-60H	NAS Point Mugu, Calif.

These squadrons were established in 1989 to provide combat SAR and special-warfare support for active and reserve operations. Each squadron flies six HH-60H Seahawk helicopters. During Operations Desert Shield/Desert Storm, these two squadrons deployed HH-60H helicopters as a joint unit into Saudi Arabia for combat SAR operations. The HH-60H is the Navy's only dedicated combat SAR helicopter; it is also being integrated into HS anti-submarine squadrons (see page 386). The Coast Guard flies the HH-60J version of the Blackhawk/Seahawk helicopter.

These squadrons took over the functions of reserve helicopter light attack squadrons HAL-4 and HAL-5, which flew the HH-1K Huey in support of riverine and special operations, and of helicopter composite squadron HC-9, which flew the HH-3A in the combat SAR role. The reserve HALs also had anti-terrorist support roles, working with SEAL units.

No helicopter squadrons are assigned to the two reserve air wings.

Historical: HAL-4 and HAL-5 were established in 1976–1977 as helicopter gunship units. The Navy's only active gunship unit was HAL-3, established in 1967 and disestablished in 1972 after extensive service in Vietnam.

HC-9 was established on 1 August 1975 and disestablished on 31 July 1990.

HELICOPTER MINE COUNTERMEASURES SQUADRONS

Squadron	Code	Aircraft	Location
HM-18	NW	RH-53D	NAS Norfolk, Va.
HM-19	NW	RH-53D	NAS Alameda, Calif.

Reserve mine countermeasure squadron HM-18 was established in 1986 and HM-19 in 1989. Each squadron flies five RH-53D Sea Stallion helicopters. Twelve MH-53E Sea Dragon helicopters are being processed for these squadrons.

HELICOPTER ANTI-SUBMARINE SQUADRONS

Squadron	Code	Aircraft	Location
HS-75*	NW	SH-3H	NAS Jacksonville, Fla.
HS-85	NW	SH-3H	NAS Alameda, Calif.

These ASW helicopters are capable of operating from carriers with the two reserve air wings, but they are not assigned to those wings.

Operational: On 3 February 1991, an SH-3H of HS-75 rescued the three surviving crewmen of an Air Force B-52 that crashed at sea while approaching Diego Garcia in the Indian Ocean. (It was the only B-52 lost during Operation Desert Storm.)

LIGHT HELICOPTER ANTI-SUBMARINE SQUADRONS

Squadron	Code	Aircraft	Location
HSL-74	NW	SH-2F	NAS South Weymouth, Mass.
HSL-84	NW	SH-2F	NAS North Island, Calif.
HSL-94	NW	SH-2F	NAS Willow Grove, Penna.

HSL-75 and HSL-84 are former reserve HS units that flew the SH-3G Sea King. They were changed to HSL for the LAMPS role on 1 January 1985 and 1 March 1984, respectively. HSL-94 was established on October 1985. They provide ASW helicopters for NRF frigates.

CHIEF OF NAVAL AIR RESERVE

The Chief of Naval Air Reserve has several aircraft assigned, mostly C-12, C-20, and CT-39D/G transports and training aircraft. These are based at various air stations.

Code	Location
6A	Washington, D.C.
6F	Jacksonville, Fla.
6G	Alameda, Calif.
6M	Memphis, Tenn.
6S	NAS Norfolk, Va.

These aircraft were formerly assigned to Naval Air Reserve Units (NARU).

MARINE AVIATION

The U.S. Marine Corps currently operates some 1,100 aircraft in three active aircraft wings plus 100 in a reserve wing. It is the only Marine force in the world with a major air arm (Britain's Royal Marines fly helicopters and light fixed-wing aircraft, while the Russian Naval Infantry has some helicopters assigned).

Marine aviation has undergone major aircraft changes in the past few years with the advanced AV-8B Harrier replacing the earlier AV-8A/C Vertical/Short Take-Off and Landing (VSTOL) aircraft, and variants of the F/A-18 Hornet replacing the A-4 Skyhawk, A-6 Intruder, and RF-4 and F-4 Phantom. Further, the cancellation of the A-12 Avenger all-weather attack aircraft and the Navy's shortfall of A-6E Intruders have led to transfer of Marine A-6Es to the Navy, with replacement by the F/A-18D. The two-place, all-weather Hornet, however, has less range and a smaller weapons capacity than the A-6E but is a more flexible aircraft.

Marine aviation had a major role in the Gulf War during January–February 1991, with most Marine aircraft flying from shore bases in Saudi Arabia. AV-8B Harriers from squadron VMA-331 flew from the assault ship NASSAU in the Persian Gulf, while Marine helicopters flew from more than 30 other U.S. Navy amphibious ships in the Gulf area. (Most Marine air strikes were flown against Iraqi positions in Kuwait, with Marine helicopters and fixed-wing aircraft providing close air support, troop transport, and logistics support to the 1st and 2nd Marine Divisions' drive into Kuwait. There was no amphibious landing in the Gulf, although Marines were flown ashore by helicopter to reinforce those divisions in the drive into Kuwait.)

During Desert Storm all Marine aircraft ashore in Saudi Arabia were assigned to the 3rd Marine Aircraft Wing, with the 4th and 5th Marine Expeditionary Brigades being assigned aircraft on board the amphibious ships in the Persian Gulf.

ORGANIZATION

The Marine aircraft wing (MAW) is the major aviation command of the Marine Corps. There are three active and one reserve Marine aircraft wings that are assigned all fixed-wing and rotary-wing aircraft except for a few utility and cargo aircraft. The wings vary in size and composition—an active wing having some 300 aircraft of all types. Unlike Navy wings, in which the principal subordinate command is the squadron, the Marine aircraft wings have several groups, as shown in the accompanying chart showing a nominal Marine aircraft wing. *Major air wing changes are being made; see Addenda.*

The Marine aircraft groups (MAG) each control specific aircraft squadron types, i.e., fighter and attack, and helicopters. Several aircraft are attached to wing headquarters and support squadrons.

NOMINAL MARINE AIRCRAFT WING[16]

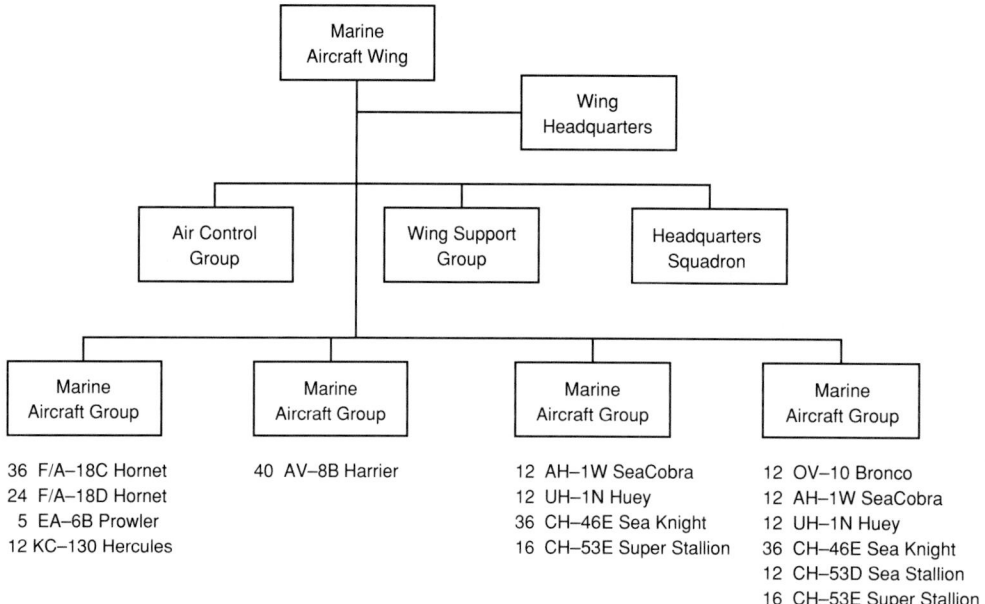

The principal components of the standard wing are:

Marine Wing Headquarters Squadron: Provides command, administration, and camp facilities for the wing headquarters.

Marine Air Control Group: Provides communications, air control, and air support squadrons for the operation of the wing; it also contains a light anti-aircraft missile battalion (with 16 Hawk missile launchers) and a low-altitude air defense battalion (with 90 Stinger missile teams). The air-support squadron provides control and coordination for aircraft operating in direct support of Marine ground forces.

Marine Wing Support Group: Provides fixed-wing and helicopter support with respect to maintenance, mess, medical, supply, and transportation, weather, and airfield services.

Marine Aerial Refueler Transport Squadron: Operates KC-130 aircraft to provide refueling and transport services for the wing. In theory, each wing is assigned one VMGR squadron.

Marine Tactical Electronic Warfare Detachment: Operates EA-6B aircraft to provide electronic warfare support and countermeasures for the wing.

The 1st MAW is based at Iwakuni, Japan, and Futenma on Okinawa, where the wing headquarters is located. However, most of

16. None of the wings exactly match this nominal organization.

its aircraft squadrons are on rotation to the Far East on a six-month basis from Marine Aircraft Group 24 at Kanehoe, Hawaii, the 2nd and 3rd MAWs. (Marine Aircraft Group 24 is assigned to the 1st Marine Expeditionary Brigade on Oahu, Hawaii.) The 2nd MAW, with headquarters at Cherry Point, N.C., has aircraft squadrons based on the East Coast, while the 3rd MAW, with headquarters at MCAS El Toro, Calif., has its squadrons on the West Coast and at Yuma, Ariz.

An aircraft wing is generally paired with a reinforced division to form a Marine Expeditionary Force (MEF), an air group with a reinforced regiment to form a Marine Expeditionary Brigade (MEB), and a composite squadron with a reinforced battalion to form a Marine Expeditionary Unit (MEU); see chapter 6.

A composite squadron generally consists of 4 CH-53E, 12 CH-46E, 4 AH-1W, and 2 UH-1N helicopters deployed on board an LHA/LHD/LPH and accompanying amphibious ships. Additionally, AV-8B Harriers may also be assigned to the squadron, depending upon mission and aircraft and ship availability.

Asterisks indicate units that participated in Operations Desert Shield/Desert Storm in 1990–1991.

UNIT DESIGNATIONS

The Marine Corps uses the standard naval squadron designation scheme except that the second letter *M* indicates Marine aviation squadrons; the suffix *T* indicates Marine training squadrons.

MARINE ATTACK SQUADRONS

Squadron	Code	Aircraft
VMAT-203	KD	AV-8B/TAV-8B
VMA-211	CF	AV-8B
VMA-214	WE	AV-8B
VMA-223	WP	AV-8B
VMA(AW)-224*	WK	A-6E
VMA-231*	CG	AV-8B
VMA-311*	WL	AV-8B
VMA-331*	VL	AV-8B
VMA(AW)-332	EA	A-6E
VMA-513*	WF	AV-8B
VMA(AW)-533*	ED	A-6E
VMA-542*	CR	AV-8B

Marine attack squadrons are being reduced, several having converted to the multi-purpose F/A-18 Hornet and redesignated as VMFA squadrons. The A-6E Intruder all-weather attack aircraft is being phased out entirely (with aircraft transferred to the Navy). VMA(AW)-121 in late 1989 became the first of several A-6E squadrons to shift to the F/A-18D, becoming VMFA(AW); see page 392. The eight other Marine attack squadrons now fly the AV-8B Harrier VSTOL attack aircraft with VMAT-203 at Cherry Point, N.C., providing Harrier readiness and transition training.

Harrier squadrons have 20 aircraft. The F/A-18 squadrons have 12 aircraft. Two AV-8B squadrons are to be deactivated by fiscal 1994.

Historical: VMA-513 was the first operational Harrier squadron, with AV-8A deliveries beginning in April 1971; all AV-8A/C models of the Harrier have been retired. The A-6E has been flown by the Marines since 1964. The last active-duty A-4M Skyhawk squadron was VMA-211, which shifted to Harriers in 1992.

MARINE ELECTRONIC WARFARE SQUADRONS

Squadron	Code	Aircraft
VMAQ-1	CB	EA-6B
VMAQ-2*	CY	EA-6B
VMAQ-3	MD	EA-6B
VMAQ-4	RM	EA-6B

The Marine Corps established four EW squadrons in 1992, replacing the single active-duty squadron (VMAQ-2 with code CY) and reserve squadron VMAQ-4 (RM). Each of the new squadrons has five EA-6B Prowlers.

Historical: The Marine Corps originally operated EW and photo-reconnaissance aircraft in three composite reconnaissance squadrons (VMCJ); they were disestablished in 1975 and their aircraft allocated to VMAQ-2 and VMFP-3. VMAQ-2 flew the EA-6A Intruder and then the EA-6B Prowler, providing detachments to the aircraft wings and occasionally to Navy carrier wings.

TABLE 28-4. MARINE AIRCRAFT WINGS

Marine Aircraft Wing	Marine Aircraft Group	Squadrons[b]	Marine Aircraft Wing	Marine Aircraft Group	Squadrons[b]
1st MAW	MAG-12 (Iwakuni)	VMA[a]	3rd MAW	MAG-11 (El Toro)	VMFA(AW)-121
		VMFA(AW)[a]			VMFA(AW)-242
		VMFA[a]			VMFA(AW)-225
		VMFA[a]			VMFA-314
	MAG-36 (Futenma)	VMGR-152			VMFA-323
		VMO[a]			VMFA-531
		HMH[a]			VMFAT-101
		HMLA[a]			VMGR-352
		HMM[a]		MAG-13 (Yuma)	VMA-211
		HMM-262			VMA-214
					VMA-311
2nd MAW	MAG-14 (Cherry Point)	VMA(AW)-224			VMA-513
		VMA(AW)-332		MAG-16 (Tustin)	HMH-268
		VMA(AW)-533			HMH-361
		VMAQ-1,2,3			HMH-363
		VMGR-252			HMH-464
		VMGRT-253			HMH-465
	MAG-26 (New River)	HMH-362			HMH-466
		HMH-461			HMM-161
		HMLA-167			HMM-163
		HMM-261			HMM-164
		HMM-264			HMM-166
		HMM-266			HMT-301
		HMT-204			HMT-302
	MAG-29 (New River)	VMO-1		MAG-39 (Camp Pendleton)	VMO-2
		HMH-464			HMLA-169
		HMLA-269			HMLA-267
		HMM-162			HMLA-367
		HMM-263			HMLA-369
		HMM-365			HMT-303
	MAG-32 (Cherry Point)	VMA-223			
		VMA-231	1st Marine Expeditionary Brigade	MAG-24 (Kanehoe)	VMFA-212
		VMA-331			VMFA-232
		VMA-542			VMFA-235
		VMAT-203			HMH-463
	MAG-31 (Beaufort)	VMFA-115			HMM-165
		VMFA-122			HMM-265
		VMFA-251			HMM-364
		VMFA-312			
		VMFA-333			
		VMFA-451			

[a]These units are deployed on a temporary basis from the 2nd and 3rd Wings and the 1st Marine Expeditionary Brigade.
[b]See specific squadron entries for units that served in Desert Shield/Desert Storm (indicated by asterisks).

MARINE FIGHTER-ATTACK SQUADRONS

Squadron	Code	Aircraft	Notes
VMFAT-101	SH	F/A-18, T-34C	
VMFA-115	VE	F/A-18A	
VMFA(AW)-121*	VK	F/A-18/D	ex-VMA(AW) 121
VMFA-122	DC	F/A-18A	
VMFA-212*	WD	F/A-18C	
VMFA(AW)-225	CE	F/A-18D	ex-VMFP-3
VMFA-232*	WT	F/A-18C	
VMFA-235*	DB	F/A-18C	
VMFA(AW)-242	DT	F/A-18D	ex-VMA(AW) 242
VMFA-251	DW	F/A-18A	
VMFA-312	DR	F/A-18C	
VMFA-314*	VW	F/A-18A	
VMFA-323	WS	F/A-18A	
VMFA-333*	DM	F/A-18A	deactivated 1992
VMFA-451*	VM	F/A-18A	
VMFA-531	EC	F/A-18A	deactivated 1992

The F/A-18 Hornet has succeeded the F-4 Phantom in Marine fighter-attack squadrons. All Marine fighter squadrons have transitioned to the F/A-18 Hornet, the first being VMFA-314 shifting to the F/A-18 in January 1983 and VMFA-323 and VMFA-531 later the same year. All of the A-6E VMA (AW) squadrons and the Marine Corps's RF-4B Phantom squadron (VMFP-3) are transitioning to a two-place F/A-18D variant. These planes also replaced OA-4M and TA-4F Skyhawks in the tactical air control role.

VMFA squadrons each have 12 aircraft. VMFAT-101 provides transition/readiness training for Marine F/A-18 pilots.

Historical: Marine fighter squadrons flew the F-4 since 1961; on 1 August 1962 these squadrons were changed from VMF(AW) to the current VMFA. Proposals to provide the F-14 Tomcat to at least four Marine squadrons were cancelled in August 1975 at the request of the Marine Corps (freeing up funds for the procurement of the AV-8A Harrier).

MARINE PHOTO-RECONNAISSANCE SQUADRONS

The last photo-reconnaissance squadron in service with the Navy or Marine Corps, VMFP-3, was disestablished on 10 August 1990. It was the only Navy or Marine squadron to fly the RF-4B Phantom (the U.S. Air Force and German Air Force still fly photo-reconnaissance variants of the Phantom).

VMFP-3 flew 21 of the reconnaissance-configured Phantoms. Detachments from the squadron were provided to the other wings (and previously to the carrier MIDWAY). The Marine recce role is being taken over by VMFA(AW) squadrons flying the F/A-18D.

Historical: The Marines took delivery of their first RF-4B in 1965.

MARINE REFUELER-TRANSPORT SQUADRONS

Squadron	Code	Aircraft
VMGR-152	QD	KC-130F
VMGR-252*	BH	KC-130F/R
VMGR-352*	QB	KC-130F/R
VMGRT-253	GR	KC-130

These squadrons fly Hercules aircraft to provide transport for ground forces and for in-flight refueling. One Marine KC-130F "Herk" supports the Navy-Marine Blue Angels flight demonstration team (named "Fat Albert").

MARINE OBSERVATION SQUADRONS

Squadron	Code	Aircraft
VMO-1*	ER	OV-10A/D
VMO-2*	UU	OV-10A/D

The two observation squadrons fly the STOL-capable OV-10 Bronco, with all surviving A models being upgraded to the OV-10D. Unlike previous Marine observation aircraft, the Bronco can be heavily armed. Twelve aircraft are assigned to each squadron. These aircraft will be deactivated by the end of fiscal 1994.

(The Navy's lone light attack squadron, VAL-4, flew Broncos during the Vietnam War.)

MARINE HEAVY HELICOPTER SQUADRONS

Squadron	Code	Aircraft
HMT-302	UT	CH-53D/E
HMH-361	YN	CH-53E
HMH-362*	YL	CH-53A/D
HMH-363	YZ	CH-53A/D
HMH-461*	CJ	CH-53E
HMH-462*	YF	CH-53A/D
HMH-463*	YH	CH-53D
HMH-464*	EN	CH-53E
HMH-465*	YJ	CH-53E
HMH-466*	YK	CH-53E

These squadrons fly the twin-engine CH-53A/D or the three-engine CH-53E. The first of six currently approved CH-53E squadrons was HMH-464, activated at New River on 27 February 1981. Sixteen E-version helicopters will be assigned to each of these squadrons. HMT-301 switched from the CH-46F to the CH-53E in October 1983 as the Super Stallion readiness squadron.

MARINE LIGHT AND ATTACK HELICOPTER SQUADRONS

Squadron	Code	Aircraft
HMLA-167	TV	AH-1W, UH-1N
HMLA-169*	SN	AH-1W, UH-1N
HMLA-267	UV	AH-1W, UH-1N
HMLA-269*	HF	AH-1W, UH-1N
HMT-303	QT	AH-1W, UH-1N
HMLA-367*	VT	AH-1W, UH-1N
HMLA-369*	SM	AH-1W, UH-1N

The Marine light (HML) and attack (HMA) helicopter squadrons have been combined to facilitate the deployment of detachments of combined troop-carrying/command UH-1N Huey helicopters and AH-1W SeaCobra gunships. The last of these squadrons transitioned from the AH-1T to the AH-1W model in 1992. HMT-303 provides helicopter readiness training for both helicopter types and also provides OV-10 training from late 1991 to mid-1992. Previously the Air Force trained Marine OV-10 pilots.

Historical: The Huey has been in Marine service since 1964 and the SeaCobra since late 1978.

MARINE MEDIUM HELICOPTER SQUADRONS

Squadron	Code	Aircraft
HMM-161*	YR	CH-46
HMM-162	YS	CH-46
HMM-163	YP	CH-46
HMM-164*	YT	CH-46
HMM-165*	YW	CH-46
HMM-166	YX	CH-46
HMT-204	GX	CH-46, CH-53
HMM-261*	EM	CH-46
HMM-262	ET	CH-46
HMM-263*	EG	CH-46
HMM-264	EH	CH-46
HMM-265*	EP	CH-46
HMM-266*	ES	CH-46
HMM-268*	YQ	CH-46
HMT-301	SU	CH-46
HMM-364	PF	CH-46
HMM-365*	YM	CH-46

Each medium squadron flies 12 Sea Knight helicopters, being reduced from 18 in some units. The CH-46 is scheduled for replacement by the MV-22 Osprey tilt-rotor aircraft in the 1990s if that aircraft is procured. HMT-204 and HMT-301 provide HMM readiness-transition training.

Historical: HMM-161 was the Marine Corps's first tactical helicopter squadron; it was established on 15 January 1951, flying the Sikorsky HRS-1.

Operational: Due to an administrative oversight, HMM-262 and Navy VQ-6 both have the same tail code—ET. VQ-6 was assigned the code after HMM-262 was inadvertently omitted from the official code assignment chart. Also, HMT-301 is assigned the code US according to official documents, but the squadron uses SU.

MARINE HELICOPTER SQUADRONS

Squadron	Code	Aircraft
HMX-1	MX	VH-3D, VH-60N, CH-46E, CH-53D/E

This squadron—sometimes incorrectly called Marine Helicopter *Experimental* Squadron 1 or Marine *Development* Squadron 1—was commissioned on 1 December 1947 to develop helicopter assault tactics for the Marine Corps. The squadron, at MCAS Quantico, Va., fulfills a variety of development and operational functions, including providing helicopter transport for the President with VH-60 Blackhawks. With the President embarked, the helicopter is designated *Marine One*.

The VH-1N helicopters previously flown by HMX-1 have been withdrawn and converted to HH-1Ns.

MARINE AIR RESERVE

The Marine Air Reserve consists of the 4th Marine Aircraft Wing plus a few detachments. The wing, organized similarly to the active MAWs, has some 100 aircraft.

Fighter readiness training squadron VMFT-401 was established on 18 March 1986 to provide adversary training aircraft for active and reserve Marine squadrons. The squadron—nicknamed "Snipers"—initially flew 13 F-21A Kfir fighters leased from Israel Aircraft Industries from June 1987 until September 1989. They were replaced by 12 F-5E Tiger II and one F-5F aircraft for adversary training.

During the late 1990s the Marines plan to delete the single heavy helicopter squadron (HMH-772) from the 4th MAW and form six HMM squadrons, providing an overall net increase in lift capacity.

In addition to the aircraft squadrons indicated for the 4th MAW, there are various wing command and support aircraft as well as a detachment of C-12 utility aircraft.

4TH MARINE AIRCRAFT WING

Group	Squadron	Code	Aircraft	Location
MAG-41	VMFA-112	MA	F/A-18A	NAS Dallas, Texas
	VMA-124	OP	A-4M	NAS Memphis, Texas
	VMGR-234*	QH	KC-130T	NAS Glenview, Ill.
	HML-776	QL	UH-1N	NAS Glenview, Ill.
	HMH-777	QM	CH-53D	NAS Dallas, Texas
MAG-42	VMFA-142	MB	F/A-18A	NAS Cecil, Fla.
	HMA-773*	MP	AH-1J	NAS Atlanta, Ga.
	HML-767*	MM	UH-1N	NAS New Orleans, La.
	HMM-774*	MQ	CH-46E	NAS Norfolk, Va.
MAG-46	VMFA-134	MF	F/A-18A	MCAS El Toro, Calif.
	VMFT-401	WB	F-5E/F	MCAS Yuma, Az.
	HMA-775*	WR	AH-1J	MCAS Camp Pendleton, Calif.
	HMM-764	ML	CH-46E	MCAS El Toro, Calif.
	HMH-769	MS	RH-53D	NAS Alameda, Calif.
MAG-49	VMFA-321	MG	F/A-18A	NAF Washington, D.C.
	VMA-131	QG	A-4M	NAS Willow Grove, Penna.
	VMGR-452	NY	KC-130	Stewart Air Force Base, N.Y.
	HML-771	QK	UH-1N	NAS South Weymouth, Mass.
	HMH-772	MT	CH-53D	NAS Willow Grove, Penna.

VMO-4 (code MU) flying the OV-10D, VMA-133 (ME) flying the A-4M, and VMA-322 (QR) flying the A-4M were decommissioned during 1992. HMLA-770 flying the AH-1W is scheduled to join MAG-49 about 1995. VMAQ-4 became an active EW squadron in 1992. Note that several Marine reserve squadrons flew in Desert Storm/Desert Shield.

VMFA-112 was the last U.S. Navy-Marine squadron to fly the versatile Phantom, the F-4S variant in this instance. The squadron—called the "Cowboys"—is converting to F/A-18s in 1992.

MARINE CORPS AIR STATION AIRCRAFT

Code	Location
5A	NAF Washington, D.C.
5B	MCAS Beaufort, N.C.
5C	MCAS Cherry Point, N.C.
5D	MCAS New River, N.C.
5F	MCAS Futenma, Okinawa
5G	MCAS Iwakuni, Japan
5T	MCAS El Toro, Calif.
5Y	MCAS Yuma, Ariz.
EZ	NAS Belle Chase, La.

These are mostly administrative and training aircraft, both fixed-wing (UC-12B, CT-39G, C-9B) and helicopter (HH-46A, UH-1N) types. Those at NAF Washington and NAS Belle Chase are operated by the 4th MAW.

CHAPTER 29

Naval Aircraft

An F-14 Tomcat from VF-24 overflies burning Kuwaiti oil wells during Operation Desert Storm. Navy fighters downed only 3 of the 44 Iraqi aircraft destroyed in air-to-air combat—two MiG-21s destroyed by F/A-18s, and an Mi-8 helicopter by an F-14A. However, naval aircraft were the first in the area and ready for combat after the Iraqi invasion of Kuwait. (Comdr. ''T-Bear'' Carson, USN, courtesy *Wings of Gold*)

This chapter describes the aircraft flown by the U.S. Navy, Marine Corps, and Coast Guard. The Navy and former Coast Guard airship programs and the Marine Corps Remotely Piloted Vehicle (RPV) or drone programs are described at the end of this chapter.

The procurement of naval aircraft, both types and numbers, has been reduced in the past few years because of the improving world situation and the severe budget constraints. Further, problems with naval aircraft programs and mismanagement of some have caused the cancellation of several—the A-12 Avenger attack aircraft, P-7 maritime patrol aircraft, and MV-22 Osprey tilt-rotor aircraft; further F-14 Tomcat fighter production as well as "remanufacture" of the F-14A to the F-14D have been halted.

There are currently ten aircraft types being procured for the Navy and Marine Corps; four are fixed-wing types and six are helicopters, including the similar CH/MH-53E series and three models of the H-60 helicopter; the C-130s are paid for with reserve funding and not aircraft procurement funds.

F/A-18C/D	Hornet
E-2C	Hawkeye
T-45A	Goshawk
HH-60H	Seahawk
SH-60F	Seahawk (CV Helo)
SH-60B	Seahawk (LAMPS III)
CH-53E	Super Stallion
MH-53E	Sea Dragon
AH-1W	SeaCobra
C-130	Hercules

The Congress, however, has made it clear to the Department of Defense that the MV-22 (and other variants of the Osprey) will be funded and eventual procurement is expected.

In addition, the Coast Guard is currently procuring the HH-60J Jayhawk variant of the ubiquitous H-60 series helicopter.

Traditionally, the Marine Corps and Coast Guard have flown Navy aircraft; however, during the 1980s both the Marines and Coast Guard sponsored procurements of aircraft that differed from Navy types, especially the AV-8 Harrier series for the Marines and the HU-25 Guardian reconnaissance aircraft and HH-65 Dolphin helicopter for the Coast Guard. All of those programs are completed, although the HH-65 helicopters are being reengined.

The Navy has attempted to reduce development costs and time by procuring a modification of the British Aerospace Hawk trainer in the form of the T-45 Goshawk; that program, however, has become a procurement nightmare.

Table 29-1 lists the current aircraft procurement for the Navy and Marine Corps. It is considered likely that the MV-22 Osprey VSTOL aircraft will also be procured in this period for the Marine Corps and Navy, as a replacement for the Marines' aging CH-46 assault helicopter and to fill several Navy roles.

The reduction of the fiscal 1993 aircraft procurement from 126 units to only 69 will cause a readjustment of future plans, which will be tempered by air wing and squadron reductions.

TABLE 29-1.   U.S. NAVY-MARINE CORPS AIRCRAFT PROCUREMENT

	FY 91 Actual	FY 92 Actual	FY 93 Actual	FY 94 Planned	FY 95 Planned	FY 96 Planned	FY 97 Planned
AV-8B	24	6	—	—	—	—	—
E-2C	6	6	—	—	—	—	—
F/A-18C/D	48	48	36	39	45	60	84
KC-130T	2	—	—	—	—	—	—
T-45A	—	12	12	36	48	48	48
HH-60H	—	7	—	8	9	—	—
SH-60F	18	12	9	12	12	12	12
SH-60B	6	13	12	12	12	12	12
CH/MH-53E	12	16	—	20	—	—	—
AH-1W	8	14	—	12	12	12	12
Total	124	128	69	139	138	144	168

A pair of Navy front-line aircraft about to be catapulted from a carrier: in the foreground is an F/A-18C Hornet from VFA-113; behind it an EA-6B Prowler from VAQ-129. The latter aircraft has "DCAG" on the electronics pod atop the tail fin indicating the plane is normally flown by the deputy air wing commander. (OS2 John Bouvia, USN)

AIRCRAFT DESIGNATIONS

The current U.S. military aircraft designation scheme, adopted in 1962, is relatively simple. Prefix and suffix letters can provide considerable detail. But confusion persists as the old and new schemes are mixed or written incorrectly. For example, the McDonnell Douglas F-4B Phantom is sometimes written incorrectly as F4B—which was a Boeing fighter of the 1920s. Similarly, the F4F Wildcat of World War II fame is often written incorrectly as F-4F, which is the U.S. designation used for F-4 Phantoms configured for West Germany.

Further, the U.S. military services do not follow the system as it was established. For example, in 1962 a new helicopter series was established, beginning with H-1 (formerly HU-1); that series reached only to H-6 before the helicopter programs began adding to the supposedly abandoned Air Force numerical series with H-54 and above. (More severe violations were performed by the Air Force, with fighter-series numbers above F-111 being assigned, although a new series had begun with the F-1 and carried through to the F-21.)

Further, modifications to aircraft, which have in the past added a new suffix numeral or letter, have instead resulted in such confusing designations as the P-3C Update III, EA-6B ICAP, and EP-3E Aires II aircraft.

Historical: From 1922 to 1962 the Navy used its own designation scheme that indicated the aircraft mission, the sequence of that aircraft type produced by the manufacturer, the manufacturer (hyphen) model, and modification. Thus, an AD-2N indicated the first series of attack aircraft built by Douglas, the second model, modified for night operation.

That scheme became unwieldy as the number of manufacturers of naval aircraft increased. For example, the letter *F* was used for Grumman (as F9F) because *G* was already assigned to Gallaudet; *Y* for Consolidated (as PBY) with *C* used by Curtiss and, later, Cessna and Culver as well; *A* for Brewster (as F2A) because *B* was previously assigned to Boeing and, later Beech and Budd Manufacturing. Also, the same aircraft flown by different services had different designations. The famed Boeing B-29 Superfortress had the Navy designation P2B, the North American B-25 was used by the Navy and Marine Corps as the PBJ, and the McDonnell Phantom II entered service as the F4H in the Navy and F-110 in the Air Force.

The U.S. Air Force and Army used different designation schemes for their respective aircraft after the Air Force was established as a separate service in 1947.

A unified scheme for U.S. military aircraft went into effect in October 1962 when all existing and new naval aircraft and all new Air Force planes were redesignated in a new, simplified series, almost all beginning with the series number one. The Navy-flown AD Skyraider became the first plane in the new attack series, the A-1. The Navy's TF Trader started the new cargo series as C-1; and FJ Fury became the F-1; the T2V Sea Star the T-1; the UC-1 Otter the U-1; and the WF Tracer became the E-1.

There was no P-1 or S-1, as the new system picked up the Navy's P2V Neptune and S2F Tracker as the P-2 and S-2, respectively. The improved P3V Orion was the obvious candidate for P-3 and the P5M Marlin, the Navy's last combat flying boat, for P-5. The designation P-4 was used, albeit briefly, for the drone versions of the Privateer (the P4Y-2K, formerly PB4Y-2). The designations P-4 and P-6 are sometimes cited as having been reserved for the P4M Mercator and the P6M Seamaster. But the last of the combination piston-turbojet Mercators were gone and the turbojet Seamaster flying boat had been cancelled before the 1963 system was established. The next patrol aircraft was to be the aborted P-7.

Variations of the previous Air Force *X* (for experimental) and *V* (for VSTOL) designations remained, but official records differ as to which aircraft were part of the old or new series. The Marine AV-8 Harrier is officially in the *V* series, but apparently the designation A-8 was avoided to reduce confusion. In the *V* series, however, the Ryan "flying jeep" had already been designated XV-8. The latter program never took off, hence the "8" spot is firmly held by the successful Harrier series.

Another naval aircraft that contributes to confusion is the F/A-18 Hornet. This aircraft began life as the F-18 in the fighter series, having evolved from the YF-17 prototype. When the decision was made to configure the aircraft as a strike fighter, the designation was changed to F/A-18 (although the two-seat trainer version remained simply TF-18).

Planes that were used by both services, as the Albatross seaplane (Navy UF), generally took on the existing Air Force numerical designation (U-16, formerly SA-16). But the Phantom was recent enough to be given a Navy designation, the now-familiar F-4, and not the Air Force F-110.

Helicopters proved a more confusing issue because the Army had still another designation series before 1962 in addition to those of the Navy–Marine Corps and Air Force. The Sea Knight was the Navy HRB, while the Army called the helicopter HC-1A (HC for helicopter-cargo). This became the H-46 in the new scheme. The Army's HU-1 Iroquois (HU for helicopter-utility) started the new helicopter series as H-1, with most of the Army and Air Force designations being merged to form the new *H* series. Navy helicopters were "stuck in" where there were gaps. The Kaman HU2K became the H-2 and the Sikorsky HSS-2 the H-3, but the Navy's HSS-1/HUS, being similar to the Army–Air Force H-34, took on that designation.

Further, after the new H-series reached H-6, the military reverted to simply adding to the larger numerical series.

The accompanying diagram explains the current aircraft designation scheme.

Explanation of symbols:

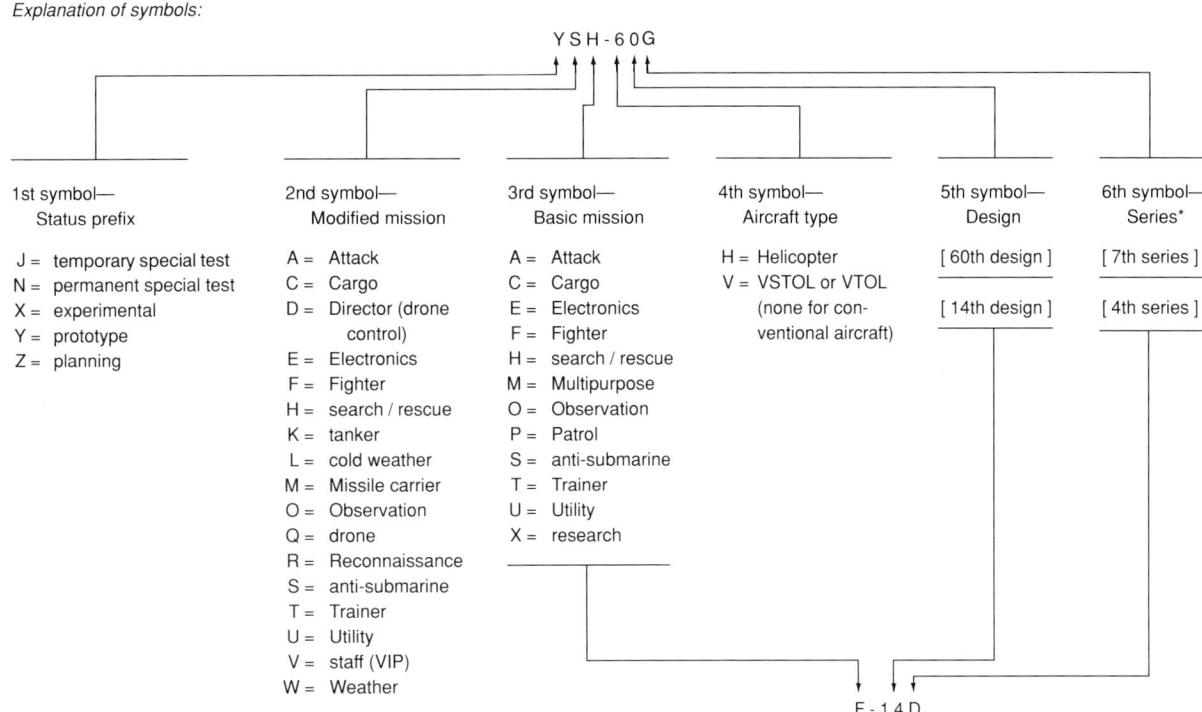

1st symbol— Status prefix	2nd symbol— Modified mission	3rd symbol— Basic mission	4th symbol— Aircraft type	5th symbol— Design	6th symbol— Series*
J = temporary special test	A = Attack	A = Attack	H = Helicopter	[60th design]	[7th series]
N = permanent special test	C = Cargo	C = Cargo	V = VSTOL or VTOL		
X = experimental	D = Director (drone	E = Electronics	(none for con-	[14th design]	[4th series]
Y = prototype	control)	F = Fighter	ventional aircraft)		
Z = planning	E = Electronics	H = search / rescue			
	F = Fighter	M = Multipurpose			
	H = search / rescue	O = Observation			
	K = tanker	P = Patrol			
	L = cold weather	S = anti-submarine			
	M = Missile carrier	T = Trainer			
	O = Observation	U = Utility			
	Q = drone	X = research			
	R = Reconnaissance				
	S = anti-submarine				
	T = Trainer				
	U = Utility				
	V = staff (VIP)				
	W = Weather				

F-14D

*Note: Letters I and O are not used to avoid confusion with numerals

AIRCRAFT MARKINGS

Unit markings—indicating wing, squadron, or base assignment—consist of letters or letter-number combinations on the tail fin or after body of the aircraft; see chapter 28 for codes.

Side numbers—generally on fuselage and upper right and lower left wings indicate the aircraft position in squadron or other unit. The side number sequence for carrier air wings is also shown in chapter 28.

Bureau numbers—assigned to all Navy and Marine Corps aircraft in sequence of their procurement. The numbers are used on the aircraft's after fuselage or tail, and on transports the last three digits are sometimes used as their side numbers. "Bureau" refers to the Bureau of Aeronautics, which directed naval aircraft procurement from 1921 to 1959, when it became the Bureau of Naval Weapons and, subsequently, the current Naval Air Systems Command.

National insignia of the United States consists of a white star within a blue circle, with white rectangles on either side, the rectangles having a red horizontal stripe and blue border. Naval aircraft have the national insignia on both sides of the fuselage, with fixed-wing aircraft also having it on the upper left and lower right wing surfaces.

Coast Guard aircraft have the national insignia or American flag on their tail fin. Some U.S. Navy COD and other transport aircraft also have the American flag on their fin. *Coast Guard* aircraft wear that services' wide orange and narrow blue stripe insignia on the forward fuselage with the Coast Guard crest on the orange stripe.

These aircraft have a four-digit side number based on their (Coast Guard) procurement sequence except for two Coast Guard executive transports, a VC-11A and VC-4A, which have the side numbers 01 and 02, respectively.

FIGHTER AIRCRAFT

When this edition of *Ships and Aircraft* went to press, it appeared that the successor to the F-14 Tomcat fighter would be the advanced F/A-18E variant of the Hornet. Because of the significance of that program, the advanced F/A-18E/F models are given a separate entry.

In selecting the F/A-18E as the next-generation carrier-based fighter over several alternatives, including the F-14D, Secretary of Defense Dick Cheney, in a letter to Senator Christopher Bond dated 29 July 1991, said that the F/A-18E "was the clear choice over the F-14" based on reliability, safety, fewer maintenance personnel, and operating costs.

"In the final analysis, the F/A-18E/F was the clear choice over the F-14. . . . It is three times more reliable, twice as easy to maintain, and has a safety record which is 50 percent better, requires about 25 [percent] fewer maintenance personnel, and costs about 25 percent less to operate per flight hour." Cheney concluded: "When combined, these factors clearly show that the F/A-18E/F is the more cost effective aircraft."

ADVANCED STOVL FIGHTER

The Navy is initiating studies of an Advanced Short Take-Off Vertical Landing (STOVL) strike-fighter aircraft. The current effort, announced early in 1992, follows several earlier, unsuccessful efforts to develop a high-performance VSTOL-type aircraft, including the aborted AV-18 Advanced Harrier and XFV-12A (see 14th Edition/ pages 403 and 443). The new aircraft would be the successor to the AV-8B Harrier, now flown by the Marine Corps.

About $10 million has been programmed by the Navy to begin the studies in 1994, which will be carried out in conjunction with the Marine Corps, the Defense Advanced Research Projects Agency (DARPA), and the National Aeronautics and Space Administration (NASA). These other agencies will also contribute to funding the studies. Full-scale development of the aircraft was estimated in 1992 to cost $600 million to $1 *billion,* depending upon the design chosen and the technologies required to be developed in support of that design.

While Great Britain is not initially participating in the U.S. effort, the British military services will closely follow the studies. If the design is successfully developed, it is envisioned that Britain will become at least a production partner.

Related to the official U.S. effort, McDonnell Douglas Aircraft and British Aerospace—producers of the Harrier series—announced on 24 February 1992 that they had reached an exclusive arrangement to pursue next-generation VSTOL aircraft. Other companies as well as McDonnell Douglas are expected to undertake development efforts in conjunction with the Navy's STOVL project, among them General Dynamics, Grumman, General Electric, Aircraft Engines, and Pratt and Whitney Government Engines.

NAVAL ADVANCED TACTICAL FIGHTER

The Naval Advanced Tactical Fighter (NATF) was originally envisioned by the Navy as a long-term replacement for the F-14 Tomcat. The NATF was to be a "navalized" version of the F-22 Lightning (ATF) being developed by a team comprising Lockheed–General Dynamics–Boeing for the U.S. Air Force. A senior official of Lockheed, whose aircraft won the competition, said that the company planned to "give the NATF a swing-wing like the F-14. The swing-wing will let us optimize the plane for the best performance in different [speed and altitude] regions." The official admitted that there would be a penalty for the swing-wing, but performance and stealth would be enhanced in combat environments. Also, Lockheed was to look at a two-seat aircraft for the Navy (the F-22 is a single-seat plane) that would carry 50 percent more fuel than the Air Force version. Other changes envisioned for the naval aircraft would be additional avionics and engines modified to resist corrosion in a

An advanced STOVL aircraft concept designed by McDonnell Douglas in collaboration with Pratt & Whitney that makes use of the mixed-flow, vectored-thrust concept. This design has twin tail "pods" and canards forward. (NASA)

This advanced STOVL design was developed by Grumman in conjunction with General Electric. Making use of the remote augmented lift system, this craft also has a twin-tail configuration with wingtip as well as under-wing and under-fuselage missile positions. (NASA)

salt-water environment. In short, said the Lockheed official, "The NATF will be designed to a completely different set of requirements."[1]

1. "Lockheed NATF design will be swing-wing," *Navy News* (4 February 1991), pp. 1–2.

A prototype F-22, the winner in the Air Force ATF competition for the next-generation Air Force fighter. The Navy could share in the F-22 program, although such participation is unlikely. (Lockheed)

By early 1991—about the time of the Air Force selection from the YF-22 and YF-23 ATF design competitors—the Navy reached the decision that development and production of a naval ATF was unaffordable.

Many in the Navy were apprehensive of the concept of adapting the Air Force ATF for carrier use—and with good reason. Historically, land-based aircraft have not been successful when employed aboard ship; the last major effort and failure was the General Dynamics F-111 of the 1960s.[2] At the time the decision was made to pursue the NATF, the initial Air Force procurement was scheduled for fiscal 1996, with the naval variant expected to join the fleet between 2001 and 2005. A buy of 546 advanced fighters through fiscal 2014 was envisioned to replace the F-14.

Following the decision not to procure the NATF, the available future Navy fighter options included an improved F/A-18 that McDonnell Douglas–Northrop labeled the Hornet 2000, an updated F-14 called the Super Tomcat 21 by Grumman, or an ATS/Missileer aircraft. However, in July 1991 the Secretary of Defense stated his preference for an advanced F/A-18 variant (see above).

Prototype YF-22 Advanced Tactical Fighter. (Lockheed)

F-21A KFIR

From 1985 to 1989 the Navy and Marine Corps leased 25 Israeli-built Kfir C1 fighter aircraft to simulate Soviet aircraft in adversary training for pilots.[3] The Kfirs were leased to the United States on a no-cost basis, with Israel Aircraft Industries being contracted to maintain the aircraft. All 25 aircraft were returned to Israel with the availability of F-16N fighters for adversary training. Squadron VF-43 flew 12 of the F-21s and VMFT-401 flew 13 aircraft.

The Kfir was a refinement of the Dassault Mirage 5 design, with a more powerful engine of American origin. IAI had produced 27 Kfir C1 aircraft, one having been lost and one being retained in Israel for museum display. After return of the 25 leased aircraft, IAI modified them to extend their service life for further foreign lease or sale.

See 14th Edition/page 395 for F-21A Kfir characteristics.

2. The reverse procedure appears to have worked quite well; recent examples include the Navy-developed F-4 Phantom and the A-7 Corsair, both employed by the U.S. Air Force in large numbers, and the A-4 Skyhawk and E-2C Hawkeye, both flown by several foreign air forces.
3. *Kfir* is Hebrew for lion cub.

Prototype YF-22 Advanced Tactical Fighter. (Lockheed)

F/A-18E/F HORNET

The advanced Hornets—the single-seat F/A-18E and two-seat F/A-18F—are proposed as carrier-based aircraft to succeed the F-14 Tomcat fighter and A-6E Intruder attack plane. In the latter role the F/A-18F would fulfill the Navy's AX requirement.

By early 1992, however, the E/F variants were being criticized for increasing costs and having less commonality with the early F/A-18s than originally envisioned. In testimony before a congressional committee in March 1992, Secretary of the Navy Lawrence Garrett estimated that development costs of the F/A-18 would be $4.9 *billion,* up from $3.3 *billion* estimated a year earlier (in fiscal 1990 dollars). Reasons for the increased costs and the reduction in F/A-18 commonality include changes in airframe and payload and the use of technology from the cancelled A-12 Avenger, including the engines. However, the F/A-18E/F and earlier C/D variants will share avionics as well as maintenance and logistics support.

The E/F models are based on a lengthened and upgraded F/A-18C/D design. The requirement for an enhanced F/A-18 was first mentioned in a 15 July 1987 memorandum from then-Secretary of Defense Caspar Weinberger to the secretaries of the Navy and Air Force noting that, because the next-generation Navy attack aircraft and a replacement for the Air Force's F-16 fighter could not be available "for many years," the Navy should study derivatives of the F/A-18 and the Air Force should study F-16 upgrades as interim replacements.

Compared to the F/A-18C/D series, the later aircraft will have a center section plug, 25 percent larger wing, and improved engines with 35 percent more thrust. The F414 engines in the aircraft are a derivative of the F404 used in the earlier F/A-18s. Two additional wing stores stations will provide a total of ten on the fuselage and wings, plus two wingtip stations for the Sidewinder AAM.

Status: In development. Proposed IOC in 1998.

F/A-18E (Provisional)

Manufacturer:	McDonnell Douglas
Crew:	(1) pilot in F/A-18E
	(2) pilot, bombardier/navigator in F/A-18F
Engines:	2 General Electric F414-GE-400 turbofan; 22,000 lbst (9,979 kgst) each
Weights:	empty 30,000 lbs (13,608 kg)
	max takeoff 63,500 lbs (28,800 kg)
Dimensions:	length overall 60 ft (18.29 m)
	wing span 44 ft 8½ in (13.63 m) with Sidewinder AAMs fitted
	wing area 500 ft² (45 m²)
	height 15 ft 10 in (4.83 m)
Speed:	
Range:	
Ceiling:	
Armament:	
Radar:	APG-73 multi-mode

An F/A-18D Hornet from VMFA(AW)-121 over Kuwait City during Desert Storm. The Navy and Marine Corps flew more F/A-18s than any other aircraft type in Desert Storm. Visible on the wingtips are Sidewinder AAMs; three 330-gallon (1,250-liter) fuel tanks are also carried. Note the wingroot Leading-Edge Extensions (LEX) that permit high angles of attack. (U.S. Marine Corps/McDonnell Douglas)

F/A-18 Hornets from CVW-1 on the AMERICA with all pylons loaded. The aircraft in the foreground carries Sidewinder and Sparrow AAMs, and at least one Harpoon anti-ship missile plus a centerline fuel tank. This aircraft, from VFA-82, is flown by the wing commander. (McDonnell Douglas)

F/A-18   HORNET

The Hornet is a strike-fighter aircraft in wide use by the Navy and Marine Corps, being flown in significantly larger numbers than any other naval aircraft. In the Navy the F/A-18 replaced the A-7E Corsair light attack aircraft; most carrier air wings have two VFA squadrons flying the F/A-18. In the Marine Corps the F/A-18 replaced the F-4S Phantom fighter, the A-6E Intruder, and A-4M Skyhawk attack aircraft, and the RF-4B Phantom and OA-4 Skyhawk special-purpose aircraft.

The F/A-18 has been a controversial program because of the initial Marine decision to procure the AV-8B Harrier instead of the F/A-18 for the attack role, higher-than-predicted F/A-18 costs, and the F/A-18 having less range than the A-7. However, the aircraft's widespread use has had positive cost and support impact, and its performance in Operation Desert Storm equaled its manufacturers' performance promises.

A twin-engine, single- or two-seat aircraft, the F/A-18 is characterized by its high maneuverability, the ability to operate in either the fighter or attack role with the push of a button, and comparatively low maintenance requirements.[4] The initial versions were the F/A-18A strike-fighter and TF-18 two-seat trainer, the latter now referred to as the F/A-18B. The F/A-18C is an improved single-seat aircraft and the F/A-18D is a two-seat aircraft with a weapons officer in the rear seat (no flight controls). The D variant is also configured for the Marine tactical air control and reconnaissance roles, and has an austere all-weather capability. F/A-18 avionics include ALR-50 and ALR-67 Radar Warning Receivers (RWR) and Head-Up Display (HUD).

The F/A-18 has wingtip Sidewinder AAM positions as well as three fuselage and four wing stations for weapons and sensor/guidance pods. A variety of bombs, missiles, and rockets can be carried, including up to four 2,000-lb (907-kg) bombs.

Initially the F/A-18 flew with a pod-mounted Forward-Looking Infrared (FLIR), developed specifically for the F/A-18 (AAS-38). The F/A-18C/D models delivered since October 1989 have a night-attack capability based on a FLIR sensor called TINS (Thermal Imaging Navigation Set) and designated ARR-50, and an improved HUD. The F/A-18s delivered through mid-1994 have the APG-65 radar; subsequent aircraft—including the E/F variants—will have the APG-73 radar.

The development of the F/A-18 came as a result of pressure by Congress for the Navy to obtain a lightweight fighter to complement the F-14 in carrier air wings. Congress originally had directed the Navy to select the winner of the Air Force's lightweight fighter competition between the General Dynamics YF-16 and Northrop YF-17 prototypes. The Air Force selected the F-16 for production; the Navy selected the YF-17, but made major modifications, leading to the F/A-18 developed jointly by McDonnell Douglas and Northrop.

4. During the Gulf War, on 17 January 1991, two Navy F/A-18 Hornets from the carrier SARATOGA on a bombing mission where each was carrying four 2,000-pound (907-kg) bombs were able to engage two Iraqi MiG-21 fighters. Both Iraqi planes were shot down with air-to-air missiles, after which the F/A-18s were able to continue their bombing mission, not having had to jettison their bombs to engage the enemy planes.

(The initial order for 11 development aircraft used the designation YF-18.) The aircraft failed to fully achieve its range/payload goals in the attack role.

The Navy–Marine Corps Blue Angels flight demonstration team began flying the F/A-18A in 1987; these were early development models of the Hornet that are not carrier capable.[5] Later A models have been provided as fleet squadrons converted to F/A-18C variants.

Operational: More F/A-18s participated in the Persian Gulf War (January–February 1991) than any other fixed-wing naval aircraft— 13 Navy VFA and 7 Marine VMFA squadrons, plus Canadian Forces. A total of some 200 F/A-18 Hornets flew more than 20,000 sorties during the conflict, averaging 3.3 hours per flight.

Status: Operational; in production. First flight on 18 November 1978. Navy-Marine IOC (VFA-125) in February 1981; Marine IOC (VMFA-314) in March 1983.

Through the end of 1991 more than 1,100 F/A-18s were delivered- —some 800 to the U.S. Navy and Marine Corps, and 300 to foreign air forces (including 73 coproduced with Aerospace Technologies of Australia).

The original F/A-18 procurement plan was for 11 development aircraft and 1,366 production planes for 24 Navy attack and 6 fighter squadrons, and 12 Marine fighter squadrons plus 332 aircraft in reserve units and 142 attrition and pipeline aircraft. The current Navy-Marine procurement is expected to total 1,168 aircraft.

Australia, Canada, Kuwait, Spain, Finland, and Switzerland are procuring the F/A-18 for land operation; South Korea planned to acquire the F/A-18 in 1989, but subsequently cancelled that order in favor of the F-16 Fighting Falcon. (A proposed Northrop F-18L land-based variant has not been ordered.)

5. See page 384 for previous Blue Angel aircraft.

F/A-18A

Manufacturer:	McDonnell Douglas and Northrop
Crew:	(1) pilot in F/A-18A/C
	(2) pilot, bombardier/navigator in F/A-18D
Engines.	2 General Electric F404-GE-400 turbofan; 16,000 lbst (7,258 kgst) each; F404-GE-402 engines with 17,700 lbst (8,029 kgst) in fiscal 1992 and later aircraft
Weights:	empty 28,000 lbs (12,700 kg)
	fighter mission normal takeoff 37,000 lbs (16,783 kg)
	attack mission normal takeoff 48,253 lbs (21,888 kg)
Dimensions:	length overall 56 ft (17.07 m)
	wing span 37 ft 6 in (11.43 m)
	40 ft 5 in (12.32 m) with Sidewinder AAMs fitted
	wing area 400 ft² (37.16 m²)
	height 15 ft 3½ in (4.66 m)
Speed:	max 1,185 mph (1,900 kmh) at 37,000 ft (11,280 m)
Ceiling:	50,000+ ft (15,244 m)
Range:	radius 415 n.miles (768 km) in fighter role
	radius 550 n.miles (1,018 km) in attack role
Armament:	1 20-mm Vulcan cannon M61 (multi-barrel; 570 rounds)
	2 Sidewinder + 4 Sparrow AAMs in fighter role, or
	2 Sidewinder AAMs + 17,000 lbs (7,711 kg) of bombs, missiles, rockets in attack role, including HARM, SLAM, Harpoon
Radar:	APG-65 multi-mode digital

An F/A-18 Hornet showing the weapons flexibility of the aircraft: Four 2,000-pound (907-kg) bombs are being carried as well as two Sidewinder AAMs and one Sparrow AAM during a Desert Storm flight. The arresting hook is positioned between the engine exhausts. (McDonnell Douglas)

An F/A-18 Hornet from VFA-87, "dirty" with wheels and hook lowered, landing aboard the THEODORE ROOSEVELT during operations in the eastern Mediterranean. (U.S. Navy)

F-16N FIGHTING FALCON

The Navy flies 26 modified F-16C Fighting Falcon fighters in the adversary training role (replacing the F-21A Kfir). The F-16 is the standard U.S. Air Force lightweight fighter, which is also flown by several allied air forces. The naval aircraft are 22 single-seat variants designated F-16N and 4 two-seat TF-16N variants.

The F-16 has a slightly swept-back, fixed-wing configuration, with long wing-root extensions to improve supersonic maneuvering. The Navy F-16s differ from the Air Force versions in not having the M61 20-mm Vulcan cannon; the Navy planes have the APG-66 radar fitted in the earlier Air Force F-16A/B aircraft and a more advanced engine than the Pratt & Whitney F100 in the F-16C.[6] The F-16Ns also have the ALR-69 radar warning receiver and ALE-40 chaff/flare dispenser.

In May 1990 the Navy discovered cracks in F-16Ns that will severely limit their service life.

Status: Operational. First flight (USAF) YF-16 on 2 February 1974. IOC (USAF) in January 1979; the Navy F-16N procurement decision was made in January 1986 with Navy IOC (VF-126) in April 1988; all F-16Ns delivered 1988–1989. Also flown by VF-43, VF-45, VFA-127, and the Navy Fighter Weapons School (Top Gun).

More than 1,900 F-16s had been delivered to the U.S. Air Force and more than 1,000 aircraft to 16 allied nations through 1991 with several hundred additional planes on order.

6. The Navy/General Electric F110 engine was formerly designated as the F101 DFE (Derivative Fighter Engine).

Manufacturer:	General Dynamics
Crew:	(1) pilot (2 in TF-16N)
Engines:	1 General Electric F110-GE-100 turbofan; 27,600 lbst (12,519 kgst) with afterburner
Weights:	empty 17,278 lbs (7,837 kg)
	fighter takeoff 25,471 lbs (11,554 kg)
	max takeoff 37,500 lbs (17,010 kg)
Dimensions:	length 49 ft 3 in (15.01 m)
	wing span 31 ft (9.45 m)
	32 ft 9¾ in (10.0 m) over missiles
	wing area 300 ft² (27.87 m²)
	height 16 ft 8½ in (5.09 m)
Speed:	max Mach 2+ at 40,000 ft (12,195 m)
Ceiling:	50,000+ ft (15,244 m)
Range:	radius 500+ n.miles (805 km)
	ferry 2,100+ n.miles (3,380 km) with drop tanks
Armament:	none except wingtip launchers for 2 practice Sidewinder AAMs
Radar:	APG-66 multi-mode

The wingroot LEXes that enhance maneuverability are evident in this view of an F-16N. (General Dynamics)

The F-16N Fighting Falcon adversary training aircraft is based on the Air Force F-16C variant. The Navy also flies several of the TF-16N two-seat variants. (U.S. Navy)

F-14 TOMCAT

The F-14 is the standard U.S. Navy carrier-based fighter, with two squadrons assigned to each carrier air wing. In several respects the F-14 remains the most-capable long-range, all-weather fighter aircraft in service with any air force. One VF squadron in each carrier can employ the F-14 in the photo-reconnaissance role with the standard F-14 fitted with the removable TARPS (Tactical Air Reconnaissance Pod System). The TARPS package can be fitted to or removed from a standard aircraft in a few hours; it contains a KS-87 frame camera, KA-99 panoramic camera, and an AAD-5 infrared line scanner.

A two-seat aircraft, the F-14 has variable-geometry wings that sweep back automatically as the aircraft maneuvers during flight; they extend for long-range flight and landings, sweeping back for high-speed flight (and carrier stowage). Normal sweep range is 20 to 68 degrees with a 75-degree "oversweep" position provided for shipboard hangar stowage; sweep speed is 7.5 degrees per second.

The F-14A has the long-range AWG-9 radar that can detect hostile aircraft out to more than 100 miles (161 km) and simultaneously track up to 24 targets, and the Phoenix missile that can engage targets more than 60 miles (96.5 km) away. The basic F-14 suite includes the ALR-45 and ALR-50 RWR, ALE-29 and ALE-39 chaff/flare dispensers, and ALQ-100 deception jamming pod. A forward-looking AXX-1 television camera is fitted for long-range visual detection.

The aircraft has a total of four fuselage missile positions (4 Sparrow or 4 Phoenix) and two wing positions (4 Sidewinder or 2 Sparrow or 2 Phoenix); alternatively, fuel tanks or a TARPS can be carried with a reduced missile load. Planned under-fuselage pallets for bombs and air-to-surface missiles were never provided; the F-14D has pylon adapters for "iron" bombs and air-to-surface missiles (HARM and Harpoon).

Only about 80 F-14A variants were originally to have been procured, with subsequent aircraft to have been the F-14B with F401-PW-400 engines and a later F-14C with upgraded avionics. In the event, only the F-14A model was produced through the mid-1980s. (The Navy had planned an F-14 upgrade with improved engines and air-to-surface weapons in the 1970s, but those programs were halted because of the lack of funds.) Engine problems plagued the F-14A, and the F-14A+ was fitted with the F110-GE-400

engines, but otherwise similar to the basic F-14A. (The F-14A+ was changed to F-14B in 1991; previously one F-14A had been reengined and designated F-14B.) The follow-on F-14D has the improved engines plus digital avionics, a new radar, ALR-67 RWR and ALQ-165 Advanced Self-Protection Jammer (ASPJ), airframe improvements to give more service life, Infrared Search and Track (IRST) sensor, and provisions for carrying air-to-surface weapons. The F110-GE-400 engine had a maximum engine thrust of 28,500 pounds (12,928 kg), resulting in an increased radius (deck-launched intercept role) from 135 to 210 n.miles (250 to 390 km), and a maximum catapult weight increase from 59,000 pounds (26,762 kg) to 74,000 pounds (33,566 kg).

The decision to procure 324 of the improved F-14D models with the F110-GE-400 engine (formerly F101 DFE) and upgraded avionics was made in early 1984. New procurement was halted by the Department of Defense in April 1989 in favor of the "remanufacture" of 400 earlier F-14A aircraft; subsequently, in 1991 the Navy decided to remanufacture only 104 F-14A to the F-14D configuration by the year 1997, the cutback made in an unsuccessful effort to garner funds for new F-14D production. This cutback, in effect, means the Navy could face a severe shortage of F-14s by the year 2005.

The F-14 was originally planned for Marine Corps use, but that service turned it down, in part because of the decision to procure the AV-8A Harrier.

Status: Operational. First flight F-14A on 21 December 1970; first flight F-14B (F-14A engine conversion) on 12 September 1973; F-14A+ on 14 November 1987. IOC F-14A (VF-124) in January 1973; F-14D IOC in November 1990.

The last F-14s were delivered in May 1992; a total of 633 aircraft were produced for the U.S. Navy: 558 F-14A (including development models), 38 F-14A+ (redesignated F-14B), and 37 F-14D variants. Subsequently, the following F-14A conversions were undertaken: 1 F-14A to F-14B (engine change only in 1973); 34 to F-14A+; 3 to F-14D electronic test bed aircraft; 18 to F-14D. An additional 80 F-14A aircraft were built for Iran; 79 were delivered in 1976–1979 with 1 retained by Grumman after the Iranian revolution.

The F-14C variant was to have been a development of the original (engine update) F-14B with improved avionics.

F-14A

Manufacturer:	Grumman
Crew:	(2) pilot, radar-intercept officer
Engines:	2 Pratt & Whitney TF30-P-414A turbofan; 20,900 lbst (9,480 kgst) each with afterburning
Weights:	empty 40,104 lbs (18,191 kg)
	"clean" takeoff 58,715 lbs (26,632 kg)
	takeoff with 6 Phoenix AAMs 70,764 lbs (32,089 kg)
	max takeoff 74,349 lbs (33,724 kg)
Dimensions:	length overall 62 ft 8 in (19.1 m)
	wing span 64 ft 1½ in (19.54 m) unswept
	38 ft 2½ in (11.65 m) swept back
	wing area 565 ft² (52.49 m²)
	height 16 ft (4.88 m)
Speed:	max Mach 2.4
Ceiling:	50,000+ ft (15,244 m)
Range:	radius approx. 500 n.miles (926 in air intercept configuration)
	ferry 1,850 n.miles (3,426 km) with 2 267-gallon (1,015-liter) drop tanks
Armament:	1 20-mm Vulcan cannon M61 (multi-barrel; 676 rounds)
	2 Phoenix + 3 Sparrow + 2 Sidewinder AAMs + 2 267-gallon drop tanks, or
	4 Phoenix + 2 Sparrow + 2 Sidewinder AAMs + 2 267-gallon drop tanks, or
	6 Phoenix + 2 Sidewinder AAMs + 2 267-gallon drop tanks, or
	6 Sparrow + 2 Sidewinder AAMs + 2 267-gallon drop tanks
Radar:	AWG-9 in F-14A
	APG-71 in F-14D

An F-14A+ Tomcat of VF-101 with its wings partially swept. The large inboard wing sections are faired into the engine intakes and house the swing-wing mechanisms. (Peter B. Mersky)

An F-14 Tomcat on the carrier SARATOGA. A TV optical system and deceptive jamming system are mounted under the nose; the 20-mm Vulcan cannon is on the port side; the in-flight refueling probe retracts into the starboard side of the nose. (U.S. Navy, PH3 Mac Thurston)

An F-14A Tomcat from VF-32 carrying a TARPS reconnaissance pod (between engine nacelles). While in the recon role over the Red Sea, the aircraft also carries two Sparrow and two Sidewinder AAMs plus two fuel tanks. (Lt. Comdr. Dave Parsons, USN)

Photographic specialists prepare a TARPS pod fitted on an F-14 Tomcat of VF-84 aboard the THEODORE ROOSEVELT in the eastern Mediterranean. The arresting hook is at right. (PH2 Joe Cina, USN)

F-5E/F TIGER II

The F-5E/F variants are flown by the Navy as an air combat maneuvering/adversary training aircraft. The aircraft was the penultimate design in a long series of trainer/fighter aircraft developed by Northrop, primarily for Third World markets. (The much-improved F-5G Tigershark was redesignated F-20.)

The F-5E Tiger is a single-seat aircraft and the F-5F a two-seat version, both with two turbojet engines. Sidewinder AAMs can be carried on wingtips, and there are one fuselage and four wing stations for ordnance.

More than 3,000 F-5 fighters and the similar T-38 Talon trainers have been built for the U.S. Air Force and some 25 foreign nations. The U.S. Navy has almost 50 F-5E and 3 F-5F fighters, plus six T-38s to simulate Soviet fighter aircraft in adversary training. The Marines fly the F-5E/F in reserve adversary training squadron VMFT-401.

The aircraft is not carrier capable.

Status: Operational. First flight F-5A on 30 July 1959; first flight F-5E on 11 August 1972.

F-5E

Manufacturer:	Northrop
Crew:	(1) pilot (2 in F-5F)
Engines:	2 General Electric J85-GE-21B turbojet; 5,000 lbst (2,268 kgst) each with afterburning
Weights:	empty F-5E 9,723 lbs (4,410 kg)
	F-5F 10,576 lbs (4,797 kg)
	max takeoff F-5E 24,722 lbs (11,214 kg)
	F-5F 25,152 lbs (11,409 kg)
Dimensions:	length overall F-5E 47 ft 4¾ in (14.45 m)
	F-5F 51 ft 4 in (15.65 m)
	wing span 26 ft 8 in (8.13 m)
	wing area 186 ft² (17.3 m²)
	height F-5E 13 ft 4 in (4.06 m)
	F-5F 13 ft 1¾ in (4.01 m)
Speed:	max Mach 1.64 at 36,000 ft (10,975 m)
Ceiling:	51,800 ft (15,790 m)
Range:	radius 570 n.miles (1,056 km) with 2 Sidewinder AAMs
	1,545 n.miles (2,861 km) with external tanks
Armament:	none
Radar:	APQ-159

An F-5E Tiger II from the Navy's Fighter Weapons School—better known as Top Gun—flies formation with an F-4 Phantom from VX-4, shortly before that squadron traded in its Phantoms for newer fighters. The Tiger II is in camouflage paint also used by some adversary training squadrons; Sidewinder missile rails are fitted to the wingtips. The Phantom has the Playboy insignia used by VX-4. (Lt. Cmdr. David Baranak, USN)

F-4 PHANTOM (formerly F4H)

Long the principal all-weather, multi-purpose fighter flown by the Navy and Marine Corps, all F-4 Phantoms have been retired from Navy and Marine squadrons, replaced by the F-14 Tomcat in Navy fighter squadrons (VF) and the F/A-18 Hornet in Marine fighter-attack squadrons (VMFA).

McDonnell Douglas produced 5,211 aircraft for U.S. and foreign service, while Japan built 138 F-4EJ variants, including 11 from parts produced by McDonnell Douglas. All production ended in 1979; the last of 1,264 aircraft delivered to the Navy and Marine Corps were completed in December 1971 (including 46 of the RF-4B reconnaissance variant); the principal U.S. naval production versions were the F-4B and F-4J, which were subsequently upgraded to the F-4N and F-4S, respectively. The Phantom remains in service with the U.S. Air Force (F-4G Wild Weasel and variants) and some 1,500 aircraft in foreign air forces.[7]

The last Navy squadron to fly the Phantom, reserve VF-202, retired its last F-4S in early 1987; the last Marine unit flying the F-4S was reserve VMFA-112, which phased out its last Phantoms in mid-1992. All RF-4B reconnaissance variants have been retired from Marine service.

See 14th Edition/pages 401–402 for characteristics.

7. The Royal Navy also flew Phantoms from aircraft carriers, with the F-4K being Britain's last non-VSTOL carrier-based fighter-attack aircraft.

ATTACK AIRCRAFT

The U.S. Navy attack squadrons currently fly the A-6E Intruder; Marine attack squadrons fly the A-6E (being phased out) and the AV-8B Harrier. In addition, several variants of the long-serving A-4 Skyhawk remain in Navy and Marine service in training and specialized roles.

The AX is under development to replace the cancelled A-12 Avenger. The latter aircraft is described in this edition of *Ships and Aircraft* to provide a record of the plane's characteristics.

The F/A-18F was a likely candidate to fulfill the AX requirement when this edition went to press.

AX   ADVANCED ATTACK AIRCRAFT

This is a proposed long-range, all-weather attack aircraft intended for carrier operation. It will succeed the aborted A-12 Avenger as the Navy's most-capable carrier attack aircraft in the next decade. Near-term alternatives include variants of the Grumman F-14D Quickstrike and the McDonnell Douglas–Northrop F/A-18. In addition, the General Dynamics–McDonnell Douglas–Northrop team is proposing a design based on the cancelled A-12 aircraft and Lockheed teamed with General Dynamics and Boeing to propose a variant of the Air Force F-22, which was selected in 1991 as the USAF Advanced Tactical Fighter (ATF).

Development and funding for the AX have been slowed following the end of the Cold War. The original IOC of 2005 has been delayed about five years based on fiscal 1992 budget revisions.

Priorities for the AX design include low-observable (stealth) characteristics and multi-mission potential—attack, electronic warfare, and possibly anti-submarine warfare with the primary missions to be (1) strike and (2) anti-surface warfare. The aircraft is to be capable of carrying all existing and planned Navy air-launched missiles except the Phoenix AAM.

Status: In development. Multiple teams of aerospace firms began design studies in early 1992 (see below). Planned IOC for the AX is 2010.

Manufacturer:	Team No. 1	Boeing-Grumman-Lockheed
	Team No. 2	McDonnell Douglas–LTV
	Team No. 3	General Dynamics–McDonnell Douglas–Northrop
	Team No. 4	Rockwell-Lockheed
Crew:	(2) pilot, bombardier/navigator	
Engines:	2	
Weights:		
Dimensions:		
Speed:		
Range:	radius 700 n.miles (1,300 km)	
Ceiling:		
Armament:	up to 12,000 lbs (5,443 kg) of bombs and missiles including 2 AAMs	
Radar:	multi-function	

A-12   AVENGER

The A-12 Avenger was intended to replace the A-6E Intruder, the "medium" all-weather strike aircraft found on all U.S. carriers. It was also to replace the A-6E in five Marine attack squadrons, but the Marine Corps early in the program decided to forego the A-12 and is giving up its remaining A-6Es to the Navy. Instead, the Marines are flying the two-seat F/A-18D in the all-weather attack role.

The Navy and Department of Defense cancelled the A-12 program on 7 January 1991, citing "the inability of the contractors to design, develop, fabricate, assemble, and test A-12 aircraft within the contract schedule and to deliver an aircraft that meets contract requirements." Also cited were major cost overruns, and misrepresentations by the Naval Air Systems Command; the latter resulted in three senior officers being censured.[8]

The design and cost of the A-12 were highly classified until 1990. In January 1990, citing a "slip" in congressional testimony, the press reported that the 620-plane program was to have a unit cost of $96.2 million, making it the most expensive Navy aircraft yet built.[9] The peak A-12 production for the run of 620 aircraft was to be 36 units in fiscal 1994. (When the Marine Corps was buying the A-12, the procurement goal was 858 aircraft.)

The Air Force had been forced by the Defense Department to join the A-12 program to develop a deep-strike aircraft to succeed the F-111 and F-15 Strike Eagle in that role. Called the Advanced Tactical Aircraft (ATA), in 1990 production of the Air Force version was deferred beyond 1997. The Air Force had planned to buy 400 ATA models.

The A-12 was to be a low-observable (stealth) aircraft with a flying-wing configuration sans major tail-fin structures. The official artist's drawings of the A-12—heavily retouched—show a classic delta flying-wing configuration with the "fuselage" extending slightly rearward from the trailing edge; the wing has a leading-edge sweep of about 48 degrees. There are two large, trapezoidal inlets for the engines just aft and below the leading edges of the wing; no afterburners are fitted. The tandem-seat cockpit is close to the nose of the aircraft, which appears to be sharply pointed and appears to "blend" into the leading edge of the wing. The aircraft was to have been fitted with a digital fly-by-wire control system. The weapons load—estimated to be up to 12,000 pounds (5,443 kg)—was to be carried internally. The A-12 had folding wings for carrier stowage. Other features were to include superior range and payload over the A-6E, a low flight-to-maintenance ratio (expected to be four times better than the A-6E ratio), and dual-function radar/FLIR search-and-tracking system.

Designation: The designation A-12 was previously assigned by the Central Intelligence Agency to the hypersonic aircraft that was the progenitor of the YF-12 fighter aircraft and SR-71 Blackbird reconnaissance aircraft.

Name: The name Avenger was assigned to honor President George Bush, who flew a TBM Avenger torpedo plane in World War II; he was reported to be the Navy's youngest wartime pilot.

Status: Cancelled. The A-12 program began in 1984 with the first of six A-12 prototypes originally scheduled to fly in June 1990; when the aircraft was cancelled in January 1991, the first flight was expected to occur in March 1992. Carrier trials were expected in late 1992 or early 1993, with an IOC of 1996.

The following data are partially estimated.

---

8. The Commander, Naval Air Systems Command was retired and the program's manager and executive officer were transferred, the two latter officers also receiving administrative letters of censure.
9. See, for example, "A-12 Disclosure," *Aviation Week & Space Technology* (15 January 1990), p. 15.

Manufacturer:	General Dynamics and McDonnell Douglas
Crew:	(2) pilot, bombardier/navigator
Engines:	2 General Electric F412-GE-400 turbofan
Weights:	max takeoff 70,000+ lbs (31,752 kg)
Dimensions:	length	38 feet (11.6 m)
	wing span	69 feet (21 m)
	wings folded	34½ feet (10.5 m)
	wing area	
	height	
Speed:	subsonic (~ Mach 0.9)
Range:	radius 750 n.miles (1,390 km) with 24,000 lbs (10,886 kg) weapons
	ferry 2,500 n.miles (4,630 km)
Ceiling:	40,000+ ft (12,195 m)
Armament:	up to 12,000 (5,443 kg) lbs of bombs and missiles
Radar:	multi-function

Details of the A-12 Avenger shows the intakes for the two F412-GE-400 turbofan engines flush beneath the wing leading edge (exhausts are below the wing, short of the trailing edge). Outboard of the intakes on the wings are hexagonal di-electric panels, presumed to be associated with the APQ-183 multi-mode radar. (General Dynamics)

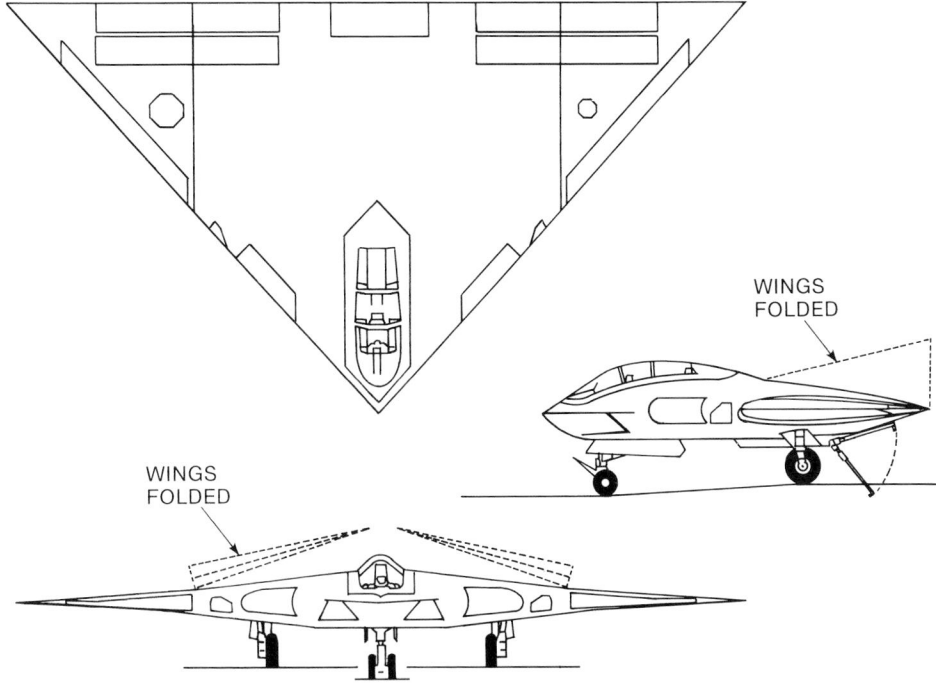

These drawings of the A-12 Avenger are based on official sketches produced by General Dynamics, courtesy American Institute of Astronautics and Aeronautics. (William Clipson)

An artist's concept of the A-12 Avenger. Control surfaces on the A-12 included "elevons" or "flaperons" and pairs of spoilers plus a single trailing-edge control surface between the elevons. With no vertical tail surfaces, the A-12 would have depended on differential use of the elevons and/or spoilers for yaw control. (General Dynamics)

AV-8B HARRIER

The AV-8B is an advanced VSTOL attack aircraft flown by eight Marine attack squadrons and one training squadron. Although not fitted with arresting gear or catapult points, these aircraft operate regularly from amphibious ships and have flown from aircraft carriers.

The AV-8B differs from the earlier AV-8A/C Harrier flown by the Marines in having a supercritical wing shape, larger trailing-edge flaps, drooped ailerons, strakes under the gun pods, redesigned engine intakes, strengthened landing gear, and a more-powerful engine, providing twice the payload of the AV-8A with up to 9,200 pounds (4,173 kg) of external stores. The aircraft carries one external 25-mm gun with the gun and ammunition in packs faired into the under fuselage, with one fuselage and six wing points available for bombs, rockets, missiles, or 300-gallon (1,140-liter) fuel tanks.

The AV-8B has replaced the A-4M and AV-8A/C aircraft in Marine VMA squadrons. During the Carter administration (1977–1981) the Department of Defense sought to have the Marines procure the F/A-18 Hornet as a replacement for the A-4M, but the Marines—with congressional support—held fast to the AV-8B program.[10] The Marine Corps originally planned to procure 336 operational AV-8B aircraft plus four full-scale development aircraft in addition to the two YAV-8B prototypes that were converted from AV-8A aircraft. This was revised to the actual production of 256 AV-8B models and 20 of the two-seat TAV-8B trainers, the last procurement being in fiscal 1991. NASA flies a YAV-8B to study integrated flight and engine controls.

The AV-8B was originally built with the Angle Rate Bombing System (ARBS), an electro-optical device limited to good weather conditions; the currently installed model is the ASB-19(V)3. Those aircraft delivered after September 1989 are night-attack capable, being fitted with nose-mounted FLIR, pilot night-vision goggles, HUD and color head-down displays, and digital moving-map systems. The 24 Harriers authorized in fiscal 1991 will be built with the APG-65 radar, those aircraft being delivered in 1993 (with the prototype radar aircraft—informally referred to as Harrier II+ variant—flying in late 1992). These aircraft will also have the improved Pegasus 408 engine. Earlier aircraft may be remanufactured to this configuration.

Also fitted are the ALR-67 RWR and the pod-mounted ALQ-164 ECM suite.

Status: Operational. First flight YAV-8B on 9 November 1978; first flight AV-8B on 5 November 1981. Marine IOC (VMA-331) in 1985.

The RAF procured essentially the same aircraft as the GR Mk 5 and the night-attack GR 7 variant; the British T Mk 10 variants are similar to the TAV-8B. Harrier variants are flown from VSTOL aircraft carriers by Italy, Spain, and India.

10. In the event, during the Reagan administration (1981–1988) then-Secretary of the Navy John Lehman procured both the AV-8B and the F/A-18 for the Marine Corps.

Manufacturer:	McDonnell Douglas and British Aerospace
Crew:	(1) pilot (2 in TAV-8B)
Engines:	1 Rolls-Royce F402-RR-406 Pegasus 11 Mk 103 turbofan; 21,700 lbst (9,843 kgst)
Weights:	empty 13,086 lbs (5,936 kg)
	max takeoff VTO 18,950 lbs (8,595 kg)
	max takeoff STO 31,000 lbs (14,061 kg) with 1,330-ft (405-m) takeoff run
Dimensions:	length 46 ft 4 in (14.12 m)
	wing span 30 ft 4 in (9.25 m)
	wing area 230 ft^2 (21.37 m^2)
	height 11 ft 7¾ in (3.55 m)
Speed:	max 668 mph (1,075 km) at sea level
Ceiling:	50,000 ft (15,244 m)
Range:	radius 150 n.miles (278 km) with 12 500-lb (227-kg) bombs with 1 hour loiter in STO takeoff
	radius 600 n.miles (1,111 km) with 7 500-lb bombs in STO mode
	ferry range 2,560 n.miles (4,741 km) with 4 300-gallon (1,140-liter) drop tanks
Armament:	1 25-mm cannon GAU-12/U (multi-barrel; 300 rounds)
	16 500-lb bombs, or
	4 Sidewinder AAMs
Radar:	APG-65 multi-mode being retrofitted

An AV-8B Harrier landing aboard the helicopter carrier SAIPAN. This ungainly aircraft design proved itself in combat in the Falkland Islands in 1982, flying from two British VSTOL carriers. The Harrier wings do not fold. (JO1 Kip Burke, USN)

A two-seat TAV-8B Harrier in hover. The TAV-8B variant has a longer fuselage and taller tail than the AV-8B and only two wing store stations for carrying training weapons. (McDonnell Douglas)

AV-8A HARRIER

The Harrier was the first VSTOL aircraft to enter first-line service with the U.S. armed forces. The British-developed Harrier was procured for three Marine attack squadrons. The Marines deemed it a success despite a high accident rate; 47 surviving AV-8A aircraft were upgraded to the AV-8C configuration, with two AV-8A Harriers being converted to YAV-8B prototypes for the Harrier II. All AV-8A/C aircraft have been discarded.

The Marine Corps took delivery of a total of 102 single-seat AV-8A (British GR 3 Mk 50) and eight two-seat TAV-8A (British T Mk 4 Mk 54) aircraft from 1971 to 1976 with McDonnell Douglas as the American support contractor.

See 14th Edition/page 403–404 for characteristics.

A-7E CORSAIR

The Corsair was a carrier-based, light attack aircraft in first-line Navy service from 1966 until 1991. It saw extensive combat in the Vietnam War, with the last two A-7E squadrons flying in the Gulf War (see chapter 28); those two A-7E squadrons flew almost 3,200 hours in that last conflict, with the units being disbanded in May 1991. The last naval air reserve units to fly the A-7E traded in their Corsairs for the F/A-18 in April 1991.

The A-7E was replaced in Navy carrier air wings by the F/A-18 Hornet; the Marine Corps did not fly the A-7. Production of the A-7 ended in 1983 with 1,551 Corsairs delivered—997 for the U.S. Navy, 459 A-7D and 30 two-seat A-7K for the U.S. Air Force, and 65 A-7H and TA-7H models for Greece; two A-7D models were upgraded to YA-7F prototypes for an improved close air support aircraft, but no mass conversion followed. Many former U.S. Navy aircraft were modified for foreign use.

Sixty U.S. Navy versions were two-seat TA-7C with dual controls (converted from A-7B and A-7C aircraft); a proposed RA-7E with reconnaissance pods was dropped in favor of the F-14/TARPS, and a proposed twin-engine A-7 variant lost out in the concept stage to the F/A-18 as the new Navy attack aircraft.

See 14th Edition/pages 404–405 for characteristics.

The Gulf War was the A-7 Corsair's finale. Here an A-7E from VA-72 on the JOHN F. KENNEDY flies low over the Saudi Arabian desert. The A-7 was previously found on all Navy attack carriers, but was not flown by the Marine Corps. (Comdr. John Leenhouts, USN)

A-6E INTRUDER (formerly A2F)

A highly versatile attack aircraft, the Intruder is the most capable carrier-based aircraft with respect to weapons payload. The A-6E is capable of all-weather, day/night strikes. The aircraft was to be replaced by the A-12 Avenger; however, with cancellation of that aircraft the A-6 is expected to remain in carrier service well into the 21st century, when it will be succeeded by the AX.

One A-6E squadron is assigned to each carrier wing; the aircraft is also flown by Marine medium attack squadrons, but those planes are being transferred to the Navy, with the last Marine A-6E scheduled to leave service in fiscal 1995.

The Intruder is a two-seat, twin-turbojet aircraft. All weapons are carried on five attachment points, each with a 6,200-lb (2,812-kg) capacity with a maximum mission payload of 18,000 lbs (8,165 kg) of ordnance and drop tanks. The A-6E can carry nuclear weapons as well as a variety of laser-guided bombs and guided missiles. The A-6E variant has the Target Recognition Attack Multisensor (TRAM), FLIR, a combination laser designator/range finder, and a laser designation receiver. The ALQ-67 RWR is also fitted as are chaff/flare dispensers.

The SWIP (Systems/Weapons Improvement Program) upgrade to 342 A-6Es further increases their attack capability, including the use of Harpoon and Maverick missiles, and improved ECM capabilities (ALR-67 and ALQ-126B). One hundred seventy-four of the SWIP aircraft are being fitted with composite wings to enable them to serve for a few more years.

An improved A-6F, with new avionics and the APQ-173 radar, the GE F404 engines, and composite-material wings, was being developed with an IOC planned for the late 1980s; that project has been cancelled as was a proposed new A-6G aircraft. As late as 1990 the Navy was requesting cost data from Grumman for 500 A-6G variants—300 new aircraft and 200 remanufactured A-6E aircraft because of delays in the A-12 program.

The KA-6D tankers (all converted from earlier aircraft) have avionics deleted from the after fuselage to provide space for a refueling hose reel; up to five 500-gallon (1,900-liter) drop tanks can be carried to permit the transfer of over 21,000 pounds (9,525 kg) of fuel immediately after takeoff or 15,000 pounds (6,804 kg) at a distance of 288 n.miles (533 km) from the carrier. The first A-6A conversion flew on 16 April 1970, designated NA-6A as land-based tanker test aircraft. All tankers will be gone by 1994.

All Intruder variants have a prominent, fixed refueling probe forward of the cockpit; wings fold for carrier stowage.

The EA-6A Intruder and EA-6B Prowler electronic warfare variants are listed separately in this edition.

Status: Operational. First flight A-6A on 19 April 1960. A-6A IOC (VA-42) in February 1963; KA-6D IOC (VA-176) in September 1970; A-6E IOC in September 1971.

More than 700 aircraft of all variants have been built for the Navy and Marine Corps, with production ending in 1991; 240 A-6A/B/C aircraft were upgraded to the A-6E variant. There are no foreign users of the aircraft.

Manufacturer:	Grumman
Crew:	(2) pilot, bombardier/navigator
Engines:	2 Pratt & Whitney J52-P-8B turbojet; 9,300 lbst (4,218 kgst) each
Weights:	empty 26,660 lbs (12,093 kg)
	max takeoff 60,400 lbs (27,397 kg)
Dimensions:	length overall 54 ft 9 in (16.69 m)
	wing span 53 ft (16.15 m)
	wing area 528.9 ft² (49.1 m²)
	height 16 ft 2 in (4.93 m)
Speed:	max 644 mph (1,036 kmh) at sea level
Ceiling:	42,400 ft (12,927 m)
Range:	880 n.miles (1,630 km) with combat load
	ferry 2,375 n.miles (4,400 km)
Armament:	30,500 lbs (13,835 kg) bombs and missiles, or
	10 1,000-lb (454-kg) bombs, or
	3 2,000-lb (907-kg) bombs + 2 300-gallon (1,140-liter) drop tanks, or
	1 B57 nuclear bomb + 4 300-gallon drop tanks, or
	HARM, Harpoon, Maverick, Sidewinder, Skipper, SLAM missiles
Radar:	APQ-148 multi-mode

An A-6E Intruder in low-visibility markings from VX-5. This aircraft is the Navy's only "medium" attack aircraft; it will probably be succeeded in Navy service by a variant of the F/A-18 Hornet. (U.S. Navy)

An upgraded (SWIP) A-6E Intruder from VA-36 being serviced. The Intruder has a fixed refueling probe and a TRAM sensor under the nose, which houses the APQ-148 multi-mode radar; note the folded wings. (Peter B. Mersky)

A KA-6D Intruder tanker from VA-34 on the Dwight D. Eisenhower. The refueling drogue is streamed from the device under the fuselage, just below the word "Navy." The KA-6D tankers are being phased out in favor of "buddy stores" carried on other aircraft, including the S-3B Viking ASW aircraft. (Cmdr. John Leenhouts, USN)

The view from the cockpit of an A-6E Intruder while refueling from a KA-6D tanker. The tanker has five 500-gallon (1,900-liter) external fuel tanks mounted under the fuselage and wings. (PH1 Paul D. Goodrich, USN)

A-4 SKYHAWK (formerly A4D)

The Skyhawk was developed in the early 1950s as a lightweight, daylight-only nuclear strike aircraft for use in large numbers from aircraft carriers. The aircraft subsequently evolved into a highly versatile attack aircraft, widely used by the Navy and Marine Corps as well as several foreign air forces. It survives in Navy service mainly as a trainer and utility aircraft, and with the Marine air reserve as a light-attack plane, with the last being replaced by the F/A-18 Hornet. (The Navy flies the Skyhawk in the adversary training squadrons as MiG stand-ins with the name Mongoose, a play on the NATO designation of Soviet trainers with M-series names.)

The basic Skyhawk is a single-seat, single-engine aircraft with a delta wing, which does not fold for carrier stowage. Two 20-mm cannon are fitted in the wing roots and there are five attachment points for up to 9,155 pounds of ordnance or external fuel tanks. A dorsal hump on the A-4M and some A-4F aircraft houses avionics equipment.

Marine A-4Ms have the Angle Rate Bombing System (ARBS), a computerized system with a dual-mode television and laser tracker that significantly increases the accuracy of weapon delivery.

Operational: The Israeli Air Force has made extensive use of A-4s in Middle East combat as did the Argentine Navy and Air Force during the 1982 conflict in the Falklands. The surviving A-4K Skyhawks of the Kuwaiti Air Force flew combat strikes from Saudi Arabia after the Iraqi invasion of Kuwait in August 1990.

Status: First flight on 22 June 1954. Navy IOC (VA-72) in September 1956. IOC A-4M (VMA-324 and VMA-513) in April 1971.

A total of 2,960 A-4s were built for U.S. and foreign use, of which 555 were two-seaters; the first was delivered in 1956 and the last, an A-4M for the Marine Corps, in 1979. This was one of the longest production runs of any combat aircraft in history. The Navy TA-4J variant will be replaced in the training role by the T-45 Goshawk, while the Marines have received the AV-8B to replace the A-4M. The Navy-Marine Blue Angels flight demonstration team flew the A-4F until transitioning to the F/A-18 in 1987. Many A-4s survive in foreign air forces.

This partially camouflaged A-4E Skyhawk from VC-1 has a red star to indicate it plays the role of an aggressor aircraft in adversary training. The diminutive Skyhawk has proven to be one of the most flexible aircraft ever built. (U.S. Navy)

A-4M

Manufacturer:	McDonnell Douglas
Crew:	(1) pilot (2 in TA-4J, OA-4M, TA-4F)
Engines:	1 Pratt & Whitney J52-P-408 turbojet; 11,200 lbst (5,080 kgst)
Weights:	empty 10,465 lbs (4,747 kg)
	max takeoff 24,500 lbs (11,113 kg)
Dimensions:	length A-4M 40 ft 3¾ in (12.27 m)
	TA-4J 42 ft 7¼ in (12.98 m)
	wing span 27 ft 6 in (8.38 m)
	wing area 260 ft² (24.16 m²)
	height A-4M 15 ft (4.57 m)
	TA-4J 15 ft 3 in (4.66 m)
Speed:	max 670 mph (1,078 kmh) at sea level
	645 mph (1,038 kmh) with 4,000 lbs (1,814 kg) weapons
	cruise 483 mph (777 kmh)
Ceiling:	42,250 ft (12,881 m)
Range:	radius 335 n.miles (620 km) with 4,000 lbs bombs, missiles, and rockets
Armament:	2 20-mm cannon Mk 12 (100 rounds each)
	14 500-lb (227-kg) bombs, or
	3 1,000-lb (454-kg) bombs, or
	1 2,000-lb (907-kg) bomb, or
	1 B57 nuclear bomb, or
	4 Maverick ASMs, or
	3 Walleye ASMs
Radar:	none

A-3B SKYWARRIOR

The few surviving EA-3B variants of the Skywarrior attack aircraft are listed under Electronic Aircraft in this chapter.

A TA-4J Skyhawk from VX-5 in low-visibility markings. Most two-seat TA-4Js are with the Naval Air Training Command and have high-visibility markings—white and international orange. (U.S. Navy)

An A-4F Skyhawk assigned to VF-43, the adversary training squadron at NAS Oceana, Va. The A-4 has a fixed refueling probe along the starboard side; the wings are too small to fold for carrier stowage. (Peter B. Mersky)

MARITIME PATROL/ANTI-SUBMARINE AIRCRAFT

The U.S. Navy has a current requirement for 443 land-based maritime patrol aircraft for active and reserve VP and other, specialized squadron use. However, the reductions in the number of VP squadrons and the number of planes per squadron will reduce the requirement to some 300 aircraft in active/reserve VP squadrons and related pipelines in 1994 plus the special-purpose aircraft (EP-3, RP-3, etc.).

Following cancellation of the P-7 LRAACA program the Navy is examining options for maritime patrol aircraft; the most probable options are to resume production of an updated P-3 Orion variant or to "remanufacture" P-3B/C aircraft into an improved P-3H configuration for U.S. service. The proposed P-3H variant would have the Update IV avionics, survivability enhancements, extended-range Harpoon capability, and larger sonobuoy capacity. A Navy cost estimate for remanufacturing in late 1991 predicted that the P-3H would cost $35 to $40 million per plane plus almost $1 *billion* in research and development costs.

The only P-3 production now under way in the United States consists of eight P-3C variants for the Republic of Korea, to be delivered in 1995. Kawasaki continues to manufacture the P-3C under license for the Japanese Maritime Self-Defense Force. However, following cancellation of the P-7, the production of additional P-3 Orions for the U.S. Navy appears likely.

P-7A LONG-RANGE AIR ANTI-SUBMARINE WARFARE CAPABLE AIRCRAFT

The P-7 LRAACA was intended as a replacement for the P-3 Orion in the maritime patrol/ASW roles. Development and procurement of the P-7 was cancelled on 20 July 1990 by the Navy because the contractor, Lockheed, "failed to make adequate progress toward completion of all contract phases, which were to have resulted in the delivery of two prototype aircraft in April and December 1992." The cancellation also affected 125 production aircraft to have been delivered from 1994 through 2001 in addition to the two prototypes.

In the mid-1980s the Navy held a competition for the P-3 replacement between the Lockheed design, the Boeing 757, and the McDonnell Douglas MD-87. The modified P-3 design submitted by Lockheed Aeronautical Systems of Burbank, Calif., was selected in October 1988 on the basis of acquisition and life-cycle costs, according to the Navy.[11] The $3.5 *billion* program was badly needed at Lockheed, with the last P-3 Orion then scheduled to come off the production line in September 1991 and with few other aircraft on the Lockheed order book. Lockheed subsequently experienced major cost problems with the P-7 program as well as some technical difficulties. The latter were particularly perplexing to observers because the Lockheed design was in several respects an enlarged P-3, with less technical innovation than either of the competitive designs.

The LRAACA bears a strong resemblance to the P-3 Orion; there was to be a large internal weapons bay plus 12 wing hard points for weapons. Up to 150 A-size and 6 B-size sonobuoys were to be carried; other sensors were to be radar and Magnetic Anomaly

11. Boeing proposed a modified version of the 757 twin-engine commercial transport and McDonnell Douglas a modified MD-87 twin-engine transport, the latter with ultra-high-bypass-ratio engines. Gulfstream Aerospace had also proposed a twin-engine, wide-body Gulfstream 4 for the LRAACA program, but it was not accepted as a viable competitor.

Detection (MAD) gear. Up to 150 additional sonobuoys to be carried in ten pylon-mounted external packs were proposed. The P-7 was to have the equivalent of the P-3 Update IV mission suite (see below) with the UYS-2 Enhanced Modular Signal Processor (EMSP), able to monitor 54 DIFAR sonobuoys at once. Other avionics included the Texas Instruments APS-137 Inverse Synthetic-Aperture Radar (ISAR), AAS-36 infrared detection system, SATCOMM receiver, inertial navigation system (INS), Omega Global Positioning Satellite (GPS) navigation, ALR-66(V)5 ESM equipment, and ALE-47 chaff/flare dispensers. An ALR-77 ESM suite, if available, may have been fitted in place of the ALR-66.

The T407 engines were estimated to have a 25 percent lower fuel consumption over the aircraft operating envelope compared with the P-3's T56 engines. The improved performance was due in part to five-bladed composite propellers.

Initial Navy planning was for 125 aircraft plus two prototypes, but more aircraft were anticipated in addition to eventual foreign orders. The German government in April 1988 announced that it planned to select the P-7 to replace its Dassault-Breguet Atlantique ASW aircraft for long-range maritime patrol duties.

Manufacturer:	Lockheed
Crew:	(10)
Engines:	4 General Electric T407-GE-400 turboprop; 5,150 shp each
Weights:	empty 105,000 lbs (47,628 kg)
	gross 165,000 lbs (74,844 kg)
	max takeoff 171,350 lbs (77,724 kg)
Dimensions:	length (fuselage) 112 ft 8 in (34.34 m)
	wing span 106 ft 7 in (32.49 m)
	wing area 1,438 ft² (129.42 m²)
	height 32 ft 11 in (10.04 m)
Speed:	
Ceiling:	
Range:	radius 1,600 n.miles (2,963 km) with 6 hours on station
Armament:	23,661 lbs (10,733 kg) of missiles and ASW torpedoes, including 7,500 lbs (3,402 kg) carried in internal weapons bay (8 Mk 50 torpedoes or four extended-range Harpoon ASM or 3 B57 nuclear depth bombs)
Radar:	APS-137 ISAR

The aborted P-7A LRAACA was a derivative of the long-serving P-3 Orion. Still, the plane ran afoul of technical problems and delays, leading to cancellation of the entire program. In this artist's concept an ASW torpedo has just been released from the weapons bay, and the parachute is opening. A variety of weapons are shown on the plane's 12 wing pylons. (Lockheed)

P-3   ORION (formerly P3V)

The Orion is a long-range maritime reconnaissance and ASW aircraft, with the Harpoon anti-ship missile providing a surface attack capability. The P-3C Orion serves in all 22 active Navy patrol squadrons (VP-VPU) and the P-3B/C models in 9 reserve VP units, with several specialized EP-3 ELINT, RP-3 reconnaissance, and utility variants also in naval service—a current total of some 440 aircraft.

The Orion was adapted from the commercial Electra transport with a lengthened fuselage and other design modifications. It is powered by four turboprop engines. Up to 15,000 pounds (6,804 kg) of rockets, missiles, mines, ASW torpedoes, or nuclear depth bombs can be carried in the internal weapons bay and on ten wing pylons. The P-3C aircraft are fitted to carry the Harpoon. (In the early 1970s some P-3B variants were fitted to carry the AGM-12 Bullpup missile.) The plane's ASW equipment includes radar, tail-mounted ASQ-81 MAD, and 48 external (fuselage) sonobuoy chutes plus 4 in-flight reloadable (internal) chutes; a total of 84 buoys are normally carried.

The P-3C variants have undergone a series of modernizations: Update I of the mid-1970s included a computer upgrade, Omega navigation system, additional tactical displays, and a new tactical program for computer-aided analysis of incoming data. Update II introduced in 1977 had additional navigation capabilities and provision for the Harpoon anti-ship missile. The latest improvement series is Update III, introduced in 1984; this provides an IBM Proteus signal processor system and new avionics. An Update IV has been developed that further improves EW, radar, and acoustic systems: APS-137(V) Inverse Synthetic Aperture Radar (ISAR), ALR-66(V)5 ESM suite, and AAS-36 Infrared (IR) detection set as well as the ASQ-81 MAD and other gear. The prototype flew in late 1991, but 140 planned upgrades were canceled in October 1992. Plans to provide an in-flight refueling capability have not been pursued.

The 31 EP-3 variants have automatic electronic and communication intercept/analysis equipment to provide fleet and task force commanders with real-time intelligence; the latest variant is the EP-3E Aries II fitted with the ALR-52 multi-band frequency-measuring receiver and/or ALR-60 Deepwell communications intercept/analysis system, and ALR-76 combined ESM/radar warning system. A few RP-3 aircraft are flown in various research configurations by the Navy. The Navy also flies 38 "bob-tailed" (sans MAD "stinger") UP-3As and five VP-3A aircraft as executive transports and support aircraft. Two WP-3D are operated by the Commerce Department/NOAA, and several UP-3A aircraft have been on loan to the Customs Service for anti-drug surveillance since October 1985 (those aircraft have been fitted with an APG-53 radar, as in the Air Force F-15 fighter); NASA flies one P-3B.

In June 1988 the Customs Service took delivery of an ex-Australian P-3B refitted with an APS-125 radar (with rotodome antenna, as in the E-2C); a second P-3B fitted with an APS-138 radar entered service in April 1989. A third modification is planned.

A planned P-3G for the U.S. Navy was to have had new engines and updated avionics. (This aircraft has been incorrectly identified as a P-3F in some official documents; six P-3F variants were produced for Iran.) The procurement of 125 P-3G models in fiscal 1990–1995 was envisioned; the P-7 LRAACA was developed in place of the P-3G. Proposals were also being considered to re-engine and upgrade the avionics of the P-3C force, with a possible enlargement of the weapons bay to internally carry extended-range Harpoon missiles; that upgrade was sometimes listed as the P-3H. Two ASW variants were converted in 1991–1992 to an EP-3J configuration.

Status: Operational; in production (for South Korea). First flight (aerodynamic airframe) on 19 August 1958; YP-3A on 25 November 1959; P-3A on 15 April 1961; YP-3C on 18 September 1968. P-3A IOC (VP-8) in August 1962; P-3C IOC in 1969.

Lockheed Burbank delivered a total of 548 Orions to the U.S. Navy and Naval Air Reserve; about 150 additional aircraft are flown by Australia, Canada, Iran, Japan, the Netherlands, New Zealand, Norway, Portugal, Spain, and Thailand. Kawasaki in Japan is producing 97 aircraft. The last U.S. Navy P-3C was delivered on 17 April 1991. Eight P-3C aircraft are being produced for South Korea with delivery in 1995.

All "straight" P-3A patrol aircraft have been discarded by U.S. Navy Patrol squadrons, the last removed in February 1991.

P-3C

Manufacturer:	Lockheed[12]
Crew:	(10) command pilot, 2 pilots, flight engineer, navigator/communications officer, tactical coordinator, 3 systems operators, technician; provisions for 2 additional observers
Engines:	4 Allison T56-A-14 turboprop; 4,910 ehp each
Weights:	empty 61,491 lbs (27,892 kg)
	normal takeoff 135,000 lbs (61,236 kg)
	max takeoff 142,000 lbs (64,411 kg)
Dimensions:	length 116 ft 10 in (35.61 m)
	wing span 99 ft 8 in (30.37 m)
	wing area 1,300 ft² (120.77 m²)
	height 33 ft 8½ in (10.29 m)
Speed:	max 473 mph (761 kmh) at 15,000 ft (4,573 m)
	cruise 380 mph (611 kmh) at 25,000 ft (7,622 m)
	loiter 230 mph (370 kmh) with two engines shut down
Ceiling:	28,300 ft (8,628 m)
Range:	radius 1,346 n.miles (2,493 km) with 13 hours on station

Armament:	weapons bay	wing points
	8 Mk 46 torpedoes	+ 4 Mk 46 torpedoes
	or 2 2,000-lb mines	+ 4 Mk 46 torpedoes
	or 4 1,000-lb mines	+ 4 Mk 46 torpedoes
	or 8 Mk 46 torpedoes	+ 16 5-inch rockets
	or 3 B57 nuclear depth bombs	
Radar:	APS-20 in EP-3B/E	
	APS-80 in P-3B	
	APS-115 in P-3C	

12. All P-3 production was carried out at the Lockheed facility in Palmdale, Calif., until 1991, when that assembly line was closed down and the tooling moved to Marietta, Ga.; the first aircraft built at the new line were the eight South Korean units.

Mechanics from reserve VP-64 work on the antenna or "stinger" for the Magnetic Anomaly Detection (MAD) gear of a P-3 Orion. During the Cold War era, reserve maritime patrol squadrons regularly flew ASW missions from bases in the United States and abroad. (U.S. Navy)

An updated P-3C Orion banks while carrying four Harpoon anti-ship missiles and several practice bombs. These aircraft pose a significant anti-ship attack and minelaying capability when there is no hostile threat. The aircraft's weapons bay is open. (U.S. Navy)

A P-3 Orion taxis at NAS Oceana. Three of the aircraft's turboprop engines are turning and one is shut down; the Orion can cruise on two engines. (Peter B. Mersky)

P-2 NEPTUNE (formerly P2V)

The last P-2/P2V Neptune patrol aircraft has been retired from U.S. naval service. Three EP-2H models survived into the early 1980s, assigned to squadron VC-8 to support target drones. Lockheed produced 1,036 Neptunes for U.S. and foreign service, and Kawasaki in Japan built another 89 P-2J variants (with 48 of the Lockheed aircraft assembled in Japan). Seven P2V-7U Neptunes were delivered to the U.S. Air Force in 1954 and flew as RB-69A electronic reconnaissance aircraft. The 12 P2V-3C variants of the late 1940s were configured for carrier launch, but not recovery, to provide the first U.S. ship-based nuclear strike capability. Japan is the only nation to currently fly Neptunes.

S-3 VIKING

The S-3 Viking is the Navy's carrier-based ASW aircraft, with one six-plane squadron serving on board each carrier. The Viking replaced the S2F/S-2 Tracker as the Navy's ship-based, fixed-wing ASW aircraft. Existing aircraft are being upgraded to the S-3B configuration.

The S-3 was designed to be within the approximate dimensions of the piston-engine Tracker, but to be faster and to carry more advanced ASW equipment. The internal weapons bay, sized to hold four Mk 44 or Mk 46 torpedoes, can carry 2,400 pounds (1,089 kg) of weapons. There are also two wing pylons, which in the S-3B are upgraded to carry the Harpoon anti-ship missile. ASW systems include the ASQ-81 MAD, FLIR, and 60 sonobuoys in fuselage chutes. The wings and tail fin fold for carrier stowage.

The S-3B has an improved acoustic processor and the improved APS-137 ISAR radar. Five preproduction and one later S-3A aircraft have been modified to a US-3A cargo configuration for operation from carriers in the Western Pacific and Indian Ocean. These planes have two pilots, a loadmaster, and room for five passengers plus 4,600 pounds (2,086 kg) of cargo, or an all-cargo load of 7,500 pounds (3,400 kg). A KS-3 tanker configuration has been proposed as well as pod tanks and a drogue system for the US-3A variant; no production has been sought by the Navy. Sixteen S-3A aircraft are being converted to the ELINT role and are designated ES-3A; see page 423.

An S-3 AEW configuration has been proposed by Lockheed; a fixed L-band phased-array radar would be fitted atop the fuselage.

An early S-3B Viking banks to show two Harpoon anti-ship missiles. The internal weapons bay (between the engine nacelles) is closed; aft are the aircraft's sonobuoy chutes, recessed into the after fuselage. (Lockheed-California)

Operational: Carrier-based S-3B aircraft served as ground attack aircraft in Operation Desert Storm, carrying out bombing missions with 500-pound (227-kg) general-purpose bombs. They also flew in the aerial tanker role, using pod-mounted refueling equipment to support other carrier aircraft (replacing the KA-6D tankers).

Status: Operational. First flight on 21 January 1972. S-3A IOC (VS-41) in February 1974.

The last of 187 S-3A aircraft was completed in 1978. Up to 160 are being upgraded to S-3B by 1994. Proposals for additional S-3 production have not come to fruition.

An S-3A Viking from VS-31 aboard the DWIGHT D. EISENHOWER with its MAD "stinger" extended; the tail boom retracts for landing and takeoff. The aircraft has electronic antennas on its wingtips. (U.S. Navy)

S-3A

Manufacturer:	Lockheed
Crew:	(4) pilot, copilot, tactical coordinator, systems operator
Engines:	2 General Electric TF34-GE-400 turbofan; 9,275 lbst (4,207 kgst) each
Weights:	empty 26,783 lbs (12,149 kg)
	max takeoff 52,539 lbs (23,832 kg)
Dimensions:	length 53 ft 4 in (16.26 m)
	wing span 68 ft 8 in (20.93 m)
	wing area 598 ft² (55.56 m²)
	height 22 ft 9 in (6.94 m)
Speed:	max 506 mph (814 kmh) at sea level
	cruise 403 mph (648.5 kmh)
	loiter 240 mph (386 kmh) at 20,000 ft (6,098 m)
Ceiling:	40,000 ft (12,195 m)
Range:	patrol 2,300+ n.miles (4,260 km)
	ferry 3,000+ n.miles (5,556 km)

Armament:	weapons bay	wing points
	4 Mk 46 torpedoes	+ 6 500-lb bombs
	or 4 500-lb bombs	+ 6 500-lb bombs
	or 1 B57 nuclear depth bomb	
Radar:	APS-116 in S-3A	
	APS-137 ISAR in S-3B	

An S-3A Viking from VS-41 when the squadron was aboard the ENTERPRISE. The wings fold asymmetrically across the fuselage, and the tail fin folds down. VS-29 is now aboard the carrier ABRAHAM LINCOLN. (Lockheed-California)

S-2 TRACKER (formerly S2F)

The last U.S. Navy S-2 series Tracker was discarded in March 1986. The aircraft, in U.S. naval service from 1954 to 1976 in the carrier-based ASW role, was the progenitor of the E-1 Tracer and C-1 Trader aircraft. The last U.S. Navy Tracker—called "Stoof" from its original S2F designation—was an ES-2D configured as a range support aircraft, retired in March 1986. The last ASW variant was an S-2G, retired from VS-37 in August 1976.

Grumman produced a total of 1,184 Trackers for U.S. and foreign service, with another 100 built in Canada; many U.S. aircraft were later transferred to other nations after Navy service, with several remaining in foreign service.

A US-3A cargo version of the Viking sits on the runway at Bahrain. The highly decorated aircraft, from VRC-50, has the ship name INDEPENDENCE below "Navy." CODs are not based aboard ship, but during sustained operations in the Indian Ocean they sometimes roost on carriers for short periods. (Lt. [jg] S. Jones, USN)

ELECTRONIC AIRCRAFT

U.S. naval electronic aircraft have two distinct types of designations: those with E-series designations that were designed specifically for an electronic mission (e.g., E-2C, E-6A), and those that have been adapted from other aircraft types and have an E-prefix to their designation (e.g., EA-6B, EC-130Q, EP-3E). In this subsection all electronic aircraft are listed in alphabetical sequence by designation, which is not their chronological order.

In addition to the electronic aircraft discussed here, the Customs Service flies AEW-configured P-3 Orions and the Coast Guard has an AEW-configured C-130 Hercules; see pages 412 and 430, respectively.

Designations: The two NKC-135A electronic simulation aircraft have a "permanent special test" designation (letter *N* prefix). It is used for a variety of Air Force, Navy, and NASA test and research aircraft, including several modified C-135s and KC-135s.

Operational: The two NKC-135A and the single EC-24 aircraft are operated by contractor personnel for the Fleet Electronic Warfare Support Group (FEWSG) to provide ECM training for naval forces. These planes have Navy markings but do not carry FEWSG's GD tail code.

Squadrons VAQ-33, VAQ-34, and VAQ-35 also operate under FEWSG.

ADVANCED TACTICAL SUPPORT AIRCRAFT

This plane is viewed by the Navy as a "totally new start"—an aircraft to replace the EA-3B Skywarrior, the E-2C Hawkeye, the EA-6B Prowler, and eventually the S-3B and ES-3A Viking, while possibly providing new capabilities to support carrier battle groups. The Advanced Tactical Support (ATS) aircraft was conceived in the late 1980s, and funding for advanced development was provided by Congress until fiscal 1991, when all ATS funding was deleted.

The V-22 Osprey VSTOL aircraft was at one point considered a viable candidate for the ATS role until Secretary of Defense Cheney cancelled the V-22 program (see page 437). In the ATS role the V-22 would have the valuable attributes of being independent of flight-deck cycles on large carriers and being capable of operating from large surface combatant and amphibious ships. (Meanwhile, British Aerospace and the Bell-Boeing team have revealed proposals for a long-range, anti-submarine version of the V-22, while potential British carrier-based airborne early-warning and other variants are being evaluated.)

The Navy had also identified two other potential roles for the ATS: (1) airborne battle management, having the computer power and other facilities to enable a force commander or tactical action officer to direct operations from above the force, and (2) the "missileer" concept. First advanced in the 1960s with the never-built Douglas F6D aircraft, the missileer provides for a relatively low-performance aircraft to remain on station for long periods with advanced air-to-air missiles to intercept incoming attackers.

When this edition went to press, it appeared that efforts would be made to extend the service life of the E-2C, EA-6B, and ES-3A, with an ATS not becoming available for service use before 2005–2010.

E-6A MERCURY

This aircraft has replaced the EC-130 Hercules in the TACAMO (Take Charge And Move Out) role of providing VLF radio relay to strategic missile submarines at sea. The E-6A is a navalized version of the Boeing 707-320B airframe, which also serves as the airframe for the E-3A AWACS (Airborne Warning And Control System); the KC-135/C-135/VC-137/EC-18/E-8A aircraft are similar.

The E-6A has the familiar lines of the Boeing 707-series commercial transports, but is fitted with four large GE/SNECMA turbofan engines. (The engine oil tanks have been enlarged to provide for increased flight endurance.)

The aircraft was developed under the designation EXC. The Navy had proposed a competition of available airframes; however, only the Boeing Company responded, proposing the modified Boeing 707-320B airframe, which also serves as the E-3 AWACS. In the TACAMO role the E-6A has essentially the same communications equipment as the EC-130Q, with two trailing-wire antennas, one almost 5,000 feet (1,524 m) and the other some 25,000 feet (7,622 m) in length; only the shorter wire is electrically charged, with energy re-radiating off of the longer wire. Wingtip pods on the E-6A contain satellite communication antennas. The aircraft are hardened against Electro-magnetic Pulse (EMP) effects. They retain the in-flight refueling receptacle for the Air Force flying-boom refueling system. Normal mission duration is 16 hours; with in-flight refueling that can be extended to 72 hours.

Status: Operational. First flight on 19 February 1987. IOC (VQ-3) in August 1989.

The E-6A program consists of one prototype aircraft that has been upgraded to full operational capability and 15 production aircraft. The prototype was delivered in 1987; that aircraft was reconfigured as a standard E-6A and "redelivered" in 1992. The remaining aircraft were delivered through 1992.

The aircraft was originally named Hermes; it was changed in 1991 to Mercury.

Manufacturer:	Boeing
Crew:	(18) 4 flight crew + 6 mission crew + 8 relief crew
Engines:	4 General Electric/SNECMA (CFM56-2A-2) F108-CF-100 turbofan; 24,000 lbst (10,886 kgst) each
Weights:	empty operating 172,795 lbs (78,380 kg)
	max takeoff 342,000 lbs (155,131 kg)
Dimensions:	length 152 ft 11 in (46.62 m)
	wing span 148 ft 2 in (45.17 m)
	wing area 3,050 ft² (283.4 m²)
	height 42 ft 5 in (12.93 m)
Speed:	cruise 508 mph (817 kmh)
	max 607 mph (977 kmh)
Ceiling:	42,000 ft (12,805 m)
Range:	6,600 n.miles (12,223 km)
	radius 1,000 n.miles (1,852 km) with 10.5 hours loiter on station
Radar:	APS-133 weather

An E-6A Mercury streams its two trailing wire antennas. The aircraft will become the nation's only strategic command/communications aircraft. The name was changed from Hermes (Greek mythology) to Mercury (Roman) to avoid confusion with the disease herpes. (Department of Defense)

An E-6A Mercury reveals its lineage to the Boeing 707/C-135/E-3 series during a roll-out at the Boeing Company plant near Seattle, Washington. Note the wingtip SATCOMM antennas. (Boeing)

E-2C HAWKEYE (formerly W2F)

The Hawkeye is an Airborne Early Warning (AEW) aircraft developed specifically for carrier operation. The E-2C variant is considered by many authorities as the most capable radar warning and aircraft control plane now in service. A four- or five-plane squadron is provided to each carrier, having replaced the piston-engine WF/E-1 Tracer in active squadrons and the two reserve AEW units.

The Hawkeye's most distinctive feature is the 24-foot (7.3-m) diameter, saucer-like radome for the APS-138 or APS-139 UHF radar. The radome revolves freely in the airstream at the rate of six revolutions per minute. It provides sufficient lift to offset its own weight in flight and on board ship can be lowered to facilitate aircraft handling. The E-2C represents primarily an avionics upgrade over the previous E-2A/B variants (which had the APS-96 radar). Beginning with the fiscal 1986 procurement, the E-2C will have the upgraded T56-427 engines, providing improved flight safety and an increase in aircraft weight.

The APS-120 radar with overland surveillance capability was initially installed in E-2C aircraft. Electronic upgrades have included the APS-125 radar with an effective aircraft detection range of some 240 n.miles (444.5 km) with an over-land/water capability; the aircraft can simultaneously track more than 250 air targets and control up to 30 interceptors. The ALR-73 passive detection system is also installed. The more-capable APS-145 radar is being developed as an update for all E-2C aircraft.

Status: Operational; in production. First flight E-2A on 21 October 1960; first flight E-2C on 20 January 1971. IOC E-2A (VAW-11) in January 1964; IOC E-2C (VAW-123) in November 1973.

The operations spaces in the E-6A Mercury will be expanded for limited command and control of U.S. strategic forces in addition to communications relay to SSBNs. (Department of Defense)

Fifty-nine E-2A aircraft were delivered from 1960 to 1967; all have been retired. The E-2B was a designation assigned but not popularly used for E-2A aircraft with upgraded computers. Two E-2A development aircraft were modified to a YE-2C configuration; these and two early-production E-2C aircraft were later employed as trainers (TE-2C). Production ended with the fiscal 1992 procurement of six aircraft.

In early 1992 the Navy had approximately 110 E-2C aircraft in service. A small number of E-2C aircraft were transferred to the Coast Guard in 1987 and to the Customs Service in 1989 for anti-drug operations; the Coast Guard lost one aircraft and the others were returned to the Navy by 1991. The aircraft is also flown by Egypt, Israel, Japan, and Singapore and is on order for Thailand. Taiwan flies the E-2B aircraft, redesignated E-2T; reportedly they are being upgraded with the APS-145 radar.

Operational: On 17–19 December 1991, a modified E-2C flying from the Naval Air Test Center at Patuxent River, Md., set 14 world flight records. All had previously been established in 1982 by a Soviet aircraft.

Manufacturer:	Grumman
Crew:	(5) pilot, copilot, combat information center officer, air controller, radar operator or technician
Engines:	2 Allison T56-A-422 turboprop; 4,591 shp each
Weights:	empty 37,678 lbs (17,090 kg)
	max takeoff 51,569 lbs (23,392 kg)
Dimensions:	length 57 ft 7 in (17.56 m)
	wing span 80 ft 7 in (24.58 m)
	wing area 700 ft² (65.03 m²)
	height 18 ft 4 in (5.59 m)
Speed:	max 375 mph (603 kmh)
	cruise 310 mph (499 kmh)
Ceiling:	service 30,800 ft (9,390 m)
	max approx. 40,000 ft (12,195 m)
Range:	radius 200 n.miles (370 km) with 6 hours on station
	ferry 1,525 n.miles
Armament:	none
Radar:	APS-138/139 (APS-120/125 in early E-2C aircraft); to be replaced by APS-145

An E-2C Hawkeye taxis on a Middle East runway during a multi-national exercise. The Hawkeye is scheduled for eventual replacement by a multi-purpose Advanced Tactical Support Aircraft (ATSA). One of the candidates for that platform is the V-22 tilt-rotor Osprey. (Department of Defense)

EA-6B   PROWLER

The EA-6B is an extensively modified Intruder with significantly more EW/ECM capabilities than previous carrier-based electronic aircraft. Four-plane VAQ squadrons flying the Prowler are normally assigned to each carrier imaging.

The Prowler has the basic Intruder configuration with an enlarged cockpit for four crew. There is a distinctive electronics pod mounted atop the tail fin, and up to five jamming pods and two fuel tanks can be carried on fuselage and wing pylons. The weight of internal avionics/EW equipment totals 8,000 pounds (3,636 kg) in addition to 950 pounds (431 kg) being carried on each of five pylons. Normally five ALQ-99 pods are carried, each with two jamming transmitters, although a 300-gallon (1,140-liter) drop tank can be substituted for each pod. Beginning in 1986, EA-6B aircraft have been configured to carry the HARM anti-radar missile, their first "hard kill" armament.

A KA-6H tanker based on the enlarged EA-6B airframe was proposed as a successor to the KA-6D, but none were procured.

The EA-6B has undergone a number of EW system upgrades since the original configuration with these modifications being given the designations EXCAP (Expanded Capability), in service from 1973 to 1985; ICAP (Improve Capability), first delivered in 1976; ICAP II, first delivered in 1984; and ADVCAP (Advanced Capability) entering service in 1994. These upgrades respond to changing foreign radar/SAM threats and have been incorporated into new-production aircraft.

The ADVCAP upgrades include adding the low-band ALQ-149 communications ECM, providing two additional ALE-39 chaff/flare dispensers (a total of four), and fitting the J52-P-409 engine to increase allowable landing weight by about 2,000 pounds (909 kg) and decrease stall speed; wing pylons are increased to seven; and the GPS (Global Positioning System) is provided. In addition, the jammer pods have been successively upgraded from the basic ALQ-99 to the A/B/C configurations, primarily to increase reliability.

An E-2C Hawkeye from VAW-125 about to touch down on the carrier SARATOGA. AEW/AWACS aircraft have become an indispensable part of U.S. air activities in combat and surveillance operations. The Hawkeye has been used extensively in anti-drug operations. (U.S. Navy)

An E-2C Hawkeye from VAW-120 on a local training flight. VAW-120 provides readiness/transition training for East Coast AEW squadrons. Note that the second tail fin from the left does not have control surfaces. (Peter B. Mersky)

E-1B   TRACER (formerly WF-2)

The E-1B Tracer AEW aircraft has been discarded from Navy service. Based on the S-2 Tracker and C-1 Trader cargo aircraft, the E-1 introduced the fixed, aerodynamically shaped radome (for the APS-82 radar) to carrier aircraft. A C-1A flew as the aerodynamic prototype for the AEW configuration, followed by the production of 88 WF-2/E-1B aircraft, with deliveries from 1958 to 1961.[13] The last was retired in 1976.

Names: The EA-6B name was changed from Intruder to Prowler in February 1972.

Status: Operational. First flight (converted A-6A) on 25 May 1968; first flight (production EA-6B) November 1970. IOC (VAQ-129) in January 1971. A total of 170 aircraft were built for the U.S. Navy and Marine Corps through July 1991 when production ended.

Three A-6A Intruder airframes were modified to serve as development aircraft for the EA-6B program.

13. The XWF-1 was Grumman Design No. 95 for an earlier AEW aircraft carrying the APS-20A radar based on the S2F initiated in 1951. Two prototypes were ordered but the project was terminated early in 1953 before either aircraft was completed. The WF-2 was initiated in early 1955.

EA-6B[14]

Manufacturer:	Grumman
Crew:	(4) pilot, 3 electronic countermeasures operators[15]
Engines:	2 Pratt & Whitney J52-P-408 turbojet; 11,200 lbst (5,080 kgst) each
Weights:	empty 32,162 lbs (14,589 kg)
	normal takeoff 54,461 lbs (24,704 kg)
	max takeoff 65,000 lbs (29,480 kg)
Dimensions:	length 59 ft 10 in (18.24 m)
	wing span 53 ft (16.15 m)
	wing area 528.9 ft² (49.1 m²)
	height 16 ft 3 in (4.95 m)
Speed:	max 613 mph (986 kmh) at sea level
	cruise 483 mph (777 kmh)
Ceiling:	41,000 ft (12,500 m)
Range:	700 n.miles (1,296 km)
Armament:	2 HARM ASM
Radar:	APQ-129

14. Normal takeoff weight, speed, ceiling, and range while carrying five jammer pods.
15. The ECMO in the right forward seat (next to the pilot) also serves as navigator.

An EA-6B Prowler from VAQ-140 aboard the DWIGHT D. EISENHOWER poses while over the eastern Mediterranean. The Prowler is easily identified by its twin cockpits, tail-fin pod and blisters, and the ECM pods mounted on wing and fuselage pylons. This Prowler has an ECM pod and a fuel tank under the port wing. (Comdr. John Leenhouts, USN).

Displaying high-visibility markings, an EA-6B Prowler from VAQ-131 is catapulted from the carrier INDEPENDENCE in the Mediterranean. VAQ-131 now flies from the RANGER in the Pacific. (U.S. Navy)

Detail of the EA-6B Prowler's cockpit arrangement, with side-by-side seating for the pilot and one ECM operator forward, and for two operators aft. The earlier EA-6A Intruder had a pilot and only one operator. (OS2 John Bouvia, USN)

EA-6A INTRUDER (formerly A2F-1H)

This version of the carrier-based Intruder has a built-in Electronic Countermeasures (ECM) suite to detect and jam hostile radars, primarily for suppressing anti-aircraft missile systems. The aircraft was developed specifically for Marine Corps use; it was succeeded in Marine service by the more-capable EA-6B Prowler beginning in 1977. The EA-6A is now flown only by Navy squadron VAQ-33. The aircraft is similar to the basic A-6 aircraft, with a distinctive pod atop the tail fin and up to five jamming pods and two fuel tanks carried on one fuselage and six wing pylons. The EA-6A can accommodate the ALQ-31B, ALQ-54, or ALQ-76 jammer pods and chaff dispensers.

The EA-6A differs from the later and larger EA-6B Prowler in having only one ECM operator (vice three in the EA-6B) and significantly less electronics equipment.

Status: Operational. First flight (A-6A conversion) on 26 April 1963. IOC (VMCJ-2) in December 1965.

Seven A-6A Intruder attack aircraft were converted to the EA-6A configuration, followed by the production of 21 EA-6A aircraft delivered by Grumman from 1965.

Manufacturer:	Grumman
Crew:	(2) pilot, electronic systems operator/navigator
Engines:	2 Pratt & Whitney J52-P-8A/B turbojet; 9,300 lbst (4,218 kgst) each
Weights:	empty 28,643 lbs (12,992 kg)
	max takeoff 58,833 lbs (26,687 kg)
Dimensions:	length 55 ft 3 in (16.84 m)
	wing span 53 ft (16.15 m)
	wing area 528.9 ft² (49.1 m²)
	height 16 ft 3 in (4.95 m)
Speed:	max 563 mph (906 kmh)
	cruise 450 mph (724 kmh)
Ceiling:	40,000 ft (12,195 m)
Range:	
Armament:	none
Radar:	APQ-92 search
	APQ-112 track

An EA-6A Intruder, at the time flown by reserve VAQ-309, is serviced at NAS Fallon, Nev. The EA-6A was never flown by Navy carrier-based VAQ squadrons, only by the Marines and Naval Reserve and by some Navy development activities. (Peter B. Mersky)

An EA-6A Intruder from VAQ-309 streaks fast and low during a training mission. (U.S. Navy)

EA-3B SKYWARRIOR (formerly A3D-2Q)

The last Skywarrior ELINT aircraft was retired from squadron VQ-2 in September 1991. The electronic variant of the "Whale" had been flown by VQ-1 and VQ-2 since 1959, operating from forward-deployed aircraft carriers until 1987. (Subsequently, the EA-3B flew from land bases until 1991, participating in Operation Desert Storm.)

The A3D/A-3 was developed as a long-range, carrier-based nuclear strike aircraft. The Skywarrior survived its intended successor, the A3J/A-5 Vigilante, being replaced in the VQ role by the ES-3 Viking. Aircraft are also used for VIP transport (VA-3B), reconnaissance (RA-3B), tankers (KA-3B), training (TA-3B), and electronic jamming (ERA-3B).

The Navy took delivery of 282 Douglas-built Skywarriors of all variants. These included 25 A3D-2Q/EA-3B EW variants, with many "straight" attack aircraft subsequently being modified to EW/ECM configurations. The Air Force flew the similar B-66 Destroyer in the bomber, electronic, reconnaissance, weather, and research roles; B-66 production totaled 206 aircraft.

See 14th Edition/pages 415–416 for characteristics.

An EA-3B Skywarrior from VQ-2 returns from an ELINT mission in the Persian Gulf area to the carrier AMERICA, steaming in the Gulf of Sidra. The plane's hook is lowered, its landing gear about to come down. There is an electronics "canoe" faired into the lower fuselage. (Lt. Comdr. Dave Parsons, USN)

An EA-3B Skywarrior from VQ-2 about to touch down on the SARATOGA in the eastern Mediterranean. Desert Storm marked the end of Skywarrior operations, ending the plane's 35-year, highly versatile career. Like the multi-faceted A4D/A-4 Skyhawk, the Skywarrior was designed by aviation genius Ed Heinemann. (PH3 Mac M. Thurston, USN)

EC-24A

The single EC-24A flown by the Navy in the electronic warfare simulation/jamming role in support of weapons development and fleet exercises was to be discarded in 1992. The aircraft, a converted commercial DC-8 series 54F, was placed in service in November 1987 and operated and supported by a contractor.

The aircraft had a flight crew of four plus six electronic systems operators. It was fitted with two ALE-43 chaff dispensers, two ALR-75 intercept receivers, two ALT-40 radar jammers, and two AQS-191 communication transceivers/jammers.

This four-turbofan transport was the only U.S. military aircraft given a C-24 series designation.

EC-130V HERCULES

The EC-130V is an Airborne Early Warning (AEW) conversion of an HC-130H Hercules aircraft developed for the U.S. Coast Guard. It has a large rotating radome (rotodome) for the APS-125 radar of the type fitted in the E-2C Hawkeye.[16]

Flight testing for the aircraft began in July 1991 with the Coast Guard referring to the project as a High-Endurance Surveillance (HES) aircraft, given the nickname "Delphi." The initial funding for the project was based on the aircraft's value in anti-drug surveillance operations.

See page 430 for basic C-130 characteristics.

16. The aircraft should properly have been redesignated EC-130H; however, that designation is already used for the U.S. Air Force "Compass Call" electronic jamming aircraft.

The lone EC-24A coming in for a landing. The former DC-8-54JT has a number of electronic blisters and other antennas. The aircraft is contractor-operated for the Navy's Fleet Tactical Readiness Group (FTRG), formerly the Fleet Electronic Warfare Support Group (FEWSG). (Harry Gann/McDonnell Douglas)

The Coast Guard's lone EC-130V Hercules on an evaluation flight. Lockheed had long proposed AEW variants of the Hercules as well as the P-3 Orion; evaluation aircraft of both concepts are now flying. (U.S. Coast Guard)

The EC-130V variant of the Hercules demonstrates the continued versatility of this aircraft, which has also flown in the gunship, tanker, SAR, communications relay (TACAMO), minelaying, and command-and-control roles. (U.S. Coast Guard)

EC-130Q HERCULES (formerly GV)

The EC-130Q aircraft are C-130 transports extensively modified during production for the TACAMO role of communications relay with strategic missile submarines (SSBN). These aircraft have the USC-13 airborne VLF communications suite with two trailing wire antennas. The E-6A Mercury is replacing the 22 TACAMO "Herks" in squadrons VQ-3 and VQ-4.

An EC-130Q Hercules TACAMO aircraft from VQ-4 streaming two VLF wire antennas. (U.S. Navy)

EP-3 ORION

These are former P-3A/B/C Orions extensively modified for Electronic Intelligence (ELINT) collection. Twelve P-3C variants are being converted to the EP-3E Aries II configuration, replacing earlier EP-3E Aries I aircraft. The Navy also flies two EP-3J aircraft.

The Japanese Maritime Self-Defense Force is acquiring six Kawasaki-produced EP-3 variants for ELINT missions.

See page 413 for basic characteristics.

An EP-3E from VQ-2 with squadron markings and Batman insignia. Note the fuselage canoes and the APS-20 surveillance radar under the forward fuselage. (U.S. Navy)

EC-121 WARNING STAR (formerly WV/PO)

The last U.S. military version of the Constellation transport, a Navy NC-121K Warning Star assigned to VAQ-33, was retired on 25 June 1982. The EC-121, originally designated PO-1W/2W and then WV-2, was acquired as part of the Navy's seaward extension of the Distant Early Warning (DEW) line established in the early 1950s to warn of Soviet bomber attack. Starting in 1954 a total of 142 Warning Stars were delivered for the DEW operation. Various models of the Lockheed Constellation and "Super Connie" were flown by the Navy and Air Force, the former also using the designations R7O/R7V for transport aircraft.

A "bob-tailed" EP-3E Aires I from VQ-1 off Mt. Fuji, Japan. The VQ surveillance squadrons rarely have their tail code or other unit identification when flying operational missions, hence no PR tail code on this aircraft. (U.S. Navy)

ES-3A VIKING

The Navy is converting 16 S-3A Viking carrier-based ASW aircraft to an ES-3A configuration to serve as electronic surveillance aircraft. They replace the long-serving EA-3B Skywarrior. Sometimes labeled TASES for Tactical Airborne Signal Exploitation System, the aircraft's mission is described as (1) electronic warfare reconnaissance (i.e., surveillance), (2) over-the-horizon targeting, and (3) airborne tactical command, control, communications, and intelligence.

The Navy began seeking an EA-3B replacement in the mid-1970s with a planned IOC of 1981. However, there was little movement, and the EA-3B "Whales" continued flying in this role until 1987 when they experienced an increase in operational accidents and were assigned exclusively to land-based operations. (They participated in the 1991 war in the Persian Gulf.)

The ES-3A is believed to be fitted with the same systems as the EA-3B; it is fitted with the APS-137 ISAR radar. See page 414 for basic characteristics.

Status: Operational. First flight prototype ES-3A conversion (NS-3A aerodynamic prototype) on 7 September 1989 (the second conversion was the first with a full electronics suite; first flight 21 January 1992). All being delivered through 1993. The 16 ES-3A aircraft will be flown by squadrons VQ-5 and VQ-6; two of their aircraft normally operate aboard each forward-deployed carrier.

NKC-135A STRATOTANKER

The Navy's two NKC-135A aircraft employed in the electronic warfare simulation/jamming role in support of weapons development and fleet exercises were to be stricken in 1992. They replaced a pair of modified EB-47E Stratojet bombers previously flown in this role; the two NKC-135A aircraft entered Navy service in 1977–1978 and were contractor-operated.

The aircraft were modified Boeing 707/Air Force KC-135A tankers, originally fitted with in-flight refueling equipment. They were modified by the Air Force for research work, with their refueling equipment removed. Further modifications by the Navy included removal of some of the body fuel cells to provide equipment bays, replacement of the weather track radar with a sea search unit, provision of wing pylons for electronic pods, and an electronic warfare office/navigator station in the cargo cabin area. Each carried about 12,500 pounds (5,670 kg) of electronic equipment on board and had two wing pylons providing a greater jamming capability than any other aircraft then flying.

See 14th Edition/page 416 for characteristics.

The ES-3A Viking is the long-delayed replacement for the EA-3B Skywarrior as the Navy's carrier-based ELINT aircraft. One or two of these aircraft are normally deployed aboard carriers operating in forward areas. (Lockheed)

OBSERVATION/RECONNAISSANCE AIRCRAFT

OV-10D BRONCO

The Bronco was developed during the Vietnam War as a multi-purpose Counterinsurgency (COIN) aircraft. It was flown in Vietnam by the Air Force, Navy, and Marine Corps, with the Navy units being subsequently disbanded. The STOL operating characteristics have permitted limited flight operations from LHD/LHA/LPH-type ships as well as aircraft carriers without the use of catapults or arresting gear. All OV-10s will be phased out of service by 1994.

With the removal of the second seat, the OV-10 can carry 3,200 pounds of cargo or five troops or two litter patients plus a medical attendant. Seventeen OV-10A aircraft were modified to the Night Observation Gunship System (NOGS)—two YOV-10D and 15 OV-10D. These aircraft have FLIR and laser target designators, and a three-barrel cannon mounted in an under-fuselage turret. Four wing attachment points each have a 600-pound (272-kg) capacity, and the fuselage attachment point has a 1,200-pound (544-kg) capacity for gun pods, rockets, bombs, or fuel tanks.

Status: Operational. First flight on 16 July 1965. Marine Corps IOC (VMO-5, later HML-267) in February 1968.

The Navy and Marine Corps took delivery of 114 aircraft from 1967 to 1969, with additional OV-10s going to the U.S. Air Force and foreign services. Some USAF OV-10s have been transferred to the Marine Corps.

Manufacturer:	Rockwell International
Crew:	(2) pilot, observer
Engines:	2 Garrett-AiResearch T76-G-420/421 turboprop; 1,040 shp each
Weights:	empty 8,353 lbs (3,789 kg)
	loaded 12,940 lbs (5,870 kg)
	max takeoff 14,444 lbs (6,552 kg)
Dimensions:	length 42 ft 3 in (12.9 m) + 1 ft 10 in (0.56 m) probe
	wing span 40 ft (12.2 m)
	wing area 291 ft² (27.03 m²)
	height 15 ft 1 in (4.62 m)
Speed:	max clean 281 mph (452 kmh) at sea level
Ceiling:	24,000 ft (7,317 m)
Range:	radius 198 n.miles (367 km) with full weapons load
	ferry 1,200 n.miles (2,222 km)
Armament:	1 20-mm cannon M97 (multi-barrel; 1,500 rounds)
	3,600 lbs (1,633 kg) of bombs, rockets, gun pods
Radar:	none

Detail of an OV-10D showing the three-barrel Gatling gun fitted under the rear fuselage; it can be removed to permit fitting other weapons or stores.

RF-8G PHOTO CRUSADER (formerly F8U-1P)

The last Navy unit flying the Crusader aircraft, Naval Air Reserve squadron VFP-206 was disestablished on 1 April 1986. The squadron flew the RF-8G photo version of the Crusader. All U.S. F-8 fighter aircraft have been discarded, although the French Navy still flies the carrier-based F-8E(FN) and the Philippine Air Force recently retired the land-based F-8H.

The Crusader was the first U.S. combat aircraft to achieve more than 1,000 mph (1,609 kmh) in level flight to enter series production. Then-Major John Glenn, later astronaut and U.S. senator, flew an F8U-1P in a speed-record flight across the United States in 1957.

LTV built 1,222 F8U/F-8 Crusaders for the U.S. Navy plus 42 for the French Navy. The photo Crusaders were originally F8U-1P, being redesignated RF-8A in 1962, and then modified to RF-8G.

RF-4B PHANTOM (formerly F4H-1P)

The Marine Corps operated one squadron of RF-4B photo-reconnaissance aircraft. These aircraft were similar to the now-discarded F-4B version of the Phantom, with 46 of this variant produced; see page 405.

The U.S. Navy never flew the reconnaissance version of the Phantom, although Marine RF-4s flew from the carrier MIDWAY. Reconnaissance variants of the F-4 were also flown by the U.S. Air Force and several foreign air forces.

An OV-10D Bronco carrying bombs, rocket pods, and fuel tanks on wing and fuselage pylons; the 20-mm Gatling gun has been removed. This Counterinsurgency (COIN) aircraft will soon be retired from Marine service. (Rockwell)

O-2A SKYMASTER

The Navy flew six former Air Force O-2A Skymaster aircraft during the 1980s as spotting aircraft out of NAS Cecil Field, Fla. The planes, since replaced in that role by T-34C Mentors, were operated by VA-122 and, subsequently, by VFA-125.

The O-2 was a high-wing monoplane with twin tail booms; it was powered by two piston engines, a puller forward and a pusher aft (between the tail booms). Rocket pods, 7.62-mm Minigun packs, or other light ordnance could be fitted. The aircraft was designed for the forward air control mission, carrying a pilot and observer, with space for two passengers.

All six naval aircraft have been discarded (two each to the National Aviation Museum in Pensacola, Fla., and the Marine Corps Air-Ground Museum in Quantico, Va.; and two to the U.S. Army). The O-2 series is no longer flown by the Air Force.

One of six ex–Air Force O-2A Skymaster spotter aircraft that were briefly operated by the Navy. The NJ tail code is used by several fleet readiness/transition squadrons, including VA-122 (shown here). (Jan C. Jacobs, courtesy *The Hook*)

UTILITY AIRCRAFT

UC-27

The Navy acquired one Fokker F-27F light transport in the 1980s for evaluation. Designated UC-27, it was used in support of the Atlantic Underwater Test and Evaluation Center (AUTEC) in the Bahamas. It was discarded in April 1988.

See 14th Edition/page 419 for characteristics.

HU-25 GUARDIAN

The Guardian is an all-weather, medium-range search and surveillance aircraft flown by the Coast Guard. It replaces the HU-16 Albatross and HC-131A Samaritan aircraft.

This aircraft is a modification of the French-developed commercial Falcon 20G. It has two turbofan engines mounted in nacelles outboard of the after fuselage, an arrangement similar to the T-39 Sabreliner. In addition to crew and passengers, 3,200 pounds (1,452 kg) of rescue supplies are carried. A galley and toilet are provided.

Seven aircraft were modified with the Aireye sensor system infrared/ultraviolet line scanners in an underwing pod and an APS-131 Side-Looking Airborne Radar (SLAR) in a fuselage pod, television camera, and other equipment for pollution reconnaissance; redesignated HU-25B in 1989.

Nine aircraft were fitted with the APG-66 multi-mode radar to provide for the detection of aircraft out to 80 n.miles (148 km), and FLIR; redesignated HU-25C in 1989.

Status: Operational. Coast Guard IOC in February 1982; the last of 41 aircraft were delivered in 1984. The Guardian Jet Corporation was a jointly owned subsidiary of Dassault Bréguet and Pan American.

Similar French-built Mystère-Falcon aircraft are flown in a variety of roles by several air forces.

The HU-25A is a multi-mission aircraft developed originally for surveillance and rescue missions. It has been upgraded in the B/C variants for pollution surveillance and anti-drug intercept operations. (U.S. Coast Guard)

Manufacturer:	Dassault-Bréguet and Guardian Jet		
Crew:	(5) pilot, copilot, drop master, avionics man, air crewman + 3 passengers + 4 litters		
Engines:	2 Garrett AiResearch ATF3-6-2C turbofan; 5,538 lbst (2,512 kgst) each		
Weights:	empty 19,000 lbs (8,618 kg)		
	max takeoff 33,510 lbs (15,200 kg)		
Dimensions:	length	56 ft 3 in (17.15 m)	
	wing span	53 ft 6 in (16.30 m)	
	wing area	440 ft² (41.00 m²)	
	height	17 ft 5 in (5.32 m)	
Speed:	max 531 mph (854 kmh) at 40,000 ft (12,195 m)		
Ceiling:	42,000 ft (12,805 m)		
Range:	2,250 n.miles (4,167 km) with 30 minutes on station		
Radar:	APS-127 search/weather radar except APG-66 in nine aircraft		

An HU-25B Guardian as upgraded with the Aireye sensor system to detect oil pollution. Russian aircraft as well as satellites have been similarly equipped for this role, which may have implications for ASW operations. (U.S. Coast Guard)

HU-16 ALBATROSS (formerly JR2F/UF)

All of these twin-engine, amphibian utility aircraft have been retired from U.S. military service, the last being a Coast Guard HU-16E retired on 10 March 1983.

Following the first flight in 1947, the Albatross entered service with the Navy and later Coast Guard (JR2F and, after 1962, UF) and Air Force (SA-16/UF). The Navy flew the Albatross until 1976 and the Coast Guard from 1951 to 1983. Grumman produced 466 Albatrosses from 1947 to 1961; no less than 22 nations in addition to the United States flew the aircraft.

U-11A AZTEC

All Navy U-11A utility aircraft have been discarded. Twenty were acquired in the 1960s for use by naval air stations. The aircraft was modified from the commercial Piper Aztec, which was also used by the U.S. Army and other countries.

See 14th Edition/page 420 for characteristics.

CARGO/TRANSPORT AIRCRAFT

C-20D GULFSTREAM III

Two Gulfstream III aircraft are flown by the Navy in the transport role.

This is a swept-wing, T-tail aircraft with twin engine pods mounted on the after fuselage. Winglets are fitted (5 ft 4¼ in high). The Air Force flies several C-20 variants as replacements for the C-140 special mission/VIP aircraft. The manufacturer has proposed a maritime patrol/ASW variant of the improved Gulfstream IV (first flight of the commercial version on 19 September 1985); the Royal Danish Navy now flies the Gulfstream III in a maritime/fisheries patrol variant.

Status: Operational. First flight Gulfstream III on 24 December 1979.

Manufacturer:	Gulfstream Aerospace	
Crew:	(2) pilot, copilot + 19 passengers	
Engines:	2 Rolls-Royce Spey (Mk 511-8) F113-RR-100 turbofan; 11,400 lbst (5,171 kgst) each	
Weights:	empty 32,000 lbs (14,515 kg)	
	max takeoff 69,700 lbs (31,616 kg)	
Dimensions:	length	83 ft 1 in (25.32 m)
	wing span	77 ft 10 in (23.72 m)
	wing area	934.6 ft² (86.83 m²)
	height	24 ft 4½ in (7.43 m)
Speed:	max cruise 576 mph (927 kmh)	
	cruise 508 mph (817 kmh)	
Ceiling:	45,000 ft (13,720 m)	
Range:	3,940 n.miles (7,302 km)	
Radar:	weather radar	

UC-12 HURON

The Navy and Marine Corps use this military version of the Super King Air 200 for transport and utility purposes; these are designated UC-12B/F/M.

The aircraft's twin turboprop engines are mounted far forward on the low wing; the aircraft has a T-tail compared with the conventional tail configuration of the smaller T-44A King Air trainer. Payload is 2,000 lbs (907 kg) of cargo or eight passengers.

More than 2,800 aircraft of this basic design have been produced, most for civilian use. This is the only fixed-wing aircraft flown by the U.S. Army, Navy, Marine Corps, and Air Force (plus the Army National Guard and Marine Corps Reserve). The Navy flies 51 of these aircraft and the Marine Corps 14 in the UC-12B configuration with additional aircraft on order.

C-12B

Manufacturer:	Beech	
Crew:	(2) pilot, copilot + 8 passengers	
Engines:	2 Pratt & Whitney Canada PT6A-41 turboprop; 850 shp each	
Weights:	empty 7,869 lbs (3,569 kg)	
	loaded 12,500 lbs (5,670 kg)	
Dimensions:	length	43 ft 9 in (13.34 m)
	wing span	54 ft 6 in (16.61 m)
	wing area	303 ft² (28.15 m²)
	height	14 ft 6 in (4.42 m)
Speed:	max cruise 310 mph (500 km)	
	cruise 261 mph (420 km)	
Ceiling:	31,000 ft (9,451 m)	
Range:	1,760 n.miles (3,260 km)	
Radar:	RC-12M surface search	

A sleek-looking C-20D Gulfstream III, one of two aircraft of this executive transport type flown by the Navy. Note the vertical wingtips, called "winglets." (Gulfstream Aerospace)

A UC-12B Huron from NAS Jacksonville being refueled at NAS Norfolk. The Army-assigned name Huron is not generally used in naval service. (Peter B. Mersky)

VC-11A GULFSTREAM II

The Coast Guard operates one Gulfstream II flown in the executive transport role. The aircraft has the military designation C-11; the Coast Guard's aircraft is the only one in government service and is based at Washington National Airport in Washington, D.C.

Developed by Grumman as an executive business jet, the Gulfstream II is a swept-wing, T-tail aircraft, with engine nacelles mounted on the after fuselage, resembling the T-39 Sabreliner configuration.

Status: Operational. First flight (Gulfstream II) on 2 October 1966. IOC (Coast Guard VC-11A) in July 1968.

Total Gulfstream II production was 256 aircraft.

Manufacturer:	Grumman
Crew:	(4) pilot, copilot, 2 crewmen + 12 passengers
Engines:	2 Rolls-Royce Spey (Mk 511-8) F113-RR-100 turbofan; 11,400 lbst (5,171 kgst) each
Weights:	loaded 59,500 lbs (26,989 kg)
Dimensions:	length 79 ft 11 in (24.35 m)
	wing span 68 ft 10 in (21.00 m)
	wing area 793.5 ft² (73.72 m²)
	height 24 ft 6 in (7.47 m)
Speed:	max 588 mph (946 km)
Ceiling:	43,000 ft (13,110 m)
Range:	2,930 n.miles (5,426 km)
Radar:	navigation

VC-11A Gulfstream II. (U.S. Coast Guard)

C-9B SKYTRAIN II

The C-9B is the naval version of the commercial DC-9 series 30 medium-range passenger/cargo aircraft and is convertible to the cargo or passenger transport roles. The Navy flies both C-9B and DC-9 variants.

This sleek-looking, swept-wing transport has a T-tail with the turbofan engines in nacelles mounted on the after fuselage. The cargo compartment can accommodate eight standard 88 × 108-inch (2.2 m × 2.7 m) cargo pallets. Payload is 32,444 lbs (14,717 kg) or 90 passengers.

Skytrains are flown by reserve Navy and active Marine units, replacing the long-serving C-118 Liftmaster (formerly R6D). The U.S. Air Force flies the C-9A Nightingale in the medical evacuation role and the VC-9C as an executive transport. McDonnell Douglas has proposed a maritime patrol/ASW variant of the aircraft (company designation P-9D); it would have General Electric Unducted Fan (UDF) turboprop-type engines.

Status: Operational. First flight DC-9 series 30 on 1 August 1966. First Flight C-9B on 7 February 1973. IOC Naval Air Reserve in 1976.

Manufacturer:	McDonnell Douglas
Crew:	(5) pilot, copilot, crew chief, 2 attendants + 90 passengers
Engines:	2 Pratt & Whitney JT8D-9 turbofan; 14,500 lbst (6,577 kgst) each
Weights:	empty 59,706 lbs (27,083 kg) in cargo configuration
	empty 65,283 lbs (29,612 kg) in transport configuration
	max takeoff 110,000 lbs (49,896 kg)
Dimensions:	length 119 ft 4 in (36.37 m)
	wing span 93 ft 5 in (28.47 m)
	wing area 1,000.7 ft² (92.97 m²)
	height 27 ft 6 in (8.38 m)
Speed:	max 576 mph (927 km)
	cruise 504 mph (811 km)
Ceiling:	37,000 ft (11,280 m)
Range:	2,538 n.miles (4,700 km) with 10,000 lbs (4,536 kg) cargo
Radar:	weather radar

C-9B Skytrain from reserve VR-56 showing the aircraft's large cargo door. Only Navy and Marine Corps Reserve squadrons fly C-9B/DC-9 aircraft. (Peter B. Mersky)

A Marine C-9B Skytrain and a Marine CT-39G Sabreliner in formation. Active Marine refueler-transport squadrons fly only the KC-130 Hercules. (Harry Gann/McDonnell Douglas)

VC-4/TC-4   GULFSTREAM I/ACADEME

The Coast Guard operates one VC-4A as an executive transport, and the Navy and Marine Corps fly eight TC-4C trainers for A-6E Intruder bombardier/navigators.

Developed as a business aircraft, the Gulfstream I is a low-wing, twin turboprop aircraft with the long nacelles common to Rolls-Royce engines. The Coast Guard aircraft retained the name Gulfstream I. The Navy-Marine TC-4C variants have a simulated A-6E cockpit with pilot and bombardier/navigator positions in the after section of the cockpit plus four identical bombardier/navigator training consoles. In addition to the A-6 radar (upgraded from the original APQ-92 and APQ-88 radars), these planes have the TRAM and FLIR fitted in the A-6Es. The TC-4C variants are named Academe.

The T-41A (later TC-4B) was a navigation training version of the Gulfstream I ordered by the Navy, but that entire program was cancelled.

Status: Operational. First flight (Gulfstream I) on 14 August 1958; first flight TC-4C on 14 June 1967. VC-4A IOC in March 1963; TC-4C IOC in June 1967.

Grumman produced 190 Gulfstream I commercial aircraft plus the single similar Coast Guard VC-4A and nine TC-4C aircraft for the Navy and Marine Corps. A second VC-4A planned for the Coast Guard was not acquired.

TC-4C

Manufacturer:	Grumman
Crew:	(4) pilot, copilot, 2 instructors + 5 students
Engines:	2 Rolls-Royce Dart Mk 529-8X turboprop; 2,210 shp each
Weights:	empty 24,575 lbs (11,147 kg)
	loaded 36,000 lbs (16,330 kg)
Dimensions:	length TC-4C 67 ft 10¾ in (20.69 m)
	VC-4A 63 ft 9 in (19.34 m)
	wing span 78 ft 4 in (23.87 m)
	wing area 610.3 ft² (185.99 m²)
	height 23 ft 4 in (7.10 m)
Speed:	max 365 mph (587 km) at 15,000 ft (4,573 m)
	cruise 250 mph (402 km)
Ceiling:	30,000 ft (9,146 m)
Range:	996 n.miles (1,845 km) at 5,000 ft (1,524 m)
	1,721 n.miles (3,187 km) at 30,000 ft (9,146 m)
Radar:	APQ-148 multi-mode

TC-4C Academe of VA-128 used for A-6E bombardier/navigator training; the Marine Corps also flies the TC-4C in this role. Note the large nose radome and TRAM sensor under the nose. (U.S. Navy)

Detail of the TC-4C Academe. (Peter B. Mersky)

The Coast Guard's lone VC-4A Gulfstream I. (U.S. Coast Guard)

C-2A GREYHOUND

The Greyhound is a second-generation, built-for-the-purpose COD aircraft, having been derived from the E-2 Hawkeye AEW aircraft.

The cargo aircraft has the E-2's wings, power plant, and tail configuration, but a larger fuselage and rear-loading ramp. This last feature permits the carrying of high-cube cargo, including some aircraft engines. Cargo capacity is 675 cubic feet (20.25 m³); payload is 10,000 lbs (4,536 kg) of cargo or 28 passengers. The wings fold for carrier stowage, although these planes are not assigned to carrier wings.

Nineteen C-2A models were originally procured. In the late 1970s the Navy developed a plan to produce 24 new COD aircraft beginning in fiscal 1983 to replace the existing C-1A and, eventually, C-2A aircraft. The principal candidate for the new COD— designated VCX for planning purposes—was a variant of the S-3A Viking, with several early aircraft having been modified to a US-3A COD configuration. The decision, however, was to procure 39 additional C-2A aircraft (with the first of these "reprocured" aircraft making its first flight on 4 February 1985); the principal difference in the later aircraft was uprated engines.

Status: Operational. First flight VC-2A on 18 November 1964. IOC (VRC-50) in December 1966. Total production was 58 aircraft. Thirty-nine C-2A aircraft remain in Navy service.

C-2A Greyhound from VRC-50 at the moment of touchdown aboard the carrier INDEPENDENCE. (OS2 John Bouvia, USN)

A C-2A from VRC-40 with its tail ramp lowered and engines turning at NAS Norfolk. Like the E-2C, one of the tail fins has no control surfaces; most Navy transport/cargo planes have a U.S. flag on the tail fin. (Peter B. Mersky)

Manufacturer:	Grumman
Crew:	(3) pilot, copilot, flight engineer + 28 passengers or 20 litters
Engines:	2 Allison T56-A-425 turboprop; 4,910 shp each
Weights:	empty 36,346 lbs (16,486 kg)
	max takeoff 57,500 lbs (26,081 kg)
Dimensions:	length 56 ft 8 in (17.27 m)
	wing span 80 ft 7 in (24.57 m)
	wing area 700 ft² (65.03 m²)
	height 15 ft 11 in (4.85 m)
Speed:	max 352 mph (566 kmh) at 30,000 ft (9,146 m)
	cruise 296 mph (476 kmh) at 30,000 ft
Ceiling:	33,500 ft (10,210 m)
Range:	normal 1,043 n.miles (1,930 km)
	max 1,562 n.miles (2,890 km)
Radar:	navigation radar

C-1A TRADER (formerly TF-1)

The Navy's first specialized Carrier Onboard Delivery (COD) aircraft, the C-1A Trader has been retired from naval service. The plane was derived from the S2F/S-2 Tracker ASW aircraft. The aircraft had twin reciprocating engines.

Grumman produced a total of 87 Traders for the U.S. Navy; four were configured as electronic training aircraft (designated TF-1Q and, after 1962, EC-1A); one was modified as the E-1B aerodynamic prototype (XTF-1W) and then reverted to a COD aircraft. The aircraft were in VR-VRC squadron service from 1955 to 1986; a C-1A was the last piston aircraft to "trap" on a U.S. carrier, coming aboard the LEXINGTON (AVT 16) on 27 September 1988.

C-131H SAMARITAN (formerly R4Y)

The last Navy-flown C-131 was retired in mid-1990. The C-131 was flown by the Navy/Naval Air Reserve as a transport and by the Coast Guard (HC-131), the latter also having been discarded.

The Convair-built, twin-engine aircraft was also flown by the Air Force as a transport and specialized trainer (T-29).

See 14th Edition/page 424 for characteristics.

C-130 HERCULES (formerly GV-1)

The Hercules or "Herk" is the most widely flown military transport in the West. The Navy flies the C-130 as a logistics aircraft and the EC-130 as a VLF strategic communications aircraft under the TACAMO (Take Charge And Move Out) program; the Marine Corps uses the KC-130 as a tactical transport and aerial tanker; and the Coast Guard employs the HC-130H as a long-range search and surveillance aircraft and is evaluating an EC-130V AEW aircraft.

The basic C-130 is a four-engine cargo aircraft with a high wing with the main landing gear in pods to provide a clear fuselage cargo space; a rear ramp provides access to the cargo compartment and can be opened in flight for parachuting troops or equipment.

Navy: The Navy flies a small number of C-130F and KC-130F variants, the latter being the first and only land-based tanker aircraft flown by the Navy (VR-22). The Navy also has two ski-fitted LC-130F and four LC-130R aircraft flown by VXE-6.[17] The Navy's DC-130 drone carriers have been discarded.

The EC-130Q TACAMO variant is discussed separately (see page 422).

Marine Corps: The Marine KC-130F/R/T are employed as cargo aircraft and tankers, flown by six VMGR/VMGRT squadrons. They can accommodate removable aluminum tanks for 3,600 gallons (13,680 liters) of fuel in the cargo area; two refueling drogues can be streamed simultaneously. Two KC-130T-30 stretched aircraft delivered in 1991 to reserve squadron VMGR-452 have two fuselage plugs adding a total of 14¾ feet (4.5 m) to the fuselage length. The KC-130R has a payload of 26,913 lbs (12,208 kg) of cargo or 92 troops or can offload 7,077 gallons (26,790 liters) of fuel.

The Marine TC-130G is equipped as a maintenance center to support the Navy-Marine Blue Angels flight demonstration team, carrying a crew of 7 plus 30 maintenance personnel; it is called "Fat Albert" for a characterization of comedian Bill Cosby. The TC-130G is a converted Navy EC-130G delivered in 1991; previously "Fat Albert" was a KC-130F.

Coast Guard: The Coast Guard's 31 HC-130H aircraft carry air-droppable rescue and salvage gear. The HC-130H has increased range, flare launchers, and other improvements over the C-130B aircraft they replaced. (Characteristics are similar to the KC-130R described below.) The HC-130H aircraft have been refitted with the APS-137 ISAR radar; they also have APN-215 weather radar, and an external Samson sensor pod containing a FLIR is being fitted to these aircraft.

KC-130R

Manufacturer:	Lockheed (Georgia)
Crew:	(5) pilot, copilot, navigator, flight engineer, radio operator/loadmaster + 92 troops
Engines:	4 Allison T56-A-15 turboprop; 4,591 shp each
Weights:	empty 79,981 lbs (36,279 kg)
	max takeoff 175,000 lbs (79,378 kg)
Dimensions:	length 97 ft 9 in (29.79 m)
	wing span 132 ft 7 in (40.42 m)
	wing area 1,745 ft² (162.12 m²)
	height 38 ft 3 in (11.66 m)
Speed:	max 348 mph (560 kmh) at 19,000 ft (5,790 m)
	cruise 331 mph (533 kmh)
Ceiling:	25,000 ft (7,622 m)
Range:	radius 2,564 n.miles (4,749 km) with maximum payload
	radius 1,000 n.miles (1,852 km) in tanker role with 32,140 lbs (14,579 kg) of fuel for transfer
Radar:	APN-59B

A single Coast Guard HC-130H Hercules has been converted to an AEW configuration for Coast Guard evaluation; redesignated EC-130V (see page 000).

Operational: A KC-130F conducted carrier landings and takeoffs from the FORRESTAL (CV 59) in 1963 without the use of arresting gear or catapults. C-130s have also been employed to evaluate aerial minelaying.

Status: Operational; in production. First flight YC-130 on 23 August 1954. Production continues of the HC-130H for the Coast Guard and the KC-130T for the Marine Corps as well as other models for other users.

The Hercules is widely used by the U.S. Air Force, with more than 50 other nations also employing military versions. Through early 1992 Lockheed had produced almost 2,000 military and commercial models of the Hercules, including over 1,200 for the U.S. military services.

---

17. LC-130F Bureau No. 148321 was recovered in 1990 after having been buried in Antarctic snow for 16 years. The aircraft began a two-year overhaul in 1991 before being returned to active service.

Over Thailand a Marine KC-130F Hercules from VMGR-152 refuels a Navy A-4E Skyhawk from VC-5. The "Herk" is streaming two refueling drogues; Air Force aircraft supporting naval air operations can stream drogues from their rigid refueling booms, a more flexible scheme. (PH1 M.D.P. Flynn, USN)

A ski-equipped LC-130F Hercules from VXE-6, a squadron dedicated to supporting U.S. scientific operations in the Antarctic. The wingtips, after fuselage, and vertical tail are painted red; the remainder of the aircraft is gray and blue. (U.S. Navy)

A Coast Guard HC-130H Hercules taking off from the Coast Guard Air Station Clearwater, Fla. (Lockheed Aeronautical)

One of only two "stretched" Hercules in U.S. military service, this is one of the KC-130T-30 "Herks" flown by reserve squadron VMGR-452. The aircraft has a 15-foot (4.57-m) extension, permitting it to carry seven cargo pallets or 128 troops or 97 litters plus 4 attendants. (Lockheed Aeronautical)

C-118B LIFTMASTER (formerly R6D-1)

The last Navy C-118B was retired in February 1985, having been flown by reserve squadron VR-46. The four-engine transport had extensive commercial as well as military service, being designated DC-6A in the former role. The aircraft was introduced into Navy service in 1951. The Navy also operated ex-Air Force C-118A aircraft.

C-117 SKYTRAIN (formerly R4D)

All of these twin-engine transports have been retired from Navy and Marine Corps service. The last C-117 flown by the U.S. Marine Corps was retired on 28 June 1982 and the last Navy "Gooney Bird" was retired on 1 July 1982.

Developed as the commercial Douglas DC-3, the aircraft was the most widely used cargo aircraft of World War II. Outside of the United States it was known as the C-47 Dakota, and, informally, as the "Gooney Bird." Douglas military production totaled 10,048 aircraft from 1938 to 1945, plus about 2,000 built in the USSR as the Li-2 and several in Japan. The U.S. naval versions were designated R4D, changed to C-47 in 1962 and, after rebuilding, C-117. Six took off from the carrier PHILIPPINE SEA (CV 47) in 1947 to land in Antarctica.

CT-39 SABRELINER (formerly T3J)

A few CT-39E/G aircraft are employed to transport high-priority cargo and passengers. The T-39D has been phased out of the training role, having been employed to train bombardier/navigators and radar intercept officers; the aircraft was fitted with the APS-94 radar for that role. The T-39N is flown in the training role; see page 000.

The low, swept-wing configuration of the T-39 has two turbojet engine nacelles mounted on the after fuselage. The aircraft is not carrier capable. The CT-39 aircraft carry a crew of three and seven passengers. These were modified commercial Sabreliner series 40 (E) and 60 (G) aircraft, acquired specifically for the transport role and never used as trainers. One T-39D was fitted as the test bed for the F/A-18 Hornet's APG-65 radar. The aircraft was also used by the Air Force.

Status: First flight of a modified commercial Sabreliner in September 1958; T-39A in June 1960; T-39D in December 1962.

Manufacturer:	North American Rockwell
Crew:	(3) pilot, copilot, crewman + 7 passengers
Engines:	2 Pratt & Whitney J60-P-3A turbojet; 3,000 lbst (1,361 kgst) each
Weights:	loaded 17,760 lbs (8,056 kg)
Dimensions:	length 43 ft 9 in (13.33 m)
	wing span 44 ft 5 in (13.53 m)
	wing area 342.6 ft² (31.83 m²)
	height 16 ft (4.88 m)
Speed:	538 mph (866 kmh)
Ceiling:	39,000 ft (11,890 m)
Range:	2,500 n.miles (4,630 km)
Radar:	APN-59 navigation

CT-39G Sabreliner from VR-24 at NAS Sigonella. The Navy's airfield on Sicily is important in supporting Sixth Fleet operations. (Lt. Comdr. E.H. Lundquist, USN)

TRAINING AIRCRAFT

T-47A CITATION

The Navy previously employed 15 T-47A aircraft for training Naval Flight Officers (NFO) in training squadrons VT-10 and VT-86. The T-47 replaced the T-39D Sabreliner in that role and, in 1991, was succeeded by the T-39N Sabreliner. The T-47 was contractor maintained and operated.

The T-47s, a modified commercial Cessna Model 500 design, have been discarded.

See 14th Edition/page 426 for characteristics.

T-45 GOSHAWK

The Goshawk is being procured as the Navy's basic undergraduate jet training aircraft to replace the T-2C and TA-4J. The T-45 is a variant of British Aerospace's Hawk series 60 trainer. Despite using this off-the-shelf aircraft, the first flight of a Goshawk took place almost five years behind the original schedule. The Navy had planned to procure 253 carrier-compatible T-45A trainers and 54 land-based T-45B variants. However, Congress directed that they all be T-45A "wet"—carrier-capable—models. Accordingly, the current program provides for a total of 300 training aircraft and two prototypes (plus 32 flight simulation devices).

Developed by Hawker Siddeley Aviation before it was merged into British Aerospace, the Hawk entered RAF service in 1976 and is also flown by several other air forces. The U.S. Navy's program was originally designated VTX-TS, the VTX for a new training aircraft and TS for Training System, i.e., the simultaneous development of simulators and related training equipment. The Goshawks have a small ventral fin, catapult attachment points, arresting hook, and modified wing, landing gear, speed brakes, and provision for external stores. Endurance is approximately four hours.

The wing and after fuselage sections of the T-45A are built in Britain by British Aerospace, and Rolls-Royce produces the engines in Britain. (The Hawk continues in production in Britain, with 358 aircraft built through the end of 1991.)

Flight tests of T-45 prototypes revealed several shortcomings; among other changes, the original Adour Mk 861/F405-RR-400 engines were replaced in production aircraft with the Adour Mk 871/F405-RR-401. Also, leading-edge slats are fitted to bring carrier approach speeds within acceptable limits.

Names: The name Goshawk was previously assigned to the Navy-Curtiss F11C fighter of the 1930s.

Operational: First carrier landings and takeoffs on the JOHN F. KENNEDY on 4 December 1991.

Status: Operational; in production. First flight T-45A on 16 April 1988. IOC (TraWing-2) in late 1992. The British-built Hawk is flown by ten air forces. (First flight of British T Mk 1 on 21 August 1974.)

Manufacturer:	British Aerospace and McDonnell Douglas
Crew:	(1) pilot + student
Engines:	1 Rolls-Royce Adour Mk 871/F405-RR-401 turbofan; 5,845 lbst (2,651 kgst)
Weights:	empty 9,399 lbs (4,263 kg)
	max takeoff 12,700 lbs (5,761 kg)
Dimensions:	length 35 ft 9 ft (10.89 m) + probe
	wing span 30 ft 9¾ in (9.39 m)
	wing area 179.6 ft² (9.39 m²)
	height 13 ft 6⅛ in (4.12 m)
Speed:	maximum 609 mph (980 km) at 8,000 ft (2,439 m)
Ceiling:	42,500 ft (12,957 m)
Range:	700 n.miles (1,296 km)
	ferry 1,600 n.miles (2,963 km) with external tanks
Radar:	none
Armament:	25-lb (11-kg) Mk 76 practice bombs and 2.75-inch (70-mm) rockets

The first carrier landing by a T-45A Goshawk aboard the carrier John F. Kennedy on 4 December 1991. This photo, taken the instant the aircraft caught an arresting wire, shows the plane's dive brakes open (just above the arresting hook). (McDonnell Douglas)

The first production model T-45A Goshawk; the T-45B was to have been a land-based variant, which the Congress has refused to fund. The underwing pylons are for practice munitions. (McDonnell Douglas)

T-45A Goshawk on the Kennedy showing the aircraft's leading-edge flaps. (McDonnell Douglas)

T-45A Goshawk aboard the Kennedy. (McDonnell Douglas)

T-44 KING AIR

The T-44 was procured as a replacement for the TS-2/US-2 Tracker in the multi-engine training role.

The aircraft is a modification of the commercial Air King 90, with a straight wing mounting twin turboprop engines relatively far forward, with a conventional tail configuration. The aircraft can be configured as a transport carrying two pilots and three passengers. During development the military version was designated VTAM(X).

Status: Operational. From 1977 on the Navy took delivery of 61 T-44A aircraft, all being assigned to VT-28 and VT-31. Five T-44B aircraft were authorized for the Navy in fiscal 1990. The U.S. Army procured unpressurized versions as the U-21A, while the Air Force obtained one as the UC-6A for special missions and a VC-6A as a VIP transport.

T-44A

Manufacturer:	Beech
Crew:	(3) pilot, copilot, instructor + 2 students
Engines:	2 Pratt & Whitney of Canada PT-6A-34B turboprop; 550 hp each
Weights:	empty 6,326 lbs (2,869 kg)
	max takeoff 9,650 lbs (4,377 kg)
Dimensions:	length 35 ft 6 in (10.82 m)
	wing span 50 ft 3 in (15.32 m)
	wing area 293.9 ft² (27.3 m²)
	height 14 ft 3 in (4.33 m)
Speed:	cruise 276 mph (444 km) at 15,000 ft (4,573 m)
Ceiling:	29,500 ft (8,994 m)
Range:	1,265 n.miles (2,343 km)
Radar:	air search

T-44A King Air from TraWing-4 (now tail code G). (U.S. Navy)

T-39N SABRELINER

The Navy operates several of the long-serving T-39s to train Naval Flight Officers (NFO) who fly in F-14, A-6E, S-3A/B, and two-seat F/A-18 aircraft. The T-39N has a low, swept-wing configuration with two turbojet engine nacelles mounted on the after fuselage. The aircraft is not carrier capable.

The T-39N is distinguished from earlier T-39s by being fitted with the Westinghouse APG-66NT radar, a modification of the APG-68 currently installed in several combat aircraft. The T-39N also has engine thrust reversers. Each aircraft carries a pilot, two instructors, and three students.

A few CT-39s serve as high-priority transport aircraft; see page 433 for basic characteristics.

Status: Operational. The first of 16 T-39N aircraft were delivered in late 1991. The aircraft are flown by Tracor Flight Services, Inc., under contract to the Navy.

T-38A TALON

The T-38 is the standard U.S. Air Force trainer, flown in small numbers by the Navy for test-pilot proficiency, currently five A models and three B models, all at the Naval Test Pilot School at Patuxent River.

The T-38 is closely related to the design of the Northrop F-5 Freedom Fighter and F-5E/F/G (now F-20) Tiger II aircraft.

Status: Operational. From 1958 to 1972 Northrop produced 1,187 T-38s for U.S. and foreign service. The Navy acquired five T-38s.

Manufacturer:	Northrop
Crew:	(1) pilot + student
Engines:	2 General Electric J85-GE-5A/J turbojet; 3,850 lbst (1,746 kgst) each with afterburner
Weights:	empty 7,410 lbs (3,361 kg)
	max takeoff 12,000 lbs (5,443 kg)
Dimensions:	length 46 ft 10 in (14.13 m)
	wing span 25 ft 3 in (7.7 m)
	wing area 170 ft² (15.80 m²)
	height 12 ft 11 in (3.92 m)
Speed:	max cruise 630 mph (1,014 kmh) at 40,000 ft (12,195 m)
	economical cruise 594 mph (956 kmh) above 40,000 ft
Ceiling:	53,600 ft (26,341 m)
Range:	1,140 n.miles (2,111 km)
Radar:	none

T-38A Talon assigned to VF-43. (Robert L. Lawson)

T-34C   MENTOR

The Mentor is the Navy's primary and basic flight training aircraft. A few T-34C aircraft are used for recruiting and utility activities, with the Light Attack Wing Atlantic employing a few for spotting duties.

The low-wing, turboprop C model has replaced the earlier piston-engine aircraft in Navy service. The plane is not carrier capable.

Status: Operational. First flight YT-34C on 21 September 1973. IOC T-34C in July 1976.

The Navy selected the Beechcraft Model 45 as a primary trainer in 1953, leading to procurement of the T-34A/B/C series. Two T-34B aircraft were converted to YT-34C prototypes (turboprop engine) in 1973. The last of 353 T-34C aircraft were delivered from 1976 to 1988.

About 350 T-34B/C aircraft are in service; all of the piston-engine T-34B models have been retired from the training role; some 50 are used in recruiting activities. Variants of the T-34 are also flown by the U.S. Air Force, U.S. Army, and several foreign air arms.

Manufacturer:	Beech	
Crew:	(1) pilot + student	
Engines:	1 Pratt & Whitney of Canada PT6A-25 turboprop; 400 shp	
Weights:	empty 2,940 lbs (1,334 kg)	
	max takeoff 4,300 lbs (1,950 kg)	
Dimensions:	length	28 ft 8½ in (8.75 m)
	wing span	33 ft 3⅞ in (10.16 m)
	wing area	179.6 ft² (16.69 m²)
	height	9 ft 7 in (2.92 m)
Speed:	max 257 mph (413 kmh) at 5,335 ft (1,627 m)	
	cruise 245 mph (394 kmh) at 15,000 ft (4,573 m)	
Ceiling:	30,000 ft (9,146 m)	
Range:	740 n.miles (1,370 km)	
Radar:	none	

T-34C Mentors from VT-2/TraWing-5. (Peter B. Mersky)

T-28   TROJAN

The last of these piston-engine primary trainers have been retired. The T-28C model of the Trojan was carrier capable.

T-2C   BUCKEYE (formerly T2J)

The Buckeye is used by the Navy for undergraduate jet-pilot training, with a few aircraft also flown by fleet readiness squadrons for spin recovery training.

The aircraft has straight wings, generally with wing tip tanks fitted, with the twin engines buried in the bottom of the fuselage (the T-2B has the J60 engine). Wing pylons can be fitted. The Buckeye is carrier capable. The aircraft's service life is being extended from 7,500 to 12,000 hours, at considerable cost, pending availability of the T-45 Goshawk for the training role.

Most T-2B/C aircraft are assigned to training squadrons (VT), with a few in fleet readiness squadrons (VF) for spin recovery training; they are assigned to the Navy Test Pilot School at NAS Patuxent River, Md.

Manufacturer:	North American Rockwell	
Crew:	(1) pilot + student	
Engines:	2 General Electric J85-GE-4 turbojet; 2,950 lbst (1,338 kg) each	
Weights:	empty 8,115 lbs (3,681 kg)	
	max takeoff 13,179 lbs (5,978 kg)	
Dimensions:	length	38 ft 4 in (11.67 m)
	wing span	38 ft 2 in (11.62 m)
	wing area	255 ft² (23.69 m²)
	height	14 ft 10 in (4.51 m)
Speed:	max 522 mph (840 kmh) at 25,000 ft (7,622 m)	
Ceiling:	40,400 ft (12,317 m)	
Range:	909 n.miles (1,683 km)	
Armament:	up to 640 lbs (290 kg) of bombs or rockets on 2 wing stations + wingtip tanks	
Radar:	none	

T-2C Buckeyes from VT-9/TraWing-1. (Peter B. Mersky)

T-2C Buckeyes from VT-10/TraWing-6. (Peter B. Mersky)

ROTARY-WING AIRCRAFT

V-22 OSPREY

The MV-22 Osprey is a high-speed, rotary-wing aircraft being developed primarily for the Marine Corps to replace the CH-53A/D and CH-46E in the amphibious assault role and for Navy use in the Search-And-Rescue (SAR) role to replace HH-60H helicopters. The Navy is considering a follow-on V-22 variant for the AEW and possibly ASW roles as well as for VERTREP operations.

The V-22, developed from the XV-15A technology-demonstration aircraft, has twin rotor-engine nacelles mounted on a connecting wing. The nacelles rotate to a horizontal position for conventional aircraft flight and are vertical for vertical takeoff and landing or hover. The basic aircraft will have an internal cargo capacity of 10,000 pounds (4,536 kg) and an external (slung) capacity of 15,000 pounds (6,804 kg). Vertical takeoffs and landings are the normal operating mode, although STOL operations are feasible. Thus, the design has the advantages of both a conventional aircraft and helicopter.

The Navy–Marine Corps had the lead in developing the aircraft under the project designation JVX. The Marine Corps initially planned to procure 552 for vertical assault and the Navy an additional 50 HV-22 variants for combat search and rescue. Other possible Navy missions could have added some 200 to 300 additional aircraft to the Navy program. (The Air Force at one point envisioned a buy of 80 CV-22 aircraft for special operations and the Army about 230 for medical evacuation as well as for Special Electronic Mission Aircraft [SEMA]). Thus, the V-22 program could have reached 900 to 1,200 aircraft.

The Army withdrew from the V-22 tilt-rotor program in the late 1980s, and on 25 April 1989 Secretary of Defense Cheney eliminated all funding for the Navy–Marine program. His staff proposed replacing a suggested force of 602 MV-22s with a combination of 376 CH-53E and 590 H-60 helicopters. The Marine Corps opposed this alternative, and the Congress has continued to support and fund the V-22 program. Research and development as well as prototype testing continue, and procurement is expected.

The Royal Navy has expressed interest in the AEW variant of the V-22 for operation from the INVINCIBLE-class VSTOL carriers. That AEW aircraft would loiter at about 15,000 feet (4,500 m) with a radius of some 200 n.miles (370 km) with 2.5 hours on station; in-flight refueling could extend the on-station time to 5.5 hours. The aircraft would carry the APS-138 or APS-145 radar. (Potential U.S. Navy AEW configurations provided for conformal-array radars on the fuselage of the aircraft.)

Armament: The Marine Corps has proposed a gunship variant of the MV-22 that could carry a variety of guns, rockets, and missiles. The proposed Navy SV-22 would carry Mk 50 ASW torpedoes and deploy dipping sonar.

Operational: The No. 4 development aircraft began shipboard flight trials on the WASP (LHD 1) on 4 December 1990; they were highly successful. The No. 5 development aircraft crashed on its initial flight on 11 June 1991; the cause was not a design flaw, but rather an assembly error.

Status: In development. First flight on 19 March 1989; first full conversion flight on 14 September 1989. Six development aircraft are being built.

MV-22

Manufacturer:	Bell-Boeing	
Crew:	(3) pilot, copilot, crewman + 24 troops	
Engines:	2 Allison T406-AD-400 turboshaft; 6,150 shp each	
Weights:	max takeoff 59,000 lbs (26,762 kg)	
Dimensions:	fuselage length	56 ft 10 in (17.33 m)
	span (over engine nacelles)	46 ft 6 in (14.18 m)
	height	17 ft 4 in (5.28 m)
	rotor diameter	36 ft (10.98 m)
	aircraft width (including rotor blades)	84 ft 6 in (25.76 m)
Speed:	dash approx. 345 mph (156 kmh)	
	max cruise approx. 300 mph (483 kmh) at 18,000 ft (5,488 m)	
Ceiling:	30,000+ ft (9,146 m)	
Range:	1,600 n.miles (2,963 km) with 4,000-lb (1,814-kg) payload	
	800 n.miles (1,482 km) with 12,000-lb (5,443-kg) payload	
	ferry 2,100 n.miles (3,889 km)	
Radar:	none	

A prototype V-22 Osprey in Marine markings. The aircraft is in the high-speed mode, with engine nacelles in the horizontal position. Despite the efficacy of the V-22 design and the Marines' need for such a medium-lift aircraft, the Secretary of Defense has opposed the program. (Bell Helicopter Textron)

A V-22 Osprey prototype on a helicopter carrier's deck-edge elevator shows the means by which the stub wing rotates and the rotor blades fold for shipboard stowage. (Bell Helicopter Textron)

A V-22 prototype during an in-flight refueling; note the "thimble" on the port side of the nose, housing the APQ-174 terrain-following, multi-mode radar. The engine nacelles are rotated to a near-vertical position. (Bell Helicopter Textron)

An artist's concept of the SV-22 Osprey in a hover mode with its dipping sonar lowered. The sponsons hold auxiliary fuel tanks and ASW torpedoes. An EV-22 AEW variant is now under investigation by the Royal Navy. (Bell Helicopter Textron)

S-92M MEDIUM-LIFT HELICOPTER

The Sikorsky S-92M has been proposed to meet the Marine Corps medium-lift helicopter requirement to replace the CH-46 Sea Knight. The S-92M was revealed in April 1992 to fill the gap in Marine assault lift being created by the failure of the Department of Defense to proceed with development of the MV-22 Osprey.

The S-92M design incorporates technology and features from the H-60 Black Hawk/Seahawk series, with more cabin volume than the H-60 and a rear ramp for loading small vehicles and palletized cargo. As a troop carrier, the S-92M could accommodate 18 to 20 troops for a 200-n.mile (370-km) lift. The four-blade main rotor folds for shipboard stowage as does the tail boom. It will have a fully retractable landing gear and be fitted for in-flight refueling.

A civilian version is envisioned (19-passenger capacity).

Status: Development.

Manufacturer:	Sikorsky
Crew:	(3) pilot, copilot, crew chief + 18–20 troops
Engines:	2 General Electric T701-GE-40X turboshaft
Weights:	empty 13,728 lbs (6,240 kg)
	max takeoff 23,000 lbs (10,350 kg)
Dimensions:	fuselage length 54 ft 2 in (16.51 m)
	overall length 66 ft 3 in (20.20 m)
	height 19 ft 10 in (6.05 m)
	main rotor diameter 53 ft 8 in (16.36 m)
Speed:	cruise 172.5 mph (278 kmh)
Ceiling:	
Range:	200-n.mile (370-km) radius with 20 troops

The S-92 mockup with rotors and tail boom folded for shipboard stowage and the stern ramp lowered. The helicopter is proposed for the medium-lift role in place of the V-22 tilt-rotor aircraft. (Sikorsky)

The mockup of the S-92 medium-lift helicopter proposed for the Marine Corps reveals a general similarity to the large CH-53 Sea Stallion/Super Stallion helicopters. Note the four-blade main rotor; the CH-53A/D has six blades and the CH-53E has seven. (Sikorsky)

HH-65A DOLPHIN

The French-designed Dolphin has been procured by the Coast Guard to replace the aging HH-52A in the short-range SAR role. It is flown in larger numbers than any other Coast Guard aircraft.

Developed by Aérospatiale as model SA 366G Dauphin, the helicopter was selected in a Coast Guard competition in 1979. The helicopter has a fan-in-fin *fenestron* (shrouded) tail rotor. The U.S. Coast Guard version has droppable rescue equipment and an infrared search system. Maximum mission endurance is four hours. However, engine problems led to a program to replace the original LTS101 with Allison-Garrett LHTEC T800-800 turboshaft engines, the first being installed in 1991. Those helicopters embarked in icebreakers are fitted with skis in addition to their standard landing gear, giving them more stability for snow and ice operations.

Status: First flight SA 360 on 2 June 1972; SA 366G/HH-65A (prior to installation of avionics) on 23 July 1980. Coast Guard IOC in November 1984.

The Coast Guard has procured 96 Dolphins, with deliveries delayed from an originally planned IOC of late 1981 because of engine problems. Several nations fly the helicopter in the military role, with some variants fitted with anti-ship missiles and ASW equipment.

For shipboard evaluation the Israeli Navy procured two additional H-65A helicopters that were funded by the United States; the procurement of 20 additional helicopters followed, all built by Aérospatiale to H-65A standards.

Manufacturer:	Aérospatiale
Crew:	(3) pilot, copilot, crewman + 3 passengers
Engines:	2 Avco Lycoming LTS101-750A-1 turboshaft; 680 shp each; being replaced by 2 Allison-Garrett LHTEC T800-800 turboshaft; 1,200 shp each
Weights:	empty 5,992 lbs (2,718 kg)
	max takeoff 8,928 lbs (4,050 kg)
Dimensions:	fuselage length 37 ft 6 in (11.43 m)
	overall length 43 ft 9 in (13.33 m)
	height 12 ft 9 in (3.89 m)
	main rotor diameter 39 ft 2 in (11.9 m)
Speed:	max 201 mph (324 kmh)
	cruise 160 mph (257 kmh)
Ceiling:	7,510 ft (2,290 m) hover IGE[18]
	5,340 ft (1,627 m) hover OGE
Range:	radius 166 n.miles (307 km) with 30 minutes loiter
	max 410 n.miles (760 km)

18. IGE = In Ground Effect; OGE = Out of Ground Effect.

An HH-65A Dolphin flying over the Potomac River. The Dolphin has a novel, 11-blade "finestron" type of ducted fan in place of the standard anti-torque tail rotor found in most helicopters. The tricycle landing gear is fully retractable. (U.S. Coast Guard)

An HH-65A from Coast Guard Air Station Mobile, Ala. (Aérospatiale)

HH-60J JAYHAWK

The H-60 series helicopter, flown in large numbers by the Army in the transport role and by the Navy in the ASW role (SH-60B/F), has been adopted by the Navy and Coast Guard for the Search-And-Rescue (SAR) role. In Coast Guard service the HH-60J Jayhawk performs medium-range SAR. The service has committed to an initial buy of 35 aircraft through 1993 to replace the HH-3F Pelican and CH-3E Sea King.

The HH-60J configuration is similar to the Navy's Seahawk variants, with generally the same characteristics, except the HH-60J can be fitted with three external fuel tanks for the 300-n.mile (556-km) mission radius with 45 minutes on station.

(There are other J variants in the H-60 series, the Coast Guard's HH-60J and the Japanese Maritime Self-Defense Force's SH-60J and UH-60J, the former a copy of the U.S. SH-60B Seahawk ASW aircraft; the latter J suffix indicates Japanese.)

Status: Operational. HH-60J IOC in July 1991 at the Coast Guard Air Station Elizabeth City, N.C. Sixteen aircraft were delivered through the end of 1991.

Manufacturer:	Sikorsky
Crew:	(4) pilot, copilot, 2 crewmen + 6 rescuees
Weights:	empty
	max takeoff 21,884 lbs (9,927 kg)
Range:	radius 300 n.miles (556 km) with 45 minutes on station
Radar:	Bendix RDR-1300C weather

See page 441 for basic characteristics.

HH-60H SEAHAWK

The HH-60H is the Navy's SAR variant of the ubiquitous H-60 helicopter. In the Navy it replaces the HH-1K Huey and HH-3A Sea King; in Coast Guard service the similar HH-60J performs medium-range SAR.

The HH-60H variants are flown by reserve squadrons HCS-4 and HCS-5 and by carrier-based HS anti-submarine squadrons. In supporting special operations these helicopters can carry eight SEALs.

The HH-60H variants have the APR-39 RWR, ALE-39 chaff/flare dispenser, and ALQ-144 infrared jammer as well as sophisticated communications gear. Although initially armed with machine guns, proposals are being considered to additionally provide these helicopters with 2.75-inch (70-mm) rockets and Hellfire air-to-surface missiles, with a growth potential for air-to-air missiles.

Status: Operational; in production. First flight on 17 August 1988. HH-60H IOC (HCS-5) in July 1989. Eighteen helicopters were delivered through the end of 1991.

Manufacturer:	Sikorsky
Crew:	(3) pilot, copilot, crewman + rescuees
Range:	radius 165 n.miles with 30 minutes loiter
	max 410 n.miles
Armament:	2 7.62-mm machine guns M60D (8,000 rounds)
Radar:	none

See page 441 for basic characteristics.

A Coast Guard HH-60J Jayhawk. The standard access door is on the starboard side; the port opening permits litters to be loaded. The nose radome houses an RDR-1300 weather radar. Up to three external fuel tanks can be fitted. (Sikorsky)

HH-60H Seahawk with low-visibility markings. The tail-wheel landing gear (with double tail wheels) is non-retracting. (Sikorsky)

An HH-60H Seahawk from reserve HCS-4. The main rotor blades are folded and an auxiliary fuel tank is fitted on the port side. Two such tanks can be carried, extending endurance one hour. Machine guns can be fitted in the port and starboard doors. (Peter B. Mersky)

SH-60B/F SEAHAWK (LAMPS III)

In naval service the Seahawk is primarily an ASW helicopter with the SH-60B the component of the Navy's ship-based LAMPS III ASW and over-the-horizon targeting system, and the SH-60F a carrier-based ASW aircraft. In 1986 the helicopter was additionally selected for the Navy combat SAR and Coast Guard medium-range SAR roles (see separate entries), and nine VH-60N variants have been procured for the Marine Corps.

The Seahawk is adapted from the UH-60A Black Hawk, the U.S. Army's basic transport helicopter. The SH-60B carries 2,000 pounds (907 kg) of avionics including the ALQ-142 ESM sensor (similar to the SLQ-32 found on most U.S. surface warships); this system permits the helicopter to provide over-the-horizon detection and missile targeting for the launching ship. It also has a 25-sonobuoy dispenser, APS-124 radar, FLIR, ASQ-81 MAD, and UYS-1(V)2 Proteus acoustic processor. No dipping sonar is fitted in the SH-60B. Beginning in 1990 the SH-60B variants were being fitted to carry the Penguin anti-ship missile.

The carrier-based SH-60F has the AQS-13F dipping sonar, with a 1,500-foot (457-m) cable; the radar, MAD, sonobuoys, and some other equipment of the SH-60B have been deleted; the UYS-1(V)2 is fitted in the F variants.

Early plans called for a crew of four in the SH-60B, but in the event the aircraft has three with only one sensor operator. Although designed to carry nuclear depth bombs, the Seahawks have not been "wired" for this weapon. The IBM Corporation was the prime contractor for the LAMPS III/SH-60B, the first time that the airframe manufacturer did not perform this role for a U.S. Navy helicopter; Sikorsky is the prime contractor for the SH-60F variant.

The SH-60B program is currently intended to provide two helicopters per ship to the following classes:

ships	class	
25	CG 47	TICONDEROGA class
31	DD 963	SPRUANCE class
26	FFG 7	OLIVER HAZARD PERRY class

The current Navy SH-60B requirement is for 260 helicopters, including pipeline and training units.

The SH-60F program is currently intended to provide six helicopters for each carrier air wing; the current Navy requirement is for 150 helicopters, down from the previous 175 sought when there were to be 15 air wings. (Each carrier HS squadron will have six SH-60F and two HH-60H helicopters.)

Status: Operational; in production. First flight YUH-60 on 17 October 1974; prototype SH-60B in December 1979. Navy SH-60B IOC (HSL-41) in September 1983; SH-60F IOC (HS-10) in June 1989.

SH-60F Seahawk from HS-2 aboard the carrier NIMITZ lowering the AQS-15F active dipping sonar. The F-model Seahawks do not have sonobuoys, the active sonar being more effective when in the area of operating ships, which reduce passive detection effectivenss. (Sikorsky)

The Navy procured 148 operational SH-60B helicopters in addition to six prototypes through the end of 1991; 48 SH-60F helicopters were delivered through the end of 1991.

Australia, Greece, and Spain have purchased the SH-60B, while Japan is producing the SH-60J for shipboard use and UH-60J for land basing. (A total of 16 nations other than the United States fly H-60 variants.)

SH-60B

Manufacturer:	IBM/Sikorsky
Crew:	(3) pilot, copilot/airborne tactical officer, sensor operator
Engines:	2 General Electric T700-GE-401 turboshaft; 1,690 shp each; helicopters procured after 1988 have 2 T700-GE-401C turboshaft; 1,900 shp each
Weights:	empty 13,648 lbs (6,191 kg)
	loaded 19,500 lbs (8,845 kg) in ASW role
	18,000 lbs (8,165 kg) in Harpoon targeting role
	21,000+ lbs (9,526 kg) in utility role
Dimensions:	fuselage length 50 ft (15.26 m)
	overall length 64 ft 10 in (19.76 m)
	height 17 ft 2 in (5.23 m)
	main rotor diameter 53 ft 8 in (16.36 m)
Speed:	max cruise 145 mph (233 kmh)
Ceiling:	19,000 ft (5,790 m)
	9,500 ft (2,896 m) hover IGE
	10,400 ft (4,390 m) hover OGE
Range:	radius 50 n.miles (92.5 km) with 3-hour loiter
	radius 150 n.miles (278 km) with 1-hour loiter
Armament:	2 Mk 46 or Mk 50 ASW torpedoes, or
	2 Penguin anti-ship missiles
Radar:	APS-124 in SH-60B (none in SH-60F)

An SH-60B Seahawk showing two dummy Mk 46 ASW torpedoes and (on the starboard side) the towed MAD antenna. The 25-chute sonobuoy dispenser is on the starboard side. This is the only H-60 variant to have the APS-124 radar (circular radome below nose). (Sikorsky)

VH-60N SEAHAWK

The Marine Corps flies nine VH-60 variants of the H-60 series as executive transports. Assigned to squadron HMX-1 at Quantico, Va., these are "white top" helicopters that provide transportation for the president and other senior national officials. They replaced VH-1A Huey helicopters previously employed in this role. When the president is embarked in one of these helicopters it is designated "Marine One."

The VH-60N is fitted with weather radar, cabin soundproofing, Electromagnetic Pulse (EMP) hardening, and a VIP interior configuration.

Status: IOC on 30 November 1988.

Manufacturer:	Sikorsky	
Crew:	(4) pilot, copilot, flight engineer, radio operator + passengers	
Engines:	2 General Electric T700-GE-700 turboshaft; 1,560 shp each	
Weights:	empty 11,284 lbs (5,118 kg)	
	loaded 16,994 lbs (7,708 kg)	
Dimensions:	fuselage length	50 ft $\frac{3}{4}$ in (15.26 m)
	overall length	64 ft 10 in (19.76 m)
	height	16 ft 10 in (5.13 m)
	main rotor diameter	53 ft 8 in (16.36 m)
Speed:	max 184 mph (296 kmh)	
	max cruise 167 mph (268 kmh)	
Ceiling:	19,000 ft (5,790 m)	
	9,500 ft (2,896 m) hover IGE	
	10,400 ft (4,390 m) hover OGE	
Range:	324 n.miles (600 km) with 30-min loiter	
Radar:	weather	

A "white top" VH-60N Seahawk, configured as a VIP transport. The weather radar is housed in a small radome under the nose. This relatively lightweight variant has only a single tail wheel, positioned farther aft than in SH-60 variants. (Sikorsky)

TH-57 SEARANGER

The SeaRanger is a training version of the commercial Bell 206 JetRanger series. The JetRanger was originally designed to compete in a U.S. Army 1961 light observation helicopter competition. Bell lost that competition, but the Model 206 was commercially successful and was later produced in large numbers for the Army as the OH-58 Kiowa. The Navy's TH-57A is fitted with dual controls; the TH-57C models have improved engines, avionics, and controls. (Fitted with Allison 250-C20J/T63-A-720 engines with 420 shp.)

Status: TH-57A IOC in 1968; TH-57C IOC in November 1982.

The Navy purchased 40 off-the-shelf commercial aircraft as the TH-57A in 1968; subsequently, 89 improved TH-57C models were ordered in the early 1980s. The latter replaced the TH-1L Hueys in the training role.

TH-57A

Manufacturer:	Bell	
Crew:	(1) pilot + 4 students	
Engines:	1 Allison T63-A-700 turboshaft; 317 shp	
Weights:	empty 1,464 lbs (664 kg)	
	max takeoff 3,000 lbs (1,361 kg)	
Dimensions:	fuselage length	32 ft 7 in (9.94 m)
	overall length	41 ft (12.5 m)
	height	9 ft 7 in (2.91 m)
	main rotor diameter	35 ft 4 in (10.78 m)
Speed:	max 138 mph (222 km)	
	cruise 117 mph (188 km)	
Ceiling:	18,900 ft (5,762 km)	
	13,600 ft (4,146 km) hover IGE	
Range:	300 n.miles (483 km)	
Radar:	none	

TH-57A SeaRanger. (Bell Helicopter Textron)

CH-53E/MH-53E SUPER STALLION/SEA DRAGON

Developed specifically for the U.S. Navy and Marine Corps, this is the heaviest lift helicopter in service outside of the former Soviet Union. It is flown by the Marines in the CH-53E assault/heavy cargo roles, by the Navy in the CH-53E cargo/VERTREP role, and by the Navy in the MH-53E mine countermeasures role. (The M prefix indicates multi-mission capability.)

The CH-53E can lift 16 tons (16,330 kg) of external load. These helicopters have the same basic configuration as the Sea Stallion, but with three engines, a seven-blade main rotor (vice six in the CH-53A/D), larger rotor blades, in-flight refueling probe, and improved transmission. Two 650-gallon (2,470-liter) external tanks can be fitted to the sponsons. The CH-53E can lift 93 percent of the heavy equipment in a Marine division compared to 38 percent for the CH-53D.

The MH-53E can handle the Mk 103 moored sweep gear, Mk 104 acoustic sweep, Mk 105 magnetic sweep, Mk 106 magnetic/acoustic sweep, and AQS-14 towed minehunting sonar. The improved AQS-20 mine-hunting sonar will be provided for these helicopters in place of the AQS-14. The MH-53E has a six-hour mission capability; its night capability is limited (the helicopters deployed to the Persian Gulf in 1991 were not certified to conduct night operations; see below).

Operational: Six MH-53E Sea Dragons were air-lifted by C-5A Galaxy transport to the Persian Gulf in early October 1990 to participate in Desert Shield/Desert Storm. They then operated from the helicopter carrier TRIPOLI (LPH 10). In doing so, of course, the MH-53Es displaced Marine helicopters and troops.

Status: Operational; in production. First flight YCH-53E on 1 March 1974; first flight CH-53E on 13 December 1980; first flight MH-53E on 1 September 1983 (a CH-53E in the MCM configuration flew on 23 December 1981). IOC CH-53E (HMH-464) in February 1981.

The current program is for 177 CH-53E helicopters to be procured for the Marine Corps and 52 MH-53E plus 15 CH-53E variants for the Navy. Through the end of 1991 the Navy had taken delivery of 15 CH-53E and 31 MH-53E variants; through the end of 1991 the Marine Corps had received some 100 CH-53Es. The MH-53E and the CH-53E remain in production for Navy and Marine use, respectively.

CH-53E

Manufacturer:	Sikorsky
Crew:	(3) pilot, copilot, crew chief + 55 troops
Engines:	3 General Electric T64-GE-416 turboshaft; 4,380 shp each
Weights:	empty CH-53E 33,228 lbs (15,072 kg)
	MH-53E 36,336 lbs (16,482 kg)
	max takeoff 73,500 lbs (33,340 kg)
Dimensions:	fuselage length 73 ft 4 in (22.33 m)
	overall length 99 ft $\frac{1}{2}$ in (30.18 m)
	height 29 ft 5 in (8.97 m)
	main rotor diameter 79 ft (24.08 m)
Speed:	max 195 mph (315 kmh) at sea level
	cruise 172 mph (278 kmh) at sea level
Ceiling:	18,500 ft (5,640 m)
	11,550 ft (3,520 m) hover IGE
	9,500 ft (2,895 m) hover OGE
Range:	radius 50 n.miles (92.5 km) with 16 tons external cargo
	radius 500 n.miles (926 km) with 10 tons external cargo
	ferry 1,120 n.miles (2,075 km)
Radar:	none

Marine CH-53E Sea Stallion helicopters in Saudi Arabia during Desert Storm/Desert Shield. The H-53E series are the heaviest-lift helicopters produced outside of Russia; the widely flown Russian Mi-26 Halo can lift a payload of some 22 tons. (U.S. Marine Corps)

Marine CH-53E Sea Stallion with the in-flight refueling probe removed (fits in right side of nose). The third engine nacelle is visible on the port side, adjacent to the large rotor head. (Sikorsky)

An MH-53E Sea Dragon lowering the AQS-14 minehunting sonar; the sonar can be towed at relatively high speeds. The mirrors projecting from the nose help the pilots keep track of the position of minesweeping gear being streamed. (Westinghouse)

Mk 105 hydrofoil sleds for MH-53E Sea Dragons are stowed in the hangar deck of the helicopter carrier TRIPOLI during Operation Desert Storm. The TRIPOLI was flagship for the Coalition mine countermeasure efforts—and was one of two U.S. warships to strike mines in the Persian Gulf during Desert Storm. (U.S. Navy)

CH-53A/D SEA STALLION

The CH-53A/D is a Marine Corps heavy assault helicopter, now being succeeded in the heavy-lift role by the CH-53E. The Naval Air Reserve flies the RH-53D as a mine countermeasures helicopter, being succeeded by the MH-53E.

These helicopters have large cargo compartments with a stern ramp. The RH-53D variants are similar to the CH-53A/D but with upgraded T64-GE-415 engines and automatic flight controls for sustained low-level flight. The MCM versions have provisions for two swivel .50-cal machine guns and can stream Mk 103 cutters for countering contact mines, Mk 104 acoustic countermeasures, Mk 105 hydrofoil sled for countering magnetic mines, Mk 106, which is the sled with acoustic sweep equipment added, and the SPU-1 Magnetic Orange Pipe (MOP) for countering shallow-water mines. The sled weighs about 6,000 pounds and is 27 feet long and 13 feet wide; the MOP is 33 feet long, 10 inches in diameter, and weighs 1,000 pounds (454 kg; filled with polystyrene). The AQS-14 dipping/towed sonar is also available for the RH-53D.

Historical: The RH-3A Sea King was the first airborne MCM helicopter approved for service. It was replaced by the CH-53A Sea Stallion in the early 1970s, with those helicopters used during the Operation End Sweep 1972–1973 mine clearance of North Vietnamese ports.

The CH-53A was succeeded by the RH-53D in 1972; these helicopters were deployed to the Suez Canal in 1974–1975 (Operations Nimbus Star/Stream); to the Red Sea/Gulf of Suez in 1984 (Operation Intense Look); and to the Persian Gulf in 1987 (Operation Earnest Will).

Operational: Eight RH-53D helicopters, flying from the carrier NIMITZ (CVN 68), were used in the aborted April 1980 attempt to rescue hostages from the American embassy in Tehran; seven of those helicopters were destroyed in the operation.

Refueling in flight five times from KC-130 tankers, an RH-53D has made an 18½-hour flight across the United States.

Status: Operational. First flight CH-53A on 14 October 1964. Marine Corps IOC (HMH-463) in November 1966.

The Navy and Marine Corps took delivery of 384 H-53A/D series helicopters; others were flown by the U.S. Air Force and foreign services. In addition to the 30 RH-53D models delivered to the U.S. Navy, six more MCM versions went to Iran in 1976.

CH-53D

Manufacturer:	Sikorsky	
Crew:	(3) pilot, copilot, crewman + 38 troops or 24 litters + 4 attendants (7 crewmen in RH-53D)	
Engines:	2 General Electric T64-GE-413 turboshaft; 3,925 shp each	
Weights:	empty 23,628 lbs (10,718 kg)	
	loaded 34,958 lbs (15,857 kg)	
	max takeoff 42,000 lbs (19,051 kg)	
Dimensions:	fuselage length	67 ft 2 in (20.48 m)
	overall length	88 ft 3 in (26.92 m)
	height	24 ft 11 in (7.59 m)
	main rotor diameter	72 ft 3 in (22.04 m)
Speed:	max 196 mph (315 kmh)	
	cruise 173 mph (278 kmh)	
Ceiling:	21,000 ft (6,402 m)	
	13,400 ft (4,085 m) hover IGE	
Range:	540 n.miles (1,000 km)	
	ferry 886 n.miles (1,641 km)	
Radar:	none	

A Marine CH-53 Sea Stallion, fitted with auxiliary fuel tanks and machine guns (one protruding from first hatch on port side). The H-53E series has a third engine, mounted on the port side, slightly behind the existing engine. (U.S. Navy)

An RH-53D airborne MCM helicopter towing a Mk 105 sled. This helicopter was assigned to HM-14 when this photo was taken; RH-53Ds are now flown only by the Naval and Marine Air Reserves. (U.S. Navy)

HH-52A SEA GUARDIAN (formerly HU2S-1G)

The HH-52A was a commercial helicopter adapted by the Coast Guard for the SAR mission; the H-52 series is not flown by any other U.S. military service. The Sikorsky-designed helicopter was in service from 1963 to 1989, with the last unit flying for the last time on 12 September 1989. Ninety-nine helicopters were procured.

The HH-52A was replaced in Coast Guard service by the HH-65A Dolphin.

See 14th Edition/pages 437–438 for characteristics.

H-46 SEA KNIGHT (formerly HRB)

The H-46 series is the Marine Corps principal assault helicopter and is flown by the Navy primarily in the VERTREP role. Plans to replace the Sea Knight with a more modern Marine "medium assault helicopter" are being held in abeyance pending the procurement decisions in the MV-22 tilt-rotor program.

The Sea Knight has a tricycle landing gear and small, wheel-housing sponsons aft, distinguishing it from the similar, widely flown CH-47 Chinook cargo helicopter. The Sea Knight is a tandem-rotor helicopter with a rear ramp for the rapid loading and unloading of cargo, including small vehicles; the rotor blades fold for shipboard stowage. The H-46 series has demonstrated the capability of remaining afloat for more than two hours in two-foot (0.6 m) waves with the rotors stopped.

The Marines have upgraded 273 CH-46A/D troop helicopters to the CH-46E configuration. Provided in the upgrade are improved engines, crash attenuating seats for pilots, a more survivable fuel system, and an improved rescue winch. The Navy flies several H-46 variants in five HC squadrons; the Navy's HH-46D helicopters are fully instrumented for night/all-weather operation and are employed in the VERTREP as well as SAR roles. (The Navy also flies CH-46D and UH-46D.)

Status: Operational. First flight YHC-1A prototype on 22 April 1958. Marine IOC (HMM-265) in June 1964.

The Navy and Marine Corps took delivery of 624 Sea Knights from 1961 to 1977.

CH-46E

Manufacturer:	Boeing Vertol
Crew:	(3) pilot, copilot, crewman + 25 troops or 15 litters + 2 attendants
Engines:	2 General Electric T58-GE-16 turboshaft; 1,870 shp each
Weights:	empty 15,198 lbs (6,894 kg)
	max takeoff 24,300 lbs (11,022 kg)
Dimensions:	fuselage length 46 ft 8 in (13.92 m)
	overall length 84 ft 4 in (25.72 m)
	main rotor diameter 25 ft 6 in (7.81 m)
	height 16 ft 8 in (5.08 m)
Speed:	max 161 mph (259 kmh)
	cruise 158 mph (254 kmh)
Ceiling:	14,000 ft (4,265 m)
Range:	radius 75 n.miles (139 km)
	ferry 600 n.miles (1,111 km)
Armament:	2 .50-cal machine guns can be fitted
Radar:	Doppler approach in HH-46D

A CH-46E Sea Knight from HMM-261 lifts off the helicopter carrier SAIPAN off the coast of Liberia in 1990. Similar to the Army's CH-46 Chinook, the Sea Knight has tandem main rotors, which alleviate the need for a stern rotor, and a rear ramp. (JO1 Kip Burke, USN)

A CH-46D Sea Knight from the HC-5 detachment from the replenishment ship SAN JOSE (AFS 7) during and UNREP operation. Most Navy Sea Knights have a rescue hoist over the starboard door. The undercarriage does not retract on the H-46 helicopters. (PHAN A.J. Kimbell, USN)

OH-6B CAYUSE

Four OH-6B Cayuse helicopters have been acquired by the Naval Test Pilot School at NAS Patuxent River, Md., on loan from the Army for use in test-pilot training.

The OH-6 (designated HO-6 before 1962) was developed for the Army's 1961 Light Observation helicopter (LOH) competition. The helicopter proved a highly versatile aircraft, and the commercial Model 500 set 23 international records for helicopters in 1966.

Status: First flight (YOH-6A) 27 February 1963. Army IOC in 1966; Navy OH-6B IOC in 1991.

The Spanish Navy flew the Cayuse (Model 500M) in the ASW role; 16 other countries in addition to the United States flew the OH-6 in a military role. Procurement totaled 1,434 helicopters.

Manufacturer:	Hughes
Crew:	(2) pilot, observer + 2 passengers
Engines:	1 Allison T63-A-5A turboshaft; 317 shp
Weights:	empty 1,229 lbs (557 kg)
	loaded 2,400 lbs (1,090 kg)
Dimensions:	fuselage length 23 ft (7.0 m)
	overall length 30 ft 3¾ in (9.24 m)
	height 8 ft 1½ in (2.47 m)
	main rotor diameter 26 ft 4 in (8.02 m)
Speed:	cruise 134 mph (216 kmh)
	max 150 mph (241 kmh)
Range:	330 n.miles (611 km)
Ceiling:	15,800 ft (4,815 m)
	11,800 ft (3,594 m) hover IGE
	7,300 ft (2,225 m) hover OGE
Radar:	none

The Navy flies four OH-6B Cayuse helicopters at the Naval Test Pilot School. The Army flew over 1,400 of the OH-6 variant, which was followed by large numbers of the improved OH-58 Kiowa version. The Hughes 500MD variant of this helicopter has been flown in an ASW configuration by several navies. (U.S. Navy)

HH-3F PELICAN

This version of the Sea King was built specifically for the U.S. Coast Guard SAR role. It is similar to the HH-3E Jolly Green Giant rescue version flown by the U.S. Air Force. The HH-3F carries droppable rescue supplies and has a modified boat-type hull and sponson-floats for water operations. FLIR has been fitted to most of the operating helicopters.

The HH-60J Jayhawk has been acquired to replace the HH-3F; however, Coast Guard helicopter requirements make it likely that these helicopters will be retained beyond the year 2000.

Status: Coast Guard IOC in 1968.

Forty of these helicopters were built for the Coast Guard.

Manufacturer:	Sikorsky
Crew:	(3 or 4) pilot, copilot, 1 or 2 crewmen + 15 passengers or 8 litters
Engines:	2 General Electric T58-GE-5 turboshaft; 1,500 shp each
Weights:	max takeoff 22,050 lbs (10,002 kg)
Dimensions:	fuselage length 57 ft 3 in (17.45 m)
	overall length 73 ft (22.25 m)
	height 18 ft 1 in (5.51 m)
	main rotor diameter 62 ft (18.9 m)
Speed:	max 162 mph (261 kmh)
	cruise 125 mph (201 kmh)
Ceiling:	11,000 ft (3,354 m)
	4,100 ft (1,250 m) hover IGE
Range:	400 n.miles (741 km)
Radar:	search-weather

A Coast Guard HH-3F Pelican with undercarriage lowered. The helicopter has a weather radar in a "thimble" nose radome. This helicopter is similar to the Air Force HH-3E Jolly Green Giant. (U.S. Coast Guard)

SH-3 SEA KING (formerly HSS-2)

The Sea King has been the U.S. Navy's standard carrier-based ASW helicopter since the early 1960s; it is being replaced aboard aircraft carriers by the SH-60F Seahawk and in the SAR and utility roles by other variants of the H-60 series.

The Navy flies the SH-3H variant in the ASW role, all having been converted from earlier models. They have AQS-13B dipping sonar, sonobuoys, APN-130 doppler radar, AQS-81 MAD, and ALE-37 chaff dispenser. The dipping sonar has a 450-foot (137-m) operating depth. A total of 145 Sea Kings have been converted to the ultimate SH-3H configuration. Two Sea Kings were used to test sensors for the SH-60B (designated YSH-3J). A large number of SH-3G utility helicopters are in Navy service, the survivors of a number of SH-3A variants with ASW equipment removed. The earlier SH-3A ASW variant, the HH-3A rescue variant, and the RH-3A mine countermeasures versions have all been discarded. The Marine Corps flies 11 VH-3D as presidential transports (squadron HMX-1).

The Sea King has a "boat" hull, but does not normally alight on the water (unlike the Coast Guard HH-3F, listed separately in this edition). The tail pylon and main rotor blades fold for carrier stowage.

Operational: During Operations Desert Shield/Desert Storm in 1990–1991, SH-3H helicopters aboard participating aircraft carriers were fitted with a flexible 7.62-mm M60 machine gun, mounted in the (starboard) door opening.

Status: First flight XHSS-2 on 11 March 1959; first flight SH-3H in April 1972. Navy IOC (HS-1) in June 1961.

The helicopter is flown by several foreign services as well as the U.S. Air Force.

SH-3H

Manufacturer:	Sikorsky
Crew:	(4) pilot, copilot, 2 systems operators
Engines:	2 General Electric T58-GE-10 turboshaft; 1,400 shp each
Weights:	empty 13,465 lbs (6,108 kg)
	max takeoff 21,000 lbs (9,526 kg)
Dimensions:	fuselage length 54 ft 9 in (16.69 m)
	overall length 72 ft 8 in (22.15 m)
	height 16 ft 10 in (5.13 m)
	main rotor diameter 62 ft (18.9 m)
Speed:	max 166 mph (267 kmh)
	cruise 136 mph (219 kmh)
Ceiling:	14,700 ft (4,482 m)
	10,500 ft (3,201 m) hover IGE
Range:	540 n.miles (1,000 km)
	ferry 647 n.miles (1,198 km)
Armament:	2 Mk 46 ASW torpedoes
Radar:	LN-66HP search

An SH-3G Sea King from HC-2, one of several squadrons that provide utility and VERTREP helicopters to the fleet, lifting off the helicopter carrier NEW ORLEANS. The SH-3D/G helicopters have been disarmed; there is a rescue hoist above the large, starboard-side door. (U.S. Navy)

An SH-3H Sea King from HS-9 and a Brazilian SH-3D both trail their AQS-13 dipping sonar during a joint naval exercise. HS-9 was with CVW-8 aboard the carrier NIMITZ at the time. (PHAA P. Silver, USN)

CH-3E SEA KING

The Coast Guard acquired nine CH-3E cargo helicopters from the Air Force in the 1980s because of the increase in rotary-wing aircraft requirements caused by drug interdiction operations.

A variant of the basic H-3 design, this helicopter was widely used by the Air Force in the cargo and transport role. The helicopter is capable of water landing and takeoff, and has a hydraulically operated rear loading ramp. Up to 8,000 lbs (3,629 kg) of cargo can be carried by sling or within the fuselage cargo compartment.

Several of the Coast Guard helicopters were modified for the SAR role, being fitted with auxiliary fuel tanks, Loran-C navigation gear, and APN-215 search radar.

Operational: The U.S. Air Force's HH-3E variant of this design gained fame in the SAR role during the Vietnam War, given the name Jolly Green Giant.

Status: Operational. First flight CH-3E in April 1967; USAF IOC in April 1967.

Manufacturer:	Sikorsky
Crew:	(3) pilot, copilot, flight mechanic + 25 troops
Engines:	2 General Electric T58-GE-5 turboshaft; 1,500 shp each
Weights:	empty 13,108 lbs (5,946 kg)
	max takeoff 22,050 lbs (10,002 kg)
Dimensions:	fuselage length　60 ft 10 in (18.55 m)
	overall length　73 ft (22.26 m)
	height　18 ft 1 in (5.51 m)
	main rotor diameter　62 ft (18.9 m)
Speed:	max 173 mph (278 kmh)
	cruise 145 mph (233 kmh)
Ceiling:	20,000 ft (6,098 m)
	10,500 ft (3,201 m) hover IGE
Range:	388 n.miles (719 km)
Radar:	none

SH-2F LAMPS I (formerly HU2K)

The LAMPS (Light Airborne Multi-Purpose System) is employed in the ASW role from surface warships that cannot accommodate the larger SH-60B LAMPS III aircraft. The Navy's need for ship-based ASW helicopters in the early 1970s led to the conversion of 20 single-engine HU2K/UH-2 Seasprite utility helicopters to the SH-2D configuration and another 85 to the SH-2F variant. The surviving D models were later upgraded to an F configuration, the last in 1983. Two conversions were further modified to a YSH-2E configuration, and one SH-2F without ASW avionics became an NHH-2D test aircraft. Subsequently, 48 additional SH-2F helicopters were procured. One HH-2D is employed in oceanographic survey work. (The principal external feature distinguishing the D from the F variant is the tailwheel, moved six feet (1.8 m) forward to facilitate handling on small ships.

The SH-2 LAMPS are employed to localize and attack submarine contacts initially made by surface ASW ships. The helicopters have no sonobuoy analysis capability. They are fitted with the LN-66 radar, a 15-sonobuoy dispenser, ASQ-81 MAD, ALR-66 ESM, and smoke markers. With the sonobuoy dispenser removed, the cabin can accommodate four passengers or two litters. In the VERTREP role the SH-2F can lift 2,000 lbs (907 kg) of cargo. The helicopter can also be employed for over-the-horizon targeting of anti-ship missiles.

In 1985 an SH-2F was provided YT700-GE-401 engines (1,723 shp); redesignated YSH-2G. The later engine provides higher performance and reduced maintenance requirements. The six fiscal 1987 helicopters were built with T700-GE-401 engines and are designated SH-2G. There is a slight increase in speed (160 mph/257 kmh), range is increased by 100 n.miles (185 km), endurance raised by almost one hour, and ceiling increased. The SH-2G has a FLIR, ALQ-144 infrared countermeasures device, ALE-39 chaff/flare dispenser, and upgraded avionics. Plans to upgrade the SH-2F variants to the G configuration were cancelled in January 1992.

These helicopters operate from ASW ships that cannot carry the larger SH-60B LAMPS III, most having been configured to operate the unmanned DSN/QH-50 DASH helicopters.[19] Those ships are (one helicopter per ship except for the FFG 7):

ships	class	
1	CGN 35	TRUXTUN
2	CG 47	TICONDEROGA class
8	CG 26	BELKNAP class
4	DDG 993	KIDD class
25	FFG 7	OLIVER HAZARD PERRY class

The SH-2F was also embarked in the KNOX (FF 1052)-class frigates when those ships were operational. The four VIRGINIA (CGN 38)-class cruisers have had their LAMPS hangar deleted; other LAMPS I ships have been discarded.

Operational: During Operation Desert Storm in 1991 SH-2F helicopters were fitted with a laser device and employed to detect naval mines in the Gulf.

Status: Operational. First flight HU2K on 2 July 1959. Navy IOC (HU-2) in December 1962. First flight SH-2D on 16 March 1971; IOC SH-2D (HC-4) in October 1971. First flight SH-2G on 28 December 1989; IOC SH-2G (HSL-33) in March 1991.

One hundred ninety UH-2 utility helicopters were built through 1965. The 54 new SH-2F helicopters produced by Kaman were the first helicopters built by that firm in 15 years and the first of this series manufactured in an ASW configuration; they were followed by the production of six SH-2G helicopters.

Pakistan and Portugal have also procured the SH-2F for shipboard use.

---

19. DASH = Drone Anti-Submarine Helicopter.

Manufacturer:	Kaman	
Crew:	(3) pilot, copilot/tactical coordinator, systems operator	
Engines:	2 General Electric T58-GE-8F turboshaft; 1,350 shp each	
Weights:	empty 6,652 lbs (3,925 kg)	
	early aircraft max 12,800 lbs (5,806 kg)	
	beginning with 28th new production SH-2F 13,500 lbs (6,124 kg)	
Dimensions:	fuselage length	38 ft 4 in (11.69 m)
	overall length	52 ft 7 in (16.04 m)
	height	15 ft 6 in (4.73 m)
	main rotor diameter	44 ft (13.42 m)
Speed:	max 152 mph (246 kmh) at sea level	
	cruise 138 mph (222 km)	
Ceiling:	17,600 ft (5,364 m)	
	14,400 ft (4,390 m) hover IGE	
	10,700 ft (3,260 m) hover OGE	
Range:	420 n.miles (778 km)	
	radius approx. 35 n.miles (65 km) on ASW patrol with 1.5 hours on station	
Armament:	2 Mk 46 or Mk 50 ASW torpedoes	
	2 7.62-mm M60 machine guns can be fitted	
Radar:	LN-66HP search	
	APN-182 Doppler navigation	

An SH-2F LAMPS I modified for Persian Gulf operations: it has an ALQ-144 jammer in the tail and a FLIR pod under the nose (starboard side); the helicopter carries a Maverick missile, a Mk 46 ASW torpedo, and a 2.72-inch rocket pod (port side). Note the retracted main landing gear (adjacent to the radome). (Kaman)

An SH-2F LAMPS I from HSL-31 with MAD gear being streamed. A Mk 46 ASW torpedo is mounted beneath the 15-chute sonobuoy dispenser. The tail wheel does not retract. (U.S. Navy)

An SH-2G LAMPS I helicopter with an auxiliary fuel tank and MAD antenna mounted on the starboard side. Upgrade of the SH-2F force to the SH-2G configuration was cancelled in 1991. (Kaman)

AH-1W   SEACOBRA

The SeaCobra is a specialized gunship helicopter that evolved from the widely used Huey series. It is flown by Marine Corps utility and attack helicopter squadrons (HMLA).

The SeaCobra has a narrow fuselage providing minimal cross section with stub wings for carrying rocket packs or gun pods, a nose turret with an M197 20-mm three-barrel cannon, and tandem seating for a gunner (forward) and pilot. The T model was formerly designated AH-1J (Improved), having been changed in August 1975. The 56 AH-1J SeaCobras have been fitted with the Army-developed Hellfire missile; the 49 AH-1T helicopters have been fitted with the TOW anti-tank missile and Sidewinder AAM, for a total of 1,000 pounds (454 kg) of weapons. The AH-1W (formerly AH-1T+) is fitted with a weapons load of 3,000 pounds (1,361 kg); this helicopter can take off on a single engine and climb at more than 800 feet (244 m) per minute. The AH-1W introduced the Hellfire missile and had a greater weapons payload than its predecessors; alternatively, external fuel tanks can be fitted. An ALE-39 chaff/flare dispenser is fitted. The 20-mm cannon has a helmet-sight system. All surviving AH-1T variants are being upgraded to AH-1W.

Status: Operational. First flight Army AH-1G on 7 September 1965; first flight AH-1T+ on 16 November 1983. IOC AH-1J in January 1971; AH-1T in October 1977; AH-1W in March 1986.

More than 2,500 Cobra gunships have been built for U.S. and foreign military services, with the AH-1S model coproduced by Mitsui in Japan.

Manufacturer:	Bell	
Crew:	(2) pilot, gunner	
Engines:	2 General Electric T700-GE-401 turboshaft; 1,690 shp each	
Weights:	empty 10,200 lbs (4,627 kg)	
	max takeoff 14,750 lbs (6,690 kg)	
Dimensions:	fuselage length	45 ft 6 in (13.87 m)
	overall length	58 ft (17.68 m)
	height	14 ft 2 in (4.32 m)
	main rotor diameter	48 ft (14.63 m)
Speed:	max 219 mph (352 kmh) at sea level	
Ceiling:	17,500 ft (5,335 m)	
	14,750 ft (4,495 m) hover IGE	
	3,000 ft (914 m) hover OGE	
Range:	343 n.miles (635 km)	
Armament:	1 20-mm cannon M197	
	(750 rounds)	
	8 TOW or Hellfire	
	missiles	
	or 38 2.75-inch rockets	
	or 32 5-inch Zuni rockets	
	plus 2 Sidewinder AAMs	
Radar:	none	

A Marine AH-1W SeaCobra crosses the Saudi Arabian desert on patrol. In addition to the three-barrel Gatling gun, the SeaCobra has eight Hellfire anti-tank missiles on sponsons. The Marine Corps has considered procurement of the Army's AH-56 Cheyenne gunship, but Marine use is unlikely. (Bell Helicopter Textron)

Crewmen ready an AH-1W SeaCobra on the helicopter carrier NEW ORLEANS during Desert Storm. The AH-1 series has a very narrow fuselage compared to its Huey progenitor. (JO1 Joe Gawlowicz, USN)

HH/UH-1N HUEY (IROQUOIS) (formerly HU-1)

The Huey series, whose name is derived from the earlier HU-1E designation, is the most widely used military helicopter in the Western world. The HH-1N and UH-1N are the only variants now flown by the Navy and Marine Corps; they are flown in the rescue and utility roles from ships and ashore.

The Navy TH-1L training and HH-1K rescue variants have been discarded as have the Marine VH-1N variants used for VIP transport. In 1991 many of the UH-1Ns employed for SAR operations aboard amphibious ships and at air stations were redesignated HH-1N.

Status: Operational. First flight XH-40 on 22 October 1956. Marine IOC (VMO-1) in March 1964.

More than 9,000 Hueys have been produced for U.S. and foreign service since the Bell design won the U.S. Army's competition for a turbine helicopter in 1955.

Manufacturer:	Bell
Crew:	(3) pilot, copilot, crewman + 12 to 15 troops
Engines:	2 United Aircraft of Canada (PT6T) T400 turboshaft; 900 shp each
Weights:	empty 5,549 lbs (2,517 kg)
	max takeoff 10,500 lbs (4,763 kg)
Dimensions:	fuselage length 42 ft 5 in (12.93 m)
	overall length 57 ft 3 in (17.47 m)
	height 14 ft 5 in (4.39 m)
	main rotor diameter 48 ft 2 in (14.7 m)
Speed:	126 mph (203 kmh)
Ceiling:	15,000 ft (4,573 m)
	12,900 ft (3,933 m) hover IGE
Range:	250 n.miles (463 km)
Armament:	various combinations of machine guns and rockets can be mounted
Radar:	none

An upgraded UH-1N Huey from readiness/transition squadron HC-16. More Hueys and the derivative models have been produced—in the United States, Italy, Japan, and Taiwan—than any other helicopter in history. (U.S. Navy)

A Marine UH-1N Huey aboard the carrier THEODORE ROOSEVELT. (PHC Denis Keske, USN)

A UH-1N Huey from VXE-6 painted red and hovering over the Antarctic ice. The Huey can operate on either its skids or on skis, the latter shown here in the stowed position. VXE-6 flies ski-equipped C-130 Hercules transports as well as Hueys in the Antarctic. (PH2 Lance Kirk, USN)

EXPERIMENTAL AIRCRAFT

X-31 ENHANCED FIGHTER MANEUVERABILITY (EFM) DEMONSTRATOR

This is an advanced research aircraft intended to demonstrate whether it is possible to exploit the high-angle-of-attack flight regime to enable a fighter to achieve tighter, faster turns, and earlier weapon-firing opportunities.

The basic aircraft design is relatively conservative with a delta wing configuration with canards (forward fuselage-mounted planes). The aircraft has a deep fuselage with a large variable-capture air intake beneath the fuselage. An F/A-18 Hornet-type HUD is provided. To the maximum extent possible off-the-shelf components were employed to reduce costs. The initial costs of developing and producing the aircraft were shared, with the United States contributing 75 percent and Germany 25 percent of the costs.

Flight testing of the two X-31A aircraft is carried out by an international test organization made up of representatives from NASA, Defense Advanced Research Projects Agency (DARPA), Navy, Air Force, Germany, and the firms of Rockwell International and Messerschmitt-Bolkow-Blöhm (MBB).[20] DARPA has overall program management, the Navy serving as DARPA's agent and providing on-site direction.

The aircraft is unarmed.

Status: Flight test. First flight on 11 October 1990. The initial test phases were carried out in 1990–1991 at Rockwell International facility in Palmdale, Calif.; in late 1991 it was moved to the NASA Ames-Dryden research facility at Edwards, Calif., to continue tests. In early 1993 the aircraft is scheduled to be moved to the Naval Air Test Center at Patuxent River, Md., for tests to demonstrate the value of thrust vectoring and other enhanced control technologies for close-in air combat maneuvering.

The designation X-31 was assigned on 23 February 1987.

20. Now part of Deutsche Aerospace.

Manufacturer:	Rockwell and Messerschmitt-Bolkow-Blöhm		
Crew:	(1) pilot		
Engines:	1 General Electric F404-GE-400 turbojet; 16,000 lbst (7,257 kgst)		
Weights:	empty 10,212 lbs (4,632 kg)		
	mission 11,830 lbs (5,366 kg)		
	max takeoff 13,968 lbs (6,335 kg)		
Dimensions:	length	43 ft 4 in (13.21 m)	
	wing span	23 ft 10 in (7.26 m)	
	wing area	226.3 ft² (20.37 m²)	
	canard area	23.6 ft² (2.12 m²)	
	height	14 ft 7 in (4.44 m)	
Speed:	max Mach 0.9 at 35,000 ft (10,670 m)		
Range:			
Ceiling:			
Radar:	none		

The first X-31 EFM demonstrator in its original markings with its sponsors—DARPA, MBB (BMVg), and Navy—emblazoned on its fuselage. A Marine pilot from the Naval Air Test Center was piloting the aircraft when this photo was taken. (U.S. Navy)

XV-15A

The XV-15A is a tilt-rotor demonstration aircraft, serving as a technology prototype for the V-22 Osprey series. Developed by Bell Helicopter Textron, the XV-15A has successfully demonstrated the ability of a rotary-wing aircraft to fully convert in flight to a conventional aircraft configuration.

The aircraft has twin rotor-engine nacelles mounted on a connecting wing; the nacelles rotate to the horizontal position for conventional aircraft flight and are vertical for takeoff and landing, or hover. Rolling takeoffs and landings are possible. Thus, the design has the advantages of both a conventional aircraft and helicopter.

Bell built two XV-15A aircraft under NASA and Army sponsorship. Subsequently, the Navy–Marine Corps gave support to the project.

Operational: The two XV-15A aircraft have achieved their flight demonstration goals in extensive testing by NASA and the services, with one having been airlifted to the Paris air show in 1982 in a C-5A Galaxy transport, where it performed for international audiences.

In a key XV-15A evaluation, one aircraft flew 54 landings and takeoffs from the helicopter carrier Tripoli during August 1982. Although not intended for shipboard operation, the tests succeeded with only minor difficulties. One of these aircraft crashed on 20 August 1992.

Status: Operational. First flight 3 May 1957.

An XV-15A during shipboard compatibility trials on the helicopter carrier Tripoli. The engine nacelles are in the vertical position, for vertical takeoff. (U.S. Navy)

Manufacturer:	Bell
Crew:	(2) pilot, copilot
Engines:	2 Avco Lycoming LTC1K-4K turboshaft; 1,800 shp each
Weights:	empty 9,670 lbs (4,386 kg)
	loaded 13,000 lbs (5,897 kg)
	max takeoff 15,000 lbs (6,804 kg)
Dimensions:	length 42 ft 2 in (12.83 m)
	wing span (over engine nacelles)
	35 ft 2 in (10.72 m)
	height 15 ft 4 in (4.67 m)
	rotor diameter 25 ft (7.62 m)
	aircraft width (including rotor blades)
	57 ft 2 in (17.4 m)
Speed:	max 382 mph (615 kmh) at 17,000 ft (5,183 m)
	max cruise 345 mph (555 kmh)
Range:	
Ceiling:	29,000 ft (8,841 m)
Radar:	none

XVF-12A

The XVF-12A was conceived as a high-performance VSTOL fighter aircraft for shipboard operation. The prototype has never flown and the program is dead.

See 12th Edition/page 318 for characteristics.

GLIDERS

Both the U.S. Navy and Marine Corps had small glider programs during World War II. The current Coast Guard program is believed to be the first maritime glider effort since the war.

RG-8A MOTORIZED GLIDERS

Two Schweizer motorized gliders were procured by the Coast Guard in the 1980s for drug-interdiction surveillance. They were obtained from the U.S. Army, which apparently employed the craft in clandestine operations.

Retaining the Army designation RG-8A, the Coast Guard craft are powered by a 235-horsepower reciprocating engine; the two-seat aircraft have been "militarized" with communications gear and FLIR. Flying out of Opa-Locka, Fla., they have a mission endurance of up to eight hours.

An XV-15A tilt-rotor technology demonstration aircraft in the horizontal flight configuration with engine nacelles in the horizontal position. The XV-15A was precursor to the V-22 Osprey. (Bell Helicopter Textron)

A Coast Guard RG-8A motorized glider off the Florida coast. The low noise level of these aircraft makes them useful in counter-drug operations. (U.S. Coast Guard)

LIGHTER-THAN-AIR

The Navy and Coast Guard airship programs have been halted. The Navy's development of a surveillance airship was cancelled in early 1992, shortly before completion of the first flight of a full-size prototype (the YEZ-2A/Sentinel 5000), while the Coast Guard's fully operational aerostat surveillance program was "grounded" on 31 December 1991 for transfer to the Army. On that date the five Coast Guard sea-based aerostat vessels were brought into the ports of Miami and Key West, Fla., pending completion of studies on the future of the program. Subsequently, the ships have returned to service, operated by civilian contract crews with uniformed Army personnel on board for technical duties (see chapter 34).

The aerostat sensors and communications gear will be upgraded.

There are two principal types of Lighter-Than-Air (LTA) aircraft——the non-rigid or "blimp" and the rigid airship. The blimp has no supporting structure to maintain its shape. The nose, however, may be stiffened by a ribbed structure similar to that of an umbrella. A rigid airship has separate gas (helium) containers held inside of a rigid metal framework covered with fabric.

The Navy and Coast Guard initiated a major airship development program in the early 1980s to develop craft suitable for surveillance and—for the Navy—anti-ship missile defense missions. A major step was taken in 1980 when the Coast Guard and NASA agreed to jointly sponsor development of a manned airship employing the latest available technology for synthetics and adhesives for the gas bag, automated controls, and ground/ship recovery systems that would reduce the large ground crews normally required to land and tether blimps. In 1983 the Coast Guard evaluated a British-built Airship Industries Skyship 500 manned airship at the Naval Air Test Center at Patuxent River, Md., with some 250 flight hours being flown in the evaluation. (The deflated Airship 500 was flown to the United States in a C-141 transport.)

By 1985 the Coast Guard was ready to award a contract to Airship Industries for lease of a larger Skyship 600 airship for operational service for at least five months. The Coast Guard effort was dubbed PACE for Patrol Airship Concept Evaluation and envisioned an eventual LTA vehicle for service use that would fly a variety of patrol/surveillance missions, carrying a crew of six on missions that would last at least 48 hours. (The French Navy also evaluated a Skyship 600.)

However, the formal entry of the Navy into the LTA program caused the Coast Guard to cancel its manned LTA efforts in September 1985. An official statement explained that the "large scale multi-year LTA program recently launched by the Navy would overshadow [the Coast Guard] project research effort. Continuation of the Coast Guard program would duplicate the Navy research and would be less comprehensive." Instead, the Coast Guard has concentrated on the development of unmanned aerostats.

The Navy airship program was launched by then-Secretary of the Navy John Lehman, who in 1985 approved a formal development effort with the goal of a large, radar-carrying airship that could provide early warning of approaching hostile aircraft and cruise missiles. Study contracts were awarded in 1985 to Goodyear, Westinghouse, and Boeing for airship concepts, and to Hughes, Westinghouse, and RCA for suitable radars. A suitable surveillance radar would require an airship at least the size of the ZPG-3W, which was in service from 1957 to 1961—a length of some 400 feet (122 m) with a gas-bag volume of about 1.5 million cubic feet (45,000 m³). But to obtain an "at sea" endurance of 30 days a much larger airship would be required, probably with a gas-bag volume of just under three million cubic feet, with a length of about 480 feet (146 m) and a diameter of 110 feet (33.5 m). Both turboprop and reciprocating engines are being considered for propulsion, providing a speed of perhaps 100 knots (185 kmh) in no-wind conditions. While their prime mission will be surveillance, both active and passive, other missions that were considered included ASW and over-the-horizon targeting for ship-launched cruise missiles.

Preliminary estimates indicated that the Navy would have a need for some 20 to 50 airships, although numbers up to 100 have been considered in some studies. A program of 20 to 50 units could have a pricetag of $3 *billion* or more (mid-1980s dollars).

This ambitious program ended after Mr. Lehman stepped down as Navy secretary in 1987 and there were severe budget cutbacks. The Navy was forced to completely cancel its airship program in mid-1990. At the time it was sponsoring the Westinghouse Sentinel 1000 airship, a one-half-scale version of the Sentinel 5000 design that the Navy was proposing for fleet operation. Subsequently, funding for the Sentinel 1000 was moved into the Air Defense Initiative (ADI) office of the Department of Defense, with the Navy continuing to manage the program. The ADI office sees the airship as a potential AEW platform, especially in defense of U.S. cities and other coastal targets against submarine-launched cruise missiles. Obviously, with the demise of the Soviet naval-strategic threat, the ADI requirements are now highly speculative.

A Coast Guard aerostat rests on its support vessel during Caribbean operations. The Coast Guard operation of the sea-based aerostat program was halted on 31 December 1991 with the craft being assigned to the Army for operation. The Army operates the U.S. land-based aerostat program, with all aerostats being used for counter-drug operations. (U.S. Coast Guard)

Coast Guard aerostat. (U.S. Coast Guard)

Characteristics of the Sentinel 1000 and 5000 airships are listed below.

Aerostats or unmanned airships for possible Navy use were being investigated under the aegis of the Coast Guard, which employed tethered aerostats for drug-interdiction surveillance.[21] A September 1985 agreement between the Coast Guard and Navy gave the latter service cognizance over manned airship development, with the Coast Guard continuing development work with unmanned aerostats.

The TCOM firm of Columbia, Md., developed the first surveillance aerostats flown by the Coast Guard.[22] These vehicles were originally fitted with a Litton 504(V)2 radar and used by the Offshore Petroleum Co. for iceberg surveillance in Arctic waters. One aerostat subsequently provided with the similar APS-140(V) radar was leased to the Coast Guard for evaluation in the Caribbean–Gulf of Mexico area.

At an altitude of 2,500 feet (762 m), the APS-140(V) radar had a 60-mile (96.5-km) detection range against small craft. While there were some problems with this "breadboard" system, the Coast Guard was "very, very enthusiastic," according to one project officer. That aerostat crashed in heavy winds on 1 March 1986. Another aerostat, with a solid-state Litton 504(V)3 radar, was delivered to the Coast Guard in September 1985, but that one was destroyed while on a dock in a freak thunderstorm.

Undismayed, and with strong congressional support, the Coast Guard put out bids for competitively developed aerostats—one from RCA, delivered in December 1986 with a modified APS-128 radar, and one from TCOM with a Litton 504(V)3 radar. The Coast Guard deployed five ship-based aerostats plus two land-based units. These aerostats could remain aloft for some two weeks without having to be recovered (mainly for helium replenishment). The ship-based units were tethered to support ships that operated in the Gulf of Mexico–Caribbean area; the ships were civilian manned by GE/RCA crews with a combined Coast Guard-civilian support team for the aerostats. The ship-based aerostats were normally kept at some 2,500 feet to provide radar surveillance of low-flying aircraft and surface craft.

A tethered aerostat is based at High Rock in the Grand Bahamas. Designated Cariball I, this aerostat is manned by Westinghouse contractor personnel. A Cariball II is operational at the abandoned Georgetown airport on Great Exuma in the Bahamas. A Cariball III is proposed—but not yet funded—for Great Inagua in the southern Bahamas. These Coast Guard aerostats provided the eastern-most coverage in a chain of aerostat sites that will stretch across the entire southern border/coast of the United States. The others are operated by the Customs Service and Air Force. As noted above, beginning in early 1992 the former Coast Guard aerostats have been operated by the Army under the aegis of that service's Intelligence and Security Command.

While most of these aerostat projects have looked into tethered craft—that can be supported from surface ships or, ashore, from trucks—untethered aerostats probably hold the most promise for fleet operations. They could have an endurance of two weeks or more, following which they could be brought to a hover over an aircraft carrier or amphibious ship for refueling or maintenance of sensors.

Historical: The U.S. Navy acquired a total of 241 non-rigid airships in 1917–1958, including 21 from allies during World War I; others were acquired from the U.S. Army. The Navy operated four rigid airships, two of which, the AKRON (ZRS-4) and MACON (ZRS-5), could launch and recover fighter aircraft while in flight, in effect serving as "flying aircraft carriers."

The U.S. Navy's last airships were AEW platforms of the EZ-1C (formerly ZPG-3W) type. The Navy's last LTA flight took place in August 1962. Several highly classified (black) surveillance programs of the Cold War era included proposals for LTA platforms, but none is known to have come to fruition. Tethered surveillance aerostats were used in the Vietnam War under a highly classified, joint project of the Air Force and Defense Advanced Research Projects Agency called Seek Skyhawk.

SENTINEL 1000 DEMONSTRATION AIRSHIP

The Sentinel 1000 was developed by Westinghouse as a technology demonstration airship for the U.S. government, a response to the Department of Defense interest in continental and fleet air defense, and counter-narcotics operations. The Sentinel is a half-scale prototype for the planned Sentinel 5000 airship that would be an operational platform. It is the world's largest airship now flying.

The 25-foot (7.6-m) antenna for the proposed ASSR-1000 radar intended for a militarized airship would be fitted within the gas bag; the radar is a modification of the military TPS-63 surveillance radar. The radar provides surface detection to the horizon (90 n.miles/167 km) and air coverage out to 200 n.miles (370 km). Avionics payload is 5,000 lbs (2,268 kg). The high thermal conductivity of helium—five times that of air—is expected to improve electronic reliability by aiding in cooling. The airship envelope, made from Dacron polyester-base cloth, is radar transparent and has a life expectancy of up to 30 years.

Propulsion is achieved through two ducted propellers (propulsors) that can be vectored from 120 degrees upward to 90 degrees downward. The airship has an X-tail configuration with a control/propulsion gondola attached to the bottom of the air bag. None of the structure is metallic, reducing the craft's radar signature; an operational airship could be made of anechoic materials.

Status: Flight test; first flight on 26 June 1991.

Manufacturer:	Westinghouse Airship Industries	
Crew:	(6)	
Engines:	2 piston engines; 2 ducted propellers	
Maximum lift:		
Dimensions:	length	221½ ft (67.53 m)
	diameter	
	height (over gondola)	65 ft (19.82 m)
	volume	353,100 ft³ (10,000 m³)
Speed:	max 67 mph (107 kmh)	
Range:	30-day mission endurance with air-to-air[23] or ship-to-air refueling at 2-day intervals	
Ceiling:		
Radar:	Westinghouse ASSR-1000	

23. The air-to-air refuellings would be from helicopters.

21. There has long been Navy interest in aerostats. "Project 2000," sponsored in 1973–1974 by then-Chief of Naval Operations Admiral E.R. Zumwalt, proposed the development of a series of remotely piloted aerostats to operate in support of surface task groups.
22. TCOM—for Tethered Communications—is a wholly owned subsidiary of Westinghouse.

The Sentinel 1000 was the world's largest airship when it flew in 1990. The advanced airship program held promise for military as well as counter-drug operations, but in 1991 became a casualty of budget reductions. (Westinghouse)

YEZ-2A SURVEILLANCE AIRSHIP (SENTINEL 5000)

A fully equipped, mission-capable airship for naval use based on the Westinghouse Sentinel 5000 is currently estimated at approximately $66,000 in small-number series production. The craft would have a payload of 25,000 lbs (11,340 kg) of electronics. Originally an E-2C electronics suite with an APS-120/125/145 radar was envisioned; if built, the YEZ-2A would most likely have a more advanced system.

The airship will normally be propelled by diesel engines, employing the gas turbine for dash speed. A tail configuration with horizontal and vertical control surfaces is envisioned. The envelope material would be similar to the Sentinel 1000 airship.

Status: Cancelled in early 1992.

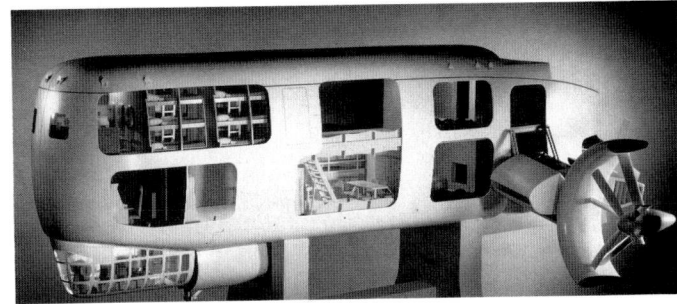

A model of the planned cupola for the aborted YEZ-2A surveillance airship. Note the shrouded propellers, crew living spaces, control room (top level, forward), and operations center (bottom level, forward). The radar antennas would be housed in the "gas bag." (Westinghouse)

Manufacturer:	Westinghouse Airship Industries
Crew:	(15)
Engines:	CODAG: 2 diesel engines (CRM BR-1/2000); 2,200 hp each + 1 turboprop (General Electric CT7-9); 1,750 shp; 2 ducted propellers
Maximum lift:	107,000 lbs (48,534 kg)

Dimensions:

	length	425 ft (129.54 m)
	diameter	105 ft
	height (over gondola)	152 ft (46.34 m)
	volume	2.5 million ft³ (70,800 m³)

Speed:	max 101 mph (163 kmh)
Range:	30-day mission endurance with air-to-air or ship-to-air refueling at 3-day intervals 60+ hours at 46 mph (74 kmh) without refueling
Ceiling:	14,000 ft (4,268 m)
Radar:	ISAR air search

REMOTELY PILOTED VEHICLES

The Department of Defense has a large, multi-faceted program of Remotely Piloted Vehicles (RPV) or aerial drones that are officially known as Unmanned Aerial Vehicles (UAV). The impetus to develop these vehicles was reinforced by the highly successful U.S. Army, Navy, and Marine Corps use of the Pioneer vehicle in the Gulf War in January–February 1991.

The current Department of Defense program seeks to provide six operational vehicles:

- close-range UAV
- short-range UAV
- medium-range UAV
- endurance UAV

This unified plan, administered by a joint (multi-service) program office within the Naval Air Systems Command, reflects an attempt to provide a family of standard aerial vehicles, applicable to several services for several roles. This coordinated program replaces a variety of separate service efforts, some of which were failures, like the Army's long-duration Aquila project, and some of which were successful, like the Navy-Marine Pioneer project.

Previously the armed forces had made extensive use of target drones as well as reconnaissance drones, the latter usually of a highly classified ("black") nature. These recce drones were used in large numbers by the Air Force in the Vietnam War.[24] Also in the 1960s, the Navy had a large drone program known as DASH (Drone Anti-Submarine Helicopter). Although the drones—designated DSN and, after 1962, QH-50—were successful aerial vehicles, problems with training and operating procedures caused a large number of losses. The DASH project was soon terminated (and U.S. ASW ships were left without helicopters until the LAMPS program was initiated in the early 1970s.) However, the Japanese Maritime Self-Defense Force continued to employ DASH vehicles after they were discarded by the U.S. Navy, and several were employed for gunfire spotting for the battleship NEW JERSEY (BB 62) during her brief service in the shore bombardment role off South Vietnam in 1968.

During the 1970s and early 1980s the U.S. Navy resisted proposals for RPV/drones except for use as target vehicles. However, following the extensive use of RPVs by the Israelis in the 1982 invasion of Lebanon, especially against anti-air gun and missile systems in the Bekaa Valley, Secretary Lehman directed that the Navy look into the pilotless aircraft. As a result, in January 1984 the Navy ordered a Mastiff III drone system produced by Tadiran Israel Electronics, Ltd., for gunfire spotting. In June 1984 the Marine Corps established the 1st RPV Platoon at Camp Lejeune, N.C., to evaluate and operate the Mastiff RPVs in support of Marine requirements. The first shipboard launching of an Israeli Mastiff (a development of the Scout) occurred in March 1984 from the helicopter carrier GUAM (LPH 9), with Israeli controllers. Marine Corps trials were carried out in February 1986 on the helicopter carrier TARAWA (LHA 1).

Subsequently, the Navy awarded a contract to provide the fleet with the Israeli-developed Pioneer RPV. This vehicle was extensively used from ashore and from the battleships MISSOURI (BB 63) and WISCONSIN (BB 64) in the Gulf War. The Marine Corps deployed all three of their RPV companies to Saudi Arabia for the Gulf War, with the Army deploying a UAV platoon to the theater. The Navy assigned detachments from squadron VC-6 to the two battleships to operate Pioneers from those ships during the conflict. Each of these six units had about five vehicles and 40 personnel assigned. According to the interim (July 1991) Department of Defense report on the Gulf conflict, "Pioneer proved to be valuable and appears to have validated the operational employment of UAVs in combat. . . ."

Also during the Gulf conflict, at the start of air operations the U.S. Air Force launched 38 Northrop BQM-74C "Chukar" target drones into Iraq, and the Navy launched a number of Tactical Air-Launched Decoys (TALD) from aircraft. These were used to get

the Iraqis to turn on air-defense radars so they could be attacked by U.S. radar suppression aircraft—Air Force F-4G Wild Weasels and Navy EA-6B Prowlers armed with HARM missiles. The BQM-74Cs were ground-launched while A-6E Intruders air-launched the TALDs.

On the ground, Marines flew a number of small, lightweight FQM-151 Pointer and Brandebury Exdrone vehicles during the Gulf War.

The basic requirements for the four new UAV programs are:

Close-range UAV: UAVs that are small, easy-to-assemble, have a minimum radius of about 18.5 miles (30 km), and are in the 200-lb (91-kg) class. Intended primarily for "over-the-hill" reconnaissance, these will be relatively inexpensive (roughly $20,000 each). The Marine Corps and Army will procure this vehicle.

Short-range UAV: These vehicles will have daytime television and FLIR, have a radius of at least 93 to 186 miles (150 to 300 km), and weigh roughly 1,000 lb (454 kg). Endurance for this UAV will be six hours. The vehicle will be used by both the Marines and Army with a total of 53 systems to be procured between fiscal 1995 and 1998.

Medium-range UAV: A vehicle with a range of more than 404 miles (650 km); designated BQM-145; see entry (below).

Endurance UAV: This will be a vehicle with at least a 24-hour loiter time.

In addition to the above vehicles, the Marines are also interested in an expendable UAV that carries a communications jammer. Currently under development by the Marine Corps, this may be a variant of the BQM-147A drone.

Navy shipboard requirements for UAVs are less clear, in part because of the demise of the four IOWA (BB 61)-class battleships, a preferred UAV launch platform. In mid-1990 the Navy stated a requirement for a maritime UAV that would have little in common with the other vehicles.

PIONEER UNMANNED AERIAL VEHICLE

The Pioneer is a highly effective unmanned, tactical reconnaissance vehicle. Following a fly-off competition of aerial vehicles, in January 1986 the Navy awarded contracts to produce 21 Pioneer RPVs to the AAI Corp. of Cockeysville, Md., and Mazlat, Ltd., the latter a joint venture of Israel Aircraft Industries (IAI) and Tadiran.

The Pioneer, modeled on the IAI Scout vehicle, carries its sensors and engines in a fuselage section fitted with twin tail booms. The vehicle is powered by a reciprocating engine with a small pusher propeller. The vehicle can be launched with rocket assistance and can be recovered on a runway or by a net; it has a fixed tricycle landing gear. The metal and fiberglass construction of the vehicle presents a low radar cross section. The Pioneer is transported in a disassembled condition and can be rapidly put together with minimum tools.

The Pioneer's payload is 100 pounds (45.4 kg). At the time of the Gulf War the Pioneer was fitted with a daylight television camera or, alternatively, a FLIR sensor. The existing control/data link is a C-band system, resistant to jamming, with a range of 100 n.miles (185 km).

Operational: The first shipboard trials of the Pioneer were held on the battleship IOWA in Chesapeake Bay in December 1986. During subsequent "proof-of-concept" tests in the Caribbean in January–February 1987, the IOWA's 16-inch (406-mm) guns fired on targets detected by the RPV. In that exercise four of the five embarked RPVs were lost in accidents.

During the Gulf conflict from 16 January to 27 February 1991 some 40 Pioneer UAVs flew 552 sorties for a total mission duration time of 1,641 hours. *At least one Pioneer was airborne at all times during Operation Desert Storm.* The vehicles were employed in adjustment of naval gunfire, battle damage assessment, reconnaissance, and force coordination. On 27 February, after a Pioneer detected two Iraqi patrol boats off Faylaka Island and naval aircraft were called in to destroy the craft, a large number of Iraqi soldiers on

---

24. From August 1964 through June 1975 the 100th Strategic Reconnaissance Wing flew 3,435 combat sorties with the Teledyne Ryan–produced AQM-34 "Buffalo Hunter" drone. Adapted from a target drone, the vehicle was employed in photographic and electronic reconnaissance.

the island surrendered to a MISSOURI-launched UAV. Apparently the soldiers knew that their detection by the drone would be followed by air or naval gunfire attack. It was history's first known surrender of enemy troops to an unmanned vehicle.

The following summary of Pioneer sorties was compiled by the Navy:

Unit	Sorties	Hours
VC-6 Det. 1 in USS WISCONSIN	100	342.9
VC-6 Det. 2 in USS MISSOURI	64	209.7
1st Marine RPV Company	94	330.3
(commenced operations 26 Sep 1990)		
2nd Marine RPV Company	69	226.6
(operations 27 Nov 1990 through 1 Mar 1991)		
3rd Marine RPV Company	147	380.6
U.S. Army UAV Platoon[25]	48	150.8
(commenced operations 1 February 1991)		

Twelve Pioneers were lost during the conflict:

airframe/engine failures	6
electromagnetic interference	3
operator error	2
enemy fire	1

Eight of the losses were from the ten Pioneers embarked in the two battleships.

In addition, 14 vehicles were damaged during Desert Storm (all repairable):

operator error	6
engine/general failure	3
enemy gunfire	3
electromagnetic interference	2

The Department of Defense final report on the Gulf War (April 1992) stated: "The Navy Pioneer UAV system's availability exceeded expectations. Established sortie rates indicated a deployed unit could sustain 60 flight hours a month."

Status: Operational. U.S. Navy IOC in May 1986.

Manufacturer:	AAI and Mazlat
Crew:	unmanned
Engines:	1 Sachs 2-stroke piston; 26 hp
Weights:	430 lbs (195 kg) max launch including
	100 lbs (45.4 kg) payload
Dimensions:	length 16 ft 3 in (4.96 m)
	wing span 16 ft 9½ in (5.12 m)
	height 3 ft 3 in (1.00 m)
Speed:	max 115 mph (185 kmh)
	cruise 55 to 81 mph (89 to 130 kmh)
Range:	8-hour endurance
Ceiling:	15,000 ft (4,573 m)

25. Assigned to the U.S. Army's 82nd Airborne Division.

Marines in the Saudi Arabian desert prepare a Pioneer RPV for a reconnaissance flight. The Pioneer is a simple system to maintain and operate. (U.S. Marine Corps)

A Pioneer RPV is launched from the battleship IOWA (BB 61). Two other battleships used Pioneers extensively in the Gulf War. Previously small RPVs had only been used in combat on a large scale by the Israelis, who originated the Pioneer design. (U.S. Navy)

A Pioneer RPV is recovered into a net on the stern of battleship. (PHC John Kristoffersen, USN)

BQM-145 UNMANNED AERIAL VEHICLE

This will be a mid-range vehicle for electro-optical and infrared reconnaissance. The Teledyne Ryan Model 350 was selected for this role in May 1989.

The BQM-145 is fabricated of fiberglass and composites; however, in 1991 the UAV Executive Committee decided that the fuselage should be all-metal. The wing has no movable control surfaces. The payload consists of FLIR, an IR line-scanning device, and meteorological sensors. In 1991 digital flight avionics were added including a radar altimeter and Mk IV Identification Friend or Foe (IFF).

The vehicle can be air- or ground-launched, with aircraft platforms including the A-6E Intruder and F/A-18 Hornet. After a mission the UAV returns to base and deploys a parachute. It can also be recovered in flight by a specially configured aircraft.

Status: Development. IOC planned for the mid-1990s. It is expected that the BQM-145 will be employed by the Army, Air Force, Marine Corps, and possibly the Navy.

Manufacturer:	Teledyne Ryan	
Crew:	unmanned	
Engines:	1 Teledyne CAE382-10 turbofan; 970 lbst (440 kgst)	
Weights:	1,950 lbs (885 kg) max launch	
Dimensions:	length	17 ft 11⅓ in (5.47 m)
	wing span	10 ft 6 in (3.20 m)
	wing area	25 ft² (2.32 m²)
	height	2 ft 10 in (0.86 m)
Speed:	max 562 mph (904 kmh)	
Range:	700 n.miles (806 miles)	
Ceiling:	13,720 ft (4,183 m)	

A YBQM-145A test vehicle is prepared for flight tests. The drone will be air-launched for high-speed reconnaissance missions. (Teledyne Ryan)

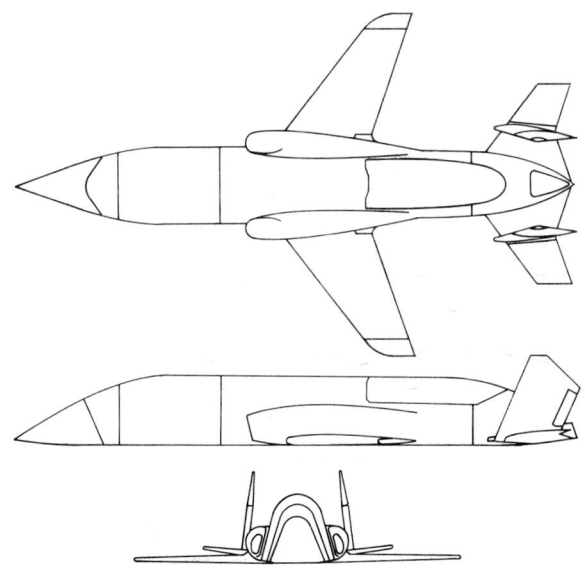

BQM-145A reconnaissance drone. (William Clipson)

FQM-151 POINTER UNMANNED AERIAL VEHICLE

The Pointer is a small, very low cost, hand-launched UAV. Resembling a model aircraft, the Pointer is man-portable, with the entire system carried in two backpacks—one carrying the air vehicle (45 lbs/20.25), and one containing the control unit (50 lbs/22.5 kg).

In 1988 the Marine Corps purchased one unit for tests. The Department of Defense joint program office procured 24 Pointers in December 1989. Several of these units were deployed to Saudi Arabia with the Marines in 1991. The Pointer's sensor payload is a black-and-white television camera using an 8-mm video cassette. It can be modified to carry a chemical agent detector.

The system can be fully prepared for flight in about five minutes. Flight endurance is over one hour. For recovery the Pointer is directed into a deep stall. The crew consists of an operator and observer.

Status: Operational.

Manufacturer:	AeroVironment (Simi Valley, Calif.)	
Crew:	unmanned	
Engines:	1 electric motor; 300 watts; 2-blade pusher propeller	
Weights:	9 lbs (4 kg)	
Dimensions:	length	6 ft (1.83 m)
	wing span	9 ft (2.74 m)
Speed:	max approx. 45 mph (72 kmh)	
	cruise approx. 23 mph (37 kmh)	
Range:		
Ceiling:		

A Marine hand-launches a Pointer, one of the smallest RPVs in existence. It is fitted with a black-and-white television camera. The mini-drone has a pusher propeller. (U.S. Marine Corps, courtesy *Marine Corps Gazette*)

FQM-151 Pointer mini-drone. (U.S. Marine Corps, courtesy *Marine Corps Gazette*)

CHAPTER 30

Weapon Systems

The war against Iraq in January–February 1991 provided the combat debut for several new naval weapons: The F/A-18 Hornet, the Tomahawk and SLAM missiles, and Pioneer and TALD drones, among others. But it was also the last combat for the Navy's A-7 Corsair, A-3 Skywarrior, and the Walleye air-to-ground missile. This A-7E from VA-72 on the carrier JOHN F. KENNEDY (CV 67) flew 23 combat missions (and 19 other sorties) in Desert Storm, delivering 50 general-purpose bombs, 73 Rockeyes, 17 HARM missiles, and 1 Walleye missile. (PH3 Paul A. Hawthorne, USN)

BOMBS AND UNGUIDED MISSILES

Navy and Marine Corps aircraft carry Mk 80-series bombs and unguided Rockeye and APAM (Anti-Personnel/Anti-Material Munitions) rockets. There are three Mk 80-series bombs in use:

Mk 82	500 lbs (227 kg)
Mk 83	1,000 lbs (454 kg)
Mk 84	2,000 lbs (907 kg)

The Mk 80 weapons have both standard (fixed) tail assemblies and low-drag tails, the latter extending upon release to slow the bomb and enable a low-level aircraft to escape damage from the bombs' explosions. In addition, Laser-Guided Bomb (LGB) kits are available to permit the aircraft or other forces to guide a bomb to its target by laser designation.[1]

U.S. Navy and Marine Corps aircraft employed the following weapons in the January–February 1991 air war in the Persian Gulf:

Mk 82 bombs	17,730
Mk 83 bombs	18,619
Mk 84 bombs	1,962
LGB	880
Rockeye/APAM	21,746

A large number of the Mk 82 and Mk 83 bombs were reportedly fitted with Destructor mine kits (Mk 36 and Mk 40, respectively) for use in attacks against airfields in Iraq. (This is in addition to mines planted in rivers; see below.)

The current Rockeye II Mk 20 is an unguided rocket that dispenses bomblets to attack "soft" targets such as anti-aircraft sites and lightly armored vehicles. Each rocket carries 247 bomblets with shaped-charge warheads; each bomblet weighs 1.02 pounds (0.46 kg). The earlier Rockeye I was the Mk 15.

The APAM is an improved rocket carrying a bomblet dispenser.

Nuclear bombs are described under the heading Nuclear Weapons in this chapter.

---

1. Laser designation can be accomplished by the launching aircraft, an accompanying aircraft or helicopter, surface ship, or troops on the ground. The last can include SEAL-type unconventional forces behind enemy lines, as was done in the 1991 war in the Persian Gulf.

An aviation ordnanceman pushes two Mk 82 low-drag bombs across the flight deck of the carrier Constellation (CV 64). The folding fins extend upon release to slow the bombs' descent, permitting the launching aircraft to escape the explosions. (U.S. Navy)

Rockeye pods on an A-6E Intruder from VA-75 on the John F. Kennedy. (PH2 William Lipski, USN)

Mk 20 Rockeye pods are stacked next to the island structure of the carrier Saratoga (CV 60) during an at-sea replenishment. They will be stowed in below-deck magazines until needed for strike aircraft. (PH1 William Shayka, USN)

An F/A-18 Hornet from the naval air test complex at Patuxent River, Md., releases a salvo of Mk 83 bombs while in a 60° dive. The F/A-18 has proven to be a versatile naval attack aircraft as well as fighter. (Randy Hepp)

NAVAL GUNS

The largest naval guns in active U.S. warships are 5-inch (127-mm) weapons. The Navy's shipboard firepower was increased dramatically in the 1980s with the reactivation of the four IOWA (BB 61)-class battleships. Those ships each carry nine 16-inch (406-mm)/50-cal guns and, as modernized in the 1980s, 12 5-inch/38-cal guns. However, with the mothballing of the MISSOURI (BB 63) in early 1992 all four of these behemoths are again laid up in reserve, with the largest guns remaining in active U.S. Navy service being 5-inch weapons.

The Marine Corps requirement for naval gunfire support has led to a renewed interest in the deployment of the 8-inch (203-mm) Major Caliber Lightweight Gun (MCLWG), which is suitable for installation in ships of cruiser and destroyer size. Austere budgets and possible adaptation of other gun and rocket systems (some already in Army or Marine use) make the deployment of the 8-inch MCLWG doubtful. The principal rocket candidate has been the ABRS (Assault Ballistic Rocket System), an unguided rocket and launcher adapted from the LTV Corporation's Multiple Launch Rocket System (MLRS) used by the U.S. Army, Marine Corps, and several NATO countries. The ABRS had been proposed for installation on the IOWA-class battleships and NEWPORT (LST 1179)-class landing ships, with one concept providing for full conversion of LSTs to "rocket monitors." (See 14th Edition/page 466 for ABRS/MLRS characteristics.)

Beyond the retiring of the battleships, there has been a steady decline of naval guns as older cruisers and destroyers have been decommissioned and newer ships generally have fewer guns of smaller caliber. All cruisers armed with 8-inch and 6-inch (152-mm) guns have been stricken, as have all pre-SPRUANCE (DD 963)-class destroyers, which carried up to six 5-inch guns. The last active U.S. ship with 8-inch/55-cal guns was the NEWPORT NEWS (CA 148), decommissioned in July 1978, and the last active ship with 6-inch/47-cal guns was the cruiser-flagship OKLAHOMA CITY (CG 5), retired in December 1979.

(The only warships in service today in foreign navies with guns larger than 5-inch are in the Russian Navy with the later KIROV-class battle cruisers, SLAVA-class missile cruisers, and SOVREMENNYY-class destroyers mounting 130-mm/70-cal dual-purpose guns. All cruisers of the SVERDLOV class mounting from 6 to 12 152-mm guns have been discarded.)

The largest guns now fitted in active U.S. Navy ships and Coast Guard cutters are the 5-inch Mk 45 lightweight gun and the 76-mm Mk 75 OTO Melara gun. The 5-inch guns are considered primarily shore-bombardment weapons and have only a limited anti-air capability; the 76-mm guns are primarily anti-aircraft weapons but have an anti-surface capability. Most Navy surface warships and several auxiliary classes are armed with the 20-mm Mk 16 Close-In Weapon System (CIWS) for defense against anti-ship cruise missiles. In addition, various types of 25-mm, 20-mm, .50-cal, and 7.62-mm machine guns are fitted in naval ships, primarily for defense against small craft in restricted waters.

Ammunition: In the following entries AP = Armor Piercing and HC = High Capacity (for shore bombardment).

Classifications: Guns are classified by their inside barrel diameter and gun-barrel length. Diameters traditionally have been listed in inches for weapons larger than one-inch diameter, and in millimeters for smaller weapons. Thus, a 5-inch/38-cal gun has a barrel length of 190 inches. The Italian-designed OTO Melara 76-mm gun retains its metric measurement in U.S. naval service.

Guns smaller than one-inch diameter are measured in millimeters or calibers, the latter being fractions of an inch (e.g., .50 cal = ½ inch).

Nomenclature: According to the Navy, "A mount is an assembled unit which includes the gun barrel (or barrels), housing(s), slide(s), carriage, stand, sight, elevating and training drives, ammunition hoists, and associated equipment. Mounts include guns from 20-mm caliber up to but not including 6-inch caliber. . . . A mount differs from a turret in that a mount does not have a barbette structure.

"Mounts are designated as single-purpose [SP], dual-purpose [DP], or anti-aircraft [AA], depending upon the elevation of which they are capable and the types of targets they are designed to take under fire."

The unmanned, unarmored mounting for the 8-inch Mk 71 MCLWG is considered a mount (rather than a turret).

Saluting guns: U.S. aircraft carriers, cruisers, missile destroyers, amphibious ships, and auxiliaries have the 40-mm Mk 11 saluting guns. This weapon is for saluting only and has no combat capability.

The forecastle of the battleship IOWA is filled with 16-inch projectiles as the dreadnought unloads munitions at the Naval Weapons Station Yorktown, Va. The four mothballed IOWA-class battleships have the largest naval guns afloat. (PH1 Jeff Hilton, USN)

16-INCH/50-CAL (406-MM) GUN

Triple gun turret. These guns, which form the main gun battery of the IOWA-class battleships, are the largest guns ever mounted in warships except for the 18.1-inch (460-mm) guns of the Japanese YAMATO-class battleships of World War II and the single 18-inch (457-mm) gun of the British carrier FURIOUS of World War I.

The U.S. 16-inch/50s were also intended for the five never-built battleships of the MONTANA (BB 67) class.

Each 16-inch round is fired with up to six 110-pound (50-kg) powder bags.

Gun barrel:	Mk 7 Mod 0
Muzzle velocity:	2,425 ft/sec AP
	2,690 ft/sec HC
Crew:	74 consisting of 27 in turret
	4 in machinery rooms
	15 in upper projectile room
	15 in lower projectile room
	13 in powder-handling room
Weight:	1,700 tons (turret)
Rate of fire:	2 rpm per barrel
Maximum range:	40,185 yds (36,755 m) AP at 45° elevation
	41,622 yds (38,069 m) HC at 45° elevation
Projectile weight:	2,700 lbs (1,225 kg) AP
	1,900 lbs (862 kg) HC
Fire control:	Mk 38 GFCS
Ships:	BB 61

The MISSOURI fires a broadside of her nine 16-inch guns. Two dreadnoughts fired their main batteries in anger during the Persian Gulf War—the NEW JERSEY (BB 62) and WISCONSIN (BB 64). (PH1 Terry Cosgrove, USN)

Details of the forward 16-inch/50-cal gun turrets in U.S. battleships. During World War II a quad 40-mm AA gun mount was fitted atop the No. 2 turret. (Giorgio Arra)

8-INCH/55-CAL (203-MM) MAJOR CALIBER LIGHTWEIGHT GUN Mk 71

Single mount. The Mk 71 Major Caliber Lightweight Gun (MCLWG) is a comparatively small and lightweight mount intended for installation in destroyer-size ships. The Navy's plan to install the 8-inch/55-cal Mk 71 MCLWG in the 31 SPRUANCE-class destroyers as well as possibly some later ship classes died with the cancellation of the gun project by then-Secretary of Defense Harold Brown in July 1978. A prototype gun had been evaluated in the FORREST SHERMAN (DD 931)-class destroyer HULL (DD 945) from 1975 to 1979. It is listed here because of historical interest and recent proposals that it be considered for deployment to provide a gunfire support capability.

It could automatically fire 75 rounds from the ready service loader. The gun was specifically designed to fire laser-guided projectiles and rocket-assisted projectiles as well as conventional rounds.

The 8-inch/55-cal MCLWG on the destroyer HULL during the gun's at-sea evaluation. The SPRUANCE-class destroyers—for which the guns were planned—are considerably larger than the HULL. (U.S. Navy)

Gun barrel:	Mk 39 Mod 2
Muzzle velocity:	2,800 ft/sec
Crew:	6
Weight:	172,895 lbs (78,425 kg)
Rate of fire:	12 rpm (guided projectiles 6 rpm)
Maximum range:	31,408 yds (28,727 m) at 45° elevation
Projectile weight:	260 lbs (118 kg)
Fire control:	Mk 86 GFCS
Ships:	(program cancelled)

8-inch/55-cal MCLWG on the destroyer HULL. (Giorgio Arra)

5-INCH/54-CAL (127-MM) GUN Mk 45

Single mount. The Mk 45 is capable of engaging air or surface targets. The gun mount is unmanned, with the gun crew stationed below deck. The mount stows up to 20 rounds of ready service ammunition that can be fired quickly by a single man at the below-deck control console. The magazine can be reloaded while the gun is firing without interrupting the firing sequence. The maximum rate of fire is 16 to 20 rounds per minute with fixed ammunition. Firing Rocket Assisted Projectiles (RAP) and other separated ammunition reduces the firing rate.

The gun is now being installed in new-construction TICON-DEROGA (CG 47) and ARLEIGH BURKE (DDG 51) surface combatants. Note that while the TARAWA (LHA 1)-class large amphibious ships mount this weapon, the successor WASP (LHD 1) class mounts 20-mm CIWS and lighter weapons.

Gun barrel:	
Muzzle velocity:	2,500 ft/sec
Crew:	6
Weight:	47,820 lbs (21,691)
Rate of fire:	16 to 20 rpm
Maximum range:	25,909 yds (23,697 m) at 47° elevation
	48,700 ft (14,848 m) at 85° elevation
Projectile weight:	70 lbs (31.75 kg)
Fire control:	Mk 86 GFCS
Ships:	CGN 38
	CGN 36
	CG 47
	DDG 51
	DDG 993
	DD 963
	LHA 1

Forward 5-inch/54-cal DP mount in the destroyer CALLAGHAN (DDG 994). The mount—all crewmen serve below decks—has won four battle efficiency "E" awards. (W. Donko)

5-INCH/54-CAL (127-MM) GUN Mk 42

Single mount. Older cruisers, destroyers, and frigates in service have the single 5-inch/54-cal Mk 42 gun mount. Several different mods are in service, most of which are limited to engaging surface targets. The guns may be fired by local or remote control.

Gun barrel:	Mk 18 Mod 0
Muzzle velocity:	2,650 ft/sec
Crew:	14
Weight:	Mods 1 thru 6 approx. 145,000 lbs (65,772 kg)
	Mod 10 139,000 lbs (63,050 kg)
Rate of fire:	20 rpm
Maximum range:	25,909 yds (23,697 m) at 47° elevation
	48,700 ft (14,848 m) at 85° elevation
Projectile weight:	70 lbs (31.75 kg)
Fire control:	Mk 68 GFCS
Ships:	CGN 35
	CG 26
	DDG 37
	FF 1052

The 5-inch/54-cal DP mount in the frigate AINSWORTH (FF 1090). This mount is fitted with one "bug-eye" local-control position. (Giorgio Arra)

5-INCH/38-CAL (127-MM) GUN Mk 30

Single mount. Installed in World War II–built ships and several classes of postwar frigates (now stricken). The nuclear-propelled missile cruiser LONG BEACH (CGN 9) was fitted with two Mk 30 single mounts after completion as a defense against small craft and aircraft (originally completed without gun armament).

Gun barrel:	Mk 12 Mod 1
Muzzle velocity:	2,500 ft/sec
Crew:	17
Weight:	approx. 45,000 lbs (20,412 kg)
Rate of fire:	20 rpm
Maximum range:	17,306 yds (15,829 m) at 45° elevation
	32,250 ft (9,832 m) at 85° elevation
Projectile weight:	55 lbs (25 kg)
Fire control:	Mk 56 GFCS
Ships:	CGN 9

The 5-inch/38-cal guns in the cruiser LONG BEACH are the last 5-inch/38s in the active fleet. Their Mk 56 GFCS are on the stub towers forward of the mounts. (Giorgio Arra)

5-INCH/38-CAL (127-MM) GUN Mk 28

Twin mount. These 5-inch/38 mounts are fitted in the IOWA-class battleships. As these ships were reactivated during the 1980s the 5-inch battery was reduced from ten twin mounts to six.

Gun barrel:	Mk 12 Mod 1
Muzzle velocity:	2,500 ft/sec
Crew:	27
Weight:	153,000 to 169,000 lbs (69,400 to 76,658 kg) (varies with Mod)
Rate of fire:	18 rpm per barrel
Maximum range:	17,306 yds (15,829 m) at 45° elevation
	32,250 ft (9,832 m) at 85° elevation
Projectile weight:	55 lbs (25 kg)
Fire control:	Mk 56 GFCS
Ships:	BB 61

The twin 5-inch/38-cal twin DP mounts in the IOWA-class battleships have been useful for short-range shore bombardment in the post–World War period. However, when reactivated in the 1980s, the ships lost four of their ten mounts. A Phalanx CIWS is seen above this mount in the IOWA. (Giorgio Arra)

76-MM/62-CAL GUN Mk 75

Single mount. The OLIVER HAZARD PERRY (FFG 7)-class frigates and PEGASUS (PHM 1)-class hydrofoil missile craft as well as Coast Guard cutters have the 76-mm/62-cal Mk 75 gun mount. The gun system was designed by OTO Melara SpA of Italy and is generally identified by the firm's name.

The 76-mm gun is specifically designed for use in ships as small as 200 tons and is capable of engaging air or surface targets. It is remotely controlled with a small, unmanned mount.

The Mk 75 gun is also used by several foreign navies.

Gun barrel:	Mk 75
Muzzle velocity:	3,000 ft/sec
Crew:	4
Weight:	13,680 lbs (6,205 kg)
Rate of fire:	75 to 85 rpm
Maximum range:	approx. 21,000 yds (19,207 m) at 45° elevation
	approx. 39,000 ft (11,890 m) at 85° elevation
Projectile weight:	14 lbs (6.35 kg)
Fire control:	Mk 92 GFCS
Ships:	FFG 7
	PHM 1
	WHEC 715
	WMEC 901

The 76-mm OTO Melara gun is found in two U.S. ship classes, but also in numerous foreign warships. This mount is in the AQUILA (PHM 4). (Giorgio Arra)

3-INCH/50-CAL (76-MM) GUN Mk 33

Twin open mount. The large number of 3-inch/50-cal anti-aircraft guns fitted from the early 1950s onward in surface combatants, amphibious ships, and fleet auxiliaries has been entirely removed from the active warships and all but two auxiliary ships; they are retained in numerous amphibious ships as well as fleet command ships (former amphibious ships).

The guns were generally ineffective and difficult to maintain. Amphibious ships and auxiliaries have been refitted with the Phalanx CIWS and/or Sea Sparrow point-defense missiles in place of some 3-inch mounts.

These are open or shielded (unarmored) mounts. They have two open, drum-type magazines for each barrel, which are hand loaded.

Gun barrel:	Mk 22	
Muzzle velocity:	2,650 ft/sec	
Crew:	12	
Weight:	approx. 33,000 lbs (14,969 kg)	
Rate of fire:	50 rpm per barrel	
Maximum range:	14,041 yds (12,842 m) at 45° elevation	
	29,367 ft (8,953 m) at 85° elevation	
Projectile weight:	7 lbs (3.2 kg)	
Fire control:	Mk 70 GFCS	
Ships:	LCC 19	LSD 36
	AGF 3	LST 1179
	AGF 11	AE 21
	LPH 2	AE 26
	LKA 113	AFS 1
	LPD 1	AO 51
	LPD 4	AS 33

Once found in most surface combatants as well as amphibious and auxiliary ships, the open-mount 3-inch/50-cal AA twin mount is rapidly disappearing from the fleet. This mount, manned by Marines and sailors, was in the SPIEGEL GROVE (LSD 32). (U.S. Marine Corps)

An enclosed 3-inch/50-cal AA twin mount on the command ship MOUNT WHITNEY (LCC 20). These guns are hand-loaded and have limited effectiveness against air targets. (U.S. Navy)

3-INCH/50-CAL (76-MM) GUN Mk 22

Single open mount. None is fitted in active U.S. Navy ships.

Gun barrel:	Mk 21 Mod 0
Muzzle velocity:	2,650 ft/sec
Crew:	11
Weight:	7,510 to 8,310 lbs (3,407 to 3,769 kg) (varies with Mod)
Rate of fire:	20 rpm
Maximum range:	14,041 yds (12,842 m) at 45° elevation
	29,367 ft (8,953 m) at 85° elevation
Projectile weight:	7 lbs (3.2 kg)
Fire control:	open sight
Ships:	WMEC 615
	WMEC 76 (some units)

The 3-inch/50-cal AA gun looks more archaic than the 47-year-old CHILULA (WMEC 153); her sister ships in Coast Guard service are older. The "3-incher" is useful for firing a shot across a ship's bow, but little more. (Giorgio Arra)

40-MM/60-CAL GUN MK 3 MOD 9

Single mount. This Bofors-type weapon is a fully automatic gun system fitted to the Mk III patrol boats. The gun may be set for full- or semi-automatic fire, being rated up to 160 rounds per minute. A magazine containing 40 rounds is fitted on the mount.

Gun barrel:	M1
Muzzle velocity:	2,800 ft/sec
Crew:	1
Weight:	3,710 lbs (1,670 kg)
Rate of fire:	120–160 rpm
Maximum range:	5,000 yds
Projectile weight:	2 lbs
Fire control:	optical
Ships:	PB Mk III (optional)

40-MM GRENADE LAUNCHER Mk 19

Numerous Navy auxiliaries and small combatants and Coast Guard cutters have the 40-mm Mk 19 grenade launcher. It is usually fitted to the Mk 64 machine gun mount. The Mk 19 is 43 inches (1.1 m) long.

The launcher is manually fired and shoots high-velocity 40-mm grenades from linked belts. The rounds are configured in an armor-piercing shape, having been initially designed to counter lightly armored vehicles. (The Mk 19 can also be mounted on land vehicles and helicopters.)

Effective range is generally cited as 1,650 yards (1,509 m).

Status: In production by Saco Defense, Inc.

Gun barrel:	
Muzzle velocity:	800 ft/sec
Crew:	1
Weight:	72.5 lbs (33 kg)
Rate of fire:	325 to 375 rpm
Maximum range:	2,400 yds (2,195 m)
Projectile weight:	
Fire control:	open sight
Ships:	small combatants, amphibious and auxiliary ships

40-mm grenade launcher Mk 19 on a tripod mount. (U.S. Marine Corps)

25-MM/87-CAL GUN Mk 38

This is a rapid-fire cannon known as the "Bushmaster" or "Chain gun." It is being provided for close-in defense in a number of Navy ships and small craft. In the larger Navy surface combatants (up to battleships) and amphibious ships the guns are installed on a temporary basis as the ships deploy to areas where they are subject to enemy small craft attack (e.g., Persian Gulf).

The gun has an M242 single barrel fitted on the M88 mounting. Different rates of fire can be selected. The Mk 88 mount is not stabilized and the gun is manually aimed. The weapon is also fitted in the Army's Bradley Armored Fighting Vehicle (AFV) and the Marine Corps' Light Armored Vehicle (LAV).

The Ex-39 is a similar mounting of the 25-mm M242 gun but with the operator seated on the mount, to the right of the gun, with complete control of the system; there is a 200-round ammunition box to the left of the gun. The system weighs about 3,000 pounds (1,360 kg). It was tested on board the IX 515 (ex-SES-200) in the fall of 1991.

Status: Navy procurement approved in 1977 but delayed because of ammunition problems. In production by McDonnell Douglas Helicopter Co. (formerly Hughes Helicopter Corp.).

Gun barrel:	M242
Muzzle velocity:	3,600 ft/sec
Crew:	2
Weight:	1,250 lbs (567 kg)
Rate of fire:	variable; single shot or 100 or 200 rpm
Maximum range:	2,500 yds (2,287 m) effective range
Projectile weight:	
Fire control:	optical
Ships:	various

25-mm/87-cal Chain gun on the landing ship MOUNT VERNON (LSD 39) in the Persian Gulf. The mount is not stabilized and is visually aimed, making its use on small craft in rough seas extremely difficult. (PH2 Jeffrey Elliott, USN)

25-MM CLOSE-IN WEAPON SYSTEM SEA VULCAN

The Sea Vulcan is an adaptation of the GAU-12/U Gatling gun fitted in the AV-8B Harrier VSTOL aircraft. Intended for small combatants, it was mounted in the Navy's surface effects ship SES-200 (now IX 515) in 1987 for shipboard evaluation.

The five-barrel CIWS uses a linkless ammunition feed system. The magazine holds more than 500 rounds. It has been evaluated with a variety of fire control systems and in conjunction with a Stinger missile pack.

Status: Development. Manufactured by General Electric.

Gun barrel:	GAU-12/U
Muzzle velocity:	4,400 ft/sec
Crew:	(unmanned)
Weight:	2,800 lbs (1,270 kg)
Rate of fire:	variable; 750 or 2,000 rpm
Maximum range:	6,560 yds (2,000 m)
Projectile weight:	6.4 lbs (2.9 kg) high explosive-incindiary
Fire control:	optical-laser on board IX 515; see text
Ships:	none

The 5-barrel, 25-mm Sea Vulcan gun system as fitted for evaluation on the research craft SES-200 (IX 515). The remote-controlled mount can be fitted with an IR detector; the off-mount laser guidance unit is shown above the gun. (U.S. Navy)

20-MM GUN Mk 68

The similar single-barrel 20-mm Mk 67 and Mk 68 cannon are fitted in auxiliary and amphibious ships, and in Coast Guard cutters for close-in defense against surface craft. These are refinements of the Oerlikon design.

Gun barrel:	Mk 16 Mod 5
Muzzle velocity:	2,740 ft/sec
Crew:	2
Weight:	900 lbs (408 kg)
Rate of fire:	800 rpm
Maximum range:	4,800 yds (4,390 m)
Projectile weight:	0.75 lbs (0.3 kg)
Fire control:	open sight
Ships:	auxiliary ships

20-MM GUN Mk 67

Earlier 20-mm guns fitted in U.S. Navy ships included the Mk 10 and Mk 24; all have been withdrawn from U.S. service.

Gun barrel:	Mk 16 Mod 5
Muzzle velocity:	2,740 ft/sec
Crew:	2
Weight:	475 lbs (215 kg)
Rate of fire:	800 rpm
Maximum range:	4,800 yds (4,390 m)
Projectile weight:	0.75 lbs (0.3 kg)
Fire control:	open sight
Ships:	amphibious and auxiliary ships

20-MM/76-CAL CLOSE-IN WEAPON SYSTEM Mk 15/Mk 16

The Phalanx Close-In Weapon System (CIWS) is intended to defeat attacking anti-ship missiles. The installation of Phalanx CIWS followed by several years the appearance of similar rapid-fire gun systems, of larger caliber, in Soviet surface warships.

The Phalanx underwent initial at-sea tests in the destroyer KING (DDG 41, then-DLG 10) from August 1973 to March 1974, with operational suitability tests in the destroyer BIGELOW (DD 942) from November 1976 to 1978. Production was initiated in December 1977.

The Phalanx CIWS is a totally integrated weapon system that includes the VPS-2 search and track radar, gun, magazine, weapon control unit, and associated electronics, all fitted into a single unit 15 feet (4.6 m) high and weighing about six tons. Thus, it is suitable for small combat craft (and is fitted in Saudi Arabian and Israeli missile craft) as well as larger warships; also, it can be rapidly installed—in 24 hours in an emergency situation. The U.S. Navy planned to fit the Phalanx in some 300 ships, from single guns in frigates to four mounts in IOWA-class battleships and some aircraft carriers. (Some Phalanx-armed ships have been mothballed.)

The CIWS "system" is designated as the Mk 15 and the individual gun groups are Mk 16; the 20-mm gun subsystem is designated Mk 26. The gun is a six-barrel Gatling gun, adopted from the Air Force M61 Vulcan gun series used in several types of aircraft and ground-mounted for airfield defense.

The gun is hydraulically powered, with a theoretical firing rate of 3,000 rounds per minute, a very low dispersion rate, and initially a 980-round magazine; later guns have a 1,550-round magazine and the earlier weapons are being upgraded. The gun fires a depleted-uranium bullet or penetrator manufactured from the waste product

A Phalanx CIWS on an Australian destroyer spews forth bullets during a test firing in the Persian Gulf. Note the enlarged magazine under the gun barrels. (Royal Australian Navy)

of nuclear energy programs; the depleted uranium penetrator is 2.5 times heavier than steel. This penetrator is being phased out in favor of a tungsten penetrator, which is slightly heavier. The diameter of the penetrator is only 12.75 millimeters and is fired in a nylon sabot with an aluminum pusher that imparts spin to the projectile. The sabot and pusher break away after the round leaves the muzzle with a velocity of 1,000 feet (305 m) per second. The built-in J-band, pule-doppler radar combines several functions and follows the bullets in flight to make corrections for the next burst being fired. Early Navy analyses indicated that about 200 rounds would be fired per gun in each engagement against a missile.

All engagement functions are performed automatically with a high-speed digital computer. When active, the CIWS will engage any incoming, high-speed target unless the operator holds fire. Reaction time for the CIWS is less than two seconds after the threat is detected and identified.

Designation: The Phalanx CIWS is designated Mk 15 and consists of one to four CIWS Weapon Groups Mk 16. The latter is the designation of the above-deck portion of the system, consisting of the actual gun, magazine, radar, and weapons control unit. The below-deck components of the Mk 15 are control panels.

Status: Operational and in production. IOC in 1980 (USS CORAL SEA/CV 43). In 1981 the Japanese destroyer KURAMA became the first foreign ship to mount the Phalanx; it is also used by Australia, Canada, Great Britain, Greece, Israel, Portugal, Saudi Arabia, and Taiwan.

Manufactured by General Dynamics, Pomona, Calif., and General Electric Corp.

Gun barrel:	Mk 26
Muzzle velocity:	3,650 ft/sec
Crew:	(unmanned)
Weight:	approx. 12,000 lbs (5,443 kg)
Rate of fire:	3,000 rpm
Maximum range:	1,625 yds (1,486 m) effective
	6,000 yds (5,488 m) maximum
Projectile weight:	8.9 ounces (1.2 kg)
Fire control:	self-contained Ku-band search radar; digital Moving Target Indicator (MTI)
Ships:	(see above)

Sailors load a Phalanx CIWS on a U.S. warship. (General Dynamics/Pomona)

At rest, a Phalanx CIWS is installed in a U.S. warship. Each above-decks weapon group is designated Mk 16; the entire Phalanx installation in a ship (one to four guns) is designated Mk 15. (General Dynamics/Pomona)

20-MM/70-CAL GUN Mk 10

Gun barrel:	Mk 2/4
Muzzle velocity:	2,730 ft/sec
Crew:	2
Weight:	700 to 1,100 lbs (varies with Mod)
Rate of fire:	450 rpm
Maximum range:	4,800 yds at 35° elevation
	10,000 ft at 90° elevation
Projectile weight:	0.2 lbs
Fire control:	open sights
Ships:	auxiliary ships

81-MM MORTAR Mk 2

This weapon is generally mounted in tandem with a .50-cal machine gun.

Gun barrel:	—
Muzzle velocity:	
Crew:	2
Weight:	580 lbs (263 kg)
Rate of fire:	10 rpm in trigger mode
	18 rpm in drop-fire mode
Maximum range:	2,200 yds (2,012 m)
Projectile weight:	10.85 lbs (4.9 kg)
Ships:	PCF
	WPC

A sailor drop-loads an 81-mm mortar of an over/under mounting of a .50-cal machine gun and a mortar. (U.S. Navy)

NAVAL MINES[2]

The U.S. Navy has a significant inventory of mines; the modern weapons are the CAPTOR (Encapsulated Torpedo) anti-submarine mine, which can be laid by aircraft and submarines; the Submarine-Launched Mobile Mines (SLMM); and the Quickstrike and Destructor series of aircraft bombs modified for use as shallow-water mines.

No mines are currently being procured, the last procurement having been CAPTOR mines in fiscal 1986. No mines are currently under development nor are advanced mines planned for procurement. (Mine warfare technology is being developed at Navy laboratories, but not for near-term application to specific programs.)

Most naval mines can be set with several influence combinations (e.g., magnetic, acoustic) and with counters that will permit a certain number of ships or submarines to pass before detonating. Timers allow a delay in activating the mines, to permit the planting submarine to depart the area or to neutralize the mine after a specific period.

The principal U.S. means of minelaying is by aircraft. The Navy's carrier-based A-6E Intruder and S-3B Viking aircraft, and the land-based P-3 Orion patrol/ASW aircraft are configured for minelaying. The Department of Defense has examined the feasibility of employing C-130, C-141, and C-5 cargo aircraft in the minelaying role under a program called CAML (Cargo Aircraft Minelaying). With the CAML rig fitted, a C-130 Hercules could carry 16 2,000-pound (907-kg) mines.

2. The author is in debt to Dr. Scott C. Truver, coauthor with Gregory Hartmann of *Weapons That Wait: Mine Warfare in the U.S. Navy* (Annapolis, Md.: Naval Institute Press, 1991), for his assistance in this section.

TABLE 30-1. AIRCRAFT MINE CAPACITIES (Mines listed by weight class)

Aircraft	Wing Pylons			Weapons Bay	
A-6E Intruder	5	2,000-lb			
S-3 Viking	2	2,000-lb	+	4	500-lb
P-3 Orion	10	500-lb	+	8	500-lb
			or		
	8	1,000-lb	+	3	1,000-lb
			or		
	6	2,000-lb	+	1	2,000-lb
B-52D Stratofortress	12	2,000-lb	+	60	500-lb
			or		
	12	2,000-lb	+	18	1,000-lb
			or		
	10	CAPTOR	+	8	CAPTOR
B-1B	—			24	CAPTOR

The Air Force's B-52D Stratofortress was the most capable minelaying aircraft; 80 of these eight-engine strategic bombers were modified to carry mines (see table 30-1). All aircraft of that type have been retired, the last in 1983; it is included for comparative purposes.

U.S. submarines are configured to launch the SLMM and CAPTOR mines. However, mines can be carried by submarines only at the expense of torpedoes, Harpoon, Tomahawk, or other internally stowed weapons. Submarines at sea when a mining decision was made would have to return to port, unload some or all of their other weapons, load mines, and then undertake the mining mission. Depending upon how many mines were carried, they could be

An Air Force C-130 Hercules releases a CAPTOR mine from its rear ramp as part of the Cargo Aircraft Minelaying (CAML) evaluation. Parachutes are fitted to air-laid mines. (U.S. Air Force)

required to return to port and rearm before undertaking anti-submarine or anti-shipping operations. Alternatively, during a period of crisis some submarines could be pre-loaded with mines, again at the expense of other weapons. The first 39 LOS ANGELES (SSN 688)-class submarines are not fitted, however, to carry mines.

No U.S. surface ships are employed to lay mines except in exercises for minesweepers or swimmers.

In the following listings shallow mines are laid to a maximum depth of approximately 600 feet (182 m), medium-depth mines to a maximum of about 1,000 feet (305 m), and deep-water mines to about 3,000 feet (915 m), i.e., CAPTOR.

Several exercise and training mines are also in Navy service.

Operational: During the Gulf War naval aircraft reportedly employed bombs modified with Destructor kits for use in attacking Iraqi airfields.

An aerial mining operation was also undertaken in an attempt to isolate Iraqi naval craft in the northern Persian Gulf from the port facilities and naval bases at Al-Basrah, Az-Zubayr, and Umm Qasr, and to prevent Iraqi naval craft from leaving those bases. On 18 January 1991 the mining operation was flown against the mouth of the Khawr Az-Zubayr River.

The mission consisted of 18 aircraft from the carrier RANGER (CV 61), including four A-6E Intruders carrying a total of 48 Destructor Mk 36 mines. Forty-two of the mines were successfully dropped at four separate locations in the river. (Six mines on one aircraft failed to release; the plane was diverted to an airfield in Bahrain, where the mines were off-loaded before the A-6E returned to the RANGER. One A-6E was lost to enemy fire during the mission.)

SLMM Mk 67

The Submarine-Launched Mobile Mine (SLMM) is a torpedo-like mine that permits covert mining by submarines in waters that are inaccessible to other means of delivery. This is also a shallow-water, bottom mine for use against surface ships. The SLMM is a Mk 37 Mod 2 torpedo modified to a mine configuration. It can use multiple influences to initiate the firing mechanism.

This is the U.S. Navy's only self-propelled mine, with an electric motor providing a range of some 10,000 yards (9,146 m). The mine can be fitted with either a magnetic/seismic or magnetic/seismic/pressure firing mechanism.

Procurement ended far short of the goals announced in the early 1980s of 2,400 weapons. Operational in 1983.

Type:	self-propelled, shallow-bottom
Targets:	surface ships and submarines
Weight:	1,765 lbs (801 kg)
Length:	13⁵⁄₁₂ ft (4.1 m)
Diameter:	21 in (533 mm)
Warhead:	high explosive
Depth:	max. 328 ft (100 m)
Delivery platform:	submarines

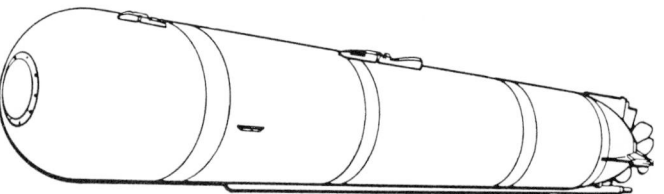

QUICKSTRIKE Mk 65

The Quickstrike mine is the latest in a series of aerial bombs modified for use against surface ships in shallow water—i.e., laid on the bottom to continental shelf depths (about 600 feet/183 m). The Mk 65 is a 2,390-pound (1,084-kg) bomb with a thin-wall mine casing. The mine is normally laid by low-flying A-6E carrier-based aircraft.

Several earlier Quickstrike mines are available: the Mk 62 converted from the Mk 82 500-pound bomb, the Mk 63 converted from the Mk 83 1,000-pound bomb, and the Mk 64 converted from the Mk 84 2,000-pound bomb. These are also shallow-water mines that are used against surface ships. All can be fitted with magnetic/seismic or magnetic/seismic/pressure firing devices.

A stockpile goal of approximately 80,000 Quickstrike weapons was identified in 1982 by a Navy official; however, procurement has fallen far short of that goal. The Quickstrike is a follow-on program to the Destructor bomb-to-mine program.

Type:	shallow-bottom
Targets:	surface ships
Weight:	2,390 lbs (1,084 kg)
Length:	9⅛ ft (2.8 m)
Diameter:	20.9 in (531 mm)
Warhead:	HBX high explosive
Depth:	max. 300 ft (91.5 m)
Delivery platform:	aircraft

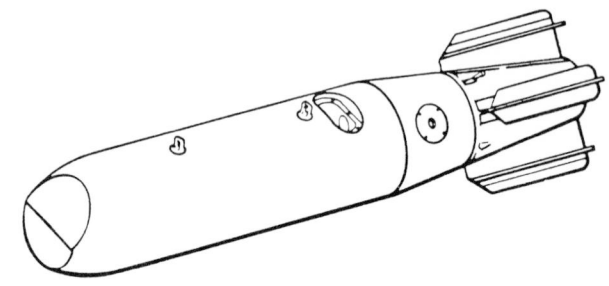

QUICKSTRIKE Mk 64

This is a modified Mk 84 bomb with a thick-walled casing.

Type:	shallow-bottom
Targets:	surface ships
Weight:	2,000 lbs (907 kg)
Length:	12⅔ ft (3.9 m)
Diameter:	18 in (457 mm)
Warhead:	H-6 high explosive
Depth:	max. 300 ft (91.5 m)
Delivery platform:	aircraft

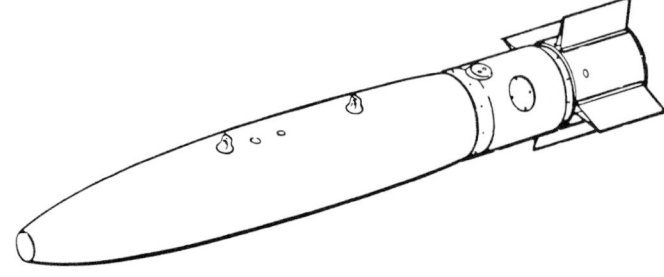

An F/A-18 Hornet dropping Mk 63 Quickstrike mines during an evaluation mission. The last U.S. military mining operation, flown in 1972, was against Haiphong and other North Vietnamese ports; it was executed by carrier-based aircraft. (Randy Hepp)

QUICKSTRIKE Mk 63

Modified Mk 83 bomb.

Type:	shallow-bottom
Targets:	surface ships
Weight:	985 lbs (447 kg) FC[3]
	1,105 lbs (501 kg) LD
Length:	9⁵⁄₁₂ ft (2.9 m)
Diameter:	14 in (355.5 mm)
Warhead:	450 lbs (204 kg) H-6 high explosive
Depth:	max. 300 ft (91.5 m)
Delivery platform:	aircraft

QUICKSTRIKE Mk 62

Modified Mk 82 bomb.

Type:	shallow-bottom
Targets:	surface ships
Weight:	531 lbs (241 kg) FC
	570 lbs (258.5 kg) LD
Length:	7⁵⁄₁₂ ft (2.3 m)
Diameter:	10.8 in (274 mm)
Warhead:	192 lbs (87 kg) H-6 high explosive
Depth:	max. 300 ft (91.5 m)
Delivery platform:	aircraft

3. CF = Conical Fixed tail assembly; LD = extending Low Drag tail assembly.

CAPTOR Mk 60

The CAPTOR (Encapsulated Torpedo), which became operational in September 1979, is the Navy's principal anti-submarine mine. It is a deep-water weapon, normally laid by aircraft or submarine. Upon being laid, the CAPTOR is anchored to the ocean floor. It acoustically detects passing submarines, ignoring surface ships; upon detecting a hostile submarine the CAPTOR launches a Mk 46 Mod 4 torpedo. Mine life in water can be for several months; detection range is reported as 1,093 yds (333 m).

The mine has suffered from significant development and operational problems. These have led to several production delays. A potential problem is the relatively small, 96-pound (43.5-kg) warhead of the Mk 46 torpedo.

Type:	deep-moored
Targets:	submarines
Weight:	2,321 lbs (1,053 kg)
Length:	12¹⁄₁₂ ft (3.7 m)
Diameter:	21 in (533 mm)
Warhead:	96 lbs (43.5 kg) high explosive
Depth:	max. 3,000 ft (915 m)
Delivery platform:	aircraft
	submarines

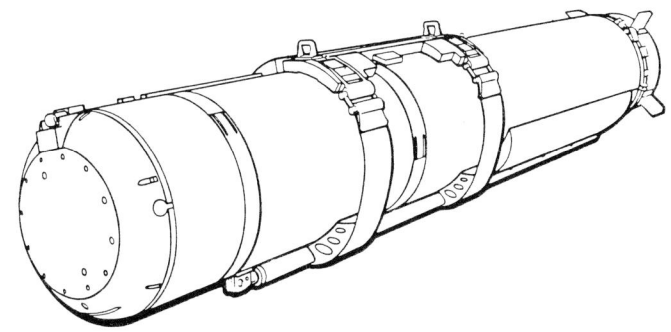

CAPTOR mine with parachute pack fitted (at right). (U.S. Navy)

CAPTOR mines mounted on wing pylons of a B-52 Stratofortress. When rigged for conventional bombing/minelaying, a B-52 could carry eight CAPTORs under its wings and 18 in its weapons bays. (U.S. Air Force)

MINE   Mk 57

An improved mine for use against high-performance submarines, the Mk 57 has a fiberglass case (compared to nonmagnetic, stainless steel for the Mk 56). The mine has a fiberglass casing (unlike the Mk 56, which has a non-magnetic steel case); fitted with a magnetic firing mechanism. It became operational in 1964.

Type:	medium-moored
Targets:	submarines
Weight:	2,059 lbs (934 kg)
Length:	10⅔ ft (3.1 m)
Diameter:	21 in (533 mm)
Warhead:	350 lbs (154 kg) HBX-3 high explosive
Depth:	max. approx. 1,200 ft (366 m)
Delivery platform:	submarines

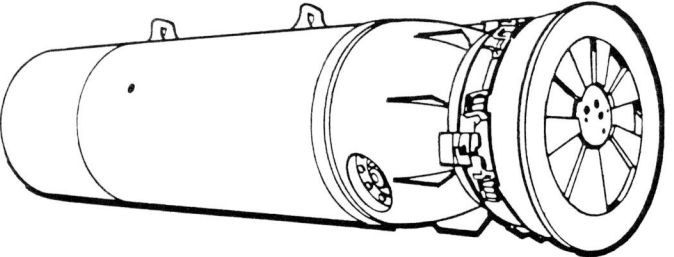

MINE   Mk 56

This mine was designed specifically for use against high-speed, deep-operating submarines, becoming operational in 1966. It has a magnetic firing mechanism.

Type:	medium-moored
Targets:	submarines
Weight:	2,135 lbs (968 kg)
Length:	9½ ft (2.9 m)
Diameter:	23.4 in (594 mm)
Warhead:	357 lbs (162 kg) HBX-3 high explosive
Depth:	max. 1,200 ft (366 m)
Delivery platform:	aircraft

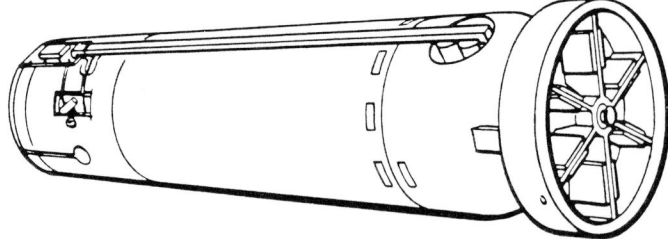

MINE   Mk 55

Modified aircraft bomb. Mods 1 through 6 are similar to the variations of the Mk 52 mine; the Mk 55 Mod 7 is similar to the Mod 2, with a dual-channel magnetic firing mechanism, making it more difficult to sweep. There is a Mod 11 with magnetic/seismic sensors.

Type:	shallow-bottom
Targets:	submarines
Weight:	2,039 lbs (925 kg) Mod 1 to 2,128 lbs (965 kg) Mod 6
Length:	6⁷⁄₁₂ ft (2.0 m)
Diameter:	23.4 in (594 mm)
Warhead:	1,290 lbs (585 kg) HBX-1 high explosive
Depth:	max. Mods 3, 5, 6 150 ft (45.7 m)
	Mods 2, 7 600 ft (183 m)
Delivery platform:	aircraft

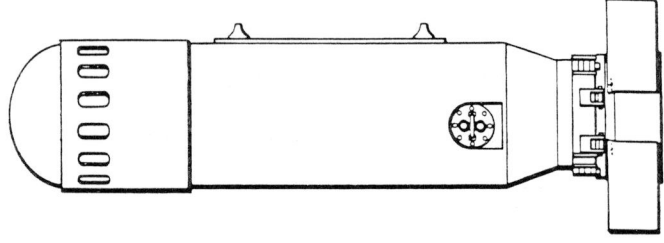

MINE Mk 52

The first of a series of post–World War II ASW mines. The Mod 1 has an acoustic firing mechanism, the Mod 2 magnetic, the Mod 3 a combination of pressure and magnetic, the Mod 5 a combination of acoustic and magnetic, the Mod 6 a combination of all three firing mechanisms, the Mod 7 dual-channel magnetic, and the Mod 11 magnetic/seismic. (There was no Mod 4; no information is available on the Mod 8 to 10.)

Type:	shallow-bottom
Targets:	submarines/surface ships
Weight:	1,130 lbs (512.5 kg) Mod 1 to 1,235 lbs (560 kg) Mod 6
Length:	5½ ft (1.7 m)
Diameter:	19 in (483 mm)
Warhead:	625 lbs (283.5 kg) HBX-1 high explosive
Depth:	max. 150 ft (45.7 m) except Mod 2 600 ft (183 m)
Delivery platform:	aircraft

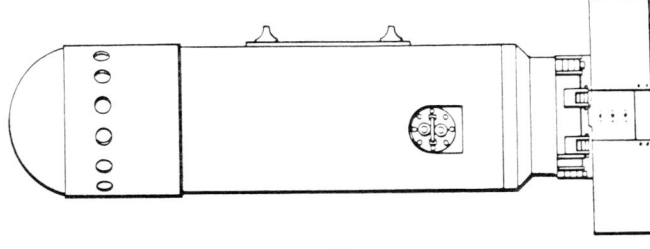

DESTRUCTOR Mk 41

The Destructor (DST) mine series are modified bombs that were introduced during the Vietnam War. The bombs are converted to mines through the installation of a modular arming kit that contains an arming device, explosive booster, and magnetic-influence firing device.

The Mk 41 is a modified Mk 84 bomb. The Mods 4–6 have magnetic/seismic firing mechanisms.

Type:	shallow-bottom
Targets:	surface ships
Weight:	2,093 lbs (949 kg) CF
Length:	12⁵⁄₁₂ ft (3.8 m)
Diameter:	25 in (635 mm)
Warhead:	990 lbs (449 kg) H-6 high explosive
Depth:	max. 300 ft (91.5 m)
Delivery platform:	aircraft

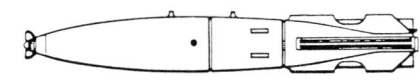

DESTRUCTOR (DST) MARK 36

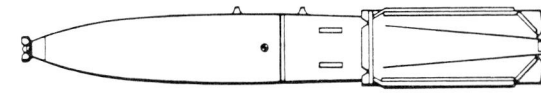

DESTRUCTOR (DST) MARK 40

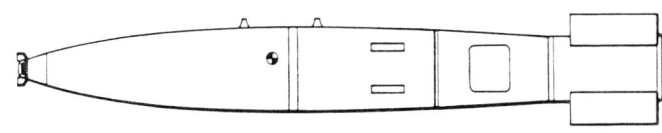

DESTRUCTOR (DST) MARK 41

DESTRUCTOR Mk 40 (also Mk 63 MINE)

Mk 83 bomb fuzed and modified for aerial minelaying. Mods 4 and 5 have magnetic/seismic firing mechanisms.

Type:	shallow-bottom
Targets:	surface ships
Weight:	985 lbs (447 kg) CF
	1,105 lbs (501 kg) LD
Length:	9¾ ft (3.0 m)
Diameter:	22.5 in (571.5 mm)
Warhead:	445 lbs (202 kg) H-6 high explosive
Depth:	max. 300 ft (91.5 m)
Delivery platform:	aircraft

DESTRUCTOR Mk 36 (also Mk 62 MINE)

Modified Mk 82 bomb. The Mods 4–6 have magnetic/seismic firing mechanisms.

Type:	shallow-bottom
Targets:	surface ships
Weight:	531 lbs (241 kg) CF
	570 lbs (258.5 kg) LD
Length:	7⁵⁄₁₂ ft (2.3 m)
Diameter:	15 in (381 mm)
Warhead:	H-6 high explosive
Depth:	max. 300 ft (91.5 m)
Delivery platform:	aircraft

MISSILE LAUNCHING SYSTEMS

Several types of missile launchers are fitted in U.S. warships. There are three generic types: (1) the traditional above-deck launchers, wherein missiles are pushed upward from below-deck magazines onto the launcher, which is then trained and elevated; (2) various "box"-like launchers, such as the Armored Box Launcher (ABL) and ASROC launcher; and (3) the below-decks Vertical Launching System (VLS). The Harpoon canisters fitted in a variety of Navy and Coast Guard ships (as well as numerous foreign ships) can be considered a variation of the box launchers.

Following completion of the last PERRY-class ships with Mk 13 Mod 4 launchers and modernization of the battleship WISCONSIN (BB 64) with Armored Box Launchers, only VLS and Harpoon canister launchers have been installed in new U.S. warships. The VLS provides a high degree of missile launch flexibility, more rapid launching, reduced maintenance requirements, and fewer crewmen in comparison with earlier above-deck surface-to-air missile launch systems. The Mk 41 VLS can accommodate Standard and Tomahawk missiles, and the Vertical-Launch ASROC (VLA), if and when that missile is deployed.

The VLS has total flexibility in missile selection, rapid reselection if a weapon fails to launch (without having to unload or jettison the missile), some protection for the missile from weather and shrapnel

in comparison with a missile on an above-deck launcher, and more efficient use of space compared to rotary below-deck magazines.

The VLS consists of a series of eight-cell launch modules plus launch control units and a missile loading/strikedown module. The strikedown module takes the space of three missile cells. Thus, the 61-missile launch system actually consists of 64 cells, with three cells devoted to the loading/strikedown module; in the 29-missile launcher there are 34 cells with a three-cell loading/strikedown module. The Mk 41 series is a system designation; there are two launcher subsystem designations, Mk 158 for 61 missiles (CG 52/DD 963/DDG 51) and Mk 159 for 29 missiles (DDG 51).

The standard eight-cell VLS module weighs 29,300 pounds (13,290 kg); each module contains two rows of four missile cells separated by an exhaust uptake. The 61-missile VLS installation (i.e., eight standard modules) is $28^7/_{12}$ feet long, $12^5/_{12}$ feet wide, and $25\frac{1}{4}$ feet high ($8.7 \times 3.8 \times 7.7$ m). The maximum missile length that can be accommodated is 22 feet (6.7 m). The launchers are manufactured by the Northern Ordnance Division of the FMC Corp., Minneapolis, Minn., and Martin Marietta, Ga.

Two new missile launcher designs have been developed for the RAM surface-to-air missile (see page 490)

TABLE 30-2. MISSILE LAUNCHERS

Designation	Missiles	Type	Operational	System Weight[a]	Ships/Class
Mk 10 Mod 0	40 Standard-ER	twin	1960	275,875 lbs	DDG 37–46
Md 10 Mod 1	40 Standard-ER	twin	1961	277,436 lbs	CGN 9
Mk 10 Mod 2	80 Standard-ER	twin	1961	450,857 lbs	CGN 9
Mk 10 Mod 5	40 Standard-ER	twin	1962	287,516 lbs	CG 16–24, CGN 25 (forward)
Mk 10 Mod 6	40 Standard-ER	twin	1962	274,938 lbs	CG 16–24, CGN 25 (aft)
Mk 10 Mod 7	60 Standard-ER/ASROC	twin	1964	361,944 lbs	CG 26–34, CGN 35 (forward)
Mk 10 Mod 8	60 Standard-ER/ASROC	twin	1967	364,197 lbs	CGN 35 (aft)
Mk 11 Mod 0	42 Standard-MR/Harpoon	twin	1962	165,240 lbs	DDG 2–14
Mk 13 Mod 0	40 Standard-MR	single	1962	132,561 lbs	DDG 15–24
Mk 13 Mod 3	40 Standard-MR	single	1974	135,012 lbs	CGN 36–37
Mk 13 Mod 4	40 Standard-MR/Harpoon	single	1978	134,704 lbs	FFG 7
Mk 16 Mods 1 to 6	8 ASROC[b]	8-tube	1961	47,782 lbs	cruisers, destroyers, frigates; some modified to launch Harpoon or Standard-ARM missiles (Mk 112 launcher box)
Mk 25 Mod 1	8 Sea Sparrow BPDMS	8-tube	1967	32,081 lbs	carriers, frigates, amphibious ships
Mk 26 Mod 0	24 Standard-MR/ASROC	twin	1976	162,028 lbs	CGN 38–41, DDG 993
Mk 26 Mod 1	44 Standard-MR/ASROC	twin	1976	208,373 lbs	CGN 38-41, CG 47–51, DDG 993
Mk 29 Mod 0	8 NATO Sea Sparrow	8-tube	1974	24,000 or 28,000 lbs[c]	carriers, destroyers, frigates, amphibious ships, auxiliaries; NATO Sea Sparrow (Mk 132 launcher box)
Mk 41	61 Standard/Tomahawk/VLA	vertical	1986	~ 188,000 lbs	CG 52, DDG 51, DD 963
Mk 41	29 Standard/Tomahawk/VLA	vertical	1991	~ 94,000 lbs	DDG 51
Mk 140 Mod 0[d]	4 Harpoon	4-tube	1976	9,000 lbs	PHM 1–6
Mk 141 Mod 1[d]	4 Harpoon	4-tube	1977	13,000 lbs	battleships, cruisers, destroyers, Coast Guard cutters
Mk 143	4 Tomahawk	quad	1980		BB 61, CGN 9, CGN 38, DD 963
Ex-31	24 RAM	24-tube	1992	11,700 lbs	LHA 1

[a]Does not include missiles and hydraulic fluids; missiles are included for Mk 16, 25, 29, 140, and 141.
[b]Does not include reloads available in some ships.
[c]One-director and two-director systems, respectively.
[d]These are launcher and not system designations.

A Standard-MR SM-2 missile is vertically launched from the cruiser BUNKER HILL (CG 52). Vertical Launching Systems (VLS) are more effective and can accommodate more missiles for a given space compared to conventional, above-deck launchers. (U.S. Navy)

A Tomahawk Land-Attack Missile (TLAM) is launched toward Iraq from an ABL on the MISSISSIPPI during Desert Storm. Most of the Tomahawks were launched from SPRUANCE-class ASW destroyers fitted with VLS. (U.S. Navy)

The forward Mk 10 SAM launcher on the cruiser HARRY E. YARNELL (CG 17) with Standard-ER SM-2 missiles on the twin rails. Access to the magazine is through the angled deck structure at left. (Stefan Terzibaschitsch)

Resembling coffins, paired Armored Box Launchers (ABL) are fitted on the stern of the cruiser MISSISSIPPI (CGN 40). At left is the ship's after Mk 26 twin-arm SAM launcher. (Giorgio Arra)

Eight Harpoon canisters in two four-tube mounts is the standard armament of most U.S. cruisers and destroyers and the PEGASUS-class missile combatants. The Harpoons are sealed in the canisters, which are also used for shipping and storing the weapons ashore. These Harpoons and 5-inch/54-cal Mk 45 gun mount are on the cruiser MOBILE BAY (CG 53). (Giorgio Arra)

Mk 13 SAM launcher on the destroyer GOLDSBOROUGH (DDG 20) with a Harpoon anti-ship missile. The Mk 13 launcher loads missiles in a vertical position from a below-deck cylindrical magazine. (OS2 John Bouvia, USN)

Eight-cell units of the Mk 41 VLS are installed in the destroyer SPRUANCE. Most SPRUANCES are receiving eight such modules, for a total of 61 missile cells plus a three-cell reload crane device. (Litton/Ingalls)

The 21-tube Ex-41 launcher for the RAM; the launcher uses components of the Phalanx CIWS. (General Dynamics/Pomona)

MISSILES[4]

The missiles currently available or under development for the Navy and Marine Corps for use from aircraft, surface ships, and submarines are listed below. (Ground- and vehicle-launched missiles used by the Marine Corps are not listed unless they are also air-launched.) The HAMILTON (WHEC 715)-class cutters, most of which are fitted with Harpoon missiles, are the only Coast Guard ships armed with guided missiles.

The missiles are arranged alphabetically by their popular names. All missiles in U.S. service or advanced development have letter-number designations explained in the accompanying chart. There is a single series for missiles and a separate series for rockets. Of the weapons described here, the ASROC RUR-5A is the only one from the latter designation series. Note that the unpowered Walleye II AGM-62 is listed in the missile series.

The term anti-radiation is officially used for missiles that home on enemy radar transmissions; because of the popular confusion over the term radiation, which is normally associated with nuclear effects, the term *anti-radar* is used throughout this volume.

4. The author is in debt to Mr. Edward L. Korb, editor of *The World's Missile Systems* (Pomona, Calif.: General Dynamics Corp., 1988), for his assistance in this section.

AAAM (Advanced Air-to-Air Missile)

The Navy was developing the AAAM to replace the Phoenix long-range AAM from the mid-1990s. The Navy awarded contracts to two firms in 1987 for technology demonstration and validation of the AAAM concept. The missile was cancelled by the Department of Defense in early 1992.

The AAAM was originally intended to counter the Soviet Backfire and Blackjack strike aircraft armed with long-range, stand-off missiles. The AAAM was also intended to counter anti-ship cruise missiles. Missile speed will be on the order of Mach 3 (i.e., faster than the Phoenix). Tentative planning provided for the F-14D variant of the Tomcat to carry up to eight AAAMs, with the F/A-18 Hornet carrying at least four AAAMs; a total U.S. Navy procurement of 4,000 missiles was envisioned. The Congress had proposed that the AAAM also be adopted by the U.S. Air Force for the F-15C/D Eagle and F-22 Advanced Tactical Fighter (ATF), although the Air Force stated that there is no requirement for the weapon on its aircraft.

The competing AAAM design groups were Hughes teamed with Raytheon and General Dynamics/Pomona teamed with Westinghouse. The Hughes/Raytheon design was based on a dual-mode active-radar/IR guidance system and ramjet propulsion; the General Dynamics/Westinghouse design had dual-band, semi-active radar/electro-optical guidance and rocket propulsion. The missile was to have a rocket booster. The winning design was to be chosen as early as 1991 with full-scale development through 1996.

The General Dynamics team believed that advanced technology can provide an AAM small enough for an F-14 to carry up to 15 missiles compared to the six Phoenix missiles now carried.

Status: Cancelled.

Weight:	approx. 660 lbs (300 kg)	
Length:		
Span:		
Diameter:	approx. 9 in (229 mm)	
Propulsion:	solid-fuel rocket	
Range:	100+ n.miles	
Guidance:	command-inertial; active terminal radar homing	
Warhead:	30–50 lbs (13.6–22.7 kg) high explosive	
Plastorms:	*aircraft*	F-14D
		F/A-18

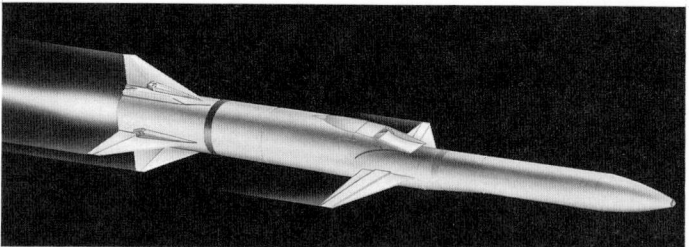

The Advanced Air-to-Air Missile (AAAM) is another victim of budget cuts, with the Navy-managed weapon having been cancelled. This will force the Navy's future fighter force to rely upon the Air Force-managed AMRAAM as its primary air-superiority weapon. This is an artist's concept of the "triple-A-M." (Hughes/Raytheon)

AIWS (Advanced Interdiction Weapon System)

This a standoff missile for use against *low-value* fixed land targets, intended as a low-cost replacement for the SLAM, Maverick, Walleye, Skipper II, and Paveway guided bombs and missiles. However, the baseline AIWS may not provide a similar capability to the weapons it is to replace. The missile is expected to be compatible with all Navy fighter and attack aircraft, as well as the S-3B Viking. Texas Instruments, selected late in 1991 over Boeing and McDonnell Douglas to develop the AIWS, plans an initial glide-bomb version with a BLU-97 submunitions warhead, and a follow-on self-propelled weapon with a unitary warhead. The initial version will be guided by a combination Global Positioning System (GPS) and inertial navigation system expected to provide accuracy on the order of 30 feet (9 m). The later version would be fitted with a datalink to send infrared images back to the launching aircraft for the weapons officer to lock-on to a target at long range for improved accuracy.

Approximately 46,000 missiles are planned for procurement for the Navy and Air Force through 2002.

In 1991 the missile was estimated to have a unit cost of $80,000; a proposed product improvement could cost as much as $170,000 per missile.

Status: In development by Texas Instruments; LTV is supporting AIWS airframe development; Aerojet is providing the submunitions; and Kearfott is developing the inertial measuring devices. Low-rate initial production is planned to begin in 1996, with development of advanced version also to begin in 1996. The missile would also be used by the U.S. Air Force (F-16 and F-111 aircraft).

Weight:	*initial*	1,050 lbs (475 kg)
Length:		
Span:		
Diameter:		
Propulsion:	*initial*	glide bomb
	follow-on	solid-propellant rocket
Range:	24 n.miles (45 km)	
Guidance:	*initial*	GPS + inertial nagivation
	follow-on	GPS + inertial navigation + infrared datalink
Warhead:	*initial*	145 BLU-97 submunitions
	follow-on	submunitions or 500-lb (227-kg) or 1,000-lb (454-kg) high explosive
Platforms:	*aircraft*	F-14D
		F/A-18
		AV-8B
		A-6E
		S-3B

Explanation of symbols:

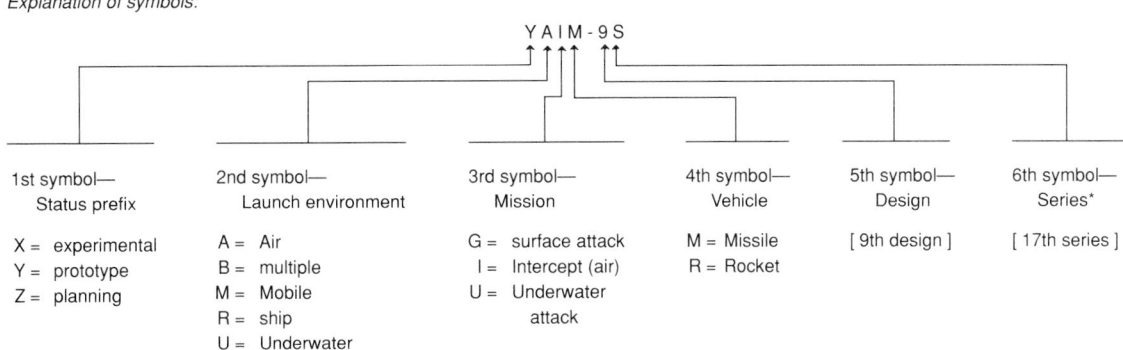

Y A I M - 9 S

1st symbol—	2nd symbol—	3rd symbol—	4th symbol—	5th symbol—	6th symbol—
Status prefix	Launch environment	Mission	Vehicle	Design	Series*
X = experimental	A = Air	G = surface attack	M = Missile	[9th design]	[17th series]
Y = prototype	B = multiple	I = Intercept (air)	R = Rocket		
Z = planning	M = Mobile	U = Underwater			
	R = ship	attack			
	U = Underwater				

*Note: Letters I and O are not used to avoid confusion with numerals.

An AIWS test missile vehicle is carried by an F-4 Phantom over Edwards Air Force Base. This vehicle was released at an altitude of 30,000 feet (9,146 m) and flew more than 20 miles (32 km) down range to point of impact. (Texas Instruments)

An artist's concept of the AIWS with wings fully extended flying toward a target. The missile design provides for a high-lift/low-drag airframe, capable of being launched from high or low altitudes, and capable of delivering a variety of warheads, including BLU-97 and, later, BLU-108 submunitions. (Texas Instruments)

AMRAAM AIM-120A

The Advanced Medium-Range Air-to-Air Missile (AMRAAM) is being developed jointly by the Navy and Air Force to succeed the Sparrow AAM. The missile is planned to have high resistance against enemy ECM and have a "snap-down" capability to engage low-flying aircraft and possibly anti-ship missiles. Its introduction is several years behind schedule, in part because of a series of mechanical problems and defective computer software.

The AMRAAM is smaller than the Sparrow and, unlike the Sparrow's semi-active radar guidance, the new missile uses a mid-course inertial reference system with a sophisticated monopulse radar seeker for terminal guidance. Maximum speed is approximately Mach 4.

Revised estimates of potential threats led to the Air force and Navy requirements for AMRAAM being reduced from 24,320 missiles to 15,450, with planned annual procurement dropping from 3,000 missiles to about 1,500. About 6,000 additional missiles had been planned for U.S. allies, with production in Europe. Hughes Aircraft is also studying the possible use of the missile from surface ships (called Sea AMRAAM).

Status: In production; 191 missiles authorized in fiscal 1992. Flight tests began in 1985, with a low rate of production approved in late 1986. Manufactured by Hughes Aircraft Co., Tucson, Ariz., and Raytheon, Lowell, Mass.

Weight:	345 lbs (156.5 kg)
Length:	12 ft (3.65 m)
Span:	20.7 in (526 mm)
Diameter:	7 in (178 mm)
Propulsion:	solid-propellant rocket
Range:	approx. 40 n.miles (74 km)
Guidance:	command-inertial + active terminal radar homing
Warhead:	30–50 lbs (13.6–22.7 kg) high explosive
Platforms:	*aircraft* F-14
	F/A-18

A just-launched Advanced Medium-Range Air-to-Missile (AMRAAM) is launched from an Air Force TF-15 Eagle over a New Mexico test range. With cancellation of the AAAM the AMRAAM will be modified to better meet Navy missile requirements. (Hughes)

An AMRAAM test missile with the *J* prefix to the designation AIM-120A indicating special test. The AMRAAM is now in production for the Navy and Air Force at Hughes Aircraft (part of GM Hughes Electronics) and Raytheon. (Hughes)

ASROC RUR-5A

The ASROC—Anti-Submarine Rocket—is a ship-launched, ballistic ASW weapon fitted with a conventional Mk 46 homing torpedo. From the early 1960s onward ASROC was fitted to all U.S. Navy cruisers, destroyers, and frigates until the advent of the PERRY-class frigates. The ASROC is a short-range weapon; almost continuous proposals for an Extended-Range (ER) ASROC have been deferred. However, a Vertical-Launch ASROC (VLA) has been developed for use in warships with Vertical Launching Systems (VLS); see below.

The standard ASROC is fired from an eight-tube "box" launcher (Mk 16) and from Mk 10 and Mk 26 surface-to-air missile launchers. It is used by 11 foreign navies with the Mk 44 or Mk 46 torpedo.

As originally delivered to the U.S. Navy, the ASROC came with two warhead options, a W44 nuclear depth bomb or a conventional homing torpedo. The last ASROC nuclear warheads were removed from the fleet in 1989.

Operational: The ASROC was tested with a nuclear warhead on only one occasion, being fired from the destroyer AGERHOLM (DD 826) on 11 May 1962 in a Pacific weapons test.

Status: Operational. IOC in 1961 (conventional with Mk 44 torpedo and nuclear). Manufactured by Honeywell with 12,000 units produced through 1970.

Weight:	1,000 lbs (453.6 kg)	
Length:	15 ft (4.6 m)	
Span:	(ballistic)	
Diameter:	12¾ in (324 mm)	
Propulsion:	solid-propellant rocket	
Range:	approx. 6 n.miles (11.1 km)	
Guidance:	ballistic (terminal acoustic homing with Mk 46 torpedo)	
Warhead:	conventional (Mk 46 Mod 1 torpedo)	
Platforms:	cruisers	CGN 9
		CG 16
		CGN 25
		CG 26
		CGN 35
		CGN 36
		CGN 38
		CG 47–51
	destroyers	DD 963 (7 ships)
		DDG 2
		DDG 37
		DDG 993
	frigates	FF 1052

An ASROC launcher on a Knox (FF 1052)-class frigate. The front of each cell has doors that open for firing; the rear of the ASROC box has blow-out panels. The "A" indicates ASROC firing excellence in exercises. (Giorgio Arra)

ASW STAND-OFF WEAPON

See Sea Lance.

HARM AGM-88A

The HARM (High-speed Anti-Radiation [radar] Missile) was developed by the Naval Weapons Center at China Lake, Calif., for attacking hostile radars. The missile is a successor to the Shrike AGM-45A and Standard-ARM AGM-78D anti-radar missiles, providing greater range, increased velocity, more frequency coverage, and additional flexibility in reacting to threats through an on-board computer. With respect to the last, HARM can automatically calculate threat priorities and engage the one that poses the greatest threat to friendly aircraft. It can also engage radiating targets detected at any angle from the launching aircraft.

Note that HARM is the only weapon carried by the EA-6B Prowler electronic jamming aircraft.

The HARM has been criticized for high costs, and in early 1986 the Navy briefly stopped accepting the missile because of manufacturing flaws.

Operational: U.S. carrier-based aircraft employed HARMs against Libyan radar sites during 1986 strikes. In the Gulf War of 1991 a total of 895 HARMs were launched by Navy and Marine aircraft, more than any other missile used by U.S. naval forces in the conflict. The Tactical Air Launched Decoy (TALD) was employed in conjunction with HARMs to entice Iraqi forces to use their radars against the decoys, marking them as HARM targets; a total of 137 TALDs were used in this manner by naval aircraft during the conflict.[5]

Status: Operational; in production, with 749 missiles authorized in fiscal 1992. IOC in 1984. The first production missiles were delivered in December 1982. A production run of some 8,000 missiles is planned for the U.S. Navy; it is also used by the U.S. Air Force, and West Germany was the first foreign user. Manufactured by Texas Instruments and Ford Aerospace.

An ASROC being fired from the "box" launcher on the frigate Brooke (FFG 1). Except for carrying the Mk 46 ASW torpedo, the ASROC has remained essentially unchanged during more than 30 years of service. (U.S. Navy)

5. In addition to attack aircraft launching TALDs, during the Gulf War they were launched by S-3B Vikings working in conjunction with HARM-armed aircraft to attack Iraqi radar sites. The TALD has an electronics designation—AN/ADM-141.

Weight:	796 lbs (361 kg)
Length:	13 ft 7 in (4.17 m)
Span:	3 ft 8 in (1.13 m)
Diameter:	approx. 10 in (253 mm)
Propulsion:	solid-propellant rocket
Range:	approx. 80 n.miles (148 km)
Guidance:	radar homing
Warhead:	145 lbs (65.8 kg) high explosive
Platforms:	*aircraft* F/A-18
	A-6E
	EA-6B

A HARM being loaded on an A-7E Corsair. The anti-radar missile was highly effective in the Gulf War. Production halted with the fiscal 1992 budget, however, as Defense officials declared that HARM inventories were sufficient for anticipated future requirements. (PH1 William Shaya, USN)

A HARM launched from an A-7E Corsair about to strike a target ship off Point Mugu, Calif. The HARM evolved from the Shrike and Standard-ARM missiles. (U.S. Navy)

HARPOON   AGM/RGM/UGM-84A

The Harpoon is a versatile, widely used anti-ship missile. It is the first U.S. Navy missile designed for shipboard launch against surface targets since the Regulus I, which was deployed in the 1950s, albeit primarily for the strategic, land-attack role. The Harpoon was initially conceived for aircraft use against surfaced Soviet Echo-class cruise missile submarines. Subsequently, the missile was developed for air, surface, and submarine launch against surface targets.

The missile is carried in most U.S. surface combatant classes, being launched from surface-to-air missile launchers (Mk 11, 13), vertical launchers (Mk 41), ASROC box launchers (Mk 29), and stand-alone canisters (Mk 140, Mk 141). For shipboard and submarine launch the missile has a solid-fuel rocket booster fitted. Submarines can launch the encapsulated Harpoon from standard 21-inch (533-mm) torpedo tubes; in submarine launch the capsule rises to the surface and the missile ignites, leaving the canister. The F/A-18, A-6E, P-3C, and S-3B aircraft can carry the Harpoon. From 1982 onward the U.S. Navy has taken delivery of the Block 1B Harpoon with improved radar guidance and a lower flight altitude. The subsequent 1C version, delivered from 1984, has improved guidance and burns a higher-density fuel, resulting in an increase in range, to almost 80 n.miles (148.2 km). The Block 1D improvements backfit of earlier missiles from 1992 enables the missile to re-attack a target by flying a clover-leaf pattern if the missile does not acquire the target on its first approach. The 1D variant also has a 23.2-inch (0.6-m) fuel tank extension to almost double the missile's range.

The maximum Harpoon flight velocity is Mach 0.85. Flight reliability is in excess of 93 percent.

The Harpoon forms the basis for the Standoff Land Attack Missile (SLAM); see separate entry. McDonnell Douglas has proposed a truck-mounted version of the Harpoon for the coastal defense role.

Operational: The first combat use of the Harpoon was by U.S. naval forces against Libyan missile craft in the Gulf of Sidra in 1986.

The only known use of the Harpoon during the January–February 1991 campaign in the Persian Gulf occurred when the Saudi Arabian missile craft FAISAL launched a single missile, which sank an Iraqi minelayer. The engagement took place early on 23 January, with the detection and missile launch being made by radar in the predawn darkness; the target ship was identified by Iraqi survivors.

Status: Operational; in production, with 749 missiles authorized in fiscal 1992. IOC 1977 in surface ships and submarines; 1979 in land-based aircraft (P-3C); and 1981 in carrier aircraft (A-6E). Twenty other nations employ the Harpoon from surface ships and submarines (with the submarine-launched Harpoon called Sub-Harpoon in foreign navies); the Coast Guard has Harpoon canisters on its larger cutters (WHEC); and the U.S. Air Force has flown B-52G and F-111 bombers armed with Harpoons in the anti-shipping role.

Through April 1992 more than 6,000 missiles were produced for the U.S. services and 20 other countries. McDonnell Douglas predicts an eventual production run of 10,000 Harpoons for all users. Manufactured by McDonnell Douglas Missile Systems Co., St. Charles, Mo.

A Harpoon fitted to the wing of a P-3C Orion maritime patrol aircraft. The letter *T* in the designation ATM-84A indicates that this is a training missile. (McDonnell Douglas)

Weight: 1,168 lbs (530 kg) for air launch
                1,470 lbs (667 kg) for Mk 11 or Mk 13 launch
                1,530 lbs (694 kg) for Mk 140, Mk 141 or SSN launch
Length: 12 ft 6 in (3.8 m) for air launch
                15 ft 2 in (4.6 m) for surface/submarine launch
Span: 3 ft (0.9 m)
Diameter: 13 in (329 mm)
Propulsion: turbojet (Teledyne CAE J402-CA-400); 600 lbst (272 kgst) + solid-
                propellant booster (12,000 lbst/5,400 kgst for 2.9 seconds) for
                surface/submarine launch
Range: 75–80 n.miles (139–148 km) except approx. 150 n.miles (278 km) in
                1D variant
Guidance: active radar
Warhead: 510 lbs (231 kg) high explosive
Platforms: *aircraft*   F/A-18
                                     A-6E
                                     P-3C
                                     S-3B
                submarines   SSN 637 and later classes
                battleships   BB 61
                cruisers   all CG/CGN
                destroyers   all DD/DDG
                frigates   all FF/FFG
                small combatants   PHM 1
                CG cutters   WHEC 715

A Harpoon blasts out of its canister after a submarine launching. The spring-loaded fins and stub wings are fully deployed in this photo. (McDonnell Douglas)

An A-6E Intruder launches an improved and lengthened Block 1D Harpoon missile during flight tests. The Harpoon is a highly flexible anti-ship missile, capable of being launched from most combat aircraft, surface ships, and submarines. (McDonnell Douglas)

An aviation ordnanceman prepares a Harpoon under the wing of a P-3C Orion. The Harpoon was designed initially for attacking surfaced Soviet cruise missile submarines. (McDonnell Douglas)

HELLFIRE AGM-114

The Hellfire (derived from Helicopter-Launched Fire and forget) is an anti-tank missile launched from Marine attack helicopters. The missile is intended to replace the wire-guided TOW, the Hellfire being a free-flight weapon with a longer range that permits launch-and-leave tactics. The missile was developed by the Army.

The Hellfire is modular, allowing a variety of sensors to be fitted. The Marines will use the laser-guided variant. The target can be designated for helicopters by ground-based or airborne laser designators; it affords additional survival to the launching helicopter by a lock-on-after-launch feature. A land-launched version has been developed. In 1990 the Army successfully demonstrated the ability of a helicopter-launched Hellfire to engage an aerial target, and in 1989 the Navy test-launched Hellfire missiles from the surface effects ship IX 515 (ex-SES-200).

When the Army initiated development of the Hellfire in the mid-1970s, Rockwell International was the prime contractor for the sole-source program, with Martin Marietta providing the laser seeker for the missile. However, from the mid-1980s Martin became a second production source for the missile. (The missile is also carried by the Army's AH-64 Apache attack helicopter; Hellfire missiles fired by AH-64s against Iraqi radar sites were the first coalition weapons launched in Operation Desert Storm in January 1991.)

Status: Operational. IOC in 1985 (U.S. Army). The missile has been adapted for the coastal defense role by Sweden. Manufactured by Rockwell International and Martin Marietta.

Weight:	99.6 lbs (45.2 kg)
Length:	5 ft 4 in (1.625 m)
Span:	1 ft 1 in (0.33 m)
Diameter:	7 in (178 mm)
Propulsion:	solid-propellant rocket
Range:	3+ n.miles (5.55 km)
Guidance:	laser tracking
Warhead:	20 lbs (9 kg) high explosive
Platforms:	*helicopters* AH-1W

A Marine AH-1J SeaCobra carrying eight Hellfire anti-tank missiles. (Bell Helicopter Textron)

An AH-1W SeaCobra flown by VX-5 fires a Hellfire anti-tank missile. U.S. Army AH-56 Apache helicopter gunships fired Hellfires to destroy Iraqi border radar installations at the start of the air war in the Gulf on the morning of 17 January 1991. (U.S. Navy)

LRDMM

The proposed LRDMM (Long-Range Dual-Mode Missile) was envisioned as a long-range (over 100-mile/161-km) missile for launching from Aegis ships. The missile would have been used against incoming anti-ship missiles launched at long ranges, attack bomber aircraft, and electronic jamming aircraft. At one point it was also envisioned that the airframe could be used for the ASW Stand-Off Weapon (SOW).

The project was not pursued because of technical difficulties and uncertainty over how to conduct the outer air battle to defend battle groups against attacking Soviet cruise missile aircraft.

MAVERICK AGM-65

This is an air-to-surface missile derived from an Air Force anti-tank missile for use by Marine aircraft in the close air support role and by the Navy in the anti-ship role.

The Marines have the AGM-65E laser-guided version, compatible with air- and ground-based laser designators; the Navy's AGM-65F combines the Imaging Infrared (I^2R) of the Air Force AGM-65D missile with the warhead and propulsion sections of the AGM-65E. These Mavericks have a 300-pound (136-kg) penetrating-blast warhead in place of the 125-pound (56.7-kg) shaped-charge used for attacking tanks in the Air Force versions.

Operational: Maverick missiles were used extensively by the Air Force and Marine Corps in the 1991 conflict in the Persian Gulf.

Status: AGM-65E IOC in 1985. Through mid-1991 approximately 2,000 missiles were delivered to the U.S. Navy and 2,000 to the Marine Corps; the U.S. Air Force and 18 other nations use the Maverick. The first Navy launch of an AGM-65F occurred in September 1983 from an A-7E Corsair aircraft, with the missile striking a discarded destroyer.

Manufactured by Hughes.

Weight:	637 lbs (289 kg)
Length:	8 ft 2 in (2.49 m)
Span:	2 ft 4½ in (0.72 m)
Diameter:	12 in (30 mm)
Propulsion:	solid-propellant rocket
Range:	12 n.miles (22.2 km)
Guidance:	AGM-65E laser
	AGM-65F infrared
Warhead:	300 lbs (136 kg) high explosive
Platforms:	*aircraft* F/A-18
	A-6E
	AV-8B

An AGM-65F infrared variant of the Maverick is checked on the pylon of an A-7E Corsair aircraft. The missile has demonstrated its effectiveness in night attacks against large and small ships during live-round tests. (Hughes)

MRASM AGM-109

The MRASM (Medium-Range Air-to-Surface Missile) was a joint Navy–Air Force program to develop an air-launched missile with a 250-n.mile range for delivering submunitions against runways. Originally to be a (shortened) variant of the Tomahawk, during early development significant changes were made to most components, reducing the commonality with Tomahawk. The Navy's interest in MRASM was minimal, while the Air Force's position was divided: the Tactical Air Command (TAC) had limited interest while the Strategic Air Command (SAC) envisioned the MRASM as a useful weapon for the B-52G strategic bomber.

The MRASM program was terminated by Congress in 1983. Other weapons that could be adapted to the MRASM role at that time included the Air Force GBU-15, an air-launched glide bomb, and the Navy's Harpoon, while the Air Force Advanced Cruise Missile (ACM)—a "stealth" weapon—could be used by strategic aircraft. Also being planned is an Army–Air Force effort to develop a common Joint Tactical Missile System (JTACMS) that could be ground-launched and carried by strategic and tactical aircraft for "deep attack."

The designation AGM-109H was intended for the Air Force airfield attack weapon and AGM-109L for a projected Navy anti-ship and land-attack version.

An AGM-65F variant of the Maverick missile is fired from a P-3C Orion during feasibility tests. Although suitable for the anti-ship role, the value of launching the missile from a large, slow, relatively vulnerable Orion is questionable at best. (U.S. Navy)

PHOENIX AIM-54

The Phoenix was developed for long-range fleet air defense against attacking Soviet bomber aircraft. It is the most sophisticated and longest-range AAM in service with any nation. The missile can be carried only by the F-14 Tomcat fighter using the AWG-9 radar/fire control system. The AWG-9 is capable of simultaneously guiding all six Phoenix missiles that can be carried by an F-14 (although six-missile loadouts are rare).

The AIM-54A, with analog electronics, has been replaced in U.S. service with the AIM-54C/C+, the latter being the current production model. The C/C+ have a digital system to allow software programming for more rapid target discrimination, improved beam attack, better resistance to electronic countermeasures, longer range, increased altitude, and increased reliability. The previously used expanding, continuous-rod warheads in early Phoenix missiles have been replaced by controlled fragmentation warheads (entering production in fiscal 1983). The AIM-54B was an interim model, similar to the AIM-54A but without the earlier missile's liquid cooling system; it did not go into production. The missile's designed range was 60 n.miles (111 km); intercepts have been made out to at least 110 n.miles (204 km). Maximum speed is approximately Mach 5. The AIM-C model was delayed in delivery to the fleet by quality-control problems that resulted in several hundred missiles being delivered but not considered acceptable by the Navy until certain modifications were made. Production will end with the fiscal 1992 order.

Hughes Aircraft Company proposed a ship-launched, short-range defensive missile system in the 1970s based on the Phoenix/AWG-9; that option was not pursued.

Operational: The AIM-54A was compromised by having been provided to the Iranian Air Force prior to the fall of the Shah in 1979.

Status: Operational; no longer in production. Procurement ended with the fiscal 1990 program. IOC in 1974. Manufactured by Hughes.

A Phoenix is launched from an F-14A Tomcat. The missile, developed to provide long-range air defense of carrier battle groups, has a limited value in tactical air situations that are likely to be encountered by U.S. naval forces in the 1990s. (Hughes)

Weight:	985 lbs (447 kg)
Length:	13 ft (4.0 m)
Span:	3 ft (0.915 m)
Diameter:	15 in (380 mm)
Propulsion:	solid-propellant rocket
Range:	110 n.miles (204 km)
Guidance:	semi-active radar in cruise phase; active terminal radar homing
Warhead:	133 lbs (60 kg) high explosive
Platforms:	*aircraft* F-14

An AIM-54C+ Phoenix missile undergoes its final inspection before delivery to the Navy. The various sections of the missile are clearly visible; the technician is working on the guidance section. (Hughes)

PENGUIN AGM-119B

The Penguin, developed by the Norwegian Navy, is an anti-ship missile that is being procured for U.S. Navy use from the SH-60B LAMPS III helicopter. The missile has also undergone U.S. Navy evaluation on small patrol craft (PB Mk III).

The missile is a "fire-and-forget" weapon with several unusual features, including an indirect flight path to target. On board ship the Penguin is fired from a storage/launcher container that weighs 1,100 pounds (499 kg). The Mk 2 Mod 7 missile being produced for U.S. LAMPS III helicopters is a modification of the Norwegian surface-launched Mk 2 Mod 3 missile.

Maximum missile speed is approximately Mach 1.2.

Status: Operational; in production, with 42 missiles authorized for the U.S. Navy in fiscal 1992. Planned U.S. Navy inventory goal is 106 missiles (reduced in 1991 from a planned 193 missiles). The original Penguin became operational on Norwegian fast attack boats in 1972; it is also used by the Greek, Swedish, and Turkish navies. The improved Mk 2 became operational in 1979 and Mk 3 in the Norwegian Air Force in 1987 (for use from F-16 strike fighters).[6]

The U.S. Navy is procuring approximately 200 missiles.

Manufactured by Norsk Forvarsteknologi A/S (Norway) and Grumman.

Weight:	820 lbs (372 kg)
Length:	10 ft 3 in (3.1 m)
Span:	3 ft 3 in (1.0 m)
Diameter:	11 in (280 mm)
Propulsion:	solid-propellant rocket + solid-propellant booster
Range:	25+ n.miles (46+ km) air launch
Guidance:	inertial + infrared homing
Warhead:	265 lbs (120 kg) high explosive
Platforms:	*helicopters* SH-60B

6. The Mk 3 was originally designated as the Mk 2 Mod 7.

A Penguin missile's rocket engine ignites moments after being released from an SH-60B Seahawk ASW helicopter from VX-1. The Norwegian-developed Penguin will give the LAMPS III helicopters a potent anti-ship capability. (PH2 Danny Lee, USN)

A Penguin missile has just been released from a VX-1 Seahawk; the missile's wings are still folded and the rocket engine has not yet ignited (see accompanying photo). (PH2 Danny Lee, USN)

POLARIS

The Polaris SLBM has been retired from U.S. Navy service. It was deployed as the U.S. sea-based strategic deterrent weapon from November 1960 with the first deterrent patrol of the GEORGE WASHINGTON (SSBN 598) with 16 A-1 missiles, to February 1981, when the THOMAS JEFFERSON (SSBN 618) completed the final U.S. Polaris A-3 patrol. The Polaris missile was produced for the U.S. Navy in three variants (A-1/2/3).

The Royal Navy procured the A-3 variant which, fitted with a British warhead, entered service in June 1968 when HMS/m RESOLUTION began the first British SSBN patrol; the Chevaline A3TK variant continues in service pending Royal Navy acquisition of the Trident C-4 system.

POSEIDON (C-3) UGM-73

All Poseidon-armed submarines were to be retired by the end of 1992, with Poseidon SSBN deployments being ended on 15 October 1991. The Poseidon SLBM was derived from the Polaris missile, with increased strike capability through a Multiple Independently targeted Reentry Vehicle (MIRV) warhead, the first strategic missile of any nation to have that feature. The Poseidon MIRV could carry up to 14 RVs, with 8 to 10 being a common loadout. The RVs could be directed at separate targets within range of the warhead's "footprint." The missile range was reduced when larger numbers of RVs were carried.

The Poseidon replaced the Polaris A-2 and A-3 missiles in the 31 LAFAYETTE (SSBN 726)-class submarines. Subsequently, 12 submarines of that class were upgraded to fire the Trident C-4 missile.

Status: No longer operational. The Poseidon C-3 missile was first deployed on 31 March 1971 in the JAMES MADISON (SSBN 627). Poseidon patrols were terminated on 15 October 1991 with a total of 1,182 Poseidon patrols having been carried out. The last launch of a Poseidon from an SSBN occurred in February 1990, from the submarine KAMEHAMEHA (SSBN 642).

See 14th Edition/page 473 for characteristics.

RAM RIM-116A

The Rolling Airframe Missile (RAM) is being developed to provide a rapid-reaction, short-range missile for shipboard defense using off-the-shelf components. The RAM is the first Navy shipboard fire-and-forget missile and the only Navy missile that rolls during flight (i.e., is not stabilized in flight).

The RAM has the infrared seeker from the Army's Stinger missile and the rocket motor, fuze, and warhead from the Sidewinder AAM; provided with multi-mode guidance. The missile is supersonic. The complete RAM round consists of the RIM-116A missile and the Ex-8 sealed canister, together being designated Ex-44. The RAM missile can be fired from a specialized, 24-missile launcher (Ex-31) or from two of the eight cells of the NATO Sea Sparrow launcher (five missiles per cell). The Ex-31 uses the mount and elevation/train assemblies from the Phalanx CIWS.

The Ex-31 launcher was evaluated in the destroyer DAVID R. RAY (DD 971) in the late 1980s. The first two production launchers were to be installed in the helicopter carrier PELELIU (LHA 5) in 1992 (the Sea Sparrow launchers having been removed). The Navy's tentative plans provide for 50 ships to have 1 or 2 launchers each for a total of 60 to 70 launchers.

The missile was originally co-sponsored by Denmark and West Germany; however, Denmark has withdrawn from the project. The RAM program suffered significant cost increases and schedule delays early in the program. A 1991 report of the U.S. General Accounting Office stated that "The basic RAM, as currently designed, will have increasing difficulties in engaging a major portion of the threat in various regions of the world."[7]

Status: In development and in production; 500 missiles were authorized in fiscal 1991. Advanced development began in 1976 and the first RAM engineering missiles were delivered in September 1981. Manufactured by General Dynamics, Rancho Cucamonga, Calif., and GmbH of Germany.

7. General Accounting Office, *Navy Budget: Potential Reductions in Weapons Procurement* (Washington, D.C.: 18 January 1991), p. 24.

Weight:	162 lbs (73.5 kg)
Length:	9 ft 2 in (2.79 m)
Span:	1.4 in (434 mm)
Diameter:	5 in (127 mm)
Propulsion:	solid-propellant rocket
Range:	approx. 5 n.miles (9 km)
Guidance:	passive RF acquisition + mid-course guidance with IR terminal or passive RF all the way
Warhead:	25 lbs (11.3 kg) high explosive
Platforms:	planned for various surface ships

The stern of the DAVID R. RAY showing, from left, NATO Sea Sparrow launcher, 5-inch/54-cal Mk 45 DP gun mount, and 24-missile RAM launcher. At its inception the RAM was envisioned for a variety of ship types of several NATO navies. (General Dynamics/Pomona)

A RAM is fired from the 24-missile launcher fitted to the destroyer DAVID R. RAY. The development of this missile has been torturous. (General Dynamics/Pomona)

SEA LANCE   UUM-125B

Formerly called the ASW Stand-Off Weapon (SOW), the Sea Lance is a planned submarine-launched weapon that provides a rocket booster for a Mk 50 anti-submarine torpedo. Although often labeled as a successor to SUBROC, the Sea Lance will have only a conventional (torpedo) warhead, whereas the SUBROC carried only a nuclear depth bomb. The Sea Lance warhead may thus inhibit its use at longer ranges because of the limited target localization capability of the Mk 50. Plans to provide a nuclear warhead for Sea Lance have been delayed indefinitely while the conventional Sea Lance has suffered a series of delays and may not be procured.

The Sea Lance was intended for attacks out to the third sonar Convergence Zone (CZ), i.e., approximately 90–100 n.miles (167–185 km). However, when fitted with the conventional Mk 50 torpedo, the effective range would probably be only the first CZ, i.e., some 30–35 n.miles (55.5–65 km). The weapon was to be stowed and launched from a standard 21-inch (533-mm) torpedo tube in a canister, much like the Harpoon anti-ship missile and the CAPTOR encapsulated mine. When the capsule reached the surface the missile booster would ignite, in effect launching the missile on a ballistic trajectory toward the target area. At a designated point the torpedo would separate from the booster, be slowed to re-enter the water and seek out the hostile submarine. Maximum speed in flight is reported in excess of Mach 1.5.

During the concept stage the Navy envisioned a common ASW stand-off weapon for surface ships and submarines. The technical and program difficulties proved too great, however, and the surface-launched weapon became the Vertical-Launch ASROC (VLA). By the late 1980s, however, the decision was made by the Navy to consider the VLA as an interim weapon (with only 300 missiles to be procured) while efforts were made to reinstate a common surface/submarine Sea Lance program.

Names: Boeing had used the name Seahawk for the weapon before the Navy designated it Sea Lance.

Status: In development. The Navy's procurement goal for Sea Lance was originally some 2,400 missiles; however, in 1989 there were reports of as many as 3,500 missiles being produced. The project was terminated for budget reasons in fiscal 1991; however, a number of technical issues may delay a restart indefinitely. Previously approval for full-scale development was expected in late 1992. Being developed by Boeing Co., Seattle, Wash.

Weight:	3,100 lbs (1,406 kg)
Length:	20½ ft (6.25 m)
Span:	(ballistic)
Diameter:	approx. 21 inch (533 mm) encapsulated
Propulsion:	solid-propellant rocket
Range:	100+ n.miles (185+ km)
Guidance:	ballistic; terminal acoustic homing with Mk 50 torpedo
Warhead:	Mk 50 torpedo
Platforms:	*submarines,* planned for SSN 688
	SSN 21

An artist's view of a Sea Lance ASW missile after an underwater launch. Note the unusual tail-fin configuration.

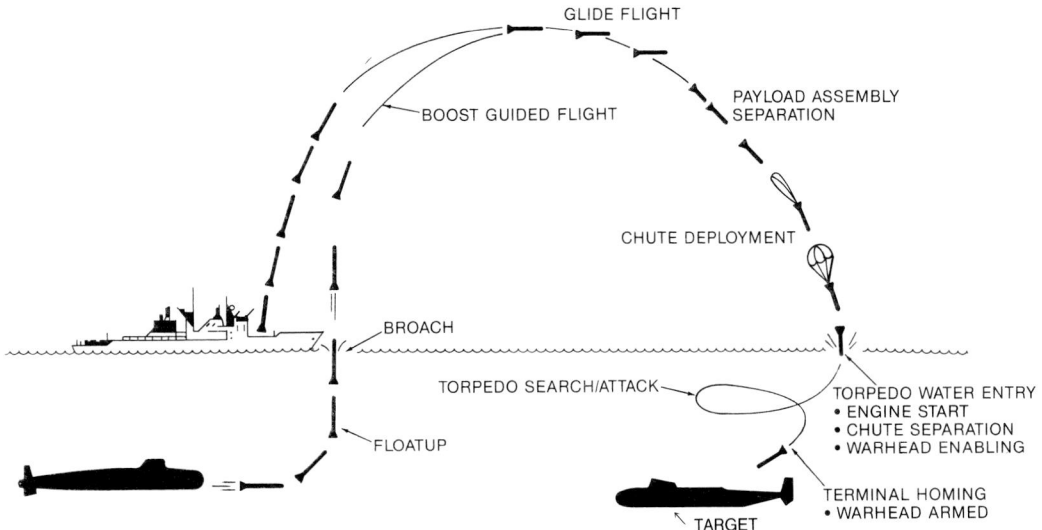

The Sea Lance launch concept showing both surface and submarine launch. The system was originally to have both a nuclear depth bomb and an ASW torpedo as warhead; the former was deferred and then cancelled, and the entire project terminated in fiscal 1991 for budgetary reasons, leaving U.S. submarines without a stand-off ASW weapon. (William Clipson)

SEA SPARROW RIM-7

The Sea Sparrow is an adaptation of the Sparrow AAM employed as an anti-ship missile defense system. The concept was developed in the 1960s to counter the threat from Soviet anti-ship weapons and is fired from the eight-tube box Mk 25 launcher of the Basic Point Defense Missile System (BPDMS) or the Mk 29 launcher of the NATO Sea Sparrow Missile (NSSM). The RIM-7H and RIM-7M missiles are used in this role. The Mk 91 missile FCS is used with the NSSM and the Mk 115 with the BPDMS. Beginning in 1980 the Mk 23 Target Acquisition System (TAS) was added to the NSSM on U.S. ships to provide a self-contained system (with TAS providing a dual-mode radar and digital processor for automatic threat detection).

The Sea Sparrow launchers are not fitted in ships that have Standard missile capabilities. The Mk 25 and Mk 29 launchers are not automatically reloaded, and many ships do not have any reloads on board. The following data apply to the RIM-7H. See listing for Sparrow missile for additional information. The weapon has been removed from LHAs, with the RAM missile being provided in its place.

Operational: The carrier SARATOGA (CV 60) accidentally launched two Sea Sparrow missiles during an exercise in the Aegean Sea on 1 October 1992. One missile struck the Turkish destroyer MAUVENET, killing five men (including the commanding officer) and injuring at least 14 others. Initial reports cited personnel failures as the cause of the accidental launches. There were no U.S. casualties in the firing.

Status: Operational. IOC in 1969; RIM-7M in 1983. Eleven other navies employ the Sea Sparrow in the missile-defense role, with the Canadian HALIFAX-class frigates having vertical-launch Sea Sparrow launchers.[8] Manufactured by Raytheon and General Dynamics.

8. Sea Sparrow VLS trials were carried out in the destroyer HURON in April 1981.

Weight:	450 lbs (204 kg)	
Length:	12 ft (3.7 m)	
Span:	3 ft 4 in (1.0 m)	
Diameter:	8 in (203 mm)	
Propulsion:	solid-propellant rocket	
Range:	approx. 10 n.miles (18.5 km)	
Guidance:	radar homing	
Warhead:	90 lbs (40.8 kg) high explosive	
Platforms:	*aircraft carriers*	CV/CVN classes
	destroyers	DD 963
	frigates	FF 1052
	command ships	LCC 19
	amphibious ships	LHD 1
		LPH 2
	auxiliaries	AOE 1
		AOE 6
		AOR 1

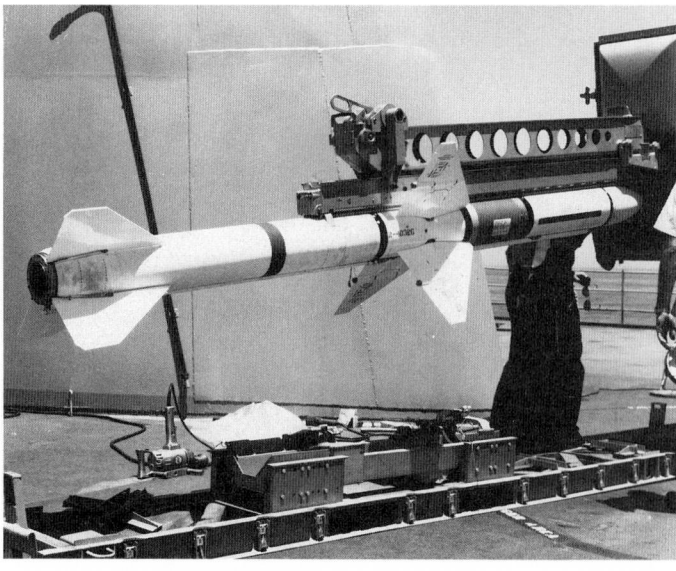

A Sea Sparrow being loaded into a launcher on board the replenishment ship KANSAS CITY A(OR)3. No U.S. ships have automatic reloading for their Sea Sparrow launchers. (U.S. Navy)

A Sea Sparrow being loaded into a test launcher. The launcher is similar to the ASROC Mk 16 box launcher, with doors in the front and blow-out panels in the rear. (U.S. Navy)

A NATO Sea Sparrow launcher on the carrier ABRAHAM LINCOLN (CVN 72) launches a missile during an exercise. F/A-18 Hornets of VFA-87/CVW-8 are on the flight deck. The Sea Sparrow provides a limited anti-missile capability. (PH2 Dennis Taylor, USN)

SHRIKE AGM-45

The Shrike was an anti-radar missile designed to home on hostile radar emissions. The missile was derived from the AIM-7 Sparrow for the U.S. Navy and was used in the Vietnam War from 1964 onward; the Royal Air Force used Shrike missiles (ineffectively) in the 1982 Falklands conflict. There are more than a dozen variants reflecting changes in the guidance seeker to counter different electronic threats. The Shrike suffered from a short range and in the mid-1980s was replaced by the HARM.

See 14th Edition/page 476 for characteristics.

SIAM

U.S. Navy interest has apparently ended in the development of technology for the SIAM (Self-Initiating Anti-aircraft Missile) for use from a submerged submarine against an ASW fixed-wing aircraft or helicopter. The weapon would be launched from special tubes in the submarine and home on the attacking aircraft. The towed acoustic arrays used by submarines could detect low-flying aircraft to initiate SIAM launch.

The concept was not new, with one earlier U.S. Navy experiment using variants of the Sidewinder missile being dubbed "Subwinder." The Royal Navy and Vickers developed the SLAM (Submarine-Launched Air Missile), in which the submarine surfaces or at least broaches its sail to extend a six-tube Blowpipe missile launcher; that system was tested at sea but not deployed. The SIAM concept calls for missile launch while the submarine remains completely submerged.

Ford Aerospace was contracted by the Defense Advanced Research Projects Agency (DARPA) to demonstrate the feasibility of the concept. During the Ford work test vehicles were successfully launched against QH-50 drone helicopters.

See 14 Edition/page 476 for tentative characteristics.

SIDEARM AGM-122A

The Sidearm is an anti-radar missile developed to counter ground-based air-defense weapons at short ranges. The new missile is based on outdated AIM-9 Sidewinder AAMs that had been placed in storage in the 1970s.

The missiles have been fitted with a relatively broad-band, passive-only, radar-homing plus active optical target-detection device from the AIM-9L missile. These, in turn, have been refitted with newer, in-production rocket motors, warheads, and fins.

Upon launch the Sidearm executes a pitch-up maneuver that permits launch from very-low altitudes, an important feature for helicopters flying in the nap-of-the-earth mode. It can be used by essentially all fixed-wing fighter and attack aircraft that can launch a Sidewinder missile. Maximum speed is Mach 2.3.

Status: Operational. The Sidearm was developed by the missile-prolific Naval Weapons Center at China Lake, Calif. Motorola is converting some 900 AIM-9 missiles to the Sidearm configuration; future new production is envisioned. An improved AGM-122B version was cancelled because of funding problems. The first production/remade Sidewinders were funded in fiscal 1986. Manufactured by Motorola of Tempe, Ariz.

Weight:	200 lbs (90.7 kg)
Length:	9 ft 6 in (2.9 m)
Span:	25 in (635 mm)
Diameter:	5 in (127 mm)
Propulsion:	solid-propellant rocket motor
Range:	18,000 yds (16,463 m)
Guidance:	radar homing + electro-optical
Warhead:	10 lb (4.5 kg) high-explosive fragmentation
Platforms:	*helicopters* AH-1W

SIDEWINDER AIM-9

The Sidewinder is the most widely used missile outside of the former Soviet Union, with several hundred thousand Sidewinder missiles having been produced for 37 nations in addition to the United States. The air-to-air weapon was used extensively by the U.S. Navy in the Vietnam War as well as by Allied forces in other conflicts. In the 1991 Persian Gulf War it was responsible for 24 percent of the air-to-air kills (see below).

Developed by the Naval Weapons Center at China Lake, Calif., the Sidewinder is a simple, effective, infrared-homing missile. The AIM-9M version is currently in production in the United States, although the AIM-9L is being built by a European consortium and by Mitsubishi in Japan. The AIM-9M features improved resistance to electronic countermeasures and can engage targets against hot backgrounds; the guidance includes digital electronics, electronic reprogramming for future software upgrades, imaging, and auto-tracking. In 1991 the Department of Defense approved full-scale development of the AIM-9R, a modified Sidewinder with tail-fin controls; however, funding problems led the Navy to cancel the 9R program in December 1991. The model designation AIM-9S was approved in November 1989 for a Sidewinder with modified guidance and controls.

Missile speed is approximately Mach 2.5. (An AIM-9C with a modified anti-radar seeker is called Sidearm; see this page.) The data below are for the AIM-9L variant.

Operational: The Sidewinder scored most of the air-to-air kills by U.S. Navy and Air Force aircraft in the Vietnam War, and by the Israeli Air Force in the 1967 and 1973 wars in the Middle East. During the 1982 fighting over Lebanon's Bekaa Valley, Israeli aircraft used Sidewinders to shoot down 51 of the 55 Syrian-flown MiG aircraft destroyed in aerial combat. The Sidewinder was also highly successfully when used by British Harrier VSTOL aircraft in the 1982 Falklands conflict.

In the 1991 Gulf War most of the Allied air-to-air kills were made with AIM-7M Sparrow missiles (see page 495); Sidewinders were responsible for 12 air-to-air kills against Iraqi aircraft—on 17 January 1991 including an Iraqi MiG-21 downed by a Navy F/A-18C Hornet and on 6 February 1991 an Iraqi Mi-8 helicopter downed by a Navy F-14A Tomcat firing AIM-9M missiles. (In addition, ten Iraqi high-performance aircraft were downed by U.S. Air Force and Saudi F-15 Eagles firing Sidewinder missiles.)

Status: Operational; in production. IOC in 1956; AIM-9M in 1983. Production will end in the mid-1990s with more than 125,000 missiles having been produced for U.S. services and some 25,000 for foreign users. Manufactured by Raytheon and Ford Aerospace.

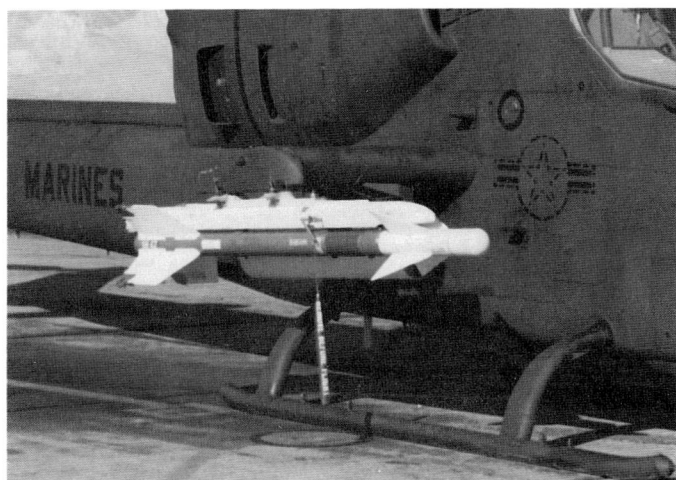

Sidearm anti-radar missile fitted on an AH-1 SeaCobra helicopter. (U.S. Navy)

Weight:	88 lbs (40 kg) for AIM-9H
	86½ lbs (39.2 kg) for AIM-9L/M
Length:	9 ft 6 in (2.87 m)
Span:	2 ft ¾ in (0.63 m) for AIM-9H
	2 ft 1 in (0.635 m) for AIM-9L/M
Diameter:	5 in (127 mm)
Propulsion:	solid-propellant rocket
Range:	approx. 10 n.miles (18.5 km)
Guidance:	infrared passive homing
Warhead:	25 lbs (11.3 kg) high explosive for AIM-9H
	20.8 lbs (9.4 kg) high explosive for AIM-9L/M
Platforms:	*aircraft* F-14
	F/A-18
	A-6E
	AV-8B
	OV-10
	helicopters AH-1W

A Sidewinder launched by a TA-4J Skyhawk from VC-10. (U.S. Navy)

AIM-9L Sidewinder missiles on the flight deck of the British VSTOL carrier HERMES. (Royal Navy)

SKIPPER II   AGM-123A

The Skipper II is a laser-guided, propelled bomb made up of off-the-shelf components; in essence it is a powered version of the Paveway II-series of unpowered Laser-Guided Bombs (LGB).[9] Created by the Naval Weapons Center at China Lake, the Skipper II was an effort to produce a low-cost weapon with a short development time for the air-to-surface role.

The missile uses a 1,000-pound (454-kg) warhead from a Mk 83 general-purpose bomb and the propulsion motor of the Shrike ARM; the laser guidance and control sections are from the Air Force Paveway II (unpowered) laser-guided bomb. There are no electrical connections to the launching aircraft, and it is not necessary to lock the missile onto the target before launch, providing a high degree of launch flexibility.

Status: Operational; in production. IOC in 1985. First launch tests of the Skipper were conducted between June and November 1984, and the first production models were delivered to the Navy in July 1985. (The Paveway II is used by 12 countries in addition to the United States.) Manufactured by Aerojet General/Emerson Electric (conversion of Mk 83 bombs).

Weight:	1,280 lbs (582 kg)
Length:	14 ft (4.27 m)
Span:	5⅛ ft (1.6 m)
Diameter:	19.7 in (500 mm)
Propulsion:	solid-propellant rocket
Range:	13.5+ n.miles (25+ km)
Guidance:	laser (improved Paveway II seeker)
Warhead:	1,000-lb (450-kg) high explosive bomb
Platforms:	*aircraft* A-6E

9. There was no Skipper I; the suffix II was adopted from the Paveway II weapon.

Skipper II laser-guided bomb fitted on the wing of an A-7E Corsair. The laser target-seeker and warhead are clearly visible at left; the remainder of this missile was painted red for flight tests. (U.S. Navy)

SLAM AGM-84E

The SLAM (Stand-off Land-Attack Missile) is a highly accurate air-to-surface missile derived from the Harpoon anti-ship missile. The weapon was originally developed by the Navy as an interim weapon, pending development of a purpose-designed missile; however, following its successful use in the 1991 Gulf War the Navy doubled its SLAM inventory objectives. The missile is normally aircraft-launched with inertial guidance and has infrared terminal guidance; a television camera returns an infrared video image to the launching aircraft for in-flight guidance corrections. In 1990 the Navy conducted trial launchings from shipboard Harpoon canisters.

The SLAM combines the airframe, propulsion, and control system of the Harpoon with a new guidance package consisting of the infrared imaging seeker of the Maverick missile, the datalink of the Walleye missile, and a Global Positioning System (GPS) receiver.

Unit cost in 1991 was approximately $910,000 per round, a relatively high unit cost.

Operational: The SLAM was employed in combat for the first time in the 1991 Gulf War, before officially reaching operational status. Navy A-6E and F/A-18 aircraft launched seven missiles during the conflict and scored four direct hits on targets. The missiles were controlled by accompanying A-7E Corsair or F/A-18 aircraft fitted with AAW-9 data-link pods. That pod was unreliable, but the missile was still considered to be highly successful against heavily defended targets. The improved AWW-13 pod is now becoming available for SLAM guidance.

Status: Operational; in production, although none was authorized in fiscal 1992. IOC in 1991. Manufactured by McDonnell Douglas Missile Systems Co., St. Charles, Mo.

Weight:	1,389 lbs (630 kg)
Length:	14 ft 9 in (4.5 m)
Span:	3 ft (0.9 m)
Diameter:	13½ in (343 mm)
Propulsion:	turbofan
Range:	60+ n.miles (111+ km)
Guidance:	inertial + command + infrared
Warhead:	485 lbs (220 kg) high explosive
Platforms:	*aircraft* F/A-18
	A-6E

SPARROW III AIM-7

The Sparrow is an all-weather, medium-range AAM. It has been adopted for surface launch in the Sea Sparrow variants for use in the anti-ship missile defense role (see page 492). The weapon had minimal use in air-to-air engagements until the 1991 Persian Gulf War when it was credited with 60 percent of the air-to-air kills (see below).

The AIM-7E/F/M variants are in wide U.S. Marine and Navy service, although production of those variants has ended. The AIM-7M combines the heavy warhead and large rocket motor introduced in the AIM-7F with an advanced monopulse seeker, better look-down shoot-down capability, and improved resistance to ECM. The early, expanding continuous-rod warhead of these missiles has been replaced by a fragmentation warhead. The AIM-7P variant is now under development by Raytheon. Missile speed is reportedly in excess of Mach 4.

The missile has been produced for U.S. and foreign air forces. In addition to the two U.S. producers, the Sparrow is manufactured in Japan by Mitsubishi. The data given below are for the AIM-7M model.

Operational: The Sparrow saw limited use in the Vietnam War; however, in the 1991 Gulf War it was used in 26 of the 44 air-to-air kills against Iraqi aircraft, although only once by naval aircraft—on 17 January 1991 an Iraqi MiG-21 was shot down by a Sidewinder from a Navy F/A-18C Hornet. (In the same engagement another F/A-18C used a Sparrow to kill a second MiG-21; U.S. Air Force F-15C Eagles used Sidewinders to shoot down 22 high-performance Iraqi aircraft and 3 helicopters.)[10]

Status: Operational. IOC in 1958; AIM-7F in 1976; AIM-7M in 1983. Manufactured by Raytheon and General Dynamics/Pomona.

10. In addition to the 26 Sparrow and 12 Sidewinder air-to-air kills, one Iraqi MiG-29 crashed while maneuvering to escape a USAF F-15C, an Iraqi Mirage F1 was forced to crash by a USAF F-15C, and a PC-9 was forced to crash by a USAF EF-111A; a hovering helicopter was destroyed by a GBU-10 guided bomb launched by an F-15E, and two helicopters were shot down by USAF A-10 Thunderbolt (Warthog) attack aircraft using 30-mm GAU-8 Gatling guns for a total of 44 air-to-air kills in the Gulf War.

An F/A-18 Hornet launches a SLAM missile. The weapon, derived from the Harpoon, was in development when the Gulf War began; reportedly, seven missiles were used with great effectiveness in that war. (McDonnell Douglas)

Weight:	500 lbs (226.8 kg)
Length:	12 ft (3.7 m)
Span:	3 ft 4 in (1.1 m)
Diameter:	8 in (203 mm)
Propulsion:	solid-propellant rocket
Range:	approx. 30 n.miles (55.5 km)
Guidance:	semi-active radar homing
Warhead:	88 lbs (40 kg) high explosive
Platforms:	*aircraft* F-14
	F/A-18

Sparrow III launched by an F-4 Phantom. The Sparrow scored 26 of the 38 air-to-air missile kills in the Gulf War. (U.S. Navy)

Sparrow III being fitted to an F-14A Tomcat. (U.S. Navy)

STANDARD-ER SM-2 RIM-67B

The ER SM-2 version of the Standard has extended range, mid-course guidance, an inertial reference system, and improved resistance to electronic countermeasures compared to earlier missiles (the range of the ER SM-2 is more than twice that of the MR SM-2 missile). This is a two-stage missile that can reach an altitude of approximately 80,000 feet (24,390 m). The production Block IV variant beginning in fiscal 1991 is 60 percent a "new" missile compared to earlier blocks; it has a new booster rocket motor 22 inches (0.56 m) in diameter plus improvements to guidance, controls, and airframe. This missile is intended specifically for the Mk 41 VLS and will have enhanced altitude and range performance.

The development of a missile with the W81 nuclear warhead—designated SM-2(N)—was approved in 1979, but cancelled in 1985. It was to have replaced the Terrier BTN missile.

Production of the less-capable ER SM-1 missile ended in 1974.

Standard missiles are fitted in 39 guided missile destroyers and frigates of Australia, Canada, France, Germany, Italy, Japan, the Netherlands, Spain, and Taiwan.

Status: Operational; in production, with 525 Standard missiles of all versions authorized in fiscal 1992. IOC in 1981. The final Block II and the first Block III missiles were ordered in fiscal 1988. Manufactured by General Dynamics/Pomona.

Weight:	2,900 lbs (1,315 kg)
Length:	26 ft 2 in (7.9 m)
Span:	5 ft 3 in (1.6 m)
Diameter:	13½ in (342 mm)
Propulsion:	solid-propellant rocket + solid-propellant booster
Range:	75–90 n.miles (139–167 km)
Guidance:	inertial with semi-active radar homing
Warhead:	high explosive
Platforms:	*cruisers* CGN 9
	CG 16
	CG 26
	CGN 35
	destroyers DDG 993
	DDG 37

Standard-ER missiles are loaded onto a Mk 10 launcher on the destroyer FARRAGUT (DDG 37). Except for the prototype GYATT (DDG 1), all other U.S. destroyer classes had the Tartar/Standard-MR missile system. The angled fittings on the deck are for jettisoning dud missiles. (Giorgio Arra)

STANDARD-MR SM-2 RIM-66C

This missile initially had increased range over the SM-1 MR (about equal to the range of the early MR SM-2 missiles) as well as the addition of mid-course guidance and enhanced resistance to electronic countermeasures. It is intended specifically for use on Aegis missile ships.

The traditional expanding, continuous-rod warheads of the Standard missiles have now been succeeded by controlled fragmentation warheads (entering production in fiscal 1983).

Status: Operational; in production. IOC in 1981. The final Block II and the first Block III missiles were ordered in fiscal 1988; the latter missiles (MR and ER variants) incorporate low-altitude intercept enhancements to defend against cruise missile attacks. Manufactured by General Dynamics/Pomona and Raytheon.

Weight:	1,400 lbs (635 kg)
Length:	14 ft (4.3 m)
Span:	3 ft 6 in (1.1 m)
Diameter:	13½ in (342 mm)
Propulsion:	solid-propellant rocket
Range:	approx. 40 n.miles (74 km) in early missiles; up to 90 n.miles (167 km) in later missiles
Guidance:	semi-active radar homing
Warhead:	high explosive
Platforms:	*cruisers* CGN 38
	CG 47
	destroyers DDG 51

A Standard-MR missile is launched from the vertical-launch system of a TICONDEROGA (CG 47)-class cruiser. Continued improvements to the single-stage Standard-MR missiles have increased their range far beyond the original Tartar weapon. (FMC)

Standard-MR missile on the Mk 13 launcher of the frigate STEPHEN W. GROVES (FFG 29). Missiles are loaded with the launcher in the vertical position, sliding up from the circular magazine beneath the launcher. (Giorgio Arra)

STANDARD-MR SM-1 RIM-66B

The Standard series of surface-to-air missiles was developed as replacement for the 3-T missiles—the Talos, Terrier, and Tartar that went to sea in the 1950s. Initially the MR (Medium Range) missiles were to replace the Tartar and the ER (Extended Range) missiles the Terrier and Talos. However, various modifications and production blocks (with varying characteristics) of Standard missiles have blurred model distinctions.

The SM-1 MR is the oldest Standard type remaining in service, being a single-stage, relatively short-range weapon.

Status: Operational. IOC in 1970. Manufactured by General Dynamics/Pomona.

Weight:	1,100 lbs (499 kg)
Length:	14 ft 8 in (4.5 m)
Span:	3 ft 6 in (1.1 m)
Diameter:	13½ in (342 mm)
Propulsion:	solid-propellant rocket
Range:	25 n.miles
Guidance:	semi-active radar homing
Warhead:	high explosive
Platforms:	*cruisers* CGN 36
	destroyers DDG 2
	frigates FFG 7

STANDARD SM-3

A Standard SM-3 missile was under consideration in the 1980s to provide a very long range missile for intercepting Soviet stand-off jamming aircraft and possibly missile-carrying aircraft at ranges greater than possible with the SM-2 ER. This is similar to the concept of the LRDMM (see above); a concept called Thor was similar.

STANDARD-ARM AGM-78

This was an Anti-Radiation (radar) Missile (ARM) adopted from the Standard RIM-66A surface-to-air missile. It was also employed briefly by the U.S. Navy as an interim surface-to-surface missile pending availability of the Harpoon. In the mid-1980s the Standard-ARM was replaced by the HARM as an air-launched weapon.

STINGER   FIM-92

The Stinger is an advanced, shoulder-held surface-to-air missile that resembles the World War II–era bazooka rocket launcher. The missile was placed aboard several U.S. naval ships in the eastern Mediterranean beginning in the winter of 1983–1984 in reaction to threatened terrorist attacks against U.S. ships. (The Russian Navy similarly uses the shoulder-held SA-7 Grail missile, formerly Strela, in various ships.)

Originally designated Redeye II, the missile is tube-launched with four pop-out vanes at the front and four folding fins at the rear.

The missile is replacing the Redeye in U.S. service. An improved Stinger-POST (Passive Optical Seeker Technique), with increased resistance to countermeasures, entered production in fiscal 1984 but was soon succeeded by the Stinger-RMP (Reprogrammable Microprocessor) version. Missile speed is Mach 1.7.

Operational: British ground forces scored successes with the missile in the 1982 war in the Falklands.

Status: Operational; in production (scheduled to end in the mid-1990s). IOC in 1981 (U.S. Army); Stinger-POST in 1987; Stinger-RMP in 1988. The Stinger is used by the U.S. Marine Corps, Army, and Air Force as well as by at least seven other countries. Manufactured by General Dynamics/Pomona.

Weight:	30 lbs (13.6 kg)
Length:	5 ft (1.5 m)
Span:	8 in (203 mm)
Diameter:	2¾ in (527 mm)
Propulsion:	solid-propellant rocket
Range:	approx. 3 n.miles (5.6 km); effective range is probably less
Guidance:	infrared homing
Warhead:	high-explosive fragmentation
Platforms:	various ships

Stinger missile in flight with fins extended. (U.S. Army)

Stinger shoulder-fired missile. (U.S. Army)

SUBROC   UUM-44A

The SUBROC (Submarine Rocket) was a rocket-propelled nuclear depth bomb that could be launched from standard 21-inch submarine torpedo tubes. The weapon was analog and hence not compatible with U.S. attack submarines that have the Mk 117 digital fire control system. Thus, only about 25 submarines of the PERMIT (SSN 594) and later classes fitted with the Mk 113 fire control system carried the weapon. The missile, which became operational in 1964, was taken out of Navy service in 1989. (The Sea Lance ASW stand-off weapon was to have replaced the SUBROC, with alternative nuclear or conventional warheads, but in the event the nuclear variant is no longer planned for development.)

See 14th Edition/pages 481–482 for SUBROC characteristics.

TACIT RAINBOW   AGM-136

Tacit Rainbow was a "loitering" anti-radar missile being developed for multi-service use. The missile, with a turbofan engine, was to have been launched from aircraft or ground vehicles toward an enemy radar emission; the missile was to "loiter" in flight if the radar was switched off (or to a non-detectable frequency) and resume its attack when the radar was again detected.

Tacit Rainbow was to be 8¼ feet (2.5 m) long, be turbofan powered, have a range of some 540 n.miles (1,000 km), and carry a high-explosive warhead.

The missile was being developed by Northrop. It was cancelled in 1991.

A test variant of the Tacit Rainbow missile. This was to have been a "loitering" anti-radar missile, capable of remaining aloft for relatively long periods to counter intermittent shutdowns of enemy radars. (Department of Defense)

TARTAR   RIM-24

The Tartar was the U.S. Navy's first surface-to-air missile developed specifically for use on destroyers and smaller warships. It was one of the 3-T missiles which, along with the now-discarded Terrier and Talos, evolved from the Bumblebee Program of World War II. U.S. ships previously armed with the Tartar have been rearmed with the Standard MR-series missiles.

See 13th Edition/page 451 for characteristics.

TERRIER   RIM-2

The Terrier was the first of the 3-T missiles to enter service. The missile entered the fleet in 1955 with the nuclear BTN (Beam-riding, Terrier, Nuclear) version becoming operational in 1962. The Terrier was subsequently replaced by the Standard-series missiles and by the early 1980s the Terrier was phased out of service in favor of the U.S. fleet, except that the Navy retained a limited number of the BTN version until 1989. The Terrier and larger Talos were the only U.S. Navy SAMs with nuclear warheads; no replacement was planned following cancellation of a nuclear version of the Standard SM-2.

The Terrier was intended for installation in cruisers (including the DLG/DLGN-type frigates) and was additionally fitted in two aircraft carriers, the KITTY HAWK (CV 63) and CONSTELLATION (CV 64), and—for evaluation—one destroyer, the GYATT (DDG 1, ex-DD 712). Ten former frigates of the FARRAGUT (DLG 6) class, reclassified as destroyers (DDG 37) in 1974, also carried the Terrier.

The Dutch and Italian navies also used the Terrier.

See 14th Edition/page 482 for Terrier characteristics.

TOMAHAWK   BGM-109

The Tomahawk is a long-range cruise missile developed for both surface and submarine launch against both surface ship and land targets. It was initially known as the Sea-Launched Cruise Missile (SLCM), but in 1979 the Navy began using the terms Tomahawk Land-Attack Missile (TLAM) and Tomahawk Anti-Ship Missile (TASM) to distinguish the principal variants.

The missile is fitted in Armored Box Launchers (ABL) on four battleships, five cruisers, and seven SPRUANCE-class destroyers; it is carried in the Mk 41 VLS of later TICONDEROGA-class cruisers, BURKE-class destroyers, and 24 SPRUANCES. It can also be fired from 21-inch submarine torpedo tubes and, in the later LOS ANGELES class, from vertical launch tubes.

An air-launched Tomahawk competed unsuccessfully with the Boeing Air-Launched Cruise Missile (ALCM) for use on B-52 strategic bombers. The Ground-Launched Cruise Missile (GLCM) version, however, was selected as a theater nuclear weapon for deployment in Western Europe under Air Force control, but those weapons were discarded under the Intermediate-range Nuclear Forces (INF) treaty of 1987 between the Soviet Union and United States.

The Block III version now in production features a smaller but more lethal warhead with an extended range permitted by additional fuel; these missiles also have a Global Positioning System (GPS) receiver for improved accuracy and time-of-arrival control to permit coordinated missile or aircraft and missile strikes. That variant also has a Williams 402 turbofan engine with a 19 percent increase in thrust and a 2 percent decrease in fuel consumption. The warhead will be reduced to 700 pounds (320 kg) but will have the same destructive power as the BGM-109C (PBXN-107 explosive).

The Navy variants are:

Mode	Type	Warhead
BGM-109A	TLAM-N	nuclear (W80 warhead)
BGM-109B	TASM	conventional (1,000-lb Bullpup)
BGM-109C	TLAM-C	conventional (1,000-lb Bullpup)
BGM-109D	TLAM-D	conventional (bomblets)

A Tomahawk in flight, showing the stub wings, air scoop for the turbofan engine, and tail fins. (U.S. Navy)

Tomahawk TASM about to strike a target ship. The Tomahawk carries a 1,000-pound conventional warhead in this role, twice the size of the U.S. Harpoon warhead and three times the size of the French Exocet missile warhead. (U.S. Navy)

The TLAM-D dispenses 168 bomblets weighing 3.4 pounds (1.5 kg) each in packets of 24; these submunitions can be armor-piercing, fragmentation, or incendiary.

In April 1992 it was revealed that a warhead containing carbon-fiber spools had also been developed for the Tomahawk. Several of the 116 missiles fired on the first day of the Gulf War carried the still-experimental warheads that, upon detonation, disrupted Iraqi electric power, helping to blind air-defense and command and control activities.

The warhead, developed under a highly classified "black" program, showered outdoor switching and transformer areas of electric generating plants with thousands of rolls of very fine carbon fibers. When released by the Tomahawks, the fiber spools unwound in the wind, the fibers then dropping onto power lines and transformers, causing massive short circuits but not permanent damage. Reportedly, each Tomahawk could spread thousands of the mini-spools over a single target when the warhead detonated to spread the spools. (They were not "dispensed" as are the BLU-97 bomblets; see below.)

General Dynamics has proposed an ASW variant of the Tomahawk as an alternative to the Sea Lance project for both surface ship and submarine use. This variant would carry several sonobuoys, a Mk 46 or Mk 50 torpedo, and an on-board acoustic processor. (Being developed in conjunction with Magnavox and Hazeltine.)

Operational: The MERRILL (DD 976) was fitted with the first Tomahawk installation in October 1982 for at-sea evaluation; the battleship NEW JERSEY (BB 62) was the second ship, receiving the Tomahawk in March 1983. The GUITARRO (SSN 665) was the first submarine armed with Tomahawk.

U.S. Navy surface ships and submarines fired 288 land-attack variants of the Tomahawk during Operation Desert Storm in January–February 1991; of those, 116 were launched during the first 24 hours of the air war. Battleships, cruisers, and destroyers launched 276 of the missiles, and submarines launched 12 (see individual ship

During the Gulf War two U.S. attack submarines fired a total of 12 Tomahawk missiles against targets in Iraq. This series shows a TLAM launch from the PITTSBURGH (SSN 720) photographed through a periscope; clockwise from upper left: A missile emerges from the water; the missile clears the water; the fins, wings, and air scoop begin to deploy; and the missile streaks toward its target. (U.S. Navy)

classes for launching ships and number fired); the first Tomahawk launch of the Gulf War was from the cruiser SAN JACINTO (CG 56), operating in the Red Sea, that launch occurring early on the morning of 17 January 1991. Tomahawks were also launched against targets in Iraq from the eastern Mediterranean and Persian Gulf.

Of the 288 missiles, 226 were launched in daylight attacks and 56 at night. Tomahawks were the only weapons used for daytime attacks against Baghdad during the entire campaign. Of the 288 missiles that were launched, 282 transitioned to a cruise profile for a successful launch rate of 98 percent. Weather conditions in the area never precluded a Tomahawk launch.

Tomahawks were employed to both destroy or specifically damage targets (in addition to the microwave warhead being used for electronic disruption activities). The TLAM-D missiles carried BLU-97 bomblets and were able to attack multiple targets; for example, one submarine-launched TLAM-D struck three separate targets and then performed a terminal dive to strike a fourth target.

According to the official Department of Defense report on the Gulf War, the Tomahawk's "demonstrated accuracy was consistent with results from pre-combat testing. The observed accuracy of TLAM, for which unambiguous target imagery is available, met or exceeded the accuracy mission planners predicted."

During the conflict an estimated 477 TLAMs were available in theater.

Status: Operational; in production, with 236 missiles authorized in fiscal 1992. IOC TASM in surface ships in 1982; TASM in submarines in 1983; TLAM in surface ships in 1984; and TLAM-N in 1987. Block III missile IOC in 1993. More than 3,000 missiles have been delivered to the Navy with an inventory goal of 4,000. Manufactured by General Dynamics/Convair of San Diego, Calif., and McDonnell Douglas Missile Systems Co., St. Louis, Mo.

Weight:	2,650 lbs (1,202 kg) + 550-lb (250-kg) booster + 1,000-lb (454-kg) capsule for submarine launch
Length:	18 ft 2 in (5.55 m) for TASM + 2 ft (0.6 m) booster
Span:	8 ft 8 in (2.6 m)
Diameter:	21 in (533 mm)
Propulsion:	turbofan (Williams International 400) + solid-propellant booster
Range:	TASM 250+ n.miles (463+ km)
	TLAM 700 n.miles (1,296 km)
	TLAM-N 1,200+ n.miles
Guidance:	active radar homing in TASM (same as Harpoon SSM) inertial and TERCOM (Terrain Contour Matching) in TLAM
Warhead:	1,000 lbs (454 kg) high explosive in TASM and TLAM; nuclear (W80) in TLAM(N)
Platforms:	*attack submarines* SSN 637
	SSN 688
	SSN 21
	battleships BB 61
	cruisers CGN 9
	CGN 38
	CG 52–73
	destroyers DDG 51
	DD 963

TOW MGM-71

The TOW—for Tube-launched, Optically tracked, Wire-guided—is an anti-tank missile fired from Army and Marine Corps helicopters as well as from ground and vehicle mounts.

Improved versions, designated Improved TOW (ITOW) and TOW2/2B, have an upgraded warhead and an upgraded warhead plus higher impulse motor, respectively. The missile has a high subsonic speed.

Marine SeaCobra helicopters carry the missile.

Status: Operational; in production. IOC in 1970. The Marine Corps has procured more than 30,000 TOWs. Manufactured by Hughes Aircraft Co., Tucson, Ariz., and Emerson Electric.

Weight:	54 lbs (24.5 kg)
Length:	3 ft 8 in (1.1 m)
Span:	3 ft 9 in (1.1 m)
Diameter:	6 in (152 mm)
Propulsion:	solid-fuel rocket + solid-fuel booster
Range:	1.5 n.miles (2.8 km); 2 n.miles (3.7 km) for TOW 2
Guidance:	optical/wire
Warhead:	8 lbs (3.6 kg) high explosive (shaped charge)
Platforms:	*helicopters* AH-1W

TOW missiles, from left: the basic TOW, Improved TOW, and TOW2. The TOW and I-TOW have 5-inch (127-mm)-diameter warheads; the TOW2 has a 6-inch (152-mm)-warhead. The spikes provide improved penetration of armor. (Hughes)

Marines fire a TOW anti-tank missile from a jeep-mounted launcher. Note the control wires; the tail fins have not yet fully extended. (U.S. Marine Corps)

A TOW2 anti-tank missile in flight. Successive variants of the TOW have increased accuracy and armor penetration. The latter has become increasingly difficult because of new tank armoring techniques. (Hughes)

TRIDENT D-5 UGM-133A

The longer-range and more accurate D-5 version of the Trident missile was approved for development by the Secretary of Defense in October 1981 and fitted in the ninth and subsequent submarines of the OHIO (SSBN 726) class. The first eight submarines of that class were to be retrofitted to fire the D-5 missile, but those plans were cancelled in 1991 because of fiscal considerations. (Submarines configured to fire the D-5 missile cannot launch the C-4 missile.)

The D-5 can carry 75 percent more payload than the C-4; however, its primary attribute is increased accuracy, approximately equivalent to that of the land-based MX or Peacekeeper ICBM. The D-5 missile carries eight warheads.

Status: Operational; in production, with 49 missiles authorized in fiscal 1992. The first Trident D-5 missiles were procured in fiscal 1987. The first D-5 test flight from Cape Canaveral on 21 March 1989 was a failure, as was the third launch on 15 August 1989. (The failures were due to a design flaw caused by the water pressure on the missiles' nozzles, which caused them to tumble after leaving the water.) The second, fourth, and later launches were successful. The first submarine-launch occurred on 22 March 1989 from the TENNESSEE (SSBN 734); that test launch failed.

President Bush cancelled production of the W88 warhead on 28 January 1992. Production had already been suspended some two years earlier because of concerns about safety at the plant producing the plutonium triggers for the weapon. Unofficial estimates indicate that about 400 W88 warheads were produced by 1990. Accordingly, the W76 warhead is being fitted in the D-5 missile.

The missile became operational with the deployment of the TENNESSEE on deterrent patrol in March 1990. Manufactured by Lockheed Missiles and Space Co., Sunnyvale, Calif.

Weight:	approx. 130,000 lbs (58,968 kg)
Length:	44 ft (13.4 m)
Span:	(ballistic)
Diameter:	83 in (2.1 m)
Propulsion:	3-stage solid-propellant rocket
Range:	approx. 4,000 n.miles (7,400 km)
Guidance:	inertial
Warhead:	nuclear Mk 5 with 8 W88 MIRVs (approx. 300–475 KT each); see text
Platforms:	*submarines* SSBN 734–743

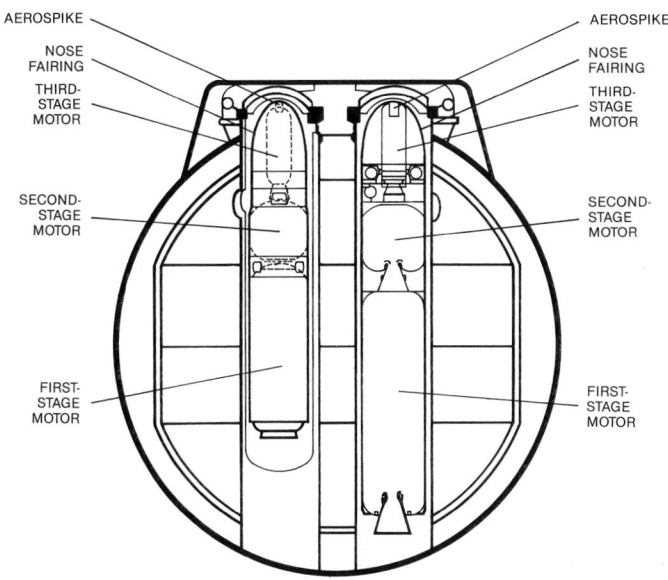

Comparison of the Trident C-4 (left) and Trident D-5 shown in cross section of an OHIO-class submarine.

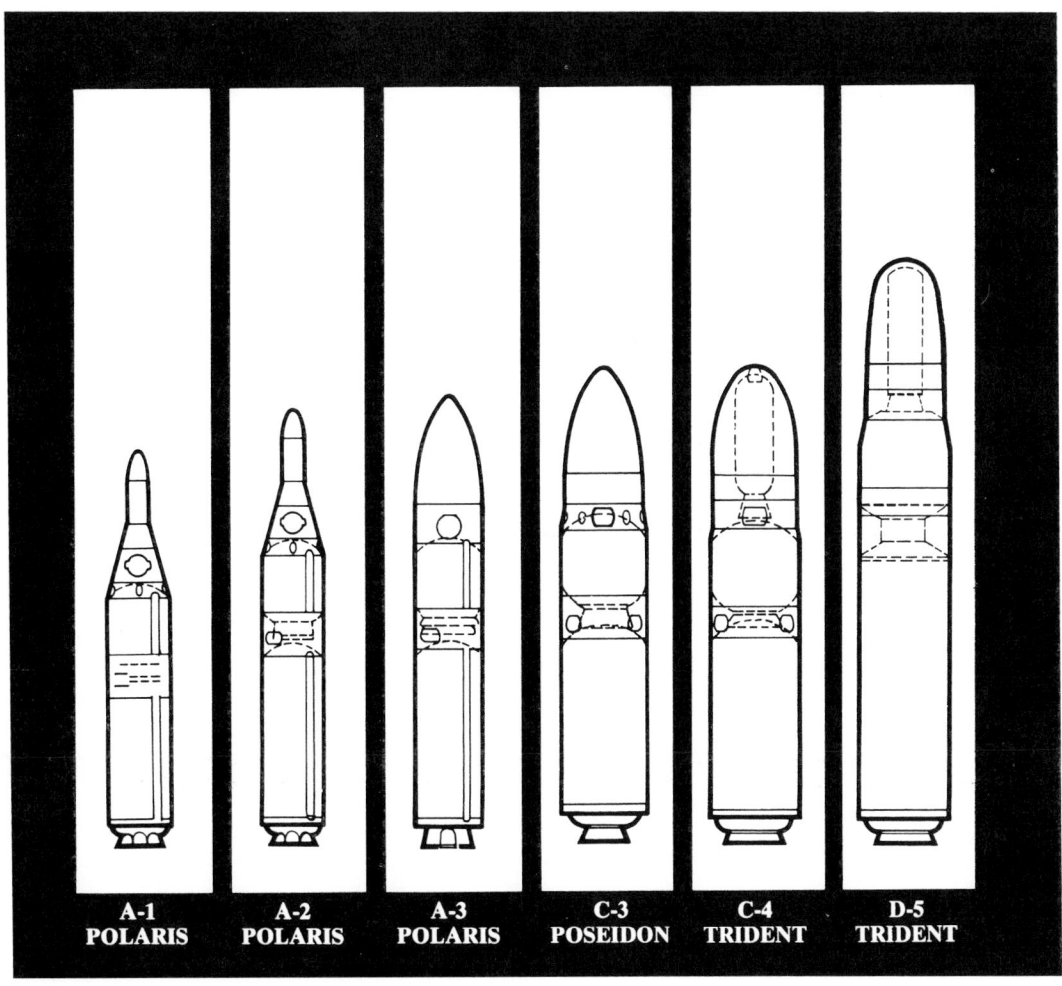

U.S. Submarine-launched ballistic missiles.

A Trident D-5 SLBM is test-launched from Cape Canaveral. In flight, an aerospike will extend from the missile's nose. Plans to arm all 18 of the OHIO-class submarines with the D-5 missile have been cancelled. (Department of Defense)

TRIDENT C-4 UGM-96

The Trident I SLBM evolved from the Department of Defense STRAT-X study of the late 1960s that proposed an advanced SLBM with a range of 6,000 n.miles (11,112 km) to be carried in a new class of submarine. Subsequently, the Navy proposed a two-phase program: the Trident C-4 (also called Trident I) based on an Extended-range Poseidon (EXPO) missile with a range of some 4,000 n.miles (7,400 km), and the later Trident D-5 (II) to be developed at a later date with the longer range.

The C-4 missile has a MIRV warhead with eight Mk 4 independently targeted reentry vehicles. It has double the yield and twice the accuracy of the previous Poseidon C-3 missile. The missile carries the Mk 4 re-entry body; it was designed to alternatively carry the Mk 500 Evader Maneuvering Reentry Vehicle (MaRV) warhead; this was designed to overcome ballistic missile defenses and is not being developed. The C-3 is a three-stage missile. After it reaches a certain altitude an aerospike extends from the nose. This spike cuts the friction of the air flowing past the missile, extending its range by about 300 n.miles (556 km).

Twelve LAFAYETTE-class submarines were refitted with the Trident missile, and the first eight of the OHIO-class submarines were armed with the missile. This missile is being procured by the Royal Navy for a new class of submarines to succeed that country's four Polaris-missile submarines of the RESOLUTION class.

Status: Operational. The last Trident C-4 missiles were procured in fiscal 1984. IOC in 1979. Manufactured by Lockheed Missiles and Space Co.

Trident C-4 engine ignites after the missile clears the water in a test launch from the submarine MICHIGAN (SSBN 727). (U.S. Navy)

Weight:	73,000 lbs (33,113 kg)
Length:	34 ft (10.4 m)
Span:	(ballistic)
Diameter:	74 in (1.9 m)
Propulsion:	3-stage solid-propellant rocket
Range:	approx. 4,000 n.miles (7,400 km)
Guidance:	inertial
Warhead:	nuclear Mk 4 with 8 W76 MIRVs (approx. 100 KT each)
Platforms:	*submarines* SSBN 616 (12 units)
	SSBN 726-733

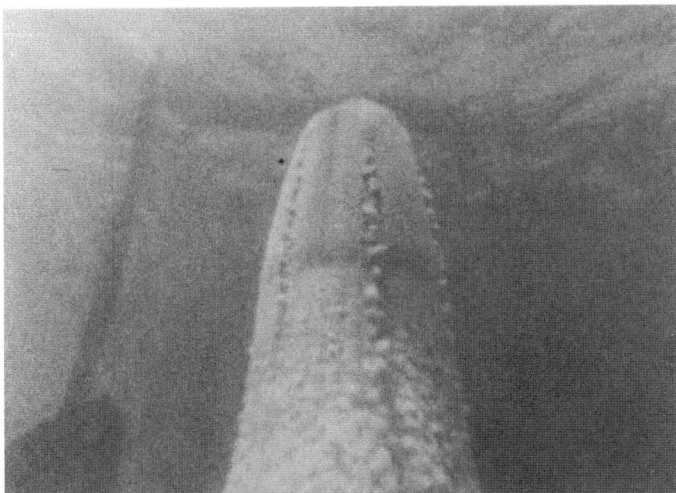

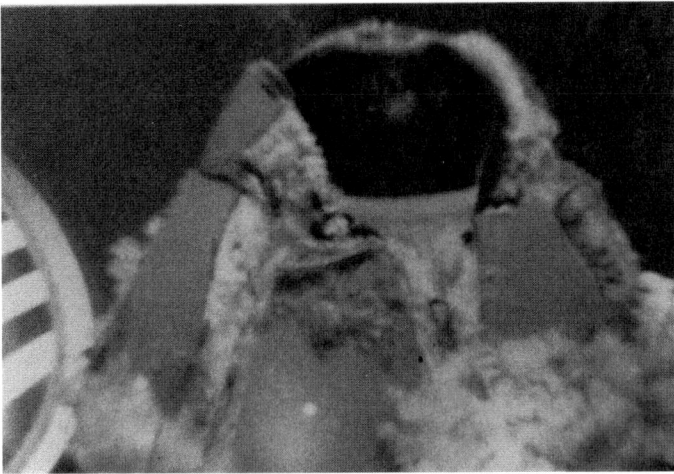

Underwater launch sequence of a Trident C-4 missile. (Courtesy Los Alamos National Laboratory)

TRI-SERVICE STANDOFF ATTACK MISSILE (TSSAM) AGM-137

Formerly a highly classified "black" program, the TSSAM was revealed by the Department of Defense in June 1991, in part to help justify procurement of the B-2 "stealth" bomber. In development since 1986, the low-observable (stealth) missile is intended to provide precision guidance with a conventional warhead to ranges of more than 100 n.miles (185 km). Apparently a variety of warheads will be available, i.e., penetrating, multiple submunitions, and conventional high explosive.

The missile will be compatible with the Army–Marine Corps Multiple Launch Rocket System (MLRS); the Air Force B-2, B-52, and F-16 Fighting Falcon aircraft; and Navy F/A-18 Hornet and A-6E Intruder aircraft as well as, presumably, the Navy AX aircraft, if built.

In June 1991 the Department of Defense estimated a TSSAM procurement of 8,650 missiles for all services at a cost of $15.1 *billion* or an average of $1.7 million, including research, tooling, support, etc.

Status: In development. The manufacturers are Northrop and Boeing.

VERTICAL-LAUNCH ASROC (VLA) RUM-139A

This is a short-range ASW missile, the successor to the ASROC for surface ship use. It was to be fitted in ships with the Mk 41 VLS—the later TICONDEROGA-class cruisers, ARLEIGH BURKE-class destroyers, and 24 of the SPRUANCE-class destroyers. The future of the missile is questionable, however, because of poor performance in tests and opposition from the Office of the Secretary of Defense.

The VLA has more than double the basic ASROC range. The VLA would also be suitable for launch from modified ASROC launchers. The VLA will carry the Mk 46 Mod 5 torpedo as warhead; in January 1992 the Department of Defense cancelled the Mk 50 torpedo as a VLA warhead.

The Navy had originally sought to combine the replacement for ASROC and SUBROC in a single weapon. This proved too difficult, however, and the VLA was to be surface launched and the Sea Lance ASW stand-off weapon submarine launched. However, in the late 1980s the VLA was labeled as an interim weapon (with only 300 to be produced) while an attempt was again made to develop the Sea Lance as a common surface/submarine ASW weapon.

Procurement began with the fiscal 1987 budget authorization.

Status: In development. Congress has approved a one-time procurement of 300 missiles in fiscal years 1987 and 1989; however, the Office of the Secretary of Defense has prohibited the Navy from proceeding with the procurement until the VLA successfully passes all tests (except for test missiles, which are being procured; up to 30 VLA test launches were planned for 1992.) Manufactured by Loral Corp.

Weight:	1,409 lbs (634 kg)
Length:	16 ft (4.9 m)
Span:	27⅖ in (0.7 m)
Diameter:	14 in (356 mm)
Propulsion:	solid-propellant rocket
Range:	approx. 15 n.miles (27.8 km)
Guidance:	ballistic; terminal acoustic homing with Mk 46 torpedo
Warhead:	Mk 46 torpedo
Platforms:	*cruisers* planned for CG 52–73
	destroyers planned for DD 963 (24 ships)
	DDG 51

Test launch of a Vertical-Launch ASROC (VLA) from the destroyer ELLIOT (DD 967). This long-delayed weapon will probably never be acquired in large numbers; rather, manned helicopters and—possibly future drones—will provide U.S. warships with a stand-off ASW attack weapon. (Loral)

VLA rising from the deck of the ELLIOT; the exhaust is being vented at left. Vertical-launch provides many advantages over conventional launchers; note that the ELLIOT retains her full ASW capability with the installation of a 61-cell VLS. (Loral)

WALLEYE II AGM-62

The Walleye is an unpowered glide bomb. However, it is listed in the missile designation series and is operationally considered as such against surface ships and hardened ground targets. Although being phased out of service, it was employed in the Gulf War with 133 being launched by Navy A-7E Corsair aircraft. With the demise of that aircraft after the Gulf War the missile is no longer in naval service.

The Navy–Marine Corps used the Walleye only with conventional warheads; the Air Force additionally had a nuclear version; it was also used by the Israeli Air Force.

Status: IOC 1967; phased out of naval service in 1991.

See 14th Edition/pages 488–489 for characteristics.

NUCLEAR WEAPONS

The U.S. Navy maintains nuclear weapons at sea in strategic missile submarines (SSBN). Following the unilateral U.S. nuclear arms reduction policy announced by President George Bush on 27 September 1991, all tactical nuclear weapons have been removed from Navy ships, while all SSBNs armed with the Poseidon missile have been disarmed. This leaves Trident missiles in the OHIO and LAFAYETTE classes as the only U.S. nuclear weapons at sea.

At the time of President Bush's statement, the Navy had the following nuclear weapons in service.

Strategic missiles: 176 Poseidon C-3 in 11 SSBNs
192 Trident C-4 in 12 SSBNs (LAFAYETTE class)
192 Trident C-4 in 8 SSBNs (OHIO class)
96 Trident D-5 in 4 SSBNs (OHIO class)

All of these submarines except for the OHIO class are being decommissioned; by the year 2000 the SSBN force is to consist of 18 submarines with 432 Trident missiles (D-4 and D-5).

Land-attack missiles: approx. 100 Tomahawk TLAM-N missiles in attack submarines, cruisers, and destroyers; all to be placed in storage ashore. The Navy's inventory goal for TLAM-N missiles prior to the President's statement was reported as 637, with 399 already funded through fiscal 1991; no additional missiles will be procured.

Bombs: Some 400 nuclear strike bombs (B57 and B61) and anti-submarine depth bombs (B57) were embarked in aircraft carriers. All are being withdrawn; most of the B61s will be placed in storage and the B57s eliminated.

Additional B57 weapons were at shore bases for use by P-3 Orion maritime patrol aircraft; these weapons will be eliminated.

Development of the advanced B90 dual-purpose bomb has been halted.

All previous naval nuclear weapons were earlier withdrawn from service. With cancellation of the B90 bomb, no nuclear weapons are under development for naval use.

During the Cold War period nuclear weapons provided three major offensive advantages over conventional weapons in war at sea. First, whereas multiple hits with high-explosive weapons would probably be required to sink a cruiser or aircraft carrier, a single nuclear weapon, of even small size, would suffice. Second, defense against nuclear weapons would require a 100 percent effectiveness since a single penetrating missile or "leaker" could destroy the target. And, third, less accuracy is required for a nuclear weapon to be effective.

In the defensive AAW role the nuclear-armed defensive missile could deter concentrated air attacks against U.S. ships as nuclear bursts might force attacking bombers to separate to greater distances, reducing the concentration of their missiles and thus enabling conventional defending systems to have a greater effectiveness. In ASW operations a nuclear weapon could compensate for the target submarine's area of uncertainty or the limited effectiveness of conventional ASW weapons. This could be especially true against high-speed and deep-diving submarines, which may give the ASW

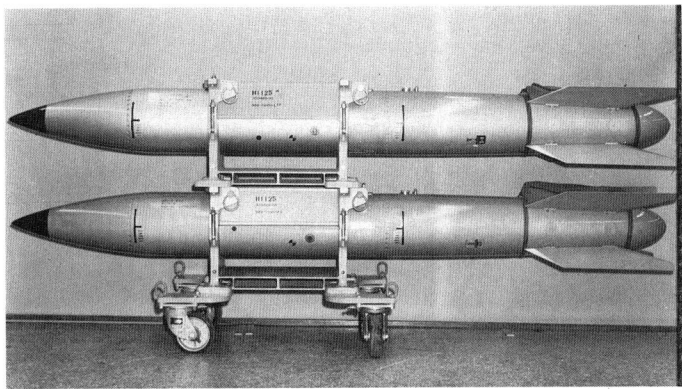

A pair of B61 nuclear bombs on a dolly. All B61s as well as other tactical and theater nuclear weapons have been removed from Navy ships and air squadrons; most B61 bombs are retained in storage depots ashore. (Los Alamos National Laboratory)

unit only a single, brief attack opportunity before the enemy submarine is beyond attack range, or has itself launched an attack.

Another consideration is the potential use of high-altitude bursts of nuclear weapons to create Electromagnetic Pulse (EMP) effects that would severely degrade electronic systems of ships and aircraft over large ocean areas. Underwater nuclear bursts could similarly degrade sonar effectiveness, creating a condition known as "blue out" over some acoustic frequencies.

Finally, being able to use tactical nuclear weapons would ease magazine constraints in surface warships and, especially, submarines. For example, if a submarine carries a weapons load of 15 percent nuclear and 85 percent conventional, with the use of conventional weapons only part of its weapons load is usable while in a nuclear situation all would be available. A related development was the Insertable Nuclear Component (INC), which could permit a conventional weapon, such as a Mk 48 torpedo, to be employed with a conventional warhead or, with a small INC being inserted, as a tactical nuclear weapon with the explosive force of one kiloton or less.[11]

The Soviet Navy had emphasized the use of nuclear weapons at sea in virtually all aspects of naval operations.[12] (In addition, to stress the offensive aspects of nuclear war at sea, Russian warships down to missile craft of the Osa class are configured to operate in a nuclear environment with survivability features that are not now found in any U.S. surface combatants.)

11. See John J. Engelhardt, "The Implications of Sub-kiloton Nuclear Torpedoes," U.S. Naval Institute *Proceedings* (August 1987), pp. 102–104, and Norman Polmar and Donald M. Kerr, "Nuclear Torpedoes," U.S. Naval Institute *Proceedings* (August 1986), pp. 62–68.
12. See Norman Polmar, *Guide to the Soviet Navy,* 5th ed. (Annapolis, Md.: Naval Institute Press, 1991), p. 393; and "The Soviet Navy: Nuclear War at Sea," *Proceedings* (July 1986), pp. 112–113.

TORPEDOES

The U.S. Navy has two series of torpedoes in service: the lightweight Mk 46 used by aircraft and surface ships, and in the CAPTOR mine; and the heavy-weight Mk 48 carried in all submarines. Both torpedoes are intended primarily for the anti-submarine role, although the Mk 48 can be used against surface ships.

The improved Mk 50 torpedo (formerly known as ALWT for Advanced Lightweight Torpedo) is in production to succeed the Mk 46 in U.S. service.

Both the current heavy and lightweight torpedo programs have encountered major problems, most related to the nature of the Soviet submarine threat. The accompanying table outlines the problems with U.S. torpedoes that have been identified publicly. It must be acknowledged that the Mk 48 ADCAP is *the best* heavy torpedo currently in service with any navy; but the requirements placed on that weapon are severe.

TABLE 30-3.   U.S. TORPEDO LIMITATIONS

Torpedo	Program	Technical	Threat
Mk 46/50	long interval until successor (Mk 50)	small warhead limited range if ship launched	Russian submarines (1) high speeds (2) large size (3) double hull (4) anechoic coatings (6) use of decoys (7) under ice operations
Mk 48	limited procurement	limited loadout in submarines	Russian submarines (1) high speeds (2) anechoic coatings (3) use of decoys (4) under ice operations

A Mk 48 torpedo is lowered to the attack submarine DRUM (SSN 677) while moored alongside a submarine tender. (U.S. Navy)

By some criteria, U.S. torpedoes have lagged behind the potential threat since the appearance of the first Soviet nuclear-powered submarines in the late 1950s. In a 1981 congressional colloquy between a senator and the Deputy Chief of Naval Operations (Surface Warfare), Vice Admiral William H. Rowden, the senator noted that then-new Soviet submarines of the Alfa class could travel at "40-plus knots and could probably outdive most of our anti-submarine torpedoes." He then asked what measures were being taken to redress this particular balance.

The admiral replied, "We have modified the Mark 48 torpedo . . . to accommodate to the increased speed and to the diving depth of those particular submarines." The admiral was less confident of the Mark 46 used by aircraft, helicopters, and surface ships: "We have recently modified that torpedo to handle what you might call the pre-Alfa. . . ."

In addition to the relatively high speeds of modern Soviet submarines—35 to 40 knots for the more modern submarines—Soviet undersea craft are difficult targets for several reasons.[13] The large size, double hull, and multiple compartments of Soviet submarines reduce the effectiveness of the small Mk 46 and Mk 50 warheads. Both heavy and light torpedo effectiveness also suffer from the Soviet use of anechoic coatings on their submarine hulls that degrade torpedo acoustic guidance, and the extensive use of acoustic decoys. Finally, the Mk 48's capability is reduced in the under-ice environment of the Arctic ice pack.

Navy officials also consider the number of Mk 48s being procured as insufficient for a major conflict. The original Navy procurement goal was about 4,000 submarine torpedoes. But that number has been reduced by more than one-quarter by the Department of Defense. If one subtracts the torpedoes used for trials and training, and those weapons in overhaul, there were hardly enough available for one complete "ship fill" of all attack and strategic missile submarines prior to the massive force level cutbacks of the early 1990s. Of course, some submarine weapon spaces would normally be taken up with Harpoon and Tomahawk missiles, and possibly by mines.

Submarines carry the Mk 48 torpedo. Modern U.S. Navy SSNs have a capacity of some 25 tube-launched weapons (4 tubes + 21 reloads). The later, improved LOS ANGELES class submarines additionally have 12 vertical-launching tubes for Tomahawk missiles, making more reload spaces available within the submarine. The SEAWOLF (SSN 21) will have space for 50 weapons (8 tubes + 42 reload spaces).

While weapon loadouts will vary with the submarine's mission and operating area, a nominal loadout is torpedoes plus four Harpoons and four Tomahawks for a standard SSN. The improved LOS ANGELES would, of course, have 12 Tomahawks in external VLS tubes.

13. The revolutionary Alfa-class SSN, designed in the late 1950s, had a maximum speed of 43 knots and an operating depth of some 1,970 to 2,500 feet (600 to 760 m). Only six of these craft became operational, the prototype having been dismantled. All were decommissioned by about 1990.

Surface ships have the Mk 46 torpedo as an ASW weapon, launched by (1) over-the-side Mk 32 torpedo tubes, (2) LAMPS helicopters, or (3) ASROC. U.S. destroyers and cruisers (DL/DLG type) had "long" torpedo tubes for launching heavy anti-ship torpedoes until the late 1950s, when it was decided they would carry only the lightweight torpedoes to counter submarines. For a brief period in the 1960s the Mk 48 was intended for tube-launch from surface warships to provide a long-range, wire-guided ASW torpedo. Several surface warships were fitted with torpedo handling gear and 21-inch tubes in their stern counter or after deckhouse. However, this aspect of the Mk 48 program was cancelled, and only Mk 32 tubes for lightweight torpedoes have been retained in U.S. cruisers, destroyers, and frigates.

The Mk 50 torpedo is scheduled to succeed the Mk 46 in U.S. service.

ASW aircraft and helicopters carry the Mk 46 torpedo, external on the SH-2F, SH-3H, and SH-60B/F helicopters, and in internal weapon bays in the S-3A/B and P-3B/C fixed-wing aircraft.

The procurement schedule for torpedoes is listed below. Fiscal 1987 was the last year of procurement of the Mk 46 torpedo (NEARTIP version), with fiscal 1988 the first year of procurement for the new Mk 50 lightweight torpedo. The Mk 48 ADCAP as well as the Mk 50 torpedo is planned for procurement for the foreseeable future.

TABLE 30-4. TORPEDO PROCUREMENT

	FY 1987	FY 1988	FY 1989	FY 1990	FY 1991	FY 1992	FY 1993
	Actual	Actual	Actual	Actual	Actual	Actual	Planned
Mk 46	500	—	—	—	—	—	—
Mk 48 ADCAP	50	320	320	260	240	108	108
Mk 50	—	140	140	200	265	218	212

In addition to these torpedoes, the firm of Honeywell in Minneapolis, Minn., is remanufacturing and improving the older Mk 37 torpedo for foreign use under the designation NT-37. This weapon is not used by the U.S. Navy.

MK 48 torpedoes are prepared for loading aboard an SSN at Port Canaveral, Fla., for test launches. (U.S. Air Force)

Rear of a Mk 48 torpedo; the guide for the control wire is at top. (Gould)

Mk 48 torpedo showing the shrouded propeller or "propulsor" design. (Gould)

Mk 48 ADCAP TORPEDO

The Mk 48 ADCAP (Advanced Capability) verson of the Mk 48 heavy torpedo has been in production since fiscal 1985 as successor to the standard Mk 48 versions. The ADCAP version was developed from 1978 onward to counter the Alfa and other advanced Soviet submarines. The ADCAP performance requirements were to: (1) improve target acquisition range, (2) reduce the effect of enemy countermeasures, (3) minimize shipboard constraints such as warm-up and reactivation time, and (4) enhance effectiveness against surface ships.

The principal changes to the Mk 48 to meet these requirements were made to the torpedo's acoustic transducer (guidance) and control system. The higher-powered active sonar enables the torpedo to search a much greater volume of water to attain a target submarine. And the sonar is electrically steered, reducing the need for the torpedo to maneuver while searching. The torpedo retains the Gould (swashplate) motor with a larger fuel capacity. In November 1986, however, the Navy began seeking proposals for a quieter, closed-cycle propulsion system for the ADCAP, an apparent requirement in view of recent Soviet submarine quieting efforts.

The ADCAP program has suffered delays and severe cost increases. In 1982 the Chief of Naval Operations, Admiral Thomas B. Hayward, said that the problems arose because: (1) the original R&D program had been significantly underestimated, (2) the scope of effort had increased because of the evolving Soviet submarine threat, (3) an attempt had been made to accelerate the IOC, (4) too little emphasis had been placed on cost control, and (5) the prime contractor (Hughes) was new to the torpedo business and underestimated the effort required. Reliability problems with the ADCAP surfaced in early 1991, but according to Navy officials, they were solved the following year.

An under-ice capability has been provided.

Status: Operational; in production. Manufactured by Westinghouse Corp. and Hughes Aircraft of Fullerton, Calif.

Weight:	3,450 lbs
Diameter:	21 in (533 mm)
Length:	19⅙ ft (5.8 m)
Propulsion:	piston engine (liquid monopropellant fuel); pump-jet
Speed:	maximum 55 knots
Range:	approx. 35,000 yds (32,012 m)
Guidance:	wire + active/passive acoustic homing
Warhead:	approx. 650 lbs (295 kg) PBXN-103 high explosive
Platforms:	*submarines* all SSBN and SSN

Mk 50 LIGHTWEIGHT TORPEDO

The Mk 50—formerly known as the Advanced Lightweight Torpedo (ALWT)—is the successor to the Mk 46 for use by ASW/patrol aircraft and helicopters, surface ships, and possibly the submarine-launched Sea Lance ASW missile. The new torpedo has enhanced kill capability over the Mk 46, but still suffers from many of the shortcomings of the older torpedo.

In January 1992 the Department of Defense cancelled the Mk 50 as a payload for the Sea Lance.

Special features of the Mk 50 include the AKY-14 programmable digital computer. The maximum weight of the torpedo will be 800 pounds (363 kg), with a length and diameter similar to the Mk 46 to permit carriage by existing helicopters and the S-3 Viking.

Status: In production. The ALWT program was initiated in August 1975, with a design competition subsequently being held between Honeywell (Ex-50 design) and McDonnell Douglas (Ex-51). The former firm was selected to develop the torpedo. During the competition the torpedo was also designated Mk XX. Concept development began in 1975 and advanced development was approved in 1979; limited production began in March 1989. Manufactured by Westinghouse Electric Corp.

Mk 50 torpedo procurement is being terminated; see addenda.

Weight:	approx. 800 lbs (363 kg)
Diameter:	12¾ in (324 mm)
Length:	9½ ft (2.9 m)
Propulsion:	Stored Chemical Energy Propulsion System (SCEPS); pump jet
Speed:	50+ knots
Range:	
Guidance:	active/passive acoustic homing
Warhead:	approx. 100 lbs conventional (shaped charge)
Platforms:	ASW aircraft (P-3, S-3)
	ASW helicopters (S-2, SH-3, SH-60)
	surface ships

Mk 48 HEAVY TORPEDO

This is the latest weapon in a long series of heavy torpedoes, 21 inches (533 mm) in diameter with a length of up to 21 feet (6.4 m). The immediate predecessor of the Mk 48 was the Mk 37, which remains in foreign naval service. The Mk 48 also replaced the Mk 45 ASTOR (Anti-Submarine Torpedo), the U.S. Navy's only nuclear torpedo, which was in service from 1958 to 1977 with a W34 warhead. The long range and improved guidance of the Mk 48 made it as effective with a large conventional warhead as the Mk 45 in most situations. Also, the Mk 48's anti-surface-ship capability was considered sufficient to cancel the purely anti-surface Mk 47 torpedo.

Operational: Although little information is publicly available on U.S. torpedo performance, the Navy did state that the SAN JUAN (SSN 751) fired 12 torpedoes during a weapon system accuracy test and scored nine hits; three torpedo failures occurred. This was said to be above the fleet average (the SAN JUAN being the first submarine to be fitted with the advanced BSY-1 sonar/fire control system).

Development of the Mk 48 began in the early 1960s as the Navy-sponsored RETORC (Research Torpedo Configuration) project of the Applied Research Laboratory of Pennsylvania State University and the Westinghouse Electric Corp. (Baltimore, Md.). The project was initially designated Ex-10. This effort led to the Mk 48 Mod 0 torpedo with a turbine propulsion system. This was subsequently refined into the Mk 48 Mod 2.

In 1967 the Gould Corp. of Cleveland, Ohio, and the Naval Surface Warfare Center (White Oak, Md.) began developing the Mod 1 with a redesigned acoustic homing guidance and a piston (swashplate) engine. This torpedo used an Otto fuel that contains its own oxidizer for combustion. After evaluation of the two versions, the Mod 1 was selected for production by Gould for fleet use.

From the outset the Mk 48 has had a guidance wire that spins out simultaneously from the submarine and the torpedo to permit the submarine to exercise control over the "fish," at least during the initial stages of its run. The Mod 3 introduced several improvements including TELECOM (Tele-Communications) to provide two-way data transmissions between submarine and torpedo; thus, the torpedo can transmit acoustic data back to the submarine for processing. See ADCAP listing above for basic characteristics.

The Mod 4 version was an upgrade to provide more capability against the Alfa-class and other advanced Soviet SSNs.

The Mk 48 is also used in Australian and Dutch submarines.

Status: Operational. Mk 48 IOC in 1972; Mk 48 ADCAP IOC in 1989. In production by Hughes Aircraft and Westinghouse Electric Corp.

Mk 46 LIGHTWEIGHT TORPEDO

The Mk 46 is a lightweight torpedo intended for use against submarines by helicopters, aircraft, and surface ships, and is fitted in the CAPTOR deep-water mine. The lightweight torpedo concept dates to the late 1940s when it was envisioned that future convoys would be protected from submarine attack by helicopters with dipping sonar and airships (blimps) with towed sonar. For this application, light weight (initially a maximum of 350 pounds/159 kg) became a primary consideration for ASW torpedoes. In addition, the concept would require large numbers of torpedoes, hence cost was also an important factor in torpedo design. Subsequently, surface combatants were fitted with "short" torpedo tubes for launching these torpedoes, and the ASROC was fitted with the lightweight torpedo.

The Navy is procuring kits for the conversion of 172 Mk 46 torpedoes to function as anti-torpedo weapons as part of the Surface Ship Torpedo Defense (SSTD) project; see chapter 31.

The first lightweight ASW torpedo to enter fleet service was the Mk 43 Mod 1 (260 lbs/118 kg) in 1951, and later the Mod 3, followed by the Mk 44 Mod 0 (425 lbs/193 kg) introduced in 1957, followed by the Mod 1. The Mk 46 is thus the third generation of lightweight ASW torpedoes.

Most U.S. surface combatants have Mk 32 triple 12.75-inch torpedo tubes; these are in the destroyer DEWEY (DDG 45), being trained outboard. These tubes can fire Mk 46 and Mk 50 torpedoes. (U.S. Navy)

The Mk 46 was developed by the Naval Ordnance Test Station (Pasadena, Calif.) and Aerojet General (Azusa, Calif.). Subsequent production was undertaken at the Naval Ordnance Plant (Forest Park, Ill.) and Honeywell, as well as Aerojet. The Mk 46 has a higher speed, twice the range, deeper operating depth, and better acoustic performance than its predecessor, the Mk 44. Propulsion was provided with a thermal piston engine, with the Mod 0 using a solid propellant grain and the Mod 1 having a liquid monopropellant fuel, the latter providing improved performance. There was no Mod 3 torpedo.

The Mod 4 version of the Mk 46 is especially configured for the CAPTOR (Encapsulated Torpedo) naval mine. In 1981 Secretary of Defense Harold Brown stated that "because the existing Mk 46 torpedo will not meet the submarine acoustic and countermeasures threat through the early 1980s, we have budgeted for a new version called the Near-Term Torpedo Improvement Program (NEARTIP)." This program included modification kits for earlier Mk 46s as well as new torpedo procurement. The NEARTIP or Mod 5 has an improved sonar transducer, new guidance and control group, and engine improvements.

The Mk 46 is extensively used by foreign navies.

Status: Operational. IOC Mod 0 in 1966; Mods 1 and 2 in 1967. The last Mk 46 Mod 5 torpedoes were delivered to the U.S. Navy in 1992; they were produced by the firm Alliant Techsystems, Inc., which was part of the defense-product spinoff from Honeywell in October 1990. In addition, the firm produced several hundred conversion kits for the Navy to upgrade earlier Mod 1 and Mod 2 torpedoes to the Mod 5 configuration.

Weight:	Mod 0	568 lbs (258 kg)
	Mods 1/2	508 lbs (230 kg)
Diameter:	12.75 inches (324 mm)	
Length:	8½ feet (2.6 m)	
Propulsion:	Mod 0	piston engine (solid propellant)
	Mods 1/2	cam engine (liquid monopropellant) contrarotating propellers
Speed:	approx. 45 knots maximum	
Range:		
Guidance:	active/passive acoustic homing	
Warhead:	approx. 95 lbs (43 kg) high explosive	
Platforms:	Mods 0/5	aircraft (P-3, S-3, SH-2, SH-3, SH-60)
	Mods 1/2/5	cruisers, destroyers, frigates
	Mod 4	mines (CAPTOR)

A Mk 46 practice torpedo is loaded aboard the Coast Guard cutter HAMILTON (WHEC 715). The cavity in the torpedo is for a lead weight used in exercise torpedoes and ejected at the end of the run to make the weapon buoyant to permit recovery. (Giorgio Arra)

Mk 46 torpedo fitted on an SH-3D Sea King helicopter; the contrarotating propellers are visible. Russian ASW helicopters carry their torpedoes in internal weapon bays. (U.S. Navy)

Mk 46 Mod 1 torpedoes in the weapons bay of a P-3 Orion patrol aircraft. Parachute packs are fitted to the rear of the torpedoes. (U.S. Navy)

ANTI-SURFACE WARFARE TORPEDO

The Navy promulgated a requirement for a low-cost, anti-surface ship torpedo on 2 December 1985 at the urging of then-Secretary of the Navy John Lehman. The torpedo was intended for use against surface ships that did not require the more complex (and higher cost) Mk 48 ADCAP torpedo, which was developed specifically for attacking maneuvering submarines, a much more difficult type of target.

Known as the "no frills" torpedo, the ASUW weapon encountered delays primarily because of the contractual restrictions placed on potential contractors, such as each finalist having to provide seven test torpedoes at its own expense for a "swim-off" competition. The torpedo was also opposed by the submarine community, which questioned the utility of such a weapon that would displace Mk 48 torpedoes and other weapons from the limited reload space in attack submarines. The program was subsequently cancelled.

The ASUW torpedo had a program goal of 2,000 weapons at a cost of $200,000 each (compared to the $2.43 million unit cost for the Mk 48 ADCAP torpedo in the fiscal 1988 budget, plus continuing research and development costs). The initial procurement was set for fiscal 1987 with 34 torpedoes.

The parachute deploys from a Mk 46 torpedo, released during an exercise from an SH-3D Sea King helicopter. Lightweight torpedoes, originally developed for use from blimps, are now the only anti-submarine weapons carried by U.S. Navy surface ships and aircraft. (U.S. Navy)

CHAPTER 31

Electronic Systems

Modern warships of all sizes increasingly rely upon electronic systems for their combat effectiveness as well as defense. A variety of antennas are evident in the frigates McCLUSKY (FFG 41) and GARY (FFG 51); an amphibious cargo ship is moored astern of the latter ship. The GARY has a Navy Mast Mounted Sight (NMMS) fitted above the bridge; the device contains television, Forward-Looking Infrared (FLIR), and a laser rangefinder, all linked to the ship's weapon control systems. (OS2 John Bouvia, USN)

ELECTRONIC DESIGNATIONS

Most U.S. Navy electronic systems are identified by the joint electronics type designation system illustrated on page 515. This was formerly called the joint Army-Navy nomenclature system, and the three letter-plus-number designations are still prefixed by the AN/ of the World War II era. In this volume the AN/ is generally omitted from three-letter designations. The electronic systems designated in various mark (Mk) series do not have the AN/ prefix.

ELECTRONIC WARFARE SYSTEMS

Electronic Warfare (EW) consists of efforts to detect, locate, exploit, reduce, or prevent an enemy's use of the electromagnetic spectrum, and actions that retain one's own use of the electromagnetic spectrum. There are several divisions of electronic warfare:

> Electronic Warfare Support Measures (ESM)
> Signals Intelligence (SIGINT)
> Electronic Countermeasures (ECM)
> Electronic Counter-Countermeasures (ECCM)

Because EW deals with electromagnetic energy and not just electronics, also included are infrared, laser, and optical systems. However, radiation produced by nuclear weapons is usually classified as nuclear effects and not EW.

ELECTRONIC WARFARE SUPPORT MEASURES (ESM)

ESM activities are the portion of EW that seeks to detect, intercept, locate, record, and analyze enemy electromagnetic radiations. Thus, ESM provides the information required to conduct electronic countermeasures and counter-countermeasures for immediate threat recognition. Generally passive, ESM seeks to detect the enemy through "listening" to an enemy's radio and radar emissions.

The U.S. Navy has a variety of ESM systems that are used in ships, submarines, aircraft, and ashore. Being passive, ESM offers a number of obvious tactical advantages; it permits the ESM collection platform to remain electronically silent, and it can detect a hostile radar's transmissions beyond the radar detection range because the radar requires much of its power to return a signal to the transmitter after it detects a target.

There are highly specialized—and highly classified—ESM systems, such as the ALR-series receivers in the Navy's ES-3 Viking and EP-3E Orion aircraft that support fleet operations. Those that have been publicly identified are:

- AAR-37   infrared receiver
- ALD-8   direction finder
- ALQ-40   ECM receiver
- ALQ-76   jammer
- ALQ-78   ECM receiver
- ALQ-108   IFF jammer
- ALQ-110   radio signal collector
- ALQ-132   infrared countermeasures set
- ALR-52   frequency-measuring receiver
- ALR-60   Deepwell communications intercept and analysis
- APA-69   radar spectrum analyzer
- APR-25   radio spectrum analyzer
- APS-20   surveillance radar
- ASQ-171   ELINT receiver

The recently modified EP-3J Orion aircraft is reported to have the following systems:

- ALE-43   chaff dispenser
- ALQ-167   jammer pod
- ALQ-170   ECM system
- AST-4/6   signal simulator
- ALT-40   jammer simulator
- USQ-113   communications deception

SLQ-32(V)2 ECM antenna in a PERRY-class frigate with the "Sidekick" antenna installed immediately below. The latter is an add-on ECM transmitter that enhances the capabilities of the SLQ-32. (Raytheon)

Other ESM capabilities are incorporated into multi-function systems. For example, according to published Navy manuals, a LOS ANGELES (SSN 688)-class submarine has the following equipment for the collection of Electromagnetic Intelligence (ELINT), including Acoustic Intelligence (ACINT) and Communications Intelligence (COMINT)

- BQQ-5 sonar system, which has a passive classification processor that can continuously evaluate low-frequency acoustic data from sonars
- BLD-1 radio direction finder
- BRD-7 radio direction finder
- WLR-8 receiver that can detect enemy fire control radars as well as radio communication frequencies (reportedly having a 50 MHz to 18 GHz frequency range)
- WLR-9 acoustic intercept receiver that can detect active search sonars and acoustic-homing torpedoes
- WLR-10 countermeasures

Several of these equipments are multi-purpose, especially the BQQ-5 system that is the submarine's tactical sonar, having both active and passive modes. Additional ESM equipment can be installed for special collection missions.

Electronic surveillance and collection equipment have special design characteristics, among them:

Wide-spectrum or bandwidth capability: Because the frequency of a foreign radar may not be known before it operates, a wide bandwidth should be covered. With modern technology, this means a frequency spectrum from 30 MHz to 50 GHz. This range is too large for a single receiver; thus, several receivers with different tuning ranges must be used or a single receiver in which different tuning units can be inserted to cover the frequency range.

SLQ-32(V)3 ECM antenna on the Aegis cruiser YORKTOWN (CG 48) with two Mk 36 launchers for Super Rapid Blooming Offboard Chaff (SRBOC) in the foreground. (N. Polmar)

The SLQ-32(V)3 ECM antenna in the cruiser MISSISSIPPI (CGN 40); the antenna at left is a telemetry receiver. The modular SLQ-32 is found in most U.S. Navy surface combatants. (Stefan Terzibaschitsch)

Wide dynamic range: The ESM receiver must be able to receive very weak and very strong signals. The receiver may be at different distances from different signals at the same time, and widely dissimilar signals could impair both collection and analysis unless the equipment is designed specifically for the role.

Unwanted signal rejection: This characteristic—also called narrow band-pass—is desirable because it enables the receiver to discriminate between the target frequency and signals at other, nearby frequencies.

Good angle-of-arrival measurement: The ability of a receiver to take bearings accurately on a distant transmitter permits different bearings (taken by the same or several surveillance platforms) to be plotted to give the precise location of the transmitter. Airborne, shipboard, or ground-based digital computers can be programmed to rapidly perform this function.

The receiver should be designed to alert the operator immediately to the presence of a signal of possible interest, to sort out the signal of interest, and to analyze the signal. The alerting and sorting are particularly important because an airborne ESM platform may be exposed to the signal for a short time compared to a ship or shore facility, or the signal may be on the air for only a very short time. The current trend in ESM is to record automatically the intercepted signal for later analysis and, if appropriate, to reproduce it for EW libraries.

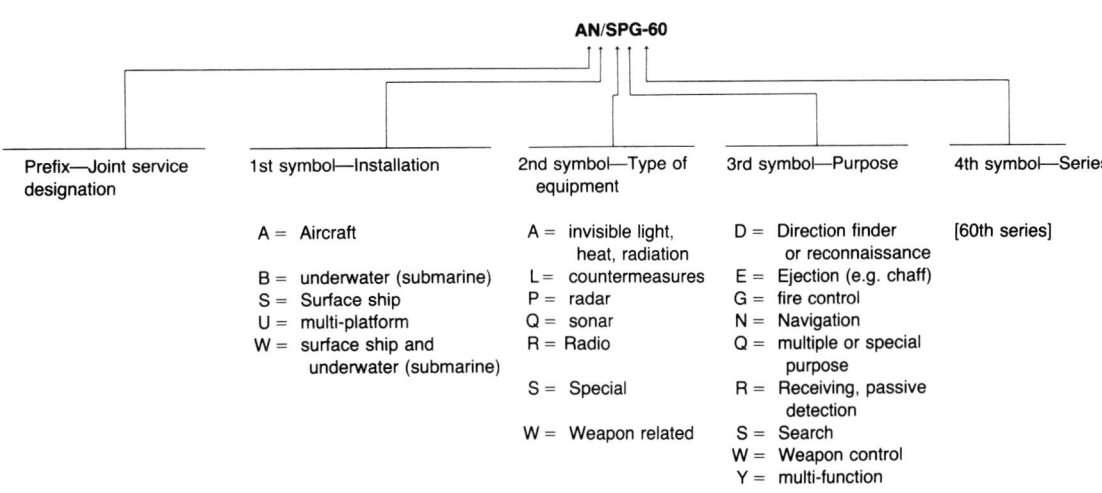

Explanation of symbols:

AN/SPG-60

Prefix—Joint service designation	1st symbol—Installation	2nd symbol—Type of equipment	3rd symbol—Purpose	4th symbol—Series
	A = Aircraft	A = invisible light, heat, radiation	D = Direction finder or reconnaissance	[60th series]
	B = underwater (submarine)	L = countermeasures	E = Ejection (e.g. chaff)	
	S = Surface ship	P = radar	G = fire control	
	U = multi-platform	Q = sonar	N = Navigation	
	W = surface ship and underwater (submarine)	R = Radio	Q = multiple or special purpose	
		S = Special	R = Receiving, passive detection	
		W = Weapon related	S = Search	
			W = Weapon control	
			Y = multi-function	

The submarine is an excellent ESM platform because it is difficult for an enemy to detect her by radar and visual means, and even by acoustic sensors under some conditions. And, of course, a submarine is not impeded by surface weather. Submarines are particularly useful in gaining acoustic intelligence on enemy submarines, and modern nuclear-powered submarines in particular are quiet and have essentially unlimited underwater endurance. The periodic press reports of U.S. and Soviet submarines "scraping" one another in close encounters in northern waters suggest that U.S. submarines are used in such surveillance missions in areas such as the Arctic and Norwegian Sea. An ACINT capability is also found in the Navy's seafloor Sound Surveillance System (SOSUS). In addition to providing a peacetime warning system of submarine movements, the SOSUS networks in the Atlantic, Pacific, and regional seas can record data on surface ship and submarine noise characteristics.

Specialized electronic reconnaissance aircraft have long conducted ESM missions along the peripheries of the Soviet Union (and now Russia), China, and North Korea. The current U.S. naval aircraft in this category are ES-3 Vikings and EP-3 Orions from fleet air reconnaissance squadrons (VQ). These aircraft, with the ES-3s able to operate from forward-deployed aircraft carriers, also provide electronic surveillance of surface ships and submarines for fleet commanders. The primary advantage of aircraft ESM platforms is their altitude, permitting them to detect distant electronic emissions, including those originating inside enemy territory.

Aircraft—and surface ships—also are used to stimulate enemy radars and communications as they near enemy territory. In turn, this stimulation permits the aircraft or ship to then record the electromagnetic responses of an enemy—that is, which of their radars they turn on, which of their communications channels they use, etc.

SIGNALS INTELLIGENCE (SIGINT)

SIGINT includes the collection of intelligence information for Navy and National requirements, including all Communications Intelligence (COMINT), Electronics Intelligence (ELINT), Acoustic Intelligence (ACINT), and Telemetry Intelligence (TELINT). The National Security Agency (NSA) is the national program manager for the collection, analysis, and dissemination of SIGINT. However, the platforms and personnel involved in SIGINT belong to the armed services, and some systems obviously have both ESM and SIGINT collection capabilities. Thus, the actual operation of SIGINT activities is conducted by the services and, in wartime, the operational control of some dedicated SIGINT platforms would be assigned to tactical commanders.

Surface warships are used extensively for SIGINT activity. Two U.S. destroyers engaged in SIGINT, the TURNER JOY (DD 951) and MADDOX (DD 731) on the so-called De Soto patrols off the North Vietnamese coast in August 1964, were involved in the Gulf of Tonkin incidents that led to a dramatic escalation of American involvement in the Vietnam conflict.[1] Because of the hostile nature of the North Vietnamese and the guerrilla war then going on, destroyers were deemed the appropriate ESM platforms.

In the supposedly more benign environment of international waters off North Korea, the U.S. Navy carried naval and National Security Agency teams on board the "passive" SIGINT surveillance ships BANNER (AGER 1) and PUEBLO (AGER 3), while the LIBERTY (AGTR 5) was used in 1967 to monitor Israeli communications during the Six-Day War. The United States and Soviet Union had long believed that such ships operated by the two superpowers were immune to hostile actions by the Third World. However, attacks on the PUEBLO and LIBERTY demonstrated that a superpower's ships are not immune. The U.S. Navy has ceased to operate such "passive" intelligence ships, although more than 50 of these intelligence collectors are still active in the Russian Navy (designated AGI by NATO).

Land-based aircraft, satellites, and land facilities also provide SIGINT collection of foreign naval activities.

1. Apparently on the night of 2 August 1964 the destroyers were, in fact, attacked by North Vietnamese motor torpedo boats and on the night of 5 August 1964 U.S. naval commanders thought the destroyers again were under torpedo boat attack.

SLQ-17(A)(V) antenna on the carrier ENTERPRISE (CVN 65). The SLQ-29, of which the SLQ-17 is a component, is being replaced aboard aircraft carriers by the SLQ-32(V)4. (Hughes)

ELECTRONIC COUNTERMEASURES (ECM)

ECM are intended primarily to (1) detect threats to friendly forces and (2) inhibit or degrade the effectiveness of enemy weapons and sensors. Most surface warships, submarines, and combat aircraft have ECM systems to help protect them against hostile detection and attack. In addition, there are specialized ECM aircraft that assist other aircraft in penetrating heavily defended areas.

Different ECM techniques are used to reduce the effectiveness of enemy radars. The three basic techniques are to (1) interfere with the radar through jamming and deception; (2) change the electrical properties of the air between the radar and (friendly) target, mainly through chaff; and (3) change the reflective properties of the (friendly) target through radar-absorbing materials or paint, and through electronic and mechanical echo (blip) enhancers or decoys.

Although the above discussion concentrated on ECM techniques against radar, to some extent the concepts are useable against electromagnetic communications and sonar. For example, shipboard noise can be reduced. Modern U.S. surface warships use the Prairie and Masker systems of creating small air bubbles around a ship's hull and wake to reduce her acoustic signature. Advanced submarine hull designs (e.g., modifications of the ALBACORE/AGSS 569 or "teardrop" configuration) reduce noise created by submarine movement, while special internal mountings reduce propulsion and auxiliary machinery noises. Of course, surface ships and, especially, submarines can slow or stop to reduce their self-generated noises.

Torpedo countermeasures also include decoys to replace the ship or submarine target in the torpedo's target-acquisition process. U.S. surface warships, amphibious ships, and certain auxiliary ships have the SLQ-25 Nixie. These are towed devices, with the effectiveness of Nixie being demonstrated in the 1982 war off the Falklands when a Nixie being towed by the British carrier HERMES attracted and was blown up by a British ASW torpedo launched against a suspected Argentine submarine contact.

An improved SLQ-36 torpedo countermeasure system is planned. After several false starts, the Surface Ship Torpedo Defense (SSTD) project is under way to provide U.S. ships with a hard-kill torpedo defense system. In the fall of 1988 the U.S. and British governments signed a Memorandum Of Understanding (MOU) to establish a four-phase, joint research SSTD project. When signed on 26 October 1988, the MOU was hailed by a U.S. Navy spokesman as providing "an excellent opportunity to improve mutual defense capabilities, reduce development and acquisition costs and to provide for increased compatibility and interoperability between the U.S. and Royal navies."[2]

The joint program, however, ran into shoal water. While the U.S. Navy has pushed for a hard-kill approach, the British believe that soft-kill is more viable for SSTD. The British fear that a convoy escort firing weapons to intercept an incoming torpedo would put other ships in the convoy at risk. More threatening to the joint effort, the U.S. House Appropriations Committee subsequently killed funding for several Anglo-American projects, among them SSTD. The House report stated that the "committee does not consider such a joint project to be feasible given the security consideration regarding the sharing of acoustic signal data and countermeasure development, which the program would ultimately require."[3] Such language was highly inflammatory and counterproductive because of the close technical and operational relationship of the U.S. and British submarine communities and the large amount of acoustic data on Soviet/Russian undersea craft provided to the United States by the Royal Navy!

In 1992 it was revealed that 172 Mk 46 ASW torpedoes were being converted to an *active* anti-torpedo system for carrier defense against Russian wake-homing torpedoes. Reportedly, by early 1992 there had been approximately 70 in-water tests of the concept against U.S. Mk 48 torpedoes simulating Russian Type 65-80 torpedoes (65 cm in diameter with an IOC of 1980).

Three American-led consortia have been formed to developed SSTD systems: General Electric teamed with Alliant Techsystems (formerly defense products of Honeywell) and Marconi Underwater Systems; Westinghouse with AT&T, Dowty Maritime, and Ferranti; and Martin Marietta worked with Hughes Ground Systems, British Aerospace Dynamics, and Frequency Engineering Laboratories (USA). After a series of initial contracts in the torpedo defense area, in early 1992 the first two teams were awarded contract extensions for the program.

U.S. attack submarines are reported to carry the Mk 23 acoustic countermeasure device that will decoy homing torpedoes, while ballistic missile submarines also can launch the Mk 70 MOSS (Mobile Submarine Simulator) from torpedo tubes to simulate a full-size submarine to hostile sonar.

There are a large number of threat warning and countermeasure systems in U.S. surface ships and submarines, mostly numbered in the SLQ and WLR series. The principal U.S. surface ship ECM equipment is the SLQ-32 "design-to-cost" EW suite. Variations of this system are fitted in most surface combatant and amphibious ships as well as several underway replenishment types. The SLQ-32 is considered a short-range, omni-directional, self-defense system that evaluates electronic emissions and can, in some variants, initiate countermeasures.

There are three variants of the SLQ-32 with modular "building blocks" for different types of ships. The (V)1 variant for frigates, some amphibious ships (LSD, LPD, LST), and auxiliary ships (AE, AFS) provides warning, identification, and bearing of radar-guided cruise missiles and their launch platforms.

The (V)2 variant for guided missile destroyers (DDG), frigates (FF/FFG), and the SPRUANCE (DD 963)-class destroyers has the (V)1 capability and expanded ESM capabilities. An add-on ECM transmitter called "Sidekick" is being fitted to OLIVER HAZARD PERRY (FFG 7)-class frigates to augment to SLQ-32(V)2. The

SLQ-32(V)1 antenna in the frigate MOINESTER (FF 1097). (Giorgio Arra)

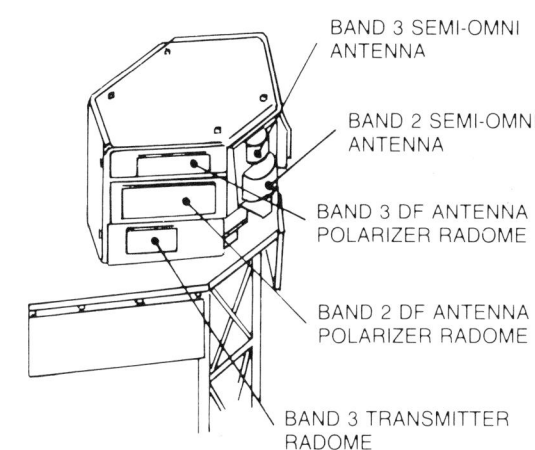

SLQ-32(V)3 antenna system.

Sidekick is an active ECM system intended to confuse enemy threats. It was developed to supplement the passive SLQ-32(V)2 system in frigates. The set was first fitted in the frigates REID (FFG 30) and HAWES (FFG 53) in 1988. Sidekick was designed, produced, and delivered by Raytheon within 11 weeks of the Navy request for the system.

The (V)3 configuration for cruisers (CG/CGN), large amphibious ships (LCC, LHA, LPH), and auxiliaries (AOE, AOR) has combined the (V)1 and (V)2 capabilities and the means to counter or deceive missile-guidance radars. The (V)3 has a quick-reaction mode that permits the initiation of jamming against a target signal before its characteristics are fully analyzed. This feature could be particularly useful against "pop-up" submarine-launched missiles or those fired by missile craft hiding in coastal shore "clutter."

The SLQ-32 antennas are fitted in two box-like enclosures, port and starboard, high in the ship's superstructure. The (V)2 and (V)3 are fitted with twin Rotman lens direction-finding receiving antennas. The SLQ-32 systems employ UYK-19 computers.

The follow-on system to the SLQ-32 series is the SLQ-54, previously known as the Advanced Integrated EW System (AIEWS). The SLQ-54 is envisioned to counter hostile threats of the twenty-first century.

The SLQ-32 and other ECM systems are used in conjunction with Mk 36 Super Rapid Blooming Offboard Chaff (SRBOC) launchers that fire either semi-automatically or on manual direction from a ship's ECM operators. Large ships have four Mk 36 launchers, and smaller ships have two, each consisting of six fixed barrels. (Infrared

2. Caleb Baker, "U.S., Royal Navy to explore torpedo defense systems," *Navy Times* (19 December 1988), p. 26.
3. "House cites 'security concerns' in cutting U.K. from SSTD," *Navy News* (21 August 1989), p. 8.

The labels on the SLQ-32(V)3 antenna system diagram read:
BAND 3 SEMI-OMNI ANTENNA
BAND 2 SEMI-OMNI ANTENNA
BAND 3 DF ANTENNA POLARIZER RADOME
BAND 2 DF ANTENNA POLARIZER RADOME
BAND 3 TRANSMITTER RADOME

Sailor holding the towed "fish" of the SLQ-25 Nixie torpedo countermeasures system; the towing cable is in the foreground. (Aerojet General)

decoys and flares can also be fired in response to detections by threat-warning devices.)

Several other, lesser EW sets are in current Navy use, principally the WLR-1, 6, 8, 9, 10, 11, 12; WLQ-4; and SLR-12 threat-warning systems; ULQ-6 deception repeater; and the SLQ-17 and BLR-14 countermeasure systems. The SLQ-17 used in carriers includes the WLR-8 and provides computer-controlled warning and jamming capabilities. The BLR-14—dubbed the Submarine Acoustic Warfare System (SAWS)—provides an integrated receiver, processor, display, and countermeasure launch system for submarines.

The principal naval ECM aircraft is the EA-6B Prowler, flown by the Navy and Marine Corps. The EA-6B is easily distinguished from the A-6 Intruder, from which it was developed, by the housing atop its tail fin and up to five jammer pods carried on its wings and fuselage. The pods are ALQ-99 tactical jammers, each with an exciter/processor and a minicomputer to detect, identify, and jam a broad spectrum of hostile radars. The aircraft also has the ALQ-100 multi-band track-breaking system and ALQ-92 communications jammer. The EA-6B is probably the most capable EW aircraft in the West (although Grumman has provided these systems in the Air Force EF-111A). The basic EA-6B aircraft has had its frequency coverage extended through a series of updates (see chapter 29).

The EA-6B aircraft are designed to provide ECM support for strike aircraft attacking defended targets. The strike aircraft can themselves carry chaff, ECM pods, and radar-homing missiles to further enhance their survivability. Each carrier air wing has a squadron of five EA-6B Prowlers, while the Marine Corps has one squadron with about 15 ECM aircraft; both the Naval and Marine Air Reserve organizations also fly the EA-6B.

A pair of Mk 70 MOSS acoustic decoys are loaded aboard an attack submarine. (U.S. Navy)

Other naval aircraft have built-in or pod-mounted ECM systems for self-defense.

Electronic countermeasures are costly, not only in resources (especially for research and development) but because of the tactical uncertainties and limitations that they impose. For example, it may be undesirable to employ ECM against an enemy's communications, for by doing so one denies communications intercept to one's own side. Or, firing chaff and decoys to defend against a possible enemy missile attack can degrade one's own radar effectiveness.

Also, ECM produces "soft kills." It is not always possible for the ECM operator to detect or determine if his efforts are successful. Further, ESM/SIGINT/ECM/ECCM are undertaken with a continuous interaction. Those who allocate resources are not always anxious to spend funds on an ECM system, for example, that may be a counter to a threat the intelligence community predicts may have a certain capability. Somehow, it seems easier to buy a new ship, or missile, or aircraft rather than a new "black box."

ELECTRONIC COUNTER-COUNTERMEASURES (ECCM)

ECCM are those actions taken to retain the effectiveness of one's own use of the electromagnetic spectrum against hostile electronic warfare efforts.

The following table lists the major electronic warfare systems in surface ships and submarines that have been identified publicly. Included in the table are two surface-ship acoustic mine neutralization systems—the SLQ-37(V) and SLQ-53. The SLQ-37(V) consists of the combined "magnetic tail" Mk 5A and the Mk 4(V) and/or Mk 6(V) acoustic sweep gear. The U.S. Navy's standard *mechanical* minesweeping gear, in use since the early 1940s, has been recently given the designation SLQ-38, while the remote-controlled Mine Neutralization System (MNS) is given the designation SLQ-48(V); see page 217 for a description of the latter.

TABLE 31-1. SHIPBOARD EW SYSTEMS

Designation	Purpose	Manufacturer	Platforms
ALR-600	radar warning	General Instrument	65-ft PB
BLQ-3/4/5	acoustic jammer	General Electric	submarines
BLQ-8	acoustic system	Bendix, Aerojet	submarines
BLR-1/10	acoustic warning	(various)	submarines
BLR-13	ECM receiver	Kollmorgan	submarines
BLR-14 SAWS*	threat warning, processor, counter-measure launcher	Sperry†	submarines
BLR-15	ESM receiver	Kollmorgan	submarines
BRD-6/7	radio direction finder	Sanders	submarines
SLQ-17	DECM‡	Hughes	carriers
SLQ-25 Nixie	towed torpedo countermeasure	Aerojet	surface ships
SLQ-32(V)1§	radar warning (H/I/J bands)	Raytheon, Hughes	surface ships
SLQ-32(V)2	radar warning (B through J bands)	Raytheon, Hughes	surface ships
SLQ-32(V)3	radar warning (B through J bands); ECM (H/I/J bands)	Raytheon, Hughes	surface ships
SLQ-37(V)	mine neutralization		surface ships
SLQ-53	deep-water mine neutralization		surface ships
SLR-12			surface ships
SRD-19 Diamond	radio direction finder	Sanders	surface ships
SSQ-74 Outboard	electronic deception	ITT Avionics	surface ships
SSQ-82 Mute	shipboard emitter monitor and control		surface ships
ULQ-6	deception repeater	General Instrument	surface ships
WLQ-4	radar countermeasures	GTE	submarines
WLR-1/1H	radar warning	(various)	surface ships
WLR-6 Waterboy	radar warning, signal collection	GTE	surface ships, submarines
WLR-8	radar warning	GTE	carriers, submarines
WLR-8(V)4/5	radar warning	GTE	submarines
WLR-9	sonar receiver	Norden	submarines
WLR-10	ECM receiver	Astro Labs	submarines
WLR-11	radar warning	ARGO Systems	surface ships
Mk 23	torpedo decoy		SSN
Mk 70 MOSS	Mobile Submarine Simulator	Gould	SSBN

*SAWS = Submarine Acoustic Warfare System.
†DECM = Deceptive ECM.
‡Sperry is now part of the Unisys Corp.
§The ALQ-142 on the SH-60B helicopter is similar to SLQ-32 with two Rotman-lens antennas; data is transmitted via data link to SLQ-32 in ships.

SHIPBOARD RADARS

U.S. Navy shipboard radars are used principally for surface and air search, height finding, weapons fire control, target illumination, and aircraft control. In a few radars two functions can overlap, with the advanced SPY-1 series providing multiple radar functions in a single system.

Many cruisers, destroyers, frigates, amphibious ships, and auxiliary ships have the Litton LN-66 commercial radar for close-in navigation; the radar has the military designation AN/SPS-59.

Aircraft control radars are unique to aviation ships (CV/CVN/LHA/LHD/LPH) and are designated in the SPN-series, referred to as "spin" radars. They are used to guide aircraft into the proper approach pattern or glide path to the ship. The SPN-41 and SPN-42 in the K band, SPN-43 in the S band, and SPN-44 in the X band are currently in service.

Several radars listed in this section are no longer in U.S. naval service but are significant because of their longevity, wide use, or technological innovation; they are given abbreviated entries.

Designations: Fire control radars were assigned mark (Mk) numbers beginning in 1941. This series ran through Mk 47, with the next radar initiating the SPG series. Subsequently, later versions of some earlier radars were given the SPG prefix, as SPG-34.

BPS-16 RADAR

Advanced submarine search and navigation sonar. Evaluated in the ATLANTA (SSN 712) in 1991–1992; that set was to go into the SEA-WOLF. The BPS-16 has an outer "sleeve" that mounts the radar and reduces problems with retraction equipment and leakage. The radar also has multiple frequencies that reduce the unique signature common to previous BPS-series radars that enabled a hostile ESM system to easily identify submarine radar emissions.

Manufactured by Sperry.

Band:	X
Operational:	1991
Ships:	SSBN 726 (3 ships; to be backfitted in first 15 units beginning about 1997)
	SSN 21

BPS-15 RADAR

Submarine search and navigation radar; the BPS-15 has replaced all older radars in U.S. submarines except for later units of the OHIO class. The principal differences among the various BPS-series radars are the pedestal mountings. Peak power is 35 kW.

Manufactured by Sperry.

Band:	X
Operational:	
Ships:	SSBN 726–740 (BPS-15B)
	SSBN 616 (BPS-15D, except BPS-15E in submarines converted to special operation role)
	SSN 688 (BPS-15A/E)
	SSN 671 (BPS-15E)
	SSN 637 (BPS-15E)

BPS-15 series radar partially raised on the submarine Lapon (SSN 661). The speckled camouflage on the other masts and periscopes makes them more difficult to sight when projecting above the water. (Giorgio Arra)

SPG-62 RADAR

This is the illumination radar for the Standard SM-2 missile in the Aegis system. The Aegis ships have three (DDG 51) or four (CG 47) Mk 99 missile control directors that use the SPG-62 illumination channel to provide radar reflections for Standard missiles. They are "slaved" to the SPY-1 radar. The antenna is 7½ feet (2.3 m) wide. Peak power is 10 kW.

Manufactured by GE-RCA.

Band:	X
Operational:	1983
Ships:	CG 47
	DDG 51

The forward SPG-62 illumination radar in the Arleigh Burke (DDG 51) is fitted above the bridge; there are two additional SPG-62s aft. From left, below the bridge, are a Phalanx CIWS, SPY-1D antenna, and SLQ-32(V)3 ECM antenna; bar-type antennas for the SPS-64 and SPS-67(V)3 radars are above the SPG-62. (Giorgio Arra)

SPG-60 RADAR

The SPG-60 radar both provides gun control data and permits Standard-MR missile tracking with the addition of an illuminator to the Mk 86 FCS. The SPG-60 is a monopulse, pulse-doppler radar, is combined with the SPQ-9A in the Mk 86 weapon control system, and can illuminate targets for the Standard and Sea Sparrow missiles. Thus, a single fire control system can serve several functions. The X-band SPG-60 is credited with a nominal range of some 50 n.miles (92.5 km).

The Separate Target Illumination Radar (STIR) using the SPG-60 antenna mount is found in the Perry-class frigates to provide two missile control channels for the Mk 86. The Mk 86 system can simultaneously track up to 120 incoming targets in a track-while-scan mode.

The antenna is 13⅓ feet (4 m) across. Peak power is 5.5 kW.

Manufactured by Lockheed Electronics.

Band:	X	
Operational:		
Ships:	CG 47	DDG 993
	CGN 38	DDG 2 (3 ships)
	CGN 36	DD 963

STIR in the PERRY-class frigates uses the SPG-60 antenna. (Giorgio Arra)

SPG-55B antennas on the destroyer FARRAGUT (DDG 37). One of the ship's two OE-82 SATCOMM antennas is fitted between them. (Giorgio Arra)

SPG-55B/C/D/F RADAR

The SPG-55 "searchlight" target acquisition and guidance radar is fitted in ships armed with the Standard-ER missile; originally developed for the Terrier missile system. Most ships have two radar sets for each missile launcher; thus a double-end (two-launcher) missile cruiser with four SPG-55s could simultaneously engage up to four aerial targets. The system was also designed for use against surface and land targets. Used with Mk 76 missile FCS.

The massive "searchlight" antennas have a reflective dish eight feet (2.4 m) in diameter. Peak power is 1 MW.

Manufactured by Sperry.

Band:	J	
Operational:		
Ships:	CGN 35	CG 16
	CG 26	CGN 9
	CGN 25	

SPG-53F RADAR

Radar for the Mk 68 GFCS for use with Mk 42 5-inch guns. This is a modified SPG-48 radar. It has been succeeded in later ships by the Mk 86 system (with SPG-60/SPQ-9A radars).

The antenna is five feet (1.5 m) in diameter. Peak power is 250 kW.

Manufactured by Western Electric.

Band:	X
Operational:	
Ships:	CGN 35
	CG 26
	DDG 2 (most ships)

SPG-53 radar mounted on Mk 68 gun director on the destroyer EDSON (DD 946). (Giorgio Arra)

SPG-51D RADAR

The SPG-51 is a pulse-doppler tracking/illumination radar used with the Standard-MR in cruisers and destroyers armed with that missile. (Originally developed for use with the Tartar missile). It is associated with the Mk 74 missile FCS. The two operating modes share a common antenna; the C-band is a pulse-doppler monopulse tracker. An SPG-51E was developed as a "universal" fire-control radar for use with the Tartar-Terrier-Talos missiles; it was not deployed in significant numbers because of the availability of more advanced radars.

The antenna is 7⅔ feet (2.3 m) in diameter. Peak power is 81 kW in tracking and 5 kW in illumination.

Manufactured by Raytheon.

Band:	C for tracking
	X for illumination
Operational:	1960
Ships:	CGN 38
	CGN 36
	DDG 993
	DDG 2

SPG-51D antennas on the after superstructure of the cruiser MISSISSIPPI. (Stefan Terzibaschitsch)

SPG-35/Mk 35 RADAR

Radar associated with the Mk 56 GFCS for 5-inch and 3-inch anti-aircraft guns. It is now found only in one older cruiser. The Mk 35 was removed from the IOWA (BB 61)-class battleships when they were reactivated in the 1980s.

Maximum tracking range is 30,000 yards (27,440 m). The radar has a 48-inch (1.2-m) parabolic scanning "dish." Peak power is 50 kW.

Manufactured by General Electric.

Band:	X
Operational:	1945
Ships:	CGN 9

SPG-35 radar antenna mounted on Mk 56 GFCS; this arrangement is now found only in the cruiser LONG BEACH (CGN 9). (U.S. Navy)

SPQ-9A RADAR

This is the fire control radar associated with the Mk 86 GFCS. It provides surface search functions as well as weapons control, operating in a high-resolution, pulse-doppler, track-while-scan mode. The SPQ-9A operates from a minimum of 150 yards (137 m) out to 20 n.miles (37 km) against aircraft-size targets. The high scan rate of 60 revolutions per minute can detect and track incoming missiles as well as aircraft and surface targets. The Mk 86 system with the SPG-60/SPQ-9 is found in new missile cruisers, the SPRUANCE-class destroyers, and the TARAWA-class helicopter ships. The battleship IOWA mounted the SPQ-9A without the Mk 86 system.

The antenna is housed in a 120-inch (3-m)-diameter plastic radome. Peak power is 1.2 kW. The MTBF is given as about 800 hours.

Manufactured by Lockheed Electronics.

Band:	X	
Operational:	1970	
Ships:	BB 61 (1 ship)	DDG 993
	CG 47	DDG 2 (3 ships)
	CGN 38	DD 963
	CGN 36	

Spherical SPQ-9A radome and SPG-60 radar antenna on destroyer ELLIOT (DD 967). Note the funnel exhaust configuration (upper right). (Giorgio Arra)

SPS-69 RADAR

Modification of commercial Raytheon R41X small-craft navigation radar.

Band:	X
Operational:	1990
Ships:	Coast Guard 47-ft motor lifeboat

SPS-66 RADAR

Surface search/navigation radar developed specifically for small craft. Based on Raytheon commercial CRP-3100.

Band:	X
Operational:	1987
Ships:	MCM 1

SPS-67(V) RADAR

Surface search/navigation radar, developed as a successor to the long-serving and widely used SPS-10 radar.

It has solid-state electronics with an MTBF in excess of 1,000 hours.

Manufactured by Norden.

Band:	C	
Operational:	1982	
Ships:	CVN 68 (3 ships)	DDG 51
	BB 61 (3 ships)	FF 1052 (some ships)
	CGN 36	LCC 19
	CGN 35	LHD 1
	CG 26	LSD 49
	CGN 25	LSD 41
	CG 16 (some ships)	AH 19
	CGN 9	AOE 6

SPS-67(V) antenna. (United Technologies/Norden)

SPS-64(V) RADAR

Surface search/navigation radar. It uses a bar-type antenna; the size of the four available antennas varies from four feet (1.2 m) to 12 feet (3.7 m), depending upon the capability/size of system. Variants have different frequency bands and operating characteristics.

The (V)1 has a single 20-kW transmitter, the (V)2 and (V)3 have two 20-kW transmitters, the (V)4 has one X-band and one S-band transmitter, the (V)5 has a tunable 20-kW transmitter, and the (V)6—for larger ships—has a 50-kW X-band transmitter.

Manufactured by Raytheon.

Band:	S and X	
Operational:		
Ships:	CVN 68 (3 ships)	PHM 1
	BB 61 (1 ship)	MHC 51
	CG 47 (25 ships)	MSO 508
	DDG 51	MSO 421
	DDG 993	AOE 6
	LCC 19	ARS 50
	LHD 1	ATS 1
	LSD 49	Coast Guard cutters
	LSD 41	service craft

SPS-64(V)9 antenna. (Raytheon)

SPS-63 RADAR

U.S. version of Italian 3RM-20N radar. It was mounted in the PEGASUS (PHM 1) class prior to the installation of the current SPS-64 radar in those ships. No U.S. ships now have the radar. X-band.

SPS-59/LN-66 RADAR

SPS-59 is the official designation for LN-66 commercial navigation radar. This is a short-range navigation radar, adopted from a commercial design. It is installed in a variety of U.S. ships, from battleships to small auxiliary ships. The radar is also fitted in the SH-2F LAMPS I ASW helicopter. Developed by Canadian Marconi.

Band:	X
Operational:	
Ships:	various

SPS-58/SPS-65(V) RADAR

Low-level, high-speed radar for both the detection of attacking anti-ship cruise missiles and target acquisition for the Sea Sparrow point-defense missile system. A pulse-doppler radar, the SPS-65 can "share" the SPS-10 antenna, while the SPS-58 has its own 16-foot (4.9-m) antenna. These radars have no integral display; in aircraft carriers the SPS-65 uses those of the ship's Naval Tactical Data System (NTDS); frigates have the SPS-58, duplexing with the SPS-10.

The SPS-65(V)1 has a specified Mean Time Between Failure (MTBF) of 400 hours.

Manufactured by Westinghouse Electric Corp.

Band:	D
Operational:	
Ships:	CVN 65
	CV 41
	FF 1052 (some ships)

SPS-65(V) antenna. (Westinghouse)

SPS-55 RADAR

Surface search radar intended as a replacement for the widely used SPS-10. The SPS-55 has a slotted-array antenna six feet (1.8 m) across. Manufactured by Cordion.

Band:	X	
Operational:		
Ships:	CG 47	DD 963
	CGN 38	FFG 7
	DDG 51	MCM 1
	DDG 993	AO 177

SPS-53 RADAR

Surface search/navigation radar. Fitted with a 60-inch (1.5-m) slotted-array antenna. Manufactured by Sperry.

Band:	X	
Operational:	1967	
Ships:	CG 47 (2 ships)	ARS 5 (some ships)
	DD 963 (some ships)	ATS 1
	FF 1052 (some ships)	ASR 21
	LHA 1	ASR 7
	AGDS 2	ATF 166
	AOE 1	Coast Guard cutters
	AOR 1	

SPS-52 RADAR

A 3-D air search radar with Frequency Scanning (FRESCAN) in elevation. Since 1963 it has been installed in several aircraft carriers plus missile-armed cruisers, destroyers, and frigates, and the five TARAWA (LHA 1)-class helicopter carriers. The carriers and LHAs used this radar for aircraft control. Most have now been replaced by the SPS-48 3-D radar.

The SPS-52 is credited with a range of 60 n.miles (111 km) against small, high-speed aerial targets, and out to much greater distances—about 250 n.miles (463 km)—against larger, high-flying aircraft. It has a high data rate and clutter rejection features including Moving Target Indicator (MTI). Later versions with solid-state components have MTBF in excess of 200 hours.

The SPS-52 is an improved SPS-39; the SPS-72 was to have been an improved version with more advanced antenna.

Manufactured by Hughes.

Band:	E
Operational:	1963
Ships:	DDG 2
	LHD 1 (1 ship)
	LHA 1

SPS-52 antenna on destroyer JOHN KING (DDG 3); an IFF antenna is fitted atop the radar. (Stefan Terzibaschitsch)

SPS-49 RADAR

The most effective rotating 2-D air search radar in the U.S. Navy is the SPS-49, a lower L-band radar. It was evaluated in 1965 on board the experimental destroyer GYATT (DD 712), and an advanced version was installed in the cruiser DALE (CG 19) in 1975. This radar features high reliability, with an MTBF reported to exceed 300 hours. It is a very long range radar and has a narrow beam, which helps to counter hostile jamming efforts. The large, 24 × 14 foot (7.3 × 4.3 m) antenna is easily identified, with a large, lower feed horn (the similar-looking SPS-40 antenna has an overhead feed horn). The SPS-49 is highly jam resistent; MTBF is in excess of 300 hours.

The SPS-49 is the principal air search radar in most U.S. warship classes and is a complementary radar to the SPY-1 in the TICON-DEROGA (CG 47) class. Note that the ARLEIGH BURKE (DDG 51) class does not have the SPS-49, deleted primarily because of cost constraints.

Several missile ships are being upgraded in their air-defense capability under the New Threat Upgrade (NTU) program, which includes provision of the improved SPS-48E and SPS-49(V)5 radars, which are linked to the SYS-2 and NTDS computer systems. The (V)5 is a digital radar with improved ECM capabilities.

The SPS-50 was a modified SPS-49 intended to replace the earlier SPS-6 and SPS-12 radars; it failed operational evaluation.

Manufactured by Raytheon.

Band:	L	
Operational:	1975	
Ships:	all CV/CVN	DDG 993
	BB 61	DDG 37
	CG 47	DD 963 (1 ship)
	CGN 38 (2 ships)	FFG 7
	CG 26	LHD 1
	CGN 25	LSD 49
	CG 16	LSD 41
	CGN 9	

SPS-49 antenna on frigate JACK WILLIAMS (FFG 24). (Giorgio Arra)

SPS-48 RADAR

The SPS-48 is a 3-D radar used for aircraft control in carriers and command ships, and to support the air defense role of missile ships. A FRESCAN radar, the older SPS-48A sets were upgraded with Automatic Detection and Tracking (ADT) features and are designated SPS-48C. This radar is more capable than the SPS-52 and can support the longer-range Standard missiles.

The rectangular antenna is $17 \times 17\frac{1}{2}$ feet (5.2×5.3 m). Maximum range is about 220 n.miles (407 km).

The SPS-48E version of the radar is being provided to missile ships under the NTU program as well as to aircraft carriers.

Manufactured by ITT Gilfillan.

Band:	E	
Operational:	1962	
Ships:	all CV/CVN	CG 16
	CGN 38	CGN 9
	CGN 36	DDG 993
	CGN 35	DDG 37
	CG 26	LCC 19
	CGN 25	LHD 1 (4 units)

SPS-48C antenna with IFF bar-type antenna (center) in the cruiser BAINBRIDGE (CGN 25). Above the SPS-48C is an SPS-67 antenna; beneath it is a cone-shaped antenna and three domes for direction-finding antennas. (Giorgio Arra)

SPS-43A RADAR

A long-range air search radar formerly mounted in aircraft carriers; an improved SPS-37, from which it was externally indistinguishable. The SPS-43 has been replaced in active aircraft carriers by the SPS-49 radar.

SPS-40 RADAR

The SPS-40 is a widely used UHF-band, 2-D air search radar capable of very long detection ranges. It is fitted in about 125 cruisers, destroyers, and frigates. It has been removed from two of the SACRAMENTO (AOE 1)-class replenishment ships and replaced on aircraft carriers by the SPS-49. One SPRUANCE-class destroyer has had the SPS-40 replaced by an SPS-49.

Older SPS-40 radars have been upgraded to the C/D configurations, which use solid-state electronics to increase reliability to some 200 hours MTBF.

The SPS-40 was developed from the SPS-31.

Manufactured by Lockheed Electronics.

Band:	B	
Operational:	1961	
Ships:	CGN 38 (2 ships)	AGF 3
	CGN 36	LHA 1
	CGN 35	LPH 2
	DDG 2	LPD 4
	DD 963 (30 ships)	LPD 1
	FF 1052	LSD 36
	LCC 19	AGFF 1
	AGF 11	AOE 1 (2 ships)

SPS-40 antenna below SPS-67 antenna. (Giorgio Arra)

SPS-39A RADAR

This 3-D search radar, previously mounted in the BAINBRIDGE (CGN 25)- and the CHARLES F. ADAMS (DDG 2)-class destroyers, has been replaced by the SPS-48 and SPS-52 radars. S-band. See SPS-26.

SPS-37A RADAR

This long-range, air search radar has been replaced by the SPS-40 and SPS-49 radars in surviving ships. A pulse-compression version of the SPS-29, it was previously fitted in the cruiser BAINBRIDGE, aircraft carriers, and various destroyer classes. (The SPS-29/37/43 used the same antenna, with the SPS-37A and SPS-43A having a larger antenna that provided longer detection ranges.)

SPS-32/SPS-33 RADARS

These early, fixed-array radars have been removed from the two ships on which they were installed. The large "billboard"-antenna SPS-32/SPS-33 were frequency-scan radars, the SPS-32 being a very long range FRESCAN 2-D radar that scanned in azimuth, with detection ranges of 400 n.miles (740 km) reported against large aerial targets under ideal conditions; the SPS-33 provided 3-D multiple-target tracking in azimuth and elevation. Each radar had four antenna "faces" paired on each side of a square superstructure in the cruiser LONG BEACH (CGN 9) and the carrier ENTERPRISE (CVAN 65), both completed in 1961 although the radar installations were not completed until 1962. During subsequent service the radars were plagued by maintenance and reliability problems, and they have been replaced during overhauls by conventional radars. The sets were too large for subsequent nuclear surface ships.

SPS-30 RADAR

A widely used height-finding radar of the 1960s and 1970s. The last U.S. Navy ship to operate with the SPS-30 was probably the carrier CORAL SEA (CV 43), with the set removed during the ship's 1983–1984 overhaul. The large ALBANY (CG 10)-class missile cruisers each had two SPS-30s, which was also found in aircraft carriers and other missile cruisers as well as specialized radar picket ships (AGR/YAGR).

SPS-29 RADAR

The long-range SPS-29 air-search radars previously installed in the FARRAGUT (DDG 37)-class ships have been replaced by the SPS-49. See SPS-37 and SPS-43 listings.

SPS-26 RADAR

The SPS-26 was the Navy's first electrically scanned, 3-D search radar; it was the forerunner of the SPS-39 and later rotating 3-D radars. The SPS-26 was laboratory tested in 1953, and the first sets went to sea in the frigate NORFOLK (DL 1) in 1957 and the nuclear radar picket submarine TRITON (SSRN 586) in 1959.

SPS-10B through F RADARS

Probably the most widely used radar in the Navy is the SPS-10 surface search, found in most surface combatants, amphibious ships, and auxiliaries. Its 11-foot (3.35-m)-wide antenna has been a familiar sight on U.S. and allied ships since late 1953. It is generally considered a horizon-range radar, although significantly longer-range detections are routinely made.

Numerous SPS-10 radars remain in U.S. Navy use. The improved I-band SPS-55, similar to the SPS-10 but with higher resolution, is being fitted in newer U.S. naval ships, while the existing SPS-10s are scheduled to be replaced by the solid-state SPS-67.

Approximately 200 U.S. naval ships continue to mount this radar, from aircraft carriers to salvage ships; the battleship NEW JERSEY (BB 62) was the only dreadnought to mount this radar (SPS-10F).

Manufactured by GTE and Raytheon.

Band:	C
Operational:	1953
Ships:	various

SPS-10 antenna above an SPS-37 antenna on the destroyer EDSON. (Giorgio Arra)

SPS-8A RADAR

This was a widely used height-finding radar, found in most carriers, battleships, cruisers, and specialized radar-picket ships (DDR/DER) in the 1950s and 1960s. It was mounted in the IOWA-class battleships prior to their 1980s reactivation. No ships now mount the radar.

SPS-6 RADAR

This air-search radar is no longer in U.S. Navy service; the last ships to carry it were the THOMASTON (LSD 28)-class amphibious ships and the SACRAMENTO-class replenishment ships. An L-band search radar, it was widely used in the 1950s and 1960s.

SPY-1 RADAR

The SPY-1 is a multi-function, phased-array (fixed-antenna) radar that is the heart of the Aegis AAW system. The SPY-1 combines the azimuth and height search, target acquisition, classification, and tracking functions, and can provide command guidance to ship-launched missiles. The replacement of several different radars with the single SPY-1 results in the reduction or elimination of several complex interfaces between specialized radars, speeds up all functions, and provides a very large target-handling capability.

The SPY-1 radar—consisting of the antenna, transmitter, signal processor, control groups, and auxiliary equipment—employs four fixed antennas ("faces") and operates in the F (formerly S) band. The antennas each contain 4,480 separate radiating elements in an octagonal face only 12½ feet (3.7 m) across. This small size facilitates ship design, with the TICONDEROGA having two antennas on a forward deckhouse (facing forward and to starboard) and two on an after deckhouse (facing aft and to port); the ARLEIGH BURKE destroyers have four antennas fitted on a single deckhouse. These four antennas each cover a 90° quadrant from the horizon to zenith for total scanning around the ship.

The SPY-1 has a wide frequency bandwidth that randomly radiates different frequencies across the bandwidth on a pulse-to-pulse basis, with very low sidelobes in comparison with its main lobe, and has extremely complex signal structures. All of these characteristics present great challenges to anti-radar missiles. The SPY-1 radar is also highly resistant to electronic countermeasures because of its frequency diversity, and it can "sense" jamming and automatically shift to different frequencies where less interference is present. Also, digital signal-processing techniques are employed to counter or suppress jamming as well as sea clutter. The latter feature is vital for an effective defense against sea-skimming missiles whose radar return is often lost to conventional radars because of sea clutter masking the target's signal.

Control of the SPY-1 is exercised by four UYK-7 digital computers that schedule and direct the beams, necessary because the SPY-1 can project hundreds of pencil-thin radar beams in rapid sequence, far too many for manual control or coordination. Beam steering is a mathematical problem that requires the calculations of a computer system. Indeed, computer capacity is a practical limitation on the number of targets that the SPY-1 can handle at one time. When a target is detected, the computers automatically schedule several more beams to "dwell" on the target within a second of the initial detection, thus initiating a track. Hundreds of targets can thus be identified and tracked simultaneously, out to ranges on the order of 200 n.miles (370 km).

In earlier missile ships the surface-to-air missiles had to be guided all the way from launch to the target. Missile ships could thus be characterized by the number of guidance channels, i.e., separate guidance radars available. The modern Standard missiles have an "autopilot" that is set at the moment of launch. The SPY-1 continuously tracks both the missiles in flight and targets, and the missile guidance can be updated while in flight. Specific radar guidance is required only for the last few seconds before the missile detonates. With this concept the TICONDEROGA's four guidance radars can handle perhaps 20 separate targets simultaneously. This provides a vast improvement over previous AAW ship capabilities.

The SPY-1 F-band covers 3100–3500 MHz with a beam measuring 1.7 × 1.7 degrees. Its peak power is four to six MW with an average power of 58 kW. Control is exercised by the UYK-7 computer in the CG 47–64 and the UYK-43/UYK-44 series in the CG 65–74 and the DDG 51 class.

There are three production versions of the SPY-1:

SPY-1A initial design (CG 47–58)
SPY-1B possessing upgraded antenna, improved transmitter and signal processor for increased effectiveness against low-flying and small radar–cross section missiles, and low sidelobe levels for enhanced ECM resistance (CG 59–73)
SPY-1C designation not used
SPY-1D single deckhouse version in ARLEIGH BURKE class

There have been proposals to install the SPY-1 radar in the NIMITZ (CVN 68)-class carriers, primarily for aircraft control, and in some nuclear-propelled cruisers. However, no installations have been made, for fiscal reasons in the carriers; the cruiser installations were opposed by the Navy's nuclear propulsion community, which sought the construction of nuclear-propelled Aegis ships.

The SPY-1 was developed from the SPG-59 phased-array radar intended for the aborted Typhon missile frigate (DLGN) program. Development of the Aegis SPY-1 began in the late 1960s. The SPY-1 (one radar face) began operation at the RCA development facility in Cherry Hill, N.J., in 1973, followed a year later by a single face being installed in the missile test ship NORTON SOUND (AVM 1).

Manufactured by GE-RCA and Unisys-Westinghouse (team).

Band:	F
Operational:	1983
Ships:	CG 47
	DDG 51

Inserting electronic elements into a SPY-1 radar. (RCA)

Two SPY-1A antennas on the after deckhouse of the cruiser SAN JACINTO (CG 56). Above the deckhouse are two SPG-62 illumination radars; at right an OE-82 SATCOMM antenna. The SPY-1 is the most powerful and flexible radar in service with any navy. (Giorgio Arra)

Reverse side of SPY-1 radar during assembly. (RCA)

VPS-2 RADAR

Radar fitted in the Mk 16 Phalanx gun system with a single transmitter supporting separate search and tracking radars mounted above the actual Gatling gun. The radar tracks both incoming targets and outgoing bullets, detects the angular error between them, and automatically corrects gun aim. It has a Moving Target Indicator (MTI) with the ability to track very high speed targets and has a very rapid reaction capability. (The radar is also used with the U.S. Army's Vulcan air-defense gun system.)

The search range is approximately 5,500 yards (5,030 m). Its band is 9200–9250 MHz with a peak power of 1.4 kW.

Manufactured by Lockheed Electronics.

Band:	Ku and X
Operational:	1980
Ships:	various

STIR   SEPARATE TARGET ILLUMINATION RADAR

Modified SPG-60 radar for use with Mk 92 gun/missile fire control system in the PERRY-class frigates.

Band:	X
Operational:	1974
Ships:	FFG 7

Mk 25 RADAR

Radar for Mk 37 GFCS intended primarily for 5-inch anti-aircraft gun control (although the Mk 25 Mod 7 was also the first U.S. missile guidance radar). They survive in the U.S. Navy only in the IOWA-class battleships.

Maximum tracking range is 100,000 yards (91,465 m). The radar has a 60-inch (1.5-m) conical scanning "dish." Peak power is 250 kW.

Manufactured by Western Electric.

Band:	X
Operational:	1948
Ships:	BB 61

Mk 25 radar fitted to Mk 37 GFCS (left) and Mk 13 radar on Mk 38 GFCS on the after superstructure of the battleship Iowa. (Giorgio Arra)

MK 13 RADAR

Range-and-bearing radar for Mk 38 and Mk 34 gun directors for main gun battery control. Previously mounted in cruisers as well as battleships.

Tracking range is 50,000 yards (45,730 m). The bar-type antenna is eight feet (2.4 m) long and two feet (0.6 m) in diameter; mounted atop the Mk 38 director in IOWA-class battleships. Peak power is 50 kW.

Manufactured by Western Electric.

Band:	X
Operational:	
Ships:	BB 61

WEAPON CONTROL SYSTEMS

In the following listings, several series are merged into a single alpha-numerical order for the convenience of users of this volume.

CCS-series COMBAT CONTROL SYSTEMS

Multiple-function control systems for weapons in LOS ANGELES-class submarines. The original Mk 1 CCS developed for the LOS ANGELES class has been replaced in some units by the upgraded Mk 2 CCS (see chapter 12). The CCS integrates the submarine's torpedo fire control system (Mk 117) with the central computer complex.

The originally CCS Mk 1 was the Mod 0; the Mod 1 (using UYK-7 computers) integrated the Tomahawk missile; the Mod 2 (using UYK-44 computers) added the vertical-launching capability; the Mod 3 adds Mk 48 ADCAP capability; and the Mods 4 and 5 add the Sea Lance missile capability.

The CCS Mk 2 has improved displays and workstations over the Mk 1. The Mod 0 was rapidly succeeded by the Mod 1, with provisions for over-the-horizon targeting (Tomahawk and Harpoon missiles); the Mod 2 intended for Trident submarines has modified consoles/controls.

The software is modular, facilitating adaptation for various submarine-weapon configurations.

Manufactured by Raytheon.

Operational:	
Ships:	SSBN 726
	SSN 688

SYS-series INTEGRATED AUTOMATIC DETECTION/TRACKING SYSTEMS

The SYS-1(V)2 and SYS-2(V) Integrated Automatic Detection and Tracking (IADT) systems integrate various radars in non-Aegis guided missile ships and large amphibious ships to facilitate command and control in high-threat environments. Each shipboard radar is fitted with a video converter, with the images passed through a processor and integrated for display in the ship's combat information center.

The SYS-1 was developed specifically for the ADAMS-class destroyers and the SYS-2 for guided missile cruisers. The latter was subsequently selected for the PERRY-class frigate upgrade and is also installed in the WASP-class amphibious ships. (The SYS-3 system is being procured for the Israeli Sa'ar V-class missile corvettes being built in the United States.)

The follow-on Integrated Radar Detection and Identification System (IRDIS) will integrate non-radar data (e.g., ESM) into the system.

Manufactured by Norden.

Operational:	SYS-1 in 1977
Ships:	CG 26 (8 ships)
	CG 16
	DDG 993
	FFG 7 (some ships)
	LHD 1

Mk 160 GFCS

Advanced gunfire control system.

Band:
Operational: 1991
Ships: DDG 51

Mk 118 TORPEDO FCS

An all-digital torpedo fire control system developed for the Trident SSBNs. It controls both torpedo launches and the release of 3-inch (76-mm) and 6-inch (152-mm) torpedo countermeasures, and the Mk 70 MOSS target simulators.

Operational: 1981
Ships: SSBN 726

Mk 117 TORPEDO FCS

The U.S. Navy's first all-digital torpedo fire control system. The system was installed in submarines of the THRESHER (SSN 593)/ PERMIT (SSN 594), STURGEON (SSN 637), and LOS ANGELES classes plus the GLENARD P. LIPSCOMB (SSN 685) and NARWHAL (SSN 671), the last being the prototype installation. Installation of the digital Mk 117 prevented use of the analog SUBROC missile; although there was an attempt to correct this interface, it had only limited use (see Mod 8, below).

The Mk 117 Mod 0 was fitted in the SSN 700–715; Mod 1 in SSN 594–596, 603–607, 612–615, and 621; Mod 2 in SSN 637–639, 646–653, 660–670, and 672–677; Mod 3 in SSN 671 and 678–687; Mod 5 (with Tomahawk capability) in SSN 596, 604–606, and 612–615; Mod 6 (Tomahawk) in SSN 637–639, 646–653, 660–670, and 662–677; Mod 7 (Tomahawk) in SSN 671 and 678–687; and Mod 8 (Tomahawk/ SUBROC/Sea Lance) for SSN 716–720.

Operational:
Ships: SSN 21
                 Improved SSN 688
                 SSN 688
                 SSN 671
                 SSN 637

Mk 116 ASW FCS

Advanced ASW weapons control system for surface ships. The all-digital system is linked to the SQS-53 sonar and controls ship-launch weapons (ASROC and Mk 32 torpedo tubes) and interfaces with the LAMPS helicopter (SH-2F/G or SH-60B).

Mods 1 through 4 are for various ship types; Mod 5 integrates the SQQ-89 sonar system; Mod 6 integrates the Vertical-Launch ASROC (VLA) potential for the later TICONDEROGA-class cruisers; and Mods 7, 8, 9, and 10 introduced the UYK-43B computer and are for use in the BURKE-class destroyers as well as non-VLS ships.

Manufactured by Librascope.

Operational:
Ships: CG 47   DDG 51
                 CGN 38   DDG 993
                 CGN 36   DD 963
                 CG 26 (1 ship)

Mk 115 FIRE CONTROL SYSTEM

The Mk 115, associated with the Sea Sparrow BPDMS, is a director/illuminator adapted from the older Mk 51 gun director mount. It also has side-by-side antennas. Tracking is manual.

Band: X
Operational:
Ships: FF 1052 (some ships)
                 LCC 19
                 LPH 2

Mk 114 ASW FCS

ASW weapons control system for surface ships. The analog, solid-state system controls ASROC and torpedo (Mk 32 tubes) in surface ships. Mods 0 through 27 were developed for various ship/sonar configurations. Succeeded by the digital Mk 116.

Operational:
Ships: CGN 35
                 CG 26 (8 ships)
                 CG 16
                 DDG 2 (some ships)
                 FF 1052

Mk 113 TORPEDO/MISSILE FCS

Widely used torpedo fire control system in SSNs and SSBNs; in attack submarines it was replaced by the Mk 117 system. The only active U.S. submarines with the Mk 113 are the remaining LAFAY-ETTE (SSBN 616)-class submarines; they were not upgraded to the Mk 117 system because of their limited sonar capabilities and limited remaining service life.

Manufactured by Librascope.

Operational:
Ships: SSBN 616

Mk 111 ASW FCS

ASW weapons control system. A solid-state digital system for launching ASROC and torpedoes (Mk 32 tubes) from surface ships. It was originally installed in FRAM destroyers from the late 1950s and subsequently in new-construction missile ships.

Mods 1 through 9 were developed for various ship/sonar configurations.

Operational:
Ships: CGN 25
                 CGN 9
                 DDG 993
                 DDG 2 (some ships)

Mk 99 MISSILE FCS

Fire control directors associated with the Aegis weapon system (Mk 7); operated in conjunction with SPG-62 radar.

The Mods 0 and 3 were fitted in the missile test ship NORTON SOUND; Mod 1 was the prototype for the TICONDEROGA class; Mod 2 the production model for that class; and Mod 4 was a production model.

Band:	X
Operational:	1983
Ships:	CG 47
	DDG 51

Mk 98 MISSILE FCS

Missile control system for Trident missile submarines.

Operational:	1981
Ships:	SSBN 726

Mk 92/Mk 94 WEAPON DIRECTION SYSTEMS

The Mk 92/Mk 94 is a combined tracking and illuminating system incorporating two antennas, one for air and surface target tracking. The Mod 2 version, in the PERRY-class frigates, is combined with the STIR radar to provide a second missile guidance channel in those ships; Mods 0 and 2 can control guns or missiles. Mods 1 and 3 through 5 versions are for gun control only, with the Mod 1 in the PEGASUS (PHM 1) class, except that the lead ship has the Mk 94 prototype, the Coast Guard's BEAR (WMEC 901) class, and the modernized Coast Guard HAMILTON (WHEC 715) class. The Mk 94 prototype is fitted in the missile ship PEGASUS and the PERRY-class frigates. In the latter ships, those refitted with the Mk 92 Mod 6 system with a Coherent Radar Transmitter (CORT) in conjunction with SYS-2(V)2 automatic target tracking system have realized an increased weapons control capability.

Manufactured by Sperry.

Band:	X
Operational:	
Ships:	FFG 7
	PHM 1
	WHEC 715
	WMEC 901

The antenna for the Mk 92 weapon direction system is fitted in radomes in these PEGASUS-class missile craft. (PH2 Mark Kettenhofen, USN)

Mk 91 WEAPON DIRECTION SYSTEM

Weapon direction system for the NATO Sea Sparrow missile system. The antenna system has side-by-side receiving and transmitting antennas; it typically has targets designated automatically by the SPS-58/SPS-65 radars or the Mk 23 TAS.

Band:	X
Operational:	
Ships:	all CV/CVN except CV 41
	DD 963
	LHD 1
	AOE 6
	AOE 1

Paired Mk 91 missile directors—with concave and convex antenna domes—on the carrier KITTY HAWK (CV 63). (Giorgio Arra)

Mk 86 GUN/MISSILE FCS

Weapons control system; fitted with SPQ-9A radar. The complete Mk 86 system includes an electro-optical sensor (closed-circuit low-light-level television) and SPG-60 tracker-illuminator radar. Reportedly, up to 120 target tracks can be monitored simultaneously.

Evaluated in 1965 in the destroyer BARRY (DD 933). Mods 0 through 10 developed with various target/tracking capabilities for various ship/radar/computer configurations.

Band:	X	
Operational:	1970	
Ships:	CG 47	DDG 2 (3 ships)
	CGN 38	DD 963
	CGN 36	LHA 1
	DDG 993	

Mk 76 MISSILE FCS

Fire control system for Standard-ER ships; fitted with SPG-55 "searchlight" illumination and guidance radar. No gunfire control capability is provided.

Mods 0 through 10 developed for various ship/radar/computer configurations.

Band:	J	
Operational:		
Ships:	CGN 35	CG 16
	CG 26	CGN 9
	CGN 25	DDG 993

Mk 74 MISSILE FCS

Weapons control system associated with Tartar/Standard-MR missiles. Fitted with SPG-51D radar.

Mods 0 through 15 developed for various ship/radar/computer configurations. Some mods fitted with low-light-level television.

Band:	G
Operational:	1960
Ships:	CGN 38
	CGN 36
	DDG 993
	DDG 2

Mk 68 GFCS

Gunfire control system for Mk 42 5-inch guns. Fitted with the SPG-53 radar.

Mods 0 through 20 developed for various ship/radar/computer configurations; some fitted with Forward-Looking Infrared (FLIR) sensor.

Band:	X
Operational:	
Ships:	CGN 35
	CG 26
	DDG 2 (most ships)
	FF 1052

Mk 56 GFCS

Fire control system for 5-inch and 3-inch guns; widely used from the 1950s, the system is now found only in one ship, the nuclear-propelled cruiser LONG BEACH. Fitted with Mk 35 radar.

Band:
Operational:
Ships: CGN 9

Mk 40 GUN DIRECTOR

Gun director fitted with Mk 27 radar. It is employed as a standby director for the Mk 38 GFCS.

Operational:
Ships: BB 61

Mk 38 GFCS

Large main battery gun director for battleships and cruisers.
 Fitted with Mk 13 radar.

Operational:
Ships: BB 61

Mk 37 GFCS

Widely used World War II–era GFCS; succeeded by Mk 67 and Mk 68 systems. Now found only in the IOWA-class battleships to control 5-inch gunfire. Fitted with Mk 25 radar.

Operational:
Ships: BB 61

Mk 25 TARGET ACQUISITION SYSTEM

Improved version of the Mk 23 Target Acquisition System (TAS).

Operational:
Ships: AOE 6

Mk 23 TARGET ACQUISITION SYSTEM

The Mk 23 Target Acquisition System (TAS) supports the NATO Sea Sparrow launcher Mk 29; the Mk 92/Mk 94 weapon FCS adopted from the Dutch M28 system; and the Mk 115 director/illuminator for the basic Sea Sparrow launcher Mk 25.

The Mk 23, intended for automatic reaction/target designation of incoming sea-skimming missiles, has a maximum range of almost 100 n.miles (185 km) and a minimum designation range of 20 n.miles (37 km). Incorporates pulse-doppler radar. Designed to operate in a high-clutter environment, it can simultaneously track up to 54 targets with a two-second scan rate. The Mk 23 first went to sea in the frigate DOWNES (FF 1070) in 1975.

Manufactured by Hughes.

Band: D
Operational: 1975
Ships: CVN 68 (2 ships)   LHD 1
      DD 963 (most ships) AOE 1 (1 ship)

The destroyer BRISCOE (DD 977) showing the Mk 23 TAS bar antenna fitted on the ship's second mast (with SPS-40 radar). (Stefan Terzibaschitsch)

Mk 14 WEAPON DIRECTION SYSTEM

Weapon direction system for guided missile ships.

Operational:
Ships:
CGN 38	CG 16
CGN 36	CGN 9
CGN 35	DDG 993
CG 26 (8 ships)	DDG 37 (1 ship)
CGN 25	

Mk 13 WEAPON DIRECTION SYSTEM

Weapon direction system. Fitted in place of the Mk 4 in three ADAMS-class destroyers that were upgraded.

Operational:
Ships: DDG 2 (3 ships)
           FFG 7

Mk 11 WEAPON DIRECTION SYSTEM

Weapon direction system. It has been replaced in ships that have an upgraded anti-air capability.

Operational:
Ships: CG 26 (1 ship)
           DDG 37 (9 ships)

Mk 4 WEAPON DIRECTION SYSTEM

Weapon direction system.

Operational:
Ships: DDG 2 (some ships)

Mk 1 TARGET DESIGNATION SYSTEM

Target designation system.

Operational:
Ships: FFG 7

SHIPBOARD SONARS

Sonar is the U.S. Navy's principal means of detecting and targeting submarines. All active U.S. cruisers, destroyers, frigates, and submarines are fitted with sonars; anti-submarine aircraft employ expendable sonobuoys, and the SH-3H and SH-60F ASW helicopters use a "dipping" sonar as well as sonobuoys; the CAPTOR sea mines employ sonar for submarine detection; mine countermeasure forces use sonars to detect mines; and ASW forces make extensive use of seafloor Sound Surveillance Systems (SOSUS). These sonars are passive or active, with some equipment capable of operating in both modes.

Submarine sonars. Contemporary U.S. submarine sonars are derived principally from German development of passive array sonars in the World War II period. These sonars have a series of fixed transducers that form beams in various directions by the electrical phasing of the transducer inputs.[4] U.S. submarines traditionally have operated in the passive mode in the era of nuclear-propelled submarines, generally being able to detect relatively noisy Soviet nuclear submarines before they themselves could be detected by their opponents. However, the appearance of quiet Soviet nuclear submarines from the early 1980s, of which the Akula class was the harbinger, has resulted in new interest in active sonar techniques. These modern, ex-Soviet diesel-electric submarines—when operating submerged on electric propulsion—have a very low acoustic signature. (Of course, operating techniques, environmental conditions, and other factors can make even the relatively noisy submarines difficult to detect.)

Although the towed-array sonars were developed by the U.S. Navy primarily for use in surface ships, they were quickly adapted to submarine use and have now been fitted in most of the current SSN and SSBN types.

BSY-2 COMBAT SYSTEM (formerly SUBACS/Fiscal 1989 System)

The BSY-2 system is an advanced sonar and fire control system designed for the attack submarine SEAWOLF. This system was originally part of the SUBACS (Submarine Advanced Combat System); see BSY-1 entry for background information.

The functions of the BSY-2 are to detect, classify, track, and launch weapons against hostile submarine targets. It is intended to permit the SEAWOLF to detect and locate targets faster, allow operators to perform multiple tasks and address multiple targets concurrently, and—ultimately—to reduce time between detecting a threat and launching weapons. The principal antennas of the BSY-2 are a large, 24-foot (7.3-m) spherical array, conformal hull array, separate active transmitter, HF mine/under-ice sonar, towed arrays, and Wide Aperture Arrays (WAA). The last consist of three large, flat arrays mounted along each side of the submarine; they employ low-frequency, passive sensing capabilities to rapidly determine the locations of targets in both azimuth and depth to provide more accurate target range and tracking data. (The BSY-1 is similar in concept although the configuration is different; see below.)

The BSY-2 has been plagued by a number of problems, including increasing costs and technical problems associated with the UYS-2 Enhanced Modular Signal Processor (EMSP), database management system, and computer network. Of particular concern has been the unprecedented number of lines of computer (software) code required for the BSY-2 system—some 3.2 million lines, of which over two million lines are in the new Ada language for which there were

4. The first "modern" array sonar installations were fitted in German submarines and surface ships beginning in the late 1930s. After the war the first U.S. array sonar developed for operational use was the BQR-4, fitted in the hunter-killer submarine K-1 (SSK 1) in 1951.

inadequate numbers of experienced programmers available.[5] The BSY-2 computer code requirement is about twice the amount needed for the BSY-1. A recent investigation of the General Accounting Office into the BSY-2 concluded:

> The risks that the Navy has allowed in the development of its BSY-2 combat system are serious. . . .
>
> In its endeavor to meet BSY-2 delivery schedules, tied closely to the submarine's delivery, the Navy is not following some sound management principles and practices, and is pushing forward not only with development of the first three systems but also for approval of three additional systems. By doing so, the Navy could find itself with combat systems that fall short of their promised capability and could cost millions to enhance.[6]

5. The only Department of Defense program known to exceed the SEAWOLF in lines of Ada code is the F-22 Advanced Tactical Fighter.
6. General Accounting Office, *Submarine Combat System: BSY-2 Development Risks Must Be Addressed and Production Schedule Reassessed* (Washington, D.C.: August 1991), p. 2.

The delays in completion of the only submarine of the design, however, could permit time to remedy some or all of these problems, many of which can be traced directly to its predecessor, the BSY-1.

The estimated cost of the BSY-2 program has *decreased* over the past few years, from about $16 *billion* to some $14 *billion.* The reduction was due mainly to the Navy's eliminating one base at which SEAWOLFs would operate (with a reduction in BSY-2 spares, training equipment, personnel, etc.). Those costs, however, were based on the procurement of 29 sets; only two sets will be procured for the truncated SEAWOLF program, although a variant of the system will probably go into the follow-on Centurion class.

Manufactured by General Electric.

Operational: 1997 (?)
Ships: SSN 21

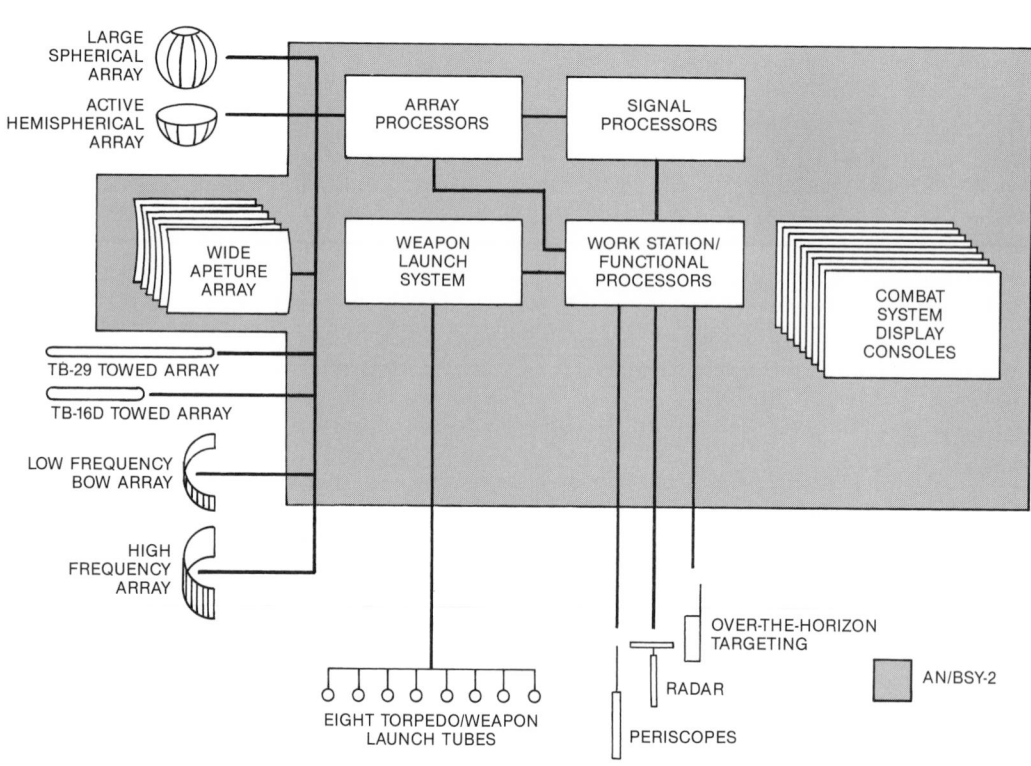

BSY-2 Combat system. (William Clipson)

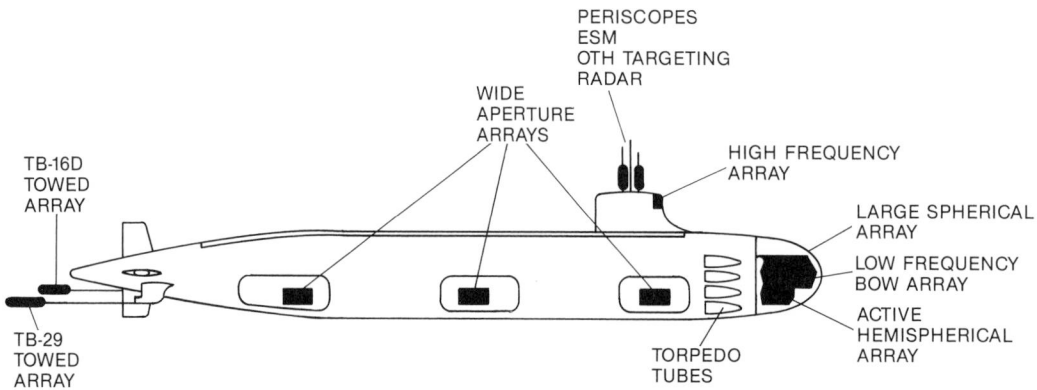

BSY-2 Combat system in SEAWOLF. (William Clipson)

The spherical, bow-mounted array housing for the BSY-2 combat system. Three systems are now being procured—one each for SSN 21 and SSN 22, plus one for software support, training, and development activities. (Newport News Shipbuilding)

BSY-1 COMBAT SYSTEM (formerly SUBACS)

The BSY-1 is an advanced sonar and fire control system intended for installation in 20 LOS ANGELES submarines beginning with the SSN 751. The system was known as SUBACS until changed to BSY-1 in 1986. As the SUBACS, the BSY-1 program was one of the most poorly run programs in recent Navy history.

Early in 1986 the Secretary of Defense told Congress that SUBACS "will maintain our [submarine] force's edge in undersea detection and targeting." Employing advanced computer hardware and software, the system is intended to exploit advanced acoustic sensors—such as Wide Aperture Arrays (WAA)—to analyze acoustic detection data, identify targets, and make fire control calculations.

When conceived in the early 1980s there were to be three versions of SUBACS: the *Basic* version for the SSN 751–759, the *B* version for the SSN 760 (fiscal 1986) and later LOS ANGELES-class submarines, and the *B-prime* variant for the SSN 21 class. The need to restructure the program because of major problems led to a two-part program, the BSY-1 for the improved LOS ANGELES class (SSN 751–773) and BSY-2 for the SEAWOLF.

The program has suffered severe technical, cost, and management problems. The planned optical data bus—using fiber-optic technology to transmit data—encountered difficulties, causing a redesign effort to employ more conventional electronic technology. Next, there were difficulties in producing the multi-layer computer circuit boards. And there were management problems, both on the part of IBM, which had been contracted to develop and produce SUBACS, and the Navy. A late 1985 congressional report on the situation stated: ". . . severe technical and management problems have significantly increased costs, delayed schedules, and degraded planned system capability." Navy and other government agency reviews of SUBACS indicated that research and development for the system would cost $2.4 *billion* and shipbuilding costs for the submarines already authorized were estimated to be 40 percent more than appropriated. The House and Senate armed services committees at the time reported: "the constrained capability of the SUBACS is no longer worth the investment."

The problems led the Secretary of the Navy and the Chief of Naval Operations to personally take over the management of the contract and renegotiate it. In late 1985 the Navy restructured the program to provide a two-track approach: The BSY-1 is being developed by IBM for the SSN 751 and later (improved) LOS ANGELES-class submarines. In January 1986 the Navy renegotiated the IBM contract to complete seven sets at a fixed price of $1.3 *billion.* In his February 1986 testimony to Congress, Admiral James Watkins, then Chief of Naval Operations, spoke of the "restructured" and "relabeled" SUBACS program becoming the BSY program. Watkins described SUBACS as originally having three steps; it was reorganized: "The middle step was not deemed necessary; it was very expensive and there was no way we could have managed the transition from step 2 to 3, which is to the SSN 21 class suite."

When installation of the first BSY-1 set began on the SAN JUAN (SSN 751) late in 1986, it was found that the cabling would not fit into the spaces allocated for the equipment in the submarine. This situation has further increased costs and delayed completion of that submarine; further, the first four installations (SSN 751–754) were not complete when fitted in submarines having only limited self-defense capabilities; they were upgraded to provide full BSY-1 capabilities after the submarines went to sea.

Manufactured by IBM and General Electric.

Operational: 1989
Ships: SSN 751–773

BQG-5 WIDE APERTURE ARRAY

The Wide Aperture Array (WAA) will enhance the fire control solutions against hostile submarines. The first BQG-5 was installed in the submarine AUGUSTA (SSN 710) in 1992 for at-sea evaluation. Apparently WAA components are also evaluated in the research ship GLOVER (T-AGFF 1).

The SEAWOLF will be fitted with the BQG-5 and probably the follow-on Centurion design.

Operational: 1992
Ships: SSN 688 (1 ship)
                SSN 21

BQQ-6 SONAR

Sonar system adopted from BQQ-5 for use in strategic missile submarines of the OHIO (SSBN 726) class. It is primarily a passive system with a limited active capability (see BQS-13); the BQQ-6 includes a bow sphere with 944 hydrophones plus flank arrays and towed array.

Manufactured by IBM.

Operational: 1981
Ships: SSBN 726

BQQ-5 SONAR

Active/passive sonar system currently fitted in all U.S. attack submarines. The BQQ-5 was built in the LOS ANGELES class (through SSN 750) and has been backfitted in the PERMIT and STURGEON classes. It is a digital system that integrates the bow-mounted array, the conformal (hull-mounted) array, and the towed array. A computer-driven signal processor is used to select the hydrophones and steer the beams. With this method the number of beams that can be formed is limited only by computer capacity. Also the digital BQQ-5 suffers far less from internal noises than the BQQ-2 with manual switching, thus enhancing the detection of weaker acoustic signals. The BQQ-5 digital computer's processing allows a reduction in the number of normal watch standers.

Developed from the BQQ-2 system, there is a large spherical bow array fitted in a 15-foot (4.6-m) sphere mounting 1,241 transducers, a "chin" array with 104 hydrophones, and TB-series towed array (see below).

BQQ-5 variants have provided improved display consoles as well as integrated towed array processing. The latest variant is the BQQ-5E modification, being fitted in all LOS ANGELES-class submarines; the improved SSN 688 class has the BQQ-5 integrated in the BSY-1 system.

Manufactured by IBM.

Operational: 1976
Ships: Improved SSN 688
                SSN 688
                SSN 671
                SSN 637

BQQ-2 SONAR

Active/passive sonar. An early version was fitted in the TULLIBEE (SSN 597), followed by the production version in the THRESHER/ PERMIT and STURGEON classes. The BQQ-2 sonar system had a 15-foot (4.6-m) diameter bow sphere mounting the BQR-7 conformal array of passive hydrophones plus the active/passive BQS-11/12/ 13 sonars.

No BQQ-2 systems remain in active SSNs, the STURGEON-class sonars having been upgraded to the BQQ-5 configuration.

BQR-21 SONAR

Passive detection sonar. The BQR-21 is a highly capable sonar, has DIMUS (Digital Multi-beam Steering). It is now found only in SSBNs. Used with BQR-24 processor.

Manufactured by Honeywell.

Operational:
Ships: SSBN 616

BQR-19 SONAR

Short-range passive navigation sonar mounted on a submarine mast; has 24 hydrophones in a cylindrical housing.

Manufactured by Raytheon.

Operational:
Ships: SSBN 726
                SSBN 616

BQR-15 TOWED ARRAY SONAR

Towed passive detection array used with the BQR-23 signal processor and BQR-7 sonar. It was the first operational towed array used by U.S. submarines.

Approximately 120 feet (37 m) long; fitted with 42 hydrophones.
Manufactured by Western Electric.

Operational: 1974
Ships: SSBN 616

BQR-7 SONAR

Conformal array sonar for passive detection. The system has 156 hydrophones that were originally scanned by mechanical means; upgraded to electronic scanning in remaining LAFAYETTE-class submarines. It is integrated with the BQR-15 towed array.

Manufactured by EDO and Raytheon.

Operational: 1955
Ships: SSBN 616

BQS-14/BQS-15 SONAR

Short-range sonar for under-ice and mine-avoidance operations. It has a cylindrical transducer housing and operates in both HF and LF ranges.

Operational:
Ships: SSBN 726 (BQS-15)
SSN 688 (BQS-15)
SSN 671 (BQS-14)
SSN 637 (BQS-14)

BQS-13 SONAR

Bow-sphere sonar of BQQ-5 and BQQ-6 systems. This is a narrow-band, active search sonar.

Operational:
Ships: SSBN 726
SSN 688
SSN 671
SSN 637

BQS-4

Active/passive sonar with seven large transducers that serve as receivers.

Manufactured by EDO.

Operational: 1955
Ships: SSBN 616

TB-SERIES TOWED ARRAY SONARS

Submarine towed array sonars are now designated in the TB-series (for Towed Body). These passive arrays are fully retractable into "sleeves" on submarine decks.

The original TB-16 array is 240 feet (73 m) long and is towed at the end of a 2,600-foot (793-m) cable and mounts 50 hydrophones. Later variants have longer arrays, with the TB-16D being a thin-line version.

The TB-23 is a thin-line array about 1,500 feet (457 m) long towed by a 2,600-foot cable. It has 98 hydrophones, the smaller diameter of the array permitting the greater length to be accommodated by the submarine.

Operational:
Ships: SSBN 726 (TB-16 being replaced by TB-29)
SSN 21 (TB-16D and TB-29)
ISSN 688 (TB-16 or TB-23)
SSN 688 (TB-16 or TB-23)
SSN 671 (TB-16)
SSN 637 (TB-16 or TB-23)

Surface ship sonars. Surface ship sonars vary considerably in type and installation. The principal hull-mounted sonars in the U.S. Navy today are the SQS-23, SQS-26/SQS-53 series, and SQS-56. The SQS-23/26/53 sonars had their origins in the early 1950s, when the first Soviet post–World War II submarines began going to sea in large numbers; these are relatively large sonars, with long-range passive and some active capabilities.

During the later 1950s the U.S. Navy developed two additional types of surface ship sonars: Variable Depth Sonar (VDS) and Towed Array Sonar (TAS). The VDS is lowered over the stern of the ship to place the sonar dome below the near-surface thermal layers that reflect sonar beams. Towed array development has led to the highly successful Tactical Towed Array Sonar (TACTAS), which consists of a passive (hydrophone) system in a cable towed behind the ship. By using convergence zone detection techniques, TACTAS has long-range capabilities against submarines, especially when employed by screening ships away from the noisy task force center. (If the ocean depth is sufficient, sound will travel down and back to the surface at an annular about 30 n.miles (55.5 km) away, i.e., to the first convergence zone. An advanced passive sonar system can be effective out to three convergence zones or some 90–100 n.miles/167–185 km.)

A further development of the towed-array concept is the Surveillance Towed Array Sonar System (SURTASS), which is a longer, more capable hydrophone array. While the TACTAS is carried by combatant ships (cruisers, destroyers, and frigates), the SURTASS is an area surveillance system, towed by slow-speed, tug-type ships designated T-AGOS (see page 243). The SURTASS/T-AGOS concept is intended for use in areas where the seafloor SOSUS detection system has been destroyed or does not exist (see below). The SURTASS AN-series designation is UQQ-2.

Sonar is also used in mine countermeasures with high-resolution sonars in minesweepers and helicopters (see below).

SQQ-89(V) ASW COMBAT SYSTEM

The SQQ-89 Surface Ship ASW Combat System is the first integrated ASW combat system for surface ships, combining sensors and weapons control systems with sophisticated data processing and display. Known as the "Squeak 89," the system correlates and manages acoustic sensor input from hull-mounted sonar and towed array, and forwards track data to the ship's combat direction system.

There are four variants of the SQQ-89; the (V)1 is going into the SPRUANCE and KIDD (DDG 993) destroyers, the (V)3 in the TICONDEROGA-class cruisers, and the (V)3 in the BURKE-class destroyers. The (V)2 was intended for the PERRY frigates, but that installation was cancelled in 1990 because of budgetary constraints; that variant was also known as the SQQ-89I, the suffix indicating "improved." It has been reinstated as the SQY-1 system. The (V)2 was to be installed in both active and Naval Reserve Force frigates of the PERRY class. In those ships the limited-capability SQS-56 sonar was to be integrated with the SQQ-89.

The large SQS-53B/C sonars of the cruisers and destroyers are integrated into the SQQ-89, as are the SQR-19 towed arrays, the SQQ-28 shipboard acoustic processing component of the LAMPS III (helicopter) system, and the ships' ASW weapons control system.

Current Navy plans call for 130 ships to be fitted with the SQQ-89 by 1995. The destroyer MOOSBRUGGER (DD 980) was the first ship fitted with the SQQ-89.

Manufactured by Westinghouse.

Operational: 1985
Ships: CG 47
DDG 51
DDG 993
DD 963
FFG 7

SQQ-32 MINEHUNTING SONAR

High-resolution mine detection and classification sonar. Provided in new-construction minesweepers and to be backfitted in early MCM ships. The sonar antenna is a "towed" body lowered through the hull of the carrying ship (the SQQ-14/SQQ-30 arrangement is similar). The sonar can be employed in a hull-mounted (retracted) mode for shallow-water operation. There are 48 acoustic arrays in a "stave" arrangement around the barrel-like towed body, with the bar-type classification antenna at the bottom of the body. Thus, the SQR-32 can display search-and-classification information simultaneously. The towed body weighs 7,845 pounds (3,530 kg).

The first operational use of the SQQ-32 was by the AVENGER (MCM 1) in the Persian Gulf in early 1991.

Manufactured by Raytheon/Thomson CSF.

Operational:	1989 (MSO test ship)
Ships:	MCM 1 (5 ships)
	MHC 51

SQQ-32 towed body. (Raytheon)

SQQ-30 MINE DETECTION SONAR

Mine detection and classification sonar developed from the SQQ-14. Cable-lowered from under minesweeper. Solid-state electronics. The SQQ-30 has limited capabilities and will be succeeded in service by the SQQ-32.

Manufactured by General Electric.

Operational:	1983
Ships:	MCM 1 (9 ships)

SQQ-28 SONOBUOY PROCESSOR

Shipboard acoustic processor and data link for LAMPS I/III anti-submarine helicopters.

Operational:	
Ships:	CG 47
	DDG 51
	DDG 993
	DD 963
	FFG 7

Artist's concept of an SQQ-32 minehunting sonar examining seafloor objects. This "hunting" technique is necessary to detect and identify objects on the seafloor that could be mines. (Raytheon)

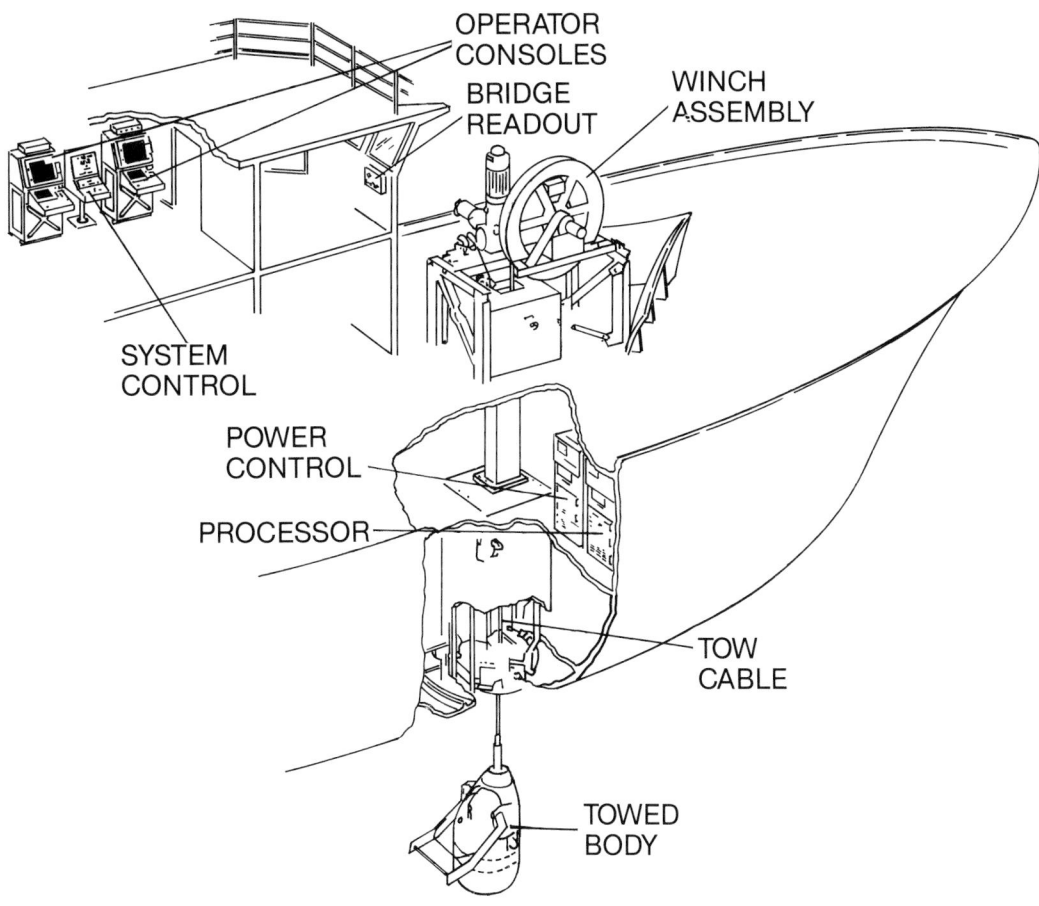

SQQ-32 arrangement in MCM/MHC. (William Clipson)

SQQ-23 PAIR SONAR

Active/passive detection sonar modified from SQS-23 sonar under the Performance And Integration Retrofit (PAIR) program. The SQQ-23 configuration generally has two domes, the second transducer for the Passive-Active Detection and Localization (PADLOC) component.

Manufactured by Sperry.

Operational:	1972
Ships:	CGN 9
	CG 16
	CGN 25
	DDG 2

SQQ-14 MINE DETECTION SONAR

Mine detection and classification sonar for minesweepers. It is lowered by cable from under the hull. Dual-frequency (80 kHz search and 350 kHz classification). Basically a UQS-1 minehunting sonar fitted with CXRP, the latter a copy of the British Type 193 high-resolution sonar. Intended primarily for use in shallow water against bottom mines.

Manufactured by General Electric.

Operational:	
Ships:	MSO

SQR-19 TACTAS

This Tactical Towed Array Sonar (TACTAS) is a passive hydrophone array deployed from cruisers, destroyers, and frigates. The towed array or "tail" locates the sonar away from ship-generated noises that could otherwise mask a target's acoustic signals. The modular construction of the array permits hydrophone components that fail or are damaged to be replaced aboard ship.

The SQR-19 is being fitted in the TICONDEROGA-class cruisers, BURKE and SPRUANCE destroyer classes, and the active PERRY-class frigates. Installation in the KIDD-class destroyers was considered but will probably not occur.

The array can be effective at relatively high ship's speed and in sea states up to 4. The SQR-19 array has a nominal diameter of 3¼ inches (82.5 mm) and is towed at the end of a 5,600-foot (1,700-m) cable. The array section weighs about 10,000 pounds (4,536 kg).

The "wet end" (cable system) of the SQR-19 is also fitted in Canadian and Spanish frigates.

Manufactured by Gould Electronics.

Operational:	
Ships:	CG 47
	DDG 51
	DD 963 (several ships)
	FFG 7 (33 ships)

SQR-18A(V) TACTAS

This version of the TACTAS is a passive hydrophone system employed by frigates. Similar to the SQR-19, there are two variants of the SQR-18: the SQR-18A(V)1 is deployed from KNOX (FF 1052)-class frigates with the array towed from the ship's variable-depth sonar, and the SQR-18A(V)2 is streamed from KNOX-class frigates without VDS and PERRY-class ships assigned to the Naval Reserve Force. On the latter ships the array—which is 730 feet (223 m) long—is towed from a 5,000-foot (1,525-m) cable rather than from the VDS towed body. The system can be effective in sea states up to 4.

The SQR-18A is fitted in Japanese ASW ships.

The basic SQR-18 was an interim towed array that evolved into the SQR-18A TACTAS. Manufactured by Gould Electronics.

Operational:	
Ships:	FFG 7 (Naval Reserve units)
	FF 1052

SQR-17A ACOUSTIC PROCESSOR

Acoustic processor for sonobuoys and related display for use with SH-2F LAMPS I helicopters. Being succeeded in newer ships by the SQQ-89. In 1986 the Congress voted funds for the procurement of 20 SQR-17A for Naval Reserve frigates.

Operational:	
Ships:	CG 26
	DDG 993
	DD 963
	FFG 7 (Naval Reserve units)
	FF 1052

SQR-15 TASS

The SQR-15 and SQR-16 were the first long-range towed sonar arrays used by the U.S. Navy. Known as Towed Array Surveillance System (TASS), the SQR-15 was installed in several GARCIA (FF 1040)-class frigates and in the BRONSTEIN (FF 1037) and MCCLOY (FF 1038) in the mid-1970s. All of those ships have been discarded. This system is supported by an equipment van on the ship's fantail, permitting it to be "cross-decked" between ships. Four SPRUANCE-class destroyers also employed the system pending the availability of the SQR-19; those were to be removed from the SPRUANCEs by the end of 1992.

A Soviet Victor III-class nuclear submarine tangled with an SQR-15 being towed by the MCCLOY in November 1983 and apparently carried off part of the array.

Manufactured by Raytheon and Gould.

Operational:	1973 (SQR-15T on converted minesweepers)
Ships:	DD 963 (4 ships)

SQS-56 SONAR

Active/passive sonar with severely limited capabilities. Ships fitted with this sonar are primarily expected to detect submarines with their towed array sonar.

The severe cost and size constraints imposed by the Chief of Naval Operations when the PERRY-class frigates were designed led to the small, higher-frequency and thus shorter-range SQS-56 being employed in this class. Raytheon had developed the SQS-56 as a totally company-funded project to provide a modern, lightweight sonar for smaller warships. The use of the SQS-56 saved perhaps 600 tons of displacement in the FFG 7, while requiring far less electrical power than the 66 kilowatts needed for the SQS-53. The cost is effective range, with the SQS-56 being capable of direct-path detections only on the order of five miles (8 km)—far too little for effective use with ship-based ASW helicopters. During the 1980s the set was modified to provide a capability for short-range mine detection; the modification is known as the "Kingfisher."

(Other factors in the decision to reduce the PERRY-class sonar effectiveness were the availability of large numbers of SQS-26/SQS-53 sonars in other ASW ships and the potential of towed array sonars.)

SQS-56 sonars have been fitted in the warships of several other navies, some with the Raytheon commercial designations DE-1160B/C.

Manufactured by Raytheon.

Operational:	1977
Ships:	FFG 7

SQS-53 SONAR

Active/passive sonar. An improved SQS-26CX sonar, the SQS-53 became the bow-mounted sonar of the SPRUANCE variants (DD 963/DDG 993/CG 47 classes) as well as the VIRGINIA (CGN 38)-class nuclear-propelled cruisers and the subsequent ARLEIGH BURKE-class destroyers.

The principal difference between the SQS-26CX and SQS-53 is the digital interface with the Mk 116 ASW weapon control system in the latter sonar. The SQS-53B has an improved, digital, solid-state display. The SQS-53C has improved active performance, multiple target capability; automatic target tracking; and a higher systems availability (2,000 hours MTBF).

The SQS-53B is being fitted in the TICONDEROGA class (beginning with CG 56) and will be backfitted in the SPRUANCE class (beginning with DD 980). The SQS-53C is being procured for the BURKE-class destroyer and will eventually be backfitted in ships with SQS-53/SQS-53B.

Manufactured by General Electric and Hughes.

Operational:	1975
Ships:	CG 47
	CGN 38
	DDG 51
	DDG 993
	DD 963

SQS-53 transducer housing on a SPRUANCE-class destroyer. (Litton/Ingalls Shipbuilding)

SQS-38 SONAR

Hull-mounted version of the SQS-35 developed for Coast Guard cutters. The solid-state sonar was developed specifically to replace the vacuum-tube SQS-36 sonar in the HAMILTON-class cutters. The sonar can operate in both active and passive modes.

This is the only sonar fitted in U.S. Coast Guard cutters.

Manufactured by EDO Corporation, College Point, N.Y., with 14 sets delivered for shipboard installation and training from 1967.

SQS-35 IVDS

Independent Variable Depth Sonar (IVDS) intended for bistatic operations with hull-mounted sonar. The ships can use their hull-mounted SQS-26 or the SQS-35 VDS, or radiate a sonar beam on one and receive its echo on the other. The VDS "fish" can be towed at relatively high speeds, and can be operated to depths of several hundred feet. It is mechanically retracted and stowed on a cradle within the stern of the ship.

The IVDS installations did not achieve the performance expected and they have been overtaken by the TACTAS.

Manufactured by EDO.

Operational:	1968
Ships:	DD 931
	FF 1052

Towed "fish" for SQS-35 variable-depth sonar in a KNOX-class frigate. (U.S. Navy)

SQS-26 SONAR

The SQS-26 is an active/passive sonar with a nominal direct-path range of 20,000 yards (18.3 km). Significantly, delays in delivery and technical problems caused the SQS-26 not to be approved for service use until November 1968. By that time more than a score of ships had been fitted with the sonar. The sonars were of limited effectiveness during this period while the ships' long-range ASW delivery capability was nil because of the short range of ASROC and the short-lived Drone Anti-Submarine Helicopter (DASH) program.

The large SQS-26 next went into the subsequent 46 ships of the KNOX class and the two nuclear cruisers of the CALIFORNIA (DLGN/CGN 36) class. With these installations a number of improvements were made to the SQS-26. A major advance was made with a shift to solid-state electronics, resulting in the new designation SQS-53. The SQS-26 variants are AXR, BX, and CX.

Manufactured by General Electric.

Operational:	1962
Ships:	CG 26
	CGN 36
	FF 1052

SQS-26 sonar dome on the frigate KNOX. (U.S. Navy)

SQS-26 sonar dome in the cruiser BELKNAP (CG 26). The stem anchor is placed specifically to reduce possible damage to the dome. (U.S. Navy)

SQS-23 SONAR

The SQS-23 is a direct-path active sonar with a range of some 10,000 yards (9.1 km), originally intended to support the ASROC weapon. In an effort to improve the capability of ships with the SQS-23, the several ships with the sonar have been fitted with a second (passive) dome under the Passive Detection and Localization (PADLOC). At sea since the mid-1970s, this arrangement is designated SQQ-23 and is reported to be highly effective. A further SQS/SQQ-23 improvement is the Performance And Integration Retrofit (PAIR), which provides a track-while-scan capability through the use of the two sonar domes. Improvements to the basic SQS-23 sonar have reached the D model.

The SQS-23 passive/active mode sonar became operational from 1958 onward in modernized, war-built FRAM destroyers, modernized FORREST SHERMAN (DD 931)-class destroyers, and then new-construction ships. Most had the SQS-23 sonar dome fitted under the hull, in the traditional position of sonars. However, one ship, the BARRY (DD 933), and the last five of the ADAMS-class ships (DDG 20–24) have bow-mounted SQS-23 domes. Moving the sonar forward to the bow had the advantage of placing the sonar as far as possible from own-ship machinery and propeller noises. But it is not without cost. The SQS-23 bow sonar weighs 28 tons and has an internal volume of 8,000 cubic feet (240 m³), resulting in a ship several hundred tons heavier than a ship with keel-mounted sonar. The bow sonar also necessitates special care in maneuvering with tugs or pulling alongside a pier, and in dry-docking the ship.

The large carrier AMERICA (CV 66) was built with an SQS-26; it was subsequently removed.

Manufactured by Raytheon.

Operational:	1958
Ships:	CG 16
	DDG 2 (5 ships)
	DD 931

SQY-1 ASW COMBAT SYSTEM

Integrated ASW combat system was intended for major ASW ships. It was to integrate all ASW sensors and fire control systems in surface combatants. The system was originally designated SQQ-89 Improved.

The SQY-1 was terminated by the Department of Defense in January 1992 as a cost-saving measure, permissible in view of the demise of the Soviet Union and the reduced threat from its submarine force. Accordingly, there will be some changes in the SQQ-89 modernization program to reflect the SQY-1 cancellation.

The initial operational capability was originally planned for the mid-1990s, but then delayed because of funding issues until after the year 2000 prior to cancellation. The system was originally intended for the 51 frigates of the PERRY class as well as cruisers and destroyers. The subsequent decision not to provide the system to ASW frigates reduced the program to some 80 ships with a related increase in unit costs.

Like the BSY-2, the SQY-1 was to incorporate the UYS-2 Enhanced Modular Signal Processor (EMSP) to handle the large amount of data processing required for the system. (When developed, the EMSP will also be used for an upgrade of the SURTASS and other ASW systems.)

Operational:	2000+	
Ships:	planned	CG 47
		DDG 51
		DDG 993
		DD 963

UQQ-2 SURTASS

The Surveillance Towed Array Sensory System (SURTASS) is a submarine detection system towed by slow surface ships to supplement the SOSUS. These ships operate where SOSUS coverage is inadequate or where the seafloor arrays are damaged or destroyed. The SURTASS data is sent via satellite link to shore facilities for processing and further transmission to ASW forces; however, the ships can provide "raw" acoustic data to ASW ships in the area. The SURTASS concept differs from the tactical TASS/TACTAS systems in that the latter are tactical hydrophone arrays towed by warships to supplement hull-mounted sonars.

The oceanographic research ship MOANA WAVE (AGOR 22) conducted sea trials of the UQQ-2 in 1979–1984; the ex-missile submarine SAM HOUSTON (SSN 609) was employed in the mid-1980s as an underwater test platform for the UQQ-2.

See page 243 for additional characteristics.

Operational:	1984
Ships:	T-AGOS 19
	T-AGOS 1

SEAFLOOR ACOUSTIC SYSTEMS

The U.S. Navy operates several seafloor Sound Surveillance Systems (SOSUS) in various parts of the Atlantic and Pacific, as well as across the Strait of Gibraltar and off the North Cape (north of Norway).[7] In the late 1960s then-Secretary of Defense Robert S. McNamara first publicly acknowledged the existence of SOSUS, although installation began in the 1950s.

SOSUS is used to detect transiting submarines and, in wartime, would be used to direct air, surface, and submarine ASW forces to their targets. However, the SOSUS arrays are vulnerable to active and passive (i.e., jamming) attacks by hostile naval and possibly merchant forces.

During World War II the American, British, and Soviet navies installed limited-capability acoustic arrays on the ocean floor in shallow waters, especially near harbors. Immediately after the war the U.S. Navy began development of deep-ocean arrays. By 1948 arrays were being tested at sea and by 1951 the first SOSUS arrays were being implanted at sea. Also termed Project Caesar, the first set of operational hydrophones was installed at Sandy Hook, south of Manhattan, followed in 1952 by a deep-water (1,200-foot/365.85-m) installation off Eleuthera in the Bahamas. That year the Chief of Naval Operations directed the establishment of six arrays in the Western Atlantic, all to be ready by the end of 1956. The first arrays in the Pacific were operational in 1958. Installations in other areas followed.

Initially a number of Naval Facilities (NAVFAC) were established as the shore terminals for SOSUS, with NAVFACs being located along both U.S. coasts, in the Caribbean, Iceland, and Japan as well as at other overseas locations. Subsequently the seafloor hydrophones have been replaced, and the NAVFACs in the United States and Caribbean have been consolidated as more capable arrays and computers have been developed.

The SOSUS system and SURTASS (T-AGOS) ships are integrated into the so-called Integrated Undersea Surveillance System (IUSS). Acoustic data from the NAVFACs and Regional Evaluation

7. The locations of U.S. SOSUS arrays have been identified in Soviet/Russian magazines.

Centers (REC) are provided through the Ocean Surveillance Information System (OSIS) to the Atlantic, Pacific, and European area Fleet Command Centers (FCC) and to the Naval Ocean Surveillance Information Center (NOSIC) in Suitland, Maryland, near Washington, D.C., as well as to the National Command Authority (NCA). Thus, SOSUS information is provided at several levels—to tactical as well as theater and national commanders, and for technical evaluation.

Published sources cite detection ranges of "hundreds" of miles by SOSUS, with arrays reported in the Atlantic and Pacific areas as well as in some regional seas. Several update programs have been announced, especially related to computer capability, which can more rapidly provide data with an improved signal-to-noise ratio.

An improved SOSUS-type system known as the Fixed Distributed System (FDS) is under development. The system is intended to detect quiet, deep-running Soviet/Russian submarines. A shallow-water FDS variant is being developed, with greater emphasis on fiber-optics than SOSUS-type systems, and possible integration of non-acoustic sensors.

These acoustic systems are to be linked into the Integrated Undersea Surveillance System (IUSS). The FDS was in advanced development in the early 1990s at the time of massive defense-funding reductions. Beginning in mid-1990, Congress began cutting the funding for the IUSS and FDS programs despite traditional congressional support for major ASW programs. At the same time, the Navy began examining the feasibility of employing FDS in coastal and shallow-water areas.

The obvious vulnerabilities of SOSUS in wartime, as well as some coverage limitations, have led to the T-AGOS/SURTASS program and to proposals for smaller arrays that could be planted by surface ships or aircraft. The latter has been an on-again, off-again program, identified by such acronyms as MSS (Moored Surveillance System) and RDSS (Rapidly Deployable Surveillance System). The RDSS was formally cancelled by the Navy on 26 December 1984. This form of sonar would have probably been quite useful, in view of increased Soviet naval operating areas predicted at that time and the growing Third World submarine forces.

HELICOPTER SONARS

The Navy's SH-3H Sea King and SH-60F Seahawk ASW helicopters are fitted with the AQS-13 active "dipping" sonar. This sonar is generally used in areas where ship-generated noises (e.g., near a carrier battle group) are high and passive sonar or sonobuoy effectiveness is limited. The latest variant to be fitted in these helicopters is the AQS-13F.

An airborne low-frequency sonar has been under development to succeed the AQS-13 series. This system was intended for use with the SH-60B LAMPS III helicopter as well as the SH-60F carrier-based variant. However, the weight of the dipping sonar would require an increase of the operating weight of the SH-60B to an estimated 23,500 pounds (10,660 kg).

In December 1991 the Navy selected the French-based Thomson-CSF firm to develop the advanced helicopter sonar, called Airborne Low Frequency Sonar (ALFS) by the Navy. The French system is known as FLASH for Folding Light Acoustic Sonar for Helicopters. The FLASH system was chosen over proposals by several U.S. firms and, when this edition went to press, the selection was being contested by some of the competitors.

The Thomson system will be developed under a subcontract from Hughes Aircraft Co. The lead systems will be delivered in the late 1990s.

AQS-13 dipping sonar being deployed from an SH-3 Sea King. (U.S. Navy)

The airborne low-frequency sonar program calls for 429 systems at a production cost of $1.2 *billion,* which includes the costs of spares, training, and fitting the system to SH-60B/F helicopters.

(A towed vice dipping helicopter array has been proposed; such a system could also be employed from airships, should they be acquired by the U.S. Navy; see chapter 29.)

The AQS-14 produced by Westinghouse is a helicopter-towed, active sonar employed by the MH-53E Sea Dragon and RH-53D Sea Stallion mine countermeasures helicopters. The AQS-14 towed body weighs 555 pounds (251 kg). The system's control console and winch are mounted on pallets and can be rapidly installed or removed from a helicopter; they can also be fitted to small surface craft.

The improved AQS-20 is now being developed by Raytheon for the mine-detecting role. It is capable of being towed at higher speeds, with a greater sonar path width and area search rate than the AQS-14.

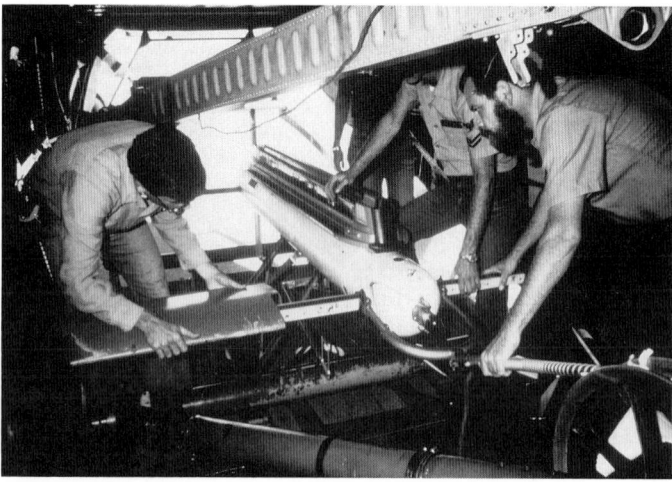

AQS-14 minehunting sonar "fish" being prepared for deployment from an MH-53E Sea Dragon helicopter. (Westinghouse)

SEA MINE SONAR

Another significant use of sonar in ASW is mine warfare, with the U.S. Navy's CAPTOR (encapsulated torpedo) being fitted with sonar to detect hostile submarines passing through the "attack envelope" of the mine's Mk 46 homing torpedo. The Mk 60 uses a passive sonar to initially detect targets and an active acoustic set to identify the hostile submarine before launching an acoustic-homing Mk 46 torpedo.

(In addition to the Mk 46 Mod 5 launched by the CAPTOR mine, other versions of the torpedo launched from surface ships [Mk 32 tubes or ASROC] and aircraft are fitted with active-passive acoustic guidance, as is the larger, submarine-launched Mk 48 torpedo.)

SONOBUOYS

Naval aircraft employ expendable, short-duration sonobuoys for the localization of submarines. Sonobuoys are generally employed after an initial submarine contact is gained by other means. However, there are sonobuoy barrier tactics in which a string of sonobuoys is periodically planted ahead of a task force. The Navy's S-3 Viking, P-3 Orion, SH-2 LAMPS I, SH-3H Sea King, and SH-60B/F Seahawk aircraft all can launch and monitor sonobuoys; the SH-2 helicopters cannot analyze sonobuoy data, but relay data back to their supporting warship.

The principal types of sonobuoys now in U.S. Navy service are listed in table 31-2. When released by aircraft, the buoys fall to the water, slowed by a retardation device or by parachute in older buoys. Upon reaching the water the buoy's battery is activated, the transmission antenna extends, and the hydrophone is lowered by cable; buoys either activate upon hitting the water or are command-activated. In table 31-2 the data are for the latest production models unless a variant is indicated; the term "depth" indicates the level to which the buoy's hydrophone (or XBT sensor) is lowered by cable. After a specified number of minutes or hours the buoy canister floods and sinks. Most current sonobuoys are of a standard "A"-size that fit launch chutes on board ASW aircraft—three feet (0.9 m) in length and 4⅞ inches (122 mm) in diameter. However, the SSQ-75 is larger—10 feet (3 m) in length with a diameter of 91 inches (2.3 m). Efforts are being made to reduce sonobuoy size, with dwarf "B" versions of the SSQ-53/77/79 being developed that will permit three sonobuoys to be carried in a standard "A"-size aircraft launcher.

Ice-penetrating sonobuoys have also been developed for use in the Arctic ice pack to detect Russian submarines operating under ice. These air-launched buoys are known to have successfully penetrated ice up to ten feet (3 m) thick. At least one concept for ice-penetrating buoys employs a two-pound (0.9-kg) lithium nose cone for penetrating the ice cover. Housed in an A-size sonobuoy, the ice-penetrator has an oversized parachute and shock absorber to reduce impact upon landing. After landing on the ice the lithium nose cone melts through the ice; the sensor deploys through the hole in the ice, the nose cone falls away, and the antenna, which remains above the ice, extends and the sonobuoy becomes operational.

Sonobuoys are used in a complementary manner, some being laid to attain initial detection of a possible submarine target while others provide shorter-range, more precise data on the target's exact depth and bearing. The SSQ-36 Expendable Bathythermograph (XBT) is used to determine the acoustic conditions of the water column, vital data in ASW operations. The principal buoys currently used in air ASW operations are the SSQ-53 Directional low-Frequency Acquisition and Ranging (DIFAR) and SSQ-62 Directional Command Activated Sonobuoy System (DICASS) types. The SSQ-77 is a deep-searching sonobuoy with a long-line array, as is the SSQ-79 Steered Vertical Line Array (SVLA). The SSQ-75 Expendable Reliable Acoustic Path Sonobuoy (ERAPS) is a command-activated buoy that actively seeks very quiet submarines; during its three-hour service life it produces about 100 active acoustic "pings." The SSQ-57 is a small, passive-detection sonobuoy intended for relatively shallow waters; the current U.S. Navy interest in regional naval operations could lead to renewed attention to this type of buoy.

The earlier SSQ-50 CASS buoy has been succeeded by the SSQ-62 DICASS. The SSQ-73 was an experimental deep-DIFAR buoy based on the SSQ-53; the SSQ-73 passive Vertical Line Array DIFAR (VLAD) was procured in its place.

A large, "B"-size active pinging buoy designated SSQ-90 is in limited production for the Navy.

The SSQ-101 is a Horizontal-Line Array (HLA) sonobuoy that holds promise of long-range submarine detections. If development is successful, the buoy would be used for long-range detections ahead of surface naval forces. Development began in the mid-1980s (as did development of the TSS and LCS buoys in response to the emergence of several Soviet quiet submarine classes).

TABLE 31-2. SONOBUOYS

Designation	Type	Manufacturer	Weight	Depth	Frequency range	Endurance
SSQ-36*	bathythermograph (water temperature profile)	Sparton		1,000 ft (305 m)	—	few minutes
SSQ-41A	omnidirectional passive detection; LOFAR (Jezebel)	Hermes, Magnavox, Sparton	21 lbs (9.5 kg)	60 or 300 ft (18 or 91 m)	10 Hz to 20 KHz	1,3, or 8 hours
SQQ-41B	same		29 lbs (13 kg)	60 or 1,000 ft (18 or 305 m)	10 Hz to 10 kHz	
SSQ-47B	active range only		29 lbs (13 kg)	60 or 800 ft (18 or 244 m)		30 minutes
SSQ-53B*	passive directional (DIFAR)	Canadian Commercial, Magnavox, Sparton	22 lbs (10 kg)	100, 400 or 1,000 ft (30.5, 122 or 305 m)	10 Hz to 2.4 kHz	1, 3, or 8 hours
SSQ-57	passive for restricted waters	Hermes, Sparton	14 lbs (6.35 kg)	60 or 400 ft (18 or 122 m)		1, 3 or 8 hours
SSQ-58	surveillance buoy	Sparton		20 ft (6.1 m)	50 Hz to 10 kHz	100 hours
SSQ-62B*	Directional Command Active Sonobuoy System (DICASS)	Raytheon	34 lbs (15.4 kg)	90, 400 or 1,500 ft (27, 122 or 457 m)		30 hours
SSQ-75	Expendable Reliable Acoustic Path Sonobuoy (ERAPS)	ERAPSCo†	325 lbs (147 kg)	60 *to* 16,500 ft (18 *to* 5,030 m)		3 hours
SSQ-77B*	passive Vertical Line Array DIFAR (VLAD)	Sparton, Magnavox	29 lbs (13 kg)	1,000 ft (305 m)	10 Hz to 2.4 kHz	1 or 8 hours
SSQ-79	Steered Vertical Line Array (SVLA)	Hazeltine		1,000 ft (305 m)		4 or 8 hours

*Currently in large-scale production.
†EARPSCo is a joint venture by Magnavox and Sparton formed in 1987 to produce the ERAPS buoy.

An advanced submarine detection program known as the SSQ-102 Tactical Surveillance Sonobuoy (TSS) was cancelled in late 1991 because of the reduced Soviet/Russian submarine threat. The TSS was to have had an onboard mini-computer to analyze and record probable submarine noises and transmit them to ASW aircraft when so directed. This transmit-on-command was necessary because of the expected service life of TSS, on the order of *five to seven days*. (In effect, the TSS would have been a scaled-down version of the MSS and RDSS concepts; see page 545.)

Although TSS has been cancelled, some of the technologies being developed under the program will be applicable to other ASW projects.

Also under development is the SSQ-103 Low-Cost Sonobuoy (LCS), a multiple-buoy device, in which an "A"-size buoy would deploy a field of six mini-buoys, each of which would suspend a hydrophone 300 feet (91 m) below the surface. The individual buoys would be 5½ inches (140 mm) in length and 4½ inches (114 mm) in diameter.

The LCS system would seek out submarine flow noises, i.e., the water flow over a submarine's hull, a gross, broad-band noise. This requires less sophisticated sensors and analyses than are needed for narrow-band noises (produced by a submarine's machinery and propellers), and are very short range against slow-moving submarines.

The SSQ-58A is a moored surveillance buoy used by the Navy's Mobile Inshore Undersea Warfare units to form surveillance barriers to detect swimmers or small craft. The buoy itself is a fiberglass float 24 inches (0.6 m) in length and 36 inches (0.9 m) in diameter, carrying a standard, omnidirectional hydrophone, up-link transmitter, antenna, etc. It can be recovered and its battery recharged; it does not sink at a predetermined time as do other buoys discussed here. (The designation SSQ-58 was previously applied to a Low-Frequency Acquisition And Ranging [LOFAR] buoy.)

The U.S. Navy also employs several communication buoys for submarine use: The BRC-6 Expendable Submarine Tactical Transceiver (XSTAT) is a two-way expendable buoy for UHF communications between a submarine and aircraft; the BRT-1 Submarine-Launched One-way Transmitter (SLOT) is ejected by a submarine to broadcast, with a preset delay, a four-minute taped message; the BRT-3/4/5 buoys transmit a signal to identify a submarine in night/bad weather; the BRT-6 is a one-way transmission buoy, to uplink prerecorded UHF transmissions to a communications satellite; and the SSQ-71 and SSQ-86 are "A"-size, two-way, aircraft-submarine communications buoys that are carried in aircraft sonobuoy dispensers.

Sonobuoys are loaded into the dispensing chutes on the starboard side of an SH-60B Seahawk helicopter. (U.S. Navy)

A technician loads an *internal* sonobuoy dispenser in a P-3 Orion; this is the only aircraft that has a sonobuoy dispenser that can be reloaded in flight (in addition to the non-reloadable chutes external to the cabin). (U.S. Navy)

A sonobuoy falls from an SH-2F helicopter of HSL-31. The retardation fins are open to slow its descent; note the sonobuoy chutes fitted in the side of the helicopter and the Mk 46 ASW torpedo. (U.S. Navy)

CHAPTER 32

Coast Guard

The Island-class patrol boat ADAK "rides shotgun" for the battleship WISCONSIN (BB 64) during an exercise. The Coast Guard's cutters, boats, and aircraft have long comprised a versatile and effective maritime force. (U.S. Coast Guard, R. Ressler)

The U.S. Coast Guard is a military service under the Department of Transportation. Federal statute states that in the national security role the Coast Guard "... shall maintain a state of readiness to function as a specialized service in the Navy in time of war, including the fulfillment of Maritime Defense Zone command responsibilities."

The Coast Guard is responsible for the enforcement of U.S. laws in coastal waters and on the high seas subject to the jurisdiction of the United States. At the direction of the president, the Coast Guard can become a part of the Navy (as during both World Wars) or it can operate in a war zone while remaining an independent service (as during the Korean and Vietnam Wars and the 1991 conflict in the Persian Gulf).

The principal peacetime missions of the Coast Guard are: (1) enforcing recreational boating safety: (2) conducting search-and-rescue operations; (3) maintaining aids to navigation, including 1 manned lighthouse at Boston, Mass., and some 450 unmanned lighthouses, and some 13,000 minor navigational lights; (4) implementing merchant marine safety; (5) carrying out environmental protection; (6) being responsible for port safety; and (7) enforcing laws and treaties.

The last mission comprises the enforcement of the nation's customs and immigration laws, including the prevention of smuggling of narcotics, and also the enforcement of fisheries laws, including international treaties related to the 200-n.mile (370-km) offshore Exclusive Economic Zone (EEZ).

In addition, as a military service, the Coast Guard carries out those military missions assigned by the Joint Chiefs of Staff (with the Commandant of the Coast Guard attending those JCS meetings that address issues of interest to the Coast Guard). Since 1985 the Coast Guard has had coastal defense responsibilities for the U.S. Atlantic coast and, since 1986, for the U.S. Pacific coast under the concept of Maritime Defense Zones (see below).

Historical: The Coast Guard was established on 4 August 1790 as the Revenue Marine of the Department of the Treasury. Subsequently, it became the Revenue Cutter Service and, from 1915, the Coast Guard. The service incorporated the Lighthouse Service in 1939. The Coast Guard was a component of the Treasury Department from its formation until being transferred to the newly established Department of Transportation in 1967.

ORGANIZATION

The major U.S. Coast Guard operating commands are the Atlantic Area (headquarters on Governors Island in New York Harbor) and the Pacific Area (headquarters in San Francisco), with ten subordinate district commands (see figure 32-1). Each area command, in addition to its assigned districts, has an assigned Maintenance and Logistics Command.

District	Headquarters	Area	Personnel[1]
1st District	Boston, Mass.	northeast	3,000
2nd District	St. Louis, Mo.	central	800
5th District	Portsmouth, Va.	middle Atlantic	2,400
7th District	Miami, Fla.	southeast	4,000
8th District	New Orleans, La.	Gulf coast	2,800
9th District	Cleveland, Ohio	northern, Great Lakes	2,100
11th District	Long Beach, Calif.	southwest	1,350
13th District	Seattle, Wash.	northwest	3,300
14th District	Honolulu, Hawaii	Hawaii	2,100
17th District	Juneau, Alaska	Alaska	2,450

The district commanders control all shore, air, and sea activities in their area of responsibility. In addition, in 1985–1986 the commanders of the Coast Guard Atlantic and Pacific areas were designated as commanders of the newly established Maritime Defense Zone (MDZ) Atlantic and Pacific, respectively. The MDZ commanders report to their respective Navy fleet commanders.[2]

The MDZ commanders are responsible for: (1) planning, conducting, and coordinating wartime operations in and around U.S. harbors and coasts; (2) ensuring an integrated defense plan for the MDZs' areas of responsibility; and (3) protecting coastal and nearby sea lines of communication. Within each MDZ are operating sectors, which are commanded by Coast Guard district or base commanders.

The MDZ organization sought to rectify a long-standing shortfall in U.S. defense policy—that of defending U.S. harbor and coastal waters from hostile activity in wartime, particularly submarine operations. However, the threat from submarine mining and the use of Coast Guard forces in forward crisis and combat areas does raise the question of whether the Coast Guard should additionally have

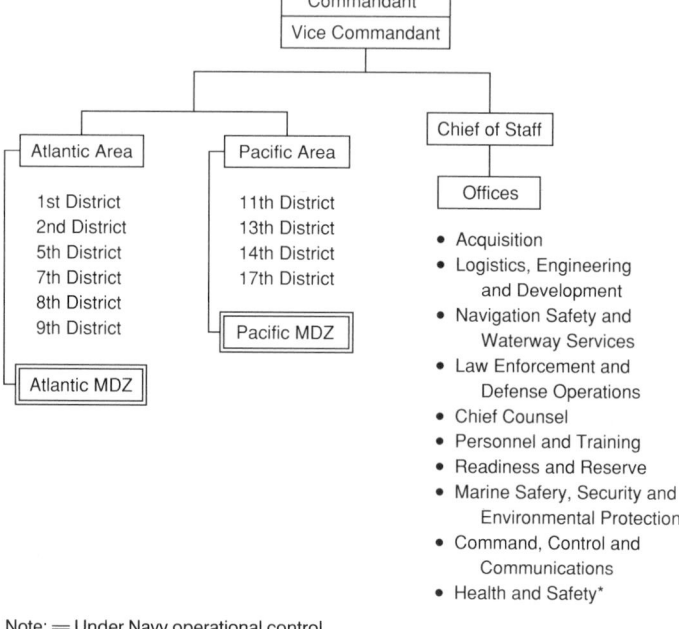

Note: ═ Under Navy operational control.
*Chief is a rear admiral in the U.S. Public Health Service.

FIGURE 32-1.   COAST GUARD ORGANIZATION

control of the surface mine countermeasure forces, which are now, of course, a Navy activity.[3]

Coast Guard Headquarters, located in Washington, D.C., provides overall supervision and support for the operating districts. The Headquarters, as shown in figure 32-1, has ten major directorates or "offices" and suffers from overlap, which results in an awkward command structure for efficient management of the Coast Guard in the rapidly changing maritime-defense environment of the 1990s.

1. Active-duty Coast Guard men and women.
2. A more detailed description of the Maritime Defense Zones is found in Comdr. Lawson W. Brigham, USCG, "U.S. Coast Guard in 1985," *Naval Institute Proceedings* [Naval Review] (May 1986), pp. 42–49.

3. This issue is examined in N. Polmar, "The U.S. Navy: Mine Warfare Problems ... And a Solution," Naval Institute *Proceedings* (December 1991), pp. 105–106.

Adm. J. William Kime, Commandant since 31 May 1990. (USCG)

OPERATIONS

The Coast Guard made major contributions to U.S. military activities in Operations Desert Shield and Desert Storm in the Persian Gulf area. The Coast Guard contribution comprised:

- Ten four-man Law Enforcement Detachments (LEDet) that were placed on board Navy ships to perform boarding of ships suspected of carrying contraband cargoes to Iraq.
- Three reserve Port Security Units (PSU), each with some 100 men and women, with patrol craft that were deployed in the Gulf.[4]
- Two HU-25C Falcon surveillance aircraft that were deployed to Bahrain to monitor the oil pollution caused by Iraqi forces.

No Coast Guard cutters were deployed to the Gulf area. (In 1987 the deployment of 110-foot/33.5-m patrol craft to the Gulf was proposed, but quickly abandoned in the face of Navy opposition.)

In the Western Hemisphere, Coast Guard activities include the service's traditional law-enforcement, safety, and merchant marine inspection activities. The Coast Guard is a major participant in drug interdiction operations with Joint Task Forces 4 and 5, the multi-agency anti-drug forces; both task forces are commanded by Coast Guard rear admirals.

---

4. These units, which were flown to the Gulf with their boats, served as port security forces in Bahrain and Saudi Arabia. It was the first time in the 50-year history of the Coast Guard Reserve that its personnel had served outside of the United States. The units were No. 301 from Buffalo, N.Y., No. 302 from Cleveland, Ohio, and No. 303 from Milwaukee, Wisc.

CUTTERS AND BOATS

The Coast Guard operates a large number of oceangoing, coastal, and inland ships and small craft for a variety of purposes.

Two major ship-procurement programs have recently been completed, the acquisition of 13 medium-endurance cutters of the Famous or BEAR class, and 49 large patrol boats of the Island class. The former ships equate to corvettes in many navies; unfortunately, those ships have a limited military capability.

Coast Guard plans to construct a larger patrol boat design known as the Heritage class have come to a full stop. It now appears that the program was not adequately thought out and has suffered severe criticism from other government agencies.

The Coast Guard is now considering designs for a smaller patrol boat to replace the popular and useful 82-foot (25-m) patrol boats of the Point class. The new design is referred to as a coastal patrol boat. All of the older 95-foot (29-m) patrol boats of the Cape class have been discarded.

Other procurement programs include a long-delayed third large icebreaker, a series of seagoing buoy tenders, and an advanced-design series of 44-foot (13.4-m) rescue boats.

The large HAMILTON-class high-endurance cutters have recently completed an extensive modernization program that will permit these ships to serve effectively in peacetime as well as wartime roles throughout this decade. There are no plans at this time to develop a replacement for these excellent ships, and if they are not replaced the Coast Guard will in fact as well as name evolve into a coastal patrol force. Unfortunately, the HAMILTON-class modernization included the removal of the ships' 5-inch/38-cal DP guns, which were very useful weapons.

Several other cutter and boat classes have undergone upgrade programs.

One former Navy floating dry dock, the YFD 83 (ex-AFDL 31) is operated by the Coast Guard at Curtis Bay, Md.; see page 370.

Most cutters are painted white; the larger icebreakers are painted red and buoy tenders and harbor tugs painted black (their superstructures remain white).

The Coast Guard insignia, a narrow blue and wide orange stripe with the Coast Guard shield superimposed on the latter, is carried on the bows of all vessels except lightships. The words "Coast Guard" are painted on the sides of all ships.

Designations: The Coast Guard uses the term *vessels* for all watercraft operated by the service. Within that classification, the term *cutter* is used for ships that have "an assigned personnel allowance and that [have] installed habitability features for the

The cutter MELLON fires a Harpoon anti-ship missile on 16 January 1990—the first guided missile ever fired by a Coast Guard ship. (U.S. Coast Guard)

TABLE 32-1 COAST GUARD CUTTERS AND PATROL BOATS

Number	Class/Ships	Class	Commissioned	Active	Building	Notes
WHEC 715	HAMILTON	378	1967–1972	10	(2)	2 being modernized
WMEC 901	BEAR	270	1983–1990	13	—	
WMEC 615	RELIANCE	210	1964–1969	16	—	
WMEC 38	STORIS	230	1942	1	—	ex-WAGB type
WMEC 6	ESCAPE	213	1943–1944	3	—	ex-Navy ARS
WMEC 153	CHILULA	205	1940–1945	3	—	ex-Navy ATF
WMEC 62	BALSAM	180	1942–1944	1	—	ex-WLB type
WSES 2	SEA HAWK	150	1982–1983	3	—	
WPB 1400	Heritage	120	suspended	—	(1)	
WPB 1301	Island	110	1986–1990	49	—	
WPB 82301	Point	82	1960–1970	43	—	
WFCI 43501	Interceptor	43	1987–	5	20	
WAGB 12	HEALY	460	1996	—	—	1 authorized
WAGB	Polar	399	1976–1978	2	—	
WAGB 83	MACKINAW	290	1944	1	—	Great Lakes
WIX 327	EAGLE	295	1936	1	—	sailing bark
WLB 62	BALSAM	180	1942–1944	24	—	
WLM	coastal buoy tenders			11	—	
WLI	inland buoy tenders			6	—	
WLIC	inland construction tenders			14	—	
WLR	river buoy tenders			18	3	
WTGB	icebreaking tugs			9	—	
WYTL	small harbor tugs			14	—	

extended support of a permanently assigned crew." In practice, this includes 65-foot (19.8-m) tugs and larger vessels, except ferries. The term "cutter" comes from the early British revenue service ships that were cutter-rigged sailing vessels, although the original U.S. revenue cutters were sailing schooners.

Craft less than 65 feet in length are officially considered "boats" and have hull numbers with the first two digits indicating the vessel's length overall. However, the designation "patrol boat" (WPB) is used for craft up to 120 feet (36.6 m).

The Coast Guard classifies all of its ships and small craft by length (in this volume shown in parentheses after the class name). The Coast Guard vessel classification scheme is derived from that of the U.S. Navy (see chapter 3). All Coast Guard cutters and boat classifications are prefixed by the letter *W* (*unofficially* for White-painted ships). The larger cutters are numbered in a single, sequential series that was initiated in 1941–1942 with new classes initiating new number blocks.

Cutter names are prefixed by USCGC for U.S. Coast Guard Cutter.

AVIATION

The Coast Guard air arm operates 222 aircraft based at 25 air stations in the continental United States, Hawaii, Alaska, and Puerto Rico.

In addition to the fixed-wing aircraft and helicopters listed below, the Coast Guard has pioneered in the development of unmanned airships or aerostats for ocean surveillance. A 1985 agreement between the Navy and Coast Guard shifted responsibility for development of manned airships to the Navy and unmanned craft to the Coast Guard. However, on 31 December 1991, all Coast Guard aerostats and their support ships were transferred to the Army; the ships are described in chapter 34 of this edition. (See chapter 29 for details of aircraft and airship programs.)

Two major aircraft procurement programs have recently been completed: 41 HU-25 Guardian Medium-Range Search (MRS) fixed-wing aircraft, acquired to replace the HU-16 Albatross amphibian and HC-131 Samaritan, and 96 HH-65A Dolphin Short-Range Recovery (SRR) helicopters, acquired to replace the HH-52A Sea Guard helicopters. Both aircraft are of French design, and are not being flown by any other U.S. military service. The Coast Guard's HH-52A is also unique to that service, but historically most Coast Guard aircraft have been of the same type as those flown by the Navy. As the HH-65As became operational, the HH-52As were mothballed at Davis-Monthan Air Force Base near Tucson, Ariz.

The Coast Guard is now procuring the HH-60J Jayhawk Medium-Range Recovery (MRR) helicopters. These are search-and-rescue variants of the widely flown H-60 series (Navy SH/HH-60 Seahawk).

All earlier HC-130B Hercules Long-Range Search (LRS) aircraft have been replaced by the more capable HC-130H variants. The Coast Guard has acquired the first EC-130V "Herk" configured for Airborne Early Warning (AEW). The radar surveillance aircraft is intended primarily for anti-drug operations. However, the AEW capability holds promise for value in other Coast Guard activities. The E-2C Hawkeye AEW aircraft previously flown by the Coast Guard were returned to the Navy in late 1991.

The cutters of the HAMILTON and BEAR classes, as well as icebreakers, regularly operate helicopters, while some of the other cutter classes have landing decks but cannot support helicopters. In wartime the HAMILTON and BEAR classes are intended to carry Navy SH-2F LAMPS I anti-submarine helicopters. Their effectiveness, however, will be limited because of the lack of towed-array sonars for the Coast Guard cutters.

The Coast Guard also operates two motorized gliders for anti-drug surveillance.

The Coast Guard also has a single CASA 212-300 turboprop transport, leased in the summer of 1990 to evaluate the aircraft for possible use in the logistics support role. The aircraft, leased from CASA Construcciones Aeronauticas of Spain, is flown by the Coast Guard with the designation CA-21.

Coast Guard aviators are Navy-trained, with specialized training being given at the Coast Guard Aviation Training Center in Mobile, Ala.

The following table lists the aircraft in active Coast Guard service. One additional HH-60J is the only aircraft requested in the Coast Guard's fiscal 1993 procurement budget. No aircraft are flown by the Coast Guard Reserve.

TABLE 32-2. COAST GUARD AIRCRAFT

Active*	Storage	Type	Mission
1	—	EC-130V Hercules	radar surveillance
30	—	HC-130H Hercules	Long-Range Search (LRS)
25	1	HU-25A Guardian	Medium-Range Search (MRS)
7	—	HU-25B Guardian	pollution surveillance
9	—	HU-25C Guardian	"interceptor"
1	—	VC-4A Gulfstream I	executive transport
1	—	VC-11A Gulfstream II	executive transport
1	—	CA-21 (CASA 212-300)	cargo aircraft (lease)
96	—	HH-65A Dolphin	Medium-Range Recovery (MRR)
35	—	HH-60J Jayhawk	Medium-Range Recovery (MRR)
34	2	HH-3F Pelican	Medium-Range Recovery (MRR)
—	9	CH-3E Sea King	Medium-Range Recovery (MRR)
2	—	RG-8A	motorized glider

*Includes about 30 aircraft that are not in operational service but are in depot-level or long-term maintenance.

HIGH-ENDURANCE CUTTERS

These are the largest ships operated by the Coast Guard except for icebreakers. All high-endurance cutters prior to the HAMILTON class have been stricken; no new construction of this type is planned. The HAMILTONs will reach the end of their nominal service life from about 2005 on.

PERSONNEL

Uniformed Coast Guard personnel operate all cutters and boats as well as aircraft. Medical personnel are provided by the U.S. Public Health Service on assignment to the Coast Guard.

Active-duty Coast Guard strength at the beginning of 1992 totaled almost 37,000—approximately 5,200 officers, 1,500 warrant officers, and 29,900 enlisted men and women. Also counted as active-duty personnel were over 900 cadets at the Coast Guard Academy in New London, Conn., and 160 medical officers of the Public Health Services who provide medical support to the Coast Guard.

Women comprise about 7 percent of the Coast Guard's active-duty personnel. The Coast Guard was the first U.S. military service to accept women at its service academy and the first to assign women as commanding officers of armed vessels (WPB patrol boats in 1988).

The Coast Guard has 12,000 selected reservists who attend periodic drills as well as summer active-duty training. There is also a civilian auxiliary of 34,000 men and women. The Coast Guard Auxiliary consists of expert boaters, amateur radio operators, or licensed aircraft pilots using their own equipment to support Coast Guard activities. Their efforts include conducting free courtesy marine inspections of recreational boats, teaching a variety of boating courses, and assisting the Coast Guard in search and rescue.

Coast Guard personnel have Navy-style ranks, with the Commandant having the rank of full admiral and the Deputy Commandant vice admiral. There are two other vice admirals (commanders Atlantic and Pacific areas with additional duty as commanders of the Atlantic and Pacific MDZs, respectively), 13 rear admirals upper half, and 12 rear admirals lower half, plus 5 rear admiral selectees.

With the cutback in active Navy frigates, the proposal has been made for some Navy FF/FFG-type ships to be transferred to the Coast Guard, with at least one to serve as a training cutter; however, such transfers are unlikely.

12 HIGH ENDURANCE CUTTERS: "HAMILTON" CLASS (378)

Number	Name	Builder	Laid down	Launched	Commissioned	Status
WHEC 715	HAMILTON	Avondale Shipyards, New Orleans, La.	4 Jan 1965	18 Dec 1965	20 Feb 1967	**PA**
WHEC 716	DALLAS	Avondale Shipyards, New Orleans, La.	7 Feb 1966	1 Oct 1966	26 Oct 1967	**AA**
WHEC 717	MELLON	Avondale Shipyards, New Orleans, La.	25 July 1966	11 Feb 1967	22 Dec 1967	**PA**
WHEC 718	CHASE	Avondale Shipyards, New Orleans, La.	15 Oct 1966	20 May 1967	1 Mar 1968	**PA**
WHEC 719	BOUTWELL	Avondale Shipyards, New Orleans, La.	12 Dec 1966	17 June 1967	24 June 1968	**PA**
WHEC 720	SHERMAN	Avondale Shipyards, New Orleans, La.	13 Feb 1967	23 Sep 1967	23 Aug 1968	**PA**
WHEC 721	GALLATIN	Avondale Shipyards, New Orleans, La.	17 Apr 1967	18 Nov 1967	20 Dec 1968	**AA**
WHEC 722	MORGENTHAU	Avondale Shipyards, New Orleans, La.	17 July 1967	10 Feb 1968	14 Feb 1969	**PA**
WHEC 723	RUSH	Avondale Shipyards, New Orleans, La.	23 Oct 1967	16 Nov 1968	3 July 1969	**PA**
WHEC 724	MUNRO	Avondale Shipyards, New Orleans, La.	18 Feb 1970	5 Dec 1970	27 Sep 1971	**PA**
WHEC 725	JARVIS	Avondale Shipyards, New Orleans, La.	9 Sep 1970	24 Apr 1971	30 Dec 1971	**PA**
WHEC 726	MIDGETT	Avondale Shipyards, New Orleans, La.	5 Apr 1971	4 Sep 1971	30 Mar 1972	**PA**

Displacement:	2,716 tons standard	Guns:	1 76-mm/62-cal DP Mk 75
	3,050 tons full load		2 40-mm grenade launchers Mk 19 (2 single)
Length:	350 feet (106.7 m) waterline		1 20-mm Phalanx close-in Mk 16 (multi-barrel)
	378 feet (115.2 m) overall		2 20-mm Mk 67 (2 single)
Beam:	42¾ feet (13.0 m)		4 .50-cal machine guns (4 single)
Draft:	20 feet (6.1 m)	ASW weapons:	6 12.75-inch (324-mm) torpedo tubes Mk 32 (2 triple)
Propulsion:	CODOG: 2 gas turbines (Pratt & Whitney FT4-A6); 28,000 shp + 2 diesel engines (Fairbanks Morse 38TD8⅛), 7,200 bhp; 2 shafts	Missiles:	8 Harpoon SSM (2 quad canisters Mk 141) in several ships (see notes)
Speed:	29 knots	Radar:	1 SPS-40B air search
Range:	2,400 n.miles (4,445 km) at 29 knots		2 SPS-64(V)6 navigation
	14,000 n.miles (25,930 km) at 11 knots	Sonars:	SQS-38 keel-mounted
Manning:	171 (17 officers + 154 enlisted)	Fire control:	1 Mk 92 weapon FCS
Helicopters:	1 SH-2F LAMPS I or HH-65 Dolphin		1 Mk 309 torpedo control panel
			1 SQR-17A(V)1 acoustic processor
		EW systems:	WLR-1C
			WLR-3

These ships are the largest cutters operated by the Coast Guard except for the Polar-class icebreakers. They are capable of long-range operations and of serving in the frigate role as ocean escorts during wartime. All have been upgraded under a Fleet Rehabilitation And Modernization (FRAM) program.

Anti-Submarine: As completed, the earlier ships of this class were fitted with two ahead-firing hedgehogs. They have been removed. These are the only Coast Guard cutters that retain ASW weapons. They can accommodate an SH-2 LAMPS I helicopter; SQR-4 and SQR-17A sonobuoy data-link and analyses equipment was fitted during FRAM; two triple torpedo mounts are installed.

Class: Originally 36 ships of this class were planned. Additional ships were deferred in favor of retaining older cutters and then dropped with construction of the smaller BEAR-class cutters.

Design: The superstructures of these ships are fabricated largely of aluminum. They are fitted with oceanographic and meteorological facilities. The helicopter hangars were used as balloon shelters prior to their modernization.

Electronics: Beginning in 1967 the original keel-mounted SQS-36 sonar was replaced in these ships by the SQS-38, a hull-mounted version of the SQS-35 variable-depth sonar.

Mk 36 SRBOC chaff launchers were fitted during FRAM upgrade. However, the previously planned SLQ-32(V)2 and SLQ-25

The DALLAS is one of two HAMILTON-class cutters remaining on the East Coast. The Harpoon canisters and Phalanx CIWS are not always fitted to all ships because of weapons availability, the ships' yard periods, and other factors. (1990, Giorgio Arra)

Detail of the HAMILTON showing the Harpoon and 76-mm gun arrangement; there is an OE-82 SATCOMM antenna between the Harpoon canisters and the bridge structure. An SPS-64(V)6 radar antenna is visible on the mast. (1991, Giorgio Arra)

Nixie installations were cancelled. (Thus, the BEAR-class cutters are the only Coast Guard units with the SLQ-32 system.)

Engineering: These were the largest U.S. combat ships to have gas-turbine propulsion until completion of the SPRUANCE (DD 963) in 1975. The gas turbines are FT4-A6, marine versions of the J75 aircraft engine. The propulsion machinery is CODOG (Combination Diesel Or Gas turbine). A 350-hp, trainable bow propeller pod is fitted.

Guns: These were the last active ships in U.S. service to mount 5-inch (127-mm)/38-cal DP guns. The 5-inch gun mount was replaced during the FRAM. (The last active U.S. Navy ship with this weapon is the nuclear-propelled missile cruiser LONG BEACH (CGN 9).

Missiles: On 16 January 1990 the MELLON became the first Coast Guard cutter to fire a guided missile, launching a Harpoon SSM. Five cutters were fitted with Harpoon through 1992, with all of the ships scheduled for eventual installation.

Modernization: These cutters have been updated under a FRAM program and the related Harpoon/CIWS weapons upgrade. The principal changes are:

- 5-inch/38-cal DP gun replaced by the 76-mm OTO Melara Mk 76
- Mk 56 GFCS replaced by Mk 92 gun FCS
- SPS-29 air search radar replaced by SPS-40 air search radar
- flight deck upgraded to accommodate SH-2F LAMPS I
- installation of telescoping helicopter hangar and TACAN
- communications equipment upgraded
- installation of Harpoon SSM
- installation of Phalanx CIWS
- installation of SQR-4 and SQR-17
- Mk 36 SRBOC chaff/flare launchers installed

With the FRAM update the manning standards for these cutters was increased from 152 (15 officers + 137 enlisted) to 171.

The FRAM work was undertaken at the Bath Iron Works, Maine, shipyard for the four East Coast ships (see Operational notes) and at the Todd Pacific yard in Seattle, Wash., for the eight West Coast ships. A large deck structure was fitted to the forecastle to mount the 76-mm gun and the Harpoon canisters; the Phalanx CIWS mount is fitted aft of the flight deck.

Cutter	Start	Completion
WHEC 715	Oct 1985	Nov 1988
WHEC 716	Nov 1986	Nov 1989
WHEC 717	Oct 1985	Feb 1989
WHEC 718	July 1989	Mar 1991
WHEC 719	Mar 1989	Aug 1990
WHEC 720	May 1986	June 1989
WHEC 721	Mar 1990	Dec 1991
WHEC 722	Nov 1989	May 1991
WHEC 723	July 1989	Dec 1990
WHEC 724	Dec 1986	Oct 1989
WHEC 725	Nov 1990	Nov 1991
WHEC 726	Mar 1991	Mar 1992

The FRAM upgrades experienced major delays and cost increases over the original estimate. The program has run about two years behind schedule, and the original cost of $30 million per ship increased to between $50 and $70 million per ship.

Names: The first nine ships were named for Secretaries of the Treasury; the last three ships honor heroes of the Coast Guard. Accordingly, the cutters have been referred to as the Hero class.

Operational: The HAMILTON and CHASE were transferred from the East Coast (Boston) to the West Coast (San Pedro, Calif.) in late 1991, bringing 10 of the 12 ships of this class to the Pacific. The DALLAS and GALLATIN remain on the East Coast, based at Governors Island, New York.

The Harpoon missiles and Phalanx CIWS are intended for combat operations in the Third World, and are obviously not related to the cutters' law-enforcement and search-and-rescue activities.

The HAMILTON showing the post-FRAM configuration for this class: 01 level extended forward, 76-mm OTO Melara gun forward, Harpoon canisters, new electronics, and a Phalanx CIWS on the fantail. These are highly capable, long-range ships. (1991, Giorgio Arra)

Stern aspect of the rejuvenated HAMILTON. The helicopter hangar is open. The Phalanx CIWS or Gatling gun is aft; the Mk 32 torpedo tubes are amidships, on the 01 level. These ships were to have received the SLQ-32(V)2 and SLQ-25 Nixie, but they were not provided. (1990, Giorgio Arra)

HIGH-ENDURANCE CUTTERS: "CASCO" CLASS (311)

The UNIMAK (WHEC 379, ex-AVP 31), the last of 18 seaplane tenders of the World War II–built BARNEGAT (AVP 10) class transferred to the Coast Guard in 1946–1948, was stricken on 29 April 1988 (returned to the Navy for disposal). The UNIMAK was completed as the Navy AVP 31 in 1943; she was transferred to the Coast Guard in 1946 as WAVP 31; changed to WHEC 379 in 1966. She operated as a training cutter (WTR 379) from 1969 until her decommissioning in May 1974. The ship had been scheduled for transfer to South Vietnam (as had other ships of this class), but with the fall of the Saigon government she was laid up in reserve. She was recommissioned as a WHEC in August 1977 to support the 200-n.mile (370-km) U.S. offshore economic zone.

During World War II ships of this class served as seaplane tenders and motor torpedo boat tenders, and one as an amphibious command ship. One ship of this class continues to serve in the Vietnamese Navy (ex-ABSECON/WHEC 374, ex-AVP 23).

See 14th Edition/page 535 for characteristics.

HIGH-ENDURANCE CUTTERS: SECRETARY CLASS (327)

All of the large, venerable cutters of the so-called Secretary class have been stricken.[5] Seven of these cutters were completed in 1936–1937; all saw service in World War II as ocean escorts (WPG) and, except for the ALEXANDER HAMILTON (WPG 34), as amphibious command ships (WAGC); the HAMILTON was sunk by a German U-boat in 1942. The six surviving ships were reclassified to high-endurance cutters (WHEC) on 1 May 1968.

The cutters were stricken from 1981 to 1988; the last were the DUANE (WHEC 33) on 1 August 1985; BIBB (WHEC 31) on 1 September 1985; TANEY (WHEC 37) on 7 December 1986; and INGHAM (WHEC 35) on 27 May 1988 (after 52 years of active service!).

See 14th Edition/pages 535–536 for characteristics.

5. They were named for Secretaries of the Treasury. Details of the World War II configuration of these cutters and other Coast Guard units will be found in Robert L. Scheina, *U.S. Coast Guard Cutters & Craft of World War II* (Annapolis, Md.: Naval Institute Press, 1982). Later cutters are described in Scheina, *U.S. Coast Guard Cutters & Craft, 1946–1990* (Annapolis, Md.: Naval Institute Press, 1990).

The TANEY at Baltimore, Md. The 327-foot cutter was at Honolulu (not Pearl Harbor) when the Japanese made their surprise air attack on 7 December 1941. This was a highly successful class of large cutters, with the TANEY surviving as a museum ship. (1989, N. Polmar)

MEDIUM-ENDURANCE CUTTERS

13 MEDIUM-ENDURANCE CUTTERS: "BEAR" CLASS (270)

Number	Name	Builder	Laid down	Launched	Commissioned	Status
WMEC 901	BEAR	Tacoma Boatbuilding, Tacoma, Wash.	23 Aug 1979	25 Sep 1980	4 Feb 1983	**AA**
WMEC 902	TAMPA	Tacoma Boatbuilding, Tacoma, Wash.	2 Apr 1980	19 Mar 1981	16 Mar 1984	**AA**
WMEC 903	HARRIET LANE	Tacoma Boatbuilding, Tacoma, Wash.	15 Oct 1980	6 Feb 1982	20 Sep 1984	**AA**
WMEC 904	NORTHLAND	Tacoma Boatbuilding, Tacoma, Wash.	9 Apr 1981	7 May 1982	17 Dec 1984	**AA**
WMEC 905	SPENCER (ex-SENECA)	Robert E. Derecktor, Middletown, R.I.	26 June 1982	17 Apr 1984	28 June 1986	**AA**
WMEC 906	SENECA (ex-ESCANABA)	Robert E. Derecktor, Middletown, R.I.	16 Sep 1982	17 Apr 1984	4 May 1987	**AA**
WMEC 907	ESCANABA (ex-TAHOMA)	Robert E. Derecktor, Middletown, R.I.	1 Apr 1983	2 June 1985	27 Aug 1987	**AA**
WMEC 908	TAHOMA (ex-SPENCER)	Robert E. Derecktor, Middletown, R.I.	28 June 1983	2 June 1985	6 Apr 1988	**AA**
WMEC 909	CAMBELL (ex-ARGUS)	Robert E. Derecktor, Middletown, R.I.	10 Aug 1984	29 Apr 1986	19 Aug 1988	**AA**
WMEC 910	THETIS (ex-TAHOMA)	Robert E. Derecktor, Middletown, R.I.	24 Aug 1984	29 Apr 1986	30 June 1989	**AA**
WMEC 911	FORWARD (ex-ERIE)	Robert E. Derecktor, Middletown, R.I.	11 July 1986	19 Aug 1987	4 Aug 1990	**AA**
WMEC 912	LEGARE (ex-McCULLOCH)	Robert E. Derecktor, Middletown, R.I.	11 July 1986	19 Aug 1987	4 Aug 1990	**AA**
WMEC 913	MOHAWK (ex-EWING)	Robert E. Derecktor, Middletown, R.I.	18 June 1987	18 May 1988	20 Mar 1991	**AA**

Displacement:	1,200 tons light		Manning:	99 (12 officers + 87 enlisted)
	1,820 tons full load		Helicopters:	landing area
Length:	255 feet (77.8 m) waterline		Guns:	1 76-mm/62-cal AA Mk 75
	270 feet (82.3 m) overall			4 .50-cal machine guns (4 single)
Beam:	38 feet (11.6 m)		ASW weapons:	none
Drafts:	14 feet (4.3 m)		Torpedoes:	none
Propulsion:	2 geared diesel engines (Alco 251); 7,000 bhp; 2 shafts		Radars:	2 SPS-64(V)1/6 navigation
Speed:	19.5 knots		Sonars:	none
Range:	3,850 n.miles (7,130 km) at 19.5 knots		Fire control:	Mk 92 weapons control system
	9,900 n.miles (18,335 km) at 12 knots		EW systems:	SLQ-32(V)1

These are multi-purpose cutters. However, their lack of ASW weapons and sensors make them unsuitable for employment in the ASW role without extensive modification. They have also been criticized for their slow speed, and they ride poorly in heavy seas.

The first four ships were ordered from Tacoma Boatbuilding with the remainder planned for procurement from the Tacoma yard; however, the Coast Guard was forced into competitive bidding. The subsequent ships were then awarded to the Derecktor yard.

The BEAR was not delivered to the Coast Guard for service until late in 1983. The entire class is based on Atlantic coast ports.

Aircraft: A landing deck and expanding hangar permit these cutters to handle any of the Coast Guard's helicopters as well as the Navy's SH-2F LAMPS I. It is intended in wartime that an SH-2F would be assigned to each ship for convoy escort. The ESCANABA conducted trials with a Navy SH-60B LAMPS III helicopter in 1988.

The Recovery Assistance, Securing, and Traversing System (RAST) is fitted to facilitate helicopter operations in rough seas.

Class: The lead ship was authorized in fiscal 1976, WMEC 902–904 in fiscal 1977, and WMEC 905–913 in fiscal 1980. The class is officially known as the Famous class, but generally referred to as the BEAR class.

Design: Design criteria for this class included 14-day law-enforcement patrols in areas out to 400 n.miles (740 km) from base. Maximum normal at-sea endurance is 21 days.

They have a very short forecastle with a large, two-level superstructure providing a humpback shape. Active fin stabilizers are fitted.

These were the first Coast Guard cutters to be completed with a contemporary EW suite since World War II. These ships are designed to be fitted with the following military systems in wartime: SH-2F LAMPS I anti-submarine helicopter, two Harpoon anti-ship quad missile canisters, one 20-mm Phalanx CIWS, Tactical Towed Array Sonar (TACTAS), and chaff launchers. The ships seem unlikely, however, to accommodate simultaneously all of these systems, in part because of the number of additional personnel required as well as the probable lack of available systems during a conflict.

Accommodations are provided for 109 personnel.

Names: The Coast Guard initially named all 13 ships of the class. Subsequently, these prematurely awarded names for WMEC 905 and later ships were withdrawn and those cutters were renamed, as indicated above.

The BEAR honors a long-serving Navy and Coast Guard screw steamer. Built in Scotland in 1874 as a sealing vessel, she was purchased by the U.S. Navy in 1884 and operated successively in the Navy, Revenue Cutter Service, and Coast Guard, and again by the Navy (designated AG 29). The BEAR was used extensively in Arctic operations and was used by Rear Admiral Richard E. Byrd during his Antarctic expedition of 1933–1935. She was decommissioned in 1944 and transferred to the Maritime Commission in 1948.

The THETIS. Her SLQ-32(V)1 ECM antenna is visible immediately behind the bridge (beneath a radio direction-finding antenna loop). There are OE-82 SATCOMM antennas atop her superstructure. (1990, Giorgio Arra)

The FORWARD with an HH-65 Dolphin helicopter on her flight deck. Although these cutters could accommodate an SH-2F LAMPS I/ASW helicopter, their lack of sonar would prevent the ships from being used effectively in an anti-submarine role. (1990, Giorgio Arra)

The THETIS with the door to her helicopter hangar partially raised. The safety nets around her helicopter deck are raised for use as a safety rail; they lower for flight operations. A rigid-hull rubber craft is on her fantail. (1990, Giorgio Arra)

16 MEDIUM-ENDURANCE CUTTERS: "RELIANCE" CLASS (210)

Number	Name	Launched	Commissioned	Status
WMEC 615	RELIANCE	25 May 1963	20 June 1964	**AA**
WMEC 616	DILIGENCE	20 July 1963	31 Aug 1964	**AA**
WMEC 617	VIGILANT	24 Dec 1963	1 Oct 1964	**AA**
WMEC 618	ACTIVE	21 July 1965	17 Sep 1966	**PA**
WMEC 619	CONFIDENCE	8 May 1965	19 Feb 1966	**AA**
WMEC 620	RESOLUTE	30 Apr 1966	8 Dec 1966	**PA**
WMEC 621	VALIANT	14 Jan 1967	28 Oct 1967	**AA**
WMEC 622	COURAGEOUS	18 Mar 1967	19 Apr 1968	**AA**
WMEC 623	STEADFAST	24 June 1967	7 Oct 1968	**AA**
WMEC 624	DAUNTLESS	21 Oct 1967	10 June 1968	**AA**
WMEC 625	VENTUROUS	11 Nov 1967	16 Aug 1968	**PA**
WMEC 626	DEPENDABLE	16 Mar 1968	22 Nov 1968	**AA**
WMEC 627	VIGOROUS	4 May 1968	23 Apr 1969	**AA**
WMEC 628	DURABLE	29 Apr 1967	8 Dec 1967	**AA**
WMEC 629	DECISIVE	14 Dec 1967	23 Aug 1968	**AA**
WMEC 630	ALERT	19 Oct 1968	28 July 1969	**AA**

Builders:	WMEC 615–617 Todd Shipyards, Houston, Texas
	WMEC 618 Christy Corp., Sturgeon Bay, Wisc.
	WMEC 619, 625, 628, 629 Coast Guard Yard, Curtis Bay, Md.
	WMEC 620–624, 626, 627, 630 American Shipbuilding, Lorain, Ohio
Displacement:	950 tons standard
	1,007 tons full load except WMEC 616–619 970 tons
Length:	210½ feet (64.2 m) overall
Beam:	34 feet (10.4 m)
Draft:	10½ feet (3.2 m)
Propulsion:	2 turbo-charged diesel engines (Alco 251B); 5,000 bhp; 2 shafts
Speed:	18 knots
Range:	A series 2,100 n.miles (3,890 km) at 18 knots
	6,100 n.miles (11,300 km) at 13 knots
	B series 2,700 n.miles (5,000 km) at 18 knots
	6,100 n.miles (11,300 km) at 13 knots
Manning:	74 (8 offices + 66 enlisted)
Helicopters:	landing area
Guns:	1 3-inch (76-mm) 50-cal Mk 22
	2 40-mm grenade launchers Mk 19 (2 single)
	4 .50-cal machine guns (4 single)
ASW weapons:	none
Radars:	2 SPS-64(V)1 navigation

Bow and bridge detail of the VIGOROUS. (1989, Giorgio Arra)

These are search-and-rescue ships. They can land helicopters but have no hangar.

Armament: No ASW armament is provided in these cutters. Their design included space and weight provisions for hedgehogs and ASW torpedo tubes.

Classification: These ships were originally classified as patrol craft (WPC); changed to WMEC with same hull numbers on 1 May 1966. The RELIANCE was changed to WTR on June 1975 (the TR indicating Training of Reserves); she reverted to WMEC on 16 August 1982.

Design: The RELIANCE design has a small island superstructure with 360° visibility from the bridge to facilitate helicopter operations and towing. The ALERT was fitted with the Canadian-developed "Beartrap" helicopter haul-down system.

Engineering: The WMEC 615–619 (A series) were built with CODAG (Combination Diesel And Gas) turbine plants to provide experience in operating mixed propulsion plants. Those cutters had a high acceleration rate from all stop; or with their engines shut down could be at full speed in a few minutes; they could make 15.25 knots on gas turbines alone. The cost factor influenced the decision to make the remaining ships all-diesel (B series).

The five A-series ships were re-engined during their mid-life modernization (see below).

Modernization: These cutters are being upgraded under a Mid-life Maintenance Availability (MMA) program. The upgrade includes an enlarged superstructure, installation of a larger, improved engine exhaust (funnel), improved living spaces, redesigned engine room, upgraded fire-fighting system, new refrigeration and air-conditioning units, and a new electronics suite.

The VIGOROUS showing the original stern configuration of these ships with twin engine exhausts in the stern counter. There is a motor lifeboat on the starboard davits and a rigid-hull rubber craft on the port side, handled by a small crane. (1991, Giorgio Arra)

The ACTIVE after undergoing the MMA upgrade. The most obvious feature of the modernization is the large, streamlined funnel, which replaces the two exhausts built into the stern counter. Only the Coast Guard retains the 3-inch/50-cal Mk 22 gun mount. (1991, L. Van Gindern Collection)

The unmodernized VIGOROUS. These are limited-capability cutters, but have proven effective in SAR and drug interdiction operations. The VIGOROUS wears "E" awards for excellence and a "DC" award for damage-control efficiency. (1991, Giorgio Arra)

1 MEDIUM-ENDURANCE CUTTER: "STORIS" (230)

Number	Name	Launched	Commissioned	Status
WMEC 38	STORIS	4 Apr 1942	30 Sep 1942	**PA**

Builders:	Toledo Shipbuilding, Ohio
Displacement:	1,715 tons standard
	1,925 tons full load
Length:	230 feet (70.1 m) overall
Beam:	43 feet (13.1 m)
Draft:	15 feet (4.6 m)
Propulsion:	diesel-electric (3 Fairbanks-Morse 38D 8¼ diesel engines); 1,800 shp; 1 shaft
Speed:	14 knots
Range:	12,000 n.miles (22,225 km) at 14 knots
	22,000 n.miles (40,745 km) at 8 knots
Manning:	72 (9 officers + 63 enlisted)
Helicopters:	no facilities
Guns:	4 .50-cal machine guns (4 single)
Radars:	2 SPS-64 navigation

The STORIS was built specifically for offshore icebreaking and patrol in the Greenland area. She has been employed in Alaskan service for search, rescue, and law enforcement since 1949. She is currently the oldest Coast Guard cutter in active service.

Classification: The STORIS originally was classified as WAGL 38 and then WAG 38; she was changed to WAGB 38 on 1 May 1966. Subsequently she was reclassified as a medium-endurance cutter (WMEC) on 1 July 1972 to emphasize her role in law enforcement off the Alaskan fishing grounds.

Design: The ship was designed specifically for operation in northern waters and for icebreaking, although she is generally similar to the Coast Guard's 180-foot (54.9-m) buoy tenders. During World War II the STORIS carried a single J2F Duck biplane scouting aircraft.

Guns: As built, the STORIS was armed with two 3-inch guns and four 20-mm guns plus ASW weapons. A single 3-inch gun was retained into the 1980s.

Names: The ship was initially named the ESKIMO, but was changed during construction to STORIS at the request of the State Department, which feared that the name might offend the natives of Greenland.

Operational: During World War II the STORIS served in the North Atlantic as an ocean escort ship.

The STORIS and the seagoing buoy tenders BRAMBLE and SPAR carried out the first circumnavigation of the North American continent and transited the Northwest Passage in 1957, departing from Unimak Pass, Alaska, on 1 July and reaching Argentia, Newfoundland, on 19 September.

The STORIS in Alaskan waters. She is a versatile cutter and the oldest cutter in Coast Guard service. Note her icebreaking prow, cargo cranes forward of the bridge and amidships, and the 3-inch gun mount aft of the funnel. In World War II she carried a second 3-inch gun (forward), 20-mm AA guns, depth charges, and Mousetrap rocket projectors plus a floatplane. (U.S. Coast Guard)

3 MEDIUM ENDURANCE CUTTERS: FORMER SALVAGE SHIPS (213)

Number	Name	Launched	Navy ARS Comm.	Status
WMEC 6 (ex-ARS 6)	ESCAPE	22 Nov 1942	20 Nov 1943	**AA**
WMEC 167 (ex-ARS 9)	ACUSHNET	1 Apr 1943	5 Feb 1944	**PA**
WMEC 168 (ex-ARS 26)	YOCONA	8 Apr 1944	3 Nov 1944	**PA**

Builders:	Basalt Rock, Napa, Calif.
Displacement:	1,557 tons standard
	1,745 tons full load
Length:	213½ feet (65.1 m) overall
Beam:	39 feet (12.8 m)
Draft:	15 feet (4.9 m)
Propulsion:	4 diesel engines (Cooper Bessemer GSB-8); 3,000 bhp; 2 shafts
Speed:	15.5 knots
Range:	9,000 n.miles (16,670 km) at 15.5 knots
	20,000 n.miles (37,040 km) at 7 knots
Manning:	77 (9 offices + 68 enlisted)
Helicopters:	no facilities
Guns:	2 40-mm grenade launchers Mk 19 (2 single)
Radars:	2 SPS-64 navigation

These are former Navy salvage ships; two were permanently transferred to the Coast Guard after World War II, the WMEC 167 on 29 June 1946 and WMEC 168 on 28 June 1946; the ESCAPE was transferred to the Coast Guard on loan on 4 December 1980.

Classification: Upon transfer to the Coast Guard, these ships were classified as tugs (WAT). They were changed to WMEC on 1 May 1966, with the ACUSHNET subsequently modified to handle environmental data buoys and changed to oceanographic cutter (WAGO 167) in 1969; she was redesignated WMEC in 1978.

Names: Two ships were renamed in Coast Guard service; their Navy names were SHACKLE (ARS 9) and SEIZE (ARS 26). The ex-ARS 6 retains her Navy name.

3 MEDIUM-ENDURANCE CUTTERS: FORMER FLEET TUGS (205)

Number	Name	Launched	Navy ATF Comm.	Status
WMEC 153 (ex-ATF 153)	CHILULA	1 Dec 1944	5 Apr 1945	**AA**
WMEC 165 (ex-ATF 66)	CHEROKEE	10 Nov 1939	26 Apr 1940	AR
WMEC 166 (ex-ATF 95)	TAMAROA	13 July 1943	9 Oct 1943	**AA**

Builders:	WMEC 153 Charleston Shipbuilding and Dry Dock, S.C.
	WMEC 165 Bethlehem Steel, Staten Island, N.Y.
	WMEC 166 Commercial Iron Works, Portland, Ore.
Displacement:	1,731 tons full load
Length:	205 feet (62.5 m) overall
Beam:	38½ feet (11.7 m)
Draft:	17 feet (5.2 m)
Propulsion:	diesel-electric (4 General Motors 12-278 diesel engines); 3,000 shp; 1 shaft
Speed:	16.2 knots
Range:	6,500 n.miles (12,040 km) at 16 knots
	15,000 n.miles (27,780 km) at 8 knots
Manning:	76 (6 officers + 70 enlisted)
Helicopters:	no facilities
Guns:	1 3-inch (76-mm) 50-cal AA Mk 22
	2 40-mm grenade launchers Mk 19 (2 single)
Radars:	2 SPS-64 navigation

These are former Navy fleet tugs. The CHEROKEE and TAMAROA were transferred from the active fleet to the Coast Guard on 29 June 1946; the CHILULA, laid up since 1947, was transferred to the Coast Guard on 9 July 1956. The CHEROKEE was decommissioned on 28 February 1991; returned to the Navy for disposal.

Class: Two additional Navy ATFs transferred to the Coast Guard on loan on 30 September 1980 also served as cutters: the UTE (WMEC 76, ex-ATF 76) and LIPAN (WMEC 85, ex-ATF 85); both were returned to the Navy, on 26 May 1988 and 9 June 1988, respectively; they have been stricken.

The ESCAPE is one of the few former Navy ships in Coast Guard service that was not renamed and retains her Navy hull number (ex-ARS 6). These cutters are almost 50 years old, but continue to operate in the patrol role. (1990, Giorgio Arra)

The ACUSHNET showing the mast rig carried by the two sister ships of the ESCAPE. The three former ARS-type ships are generally similar, although the ESCAPE retains the "notched" bow of a salvage ship (provided for four-point mooring over sunken ships). (1989, Giorgio Arra)

The CHEROKEE in New York harbor with her crew manning the rail. The words "Coast Guard" on her sides are smaller than the standard markings. The former ATFs retain their 3-inch gun, which was beached by the ARS-type ships. (1990, Giorgio Arra)

Classification: These ships were classified ATF by the Navy; upon transfer to the Coast Guard the ships became WAT, with two having new hull numbers assigned. All three were changed to WMEC on 1 May 1966.

Names: The TAMAROA was named ZUNI in Navy service. The others retain their Navy names.

MEDIUM-ENDURANCE CUTTERS: "BALSAM" CLASS (180)

The CITRUS (WMEC 300), a buoy tender of the BALSAM (WLB 62) class, is employed as a medium-endurance cutter; see page 572.

SURFACE EFFECT SHIPS

3 SES CUTTERS: SEA HAWK CLASS

Number	Name	Commissioned	Status
WSES 2	SEA HAWK	17 Nov 1982	AA
WSES 3	SHEARWATER	17 Nov 1982	AA
WSES 4	PETREL	8 July 1983	AA

Builders:	Bell Halter, New Orleans, La.
Displacement:	110 tons light
	150 tons full load
Length:	110 feet (33.5 m) overall
Beam:	39 feet (11.9 m)
Draft:	5½ feet (1.7 m) on cushion
	8¼ feet (2.5 m) off cushion
Propulsion:	2 diesel engines (General Motors 16V149TI); 3,600 bhp; 2 shafts
Lift:	2 diesel engines (General Motors 8V92TI); 890 bhp; 2 fans
Speed:	33 knots on cushion in sea state 0
	30 knots on cushion in sea state 3
	19 knots off cushion in sea state 0
	15 knots off cushion in sea state 3
Range:	1,000 n.miles (1,850 km) at 30 knots on cushion in sea state 3
Manning:	17 (1 officer + 16 enlisted)
Helicopters:	no facilities
Guns:	2 .50-cal machine guns (2 single)
Radars:	2 Decca 914 navigation
Sonars:	none

All three craft were acquired by the Coast Guard primarily for use in the drug-enforcement role. They were obtained after evaluation of a prototype ship, the DORADO (designated WSES 1), which was commissioned in the Coast Guard in 1981 and, after extensive trials, retransferred to the Navy.

Mission endurance of the WSES type is seven days.

The SEAWATER at rest. The Coast Guard has pioneered in the development and evaluation of advanced technology vehicles and systems, including SES, hydrofoils, helicopters, and gas turbines. (1990, L. Van Ginderen Collection)

The SEA HAWK at slow speed off Miami, Fla. These craft have been highly effective in offshore operations, including anti-drug and rescue operations. There are life-raft canisters amidships, a rigid-hull rubber craft aft. (1990, Giorgio Arra)

The SEA HAWK shows the step-down stern of this class, which facilitates handling small boats alongside. These are the fastest cutters in Coast Guard service. (U.S. Coast Guard)

PATROL BOATS

(1) PATROL BOAT: HERITAGE CLASS (120)

Number	Name	Launch	Complete	Status
WPB 1400	LEOPOLD		(1993)	suspended

Builders:	Coast Guard Yard, Curtis Bay, Md.
Displacement:	157 tons full load
Length:	118 feet (36.0 m) overall
Beam:	23 feet (7.0 m)
Draft:	8 feet (2.5 m)
Propulsion:	2 diesel engines; 2 shafts
Speed:	30 knots
Range:	720 n.miles (1,333 km) at 30 knots
Manning:	17 (2 officers + 15 enlisted)
Guns:	1 20-mm cannon
	2 .50-cal machine guns (2 single)
Radars:	1 SPS-64(V)1 navigation

This class of Coast Guard patrol boats was intended to replace the older and smaller Cape-class and Point-class patrol boats. The Heritage-class design was to be faster, longer-lived, and less expensive to build and maintain than the Island class.

The LEOPOLD was ordered in March 1989 and was laid down on 27 August 1990. Series production of 35 follow-on units was expected to begin in 1992 if the prototype proved successful; long-range plans called for a total of up to 96 units. However, the Coast Guard halted work on the LEOPOLD on 25 November 1991 because of the rapidly changing world situation. A Coast Guard spokesman stated: "The reason that we're suspending it at this point—and most likely it will be cancelled—is basically times have changed."

The Coast Guard decision came four months after a report from the General Accounting Office questioned the need for the craft; the reported summary stated: "There were weaknesses in identifying mission needs and the capabilities the replacement vessels [Heritage class] would require to meet these needs. The Coast Guard also could not support its decision for the number of patrol boats needed because agency officials could not provide support for the calculations of the computer model used to determine the need for 96 vessels."[6] The GAO report also noted that the Coast Guard underestimated the time and cost required to acquire the Heritage class.

6. General Accounting Office, *Coast Guard: Adequacy of the Justification for Heritage Patrol Boats* (Washington, D.C.: 12 July 1991), pp. 1–2.

Classification: The class is rated at 120 feet, although the actual length is 118 feet.

Cost: In October 1991 a government report revealed an expected cost of $13 million for the lead unit, or almost double the initial estimate of $7.7 million; in comparison, the Island-class boats are about $6.5 million each. In series production the Heritage class was expected to cost some $6 million per unit.

Design: The design's "deep-V" hull has a raked bow, low bow bulwark, and a full hull form farther aft. The forward half of the deckhouse is protected by a full-beam shield with a ladder in its face that leads to bridge wings. A tripod mast is stepped abaft the bridge, which has 360° visibility; the design provided for a steel hull with an aluminum deckhouse.

The new class was to have the towing capability that the Island class lacks.

The new boats were expected to have an estimated life of 30 years vice the 15 to 20 years of the Island class because the heavier hull plating will take longer to wear from corrosion.

Names: These craft were to be named for former Coast Guard cutters that were part of the service's heritage.

Artist's concept of the LEOPOLD. She was to have had a streamlined superstructure compared to the boxy appearance of the Island class. (U.S. Coast Guard, T. Freeman)

49 PATROL BOATS: ISLAND CLASS (110)

Number	Name	Commissioned	Status
A series			
WPB 1301	FARALLON	21 Feb 1986	AA
WPB 1302	MANITOU	28 Feb 1986	AA
WPB 1303	MATAGORDA	25 Apr 1986	AA
WPB 1304	MAUI	9 May 1986	AA
WPB 1305	MONHEGAN	16 June 1986	AA
WPB 1306	NUNIVAK	4 July 1986	AA
WPB 1307	OCRACOKE	4 Aug 1986	AA
WPB 1308	VASHON	15 Aug 1986	AA
WPB 1309	AQUIDNECK	26 Sep 1986	AA
WPB 1310	MUSTANG	29 Aug 1986	PA
WPB 1311	NAUSHON	3 Oct 1986	PA
WPB 1312	SANIBEL	14 Nov 1986	AA
WPB 1313	EDISTO	7 Jan 1987	PA
WPB 1314	SAPELO	24 Feb 1987	PA
WPB 1315	MATINICUS	16 Apr 1987	AA
WPB 1316	NANTUCKET	4 June 1987	AA
B series			
WPB 1317	ATTU	9 May 1988	AA
WPB 1318	BARANOF	20 May 1988	AA
WPB 1319	CHANDELEUR	8 June 1988	AA
WPB 1320	CHINCOTEAGUE	8 Aug 1988	AA
WPB 1321	CUSHING	8 Aug 1988	AA
WPB 1322	CUTTYHUNK	15 Oct 1988	PA
WPB 1323	DRUMMOND	19 Oct 1988	AA
WPB 1324	KEY LARGO	24 Dec 1988	AA
WPB 1325	METOMKIN	12 Jan 1989	AA
WPB 1326	MONOMOY	16 Dec 1988	AA
WPB 1327	ORCAS	14 Apr 1989	PA
WPB 1328	PADRE	24 Feb 1989	AA
WPB 1329	SITKINAK	31 Mar 1989	AA
WPB 1330	TYBEE	9 May 1989	PA
WPB 1331	WASHINGTON	9 June 1989	PA
WPB 1332	WRANGELL	24 June 1989	AA
WPB 1333	ADAK	17 Nov 1989	AA
WPB 1334	LIBERTY	22 Sep 1989	PA
WPB 1335	ANACAPA	13 Jan 1990	PA
WPB 1336	KISKA	1 Dec 1989	PA
WPB 1337	ASSATEAGUE	15 June 1990	PA
C series			
WPB 1338	GRAND ISLE	19 Apr 1991	AA
WPB 1339	KEY BISCAYNE	27 Apr 1991	AA
WPB 1340	JEFFERSON ISLAND	16 Aug 1991	AA
WPB 1341	KODIAK ISLAND	21 June 1991	AA
WPB 1342	LONG ISLAND	27 Aug 1991	PA
WPB 1343	BAINBRIDGE ISLAND	1991	AA
WPB 1344	BLOCK ISLAND	22 Nov 1991	AA
WPB 1345	STATEN ISLAND	22 Nov 1991	AA
WPB 1346	ROANOKE ISLAND	8 Feb 1992	PA
WPB 1347	KNIGHT ISLAND	1992	AA
WPB 1348	PEA ISLAND	12 Dec 1991	AA
WPB 1349	GALVESTON ISLAND	1992	PA

Builders:	Bollinger Shipyard, Lockport, La.
Displacement:	136 tons standard
	A series 163 tons full load
	B series 157 tons full load
	C series 153 tons full load
Length:	110 feet (33.5 m) overall
Beam:	21 feet (6.4 m)
Draft:	7⅓ feet (2.2 m)
Propulsion:	2 diesel engines (Alco-Paxman Valenta 16 RP200); 5,820 bhp, except C series 5,324 bhp; 2 shafts
Speed:	30 knots
Range:	A series 900 n.miles (1,670 km) at 30 knots
	2,700 n.miles (5,000 km) at 12 knots
	B and C series 840 n.miles (1,555 km) at 30 knots
	2,400 n.miles (4,445 km) at 12 knots
Manning:	16 (2 officers + 14 enlisted)
Guns:	1 20-mm cannon Mk 16
	2 .50-cal machine guns (2 single)
	2 40-mm grenade launchers Mk 19 (2 single)
Radar:	1 SPS-64(V)1 navigation

The Coast Guard has acquired this class for offshore surveillance and search-and-rescue operations, replacing the 95-foot (29-m) and 82-foot (25-m) WPBs; however, some ports for those smaller craft cannot accommodate the Island-class WPBs.

The contract for these boats was originally awarded in May 1984 to the Marine Power and Equipment Co., Seattle, Wash., for 16 boats; however, a U.S. District Court set aside the award because of irregularities in the procurement process. Subsequently, Bollinger was awarded a contract for the first 16 units in August 1984.

The design was 20 years old when the contract was awarded, and critics have claimed that more capable designs were available. Also, early operational experience with the Island-class WPBs revealed hull problems, i.e., cracks developing in heavy seas.

The FARALLON was delivered on 15 November 1985, with the remainder being completed through 1992.

Design: The design is based on an existing patrol boat developed by Vosper Thornycroft in Britain to minimize cost and reduce technical risks. The craft have a steel hull with aluminum deck and superstructure; they have a flush-deck, round-bilge hull with some bow sheer, and a low bow coaming. The WPB 1317 and later units have heavier bow plating to correct a hull-cracking problem. A quadripod mast is fitted.

Names: WPB 1324 originally named LARGO; changed during construction.

The BARANOF at high speed showing the lines of a Vosper Thornycroft design. These patrol boats are easily identified by their large deck structure and lattice mast. There is a 20-mm cannon forward (under canvas in this view). (1992, Giorgio Arra)

THE BARANOF. There is an amidships crane for handling the rigid-hull rubber craft and considerable working space aft. (1992, Giorgio Arra)

The TYBEE barely under way. Her 20-mm cannon has been unshipped, and her rubber boat is over the side. There are life-raft canisters amidships. (1989, Giorgio Arra)

PATROL BOATS: CAPE CLASS (95)

Number	Name	Status
WPB 95300	CAPE SMALL	decomm. 13 Apr 1987; to Marshall Is. 1987
WPB 95302	CAPE HIGGON	decomm. Jan 1990; to Uruguay 1990
WPB 95303	CAPE UPRIGHT	decomm. 6 Jan 1989; to Bahamas 1989
WPB95304	CAPE GULL	decomm. 15 May 1988
WPB 95305	CAPE HATTERAS	decomm. 14 Mar 1991
WPB 95306	CAPE GEORGE	decomm. 3 Sep 1989
WPB 95307	CAPE CURRENT	decomm. 1 May 1989; to Bahamas 1989
WPB 95308	CAPE STRAIT	decomm. 21 Jan 1983
WPB 95309	CAPE CARTER	decomm. 19 Jan 1990; to Mexico 1990
WPB 95310	CAPE WASH	decomm. 1 June 1987
WPB 95311	CAPE HEDGE	decomm. 7 Jan 1987; to Mexico 1990
WPB 95312	CAPE KNOX	decomm. 10 Feb 1989
WPB 95313	CAPE MORGAN	decomm. 20 Oct 1989; to Bahamas 1989
WPB 95316	CAPE FOX	decomm. 30 June 1989; to Bahamas 1989
WPB 95317	CAPE JELLISON	decomm. 12 Dec 1986
WPB 95319	CAPE ROMAIN	decomm. 11 Aug 1989; to U.S. Navy 1989
WPB 95320	CAPE STARR	decomm. 16 Jan 1987
WPB 95321	CAPE CROSS	decomm. 20 Mar 1990; to Micronesia 1990
WPB 95322	CAPE HORN	decomm. 25 Jan 1990; to Uruguay 1990
WPB 95324	CAPE SHOALWATER	decomm. 9 Dec 1988; to Bahamas 1989
WPB 95326	CAPE CORWIN	decomm. 6 Apr 1990; to Micronesia 1990
WPB 95328	CAPE HENLOPEN	decomm. 28 Sep 1989; to Costa Rica 1989
WPB 95332	CAPE YORK	decomm. 26 May 1989; to Bahamas 1989

All 95-foot (29-m), steel-hull patrol boats of the Cape class have been discarded, with many having been transferred to other navies and coastal patrol agencies. The above units were those in service when the last edition of *Ships and Aircraft* was published; see appendix D for details on foreign transfers. Previous transfers of this class went to Ethiopia, Haiti, South Korea, Saudi Arabia, and Thailand.

The CAPE HEDGE (WPB 95311) was transferred to the Navy on 7 January 1987 and served as a pilot boat in 1987–1989 (renamed VANGUARD); she was subsequently transferred to Mexico in January 1990. CAPE ROMAIN (WPB 95319) went to the U.S. Navy as a pilot boat on 11 August 1989.

These craft, originally intended primarily for harbor patrol and coastal ASW, were constructed between 1953 and 1959. Plans to discard this class in the 1970s in favor of new construction were delayed, and all surviving units were modernized. Subsequently they were replaced from the mid-1980s by the Island-class WPBs.

See 14th Edition/page 544 for characteristics.

The former patrol boat CAPE HEDGE (WPB 95311) while in service as the Navy pilot boat VANGUARD at San Francisco. She was subsequently transferred to Mexico in 1990. (1989, Giorgio Arra)

43 PATROL BOATS: POINT CLASS (82)

Number	Name	Commissioned	Status
A series			
WPB 82302	POINT HOPE	5 Oct 1960	to Costa Rica 1991
WPB 82311	POINT VERDE	15 Mar 1961	decomm. July 1991
WPB 82312	POINT SWIFT	22 Mar 1961	AA
WPB 82314	POINT THATCHER	13 Sep 1961	decomm. Mar 1992
C series			
WPB 82318	POINT HERRON	14 June 1961	AA
WPB 82332	POINT ROBERTS	6 June 1962	decomm. Feb 1992
WPB 82333	POINT HIGHLAND	27 June 1962	AA
WPB 82334	POINT LEDGE	18 July 1962	PA
WPB 82335	POINT COUNTESS	8 Aug 1962	PA
WPB 82336	POINT GLASS	29 Aug 1962	AA
WPB 82337	POINT DIVIDE	19 Sep 1962	PA
WPB 82338	POINT BRIDGE	10 Oct 1962	PA
WPB 82339	POINT CHICO	29 Oct 1962	PA
WPB 82340	POINT BATAN	21 Nov 1962	AA
WPB 82341	POINT LOOKOUT	12 Dec 1962	AA
WPB 82342	POINT BAKER	30 Oct 1963	AA
WPB 82343	POINT WELLS	20 Nov 1963	AA
WPB 82344	POINT ESTERO	11 Dec 1966	AA
WPB 82345	POINT JUDITH	26 July 1966	decomm. Jan 1992
WPB 82346	POINT ARENA	26 Aug 1966	AA
WPB 82347	POINT BONITA	12 Sep 1966	AA
WPB 82348	POINT BARROW	4 Oct 1966	to Panama 1991
WPB 82349	POINT SPENCER	25 Oct 1966	AA
WPB 82350	POINT FRANKLIN	14 Nov 1966	AA
WPB 82351	POINT BENNETT	19 Dec 1966	PA
WPB 82352	POINT SAL	5 Dec 1966	AA
WPB 82353	POINT MONROE	27 Dec 1966	AA
WPB 82354	POINT EVANS	10 Jan 1967	PA
WPB 82355	POINT HANNON	23 Jan 1967	AA
WPB 82356	POINT FRANCIS	3 Feb 1967	AA
WPB 82357	POINT HURON	17 Feb 1967	AA
WPB 82358	POINT STUART	17 Mar 1967	PA
WPB 82359	POINT STEELE	26 Apr 1967	AA
WPB 82360	POINT WINSLOW	3 Mar 1967	PA
WPB 82361	POINT CHARLES	15 May 1967	decomm. Dec 1991
WPB 82362	POINT BROWN	30 Mar 1967	decomm. Oct 1991
WPB 82363	POINT NOWELL	1 June 1967	AA
WPB 82364	POINT WHITEHORN	13 July 1967	AA
WPB 82365	POINT TURNER	14 Apr 1967	AA
WPB 82366	POINT LOBOS	29 May 1967	AA
WPB 82367	POINT KNOLL	27 June 1967	decomm. Oct 1991
WPB 82368	POINT WARDE	14 Aug 1967	AA
WPB 82369	POINT HEYER	3 Aug 1967	PA
WPB 82370	POINT RICHMOND	25 Aug 1967	PA
D series			
WPB 82371	POINT BARNES	21 Apr 1970	AA
WPB 82372	POINT BROWER	21 Apr 1970	PA
WPB 82373	POINT CAMDEN	4 May 1970	PA
WPB 82374	POINT CARREW	18 May 1970	PA
WPB 82375	POINT DORAN	1 June 1970	PA
WPB 82376	POINT HARRIS	22 June 1970	decomm. May 1992
WPB 82377	POINT HOBART	13 July 1970	PA
WPB 82378	POINT JACKSON	3 Aug 1970	AA
WPB 82379	POINT MARTIN	20 Aug 1970	AA

Builders:	Coast Guard Yard, Curtis Bay, Md., except WPB 82345–82349 J. Martinac Shipbuilding, Tacoma, Wash.
Displacement:	A series 67 tons full load
	C series 66 tons full load
	D series 69 full load
Length:	83 feet (25.3 m) overall
Beam:	17⅙ feet (5.2 m)
Draft:	5¾ feet (1.8 m)
Propulsion:	2 diesel engines (Cummins VT-12-M); 1,600 bhp; 2 shafts (see notes)
Speed:	A series 23.5 knots
	C series 23.7 knots
	D series 22.6 knots
Range:	A and C series 490 n.miles (910 km) at 20 knots
	1,500 n.miles (2,780 km) at 8 knots
	D series 320 n.miles (590 km) at 20 knots
	1,200 n.miles (2,220 km) at 6 knots
Manning:	10 (see notes)
Guns:	2 40-mm grenade launchers Mk 19 (2 single)
	2 .50-cal machine guns (2 single)
Radars:	SPS-64(V)1 navigation

These are 83-foot cutters used for port security and search and rescue.

Class: Originally a class of 78 units; 26 units were transferred to South Vietnam in 1969–1970. Recent disposals are listed above; see appendix E for details. The survivors are being re-engined (see below); some will serve beyond the year 2000.

Design: These patrol boats have steel hulls with aluminum superstructures. There are no noticeable differences among the various series of the Point class. A tripod mast is fitted atop the bridge roof.

Engineering: The POINT THATCHER originally had two gas turbines generating 1,000 shp and capable of making 27 knots; fitted with controllable-pitch propellers. She was refitted with diesels.

The Coast Guard had planned to re-engine 43 of these craft beginning in the late 1980s to extend their service lives. All were completed with two Cummins VT-12-M diesel engines; beginning in 1989, the 43 units were to be refitted with two 750-bhp Caterpillar 3412 V-12 diesel engines, but that effort is behind schedule and fewer units will be upgraded. The POINT HIGHLAND was the first unit to be re-engined.

Guns: Earlier these WPBs had a single 20-mm gun forward of the deckhouse. During the 1960s and 1970s many units instead carried two .50-cal machine guns or an 81-mm mortar mounted "piggyback" with a .50-cal machine gun. Subsequently they carried only the single machine guns. Only small arms are now carried.

Manning: About half of the Point-class WPBs are commanded by commissioned officers and the remainder by an officer-in-charge, normally a chief petty officer; the remainder of the crew is enlisted.

Names: The WPB 82301–82344 were assigned geographical point names in January 1964; later cutters were named as built.

The POINT CHARLES with two .50-cal machine guns mounted forward under canvas covers. Some WPBs have "U.S." prefixing Coast Guard on their sides. (1991, Giorgio Arra)

The POINT CHARLES, mounting a small commercial navigation radar above the bridge as well as the SPS-64(V)1 navigation radar atop her mast. (1990, Giorgio Arra)

The fast coastal interceptor WFCI 43505. Note the commercial navigation radar atop her "roll bar." (1990, Giorgio Arra)

5 + 20(?) FAST COASTAL INTERCEPTORS (43)

Number	Number	Number
WFCI 43501	WFCI 43503	WFCI 43505
WFCI 43502	WFCI 43504	

Builders:	Tempest Marine, North Miami Beach, Fla.
Displacement:	7 tons standard
Length:	43½ feet (13.3 m) overall
Beam:	9½ feet (2.9 m)
Draft:	3⅙ feet (1.0 m)
Propulsion:	2 diesel engines (Caterpillar 3208-TA); 750 bhp; 2 shafts
Speed:	50+ knots; approx. 40 knots sustained
Range:	
Manning:	4 to 6
Guns:	small arms
Radars:	1 Raytheon 1900 navigation

These are small, high-speed boats built specifically for Coast Guard use in intercepting drug smugglers off the Florida coasts. They are based on the design of the Riviera-class "cigarette boats," but have diesel engines in lieu of the gasoline engines normally found in those craft.

The first four units were completed in April 1987; the fifth was delivered in 1988; 20 additional units have been authorized.

Design: They have a 25° V-bottom monohull fabricated of fiberglass. These are extremely stable craft at high speeds and in heavy sea conditions. They are fitted with fixed-pitch, super-cavitating propellers.

Operations: All are based in Florida.

ICEBREAKERS

Coast Guard icebreakers operate in the Arctic and Antarctic regions in support of U.S. national requirements for military and scientific activities. The Coast Guard had long planned to construct two additional Polar-class icebreakers to replace the GLACIER and two Wind-class icebreakers to provide a force of four modern icebreakers to meet national requirements. But the GLACIER and two surviving Wind-class ships were decommissioned without replacements.

In late 1986 the Coast Guard expressed interest in leasing two large polar icebreakers as an alternative to building and operating government-owned ships. Such a build-and-charter concept was similar to that used by the Navy for tankers and maritime prepositioning ships. The concept, however, has been rejected in favor of a single new-construction ship. Named HEALEY, the new ship will be larger and more powerful than the Polar class.

(1) ICEBREAKER "HEALY" (460)

Number	Name	FY	Launch	Commission	Status
WAGB 12	HEALY	90		(1997)	Authorized

Builders:	
Displacement:	17,710 tons full load
Length:	400 feet (121.95 m) waterline
	460 feet (140.2 m) overall
Beam:	94½ feet (28.8 m)
Draft:	32 feet (9.75 m)
Propulsion:	diesel-electric: 4 diesel engines; 40,000 bhp + electric motors; 30,000 shp; 2 shafts
Speed:	12.5 knots
Range:	34,500 n.miles (63,900 km) at 12.5 knots
	37,000 n.miles (68,525 km) at 9.25 knots
Manning:	133 (19 officers + 114 enlisted) + 30 scientists
Helicopters:	2 HH-65A Dolphin
Guns:	2 .50-cal machine guns (2 single)
Radars:	2 navigation

The Congress voted $275 million in the fiscal 1990 budget for construction of this ship; the remainder of the necessary funding, $60 million, was authorized by Congress in fiscal 1992. Although a second ship is planned, no authorization was proposed when this edition went to press.

Cancellation of the planned shipyard selection and award of a contract for construction of the HEALY was announced on 20 March 1992. The Naval Sea Systems Command, procurement agent for the Coast Guard for icebreakers, cancelled the procurement because the responses received from shipyards were in excess of appropriated funds. The Coast Guard and Navy stated that they would "continue to examine alternatives for procuring the icebreaker. . . ."

Design: Intended to break ice 4½ feet (1.4 m) thick at a continuous speed of three knots.

Engineering: The ship would have had an endurance of 180 days.

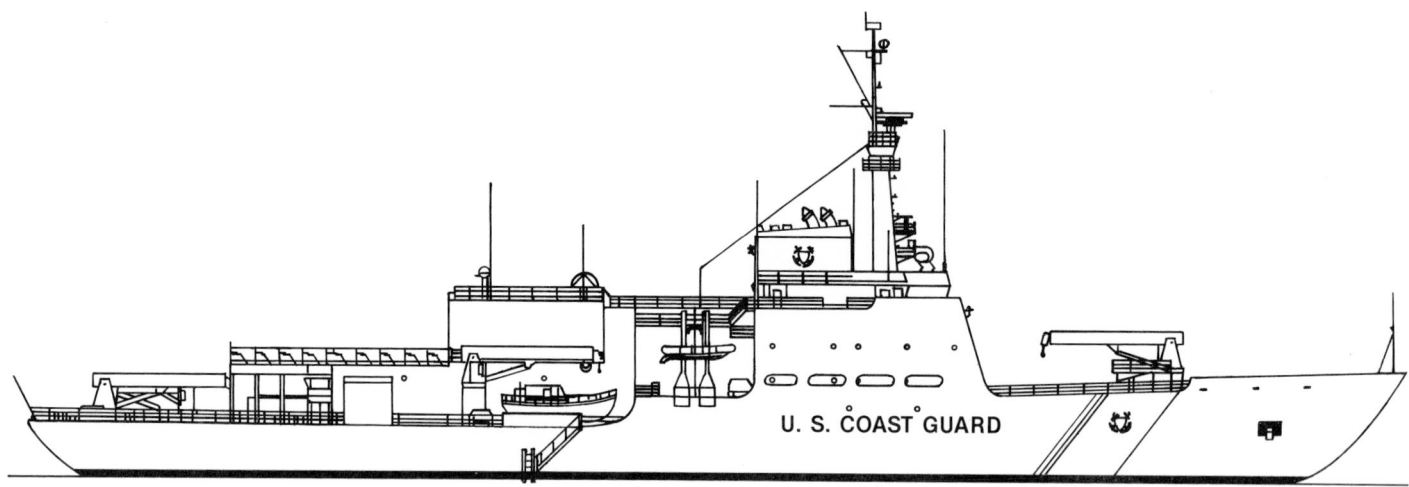

Line drawing of the planned icebreaker HEALY. After a prolonged gestation period, the Navy cancelled acquisition of the ship in March 1992 because of higher-than-expected cost estimates from U.S. shipyards. The ship is needed to support U.S. Arctic and Antarctic activities. (William Clipson)

2 ICEBREAKERS: POLAR CLASS (399)

Number	Name	Launched	Commissioned	Status
WAGB 10	POLAR STAR	17 Nov 1973	17 Jan 1976	PA
WAGB 11	POLAR SEA	24 June 1975	26 Sep 1976	PA

Builders:	Lockheed Shipbuilding, Seattle Wash.
Displacement:	10,430 tons standard
	13,190 tons full load
Length:	399 feet (12.6 m) overall
Beam:	83½ feet (25.5 m)
Draft:	33½ feet (10.2 m)
Propulsion:	CODOG: 6 diesel engines (Alco); 18,000 bhp + 3 gas turbines (Pratt & Whitney); 60,000 shp; 3 shafts
Speed:	18 knots
Range:	16,000 n.miles (2,963 km) at 18 knots
	28,000 n.miles (51,855 km) at 13 knots
Manning:	139 (14 officers + 125 enlisted)
Helicopters:	2 HH-65A Dolphin
Guns:	2 40-mm grenade launchers Mk 19 (2 single)
Radars:	2 SPS-64 navigation

These are the largest icebreakers now in service outside of Russia. Several ships were originally planned in this class as replacements for the Wind-class icebreakers. No more ships of this class were built, in part because of the higher-than-anticipated construction costs.

Design: These ships have conventional icebreaker hull forms. A hangar and flight deck are fitted aft and two 15-ton-capacity cranes are abaft the hangar. Arctic and oceanographic laboratories are provided.

Engineering: CODOG (Combination Diesel Or Gas turbine) propulsion is provided, with diesel engines for cruising and rapid-reaction gas turbines available for surge-power requirements. Controllable-pitch propellers allow propeller thrust to be reversed by reversing the direction of shaft rotation. Both ships have experienced problems with their controllable-pitch propellers and control systems.

The original design provided for a speed of 21 knots; it has not been achieved in service.

Operational: The POLAR SEA circumnavigated the North American continent in 1985. The icebreaker departed Seattle, Wash., on 6 June, sailed through the Panama Canal, up the East Coast to Greenland, and through the Northwest Passage to pass into the Bering Sea and into the Pacific, returning to Seattle on 2 October. The ship required just under seven days, including a brief stop at the village of Resolute, to transit the 850-n.mile (1,575-m) Northwest Passage.

The POLAR SEA off New York. The POLAR SEA and POLAR STAR are the only oceangoing icebreakers in U.S. service; they are painted red for easy recognition in ice. The ships have suffered numerous mechanical problems. (1990, Giorgio Arra)

The POLAR STAR with an HH-65 Dolphin helicopter on her flight deck. These ships normally embark two HH-65s when deployed, the hangar being large enough to house both of them. (U.S. Coast Guard)

ICEBREAKER: "GLACIER"

The one-of-a-kind icebreaker GLACIER (WAGB 4, ex-AGB 4) was decommissioned on 17 June 1987 and, when this edition went to press, was laid up at the Mare Island Naval Shipyard awaiting disposal.

The GLACIER was the only icebreaker built for U.S. naval service after World War II, being commissioned as the AGB 4 on 27 May 1955. She was transferred to the Coast Guard on 30 June 1966 (and stricken from the Navy Register on 1 July 1966, the day after her transfer to the Coast Guard).

See 14th Edition/page 547 for characteristics.

1 ICEBREAKER: "MACKINAW" (290)

Number	Name	Launched	Commissioned	Status
WAGB 83	MACKINAW	4 Mar 1944	20 Dec 1944	**GL**

Builders:	Toledo Shipbuilding, Ohio
Displacement:	5,320 tons full load
Length:	290 feet (88.4 m) overall
Beam:	75 feet (22.9 m)
Draft:	19 feet (5.8 m)
Propulsion:	diesel-electric (Fairbanks-Morse diesel engines, Westinghouse electric motors); 10,000 shp aft + 3,000 shp forward; 2 shafts aft + 1 shaft forward
Speed:	18.7 knots
Range:	10,000 n.miles (18,520 km) at 18.7 knots
	41,000 n.miles (75,930 km) at 9 knots
Manning:	75 (8 officers + 67 enlisted)
Helicopters:	landing area
Guns:	none

The MACKINAW was designed and constructed specifically for Coast Guard use on the Great Lakes. The ship is home-ported in Cheboygan, Mich.

Classification: The ship originally was classified WAG 83; she was changed in WAGB on 1 May 1966.

Design: The MACKINAW has many features of the Wind class; however, being designed for the Great Lakes, the ship is longer and wider than the oceangoing ships with significantly less draft. Two 12-ton-capacity cranes are fitted. The ship has a clear deck aft for a helicopter, but no hangar is provided.

Name: Originally named MANITOWOC.

The MACKINAW and a Bay-class icebreaking tug in Great Lakes ice. The MACKINAW was designed specifically for Great Lakes operation, no armament was planned because of the U.S.–Canadian agreement on demilitarization of their common border. (U.S. Coast Guard)

ICEBREAKERS: WIND CLASS (269)

The Wind-class icebreakers WESTWIND (WAGB 281, ex-Navy AGB 6) and NORTHWIND (WAGB 282) were decommissioned on 29 February 1988 and 20 January 1989, respectively. These were the last of seven sister ships, two built for the Navy and the remaining five to Coast Guard specifications; three of the latter ships served with the Soviet Navy after World War II. A table showing their service assignments and designations is found in the 14th edition of *Ships and Aircraft*.

These were highly effective icebreakers; they were built with a relatively heavy gun armament and could carry a floatplane (later provided with a helicopter capability).

See 14th Edition/pages 547–549 for characteristics.

TRAINING CUTTERS

1 TRAINING BARK: "EAGLE"

Number	Name	Launched	USCG Comm.	Status
WIX 327	EAGLE	13 June 1936	Jan 1946	**TRA-A**

Builders:	Blohm and Voss, Hamburg (Germany)
Displacement:	1,519 tons light
	1,784 tons full load
Length:	231 feet (90.0 m) waterline
	295 feet (89.9 m) over bowsprit
Beam:	39½ feet (11.9 m)
Draft:	17 feet (5.2 m)
Masts:	fore and main 150½ feet (45.7 m)
	mizzen 132 feet (40.2 m)
Propulsion:	1 auxiliary diesel engine (Caterpillar); 1,000 bhp; 1 shaft
Speed:	up to 18 knots under sail; 10 knots on auxiliary diesel engine
Allowance:	65 (19 officers + 46 enlisted) + 175 cadets and instructors
Guns:	none
Radars:	1 SPS-64(V) navigation

The EAGLE is the former German naval training bark HORST WESSEL. Taken by the United States as a reparation after World War II, she was acquired in January 1946 at Bremerhaven and assigned to the Coast Guard. Based at the Coast Guard Academy in New London, Conn., she is employed to train Coast Guard cadets on summer practice cruises.

Class: The similar ALBERT LEO SCHLAGETER (launched 1937) was also taken over by the United States in 1945 but was sold to Brazil in 1948 and re-sold to Portugal in 1962 (now in service as the SAGRES). A third ship of this basic design, the GORCH FOCK (1933), was taken over by the Soviet Union in 1946 and renamed the TOVARISH; she remains in Russian service.[7] The similar MIRECA was built for Romania and also remains in service.

A later ship of the same general design, also named the GORCH FOCK, was built at the same German yard for the West German Navy (launched in 1958).

Design: The EAGLE is steel-hulled. She carries up to 21,350 square feet (1,921.5 m²) of sail.

Engineering: Original MAN diesel auxiliary engine replaced in the early 1980s.

---

7. The TOVARISCH is employed as a sail training ship for the Russian merchant marine; see N. Polmar, *Guide to the Soviet Navy,* 5th edition (Annapolis, Md.: Naval Institute Press, 1991). pp. 332–333.

The training bark EAGLE under way on auxiliary propulsion off Miami. In the 1980s then-Secretary of the Navy John Lehman proposed the construction of a sail training ship for the Navy; see page 284. (1988, Giorgio Arra)

Training bark EAGLE. (U.S. Coast Guard)

BUOY TENDERS

(APPROX. 28) SEAGOING BUOY TENDERS: NEW CONSTRUCTION

Displacement:	
Length:	approx. 200 feet (61 m) overall
Beam:	
Draft:	
Propulsion:	
Speed:	15 knots
Range:	6,000 n.miles (11,110 km) at 12 knots
Manning:	40 (6 officers + 34 enlisted)
Guns:	
Radars:	

These will be the first seagoing buoy tenders built for the U.S. Coast Guard since the BALSAM class of World War II. In 1991 the Coast Guard awarded contracts for the design of these ships to several shipyards. In August 1992 one of the yards was to be chosen to construct the lead tender. Delivery of the lead ship is planned for mid-1995.

The number of tenders to be built is the subject of an ongoing Coast Guard analysis; the 28-unit estimate is unofficial.

Design: Endurance will be 21 days.

The tenders are to have a 30,000-pound (13,605-kg) lift capacity, a large deck area for handling buoys, and the ability to work buoys in eight-foot (2.4-m) seas.

1 MEDIUM-ENDURANCE CUTTER ⎫
24 SEAGOING BUOY TENDERS ⎬ "BALSAM" CLASS (180)

Number	Name	Builder	Launched	Commissioned	Status
A series					
WLB 277	COWSLIP	MI	11 Apr 1942	17 Oct 1942	**AA**
WLB 290	GENTIAN	ZD	23 May 1942	3 Nov 1942	**AA**
WLB 291	LAUREL	ZD	4 Aug 1942	24 Nov 1942	**AA**
WLB 296	SORREL	ZD	28 Sep 1942	15 Apr 1943	**AA**
WMEC 300	CITRUS	MI	15 Aug 1942	30 May 1943	**PA**
WLB 301	CONIFER	MI	3 Nov 1942	1 July 1943	**PA**
WLB 302	MADRONA	ZD	11 Nov 1942	30 May 1943	**AA**
B series					
WLB 297	IRONWOOD	CG	16 Mar 1943	4 Aug 1943	**PA**
WLB 306	BUTTONWOOD	MI	30 Nov 1942	24 Sep 1943	**AA**
WLB 307	PLANETREE	MI	20 Mar 1943	4 Nov 1943	**PA**
C series					
WLB 388	BLASSWOOD	MI	20 May 1943	12 Jan 1944	**PA**
WLB 389	BITTERSWEET	ZD	11 Nov 1943	11 May 1944	**AA**
WLB 390	BLACKHAW	MI	18 June 1943	17 Feb 1944	**PA**
WLB 392	BRAMBLE	ZD	23 Oct 1943	22 Apr 1944	**GL**
WLB 393	FIREBUSH	ZD	3 Feb 1944	20 July 1944	**PA**
WLB 394	HORNBEAM	MI	14 Aug 1943	14 Apr 1944	**AA**
WLB 395	IRIS	ZD	18 May 1944	11 Aug 1944	**PA**
WLB 396	MALLOW	ZD	9 Dec 1943	6 June 1944	**PA**
WLB 397	MARIPOSA	ZD	14 Jan 1944	1 July 1944	**GL**
WLB 400	SALVIA	ZD	15 Sep 1943	19 Feb 1944	**AA**
WLB 401	SASSAFRAS	MI	5 Oct 1943	23 May 1944	**PA**
WLB 402	SEDGE	MI	27 Nov 1943	5 July 1944	**PA**
WLB 403	SPAR	MI	2 Nov 1943	12 June 1944	**PA**
WLB 404	SUNDEW	MI	8 Feb 1944	24 Aug 1944	**GL**
WLB 405	SWEETBRIER	MI	30 Dec 1943	26 July 1944	**PA**
WLB 406	ACACIA	ZD	7 Apr 1944	1 Sep 1944	**GL**
WLB 407	WOODRUSH	ZD	28 Apr 1944	22 Sep 1944	**PA**

Builders:	ZD = Zenith Dredge, Duluth, Minn.
	MI = Marine Iron and Shipbuilding Co., Duluth, Minn.
	CG = Coast Guard Yard, Curtis Bay, Md.
Displacement:	935 tons standard
	1,025 tons full load
Length:	180 feet (54.9 m) overall
Beam:	37 feet (11.3 m)
Draft:	13 feet (4.0 m)
Propulsion:	diesel-electric (2 General Motors 8-645E6A diesel engines); 1,200 shp; 1 shaft
Speed:	13 knots
Range:	4,500 n.miles (8,335 km) at 13 knots
	13,500 n.miles (25,000 km) at 7.5 knots
Manning:	48 (6 officers + 42 enlisted)
Guns:	2 40-mm grenade launchers Mk 19 (2 single) in most units; others are unarmed

These are tenders that service navigation buoys and other aids to navigation in coastal waters. They have proven to be highly versatile ships, having served as convoys escorts, in the SAR role, assisting in constructing and servicing LORAN navigation stations, and as salvage ships; some have a light icebreaking capability.

Class: Thirty-nine ships of this design were completed in 1942–1944.

The COWSLIP (WLB 277) was stricken on 23 March 1973 (sold); she was repurchased by the Coast Guard in January 1981 and recommissioned in November 1981. She replaced the BLACKTHORN (WLB 391), which was rammed and sunk on 28 January 1980.

CLOVER (WLB/WMEC 292) decommissioned in June 1990.

EVERGREEN (WLB/WAGO/WMEC 295) decommissioned on 13 June 1990.

The MESQUITE (WLB 305) ran aground in Lake Superior on 4 December 1989 and was a total loss; none of her crew was lost.

Classification: Several ships were temporarily reclassified as medium-endurance cutters (WMEC) and engaged in patrol work during the 1970s and 1980s. The EVERGREEN was refitted as an

The seagoing buoy tender MADRONA. The WLBs are the only seagoing Coast Guard cutters with black hulls. Note the boom arrangement; these were the first buoy tenders to be provided with SAR features. They have also served in the escort and law-enforcement roles. (1990, Giorgio Arra)

The COWSLIP, oldest of the BALSAM-class seagoing tenders, steaming off Norfolk. There is an empty 3-inch gun "tub" aft of the funnel. Several large buoys are being carried forward. (1988, Giorgio Arra)

oceanographic cutter in 1973 and reclassified WAGO; she was changed to WMEC on 1 May 1982. The only BALSAM-class WMEC at this time is the CITRUS, changed in WMEC in June 1979.

Design: The WLB 296, 300, 390, 392, and 402–404 have strengthened hulls for icebreaking. Fitted with 20-ton-capacity boom. (In SLEP ships a hydraulically powered system replaces the electrically powered boom.) These ships are highly effective for breaking through light ice.

Engineering: The WLB 277, 389, 394, and 395 are fitted with controllable-pitch, bow-thrust propellers.

Guns: As completed, these tenders had one 3-inch/50-cal AA gun and four 20-mm AA guns (two in A-series ships); the 3-inch gun was fitted in a raised "tub" aft of the funnel. They additionally carried depth charges, with some ships having ahead-throwing Mousetrap ASW projectors.

Modernization: All surviving units have been upgraded under a Service-Life Extension Program (SLEP). They were fitted with new main engines, electronics, and other systems plus improved habitability. The SORREL was the first ship, with her 16-month SLEP being completed in January 1983.

Names: The ACACIA originally was named THISTLE; her name was changed in 1944 because that former name was also carried at the time by an Army hospital ship.

The CITRUS was one of several seagoing buoy tenders employed as medium-endurance cutters. The superstructure has an unusual appearance with the removal of the bridge boom. The EVERGREEN was also painted white when employed as an oceanographic ship. (1986, Giorgio Arra)

COASTAL BUOY TENDERS: NEW CONSTRUCTION

A new class of coastal buoy tenders (WLM) is planned to replace the existing, outdated craft.

5 COASTAL BUOY TENDERS: RED CLASS (157)

Number	Name	Launched	Commissioned	Status
WLM 685	RED WOOD	4 Apr 1964	6 Aug 1964	AA
WLM 686	RED BEECH	6 June 1964	20 Nov 1964	AA
WLM 687	RED BIRCH	19 Feb 1965	7 June 1965	AA
WLM 688	RED CEDAR	1 Aug 1970	18 Dec 1970	AA
WLM 689	RED OAK	19 June 1971	10 Dec 1971	AA

Builders:	Coast Guard Yard, Curtis Bay, Md.
Displacement:	471 tons standard
	512 tons full load
Length:	157 feet (47.8 m) overall
Beam:	33 feet (10.1 m)
Draft:	6 feet (1.8 m)
Propulsion:	2 diesel engines (Caterpillar); 1,800 bhp; 2 shafts
Speed:	12.8 knots
Manning:	31 (4 officers + 27 enlisted)

These buoy and navigation aid tenders have strengthened steel hulls for light icebreaking and are fitted with bow thrusters.

Armament: No coastal or small buoy tenders are armed.

The RED CEDAR breaking through light ice. Most buoy tenders have a limited icebreaking capability. (U.S. Coast Guard)

6 COASTAL BUOY TENDERS: WHITE CLASS (133)

Number	Name	Launched	Commissioned	Status
WLM 540 (ex-YF 416)	WHITE SUMAC	14 June 1943	6 Nov 1943	AA
WLM 543 (ex-YF 341)	WHITE HOLLY	8 Apr 1944	6 June 1944	AA
WLM 544 (ex-YF 444)	WHITE SAGE	9 June 1943	29 May 1944	AA
WLM 545 (ex-YF 445)	WHITE HEATH	21 July 1943	9 Aug 1944	AA
WLM 546 (ex-YF 446)	WHITE LUPINE	28 July 1943	31 May 1944	AA
WLM 547 (ex-YF 448)	WHITE PINE	28 Aug 1943	11 July 1944	AA

Builders:	Erie Concrete and Steel Supply, Penna., except WHITE SUMAC by Niagara Shipbuilding, Buffalo, N.Y., and WHITE HOLLY by Basalt Rock, Napa, Calif.
Displacement:	435 tons standard
	600 tons full load
Length:	133 feet (40.5 m) overall
Beam:	31 feet (9.4 m)
Draft:	9 feet (2.7 m)
Propulsion:	2 diesel engines (Union); 600 bhp; 2 shafts
Speed:	9.8 knots
Manning:	23 (1 officer + 22 enlisted)

These tenders are converted Navy self-propelled lighters (YF); they were transferred to the Coast Guard in August–September 1947.

Class: WHITE BUSH (WLM 542) decommissioned on 16 September 1985.

The WHITE SUMAC shows the typical buoy tender configuration: working space forward with a heavy boom to lift buoys and other navigation markers. There is a rigid-hull rubber launch aft of the deckhouse and a life-raft canister aft. (1992, Giorgio Arra)

COASTAL BUOY TENDERS: "HOLLYHOCK" CLASS (175)

The last of three tenders of this class, the FIR (WLM 212), was decommissioned on 1 October 1991. Her sister ships HOLLYHOCK (WLM 220) and WALNUT (WLM 252) were decommissioned on 31 March 1982 and 15 June 1982, respectively.

See 14th Edition/page 551 for characteristics.

1 INLAND BUOY TENDER
3 INLAND CONSTRUCTION TENDERS } "COSMOS" CLASS (100)

Number	Name	Launched	Commissioned
WLIC 298	RAMBLER	6 May 1943	26 May 1943
WLI 313	BLUEBELL	28 Sep 1944	24 Mar 1945
WLIC 315	SMILAX	18 Aug 1944	1 Nov 1944
WLIC 316	PRIMROSE	18 Aug 1944	23 Oct 1944

Builders:	Dubuque Boat & Builder, Iowa, except BLUEBELL, Birchfield Boiler, Tacoma, Wash.
Displacement:	178 tons full load
Length:	100 feet (30.5 m) overall
Beam:	24 feet (7.3 m)
Draft:	5 feet (1.5 m)
Propulsion:	2 diesel engines: 600 bhp; 2 shafts
Speed:	10.5 knots
Range:	2,700 n.miles (5,000 km) at 7 knots
Manning:	14 (1 officer + 13 enlisted)

All were formerly designated WLI; three of these tenders were changed to inland construction tenders (WLIC) on 1 October 1979.

This was originally a class of eight tenders. COSMOS (WLI 293) was decommissioned on 16 August 1985.

RAMBLER. (1983, Giorgio Arra)

1 INLAND BUOY TENDER: "BUCKTHORN" (100)

Number	Name	Commissioned
WLI 642	BUCKTHORN	17 July 1964

Builders:	Mobile Ship Repair, Ala.
Displacement:	200 tons full load
Length:	100 feet (30.5 m) overall
Beam:	24 feet (7.3 m)
Draft:	4 feet (1.2 m)
Propulsion:	2 diesel engines; 600 bhp; 2 shafts
Speed:	11.9 knots
Manning:	15 (1 officer + 14 enlisted)

The BUCKTHORN operates on the Great Lakes. A single-ship design.

BUCKTHORN. (1989, L. Van Ginderen Collection)

2 INLAND BUOY TENDERS: IMPROVED BERRY CLASS (65)

Number	Name	Launched	Commissioned
WLI 65400	BAYBERRY	2 June 1954	28 June 1954
WLI 65401	ELDERBERRY	2 June 1954	28 June 1954

Builders:	Reliable Welding Works, Olympia, Wash.
Displacement:	68 tons full load
Length:	65 feet (19.8 m) overall
Beam:	17 feet (5.2 m)
Draft:	4 feet (1.2 m)
Propulsion:	2 diesel engines; 400 bhp; 2 shafts
Speed:	11.3 knots
Range:	1,700 n.miles (3,150 km) at 6 knots
Manning:	8 (enlisted)

Similar to the basic Berry-class design but with a more powerful propulsion plant. Originally designed for freshwater operation, they have been modified for saltwater operation.

Names: Inland tenders were named in 1963.

ELDERBERRY. (U.S. Coast Guard)

2 INLAND BUOY TENDERS: BERRY CLASS (65)

Number	Name	Launched	Commissioned
WLI 65303	BLACKBERRY		24 Aug 1946
WLI 65304	CHOKEBERRY	23 May 1946	30 Aug 1946

Builders:	Dubuque Boat & Boiler, Iowa
Displacement:	68 tons full load
Length:	65 feet (19.8 m) overall
Beam:	17 feet (5.2 m)
Draft:	4 feet (1.2 m)
Propulsion:	1 diesel (General Motors); 220 bhp; 1 shaft
Speed:	9 knots
Range:	1,500 n.miles (2,780 km) at 5 knots
Manning:	8 (enlisted)

The third tender of this craft, the LOGANBERRY (WLI 65305), was decommissioned in 1977.

9 INLAND CONSTRUCTION TENDERS: "ANVIL" CLASS (75)

Number	Name	Number	Name
A series		*C series*	
WLIC 75301	ANVIL	WLIC 75306	CLAMP
WLIC 75302	HAMMER	WLIC 75307	WEDGE
B series		WLIC 75309	HATCHET
WLIC 75303	SLEDGE	WLIC 75310	AXE
WLIC 75304	MALLET		
WLIC 75305	VISE		

Builders:	WLIC 75301, 75302 Gibbs Shipyard, Jacksonville, Fla.
	WLIC 75303-75735 McDermott, Morgan City, Mich.
	WLIC 75306, 75307 Sturgeon Bay Shipbuilding, Wisc.
	WLIC 75309, 75310 Dorchester Shipbuilding, Dorchester, N.J.
Displacement:	145 tons
Length:	75 feet (22.9 m) overall, except C series 76 feet (23.2 m) overall
Beam:	22 feet (6.7 m)
Draft:	4 feet (1.2 m)
Propulsion:	2 diesel engines; 600 bhp; 2 shafts
Speed:	A series 8.6 knots
	B series 9.1 knots
	C series 9.4 knots
Range:	approx. 1,000 n.miles (1,850 km) at 9 knots
Manning:	13 (enlisted)

These tenders were completed in 1962–1966. The SPIKE (WLIC 75308) was decommissioned on 30 May 1986.

1 RIVER BUOY TENDER: "SUMAC" (115)

Number	Name	Launched	Commissioned
WLR 311	SUMAC	14 Oct 1944	11 Nov 1944

Builders:	Peterson and Haecker, Blair, Neb.
Displacement:	478 tons full load
Length:	115 feet (35.0 m) overall
Beam:	30 feet (9.1 m)
Draft:	6 feet (1.8 m)
Propulsion:	3 diesel engines (General Motors); 2,250 bhp; 3 shafts
Speed:	10.6 knots
Manning:	22 (enlisted)

A single tender of this type was built.

RIVER BUOY TENDERS: "DOGWOOD" CLASS (114)

The three tenders of this class, completed 1941–1943, have been discarded: FORSYTHIA (WLR 63) decommissioned on 12 August 1977; DOGWOOD (WLR 259) decommissioned on 11 August 1989; and SYCAMORE (WLIC 268) decommissioned on 30 June 1977.

See 14th Edition/page 555 for characteristics.

RIVER BUOY TENDER: "LANTANA" (80)

The LANTANA (WLR 80310), the single tender of this design, completed 1943, was decommissioned on 27 October 1991.

See 14th Edition/page 555 for characteristics.

HATCHET pushing a work barge. (U.S. Coast Guard)

The one-of-a-kind SUMAC. The Coast Guard also has a buoy tender named WHITE SUMAC. (U.S. Coast Guard)

2 + 3 RIVER BUOY TENDERS: "KANKAKEE" CLASS (75)

Number	Name	Commissioned
WLR 75500	KANKAKEE	1990
WLR 75501	GREENBRIER	1991

Builders:	Avondale Industries (Small Boat Division), New Orleans, La.
Displacement:	172 tons full load
Length:	75 feet (22.9 m) overall
Beam:	24 feet (7.3 m)
Draft:	5 feet (1.5 m)
Propulsion:	2 diesel engines: 1,080 bhp; 2 shafts
Speed:	12 knots
Manning:	19 (enlisted)

Improved river tenders; they push 130-foot (96.6-m) work barges. The first two units support navigation aids on the Arkansas River, replacing the LANTANA and DOGWOOD. Three additional units are planned.

The GREENBRIER, resembling a houseboat. There are twin engine exhausts on the upper deck, behind the bridge. The mast is offset to port. (1990, Avondale Shipyards)

4 INLAND CONSTRUCTION TENDERS: "PAMLICO" CLASS (160)

Number	Name	Number	Name
WLIC 800	PAMLICO	WLIC 802	KENNEBEC
WLIC 801	HUDSON	WLIC 803	SAGINAW

Builders:	Coast Guard Yard, Curtis Bay, Md.
Displacement:	416 tons
Length:	160 feet (48.8 m) overall
Beam:	30 feet (9.1 m)
Draft:	4 feet (1.2 m)
Propulsion:	2 diesel engines (Cummings); 1,000 bhp; 2 shafts
Speed:	10 knots
Manning:	14 (1 officer + 13 enlisted)

These large inland tenders were completed in 1976–1977.

The HUDSON; note the large crane on her forecastle. (1989, Giorgio Arra)

INLAND BUOY TENDER: "TERN" (80)

The single tender of this design, the TERN (WLI 8080), was decommissioned in July 1977. Completed in 1969, the TERN had a unique stern–crane configuration for buoy handling; after evaluation and service use, the concept was discarded.

See 14th Edition/page 586 for characteristics.

The KANKAKEE at high speed. This type of river buoy tender operates as a pusher for a work barge that carries buoys and other navigation aids, and has a crane fitted. (1990, Avondale Shipyards)

9 RIVER BUOY TENDERS: "GASCONADE" CLASS (75)

Number	Name	Number	Name
WLR 75401	GASCONADE	WLR 75406	KICKAPOO
WLR 75402	MUSKINGUM	WLR 75407	KANAWHA
WLR 75403	WYACONDA	WLR 75408	PATOKA
WLR 75404	CHIPPEWA	WLR 75409	CHENA
WLR 75405	CHEYENNE		

Builders:	WLR 75401	St. Louis Shipbuilding & Dry Dock, Mo.
	WLR 75402–75405	Maxon Construction, Tell City, Ind.
	WLR 75406–75409	Halter Marine, New Orleans, La.
Displacement:	141 tons full load	
Length:	75 feet (22.9 m) overall	
Beam:	22 feet (6.7 m)	
Draft:	4 feet (1.2 m)	
Propulsion:	2 diesel engines (Caterpillar); 600 bhp; 2 shafts	
Speed:	7.6 or 8.7 knots	
Manning:	19 (enlisted)	

These tenders were completed from 1964 to 1970. They work in tandem with a 90-foot (27.4-m) barge.

CHEYENNE with buoy barge. (U.S. Coast Guard)

6 RIVER BUOY TENDERS: "OUACHITA" CLASS (65)

Number	Name	Number	Name
WLR 65501	OUACHITA	WLR 65504	SCIOTO
WLR 65502	CIMARRON	WLR 65505	OSAGE
WLR 65503	OBION	WLR 65506	SANGAMON

Builders:	Gibbs Corp., Jacksonville, Fla., except WLR 66501, 66502 Platzer Shipyard, Houston, Texas
Displacement:	143 tons
Length:	65½ feet (20.0 m) overall
Beam:	21 feet (6.4 m)
Draft:	5 feet (1.5 m)
Propulsion:	2 diesel engines; 600 bhp; 2 shafts
Speed:	10.5 knots
Manning:	12 (enlisted)

These tenders were completed in 1960–1962. They were designed specifically to operate with work barges on western rivers.

OSAGE with buoy barge. (U.S. Coast Guard)

TUGS

9 ICEBREAKING TUGS: BAY CLASS (140)

Number	Name	Launched	Commissioned	Status
WTGB 101	KATMAI BAY	8 Apr 1978	8 Jan 1979	GL
WTGB 102	BRISTOL BAY	22 July 1978	5 Apr 1979	GL
WTGB 103	MOBILE BAY	11 Nov 1978	6 May 1979	GL
WTGB 104	BISCAYNE BAY	3 Feb 1979	8 Dec 1979	GL
WTGB 105	NEAH BAY	2 Feb 1980	18 Aug 1980	GL
WTGB 106	MORRO BAY	11 July 1980	25 Jan 1981	AA
WTGB 107	PENOBSCOT BAY	27 July 1984	2 Jan 1985	AA
WTGB 108	THUNDER BAY	15 Aug 1985	4 Nov 1985	AA
WTGB 109	STURGEON BAY	12 Sep 1987	20 Aug 1988	AA

Builders:	Tacoma Boatbuilding, Wash., except WTGB 107, 109, Bay City Marine, Tacoma, Wash.
Displacement:	662 tons full load
Length:	140 feet (42.7 m) overall
Beam:	37 feet (11.3 m)
Draft:	12 feet (3.7 m)
Propulsion:	diesel-electric (2 Fairbanks-Morse 38D8 ⅛ diesel engines); electric drive (Westinghouse); 2,500 shp; 1 shaft
Speed:	14.7 knots
Range:	1,800 n.miles (3,333 km) at 14.7 knots
	4,000 n.miles (7,410 km) at 12 knots
Manning:	17 (3 officers + 14 enlisted)
Radar:	SPS-64(V)1 navigation

These were the largest tugs to be constructed specifically for Coast Guard service. They are designed to provide general towing and support services, and can break through ice up to 20 inches (2 m) thick.

A planned tenth unit was not built.

Classification: These tugs were originally designated WYTM. The KATMAI BAY was changed to WTGB on 5 February 1979; the others were changed to WTGB upon completion.

Design: Fitted with a hull air-lubrication system to enhance icebreaking capability.

MOBILE BAY. (1989, L. Van Ginderen Collection)

STURGEON BAY. (1991, Giorgio Arra)

14 SMALL HARBOR TUGS: 65-FT TYPE

Number	Name	Commissioned	Status
WYTL 65601	CAPSTAN	19 July 1961	AA
WYTL 65602	CHOCK	12 Sep 1962	AA
WYTL 65603	SWIVEL	27 Oct 1961	AA
WYTL 65604	TACKLE	1962	AA
WYTL 65605	TOWLINE	27 Mar 1963	AA
WYTL 65606	CATENARY	Apr 1962	AA
WYTL 65607	BRIDLE	3 Apr 1963	AA
WYTL 65608	PENDANT	Aug 1963	AA
WYTL 65609	SHACKLE	7 May 1963	AA
WYTL 65610	HAWSER	17 Jan 1963	AA
WYTL 65611	LINE	21 Feb 1963	AA
WYTL 65612	WIRE	19 Mar 1963	AA
WYTL 65614	BOLLARD	10 Apr 1967	AA
WYTL 65615	CLEAT	10 May 1967	AA

Builders:	WYTL 65601–65606 Gibbs Corp., Jacksonville, Fla.
	WYTL 65607–65612 Barbour Boat Works, New Bern, N.C.
	WYTL 65614, 65615 Western Boatbuilding, Tacoma, Wash.
Displacement:	72 tons full load
Length:	65 feet (19.8 m) overall
Beam:	19 feet (5.8 m)
Draft:	7 feet (2.1 m)
Propulsion:	1 diesel engine; 400 bhp; 1 shaft
Speed:	10.5 knots except WYTL 65607–65609 9.8 knots
Range:	3,600 n.miles (6,670 km) at 6 knots, except WYTL 65607–65609 2,700 n.miles (5,000 km) at 5.8 knots
Manning:	8 (enlisted)

Steel-hull tugs. Originally a class of 15 tugs; the BITT (WYTL 65613) decommissioned on 4 October 1982.

LINE. (1991, Giorgio Arra)

HAWSER. (1990, Giorgio Arra)

FERRIES

These ferries are used to transport personnel and vehicles between lower Manhattan and Governors Island, N.Y. Located off the southern tip of Manhattan, the island has been the site of a major Coast Guard station since 1966 and serves as headquarters for the Commander, Atlantic Area; previously it was also headquarters for the 3rd Coast Guard District. (Both Atlantic area HAMILTON-class cutters and several other vessels are home-ported there.)

These ferries are civilian-manned. They do not have Coast Guard hull numbers assigned and are not in commission.

1 FERRY: "GOVERNOR"

Number	Name	USCG in service
(none)	GOVERNOR	22 Feb 1985

Builders:	Moore Drydock, Oakland, Calif.
Displacement:	1,600 tons standard
Length:	242⅔ feet (74.0 m) overall
Beam:	65⅙ feet (19.85 m)
Draft:	12¼ feet (5.9 m)
Propulsion:	diesel-electric (2 diesel engines); 1,000 bhp; 2 shafts
Speed:	14.5 knots
Manning:	6 civilian

The ship was built in 1954 and as the CROWN CITY was used by the Navy in San Diego; she was subsequently sold to the state of Washington, renamed KULSHAN, and employed in the Puget Sound area. She was acquired by the Coast Guard in 1982 and rehabilitated by the Coast Guard yard at Curtis Bay from late 1982 until early 1985.

The GOVERNOR can carry 55 automobiles and 500 passengers.

The GOVERNOR transiting between Manhattan and Governors Island, with Brooklyn in the background. The GOVERNOR did not have the Coast Guard's shield on her blue-and-red stripes when this photo was taken, nor do the ferries have "Coast Guard" on their sides. (1991, Giorgio Arra)

2 FERRIES: EX-U.S. ARMY

Number	Name	USCG in service
(ex-FB 812)	LT SAMUEL S. COURSEN	1966
(ex-FB 813)	PVT NICHOLAS MINUE	1966

Builders:	John H. Mathis, Camden, N.J.
Displacement:	869 tons full load
Length:	180⅙ feet (54.9 m) overall
Beam:	60 feet (18.3 m)
Draft:	14 feet (4.3 m)
Propulsion:	diesel-electric (2 diesel engines); 1,000 bhp; 2 shafts
Speed:	12 knots
Manning:	6 civilian

Both are former U.S. Army ferries completed in 1955. They can each accommodate 30 automobiles and 1,100 passengers.

LT SAMUEL S. COURSEN. (1990, Giorgio Arra)

1 FERRY: "THE TIDES"

Number	Name	USCG in service
(none)	THE TIDES	1966

Builders:	
Displacement:	774 tons full load
Length:	185⅙ feet (56.45 m) overall
Beam:	55 feet (16.8 m)
Draft:	9½ feet (2.9 m)
Propulsion:	diesel-electric (2 diesel engines); 1,350 shp; 2 shafts
Speed:	12 knots
Manning:	

THE TIDES is a former commercial ferry launched in 1947. She can carry 42 automobiles and 500 passengers.

THE TIDES. (1991, Giorgio Arra)

LIGHTSHIPS

The last of the Coast Guard lightships have been stricken, the LIGHTSHIP I (WLV 612) on 29 March 1985 and the LIGHTSHIP II (WLV 613) on 18 October 1984.

See 13th Edition/page 525.

SMALL CRAFT

The Coast Guard operates several hundred small craft in the patrol, search, rescue, oil cleanup, and navigation support roles. The larger series are listed below.

The Raider-type patrol craft are the only units normally armed and are listed first in this section.

24 PATROL CRAFT: 22-FT RAIDER TYPE

Builders:	NAPCO International, Hopkins, Minn.
Displacement:	1.5 tons light
	2 tons full load
Length:	22⅓ feet (6.8 m) overall plus engines
Beam:	7⁵⁄₁₂ feet (2.25 m)
Draft:	2⅚ feet (0.86 m) with engines
Propulsion:	2 outboard gasoline engines; 360 hp
Speed:	40 knots
Range:	165 n.miles (305 km) at 40 knots
	225 n.miles (420 km) at cruise
Manning:	3
Guns:	1 .50-cal machine gun M2HB
	1 7.62-mm machine gun
	small arms
Radars:	1 navigation

These are modified Boston Whalers built of Glass-Reinforced Plastic (GRP). They are "unsinkable" as they will float when swamped. Delivered 1987–1989.

They are craft operated by reserve Port Security Units; several were airlifted to the Persian Gulf during Operation Desert Shield (1990).

A modified 22-foot Boston Whaler employed by the Coast Guard passes the flagship LA SALLE (AGF 3) in the Persian Gulf. These small, high-speed craft have radar, a high degree of maneuverability, and can carry several machine guns, making them potent patrol craft. (1991, CWO2 Ed Bailey, USN)

A 22-foot raider craft of the type used by the Coast Guard. Note the "skate ring" around the craft for mounting machine guns. The fiberglass-hulled craft is "unsinkable," being able to float when swamped. (NAPCO International)

20 AIDS-TO-NAVIGATION BOATS: 55-FT TYPE

Builders:	Robert E. Derecktor, Mamaroneck, N.Y.
Displacement:	28.8 tons full load
Length:	58 feet (17.68 m) overall
Beam:	17 feet (5.2 m)
Draft:	5 feet (1.5 m)
Propulsion:	2 diesel engines (General Motors 12V71 T1); 1,080 bhp; 2 shafts
Speed:	22 knots
Manning:	4 (enlisted)
Radars:	1 Raytheon 1900 navigation

These are aluminum-hull craft that support navigation aids on inland waterways. Numbered from 55100, the number reflecting their waterline length. Aluminum construction.

A 58-foot aids-to-navigation boat at San Francisco. Although 58 feet long, these craft are designated as 55-footers by the Coast Guard. (1988, Giorgio Arra)

SEVERAL MOTOR LIFEBOATS: 52-FT TYPE

Builders:	
Displacement:	35 tons
Length:	52 feet (15.85 m) overall
Beam:	14½ feet (4.4 m)
Draft:	6¼ feet (1.9 m)
Propulsion:	2 diesel engines (General Motors 6-71); 340 bhp; 2 shafts
Speed:	11 knots
Range:	495 n.miles (920 km) at 11 knots
Manning:	5 (enlisted) + 35 survivors
Radar:	1 navigation

"Self-righting" lifeboats with steel hulls and aluminum superstructures. Built in early 1960s.

1 + 105(?) MOTOR LIFEBOATS: 47-FT TYPE

Builders:	Textron Marine Systems, New Orleans, La.
Displacement:	17.9 tons full load
Length:	47 feet (14.33 m) overall
Beam:	14 feet (4.3 m)
Draft:	4 feet (1.2 m)
Propulsion:	2 diesel engines (Detroit Diesel 6V92); 850 bhp; 2 shafts
Speed:	28 knots
Range:	220 n.miles (410 km) at 27 knots
Manning:	4 (enlisted) + 5 survivors
Radars:	1 SPS-69 navigation

Aluminum construction. These are "self-righting" lifeboats, capable of flipping end-over-end or rolling up to 360° and self-righting in 30 seconds or less. They can withstand 20-foot (6.1-m) breaking waves.

The lead boat was delivered in August 1990; five additional prototypes are being built, with production of about 100 more units planned for delivery by the end of 1996. They will replace the surviving 44-foot motor lifeboats.

The prototype 47-foot motor lifeboat. The craft has the hull number 47200—the second zero had fallen off when this photo was taken. On her trials off the coast of Oregon, the craft rescued four fishermen when their ship sank in 20-foot seas. (Textron Marine Systems)

The prototype 47-foot motor lifeboat successfully self-righted in 5.3 seconds during rollover tests. This is the Coast Guard's first all-aluminum rescue craft. (1990, Textron Marine Systems)

SEVERAL BUOY SERVICING BOATS: 46-FT TYPE

Builders:	
Displacement:	27 tons
Length:	46⅓ feet (14.1 m) overall
Beam:	16⅙ feet (4.9 m)
Draft:	5⅔ feet (1.7 m)
Propulsion:	1 diesel engine (General Motors 6-71); 180 bhp; Schottel rudder-propeller unit
Speed:	9 knots
Range:	440 n.miles (815 km) at 9 knots
Manning:	4 (enlisted)

These craft have steel hulls and superstructures. The above data are for later units; the initial 46301–46306 have reduced fuel capacities with a range of only 320 n.miles (590 km).

Cargo capacity is 7¼ tons of buoys and navigation aids; there is a 4,000-pound (1,800-kg) lifting frame aft.

46-foot buoy boat 46314, based in New York. (1990, Giorgio Arra)

45-foot buoy boat 45306. (1988, L. Van Ginderen Collection)

SEVERAL BUOY SERVICING BOATS: 45-FT TYPE

Builders:	
Displacement:	31.27 tons full load
Length:	45¼ feet (13.8 m) overall
Beam:	15 feet (4.6 m)
Draft:	3 feet (0.9 m)
Propulsion:	1 diesel engine (General Motors 6-71); 150 bhp; 1 shaft
Speed:	8.5 knots
Range:	550 n.miles (1,020 km) at 8.5 knots
Manning:	4 (enlisted)

These are steel-hulled craft with steel superstructures. The above characteristics relate to units 45302–45312; the similar 45313–45316 carry less fuel, but their GM 6-71 engine is rated at 180 bhp, with a range reduction to 520 n.miles (960 km).

These boats can carry about 9½ tons of buoys and navigation aids.

100+ MOTOR LIFEBOATS: 44-FT TYPE

Builders:	Coast Guard Yard, Curtis Bay, Md.
Displacement:	14.9 tons light
	17.7 tons full load
Length:	44 feet (13.4 m) overall
Beam:	12⅔ feet (3.9 m)
Draft:	3¹¹⁄₁₂ feet (1.2 m)
Propulsion:	2 diesel engines (General Motors 6-71); 372 bhp; 2 shafts
Speed:	13 knots
Range:	185 n.miles (340 km) at 11.8 knots
Manning:	4 (enlisted) + 21 survivors
Radars:	1 navigation

These are "unsinkable" lifeboats; numbers begin with 44300. Delivered from 1963 to 1972. Sustained speed is 11.8 knots. They have steel hulls.

These craft will be replaced by the 47-foot (14.3-m) design.

Lifesaving in coastal waters as well as on the high seas is one of the Coast Guard's primary missions. This 44-foot motor lifeboat is typical of the large number of small patrol and lifesaving craft operated by the service. (U.S. Coast Guard)

The 44-ft motor lifeboat 44306. These craft are constructed of alloy steel. They can carry 20 survivors. (U.S. Coast Guard)

The 41-foot utility boat 41352 off Fort Lauderdale, Fla. (1990, Giorgio Arra)

200+ UTILITY BOATS: 41-FT TYPE

Builders:	Coast Guard Yard, Curtis Bay, Md.
Displacement:	13–14 tons full load
Length:	40⅔ feet (12.4 m) overall
Beam:	13½ feet (4.1 m)
Draft:	4 feet (1.2 m)
Propulsion:	2 diesel engines (Cummins V903M or VT903M); 560 or 636 bhp; 2 shafts
Speed:	22–26 knots (see notes)
Manning:	3 (enlisted) + 22 survivors
Radars:	1 Raytheon 1900 navigation

These are aluminum utility craft. Completed 1973–1978. Numbers begin with 41300. The 43400 and later units have vanes on the propeller shafts, adding 2.5 knots.

365 PORTS AND WATERWAYS BOATS: 32-FT TYPE

Builders:	
Displacement:	8.6 tons full load
Length:	33⅓ feet (10.2 m) overall
Beam:	11¾ feet (3.6 m)
Draft:	2⅚ feet (0.9 m)
Propulsion:	2 diesel engines (Caterpillar 3208); 406 bhp; 2 shafts
Speed:	20 knots
Manning:	3
Radars:	1 Raytheon 1900 navigation

GRP construction. Built in the late 1970s. Equipped for fire fighting. Numbers began with 32301.

A covey of 41-foot utility boats. These aluminum-hull craft with fiberglass superstructures are employed in the SAR and law-enforcement roles. They can carry up to 22 survivors. (U.S. Coast Guard)

The 32-foot port and waterways boat 32328 based in New York. (1990, Giorgio Arra)

Port and waterways boat 32328. (1990, Giorgio Arra)

20+ PORT SECURITY BOATS: 31-FT TYPES

Builders:	Coast Guard Yard, Curtis Bay, Md.
Displacement:	7.4 tons full load
Length:	30⅚ feet (9.27 m) overall
Beam:	11½ feet (3.5 m)
Draft:	3¹¹⁄₁₂ feet (1.2 m)
Propulsion:	1 diesel engine (General Motors); 197 bhp; 2 shafts
Speed:	14 knots
Range:	165 n.miles (305 km) at 12.5 knots
Manning:	3 (enlisted)
Radars:	1 navigation

Numbered from 31001. GRP construction. Completed in the 1960s, these craft are used primarily for training.

19 SURF RESCUE BOATS: 30-FT TYPE

Builders:	Coast Guard Yard, Curtis Bay, Md.
Displacement:	4.6 tons full load
Length:	30⅓ feet (9.25 m) overall
Beam:	9⅓ feet (2.8 m)
Draft:	3⅔ feet (1.1 m)
Propulsion:	2 diesel engines (General Motors 6VT92T); 375 bhp; 1 shaft
Speed:	28 knots
Range:	150 n.miles (280 km) at 25 knots
Manning:	2 (enlisted) + 6 survivors
Radars:	none

Rescue boats employed in short-distance operations. GRP construction. Hull numbers begin with 30201. Placed in service 1986–1990.

30-foot surf rescue boat. (U.S. Coast Guard)

200+ SURF BOATS / 41 CARGO BOATS } 25-FT TYPE

Builders:	Coast Guard Yard, Curtis Bay, Md.
Displacement:	3.3 tons full load
Length:	25⅔ feet (7.8 m) overall
Beam:	7¹⁄₁₂ feet (2.15 m)
Draft:	2¹⁄₁₂ feet (0.63 m)
Propulsion:	1 diesel engine (General Motors); 80 bhp; 1 shaft
Speed:	11 knots
Range:	60 n.miles (111 km) at 11 knots
Manning:	surf boats: 3 (enlisted) + 13 survivors

More than 200 surf boats of this design plus 41 similar cargo craft entered Coast Guard service from 1969 to 1970. They are of GRP construction. Numbered from 253301.

Several additional small craft are in Coast Guard service, including this new 38-foot utility boat 380502. (1991, Giorgio Arra)

25-foot utility boat 252511. Note the twin outboard engines. (1989, Giorgio Arra)

The one-of-a-kind, search-and-rescue boat 502001 at high speed in Chesapeake Bay, Md. The boat is being evaluated for a new operating procedure at small Coast Guard stations. (U.S. Coast Guard, PA3 Richard Matthews)

1 SEARCH AND RESCUE BOAT: NEW DESIGN

Builders:	
Displacement:	
Length:	50 feet (15.2 m) overall
Beam:	
Draft:	5 feet (1.5 m)
Propulsion:	2 diesel engines
Speed:	26 knots
Range:	300 n.miles (555 km) at 18 knots
	200 n.miles (370 km) at 26 knots
Manning:	4 (enlisted)

The 502001 is a small SAR craft, procured in record time by the Coast Guard to evaluate the potential for a live-aboard boat to replace small shore stations. The craft was placed in service on 1 May 1992 at Station Taylors Island in Chesapeake Bay, Md. With the 502001, the station's personnel was reduced from 19 to eight.

The craft was adopted from a commercial design; its cost was $550,000.

The new 502001 at rest. There is a stern gate to assist in rescue operations; a life raft canister and navigation radar are fitted atop the bridge. (U.S. Coast Guard, PA3 Richard Matthews)

CHAPTER 33

National Oceanic and Atmospheric Administration

The OCEANOGRAPHER, one of the two largest ships in NOAA service. She is now in the yard undergoing a needed upgrade. Many of NOAA's ships are suffering "functional obsolescence" as they reach 25 years of age. Prior to her modernization the OCEANOGRAPHER differed in appearance from the DISCOVERER principally in the radome at the after end of her superstructure. (NOAA)

The National Oceanic and Atmospheric Administration (NOAA), an agency within the Department of Commerce, conducts ocean surveys and other research and surveying activities for the U.S. government. These activities are of a nonmilitary nature, with research operations in U.S. coastal waters as well as overseas. However, NOAA maps and charts are used by the armed forces, and during time of war or national emergency the president may transfer NOAA ships, shore stations, and personnel to the Navy (or to other military services).

NOAA's National Ocean Survey currently has 23 ships, most in an operating status. All but two ships are more than 20 years of age. A new construction program has been proposed to Congress for replacing all existing NOAA ships over the next 10 to 15 years.

Several Navy ocean surveillance ships (T-AGOS) are being transferred to NOAA for use in the research role; see Addenda.

Historical. The Survey of the Coast was established as a U.S. government agency by an act of Congress on 10 February 1807; its name was changed to the Coast Survey in 1834 and Coast and Geodetic Survey in 1878.

The commissioned officer corps was established in 1917. The Coast and Geodetic Survey was made a component of the Environmental Science Services Administration (ESSA) on 13 July 1965, when that agency was established within the Department of Commerce. ESSA subsequently became the National Oceanic and Atmospheric Administration in October 1970, with the Coast and Geodetic Survey being renamed the National Ocean Survey, which is today the ship-operating branch of NOAA.

SHIPS

The status of ships varies slightly from year to year, with research and survey operations dependent upon specific budget allocations. Several NOAA ships, beginning with the OCEANOGRAPHER, will undergo extensive upgrades during the next few years to extend their service life.

These ships are supported by the NOAA Atlantic Marine Center at Norfolk, Va., and the Pacific Marine Center at Puget Sound, Wash.

NOAA ships are unarmed.

Designations. All NOAA ships are designated by a three-digit number preceded by the letter *R* for Research and *S* for Survey, with the first digit indicating the Horsepower Tonnage (HPT) class. The HPT is the numerical sum of the vessel's shaft horsepower plus her gross tonnage.

Class I ships are 5501–9000 HPT; Class II are 3501–5500 HPT; Class III are 2001–3500 HPT; Class IV are 1001–2000 HPT; Class V are 501–1000 HPT; and Class VI are up to 500 HPT.

Table 33-1 lists the NOAA research and survey ships, their HPT class, current hull numbers, and previous designations.

Helicopters. Only the large MALCOLM BALDRIGE and SURVEYOR have helicopter platforms. Helicopters are not normally operated from these ships.

TABLE 33-1. NOAA SHIP DESIGNATIONS

Class	Number	Name	Former Number
I	R101	OCEANOGRAPHER	OSS 01
I	R102	DISCOVERER	OSS 02
I	R103	MALCOLM BALDRIGE	OSS 03
I	R132	SURVEYOR	OSS 32
II	R223	MILLER FREEMAN	
II	S220	FAIRWEATHER	MSS 20
II	S221	RAINIER	MSS 21
II	S222	MT. MITCHELL	MSS 22
III	S328	PEIRCE	CSS 28
III	S329	WHITING	CSS 29
III	S330	MCARTHUR	CSS 30
III	S331	DAVIDSON	CSS 31
III	R332	OREGON II	
III	R342	ALBATROSS IV	
IV	R443	TOWNSEND CROMWELL	
IV	R444	DAVID STARR JORDAN	
IV	R445	DELAWARE II	
IV	R446	CHAPMAN	
IV	S492	FERREL	ASV 92
V	R552	JOHN N. COBB	
V	S590	RUDE	ASV 90
V	S591	HECK	ASV 91

AVIATION

The NOAA operates eight light aircraft and three helicopters plus two Lockheed WP-3D Orion weather reconnaissance aircraft. These aircraft fly from airports throughout the United States, although most are based at the Miami International Airport.

The WP-3D Orions normally fly with a crew of 8: 2 pilots, 1 flight engineer, 1 navigator, 1 chief scientist, 1 camera operator, 1 flight director, and 1 mission scientist.

PERSONNEL

NOAA has 400 commissioned officers, of whom approximately 110 are assigned to ships. The first female officer to captain a NOAA ship took command of the MCARTHUR in February 1989. About 25 commissioned officers are assigned to flying duties.

Sixty licensed civil service personnel and about 400 unlicensed personnel are also assigned to ships. Medical officers from the U.S. Public Health Service are provided to ships when necessary.

NOAA is commanded by a rear admiral of the NOAA Commissioned Corps.

NOAA flies two WP-3D variants of the Orion, aircraft especially configured for weather research. The aircraft are easily identified by their nose probes and instrumented tail cones. Their markings including "United States Dept. of Commerce" on their fuselage and the NOAA insignia on their tail fin. (NOAA)

Rear Adm. Sigmund R. Petersen, Director, Office of NOAA Corps Operations since 1991.

2 RESEARCH SHIPS: "OCEANOGRAPHER" CLASS (S2-MET-MA62a)

Number	Name	Launched	Commissioned	Status
R101	OCEANOGRAPHER	18 Apr 1964	13 July 1966	Yard
R102	DISCOVERER	29 Oct 1984	29 Apr 1967	**PA**

Builders:	Aerojet-General Corp., Jacksonville, Fla.
Displacement:	4,033 tons full load
Length:	303½ feet (92.4 m) overall
Beam:	52 feet (15.8 m)
Draft:	18½ feet (5.6 m)
Propulsion:	diesel-electric (4 diesel engines); 5,000 shp; 2 shafts
Speed:	18 knots
Range:	12,250 n.miles (22,690 km) at 15 knots
Manning:	R101 59 (10 officers + 49 civilians) + 30 scientists
	R102 60 (10 officers + 50 civilians) + 24 scientists

These are NOAA's largest ships. The R-series, Class I ships conduct worldwide oceanographic research, primarily in physical and chemical oceanography, air-sea interactions, and marine geology.

The ships have graceful, yacht-like lines.

Engineering: These ships have a 400-hp through-bow thruster.

Modernization: The OCEANOGRAPHER is undergoing an extensive modernization in 1992–1994. Major systems are being upgraded, including main engines, sonar, scientific-laboratory facilities, and electrical. The work will add some seven to ten years to the ship's useful operating life.

It is anticipated that modernization of the DISCOVERER will follow.

Operational: The OCEANOGRAPHER became the first U.S. government ship to visit China in 30 years when the ship called at the ports of Shanghai and Xiamen in June 1990.

DISCOVERER. (NOAA)

1 RESEARCH SHIP: "MALCOLM BALDRIGE" (S2-MT-MA7a)

Number	Name	Launched	Commissioned	Status
R103	MALCOLM BALDRIGE	5 Oct 1968	8 Oct 1970	**AA**

Builders:	American Shipbuilding, Lorain, Ohio
Displacement:	2,875 tons full load
Length:	278¼ feet (84.8 m) overall
Beam:	51 feet (15.5 m)
Draft:	16¼ feet (5.0 m)
Propulsion:	2 diesel engines; 3,200 bhp; 2 shafts
Speed:	16 knots
Range:	10,800 n.miles (20,000 km) at 12.5 knots
Manning:	59 (10 officers + 49 civilians) + 14 scientists

Fitted with a bow sonar dome. A helicopter platform is fitted, one of only two NOAA ships with this feature.

Engineering: The BALDRIGE is fitted with a 450-hp 360° retractable bow thruster for precise maneuvering and "creeping" speeds up to seven knots.

Names: Originally named RESEARCHER; changed on 5 March 1988.

MALCOLM BALDRIGE, formerly RESEARCHER. (1989, Giorgio Arra)

MALCOLM BALDRIGE. (1990, L. Van Ginderen Collection)

1 SURVEY SHIP: "SURVEYOR" (S2-S-RM28a)

Number	Name	Launched	Commissioned	Status
S132	SURVEYOR	25 Apr 1959	30 Apr 1960	**PA**

Builders:	National Steel, San Diego, Calif.
Displacement:	3,150 tons full load
Length:	292⅓ feet (88.8 m) overall
Beam:	46 feet (14.0 m)
Draft:	18 feet (5.5 m)
Propulsion:	2 steam turbines (De Laval); 3,200 shp; 1 shaft
Boilers:	2 (Combustion Engineering)
Speed:	16 knots
Range:	13,680 n.miles (25,335 km) at 15 knots
Manning:	61 (10 officers + 51 civilians) + 16 scientists

A helicopter platform has been fitted aft.

Engineering: The SURVEYOR is the only steam-powered ship remaining in NOAA service. There is a 200-hp electric auxiliary propulsion motor installed aft.

SURVEYOR. (NOAA)

3 SURVEY SHIPS: "FAIRWEATHER" CLASS (S1-MT-MA72a)

Number	Name	Launched	Commissioned	Status
S220	FAIRWEATHER	15 Mar 1967	2 Oct 1968	PR
S221	RAINIER	15 Mar 1967	2 Oct 1968	**PA**
S222	MT. MITCHELL	29 Nov 1966	23 Mar 1968	**AA**

Builders:	Aerojet-General Corp., Jacksonville, Fla.
Displacement:	1,798 tons full load
Length:	231 feet (70.4 m) overall
Beam:	42 feet (12.8 m)
Draft:	13⅝ feet (4.2 m)
Propulsion:	2 diesel engines; 2,400 bhp; 2 shafts
Speed:	14.5 knots
Range	7,000 n.miles (12,965 km) at 13 knots
Manning:	S220, S221 63 (10 officers + 53 civilians) + 4 scientists
	S222 54 (10 officers + 44 civilians)

The Class II ships are outfitted primarily for hydrographic surveys involving charting operations.

Engineering: These ships have a 200-shp through-bow thruster.

FAIRWEATHER. (NOAA)

1 RESEARCH SHIP: "MILLER FREEMAN"

Number	Name	Launched	Completed	Status
R223	MILLER FREEMAN	1967	1974	**PA**

Builders:	American Shipbuilding, Lorain, Ohio
Displacement:	1,920 tons full load
Length:	216½ feet (66.0 m) overall
Beam:	41 feet (12.5 m)
Draft:	20 feet (6.1 m)
Propulsion:	1 diesel engine (General Motors); 3,200 bhp; 1 shaft
Speed:	14 knots
Range:	13,800 n.miles (25,560 km) at 14 knots
Manning:	39 (7 officers + 32 enlisted) + 11 scientists

Fisheries research ship.

MILLER FREEMAN. (1985, NOAA)

2 SURVEY SHIPS: "PEIRCE" CLASS (S1-MT-59a)

Number	Name	Launched	Commissioned	Status
S328	PEIRCE	15 Oct 1962	6 May 1963	AR
S329	WHITING	20 Nov 1962	8 July 1963	**AA**

Builders:	Marietta Manufacturing, Point Pleasant, W.Va.
Displacement:	760 tons full load
Length:	164 feet (50.0 m) overall
Beam:	33 feet (10.1 m)
Draft:	10 feet (3.0 m)
Propulsion:	2 diesel engines; 1,600 bhp; 2 shafts
Speed:	12.5 knots
Range:	5,700 n.miles (10,555 km) at 12 knots
Manning:	34 (7 officers + 27 civilians) + 2 scientists

These ships primarily conduct hydrographic surveys of the 200-mile exclusive economic zone for bathymetric maps and nautical charts. The PEIRCE was inactive at Norfolk, Va., when this edition went to press. The ship will be scrapped in the near future.

PEIRCE; to be scrapped in near future. (NOAA)

WHITING; note satellite antenna dome on superstructure. (1990, L. Van Ginderen Collection)

2 SURVEY SHIPS: "McARTHUR" CLASS (S1-MT-MA70a)

Number	Name	Launched	Commissioned	Status
S330	MCARTHUR	15 Nov 1965	15 Dec 1956	**PA**
S331	DAVIDSON	7 May 1966	10 Mar 1967	PR

Builders:	Norfolk Shipbuilding and Dry Dock, Va.
Displacement:	995 tons full load
Length:	175 feet (53.3 m) overall
Beam:	38 feet (11.5 m)
Draft:	11½ feet (3.5 m)
Propulsion:	2 diesel engines; 1,600 bhp; 2 shafts
Speed:	13 knots
Range:	6,000 n.miles (11,111 km) at 12 knots
Manning:	S330 30 (6 officers + 24 civilians) + 2 scientists
	S331 34 (7 officers + 27 civilians)

McARTHUR. (NOAA)

1 RESEARCH SHIP: "OREGON II"

Number	Name	Launched	Completed	Status
R332	OREGON II	1967	1967	**AA**

Builders:	Ingalls Shipbuilding, Pascagoula, Miss.
Displacement:	952 tons full load
Length:	169¹¹⁄₁₂ feet (51.8 m) overall
Beam:	34¹⁄₁₂ feet (10.4 m)
Draft:	14¹⁄₁₂ feet (4.3 m)
Propulsion:	2 diesel engines (Fairbanks-Morse); 1,600 bhp; 1 shaft
Speed:	12 knots
Range:	9,500 n.miles (17,600 km) at 12 knots
Manning:	18 (3 officers + 15 civilians) + 6 scientists

OREGON II. (NOAA)

1 RESEARCH SHIP: "ALBATROSS IV"

Number	Name	Launched	Completed	Status
R342	ALBATROSS IV	1962	1963	**AA**

Builders:	Southern Shipbuilding, Slidell, La.
Displacement:	1,089 tons full load
Length:	187 feet (57.0 m) overall
Beam:	32⅝ feet (10.0 m)
Draft:	16 feet (4.9 m)
Propulsion:	2 diesel engines (Caterpillar); 1,130 bhp; 1 Kort-nozzle
Speed:	12 knots
Range:	4,300 n.miles (7,965 km) at 12 knots
Manning:	20 (4 officers + 16 civilians) + 15 scientists

Fisheries research ship.

ALBATROSS IV. (NOAA)

1 RESEARCH SHIP: "TOWNSEND CROMWELL"

Number	Name	Launched	Completed	Status
R443	TOWNSEND CROMWELL	1963	1963	**PA**

Builders:	J. Ray McDermott, Morgan City, La.
Displacement:	652 tons full load
Length:	163 feet (49.7 m) overall
Beam:	32⅝ feet (10.0 m)
Draft:	12⅝ feet (3.9 m)
Propulsion:	2 diesel engines (White Superior); 800 bhp; 2 shafts
Speed:	11.5 knots
Range:	8,300 n.miles (15,370 km) at 11.5 knots
Manning:	18 (4 officers + 14 civilians) + 9 scientists

Fisheries research ship.

TOWNSEND CROMWELL. (NOAA)

1 RESEARCH SHIP: "DAVID STARR JORDAN"

Number	Name	Launched	Completed	Status
R444	DAVID STARR JORDAN	1964	1966	**PA**

Builders:	Christy Corp., Sturgeon Bay, Wisc.
Displacement:	993 tons full load
Length:	170¹¹⁄₁₂ feet (52.1 m) overall
Beam:	36¾ feet (11.2 m)
Draft:	15¾ feet (4.8 m)
Propulsion:	2 diesel engines (White Superior); 1,086 bhp; 2 shafts
Speed:	11.5 knots
Range:	8,560 n.miles (15,850 km) at 11.5 knots
Manning:	18 (3 officers + 15 civilians) + 13 scientists

Fisheries research ship.

DAVID STARR JORDAN. (NOAA)

1 RESEARCH SHIP: "DELAWARE II"

Number	Name	Launched	Completed	Status
R445	DELAWARE II	1967	1968	AR

Builders:	South Portland Engineering, Maine
Displacement:	758 tons full load
Length:	154⅝ feet (47.2 m) overall
Beam:	30⅙ feet (9.2 m)
Draft:	14¾ feet (4.5 m)
Propulsion:	1 diesel engine (General Motors); 1,230 bhp; 1 shaft
Speed:	11.5 knots
Range:	6,600 n.miles (12,200 km) at 11.5 knots
Manning:	17 civilian + 9 scientists

Fisheries research ship. Currently laid up.

DELAWARE II. (NOAA)

1 RESEARCH SHIP: "CHAPMAN"

Number	Name	Launched	Completed	Status
R446	CHAPMAN	1979	1980	**AA**

Builders:	Bender Shipbuilding, Wash.
Displacement:	520 tons full load
Length:	126¹¹⁄₁₂ feet (38.7 m) overall
Beam:	29⅝ feet (9.1 m)
Draft:	14¹⁄₁₂ feet (4.3 m)
Propulsion:	1 diesel engine (Caterpillar); 1,250 bhp; 1 shaft
Speed:	11 knots
Range:	6,000 n.miles (11,111 km) at 11 knots
Manning:	13 (3 officers + 10 civilians) + 6 scientists

Fisheries research ship.

CHAPMAN. (NOAA)

1 RESEARCH SHIP: "JOHN N. COBB"

Number	Name	Launched	Completed	Status
R552	JOHN N. COBB	1950	1950	**PA**

Builders:	Western Boatbuilding, Tacoma, Wash.
Displacement:	250 tons full load
Length:	92⅝ feet (28.3 m) overall
Beam:	25¹¹⁄₁₂ feet (7.9 m)
Draft:	10⅝ (3.3 m)
Propulsion:	1 diesel engine (Fairbanks-Morse); 325 bhp; 1 shaft
Speed:	9.3 knots
Range:	2,900 n.miles (5,370 km) at 9.3 knots
Manning:	7 (2 officers + 5 civilians) + 4 scientists

Fisheries research ship.

JOHN N. COBB (NOAA)

1 SURVEY SHIP: "FERREL" (S1-MT-MA83a)

Number	Name	Launched	Commissioned	Status
S492	FERREL	4 Apr 1968	4 June 1968	**AA**

Builders:	Zigler Shipyard, Jennings, La.
Displacement:	363 tons full load
Length:	133¼ feet (40.5 m) overall
Beam:	32 feet (9.7 m)
Draft:	7 feet (2.1 m)
Propulsion:	2 diesel engines (Caterpillar); 750 bhp; 2 shafts
Speed:	10.6 knots
Range:	2,200 n.miles (4,075 km) at 10 knots
Manning:	16 (4 officers + 12 civilians)

The FERREL conducts near-shore and estuarine-current surveys. She employs data-collection buoys in her work; there is a large, open buoy-stowage area aft as well as a comprehensive workshop.

Engineering: Fitted with a 100-hp through-bow thruster.

FERREL. (NOAA)

2 SURVEY SHIPS: "RUDE" CLASS (S1-MT-MA71a)

Number	Name	Launched	Commissioned	Status
S590	RUDE	17 Aug 1966	29 Mar 1967	**AA**
S591	HECK	1 Nov 1966	29 Mar 1967	**AA**

Builders:	Jakobson Shipyard, Oyster Bay, N.Y.
Displacement:	214 tons full load
Length:	90 feet (27.4 m) overall
Beam:	22 feet (6.7 m)
Draft:	7 feet (2.1 m)
Propulsion:	2 diesel engines (Cummins); 800 bhp; 2 Kort-nozzles
Speed:	11.5 knots
Range:	800 n.miles (1,480 km) at 10 knots
Manning:	11 (4 officers + 7 civilians)

Surveying ships. These ships formerly worked as a pair, using wire drags to locate underwater navigational hazards. In that role one commanding officer was assigned to the two vessels; he normally rode one ship and the executive officer the other. They now operate separately, each with a commanding officer.

Side-scanning sonar is installed.

Engineering: The propellers on these ships are protected by shrouds, similar to Kort-nozzles. Auxiliary propulsion provides 70 hp to each propeller for slow-speed dragging operations.

RUDE. (NOAA)

HECK. (1988, L. Van Ginderen Collection)

RESEARCH SHIP: "MURRE II"

The fishery research and logistic support ship MURRE II (R663), a former Army craft, was sold in 1991 for private use. She operated in Alaskan waters.

See 14th Edition/page 565 for characteristics.

RESEARCH CRAFT

NOAA laboratories operate some 20 small research craft that are 65 feet (19.8 m) or less in length.

CHAPTER 34

Miscellaneous U.S. Ships

The vehicle landing ship GEN FRANK S. BESSON, JR, is typical of the new landing ships and craft being constructed by the Army to support coastal operations as well as the unloading of maritime prepositioning and merchant ships in forward areas. (1988, Georgio Arra)

Several U.S. agencies in addition to the Navy, Coast Guard, and NOAA operate a variety of ships and craft. The more significant ships as well as landing craft and vehicles are listed in this chapter. In addition, under Navy sponsorship, several universities operate research ships in addition to those specifically built by the Navy and described in chapter 23 (with the status of **Academic**).

ENVIRONMENTAL PROTECTION AGENCY

The Environmental Protection Agency (EPA) operates two major research ships.

1 RESEARCH SHIP: EX-NAVY GUNBOAT

Number	Name	FY	Launched	Commissioned
ex-PG 86	PETER W. ANDERSON	63	18 June 1966	4 Nov 1967

Builders:	Tacoma Boatbuilding, Wash.
Displacement:	approx. 250 tons full load
Length:	164½ feet (50.2 m) overall
Beam:	23¾ feet (7.28 m)
Draft:	9½ feet (2.9 m)
Propulsion:	2 diesel engines (Cummins VT12-875M); 1,400 bhp; 2 shafts
Speed:	16 knots
Range:	2,400 n.miles (4,445 km) at 14 knots on diesel engines
	325 n.miles (602 km) at 37 knots on gas turbines
Manning:	30 (civilian contractor)

The ANDERSON is a former ASHEVILLE-class patrol combatant/gunboat now employed in the pollution-research role. Three sister ships serve as Navy research ships with the David Taylor Research Center (see chapter 25).

The ship was decommissioned as a Navy gunboat on 1 October 1977; transferred to EPA on 17 January 1978.

All weapons have been removed.

Class: Originally a class of 17 units; see page 199. The Crockett (PG 88), also operated by the EPA, is now a museum at Muskegon, Mich.

Design: Aluminum hull with fiberglass superstructure. For the research role the ship has been fitted with three laboratories and a computer center.

Names: The ANDERSON was the ANTELOPE (PG 86) in naval service.

Operational: Under EPA the ship originally operated on the Great Lakes; now based at Annapolis, Md.

Propulsion: Originally a CODOG-propelled ship; the gas turbine has been removed.

PETER W. ANDERSON. (1990, Giorgio Arra)

1 RESEARCH SHIP: EX-COAST GUARD BUOY TENDER

Number	Name	Launched	Commissioned
ex-WAGL 234	ROGER R. SIMONS	29 Apr 1939	June 1939

Builders:	Marine Iron and Shipbuilding, Duluth, Minn.
Displacement:	342 tons full load
Length:	122¼ feet (37.26 m) overall
Beam:	27 feet (8.23 m)
Draft:	7½ feet (2.29 m)
Propulsion:	2 diesel engines (Superior); 430 bhp; 2 shafts
Speed:	10 knots
Range:	3,500 n.miles (6,480 km) at 6 knots
Manning:	

Former Coast Guard buoy tender employed by EPA in pollution survey and water studies. She was decommissioned and stricken by the Coast Guard on 1 June 1973 and transferred to the U.S. Navy on 8 August 1973; transferred to EPA in 1974.

Names: Coast Guard name was MAPLE (WAGL 234).

Operational: Based at Cleveland, Ohio, on Lake Erie.

PETER W. ANDERSON. (1989, Giorgio Arra)

GEOLOGICAL SURVEY

The Geological Survey of the Department of Interior operates one major research ship, the former Navy survey ship S.P. LEE.

1 SURVEY SHIP: "KELLER" CLASS

Number	Name	FY	Launched	In service
ex-AG 192	SAMUEL P. LEE	65	19 Oct 1967	2 Dec 1968

Builders:	Defoe Shipbuilding, Bay City, Mich.
Displacement:	1,297 tons full load
Length:	208⅓ feet (63.5 m) overall
Beam:	39 feet (11.9 m)
Draft:	14⅙ feet (4.3 m)
Propulsion:	diesel-electric; 1,000 bhp; 1 shaft
Speed:	12 knots
Range:	12,000 n.miles at 12 knots
Manning:	approx. 55 civilian

The ship was built as a naval surveying ship, placed in service with the Military Sealift Command (USNS) upon completion in 1968 and designated T-AGS 31. Although intended to operate under the Oceanographer of the Navy, the ship was assigned to support the Naval Underwater Research and Development Center in San Diego. (In that role the ship conducted acoustic tests in the Atlantic, Mediterranean, and Pacific areas.)

The LEE was reclassified as a miscellaneous research ship (AG 192) on 25 September 1970. She was taken out of naval service on 29 January 1973 and was transferred on indefinite loan to the National Geological Survey on 27 February 1974.

Under the Geological Survey the LEE conducts deep-sea seismic surveys, seafloor coring, and seafloor bottom sampling.

Class: The LEE and a sister ship, the KELLER (T-AGS 25), were built to a modified CONRAD (AGOR 3) design. The KELLER was transferred to Portugal on 21 January 1972.

Names: In naval service the ship's name was S.P. LEE.

SAMUEL P. LEE. (1983, L. Van Ginderen Collection)

NATIONAL SCIENCE FOUNDATION

The National Science Foundation (NSF) operates two large research ships. Both ships have extensive laboratory complexes.

1 ARCTIC RESEARCH SHIP: "NATHANIEL B. PALMER"

Number	Name	Launched	Completed
(none)	NATHANIEL B. PALMER	1991	May 1992

Builders:	North American Shipbuilding, Larose, La.
Displacement:	6,800 tons full load
Length:	308 feet (93.9 m) overall
Beam:	60 feet (18.29 m)
Draft:	22½ feet (6.86 m)
Propulsion:	4 diesel engines (Caterpillar); 13,200 bhp; 2 shafts
Speed:	15 knots
Range:	
Manning:	approx. 25 + 37 scientists

This ship was built specifically for NSF operation.

Design: Icebreaking hull. A helicopter deck and hangar are provided.

NATHANIEL B. PALMER.

1 ARCTIC RESEARCH SHIP: "POLAR DUKE"

Number	Name	Launched	Completed
(none)	POLAR DUKE	1983	1983

Builders:	Vaagen Verft (Norway)
Displacement:	1,645 tons full load
Length:	219 feet (66.77 m) overall
Beam:	43 feet (13.1 m)
Draft:	19 feet (5.79 m)
Propulsion:	2 diesel engines; 4,500 bhp; 2 shafts (Kort-nozzle propellers)
Speed:	12 knots
Range:	29,950 n.miles (55,470 km) at 12 knots
Manning:	14 civilian + 23 scientists

The POLAR DUKE was constructed specifically for the NSF; she is a Norwegian-flag vessel under charter. The ship supports multi-discipline research in the Antarctic area.

Design: Icebreaking hull. Fitted with a helicopter deck but no hangar. Endurance is 90 days.

POLAR DUKE. (National Science Foundation)

ARMY

The Army operates logistic support ships, landing craft, and small tugs under the Transportation Corps, and a number of dredges under the Corps of Engineers; there are also numerous motor boats used by engineer units to assist in the assembly of pontoon bridges. Only self-propelled ships and craft of the Transportation Corps are listed in this chapter. Also listed are the former Coast Guard–operated Mobile Aerostat Program (MAP) vessels.

The Army Transportation Corps operated a large number of oceangoing troop transports, cargo and supply ships, minelayers, and large tugs until 1950. The troop transports and some cargo ships and tugs were transferred to the newly established Military Sea Transportation Service (now Military Sealift Command). Other ships were transferred to the Navy. A few ex-Army transports, barges, and one tug remain on the Naval Vessel Register as service craft (see chapter 25). No Army ships are armed.

Designations. The Army uses a ship and craft designation series derived in part from the Navy's designation scheme. They are:

BC	barge, dry cargo (non-self-propelled)
BCDX	barge, deck enclosure
BD	floating crane
BDL	beach discharge lighter
BG	barge, liquid cargo (non-self-propelled)
BK	barge, dry cargo (non-self-propelled)
BPL	barge, pier, self-elevating
BR	barge, refrigerated (non-self-propelled)
FMS	floating marine repair shop (non-self-propelled)
FS	freight and supply vessel (over 100 ft/30.48 m)
FSR	freight and supply vessel, refrigerated
HLS	heavy lift ship
J	work boat (under 50 ft/15.24 m)
LARC	lighter, amphibious, resupply, cargo (amphibious)
LCM	landing craft, mechanized
LCU	landing craft, utility
LCV	landing craft, vehicle
LSV	landing ship, vehicle
LT	large tug (over 100 ft/30.48 m)
Q	work boat (over 50 ft/15.24 m)
ST	small tug (under 100 ft/30.48 m)
T	small freight and supply vessel (under 100 ft/30.48 m)
Y	liquid cargo vessel

Names. Army ships and craft are generally named for campaigns and battles in which the Army participated, except that the LT 130-series large tugs are named for signers of the United States Constitution who had a military affiliation. Several battle names are carried by both Navy ships and Army craft.

Operational. Four LCUs, three LT-series tugs, and ten LCMs plus floating cranes are on board the Military Sealift Command–operated prepositioning ship AMERICAN CORMORANT (T-AK 2062) at Diego Garcia in the Indian Ocean (see page 303).

A large number of Army ships and craft are based at the Army Transportation Center at Ft. Eustis, Va.

HEAVY LIFT SHIPS

1 HEAVY LIFT SHIP: C1-MT-123a TYPE

Number	Name	Launched	In service
HLS 01	JAMES McHENRY		1978

Builders:	Peterson Builders, Sturgeon Bay, Wisc.
Displacement:	5,453 tons full load
Tonnage:	2,640 DWT
Length:	278¹¹⁄₁₂ feet (85.01 m) waterline
	300⅙ feet (91.49 m) overall
Beam:	55⅙ feet (16.82 m)
Draft:	16¹¹⁄₁₂ feet (5.16 m)
Propulsion:	2 diesel engines (General Motors 16-645-E2); 5,750 bhp; 2 shafts
Speed:	14 knots
Range:	10,100 n.miles (18,700 km) at 11 knots
Manning:	approx. 30

The JAMES McHENRY is a unique heavy lift ship, employed by the Army primarily as a training ship for cargo handlers at Fort Story, Va. The ship has a vehicle ramp aft, with a drive-through tunnel in the superstructure to provide access to the cargo deck forward. (1990, Giorgio Arra)

JAMES McHENRY. (1990, Giorgio Arra)

VEHICLE LANDING SHIPS

5 VEHICLE LANDING SHIPS: "BESSON" CLASS

Number	Name	Launched	In service
LSV 01	GEN. FRANK S. BESSON, JR.	30 June 1987	20 Jan 1988
LSV 02	CW3 HAROLD C. CLINGER	16 Sep 1987	20 Apr 1988
LSV 03	GEN. BEHON B. SOMERVELL	18 Nov 1987	26 July 1988
LSV 04	LT. GEN. WILLIAM B. BUNKER	11 Jan 1988	1 Sep 1988
LSV 05	MAJ. GEN. CHARLES P. GROSS	11 Jul 1990	12 Dec 1990

Builders:	Halter-Moss Point Marine, Escatawpa, Miss.
Displacement:	1,612 tons light
	4,199 tons full load
Tonnage:	1,800 DWT
Length:	256 feet (78.03 m) waterline
	272⅔ feet (83.14 m) overall
Beam:	60 feet (18.28 m)
Draft:	12 feet (3.66 m)
Propulsion:	2 diesel engines (General Motors EMD 16-645-E2); 3,900 bhp; 2 shafts
Speed:	12 knots
Range:	5,500 n.miles (10,185 km) at 11 knots
Manning:	29 (6 officers + 23 crew)
Radars:	2 SPS-64(V) navigation

These ships are based on the Australian roll-on/roll-off ship FRANCES BAY. Four units were ordered in 1986 and one in 1990 to transport vehicles and containers (48 TEU) or 1,815 tons of vehicles or other cargo.

Design: These ships have an LST-like design with a superstructure aft; there is a tunnel under the superstructure to permit vehicles to drive through from the stern ramp into the open cargo well. A bow ramp is fitted. Built to commercial shipbuilding standards.

GEN FRANK S. BESSON, JR. (1988, Giorgio Arra)

GEN FRANK S. BESSON, JR. (1988, Giorgio Arra)

BEACH DISCHARGE LIGHTERS

This classification was for ships intended to unload large naval vehicle cargo ships (T-AKR) that could not unload their cargo directly onto piers. Only one ship was built to test the concept; proposed follow-on production did not occur.

1 BEACH DISCHARGE LIGHTER

Number	Name	Launched	In service
BDL 1	LT. COL. JOHN D. PAGE	1958	1958

Builders:	National Steel and Shipbuilding, San Diego, Calif.
Displacement:	1,548 tons light
	4,126 tons full load
Length:	338⅛ feet (103.09 m) overall
Beam:	65 feet (19.83 m)
Draft:	13⅔ feet (4.17 m)
Propulsion:	2 diesel engines (Fairbanks Morse); 2,400 bhp; 2 vertical cycloidal propellers
Speed:	10 knots
Range:	7,780 n.miles (14,410 km) at 9 knots
Manning:	49
Troops:	200

Large open-deck ferry designed specifically to mate with the USNS COMET (T-AKR 7/now T-AKR 0007). The Army ship has bow and stern ramps. The PAGE was laid up in 1989 and is unlikely to be returned to service.

Cargo capacity is 2,200 tons. For over-the-beach operations the maximum load is about 600 tons.

UTILITY LANDING CRAFT

The earlier classes are almost identical to their Navy counterparts; the LCU 200-series was built to an Army design.

35 LCU 2000 TYPE

Number	Name	Number	Name
LCU 2001	RUNNYMEDE	LCU 2019	FORT DENELSON
LCU 2002	KENESAW MOUNTAIN	LCU 2020	FORT MCHENRY
LCU 2003	MACON	LCU 2021	GREAT BRIDGE
LCU 2004	ALDIE	LCU 2022	HARPERS FERRY
LCU 2005	BRANDY STATION	LCU 2023	HOBKIRK
LCU 2006	BRISTOE STATION	LCU 2024	HORMIGUEROS
LCU 2007	BROAD RUN	LCU 2025	MALVERN HILL
LCU 2008	BUENA VISTA	LCU 2026	MATAMOROS
LCU 2009	SPRINGFIELD	LCU 2027	MECHANICSVILLE
LCU 2010	CEDAR RUN	LCU 2028	MISSIONARY RIDGE
LCU 2011	CHICKAHOMINY	LCU 2029	MOLINO DEL REY
LCU 2012	CHICKASAW BAYOU	LCU 2030	MONTEREY
LCU 2013	CHURUBUSCO	LCU 2031	NEW ORLEANS
LCU 2014	COAMO	LCU 2032	PALO ALTO
LCU 2015	CONTRERES	LCU 2033	PAULUS HOOK
LCU 2016	CORINTH	LCU 2034	PERRYVILLE
LCU 2017	EL CANEY	LCU 2035	PORT HUDSON
LCU 2018	FIVE FORKS		

Builders:	LCU 2001–2003 Lockheed Shipbuilding, Savannah, Ga.
	LCU 2004–2035 Trinity-Moss Point Marine, Escatawpa, Miss.
Displacement:	672 tons light
	1,102 tons full load
Length:	156 feet (47.55 m) waterline
	174 feet (53.03 m) overall
Beam:	42 feet (12.8 m)
Draft:	8½ feet (2.6 m)
Propulsion:	2 diesel engines (Cummins KTA-50M); 2,500 bhp; 2 Kort-nozzles
Speed:	11.5 knots
Range:	4,500 n.miles (8,333 km) at 11.5 knots empty
Manning:	12 (2 officers + 10 enlisted)

Lᴛ Cᴏʟ Jᴏʜɴ D. Pᴀɢᴇ. (1986, W. Donko)

These are large landing craft with a deckhouse aft; they are too large to be carried by Navy amphibious ships with docking wells (as can the smaller LCU designs). Completed in 1990–1992, these ships are intended to replace the LCU 1466-class landing craft.

These ships have a bow ramp for unloading onto the beach (beaching draft forward is 4 feet/1.2 m).

The first three units were completed at Trinity Marine after the demise of the Lockheed shipbuilding yard.

Class: LCU 2001–2007 ordered in 1986; LCU 2008–2017 in 1987; LCU 2018–2023 in 1988; and LCU 2024–2035 in 1989. Two additional craft were authorized but not ordered; to have been named Sᴀᴄᴋᴇᴛᴛ's Hᴀʀʙᴏʀ and Sᴀʏʟᴇʀ's Cʀᴇᴇᴋ.

Design: Built to commercial shipbuilding standards.

Engineering: These craft have a 300-shp bow thruster.

Names: The LCU 2009 was originally named Cᴀʟᴀʙᴏᴢᴀ.

Bʀɪsᴛᴏᴇ Sᴛᴀᴛɪᴏɴ. (1990, Giorgio Arra)

13 UTILITY LANDING CRAFT: "LCU 1610" CLASS

Number	Name	Number	Name
LCU 1667	Mᴀɴᴀssᴀs	LCU 1674	Sᴛ. Mɪᴄʜɪᴇʟ
LCU 1668	Bᴇʟʟᴇᴀᴜ-Wᴏᴏᴅ	LCU 1675	Cᴏᴍᴍᴀɴᴅᴏ
LCU 1669	Mᴀʀsᴇɪʟʟᴇs	LCU 1676	Bɪʀᴍɪɴɢʜᴀᴍ
LCU 1670	Sᴀɴ Isɪᴅʀᴏ	LCU 1677	Bʀᴀɴᴅʏᴡɪɴᴇ
LCU 1671	Cᴀᴛᴀᴡʙᴀ Fᴏʀᴅ	LCU 1678	Nᴀʜᴀ
LCU 1672	Bᴜsʜ Mᴀsᴛᴇʀ	LCU 1679	Cʜᴀᴛᴇᴀᴜ-Tʜɪᴇʀʀʏ
LCU 1673	Dᴏᴜʙʟᴇ Eᴀɢʟᴇ		

Builders:	General Ship & Engine Works, East Boston, Mass.
Displacement:	190 tons light
	390 tons full load
Length:	134¾ feet (41.1 m) overall
Beam:	29¾ feet (9.1 m)
Draft:	6¹¹⁄₁₂ feet (2.1 m)
Propulsion:	4 diesel engines (General Motors Detroit 6-71); 1,200 bhp; 2 Kort-nozzle propellers
Speed:	11 knots
Range:	1,200 n.miles (2,222 km) at 11 knots empty
	1,200 n.miles (2,222 km) at 8 knots loaded
Manning:	6 (enlisted)
Troops:	8
Radars:	LN-66 or SPS-53 navigation

These are Navy-designed LCUs completed in 1976–1978.

Class: This class originally consisted of hull numbers LCU 1610–1624 and 1627–1681; many serve in the Navy (see chapter 20).

Design: These craft have unloading ramps forward and aft.

Sᴀɴ Isɪᴅʀᴏ. (1989, L. Van Ginderen Collection)

The Naha carrying Army cranes and trucks; note the stern ramp and starboard island structure. (1983, Giorgio Arra)

42 UTILITY LANDING CRAFT: "LCU 1466" CLASS

Number	Name	Number	Name
LCU 1466	Casablanca	LCU 1542	Malolos
LCU 1469	Fort Apache	LCU 1543	Carolina
LCU 1504	Hampton Roads	LCU 1545	Meuse-Argonne
LCU 1507	Chippewa	LCU 1547	Solomon Islands
LCU 1508	Attu	LCU 1549	Guam
LCU 1509	Antietam	LCU 1550	White Wing
LCU 1510	Atlanta	LCU 1557	Zapopte River
LCU 1511	Cumberland	LCU 1560	Rhineland
LCU 1512	Cerro Gordo	LCU 1561	Manila
LCU 1514	Delaware	LCU 1562	Inchon
LCU 1516	Shenandoah	LCU 1566	Cadgel
LCU 1519	El Paso	LCU 1574	Cold Harbor
LCU 1521	Eniwetok	LCU 1575	Junction City
LCU 1522	Lorraine	LCU 1579	Bull Run
LCU 1524	Chapultepec	LCU 1580	Vera Cruz
LCU 1525	Hollandia	LCU 1583	Chattanooga
LCU 1526	Leyte	LCU 1586	Tunisia
LCU 1527	Guadalcanal	LCU 1587	Chickamauga
LCU 1528	Lingayen Gulf	LCU 1590	Spotsylvania
LCU 1534	Saipan	LCU 1591	Viper
LCU 1540	Pusan	LCU 1592	Fort Reno

Builders:
Displacement:	180 tons light
	360 tons full load
Length:	119 feet (39.0 m) overall
Beam:	34 feet (10.4 m)
Draft:	6 feet (1.8 m)
Propulsion:	3 geared diesel engines (Gray Marine 64 YTL); 675 bhp; 3 shafts
Speed:	8 knots
Range:	700 n.miles (1,300 km) at 7 knots with payload
	1,200 n.miles (2,222 km) at 6 knots empty
Manning:	11 (enlisted)
Troops:	8
Radars:	1 navigation

These are the survivors of a large series of Navy-designed LCUs. Two still serve in the Navy. They can carry 300 tons of cargo or, for short distances, 300 troops.

Completed in 1954.

Class: This class covered hull numbers LCU 1466–1609, with 14 units constructed in Japan. Numerous units were transferred to other nations; others became Navy service craft (YFU).

Classification: The LCU 1466–1503 were ordered as utility landing ships (LSU) on 31 October 1951; they were reclassified as LCUs on 15 April 1952.

Design: Navy SCB-25. These craft are smaller than the later LCU 1610 and have a deckhouse-aft configuration with a bow ramp.

Operational: Four units are in storage at Charleston, S.C.: LCU 1519, 1579, 1583, and 1586.

Cold Harbor. (1986, Giorgio Arra)

The Solomon Islands carrying an Army crane. These LCUs have a superstructure-aft configuration; a stern anchor is fitted for retracting off the beach. (1983, L. Van Ginderen Collection)

126 MECHANIZED LANDING CRAFT: LCM(8) TYPE

Weight:	varies 34–36.5 tons light
	111–121 tons full load
Length:	$73^{7}/_{12}$ feet (22.4 m) overall
Beam:	21 feet (6.4 m)
Draft:	$4^{7}/_{12}$ feet (1.4 m) aft
Propulsion:	2 diesel engines (General Motors Detroit 6-71); 600 bhp; 2 shafts
Speed:	12 knots empty
	9.2 knots loaded
Range:	150 n.miles (278 km) at 12 knots empty
	150 n.miles (278 km) at 9.2 knots loaded
Manning:	2–4 (enlisted)

These are standard landing craft intended to carry vehicles and cargo. Capacity is one M60-series Abrams tank or about 60 tons of cargo. No accommodations are provided in these craft.

Completed 1954–1972. Eighteen of these craft are in reserve.

LCM (8). (1986, L. Van Ginderen Collection)

AIR-CUSHION LANDING CRAFT

These craft, based at Ft. Story, Va., are intended for the ship-to-shore movement of troops and equipment; the Army uses the term Logistics-Over-The-Shore (LOTS) for this evolution.

(1+) AIR-CUSHION LANDING CRAFT: LAMP-H TYPE

Builders:	
Weight:	86.9 tons light
	177.6 tons loaded
Length:	70 feet (21.34 m) hull
	79⅝ feet (24.33 m) over cushion
Beam:	49½ feet (15.09 m) hull
	59 feet (17.97 m) over cushion
Propulsion:	2 gas turbines (Pratt & Whitney AVCD TF40B); 7,840 shp; 2 airscrews + 2 centrifugal lift fans
Speed:	45 knots empty
	14 knots loaded
Range:	
Manning:	4 (enlisted)

An enlarged, advanced LOTS prototype vehicle capable of carrying 89 tons of cargo; to be fitted with stern ramp.
Ordered in 1990.

26 AIR-CUSHION LANDING CRAFT: LACV 30 TYPE

Builders:	Textron Marine, New Orleans, La.
Weight:	52 tons loaded
Length:	76⁵⁄₁₂ feet (23.29 m) over cushion
Beam:	36¾ feet (11.2 m) over cushion
Propulsion:	4 gas turbines (Pratt & Whitney ST6T); 7,200 shp; 2 airscrews + 2 centrifugal lift fans
Speed:	40 knots empty
Range:	
Manning:	4 (enlisted)

Air-cushion LOTS vehicles that can accommodate 2 TEU containers or 35 tons of vehicles and cargo. The vehicles can be broken down for transport by truck, train, or helicopter.
Completed 1976–1987.
Designation: The vehicles are designated LACV 01–26.

Bow view of LACV 30. (U.S. Army)

LACV 30 carrying two containers, a 30-ton payload. (Textron Marine Systems)

AMPHIBIOUS VEHICLES

These wheel propeller-driven vehicles are the successors to the DUKW "duck" amphibious trucks of World War II fame. They were introduced into amphibious landings by the U.S. Army in Operation Huskey, the 1943 Allied landings on Sicily.

38 LARC XV TYPE

Builders:	
Weight:	20.8 tons empty
	35.7 tons loaded
Length:	45 feet (13.72 m) overall
Beam:	14½ feet (4.42 m)
Propulsion:	2 diesel engines; 600 bhp; 1 propeller
Speed:	8.25 knots water
	29.5 mph land
Range:	45 n.miles (83 km) water at 8.25 knots
	300 miles (483 km) land at 29.5 mph
Manning:	2 (enlisted)
Troops:	50+

These are large, four-wheel cargo vehicles; they can carry a 15-ton cargo load, unloading over a stern ramp. Aluminum hull.

19 LARC LX TYPE

Builders:	
Weight:	88 tons empty
	190 tons loaded
Length:	62½ feet (19.07 m) overall
Beam:	26⁷⁄₁₂ feet (8.1 m)
Propulsion:	4 diesel engines; 660 bhp; 2 propellers
Speed:	6.5 knots water
	15 mph land
Range:	75 n.miles (139 km) water at 6 knots
	150 miles (241 km) land at 15 mph
Manning:	8 (enlisted)
Troops:	125

Very large, four-wheel cargo vehicles. They can normally carry 60 tons of cargo or an overload of up to 90 tons; fitted with a bow ramp. The craft has limited maneuverability.

The LARC LX 16 carrying a fuel truck while traversing shallow water. (U.S. Army)

3 LARC V DESIGN

Builders:	
Weight:	8.9 tons empty
	13.4 tons loaded
Length:	35 feet (10.67 m) overall
Beam:	10 feet (3.05 m)
Propulsion:	1 diesel engine; 300 bhp; 1 propeller
Speed:	9 knots water
	29.5 mph land
Range:	60 n.miles (111 km) water at 9 knots
	200 miles (322 km) land at 29 mph
Manning:	2 (enlisted)
Troops:	20

Four-wheeled cargo vehicles with a five-ton cargo capacity; fitted with a bow ramp. Aluminum hull. Troops are not normally carried in these vehicles.

HARBOR TUGS

The former Army tug LT 535 serves in the U.S. Navy as the PACIFIC ESCORT (No. 143WB8401); see chapter 25. Several other ex-Army tugs transferred to the Navy have been stricken.

1 + 7 LARGE TUGS: LT 130 DESIGN

Number	Name
LT 801	MAJ. GEN. NATHANAEL GREENE
LT 802	MAJ. GEN. HENRY KNOW
LT 803	MAJ. GEN. ANTHONY WAYNE
LT 804	BRIG. GEN. ZEBULON PIKE
LT 805	MAJ. GEN. WINFIELD SCOTT
LT 806	COL. SETH WARNER
LT 807	SGT. MAJ. JOHN CHAMPE
LT 808	MAJ. GEN. JACOB BROWN

Builders:	Robert E. Derecktor, Middletown, R.I.
Displacement:	710 tons light
	1,000 tons full load
Length:	128 feet (39.0 m) overall
Beam:	36 feet (11.0 m)
Draft:	16 feet (4.9 m)
Propulsion:	2 diesel engines (General Motors EMD 12-645FMB); 2,550 bhp; 2 shafts
Speed:	12 knots
Range:	5,000 n.miles (9,260 km) at 12 knots
Manning:	24 (4 officers + 20 enlisted)

A series of large tugs were awarded beginning in 1988 by the Navy to the Derecktor yard on behalf of the Army. The lead unit was "conditionally" delivered to the Army on 30 August 1991, with the yard responsible for correcting certain deficiencies.

Subsequently, on 3 January 1992 the Derecktor yard filed for bankruptcy protection under Chapter 11. Thus, the status of the class is not clear. Up to 14 tugs of this design were planned.

The MAJ GEN NATHANAEL GREENE is the first of a series of large tugs being acquired by the Army—the largest tugs yet operated by that service. Army tugs are intended to help maneuver merchant ships and landing ships in overseas ports. (U.S. Army)

25 LARGE HARBOR TUGS

Number	Name	Number	Name
LT 1937	SGT. WILLIAM W. SEAY	LT 2076	NEW GUINEA
LT 1953	SALERNO	LT 2080	(unnamed)
LT 1956	FREDERICKSBURG	LT 2081	SAN SAPOR
LT 1959	MURFREESBORO	LT 2085	ANZIO
LT 1960	LUNDY'S LANE	LT 1086	BATAAN
LT 1961	(unnamed)	LT 2087	KWAJALEIN
LT 1967	(unnamed)	LT 2088	PETERSBURG
LT 1970	OKINAWA	LT 2090	SP4 LARRY G. DAHL
LT 1971	NORMANDY	LT 2092	NORTH AFRICA
LT 1972	GETTYSBURG	LT 2094	CHANCELLORSVILLE
LT 1973	SHILOH	LT 2096	VALLEY FORGE
LT 1974	CHAMPAGNE-MARNE	LT 2202	(unnamed)
LT 1977	ATTLEBORO		

Builders:	
Displacement:	295 tons light
	390 tons full load
Length:	107 feet (32.61 m) overall
Beam:	26½ feet (8.08 m)
Draft:	12⅙ feet (3.71 m)
Propulsion:	1 diesel engine (Fairbanks Morse); 1,200 bhp; 1 shaft
Speed:	12.75 knots
Range:	3,325 n.miles (6,160 km) at 12 knots
Manning:	16 (enlisted)

Sixty-five tugs of this design were built in the 1950s (LT 1936–1977, 2202, and 2075–2096).

NORTH AFRICA. (1989, L. Van Ginderen Collection)

28 SMALL TUGS

Number	Name	Number	Name
ST 1979	FORT STANWIX	ST 2116	KING'S MOUNTAIN
ST 1981	RIDGEFIELD	ST 2118	GUILFORD COURT HOUSE
ST 1982	GROTON	ST 2119	BENNINGTON
ST 1983	GREEN SPRINGS	ST 2123	NINETY-SIX
ST 1984	SCHOHARIE	ST 2124	QUAKER HILL
ST 1988	BEMIS HEIGHTS	ST 2125	SAG HARBOR
ST 1989	EUTAW SPRINGS	ST 2126	STONY POINT
ST 1990	MOHAWK VALLEY	ST 2127	APPOMATTOX
ST 1991	ORISKANY	ST 2128	DORCHESTER HEIGHTS
ST 1993	COWPENS	ST 2129	BUNKER HILL
ST 2104	MONMOUTH	ST 2130	FORT MIFFLIN
ST 2113	CHARLESTOWN	ST 2199	VALCOUR ISLAND
ST 2114	VINCENNES	ST 2200	PELHAM POINT
ST 2115	FORT MOULTRIE	ST 2201	FALMOUTH

Builders:
Displacement:	100 tons light
	122 tons full load
Length:	69¹¹⁄₁₂ feet (21.31 m) overall
Beam:	19½ feet (5.94 m)
Draft:	8⅛ feet (2.5 m)
Propulsion:	1 diesel engine: 600 bhp; 1 shaft
Speed:	12 knots
Range:	3,500 n.miles (6,480 km) at 12 knots
Manning:	6 (enlisted)

These are the survivors of a large class of Army tugs built in the 1950s. Four units are in storage at Hythe (Kent) in England and one at Charleston, S.C.

VALCOUR ISLAND. (1986, L. Van Ginderen Collection)

1 SMALL TUG

Number	Name
ST 2028	SANTIAGO

Builders:
Displacement:	25.2 tons light
	29 tons full load
Length:	45⅛ feet (13.77 m) overall
Beam:	12⅝ feet (3.91 m)
Draft:	6 feet (1.83 m)
Propulsion:	1 diesel engine; 170 bhp; 1 shaft
Speed:	10 knots
Range:	700 n.miles (1,300 km) at 10 knots
Manning:	4 (enlisted)

Last of a series of small tugs built in the 1950s.

SERVICE CRAFT

The Army's Transportation Corps and Corps of Engineers operate a large number of small self-propelled craft for local transportation and supply; they also operate dredges and barges of various types.

MOBILE AEROSTAT PROGRAM VESSELS

The Coast Guard owned one Mobile Aerostat Program (MAP) vessel and leased four others to support the radar surveillance aerostats (see page 453). The ships are similar in general design.

The aerostat program was "grounded" on 31 December 1991 pending transfer from the Coast Guard to the Army. See page 552 for details of the program and transfer.

They were operated in Coast Guard service under contract by General Electric Government Services. A Coast Guard team of nine personnel are embarked to maintain the aerostat and monitor the equipment. The ATLANTIC SENTRY and CARIBBEAN SENTRY are based at Key West, Fla., and the GULF SENTRY, PACIFIC SENTRY, and WINDWARD SENTRY at Miami, Fla.

These ships were not in commission. Their Coast Guard hull numbers were not in the length series of other cutters and boats; SBA indicated for sea-based aerostat and relates to their "balloon."

1 AEROSTAT TENDER: "WINDWARD SENTRY"

Number	Name	Completed	USCG in service
SBA 5	WINDWARD SENTRY	1979	Nov 1989

Builders:	McDermott Shipyard, New Iberia, La.
Displacement:	approx. 1,770 tons full load
Length:	192 feet (58.5 m) overall
Beam:	40 feet (12.2 m)
Draft:	13⅔ feet (4.2 m)
Propulsion:	2 diesel engines (General Motors); 2,520 bhp; 2 shafts
Speed:	12 knots
Range:	7,000 n.miles (12,965 km) at 10 knots
Manning:	10 civilian + 9 Coast Guard
Radars:	2 navigation

A former oilfield supply tug modified to support a surveillance aerostat; home-ported at Key West, Fla. The ship is similar to the CARIBBEAN SENTRY class.

The WINDWARD SENTRY was the only ship of this type owned by the Coast Guard. The ship was acquired from the Maritime Administration on 10 January 1989 and converted to an aerostat tender by Halter Marine (which constructed and converted the CARIBBEAN SENTRY class).

Names: Previous commercial names were LIBERATOR and MARK BRILEY.

3 AEROSTAT TENDERS: "CARIBBEAN SENTRY" CLASS

Number	Name	Completed	USCG in service
SBA 2	CARIBBEAN SENTRY	1987	20 Dec 1988
SBA 3	GULF SENTRY	1984	30 Dec 1988
SBA 4	PACIFIC SENTRY	1983	6 Mar 1989

Builders:	Halter Marine, Lockport, La.
Displacement:	approx. 2,140 tons full load
Length:	192 feet (58.5 m) overall
Beam:	44 feet (13.4 m)
Draft:	15 feet (4.6 m)
Propulsion:	2 diesel engines (General Motors 16-645E6); 3,900 bhp; 2 shafts
Speed:	12 knots
Range:	7,000 n.miles (12,965 km) at 10 knots
Manning:	10 civilian + 9 Coast Guard
Radars:	2 navigation

1 AEROSTAT TENDER: "ATLANTIC SENTRY"

Number	Name	Completed	USCG in service
SBA 1	ATLANTIC SENTRY	1986	Apr 1987

Builders:	Steiner Marine Corp., Bayou La Batre, Ala.
Displacement:	approx. 1,820 tons full load
Length:	192 feet (58.5 m) overall
Beam:	40 feet (12.2 m)
Draft:	14¼ feet (4.3 m)
Propulsion:	2 diesel engines (General Motors 16-645E6); 3,900 bhp; 2 shafts
Speed:	12 knots
Range:	7,000 n.miles (12,965 km) at 10 knots
Manning:	10 civilian + 9 Coast Guard

These are former oilfield supply tugs modified by Halter Marine to serve as tenders for aerostats.

Names: Previous names were JUANITA CANDIES, ASHLEY CANDIES, and AGNES CANDIES, respectively.

The CARIBBEAN SENTRY carrying her aerostat. The design of all former Coast Guard aerostat tenders is similar. The program encountered several technical problems, causing Congress to order the program transferred to the Army. Its future was uncertain when this edition went to press. (1990, Giorgio Arra)

CARIBBEAN SENTRY. (1990, Giorgio Arra)

AIR FORCE

The Air Force operates a large number of small craft, all managed by the San Antonio Air Logistics Center at Kelly Air Force Base (AFB) in Texas. In addition to the craft listed here, the Air Force operates several small personnel craft, utility boats, and miscellaneous barges, plus one Army LARC V-type amphibious craft (designated L-35-2212).

Designations: Air Force craft are designated by their length (rounded).

MISSILE RECOVERY CRAFT

5 MISSILE RETRIEVERS: 120-FT TYPE

Number
MR-120-8801
MR-120-8802
MR-120-8803
MR-120-8804
MR-120-8805

Builders:	Swiftships, Morgan City, La.
Displacement:	91 tons light
	133 tons full load
Length:	117⅓ feet (35.78 m) overall
Beam:	24⅔ feet (7.51 m)
Draft:	6¾ feet (2.06 m)
Propulsion:	4 diesel engines (Detroit Diesel 16V92 MTA); 5,600 bhp; 4 shafts
Speed:	30 knots
Range:	600 n.miles (1,111 km) at 27 knots
Manning:	10 civilian

Retrieval craft employed to recover practice missiles. They can carry 20 tons of deck cargo. Aluminum construction. Completed in 1988–1989.

A pair of 120-foot missile retrievers at Tyndall Air Force Base near Panama City, Fla. Air Force craft wear aircraft-type insignia. (1991, Staff Sgt. Rick Fligort, USAF)

3 MISSILE RETRIEVERS: 85-FT TYPE

Number
MR-85-1602
MR-85-1603
MR-85-1604

Builders:	
Displacement:	90 tons full load
Length:	85 feet (25.91 m) overall
Beam:	18 feet (5.49 m)
Draft:	5⅙ feet (1.57 m)
Propulsion:	2 diesel engines (Detroit 16V92); 2 shafts
Speed:	17 knots
Range:	400 n.miles (740 km) at 17 knots
Manning:	10 civilian

Completed 1967–1968.

The 85-foot missile retriever craft MR-85-1603 at Tyndall AFB. (1991, Staff Sgt. Rick Fligort, USAF)

3 MISSILE RETRIEVERS: 65-FT TYPE

Number
MR-65-2068
MR-65-2109
MR-65-2110

These small missile retrievers were completed in 1967–1970; they are expected to be stricken in the near future.

HARBOR TUGS

2 SMALL TUGS

Number
TG-45-1919
TG-45-2215

Builders:	
Displacement:	25.2 tons light
	29 tons full load
Length:	45⅙ feet (13.77 m) overall
Beam:	12⅝ feet (3.91 m)
Draft:	6 feet (1.83 m)
Propulsion:	1 diesel engine; 170 bhp; 1 shaft
Speed:	10 knots
Range:	700 n.miles (1,300 km) at 10 knots
Manning:	4 (enlisted)

Similar to the Army ST-series tugs. Completed in 1953.

Operational: Both tugs are based at Thule, Greenland, to assist cargo ships and barges supporting the Air Force base there.

LANDING CRAFT

8 MECHANIZED LANDING CRAFT: LCM(8) TYPE

Number	Number
C-74-1866	C-74-2206
C-74-2167	C-74-8701
C-74-2168	C-74A-1938
C-74-2205	C-74A-2113

Displacement:	116 tons full load
Length:	73⁷⁄₁₂ feet (22.4 m) overall
Beam:	21 feet (6.4 m)
Draft:	4⁷⁄₁₂ feet (1.4 m) aft
Propulsion:	2 diesel engines (General Motors Detroit 6-71); 600 bhp; 2 shafts
Speed:	12 knots empty
	9.2 knots loaded
Range:	150 n.miles (278 km) at 12 knots empty
	150 n.miles (278 km) at 9.2 knots loaded
Manning:	2–4 (enlisted)

Cargo capacity is 57 tons. Completed from 1954 to 1987.

APPENDIX A

Advanced Technology Ships

The U.S. Navy and Coast Guard have been world leaders in the development of advanced-technology surface ships and craft. Several major production projects have been initiated, most of which, however, encountered major development problems. Four advanced technology ships have reached series production:

- hydrofoil missile craft for the Navy (page 197)
- Surface Effects Ship (SES) patrol craft for the Coast Guard (see page 563)
- Air Cushion Vehicle (ACV) landing craft for the Navy (see page 183)
- Small Waterplane-Area Twin Hull (SWATH) surveillance ships for the Navy (page 243)

This first series production of advanced technology ships for the U.S. Navy was the hydrofoil missile program initiated in the early 1970s by Admiral Elmo R. Zumwalt, Jr., USN, the Chief of Naval Operations.[1] Initially planned at 30 units, this evolved into the PEGASUS (PHM 1) class of six units that are now in service. That program suffered technical and cost difficulties, the former related to the complex transmissions for the craft. The six PHMs are fully operational and are considered successful and highly useful craft, although they have not been forward-deployed and have been used primarily in drug interdiction operations.

Subsequently, in the early 1980s the U.S. Navy initiated five other advanced technology ship programs:

(1) air-cushion landing craft (LCAC): More than 100 of these craft were initially planned, the number later reduced to 84 units. These craft are now in series production. They have encountered some mechanical difficulties, but those have been solved and the craft have been highly successful.

(2) special-warfare craft medium (SWCM), a multi-purpose patrol boat (PBM): The Navy planned to construct 19 of these air-cushion craft with the popular name Sea Viking. The craft was to have been multi-purpose in the context of supporting Sea-Air-Land

(SEAL) swimmer/commando teams as well as being capable of offshore patrol and interdiction operations.

Construction of the lead craft was begun, but the design was flawed and construction halted before completion. A more conventional patrol-type craft has been substituted to support SEAL and coastal interdiction operations.

(3) coastal minehunter (MSH): A class of 17 of these slow, air-cushion vehicle mine-countermeasure craft was initiated, but before the lead craft was launched, testing of hull sections revealed major flaws in workmanship and design. Accordingly, that program was cancelled in 1986 with a conventional mine-countermeasures craft (OSPREY class/MHC 51) being procured in its place.

(4) Small Waterplane Area Twin-Hull (SWATH) ocean surveillance ship (AGOS): The ships of the VICTORIOUS (T-AGOS 19) class have a SWATH configuration to provide increased seakeeping capabilities in northern latitudes. The prototype SWATH built for the U.S. Navy, the KAIMALINO, built at the Coast Guard Yard, has been most successful as a range support ship.

In addition, the Navy continues to evaluate a medium-size SES. The 210-ton craft is now in Navy service as a test craft (designated IX 515). The craft was previously evaluated by the Coast Guard as the DORADO (WSES 1) from September 1980 to September 1982, after which the Coast Guard procured three similar craft for operational use (designated WSES). There is no Navy interest in obtaining such craft for operational use at this time. Navy consideration of a larger, approximately 3,000-ton SES frigate has ended.[2]

The following tables list the major advanced technology prototypes built by the U.S. Navy. The data are full-load displacement, length overall (not over foils for hydrofoils), and maximum speed. Where craft have undergone major modifications, the later displacement and length are given.

2. The Soviet Union pursued this concept, producing the 760-ton Dergach SES corvette; that ship carries eight anti-ship missiles in addition to a 76.2-mm rapid-fire gun and defensive weapons. See N. Polmar, *Guide to the Soviet Navy*, 5th Edition (Annapolis, Md.: Naval Institute Press, 1991), p. 192.

1. Adm. Zumwalt served as CNO from July 1970 to June 1974.

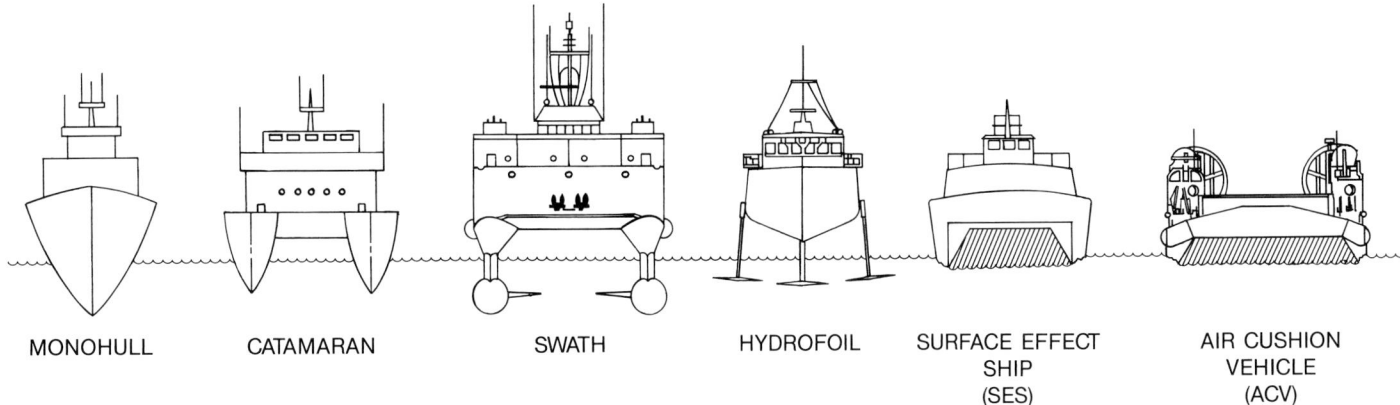

MONOHULL CATAMARAN SWATH HYDROFOIL SURFACE EFFECT SHIP (SES) AIR CUSHION VEHICLE (ACV)

(Drawings by William Clipson)

HYDROFOILS

Hydrofoils use submerged foils or wing-like structures to lift the hull above the water to reduce drag, thus achieving high speed and stability. Several prototype hydrofoil combat craft have been built and, as noted above, six PEGASUS-class hydrofoil missile craft are in service.

In addition to the ships and craft listed here, during the 1960s the Navy experimented with landing vehicles (LVHX) and landing craft (LVCP(H)) fitted with hydrofoils. The latter craft were given the nicknames HIGH POCKET and HIGH LANDER.

FRESH-1 twin-hull hydrofoil. (Boeing)

Number	Name/Designation	Displacement	Length	Speed	Completed	Status/Remarks
—	DENISON	80 tons	104 ft	62 knots	1960	Maritime Administration test craft developed with Navy assistance; built by Grumman-Jakobson's Shipyard; disposed of after trials.
—	FRESH-1	20 tons	47 ft	84 knots	1963	In storage since 1964 following Navy evaluation.
PCH 1	HIGH POINT	110 tons	115 ft	45 knots	1963	Evaluated by Navy and Coast Guard (WMEH 1) until 1978; sold in 1990.
PGH 1	FLAGSTAFF	67 tons	74⅓ ft	40+ knots	1968	Grumman competitive prototype for PHM; to Coast Guard for evaluation (WPBH 1) and subsequently stricken.
PGH 2	TUCUMCARI	57 tons	71¾ ft	40+ knots	1968	Boeing competitive prototype for PHM; wrecked on reef in November 1972 and stricken in October 1973.
AGEH 1	PLAINVIEW	320 tons	212 ft	50 knots	1969	The world's largest hydrofoil; stricken after evaluation by Navy; fitted with Mk 32 torpedo tubes.

HIGH POINT hydrofoil. (Boeing)

FLAGSTAFF with foils raised. (Boeing)

FLAGSTAFF hydrofoil. (U.S. Navy)

TUCUMCARI hydrofoil. (U.S. Navy)

PLAINVIEW and HIGH POINT hydrofoils. (U.S. Navy)

SMALL WATERPLANE-AREA TWIN-HULL

The SWATH concept provides for twin, torpedo-shaped hulls that are fully submerged to provide a very high degree of ship stability. The twin hulls accommodate machinery, with the main ship structure being above water. Unlike most other advanced technology designs, these are not high-speed craft. Rather, the SWATH advantages are good seakeeping in rough seas (facilitating the operation of aircraft and other sea-sensitive systems) and a relatively large deck area for equipment (facilitating the use of modular weapon and sensor systems, or otherwise rapidly changing ship mission configuration).

Number	Name/Designation	Displacement	Length	Speed	Completed	Status/Remarks
—	KAIMALINO	228 tons	88 ft	25 knots	1973	In Navy service; see page 350 for details.

SURFACE EFFECT SHIPS

The SES ships and craft ride on a "bubble" of air that is contained by flexible "skirts" forward and aft and with rigid, fixed sidewalls. These sidewalls penetrate the water surface, providing stability in rough seas.

The SES-100B conducted the first U.S. missile launch tests from an SES with Standard SM-1 vertical-launch firings in 1977.

Number	Name/Designation	Displacement	Length	Speed	Completed	Status/Remarks
—	XR-1	17 tons		34 knots	1963	Disposed of after evaluation by Navy; there were several X-craft variants.
—	SES-100A	110 tons	80 ft	75+ knots	1972	Scrapped after evaluation by Navy.
—	SES-100B	100 tons	77¾ ft	91.9 knots	1972	Following Navy evaluation placed on static display at Naval Ship Research and Development Center, Annapolis, Md.
—	SES-200	200 tons	160 ft	32 knots	1982	In Navy service (now IX 515); evaluated by Coast Guard as WSES 1; see chapter 25.

SES-100A surface effect ship. (Aerojet-General)

SES-100B surface effect ship. (U.S. Navy).

AIR-CUSHION VEHICLES

The ACV similarly rides on a bubble of air that is entirely contained by flexible skirts, permitting such craft to operate *above* the water and to travel at high speeds over marshes and solid ground. As noted above, the LCAC landing craft is in series production for the Navy.

Number	Name/Designation	Displacement	Length	Speed	Completed	Status/Remarks
—	SKMR-1	20 tons	65½ ft	70 knots	1963	Bell Aerospace research craft; disposed of after Navy evaluation.
—	PACV 1	8.5 tons	38¾ ft	60 knots	1965	British-developed SR.N5 hovercraft built by Bell; evaluated by
—	PACV 2	8.5 tons	38¾ ft	60 knots	1965	U.S. Navy and used in combat in Vietnam in 1966–1969; to
—	PACV 3	8.5 tons	38¾ ft	60 knots	1965	Coast Guard for evaluation in 1969 as HOVER 01, 01, 03; all stricken.
—	JEFF-A	162.56 tons	100 ft	50 knots	1977	Aerojet-General competitive prototype for LCAC; disposed of after trials.
—	JEFF-B	160 tons	87 ft	50 knots	1977	Bell Aerospace competitive prototype for LCAC; disposed of after trials.

SKMR-1 air-cushion vehicle. (U.S. Navy)

PACV 1 air-cushion vehicle in South Vietnam. (U.S. Navy)

APPENDIX B

Force Levels, 1945–1990

The following are ships in active commission as of the end of the fiscal year indicated; beginning in 1965 operational Naval Reserve/ Naval Reserve Force (NRF) ships manned by composite active-reserve crews are indicated by the plus symbol.

Large frigate-type ships (DL-DLG-DLGN) are listed separately prior to 1975; from that year they are included with missile cruisers and destroyers.

Ship Type	1945	1950	1953[1]	1955	1960	1965	1970	1975	1980	1985	1990
Submarines—*conventional*											
SS-SSK-SSR	237	73	122	121	113	83	59	11	6	4	—
SSG	—	—	1	2	4	—	—	—	—	—	—
auxiliary[2]	—	—	7	18	20	15	26	2	1	1	1
Submarines—*nuclear*											
SSN-SSRN	—	—	—	1	7	22	48	64	73	94	87
SSGN	—	—	—	—	1	—	—	—	—	—	—
SSBN	—	—	—	—	2	29	41	41	40	37	34
auxiliary[3]	—	—	—	—	—	—	—	—	—	2	2
(total submarines)	(237)	(73)	(130)	(142)	(147)	(149)	(174)	(118)	(120)	(138)	(124)
Aircraft carriers											
CVB-CVA-CVAN-CV-CVN	20	7	17	16	14	16	15	15	13	13	12
CVS	—	—	—	5	9	9	4	—	—	—	—
CVL	8	4	5	1	—	—	—	—	—	—	—
CVE	70	4	17	3	—	—	—	—	—	—	—
Battleships											
BB	25[4]	1	4	3	—	—	—	—	—	2	3
Cruisers											
CAG-CG-CLG-CGN	—	—	—	—	6	12	10	27	27	30	43
CA (8-inch guns)	24	9	15	10	6	2	2	—	—	—	—
CL (6-inch guns)	42	3	3	3	—	—	—	—	—	—	—
CLAA (5-inch guns)	6	1	1	—	—	—	—	—	—	—	—
Frigates[5]											
DL	—	—	—	5	5	5	—	—	—	—	—
DLG-DLGN	—	—	—	—	4	20	20	—	—	—	—
Destroyers[6]											
DD-DDE-DDK-DDR	372	142	246	244	211	189+17	122	32	43	31+1	31
DDG	—	—	—	—	—	33	37	38	37	37	22
Escort Ships/Frigates											
DE-DER/FF-FFR[7]	365	11	89	64	41	39+21	41	58	59	53+6	36+12
DEG/FFG	—	—	—	—	—	—	6	6	13	47+4	35+16
Flagships/Command Ships											
AGC-CC-CLC-LCC-AGF	18[8]	6	} 226[9]	} 175[9]	} 113[9]	7	3	3	3	4	4
AMPHIBIOUS SHIPS	~3,300	83				132	95	62	58+5	58+2	59+3

[1]End of Korean War (June 1953).
[2]Does not include nuclear-propelled research vehicle NR-1, completed in 1969. Does include two SSNs employed as special operations transports.
[3]Includes transport submarines.
[4]The 1945 force included two large cruisers (designated CB); they were often referred to as battle cruisers (armed with 12-inch guns).
[5]Frigates (DL-DLG-DLGN) were reclassified as CG-CGN-DDG in 1975.
[6]Additional destroyer-type ships were employed as mine warfare ships (DM-DMS-MMD) until 1958; they retained most of their guns and some ASW weapons.
[7]Includes one AGDE-AGFF from 1966 until classified as an FF in 1975.
[8]In addition, six large Coast Guard cutters were configured as amphibious force flagships.
[9]Includes amphibious force flagships (AGC).

APPENDIX C

Navy Shipbuilding Programs, Fiscal 1947–1992

This appendix lists U.S. Navy shipbuilding programs since World War II. Only those ships actually constructed are listed except where noted; ships transferred to other navies upon completion are not included.

See Addenda for FY 1993 and later shipbuilding plan.

Number	Class name	SCB No.	Notes
Fiscal Year 1947			
2 SS 563, 564	Tang	2	
Fiscal Year 1948			
2 SS 565, 566	Tang	2	
1 SSK 1	K-1	35	
(1)CVA 58	United States	6A	construction cancelled
1 CLK 1	Norfolk	1	completed as DL 1
(1)CLK 2	Norfolk	1	construction cancelled
4 DD 927–930	Mitscher	5	completed as DL 2–5
Fiscal Year 1949			
2 SS 567, 568	Tang	2	
2 SSK 2, 3	K-1	35	
Fiscal Year 1950			
1 AGSS 569	Albacore	56	
1 MSO 421	Agile	45A	
Fiscal Year 1951			
2 SST 1	Mackerel	68	
28 MSO 422–449	Agile	45A	
Fiscal Year 1952			
1 SSN 571	Nautilus	64	
2 SSR 572, 573	Salmon	84	changed to SS
1 SST 2	Mackerel	68	
1 CVA 59	Forrestal	80	changed to CV/AVT 59
1 DE 1006	Dealey	72	
1 IFS 1	Carronade	37	changed to LFS 1
4 LSD 28–31	Thomaston	75	
15 LST 1156–1170	Terrebonne Parish	9	
20 MSO 455–474	Agile	45A	
2 MSC 121, 122	Bluebird	69	
1 AGB 4	Glacier	11A	changed to WAGB 4
6 AO 143–148	Neosho	82	
Fiscal Year 1953			
1 SSG 574	Grayback	161	changed to LPSS 574
1 SSN 575	Seawolf	64A	
1 CVA 60	Forrestal	80	changed to CV 60
3 DD 931–933	Forrest Sherman	85	
2 DE 1014, 1015	Dealey	72	
9 MSO 488–496	Agile	45A	
20 MSC 190–199, 201, 203–209 289, 290	Bluebird	69	
2 AF 58, 59	Rigel	97	
Fiscal Year 1954			
1 SS 576	Darter	116	
1 CVA 61	Forrestal	80	changed to CV 61
3 DD 936–938	Forrest Sherman	85	
2 DE 1021, 1022	Dealey	72	
2 LSD 32, 33	Thomaston	75	
1 LST 1171	De Soto County	119	
1 MHC 43	Bittern	109	
4 MSO 508–511	Acme	45A	
2 AE 21, 22	Suribachi	114	
Fiscal Year 1955			
1 SSG 577	Grayback	161	
2 SSN 578, 579	Skate	121	
1 CVA 62	Forrestal	80	changed to CV 62
5 DD 940–944	Forrest Sherman	85	
8 DE 1023–1030	Dealey	72	
2 LSD 34, 35	Thomaston	75	
6 LST 1173–1178	De Soto County	119	
2 T-AOG 81, 82	Alatna	—	
Fiscal Year 1956			
3 SS 580–582	Barbel	150	
2 SSN 583, 584	Skate	121	
1 SSN 585	Skipjack	154	
1 SSRN 586	Triton	132	changed to SS 586
1 SSGN 587	Halibut	137A	changed to SS 587
1 CVA 63	Kitty Hawk	127	changed to CV 63
6 DLG 6–11	Coontz	142	changed to DDG 37–42
7 DD 945–951	Forrest Sherman	85	
2 DE 1033, 1034	Claud Jones	131	
2 AE 23, 24	Suribachi	114A	
Fiscal Year 1957			
5 SSN 588–592	Skipjack	154	
1 SSN 593	Thresher	188	
1 CVA 64	Kitty Hawk	127A	changed to CV 64
1 CLGN 160	Long Beach	169	completed as CGN 9
4 DLG 12–15	Coontz	142	changed to DDG 43–46
8 DD 952–959	Charles F. Adams	155	completed as DDG 2–9
2 DE 1035	Claud Jones	131	
1 AE 25	Suribachi	114A	

Number	Class name	SCB No.	Notes
Fiscal Year 1958			
3 SSN 594–596	Thresher[1]	188	originally ordered as SSGN 594–596 (SCB-166A)
1 SSN 597	Tullibee	178	
3 SSBN 598–600	George Washington	180A	
1 CVAN 65	Enterprise	160	changed to CVN 65
3 DLG 16–18	Leahy	172	changed to CG 16–18
5 DDG 10–14	Adams	155	
1 LPH 2	Iwo Jima	157	
Fiscal Year 1959			
2 SSBN 601, 602	George Washington	180A	
5 SSN 603–607	Thresher	188	1 unit originally planned as SSGN (SCB-166A)
4 SSBN 608–611	Ethan Allen	180	
6 DLG 19–24	Leahy	172	changed to CG 19–24
1 DLGN 25	Bainbridge	189	changed to CGN 25
5 DDG 15–19	Adams	155	
1 LPD 1	Raleigh	187	
1 LPH 3	Iwo Jima	157	
Fiscal Year 1960			
4 SSN 612–615	Thresher	188	
3 DDG 20–22	Adams	155	
2 DE 1037, 1038	Bronstein	199	changed to FF 1037, 1038
1 PCH 1	High Point	202	
1 LPD 2	Raleigh	187	
1 LPH 7	Iwo Jima	157	
2 AGOR 3, 4	Conrad	185	academic ships
1 AS 31	Hunley	194	
Fiscal Year 1961			
1 SSBN 618	Ethan Allen	180	
4 SSBN 616, 617, 619, 620	Lafayette	216	
1 SSN 621	Thresher	188	
5 SSBN 622–626	Lafayette	216	FY 1961 supplemental
1 AGSS 555	Dolphin	207	
1 CVA 66	Kitty Hawk	127B	changed to CV 66
3 DLG 26–28	Belknap	212	changed to CG 26–28
2 DDG 23, 24	Adams	155	
2 DE 1040, 1041	Garcia	199A	changed to FF 1040, 1041
1 LPD 3	Raleigh	187	changed to AGF 3
1 AG 163	Glover	198	completed as AGDE 1; changed to FF 1098/AGFF 1
1 AFS 1	Mars	208	
2 T-AGOR 5, 6	Conrad	185	academic ships
1 AOE 1	Sacramento	196	
Fiscal Year 1962			
3 SSN 637–639	Sturgeon	188A	
10 SSBN 627–636	Lafayette	216	
6 DLG 29–34	Belknap	212	changed to CG 29–34
1 DLGN 35	Truxtun	222	changed to CGN 35
3 DE 1043–1045	Garcia	199A	changed to FF 1043–1045
3 DEG 1–3	Brooke	199B	changed to FFG 1–3
3 LPD 4–6	Austin	187B	
1 LPH 9	Iwo Jima	157	
1 AFS 2	Mars	208	
1 AGEH 1	Plainview	219	
1 T-AGOR 7	Conrad	185	
1 T-AGS 25	Kellar	214	
1 AS 32	Hunley	194	

Number	Class name	SCB No.	Notes
Fiscal Year 1963			
8 SSN 646–653	Sturgeon	188A	
6 SSBN 640–645	Lafayette	216	
1 CVA 67	John F. Kennedy	127C	
5 DE 1047–1051	Garcia	199A	changed to FF 1047–1051
3 DEG 4–6	Brooke	199B	changed to FFG 4–6
4 LPD 7–10	Austin	187B	
1 LPH 10	Iwo Jima	157	
1 T-AK 278	Meteor	236	changed to T-LSV/T-AKR 9
2 PGM 84, 85	Asheville	229	changed to PG 84, 85
2 AGOR 9, 10	Conrad	185	academic ships
1 T-AGS 26	Silas Bent	226	
1 AOE 2	Sacramento	196	
1 AS 33	Simon Lake	238	
Fiscal Year 1964			
5 SSN 660–664	Sturgeon	188A	
1 SSN 671	Narwhal	245	
6 SSBN 654–659	Lafayette	216	
10 DE 1052–1061	Knox	199C	changed to FF 1052–1061
3 LPD 11–13	Austin	187C	LPD 11 changed to AGF 11
2 PGM 86, 87	Asheville	229	changed to PG 86, 87
1 AD 37	Samuel Gompers	244	
1 AFS 3	Mars	208	
1 T-AGS 27	Silas Bent	226	
1 AS 34	Simon Lake	238	
Fiscal Year 1965			
6 SSN 665–670	Sturgeon	188M	
16 DE 1062–1077	Knox	200	new SCB series; changed to FF 1062–1077
1 AGC 19	Blue Ridge	400	changed to LCC 19
4 AKA 113–116	Charleston	403	changed to LKA 113–116
2 LPD 14, 15	Austin	402	new SCB series
1 LPH 11	Iwo Jima	157	
1 LSD 36	Anchorage	404	new SCB series
1 LST 1179	Newport	405	new SCB series
3 PGM 88–90	Asheville	600	new SCB series; changed to PG 88–90
1 AD 38	Samuel Gompers	700	new SCB series
2 AE 26, 27	Kilauea	703	new SCB series
2 AFS 4, 5	Mars	705	new SCB series
2 T-AGOR 12, 13	Conrad	710	new SCB series
1 AGS 29	Chauvenet	723	built in Scotland
1 T-AGS 31	Kellar	709	
1 AOE 3	Sacramento	196	
2 AOR 1, 2	Wichita	707	
(1)AS 35	Simon Lake	738	*cancelled*
1 AS 36	L.Y. Spear	702	
Fiscal Year 1966			
6 SSN 672–677	Sturgeon	188M	
10 DE 1078–1087	Knox	200	changed to FF 1078–1087
1 AGC 20	Mount Whitney	400	changed to LCC 20
1 LKA 117	Charleston	403	changed to LKA 117
1 LPH 12	Iwo Jima	157	
3 LSD 37–39	Anchorage	404	
8 LST 1180–1187	Newport	405	
2 PGH 1, 2	Flagstaff/Tucumcari	601	competitive prototypes
10 PGM 92–101	Asheville	600	changed to PG 92–101
2 AE 28, 29	Kilauea	703	
1 AFS 6	Mars	705	
2 AGOR 14, 15	Melville	710	academic ships
1 T-AGS 32	Chauvenet	723	built in Scotland
1 AOE 4	Sacramento	196	
2 AOR 3, 4	Wichita	707	
1 AS 37	L.Y. Spear	702	
1 ATS 1	Edenton	719	built in England

Number	Class name	SCB No.	Notes
Fiscal Year 1967			
5 SSN 678–682			
1 CVAN 68	Nimitz	102	changed to CVN 68
1 DLGN 36	California	241	changed to CGN 36
10 DE 1088–1097	Knox	200	changed to FF 1088–1097
1 LSD 40	Anchorage	404	
11 LST 1188–1198	Newport	405	
2 AE 32, 33	Kilauea	703	
1 AFS 7	Mars	705	
1 T-AGOR 16	Hayes	726	changed to T-AG 195
1 T-AGS 33, 34	Silas Bent	725/728	
2 AOR 5, 6	Wichita	707	
1 ASR 21	Pigeon	721	
2 ATS 2, 3	Edenton	719	built in England
Fiscal Year 1968			
2 SSN 683, 684	Sturgeon	188M	
1 SSN 685	Glenard P. Lipscomb	302	new SCB series
1 DLGN 37	California	241	changed to CGN 37
(10)DE 1098–1107	Knox	200	*cancelled;* No. 1098 assigned to the Glover
7 MSO			
2 AE 34, 35	Kilauea	703	
(2)AGOR 19, 20	Melville	710	*cancelled*
1 ASR 22	Pigeon	721	
Fiscal Year 1969			
2 SSN 686, 687	Sturgeon	188M	
1 LHA 1	Tarawa	410	
Fiscal Year 1970			
3 SSN 688–690	Los Angeles	303	
1 CVAN 69	Nimitz	102	changed to CVN 69
1 DLGN 38	Virginia	—	changed to CGN 38
3 DD 963–965	Spruance	224	
2 LHA 2, 3	Tarawa	410	
Fiscal Year 1971			
4 SSN 691–694	Los Angeles	303	
1 DLGN 39	Virginia		changed to CGN 39
6 DD 966–971	Spruance	224	
2 LHA 4, 5	Tarawa	410	
2 AGOR 21, 22	Gyre	734	academic ships
Fiscal Year 1972			
5 SSN 695–699	Los Angeles	303	
1 DLGN 40	Virginia	—	changed to CGN 40
7 DD 972–978	Spruance	224	
1 AOR 7	Wichita	707	
1 AS 39	Emory S. Land	737	
Fiscal Year 1973			
6 SSN 700–705	Los Angeles	303	
1 PF 109	Oliver Hazard Perry	261	changed to FFG 7
1 PHM 1	Pegasus	602	
(1)PHM 2	Pegasus	602	*cancelled;* reauthorized in FY 1976
1 AS 40	Emory S. Land	737	
Fiscal Year 1974			
5 SSN 706–710	Los Angeles	303	
1 SSBN 726	Ohio	304	
1 CVN 70	Nimitz	102	
7 DD 979–985	Spruance	224	
Fiscal Year 1975			
3 SSN 711–713	Los Angeles	303	
2 SSBN 727, 728	Ohio	304	
1 CGN 41	Virginia	—	
7 DD 986–992	Spruance	224	
3 FFG 8–10	Perry	261	
4 PHM 3–6	Pegasus	602	
1 AD 41	Samuel Gompers	700	

Number	Class name	SCB No.	Notes
Fiscal Year 1976			
2 SSN 714, 715	Los Angeles	303	
1 SSBN 729	Ohio	304	
6 FFG 11–16	Perry	226	
1 PHM 2	Pegasus	602	
1 AD 42	Samuel Gompers	700	
2 AO 177, 178	Cimarron	739	
3 T-ATF 166–169	Powhatan	744	
Fiscal Year 1977			
3 SSN 716–718	Los Angeles	303	
1 SSBN 730	Ohio	304	
8 FFG 19–26	Perry	261	
1 AD 43	Samuel Gompers	700	
1 AO 179	Cimarron	739	
1 AS 41	McKee	737	
Fiscal Year 1978			
1 SSN 719	Los Angeles	303	
2 SSBN 731, 732	Ohio	304	
1 DDG 47	Ticonderoga	226	changed to CG 47
1 DD 997	Spruance[2]	224	
8 FFG 27–34	Perry	261	
2 AO 180, 186	Cimarron	739	
3 T-ATF 170–172	Powhatan	744	
Fiscal Year 1979			
1 SSN 720	Los Angeles	303	
4 DDG 993–996	Kidd[3]	—	
8 FFG 36–43	Perry	261	
1 AD 44	Samuel Gompers	700	
2 T-AGOS 1, 2	Stalwart	—	
1 T-ARC 7	Zeus	—	
Fiscal Year 1980			
2 SSN 721, 722	Los Angeles	303	
1 SSBN 733	Ohio	304	
1 CVN 71	Nimitz	102	
1 CG 48	Ticonderoga	226	
5 FFG 45–49	Perry	261	
1 T-AGOS 3	Stalwart	—	
Fiscal Year 1981			
2 SSN 723, 724	Los Angeles	303	
1 SSBN 734	Ohio	304	
2 CG 49, 50	Ticonderoga	226	
6 FFG 50–55	Perry	261	
1 LSD 41	Whidbey Island	—	
1 ARS 50	Safeguard	—	
5 T-AGOS 4–8	Stalwart	—	
Fiscal Year 1982			
3 SSN 725, 750	Los Angeles	303	
3 CG 51–53	Ticonderoga	226	
3 FFG 56–58	Perry	261	
1 LSD 42	Whidbey Island	—	
1 MCM 1	Avenger	—	
4 T-AGOS 9–12	Stalwart	—	
1 T-AO 187	Henry J. Kaiser	—	
2 ARS 51, 52	Safeguard	—	
Fiscal Year 1983			
1 SSBN 735	Ohio	304	
2 SSN 751, 752	Los Angeles	303	improved design
2 CVN 72, 73	Nimitz		
3 CG 54–56	Ticonderoga	226	
2 FFG 59, 60	Perry	261	
1 LSD 43	Whidbey Island	—	
1 MCM 2	Avenger	—	
1 T-AO 188	Henry J. Kaiser	—	
1 ARS 53	Safeguard	—	

Number	Class name	SCB No.	Notes
Fiscal Year 1984			
1 SSBN 736	OHIO	304	
3 SSN 753–755	LOS ANGELES	303	improved design
3 CG 57–59	TICONDEROGA	226	
1 FFG 61	PERRY	261	
1 LHD 1	WASP	—	
1 LSD 44	WHIDBEY ISLAND	—	
(1)SWCM 1	(Sea Viking class)	—	*cancelled*
3 MCM 3–5	AVENGER	—	
(1)MSH 1	CARDINAL	—	*cancelled*
2 T-AO 189, 190	HENRY J. KAISER	—	
Fiscal Year 1985			
1 SSBN 737	OHIO	304	
4 SSN 756–759	LOS ANGELES	303	improved design
3 CG 60–62	TICONDEROGA	226	
1 DDG 51	ARLEIGH BURKE	—	
2 LSD 45, 46	WHIDBEY ISLAND	—	
4 MCM 6–9	AVENGER	—	
2 T-AGOS 13, 14	STALWART	—	
2 T-AGS 39, 40	MAURY	—	
3 T-AO 191–193	HENRY J. KAISER	—	
Fiscal Year 1986			
1 SSBN 738	OHIO	304	
4 SSN 760–763	LOS ANGELES	303	improved design
3 CG 63–65	TICONDEROGA	226	
1 LHD 2	WASP	—	
2 LSD 47, 48	WHIDBEY ISLAND	—	
2 MC 10, 11	AVENGER	—	
1 MHC 51	OSPREY	—	
2 T-AGOS 15, 16	STALWART	—	
2 T-AO 194, 195	HENRY J. KAISER	—	
Fiscal Year 1987			
1 SSBN 739	OHIO	304	
4 SSN 764–767	LOS ANGELES	303	improved design
3 CG 66–68	TICONDEROGA	226	
2 DDG 52, 53	ARLEIGH BURKE	—	
(1)SWCM 1	(Sea Viking class)	—	*cancelled*[4]
1 AOE 6	SUPPLY	—	
1 AGOR 23	THOMAS G. WASHINGTON	—	academic ship
2 T-AGOS 17, 18	STALWART	—	
1 T-AGOS 19	VICTORIOUS	—	
2 T-AO 196, 197	HENRY J. KAISER	—	
Fiscal Year 1988			
1 SSBN 740	OHIO	304	
3 SSN 768–770	LOS ANGELES	303	improved design
2 CVN 74, 75	NIMITZ	102	
5 CG 69–73	TICONDEROGA	226	
1 LHD 3	WASP	—	
1 LSD 49	HARPERS FERRY	—	
3 MCM 12–14	AVENGER	—	
2 T-AO 198, 199	HENRY J. KAISER	—	

Number	Class name	SCB No.	Notes
Fiscal Year 1989			
1 SSBN 741	OHIO	304	
1 SSN 21	SEAWOLF	—	
2 SSN 771, 772	LOS ANGELES	303	improved design
5 DDG 54–58	ARLEIGH BURKE	—	
1 LHD 4	WASP	—	
2 MHC 52, 53	OSPREY	—	
3 T-AGOS 20–22	VICTORIOUS	—	
5 T-AO 200–204	HENRY J. KAISER	—	
1 AOE 7	SUPPLY	—	
Fiscal Year 1990			
1 SSBN 742	OHIO	304	
1 SSN 773	LOS ANGELES	303	improved design
5 DDG 59–63	ARLEIGH BURKE	—	
1 LSD 50	HARPERS FERRY	—	
2 MHC 54, 55	OSPREY	—	
3 AGOR 24–26	THOMAS G. WASHINGTON	—	2 academic ships
1 T-AGOS 23	IMPECCABLE	—	
1 AOE 8	SUPPLY	—	
1 WAGB 12	HEALY	—	for Coast Guard operation; deferred in March 1992
Fiscal Year 1991			
1 SSBN 743	OHIO	304	
1 SSN 22	SEAWOLF	—	
4 DDG 64–67	ARLEIGH BURKE	—	
1 LHD 5	WASP	—	
1 LSD 51	HARPERS FERRY	—	
2 MHC 56, 57	OSPREY	—	
Fiscal Year 1992			
(1)SSN 23	SEAWOLF	—	*cancelled* in January 1992
5 DDG 68–72	ARLEIGH BURKE	—	
3 MHC 56–58	OSPREY	—	
1 AOE 9	SUPPLY	—	
2 AGOR 27, 28	THOMAS G. WASHINGTON	—	

[1]Class renamed for PERMIT (SSN 594) after loss of the USS THRESHER in April 1963.

[2]The Congress authorized two improved SPRUANCE-class destroyers with enhanced aviation capabilities; in the event, the Navy ordered only one ship, to a standard SPRUANCE configuration.

[3]Taken over while under construction for Iran.

[4]The SWCM/Sea Viking program was restructured in 1987 with the lead ship reordered in 1987; no ships of this design were completed.

APPENDIX D

Foreign Ship Transfers, 1987–1991

Number	Name	Recipient	Date
Destroyers			
DDG 16	JOSEPH STRAUUS	Greece	1992
DDG 18	SEMMES	Greece	12 Sep 1991
DDG 23	RICHARD BYRD	Greece	1992
DDG 24	WADDELL	Greece	1992
Frigates[1]			
FFG 1	BROOKE	Pakistan	1 Feb 1989
FFG 4	TALBOT	Pakistan	31 Apr 1989
FFG 5	RICHARD L. PAGE	Pakistan	31 Mar 1989
FFG 6	JULIUS A. FURER	Pakistan	31 Jan 1989
FF 1040	GARCIA	Pakistan	30 Jan 1989
FF 1041	BRADLEY	Brazil	25 Sep 1989
FF 1044	BRUMBY	Pakistan	31 Mar 1989
FF 1045	DAVIDSON	Brazil	18 Sep 1989
FF 1048	SAMPLE	Brazil	24 Aug 1989
FF 1049	KOELSCH	Pakistan	31 May 1989
FF 1050	ALBERT DAVID	Brazil	18 Sep 1989
FF 1051	O'CALLAHAN	Pakistan	8 Feb 1989
Amphibious Ships			
LSD 33	ALAMO	Brazil	28 Sep 1990
LSD 34	HERMITAGE	Brazil	28 Nov 1989
Patrol Combatants			
PG 99	BEACON	Greece	22 Nov 1989
PG 101	GREEN BAY	Greece	22 Nov 1989
Auxiliary Ships			
AR 7	HECTOR	Pakistan	20 Apr 1989
Coast Guard Cutters			
WPB 95300	CAPE SMALL	Marshall Is.	10 Dec 1987
WPB 95302	CAPE HIGGON	Palau	May 1990
WPB 95303	CAPE UPRIGHT	Bahamas	30 June 1989
WPB 95305	CAPE HATTERAS	Mexico	Mar 1991
WPB 95307	CAPE CURRENT	Bahamas	30 June 1989
WPB 95309	CAPE CARTER	Mexico	June 1991
WPB 95311	CAPE HEDGE	Mexico	Jan 1990
WPB 95313	CAPE MORGAN	Bahamas	20 Oct 1989
WPB 95316	CAPE FOX	Bahamas	30 June 1989
WPB 95318	CAPE HERRON	Mexico	June 1991
WPB 95321	CAPE CROSS	Micronesia	1990
WPB 95322	CAPE HORN	Uruguay	Jan 1990
WPB 95324	CAPE SHOALWATER	Bahamas	30 June 1989
WPB 95326	CAPE CORWIN	Micronesia	1990
WPB 95328	CAPE HENLOPEN	Costa Rica	Oct 1989
WPB 95332	CAPE YORK	Bahamas	30 June 1989
WPB 82302	POINT HOPE	Costa Rica	1991
WPB 82345	POINT JUDITH	Venezuela	Dec 1991
WPB 82348	POINT BARROW	Panama	June 1991
WPB 82367	POINT KNOLL	Venezuela	Sep 1991

[1]The RAMSEY (FFG 2) and SCHOFIELD (FFG 3) were to have been transferred to Turkey in 1989 but were rejected.

APPENDIX E

Navy and Coast Guard Ships Preserved as Memorials and Museums

These ships are arranged alphabetically by name. Also of significance, the U.S. nuclear-propelled merchant ship SAVANNAH is located at Patriots Point, Mt. Pleasant, S.C. The world's first civilian nuclear ship, the SAVANNAH was launched in 1959 and went to sea in 1962 to demonstrate peaceful uses for nuclear power. She was retired from service in 1971.

Number	Name	Completed	Location
BB 60	ALABAMA	1942	Battleship Memorial Park, Mobile, Ala.
AGSS 569	ALBACORE	1953	Portsmouth Naval Shipyard, N.H.
BB 39	ARIZONA	1916	Sunken remains and memorial off Ford Island, Pearl Harbor, Hawaii
DD 933	BARRY	1956	Navy Yard, Washington, D.C.
SS 310	BATFISH	1943	Muskogee War Memorial, Okla.
SS 319	BECUNA	1944	Cruiser OLYMPIA Association, Philadelphia, Penna.
SS 287	BOWFIN	1943	Submarine Memorial Park, Honolulu, Hawaii
CVL 28	CABOT	1943	CABOT/DEDALO Museum, New Orleans, La.
	CAIRO[1]	1862	Vicksburg National Park, Vicksburg, Miss.
DD 793	CASSIN YOUNG	1943	Boston Historical National Park, Boston, Mass.
SS 244	CAVALLA	1944	U.S. Submarine Veterans, Galveston, Texas
SS 343	CLAMAGORE	1945	Patriots Point, Mt. Pleasant, S.C.[2]
SS 245	COBIA	1944	Manitowoc Maritime Museum, Wisc.
SS 224	COD	1943	Cleveland, Ohio
IX 20	CONSTELLATION[3]	1853	Constellation Dock, Baltimore, Md.
IX 21	CONSTITUTION	1798	Boston National Historical Park, Boston, Mass.
SS 246	CROAKER	1944	Buffalo Naval and Servicemen's Park, N.Y.
PG 88	CROCKETT	1967	Great Lakes Naval and Maritime Museum, Muskegon, Mich.
SS 228	DRUM	1941	Battleship Memorial Park, Mobile, Ala.
DD 946	EDSON	1958	Sea-Air-Space Museum, New York, N.Y.
SSG 577	GROWLER	1958	Sea-Air-Space Museum, New York, N.Y.
AM 240	HAZARD	1944	Omaha Military Historical Society, Omaha, Neb.
AM 242	INAUGURAL	1944	Gateway Arch, St. Louis, Mo.
WPG 35	INGHAM	1936	Patriots Point, Mt. Pleasant, S.C.
	INTELLIGENT WHALE[4]	1863	Navy Museum, Navy Yard, Washington, D.C.
CVS 11	INTREPID (ex-CV 11)	1943	Sea-Air-Space Museum, New York, N.Y.
DD 850	JOSEPH P. KENNEDY, JR.	1945	Battleship Cove, Fall River, Mass.
DD 661	KIDD	1943	Louisiana War Memorial, Baton Rouge, La.
DD 724	LAFFEY	1944	Patriots Point, Mt. Pleasant, S.C.
AVT 16	LEXINGTON (ex-CV 16)	1943	Corpus Christi, Texas
SS 297	LING	1945	Submarine Memorial, Hackensack, N.J.
SS 298	LIONFISH	1944	Battleship Cove, Fall River, Mass.
CLG 4	LITTLE ROCK (ex-CL 92)	1945	Buffalo Naval and Servicemen's Park, N.Y.
SST 2	MARLIN	1953	Omaha Military Historical Society, Omaha, Neb.
BB 59	MASSACHUSETTS	1942	Battleship Cove, Fall River, Mass.
WPG 78	MOHAWK	1934	City piers, Wilmington, Del.
	MSB 5		Pate Museum of Transportation, Fort Worth, Texas
SSN 571	NAUTILUS	1954	Naval Submarine Base, New London, Conn.
	NEUSE[5]	1864	Caswell-Neuse State Historic Site, Kingston, N.C.
	NIAGARA[6]	1813	Erie, Penna.
BB 55	NORTH CAROLINA	1941	Memorial, Wilmington, N.C.
CA 15	OLYMPIA	1895	Cruiser OLYMPIA Association, Philadelphia, Penna.
SS 383	PAMPANITO	1943	Fisherman's Wharf, San Francisco, Calif.
	PHILADELPHIA[7]	1776	Smithsonian Institution, Washington, D.C.
	PIONEER[8]	1862	CABOT/DEDALO Museum, New Orleans, La.
	PT 617	1945	Battleship Cove, Fall River, Mass.
	PT 796	1945	Battleship Cove, Fall River, Mass.
	PTF 17	1968	Buffalo Naval and Servicemen's Park, N.Y.

Number	Name	Completed	Location
SSR 481	REQUIN	1945	Carnegie Science Center, Pittsburgh, Penna.
SS 236	SILVERSIDES	1941	Great Lakes Naval and Maritime Museum, Muskegon, Mich.
DE 238	STEWART	1943	U.S. Submarine Veterans, Galveston, Texas
WPG 37	TANEY	1936	Baltimore Maritime Museum, Baltimore, Md.
BB 35	TEXAS	1914	Battleship TEXAS State Historical Park, Laporte, Texas
DD 537	THE SULLIVANS	1943	Buffalo Naval and Servicemen's Park, N.Y.
SS 423	TORSK	1944	Baltimore Maritime Museum, Baltimore, Md.
	TRIESTE I[9]	1958	Navy Museum, Navy Yard, Washington, D.C.
	TRIESTE II[10]	1964	Naval Undersea Museum, Keyport, Wash.
DD 951	TURNER JOY	1959	Puget Sound Naval Shipyard, Bremerton, Wash.
	U-505[11]	1941	Museum of Science and Industry, Chicago, Ill.
AG 16	UTAH (ex-BB 31)	1911	Sunken remains off Ford Island, Pearl Harbor, Hawaii
	X-1	1955	Naval Academy, Annapolis, Md.
CV 10	YORKTOWN	1943	Patriots Point, Mt. Pleasant, S.C.

[1]Union ironclad, paddlewheel gunboat.
[2]The nuclear-propelled merchant ship SAVANNAH is also moored at Patriots Point.
[3] Not the original ship built in 1797, but a ship constructed at the Gosport (Norfolk) Navy Yard (Va.) in 1853; see chapter 25.
[4]Submersible.
[5]Confederate ironclad ram.
[6]American brig from Battle of Lake Erie.
[7]Gondola gunboat built on Lake Champlain during the American Revolution.
[8]Confederate submersible.
[9]Bathyscaph; built in 1953.
[10]Bathyscaph.
[11]Former German submarine captured at sea during World War II.

General Index

Ship Name and Class Index

Individual ships are indexed by their entire class entry. A few ships without names are indexed by their designations when they are not part of the standard ship designation scheme, e.g., DR-1, NR-1, SES-200, RSB-1. Non-U.S. ships are identified by nationality and type.

Weapons and electronics tables and the list of shipbuilding programs (Appendix C) are not indexed.